African American National Biography

African American National Biography

SECOND EDITION

HENRY LOUIS GATES JR.

EVELYN BROOKS HIGGINBOTHAM

Editors in Chief

VOLUME 9: PATTERSON, JAMES OGLETHORPE – RUGGLES, DAVID

OXFORD
UNIVERSITY PRESS

OXFORD
UNIVERSITY PRESS

Oxford University Press is a department of the University of Oxford.
It furthers the University's objective of excellence in research, scholarship,
and education by publishing worldwide.

Oxford   New York
Auckland   Cape Town   Dar es Salaam   Hong Kong   Karachi
Kuala Lumpur   Madrid   Melbourne   Mexico City   Nairobi
New Delhi   Shanghai   Taipei   Toronto

With offices in
Argentina   Austria   Brazil   Chile   Czech Republic   France   Greece
Guatemala   Hungary   Italy   Japan   Poland   Portugal   Singapore
South Korea   Switzerland   Thailand   Turkey   Ukraine   Vietnam

Oxford is a registered trademark of Oxford University Press in the UK and certain other countries.

Published in the United States of America by
Oxford University Press
198 Madison Avenue, New York, NY 10016

Library of Congress Cataloging-in-Publication Data
African American national biography / editors in chief Henry Louis Gates Jr., Evelyn Brooks Higginbotham. – 2nd ed.
p. cm.
Includes bibliographical references and index.
ISBN 978-0-19-999036-8 (volume 1; hdbk.); ISBN 978-0-19-999037-5 (volume 2; hdbk.); ISBN 978-0-19-999038-2 (volume 3; hdbk.);
ISBN 978-0-19-999039-9 (volume 4; hdbk.); ISBN 978-0-19-999040-5 (volume 5; hdbk.); ISBN 978-0-19-999041-2 (volume 6; hdbk.);
ISBN 978-0-19-999042-9 (volume 7; hdbk.); ISBN 978-0-19-999043-6 (volume 8; hdbk.); ISBN 978-0-19-999044-3 (volume 9; hdbk.);
ISBN 978-0-19-999045-0 (volume 10; hdbk.); ISBN 978-0-19-999046-7 (volume 11; hdbk.); ISBN 978-0-19-999047-4 (volume 12;
hdbk.); ISBN 978-0-19-992077-8 (12-volume set; hdbk.)
1. African Americans – Biography – Encyclopedias.   2. African Americans – History – Encyclopedias.
I. Gates, Henry Louis.   II. Higginbotham, Evelyn Brooks, 1945-
E185.96.A4466 2012
920'.009296073 – dc23
[B]
2011043281

1 3 5 7 9 8 6 4 2
Printed in the United States of America
on acid-free paper

African American National Biography

P CONTINUED

Patterson, James Oglethorpe (21 July 1912–29 Dec. 1989), minister and Church of God in Christ leader, was born in Derma, Mississippi, to William and Mollie Patterson. One of four children, James grew up in Heath, Arkansas, and Memphis, Tennessee. In Memphis he attended public schools and the Howe School of Religion, which later merged with LeMoyne-Owen College. On 4 July 1934 he married Deborah Mason, with whom he had two children, James Oglethorpe Jr. and Janet Laverne. A year later Patterson was ordained an elder in the Church of God in Christ (COGIC) and took his first charge in Gates, Tennessee. He pastored other churches in Brownsville and Memphis, Tennessee, and in East Orange, New Jersey, before moving to Memphis to found the Pentecostal Temple Institutional COGIC in 1941. Patterson remained a lifetime resident of Memphis, where the COGIC maintained its headquarters for more than a century.

As a local pastor, Patterson became a quiet yet effective social activist. In the 1950s he supported student sit-ins. In September 1955 Patterson's Pentecostal Temple hosted a meeting that drew two hundred ministers and community leaders who organized the Ministers and Citizens League. This new organization, of which Patterson served on the executive committee, approved a registration budget of two thousand dollars and the hiring of three full-time secretaries, and it set a goal to register up to sixty thousand new black voters. By November 1955 the league already had managed to register five thousand new black voters. During the 1955 mayoral race, the Ministers and Citizens League helped secure the black vote for Edmund

Orgill, who would lead Memphis for three years (1956–1959).

Patterson's leadership extended well beyond the walls of his local church. The COGIC looked for his leadership and in 1952 appointed him a member of its Special Committee—later called the Special Commission and Executive Commission—to help run the growing denomination. By including Patterson, his son-in-law, within his inner circle, Bishop C. H. Mason set the stage for Patterson later to be elected presiding bishop. Mason also entrusted Patterson with the position of assistant general secretary (1953) and bishop over the Second Ecclesiastical Jurisdiction of Tennessee (1955).

Mason died in 1961 and was replaced a year later by Bishop Ozro Thurston Jones, who was appointed by the Executive Commission. Although Jones was the new senior bishop, he was unable to dismiss the Executive Commission—now the Executive Board—which gave itself the right to counter Jones's decisions. Jones's leadership was significantly hindered because the COGIC constitution did not establish clear guidelines for the election of the successor to the founding bishop. Jones could not hold the denomination together and was removed by court action in 1966. Meanwhile Patterson's power had grown within the COGIC since he had been appointed general secretary in 1963. By popular vote the members and ministers of the COGIC in 1968 elected Patterson to be the presiding bishop for a term of four years. Patterson was reelected every four years until he died.

Now the leader of a denomination with 3 million members, Bishop Patterson worked tirelessly to develop a progressive agenda, founding the C. H. Mason Theological Seminary in Atlanta in 1970; the Charles Harrison Mason Foundation, to provide scholarships to COGIC students; the C. H. Mason System of Bible Colleges in 1970; the J. O. Patterson Fine Arts Department; the Historical Museum and Fine Arts Center; and the Department of Research and Survey. The C. H. Mason Theological Seminary, the first fully accredited Pentecostal seminary, allowed the COGIC to initiate chaplaincy ministries within the U.S. military. Bishop Patterson reorganized the publishing house and merged various programs into the United National Auxiliaries Convention, an annual assembly for the youth, missions, Sunday school, music, and evangelism departments.

In 1972 Robert Snowden and his sister Mary Todd, two local white philanthropists, gave Patterson Memphis's Chisca Plaza Hotel, worth $3 million, as a personal gift; but concerned for the progress of his denomination, Patterson donated the hotel to the COGIC, which used it as headquarters for many years. Patterson also intended to use the Chisca property for a proposed All Saints University, a four-year liberal arts university to include schools of theology, education, sciences, and fine arts. Millions of dollars were raised for this project, but it was never realized. In 1976 Patterson closed Saints Junior College, though its private academy continued to operate until 1983.

Patterson also worked hard to connect the COGIC with other black denominations. He affiliated the COGIC with the Congress of National Black Churches and served as the founding president of the World Fellowship of Black Pentecostal Churches. He was welcome in white organizations and participated in the North American Congress on the Holy Spirit and the National Association of Evangelicals. Politically, Patterson supported JESSE JACKSON's first presidential run by allowing him to speak at the 1984 annual COGIC convocation.

Patterson's wife died in 1984, and five years later he married the former Mary Peak, a COGIC member. The same year, Patterson was stricken with pancreatic cancer, which is nearly always fatal, but because of his faith in divine healing he refused chemotherapy. Patterson died in Memphis, but his legacy lives on through the Pentecostal Temple, which had grown into a congregation with three thousand members, and through the numerous institutions he founded that continue to serve COGIC members.

FURTHER READING

Bean, Bobby. *This Is the Church of God in Christ* (2001).

Kelly, Frances Burnett. *Here Am I, Send Me: The Dramatic Story of Presiding Bishop J. O. Patterson* (1970).

Tucker, David M. *Black Pastors and Leaders: Memphis 1819–1972* (1986).

DAVID MICHEL

Patterson, Louise Thompson. *See* Thompson Patterson, Louise.

Patterson, Mary Jane (1840–24 Sept. 1894), educator and school administrator, was born in Raleigh, North Carolina, to Henry I. Patterson, a brick mason, and Emmeline Eliza Taylor, both free blacks. Mary Jane was probably the first of ten or more children born to the Pattersons. In the early 1850s, when Patterson was in her teens, the family moved to Ohio, living first in Brunswick, Medina County, before moving in 1856 to Oberlin, Lorain County. Records show that in 1859, 344 blacks, including twenty-six fugitive slaves, were living in Oberlin. The Pattersons, according to the 1860 Oberlin census, were comparatively comfortable, with real estate holdings estimated at fifteen hundred dollars and their personal worth at about two hundred dollars. The Pattersons attended the integrated First Congregational Church in Oberlin, where Charles G. Finney was minister. First Church received Patterson and her younger brother John into the congregation by letter of transfer in early March 1856.

Like a number of other black families who had moved to racially integrated Oberlin, the Pattersons chose the town so that their children would have access to a higher education at coeducational Oberlin College (called Collegiate Institute before 1850), where students of color had been enrolling since 1835. By the 1861–1862 school year, Oberlin had an enrollment of 1,071 students, of whom about forty, or 3.7 percent, were black.

Patterson first took one year of study, 1857–1858, in Oberlin College's preparatory course before enrolling in the classical or college course leading to an AB degree. Up until this time black women who enrolled at Oberlin had attended or graduated from either the Preparatory Department or the four-year Ladies Department, which carried only a literary certificate and not a bachelor's degree. Other notable black students during Patterson's time were EMMA V. BROWN, FANNY JACKSON (COPPIN), and EDMONIA LEWIS. By living at her family's home on East Lorain Street, Patterson reduced the cost of her education. She also held a twenty-five-dollar scholarship, which easily paid for her thirteen-dollar tuition and her incidental expenses of two dollars and twenty-five cents. Her college course work included advanced mathematics, ancient Greek, and Latin prose composition. In the latter course she read Cicero, Horace, Livy, Tacitus, Agricola, and Virgil. Despite the fact that Patterson undoubtedly found herself the only female student of color in many of her classes, she earned excellent grades.

Little is known of Patterson's involvement in student life, including whether she was a member of the Ladies Literary Society or the Young Ladies Anti-Slavery Society. Both Oberlin College and the town were steeped in antislavery activity in the 1850s and early 1860s. A number of college faculty and students joined the town's black and white citizens in the celebrated rescue of the fugitive slave John Price in September 1858 in Wellington, Ohio. Patterson's first cousin, Mary S. Patterson, from Oberlin, married a harness maker named Lewis Sheridan Leary, who with two other blacks from Oberlin joined John Brown in 1859 and lost their lives during the raid on Harpers Ferry. Like other black Oberlin families headed by artisan fathers, the Pattersons exhibited black consciousness, and they were caught up in a charged antislavery and freedom environment that affected their daily lives.

When Patterson completed her college course in 1862, she became the first black woman to receive a bachelor's degree in the United States. Her graduation photograph shows her wearing a plain Garibaldi shirt, which would have been of black or red wool, and a black and white checked woolen skirt finished with black silk. As part of her commencement exercises, she was one of several students selected by her classmates to read their essays. Patterson's essay about Giuseppe Garibaldi, "The Hero of Italy," attracted much attention in area newspapers.

Following Patterson's graduation, Edward H. Fairchild, the principal of the Oberlin preparatory course, recommended her for a teaching position at a school for black children in Norfolk, Virginia, describing her as "a light quadroon" and avowing that she was "a superior scholar, a good singer, faithful Christian, and a genteel lady" (A.M.A. Manuscripts [on microfilm], Roll 13). The onset of the Civil War undoubtedly prevented her from obtaining the Norfolk appointment. After the war, however, Patterson accepted a position at Philadelphia, Pennsylvania's Institute for Colored Youth, where she served for five years as an assistant to Fanny Jackson (later Coppin) in the Female Department.

Patterson taught with distinction at the institute, where classical languages and mathematics as well as industrial and vocational classes made up the curriculum. In 1869 she left for Washington, D.C., where she accepted a more demanding teaching and administrative position as the first black principal at the newly established Preparatory School for Negroes, later known as the M Street School and still later as Paul Laurence Dunbar High School. After one year, RICHARD THEODORE GREENER, the first black man to graduate from Harvard University, replaced her. Greener had been a classmate of Patterson's in Oberlin's preparatory course as well as a teaching colleague at the Institute for Colored Youth in Philadelphia. When Patterson stepped down she became the school's assistant principal, but again for only one year. In 1873 Greener left for Howard University, and Patterson was once again named principal. Pragmatic and disciplined, she served in this role until 1884, greatly improving the school's image and standing in the community. Among her many achievements were dropping the designation "Preparatory" from the school's name and instituting a highly regarded curricular teacher-training department. Throughout her career, she encouraged her students to seize every educational opportunity they could find.

Patterson's sisters, Chanie and Emma, also teachers, joined her in Washington during the fall of 1871, perhaps because Patterson was experiencing health problems. Declining health may have influenced her to retire as principal in 1884 when she was only forty-four years old. By then the school's greatly increased enrollment also led the school authorities to replace Patterson with a prominent male member of Washington's elite black community, FRANCIS LOUIS CARDOZO. Student-centered and unpretentious, Patterson gracefully accepted being displaced a second time and agreed to stay on at the school and teach. Less than a year later, however, Patterson stopped teaching, apparently because she and her sisters undertook the care of their aging and poor parents who had come to live with them in Washington, D.C.

Patterson devoted time and financial gifts to other black District of Columbia institutions, such as the Home for Aged and Infirm Colored People. She also supported industrial schools for young black women—always with an eye toward using education for social uplift of her race. She was a member of the Bethel Literary and Historical Association and a charter member of the National

Colored Women's League. Neither Patterson nor her sisters ever married.

When Mary Jane Patterson died at the age of fifty-four, newspaper headlines read, "Worked for Her Race" and "One of the Well-Known Teachers in the Colored Schools" (*Evening Star* [Washington, D.C.], 25 Sept. 1894; *Oberlin News*, 27 Sept. 1894). She had been one of the ablest and best-known school administrators and teachers in Washington, D.C., and her years of devoted service advanced the education of a great many African American children.

FURTHER READING

Bigglestone, William E. *They Stopped in Oberlin: Black Residents and Visitors of the Nineteenth Century* (1981).

Chesnutt, Helen M. *Charles Waddell Chesnutt: Pioneer of the Color Line* (1952).

Fletcher, Robert Samuel. *A History of Oberlin College: From Its Foundation through the Civil War*, 2 vols. (1943).

Lawson, Ellen N., and Marlene D. Merrill. "The Antebellum 'Talented Thousandth': Black College Students at Oberlin before the Civil War," *Journal of Negro Education* 52 (Spring 1983).

Perkins, Linda M. "Quaker Beneficence and Black Control: The Institute for Colored Youth, 1852–1903," in *New Perspectives on Black Educational History*, eds. Vincent P. Franklin and James D. Anderson (1978).

Terrell, Mary Church. "History of the High School for Negroes in Washington," *Journal of Negro History* 2 (July 1917).

Obituaries: *Evening Star* (Washington, D.C.), 25 Sept. 1894; *Oberlin News*, 27 Sept. 1894.

ROLAND M. BAUMANN

Patterson, Orlando (5 June 1940–), sociologist, novelist, and Harvard professor, was born near Frome, Westmoreland, Jamaica, and spent most of his childhood in May Pen, Clarendon, Jamaica. His father, Charles Patterson, was a detective in the colonial police force who became radicalized while spying on MARCUS GARVEY for the government, and his mother, Almina Morris, was a seamstress who took a keen interest in her son's education. In 1953 Patterson moved to Kingston to attend high school at Kingston College. He won an Exhibition Scholarship to the University College of the West Indies (then a Jamaica-based college of the University of London) and was active on campus, chairing the literary and economics societies and editing the campus magazine. He graduated with a B.S. in Economics in 1962, the same year Jamaica achieved independence from Britain. Some months later Patterson took up a Commonwealth Scholarship for graduate research in sociology at the London School of Economics (LSE), from which he received a Ph.D.

London at this time was vibrant with students from former colonies as well as a maturing generation of West Indians who had moved during the heyday of colonial migration in the 1950s. Patterson joined this milieu through the Caribbean Artists Movement (CAM), at whose first meeting he presented a paper. He also attended study sessions at the North London flat of C. L. R. JAMES, joining his West Indian student friends at the feet of the magisterial Marxist thinker. While in London, Patterson was also active in British leftist and cultural circles, most notably on the editorial board of *New Left Review*. He met Nerys Thomas, a fellow LSE graduate student and subsequent specialist in Celtic history. They married in 1965 and had two daughters before they divorced in 1994.

In 1965 Patterson completed his dissertation, which was later published as *The Sociology of Slavery: An Analysis of the Origins, Development, and Structure of Negro Slave Society in Jamaica, 1655–1838* (1967). He was invited to stay at LSE as a lecturer. Torn between taking that position and returning to the Caribbean, he signed on to teach at LSE but left after two years to take a position in the sociology department at his alma mater, the now independent degree-granting University of the West Indies, Mona (UWI). Patterson eventually became disenchanted with postindependence life and politics. The Jamaican government's refusal to allow reentry to the Guyanese UWI professor Walter Rodney for alleged sedition was an important catalyst in Patterson's decision to leave. In 1970 he took a visiting fellowship in Harvard's newly formed Afro-American studies department. Following disagreements with that department's chair, Professor Ewart Guinier, Patterson completed his fellowship in the university's sociology department, which offered him a permanent position the next year. He was named John Cowles Professor of Sociology in 1993.

Patterson published three novels. His first, *Children of Sisyphus* (1964), considered a Jamaican classic, was actually submitted to its publisher by James, Patterson's mentor. The book explores the relationship between the marginalized poor squatting on the wastelands of the Dungle and the freshly consolidated black middle class in the suburbs of Kingston. It was influenced as much by French existentialism (with its themes of will and desperation) as by Caribbean sociology (with its issues of class and sexuality). His campus novel, *An Absence of Ruins* (1967), highlights the ennui and absurdity among a group of middle-class intellectuals in Jamaica. Patterson's last novel, *Die the Long Day* (1972), is historical fiction that resonates with his academic work on the social lives of slaves. The narrative unfolds after a slave mother attacks the syphilitic overseer who fixates on her daughter. Patterson's fiction was acclaimed in some circles and chastised in others—most famously perhaps by the Jamaican writer John Hearne, who charged Patterson with importing the forms and discourse of sociology into the realm of art. Patterson was steadfast in his fundamental disagreement with Hearne about the nature of fiction; nevertheless he found that he could not focus both on academic work and art and chose to give up writing novels.

Patterson had numerous academic publications and a reputation for masterful works of historical sociology. He was also well known for more specifically located work on American ethnicity. *Ethnic Chauvinism: The Reactionary Impulse* (1977) combined both of these tendencies and intimated future directions in his scholarship. It explores the historical foundations of group identity and presents case studies of ethnic arrangements in the Caribbean and the United States. Patterson argued that ethnic identities are social constructs that last only as long as they are socially and economically necessary.

Slavery and Social Death (1982) was a comparative study of the nature and logic of slavery the world over, from classical antiquity to the nineteenth century. It was arguably Patterson's most famous book, and the concepts of "natal alienation" was its most enduring. Patterson argued that the slave is defined by his or her alienation "from all 'rights' or claims of birth" in the society in which he or she is enslaved, that he or she ceases "to belong in his own right to any legitimate social order" (5). This genealogical and social isolation, combined with the brute force of slavery and its generalized dishonor, function to make the slave a "social non-person" (5). In 1983 *Slavery and Social Death* won the Ralph Bunche Award of the American Political Science Association and the Distinguished Contribution to Scholarship Award of the American Sociological Association.

Patterson also embarked on two separate multi-volume projects. *Freedom in the Making of Western Culture* (1991) was the first of his two-volume meditation on what he called "the shadow concept of slavery." The volume covers the period from ancient Greece to the Middle Ages, aiming to be historically comprehensive but also to shed new light on the neglected role of women in understandings of freedom (in a chapter on Greek drama) and on the importance of versions of freedom in the medieval period. *Freedom* won the National Book Award in 1991.

The Ordeal of Integration: Progress and Resentment in America's "Racial" Crisis (1997) was the first in a trilogy of works on American race relations (the quotation marks in the title indicate Patterson's preference for the term *ethnic* in this context). In a series of essays, the book tackles the discourse on racism in America, arguing that African Americans have made real social, economic, and political gains since the civil rights movement and that race relations have improved considerably. He argues that commentary across the political spectrum tends not to differentiate among African Americans as a group, tends to overestimate urban black poverty, and tends to share an investment in the flawed principles of determinism. To improve upon the gains won in the twentieth century, Patterson favors more focused social programs, including an evolving and eventually phased-out affirmative action policy, and eliminating taboos on ethnic intermarriage and assimilation. The second in the trilogy, *Rituals of Blood: Consequences of Slavery in Two American Centuries* (1998), argues that gender relations frame the most dire problems facing African Americans. Patterson argued that there is a crisis in long-term partnership among African Americans and that this crisis was intimately connected to African American masculine identity. Male identity suffered from the blood ritual of lynching during Reconstruction and continued to work itself out in the Dionysian spectacle of African American male self-destruction.

As Patterson worked to complete both projects, he earned an esteemed place in the scholarly community, but he was not wholly free of controversy. His writing on American ethnicity and his editorials for such publications as the *New York Times* and the *Washington Post* were hotly debated. Commentators sometimes sought to place him in one political camp or another, but Patterson's diverse influences, evolving ideas, and avowedly questioning style made him difficult to pigeonhole. In 1995 he married Anita Haya Goldman, an associate professor of English at Boston University; they had one daughter.

FURTHER READING
Davis, David Brion. "Of Human Bondage," *New York Review of Books* (17 Feb. 1983).

Fredrickson, George M. "America's Caste System: Will It Change?" *New York Review of Books* (23 Oct. 1997).

Holmes, Stephen A. "Challenging Everyone's Conceptions about Blacks," *New York Times*, 1 May 1999.

James, C. L. R. "Rastafari at Home and Abroad," *New Left Review* (May–June 1964).

Jones, Bridget. "Orlando Patterson," in *Fifty Caribbean Writers: A Bio-Bibliographical Critical Sourcebook*, ed. Daryl Cumber Dance (1986).

Walmsley, Anne. *The Caribbean Artists Movement, 1966–1972* (1992).

Williams, Richard. "Orlando Patterson Interview," *Sociological Forum* 10.4 (Dec. 1995): 653–671.

NADIA ELLIS

Patterson, William L. (27 Aug. 1891–5 Mar. 1980), writer, attorney, and leader of the American Communist Party, was born William Lorenzo Patterson in San Francisco, California, the son of James Edward Patterson, a ship's cook and dentist, and Mary Galt, a domestic. After his father left the family to become a missionary as a Seventh-day Adventist, his mother worked to support the family. Failure to pay the rent resulted in numerous evictions, but Patterson managed to attend Tamalpais High School in California by working first as a newsboy and later as a racetrack hand. He graduated from high school in 1911 and studied at the University of California, Berkeley, to be a mining engineer, but he had to drop out because he could not afford tuition. No scholarships were available, and he objected to Berkeley's compulsory military training. Later Patterson refused to participate in World War I because he felt that it was being fought for a democratic tradition that did not extend to blacks. He was arrested and held for five days in Oakland for declaring the conflict a "white man's war."

Patterson decided to study law in 1915. He took jobs as a night clerk and elevator operator to attend the Hastings College of Law at the University of California in San Francisco. While there he joined radical political activists in protesting discrimination against blacks. He graduated in 1919, but when he failed to be admitted to the California bar, he suspected that this failure was the result of his political activism. In the same year he was chairman of the National Association for the Advancement of Colored People (NAACP) branch in Oakland.

Patterson then took a job as cook on the SS *Barracuda*, which was headed for England. In London he introduced himself to the editor and publisher of the *Daily Herald*, George Lansbury, who was also a leading figure of the British Labour Party. Lansbury published an article written by Patterson on "the Negro's problem" in the United States. After a short-lived plan to settle in Liberia, Patterson moved to New York City and in 1923 opened a law firm in Harlem, Dyett, Hall, and Patterson, with two friends. In 1924 he was admitted to the New York bar. Patterson married Minnie Summer, a fashion designer and dressmaker, in 1926; they had no children and divorced within two years.

Patterson was appalled in 1926 by the legal treatment of the Italian immigrant anarchists Nicola Sacco and Bartolomeo Vanzetti, accused of murder and executed in 1927 despite questionable evidence and international protest. Patterson was arrested in Boston during a protest as part of the Sacco-Vanzetti Freedom Delegation. Upton Sinclair, in his semifictional account of the Sacco-Vanzetti case in his novel *Boston* (1928), describes "William Patterson, a Negro lawyer from New York, running the greatest risk of any of [the protesters], with his black face not to be disguised" (682). Communist friends helped persuade Patterson that black oppression was caused by class exploitation as well as racism. Patterson left his law practice in 1927 to enroll in the Communist Party Workers School. Along with LANGSTON HUGHES, Patterson was one of the first black men attracted to the American Communist Party. His efforts resulted in a fifty-year career as a leader in the party and as an activist for human rights.

The American Communist Party sent Patterson to the Soviet Union to attend the University of Toiling People of the Far East, in Moscow. Patterson's experiences in the Soviet Union persuaded him that socialism precluded the need for prejudice based on race, class, or religious creed. He joined the International Organization to Help Workers in Moscow. While in Moscow in 1928, Patterson married Vera Gorohovskaya; they had two children and amicably divorced in 1930 when Patterson returned to the United States.

In New York City Patterson became a Communist organizer, teacher, and public speaker. As a lawyer he defended blacks who he felt were wrongly accused or not given a fair trial. In 1931 he accepted the position of national secretary of the International Labor Defense. His first assignment was to defend the SCOTTSBORO BOYS, nine black youths aged thirteen to nineteen who had been charged in Scottsdale, Alabama, again on questionable evidence, with allegedly raping and assaulting two white women on a freight train. Eight of the boys were sentenced to death, despite the revelation that Alabama state police had obstructed justice. In 1930 Patterson participated in the World Conference against Racism and Anti-Semitism in Paris. The same year he helped plan the First International Negro Workers Congress. In 1932 he was elected to the party's Central Committee and was chosen as its Communist candidate for mayor of New York City, the year that Democrat John O'Brien won.

Patterson firmly believed that journalists and historians obscured the truth about blacks, black history, and blacks' contributions to the development of the United States, and he believed that Americans needed to be educated about how the negative effects of racism reached beyond blacks to whites—ideas that he addressed in his many writings. He was associate editor of the *Daily Record* in Chicago from 1938 to 1940, and he contributed articles to the *Daily World, Daily Worker, Worker, New Times, African Communist, New World Review, Negro Worker,* and *Marxist Review.*

Patterson was an active leader of other communist organizations, such as the International Labor Defense, for which he served as the national executive secretary from 1931 to 1949. He held the same position for the Civil Rights Congress (CRC) in 1949. In 1950 he was prosecuted by the federal government and sentenced to three months in prison for failure to turn over to the Internal Revenue Service the Civil Rights Congress's list of contributors. The sentence was reversed on appeal. Patterson engaged in a number of political and legal battles in which he protested what he termed genocide, the unconstitutional treatment of blacks. As a member of the Civil Rights Congress, Patterson aided in the legal appeals for Willie McGee, veteran and father of four, wrongly accused of rape by a white woman in Laurel, Mississippi, and the Martinsville Seven, seven men also charged with raping a white woman. All eight victims were forced to confess to the crimes, convicted by an all-white jury, and in 1951 executed despite CRC appeals to the state and federal supreme courts.

The climactic moment of Patterson's career came in 1951 when he joined the actor and activist PAUL ROBESON, whom he had met in Harlem in 1920, and presented to the United Nations his petition *We Charge Genocide: The Crime of Government against the Negro People,* accusing the U.S. government of committing acts of genocide, which include killing or harming mentally or physically with the intent to destroy in part or in whole. The petition was signed by many notable figures, including the activist and writer W. E. B. DuBois, and was resubmitted in 1970 with

the signatures of OSSIE DAVIS, actor and civil rights activist; RALPH ABERNATHY, leader of the Southern Christian Leadership Conference after MARTIN LUTHER KING JR.'s death; SHIRLEY CHISHOLM, U.S. representative of the Twelfth Congressional District in New York; and HUEY NEWTON, cofounder with BOBBY SEALE of the Black Panther Party.

Patterson had married Louise Thompson in 1940; they had one child. In 1971 he received the Lenin Anniversary Medal from the Union of Soviet Socialist Republics. The Academy of Arts of the German Democratic Republic in 1978 bestowed on him the honor of the Paul Robeson Memorial Medal. Patterson died in the Bronx, New York.

FURTHER READING

Patterson, William L. *The Man Who Cried Genocide* (1971).

Patterson, William L. *We Charge Genocide: The Crime of Government against the Negro People* (1951; repr. 1970, 2001).

Howe, Irving. *The American Communist Party: A Critical History, 1919–1957* (1957).

Ottanelli, Fraser. *The Communist Party of the United States: From the Depression to World War II* (1991).

Obituary: *New York Times,* 7 Mar. 1980.

This entry is taken from the *American National Biography* and is published here with the permission of the American Council of Learned Societies.

BARBARA L. CICCARELLI

Pattillo, Walter Alexander (9 Nov. 1850–12 May 1908), Baptist minister, educator, and independent political leader, was born into slavery in North Carolina. Pattillo's father was a white farmer, his mother a black slave. During Reconstruction Pattillo drove wagons and worked in a sawmill factory to support his mother in Granville County, North Carolina. At the age of seventeen Pattillo joined the General Association of the Colored Baptists of North Carolina to expand the black-led church, which only after Emancipation had become a visible institution in the South. In 1870 he met and then married Mary Ida Hart, who came from an antebellum free African American family in an adjacent county. The couple, both of whose names appear on titles for land they purchased, went on to rear twelve children.

Having taught himself how to read and write, Pattillo received a permit to preach in 1874 and quickly gained a reputation as a "convention stalwart" of the black Baptist Church. Over the course of his lifetime he preached before dozens of congregations, including Antioch Baptist and First

Baptist in Oxford, his hometown, and later traveled to Virginia to serve the Mount Olive congregation. In 1876 Pattillo entered Shaw University in Raleigh to study theology after raising funds from black and white friends and family for his tuition and boarding. At Shaw he befriended leading members of black Baptist congregations, further raising his profile in the state. After graduation Pattillo served the Home Mission Board of the Baptist State Convention and was elected president of the Middle Baptist Association. According to one of his sons Pattillo delivered nearly 3,000 sermons and baptized more than 3,100 people throughout his life.

Pattillo's work with black Baptist congregations also brought him into contact with farmers, sharecroppers, and agrarian workers across the state. In the early 1880s Pattillo ran in Granville County unsuccessfully for register of deeds as a Republican. He was defeated after his white opponent warned that, if elected, the "sleek, oily negro," would have the authority to issue marriage licenses to white couples—thereby violating the sanctity of marriage. Such attacks did not deter Pattillo from continuing to reach out to all members of the community. He became actively involved in public education, teaching classes and serving as superintendent of schools in Granville and surrounding counties. He helped to raise funds for what would become the state's only black orphanage, based in Oxford, serving as its general agent in 1882. Between 1886 and 1887 Pattillo directed the construction of the orphanage as its superintendent and shaped the institution's unique character as nondenominational. For his contributions he was later described by the orphanage as its "magnanimous spirit."

In the 1880s, as economic and political conditions deteriorated for African Americans—with rising debt, low prices, and spiraling interest rates—Pattillo turned his attention to building what would become the largest network of black farmers in the nation, the Colored Farmers Alliance. The Colored Alliance was the chief organization in the early period of Black Populism, the largest political movement of African Americans in the rural South until the modern civil rights movement. Colored Alliances initially functioned as nonpartisan social organizations, paralleling the all-white Farmers Alliances. Members paid dues and attended local chapter meetings. Like the black churches, Colored Alliance chapters helped to raise money for the community's poorest members. The Colored Alliance also organized economic cooperatives and called for a national subsidy program, a reform of the credit system, and enforcement mechanisms to regulate railroads.

In 1890, in his capacity as state organizer and lecturer for the Colored Alliance, Pattillo traveled across the state recruiting members. During this period he edited two newspapers, the *Alliance Advocate* and the *Baptist Pilot*. Pattillo was a particularly effective organizer, combining his skills as an orator and organization builder. His success was reflected in part in the phenomenal growth of the Colored Alliance, which by the early 1890s claimed a membership of 55,000 men and women in North Carolina; nationally, the organization claimed a membership of 1.2 million black farmers, sharecroppers, and agrarian workers.

Recognizing the limits of the southern branch of the Republican Party in the face of planter- and business-dominated Democratic Party control of the electoral process, Pattillo called for the formation of an independent political party that could unite disaffected poor white southern Democrats and black Republicans into a third political force. In January of 1891 Pattillo traveled to Washington, D.C., as a Colored Alliance delegate for the Confederation of Industrial Organizations, comprising delegates from the black and white Alliances, the Knights of Labor, and the Woman's Christian Temperance Union. The Confederation issued a call for a convention to be held in St. Louis, Missouri, the following year, where "all interested groups were to discuss the issue of a national third party." Pattillo served as one of three national representatives of the Colored Alliance on the credentials committee of the St. Louis convention. The third party he called for would soon come to be organized as the People's Party.

In 1892 the People's Party (also known as the Populist Party) competed directly against the Democratic Party, receiving more than 1 million votes nationally for its candidate, James B. Weaver. By 1894, in coalition with the Republican Party, the North Carolina People's Party gained a majority of seats in its state legislature; in 1895 Populists in the state captured the governor's office. Over the next three years, however, the Democratic Party, aided by local law enforcement and vigilante groups, effectively destroyed the independent movement through violence.

Pattillo returned to his work as a minister and educator in 1896. That year the 10 January issue of the *Oxford Public Ledger* reported that Pattillo had just returned to Granville, whereupon he was appointed principal of Oxford High School. He would go on preaching and teaching up until his death in 1908, debt-ridden from overextending himself. Two years before he died, his alma mater, Shaw University, honored him for his life's work with a doctor of divinity degree.

FURTHER READING

Ali, Omar H. "Independent Black Voices from the Late 19th Century: Black Populists and the Struggle against the Southern Democracy," *Souls: A Critical Journal of Black Politics, Culture, and Society*, vol. 7, no. 2 (Spring, 2005).

Ali, Omar H. "The Making of a Black Populist: A Tribute to the Rev. Walter A. Pattillo," *Oxford Public Ledger*, vol. 121, no. 25, 28 Mar. 2002.

Williams, Moses W., and George W. Watkins. "Walter A. Pattillo," in *Who's Who among North Carolina Negro Baptists* (1940).

OMAR H. ALI

Patton, Charley (Apr. 1891–28 Apr. 1934), blues singer and guitarist, was born on Heron's Place between Bolton and Edwards, Mississippi, the eldest son of William Patton and Annie Martin, farmers. Patton was of mixed descent, with white, black, and Native American forebears. His name is sometimes spelled "Charlie." The nature of his formal schooling is uncertain but may have included some elementary school education. During Patton's early teen years, his family moved to the Will Dockery plantation between Cleveland and Ruleville, which in time became the base of his musical activities.

There Patton began acquiring the necessary musical skills that would enable him to perform alone or with bands. It is believed that Patton started with basic guitar chords shown to him by Henry Sloan. By 1908 Patton was an itinerant blues musician, performing mostly in the Mississippi Delta region between Vicksburg, Mississippi, and Memphis, Tennessee, in juke joints and stores, or at picnics and house parties.

Certainly before World War I Patton codified his musical art with three songs: "Pony Blues," "Banty Rooster Blues," and "Maggie." Patton would affix new lyrics to these songs for a new subject or occasion and also developed secondary themes for musical variety. A substantial portion of the repertoire recorded by Patton later in his career can be traced to these three songs. Other early pieces from this time were "Mississippi Boweevil Blues" and "Green River Blues."

With this early repertoire Patton made an impact on regional musicians from 1910 to 1915. Among those who traded melodies and lyrics with Patton were Willie Lee Brown, TOMMY JOHNSON, Dick Bankston, and Jake Martin, who met often in Drew, Mississippi, a central location in the upper Delta. After 1915 they separated to develop their respective styles. However, some fifteen years later, Patton, Brown, and Johnson recorded their respective variants of "Pony Blues" and "Maggie," revealing their close musical ties.

During World War I Patton was called for the army but failed to pass the physical, probably because of a heart disorder that would eventually end his life. He played on, however, making his musical rounds in the Mississippi Delta. With his distinctive hoarse voice and flashy performing antics, such as throwing his guitar and playing it behind his head, Patton came to be a leading draw for black sharecroppers and white landowners alike. Sometimes he would perform on Sundays, even preaching a little, a sample of which he recorded in late 1929 as "You're Gonna Need Somebody When You Die."

Throughout the 1920s Patton continued to return to the Dockery plantation from time to time, but he often stayed with friends and lovers in other Mississippi Delta towns and hamlets, including Cottondale, the Osa Pepper plantation, Mound Bayou, and Merigold. Sometimes his playing dates would take him to Lula, Lake Cormorant, and across the state border to Memphis. In 1927 the Mississippi River overflowed its banks and inundated many Delta communities; Patton chronicled the disaster in his song "High Water Everywhere," sprinkling his narrative with many Mississippi place names. His contact with and influence on younger musicians continued with the likes of BOOKER WASHINGTON "BUKKA" WHITE, HOWLIN' WOLF, Booker Miller, and Willie Moore.

Meanwhile, record companies began producing "race records" by black artists for black listeners. Although urban singers established the "race" market, the first hit records by the rural Texas musician BLIND LEMON JEFFERSON in 1926 made it possible for other country blues performers to record. On the recommendation of the Jackson, Mississippi, talent scout H. C. Speir, Paramount Records engaged Patton for a session on 14 June 1929. Performing in the Gennett Records studio in Richmond, Indiana, Patton made fourteen three-minute, 78-rpm sides, among them his signature tunes "Pony Blues" and "Banty Rooster Blues," whose back-to-back release on one record enjoyed high sales. Recognizing a new record star, Paramount quickly brought him north in late 1929 for a second session, this time in its newly completed studios in Grafton, Wisconsin. Bringing along Henry "Son" Sims, a fiddler from Farrell, Mississippi, Patton laid down twenty-six performances acceptable for commercial release. "High Water Everywhere" was the big hit of the session, retaining the label's interest in him.

Throughout his life Patton took a number of wives, many of whom were commonlaw, but a few he legally married. Researchers agree that Patton had eight or nine wives, and four spouses should be noted. In 1908 Patton married Mille Barnes (or Bonds), and they had a daughter known either as Willie Mae or China Lou. Ten years later he took Roxie Morrow as a wife; they did not have children. In 1922 Patton formally married Mandy France on the Pepper plantation. The best known of Patton's wives, however, was Bertha Lee Pate, who met Patton in Lula around 1930 and stayed with him through much of his remaining life, moving with him to the Heathman-Dedham plantation near Holly Ridge and Indianola, Mississippi.

With the commercial success of "High Water Everywhere," Patton was contacted in May 1930 for a third Paramount Records session, and like his second session, he was allowed to bring any musicians he felt talented enough to record. This time he asked Willie Brown, the singer and guitarist EDDIE "SON" HOUSE JR., and the pianist Louise Johnson to join him. In the studio the four musicians took their respective turns at the microphone; Patton waited until the others were finished before recording four songs, one of which was "Dry Well Blues," about a drought then ravaging the South.

During the worst years of the Depression, Patton stayed near Indianola, but he still traveled throughout the Delta to play for black and white audiences. Occasionally he would perform with Brown and House, and in 1933 the three musicians approached Speir in Jackson, hoping for a formal session to record some spirituals. Vocalion Records heard the test disc that resulted and invited Patton to a session in New York City on 30 and 31 January and 1 February 1934. His wife, Bertha Lee, traveled with Patton to the session and even sang on several sides. Although in poor health by this time, Patton successfully played through his latest blues, "34 Blues" and "High Sheriff Blues," but he also recorded "Oh Death" and "Troubled 'bout My Mother," songs that reflect his premonitions of his approaching death.

After returning to the Indianola area, Patton continued to perform despite his weakening physical condition. He succumbed in Indianola to the mitral heart valve disorder that he had had since his youth. Over the years, memories of Patton were kept alive by Bertha Lee Patton, House, Moore, Howlin' Wolf, and other musicians and relatives. In 2003 the Revenant Records reissue of Patton's complete recordings won three Grammy awards, including Best Historical Album and Best Liner Notes.

FURTHER READING

Calt, Stephen, and Gayle Wardlow. *King of the Delta Blues: The Life and Music of Charlie Patton* (1988).

Evans, David. Liner notes to *Screamin' and Hollerin' the Blues: The Worlds of Charley Patton* (Revenant Records 212, 2001).

Fahey, John. *Charley Patton* (1970).

DISCOGRAPHY

Charlie Patton: Complete Recorded Works in Chronological Order (vols. 1–3, Document Records 5009, 5010, 5011).

Charlie Patton: Founder of the Delta Blues 1929–34 (Yazoo Records 1020).

Screamin' and Hollerin' the Blues: The Worlds of Charley Patton (Revenant Records 212).

This entry is taken from the *American National Biography* and is published here with the permission of the American Council of Learned Societies.

EDWARD KOMARA

Patton, Georgia E. L. (16 Apr. 1864–8 Nov. 1900), physician and religious worker, was born Georgia Esther Lee Patton into slavery in mountainous Grundy County, southeast Tennessee, the youngest of her parents' many children. Little is known about her mother and father, both of whom were born into slavery in Tennessee. Georgia's mother was widowed while pregnant with her. When Georgia was two, the family settled nearby in Coffee County, where her mother took in laundry. The local school opened only a few weeks each year, if at all. Between her ninth and seventeenth years, Georgia's formal education totaled a mere twenty-six months.

When Georgia was sixteen her mother died and her siblings took over her care. They pooled their resources and sent her to Nashville's Central Tennessee College (later Walden University) in February 1882. However, she had to spend most of each year earning her living expenses instead of attending classes. By 1890 she completed the entire normal (teacher) curriculum. Patton then excelled in the College's Meharry Medical Department (later a freestanding medical school) and earned her M.D. on 7 February 1893, becoming—with Annie Gregg—one of Meharry's first two women medical graduates.

According to the journalist and anti-lynching crusader Ida B. Wells, Patton was "early imbued with the desire to go to Africa as a medical missionary" (Wells, 88). Her aspiration meshed with the American Colonization Society's recently declared (1892) refocus on Liberian nation-building instead of mass emigration. Few other African American doctors besides ALICE WOODBY-MCKANE sought to practice in Liberia (or elsewhere in Africa, for that matter). When Patton's Methodist Episcopal Church missionary society rejected her funding appeal, she paid her own way, explaining, "I go to Liberia for the good I want to do for others, to relieve the suffering, and to assist in radiating the light of Christianity and civilization to other parts of Africa....After two years I hope to return to this country, to take a post-graduate course in medicine, and then return to Liberia able to do better work in the line of medicine. I look forward to a long life to do good and help build up Africa" (Patton, 78).

On 5 April 1893 Patton boarded a steamer to Liverpool, England, sharing a stateroom with Ida B. Wells-Barnett, on her way to a British speaking tour. At first, Wells-Barnett triumphantly declared her lack of seasickness and her confidence in Patton's medical skill if she should take ill. Three days out, however, Wells-Barnett wrote: "Seasick. So is Georgia E. L. Patton. We...lie in the two lower berths looking at each other. Ugh" (Wells, 88). After nine days they landed in Liverpool and stayed together at the Shaftsbury Hotel until Patton shipped out to Monrovia, the Liberian capital. Despite her missionary beliefs, Patton earned the respect and trust of the Liberians she treated. Initially uncertain how to practice her profession without familiar drugs, instruments, and operating rooms, she adapted rapidly and skillfully, even saving the lives of patients deemed hopeless cases in the local community. She wrote Meharry dean George W. Hubbard that she lost only four patients out of a hundred. After two years she returned to the United States, but not for further medical training as she had planned. She was running out of money and suffering from tuberculosis. She never fully regained her previous vigor.

In 1895 Patton opened a private practice in Memphis, Tennessee. She was the first black woman to hold a Tennessee physician and surgeon's license and to practice medicine in Memphis. Patton married David W. Washington on 29 December 1897. Washington, then forty-five years old and himself an emancipated slave, was the first black postal carrier in the city. Both spouses were active church members and generous philanthropists. The Freedman's Aid Society nicknamed Patton Washington "the Gold Lady" for her regular donations. Nevertheless she once received a thank-you letter addressed "Dear Brother." She wrote back that she was not a brother, enclosed an additional sum, and asked to be addressed as "Dear Sister."

On 14 February 1899 she gave birth to her first child, Willie Patton Washington. He lived less than a day. On 11 July 1900 she had a second son, David W. Washington. Four months later Washington passed away in her home at the age of thirty-six. On 23 November 1900, the infant died. In Zion Christian Cemetery, the original black burial ground in Memphis, Washington and her two babies were laid to rest together under a magnolia tree. Her widower later married a schoolteacher and became a prosperous landowner and businessman. He died in 1930 and was himself buried in Zion.

Ida B. Wells-Barnett lamented that Patton Washington, like her children, never "reached the noonday of life" (Wells, 89). Zion's 22,000 graves on fifteen acres were carefully tended until the 1940s, when the headstones disappeared under tall, profuse brush. During the 1980s the African public health expert HILDRUS AUGUSTUS POINDEXTER testified that Patton Washington was "still remembered among the elders in Liberia" (*Global Dimensions of the African Diaspora, Second Edition*, ed. Joseph L. Harris, 1993, 117). During the early 2000s volunteers from Memphis and from Kent State University in Ohio began to cut away Zion's six decades of woody overgrowth and to revive the names and stories underneath. Citing Patton Washington as their inspiration, some black medical students joined the effort. In January 2005 the graves of Patton Washington and her children were uncovered beneath the still-living magnolia tree.

FURTHER READING

Meharry Medical College holds some archival materials on Georgia E. L. Patton.

Patton, Georgia E. L. "Brief Autobiography of a Colored Woman Who Has Recently Emigrated to Liberia," *Liberia* 3 (Nov. 1893).

DeCosta-Willis, Miriam. "Georgia E. L. Patton," in *Notable Black American Women, Volume One*, ed. Jessie Carney Smith (1992).

Summerville, James. *Educating Black Doctors: A History of Meharry Medical College* (1983).

"Uncovering the Past: Volunteers Tackle Undergrowth at Historic Memphis Cemetery," *Memphis Commercial Appeal*, 25 Mar. 2005.

Wells, Ida B. *Crusade for Justice: The Autobiography of Ida B. Wells*, Alfreda M. Duster, ed. (1970).

MARY KRANE DERR

Patton, Gwen (14 Oct. 1943–), veteran activist in the Black Freedom movement, was born Gwendolyn M. Patton in Inkster, Michigan, the elder of two children of C. Robert Patton Sr., a longtime auto-worker, and Jeanetta Bolden Patton, a homemaker. Her parents migrated from Alabama to the industrial North in order to increase their employment opportunities and raise their children in a freer environment. As a child, Patton looked forward to her annual summer vacations spent with her brother Robert at the home of her paternal grandparents, Sam and Mary Jane Patton, in Montgomery. Following her mother's early death in 1958, she went to live permanently with her grandparents in 1960. She graduated from Carver High School in Montgomery in 1961.

It was during her childhood visits to Montgomery that she first became aware of the system of segregation, which she resisted even as a young person. Although she was required to ride in the back of the public city bus, she was far more offended at not being allowed to drink a glass of water in a downtown restaurant. At age nine, in her first act of public disobedience, she dumped a glass of water onto the counter of the restaurant and stormed out with her brother and cousin in tow.

In the summer of 1956 Patton participated along with her grandparents in the Montgomery bus boycott, which had begun with ROSA PARKS's refusal to give up her seat in December 1955. The Pattons were devoted members of Hutchinson Missionary Baptist Church, one of the activist churches of the boycott, combining their understanding of Christian faith with their membership in the Montgomery Improvement Association (MIA). Sam Patton was among those who traveled to Washington, D.C., to hear the MIA's bus desegregation case then before the Supreme Court. On 13 November 1956 in the historic case of *Browder v. Gayle* the Supreme Court upheld a U.S. District Court ruling against the system of bus segregation. In the meantime, the teenage Patton had witnessed her family and community's commitment to black equality assertively maintained even in the face of black church bombings (including her grandparents' church) and local white intransigence. Patton joined the Black Freedom movement as a consequence of her family's fundamental beliefs and enjoyed their full support throughout her years of activism.

Patton volunteered as an MIA youth worker while still in high school, assisting Montgomery residents in becoming registered voters. She worked as a literacy instructor, which included teaching the Alabama State Constitution geared to help pre–Voting Rights Act (1965) registrants pass Alabama's literacy tests. Patton also worked closely with the Montgomery chapter of the Southern Christian Leadership Conference (SCLC), assisting JAMES BEVEL and James Orange in their youth organizing. She was instrumental in gaining her family's permission to use one of their properties as an office and living space for the SCLC workers. When the Freedom Riders came through Montgomery in the spring of 1961, Patton was there to help receive and rescue them from almost two days of mob violence.

In the fall of 1961 Patton entered college at nearby Tuskegee Institute where she developed her organizing skills in a number of areas. She continued to work closely with the SCLC on weekends in Montgomery, and by her sophomore year had joined the Student Nonviolent Coordinating Committee (SNCC). In her junior year, Patton was elected the first woman student body president and formed her own student cabinet. She and her cabinet met regularly with Tuskegee's president Luther Foster and several of his administrators in order to increase the weight and influence of student voices in school policy. Patton rallied SNCC and other students to a variety of movement activities, including voter registration work in Montgomery and Macon counties. She spearheaded the push to bring the U.S. Communist Party chairman Gus Hall, the radical historian Herbert Aptheker, the Nation of Islam leader ELIJAH MUHAMMAD, and MALCOLM X to speak on campus against stiff administration opposition. She and the other students kept pressure on the administration, which ultimately resulted in Malcolm X's visit to Tuskegee on 3 February 1965 where nearly three thousand students jammed Logan Hall to hear him. At the invitation of SNCC organizers, Malcolm X went on to Selma to speak at Brown Chapel in the run-up to the first attempted Selma-to-Montgomery march (7 March 1965). By its successful conclusion on 25 March 1965 Patton had helped organize some 1,500 Tuskegee student participants.

Working with students affiliated with the Tuskegee Institute Advancement League in 1965 and 1966, Patton and other students, including George Ware, Wendy Paris, and SAMMY YOUNGE JR., led demonstrations and pickets against segregated businesses in the town of Tuskegee. When Foster asked Patton to convince students to cease their picketing, Patton refused and instead invited Foster to participate in the protests, which he declined. She also asked future SNCC leader H. RAP BROWN to help protect Tuskegee students and other demonstrators by calling on the Deacons for Defense and Justice, an armed self-defense organization out of Louisiana. Although the battle to finally integrate Tuskegee businesses and public spaces continued through 1967 and 1968, the large contingent of SNCC and

Tuskegee students had stepped up the pace of black demands while exposing the town's intransigence and calling for more meaningful changes.

Patton also counseled students about the Vietnam War and their potential service in it. In 1965 a campus poll revealed that the majority of students were not in favor of U.S. involvement in Vietnam. However, many students routinely joined the ROTC as a way to afford college tuition. Patton recognized this tendency among the student body and argued in their defense with Bettina Aptheker, a Free Speech movement activist at the University of California Berkeley and antiwar advocate, who was attempting to organize opposition to the ROTC at Tuskegee. Patton continued her draft counseling after graduating with a B.A. in English in 1965.

During the period following graduation Patton was based at various times in Atlanta, Washington, D.C., and New York. In the summer of 1966, Patton helped lead a demonstration against South African apartheid at the South African embassy in Washington, D.C., thus beginning her long involvement with antiapartheid work. Also in 1966 Patton worked for the Southern Student Human Relations Project in Atlanta writing funding grants for SNCC and rooming with STOKELY CARMICHAEL. She found rooming with Carmichael to be an exercise in resisting sexism which she felt plagued the movement by the time of its more nationalist turn in the late 1960s. In the summer of 1967 her antiwar and movement activities were interrupted by a serious automobile accident that cost her full use of her left leg. While undergoing a series of complicated surgeries at New York's Hospital for Bone and Joint Disease, Patton helped organize the formation of Local 1199 of the Hospital Workers Union in the fall of 1967. Allied to her organizing among black workers, she formed an especially close bond at this same time with James Forman, one of the founders of the League of Revolutionary Black Workers and SNCC's former executive secretary. Continuing her convalescence in New York, Patton also worked for a time with George Wiley and the Welfare Rights movement.

Between 1967 and 1971 Patton continued her work in antiwar and student movement organizations despite the occurrence of a second bad accident in 1968 in which she reinjured her left leg. Spending part of her rehabilitation in Harlem, Patton served on the national board of the Student Mobilization Committee, and urged black organizations to speak and act more forcefully against the war in Vietnam. She also suggested that SNCC be more vigorous in forming its antiwar agenda, but contrary to what she expected, did not see it take a leadership position on the issue. In 1968 Patton helped organize the National Black Anti-War Anti-Draft Organization in an effort to develop a locus of activity in the black community similar to her previous organizing around voter registration in Alabama. The organizers, based largely in Northern cities, helped students with deferments, scholarships, and counseling while also educating the wider black community in churches, schools, and community centers about what they saw as the imperialist nature of the U.S.-led war against the Vietnamese. It was important to Patton and the other organizers that black people were able to make the ideological links between themselves and other African, Asian, and Latin American liberation struggles.

Working from within the National Student Association, Patton led other black members in the formation of the National Association of Black Students (NABS) and was elected that body's first president in 1970. In keeping with the current trend of black student union demands across the country at that time, NABS objectives included promoting significantly increased enrollments of black students, particularly on predominantly white college campuses, and enlarged work-study and scholarship opportunities and programs. Also in 1970 Patton published an essay calling for the elimination of the "Victorian Philosophy" from male/female relations in TONI CADE BAMBARA's groundbreaking anthology, *The Black Woman*.

In 1971 Patton left the NABS and earned a master's degree in education from a branch division of Antioch College then located in Washington, D.C. In that same year she also married Jerry Woods, but the marriage was short-lived and ended by 1973. Patton also began teaching English courses at Brooklyn College in 1973. While in New York she worked for a brief period with ANGELA DAVIS and Charlene Mitchell at the National Alliance Against Racism and Political Repression. She traveled with the World Federation of Democratic Youth to Chile in 1971 and to Cuba with the Venceremos Brigades in 1972. Before leaving New York in 1977, Patton had again become involved in antiapartheid work, especially after the students' uprising in Soweto in 1976. During her time in New York, Patton had begun work on a doctorate in political history and higher education administration at the Maryknoll Consortium in Tarrytown, completing all requirements but the dissertation (ABD) in 1979.

Patton returned to Alabama in 1977, intending to help organize Tuskegee Institute's centennial celebration, in which she participated for about six months before beginning a job at Alabama State College. In late 1977 she developed breast cancer, which sidelined her for the period of her recovery. Facing what she saw as sexism and opposition to her brand of progressive politics at Alabama State she fought almost continually to have her contract renewed between 1980 and 1986. In the meantime her political visibility increased. In 1980 Patton joined the Montgomery Board of the League of Women Voters, and in 1981 she became a state Board Member of the Coalition of 100 Black Women. In 1983 she became a member of the National Committee for Independent Political Action, and in 1984 Patton won election as a JESSE JACKSON delegate to the National Democratic Convention in San Francisco. She was a founding member of the Alabama New South Coalition in 1986 and ran for state representative as part of a slate of ANSC candidates in the June 1986 Democratic primary. Also that same year she served on the National Executive Board of the National Political Congress of Black Women.

Patton became the principal archivist at Trenholm State Technical College in Montgomery in 1993. At Trenholm she focused the library's attention and resources on enlarging its collection of Alabama and Montgomery's history of the Black Freedom struggle. In 1996 she became a member of the Friends of the Selma-to-Montgomery National Voting Rights Trail and has been a member of the Advisory Council to the National Historic Trail since its inception in 1998. In 2005 she was one of the principal organizers of the fortieth anniversary celebration of the 1965 Selma-to-Montgomery voting rights march.

FURTHER READING

Patton, Gwen. "Black People and the Victorian Ethos," in *The Black Woman: An Anthology*, ed. Toni Cade (1970).

Gibson Robinson, Jo Ann, with David J. Garrow, eds. *The Montgomery Bus Boycott and the Women Who Started It* (1987).

Norrell, Robert J. *Reaping the Whirlwind: The Civil Rights Movement in Tuskegee* (1985).

PAMELA E. BROOKS

Paul, Emmanuel (2 Feb. 1904–23 May 1988), jazz tenor saxophonist, was born in New Orleans, Louisiana. Nothing is known of his parents, including their names or occupations. The self-taught Emmanuel played various instruments, borrowing, purchasing, and pawning them as circumstances allowed, and sometimes losing them to theft. He began on violin at age eighteen, taking his training in an orchestra organized by a church foundation until the deacon and preacher expelled him for playing at dances and picnics.

Paul worked at a bank for twelve years until 1933, when the bank closed. His first wife—details of the marriage are unknown—disliked the violin and in 1928 bought him a banjo, with which he performed regularly in local bands until around 1935, when he was a member of the trumpeter Louis Dumaine's group. He played with John Robichaux's band at country dances between roughly 1934 and 1939. In 1936 he took up soprano saxophone to join a Works Progress Administration (WPA) band, with which he remained until 1938. At this point he began to hold various day jobs involving manual labor. In about 1939 he joined the local musicians' union to work in a trio with the banjoist Albert French and the drummer Sam Mossey at the Shadowland, and he became an alto saxophonist in the saxophonist Henry Harding's ten-piece band.

Around 1940 Paul switched permanently to tenor saxophone when an opening for that instrument developed in another WPA orchestra. He joined the trumpeter Dominique "T-Boy" Remy's band in 1940, and through Remy he secured his first job of lasting significance, as a member of the Eureka Brass Band, the leadership of which passed from Remy to the trumpeter Percy Humphrey. Paul took over on tenor sax the parts usually played by the baritone horn, as in "Westlawn Dirge," taped at a rehearsal of the Eureka band in 1951. Paul remained with this brass band for more than three decades and during this time participated in the making of their few issued recordings, including the album *Jazz at Preservation Hall, I: The Eureka Brass Band of New Orleans* (1962).

From 1943 to 1947 Paul played three nights a week at the Moulin Rouge in New Orleans in the trumpeter KID THOMAS VALENTINE's band. At first he worked by day sewing and stacking food sacks for the navy, but after suffering from a stomach illness and losing all of his upper teeth in 1945 he gave up all work except music. "'Good old days?' Hard time days. They wasn't good for me, not all of them. Bad, tough coming up," he told the writer William Carter (77).

In 1948 Paul's appendix ruptured, and he was never quite well afterward, experiencing chronic back pain and becoming fatigued easily. Nonetheless his musical career flourished. Permanent work with Valentine included regular performances at Preservation Hall, from its opening in 1961 into the 1980s, and numerous albums, including *New Orleans Today: A Jazz Document* (1957), *Kid Thomas Valentine's Creole Jazz Band* (1959), and *Kid Thomas Valentine and His Algiers Stompers in Lugano* (1983).

Paul recorded with the trumpeter PAPA CELESTIN in 1953 and with the banjoist and guitarist Emanuel Sayles in 1961, and at an unknown time he played in the band of the trumpeter George "Kid Sheik" Colar. While with Valentine he doubled from at least 1966 to 1976 with Harold Dejan's Olympia Brass Band, making several recordings and touring Europe in 1967 and 1968. In 1979 he performed in the Soviet Union on a tour sponsored by the U.S. State Department.

Paul died in New Orleans. He was survived by his second wife and two children; details of his second marriage and of whether these children were from his first or second marriage are unknown.

The writer Paige Van Vorst recalled that "Paul was one of the most cheerful, easy-to-get-along-with musicians in the business. One always felt he was glad to see you. He always seemed 'on' and never appeared to coast or play less than well....He was a good cook and loved good food" (*Mississippi Rag*, July 1988).

Although the stereotypical "front line" of instrumentalists in the New Orleans jazz revival comprises trumpet (or cornet), clarinet, and trombone, assorted saxophones have made their own substantial contributions. In this setting Paul was the leading exponent of the tenor saxophone. Characteristically, he used his instrument as a substitute for the trombone (and in brass bands, for the baritone horn), or he supplied an additional part, adding density to collective improvisations and taking solos. Like that of numerous other New Orleans reed players, Paul's sound featured a heavily pronounced, rapidly quavering vibrato. His devotedly simple and old-fashioned approach to melody was largely independent of the principal traditions of jazz tenor saxophone playing.

FURTHER READING

Carter, William. *Preservation Hall: Music from the Heart* (1991).

Charters, Samuel B. *Jazz: New Orleans 1885–1963, An Index to the Negro Musicians of New Orleans*, rev. ed. (1983).

Obituaries: *New York Times*, 23 May 1988; *Mississippi Rag* 15 (July 1988); *Footnote* 19 (Aug.–Sept. 1988).

This entry is taken from the *American National Biography* and is published here with the permission of the American Council of Learned Societies.

BARRY KERNFELD

Paul, Nathaniel (?–18 Sept. 1839), abolitionist and minister, was born in New Hampshire, probably in Exeter, Rockingham County, to unidentified parents. His brother, THOMAS PAUL, became a minister and community leader in Boston, Massachusetts. The Free Will Baptist Church educated both black and white youths, and Paul may have been a student with his brother at its academy in Hollis, New Hampshire. In 1820 he became pastor of the First African Baptist Church in Albany, New York. Influenced by evangelicals and reformers, northern New York was a hotbed of abolitionist activity on the part of both blacks and whites. New York had extirpated slavery gradually, first, in 1799, legislating that all blacks born to slave mothers on or after 4 July 1799 would be indentured servants and then, in 1817, declaring that all slaves born before 4 July 1799 would be freed on 4 July 1827.

In an 1827 address Paul criticized the slave trade and slavery, celebrated the 1817 law, and named all ninety-five elected New York State officials who had voted for the emancipation act. Like many African Americans in the 1820s, he supported the resettlement of free blacks when it seemed likely to foster social and economic progress, but he opposed the American Colonization Society (ACS), which promoted the expatriation of manumitted slaves to Liberia—an action that most abolitionists believed fortified American slavery. In 1824 Thomas Paul visited Haiti, which was then being touted as a place African Americans might relocate, but he returned to Boston. In 1830 Nathaniel Paul, with his brother Benjamin, resettled in a free black community, Wilberforce, being constructed in Lucan, Ontario, Canada. In 1832 he commenced a speaking tour of England, Ireland, and Scotland, seeking funds for a manual labor academy at Wilberforce and countering propaganda spread by an ACS agent, Elliott Cresson. Cresson was exaggerating the antislavery thrust of the ACS as he sought to gain support for colonization in British abolitionist and political circles.

Paul cooperated with the noted abolitionist William Lloyd Garrison, another opponent of the ACS, in touring Britain, but a rift between the two men occurred when Paul provided funds for Garrison's journey home to the United States. Paul considered the money a personal loan, while Garrison insisted that it was an expense of their joint abolitionist activities. Paul remained in Britain until 1836, marrying an Englishwoman in 1833 and meeting the most prominent figures in British abolitionism. Upon returning to Wilberforce, at the request of its leader, AUSTIN STEWARD, Paul revealed that although he had collected more than $8,000 in British donations, he had nothing to remit, since his expenses of $7,000 and his $50 monthly salary totaled more than $9,000. In 1836 Paul returned to Albany, where he became pastor of the Hamilton Street Baptist Church. Poverty marked the last three years of his life.

Several addresses and letters written by Paul survive. His *Address, Delivered on the Celebration of the Abolition of Slavery, in the State of New York* (1827) noted the oppression and the pernicious influence on society of slaveholding. Paul denounced the persistence of slavery in a republican nation that had been forged in revolution. He praised the American revolutionaries, arguing that slavery was a legacy of colonialism that had improperly survived in the new nation. Addresses, letters, and reports recounting his experience in Britain suggest that he was a gifted author and dynamic orator who effectively countered ACS propaganda as well as soliciting donations for what seemed to be the benefit of African Americans. He proved to be a popular lecturer, and he claimed to prefer English to American life. In this he was not alone, for Henry Nell, the African Canadian sent from Wilberforce by Steward to demand Paul's return, did not himself leave England after accomplishing his errand. Moreover, Paul was in England during parliamentary discussion of West Indian emancipation and the enactment of the Emancipation Act of 1833; his letters to American abolitionists provided information about these momentous events.

Although he was a celebrated figure in the transatlantic abolitionist movement, Paul was also a citizen of Wilberforce and should be viewed in its context. In 1829 black residents of Cincinnati, Ohio, began plans for a mass exodus to Canada. Discriminatory state laws and antiblack riots in 1829 had made many of them pessimistic about their future in the United States. Ohio and Indiana Quakers donated funds for the purchase of land, and the first settlers arrived in Wilberforce in October 1829, followed by members of the Paul family in 1830. Although the settlement was praised at a distance by leading abolitionists, it probably never held more than two hundred inhabitants (one thousand blacks left Cincinnati in 1829–1830, but many settled instead in nearby towns), and it

seemed a failure to most sympathetic people who visited it.

Expectations of settlers and abolitionists alike were high, but Wilberforce itself faltered. Schools were open only irregularly. Emigrants from the city of Cincinnati proved unable to farm productively. The officials of the settlement continually bickered over allegations of misuse of funds, questions of representation of the settlers for the purpose of fund-raising, and accusations of moral improprieties. By the 1850s Wilberforce was home to only about fifty people. The lack of a monetary return from Paul's tour and his retreat to Albany in 1836 were symptomatic of the larger problems of resettling people who had been harassed from their homes and of securing competent leadership for a community attempting to reconstitute itself as it fled from racism, inequality, and violence. Paul was a gifted man who fought racism and slavery but who was unable to square his self-interest and the needs of the black community that employed him.

FURTHER READING

Transcriptions of Nathaniel Paul's speeches and his letters from Britain, in which he relayed information about his speaking tour, appeared in the *Liberator* (1831–1865), William Lloyd Garrison's abolitionist newspaper, published in Boston. His speeches and letters have been reprinted in *The Black Abolitionist Papers, Volume 1: The British Isles, 1830–1865*, ed. C. Peter Ripley, et al.(1985): 42–59.

Mitchell, J. Marcus. "The Paul Family," in *Old-Time New England* (1973), 73–77.

Pease, William H., and Jane H. Pease. *Black Utopia: Negro Communal Experiments in America* (1963), 46–62.

Taylor, Nikki. "Reconsidering the 'Forced' Exodus of 1829: Free Black Emigration from Cincinnati, Ohio, to Wilberforce, Canada," *Journal of African American History* 87 (Summer 2002): 283–302.

JOHN SAILLANT

Paul, Robert Austin (3 Nov. 1846–1902), soldier and politician, was born to literate slaves in Nelson County, Virginia. As a young man Paul was taught how to read by his mother, father, and grandfather, Richard Madison. In 1852 he was sold to a neighboring slave owner, abruptly ending his lessons until after the Civil War. Following the Civil War Paul took a job in a hotel (perhaps in Richmond or Petersburg) but managed to pursue informal studies under the supervision of his mother; within a short time Paul was reading on such subjects as ancient history and pursuing law through *Blackstone's Commentaries*. All the while he expressed an interest in a political career.

Paul eventually joined the Republican Party, though he played no active role until 1874, when he ran unsuccessfully for Congress against Virginia's former Democratic governor, Gilbert C. Walker. Even as Republicans struggled to counter Virginia's Conservative Party, Paul remained active by supporting Rutherford B. Hayes against Samuel Tilden in the presidential election of 1876. Two years later he supported W. W. Newman in his unsuccessful bid for Congress against the former Confederate general Joseph E. Johnston. In addition Paul was appointed bailiff in 1877 and commissioned U.S. deputy marshall in 1880.

Paul's political and public prominence was due in large part to the formation and success of the Readjuster Party in 1879, led by the former Confederate major general William Mahone. The rise of the Readjusters was spurred by the question of what to do about Virginia's state debt, which totaled $45 million in 1870—the result of internal improvements made during the antebellum years. The Readjusters included black and white Republicans along with disgruntled Democrats like Mahone. They advocated scaling back the debt (or readjusting it) and supporting the state's commitment to public education. By 1881 the Readjusters had control of the legislature and elected their own governor. Paul was slow to speak out in support of the Readjusters, but after election to the Republican State Convention in 1880 called for a union with the biracial party. On 14 March 1881 Virginia's black Republicans, including Paul, met in Petersburg and decided to support the Readjusters. In June of that year Paul served as a delegate to the Readjuster State Convention in Richmond and supported William Cameron for governor. In addition, the State Executive Committee appointed Paul to the position of campaign orator—one of only a handful of black Readjusters appointed to such a position.

Once in power the Readjusters adjusted the state debt downward to $21 million, leaving sufficient funds for public schools, the hiring of black teachers, and even a hospital for mentally ill African Americans in Petersburg. In 1882 Paul was appointed by Governor Cameron to the position of "Doorkeeper to the Executive or Messenger to the Governor and Secretary of the Commonwealth." He was the first black man to occupy this position. That same year Paul campaigned vigorously for the Readjusters in the congressional elections on a platform calling for black suffrage, free education, and acknowledgment of the provisions contained in the Fourteenth Amendment. Along with the rest of the Readjusters he worked to abolish the poll tax and the whipping post, both of which had been used to limit the black vote. The General Assembly passed legislation supporting a Literary Fund and appropriated funds for black public schools. In 1882 Paul was elected to the Richmond school board. Under his leadership black enrollment soared between 1881 and 1884, and the state mandated equal pay for black and white teachers. In addition, Paul helped appoint three black men to the position of principal, and thirty-four new black teachers were selected to fill schools previously occupied by white teachers.

The end of Readjuster control of Virginia's state government in 1883 also ended Paul's political influence. Paul participated in the Readjuster Convention of 1884 and joined with others in aligning themselves with the Republican Party; in 1888 Paul joined the "Anti-Mahone" faction at the Republican State Convention. With the demise of the Readjuster Party, Paul continued to work to improve the social standing of Virginia's African American population. In 1883 Paul helped subsidize the *Richmond Planet*, which was in publication for forty-five years and edited by JOHN MITCHELL JR. Paul also remained involved with Lodge no. 2 of the black Knights of Pythias, which he founded in 1882 in Richmond. In addition to these roles, Paul commanded the black militia unit, the Richmond State Guard, from 1878 to 1891. The unit was deployed by Governor Fitzhugh Lee in 1878 to Newport News to put down a strike that included black longshoremen.

Paul's brief but active political career serves as a reminder that Virginia's black population achieved notable success in the public sphere between Reconstruction and the more stringent segregation codes and practices that would define the Jim Crow South by the turn of the century.

FURTHER READING

Alexander, Anne F. *Race Man: The Rise and Fall of the "Fighting Editor" John Mitchell Jr.* (2002).

Blake, Nelson M. *William Mahone of Virginia: Soldier and Political Insurgent* (1935).

Dailey, Jane. *Before Jim Crow: The Politics of Race in Postemancipation Virginia* (2000).

Williams, D. B. *A Sketch of the Life and Times of Capt. R. A. Paul* (1885).

KEVIN M. LEVIN

Paul, Susan (1809–19 Apr. 1841), activist, author, and educator, was born in Boston to the minister Thomas Paul and the teacher Catherine Waterhouse. Her father, whose brothers Nathaniel and Benjamin were also activist clergymen, was the pastor of Boston's first black church (on Belknap Street), and his religious and abolitionist fervor sent him as far as Haiti to advance these causes. It also linked him with both prominent blacks such as DAVID WALKER and MARIA STEWART and important white abolitionists such as William Lloyd Garrison. Her mother, Catherine Waterhouse Paul, became the director of Boston's African School Number 2 (later Boston Primary School Number 6) in 1824 and was a force both in and for black education.

Given her parents' positions of leadership in the community, the Paul family was solidly middle class. That changed abruptly when Thomas Paul died of tuberculosis in 1831. For the rest of Paul's life, the family struggled financially, and depended greatly on Paul, the eldest daughter, for economic support. Although she did not receive as much education as her younger brother Thomas Jr., who earned a degree from Dartmouth, Paul had, by this time, gained both a rich love of reading, writing, and music and a solid foundation in activism. She was also already teaching by the early 1820s; it seems most likely that she started such work as a kind of apprentice to her mother, whom she eventually succeeded at the African School. In addition to teaching in black primary schools, both she and her sister, Anne Catherine, were active in the Sabbath School at the Belknap Street Church.

For Paul, education, faith, abolition, and community uplift were deeply intertwined, as was evidenced by her formation in 1832 of a Juvenile Choir, which was largely made up of her students at Boston Primary School Number 6. The group performed at least seven times over the next three years to raise funds for the Garrisonian New England Anti-Slavery Society as well as to promote relief efforts for the Mashpee tribe of Native Americans.

Paul's educational philosophy seems to have emphasized such linkages, too. When, in the summer of 1833, she allowed a group from the New England Anti-Slavery Society to observe her classroom, it was with the clear hope that their reports could aid black education. Paul's activism went beyond her teaching. Within the black community, in addition to a number of church activities, she served as the first secretary of the all-black Ladies Temperance Society. Her intellect and connections within the abolitionist community also led her to participate in efforts that crossed racial lines. In 1833, the same year that the New England Anti-Slavery Society group visited her classes, she became the first woman—white or black—to purchase a lifetime membership in the Society (at the notable cost of $15).

The next year, when the Boston Female Anti-Slavery Society made the decision to integrate—under pressure from Garrison—Paul was the first African American invited to join. Soon after she was appointed "counselor." Her most long-lasting contribution to the struggle was the eighty-eight-page *Memoir of James Jackson, the Attentive and Obedient Scholar who Died in Boston, October 31, 1833, Aged Six Years and Eleven Months*, published in 1835 by the abolitionist James Loring. The volume opened with the bold assertion that "the design of this Memoir is, to present the incidents in the life of a little colored boy" hoping to "do something towards breaking down that unholy prejudice which exists against color." The book also aimed to provide young black students with a text that demonstrated that they could be the equals of white children. In all of these goals, Paul was probably consciously responding not only to generalized racism but also to the specific events surrounding Prudence Crandall's work to educate black children (Crandall and Paul, both members of the NEAAS, undoubtedly met at NEAAS events). Excerpts from the *Memoir* were published in the *Liberator*.

In 1837 Paul was chosen as a delegate to the Women's Anti-Slavery Convention, a group that elected her a vice president the next year. Her Juvenile Choir also returned to the stage at least twice in 1837, and the concerts were covered by Garrison's abolitionist newspaper the *Liberator* and seem to have been both popular and challenging for audiences: Paul's choir forthrightly sang not just abolitionist songs but also songs like "The Little Wanderer's Song" that idealized domesticity and drew clear links to the period's representations of white childhood. In 1840 she was a BFASS delegate to the American Anti-Slavery Society's annual meeting, a role she shared with, among others, well-known abolitionist writer Lydia Maria Child. While the BFASS was consistently troubled by the question of integration and by factional splits around Garrisonian politics, Paul seems to have consistently maintained the respect of her white colleagues without changing her principles. She stood with white members of the society in 1835 when a mob threatened them on the eve of a lecture by British abolitionist George Thompson (an event that some historians have suggested nearly led to the lynching of Garrison)—even though her race would have placed her in heightened danger.

As Paul's prominence in the movement increased, though, her home life worsened. Her sister Anne died in June 1835, leaving Paul and her aging mother to care for Anne's four children. In addition to teaching, she began to take in sewing, but consistently struggled for basic sustenance. Sometime during the late 1830s, she was engaged—though her fiancé's name has not yet been discovered—but her fiancé died of tuberculosis in 1840. Paul's health was also in decline: while working a table at the December 1840 BFASS Fair, she had to be carried from the floor to the sickroom. She never recovered, and she herself died from tuberculosis months later.

FURTHER READING

Paul, Susan. *Memoir of James Jackson* (2000).

Brown, Lois. "Out of the Mouths of Babes: The Abolitionist Campaign of Susan Paul and the Juvenile Choir of Boston," *New England Quarterly* (Mar. 2002).

Hansen, Debra Gold. *Strained Sisterhood: Gender and Class in the Boston Female Anti-Slavery Society* (1993).

Obituary: The *Liberator*, 23 Apr. 1841.

ERIC GARDNER

Paul, Thomas (3 Sept. 1773–13 Apr. 1831), Baptist minister and community leader, was born in Exeter, New Hampshire. The names of his parents are unknown. Converted and baptized at age sixteen Paul began preaching when he was about twenty-eight and conducted an itinerant ministry. In 1804 he settled in Boston. He was ordained on 1 May 1805 at Nottingham West, New Hampshire, and later the same year married Catherine Waterhouse. The couple had three children.

A number of African Americans in Boston attended white Baptist churches, but they were assigned seats in the galleries and could not vote on church affairs. Recognizing their desire for more religious freedom Paul conducted nondenominational meetings for them first in Franklin Hall on Nassau Street and later in historic Faneuil Hall.

In 1805 these black Baptists decided to form an independent congregation that became known variously as the African Church and First African. Twenty-four members met on 8 August in Master Vinal's schoolhouse and formed the earliest independent black Baptist church in the North. Boston's two white Baptist churches assisted the African Church in its early stage of development. The congregation occupied a three-story brick building in Smith Court near Belknap Street. The church was dedicated two days after Paul's installation as pastor on 4 December 1806. In 1812 the church, now known as First African, became a charter member of the Boston Baptist Association. By 1819 First African had more than one hundred members.

Paul also assisted other congregations and worked to improve the conditions of African Americans in Boston and elsewhere. He went to New York City to help organize the Abyssinian Baptist Church, the first independent black Baptist congregation in that city. He conducted revivals for the Home Mission Society and traveled as far as Haiti to preach and do missionary work. Paul's own congregation apparently enjoyed good relations with white Baptists in Boston during his ministry, and overt discrimination against the church seems to have been minimal. The First African Church was an important center of religious and civic activity for Boston's African American community. Paul's congregation hosted the abolitionist William Lloyd Garrison and other social reformers active in the Boston area.

Paul served the church for twenty-five years, resigning in 1829 because of ill health. One hundred persons were baptized during his tenure. The membership had reached 139 by the time of his resignation. Invoking the language of 1 Corinthians 3:6 [AV], Paul said of the early history of the African Church, "I planted the seed and Apollos watered it, but God made it grow." Internal controversy erupted in about 1835 between church conservatives and activists over involvement in the abolitionist cause. The controversy had been precipitated in part by disagreement over the publication in 1829 of DAVID WALKER's *Appeal*. Walker, a member of Boston's black Baptist community, advocated armed insurrection on the part of the slaves and was especially critical of the Christian churches and clergy for not taking a stronger stance against slavery. Paul, already retired, avoided taking a stand on his friend Walker's *Appeal*.

The exact nature of the difficulties that Paul encountered near the end of his pastorate may never be known. Some sources suggest that members of First African became troubled by Paul's frequent absences on missionary trips. Others surmise that pastor and people had differences over how strongly to become involved in radical protest politics. Some members apparently favored integration, while others advocated separation and the creation of more black-controlled institutions. Because Paul retired from active involvement in the church, he was not a principal in the split in 1840 that resulted in the formation of what became known as Twelfth Baptist Church.

Paul died in Boston. An obituary in Garrison's abolitionist paper, the *Liberator*, read, "His fame, as a preacher, is exceedingly prevalent; for his eloquence charmed the ear, and his piety commended itself to his hearers." Despite his resignation apparently under fire, Paul is remembered as the father of Boston's black Baptist community and as a pioneering leader in the creation of independent black Baptist churches in the North.

FURTHER READING

Horton, Oliver, and Lois E. Horton. *Black Bostonians: Family Life and Community Struggle in the Antebellum North* (1979).

Levesque, George A. *Black Boston: African American Life and Culture in Urban America, 1750–1860* (1994).

Levesque, George A. "Inherent Reformers—Inherited Orthodoxy: Black Baptists in Boston, 1800–1873," *Journal of Negro History* 60 (Oct. 1975).

Piersen, William D. *Black Yankees: The Development of an Afro-American Subculture in Eighteenth-Century New England* (1988).

Obituaries: *Liberator*, 16 Apr. 1831; *American Baptist Magazine* (July 1831).

This entry is taken from the *American National Biography* and is published here with the permission of the American Council of Learned Societies.

MILTON C. SERNETT

Payne, Adam (1843–1 Jan. 1877), Seminole Negro Scout and Medal of Honor Recipient, was a native of Florida. While nothing specific is known about Payne's life prior to his military service, his ancestors were formerly enslaved before running away and seeking refuge with the friendly Seminole Tribe in Florida. Indeed, the Seminoles treated the large number of black runaways that sought freedom so well that many became assimilated within the tribe, adopting its language and culture. When Payne left Florida for the southwest is unknown; he may, as several biographers claim, have been among the last group of native peoples that traveled on the Trail of Tears after 1842 when the U.S. government forcibly expelled most of the remaining Seminole Tribe after the end of the long-running Seminole War to territory in what is now Oklahoma.

Payne began his military service on 12 November 1873, enlisting in the U.S. Army as an Indian Scout at Fort Duncan, Texas, for a period of six months. The Seminole Negro Scouts were a unique unit in the army; as their name implies, the majority of the men had a mixed African American and Seminole heritage. Though scouts like Payne did not always conform to traditional army discipline and preferred short enlistment periods, they were excellent trackers, horsemen, and fighters, and were vital in the army's efforts to subdue the Native American tribes of the southwest during a period of major westward expansion. Payne's military service would be brief—in fact one of the shortest among all African American Medal of Honor recipients—and he quickly earned not only a reputation as a "Bad Man" (Schubert, p. 32), but also as a brave and valiant soldier.

On 1 June 1874 Payne signed up for a final six months of service at Fort Clark, Texas. On 20 September of that year Payne was serving with Colonel Ranald Mackenzie's 4th Cavalry Regiment, performing advance scouting duties at Canyon Blanco, Texas, when he and three or four (accounts vary) other scouts were attacked by a group of twenty-five Comanche Indians. During this engagement, Payne, who was wearing a buffalo horn headdress, led the fight by killing one warrior on the first attack, and later fought six Comanche warriors at one time before the scouts could finally break free and return back to camp. Calling Payne "a scout of great courage" (Hanna, p. 79), Colonel Mackenzie recommended Payne for the Medal of Honor (misspelling his last name as "Paine").

The service of Seminole Negro Scouts, men like Adam Payne, ISAAC PAYNE, and JOHN WARRIOR, has been largely forgotten, but deserves wider recognition. The valorous deeds that earned them the Medal of Honor on their own makes them worthy of remembrance, and the overall service of these scouts to army operations during the period of the Indian Wars from the 1870s to 1890 was extremely valuable. However, the service of the Seminole Negro Scouts has also been viewed as culturally contradictive by modern historians; how is one to explain the scout's participation in the subjugation and removal of native peoples from their homeland, a traumatic event that the families of the Seminole Negro Scouts themselves had suffered some thirty years earlier? There is no easy explanation as the thoughts of the scouts on this matter, if voiced at all, have not been recorded for posterity.

Payne left the army for good when his second term of service expired on 19 February 1875, a short time after his Medal of Honor heroics. By the following year Payne was a wanted man, accused of murdering another black soldier in Brownsville, Texas. Payne was subsequently killed in Brackettsville, Texas, the home community of the Seminole Negro Scouts, by a sheriff's deputy while attending a New Year's Eve party. The deputy, who had been searching for Payne after the Brownsville murder, made no attempt to capture Payne, who was executed at close range, shot in the back with a double-barrel shotgun. Adam Payne is buried in the Seminole Indian Scout Cemetery in Brackettville, Texas.

FURTHER READING

Hanna, Charles W. *African American Recipients of the Medal of Honor* (2002).

Schubert, Frank N. *Black Valor: Buffalo Soldiers and the Medal of Honor, 1870–1898* (1997).

GLENN ALLEN KNOBLOCK

Payne, Christopher Harrison (7 Sept. 1848–5 Dec. 1925), minister, educator, editor, and West Virginia's first black legislator, was born near Red Sulfur Springs in Monroe County, Virginia. His father, Thomas Payne, was freeborn, and his mother, Bersheba, was a former slave who was set free by her owner and rumored father, James Ellison, before her marriage. Christopher was their only child; Thomas died from smallpox after taking a drove of cattle to Baltimore, Maryland, when Christopher was still young.

Payne's mother provided his early education. He worked as a farmhand, but when the Civil War began, Payne—as a free, unprotected black in a slave state—found himself forced to become a servant in the Confederate army. He left the service in 1864 and went to the southern part of Monroe County (later Summers) and worked for Mr. Vincent Swinney until the war ended. It was there that he met and married his wife, Ann Hargo. In 1866 Payne left home and family to seek better wages in nearby Charleston, West Virginia. He took a job working on steamboats, traveling to Ohio and Kentucky for several months and then returning to Charleston to work and attend night school. After almost fifteen months of absence, Payne returned to his family in Monroe County and began teaching school during the winters in Monroe, Mercer, and Summers counties and farming in the summer.

A Baptist, Payne obtained a license to preach in February 1876 and was ordained in May 1877. That September Payne passed his preliminary exams at Richmond Theological Institute in Richmond, Virginia, and entered the senior class of the Preparatory Department. After his first year at the institute, in the spring of 1878 Payne returned to West Virginia and spent the next several years working as well as preaching. During that time, Payne organized Baptist churches and Sunday schools. In the fall of 1880 he returned to the Richmond Theological Institute, where he remained for three years. Payne preached at the Moore Street Baptist Church in Richmond and attended classes during the week, while supporting his wife, his five children, his mother, and his grandmother. While he was in Richmond, the American Baptist Publication Society of Philadelphia, Pennsylvania, appointed Payne missionary for the eastern district of Virginia.

Payne graduated from the institute in 1883 and spent the next nine months preaching, lecturing, and organizing Sunday schools and Sunday school unions across Virginia in major cities including Norfolk, Alexandria, Danville, and Staunton. In January 1884, overworked and ill, Payne resigned from the Society position, and in the spring returned to West Virginia, where he took charge of the First Baptist Church in Coal Valley. He played a key role in the organization of the West Virginia Baptist State Convention and served as its first president. Appointed corresponding secretary and agent for the convention, Payne planned to establish higher education for African Americans in the state and worked to raise money and secure property for a school.

In addition to his ministerial duties, Payne founded or edited three weekly newspapers in West Virginia. In 1885 Payne co-founded the *West Virginia Enterprise,* published in Charleston. His other two papers were the *Pioneer*, published in Huntington, and the *Mountain Eagle*, published in Montgomery. All of the papers were politically Republican and were short-lived.

Payne's own political career began when he served as an alternate delegate to the Republican National Convention in 1884. In 1888 Payne represented West Virginia at the Republican National Convention, and later served as a delegate to three other Republican National Conventions. After he was appointed the deputy collector of internal revenue at Charleston, West Virginia, in 1890, Fayette County voters elected Payne to serve as their representative to the West Virginia legislature in 1896;

he thus became the first black to serve in the West Virginia House of Delegates. Republican Party leaders rewarded Payne for his work and loyalty with two federal patronage jobs.

Payne also earned a law degree in Washington, D.C., while serving as deputy collector of internal revenue, and in 1903 President Theodore Roosevelt appointed him as consul general to the Danish West Indies (later the U.S. Virgin Islands). Payne held this position until 1917 when the United States purchased the islands. Following his retirement from federal service, the citizens of St. Thomas elected Payne prosecuting attorney and judge advocate, and he remained in the islands until his death.

FURTHER READING

There are no manuscript collections available on Payne. His letters appear in the collections of West Virginia governors and in the pages of the *Richmond Examiner*, published by John Mitchell, and the *McDowell Times*, published by Matthew T. Whittico and Tyler Edward Hill.

Posey, Thomas E. *The Negro Citizen of West Virginia* (1934).

Simmons, William J. *Men of Mark* (1887).

CONNIE PARK RICE

Payne, Daniel Alexander (24 Feb. 1811–2 Nov. 1893), minister and educator, was born in Charleston, South Carolina, the son of London Payne, a free African American, and Martha (maiden name unknown), a Catawba Indian, both of whom died in the early 1820s. For two years he attended the Minor's Moralist Society School; he then continued his education with a tutor and through extensive independent reading. He joined the Methodist Episcopal Church in 1826.

Payne established a school for blacks in 1828 but closed it in 1834 when South Carolina outlawed education for slaves. Moving to Gettysburg, Pennsylvania, in 1835, Payne studied on a scholarship at the Lutheran Theological Seminary, but failing eyesight forced him to leave before graduation. He was licensed to preach in 1837 and ordained in 1839, thus becoming the first African American minister in the Franckean Evangelical Lutheran Synod. In 1840 he opened a second school for African Americans, through which he was introduced to the African Methodist Episcopal (AME) Church. He left the Franckean Church in 1841— partly because of its reluctance to give an African American minister the responsibility for a parish— and joined the AME Church.

Serious ideological differences quickly became evident between Payne and the AME Church; he favored a formal service conducted by educated ministers, while many of the AME's members opposed an educated clergy and preferred an emotional, evangelical style of worship. Payne was assigned first to the Israel Bethel Church in Washington, D.C., then to the Bethel Church and later the Ebenezer Church in Baltimore. In addition to the usual duties of a pastor, he worked to standardize the AME service, to keep records of church history, and to improve religious education. Although initial resistance to his attempts to educate the clergy was strong, by 1844 the General Conference had accepted his recommendation to standardize a course of study for all ministers.

In 1850 Payne published *Pleasures and Other Miscellaneous Poems*. Elected a bishop in 1852, Payne worked to expand the church's home and overseas mission programs, especially those involving newly freed slaves. This later led to rapid growth in the church's membership in the postwar South. Payne had married Julia A. Ferris in 1847. After her death, he married Eliza J. Clark in 1853.

In 1863 Payne purchased and became president of Wilberforce University in Ohio, the first African American–controlled college in the United States. He facilitated the growth of the university by raising standards for both students and faculty and by improving its financial stability. While visiting South Carolina in 1865, Payne founded the South Carolina Conference of the AME Church, which was to play an important role in the denomination's expansion in the South. In 1866 he published his church history, *Semi-Centenary and the Retrospection of the African Methodist Episcopal Church in the United States of America*. He resigned the presidency of Wilberforce in 1876 and became chancellor and dean of the theological school, positions he held until his death.

A prolific author, Payne wrote numerous poems, essays, speeches, and sermons. In later life he published his autobiography, *Recollections of Seventy Years* (1888), as well as *Treatise on Domestic Education* (1885) and *History of the African Methodist Episcopal Church* (1891). His last public appearance was at the World Parliament of Religions at the World's Columbian Exposition in Chicago in 1893. He died in Xenia, Ohio, a few weeks later.

Payne's importance lies in his contributions to the history of African Americans in the nineteenth century and the history of the African Methodist

Episcopal Church. He also played a significant role in the expansion of educational opportunities for African Americans, both before and after emancipation.

FURTHER READING

Payne, Daniel Alexander. *Recollections of Seventy Years* (1888).

Coan, Josephus R. *Daniel Alexander Payne: Christian Educator* (1935).

Smith, C. S. *The Life of Daniel Alexander Payne* (1891).

This entry is taken from the *American National Biography* and is published here with the permission of the American Council of Learned Societies.

ELIZABETH ZOE VICARY

Payne, Donald Milford (16 July 1934–3 Mar. 2012), politician, financial executive, and educator, was born in Newark, New Jersey, the son of William Evander, a dock worker, and Norma Garrett Payne. Payne completed high school at Barringer High School in Newark, New Jersey, graduating in 1952. During Payne's childhood he lived in a predominately white area of Newark where the sight of a professional black man was rare. As Payne commented to Joseph F. Sullivan in a *New York Times* article, "I didn't have a black teacher all through elementary and high school until my senior year." Growing up in a working-class family Payne became aware of the limited economic opportunities for minorities. That experience influenced his desire to improve the economic condition, not only of his neighbors in Newark, but also of people throughout the world. Payne went on to graduate from Seton Hall University with a Bachelor's in Social Studies degree in 1957. He later pursued a graduate degree at Springfield College in Massachusetts. Payne did not complete the graduate program at Springfield College; however, he holds honorary doctorates from Chicago State University in Illinois, Drew University in New Jersey, Essex County College in New Jersey, and William Patterson University in New Jersey.

In the early 1960s Payne began doing community work with the Young Men's Christian Association (YMCA). He organized self-help projects geared toward creating leaders within the Newark community. Payne brought together local gang members and adult volunteers in an effort to strengthen and unite the community. During this time Payne's wife, Hazel Payne, died of cancer (1963). Payne raised his two children, Donald Milford Payne Jr. and Wanda. He did not remarry.

In 1970 Payne became the first black President of the YMCA. Three years later, in 1973, he was elected chairman of the YMCA's World Refugee and Rehabilitation Committee, a position that allowed him to instill leadership qualities through the creation of self-help projects spanning over more than eighty countries. His political career began in 1972 when he was elected to the Essex County Board of Chosen Freeholders, where he served three terms. He also served three terms on the Newark Municipal Council between 1982 and 1988.

In 1980 and 1986 he ran against longtime Congressional incumbent Peter W. Rodino Jr. in the Democratic primary but was defeated both times. When Rodino retired in 1988 after forty years in Congress Payne defeated Ralph T. Grant Jr., a fellow Newark councilman in the Democratic primary, for New Jersey's 10th District and made history by being the first African American elected to Congress from New Jersey. In subsequent elections he was reelected to Congress by wide margins.

In 2002 Payne ran against a Republican opponent, gaining 84.5 percent of the vote, winning the highest margin of the vote in any New Jersey Congressional race. In 2002 House Minority Leader Nancy Pelosi chose Payne as a member of the Democratic Steering Committee. The Democratic Steering Committee seeks to foster dialogue between Senate Democrats and community leaders on critical issues such as but not limited to energy independence, affordable health care, and quality education. The Democratic Steering Committee also plays a pivotal role in Democratic legislative agenda. In Congress, Payne secured billions of dollars for economic development and other essential programs for his constituents in Essex, Hudson, and Union counties.

Both inside and outside of Congress Payne was active and influential in international relations, particularly issues related to Africa. In 2003 President George W. Bush appointed Payne to serve as a Congressional delegate to the United Nations. He was reappointed in 2005 to a second term. In his role as a Congressional delegate to the United Nations, Payne regularly attended United Nations sessions, General Assembly sessions, and other high-level meetings. In 2007 he authored the House bill, HR-2003 (Ethiopia Democracy and Accountability Act). The bill's main goal was to promote human rights and accountability in Ethiopia but it was regarded by many, including the President of Addis Ababa University in Ethiopia, Andreas

Eshete, as unfair and based on misconceptions about Ethiopia. However, Payne was determined to pass the bill and delivered an impassioned speech on the floor of the House, in which he outlined the lack of democracy and the history of human rights abuses in Ethiopia. In October 2007 the bill passed on a unanimous vote. Payne has also been a powerful advocate for human rights and democracy in South Africa, Namibia, Haiti, Zaire, Nigeria, China, Eastern Europe, Darfur, and Northern Ireland.

In 2008 Payne became the sixteenth member of the Congressional Black Caucus (CBC) to endorse Senator Hillary Rodham Clinton (D-NY) in the Democratic primary where she faced African American U.S. Senator Barack Obama (D-IL). Like many of his CBC colleagues Payne admired Clinton's thirty-five-year track record of fighting for children and families. He later switched support to Obama.

In September 2008 Essex County Executive Joseph N. DiVincenzo Jr. announced a proposal to name the walkway between the Essex County Veterans Courthouse and the LeRoy F. Smith Public Safety Building the "Congressman Donald M. Payne Plaza" in honor of Payne. DiVincenzo expressed that Payne holds a significant place in not only American, but also African American history as the first black congressman elected in New Jersey.

Payne's commitment to Africa has also been recognized by his role in promoting peace in Somalia. That commitment was tested in April 2009 when Somali fighters fired mortars at the Mogadishu airport just as a plane carrying Payne was departing from the Somali capital. Neither Payne nor his colleagues were injured during the attack but about a dozen civilians were wounded. Payne felt it was important to go to Mogadishu to better serve and assess the needs of Africa. U.S. support in Africa was not without opposition. In a 2009 interview on National Public Radio Payne said this of the Somali fighters: "They are a group that wants to see the new government fail. And so, it's sort of an act of desperation. They want to send a message that American officials, aid workers should be fearful and stay away. That's because I think they, too, know that with some support, the new government can succeed."

Payne remained active inside and outside of Congress. In 2009 he was a member of the House Committee on Education and Labor, where he served on the Subcommittee on Workforce Protections and the Subcommittee on Early Childhood, Elementary and Secondary Education. On an international level, he served as Chairman of the Subcommittee on Africa and Global health and as a member of the Subcommittee on the Western Hemisphere and the Subcommittee on International Organizations, Human Rights and Oversight.

In February 2012, Payne announced that he was undergoing treatment for colon cancer. A month later, Payne's condition rapidly deteriorated, and he was flown via medical transport from Washington to New Jersey. There, he was placed in hospice care at the Saint Barnabas Medical Center in Livingston. He died shortly thereafter, at the age of 77.

FURTHER READING

"Congressman Donald Payne. Proudly Serving New Jersey's 10th Congressional District." http://www.house.gov/payne/biography.shtml (2009).

Gettleman, J. "Welcome Back, Son. Now Don't Forget Us." *New York Times*, 12 July 2009, 3.

Sullivan, J. "A Victor in Jersey's Primary: From Coach to Congress Race." *New York Times*, 9 June 1988, p. 1.

Sullivan, J. "2 Vie to Be First Jersey Black in Congress." *New York Times*, 10 November 1988, 1.

Obituary: NJ.com, 6 March 2012. http://www.nj.com/news/index.ssf/2012/03/hold_donald_payne.html.

SHEENA C. HOWARD

Payne, Ethel Lois (14 Aug. 1911–28 May 1991), journalist, was born in Chicago, the daughter of William Payne, a Pullman car porter, and Bessie Austin Payne, who taught high school Latin before her marriage. Ethel Payne's father died when she was twelve years old, and her mother raised six children by taking in boarders and working as a domestic. Her mother was also a Republican precinct captain. Payne never married. In an oral history she said she turned down one proposal because she wanted to "do something" and not get "caught in the humdrum routine" (Ethel Payne oral history, 18).

Payne attended Crane Junior College and the Garrett Biblical Institute, and she worked as a warden at a juvenile girl's facility and a librarian at the Chicago Public Library. When her application to the University of Chicago Law School was rejected, she went to Japan in 1948 as a hostess for the Army Special Services Club, a job that involved planning recreational activities for African American troops. In her diary she recorded her observations on the persistence of segregation within the army and on the relations between African American soldiers and the Japanese. After the Korean War started in 1950, Alex Wilson, a reporter for the *Chicago Defender*, persuaded Payne to let him send portions of her diary to his paper, and when the stories appeared under her byline, the army blamed her for damaging troop morale. At that juncture LOUIS MARTIN, editor of the *Chicago Defender*, called to offer her a job as a feature writer.

Returning to Chicago in 1951, Payne produced a series of articles on the adoption of African American children, which won an award from the Illinois Press Association as the year's best news story. During this time, she also took night courses from the Medill School of Journalism at Northwestern University. When she was offered a reporting job at a higher salary from another paper, the *Chicago Defender* bid to keep her on its staff by making her its Washington correspondent in 1953. The paper also invited her to contribute unsigned editorials on government and politics.

John Sengstacke, publisher of the *Chicago Defender*, had taken the lead in creating the National Negro Publishers Association (NNPA), a news service for the black press. Payne's Washington reports were therefore carried by the *Chicago Defender* and by many of the member papers of the NNPA. In Washington she ran a one-person bureau, covering the White House, Congress, State Department, and Pentagon, and focusing on civil rights, poverty, and social policy. Since the black press had limited financial resources, its reporters often had to rely on information they gleaned from the general press. Disturbed by this practice, Payne later wrote that she became a "stickler for the original, not the warmed over" (Ethel Payne oral history, 57). She cultivated sources in the various agencies who provided her with stories and tips, and thereby compensated for her lack of staff assistance.

Whenever possible, Payne took her reporting beyond the confines of Washington. In 1955 the *Chicago Defender* sent her to Indonesia to cover the first conference of nonaligned nations, and in 1966 she spent three months reporting from Vietnam. She covered the Nigerian civil war in 1969, went to China in 1973, and was part of the press contingent on Secretary of State Henry Kissinger's mission to Africa in 1976. She also traveled repeatedly throughout the American South, reporting on many events during the civil rights movement, from the Montgomery bus boycott in 1956 to the Selma-to-Montgomery march in 1965. Her editors had an insatiable appetite for civil rights stories, and Payne developed a knack for making her stories more personal through anecdotes, rather than doing straight reporting. The editors of the *Chicago Defender* displayed her name and photograph prominently, in recognition of the power of her reporting to sell papers.

Rather than a neutral, objective reporter, Ethel Payne saw herself "as an advocate as much as being a newspaper person" (Ethel Payne oral history, 50). At President Dwight D. Eisenhower's press conferences, Payne often raised questions planted by the NAACP's Washington lobbyist, CLARENCE MITCHELL JR. On 7 July 1954 Payne asked whether the administration planned to support legislation banning segregation in interstate travel. Showing his annoyance, Eisenhower snapped that he would do what was fair but would support no "special group of any kind." The president's angry tone earned the confrontation a front-page story the same day in the *Washington Star*. Some of the black newspapers that carried Payne's reports editorially criticized her. "I was pilloried by the black press as being over-assertive," she recalled (Ethel Payne oral history, 48). But Sherman Briscoe, director of the NNPA, reassured her that the president was now "aware there is a problem here, and you have done your job" (Payne, "A Tribute to Sherman Briscoe," Ethel Payne Papers, Library of Congress).

The White House press office challenged Payne for writing on the side for the AFL-CIO, in violation of the rule that reporters not work for organizations that lobbied the government, and threatened to revoke her press pass. Drew Pearson defended her in his widely syndicated "Washington Merry-Go-Round" column, and accused the administration of trying to suppress the freedom of the press. The White House backed down, and Payne continued to attend press conferences, but President Eisenhower rarely again took questions from her. At his first presidential press conference, John F. Kennedy pointedly called on Payne and ALICE DUNNIGAN, who reported for the rival Associated Negro Press, as a sign that he planned to address civil rights issues more openly.

In 1972 the *Chicago Defender* called Payne back as associate editor, but she felt out of her element dealing with local news and longed to return to Washington. In 1978 she agreed to serve on a selection board for the U.S. Information Agency, an assignment that required her to spend considerable time in Washington. This caused John Sengstacke to accuse her of losing interest in his paper and terminate her position. She did some freelance writing and then returned to Washington in 1980 to write a self-syndicated column that ran mostly in black newspapers. By then she had also branched out into radio and television, doing commentary on the CBS series *Spectrum* from 1972 to 1978, and on the Chicago program *Matters of Opinion* from

1979 until 1982. Payne was also involved in education as a writer-in-residence at George Washington University and Jackson State College in Mississippi, a Ford Foundation fellow in educational journalism, and a visiting professor of journalism at Fisk University in Nashville, Tennessee.

Payne died of a heart attack at her home in Washington. In 2002 the U.S. Postal Service issued a postage stamp in her honor as part of its "Women in Journalism" series. Known widely as the "first lady of the black press," she was an aggressive reporter who prided herself on her refusal to acquiesce to injustice and her willingness to "raise the questions that needed to be raised" (Ethel Payne oral history, 50).

FURTHER READING

Payne, Ethel. "Loneliness in the Capital: The Black National Correspondent," in *Perspectives of the Black Press*, ed. Henry G. La Brie III (1974).

Ritchie, Donald A. *American Journalists: Getting the Story* (1997).

Streitmatter, Rodger. *Raising Her Voice: African-American Women Journalists Who Changed History* (1994).

Obituaries: *New York Times* and *Washington Post*, 1 June 1991; *Chicago Tribune*, 2 June 1991; *Chicago Defender*, 12 Oct. 1991.

DONALD A. RITCHIE

Payne, Isaac (1854–12 Jan. 1904), Seminole Negro Scout and Medal of Honor Recipient, was born in Santa Rosa, Mexico. His father may have been Caesor Payne, a native of Florida. Based on his military service, it is highly probable that Isaac Payne's family, perhaps his father, was one of the many runaway slaves in Florida that sought refuge with the Seminole Tribe, subsequently adopting their culture and way of life. After the end of the Seminole War with the U.S. government in 1842, many Black Seminoles traveled the Trail of Tears to the Indian Territory in the southwest after being forcibly removed from their native land in Florida. Wary of further troubles and the possibility of being captured and reenslaved, many Black Seminoles subsequently moved further south into Mexico to start life anew. Nothing is known about Isaac Payne's family and life in Mexico as a youth prior to 1871.

On 7 October 1871, Payne enlisted in the U.S. Army as an Indian Scout at Fort Duncan, Texas, for a period of six months. Among those that enlisted in the scouts with him at the same time were Caesor Payne (born c. 1825) and Titus Payne (born c. 1831). Both men were born in Florida and their first names, common among slaves, are indicators that they were likely enslaved early in their life. It is probable that, given his age, Caesor Payne was Isaac Payne's father, while Titus may have been his uncle. It is easy to imagine these older men accompanying young Isaac Payne to Fort Duncan, offering encouragement and support as he entered a new phase of life. Whatever their relation, the Payne surname soon became a common one among the Seminole Negro Scouts.

Though diminutive in stature, standing but five feet, five inches tall, Payne excelled as a soldier; to serve in the scouts, a soldier had to be a good tracker and horseman, as well as handy with a rifle. Payne was all of these and more, often being listed as a trumpeter. Whether Payne learned to play the trumpet in the army or had previous musical experience is unknown. However, the trumpeter was important during the conduct of field operations by cavalry units, his playing serving as part of the signaling system to direct coordinated moves as needed. Apparently finding the life of a scout to his liking, Isaac Payne subsequently reenlisted for further terms of service in 1872 and 1874, often in six-month increments.

Payne's skills as a scout, as well as those of JOHN WARRIOR and POMPEY FACTOR, were severely tested during a scouting patrol on the Pecos River in Texas on 25 April 1875. Under the command of Lieutenant John Bullis, Payne and his fellow scouts were on patrol, having left Fort Clark nine days earlier in company with the 25th Infantry, when they encountered a large force, perhaps thirty strong, of Comanche warriors. The scouts fired on the Comanches, surprising them as they were crossing the Pecos River and subsequently held favorable ground for nearly an hour before the situation turned dire. Not only were the scouts heavily outmanned, but they soon noticed that the warriors were moving to cut them off from their horses. The scouts made it back to their horses safely in an attempt to keep from getting trapped, but as they were about ready to leave Lieutenant Bullis's horse became frightened due to the noise of battle and could not be mounted. The lieutenant might have been lost had it not been for the actions of his scouts: led by Sergeant John Warrior, the men galloped back to Bullis, with Payne and Factor providing gunfire support. Bullis was able to jump on Warrior's horse, and the party made a dash to escape. During their gallop to safety, Bullis rode behind Payne on his horse, alternating between him and Factor so that no one horse would be overtaxed. For their heroic actions, Bullis recommended all his scouts, Payne included, for the Medal of Honor, which was subsequently awarded in March 1876.

The service of men like Isaac Payne, ADAM PAYNE, and Pompey Factor in the Seminole Negro Scouts in the U.S. Army is important for a variety of reasons; their Medal of Honor heroics alone makes these men worthy of remembrance. However, in the broader scope of history their service in the Seminole Negro Scouts is indicative of the important contributions made by this unique cultural group from 1870 to 1914 during the time of America's great westward expansion. The scouts were a rugged and fearless group of men who were expert, as the historian Frank Schubert notes, in "helping the Army find and fight an enemy that regular troops had difficulty locating and bringing to battle" (Schubert, p. 40).

Following the receipt of his Medal of Honor, Isaac Payne remained an army scout for most of his remaining life, reenlisting for additional short terms of service every year from 1877 to 1883, the years from 1885–1888 and 1893–94, and for longer terms of service in 1895 and 1898. Just a month after his final enlistment in January 1898, his son Charles Payne, born in 1871 and a farmer by trade, enlisted in the scouts for a period of three years. Worn out by his years of hard-riding, Payne retired as a soldier on 21 January 1901. He spent the remainder of his life with his family at the Seminole Negro settlement in Brackettville, Texas, and applied for a government pension, unable to work due to severe rheumatism. He died in Mexico and was subsequently buried at the Seminole Indian Scout Cemetery in Brackettville.

FURTHER READING

Hanna, Charles W. *African American Recipients of the Medal of Honor* (2002).
Schubert, Frank N. *Black Valor: Buffalo Soldiers and the Medal of Honor, 1870-1898* (1997).

GLENN ALLEN KNOBLOCK

Payne, Rufus "Tee Tot" (1884–17 Mar. 1939), musician, was born on the Payne Plantation in Sandy Ridge, Lowndes County, Alabama, on which his parents had been slaves. The family moved to New Orleans in 1890, where his father worked as a mule skinner (no further information is known about his parents). By 1915 Payne had returned to Alabama, settling in Greenville.

Payne's first name frequently was recorded as Rufe, but in most accounts he was referred to by the nickname "Tee Tot," an ironic and somewhat disparaging abbreviation of "teetotaler," derived from his reputation as a tippler. No record of his years in New Orleans exists, but presumably he gained a formative musical education during this period. In the Crescent City he probably heard the emerging modern musical forms of ragtime, jazz, and blues, as well as older rural song styles, such as ballads and the music of string and jug bands. In 1921 he fathered a son, Henderson, with seventeen-year-old Bea Williamson, though he was married to someone else. This situation led to his estrangement from his family.

Payne never recorded, and descriptions of his repertoire and performances are vague and contradictory. Most accounts of his life and music have centered on his early influence on a young Hank Williams in Alabama. The interaction between the two occurred in Greenville and neighboring Georgiana. Payne is often described as a street singer and blues musician who provided Williams, a future country music superstar, with the musical outlook that eventually made him famous. In later interviews, Williams often declared that everything he learned about musical performance he learned from Payne.

Williams's assertion indicated that Payne represented a largely unacknowledged aspect of country music history, that of African American country performers. His example provided a critical window into the context of interracial exchange that characterized much early rural American music, especially in the South. At the same time, Payne's relative obscurity also highlighted the segregationist logic that has undergirded historical narratives of country music's development. The direct participation of African American musicians in a musical tradition that has been construed as "white" has often been minimized. The details of Payne's influence on Williams—and thus on much of the commercial country music that followed—have remained unclear. By some accounts, Payne gave Williams lessons, either for food or for money; others have suggested that the two performed together on the street and at parties. One of Williams's band members stated flatly that Payne and the church provided the singer with virtually all of his musical influences. Biographers have disagreed as to whether Williams learned any songs from Payne, although many have identified him as the source of at least one number from the country performer's recording catalog, "My Bucket's Got a Hole in It" (1949). This song had clear antecedents in African American musical traditions, including the lines, "Well there ain't no use in me workin' so hard / 'Cause I got a woman in the boss man's yard," which occurred in recordings by such African American artists as LEAD BELLY and BLIND WILLIE MCTELL. A number of African American musicians recorded various versions of the song with different lyrics throughout the 1920s and 1930s. LOUIS ARMSTRONG recorded the song some seven years following the Williams rendition. Many also have speculated that Williams learned another of his hits, "Lovesick Blues," from Payne. The song was copyrighted in the 1920s, and it could have been part of Payne's repertoire. He probably was familiar with the song, since it had been recorded a number of times. Williams adapted it in 1949.

Accounts of Payne's performances and musical styles have varied widely. The most disparaging have described him as a talented musical beggar, who played on the street for tips from passersby. Later accounts indicated that he was a polished performer who played with a small combo at white society functions. Williams in a 1952 interview recalled that Payne played in an African American street band that included a washtub bass. Each of these possibilities seems likely. As a professional or semiprofessional musician in segregated Alabama, Payne probably was adept at a range of styles, not only blues or other styles derived from folk tradition but also dance numbers and the popular hits of the day. He could play whatever it was that his diverse audiences wanted to hear. The diversity of Payne's style and repertoire was evident in Williams's recorded work, and it suggested that the generic and racial divisions between the music of blacks and whites may have owed more to the marketing efforts of record companies than to actual performance practices in the South during the 1920s and 1930s.

Even such mundane details as descriptions of Payne's physical appearance were contradictory. Caricature often distorted the characterizations. Williams's cousins described Payne as hunchbacked, with long arms reaching almost to his knees. Payne's son Henderson denied such a description, emphasizing that Payne appeared compact and handsome. Opposed to this grotesque image of Payne as a hunchbacked, shuffling figure were deeply romanticized and probably entirely fictional depictions of him as a sort of saintly Uncle Remus figure. Such descriptions were common in depicting relationships between black musicians and their white protégés, especially in country music. The somewhat absurd apotheosis of this version of Payne was seen in the highly fictionalized 1964

film version of Williams's life, in which Payne was depicted as dying in his arms. In fact, Payne had died in 1939 in a charity hospital in Montgomery, Alabama, where he had moved two years previously. Thanks to the efforts of local historian Alice Harp, Payne's grave site in Montgomery's Lincoln cemetery was located in 1999, and a grave marker was erected a few years later.

FURTHER READING

Escott, Colin. *Hank Williams: The Biography* (2004).
Gleason, Ralph J. "Hank Williams, Roy Acuff, and Then God!!" *Rolling Stone* (28 June 1969).
Koon, George William. *Hank Williams: A Bio-Bibliography* (1983).
Koon, George William. *Hank Williams: So Lonesome* (2001).

ERICH NUNN

Payton, Carolyn Robertson (13 May 1925–11 Apr. 2001), psychologist, activist, and Peace Corps director, was born Carolyn Robertson in Norfolk, Virginia, the second of two daughters of Leroy Solomon Robertson, a ship steward, and Bertha Flanagan Robertson, a seamstress. Robertson grew up during the Depression, but her family was relatively comfortable. They were also close-knit, and all of the adults in her family—her grandfather, a former slave, in particular—emphasized the value of education.

On her parents' wishes, Robertson matriculated at Bennett College, a small, historically black women's college located in Greensboro, North Carolina. Payton adored her time at Bennett, and she particularly appreciated the opportunity it afforded her to know African American women who worked in significant leadership roles there. She was thrilled to see the many female luminaries who came to speak on the Bennett campus; while a student, she got to meet, among others, Eleanor Roosevelt, who became and would remain one of Payton's greatest role models. Upon receiving her B.A. in Home Economics from Bennett in 1945, she decided to continue her studies.

Although she had not studied psychology extensively in college, Robertson decided to obtain a graduate degree in that field because it qualified her for state funding under Virginia's separate-but-equal voucher system. In that system, if a course of study was available to whites at the state's white institutions but not available to blacks at the state's black institutions, the State of Virginia would pay all of the expenses for a black student to pursue that course of study out-of-state. So Robertson enrolled at the University of Wisconsin at Madison and received her M.S. in Clinical Psychology in 1948.

Robertson's time in Madison was challenging and often grim. Thrust from an African American school into a place where she was one of very few blacks and where her classes were often white-supremacist in tone, Robertson felt isolated and angered—particularly during class discussions about the intellectual superiority of whites. She brought this anger to bear in her work; her master's thesis critically analyzed the Wechsler-Bellevue Intelligence Scale, in order to show that the test inaccurately measured the aptitudes of blacks.

While she was a student at the university, she moved into one of Madison's black neighborhoods, where she met and married Raymond Rudolph Payton, a police detective. While the relationship increased her feeling of belonging in the community, their union was short-lived. They divorced in 1951 after four years of matrimony.

After finishing her degree, Payton took a position as a psychologist at Livingston College in Salisbury, North Carolina, where she worked for five years before being hired as the dean of women and as a psychology instructor at Elizabeth City State Teachers College in Elizabeth City, North Carolina. Payton found that she was a talented administrator, but she left the school in 1956 to become an associate professor of psychology at Virginia State College in Petersburg, Virginia.

During most of this time, Payton had been taking summer courses at Columbia University's Teachers College. Although she had not intended to obtain another degree, by 1958 Payton had acquired enough credits to put a doctorate within easy reach. She enrolled in Columbia's doctoral program and received her doctorate in Counseling and School Administration in 1962.

Beginning in 1959 she was also an assistant professor at Howard University in Washington, D.C. Her work in a primate laboratory, in which she sought to study perception with a goal of ultimately studying racial perception, won her national-level grants and the esteem of her colleagues.

In 1964 Payton left Howard after she was nominated to help design the selection criteria for President John F. Kennedy's nascent Peace Corps. Her early work for the organization was enthusiastic and varied; she began as a field assessment officer, visited Peace Corps sites, and by 1966 she became the director for the Caribbean region.

Payton rejoined the Howard faculty in 1970 to direct the Howard University Counseling Service

(HUCS). Greatly expanding the scope of counseling services and establishing a supervision program for graduate students, Payton advocated postgraduate training for her own staff and promoted the use of counseling services on the campus. This made her one of the first university officials in the nation to recognize that students often needed support services that were emotional and psychological, not merely academic. To provide these services to as many people as possible without great expense, Payton advocated the kind of short-term group therapy that has since become a standard form of treatment. She insisted that HUCS focus not only on standard clinical ideas, but also on the particular therapeutic needs of African Americans. Her HUCS program eventually developed into the American Psychological Association (APA)–approved Clinical and Counseling Psychology Pre-Doctoral Internship.

In 1977 President Jimmy Carter nominated Payton to head the Peace Corps, making her both the first African American and the first woman to hold the position. She spent a thirteen-month tenure as the leader of that organization, where she made a concerted effort to recruit more minority volunteers. But Payton ran into a series of difficulties. Funding was low, so many of her more ambitious goals ran against budget constraints. Payton also clashed with the leaders of ACTION, an umbrella organization that President Richard Nixon had created in 1971 to administer the Peace Corps, so she resigned the post in 1979.

Payton again returned to Howard, where she became dean of counseling and career development, a position she would hold until her retirement in 1995. During that time, Payton grew increasingly prominent within the psychological community. Perhaps her most well-known scholarly work was a 1984 article in *American Psychologist* entitled "Who Must Do the Hard Things?" in which she argued that psychology could not survive as a science if psychologists continued to ignore the social implications of their work.

Even on the national level, she was committed to professional service. Payton sat on several of the APA's committees, including the Policy and Planning Board, Committee on Women in Psychology, Committee on Lesbian, Gay, and Bisexual Concerns, and Public Policy Committee. She received several major awards from the APA, including the Distinguished Professional Contributions to Public Service Award in 1982, the Committee on Women in Psychology Leadership

Citation in 1985, and the Award for Outstanding Lifetime Contribution to Psychology in 1997. Payton was seventy-five when she died of a heart attack, at home.

FURTHER READING

Payton, Carolyn Robertson. "Who Must Do the Hard Things?" *American Psychologist* (1984).

Keita, Gwendolyn Puryear, and Tressie Muldrow. "Carolyn Robertson Payton," in *Women in Psychology: A Bio-Bibliographic Sourcebook* (1990).

O'Connell, Agnes N., and Nancy Felipe Russo, eds. "C. R. Payton," in *Models of Achievement: Reflections of Eminent Women in Psychology* (1983).

Redmond, Coates. *Come As You Are: The Peace Corps Story* (1986).

Smith, J. C., ed. "Carolyn Robertson Payton" in *Notable Black American Women* (1991).

SUSAN J. MCWILLIAMS

Payton, Philip A., Jr. (27 Feb. 1876–29 Aug. 1917), Harlem real estate agent, was born in Westfield, Massachusetts, the son of Philip Payton Sr., a barber and tea merchant, and Anna Marie Rynes. Payton's father was a graduate of Wayland Seminary in Washington, D.C., and his shop was an important gathering place for Westfield's small black community. The younger Payton went to public schools in Westfield and in 1899 obtained a degree from Livingston College in Salisbury, North Carolina. Payton married Maggie (maiden name unknown) that same year and relocated to New York City, where he held odd jobs, including department store attendant and barber. As a janitor to a real estate firm, Payton became intrigued with real estate and decided to go into business for himself.

Payton's entrance into the real estate field was well timed. In 1900 New York was a mecca for black migrants from the South. Decent-paying jobs were more plentiful, and the racial climate was more tolerant. Migrants, however, found that the housing market in Harlem was closed to them, as it was in most of the city. Many middle-class blacks felt intense frustration about their lack of access to decent housing. White real estate agents and landlords refused to sell or rent to blacks and confined them to a dilapidated stretch of Manhattan between Thirty-seventh and Fifty-eighth streets and other rundown areas.

Overspeculation in Harlem in the 1890s and early 1900s created an unusual opportunity for blacks to gain access to decent housing in other sections of the city. In the late nineteenth century Harlem became a fashionable neighborhood for successful New Yorkers. White landowners bought up property and built high-grade apartments with the expectation that the area would prosper. However, real estate developers were overconfident about the area's future and drove up land prices out of proportion to their actual value. When the housing market collapsed in 1904–1905, many owners had difficulty locating white tenants willing to pay the high rents the owners had to charge to meet their financial obligations. Payton, along with other black and white real estate agents, exploited this collapse in values and opened large areas of Harlem to black tenants.

Earlier, in 1900, Payton and a partner had opened an office on West Thirty-second Street specializing in managing "colored" tenements. For a while Payton struggled; his partner quit, and he was evicted from his offices more than once. Payton received his first break when owners of an apartment building on 134th Street could not find new tenants. They turned the building over to Payton to rent to blacks. He was successful and between 1900 and 1907 expanded his operation to become a wealthy, nationally recognized black business leader.

Payton's success was based on his audacity as a businessman, his skill as a promoter, and his reputation as an advocate of black-owned businesses in New York and elsewhere. He formed a limited partnership with a group of ten black businessmen and specialized in five-year leases on white-owned property rented to blacks. After 1904 Payton's creation, the Afro-American Realty Company, proceeded to attract new investors and tenants through extensive advertising in local and national black newspapers and on billboards, trains, and in subway stations. Payton also attracted attention by successfully confronting white realty companies that opposed his business strategy. He was aided by strong relationships with a small group of white real estate agents and bankers who tacitly supported his efforts.

Payton's activities in promoting black-owned enterprises in New York and in other urban centers included becoming a manager of the National Negro Business League, and in 1905 he organized a local black defense society to protest police brutality. Payton was also closely allied with prominent black leaders such as FREDERICK R. MOORE, the editor of the *New York Age*, and associates of BOOKER T. WASHINGTON such as CHARLES W. ANDERSON and EMMETT JAY SCOTT. While Payton counted Washington himself among his network of associates, their relationship was often troubled by philosophical differences and Payton's reluctance to fully endorse Washington's efforts to expand his influence in New York City. Payton drew together a group of black real estate agents and other businessmen, including John M. Royall, JOHN E. NAIL, and Henry C. Parker, who adopted Payton's methods to advance black expansion in Harlem even after Payton's own fortunes began to decline in 1907–1908.

After a series of organizational shake-ups, Afro-American Realty Company stockholders began to question Payton's high-risk speculating policies as well as his autocratic management style. In 1906 the stockholders sued Payton on the grounds that he ran the company without any input from the board of directors and was therefore responsible for any losses the company might accrue. Because the company claimed that it owned property free and clear when actually all of it was heavily mortgaged, the courts found the company guilty of misrepresentation (although Payton himself was cleared). Banking on his friends and his reputation, Payton kept the company afloat for another two years. However, the bad press created by the lawsuit and Payton's own speculations made obtaining credit increasingly difficult, and by 1908 the company had failed. Payton remained personally active in Harlem properties. In the summer of 1917 he obtained six apartment buildings on West 141st Street valued at $1.5 million, the biggest deal of his career. In late August, however, he became ill and died at his summer home in Allenhurst, New Jersey.

Philip A. Payton Jr. was a prominent black real estate entrepreneur who helped open the housing market in the Harlem section of New York City to blacks in the early twentieth century. He provided quality housing to black New Yorkers of all classes, became an influential business leader, an associate of national black leaders, and a symbol to black entrepreneurs and home seekers who referred to him as the "Father of Colored Harlem."

FURTHER READING

Many important documents relating to Payton can be found in the Booker T. Washington Papers at the Library of Congress and at the New York City Hall of Records.

Dailey, Maceo. "Booker T. Washington and the Afro-American Realty Company," *Review of Black Political Economy* (Winter 1978): 184–201.

Ingham, John, and Lynne B. Feldman. *African American Business Leaders* (1994).

Johnson, James Weldon. *Black Manhattan* (1930).

Osofsky, Gilbert. *Harlem: The Making of a Ghetto* (1971, 1996).

Richardson, Clement. *National Cyclopedia of the Colored Race* (1919).

This entry is taken from the *American National Biography* and is published here with the permission of the American Council of Learned Societies.

JARED N. DAY

Payton, Walter (25 July 1954–1 Nov. 1999), Hall of Fame football running back, was born in Columbia, Mississippi, the youngest of three children of Edward, a laborer, and Alyne Payton. Payton did not begin his football career until his junior year in high school. Before joining his brother, Eddie, in the backfield at segregated John J. Jefferson High School, Payton played drums in the marching band. He graduated from Columbia High School in 1970, following the integration of the Columbia public school system. Payton's two long touchdown runs in Columbia's 14–7 season-opening victory over rival Prentis High School are said to have silenced critics of school desegregation in his hometown.

Payton played college football at Jackson State University, from which he graduated with a degree in Special Education. At Jackson, Walter was reunited with his sister, Pam, and his brother, Eddie, and he lined up with Eddie in a backfield that came to be known as "Payton's place." Rushing for 3,563 yards and scoring 66 touchdowns, Payton helped lead the Tigers to two Southwestern Athletic Conference (SWAC) championships. Shredding defenses throughout the SWAC, Payton finished his college career with 464 points, a record in the National Collegiate Athletic Association. This total included a 46-point game and a 160-point season, which led the nation in 1973. Despite playing for a small, historically black college that received little press attention and no television coverage, Payton finished fourth in the balloting for the 1974 Heisman Trophy, awarded annually to the nation's outstanding college football player. His dazzling collegiate scores are especially impressive considering the high level of competition he faced in the SWAC. Well into the 1970s historically white southern universities did not recruit black athletes in great numbers, making black colleges and universities a vast source of draftable football talent.

The Chicago Bears made Payton their first-round pick in the 1975 National Football League (NFL) draft. A powerfully effective combination of

Walter Payton on 8 Oct. 1984. during a game against the New Orleans Saints in which he picked up 154 yards to become the National Football League's top rusher. (AP Images.)

balance, speed, and strength defined Payton's physical style of running. Small compared with other running backs of his era, at just five feet ten inches tall and 195 pounds, he was as likely to bounce off would-be tacklers as to go down. Payton rushed for 16,726 yards in the course of a thirteen-year professional career, making him the NFL's all-time leading rusher at the time of his retirement. A dynamic offensive force, he was also a punishing blocker and dependable receiver as well as a fearless runner. He led the league in rushing five consecutive times from 1976 to 1980 while posting ten seasons in which he gained more than a thousand yards. Known as "Sweetness," he was named All-Pro seven times and played in nine Pro Bowls. In 1977 he became the youngest NFL Most Valuable Player (MVP) while leading the Bears to their first trip to the play-offs in fourteen years. During that season Payton set a league record for single-game rushing, gaining 275 yards against the Minnesota Vikings. This performance was one of the record seventy-seven games in which Payton gained a hundred or more yards.

A dedicated and disciplined athlete, Payton did not possess the blazing speed of GALE SAYERS or the raw power of JIM BROWN. As a result, much of his success in the NFL can be attributed to a grueling off-season regimen he conducted on his

legendary Mississippi training course, which featured a steep vertical incline known as "the Hill." Payton's conditioning program helped him play in 188 consecutive games, missing only one contest— during his rookie season—in the course of his long career. Combining his desire to excel with a tenacious work ethic, Payton established his reputation as a consummate teammate. This made him one of Chicago's most beloved sports figures long before the Bears brought the city its first major professional sports championship in more than two decades. Payton was named the NFL's MVP for the second time during the 1985 season, as the Bears posted a 15-1 regular-season record and went on to win Super Bowl XX with a lopsided 42-6 victory over the New England Patriots.

Payton's NFL career concluded at the end of the 1987 season. His uniform number 34 was retired in a ceremony at Chicago's Soldier Field during the Bears' final regular-season home game of that year. Following his retirement Payton maintained contact with the game by serving as a member of the Bears' board of directors. However, he was not content to serve in this largely symbolic capacity. Always one to aim high, he aspired to become the first African American owner of an NFL franchise. Lacking the capital necessary to become a majority owner, Payton entered into a partnership with an investment group bidding for a proposed expansion franchise based in St. Louis. He waged a four-year campaign to make this dream a reality. When league officials awarded new teams to Jacksonville and Charlotte instead of St. Louis, Payton was deeply disappointed. In the wake of this decision, he cut many of his ties with the league. In 1993, the same year that the expansion decision was made, Payton was elected to the Pro Football Hall of Fame. His twelve-year-old son, Jarrett, delivered his induction speech.

The transition to life after football was not easy for Payton. In his memoir he describes it as a process of "withdrawal" (Payton, 2000, 138–139). Seeking to fill the void left by the game, Payton shifted his focus to auto racing. Payton raced cars on a number of levels, including the Sports 2000, GT-3, and Trans-Am circuits. Payton's days as a driver ended following a wreck in Elkhart, Wisconsin. His lifelong passion for speed and competition continued when he became the owner of an Indycar and CART racing team. During the mid-1990s Payton also began taking an active interest in the business ventures undertaken by Walter Payton Incorporated. The good fortune that he enjoyed in the business world helped underwrite the numerous charitable activities that Payton and his wife, Connie, undertook through the Walter Payton Foundation, assisting needy children and improving education in Chicago.

In January 1999 Payton was told he had primary sclerosing cholangitis, a rare form of liver disease. Amid wild speculation about his health, Payton held a press conference on 2 February 1999. He revealed his need for a liver transplant and that he had been given less than two years to live. This emotional event sent shock waves through Chicago and the sports world at large. Soon after, it was also discovered that Payton had cancer of the bile duct, which quickly spread to his lymph nodes. These conditions forced him to withdraw his name from the organ transplant list. A man of deep faith, Payton battled his illnesses valiantly, choosing to let his health struggle become a focal point in the campaign to increase awareness about organ donation.

On 6 November 1999 two thousand people gathered at Soldier Field for a public celebration of Payton's life and legacy. An array of speakers, including the Reverend JESSE JACKSON and Payton's Hall of Fame teammate the linebacker MIKE SINGLETARY recalled his greatness on and off the field. In 2000 the city of Chicago honored Payton's commitment to excellence and the work of the Walter and Connie Payton Foundation by naming its state-of-the-art, selective-enrollment math, science, and world language high school the Walter Payton College Preparatory High School.

FURTHER READING

Payton, Walter, with Don Yaeger. *Never Die Easy* (2000).

Payton, Walter, with Jerry B. Jenkins. *Sweetness* (1978).

LeGere, Bob, et al. *Sweetness: The Courage and Heart of Walter Payton* (1999).

Obituary: *Chicago Tribune*, 2 Nov. 1999.

MICHAEL A. ANTONUCCI

Peacock, Wazir (5 Sept. 1937–), civil rights worker, was born Willie B. Peacock in Charleston, Mississippi, to George W. Peacock, a farmer and millwright, and Della Martin Peacock, a domestic worker. He attended Rust College in Holly Springs, Mississippi, where he was a pre-med major. Peacock's first involvement in civil rights came when he joined other students seeking to desegregate the Holly Springs movie theater. He also teamed up with the Student Nonviolent Coordinating Committee (SNCC) field secretary Frank Smith to work on voter registration in Marshall County.

After graduation Peacock returned to Charleston to earn money for medical school. He applied for a teaching job but was refused because of his civil rights record. He was preparing to leave for Detroit when he was recruited by ROBERT P. MOSES and AMZIE MOORE to do voter registration work in the Mississippi Delta. After receiving an emergency call from SAMUEL BLOCK in Greenwood, Moses assigned Peacock there. Peacock and Block spent the summer and fall of 1962 building grass-roots support for voter registration. An early history of SNCC quotes Peacock's description of those days:

We were hungry one day and didn't have anything to eat and didn't even have a pair of shoes hardly, and we went down and started hustling and a fellow gave me a pair of shoes. Then we had to ride a mule…Didn't even have transportation. But we kept begging for transportation….But we're not worrying. We ain't complaining. We just go on and raise hell all the time. We don't have to ride, we can walk, we don't care (Zinn).

The persistence and dedication of the young SNCC workers gradually wore down the initial suspicions of Greenwood's African American community. The pair held mass meetings and built support for the movement by leading the singing of freedom songs. They began escorting local blacks to the courthouse where they attempted to register.

White authorities began harassing the young civil rights workers. Police cars conspicuously trailed them. Block was beaten shortly after his arrival in Greenwood and the SNCC office was vandalized. In October 1962 the Leflore County commissioners suspended distribution of federal surplus food to punish voter registration activities, prompting SNCC workers to appeal to northern supporters for donations of food and clothing. When several truckloads of supplies arrived, Peacock supervised their distribution. This brought him face-to-face with the region's heartbreaking poverty. In a report to SNCC's Atlanta office, Peacock and Block described the plight of one family. Their eleven children stayed out of school because they had "no money, no food, no clothes, and no wood to keep warm by…. The house they are living in has no paper or nothing on the walls and you can look at the ground through the floor" (Payne). On 13 February 1963 Peacock handed out 400 boxes of food and then

561 more on 20 February. Each time hundreds more remained standing in line.

The relief efforts were a stimulus to the voter registration drive. They also triggered violent reprisals. On 20 February 1963 four buildings near the SNCC office were burned. On 28 February a car without license plates fired at a carload of SNCC workers, seriously wounding Jimmy Travis. On 6 March a shotgun blast struck the car in which Peacock, Block, and two young women were sitting. Miraculously, they were only slightly injured. On 26 March at the home of Dewey Green, an early supporter of the movement, was fired upon. The next day more than a hundred angry blacks marched on the courthouse. Greenwood police attacked with dogs. Eight SNCC workers, including Peacock, were arrested. They refused bail and remained in jail for two weeks. Despite this repression, voter registration activity increased. During March more than 250 blacks went to the courthouse to register, but few were successful. Only twenty-three of 1,013 black applicants between August 1961 and June 1963 were registered. After Greenwood, Peacock continued voter registration work in Holmes and Humphreys Counties.

When the Freedom Summer project was proposed for 1964, Peacock opposed bringing outside volunteers into Mississippi. He felt that the influx of inexperienced students would undermine the local organization he had built. In June 1964, while driving to Oxford, Ohio, Peacock and four other SNCC staff members were arrested outside Columbus, Mississippi, jailed, and severely beaten. Peacock spent the summer of 1964 in New York receiving treatment for "battle fatigue."

That fall Peacock enrolled in graduate school at Tuskegee Institute. There he continued voter registration work in Selma and Macon County, Alabama. He returned to Mississippi in 1965 where he organized cultural festivals before moving to California. In 1970 he went back to Mississippi and was employed as a hemodialysis technician at the University of Mississippi Medical Center. His marriage to Elaine Anderson, which produced two sons, ended in divorce. In 1989 he went to California where he worked with developmentally disabled children and adults at the Stepping Stones Growth Center. He often spoke to high school and college students about the civil rights movement.

Wazir Peacock belonged to the "EMMETT LOUIS TILL generation"—those young African Americans raised under the last decade of Jim Crow's harsh rule who dedicated themselves to the black freedom struggle. During the 1960s they slipped into southern towns like guerrilla warriors, risking their lives to fight for basic civil rights. Their many sacrifices resulted in lasting change.

FURTHER READING

Dittmer, John. *Local People: The Struggle for Civil Rights in Mississippi* (1994).

Payne, Charles M. *I've Got the Light of Freedom: The Organizing Tradition and the Mississippi Freedom Struggle* (1995).

Zinn, Howard. *SNCC: The New Abolitionists* (1964).

PAUL T. MURRAY

Peagler, Robert J. (27 Nov. 1917–24 June 1945), World War II soldier and Distinguished Service Cross medalist, was born in Maryland, the son of Robert and Myrtle Peagler. His mother was a native of Virginia; his father, born in Alabama, was a farm laborer, and later a teamster in a coal yard. By 1920 the Peaglers, including son Robert and daughters Mabel and Francis, had moved to Connecticut. Little is known about the younger Robert Peagler's early life, but he probably graduated from high school, and is later known to have attended college for four years at an unknown trade institution, studying to be a plumber and gas or steam fitter. Whether or not Peagler graduated with a higher degree is unknown, but seems likely.

On 21 January 1942 Robert Peagler began his military service, leaving his home in Litchfield, Connecticut, to join the army at Fort Devens, Massachusetts. After completing his boot camp training, Peagler was assigned to the 870th Anti-Aircraft Artillery Battalion, part of the 369th Coastal Artillery Regiment. While the full details of Peagler's army service are not known, he was likely chosen for service as a junior officer in his unit due to his higher education and the leadership qualities that he would later demonstrate to the fullest measure.

The unit in which Robert Peagler served during World War II was one of many artillery, transportation, construction, quartermaster, and other support units in the army that was manned entirely by African American enlisted personnel. However, of the approximately 800,000 African American troops employed during the war, less than five percent of these men were assigned to combat duty. While the first black troops arrived overseas by early 1942, over a year later 85 percent of the over 500,000 black troops then in the army were still stationed in the United States. Indeed, by 1943 the

War Department's Advisory Committee on Negro Troop Policies, established in August 1942, affirmed these men "could not be wasted by leaving them to train endlessly in camps around the country" (MacGregor, p. 43) and continued to advise that these troops be utilized to their fullest potential. Nevertheless, the committee's recommendations were largely ignored until 1944. Despite the fact that such men were underutilized for most of the war, the service of African Americans like Peagler, ISAAC SERMON, and WAVERLY B. WOODSON JR. was critical to the war effort and should not be overlooked.

Peagler and his 870th Anti-Aircraft Artillery Battalion were sent overseas in June 1942, stationed in Hawaii for nearly three years. However, in 1945, with the Battle for Okinawa in full swing, the 870th was sent to the embattled island chain, arriving on 10 May. Here, these artillery-trained soldiers, including their black officers, were quickly converted to infantry troops and assigned garrison duty on Kerama Island, arriving there on 22 May. On Kerama, the men of the 870th were given new weapons and a quick lesson in infantry tactics training, and within a day were sending their first units out on combat patrol. Just over a month later, on 24 June 1945, three platoons from the 870th, with artillery and naval gunfire support, were ordered to take a Japanese position on high ground overlooking a village held by American forces. Leading the assault was First Lieutenant Robert Peagler and the 1st Platoon of Battery B. The first to arrive at the crest of the hill, Peagler subsequently directed automatic weapon fire on the Japanese emplacements and, when the platoon's Browning Automatic Rifle (BAR) malfunctioned, he charged forward with his rifle and hand grenades toward an enemy pillbox. Peagler succeeded in killing six Japanese soldiers and capturing a grenade launcher before he was shot in the temple by a Japanese sniper and instantly killed while directing bazooka fire. Despite his death, Peagler's heroism under fire encouraged his men to continue the advance and capture the position. Robert Peagler's actions were quickly recognized by his superior officers, and he was recommended for a combat decoration, probably the Silver Star at first, until the full extent of his actions became known. On 17 December 1945, Robert Peagler was posthumously awarded the Distinguished Service Cross by the United States Army Forces Pacific, one of just nine African American soldiers to be awarded the army's second highest military decoration during the war, exceeded in stature only by the Medal of Honor.

While the deeds of Robert Peagler have been largely forgotten, they briefly came to light in the 1990s when the army began to assess its awards decoration policies from the World War II era in regard to African American soldiers. Through the demands of individuals, civic groups, and historians alike, all questioning why no black soldier had been awarded the Medal of Honor during that conflict, in 1992 the army commissioned a study to be completed by an outside organization on the issue. Scholars at Shaw University in Raleigh, North Carolina, were chosen for the task, and in January 1995 submitted their results to the army. Researchers identified and documented the service and heroism of a number of African American soldiers, including Robert Peagler, Dowden, GEORGE WATSON, and WILLY JAMES JR. Indeed, the Shaw University study included all nine of the Distinguished Service Cross medalists as men potentially deserving of an upgrade to the Medal of Honor, as well as one other man, RUBEN RIVERS. However, after reviewing the data, army officials reduced the list to seven names, all of whom were subsequently awarded the Medal of Honor. Among the three men who were not included was Robert Peagler; the reason for his exclusion remains unknown.

FURTHER READING

Converse, Elliott V., III, Daniel K. Gibran, John A. Cash, Robert K. Griffith Jr., and Richard H. Kohn. *The Exclusion of Black Soldiers from the Medal of Honor in World War II* (1997).

Lee, Ulysses. *The Employment of Negro Troops, United States Army in World War II* (1966).

MacGregor, Morris J., Jr. *Integration of the Armed Forces, 1940–1965* (1981).

GLENN ALLEN KNOBLOCK

Peake, Mary S. (1823–22 Feb. 1862), educator, was born Mary Smith Kelsey in Norfolk, Virginia, to parents whose names, occupations, and marital status are unknown. Peake's 1863 biographer, Lewis C. Lockwood, described her mother as "a free colored woman, very light" and her father as "an Englishman of rank and culture" (Lockwood and Forten, 6). At the age of six Mary was sent to live in Alexandria, Virginia, in order to obtain an education. She resided with her aunt and uncle, Mary and John Paine, for ten years during which time she received formal schooling and training in needlework and dressmaking. Mary attended two different schools for African American children, where she was under the tutelage of both black and white teachers.

While education for blacks was generally illegal throughout the South, Mary was able to receive schooling in nearby District of Columbia. Blacks were allowed this right until the adoption of a bill in 1838 that placed the district's free black population under the laws of Virginia, thereby excluding African American children from educational opportunities. After ten years of schooling, Mary returned to Norfolk where she worked as a seamstress and joined the First Baptist Church. In 1847 her mother married Thompson Walker, and the family relocated to Hampton, Virginia.

While living in Hampton Mary Kelsey established the Daughters of Zion, a benevolent society that provided aid to the poor and the sick. In 1851 Kelsey married a former slave, Thomas Peake. The couple's only child was a daughter, Hattie, whom they nicknamed Daisy. The couple was forced to relocate during the Civil War, in 1861, after Confederate soldiers burned Hampton in an effort to eradicate the widespread support for the Union that came from the black community there. The Peakes settled across the Hampton River at "Brown Cottage," the home where the family lived on the second floor and Peake taught in the first floor classroom, near Fortress Monroe.

On 17 September 1861 Peake began a school for the contraband—freed and runaway slaves emancipated by the Civil War—and their children living near the fort, an effort that gained the attention of the Reverend Lewis C. Lockwood, a representative of the American Missionary Association (AMA). Lockwood brought Peake's school under the auspices of the AMA, raising financial support for her efforts. Funds collected by the AMA paid Peake's salary of $17.89 in October 1861. Peake's school grew to include fifty children during the daytime and twenty adults in evening classes. The lessons included spelling, arithmetic, writing, singing, and religion, including the Lord's Prayer and the Ten Commandments. Peake also founded a Sunday school there.

Peake died of tuberculosis in 1862 at the age of thirty-nine, but her work educating African Americans continued. In 1865 Peake's school and other similar efforts in the area combined to form the Butler School, which was supported by the AMA. In 1868 classes began at a new school located on Hampton Creek and run by General Samuel Chapman Armstrong. In 1869 the school was chartered as the Hampton Institute, a center of learning for African Americans that also began admitting Native American students in 1878. Peake became the first African American recipient of the American Tract Society's Medal of Praise. Her contributions to Virginia also gained recognition in 1941 when a housing development in Norfolk was named Peake's Point in her honor.

FURTHER READING

Fen, Sing-Nan. "Mary S. Peake, 1823–62," *School & Society* (6 April 1963).

Lockwood, Lewis C., and Charlotte Forten. *Two Black Teachers during the Civil War: Mary S. Peake, The Colored Teacher at Fortress Monroe* and *Life on the Sea Islands* (1969).

Virginia Writers' Program. *The Negro in Virginia* (1940).

TONIA M. COMPTON

Pearse, Abraham (?–1673), also spelled Pearce or Pierce, was an early settler in Plimoth Plantations (Plymouth Colony) in what is now the state of Massachusetts, who, according to a good deal of research from contemporary documents, was probably African or of African descent. Some commentators vigorously insist that this is unlikely.

Whatever his national origin, complexion, or standing in the Plymouth community, most sources agree that an Abraham Pearse settled in the colony of New Plymouth around 1623, most likely arriving on the *Anne*, from England, as one of two servants of another "Mr. Perce," both of whom were granted land that year. Plymouth scholar Robert Marten concluded that Pearse had most likely gone to England after working as an indentured servant in the British colony of Barbados, at that time devoted to growing tobacco with indentured labor, although most plantations later converted to sugar production using slave labor sold by Dutch merchants. A power of attorney signed by Caleb Pearse in 1739refers to an interest in a plantation in Barbados left to him by his great-grandfather, Abraham Pearse (*The Mayflower Descendant* 9 [1907]: 162).

In 1627, when the colony's communal farm was broken up into private landholdings, Pearse was among those who received cattle in the division of the settlement's herd. By 1633 he was a freeholder and a taxpayer, served on a coroner's jury in 1636, was listed as a householder in 1637, and was granted forty acres of upland and meadow at North River in 1640, the area that later became Duxbury.

The list of persons "Able to Bear Arms" (ATBA) compiled in 1643 provides the earliest cited evidence of Pearse's origins. According to a copy published by Nathaniel B. Shurtleff, M.D., between 1855 and 1861, based on a copy made from one taken in 1813 by the commissioners appointed by the General Court of Massachusetts, he was listed on the muster roll as "Abraham Pearse the blackamore." This may have been the source for Senator Charles Sumner's reference in 1860 to Pearse as a free black man ("Example of Massachusetts against Slavery," *Works of Charles Sumner* 5 [1874]: 280). The 1643 roster was also cited by John Gorham Palfrey and Francis Winthrop Palfrey in 1899 (*History of New England* 2, p. 30), "from which we infer, both that Negroes were not dispensed from military service in that Colony, and that their number was extremely small."

Pearse married Rebecca, sister of John Scudder's wife Hannah, with whom he had five children between 1638 and 1661: Abraham, Rebecca, Mary, Alice, and Isaac. Their daughter Mary married Nathaniel or William Baker, their daughter Alice married John Baker, and their son Abraham married Hannah Baker. Some of the Plymouth Bakers were among the ancestors of the British prime minister Winston Churchill's American mother, Jennie Jerome. In Germany, the Nazi ministry of progaganda in fact made use of this connection, the long-known evidence of Pearse's African origins, and the Jerome family tradition of unspecified native American connections, to tweak Churchill during World War II.

Pearse was one of the first three settlers in Duxbury. Another of the three, Dolar Davis, described his companion on a previous exploration of the area as a Negro, who may or may not have been Pearse. A proprietor in Bridgewater in 1645, Pearse was charged in court in March 1652 with "slothfull and negligent spending the Sabath, and not frequenting the publick assembly" (Bush, Barbara, *Imperialism, Race, and Resistance: African and Britain, 1919–1945*, p. 328, fn.50), being excused on that occasion with a warning. Failing to attend church would have been a much greater concern to the Pilgrim community than skin color. Pearse purchased, or was granted, additional lands up to the early 1660s.

Commentaries denying Pearse's African derivation express one of two biases. Some are shocked that old New England families might have an African in their family tree. With so many intervening generations of marriages, this includes a large portion of the "old families" constituting a kind of social aristocracy—who by strict application of the notorious "one drop rule" would therefore be black.

Others are so intent on highlighting the horror and degradation of American racism that any possibility of people with dark complexion having ever been accepted on any basis remotely resembling equality is reflexively denied.

What is certain is that scholars claiming African descent for Abraham Pearse have met strong opposition. Robert Marten, director of programs at the Plimoth Plantation historical center for eighteen years, was fired in 1981, after completing research supporting the thesis and hiring an African American actor to play the role of Pearse in the center's reenactment of Pilgrim life. In May 1983, *The Mayflower Quarterly* (p. 57) published a study commissioned by Plimoth Plantation after Marten was fired. Richard L. Ehrlich and James W. Baker acknowledged that a survey of English records failed to shed any light on Pearse's racial identity, then devoted nine pages to the "clear-cut" conclusion that the documentary evidence is "inadequate" to support the hypothesis that Pearse was of African origin. In the absence of any proof of Anglo-Saxon origin, they rely heavily on the assumption, cited from several previous books, that English colonists had intense prejudices against dark-skinned people before even leaving Britain.

Eugene Aubrey Stratton, in *Plymouth Colony, Its History and People, 1620–1691* (1986, p. 337), relies on Ehrlich and Baker to assert that the name "Abraham Pearse" and the words "the blackamore" may have been erroneously linked by Shurtleff because he put all four words on a single line, whereas in the original they were on two successive lines. Stratton does not explain why a list of males able to bear arms would refer to one unspecified person as "the blackamore" and all others by their given and family names. Overlooking both Sumner in 1860 and Palfrey in 1899, he observes that "In recent years Shurtleff's error was taken by some groups to mean that Pierce was a black" and tepidly concludes, that "there is insufficient evidence for believing that Abraham Pearce was a black."

In *History of the Negro Race in America from 1619 to 1880, Vol. 1* (2007, p. 289, fn. 337), GEORGE WASHINGTON WILLIAMS opines "Mr. Palfrey is disposed to hang a very weighty matter on a very slender thread of authority....This single case is borne down by the laws and usages of the colonists on this subject. Negroes as a class were absolutely excluded from the military service, from the commencement of the colony down to the war with Great Britain." Williams, like Ehrlich and Baker, overlooks both the widely varied laws on militia service in the colonies, over time and between colonies, and the substantial presence of African Americans in the Massachusetts militia at Lexington and Concord, and in the ranks of the Continental Army, much to George Washington's initial chagrin (Baird, Henry Carey, *General Washington and General Jackson, on Negro Soldiers*, 1863, pp. 4–5). A 1652 Massachusetts act provides that "All Negroes and Indians from sixteen to sixty years of age, inhabitants or servants to the English, be listed and hereby enjoined to attend trainings as well as the English" (Wilkes, Laura Elizabeth, *Missing Pages in American History: Revealing the Services of Negroes in the Early Wars in the United States of America, 1641–1815*, 1973, p. 9); significantly, the term "white" is not used.

Virginia, a colony with a much larger and more commonly enslaved black population, did not prohibit free men of African descent from bearing arms in the militia until 1738—and then still ordered them to appear for unarmed duty (Breen, T. H., and Stephen Innes, *"Myne Owne Ground": Race and Freedom on Virginia's Eastern Shore, 1640–1676*, 2005, p. 27). There are individuals in Virginia, contemporary to Pearse, distinctly documented as "Negro," who were landowners and respected members of the community (Breen and Innes, pp. 26–31). It is by no means certain that Abraham Pearse's contemporaries would have shared their descendants' distaste for a man of African ancestry. Upon his death, his son Abraham was appointed by the court to administer the estate and received all the land, except twenty-two acres assigned to his younger brother Isaac, while their sisters received twenty shillings each.

FURTHER READING

Kilgore, Kathleen. "Plimoth Plantation: An Interpreter's Tale." *Yankee Magazine*, Nov. 1983.

Snow, Stephen Eddy, and Barbara Kirshenblatt-Gimblett. *Performing the Pilgrims: A Study of Ethnohistorical Role-Playing at Plimoth Plantation* (1993).

"Plymouth Historian Says a Black Settled at Pilgrim's Colony," *New York Times*, 20 Aug. 1981.

"Pilgrim Surprises Tourists." *The Day* (New London, Conn.), 16 Sept. 1981.

"Experts Believe There Was a Black Pilgrim." *Jet*, 10 Sept. 1981.

CHARLES ROSENBERG

Pearson, Conrad Odell (2 Mar. 1902–26 June 1984), lawyer and civil rights activist, was born in Greensboro, North Carolina, the son of George Washington Pearson, minister of Bethel African Methodist Episcopal (AME) Church, and Frances Smith. After his father died in 1904, Pearson and his mother moved to Durham where they lived with Conrad's grandmother, Cynthia Pearson. The Pearsons also lived with Conrad's uncle, William G. Pearson, a prominent Durham businessman and educator, who helped start the North Carolina Mutual Life Insurance Company and the Mechanics and Farmers Bank.

In Durham, Conrad Pearson graduated from the Whitted School in 1918. In 1924 he earned an AB at Wilberforce University and received his law degree from Howard University in 1932. He married Mildred Harris, a public school teacher, and was a member of St. Joseph's AME Church in Durham.

At Howard, the prospective lawyer was trained by such eminent advocates for constitutional change as CHARLES HAMILTON HOUSTON, dean of Howard University Law School, and WILLIAM H. HASTIE, future federal judge. Led by Houston, Howard became a virtual factory for the production of civil rights attorneys during these and subsequent years. Pearson was among this group of Howard graduates, including THURGOOD MARSHALL, who became powerful advocates for the rights of African Americans.

After earning his law degree at Howard University, Pearson returned to Durham to practice law and fight for civil rights for African Americans. He did so during a time when there were fewer than thirty black attorneys in North Carolina, of which it is likely that only a dozen or so maintained a full-time practice. Pearson was one of the few black law school graduates who decided to practice law in the South despite the region's racially oppressive atmosphere. Within this small group of black southern lawyers, Pearson was one of a handful who embraced the chance and accepted the risks involved in using the courts to battle against racial oppression. For over fifty years, Pearson, who once said, "I was born to be a fighter," agitated for equal justice, political rights, economic opportunity, and racial integration (Pearson Interview, 1979).

In 1933 Pearson, along with fellow attorney Cecil A. McCoy, and the editor of the *Carolina Times* LOUIS AUSTIN, mounted the first legal challenge to the racial segregation of a public institution of higher learning in the South. The three young black activists tried to enroll Thomas Raymond Hocutt in the pharmacy school at the University of North Carolina in Chapel Hill. When the registrar turned Hocutt down because he was black, Pearson and

McCoy filed *Hocutt v. Wilson and the University of North Carolina* (1933). With the assistance of NAACP attorney William Hastie, Pearson and McCoy pursued the suit despite broad opposition, even from some prominent blacks, notably the North Carolina College president JAMES SHEPARD. Pearson played the leading role in the genesis of the *Hocutt* case. He formulated the case, located a plaintiff, obtained NAACP support, and enlisted support from the leading black businessman in the community. Based on a legal technicality and Hocutt's failure to present his college transcript, which NCC president Shepard denied to him, the court ruled against Hocutt.

Despite this defeat, Pearson continued to fight for legal and political gains for African Americans in North Carolina. In 1935 Pearson helped found the Durham Committee on Negro Affairs (later the Durham Committee on the Affairs of Black People), which registered black voters, organized bloc voting for sympathetic candidates for office, and lobbied for legislation favorable to the black community. For many years he served as the chairman of the Durham Committee's political committee. In 1936 Pearson helped organize the statewide counterpart to the Durham Committee, the North Carolina Committee on Negro Affairs (NCCNA).

From the 1950s through the 1970s, as the first head of the North Carolina chapter of the NAACP Legal Defense and Education Fund, Pearson took an active role in the modern civil rights movement, acting as co-counsel on many civil rights cases that succeeded in desegregating public schools, universities, and other public facilities. In *McKissick et al. v. Carmichael* (1951), Pearson helped desegregate the graduate and professional programs at the University of North Carolina. In that case, the federal court, following the precedent set in *Sweatt v. Painter* (1950), ruled that states must provide equal professional and graduate programs for blacks and whites, or failing that, admit black students to the white programs. After determining that North Carolina College School of Law was "clearly inferior" to the University of North Carolina (UNC) Law School, the court decreed that UNC must admit black students to its law school. In 1951 the first black students entered UNC, enrolling in the law school.

Pearson also succeeded in desegregating UNC's undergraduate programs. In *Frasier v. UNC Board of Trustees* (1955), a federal court ruled that based on the reasoning in *Brown v. Board of Education* (1954), if segregated public schools were unconstitutional, so were segregated public colleges and universities. The U.S. Supreme Court affirmed the Frasier ruling in *UNC Board of Trustees v. Frasier* (1956).

In 1962 Pearson represented the plaintiffs in a case to desegregate Moses H. Cone Memorial Hospital in Greensboro, North Carolina. In *Simkins v. Moses H. Cone Memorial Hospital*, Pearson relied on the due process clause of the Fifth Amendment and the equal protection clause of the Fourteenth Amendment to argue that hospitals—like Cone—that received federal funds under the Hill-Burton Act could not exclude black doctors or black patients based on race. After an adverse ruling by the district court in 1962, in 1963 the Fourth Circuit Court of Appeals, in an appeal filed by NAACP lawyer Jack Greenberg, reversed the district court and ruled that the Hill-Burton Act's separate-but-equal clause was unconstitutional. Although the U.S. Supreme Court denied certiorari, the U.S. surgeon general issued regulations in 1964, which reinforced the Court of Appeals decision. As a result, hospitals that received federal funds were required to integrate.

Pearson served as co-counsel in several North Carolina public school desegregation suits, notably in the Durham cases, *McKissick v. Durham* (1958) and *Wheeler and Spaulding v. Durham City Board of Education* (1962). Despite the Supreme Court ruling in *Brown v. Board of Education* (1954) that segregated public schools were unconstitutional, southern states like North Carolina continued their policy of segregating students by race in public schools. Consequently it fell to local attorneys and parents backed by the NAACP to force local school boards to desegregate schools.

In Durham, Pearson was lead counsel for hundreds of black parents and their children who beginning in 1955 sought to compel the Durham City School Board to desegregate the city schools. For years, Pearson and his co-counsels pursued integrated schools while the school board stonewalled and delayed. In 1959 the school board was compelled to admit twelve black students to two historically white schools. When the school board rejected the black parents' applications for large-scale transfers of black students to the white schools, Pearson, joined by NAACP attorney Jack Greenberg, among others, filed a lawsuit, which was delayed for over seven years by nine district court trials and numerous appeals. In 1966 Pearson and his colleagues won a U.S. Court of Appeals ruling in favor of student and faculty reassignment to schools where the students and teachers were mostly of another race. This victory speeded up the pace of desegregation.

Pearson played an important role in ensuring that southern employers abided by Title VII of the Civil Rights Act of 1964, which banned racial discrimination in hiring and promotion. Pearson served as plaintiff's co-counsel on numerous suits challenging companies throughout North Carolina, including banks, grocery stores, and manufacturing firms that excluded blacks from employment. He was one of the attorneys on the landmark employment discrimination case, *Griggs v. Duke Power Co.* (1971). In that case the Supreme Court ruled that tests to determine promotion were unconstitutional and violated Title VII if they resulted in limiting blacks' economic opportunity for promotion, even if the tests were not overtly racist. Pearson was also co-counsel on *Albemarle Paper Co. v. Moody* (1975), another key Title VII case, in which the plaintiffs showed that a Roanoke Rapids, North Carolina, paper mill had violated the Civil Rights Act by refusing to promote black employees to higher wage positions at the mill.

During the sit-in movement in North Carolina, Pearson actively worked for the integration of public facilities. In 1957 Pearson defended seven black activists, led by Reverend Douglas Moore, who sought unsuccessfully to desegregate the Royal Ice Cream Parlor in Durham. During the 1960s Pearson defended hundreds of civil rights demonstrators in Greensboro, Durham, and other North Carolina cities, who were arrested for their part in sit-ins and picketing to desegregate lunch counters, restaurants, hotels, and movie theaters.

In addition to his work in private practice, Pearson taught at North Carolina Central University Law School from 1968 to 1969 and served as one of the first African American assistant attorneys general of North Carolina from 1973–1976 under Attorneys General Robert Morgan and Rufus Edmisten. Pearson remained active with the NAACP until his death in 1984.

FURTHER READING

A small collection of Conrad O. Pearson's papers are housed in the Special Collections Department, William R. Perkins Library, Duke University, Durham, North Carolina.

Pearson, Conrad Odell. Interview by Walter Weare, Durham, North Carolina, 18 Apr. 1979, H-218, Southern Oral History Program, University of North Carolina at Chapel Hill.

Ballance, Vershenia M. "Conrad Odell Pearson: Pioneer Defender of Civil Rights," *North Carolina State Bar Quarterly* 41 (Fall 1994).

Reynolds, P. Preston. "Hospitals and Civil Rights, 1945–1963: The Case of *Simpkins v. Moses H. Cone Memorial Hospital*," *Annals of Internal Medicine* 126 (1 June 1997): 899–900.

Obituary: *Durham Morning Herald*, 27 June 1984.

JERRY GERSHENHORN

Pearson, Lennie (23 May 1918–7 Dec. 1980), Negro Leagues baseball player, was born Leonard Curtis Pearson in Akron, Ohio. One of ten children, his large family relocated to New Jersey when Lennie was a youngster.

Early on Lennie excelled as an athlete in basketball, football, and baseball. He further honed his athletic skills while he was a student at East Orange High School. He and high school friend MONTE IRVIN (future Newark Eagle teammate and Hall of Famer) developed their talents taking turns pitching and catching each other. A football-related arm injury forced Pearson to give up his dreams as a pitcher. Consequently, he sharpened his dexterity playing first base, where he became a fixture throughout his career, while occasionally filling in at third base and in the outfield.

After dropping out of high school, Pearson got a job and played baseball with the Orange Triangles, a local black semi-pro team. By 1937 he had signed with the Newark Eagles, where he remained a key presence in their lineup for twelve consecutive seasons. He struggled during his rookie season, batting a meager .214. But his sophomore outing proved far better, hitting a career high of .382 and ranking third in Negro National League averages behind future Hall of Famers WILLIE WELLS and BUCK LEONARD. In 1939 he spent the season playing third base and was a part of the dominant "million dollar infield," hitting a staggering .351.

Possessing a formidable combination of flashy fielding and explosive batting, Pearson's talents led him to appear in five East—West All Stars games. Although his performance at each classic was less than stellar, his best outing came at the first of two 1942 contests when he batted .333 and delivered a pinch-hit double off of the legendary SATCHEL PAIGE and scored the go-ahead run on a SAM BANKHEAD sacrifice fly in a 5–2 win for the East.

Late in the 1942 season, Pearson, along with Ed Stone, Bus Clark, and Hall of Fame hurler LeonDay, was recruited by Homestead Grays owner CUM POSEY to beef up the squad for that year's Negro Leagues World Series against the Kansas City Monarchs. The Monarchs' protest of Posey's tactics caused game one of the series to be stricken from the books, and the Monarchs went on to sweep the series in four games.

In 1944 Pearson hit an impressive .326 average and spent the winter playing basketball with the Harlem Renaissance Big Five. In 1945 the Newark first sacker hit a solid .309 and was one in four in an exhibition game against white major leaguers.

Handsome, fiercely competitive, yet soft spoken, Pearson made an impression on Eagles co-owner (and Hall of Famer) Effa Manley, which allegedly developed into an on-again/off-again affair for many years, although both were married. For Manley, however, when it came to business, matters of the heart took a back seat. In 1940, after discovering Pearson's plans to join the ever-growing flight of black players "jumping" to play baseball in Mexico, Manley took legal action against him by asking the State Department to uphold issuance of his passport on the grounds that he had "defrauded his employer." He did, however, manage to play winter ball in Puerto Rico for the Caguas team that year. In keeping with her possessiveness regarding Pearson, in 1942 Manley went to bat for Pearson by writing a letter on his behalf to the draft board, noting that his bad knee qualified him as "unacceptable" for service. Her plea added that his presence on the ball club was important "because of the big part the baseball team plays in the lives of the Negroes of New Jersey." In part because of Manley's petition, Pearson averted military service.

Led by the reliable Pearson, 1946 was a banner year for the Newark Eagles franchise as they won their only Negro League World championship. Pearson, who had become a beloved figure in the hearts of Eagles fans, was now earning as much as $300 a month and was considered one of the "Big Four" sluggers in the Eagles lineup. He batted a solid .276 for the season and a whopping .393 average during the World Series victory over the Kansas City Monarchs. In his last season as a Newark Eagle, the ever-dependable veteran had a league-leading eighteen doubles in 1948.

In 1949 the Eagles' franchise moved to Houston, Texas. Pearson, choosing to stay on the East Coast, became player-manager of the Baltimore Elite Giants. In his final year as a Negro Leaguer, in what might arguably be his most prolific season,

he batted .332 and guided the Elites to the Negro League World Series pennant.

With the onslaught of major league integration and the ensuing demise of the Negro National League, Pearson spent the 1950 and 1951 seasons in the minors with the Class AAA Milwaukee Brewers of the American Association, becoming that organization's first black player. He also played in the Cuban Winter League for five seasons. The aging slugger struggled in AAA, batting .111 in only five at-bats in his last year in 1951. However, in Cuba he shined, becoming a two-time All Star and leading the league in doubles and runs batted in (RBIs). He also became the first player to lead the league three times in RBIs. Before retiring completely, he played with the Class A affiliate Hartford Chiefs and finished his career at the age of thirty-five with the Drummondville Royals (Class C) of the Canadian Provincial League, batting a respectful .293.

Upon his retirement from baseball, Pearson opened a tavern in Newark, with Effa Manley providing some of the financing. He died in East Orange, New Jersey, and was survived by his daughter.

FURTHER READING
Irvin, Monte, with James A Riley. *Nice Guys Finish First—The Autobiography of Monte Irvin* (1996).
Overmyer, James. *Queen of the Negro Leagues* (1998).
Riley, James A. *The Biographical Encyclopedia of The Negro Baseball Leagues* (1994).

BYRON MOTLEY

Pearson, William Gaston (1859? 1940?), social reformer, teacher, and businessman, was born a slave in Durham, North Carolina, to George Pearson and Cynthia Pearson (maiden name unknown). By the time he was old enough to attend school, the Civil War was over and the slaves had been freed. Pearson attended public school six months out of the year, and taught himself in his free time.

When Pearson was twenty-one, he enrolled in Shaw University, a historically black university in Raleigh, North Carolina, and earned a B.S. in 1886 and an honorary M.A. in 1890. While there he joined the Kappa Alpha Psi Fraternity, even earning "The Laurel Leaf," a national award within the fraternity in appreciation of his "[contributing] to the fraternity every possible favor." Pearson also won the Orator's medal at Shaw in 1883. He was later awarded an honorary Ph.D. from Kittrell College in North Carolina and Wilberforce University in Ohio. After graduating from Shaw, Pearson and other black contemporaries in Durham, including the businessman CHARLES CLINTON SPAULDING and educator JAMES E. SHEPARD, started The Royal Knights of King David, a progressive reform group that focused on helping southern African Americans advance socially and economically. He served as secretary of this club for most of his remaining years. Pearson married Minnie R. Sumner in 1893 in a ceremony in Charlotte.

In 1895 Pearson and other black activists in Durham realized the lack of businesses to provide local African Americans with the products and services they needed. This encouraged them to start the region's very first black-owned drug store, the Durham Drug Company. Three years later, Pearson and his partners founded the North Carolina Mutual Life Insurance Company. The company offered life insurance to African Americans, who were excluded from white-owned companies. The company came to be recognized as the largest and most successful black owned businesses in the nation, and continued as a leading insurance company into the twenty-first century. In 1908 Pearson saw the need for yet another pharmacy in Durham, so he and some partners broke off from Durham Drug Company to create the Bull City Drug Company. Pearson also served as the president of Bankers Fire Insurance Company (which he founded in 1920) and the People's Building and Loan Association, the grand endowment secretary of the Masons of North Carolina, and the treasurer of Kittrell University. At one point, his collective businesses were worth over $5 million dollars.

Pearson believed that "Negro business languishes not because of lack of capital or want of opportunity, but because of the scarcity of young men with the training and character necessary to become successful." Pearson also took and published a survey that showed that white-run businesses were generally more financially sound than those businesses run by blacks. This survey was intended as a means to get black business leaders to match or exceed the professionalism of similar white businesses.

Pearson's belief that African American institutions needed to professionalize and meet the highest standards also inspired him in the field of education. Pearson began teaching the middle school at the Whitted School in Durham, one of the largest black schools in the area, in the 1890s. The school eventually became Hillside Park High School, and Pearson became the principal. In his eighteen years in the position, he drastically increased enrollment and achievement at the school. He recruited the best teachers and had stern demands for the quality of education at the school. Despite his reputation for strictness he was beloved by students and faculty, who regularly held birthday and honorary celebrations for their principal. When Pearson retired, he had spent over fifty years involved in the Durham City School System.

Throughout his life, Pearson was widely recognized and honored for his tremendous work in the advancement and education of African Americans in Durham, in North Carolina, and the entire South. Pearson was awarded the prestigious Harmon Award for Business in 1925, and in 1927 he was honored by both white and black citizens of Durham for his extensive work in the city schools. In 1928 Durham City Schools named a new, brick, three-story elementary school in his honor. In 1929 President Herbert Hoover appointed Pearson as a member of the National Memorial Commission. Pearson was instrumental in creating almost all of the businesses on "Black Wall Street," a collection of successful black-owned businesses on Parrish Street in Durham. At his death, it was claimed that that Pearson "contributed more to the development of his race in this city than any other individual."

W. G. Pearson was a devoted member of the AME Church and donated thousands of dollars to the church. It is also estimated that he contributed over $25,000 to Kittrell College, where he volunteered as secretary. He was also a close acquaintance of Washington Duke, the white founder of the Duke tobacco fortune and noted philanthropist.

Throughout his life, William Gaston Pearson played a major role in improving economic opportunities for blacks in the South. He helped found and support countless successful black-owned businesses that existed solely to help a struggling black community. After he helped jump-start the floundering postslavery economy, he devoted his life to helping young black children learn the basics of life as well as the education required for African American progress.

FURTHER READING

Weare, Walter B. *Black Business in the New South: A Social History of the NC Mutual Life Insurance Company* (1993).

Anderson, Jean Bradley. *Durham County: A History of Durham County, North Carolina*, 2nd ed. (2011).

Vann, Andre D., and Beverly Washington Jones. *Durham's Hayti* (1999).

CONNOR KILLIAN

Pease, Joachim (1842–?), Civil War sailor and Medal of Honor recipient, was a man whose heroism shone bright for one brief moment. The rest of his life has largely been lost to history. According to military records Pease was born in 1842 on the "island of Togo" and was living in New York, perhaps on Long Island, at the time of his enlistment in the U.S. Navy. It is uncertain whether Pease was brought to this country as a slave while a young boy from the West African nation of Togo. The idea is not inconceivable, as the country, nestled between Ghana and Benin, is located in one of the major areas on the Guinea Coast where American slavers operated. The only problem with this interpretation is that Togo is not an island. Perhaps the navy muster master got it wrong, or maybe Pease himself called his home country an island based on his youthful recollections. If Pease did come to this country as a slave, he either escaped from bondage, perhaps by running off to sea, or he was manumitted at an early age. However, there is no evidence that confirms exactly what happened.

What is known for certain is that Joachim Pease enlisted in the U.S. Navy during the Civil War on 13 January 1862 at New Bedford, Massachusetts, at the age of twenty. Described as a "negro," Pease was five feet six inches tall and was rated an ordinary seaman. His service was credited to the State of New York, meaning only that Pease was a resident there at the time he enlisted. The rating that Joachim Pease was granted is also an indicator of his previous history. The majority of black sailors enlisting in the Union navy, including men such as JOHN LAWSON and AARON ANDERSON, were rated as landsmen, implying that such men had no previous maritime experience. The fact that Pease was rated an ordinary seaman meant that he had been to sea before. Given the fact that Pease enlisted from New Bedford, it may be speculated that he had previously shipped out from that port, possibly in the crew of a whaler.

Upon his enlistment Pease was sent to New Hampshire to serve on a new Union sloop of war, USS *Kearsarge*. This 1,550-ton warship had previously been launched on 11 September 1861 and was now preparing for its first cruise. Under the command of Captain Charles Pickering, the *Kearsarge*, with Joachim Pease and 162 other men aboard, departed Portsmouth, New Hampshire, for Spain on 5 February 1862. From Spain the *Kearsarge* and its men were sent to Gibraltar to help blockade the Confederate raider *Sumter*. Their efforts finally paid off in December 1862 when the *Sumter's*

commander, Captain Raphael Semmes, burned his ship rather than let it fall into Union hands. The *Kearsarge*, however, had not seen the last of Semmes. He subsequently made his way to England and commissioned a new raider, the soon-to-be-famous CSS *Alabama*. Semmes then commenced a devastating series of raids on Union shipping in nearly every part of the globe, resulting in losses from which the U.S. maritime trade would never fully recover.

Semmes and the *Alabama* had to be stopped, and the task fell to the *Kearsarge* and its men. In March 1863 the Union warship departed Spain in search of the *Alabama*. On station with the North Atlantic Squadron, it patrolled from northern Europe to the Canary Islands in search of its nemesis. That the *Kearsarge* would eventually cross paths with the *Alabama* was almost inevitable. Despite its far-flung travels, the raider would have to return to neutral ports in Europe for refit and re-supply, as Confederate ports in the states were heavily blockaded. By June 1864 the *Alabama* was back in Europe, taking refuge at Cherbourg, France. The *Kearsarge* was not far away and began its approach to Cherbourg in hopes of engaging the Confederate raider. On 14 June, just one day from Cherbourg, Captain John Winslow, the ship's new commander, received a note from Semmes stating that "he intended to fight her and would not delay her but a day or two" (Winslow, 1). On the morning of 19 June 1864, when the *Alabama* departed Cherbourg to do battle with the *Kearsarge*, Joachim Pease was stationed in the gun crew of Robert Strahan. As the loader of gun no. 1, Pease had by this time "the reputation as one of the best men in the ship," according to Acting Master David Sumner, the commander of gun division 3 of the *Kearsarge* (Winslow, 10).

The two ships were evenly matched, and the battle was a hard-fought but rather one-sided affair. Within an hour the *Alabama* had struck its colors and soon after sank, while the *Kearsarge* suffered only three casualties. Not only was it one of the greatest Union naval victories of the war, but several men were distinguished for their heroism during the battle. One of these was Ordinary Seaman Joachim Pease, who was later awarded the Congressional Medal of Honor because he "exhibited marked coolness and good conduct and was highly recommended by his divisional officer for gallantry under fire" (United States Bureau of Naval Personnel, 43).

Pease was one of eight black sailors in the Union navy to be awarded the Medal of Honor, and his service is a shining example of the vital role played by African Americans in helping to win the war at sea. However, Pease never received his medal and may not have even known of the honor he was accorded. By late 1864 the *Kearsarge* was back in the States, and Pease's service was over. The rest of his life is a mystery. He is not listed in any U.S. census records. An experienced sailor by now if there ever was one, perhaps Pease continued to follow the sea and whatever ship he was on became his home. No matter what the case may be, his Medal of Honor still rests in navy archives to this day, waiting to be claimed by his descendants.

FURTHER READING

Quarles, Benjamin Arthur. *The Negro in the Civil War* (1953).

Reidy, Joseph P. "Black Men in Navy Blue during the Civil War," *Prologue* (Fall, 2001).

United States Bureau of Naval Personnel. *Medal of Honor, 1861–1949, The Navy* (1950).

Winslow, Captain John. "The U.S.S. *Kearsarge*'s Duel with the C.S.S. *Alabama* Official Records." http://www.civilwarhome.com/kearsargeors.htm

GLENN ALLEN KNOBLOCK

Peck, Carolyn (22 Jan. 1966–), collegiate and professional basketball head coach and television sports analyst, was born Carolyn Arlene Peck in Jefferson City, Tennessee. She was the middle of three children, between an older brother, Steve, and a younger brother, Michael. Peck attended Jefferson County High School, and was a two-time prep All-American during her high school basketball career. In 1984 she was named Tennessee's Miss Basketball.

After graduating from Jefferson County High School in 1984, Peck attended Vanderbilt University in Nashville, Tennessee, on a basketball scholarship. During her four-year career, Peck averaged 10.6 points and 5.8 rebounds. She totaled 1,240 points, 679 rebounds, and 180 blocks, helping the Commodores to a 77–42 record and appearances in the 1986 and 1987 NCAA Tournament. Peck was named team captain in her final two years and she earned Second Team All-SEC honors her final season. Peck earned her B.A. degree in Communications in 1988.

Not ready to give up her basketball pursuits, Peck returned to the court as a professional player in Japan from 1991 to 1993 with the Nippondenso Corporation. She was the league's leading rebounder her final two years and helped her team win the league championship her last season. After a two-year professional career, Peck begin her coaching career at the University of Tennessee in 1994. She remained at Tennessee for two years and, as an assistant coach under the head coach Pat Summit, helped lead the Lady Volunteers to two first-place finishes in the SEC and also reached the championship game in the 1995 NCAA.

After leaving Tennessee, Peck became an assistant coach at the University of Kentucky for one year, and moved on to become an assistant coach at Purdue University for one year before becoming head coach of Purdue in 1998. As head coach at Purdue University, Peck led her team to a Big Ten regular season undefeated championship, and NCAA Championship in 1999. That year, Peck was named Big Ten Coach of the Year, and the Associated Press and the WBCA Division I National Coach of the Year. The Purdue Boilermakers posted a 74–22 record in three years with Peck, including a 57–11 mark in her two seasons as head coach.

The summer before leading Purdue to the National Championship title, on 6 July 1998 Peck agreed to become the head coach and general manager of the Orlando Miracle, a new expansion team for the WNBA. Four days after leading Purdue to a collegiate championship, Peck began her duties as a professional basketball head coach.

As general manager and head coach of the Miracle, Peck led the Miracle to a 44–52 record in three seasons, including a trip to the 2000 playoffs. During the off-season in Orlando, Peck worked as a sports analyst for Sunshine Network. She served in a similar position for ESPN's coverage of the 2002 NCAA Championship.

In October 2002, the Orlando Miracle announced their decision to relocate their WNBA franchise out of Orlando, Florida. A few months later, on 3 April 2002 Carolyn Peck was named the University of Florida's eighth women's basketball head coach in the history of the school. At the University of Florida, Peck led the Lady Gators to the greatest season turnaround in history during the 2003–2004 season. That year, Peck led the Lady Gators to a 19-11 record. The year prior, the Lady Gators finished 9-19. After five seasons with the University of Florida, Peck returned to ESPN as a basketball analyst for women's college basketball and the WNBA in 2007.

FURTHER READING

"Peck Leaving Miracle for College Scene at Florida." *Orlando Sentinel*, 2 April 2002.

"Miracle Worker." *Sports Illustrated*, 14 June 1999.

DANIELLE D. MELVIN

Peck, David Jones (1826 or 1827–?), physician, was born in Hagerstown, Maryland, the son of John C. Peck and Sally or Sarah (maiden name unknown), free blacks who lived in Carlisle, Pennsylvania. John Peck, who worked as a preacher, wig maker, and barber, campaigned against slavery and worked with the Underground Railroad. Peck's mother was a member of the Carlisle Methodist Church. He had at least one sibling, Mary, born in 1837. That same year the family moved to Pittsburgh, Pennsylvania. From 1841 to 1844 Peck attended the Collegiate Institute at Oberlin, Ohio.

During the 1840s medicine was a virtually all-white profession. The first African American to receive a formal medical degree, JAMES MCCUNE SMITH, had obtained his M.D. in 1837 from the University of Glasgow in Scotland. Peck was the first African American to receive a medical degree at a recognized American medical school.

In 1843 Rush Medical College in Chicago began training students. The *Chicago Democrat* called the school "an ornament to the city." In 1846 school officials admitted Peck as a student with the full backing of the faculty. However, several students opposed Peck's presence, and at least one white doctor sneered that Rush was a "Nigger School" (Fishbein). School president Daniel Brainard allowed the students to decide Peck's future. Brainard "then left the hall, and the students after talking the matter over put it to a vote and we admitted the darkey whooping," class member John Ingersoll recorded (Harris, 601).

Peck's medical training consisted of two eight-week sessions. The school cost "$10 a course, or $60 a term, plus a $20 graduation fee and $5 to cover dissection costs if the student were so inclined" (Bowman, 5). His preceptor was Charles V. Dyer, an outspoken abolitionist and "station chief" in the Underground Railroad" (Kinney, 79).

Peck received his medical degree in the spring of 1847. That summer he joined William Lloyd Garrison and FREDERICK DOUGLASS on their abolition crusade in Ohio. On 16 August 1847 Garrison wrote to his wife that he was accompanied by a "Dr. Peck (he is a fine, promising colored young man, son of my old friend, John Peck, now of Pittsburgh and formerly of Carlyle [sic]) who has lately graduated at the Rush Medical School at Chicago" (Garrison and Garrison, 195). On 25 August, in Richfield, Ohio, they checked into a lodge where, Garrison recorded, the landlord—the brother of the Massachusetts governor—said "that no nigger could be allowed to sit at his table, and

that if any such attempt were made, there would be a mess" (Harris, 601).

In 1848 Peck started a medical-surgical practice in Philadelphia, Pennsylvania. In February of that year he tried to buy medical books at Thomas' Auction Store and was evicted. The *Pittsburgh Gazette* charged "this gross insult was perpetrated on a young man of education, simply to curry favor with the southern students who were in attendance" (Harris, 601). The next year Peck posted a newspaper advertisement: "Dr. D.J. Peck, Physician and Surgeon, Philadelphia Institute, Lombard Street above Seventh" (*Bulletin*, Oct. 1849).

Peck married Mary E. Lewis at a Presbyterian church in Chicago on 24 July 1849. Until late 1850 the couple lived at 223 Lombard Street in Philadelphia. By that time Peck had given up his plans for a medical career in Philadelphia and initially planned to settle in California. Instead, he moved to Nicaragua, where he and his friend and fellow physician MARTIN ROBINSON DELANY tried unsuccessfully to start a black republic. Unfortunately, the rest of Peck's life is veiled in mystery. It has been speculated that after the Civil War he returned to the United States and worked with the Equal Rights League in Pennsylvania.

Until the 1940s scholars assumed that the first black Americans to receive medical degrees at American schools were JOHN VAN SURLY DEGRASSE and Thomas J. White; both received MDs at Bowdoin College in 1849. Peck's identification as the first African American to earn an American medical degree was not generally appreciated until 1949. That year researchers reported finding a record of Peck's medical degree at Rush, according to notices in the February and October 1949 issues of the *Bulletin of the Medico-Chirurgical Society of the District of Columbia*. The Rush student records showed that a David J. Peck graduated in the fourth commencement in 1847. (By then the records had been transferred to the University of Chicago.) In the student catalog a penciled notation by Peck's name noted the then unusual fact: "a colored man." What is known is that Peck pioneered an important profession for African Americans at a time when many were literally shackled to slavery.

FURTHER READING

Bowman, Jim. *Good Medicine: The First 150 Years of Rush–Presbyterian–St. Luke's Medical Center* (1987).
Curtis, James L. *Blacks, Medical Schools, and Society* (1971).

Fishbein, Morris, ed. *Bulletin of the Society of Medical History of Chicago.* Vol. 3, 1923–1925.

Garrison, Wendell Phillips, and Francis Jackson Garrison. *William Lloyd Garrison, 1805–1879: The Story of His Life Told by His Children*, 4 vols. (1885–1889).

Harris, Michael J. "David Jones Peck, MD: A Dream Denied," *Journal of the National Medical Association* 88, no. 9 (Sept. 1996): 600–604.

Kinney, Janet. *Saga of a Surgeon: The Life of Daniel Brainard, M.D.* (1987).

Morais, Herbert M. *The History of the Negro in Medicine* (1968).

This entry is taken from the *American National Biography* and is published here with the permission of the American Council of Learned Societies.

KEAY DAVIDSON

Peeples, Nat (29 June 1926–   ), baseball player, was born Nathaniel Peeples in Memphis, Tennessee, the youngest of seven children of a barber and a housewife, whose names are not known. He grew up in Memphis and in 1944 graduated from Booker T. Washington High School, where he excelled in sports. From 1944 to 1946 Peeples served in the U.S. Navy at Pearl Harbor, where he played baseball against numerous major leaguers. For the next three years he attended LeMoyne College in Memphis, where he majored in mathematics and starred as a halfback on the football team. In 1948 he dropped out of school after signing a contract to play professional baseball with the Memphis Red Sox of the Negro American League. From 1949 to 1951 he was a reserve catcher and outfielder with two legendary Negro League teams, the Kansas City Monarchs and the Indianapolis Clowns.

In June 1951 the Brooklyn Dodgers bought Peeples's contract from the Clowns. For the next three years he played well in the minors but failed in three attempts to hit Class A pitching. He had a breakout season in 1953 in the Class B Three I League, a well-established circuit of eight teams in Illinois, Indiana, and Iowa. He demonstrated that rare combination of hitting for power, a high batting average, and excellent running speed. His performance earned Peeples a promotion to the Atlanta Crackers, where, if he made the team in 1954, he would break the color line in the venerable Class AA Southern Association.

Peeples reported to the Cracker spring training camp in Jacksonville, Florida, on 11 March 1954.

The Cracker owner Earl Mann, his teammates, and his manager Whitlow Wyatt treated him fairly. Wyatt gave Peeples more chances to earn a spot on the roster than any other outfield candidate. In spring training games Peeples batted .340, third highest on the team, and he hit six home runs to lead the club. Because of his excellent performance, Peeples won a position on the opening-day roster. He traveled with the Crackers to Mobile, Alabama, to begin the season on 9 April 1954. At 10:30 that evening, Peeples made history by breaking the color line in the Southern Association. In the fifth inning of the game, he appeared as a pinch hitter. He hit a weak grounder back to the pitcher. The next night Peeples started in left field. In four plate appearances, he walked once and grounded out three times. Peeples did not play in another game, and on 17 April 1954 the Crackers demoted him to Jacksonville of the Class A South Atlantic League. He was the first and only African American to play in the Southern Association.

Several journalists and historians have argued that the Crackers demoted Peeples because of racism. According to this interpretation, the league's other team owners wanted to restore the racial purity of the league. They pressured Mann to end his bold experiment in integration, and he capitulated. This interpretation is untenable. The Crackers sent Peeples to Jacksonville because his baseball skills were deficient, not because Mann yielded to any outside pressure. Mann had introduced integrated baseball games to the Deep South in 1949, when he brought JACKIE ROBINSON and the Dodgers to Atlanta's Ponce de Leon Park for a three-game extravaganza against the Crackers. He defied the Ku Klux Klan, which threatened to shut him down if he proceeded with these games. Subsequently Mann ignored the bitter protests of the other owners when he decided to televise Cracker home games.

Another difficulty with the thesis that Mann demoted Peeples because of outside pressure is that the sources of that pressure—the fans, the league, and the owners—either supported integration or remained largely neutral about it. Between 1949 and 1954 every city in the Southern Association hosted integrated baseball games. More than four hundred thousand fans attended these games, including almost 115,000 in 1954. When Peeples appeared in an exhibition game at Atlanta's Ponce de Leon Park, the fans gave him a longer and louder round of applause than any other Cracker player. In Mobile he received an equally warm and enthusiastic welcome from the fans. At its annual meeting in the winter of 1953, the league adopted a policy of strict neutrality on integration: a team could use African American players or not use them, and the league would not interfere. The other owners supported Mann's effort to integrate the league because they expected to benefit economically from it.

In 1954 Peeples was not ready to play in the Class AA Southern Association. His spring training performance, though impressive statistically, was suspect. He made most of his base hits in the first half of the spring training season, when the opposing pitchers were getting into shape and before they threw all the different pitches in their repertoires. In the second half of spring training, when he faced quality pitching, Peeples's performance declined dramatically. Moreover, he hit four of his six home runs off pitchers who were not ready for AA baseball.

On 17 May 1954, exactly one month after Peeples's demotion, the U.S. Supreme Court ruled school segregation unconstitutional in its *Brown v. Board of Education* decision. In Birmingham, a Southern Association city, segregationists exploited the anger and hard feelings throughout much of the South over the ruling to reestablish the sports color line. On 1 June 1954 the city's white citizens voted by a 3 to 1 margin to restore a law banning mixed-race sports that had been repealed only six months earlier. In 1956 integrated sports competition became illegal in New Orleans, another Southern Association city. In the meantime whites in Chattanooga, Nashville, and Little Rock, all Southern Association members, reacted to the *Brown* decision with violence. The integration that baseball fans had been willing to countenance before *Brown* was now no longer acceptable.

Peeples played the 1954 season in Jacksonville, and for the first time in four tries, he finally hit Class A pitching. His performance was respectable but not outstanding. He began the 1956 season in AA but was still not ready for this level of play and finished the season back in Jacksonville. Peeples's first and only successful year at AA came in 1958, when he played for Austin in the Texas League. After playing in only two games for the Mexico City Reds of the Mexican League in 1960, Peeples suffered a severe knee injury and retired from baseball. He returned to his native Memphis, where he worked as a cab driver. He married in 1964 but had no children. In 1993 the Memphis Chicks, a former Southern Association team, honored the man who broke the color line in the league by having Peeples throw out the ceremonial first ball at its opening home game of the season.

FURTHER READING

A videotaped interview with Peeples and a typed transcript and other materials are in the Southern Bases Collection, MS 735, Atlanta History Center, Atlanta, Georgia.

Adelson, Bruce. *Brushing Back Jim Crow: The Integration of Minor League Baseball in the American South* (1999).

Fenster, Kenneth R. "Earl Mann, Nat Peeples, and the Failed Attempt of Integration in the Southern Association," *Nine: A Journal of Baseball History and Culture* 12 (2004): 73–101.

Hays, Sam. "South's Jackie Robinson: The Atlanta Crackers Gave Nat Peeples a Chance—for Two Games," *Atlanta Journal-Constitution*, 1 Sept. 1985.

KENNETH R. FENSTER

Peery, Benjamin Franklin (16 Sept. 1892–6 Oct. 1971), businessman and community leader, was born to Luther C. Peery and Catherine B. Peery in St. Joseph, Missouri. His father and paternal grandparents were from Missouri, whereas his mother was born in Kentucky. Returning from military service in Europe after World War I, he lived with his parents for a few years, working as a construction laborer. His wife Carolyn, whom he married in the early 1920s, was born in Kansas to parents from Kentucky. They had seven sons between 1921 and the early 1930s: Benjamin Jr., Nelson, Alvin, Carroll, Ross, Norman, and Richard.

When Peery and another black veteran passed the civil service exam for the previously segregated Railway Mail Service, a district supervisor transferred him from Missouri to Minneapolis, Minnesota, where another supervisor responded to complaints about discrimination by transferring him to the rural community of Wabasha. His family were the only blacks in town (Peery, *Black Fire*, p. 4). Every year he requested a transfer back to Minneapolis, which was routinely ignored. Eventually he wrote directly to the postmaster general that his oldest sons were reaching puberty and associating with white girls because there were no girls their own color. His transfer came through in less than a month (Peery, *Black Fire*, p. 18).

Peery was a carefully self-conscious man, who would severely discipline his sons for the slightest prank involving a girl considered white—for fear of provoking an incident—but a proud man, who also instructed his sons to beat up anyone who called them "nigger." After knocking out a drunken man who had punched his son, NELSON PEERY, Peery faced down a half-hearted lynch mob outside a bar with a .30-06 rifle, a shotgun, and his World War I service revolver, until someone said "I don't think anybody is going to respect a man who doesn't protect his family" and invited him over for a drink (Peery, *Black Fire*, pp. 160–161).

Employed during the worst years of the Depression, he suffered repeated pay cuts, even while neighbors came to him for small loans, and his wife fed every transient who came to their house for a meal. In 1938 when a reported rape of a white woman by an unidentified Negro led to talk of a vigilante mob to "assist the police," Peery called the local police chief. He announced that his segregated American Legion post intended to assist the police in keeping a lynch mob out of the neighborhood. After a visit from a police public relations sergeant, he agreed that he and the other veterans would carry only clubs, keeping their rifles in cars parked in nearby alleys. After a tense night with no violence, the woman confessed she had actually been with a white lover. Peery proudly observed, "We let the police know, and they let the mob know" (Peery, *Black Fire*, pp. 197–198).

Peery wrote a column for the *Twin Cities Herald*, one of two prominent Negro periodicals in the Minneapolis area. Active in the local chapter of the National Association for the Advancement of Colored People, he urged support for Democratic Party candidates in 1944. As a series of red scares swept the United States in the years following World War II, Peery assiduously broke all ambivalent sympathies he had held toward American communism. His Filipino brother-in-law had been an early Communist Party member, and his older sons came home from military service convinced communists; four sons joined the party for various periods of time. He began making passionate speeches to his American Legion post that he had been forced to choose between patriotism and his sons.

In 1948 Peery developed an affair with Dollie L. Latimer, a woman sixteen years younger than himself, born in South Carolina in 1908. They married after Peery divorced his wife Carolyn, who subsequently joined the Women's International League for Peace and Freedom. Peery moved to Los Angeles, where by 1953 he was president of the fifty-fifth state assembly district Republican Assembly.

In 1958, serving as twenty-third congressional district Republican leader, he took a seat on the executive committee of the California Republican State Central Committee, a body with an ironically Leninist sound to its name. That year, he advocated that the Republican Western Conference abolish "every civil rights committee, wherever they exist within the framework" of the party, replacing them with "Committees on Constitutional Rights, Human Rights, or whatever name may be best suited" (*California Eagle*, 19 Nov. 1959). He urged that the term "civil rights" had become a "meaningless cliché" unsuited to "describe or fit the issues of our time" (*California Eagle*, 19 Nov. 1959).

Peery was not attempting to liquidate the cause of civil rights. He put Ronald Reagan in an embarrassing spotlight in April 1966, pointedly asking the candidate for California governor, at a debate with primary rival George Christopher before an audience of black Republicans, "How are Negro Republicans going to encourage other Negroes to vote for you, after your statement that you would not have voted for the civil rights bill?" (Dallek, p. 201). Reagan stumbled badly trying to answer, maintaining that he supported the principles involved, but the bill was "a bad piece of legislation." Reagan aide Stu Spencer later observed, "We knew Ron wasn't going to get anywhere with Negroes, but he had to go anyway because it would look bad if he stayed away" (Dallek, p. 201).

By that time Americans of African descent were in any case a miniscule portion of Republican voters. In 1968, following the assassination of Rev. Martin Luther King Jr., Perry offered the proposal that Watts be renamed in honor of Dr. King (*Jet*, 25 Apr. 1968). He also served as president of the Watts Community Symphony Orchestra during the late 1960s and testified as a Watts resident to the commission examining the Watts uprising of 1965.

Peery ran twice as a Republican for the state assembly to represent the fifty-fifth district. The first time, in 1960, he received the endorsement of Los Angeles's largest circulation Negro paper, the *California Eagle*, running against "white" Democrat Vernon Kilpatrick. "California Negroes got on the Democratic bandwagon in 1934," the *Eagle* editorialized, and had voted overwhelmingly for Democratic candidates ever since. "The faithful party voter, like the faithful wife, gets too much taken for granted. Republicans had the Negro vote in their vest pocket for more than 60 years and were so sure of his allegiance that they didn't bother to worry about his problems or consult him on what he wanted. Some of that attitude is beginning to creep into the Democratic party." Although "Negroes can hardly afford the luxury of voting the Republican ticket solely for the purpose of proving their independence," they could certainly "make exceptions where the GOP nominates a Negro and Democrats refuse to do so" (*Eagle*, 16 June 1960).

Few voters followed this advice. Peery lost with 19.3 percent of the vote, but the *Eagle's* sampling of Watts precincts to measure "How Negroes Voted" showed he ran ahead of Republican presidential candidate Richard M. Nixon, who received about 11.5 percent. In 1968, running against Leon D. Ralph, a Democrat who, like Perry, was African American, he received 13.5 percent of the vote. Peery died in 1971, survived by his first wife Carolyn, who died in 2000, and his second wife Dollie, who died in 1981.

FURTHER READING

Dallek, Matthew. *The Right Moment: Ronald Reagan's First Victory and the Decisive Turning Point in American Politics* (2001).

Peery, Nelson. *Black Fire: The Making of an American Revolutionary* (1994).

Peery, Nelson. *Black Radical: The Education of an American Revolutionary* (2007).

Terkel, Studs. "Carolyn Peery," *Coming of Age: The Story of Our Century by Those Who've Lived It* (1995).

CHARLES ROSENBERG

Peery, Nelson (22 June 1923–), a veteran of the segregated U.S. military in World War II and communist activist, was born in St. Joseph, Missouri, the son of BENJAMIN FRANKLIN PEERY, a railway mail service clerk, and Carolyn Peery, a charter member of the Women's International League for Peace and Freedom.

Peery's family moved to Wabasha, Minnesota, in 1928, where they were the only black family. Young Nelson had friends and learned that if nobody else involved in mischief was identified, he would be. His father secured a transfer to Minneapolis, where there was a small African American community. While Peery acquired black friends, they all had friends thought of as "white" and fought alongside or against Irish and Italian gangs. In an early display of militancy, Peery and his closest friends targeted a White Castle hamburger joint that refused to serve blacks, breaking the windows several times (Hynes, p. 170).

In 1941 Perry volunteered for Civilian Military Training Camp, with one eye on helping to contain the rise of fascism abroad and the other on helping African Americans become proficient in firearms. He reported to Fort Riley, Kansas, on 1 July 1941. The program was racially segregated, "and God help any black trooper who struck a white one" (Peery, *Black Fire*, p. 89). He qualified as an expert rifleman. After a few months riding freight trains out west, seeking work, a hobo named West Coast told Peery to go home.

Back in Minneapolis, Peery entered the writing class of Abigail O'Leary, a Christian socialist who supervised a quarterly literary magazine, *Quest* (Hynes, p. 244). Peery served as literary co-editor; many of his corner gang held editorial positions, as did four young white women. The magazine swept at least six National Scholastic prizes, with Peery taking first in autobiographical sketch, short story, and essay. Peery found his way into Young Communist League (YCL) activities—he had classmates in YCL, whose mothers regularly distributed the *Daily Worker* door to door—but was never formally a member.

After Pearl Harbor, Peery enlisted. "I wanted it to be my own decision to go fight along with the people of the world" (Peery, *Black Fire*, p. 127). Receiving his high school diploma 12 June 1942, he reported to Fort Huachuca, Arizona, assigned to the segregated Ninety-Third Infantry Division. Peery recalled that he was constantly under surveillance by military intelligence (G-2). He organized literacy classes for recruits and draftees. He led a small group planning armed response to race riots against black civilians and soldiers and also helped organize a brief strike, securing an apology from one Major Betha, who called an enlisted man "black boy."

Promoted to staff sergeant, in July 1943 Perry was shipped with the Ninety-Third to the Mojave desert and then in early 1944 to Guadalcanal in the Pacific Theater. His most intense combat experience was in the fighting for Bougainville, a small island attached to present day Papua New Guinea. After the Japanese surrendered in 1945, the Ninety-Third was assigned to the Philippines. Contacted by Hukbalahap guerillas, led by Philippine communists who had fought the Japanese independently of U.S.-aligned Filipino forces, Peery aided them in securing army supplies and training manuals and considered joining them when his division was shipped home, but was persuaded by his Huk comrades that he could be more useful to them in America.

Returning home, determined to "move from first-class soldier to first-class citizen," he joined the Communist Party. Enrolling in the University of Minnesota, he led a campaign to hire black faculty, cheerfully signing a letter "For the combined communist clubs, Nelson Peery." The first African American, Forrest Williams, was hired almost immediately in the philosophy department. Recognized for his campus leadership with induction into the prestigious Grey Friars Club, he saw a trap offering comfort and privilege in exchange for abandoning his politics and quit school, joining Local 544, Hodcarriers and Construction Laborer's Union. Soon after, he obtained membership in the Bricklayers, Masons, and Plasterers International Union, Local 2, despite a clause declaring membership "open to white men of high moral caliber."

In 1948 Peery was nearly expelled from the party over a paper he authored questioning Prime Minister Josip Broz Tito's policy in Yugoslavia—before Stalin condemned Tito. When criticism turned to praise, Peery pondered, "Comrades I respected, swung 180 degrees, on the basis of statements of leaders rather than thinking things through." Moving to Cleveland, Ohio, on party assignment, he married a woman named Roberta, whose family was an amalgam of every ethnic group in Tennessee's hill country, and got bricklaying work, despite the Federal Bureau of Investigation routinely tracking down his employer. Tom Snavely, his boss, observed, "I don't know much about communism, but if communists are trying to destroy democracy, I don't think we should help them." Peery was expelled from the party in March 1953. Although neither he nor the party made the reasons public, Peery favored open confrontation with the anti-communist red scare of the 1950s, sharply opposed a decision that "party forces are to pull out of the National Negro Labor Congress," and was contemptuous of the way black FBI informers, whom he readily recognized as agents, could charm their way into inner party circles on their skin color. Peery was invited in 1958 by veteran black communists ADMIRAL KILPATRICK and Jimmy Jackson to join the Provisional Organizing Committee (POC) to reconstitute a Marxist—Leninist Party in the United States. He moved to New York City, leaving Roberta ownership of the couple's house in an agreed divorce. Later that year, he married Sue Ying Hoyate, the daughter of a Chinese father and a Norwegian mother. Their first son, born in January 1961, was named Patrice, after the recently murdered Patrice Lumumba, prime minister of the First Republic of the Congo.

In late 1964 a small group in Los Angeles led by Michael Laski and Arnold Hoffman asked to join POC. Moving to the West Coast, Peery was unimpressed. The local group sought and got a good deal of attention in the local press, whereas Peery's experience taught that the press was silent about serious revolutionaries. He also found Laski and Hoffman patronizing toward non-white comrades—and POC by this time was almost entirely black and Hispanic. Although he considered the color of leadership of no consequence, he would not tolerate working-class black communists being blocked from participation by educated middle-class white communists. Peery also disagreed with POC's New York leadership characterizing events in Watts in 1965 as a riot. He saw a people's response to "an army of occupation," citing daily arrests and beatings over misdemeanors, black motorists stopped and humiliated, and black women raped by police who were never prosecuted (Boyd, p. 211).

Expelled from the POC in 1968, Peery led the formation of the California Communist League (Kelley, p. 100), merging in 1970 with a splinter of Students for a Democratic Society to form the Communist League, which two years later adopted the name Communist Labor Party (CLP). In 1971 they were joined by GENERAL BAKER and other veterans of the Dodge Revolutionary Union Movement (Wei-Han and Mullen, p. 121). Peery, an intellectually skilled World War II veteran and bricklayer, was a marked contrast to the post-New Left radical Maoists (Elbaum, p. 103). Enthralled with armed struggles taking place half way around the world, few had served in the military. Whether from working class families or more prosperous professional backgrounds, none had lived through the Depression. Some had heard second-hand about the repression of the McCarthy era, but none had lost one job after another to FBI harassment of their employer. Intoxicated on communist literature, none had experience with living for years as part of a disciplined party of any real substance.

Chicano filmmaker Jesús Salvador Treviño recalled Peery in 1974 as "a fifty year old African American with a distinguished gray beard" who dressed in modest work clothes, had a broad smile, and laughed deeply. Treviño said, "He reflected a profound faith in humankind, believing that all races could pull together for a better world." Treviño liked Peery, but, recalling James Baldwin's disenchantment with the Communist Party in the 1940s, resisted subordinating his art to any political supervision (Treviño, p. 342–343). When the CLP formally dissolved in 1993, Peery and other former CLP members formed the League of Revolutionaries for a New America, reflecting Peery's conclusion that the vanguard organization advocated by Lenin could not work in an industrialized nation because it is too easily penetrated and controlled by the political police.

After Sue Ying died on Christmas Eve 2002, their younger son Steve took up farming in northern Minnesota; their older son Patrice worked as a longshoreman in Los Angeles. Speaking to a variety of audiences and still a prolific writer, Peery lived long enough to share on YouTube (http://www.youtube.com/watch?v=S33j7YdrC Oc) the perspective of growing up dark-skinned in the Great Depression. Looking back on his life, Peery observed, "an American revolutionary can truthfully sing, 'Oh beautiful for spacious skies' with the same emotion that he or she sings 'Arise ye wretched of the earth.'" That echoed the words of a hobo named Ace, who told Peery in 1941, "Any farmer knows you can't hate the land...I hates some of the people in it, but you can't hate the country."

FURTHER READING

Peery, Nelson. *Black Fire: The Making of an American Revolutionary* (1994).

Peery, Nelson. *Black Radical: The Education of an American Revolutionary* (2007).

Boyd, Herb. *We shall overcome* (2004).

Elbaum, Max. *Revolution in the Air: Sixties Radicals Turn to Lenin, Mao and Che* (2002).

Hynes, Samuel. *The Growing Seasons: An American Boyhood before the War* (2004).

Kelley, Robin D.G. *Freedom Dreams: The Black Radical Imagination* (2002).

Treviño, Jesús Salvador. *Eyewitness: A Filmmaker's Memoir of the Chicano Movement* (2001).

Wei-Han, Fred, and Bill Mullen. *Afro Asia: Revolutionary Political and Cultural Connections between African Americans and Asian Americans* (2008).

CHARLES ROSENBERG

Peete, Calvin (18 July 1943–), professional golfer, was born in Detroit, Michigan, one of nine children, to Dennis Peete and Irene Bridgeport. When he was eleven, his parents split up and he was sent to live with his grandmother in rural Hayti, Missouri, supposedly temporarily. Instead Peete and two of his sisters ended up there permanently, eventually abandoned by their mother. A future master of a game played in a pastoral setting, Peete wished he was out of the countryside and back in Detroit. At the age of twelve he fell out of a tree and shattered his left elbow. Though he received proper medical attention, he would never be able to fully straighten his left arm. It is widely believed, however, that this misfortune proved to be a great advantage in his golf career.

Arguably the straightest hitter in golf history and a star of the 1980s, Peete, who suffered from Tourette's Syndrome, was an extraordinary anomaly in golf history, since he did not start playing the game until the relatively late age of twenty-three. Also, unlike most professional golfers, black or white, Peete never caddied as a young man. Caddying was a common occupation for economically underprivileged young golfers because, aside from being a well-paying part-time job, it was common for golfers to extend (limited) playing opportunities to caddies at otherwise inaccessible, private golf clubs, thus allowing them to practice. Even professional golfers (or amateurs) who come from more privileged backgrounds often learn how to caddy at some point because it is considered one of the best pedagogical methods for learning the rules and decorum of the game and also for the widest possible understanding of the game.

When Peete was a young man he fell into a life of gambling involving dice, pool, and numbers running. By his early twenties, he was involved with hustling and gambling with black, migrant workers up and down the East Coast, sometimes finding himself in violent situations. It was during this time, in Rochester, New York, that he was introduced to golf by underworld acquaintances. He soon found that he had a flair for the game. As improbable as his introduction to the game sounds, there was indeed a black subculture in which golf and illicit activities were connected. Many full-time black caddies migrated seasonally. Caddies were paid in cash on a daily basis, a situation which led to some overlap between golf and gambling.

Peete often said that his inspiration to become a professional golfer (as opposed to remaining a skilled amateur) came from watching ROBERT LEE ELDER play against Jack Nicklaus in 1968. Elder, who joined the Professional Golfers Association (PGA) Tour in 1967, was one of the first black professional golfers (CHARLIE SIFFORD integrated the PGA Tour in 1961).

In 1974 Peete married his first wife, Christine, whom he divorced in 1987. They had five children. Peete first qualified for the PGA Tour in 1975 and hit his stride in the 1980s, winning twelve PGA Tour events and playing on the U.S. Ryder Cup teams in 1983 and 1985. The crowning achievement of his career was his win in the 1985 Tournament Players Championship (his win in this tournament earned him a lifetime membership at the club where the tournament was played, Tournament Players Club, Sawgrass, in his home of Ponte Vedra Beach, Florida). That year he finished third on the PGA's all-important "money list."

Peete led the PGA Tour in drive accuracy (meaning how often he hit fairways from tees) from 1981 until 1991 and put up an array of astonishing accuracy-related statistics. The eminent golf television commentator Johnny Miller called Peete "the straightest hitter that ever lived" (*Golf Digest*, Mar. 2005). It is thought that Peete's childhood elbow injury enabled him to have a geometrically and synchronically perfect swing. Though this may be the case, it cannot explain all or even most of his success. There is an expression in golf that says "you drive for show, but putt for dough," meaning that while an impressive drive can be exhilarating to watch, the delicate putt (which often needs to curve) is what wins matches.

In fact, any advantage gained by the condition of his elbow was offset by his case of the neurological disorder Tourette's Syndrome, which causes uncontrollable muscle movements and vocal expressions. Though he was always afflicted by neck spasms, his case of Tourette's became severe during the mid-1980s and was only diagnosed in 1999. Peete went to great lengths to hide his affliction, which was not at all apparent, especially off the golf course, where he had a smooth demeanor that masked his struggle.

Peete married his second wife, Pepper Bolden, who worked for First Tee, an educational golf initiative, in 1992. He credited Pepper with encouraging him to get treatment for his Tourette's. They had two daughters. Peete joined the Senior PGA Tour (later the Champions Tour) in 1994. He retired in 2001. Still, Peete remained peripherally involved with golf, playing occasionally in charity events and serving on the board of Tournament Gifts of America, a golf tournament merchandise manufacturer.

Peete was the most visible and successful black golfer between the era of Sifford and Elder and that of TIGER WOODS. In terms of racism or discrimination, Peete never claimed to have had any trouble and he credited Elder and Sifford with paving the way for him. He once referred to his experience on the PGA Tour as "a cakewalk" (*Los Angeles Times*, 12 Mar. 1998). Though the doors of professional golf were open when he arrived, he believed that he opened doors in the black community at large by introducing young people to the game. Peete strongly believed in golf as a conduit or connection to success, an opportunity for disadvantaged children to make contact with leading figures in their communities.

FURTHER READING

Adande, J. A. "Before There Was a Tiger, Peete Held Flame for Many," *Los Angeles Times*, 12 Mar. 1998.

Adande, J. A. "Teeing Off: History of Blacks in Golf," *Black Enterprise* (Sept. 1994).

McDaniel, Pete. *Uneven Lies: The Heroic Story of African-Americans in Golf* (2000).

McDaniel, Pete. "Whatever Happened to Calvin Peete?" *Golf Digest* (Mar. 2005).

Sinnette, Calvin H. *Forbidden Fairways* (1998).

PAUL DEVLIN

Pelham, Benjamin B. (1862–7 Oct. 1948), newspaper publisher, municipal official, and politician, was born in Detroit, Michigan, the son of Robert Pelham, a plasterer and mason, and Frances Butcher. The Pelhams were a prosperous free black family who at one time owned a farm in Petersburg, Virginia. They were forced to sell, however, because of the harassment of townspeople, who were probably jealous of the family's success. The need to leave Virginia became apparent when the Pelhams attempted to purchase a license for their pet dog but were turned down by local authorities, who claimed that only whites and slaves could purchase dog licenses. The family decided to head north, and around 1862, after brief stops in Columbus, Ohio, and Philadelphia, Pennsylvania, the Pelhams settled in Detroit shortly after Benjamin's birth.

Pelham attended Detroit public schools and the fashionable Barstow private school. While still a student he became a newsboy for the *Detroit Post*, later known as the *Post-Tribune*, Michigan's leading Republican daily. He developed an interest in the mechanical aspect of typesetting and upon his graduation from Detroit High School became an apprentice typesetter for the paper.

In 1879 Pelham's older brother, ROBERT PELHAM JR., who had joined him as an apprentice typesetter at the *Post-Tribune*, started his own eight-page newspaper, the *Venture*. In 1883 W. H. Anderson and Walter H. Stowers joined the Pelham brothers in founding the successor to the *Venture*, a weekly they called the *Plaindealer*. The four men and an additional five-member staff published the *Plaindealer* in offices located in the *Post-Tribune* building. Both Pelham and his brother continued working for the *Post-Tribune* even while publishing their own paper.

The *Plaindealer*, whose widely read articles were written by important black figures of the era, became one of the country's leading African American newspapers. In 1884 the paper's editorial board championed the Colored Men's State Convention, which provided a medium for the political voice of blacks throughout the Midwest. Owing to the wide coverage that the paper gave to such issues, Pelham gained political influence on a national level. Later that year he headed a campaign that successfully elected a black man as an at-large delegate to the Republican National Convention in Chicago.

In 1893, in the eleventh year of publication of the *Plaindealer*, the partners ended operations because of financial problems. At that time Pelham was appointed a clerk in the Internal Revenue Office by its director, James H. Stone, who at one time had owned the *Post-Tribune*. In 1895 Pelham got a job as a clerk in the Office of the Treasurer in Detroit. That year he married Laura Montgomery; the couple had two children.

In 1900 Pelham moved on to a position in the Office of the Registrar of Deeds in Detroit, where he worked until 1906. In the election that year Charles Buhrer, a former printer at the *Post-Tribune*, was elected auditor of Wayne County, which includes Detroit. Buhrer named Pelham chief accountant of the Board of Supervisors of Wayne County, the highest nonelective office in county government. Pelham was soon recognized as an expert on county government administration and was appointed to serve simultaneously as clerk to the board of auditors, Detroit's governing body, with responsibility for setting the agenda for the board.

By 1906, having earned the reputation in Detroit political circles as a shrewd politician, Pelham, a lifelong Republican, had formed his own black political machine. Since the community had no white machine to oppose it, his organization became the dominant political force surrounding Detroit. Wade H. McCree Jr. wrote, "During the period of Ben Pelham's administration curiously enough no other Negro emerged into prominence in Michigan politics....[It was Pelham alone who] made and broke political figures and dominated Wayne County government as no person did before or has since his political retirement before

World War I." The onset of the war, coupled with the influx of new European immigrants, caused Pelham to lose control of his tightly knit organization, thereby signaling the end of his political machine.

Pelham continued to work in municipal government and retained his position as county accountant after a Democrat was elected mayor in 1934. Observers speculated that he kept his job because of his unique knowledge of how the city ran. Pelham retired as county accountant in 1942, following forty-seven years of continuous public service. During his tenure Wayne County had become the fourth most populous county in the United States. Pelham died in Detroit.

FURTHER READING

Mallas, Aris A., Jr., et al. *Forty Years in Politics: The Story of Ben Pelham* (1957).

McCree, Wade H., Jr. "The Negro Renaissance in Michigan Politics," *Negro History Bulletin* 26 (Oct. 1962).

Penn, Irvine Garland. *The Afro-American Press and Its Editors* (1891).

Walton, Hanes, Jr. *Black Politics* (1972).

This entry is taken from the *American National Biography* and is published here with the permission of the American Council of Learned Societies.

FRANCESCO L. NEPA

Pelham, Robert A., Jr. (4 Jan. 1859–June 1943), inventor, newspaper publisher, and editor, was born the second son and fifth child to Robert and Frances Pelham near Petersburg, Virginia. In the year of his birth his family moved to Detroit, Michigan, seeking better educational and economic opportunities. Pelham attended the public schools of Detroit and managed to finish a twelve-year educational course in nine years.

In 1871, while still in high school, Pelham sharpened his journalistic skills while working at the *Daily Post*, a leading Republican newspaper of the time. At the *Daily Post* Pelham worked under Zachariah Chandler, who not only was the owner of the *Daily Post* but also was a prominent Republican who went on to become mayor of Detroit and a U.S. senator. This close working relationship probably explains Pelham's later involvement with the Republican Party.

Pelham wrote for the *Detroit Daily* from 1883 to 1891. While in this position he created, edited, and managed the *Detroit Plaindealer*, a black weekly newspaper that went on to become the most successful black newspaper in the Midwest. Although the newspaper had closed by 1894, Pelham still benefited from its success. He then became active in the Republican Party and served as the Republican National Convention sergeant-at-arms in 1896. Pelham also held a number of significant jobs, such as deputy oil inspector for the state of Michigan from 1887 to 1891. From 1893 to 1898 Pelham was active as inspector for the Detroit water department, and in 1899 he was given the title special agent for the United States Land Office.

In 1893 Pelham wed Gabrielle Lewis of Adrian, Michigan. Gabrielle Lewis was influential in the musical world of Washington, D.C., and was also the first black person to hold an official position in the Michigan State Music Teacher's Association. Robert Pelham and Gabrielle Lewis had three children; their eldest son went on to carry out experiments in wireless telegraphy, becoming one of the few blacks in Washington, D.C., to hold a license for operating a wireless telegraph. The Pelhams moved their family to Washington, D.C., in 1900, where for thirty years Robert Pelham worked as a clerk for the U.S. Census Bureau. While in Washington, D.C., Pelham also studied law at Howard University and received his law degree in 1904.

As a clerk for the U.S. Census Bureau, Pelham compiled groups of statistics on sheets that included data sent in from manufacturers all over the country. Clerks also had to paste statistical slips manually onto sheets and then organize them. This process was labor-intensive and required many clerks. To speed up the process Pelham invented a prototype pasting machine using two cigar boxes, a wooden rolling pin, some curtain fixtures, two wood screws, a piece of tin, and a strip of sheet rubber. The pasting machine was a tabulator that automated the process of the clerks and was used in the census count of manufacturers. The machine was patented in 1905, and the U.S. government leased the machine from Pelham, paying Pelham a royalty in addition to his regular salary. By using the pasting machine the U.S. Census Bureau saved more than three thousand dollars just in 1905. The machine made the census count quicker and required fewer clerks to operate it than the old method used to organize data sent from manufacturers. In 1913 Pelham invented a tallying machine, which assisted in the tabulation of census information. Like the pasting machine, the tallying machine saved much time and money.

After retiring from the U.S. Census Bureau, Pelham purchased the *Washington Tribune*, a black newspaper, from the Murray Brothers Publishing Company. Pelham served as editor and publisher of the paper until he resold it back to Murray Brothers. While in retirement Pelham also created the *Capital News Services*, a news agency that was dedicated to addressing African American issues. At age eighty-four Robert Pelham died in Washington, D.C., leaving behind a long trail of accomplishments. He was an intellectual who left his mark on the fields of both journalism and politics. One of his greatest contributions, however, was his tallying device, which ultimately led to the invention of the calculating machine.

FURTHER READING
Baker, Henry E. *The Colored Inventor* (1913).
Brodie, James Michael. *Created Equal: The Lives and Ideas of Black American Innovators* (1993).
Warren, Francis H., ed. *Michigan Manual of Freedmen's Progress* (1915).
Obituary: *Chicago Defender*, 26 June 1943.

JACQUELINE-BETHEL MOUGOUÉ

Pendergrass, Teddy (26 Mar. 1950–13 Jan. 2010), composer, drummer, and singer, was born Theodore DeReese Pendergrass in Philadelphia, Pennsylvania, the son of Ida Geraldine Epps and Jesse Pendergrass, both of whom were the children of South Carolina sharecroppers. Jesse Pendergrass mysteriously abandoned his original family and remarried when Teddy was a small child. Teddy did not see his biological father again until 1961, one year before Jesse was murdered by a neighborhood "friend" over a supposed gambling debt. Despite being fatherless and an only child, Teddy's early childhood years were filled with the constant love and affection of his mother and several aunts, especially his aunt Ila David (Aunt Dee), who bestowed on him the nickname "Teddy the Bear" when he was two years old. During these years Ida Pendergrass instilled in her son the belief that God had chosen him to achieve greatness.

Pendergrass first exhibited signs of his musical talent at age two, when his mother encouraged him to sing a solo at their local church. When he was ten years old he was baptized and ordained as a youth minister. However, it was his experience singing with the citywide McIntyre Elementary School Choir, and later with the acclaimed Stetson Junior High School Choir, that led Pendergrass to discover his ability to sing in front of a large audience.

As a teenager Pendergrass spent most of his evenings doing homework, singing gospel songs, and

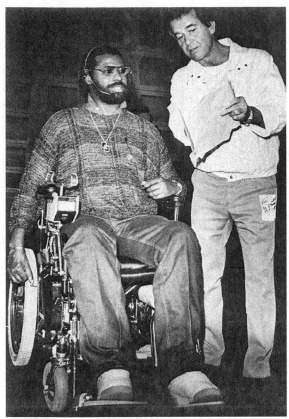

Teddy Pendergrass with Dick Clark, executive producer of the "American Music Awards" telecast, in Los Angeles on 25 Jan. 1986. (AP Images.)

teaching himself to play the drums. At fifteen he was given his first drum set by his mother, which he retained until he joined the group HAROLD MELVIN and the Blue Notes. In 1968, at the age of eighteen, his singing career was going nowhere so he took a job as a drummer for a local vocal group called the Cadillacs. At the time, the Cadillacs and Harold Melvin and the Blue Notes were the best-known R&B acts in the city. Eventually the two merged into one group, with Pendergrass remaining as the drummer. In 1970, while the Blue Notes were on tour in the Caribbean Islands, Pendergrass was asked to become a lead singer in the group. The result was a new and lucrative contract for the entire group with the recently created Philadelphia International Records (later known as PIR), led by Kenny Gamble and LEON HUFF, who had produced hit records for national artists such as WILSON PICKETT JR. and Dusty Springfield. The first song that the Blue Notes released with this new arrangement was "I Miss You," which became an instant

hit on the pop and R&B charts. The collaboration between the powerful lead vocals of Pendergrass and Harold Melvin, combined with the superb writing and production team of Gamble and Huff, made Harold Melvin and the Blue Notes nationwide celebrities with a series of hits such as "Bad Luck," "The Love I Lost," "To Be True," and "Wake Up Everybody." However, behind the scenes, Pendergrass and Melvin began to have differences. Finally, in 1976, they parted company.

For a time there were two groups called the Blue Notes, one led by Pendergrass and the other by Melvin. The arrangement made it quite difficult for the public to distinguish between the "Blue Notes Featuring Teddy Pendergrass" on one hand and "Harold Melvin and the Blue Notes" on the other. This problem was resolved when Pendergrass officially started his solo career in early 1977, with the release of his first album, *Teddy Pendergrass*. This record generated several number-one hit singles: "I Don't Love You Anymore," "You Can't Hide from Yourself," and "The More I Get, the More I Want." More importantly, despite some missteps and the tragic murder of his close friend and business manager, Taaz Lang, the subsequent concerts that supported the album announced to the music industry that Pendergrass was a powerful force as a solo artist.

During the rest of the 1970s and early 1980s Pendergrass's status as a celebrated and critically acclaimed R&B singer was crystallized with five solo albums—*Life Is a Song Worth Singing* (1978), *Teddy* (1979), *Teddy Live* (1979), *TP* (1980), and *It's Time for Love* (1981)—that either went gold or platinum and produced a series of hit songs such as "Close the Door," "Turn Off the Lights," "If You Don't Know Me by Now," "Take Me in Your Arms Tonight" (with Stephanie Mills), and "Love TKO." This recording success was accompanied by a series of national awards, including the Billboard New Artist Award in 1977, two Grammy nominations in 1977 and 1978, and an American Music Award in 1978, as well as honors for performance achievement and charitable contribution from organizations such as the NAACP, the Afro-American Historical and Cultural Museum Association, and *Ebony* magazine.

It seemed that the sky was the limit for Pendergrass. In 1979 he agreed to star in the film *The Otis Redding Story*, though the film was never made. One year later, in 1980, he started a clothing line called Teddy Bear Productions. At the same time, Pendergrass continued to sell out concerts throughout the United States and abroad. Even after a minor car accident in early 1981, his nonstop tour in Europe went on and ended in London with a duet with his childhood idol, STEVIE WONDER. However, the following year, on 18 March 1982, a near-fatal car accident in Philadelphia left Pendergrass a quadriplegic with only limited use of his arms. After years of physical and psychological therapy, as well as several surgeries, Pendergrass decided to restart his career from a wheelchair. In 1984 he released his gold album *Love Language*. The following year he returned to the concert stage for the first time since his accident, performing at Live Aid. In 1988 his album *Joy* brought him much acclaim from his many friends and colleagues both inside and outside the music industry and was nominated for a Grammy Award. Despite the release of several more albums throughout the rest of the 1980s and 1990s, Pendergrass never regained the prestige and fame he once enjoyed during the late 1970s and early 1980s. By the late 2000s, much of his energy was devoted to serving as an advocate for spinal cord injury research and to administering the Teddy Pendergrass Alliance, an organization devoted to improving quality of life for people with spinal cord injuries. Pendergrass died on 13 January 2010 from colon cancer, in Bryn Mawr, Pennsylvania.

FURTHER READING

Pendergrass, Teddy, and Patricia Romanowski. *Truly Blessed* (1998).

Mallegg, Kristen, B. *Who's Who among African Americans* (2006).

New York Times, 19 Mar. 1982.

Obituary: *The Telegraph*, 14 Jan. 2010.

ERIC R. JACKSON

Penn, Irvine Garland (7 Oct. 1867–22 July 1930), educator, journalist, and religious activist, was born in New Glasgow in Amherst County, Virginia, to Isham (or Isom) Irvine Penn, a farmer, blacksmith, grocer, and mechanic-brakeman, and Maria (or Mariah) Levine, a seamstress. His parents instilled in their son the value of education when they moved to Lynchburg, Virginia, so that the five-year-old could attend a good school. He attended Jackson Street Methodist Episcopal Church School, the first high school for blacks in Lynchburg, for one year before financial difficulties forced his departure in 1883. Although a young teen, Penn taught in Bedford County to earn the money necessary for his return to the Jackson Street School.

He graduated in 1886, along with four others, in the school's first graduating class. From 1886 to 1887 he served as superintendent of a public school in Amherst County. In 1887 he became a teacher at Payne School, a public school in Lynchburg where he later became principal. In 1890 Penn received an M.A. from Rust College, a school sponsored by the Methodist Episcopal Church in Holly Springs, Mississippi. He also received an honorary doctorate in 1908 from Wiley College in Marshall, Texas.

Penn's interest in journalism helped him advocate African American education and racial uplift. While still in high school he joined the editorial staff of the first black newspaper in Lynchburg, the *Lynchburg Laborer*. In 1886, after graduation, he became editor and co-owner of the paper with P. H. Johnson. The paper was renamed the *Laboring Man* in 1887, but financial difficulties forced its termination. Penn also wrote for several other newspapers, including the *Knoxville Negro World*, the *New York Age*, the *Richmond Planet*, and the *Virginia Lancet*, receiving praise from both the black and white presses.

On 26 December 1889 Penn married Anna Belle Rhodes, a graduate of Shaw University who taught at the Payne School, and they had seven children. Anna Belle Rhodes published some essays and poetry and assisted her husband in his most renowned work, *The Afro-American Press and Its Editors* (1891), a comprehensive history of the black press from 1827 to 1891. It begins with *Freedom's Journal* and includes sketches of numerous editors as well as a section on nineteen African American women in journalism. Religion played a central role in Penn's life and work. He was elected lay delegate to the General Conference of the Methodist Episcopal (ME) Church ten consecutive times between 1892 and 1928. Even though Penn apparently was not ordained, he acquired the title of reverend.

In 1889 Penn lectured in Charlottesville, Virginia, at the Annual Conference of the Colored ME Church, calling for the creation of a theological and normal school in Virginia. The Virginia Collegiate and Industrial Institute was established soon afterward in 1893. The link between education and religion in Penn's work is further evident in his "Lynchburg Plan," published in Jesse Lyman Hurlbut's *Seven Graded Sunday Schools* (1893). In this essay Penn responded to what he viewed as the degenerate condition of the Sunday school system, proposing systematic and progressively rigorous religious instruction.

In his role as assistant general secretary for the Epworth League, a position he held from 1897 to 1912, Penn gave numerous lectures supporting the ME Church's national effort to further African American education. Penn also asserted the importance of the church as a positive socializing space for African American youth, insisting that the church must become a place where black youth could develop their intellectual and physical identities, as well as their spiritual lives. Penn worked hard in the Colored ME and ME Churches to ensure black youths' exposure to positive reinforcement, as illustrated by his invitation to his friend FREDERICK DOUGLASS to speak at a meeting of the American Association of Educators of Colored Youth.

Penn's business interests also reflect his support for African American advancement. He was a member of the Grand Fountain United Order of True Reformers, which created the True Reformers Bank, identified by some as the "first black owned and operated bank chartered in the United States" (Harrison, 50). Penn was also a member of the board of directors of the Lynchburg Loan and Trust Company, which advanced money on real estate and assisted poor families with obtaining homes. Moreover, in 1895 Penn worked with twelve African American doctors to create the National Medical Association, a professional organization for black doctors, dentists, and pharmacists.

Penn's educational and racial uplift commitments assumed an even broader context through his work. The College of Life, or Practical Self-Educator: A Manual of Self-Improvement for the Colored Race (1895), which he wrote with Henry Davenport Northrup and Joseph R. Gay. This comprehensive self-help manual was an invaluable resource, containing writings on a range of topics related to etiquette, health, business, literature, and domestic life, even including an essay on "Suitable Rules for Love-Making." Copies of this book were circulated at the Atlanta Cotton States and International Exposition in 1895, where Penn was the National Commissioner of Negro Exhibits, for which he won the gold medal for excellence.

African American participation in this event occurred shortly after the Chicago 1893 World's Columbian Exposition. It marked an attempt to celebrate the experiences and contributions of African Americans, something that many claimed did not occur at the Chicago exposition. Penn, along with IDA B. WELLS and Frederick Douglass, affirmed this view in their pamphlet The Reasons Why the Colored American Is Not in the World's Columbian Exposition (1893). Penn is also credited with inviting BOOKER T. WASHINGTON to speak at the Cotton States and International Exposition in 1895. This speech later became known as Washington's Atlanta Compromise speech, one of the exposition's most memorable events.

After the exposition Penn moved permanently to Atlanta from Lynchburg with his family. Living near Gammon Theological Seminary and Clark University enabled Penn to pursue his interests in racial uplift through religious and academic activities, as demonstrated through his becoming a trustee at both institutions. He further advanced these interests through the publication of The United Negro: His Problems and His Progress (1902), which he co-edited with J. W. E. Bowen, a professor at Gammon Theological Seminary. This text compiles the proceedings of the Negro Young People's Christian Educational Congress, which Penn organized as corresponding secretary of the congress. The volume contains numerous writings about African American life, including an essay by Penn's wife, Anna Belle Rhodes.

In 1912 Penn and his family moved to Cincinnati, Ohio, after he became co–corresponding secretary of the Freedman's Aid Society (later known as the ME Board of Education for Negroes) and the Southern Education Society. He continued to enjoy national recognition as he traveled throughout the country in his role as a ME educational leader. Penn remained committed to African American education, as demonstrated by his assistance to Wiley College during its recovery from a fire in 1918, as well as through his position as secretary of the endowments and field promotion department of the ME board of education. During this period Penn was also instrumental in the merging of Cookman Institute, an ME Church school, with Daytona Normal and Industrial School for Girls. MARY McLEOD BETHUNE was principal of the new institute, called Daytona-Cookman Collegiate Institute, which later became Bethune-Cookman College.

Anna Belle Rhodes died almost a month before Penn himself did in Cincinnati. Hospitalization for heart disease prevented Penn from attending his wife's funeral. Penn died of heart disease after suffering from this illness for sometime. One of his daughters also attributed his death to Penn's "rigorous life-style" as well as the racist treatment he experienced as he traveled throughout the country on the train (Harrison, 213). His immense contributions to the enhancement of African American life reveal the value of cultivating intersections of religious and secular spheres of activity, something he continued to do as a writer for the ME publication the *Christian Educator*. Moreover, his work illuminates the importance of one who can affirm black communal concerns as well as mediate the relations between African Americans and other communities. Penn affirmed this latter role through his participation on the Joint High Commission on the Unification of the ME Church, which after several years succeeded in uniting the ME Church North, the ME Church South, and the Colored ME factions that initially split because of their different views on slavery.

FURTHER READING

The Irvine Garland Penn Collection of visual material is available at the Cincinnati Historical Society Library. The online edition of the Booker T. Washington Papers by the University of Illinois Press contains correspondence between Penn and Washington and can be found at http://www. historycooperative.org/btw/.

Harrison, Joanne K., and Grant Harrison. *The Life and Times of Irvine Garland Penn* (2000).

JENNIFER R. THOMAS

Penn, Robert (10 Oct. 1872–8 June 1912), U.S. Navy sailor and Medal of Honor recipient, was a native of City Point, Virginia. Little regarding his family or early life prior to joining the navy is known for certain, except that he worked on a farm as a young man. Federal Census records indicate that he was likely raised in the Horse Pasture District of Ridgeway, Virginia, in Henry County, where the Penn surname was common among African Americans. While Penn's parentage is uncertain, two possibilities present themselves, either Liberty and Eliza Penn, or Robert Jr. and Critty Penn. Both families made their living as farmers in Ridgeway and both had a child named Robert.

It is not clear when Robert Penn joined the navy, but he probably did so in the early 1890s; by the time of his service in the Spanish American War in 1898 he had attained the rate of a fireman first class and was an experienced member of the ship's engine-room crew. Given his probable lack of seafaring experience prior to joining the navy, it seems likely that it took Penn some time to gain the training and experience to become skilled at tending to a ship's boilers and other related tasks that marked the job of a fireman. Penn was probably assigned to

the battleship *U.S.S. Iowa*, the navy's most modern warship, when it was commissioned at Philadelphia in June 1897, continuing aboard the ship when it was assigned to blockade duty off Santiago, Cuba, in May 1898, a month after the outbreak of the Spanish American War. On 3 July the *Iowa* and its crew of over seven hundred men, Penn included, took part in the naval Battle of Santiago, in which the battleship played a major part in the sinking of six warships of the Spanish Fleet. While the *Iowa* was stationed off Santiago in the weeks after the battle on 20 July 1898, it suffered an explosion in its boiler room. Stationed in the compartment adjacent to the boiler room, Penn quickly made his way to the blast and found the floor covered with boiling water and the air filled with scalding steam. Penn not only rescued an injured shipmate and carried him to safety, but returned to the boiler room to combat the fire danger. He laid a plank supported by two buckets just above the scalding water on the floor, and from this precarious perch ferried multiple loads of flaming coals out of the compartment. By these actions, Penn not only saved a shipmate from being scalded to death, but also saved the ship from suffering further fire damage. He was soon thereafter recommended for the Medal of Honor, and was approved for the award 14 December 1898.

Some accounts of Penn's Medal of Honor heroics state that they took place in combat conditions during the Battle of Santiago, but this is incorrect; however, because he performed his deeds while the *Iowa* was on active duty in a war zone, he *is* classified as a Spanish American War Medal of Honor recipient. Additionally, it seems likely that Robert Penn's actions, had they taken place outside the war zone, would still have merited the award of the Medal of Honor, based on the previous peacetime awards made to other African American sailors such as ROBERT SWEENEY, AND DANIEL ATKINS. The heroics of black sailors like Robert Penn are notable in and of themselves not only because they resulted in the Medal of Honor but also because they are indicative of the vital contributions made by African American sailors to the U.S. Navy during the time period from the Civil War through the Spanish American War. Soon after the war, black sailors would be relegated to a servant status in the navy due to the influence of Jim Crow laws ashore, and would not be able to hold ratings such as that of fireman until the time of World War II.

After the Spanish American War, most of the details of Robert Penn's naval career and subsequent civilian life are uncertain. Whether he may have left the service on his own, or was forced out due to the increasing racism and limiting of black sailor's duties that occurred in the first decade of the twentieth century is unknown. In 1901 Penn married a woman named Hattie Washington, and by 1910 was out of the navy and residing in Philadelphia, where he put his fireman's skills to good use working in a machine shop. A short time later, under unknown circumstances, Penn went westward to Colorado. It is speculated that Penn may have gained employment with a railroad company, perhaps influenced by his brother-in-law, Cornelius Washington, who worked as a railroad porter. In any event, Penn's stay out West was short as he died at Las Animas, Colorado, due to unknown causes. His body is said to have been returned to Philadelphia, but the cemetery in which he was buried is unknown.

FURTHER READING

Hanna, Charles W. *African American Recipients of the Medal of Honor* (2002).

GLENN ALLEN KNOBLOCK

Penniman, Richard. *See* Little Richard.

Pennington, James William Charles (15 Jan. 1809–20 Oct. 1870), escaped slave, minister, and abolitionist, was born James Pembroke in Hagerstown, Maryland, to Bazil, a handyman and shepherd, and a woman named Nelly. Both his parents were slaves. James Tighlman, their owner, gave James's mother and an older brother to his son, Frisbie Tighlman. The family was reunited when Frisbie Tighlman purchased Bazil, though they were relocated to an area some two hundred miles from Maryland's Eastern Shore.

Even though the family had been reunited, as slaves Pembroke's parents were still unable to provide the nurturing attention he required. On one occasion Tighlman beat Bazil in Pembroke's presence, and his remarks to Bazil had a lasting impact on the young boy: "I will make you know that I am master of your tongue as well as of your time" (Pennington, 7). While he did not immediately escape, Pembroke was committed to striking for freedom; in his mind he was never a "slave" after this incident. Although he, too, would experience the "tyranny and abuse of the overseers" (3), he managed to equip himself with skills requisite for life as a freeman. At age eleven he became a trained stonemason, and he worked as a certified blacksmith for more than nine years. But the expert blacksmith yearned for freedom and would become

a fugitive. "The hour was come," and he determined that he had to act "or remain a slave for ever" (7).

One afternoon in November 1827, he struck for freedom and, several days later, arrived in Pennsylvania, where the first person he met was a Quaker woman. He lived and worked for a while with a Quaker couple, Phebe and William Wright, who taught him to read. To protect himself, he adopted the name James William Charles Pennington. (Pennington was a common name among Pennsylvania Quakers.) After living with and working for Quaker families, he settled in Newtown, Long Island, New York. He became a Christian, and this intensified his concern for his parents and eleven siblings, as well as others in slavery.

Pennington decided to fight against the institution of slavery from northern soil. With the guidance of the Presbyterian family with whom he resided in Newtown, Pennington began formal preparation for the ministry in 1835. He moved to New Haven, Connecticut, where he taught in a black school and assisted the pastor of Temple Street Congregational Church. Although Pennington could not formally register at Yale Divinity School, he was allowed to sit in the hallway and listen to lectures. Three years later he returned to Newtown, was ordained as a Presbyterian minister, and served as pastor of the black Presbyterian church from 1838 to 1840. During the next thirty-two years Pennington served seven churches in three denominations (Presbyterian, Congregational, and African Methodist Episcopal Zion) and five states.

On 16 July 1840 Pennington was called to serve at the Talcott Street (Fifth) Congregational Church in Hartford, Connecticut, and he came to play a role in the celebrated *Amistad* case, examining whether captured Africans who had rebelled and taken over the ship (the *Amistad*) they were being transported in were legally slaves. Most of the captives were from the Mende region of West Africa, in present-day Nigeria, and in April 1840 Judge Andrew T. Judson ruled that their leader CINQUÉ and the others be freed, delivered to the president of the United States, and returned to Africa.

In July 1840 Pennington helped raise money for the captives, whose case had been appealed to the U.S. Supreme Court, where the former president John Quincy Adams argued the captives' case. While the U.S. Supreme Court reaffirmed that they be freed, it did not require that the president return them to Africa. Along with his wealthy friend, the New York merchant Lewis Tappan, Pennington raised enough funds for the return of the *Amistad* victims. In September 1841 Pennington organized and was elected president of the Union Missionary Society. Hosted by Pennington's church, the society sent the first two missionaries from an African American mission society to the interior of Africa.

Pennington's role in helping the *Amistad* captives and in sending African American missionaries to Africa enhanced his popularity in Connecticut. In 1843 he was selected to represent the Connecticut Anti-Slavery Society at the World Anti-Slavery Society Convention in London. He also represented the American Peace Society and his own Union Missionary Society at the World Peace Convention meeting in London that year. He then returned to Hartford, where he was twice elected president of the Hartford Central Association of Congregational ministers.

Still legally a fugitive slave, Pennington tried to secure his freedom. As of 1844 he had not even told his wife, Harriet, that he had escaped from slavery. (It is not known when Pennington married Harriet—who died in 1846—and there is no record that the couple had children.) He did not reveal his status to his congregation until 1846, when he traveled to Jamaica, in part to raise funds to purchase his freedom. After his return later that year, Pennington played a major role in the creation of the American Missionary Association, which absorbed his Union Missionary Society. Pennington was appointed to the executive committee of the new organization.

Following the death of THEODORE S. WRIGHT, in 1847, Pennington was invited to become the new pastor of Shiloh Presbyterian Church in New York City, the most influential African American Presbyterian congregation in the nation. After concluding a promised return to Talcott and becoming vice president of the National Negro Convention Movement, a northern association of blacks committed to improving the condition of freemen and working for the abolition of slavery in the South, Pennington began his duties as pastor at Shiloh. While settling in as the pastor of his new congregation, Pennington married Almira Way at the home of a Mr. Goodwin, the former editor of the *Hartford Courant* newspaper. It is not known whether the couple had children.

In 1849 Pennington made a second European tour to promote the cause of peace and abolitionism. On this visit the University of Heidelberg in Germany awarded him the doctor of divinity degree. He was the first African American to receive this honor.

Conferred on 19 December 1849, it acknowledged Pennington foremost as a leader of his people as well as one who had published distinguished literary works while still legally a slave. Passage of the Fugitive Slave Law in 1850 prompted Pennington to more assiduously pursue the legal purchase of his freedom. From Scotland, where he was lecturing as a guest of the Glasgow Female Anti-Slavery Society, Pennington inquired whether he should return. His friend John Hooker of Farmington, Connecticut, advised Pennington to stay abroad while Hooker negotiated his purchase. On 3 June 1851 Hooker paid the Tighlman estate $150, making Pennington the property of Hooker. After contemplating the irony of "owning" a man with a doctor of divinity degree, Hooker executed the documents making Pennington a freeman. James Pembroke had been transformed into James Pennington.

Now free, Pennington later purchased the freedom of his brother Stephen. Both of his parents had died in slavery, as had a sister. Several of his other siblings tasted freedom, though some were sold south. Legally free and armed with a doctorate in divinity, Pennington became even bolder. In June 1855 he defied the New York City law that prohibited African Americans from riding on the inside of a horse-drawn car. He was arrested and charged with violent resistance, but the New York Supreme Court, on appeal, ruled in Pennington's favor; segregation was subsequently made illegal on public transportation in New York City, one hundred years before ROSA PARKS initiated the Montgomery bus boycott in Alabama.

In addition to his activism, Pennington also contributed to African American scholarship, publishing twenty-four articles and sermons, including *An Address Delivered at Newark, New Jersey, at the First Anniversary of West Indian Emancipation, August 1, 1839*, and "The Self-Redeeming Power of the Colored Races of the World" in the *Anglo-African Magazine* (1859). He also published two books: his autobiography, *The Fugitive Blacksmith* (1850), and *A Textbook History of the Origin and History of the Colored People* (1841), which was one of the earliest works of African American historical scholarship.

Yet despite his many achievements, Pennington appears to have succumbed to alcohol addiction in the 1850s, perhaps brought on by the pressures of service. After 1865 he was no longer the spiritual leader of Shiloh. While he recovered from alcoholism, Pennington wrote several significant articles on the future of the black race, though he would never recapture the fame he had once known. He served as an ordained African Methodist Episcopal (AME) minister in Natchez, Mississippi, in 1865 and was pastor of a Congregational church in Portland, Maine, in 1868 before going to a Presbyterian church in Jacksonville, Florida, where he died in October 1870.

FURTHER READING

Nineteen unpublished letters, written by James W. C. Pennington between 1840 and 1870, are held at the American Missionary Association Archives, Amistad Research Center, Tulane University, New Orleans, Louisiana.

Pennington, James W. C. *The Fugitive Blacksmith; or, Events in the History of James W. C. Pennington, Pastor of a Presbyterian Church, New York, Formerly a Slave in the State of Maryland, United States* (1849), reprinted in *Five Slave Narratives*, ed. William L. Katz (1969).

Thomas, Herman E. *James W. C. Pennington: African American Churchman and Abolitionist* (1995).

Washington, Joseph R. *The First Fugitive and Foreign and Domestic Doctor of Divinity* (1990).

HERMAN E. THOMAS

Percy, Leonard (1807–1 Aug. 1864), a laborer, shoemaker, and member of the Union Army, was born in 1807 in Granby, Connecticut. He was the son of a newly freed black slave, Earl Percy, who served under Ozias Pettibone, a colonel in the Revolutionary War. Colonel Pettibone was one of the richest men in Granby and one of only a few slave owners. A 1790 census showed that Pettibone had five slaves, three of whom were children. One of these slaves was a thirty-six-year-old woman. This original census does not list an adult male or father among Pettibone's slaves; a later census lists the children as "mulatto," but does not provide the name of the father. One of the children, Earl Pettibone, was born in 1784, the year in which the legislature passed an act ending lifetime slavery for children born to slave women after 1 March of that year. These children would still have to work twenty-five years for the owner of their mother before being freed. Later, in 1797 the legislation was changed again; the age of service was reduced from twenty-five years to twenty-one years. Earl was freed somewhere between 1805, when he would be twenty-one, and 1810, when he would have been twenty-six.

After he was freed, Earl took on the last name Percy, and by 1807 he had a wife and two children, one of whom was Leonard Percy. Leonard Percy

was later described by William C. Case, a local town lawyer and judge, as, "poor and ignorant and black, hovering on the outskirts of the village, the enemy of all thrift, but the friend and delight of all the boys, his sole business to own the worst horse and the most dogs" (Case, p. 3). As the son of a slave, Percy wasn't wealthy or well educated, but nor was he a court jester. In his speech Case noted that he remembered a day when he and his friends were discussing whether or not they believed the day would come that a Negro had the right to vote. Percy, nearby, overheard the conversation and said, "Do you believe that? I would die to have that day come" (Case, p. 3).

In 1827 Leonard Percy sold four acres of land to Calvin Dibble for $15. Earl died in 1829, and Leonard inherited the land given to his father, Earl, by Pettibone. Ten years later, Leonard married his first wife Nancy Peterson, and they had eleven children, six of whom were twins. Granby school censuses show that Leonard's children actually attended the town's free school, at least for a few years. In 1854, to pay off growing debts, Leonard sold eight acres of land with all of his crops to David Latham for $20. Two years later Nancy died of tuberculosis. Leonard was left with no land to farm, and eight children to raise without Nancy. He moved to Hartford with four of his sons to try to find work. He left the other children in Windsor and Tariffville, in hopes that they, too, would find work.

In the 1860s, Leonard's sons enlisted in the 29th Regiment U.S. Colored Infantry. In January 1864, Leonard Percy, at the age of fifty-seven, enlisted in the 30th Regiment U.S. Colored Infantry. He had the opportunity to finally fight for the one thing he considered worth dying for, the right for Negroes to vote. African Americans were prohibited from voting in the state in 1818, and weren't allowed to vote in Connecticut before the enactment of the fifteenth amendment in 1870. Before leaving for the war in 1864, he remarried. His wife, Mary Kennedy, is recorded in the census as a thirty-five-year-old white woman.

Percy's regiment was sent to Virginia that summer to march with the Army of the Potomac. On 30 July 1864, Pennsylvania Union miners dug underneath the Confederate lines, and ignited four tons of gunpowder, instantly killing approximately three hundred confederate soldiers. The explosion left a massive crater in Petersburg, Virginia. Leonard Percy, his regiment, and other soldiers then charged the Confederates, running through, rather than around the crater. By that time, the Confederates had regrouped, and they successfully massacred 136 of the men charging through the crater. Later, this became know, as "the Battle of the Crater." In this battle Percy was wounded and died shortly afterward. All of his sons, however, survived the war. A year after Leonard's death his new wife, Mary, died in September 1865. Their assets were then divided among the children, and each child received $33.05.

FURTHER READING

Information on Percy and his family can be found in the Granby, Connecticut, Vital Records; the Granby town census records; and the Granby school census records.

Case, William C. "Memorial Day Speech." *Hartford Post*, 4 June 1888.

Laun, Carol. "Glory in Granby." *Farmington Valley Herald*, March 1990.

Williams, Mark. *Tempest in a Small Town: The Myth and Reality of Country Life; Granby, Connecticut 1680–1940* (1996).

STORM BUTLER

Perez, Manuel (28 Dec. 1871–1946), brass band and dance band cornetist, was born Emile Emanuel Perez in New Orleans, Louisiana. A Catholic and a Creole, he was the son of a Hispanic father and an African American mother, whose names are unknown. His parents ran a grocery on Touro Street, and his father was also a cigar maker. Manuel was educated in a French-speaking grammar school, and he was raised on European classical and popular music. He took up cornet at age twelve, after which he entered the emerging world of syncopated music that later became ragtime and jazz.

While working steadily as a cigar maker Perez played in brass bands and dance bands in New Orleans, and he recalled that he was already playing ragtime on cornet in 1898. He married Lena (maiden name unknown) in 1900; they had at least one child. That same year he joined the Onward Brass Band, a group of ten to twelve instrumentalists whom he subsequently led from 1903 to 1930. He also led the Imperial Orchestra, a five- to seven-piece dance band, from 1901 to 1908. During this time Perez was a rival of the legendary cornetist BUDDY BOLDEN, and their bands sometimes appeared together at Johnson Park, competing for an audience. Unlike Bolden, Perez was known for his dignified and classical style of playing; at the same time, the Onward gained a reputation as the most consistent and exciting of the early New Orleans brass bands.

Accounts of Perez's move to Chicago in 1915 are confusing. Evidently the bandleader Charles Elgar promised him work, but Perez found only an unsuitable job that required him to fire the drummer Louis Cottrell and to use a xylophone rather than a piano. Somehow the situation was resolved. According to the cornetist Natty Dominique, Perez brought his family to Chicago and stayed about two years, with his family returning first and then Perez himself going home after his job ended. The Chicago venue was probably the Arsonia Café, and perhaps both Elgar and Perez led bands there at different times. During this period Perez's only extended foray away from New Orleans, his fellow band members included Cottrell, the clarinetist LORENZO TIO JR., and the trombonist George Filhe (according to Dominique) or Eddie Atkins (according to Perez himself; probably each trombonist played at some point).

Perez resumed his work with the Onward Brass Band while also performing on the riverboat SS *Capitol* in the summer of 1918 and then leading a dance band whose engagements included residencies at the Oasis Cabaret in 1921–1922 and at the Pythian Temple Roof Gardens from around 1924 through the remainder of the decade. Perez is said to have returned to Chicago in 1928 to perform with Elgar at the Savoy, but in his interview with Robert Goffin, Perez contradicted this claim: "*Depuis lors, je n'ai plus bougé du quartier créole!*" ("Since then [the earlier Chicago trip], I haven't left the Creole quarter!")

Perez was also a renowned teacher who gave private lessons on cornet to Sidney Desvigne, Willie Pajeaud, Alvin Alcorn, and Natty Dominique, all of whom made careers in jazz, dance, and brass bands. Dominique recalled: All of his pupils that he taught music, they didn't pay him one nickel....Manuel Perez see a kid that he liked in the streets, he'd call him, "Hey"—"Come here." He'd say, "I'm gonna make a cornet player out of you...Manuel Perez was a very patient man giving lessons....If you didn't know all of your lesson, you missed one measure, he'd send you back home and give you that same lesson over." Perez retired from music in 1937, but he continued his career as a cigar maker until suffering a series of strokes. He died in New Orleans.

Dominique described Perez as "short and stocky. Very good looking. Coal black hair....And very nice man and good hearted." The writer Samuel Charters reported that "in his later years he resented the emphasis placed on the city's jazz musicians, and refused to talk with anyone doing research in New

Orleans." The researcher Lawrence Gushee disputed this claim upon discovering that the problem was language, not attitude: Perez had been happy to talk to the writer Robert Goffin, who conducted his interview in French rather than in English.

In New Orleans parlance Perez was a "musicianer," gifted with prodigious technical skills, able to sight-read notated music flawlessly, and famous for his solo playing in funeral dirges. Dominique heard him "play first sight *Il Trovatore* in the dance band at the De Luxe Cafe," and the guitarist DANNY BARKER called him

> the idol of the downtown Creole colored people. To them nobody could master the cornet like Mr. Perez. When this brass band played a march, dirge or hymn it was played to perfection—no blunders….These brass bands were highly competitive….But everybody acknowledged the fact that the king could be heard all day from ten in the morning until the parade disbanded, screaming in the upper register of his cornet—Mr. Manuel Perez.

FURTHER READING
Barker, Danny, and Alyn Shipton. *A Life in Jazz* (1986).
Charters, Samuel B. *Jazz: New Orleans 1885–1963, An Index to the Negro Musicians of New Orleans*, rev. ed. (1983).
Goffin, Robert. *La Nouvelle-Orléans: Capitale du jazz* (1946).
Marquis, Donald M. *In Search of Buddy Bolden: First Man of Jazz*, rev. ed. (1991).

This entry is taken from the *American National Biography* and is published here with the permission of the American Council of Learned Societies.

BARRY KERNFELD

Pérez, Tony (14 May 1942–), baseball player, was born Atanasio Pérez Rigal in Ciego de Avila, Cuba, to Jose Pérez, a sugar cane worker, and Teodora Rigal. Raised in the eastern Cuban town of Camaguey, Pérez grew up idolizing Minnie Miñoso and other Latin stars, while working with his five siblings and father in a sugar cane mill. When he began to play baseball with the company league as a teenager, the tall, thin Pérez hit well enough to garner major league clubs' attention. Tony Pacheco, a Cincinnati Reds scout, signed him at sixteen to play for an instructional program with the Reds' Cuban affiliate, the Havana Sugar Kings. The following spring, Pérez signed with the big-league club for a bonus of just $2.50, the cost of a visa.

Sent to Geneva, New York, to play for the Reds' rookie league affiliate, Pérez underwent a difficult transition. Struggling with English, he faced language barriers on and off the field. He soon bonded with two other Latin players on the team, one of whom was the son of future Hall-of-Famer Martin Dihigo Sr. With Cuba under a new regime following the 1959 revolution, Pérez made his last extended visit to his family before spring training in 1963.

After four-and-a-half years in the minor leagues, Pérez debuted in the majors briefly in 1964, but returned to Triple-A, where he hit .309 with thirty-four home runs and 107 RBIs. The following season, Pérez stayed with the club as a part-time first baseman the entire season. His breakout season came in 1967, when he shifted to third base, hit twenty-six home runs, and topped one hundred RBIs for the first time, while earning his first of seven All-Star appearances. Pérez's game-winning home run off Catfish Hunter in the bottom of the fifteenth inning earned him the All-Star MVP and established him as one of the best clutch performers in baseball.

Pérez combined with Johnny Bench, Dave Concepcíon, Pete Rose, and Joe Morgan to give the "Big Red Machine" one of the most formidable infields in major league history. Pérez was a much-loved member of the Cincinnati dynasty; while the media called him "the Mayor of Riverfront," it was another nickname that stuck. Initially dubbed "Dog" for his intensity with pitchers, the humble and genial Pérez soon became "Big Doggie." Though pushed to the shadows by the gaudier statistics of his teammates, he was a consistent run-producer in the middle of the order. Starting with his 102 RBIs in 1967, Pérez would top ninety RBIs for eleven consecutive years. His best season came in 1970, when he established career highs in home runs, runs scored, and RBIs, and was named to his fourth of seven All-Star teams en route to a third-place finish in MVP voting. It was Pérez's bad luck that he happened to locker next to Morgan and Bench, who both won two MVP awards during the Reds dynasty, and the fiery Rose, who won one.

Pérez's light perhaps shined brightest in the 1975 postseason. After batting .417 in the NLCS against the Pittsburgh Pirates, he hit two home runs in Game Five of the World Series against the Boston Red Sox, and added a key two-run shot in game seven, helping the Reds win their first of back-to-back championships.

Just two months after the 1976 World Series victory, Pérez was traded to the Montreal Expos, an unpopular transaction with both the fans and players. Some years later Bob Howsam, Cincinnati's former general manager, called it his worst move, saying, "When we traded (Pérez) away, I feel in my heart that was one of the reasons we didn't win a third World Series title in a row" (*Associated Press*, 11 Jan. 2000).

Pérez put up almost identical numbers his first year with the Expos in 1977, but dipped in his remaining two seasons in Montreal. He signed with the Red Sox before 1980, and bounced back, topping one hundred RBIs for the seventh and final time. He signed with the Philadelphia Phillies after 1982, reuniting with former teammates Rose and Morgan. At the end of 1983 the Reds brought Pérez back. Used primarily off the bench, he played his final three seasons with Cincinnati. When Pérez retired, his 379 home runs and 1,652 RBIs were records for Latin ballplayers (he shared the home run title with the Puerto Rican ORLANDO CEPEDA).

Pérez stayed with Cincinnati in retirement, serving as a first base and hitting coach, and he was then promoted at the end of 1992 to be manager. But just forty-four games into the 1993 season, Pérez was fired, raising speculation that he had been hired solely to subdue criticism of owner Marge Schott, who had earned a one-year suspension for derogatory and racist remarks.

After eight years of rejection, Pérez was chosen to the Hall of Fame in January 2000, after campaigning not only from friends within baseball but also from friends without, who started a Cuban-American committee that inundated the Baseball Writers Association of America with letters and T-shirts bearing Tony Pérez's statistics. Coincidentally, Pérez was inaugurated with three others associated with the Big Red Machine—manager Sparky Anderson, catcher Carlton Fisk (whose Red Sox had lost to them in 1975), and Reds radio announcer Marty Brennaman. In attendance with his wife, Pituka, whom he had met playing in the Puerto Rican Winter League of 1964, were his two sons, Victor and Eduardo, then a first baseman for the St. Louis Cardinals. During his speech Pérez paid homage to the three countries he called home, Cuba, Puerto Rico, and the United States. An ambassador for the sport, during his Hall-of-Fame induction speech in 2000 he also issued a directive to young players to "respect your fans and, more important, respect the game of baseball."

Pérez's journey was an example of the broadening integration America experienced following JACKIE ROBINSON's debut in 1947. Once the color line was broken, baseball owners turned to the Caribbean for talent, finding a wealth of it in the sugar and fruit company leagues. Pérez's transition dealing with language barriers and racially charged episodes in a still-segregated America was typical for emigrated Latin ballplayers. His perseverance and rise to stardom made him a role model for the next generation of ballplayers. Pérez was one of the few athletes to join an American sports league before Fidel Castro's revolution; future Cuban athletes were forced to defect from their country, leaving for America by any means necessary.

FURTHER READING

Capozzi, Joe. "A Friend's Gift," *Palm Beach Post* (23 July 2000).

Kay, Joe. "Perez Was the 'Glue' of the Big Red Machine," *Associated Press* (11 Jan. 2000).

Oleksak, Michael M., and Mary Adams Oleksak. *Beisbol: Latin Americans and the Grand Old Game* (1991).

ADAM W. GREEN

Perkins, John M. (8 June 1930–), community activist, minister, author, lecturer, and racial reconciler, was the last child born to Maggie and Jasper Perkins in New Hebron, Mississippi, sharecroppers whose family worked on cotton farms on the smaller white plantations of south central Mississippi. Perkins's mother died of pellagra—a vitamin deficiency disease that ravaged poor families in the Deep South, seven months after his birth. Little is known of the circumstances of his father's life except that he was an itinerant sharecropper and bootlegger.

Perkins's early life was shaped by the brutal murder of his brother, Clyde, after arriving home from World War II. Clyde was shot by a white police officer outside a theater after he reached for the officer's baton when the policeman threatened him. Perkins graduated from Wiggins Vocational School and soon afterward decided to move to California where he married his childhood friend, Vera Mae Buckley, in 1951. Perkins became a steward in an iron factory, where he organized a worker's union, before he was drafted to fight in the Korean War.

Soon after his return from the war Perkins made a public profession of Christian faith and became an ordained Baptist minister in Monrovia, California. After this profession the Perkins family decided to return to Mississippi, where he became the organizing pastor of Berean Bible Church in Mendenhall, Mississippi, a small town outside the capital city of

Jackson. It was in this town that Perkins began his first extensive community outreach program titled Mendenhall Ministries, which continued to thrive even into the beginning of the twenty-first century. Under Perkins's guidance, within a short time the ministries had instituted numerous services and programs, including child care, legal assistance, youth development programs, Mendenhall Bible Church, an adult education program, a cooperative farm, a thrift store, housing development, Genesis One School, a health center, and a senior citizen facility. In some sense, Perkins became the de facto city renewal organizer and consummate activist. His highly effective organizational skills also led to his growing reputation as a noted black leader in a highly volatile period of Mississippi racial history, notice that would eventually make him a target for white racists and local Ku Klux Klansmen.

During the height of the civil rights era (1964–1972), Perkins allowed his church to be used as a central meeting place for civil rights workers and lent his aid to a Head Start program, the Federation of Southern Cooperatives, and along with his wife arranged rides for black workers during the successful 1969 boycott of white merchants who had been discriminating against blacks in Mendenhall. It was during this time that Perkins was picked up by the local police and severely beaten as a warning against future organizing activities. These overt acts of intimidation only served to embolden Perkins for what he believed was his calling from the Lord—to lead his people out of this stormy period of racial violence and into an era of racial reconciliation.

In 1972 Perkins and his wife made the decision to move to Jackson, Mississippi, to begin the arduous task of racial reconciliation by founding The Voice of Calvary Church and community outreach programs. Taking his model of holistic community activism and organizing principles from Mendenhall, Perkins took it a step further by reaching out to white people in the capital who were sympathetic to the models of ministry and leadership that Perkins had engineered. Voice of Calvary became the most significant model of church racial integration and reconciliation in the Deep South. After ten years of exhausting service to his native state, Perkins decided to begin a new ministry in Pasadena, California, in 1982.

The Perkins family felt called to move into one of the highest crime areas in the city and began the Harambee Christian Family Center. It served a twelve-block area and became a multicultural center for the growing Latino population as well as the African American community. By 1983 Perkins had decided to form an umbrella organization in order to do more systematic fund-raising for these collective endeavors. Thus was born the John M. Perkins Foundation for Reconciliation and Development that made its headquarters in Jackson, Mississippi. By 1989 Perkins had convened a group of national Christian leaders to form the Christian Development Association, that would eventually grow into a network of more than seven hundred such organizations around the world.

As a result of his life work John Perkins received honorary doctorates from Wheaton College, Gordon College, Huntington College, Spring Arbor College, Geneva College, North Park College, and Belhaven College. He lectured at Stanford, Harvard, Oxford, the University of Berlin, Howard University, Wheaton College, and more than two hundred other higher educational institutions. He was the author of eleven books—all of which focused on his lifework of racial reconciliation and community development. He was a contributing writer to *Sojourners*, *Christianity Today*, *Decision*, *Eternity*, *Time*, and numerous other journals. He was awarded a Ford Foundation Fellowship, the Dixon Outstanding Community Service Award, NAACP's Ruby McKnight Award, Mississippi Religious Leadership Man of the Year, and was a conference speaker to Promise Keepers and the National Association of Evangelicals. He was appointed by President Ronald Reagan to the Presidential Task Force on Food Assistance and has appeared on C-SPAN and ABC *World News Tonight*.

John and Vera Mae Perkins were married for more than fifty years and raised eight children, many of whom were directly involved in the direction, oversight, and supervision of the various ministries begun by Perkins. In the context of the civil rights era of United States history, it is safe to conclude that John Perkins was and remains a pivotal leader in the ensuing pursuit of racial reconciliation. He is, arguably, the key evangelical African American leader of the twentieth century, as well as an expert on community development and racial reconciliation.

FURTHER READING
Perkins, John M. *Let Justice Roll Down* (1976).
Berk, Stephen E. *A Time to Heal: John Perkins, Community Development and Racial Reconciliation* (1997).

LOUIS B. GALLIEN JR.

Perry, Carrie Saxon (31 Aug. 1931–), politician and social worker, was born Carrie Saxon in Hartford, Connecticut, the only child of Mabel Lee Saxon. Growing up in Hartford's housing projects exposed Perry to the crushing effects of poverty and crime. But rather than being defeated by it, Perry persevered and went on to become a force for change. Perry graduated from high school in 1949 and then attended Howard University, where she earned a bachelor of science in Political Science in 1953. During this time she married James Perry Sr. They had one child, James Perry Jr. Perry entered Howard's School of Law that same year, but did not complete the law program. Instead she returned in 1955 to Hartford, where she became a social worker. While she served in many professions, they all had one element in common. The positions involved helping the people of Hartford to have better lives. Some might say that Perry's biggest victory was achieved in 1980 when Perry was the "only Black woman elected by popular vote in a city of more than 50,000 people" (Marshall). Perry served as a social worker in Hartford during the 1950s, before being appointed administrator of the Community Renewal Team (CRT) of Greater Hartford in the 1960s. The organization's mission was to address the needs of the poor of Hartford. Perry served in this capacity until the 1970s, when she became executive director of Amistad House, a Hartford girl's group home. One thing quickly became clear to Perry, in order to help the poor of Hartford, Perry needed to cultivate political connections. To this end, Perry entered the political arena running for a seat in the Connecticut State Legislature in 1978. This first attempt ended in defeat, but Perry ran again and was elected in 1980, thus becoming the Connecticut State Representative for District 7. In 1986 Perry, two other Connecticut Democratic legislators, and a Republican Hartford councilwoman took part in the Colt-45 sit-in in support of striking United Auto Worker members. While serving in state government Perry served as majority leader, on the Education and Finance and on the Education and Bonding Committees.

At the start of her fourth term as a state legislator, Perry announced she would be running for the office of mayor in Hartford. Perry was backed by then-mayor Richard Milne. Perry based her platform on the division between the downtown area and the deteriorating inner-city neighborhoods, which were predominantly black and Hispanic. Perry won the mayoralty by 16 percent points in 1987 thus becoming the 60th mayor of Hartford and the first African American woman mayor of a large city in the United States. While the mayoralty in Harford is largely ceremonial, Perry did not let that stop her from attempting to help Hartford's poor. One of the first things Perry did was to form a task force that focused on reducing unemployment and crime. Perry stressed the need for job training. Perry instituted weekly telephone logs that documented complaints ranging from homelessness, crime, and housing to parking tickets. In 1989 Perry set aside funds for after-school and weekend programs designed to give poor children a place to go for safe fun activities. Other programs developed by Perry included Operation Bridge, a tutorial program, funded by the Rockefeller Foundation, that paired Hartford's middle class with potential inner-city teen dropouts. The program proved very successful. Perry was also responsible for implementing Operation Break, which trained poor people to work in jobs that provided a living wage. The program also provided drug rehabilitation, day care, remedial education, and English as a Second Language classes. In 1992, in a surprise defeat, Perry lost her fourth mayoral reelection bid to a Hartford fireman, Michael C. Peters, who took office in 1993.

Loss of the mayoral office did not stop Perry from working for the poor and disadvantaged of Hartford. Working as a for-contract social worker, Perry developed and conducted business workshops and training programs for participants in Connecticut's welfare-to-work program and for Hartford's public housing residents. Perry also served as chairperson for Hartford Black History Project. The project featured Hartford African Americans from the late nineteenth and twentieth centuries. In December 2003, Perry along with eleven others was asked to serve on the Connecticut Health Foundation Panel on eliminating racial and ethnic disparities. The group was charged with reviewing national, state, and local literature and holding public forums. This was carried out over the course of a year. Based on the information garnered, the group recommended changes related to social and environmental factors, data collection, language barriers, and workforce diversity.

Perry, represented Connecticut as the alternate delegate to the 1984 Democratic National Convention and as the delegate to the National Convention in 1988. Perry also served as regional director for the National Organization of Black Elected Women Legislatures and was appointed to the National Conference of State Legislatures. Perry served as treasurer for the National Conference of Black Mayors and chairperson of the 1987 conference of the National Black Caucus of State Legislatures.

Throughout her lifetime Perry has been involved in many groups. She is a lifetime member of the NAACP. Perry has served on a number of executive boards, including the Greater Hartford Black Democrats and the community labor coalition Organized North Easterners. Perry served as president of the Hartford Chapter of 100 Black Women. Perry is a member of the Connecticut caucus of Black Women for Political Action and the Hartford Federation of Democratic Women. Perry served as nominating chairman for the Permanent Community on the Status of Hartford Women and as comptroller of the Connecticut Center Authority, the Hartford Public Library, and the Connecticut Black and Hispanic Urban Institute Incorporated. Perry also served as corporator for the Oak Hill School for the Blind.

Perry has been honored many times during her career. These honors include, but are not limited to WKND's and Connecticut Mutual's Leader of the Month Award, the University of Hartford Outstanding Community Service Award, Greater Hartford Young Women's Christian Chapter, and a Certificate of Merit from the Ancient and Accepted Scottish Rite of Freemasonry; and she was saluted by the Connecticut Minority Business Association. In 2007 Perry, age seventy-three, was named by The Black Pages of New England as one of the 100 Most Influential People of African Descent in New England.

FURTHER READING

"Carrie Saxon Perry." *Notable Black American Women, Book 1* (1992).

Marshall, Marilyn. "Carrie Saxon Perry: More Than a Pretty Hat." *Ebony* 43 (1988): 60–64, 84.

ANNE K. DRISCOLL

Perry, Fredericka Douglass Sprague (Aug. 1872–Oct. 1943), activist, was born in Rochester, New York, to Nathan Sprague and Rosetta Douglass (the eldest daughter of FREDERICK DOUGLASS, for whom Fredericka was named). Nathan Sprague had great difficulty holding a job, and the family—which included Fredericka's five sisters and one brother—often depended on Frederick Douglass for support. Rosetta and Nathan moved to Washington in 1877.

Most of Sprague's childhood was spent in Washington, D.C., where her mother sometimes worked as a government clerk. She attended public schools and witnessed her mother's growing participation in the clubwoman's movement, which undoubtedly influenced her own later engagement with the National Association of Colored Women and a range of other groups. Around the turn of the century, she returned to Rochester as a student at the Rochester Athenaeum and Mechanics Institute (later the Rochester Institute of Technology). By 1900 she was teaching in the Washington area, though she was still living at home. In 1906 she moved to Missouri to accept a teaching position. Over the next six years she worked at a number of schools, including the Lincoln Institute (later Lincoln University) and Lincoln High School in Kansas City, where she was employed by 1910; her focus was on home economics.

In Kansas City, Sprague met John Edward Perry, a Texas-born African American physician who had graduated from the medical department of Nashville's Central Tennessee College (which later split off and became Meharry Medical College) in 1895, served in the Spanish-American War, and relocated to Kansas City in 1903. Perry probably had been previously married (in about 1901), but no further record seems extant. Perry had successfully established a sanatorium for black patients that grew into Kansas City's first private hospital for African Americans and became Wheatley Provident Hospital in 1916. The couple married in 1912 and soon after had their only son, Eugene Boone Perry, who would later become a physician in Houston, Texas, and a leader of the black Catholic service organization, the Knights of Peter Claver, which was founded when the Knights of Columbus denied blacks membership. Though Perry stopped teaching, she continued to volunteer with the school system; her sister Harriet Bailey Sprague, who never married, lived with John and Fredericka for over a decade and worked as a teacher. Perry's energies shifted toward the growing hospital, where she initially provided some nursing care services.

Throughout the first decades of the twentieth century the Perrys prospered economically—by 1930 federal census takers estimated their home was worth $10,000—and their prominence in the community grew. During the 1920s Perry was active in support efforts for the hospital—especially through the Wheatley Provident Hospital Auxiliary, which did work ranging from patient care to fund-raising and was headed by the formidable Minnie Lee Crosthwaite, whose husband had taught with Fredericka at Lincoln High School and who was one of the first black social workers in Missouri. The organization was especially active in fundraising and established an annual ball and fashion show that later featured bands from the DUKE ELLINGTON Orchestra to the CAB CALLOWAY Orchestra.

A longtime clubwoman Perry founded the Missouri State Association of Colored Girls in 1923; this youth service organization eventually joined with the National Association of Colored Girls (NACG), an affiliate of the National Association of Colored Women's Clubs. Perry later served as chairperson of the NACG. She wrote the lyrics for the state association song and the motto, "Learning as We Climb." Her concern for young black women broadened into a range of social activism. She worked for years with the Civic Protection Association, a forerunner of the NAACP Legal Defense Fund, and helped found the Colored Big Sister Association of Kansas City in 1934. This latter organization ran a home for girls for nine years—the first entity established to help young African American women who left the Niles Orphan Home at the required age of twelve to stay out of the juvenile justice system (generally, they were institutionalized in facilities for juvenile delinquents until they turned seventeen). Perry helped teach residents—using her background in home economics—and then eventually aided them when they left the home.

In addition to her sister Harriet, Perry remained close to her youngest sister, Rosabelle Douglass Jones, who also moved to Kansas City. Both Fredericka and Rosabelle were active in the National Association of Colored Women; Rosabelle was the Kansas City Association's president in 1929 and 1930. Both were involved in the Children's Improvement Association and the city "Book Lover's Club." Perry also served as a trustee of the Frederick Douglass Memorial and Historical Association. She died in Kansas City.

Fredericka Douglass Sprague Perry had a lasting effect on African American Missouri that her namesake would have been proud of. Her social service efforts were prototypes for later work, the hospital she helped build served the black community in Kansas City until its closure in 1972, and her work with the Colored Girls Clubs helped a generation of young African American women gain education and a sense of community.

FURTHER READING

Primary sources relating to Perry are kept in the Frederick Douglass Papers at the Library of Congress and the papers of the National Association of Colored Women.

Peebles-Wilkins, Wilma. "Black Women and American Social Welfare: The Life of Fredericka Douglass Sprague Perry," *Afflia* 4.1 (Spring 1989).

Peebles-Wilkins, Wilma. "Fredericka Douglass Sprague Perry and Rosabelle Douglass Sprague Jones," in *Black Women in America: An Historical Encyclopedia*, ed. Darlene Clark Hine (1993).

Perry, John Edward. *Forty Cords of Wood: Memoirs of a Medical Doctor* (1947).

Obituary: *Kansas City Times*, 25 Oct. 1943.

ERIC GARDNER

Perry, Harold Robert (9 Oct. 1916–17 July 1991), clergyman, was born in Lake Charles, Louisiana, the eldest of six children born to Frank and Josephine Perry. Neither of the parents were high school graduates, but they placed value on education; all of the children attended college. As a family they worshipped together at Sacred Heart of Jesus Catholic Church on Mill Street.

Perry began studying for the priesthood at age thirteen as a member of the Society of the Divine Word, an international organization of missionary priests and brothers founded in 1875 to minister to populations among whom the Catholic Church did not have a strong presence. In the United States the society served mostly blacks and Indians. Perry entered the seminary at St. Augustine Divine Word Seminary in Bay St. Louis, Mississippi. He made his novitiate in East Troy, Wisconsin, and studied toward ordination at Divine Word Seminary in Techny, Illinois. After ordination in 1944 he served as an assistant pastor at parishes in Louisiana, Arkansas, and Mississippi.

Perry was ordained a priest on the Feast of the Epiphany in 1944. In 1952 he founded a parish and school in Broussard, Louisiana. Over the next six years Perry built a church, rectory, and school. His superiors viewed that as a sign of his leadership; afterward the relatively young priest was launched on a series of challenging firsts.

In 1958 Perry was named rector, or head, of his alma mater, St. Augustine's Seminary in Bay St. Louis. He became the first African American to administer an institution that trained U.S. Catholic priests. Afterward he was elected head of the religious community's southern province. Perry was also the first African American to be chosen as leader of a male religious order. He was also the first African American minister to lead the opening prayer at a session of the U.S. House of Representatives, which took place on 8 July 1963. Bishop Perry was invited on 30 March 1966, by then–House Speaker John McCormick, to return as guest chaplain of Congress to pray at the session's opening.

In 1965 Pope Paul IV and two U.S. archbishops announced in a joint international statement that the forty-nine-year-old Louisiana native would be the first acknowledged African American to become a member of the United States Roman Catholic Bishops. He was consecrated as an auxiliary bishop of the Archdiocese of New Orleans on 6 January 1966. The ceremony drew international scrutiny and acclaim, the appointment seen as a sign of the Roman Catholic stance on the U.S. civil rights movement.

Archbishop John Patrick Cody, who left his post as spiritual leader of the New Orleans archdiocese in June 1965 to head the Archdiocese of Chicago, once told a reporter that U.S. Catholics, particularly those in the South, might see Perry's ordination as a "special mark of affection of the Holy Father" toward Americans. Years earlier, the noted television preacher Archbishop Fulton J. Sheen, then bishop of Rochester, New York, said the consecration of a black U.S. bishop, as symbol, would be a "better answer to the problem of civil rights than many a letter." In fact, in 1956, as an auxiliary bishop of the Archdiocese of New York, Sheen published a short list of African American candidates. Perry's name was at the top. After over forty seven years in ministry, Perry had witnessed the evolution of the Catholic community in the United States from segregation to cultural diversity. New Orleans was the portrait of the new South and a changed Church with offices to administer specialized ministries to Korean, Filipino, black, Vietnamese, and Hispanic communities. Perry lived long enough to see the appointment of more than ten African American bishops and two archbishops. His role as the first acknowledged black U.S. Roman Catholic bishop was a giant step in the effort to expand the church's ministry.

FURTHER READING

Crider, Bill. "Perry's No Catholic Dr. King," *Washington Post, Times Herald. Outlook,* 30 January 1966.

Roberts, Gene. "Negro Is Installed as a Bishop in New Orleans; Catholics Consecrate Perry, Segregationists Picket Ceremony at Cathedral," *New York Times,* 7 January 1966.

VINCENT F. A. GOLPHIN

Perry, Heman Edward (5 Mar. 1873–3 Jan. 1929), entrepreneur and founder of a bank and an insurance company, was born in Houston, Texas, the son of John Perry and Lucy Compton. Heman Perry, the second of nine children, grew to manhood in post-Reconstruction Texas. His father, a former Georgia slave, reputedly ran away to Texas, where he dabbled in various entrepreneurial activities; at times he operated a farm, traded cotton and other commodities, rented out drays, and worked as an insurance agent. Although without formal training himself, John Perry believed firmly in the value of education for his children. Heman completed only a few years of formal schooling, but his father encouraged his self-education through reading and practical business experience.

As a youth Perry helped his father with his various entrepreneurial endeavors, often peddling farm products, providing clerical help in the insurance work, or assisting with buying and selling cotton. These experiences and his father's example served to provide Perry with an early exposure to the business world and, it may be surmised, also laid the foundation for his later efforts to achieve an enormous and passionate dream of African American enterprise.

Sometime in the 1890s, after a variety of work experiences in Houston and elsewhere, Perry ventured to New York City, where he worked as an agent for several large white insurance firms, including the Equitable and Manhattan Life companies. After about twelve years in New York, having made a few hundred dollars in the stock market and having lost it all again, he left for Savannah, Georgia, with absolutely no money but with the intention of initiating a cotton trading business. In 1908 he migrated to Atlanta, where he turned his attention again to insurance, convinced that a market existed for whole or ordinary life insurance among African Americans. His confidence was bolstered by the knowledge that in 1908 no black company operated in that arena and that most white firms served African Americans poorly, if at all. Intimately familiar with the disadvantages under which most existing black insurance firms operated, offering small sick and burial policies, Perry dreamed of putting black insurance on a sound, more reputable basis. He hoped to establish a firm that would operate under state-established legal reserve requirements and that would provide a stronger basis for African American financial advancement.

In 1909 Perry put his proposal before Atlanta's most prominent black citizens, from whom, as an outsider, he received a mixed reception. Moving ahead nevertheless, he secured a charter for a new corporation, the Standard Life Insurance Company, and began efforts to raise the requisite one hundred thousand dollars in capitalization needed to launch the enterprise. This was a mammoth sum to be raised among African Americans; to make the situation more difficult, it was stipulated that these funds must be raised within two years or the charter would be forfeited to the state. After two years of tirelessly selling his idea to African Americans throughout the country, Perry acknowledged failure and returned the nearly seventy thousand dollars he had collected to the investors. Within a short time, however, he reinitiated the project, and by early 1913 he had secured the necessary capitalization for the firm through both private investors and bank loans. Perry obtained a new charter on 22 March 1913 and began operating the company that June.

The firm progressed rapidly under Perry's leadership, aggregating in the first year some $700,000 in ordinary insurance sales. Over the next ten years, Standard Life expanded into twelve states and the District of Columbia. By 1924 the company had increased capitalization to $250,000, held assets of $2.25 million, and reported insurance in force in excess of $22 million.

The success of Standard Life propelled Perry to the next stage of his plan for promoting business development among African Americans. In August 1921 he opened the Citizens Trust Company Bank in Atlanta. This venture was followed by the rapid organization of other business operations, known as the Service Enterprises. Diverse, they included a realty company, pharmacy, printing company, laundry, construction company, and several other concerns. A total of eleven such enterprises, with interlocking directorates, operated as subsidiaries of the Service Company, which Perry had organized in 1917 with capital borrowed from the insurance company.

Through Perry's initiatives, a substantial part of the business and economic foundation of the modern black community in Atlanta was created. His enterprises focused on various issues central to the needs and welfare of African Americans, including housing, education, recreation, farming, and financial development. Through the Service Enterprises, he built some five hundred new homes in an area in west Atlanta. The realty company also sold land to the city as a site for Booker T. Washington High School, the first public high school for African Americans in Atlanta, and the construction company won the $212,000 contract to build the David T. Howard Junior High School for this community. Perry's efforts also resulted in the city setting up segregated Washington Park for African Americans.

Other socially useful enterprises included publishing services for churches and colleges in the Southeast, a chain of drugstores, and a farm bureau, which sought to deal with problems of black farmers. The centerpiece of these enterprises, the bank, engaged in full-scale commercial banking, providing financing for the purchase of homes and the establishment of businesses. Emboldened by his success in Atlanta, Perry talked of establishing branches of these enterprises in other cities and promoting additional efforts to harness the financial resources of African Americans. It is said that he envisioned creating nothing less than a self-sufficient national black economy.

After 1924 Perry's unusual success was followed by severe difficulties; by 1925 most of the companies had been dismantled. Complex financial problems, resulting from overexpansion and mismanagement, drained the resources of the insurance company, causing its impairment and the eventual loss of what was Perry's most important entrepreneurial creation. Through a series of mergers and sales, the insurance firm passed out of the hands of African Americans, with major losses incurred by the community. Citizens Trust also ended its affiliation with Perry and was reorganized in 1924. The other subsidiaries, including the realty company, drug chain, and printing enterprise, were later reincarnated in new firms.

Perry left Atlanta in the wake of this disaster, which had reached national proportions. Moving to Kansas City, Missouri, he attempted to rebuild his insurance career, and he was in the process of organizing a new firm when he died there of heart failure. Although assessments of Perry vary, it is generally agreed that through extraordinary boldness and insight he helped advance black entrepreneurial standing in the country. His efforts and surging spirit were particularly important to the economic development of Atlanta's black community, where he left an indelible imprint through the many firms that were either direct or indirect heirs of Perry's legacy.

FURTHER READING
Henderson, Alexa Benson. "Heman E. Perry and Black Enterprise in Atlanta, 1908–1925," *Business History Review* 61 (Summer 1987): 216–42.

Ingham, John N., and Lynne B. Feldman. *African-American Business Leaders: A Biographical Dictionary* (1994).

Simmons, Judy C. "Heman Perry: The Commercial Booker T. Washington," *Black Enterprise*, Apr. 1978, 41–48.

Stewart, M. S. *An Economic Detour: A History of Life Insurance in the Lives of American Negroes* (1940).

This entry is taken from the *American National Biography* and is published here with the permission of the American Council of Learned Societies.

ALEXA B. HENDERSON

Perry, Ivory (5 May 1930–15 Feb. 1989), social advocate and civil rights activist, was born in Desha County, Arkansas, to the sharecroppers Pearl Barnes Perry and Ivory Perry Sr. Soon after his father left them, the family moved to Pine Bluff, Arkansas. When Perry was sixteen, his mother contracted bronchial pneumonia, had a stroke, and died at the age of forty-two. After his mother's death, Perry dropped out of school and joined the U.S. Army on 2 November 1948. He was assigned to Japan with the all-black Twenty-fourth Infantry Regiment. However, Perry found that racism still existed all those miles away from home. White soldiers made life almost unbearable for the blacks.

During a visit home in 1951, Perry realized just how little things had changed in American race relations. When he and two white soldiers entered a restaurant, the owner offered them a table in the broom closet next to the kitchen. Perry opted to reenlist in the military in November 1951. In March 1953 Perry was court-martialed and convicted of disobeying an order from a superior officer. Although Perry maintained his innocence, he was found guilty and sentenced to two years of hard labor in the stockade and was given a dishonorable discharge.

After his release from prison, Perry moved to St. Louis, Missouri. In 1955 Perry read about the murder of EMMETT TILL, a black teenager from Chicago who was lynched while visiting relatives in Mississippi. Moved, Perry soon joined the Congress of Racial Equality (CORE), a nonviolent organization devoted to the civil rights movement. Perry assisted demonstrations at the Fox Theater in St. Louis to pressure the management to admit black customers. Eventually, CORE worked out an agreement to allow blacks. Perry threw himself into the civil rights struggle, fighting for better employment opportunities and access to service in stores and restaurants.

In 1963 Perry met and married Anna Cox, who agreed with his views on racism. The couple joined in the demonstration at the Jefferson Bank, on Washington Ave. in St. Louis, to persuade the bank to hire black tellers and give them management opportunities. After many months, and jail time for many of the demonstrators—including Perry for sitting in front of a bus, stopping traffic—the bank hired its first black employees. Other banks in the city soon followed suit.

With Perry's help, CORE went on to organize protests at the Old Courthouse, to lock in five hundred Southwestern Bell employees to protest the firm's reluctance to hire black employees, and to picket at the Gateway Arch to secure jobs for black workers on federal projects.

In March 1965 Perry was responsible for causing a large traffic jam by blocking the road with a rented yellow U-Haul truck to force St. Louis whites to confront the violence and brutality leveled against the civil rights movement. When a cab tried to pass his parked truck, Perry threw himself in front of the moving vehicle. Perry's activities spread beyond St. Louis. He also traveled to Bogalusa, Louisiana, to help with the voter registration drives in 1965. The climate in Bogalusa was hostile; however, the governor, John McKeithen, claimed that he knew of no reason for African Americans there to stage demonstrations. In April, black children walked out of their classes and marched to downtown Bogalusa, at the direction of CORE. After several more demonstrations, the mayor finally met with representatives from the Civic and Voters League.

Returning home from Bogalusa, Perry took it upon himself to fight police brutality in St. Louis, when police officers shot and killed seventeen-year-old Melvin Cravens. He marched protestors to the police station where they picketed, stopping traffic when Perry threw himself under a car. This brought more attention to the cause; however, all officers were cleared of the charges.

Also in 1965 Perry began working for the Human Development Corporation (HDC), where he quickly earned respect for his actions and dedication. Later the police were accused of killing nineteen-year-old Russell Hayes and sixteen-year-old Timothy Walsh, a white youth. Perry saw this as a great opportunity to work through race relations among the poor. After meeting with him, the mayor expressed regret over the shootings and agreed to revise police procedures.

In 1967 Dr. MARTIN LUTHER KING JR. announced a "poor people's movement" and Perry became one of the coordinators. Perry was working on the project when he heard about King's death the following year. This troubled Perry greatly and soon doctors diagnosed him as manic depressive and he was hospitalized. Later, in 1969, Perry became housing coordinator for HDC, where he led rent strikes and obstructive demonstrations. He eventually won lower rents, better maintenance, and police protection for many tenants.

On a home visit for HDC Perry noticed two sickly children eating the chipped paint from a wall. After testing, he learned that their conditions—skin problems, watery eyes, runny noses, and nasal congestion—were a direct relation to lead-based paint used in many of the older homes. Perry hired a Legal Aid attorney, and in April 1970 Stolar's bill, which forced landlords to detoxify lead buildings, became law.

Later, in 1976, Perry joined the fight against big business politics that affected the poor: he participated in actions against the Missouri Public Service Commission, Laclede Gas Company, and many more. However, of all his accomplishments, Perry considered his fight against lead poisoning the most satisfying.

In 1989 Ivory was killed by his son during a domestic quarrel. As tragic as Perry's death was, it brought the issue of violence in the inner city to the forefront, helping to open up discussions about St. Louis's ever-growing crime problem. Fighting for the nameless, faceless poor was certainly no easy task. However, Ivory Perry was able to overcome many personal difficulties to lead the charge against multiple injustices for all underprivileged people—both black and white.

FURTHER READING

Greene, Lorenzo Johnston, Gary R. Kremer, and Antonio F. Holland. *Missouri's Black Heritage* (May 1993).

Lipsitz, George. *A Life in the Struggle: Ivory Perry and the Culture of Opposition* (1988).

Obituary: *St. Louis Post-Dispatch*, 16 Feb. 1989.

CHESYA BURKE

Perry, Joe (22 Jan. 1927–25 Apr. 2011), professional football player, was born Fletcher Joseph Perry in Stephens, Arkansas, the son of Fletcher Perry and Laura Wheeler Perry, whose occupations are unknown. Perry grew up in Los Angeles, graduating in 1944 from Jordan High School, where he starred in football, baseball, basketball, and track and field. He was a star running back during 1944–1945 at Compton Junior College, scoring twenty-two touchdowns in his first season.

After college Perry joined the U.S. Navy and played for the Alameda Naval Air Station football team in 1947. The San Francisco 49ers tackle John Woudenberg saw Perry play and told 49ers owner Anthony J. Morabito and coach Lawrence T. "Buck" Shaw about the six-foot, two-hundred-pound running back. Perry reportedly turned down offers from fourteen colleges to sign a contract with the 49ers.

The 49ers began playing in 1946 during the initial season of the All-America Football Conference, created to compete with the long-established National Football League (NFL). Perry started his professional football career with a fifty-eight-yard run on his first play from scrimmage. He finished the 1948 season with 562 yards in seventy-seven carries, leading the league with an average of 7.3 yards per rushing attempt and scoring ten touchdowns. Quarterback Frankie Albert called Perry "the Jet" because of his quick acceleration from the fullback position, and he was known as Joe "the Jet" Perry thereafter. Despite his great speed and his relative small size for a fullback, he was essentially a straight-ahead runner, combining power and quickness to slash through tacklers.

The only black player on the team, Perry described the 49ers, whose ranks included many players from the South, as being like a big, happy family. Opposing players, however, frequently hurled racial epithets and punches at the rookie. When Perry first went to Baltimore to play the Colts, the Lord Baltimore Hotel refused to give him a room, so he stayed with a local black doctor. He walked from the physician's house to the stadium because no taxi would pick him up. Years later the hotel issued an apology to Perry. A second black player, Bob Mike, joined the 49ers in 1948 only to be released when Morabito saw him with a light-skinned woman he wrongly assumed to be white. The NFL had a handful of black players from its origin in 1920 until 1933, but there were no others until 1946. Most professional football teams had only a handful of African American players until the 1960s.

Perry led the All-America Football Conference in rushing in 1949, with 783 yards, an average of 6.8 yards per carry, and was named the all-league fullback. The 49ers played the Browns for the All-America Football Conference championship that season, losing to Paul Brown's dominating team 21–17 before a crowd of 82,769. After the season the Browns played an all-star team drawn from the conference's remaining teams in Houston. The five black players, including Perry, on the two teams were housed in private residences in the segregated city, and the Cleveland and Houston branches of the NAACP pressured the game's organizers to sell tickets to African American spectators. The All-America Football Conference then folded, and the 49ers joined the Browns and the Baltimore Colts in moving to the NFL. Perry had many distinguished teammates during his NFL career, including Pro Football Hall of Fame quarterbacks Y. A. Tittle and John Brodie. In 1952 rookie Hugh McElhenny was rookie of the year. Joining Perry and McElhenny in the back-field in 1954 was a second black star, JOHN HENRY JOHNSON, imported from the Canadian Football League. Perry led the league in rushing, with Johnson finishing second. Perry, Johnson, and McElhenny became known as the "Million Dollar Backfield" for their value to the team, not for their low salaries in this era long before free agency. All three would be elected to the Hall of Fame.

After Perry ran for 1,018 yards in 1953, Morabito awarded him a bonus of $5,090 or $5 for each yard. Perry gained 1,049 yards the next year, becoming the first professional player to rush for over 1,000 yards (a benchmark of excellence) for two consecutive seasons. His average gain per rushing attempt of 6.1 yards in 1954, matched in 1958, remained a team record until broken by Steve Young's 6.3 yards per carry in 1991.

The 49ers had their best season of Perry's tenure in 1957 only to blow a 27–7 halftime lead and lose to the Detroit Lions 31–27, missing the NFL championship game with the Browns. Perry left San Francisco after 1960 to play two years with the Colts but returned to the 49ers for his final season in 1963. He hoped to play three games that season to qualify for an NFL pension but surprised many by appearing in nine games. After retiring, Perry worked as an automobile and wine salesman in the San Francisco area.

Because All-America Football Conference statistics are included in NFL records, Perry finished his career with 9,723 yards rushing, a record broken by JIM BROWN of Cleveland in 1964. He averaged 4.9 yards per carry, a high figure for someone who played sixteen seasons, unusual longevity for a running back. Perry also caught 260 passes, scored 513 points, and played in three Pro Bowls, the NFL's

all-star game. Perry was elected to the Pro Football Hall of Fame in 1969, becoming the first 49er so honored.

In recognition of the team's sixtieth anniversary in 2006, the 49ers announced the Joe Perry/Wally Yonamine Unity award. This honor, also named for Perry's 1947 teammate, the first professional football player of Asian descent, is bestowed upon a 49ers player, a youth football coach, and a San Francisco business exhibiting volunteerism and ties in the community. Perry's own volunteerism included feeding Thanksgiving meals to the needy. He died in Tempe, Arizona, at the age of 84.

FURTHER READING

LaBlanc, Michael L., ed. *Professional Sports Team Histories* (1994).

Porter, David L., ed. *African-American Sports Greats: A Biographical Dictionary* (1995).

Ross, Charles K. *Outside the Lines: African Americans and the Integration of the National Football League* (1999).

MICHAEL ADAMS

Perry, Julia (24 Mar. 1924–24 Apr. 1979), composer and conductor, was born Julia Amanda Perry in Lexington, Kentucky. Her parents' names are unknown; her father was a physician and amateur pianist. Perry and her sisters were encouraged in their musical interests, and they continued their studies when the family moved to Akron, Ohio. Perry followed her musical studies at the University of Akron with degree work at the Westminster Choir College. Her BMus, earned in 1947, was in Voice, and she was highly praised as a mezzo-soprano. The next year she secured her MMus in Composition, followed by a year at the Juilliard School and the summer of 1951 at the Berkshire Music Center.

For the next nine years Perry studied composition in the United States with Henry Switten and in Europe with Nadia Boulanger and Luigi Dallapiccola and conducting with Emanuel Balaban and Alceo Galliera at the Accademia Musicale Chigiana in Siena. During this period she also lectured on a tour sponsored by the U.S. Information Service and presented a series of concerts in 1957. Two Guggenheim fellowships (in 1954, for *The Cask of Amontillado*, and in 1956) and the Boulanger Grand Prix (in 1952, for her violin sonata) facilitated her European residence. In 1965 she received an award from the National Institute of Arts and Letters. For the school year 1967–1968 she served on the faculty of Florida A&M University in Tallahassee; the following year she taught at Atlanta University in Georgia.

Perry's recognition as a gifted composer then evolved rather quickly through recordings, publications, and performances, but her career was essentially terminated by strokes starting in 1973. She continued to compose from her home in Akron, but these efforts bore evidence of more than the paralysis of her right side. Until her death in Akron, she continuously planned on recovery and optimistically projected major performances and tours as a conductor.

Among her works are three operas: *The Bottle*, in one act, set to her own libretto (1953); *The Cask of Amontillado*, after Edgar Allan Poe and first performed at Columbia University (1954); and *The Selfish Giant* (1964), after Oscar Wilde. Her larger works include two piano concertos (the second in 1965), two violin concertos (1963, 1975), two masses (one an orchestral requiem setting), and several cantatas. The majority of her compositions reflect her neoclassical education with respect to style and content, with occasional reference to her African American background, particularly in settings of spirituals. Recorded and frequently performed were her *Carillon Heigh-ho* (1947, for chorus), *Homunculus C. F.* (1960, for ten percussion instruments and harp [C. F. meaning "chord of the fifteenth"]), *Stabat Mater* (1951, for mezzo-soprano and string quartet or orchestra), and the orchestral *Short Piece* (1952). The last four of Perry's thirteen symphonies were written after her first stroke, and copies of these, with correspondence from her final decade, are available at Fisk University in Tennessee.

Stylistically Perry's music is eclectic, sometimes harshly dissonant and sometimes quite harmonically traditional. In either style, her thinking was not consciously within the feminist movement. Interest in her works was evident on international programs until the time of her stroke, after which only her vocal music was performed with any frequency.

FURTHER READING

Green, Mildred. *A Study of the Lives and Works of Five Black Women Composers* (1975).

Obituary: *The Black Perspective in Music* 7, no. 2 (Fall 1979; death date correction in 8, no. 2 [Fall 1980]).

DISCOGRAPHY

de Lerma, Dominique-René. *The Black Composer: A Discography* (1997).

This entry is taken from the *American National Biography* and is published here with the permission of the American Council of Learned Societies.

DOMINIQUE-RENÉ DE LERMA

Perry, Lincoln. *See* Fetchit, Stepin.

Perry, Matthew James, Jr. (3 Aug. 1921–29 July 2011), lawyer, civil rights leader, and federal jurist, was one of three children born to Matthew Perry, a tailor, and Jennie Lyles in Columbia, South Carolina. He grew up in the Jim Crow era and his parents, who had a limited education, passionately wanted their children to have more opportunities. His father served in World War I and his exposure to mustard gas left him with a debilitating illness. While Perry Sr. received treatment in a Veterans Hospital in Tuskegee, Alabama, the family lived there and in Columbia. Matthew was twelve when his father died, and the children were then raised in Columbia by their maternal grandfather, William Lyles, a brakeman on the Southern Railroad. During the Depression Perry helped support the family by working after school digging ditches, among other jobs, while his mother found work in New York as a seamstress.

He attended segregated schools—Little Red Schoolhouse in Tuskegee, and Waverley Elementary in Columbia. At Booker T. Washington High School, where he graduated in the Class of 1939, he was inspired by J. Andrew Simmons, the principal, to do well academically and in the arts. Perry's rich baritone voice was an asset in the school's revered chorus and its performances of spirituals and operettas.

During his sophomore year at Colored Normal, Industrial, Agricultural and Mechanical College (later South Carolina State College), he enlisted to fight in World War II. From 1943 until 1946 he served with the segregated U.S. Army Quartermaster Corps—where soldiers were black and officers white—in England, France, and Germany, achieving the rank of sergeant. A defining experience occurred after basic training in Mississippi. On a segregated train en route to Camp Shanks, New York, the final staging area for combat in Europe, the train stopped in Alabama. There Perry saw Italian prisoners of war eating in a restaurant near white American soldiers, while black soldiers in uniform were forced to order food through a window and eat outside in the cold. "It was shocking," he said, "and I felt an insult that I've never forgotten" (Bernstein [2007], 1). In time he determined that a career in law was the way to fight for changes that had to take place.

Perry's resolve was strengthened in 1946 when, as an undergraduate, he watched two trials presided over by Judge J. Waties Waring, a white South Carolinian who soon became well known for his liberal views. These early "separate but equal" school cases led, from 1948 through 1951, to *Briggs v. Elliott*, a series of school desegregation cases in Clarendon County, South Carolina. Two of the judges on the three-man court voted against the black plaintiffs and upheld school segregation in South Carolina. But Judge Waring dissented from the majority in *Briggs v. Elliott* (1951), and wrote that "segregation is *per se* inequality." Waring inspired Perry and many others, and though death threats soon forced the judge to flee the state, he and the NAACP had set the stage for major changes to the nation's social landscape. The NAACP attorneys Harold Boulware, ROBERT CARTER, and chief counsel THURGOOD MARSHALL, soon combined *Briggs v. Elliott* with four other school desegregation cases, which they argued collectively before the Supreme Court as *Brown v. Board of Education*.

Perry graduated in 1948 from South Carolina State College with a bachelor of science degree in Business Administration. That June he married a schoolteacher, Hallie Bacote, of Timmonsville. Their son Michael was born in 1961. After he graduated from South Carolina State Law School in 1951 the Perrys moved to Spartanburg. There he opened his own practice (no white law firm would hire him), and began a career as courageous as it was financially unrewarding. During that time Mrs. Perry supported the family by teaching.

Perry's work in civil rights litigation began in the trenches and continued there, despite death threats. In 1957 he became state chairman of the NAACP Legal Committee. He moved his practice to Columbia in 1961 and became chief counsel of South Carolina's NAACP conference, working with national leaders, including Thurgood Marshall, Jack Greenberg, and CONSTANCE BAKER MOTLEY. He argued cases for voting rights and the desegregation of public schools, colleges, hospital waiting rooms, restaurants, parks, and beaches. He was responsible for the release on bail of 7,000 people arrested during sit-ins. Though most were convicted at trial, after appeals these convictions were reversed at the federal and state Supreme Court level. Perry's representation of protesters established precedents for the right of assembly and free speech. A 1963 case litigated by Perry forced Clemson University to admit the first African American in modern times, HARVEY GANTT; and in another case he forced the University of South Carolina to admit black students. Perry also represented peaceful marchers arrested in 1963 at the State House—*Edwards v. South Carolina*—which led to a groundbreaking U.S. Supreme Court decision that scholars consider one of the greatest First Amendment cases in history.

Perry was the lead attorney in *Stevenson v. West* (1973), a case considered of vital importance in the state's history by civil rights leader I. DeQUINCEY NEWMAN, the first black South Carolina State Senator in modern times. Backed by the U.S. Supreme Court, this case mandated the reapportionment of the South Carolina House of Representatives, enabling blacks to be elected to state and local government for the first time since Reconstruction. Though Perry himself ran unsuccessfully for pubic office, he was highly regarded by Republicans and Democrats, black and white. Astonishingly, in 1976 longtime segregationist U.S. Senator Strom Thurmond supported Perry's appointment to a federal judgeship. President Gerald Ford appointed Perry to the U.S. Military Court of Appeals in Washington, D.C.—thus making him the first black lawyer from the Deep South appointed to the federal judiciary. In 1979 President Jimmy Carter named him U.S. District Judge for South Carolina, the first African American to serve in that capacity.

Perry was honored in 2004 when a new U.S. Courthouse in Columbia, South Carolina, was named for him, and he presided there as a senior judge. In 2007 Judge Perry was inducted into the South Carolina Hall of Fame and the National Black College Alumni Hall of Fame—testaments to his lifelong dedication to justice for all people. He died in Columbia, South Carolina, at the age of 89.

FURTHER READING

Some information on Perry's life is from unpublished interviews by Alice Bernstein (11 July 2005 in Charleston; 23 Feb. 2007 by telephone).
Burke, W. Lewis, and Belinda F. Gergel, eds. *Matthew J. Perry: The Man, His Times, and His Legacy* (2004).
Clyburn, James E. "Induction of Judge Matthew J. Perry, Jr. into the South Carolina Hall of Fame," speech (2007).
Gergel, Richard Mark. "Matthew J. Perry Jr.," in *South Carolina Encyclopedia*, ed. Edgar Walter (2006), 714.

ALICE BERNSTEIN

Perry, Pettis (4 Jan. 1897–24 July 1965), Communist Party leader, was born near Marion, Alabama, on a tenant farm worked by his parents, whose names are unknown. His father died when Perry was a small child, and he was raised by his uncle, Stokes King, and an aunt. He attended a rural school sporadically, receiving about fifteen months of formal education. By the time he was ten, he was working in the cotton fields. He moved on to a sawmill and then a pipe foundry before deciding to leave the South when he was eighteen.

Perry embarked on the life of an itinerant worker, traveling around the United States in search of work. He reached California in 1920 and used it as his base for the next twelve years. Most winters he worked at a cottonseed oil mill in Los Angeles. In the summers he went on the road as a harvest hand, following the crops throughout the western, southwestern, and midwestern states. The Communist-dominated Agricultural Workers Industrial Union was active in California in the early 1930s, and Perry joined during one of the numerous strikes the union led among migratory workers.

Perry's life was transformed in April 1932 when he heard about the SCOTTSBORO BOYS, nine young black men sentenced to death in Alabama for raping two white women. Like him, the Scottsboro Boys were poor, southern blacks. The Communist-dominated International Labor Defense (ILD) had mounted a campaign to save the youths, and Perry joined the ILD in Los Angeles and participated in rallies on behalf of the defendants. By October he had joined the Communist Party of the United States of America (CPUSA). Inspired by its political activities and analyses, Perry painstakingly developed his meager reading abilities by studying *The Communist Manifesto* and *Capital* with the aid of a dictionary, demonstrating the perseverance and discipline that were characteristic of his party service.

The Communist Party was eager to recruit African Americans like Perry and to push them into prominent positions as a demonstration of its commitment to racial equality. In April 1932 he was elected as a delegate from Southern California to a conference in Chicago demanding the release of Tom Mooney, a white radical imprisoned since World War I for his alleged role in a San Francisco bombing that had killed ten people. Left-wing groups had long asserted Mooney's innocence. Perry began to move up in the party hierarchy, running for statewide office in California three times.

In 1934 as a candidate for lieutenant governor he received some 10,000 votes; in 1938 he received more than 50,000 votes for the State Board of Equalization; and in 1942 he secured a creditable 40,000 votes as the party's nominee for secretary of state. During World War II he was in charge of Communist work among blacks in Los Angeles, supervising efforts to recruit blacks, organizing and coordinating civil rights campaigns, and dealing with party relationships with non-Communist black organizations.

Late in 1948 Perry moved to New York City to become secretary of the CPUSA's National Negro Commission; he later also was in charge of the National Farm Commission, overseeing party work among these two constituencies. He wrote an article in 1949 for *Political Affairs*, the party's theoretical journal, calling for a renewed effort to root out racism in the party, inaugurating what many party cadres later recalled as the most disruptive episode in party history. Hundreds of Communists were charged with being insensitive or hostile to blacks in the CPUSA and were expelled. Many more were pressured into confessing their failings. Perry traveled around the country to press the campaign. Any perceived slight to a black Communist was vigorously attacked. Use of words like "whitewash" or "black sheep" led to charges of racism. Perry and his allies argued that until the party cleansed itself of all vestiges of racism, it would be unable to lead the black struggle for equal rights. Opponents retorted that the campaign left the impression that the party was a hotbed of racism, focused its attention inward rather than on the broader problems facing American society, and alienated many loyal Communists. Not until the party leader William Z. Foster warned in 1953 that the attack on racism had led to "left-sectarian errors" did the campaign end.

At the 1950 CPUSA convention Perry was elected as an alternate member of the National Committee. When the party leadership convicted at the first Smith Act trial in 1948 was jailed or went underground in 1951, Perry and Betty Gannett became the party's interim leaders. Perry himself was arrested in June 1951 and was tried the following year in another Smith Act trial in New York. The defendants were divided about courtroom tactics; Perry summed up the defense case with an orthodox Communist argument defending the party's program and Marxist-Leninist doctrine. Sentenced to three years in federal prison in Danbury, Connecticut, he served two and a half before being released in May 1957. Perry never regained such a prominent role in the CPUSA. He died of heart disease in Moscow, where he had gone for medical attention. He was survived by his second wife, Rose Manosa, whom he married in 1949, and by two sons and a stepson from that marriage.

FURTHER READING
Pettis Perry's papers are housed at the Manuscripts, Archives and Rare Books Division, Schomburg Center for Research in Black Culture, at the New York Public Library in New York City.
Boyer, Richard. *Pettis Perry: The Story of a Working Class Leader* (1952).
Obituary: *New York Times*, 28 July 1965.
This entry is taken from the *American National Biography* and is published here with the permission of the American Council of Learned Societies.

HARVEY KLEHR

Perry, Phyllis Alesia (8 Mar. 1961–), journalist and writer, was born in Atlanta, Georgia, to Arcola J. Perry and Harmon Perry, the latter an award-winning photojournalist, editor of *Jet* magazine from 1973 to 1981, and founder of the Atlanta Association of Black Journalists (AABJ).

Though she was a member of the Black Baptist Church and baptized by her grandfather, the Reverend Sterling Johnson, Perry's primary education was in a Catholic school, which she attended for nine years. There Perry developed an interest in stigmata, a subject that she would explore in her literary work. She studied communications at the University of Alabama and was awarded a degree in 1982.

After her graduation Perry began working at the *Tuskegee News*. This was followed by a period of work as an editor and reporter for newspapers in Tupelo, Mississippi, and Montgomery. In 1988, while working as a city editor for the *Alabama Journal* (later the *Montgomery Advertiser*), Perry was a member of the team which won the Pulitzer Prize for its investigation of Alabama's extraordinarily high infant-mortality rate. The series of twenty articles published over five days prompted legislation to tackle the problem and also won the Distinguished Service Award from the Society of Professional Journalists.

Throughout her career as a journalist Perry kept a record of ideas for writing fiction in her journals, keeping alive her childhood ambition of becoming a creative writer. It was in the pages of these journals that her first novel, *Stigmata* (1998), began to take shape. Combining her work as a novelist with that of editor and reporter for the *Atlanta Journal-Constitution*, Perry created the character of Lizzie, who upon receiving a trunk containing, among other things, the diary of her great-great-grandmother and a quilt sewn by her grandmother, begins a journey into these women's pasts. The trunk functions in the narrative as a kind of Pandora's box, the contents of which need to be interpreted and understood so that the released sorrowful past can become a force of regeneration. In *Stigmata*, the device of time travel does not imply that a character becomes a mere observer or participant in the events of another era. Lizzie does not witness her foremothers' lives from a distance; rather, she becomes Ayo and Grace, occupying not only their historical realms but also their bodies. This psychological imprint of slavery is reinforced by Lizzie's stigmata, which appear on her wrists as a tangible manifestation of her ancestor's slave past. Thus, in Perry's novels the scarred body is a central signifier in the reconstruction of African American history, functioning as a textual record of slavery. Perry's representation of the supernatural reworks the narrative models presented by OCTAVIA BUTLER's *Kindred* (1979) and TONI MORRISON's *Beloved* (1987) in order to re-create the partially lost history of the female slave.

In her work Perry investigates both the nature of reality and its representation, introducing an innovative narrative form that reflects a world where the boundaries between the earthly and the ghostly become blurred. In this context the ancestral spectre can function as a means of translating the absences of African American history into tangible presences, revising the African American tradition of the ghost tale. These are strategies that Perry also used in her second novel, *A Sunday in June* (2004), a prequel to *Stigmata*.

A Sunday in June chronicles the lives of the three Mobley sisters from childhood to maturity in the first decades of the twentieth century, revealing the deep racial divisions of the Jim Crow era. The two younger sisters, Mary Nell and Eva, have the gift of second sight and can see into the future, while Grace is haunted by the ghost of her grandmother, frequently reliving her Atlantic crossing to the New World and her life in slavery. Without the supernatural as an essential narrative device in the resurfacing of history, Perry suggests, the memories of the Mobley women would have been disrupted and so, too, would the connection to the beginning of African American history. Perry's narrative also suggests the crucial importance of remembering the history of those buried in the Atlantic Ocean, while evoking the memories of Africa as the homeland, the horrific experience of kidnap, and the African way of life.

In her novels Perry recovered the role of women's folk traditions such as religious rituals, herbal medicine, storytelling, and food- and quilt-making as an effective means of imparting a sense of identity, community, history, and the valuable life skills essential for the survival of an oppressed group. The novelist established a link between quilting and storytelling as a means of recovering history and actualizing the past via cultural practice. The present is, therefore, embedded in the past, and the quilts made both by Lizzie and Grace present a form where past and present merge in a graphic space.

The novel *Stigmata*, which won the Georgia Author of the Year Award, was selected for the Book of the Month Club/Quality Paperback Book Club, and was a finalist for the Quality Paperback Club New Voices Award, had a curious publishing history. It was first published in Germany by Ullstein in a German-language translation in the spring of 1998, while Perry was still revising her manuscript with her U.S. editor. This accounts for the fact that the ending to the German version of *Stigmata* differs from that of subsequent editions. The novel was published in English in the autumn of 1998 by Hyperion. It was later translated into several languages, including Spanish and Dutch.

An excerpt from *Stigmata* was also published in *Step into a World: A Global Anthology of the New Black Literature* (2000), an anthology of new black writers edited by Kevin Powell. Other works by Perry included "The First Place," an essay in which the writer celebrated her grandmother, published in *The Remembered Gate: Memoirs by Alabama Writers* (2002).

FURTHER READING

Moore, Shirley Walker. "Phyllis Alesia Perry," in *Writing African American Women: An Encyclopedia of Literature by and about Women of Color*, ed. Elizabeth Ann Beaulieu (2006).

ANA NUNES

Perry, Rufus Lewis (11 Mar. 1834–18 June 1895), Baptist minister and editor, was born a slave on the plantation of Archibald W. Overton in Smith County, Tennessee, the son of Lewis Perry and Maria (maiden name unknown). His father, an able mechanic and cabinetmaker, was able to hire his own time from his owner and moved his family to Nashville, where Perry was ranked as a free child and was allowed to attend a school for free blacks. But when his father fled to freedom in Canada in 1841, the family was forced to return to Overton's plantation.

The education that the young Perry had received and his continued self-education were sufficient to elicit the contempt of fellow slaves and the alarm of white people, and, as a result, he was sold in August 1852 to a slave trader who intended to take him to Mississippi. Perry, however, remained with the trader only three weeks before he made his own escape to freedom in Canada. He ended up in Windsor, Ontario, where he continued his studies and taught other fugitive slaves. In 1854 he experienced a call to the ministry. He then studied at the Kalamazoo Seminary in Michigan and was ordained on 9 October 1861 as the pastor of the Second Baptist Church in Ann Arbor, Michigan. He later served churches in St. Catharines, Ontario, and Buffalo, New York, until he moved around 1870 to Brooklyn, New York, where he organized the Messiah Baptist Church and served as pastor until his death. Perry married Charlotte Handy; they had seven children.

Perry served from 1867 to 1879 as corresponding secretary of the Consolidated American Baptist Missionary Convention (CABMC), which was organized in 1867 following the merger of two regional African American Baptist bodies. Through the CABMC and its affiliate, the American Educational Association, Perry offered a powerful countervailing voice for African Americans in response to the paternalism of the predominantly white American Baptist Home Mission Society, which sought to dominate Baptist missionary and educational efforts among the freedmen. He was coeditor of CABMC-sponsored publications, the *American Baptist*, from 1869 to 1871, and the *National Monitor*, from 1872 to 1879, becoming editor of the latter in 1879. He argued that the existence of the CABMC was necessary because of racial prejudice and that this black organization should have primary responsibility for work among black southerners. He framed the issue as nothing less than true faith versus idolatry, maintaining that black missionaries were necessary; otherwise "strangers will come in and introduce strange gods."

Perry served from 1867 to 1879 as vice president of the board of managers of the National Theological Institute and University, founded in

1864 in Washington, D.C., to train black Baptist ministers. The school failed, however, in 1872 because of infighting between the black administrators and the white sponsors. Justin D. Fulton, one of the sponsors, joined the executive board of the CABMC in 1877, hoping to remove Perry, who was implicated in some questionable financial practices; the allegations were never proved, and Perry was cleared of suspicion. Nevertheless, the CABMC disbanded in 1879. The successful consolidation of African American Baptists on a national scale would not occur until the National Baptist Convention was formed in 1895, shortly after Perry's death in Brooklyn.

Although Perry lost much of his national influence over black Baptist life with the dissolution of the CABMC, he continued to be a voice for racial justice and activism, using the remaining CABMC assets to support publications and mission work in Haiti. He also remained corresponding secretary of the abolitionist American Baptist Free Mission Society, which was a "paper organization," having effectively dissolved in 1872 following the emancipation of the slaves.

Perry's literary efforts also included editing the *Sunbeam* and the *People's Journal*, occasional publications for black Baptists. In his only book, *The Cushite; or, The Descendants of Ham as Seen by Ancient Historians* (1893), he drew upon his interest in African history, classics, and black Masonry to produce a defense of black cultural nationalism, arguing that the ancient Ethiopians and Egyptians were the black descendants of Ham and were destined for "a return of racial celebrity, when in the light of a Christian civilization, Ethiopia shall stretch out her hands unto God." This book, along with his other writings and his leadership among Baptists, earned for Perry a place as one of the most articulate religious spokespersons for African American causes in the second half of the nineteenth century.

FURTHER READING
Cathcart, William. *The Baptist Encyclopedia* (1881).
Pegues, Albert W. *Our Baptist Ministers and Schools* (1892).
Simmons, William. J. *Men of Mark* (1887).
Washington, James M. *Frustrated Fellowship: The Black Baptist Quest for Social Power* (1986).
This entry is taken from the *American National Biography* and is published here with the permission of the American Council of Learned Societies.

TIMOTHY E. FULOP

Peters, Brock (2 July 1927–23 August 2005), actor, was born George Fisher in Harlem, New York to Alma A. Norford Fisher and Sonnie Peters. By age ten he knew he wanted to be an actor. He attended the Music and Arts High School in New York and made his stage debut at fifteen as Jim, one of the Catfish Row children, in a 1943 Broadway revival of Gershwin's *Porgy and Bess*. His family was poor, and while he continued to study acting, he also worked as a hospital orderly and shipping clerk. At one point, despairing of his prospects, he enrolled at the City College of New York to pursue a degree in physical education. But in 1949 he won a stage role in a touring production of *Porgy and Bess* and left college to embark upon his acting career.

In 1953 George Fisher changed his name to Brock Peters and made his television debut on Arthur Godfrey's *Talent Scouts*. In 1954 he was cast as the intimidating Sergeant Brown in Otto Preminger's film version of *Carmen Jones*, and was further called upon to dub the song "Whizzin' Away Along De Track" for actor Roy Glenn. Stage roles followed in *Mister Johnson* (1956) and the musical *The Body Beautiful* (1958), before Preminger cast him again in his 1959 screen version of *Porgy and Bess*. Portraying Crown in that film, he sang the duet "What You Want Wid Bess?" with DOROTHY DANDRIDGE (whose voice was, however, dubbed in by Adele Addison). Peters was cast in another short-lived musical, *Kwamina*, in 1961, before landing the role of his career—accused rapist Tom Robinson, the man defended by Gregory Peck's Atticus Finch in the film *To Kill a Mockingbird* (1962).

Having gone through the usual audition process for the role, he ended up as one of two finalists alongside a formidable competitor, James Earl Jones. According to Peters, the final interview with director Robert Mulligan and the producers—which he attended in a suit and tie—occasioned him considerable nervousness since he needed to speak professionally, while still giving the impression that he could play the part compellingly. After he did win the role, he was charmed by an early morning phone call from Gregory Peck welcoming him to the production (a unique experience that, he said, never again came his way). Once on the set, Peters was required to cry often on cue, which he successfully did by mentally revisiting "places of pain, remembered pain, experienced pain." He recalled the shooting of the film as one of his happiest times, and much later in life the film still had resonance for him: he read the eulogy at Peck's funeral on 16 June 2003, and later appeared with seldom-seen author of *To Kill a Mockingbird*, Harper Lee, when she was honored by the Los Angeles Public Library.

The *Los Angeles Times* characterized Peters in 1990 as a "geyser of an actor who never errs on the side of restraint." Six feet three inches in height, with intense eyes and a strong deep voice, Peters for a time despaired of being cast as anything other than a villain. His 1962 portrayal of a gay jazz trumpet player in the British film *The L-Shaped Room* helped to dispel that image. He played Othello onstage in 1963, and in 1965 he returned to the United States—and to his typical casting—to portray an unusually cruel pimp in Sidney Lumet's *The Pawnbroker*. In the same year he led a troop of black soldiers in Sam Peckinpah's *Major Dundee*. In *The Incident* (1967), he played one of several passengers menaced by two teenagers on a subway train. All of these were supporting roles, but in 1970 Peters was given a rare leading role in a Western called *The McMasters*, where he portrayed a former slave who becomes a property owner. In 1972 Peters returned to the Broadway stage as Reverend Stephen Kumalo in *Lost in the Stars*, the Kurt Weill musical set in apartheid South Africa. He was nominated for a Tony award for the role and also played the same character in the film version a year later, which was released in 1974. In 1973 he appeared in the bleak science fiction classic *Soylent Green*.

Peters's television experience was fascinatingly wide-ranging. He appeared in projects as diverse as *Roots: The Next Generations* (1979), *Voices of Our People* (Emmy Award, 1982), the soap opera *The Young and The Restless* (1982–1989), and *Star Trek: Deep Space Nine* (1995–1999). His television credits dating back to the 1950s include episodes of *As the World Turns, Rawhide, Mission: Impossible, It Takes a Thief, Mannix, The Virginian, Longstreet, The Mod Squad, Night Gallery, Gunsmoke, The Streets of San Francisco, McCloud, Medical Center, Baretta, Police Story, The Bionic Woman, Quincy M.E., Battlestar Galactica, Magnum, P.I., Cagney & Lacey, Murder, She Wrote, The Pretender, Dark Sentinel*, and *JAG*, along with a legion of lesser known shows.

Peters remained active on the stage, starring with Julie Harris in *Driving Miss Daisy* in Los Angeles in 1989, and as a teacher in Athol Fugard's apartheid drama *My Children! My Africa!* in 1990. He became familiar to a younger generation of science fiction movie fans when he starred as Admiral Cartwright in *Star Trek IV: The Voyage Home* (1986) and *Star Trek VI: The Undiscovered Country* (1991). He played Darth Vader in the National Public Radio adaptations of *Star Wars, The Empire Strikes Back*, and *Return of the Jedi*. He also appeared in *Ghosts of Mississippi* (1996), a film about the civil rights struggle in the South.

Peters involved himself in many diverse projects, including singing background vocals on HARRY BELAFONTE's hits *Banana Boat (Day-O)* and *Mama Look At Bubu*, doing voiceovers for many animated projects including *Batman: The Animated Series* (1992–1995), and using his arresting bass voice as General Mi'Qogh in the videogame *Star Trek: Starfleet Command III* (2002). In addition to his 1973 Tony award, Peters received a National Film Society Award, Life Achievement Awards from both the Screen Actors Guild and the National Film Society, and he was inducted into the Black Filmmakers Hall of Fame in 1976.

Brock Peters married television producer Dolores Mae (DiDi) Daniels on 29 July 1961 and they had one child, a daughter, Lise Jo. Didi died in 1988. Peters was diagnosed with pancreatic cancer at age seventy-eight in January 2005 and received chemotherapy. His condition worsened and he died peacefully, surrounded by family, on 23 August in Los Angeles. At the time of his death, he had a longtime companion named Marilyn Darby. He is buried next to DiDi at Forest Lawn Cemetery in Glendale, California, overlooking Griffith Park and Hollywood.

FURTHER READING

Bogle, Donald. *Toms, Coons, Mulattoes, Mammies, and Bucks: An Interpretive History of Blacks in American Films* (2001).

Obituary: *New York Times*, 24 August 2005.

DAVID BORSVOLD

Peters, Margaret and Matilda Roumania Peters

(1915–3 Nov. 2004) and (1917–16 May 2003), tennis players, were born in Washington, D.C. Margaret and Roumania, who were often referred to as "Pete" and "Repeat," gained local distinction playing tennis on the clay courts at the Rose Park playground across the street from their homes in the Georgetown section of Washington, D.C. They played in an era when blacks were segregated from whites in both national and international competitions. In 1936 both sisters were invited to play in the ATA national championships in Wilberforce University in Ohio. The ATA had been founded in 1916 by a group of African American businessmen, college professors, and physicians who wanted to promote the game of tennis and provide a forum for competition at the national level. The ATA provided the finest competition for blacks in the United States at the time. Roumania played exceptionally well in her first national level tournament, making it to the finals before falling to three-time champion Lulu Ballard in 1936.

As teenagers the Peters sisters attracted the attention of Cleve Abbott, the tennis coach at Tuskegee, who offered them both four-year scholarships. Margaret, feeling a bit uneasy about traveling so far away from home, deferred for a year while waiting for her sister to graduate from high school in Washington, D.C. In 1937 the Peters sisters entered Tuskegee together where they would become the best African American tennis players in the nation at the time. The sisters were feared by their opponents for their excellent slice serves (a form of under-spin put on the ball to keep it low to the ground), chop shots (a shot rarely taught today in which under-spin is put on the ball during a return of serve), and strong backhands.

Both sisters played basketball and tennis while at Tuskegee and both were members of Who's Who in American Colleges and Universities. Roumania became the Southern Intercollegiate Athletic Conference tennis champion. Their fame on the tennis court largely derives from the fourteen doubles titles they won between 1938 and 1941 and between 1944 and 1953. Roumania also won ATA national singles titles in 1944 and 1946. In her second title she defeated ALTHEA GIBSON, who won ten ATA national singles titles before playing a pioneering role in integrating tennis in the United States and around the world.

After graduating from Tuskegee in 1941 with degrees in physical education the Peters sisters continued to play amateur tennis in regional and national ATA tournaments. As amateurs they had to pay for their own equipment, entry fees, and travel expenses. Their success at ATA events led to some fame. They played matches in front of British royalty and celebrities such as the actor Gene Kelly practiced with both Roumania and Margaret while in the Washington, D.C., area.

Margaret, who never married, briefly moved to New York after graduation and earned a master's degree in physical education from New York University. She later returned to Washington, D.C., to work as a special education teacher. She earned a second master's degree in special education from Coppin State College in Baltimore, Maryland.

Like her sister, Roumania also earned a master's degree in physical education from New York University after graduating from Tuskegee. In 1957 she married James Walker, a math professor from Tuskegee who came to the college after seeing a picture of Roumania in a newspaper. They had a daughter named Frances Della and a son named James George together. Roumania worked as a teacher at Howard University in the 1950s and in the D.C. public school system from 1964 until 1981. Roumania taught tennis to underprivileged children through the department of recreation. In 1977 both sisters were inducted into the Tuskegee Hall of Fame. Roumania died in 2003 from pneumonia.

Margaret and Roumania only recently began to receive national acclaim for their accomplishments on the tennis court. But the league that previously banned them from competing, the United States Tennis Association (USTA), only began to recognize the Peters sisters in 2003. The USTA presented Margaret and Roumania with an "achievement award" prior to a Federation Cup match and in 2003 the USTA inducted both sisters into the Mid-Atlantic Section Hall of Fame.

FURTHER READING
The Tuskegee University Hall of Fame possesses a few short articles on the Peters sisters.
Anonymous. "U.S. Tennis Association Honors Pioneering Black Female Athletes." *Black Issues in Higher Education* (28 Aug. 2003).
Djata, Sundiata. *Blacks at the Net: Black Achievement in the History of Tennis* (2006).
Mosley, Camille Riggs. Federation Cup Souvenir Program (2003)

KEITH R. BROWN

Peters, Thomas (1738?–25 Jun. 1792), slave, Black Loyalist, and community leader, was most likely born in present day Nigeria in West Africa. Little is known about the early stages of his life. It is unclear what his occupation or family size might have been or how Peters might have been captured in 1760. French slave traders purchased Peters and brought him to Louisiana, probably to work in the brutal sugar fields. Unwilling to reconcile himself to his new status, Peters attempted to escape several times. As a result, his master sold him to the British American colonies. By the 1770s he had become the property of William Campbell of Wilmington, North Carolina.

During the early 1770s, Peters's life started to change dramatically. First, he probably married a fellow slave named Sally and within a year became a father. Second, the impending conflict between the

American colonies and the British Empire would offer several opportunities for Peters to claim freedom for himself and his family. Peters may have become familiar with the problems between the British and Americans through his owner, an outspoken member of the Sons of Liberty. Perhaps he realized that war between Britain and the colonies might create a possibility for his family to gain freedom. As hostilities became unavoidable in 1775, the white citizens of North Carolina became increasingly fearful that political uncertainty and the disruption of authority might increase slave restiveness and lead to various forms of open resistance. Their fears proved in many cases prophetic. The confusion of warfare soon presented an opportunity for African Americans to escape the chains of slavery in areas ranging from Boston to Savannah.

The American Revolution caused the British leadership in Virginia to turn to sources of manpower it might rather have avoided. On 7 November 1775, the royal governor, Lord Dunmore, offered freedom to black slaves willing to desert their rebel owners. For Dunmore, this proclamation was a matter of military necessity as opposed to abolitionist sentiments. He also offered to arm any able-bodied men to help put down the rebellion. According to George Washington and several others, Dunmore had become the most dangerous man in America by arming former slaves. But, for Thomas Peters and his enslaved brethren, rumors of Dunmore's proclamation might have made freedom seem an immediate possibility, and the British suddenly an antislavery force. Thousands of African Americans made their way to the safety of British lines. In early 1776, when the "Patriots" evacuated Wilmington in the face of British military strength, Peters escaped from his owner. Along with other former slaves Peters joined the Black Pioneers, a newly formed regiment of the British army, and saw action in South Carolina and Pennsylvania. As a result of his meritorious service, the British promoted him to the rank of sergeant. Peters's certificate of service stated that he had "served faithfully and honestly—and in every respect becoming the character of a good and faithful subject of Great Britain" (Wilson, first page of illustrations, opposite 226). By the end of the war in 1783, Peters and at least thirty-five hundred Black Loyalists evacuated New York for other parts of British North America.

The British decided to transport a large contingent of American Loyalists to the British North American colonies of Prince Edward Island, Nova Scotia, and New Brunswick. In total, more than thirty thousand Americans, black and white, settled in these sparsely populated colonies. Thomas Peters settled on the western shore of Nova Scotia in Brindley Town. The British had promised the Loyalists (black and white) land and support, but the sheer numbers turned surveying and the granting of rations into an unbelievable hardship. Many of the Black Loyalists, Thomas Peters and his family included, either did not receive land, or obtained small and useless farms. Thus they had to search for menial work. They often competed for jobs with poor whites, which resulted in a race riot in 1784 in Birchtown—another settlement of Black Loyalists on the southern shore of Nova Scotia. In addition to economic problems, the Black Loyalists encountered severe racism in the form of economic and social obstacles that sharply curtailed their freedom. Indeed one British writer lamented that it "is not in my power to describe the scandalous and shameful conduct shewn to the free blacks by many of the White people" (Clarkson, *Clarkson's Mission to America, 1791–92*, 46). His hunger for freedom unquenched by settlement in Nova Scotia, Peters resolved in 1790 to find a better home for the Black Loyalists, possibly on the coast of Africa.

In 1790 Peters traveled to London with a petition from black families in Nova Scotia and New Brunswick. In this petition, Peters had hoped to obtain a better situation for blacks in Nova Scotia by resettling them possibly in West Africa. The petition contained an accurate assessment of the situation of both free and enslaved blacks in Nova Scotia. Peters stated that free blacks were "refused the common Rights and Privileges of other Inhabitants, not being permitted to vote at any Election nor serve on Juries" (Wilson, 180). In England, Peters stayed with the local black community, partially composed of Black Loyalists, and was introduced to leading white antislavery advocates including Granville Sharp, William Wilberforce, and Thomas Clarkson. He socialized within antislavery circles and became quite well known. After making contact with his former military commanders from the Revolutionary War, Peters spoke with Henry Dundas, the Home Department's secretary of state, and informed him that the Black Loyalists had been treated with disdain and indifference in Nova Scotia. He suggested that settlement in another colony might be the best option. Shortly thereafter, in 1791, the British Parliament granted the Sierra Leone Company (a company supposedly specializing in resettling free blacks) a charter for economic opportunities and settlement on the West African coast. The British government decided to encourage Thomas Peters and the Black Loyalists to become the Sierra Leone Company's new colonists.

Peters returned to Nova Scotia armed with British promises of passage to Sierra Leone, free land, and support from the future governor of the Sierra Leone colony, the noted abolitionist John Clarkson. Peters's campaign to encourage black migration to Sierra Leone found enthusiastic support among African American settlers who had tired of the poor economic and social climate of Nova Scotia. However, some of the Black Loyalists did not wish to remove from places where they had forged families and the bonds of community. Many white Nova Scotians also resented Peters's effort because it promised to deprive the colony of a cheap labor supply. In the end, Peters succeeded in convincing about twelve hundred Black Loyalists to join him in migrating to Sierra Leone. On 15 January 1792, they sailed from Halifax for the coast of West Africa.

Thus, in the spring of 1792, some years after he left under duress, Peters finally returned to the shores of Africa. It should have been a triumphant time for the community leader, but the fledgling colony's overbearing white leadership and the difficulties associated with settlement created a difficult atmosphere, and he quickly became a persistent critic of Governor Clarkson. Peters positioned himself as the leader of an opposition to the white government, but the majority of black settlers supported Clarkson. Shortly before Peters's untimely death, he was accused of theft and endured the embarrassment of a public reprimand. On 25 June 1792, Peters died from an intense fever.

Peters's life engaged with and transcended some of the most important events in Atlantic World history including the slave trade and the American Revolutionary War. He had moved from freedom in Africa to slavery in the Americas to freedom in Nova Scotia and Sierra Leone. As a community leader, he brought the grievances of a substantial group of black people to the epicenter of power in the British Empire. Peters ceaselessly fought to improve the situation of people of African descent in North America and Africa. His life is a reminder of the interconnectedness of black history from Africa to North America to Europe.

FURTHER READING

Several documents related to the Black Loyalists and Thomas Peters are housed at the Nova Scotia Archives and Records Management, Halifax, Nova Scotia; and the Public Record Office, London.

Fyfe, Christopher H. "Thomas Peters: History and Legend," *Sierra Leone Studies*, no. 1 (1953).

Hodges, Graham Russell, ed., *The Black Loyalist Directory: African Americans in Exile after the American Revolution* (1995).

Nash, Gary B. "Thomas Peters: Millwright and Deliverer," in *Struggle and Survival in Colonial America* (1981).

Pybus, Cassandra. *Epic Journeys of Freedom: Runaway Slaves of the American Revolution and their Global Quest for Liberty* (2006).

Schama, Simon. *Rough Crossings: Britain, the Slaves and the American Revolution* (2005).

Walker, James W. St. G. *The Black Loyalists: The Search for a Promised Land in Nova Scotia and Sierra Leone, 1783–1870* (1976).

Wilson, Ellen Gibson. *The Loyal Blacks* (1976).

HARVEY AMANI WHITFIELD

Peterson, Joseph P. (13 July 1949–), U.S. Naval officer and submarine commander, was born in Washington, D.C., the son of Theodore and Louvenia Peterson. Raised in rural Bluemont, Virginia, Joe Peterson's father was a stonemason, while his mother was a homemaker. The Petersons lived on a small plot of land and cultivated a variety of vegetables for their own use. However Joe knew that he wanted to gain a wider experience and, as Peterson noted in an interview, "the navy was the ticket" for a new life (phone interview, 19 Mar. 2007). His interest piqued by the naval movies he had watched from his childhood, after his graduation from Douglass High School in Leesburg, Virginia, Peterson enlisted in the navy in October 1968.

Upon completing boot camp, Peterson volunteered for submarine duty and attended submarine school in Connecticut. Rated an electronics technician, Peterson saw his first sea duty on the missile boat *Mariano G. Vallejo*. Although he was one of the few African Americans in the crew, Peterson was guided in this new environment by the boat's longtime steward, a man from Waco, Texas, known by the nickname "Smitty," who befriended him. Despite the overall lack of African Americans in the submarine service, Peterson recalled that the racial difficulties experienced by others in the navy was "something I didn't see" (phone interview, Mar. 2007), and that he was always treated with respect by his fellow submariners. On the *Vallejo*, Peterson made a number of routine "deterrent" patrols and rose to chief, serving as navigation leading petty officer. In 1976 he left the boat for shore duty at the Naval Ordinance Test Unit at Cape Canaveral, Florida, as Strategic Missile Test Instrumentation Supervisor.

Having reached chief petty officer status relatively early in his career, Peterson "was ready to get out of the navy" (phone interview, Mar. 2007). However, he decided to persevere despite the attraction of greater pay in the private sector and attended night school at Rollins College in Winter Park, Florida, to gain a B.S. in Economics. Peterson's experience and continued education, combined with the navy's increased need for submarine officers, made him ideal as a candidate for the Officer's Candidate School (OCS) in Newport, Rhode Island.

In 1980 Ensign Joseph Peterson was commissioned as an officer in the U.S. Navy. He returned to the *Mariano G. Vallejo* as assistant weapons officer and served on the boat for two years. Following this duty, he returned ashore to an assignment in Washington, D.C., at the Strategic Systems Programs (SSP) as strategic weapons project officer, in charge of weapons acquisitions from 1983 until 1985, Peterson's first of three tours of duty there in his career. Following this duty, after a further period of advanced submarine training, Peterson was posted to the missile boat *John C. Calhoun* as weapons officer. Peterson first joined the ship as it was coming out of an overhaul period and working to gain its nuclear weapons certification. His experience proved to be vital in this important process and, as he related in an interview, "we did so well in our practice inspection that we got certified right then and did not need another inspection....At that point I was the 'golden boy' and enjoyed my time on the boat" (phone interview, 19 Mar. 2007). From here, Peterson went back to Strategic Systems Programs (SSP) from 1988 to 1990 as test and evaluation team leader for Strategic Weapons Systems Demonstration and Shakedown Operations. Here it was that Peterson was on the other side of the fence, it being his job to certify submarine nuclear weapons systems operations for newly commissioned boats or those coming off overhaul, work that was often unheralded but vital. As Peterson said, "the ugliest thing I had to do was to fail a ship in the qualifying inspection, but sometimes this had to be done to prevent an incident which might lead to an accident" (phone interview, 19 Mar. 2007).

In the following years Peterson earned his master's degree in National Security Affairs at the Naval Postgraduate School in Monterey, California, in 1991, and underwent further training before his assignment in 1993 as executive officer on the *Dolphin*, the navy's lone remaining diesel submarine. Because Peterson was not a nuclear power trained officer, regulations dictated that he could only command a diesel submarine. However, when the navy decommissioned all but one of its diesel boats beginning in 1989, Peterson and others with his background became concerned. In fact, Peterson recalled that "a lot of guys bailed out and left the navy, but I stuck with it....I had gotten this far and was supposed to be the 'hot shot,' so I just kept going." Indeed, that is just what Joe Peterson did, excelling as executive officer aboard the *Dolphin* during tough times when the submarine's old diesel engines often failed and "things were not pretty" (phone interview, 19 Mar. 2007).

In 1994 Lieutenant Commander Joseph Peterson was named skipper of the *Dolphin*, just the fifth African American submarine commander ever, following in the wake of "PETE" TZOMES, ANTHONY WATSON, WILLIAM BUNDY, and MELVIN WILLIAMS JR., and joining that group of men that would later come to be known, with the addition of several others, as the Centennial 7. Peterson could especially relate to his mentor and friend, William Bundy, who was the first black submarine commander to come from the enlisted man's ranks and command a diesel submarine.

Peterson's time on the *Dolphin* from 1994 to 1997 was both challenging and rewarding; a boat that "mixed old and new technology, including the old diesel engines and DC generators with prototype systems being tested for the new SSN [fast attack] boats"(phone interview, 19 Mar 2007). Peterson also mentioned that he "had a good command tour" (phone interview, 19 Mar. 2007). Indeed, his successful duty on the *Dolphin* was extremely important in the area of research and development in the Submarine Force, and some of the modern systems used on later nuclear submarines were first tested on Peterson's diesel submarine.

Following his time on *Dolphin*, Peterson subsequently returned to SSP for a third tour, this time as both Research and Development and Launcher Systems Branch Head. By this time Peterson was one of the Submarine Force's premier experts on weapons systems and was heavily involved in developing the program still under way to convert four of the navy's Ohio-class submarines from the Trident missile to the Tomahawk cruise missile platform. Following his promotion to captain in 2001, Peterson headed the Naval Sea Systems Command's Fleet Readiness Office and, with his recognized expertise in diesel submarines, he would later be tapped to lead the navy's cooperative ventures building diesel submarines for the governments of Taiwan and Australia.

Peterson retired from the navy in 2004, but he remained actively involved with the submarine force. Employed by American Systems in 2005 as a contract consultant, he continued to work closely with the navy on a variety of national defense and international related submarine programs. He also worked with other members of the Centennial 7 to provide midshipmen at the Naval Academy guidance in a yearly forum held in Baltimore, and he served as a member of the board of trustees for the Washington Mathematics, Science, and Technology Public Charter High school. He married the former Alma Jones (date unknown) and had two children, daughter LaRonda and son Andrew. Reflecting on his navy career in an interview in 2007, Peterson declared that he was justly "proud of just being in the Submarine Force" and of his role in mentoring others.

FURTHER READING

The quoted material herein comes from the author's phone interview with Captain Joseph Peterson on 19 Mar. 2007 and subsequent e-mail exchanges.

GLENN ALLEN KNOBLOCK

Peterson, Oscar (15 Aug. 1925–23 Dec. 2007), jazz pianist, composer, and trio leader, was born Oscar Emmanuel Peterson, in Montreal, Canada, the son of Daniel Peterson, an immigrant from Tortola in the British Virgin Islands, and Kathleen Olivia John, a housecleaner from Saint Kitts. Daniel Peterson worked as a sleeping-car porter on the Canadian trains, and unable to realize his own dream of becoming a pianist, he made sure his five children had musical training. He recognized Oscar's talent in particular and worked hard to give the boy lessons from age six. Oscar's sister Daisy became a well-known piano teacher. She and Oscar studied with Paul de Marky, a protégé of Franz Liszt, thus receiving a thorough classical training.

At fourteen, Peterson won a Canadian Broadcasting Corporation contest and got his own weekly fifteen-minute radio program in 1939. His early playing revealed the strong influence of the harmonies of EARL "FATHA" HINES and TEDDY WILSON. In 1944 Peterson played with the Johnny Holmes dance band, and that same year he married Lillie Fraser, with whom he had five children before they divorced some years later.

In 1945, after signing with Canadian RCA Victor, Peterson showed off his deftness at playing boogie-woogie, but this did not really reflect his true style or musical education. Peterson always emphasized how much he delighted in the music of NAT KING COLE, and this is reflected in his earliest recordings. But it wasn't just Cole's piano style that held Peterson in thrall: Peterson had a distinctive singing voice that was also reminiscent of Cole's.

Peterson first caught the attention of American impresario Norman Granz, founder of Jazz at the Philharmonic (JATP), when Granz heard him playing on a broadcast from the Alberta Lounge in Montreal in 1949. Granz raced to the club and booked Peterson to appear at Carnegie Hall with Jazz at the Philharmonic, backed by bassist Ray Brown Jr. and drummer Buddy Rich. Granz became Peterson's manager for virtually his entire career. In 1950 he won the *Down Beat* magazine Readers' Poll. Peterson began touring regularly with JATP as leader of a trio, known as the Oscar Peterson Trio, which became one of the most celebrated in jazz history. At various times the trio included guitarists IRVING ASHBY, Barney Kessel, and Herb Ellis. Drummer Ed Thigpen replaced Ellis in 1958 or 1959 for another great trio until 1965. Many other peerless rhythm section players and soloists joined the Peterson trio between 1966 and 1970.

In 1950 Granz formed Verve Records and featured Peterson above all on this label as well as on the subsidiary labels of Norgran, Clef, and Mercury. Most, but not all, of Peterson's hundred-plus albums as a leader were done for Granz labels. Granz had a special knack for taking clients such as Peterson and ELLA FITZGERALD and making them millionaires.

Peterson, Brown, and Thigpen, along with trombonist Butch Watanabe and composer Phil Nimmons, founded a jazz school: the Advanced School of Contemporary Music, in Toronto in 1960. The school lasted only until 1963, but it educated a number of musicians who became well known and highly regarded in the United States; among them are pianists Mike Longo and Carol Britto, as well as bassist, singer, and composer Jay Leonhart.

In 1966 Peterson married Sandra King; they would divorce ten years later. Peterson worked on the MPS/BASF label in the late 1960s and early 1970s, but in 1972, when Granz formed Pablo Records, Peterson went back to Granz, who teamed him up with the strong European bassist Niels-Henning

Oscar Peterson with his Grammy for best jazz instrumental performance at the 21 annual Grammy Awards presentation in Los Angeles, Ca., on 16 Feb. 1979. (AP Images.)

Orsted Pedersen and virtuosic guitarist Joe Pass. Peterson participated in all-star jazz sessions at the Montreux Jazz Festival in 1975 and 1977. Also in 1977 he married Charlotte Huber, with whom he had a son before they, too, later divorced. Martin Drew became his regular drummer in 1980.

In the late 1980s Peterson began playing in reunion groups and on recordings with Brown, Ellis, and drummer Bobby Durham, who had played with the group from 1967 to 1970. Peterson's performances always drew a crowd and provoked standing ovations and cries for encores. As he grew older, he continued to play with amazing dexterity at breakneck speed, while the emotional depth of his playing deepened. It seemed as if he would never meet his match and that nothing could diminish the luster of his playing. He was invested as a Companion of the Order of Canada in 1983.

In 1991 Peterson married his fourth wife, Kelly (maiden name unknown), and they had one daughter. In May 1993 the overweight Peterson, already afflicted with arthritis in his hands, suffered a stroke and lost the use of his left hand. He endured extensive therapy for a couple of years and began using his sidemen, particularly the guitarists, to compensate for his disability. But his dazzling right hand remained so strong that it added chordal luster to the polished single note lines for which he had always been lionized, and he continued to play in festivals and concerts and to record excellent music.

Peterson won countless awards, including seven Grammy Awards and a score of honorary doctorates, as well as the medal of Service of the Order of Canada. Peterson's work comprises a melding of early and late piano styles, from stride and boogie-woogie to bebop and beyond, encompassing the whole of jazz history, including some of the harmonic innovations of pianist Bill Evans. Peterson has composed notable music, such as the *Canadian Suite* and *Hymn to Freedom*, and, for Les Ballets Jazz de Montréal, a waltz in honor of the city of Toronto called *City Lights*. Other musicians have hailed him consistently as one of the greatest jazz pianists in the world. Though some have criticized his cerebral, sometimes seemingly chilly style and his tremendous speed and facility, which can seem to dilute his soul, nobody has ever suggested that he lacked genius.

FURTHER READING

Peterson, Oscar. *A Jazz Odyssey: The Life of Oscar Peterson* (2002).

Bogdanov, Vladimir, et al. *The All Music Guide to Jazz: The Definitive Guide to Jazz*, 4th ed. (2002).

Lees, Gene. *Oscar Peterson: The Will to Swing* (1990).

Lord, Tom. *The Jazz Discography* (1992).

Obituary: *New York Times*, 25 Dec. 2007.

LESLIE GOURSE

Petioni, Charles Augustin (27 Aug. 1883–15 Oct. 1951), journalist, physician, business and civic leader, and Caribbean independence activist, was born to the reformer Charles Edgar Petioni and Alicia Martin Petioni in Port-of-Spain, Trinidad, British-occupied West Indies. Charles Augustin Petioni graduated from the Boys' Model School, the Government College for Teachers (1900), and the Royal Victoria Institute (Commercial Business Course, 1902). Between the ages of sixteen and twenty-three he was employed as clerk and manager for Felix Potin and Company, a French distributor of specialty foods such as chocolates. He then distinguished himself as chief reporter and sub-editor of Port-of-Spain's *Daily Morning Mirror* (1908–1916) and editor of the bilingual (Spanish-English) *Daily Evening Argos* (1917–1918). He also served as an official government reporter for Trinidad's Supreme Court and Legislative Council.

As a journalist, Petioni critiqued British rule. He took further anticolonial action as founder and officer of the Metropolitan Benefit Insurance Society, Ltd., Trinidad Building and Loan Association, Trinidad Fire Insurance Company, and Trinidad Cooperative Bank, Ltd., nicknamed "the Penny Bank" (1914). These financial institutions promoted black economic self-determination. Petioni also started and led the Inter-Colonial Literary League of the West India Islands, the Model Ex-Pupils Association, the Trinidad Theosophical Society, and the Trinidad Phonographic Society.

In 1913 Petioni wed Rosa Alling (sometimes spelled Allen), a Port-of-Spain department store clerk and apprentice dressmaker. Born in 1887 in British Guiana, she had a South American Indian mother and a Hong Kong Chinese father. The couple's first child, born in 1914, was MURIEL MARJORIE PETIONI, future physician and community health activist. Their second daughter, Marguerite (also called Margaret), arrived three years later. Because of his vocal anticolonialism, Petioni faced harassment from Trinidad's British administration. As Muriel Petioni recalled later, he decided to leave for the

United States so he could "be an independent person" who "could not be silenced" (Rimer, 36). In 1918 he moved to New York City and prepared for his wife and children to arrive later. The Petionis sustained their ties to their homeland while joining Harlem's rich social networks of Caribbean immigrants. Rosa Petioni turned to the garment industry, and Charles Petioni found work as a porter, elevator operator, and stocker. He decided to become a doctor despite the institutional and financial barriers that thwarted black Americans from seeking medical careers. At night he completed the premedical course at the City College of New York (1918–1921) and then enrolled in Howard University Medical School. During this period he returned to journalism—at the *New Negro* (associate editor, 1918), *Business World* (Washington, D.C., representative, 1921–1922), the Howard Medical School *Morgue* (associate editor, 1925), and especially the *Negro World*, the newspaper of the international MARCUS GARVEY Pan-Africanist movement. He served as its Washington, D.C., correspondent from 1921 to 1925. Petioni endorsed the Universal Negro Improvement Association's "Declaration of Rights of the Negro People of the World" at Liberty Hall, New York City, August 1920. The Declaration affirmed the unity of all people of African descent worldwide in the face of colonialism, and it established the colors black, green, and red as the Pan-Africanist colors.

Petioni graduated from Howard and passed the New York State board examination in 1925, the same year that the U.S. Congress placed eugenics-driven restrictions on West Indian and other non-Anglo immigration. After he interned at St. Agnes Hospital, Raleigh, North Carolina, the family purchased a brownstone on 131st Street in Harlem, and they partitioned it into medical practice space and living quarters. Private practice was often the most feasible option for black physicians such as Petioni who aspired to economic independence and security while aiding their underserved communities. Rosa Petioni worked as her husband's receptionist; their daughter Muriel often assisted as well. Petioni also applied his hard-won medical skills as a clinical reports recorder (1926–1927), overseeing the written recording of physicians' case reports, a task that he as a journalist-turned-physician would have handled skillfully. He was also an examiner for the Victory Life Insurance Company (1927), and assistant physician and adjunct visiting officer, Outpatient Department, Harlem Hospital. He also participated in many other civic-minded activities. He was an executive board member of the National Negro Business League, New York City (1928–1929);

vice president of the West Indies Societies Protective League; founder and president of the Trinidad Benevolent Society of New York; founder of the Lupetner Financial Corporation; and cofounder of the George Washington Carver Bank (Harlem, 1948). He belonged to the Roman Catholic Church, the Democratic Party, Phi Beta Sigma Fraternity, Howard Medical Reading Club, American Medical Association, National Medical Association, New York Medical Association, North Harlem Medical Society, the Odd Fellows, Foresters, Karma, and Moses' Shepherds. However, just as in Trinidad, Petioni gained most attention for his anticolonialism, especially as president of the West Indies National Council (later renamed the Caribbean Union). He asserted that "the only hope for betterment in the West Indies is continued organization of West Indians abroad and persistent agitation" (Frazier, 35). In June 1945 Petioni helped to bring a seven-point demand for Caribbean self-government before the United Nations World Security Conference. His concern for self-government extended to all people in the United States and elsewhere who were denied it. In 1940 Petioni attended the American Committee for Protection of Foreign Born national conference at the Hotel Annapolis, Washington, D.C. The multiethnic conference strongly condemned the hotel management after it forced him to ride the service elevator.

In 1950, because her father was ailing, Muriel Petioni began to take over his practice, which was still in the family brownstone on 131st Street. Charles Augustin Petioni died at age sixty-six, just as the postwar movement toward worldwide decolonization gained momentum. He did not live to witness the joint independence of his native Trinidad and neighboring Tobago from Great Britain on 31 August 1962. Rosa Petioni died in December 1969. As of early 2007 Muriel Petioni still owned the 131st Street brownstone and remained active in medicine, although she retired from the private practice in 1990. Her father's example inspired at least nine family members to become physicians. Charles Augustin Petioni's contributions were far-reaching and forward-looking, including his leadership in the Caribbean independence struggle, his focus on economic self-determination, and his ability to foster cooperation among oppressed groups.

FURTHER READING

The Schomburg Center for the Study of Black Culture, New York Public Library, contains archival materials on Charles Augustin Petioni.

Frazier, Williams. *The Economic Future of the Caribbean* (1944).

McGuire, Robert G., III. "Petioni, Charles Augustin," in *Dictionary of American Negro Biography* (1982).

Rimer, Sara. "Where the World Was New: Immigrants Recall Ellis Island," *New York Times* (9 Sept. 1990).

Watkins-Owens, Irma. *Blood Relations: Caribbean Immigrants and the Harlem Community, 1900–1930* (1996).

Yenser, Thomas. "Petioni, Charles Augustin," *Who's Who in Colored America 1930–1932*, 3rd ed. (1932).

MARY KRANE DERR

Petioni, Muriel Marjorie (1 Jan. 1914–6 Dec. 2007), physician, educator, mentor, and community health and welfare leader, was born in Port of Spain, Trinidad, one of two children from the marriage of Rose Alling, a department store clerk, and CHARLES AUGUSTIN PETIONI, a prominent newspaper reporter and outspoken advocate of Caribbean independence. Because of harassment from Trinidad and Tobago's colonial government, Charles Petioni left for New York City in 1917. Two years later, when Muriel Petioni was five, the rest of the family settled with him in Harlem. Despite the ever-present realities of racism and sexism, Harlem's close-knit, vibrant population of Caribbean blacks gave the young girl a robust sense of belonging and confidence, as did her family.

Petioni's mother worked in the garment industry, while her father worked jobs available to Caribbean immigrant men, such as a porter, an elevator operator, and a stocker. He persisted in anticolonial politics, working for MARCUS GARVEY on Garvey's newspaper, *The Negro World*, during the 1920s, and endorsing Garvey & the Universal Negro Improvement Association's 1920 "Declaration of the Rights of the Negro Peoples of the World." He also made the decision—a radical one for a black person of that time—to become a physician, starting with premed studies at the City College of New York. After graduating from Howard University Medical School he set up practice in the family brownstone on 131st Street. At twelve Muriel Petioni, who often answered the door and the phone for her father, decided to pursue a medical career herself, becoming one of at least nine doctors in the extended family.

Muriel attended Harlem's PS 68 and PS 136 elementary schools and Wadleigh High School. After a premed program at New York University (1930–1932), she transferred to Howard for an accelerated course of study, earning her B.S. in 1934 and

M.D. in 1937; she then went to Harlem Hospital for her medical internship (1937–1939). Over the next decade she gained notice as a community health educator during stints as a resident physician at Alabama State Teachers College, Bennett College, and Wilberforce University.

While working in the South, Petioni met Mallalieu S. Woolfolk and married him in 1942. After his return from U.S. Air Force service in Italy, the couple moved to Chicago, where Woolfolk attended law school. He became a legal adviser to black politicians. The couple's one child, the future media executive Charles Woolfolk, was born in 1947. For three years Petioni left medicine to be home with her son.

In 1950 the couple moved to Harlem with their young son, and Petioni resumed her practice. When her father died the next year, she inherited his practice, still in his 131st Street brownstone. For the next four decades, whatever other commitments she took on, Petioni continued to work there. Her patients were largely poor, in contrast to the largely middle-class college students she had treated previously. She maintained the 131st Street practice from 1955 into the early 1970s, when the family moved to Teaneck, New Jersey, an emerging suburban haven for black professionals. She also remained committed to extending her skills outside her office walls. She served on Harlem Hospital's clinical staff (1960–1980) and also in the city health department (1950–1984) as a school physician, then school physician supervisor for central and eastern Harlem.

From 1969 to 1970 Petioni suffered her mother's death and the collapse of her marriage. After the divorce she moved her residence back to Harlem and took up travel to East Asia, Senegal, Brazil, and Puerto Rico. Her family had always sustained their ties with their Caribbean homeland, and she was eager to learn more about peoples of color worldwide.

At Harlem Hospital she pioneered methadone treatment for heroin addiction. Unlike many doctors at the time, Petioni refused to ignore those with drug addictions. She saw rising heroin abuse as both a cause and a symptom of wide-scale disintegration in Harlem's once thriving social networks. Later she supervised and consulted with the hospital's pediatric department.

In 1974 Petioni founded the SUSAN SMITH McKINNEY STEWARD Medical Society and served as its president for the next decade. Named for the third African American woman physician to complete a formal medical education and New York

State's first, this group serves, recruits, and mentors black female doctors. In 1977 Petioni began, and chaired through 1983, the Medical Women of the National Medical Association, the black physicians' professional society. During the early 1980s Petioni taught clinical pediatrics at Columbia University. In 1987 she founded and for many years chaired the Friends of Harlem Hospital, a fund-raising and publicity group whose mission was and is the institution's long-term financial health.

Petioni retired from her brownstone practice in 1990 but held onto the building and persisted in her intensive, acclaimed public service. Accepting a Black History Month recognition from the City of New York in 2005 with four other distinguished women, she recalled past racial and gender barriers: "It's just wonderful to have lived through those years and to be able to say now, 'We've come a long way, baby!' We've come to this point where we women have achieved great heights" (*Greenwich Village Gazette*, 18 Feb. 2005).

Petioni's energetic, wide-ranging efforts to open up health-care access and nurture other black women doctors brought enduring benefits to Harlem and other poor communities of color. In 2006 Columbia University's first Annual Conference on Health Disparities launched the Muriel Petioni Award for Outstanding Service and Mentoring to Eliminate Health Disparities. The conference underscored Petioni's contributions by naming her the award's first recipient. Petioni died in Manhattan at the age of 97.

FURTHER READING

Forde, E. Donnie. *Caribbean Americans in New York City, 1895–1975* (2002).

Richardson, Lynda. "At a Bastion of Harlem Health, the Matron Is Still In," *New York Times*, 26 Dec. 2001.

Wilson, Basil. "Dr. Muriel Petioni, a Godmother in Harlem," *Everybody's Magazine* (June/July 1979).

Obituary: *New York Times*, 10 Dec. 2011.

MARY KRANE DERR

Petry, Ann (12 Oct. 1908–30 Apr. 1997), author and pharmacist, was born Ann Lane in Old Saybrook, Connecticut. The youngest daughter of Peter C. Lane, a pharmacist and proprietor of two drugstores, and Bertha James, a licensed podiatrist, Ann Lane grew up in a financially secure and intellectually stimulating family environment. After graduating from Old Saybrook High School, she studied at the Connecticut College of Pharmacy (now the University of Connecticut School of Pharmacy) and earned her graduate in pharmacy degree in 1931.

Ann Petry in New York City on 6 Feb. 1946. (AP Images.)

For the next seven years Lane worked as a pharmacist in the family business. Her family's long history of personal and professional success served as the foundation for her own professional accomplishments. She cherished the family's stories of triumph over racism and credited them with having "a message that would help a young black child survive, help convince a young black child that black is truly beautiful" (Petry, 257). These family narratives and their message of empowerment enabled her to persevere in the sometimes-hostile racial environment of New England.

After Lane's marriage on 22 February 1938 to George D. Petry of New Iberia, Louisiana, she and her husband relocated to Harlem, New York. Harlem provided her with the environment in which to expand her creative talents and source material for her future fiction. From 1938 to 1944 Petry explored a variety of creative outlets: performing as Tillie Petunia in ABRAM HILL's play *On Strivers Row* at the American Negro Theater, taking painting and drawing classes at the Harlem Art Center, and studying creative writing at Columbia University. She also served as an editor and reporter for *People's Voice* from 1941 to 1944. Equally important for her creative work, however, was the time Petry spent organizing the women in her community for Negro Women Inc., a consumer advocacy group, and running an after-school program at a grade school in Harlem. These experiences gave Petry insight into the harsh realities facing working-class black Americans and offered her a distinct contrast to the financially comfortable world in which she was raised. Witnessing the struggles of impoverished black families in Harlem and observing the social codes of more affluent communities, such as Old Saybrook, enriched Petry's fiction, which explores the ways in which social expectations, along with the forces of racism and sexism, can constrain individual lives.

Petry published her first short story shortly after moving to Harlem. "Marie of the Cabin Club" (1939) appeared in an issue of *Afro-American*, a Baltimore newspaper, under the pseudonym Arnold Petri. In 1943, under her own name, Petry published "On Saturday the Siren Sounds at Noon" in the *Crisis*. An important turning point in her career came when this publication caught the attention of an editor who suggested that she apply for the Houghton-Mifflin Literary Fellowship Award. She submitted the first chapters and an outline of what would become her most famous novel, *The Street*, and won the fellowship in 1945. Funded by a $2,400 stipend, Petry finished the novel in 1946.

The Street garnered immediate critical and popular acclaim. Twenty thousand copies sold in advance of its release, and the novel's sales surpassed 1.5 million copies, making it the first novel by a black woman to sell more than a million copies. The story of Lutie Johnson, an ambitious black woman trying to work toward financial security, *The Street* uses the bleak landscape of an impoverished Harlem street to personify the relentlessness of racism. In its use of some elements of urban realism, *The Street* evokes comparison to RICHARD WRIGHT's *Native Son*, in which Bigger Thomas's social position—poor, black, and uneducated—inevitably leads to violence and tragedy. But Petry's novel offers what some critics consider a more nuanced examination of the way in which racism shapes black experience. Lutie Johnson not only contends with racism but also confronts sexism from white and black communities alike on an almost daily basis. Furthermore, unlike Bigger Thomas, she is a reasonably well-educated and ambitious woman, driven by the mythology of the American dream and convinced that her hard work will ultimately be rewarded. Lutie's tragic failure to achieve her goals indicts not only the racism of American society but also the deceptive mythologies that encourage people like Lutie to believe that they have an equal chance at success.

The Street's enthusiastic reception made Petry a public figure. Seeking privacy, she and her husband returned in 1947 to Old Saybrook, where they lived for the rest of Petry's life. In the same year, Petry published *Country Place*, a novel that also explores the role of environment and community on individuals, though it does not deal explicitly with black characters or experiences. In 1949 Petry gave birth to the couple's only child, Elisabeth Ann Petry, and published the first of what would be several books for children and young adults, *The Drugstore Cat*.

While it is not as well known as *The Street, The Narrows*, published in 1953, further complicates the issues Petry raises in her first novel. Set in a fictional New England city, *The Narrows* explores the repercussions of a love affair between a black man and a white woman. The nearly inevitable downfall of Link Williams in *The Narrows* revisits Lutie Johnson's situation in *The Street*. Both characters are ambitious and intelligent, yet constrained by the mechanisms of racism, which prevent them from ever really succeeding. *The Narrows* offers a pointed commentary on social behavior, not only interracial romance but also excessive class consciousness. Within this frame, Petry suggests that social codes and behavioral expectations are damaging to black and white communities alike.

Petry's themes of community relationships and the complexity of black experience in the United States continued in her later publications, including the nonfiction children's books HARRIET TUBMAN, Conductor on the Underground Railroad (1955), *Tituba of Salem Village* (1964), and *Legends of the Saints* (1970). In 1971 Petry published *Miss Muriel and Other Stories*. A compilation of stories from the 1940s through 1971, the collection draws on Petry's experiences in Harlem as well as in small-town America. In addition to writing, Petry undertook several visiting lectureships, earned a National Endowment of the Arts creative writing grant in 1978, and was awarded several honorary degrees, including an honorary DLitt from Suffolk University in 1983 and honorary degrees from the University of Connecticut in 1988 and Mount Holyoke College in 1989. Petry died in Old Saybrook on 30 April 1997.

As the first best-selling African American woman writer, Ann Petry holds a firm place in American literary history as both a groundbreaker and a literary predecessor to some of the twentieth century's most significant black women novelists.

The works of GLORIA NAYLOR, ALICE WALKER, and TONI MORRISON continue to explore the complicated interplay of race, gender, and socioeconomic status that Petry illuminated so well in her fiction.

FURTHER READING

First editions of Petry's work, correspondence, and critical reviews are housed in the Ann Petry Collection at the African American Research Center, Shaw University, Raleigh, North Carolina. Additional manuscript materials may be found at the Mugar Memorial Library at Boston University; the Beinecke Rare Book and Manuscript Library at Yale University, New Haven, Connecticut; the Woodruff Library at Atlanta University; and the Moorland-Springarn Research Center at Howard University, Washington, D.C.

Petry, Ann. "Ann Petry," *Contemporary Authors Autobiography Series* (1988).

Ervin, Hazel Arnett. *Ann Petry: A Bio-Bibliography* (1993).

Holladay, Hilary. *Ann Petry* (1996).

Obituary: *New York Times*, 30 Apr. 1997.

CYNTHIA A. CALLAHAN

Pettey, Sarah Dudley (9 Nov. 1869?–1906), educator, journalist, and feminist, was born Sarah E. C. Dudley in New Bern, North Carolina, one of the nine children of Edward Dudley, a politician, and Caroline Dudley, a teacher, whose maiden name is unknown. Both of Sarah's parents had been born in slavery, but both had learned to read and write and were determined that their daughter should learn to do so at the earliest opportunity. Alongside her mother-in-law—for whom Sarah had been named—Caroline Dudley began educating Sarah in her home, teaching the child how to read and write by the time she was six. As a Republican representative in the North Carolina state legislature from 1870 to 1874, Edward Dudley worked to make such opportunities available to all black children, as well as his own daughter. By the time Sarah was of school age, the legislature had established a new graded public school system; at the New Bern school, which Sarah Dudley attended between 1874 and 1880, she was taught by both black and white teachers. Having completed the full six grades, she spent a year at the State Colored Normal School in New Bern, where she was taught by GEORGE H. WHITE, who was later elected to the U.S. Congress.

In 1881, when she was thirteen, Dudley's parents sent her to board and study at Scotia Seminary (now Barber-Scotia College), a Presbyterian women's college two hundred miles west of New Bern, in Concord, North Carolina. Instruction at Scotia, which was also the alma mater of MARY MCLEOD BETHUNE, was both academically rigorous and practical. In addition to Latin, Greek, algebra, and music, Dudley learned needlework and cooking, though Scotia's biracial faculty expected their students to make use of the domestic arts in their own homes, not in the households of whites. Upon graduating from Scotia with first-class honors in 1883, Dudley returned to New Bern, where she served first as assistant principal of the black graded public school and as associate principal of the State Colored Normal School. At a time when opportunities for African American women were few, Sarah Dudley was one of only a handful of black women of independent means in New Bern.

She was also one of the most eligible; and in 1889 she married Charles Calvin Pettey, a bishop in the African Methodist Episcopal (AME) Zion church, whose deceased wife, Lula Pickenpack, had been Sarah's best friend at Scotia Seminary. The couple soon became among the most prominent black families in New Bern. Like Victorian-era whites of similar wealth, the Petteys were not averse to displays of their high class and status. They traveled through New Bern in the latest model of carriages, pulled by the most stylish of horses, and they shopped at the town's best stores. Charles Pettey cut a dash in his silk top hats. Sarah Dudley Pettey's dinner parties were legendary; true to Scotia's teachings she served the latest in foreign cuisine and ensured that her guests were supplied with finger bowls.

Pettey's principal biographer suggests that many white North Carolinians resented such behavior, terming it "colored swelldom" (Gilmore, 69). The Petteys, for their part, merely expected to be treated in the stores and hotels of Wilmington and New Bern with the same degree of respect that they had enjoyed on their trips to Europe, where they had visited Ireland and Paris and had been received in London by the archbishop of Canterbury and the American ambassador to the Court of St. James's. Sarah Pettey and her husband may have been among the most conspicuous consumers in eastern North Carolina in the 1880s and 1890s, but below them was a growing black middle class of entrepreneurs and property owners who aspired to the wealth and respectability enjoyed by the Petteys. This state of affairs largely depended on the persistence of black political participation in North Carolina, even after the end of Reconstruction.

Pettey, the daughter of a Reconstruction-era politician, had strong political views, and she felt no compunction about expressing them while working to raise her five children: Theophytra, Elveta, Ethel, Calvin, and Charles, as well Sarah and Mamie, the two daughters from her husband's first marriage. In this task she was assisted by members of her extended family who lived nearby and shared parenting responsibilities. She was also supported in her outspokenness in politics and other matters by her husband, who endorsed woman suffrage and encouraged his wife to talk about that topic from pulpits throughout the South. Like the spouses of other religious leaders, Pettey was active in her church, and she was elected national treasurer of the Woman's Home and Foreign Missionary Society of the AME Zion denomination in May 1892. She also supported her husband's controversial decision to ordain women as elders.

However, Pettey's political philosophy found its clearest expression in the "Woman's Column" she began writing in August 1896. The column appeared bimonthly in *The Star of Zion*, an AME Zion publication founded by her husband, which was one of the most widely read black newspapers in the nation. In these columns, which some in her denomination found mildly controversial, she addressed herself to a broad range of topics. In October 1896, for instance, she hailed the cause of Afro-Cuban revolutionaries seeking independence from Spanish imperial rule (in speaking of blacks in her own nation Pettey favored the term "Afro-American," rejecting both "Negro" and "colored" as derogatory). To those who argued that blacks in the United States were "Americans, plain and simple," she retorted that were that so, there "would be no class legislation against us; there would be no need of separate schools and churches" (Gilmore, 66). Although women could not vote in North Carolina, Pettey used her column to encourage black women, and especially working-class black women, to participate in electoral politics by persuading their husbands, brothers, and sons to vote. In 1896, as a result of the exertions of Pettey and others, the Democrats were denied a majority in the North Carolina legislature for the first time since Reconstruction. Supported by a coalition, commonly known as a "Fusion" with white Populists, black Republicans were elected to a score of state and local offices in New Bern and throughout the state.

Pettey's hope that black women as well as black men would soon vote in North Carolina was short-lived. In 1898, whites burned down the

Wilmington *Daily Record* newspaper offices run by her friend ALEXANDER MANLY after he pointed out the hypocrisy of white claims that there was an epidemic of rapes of white women by black men in the South. A few weeks later, a violent coup d'état removed Republicans from elected office in Wilmington. Official reports stated that twenty-five African American were killed by rampaging whites, many of them "respectable" businessmen, but historians now believe that the death toll was considerably higher. Two years later Democrats launched a vicious and highly successful disfranchisement campaign that effectively ended black political participation in the state until after World War II. Pettey was uncharacteristically mute on these developments, in part because she did not wish to meet the same fate as IDA WELLS-BARNETT, who was forced to leave her native South for condemning lynching. A yellow fever epidemic, which struck down ten members of the Petteys' extended family in 1900, including her husband and three children, no doubt also contributed to her silence.

Her husband's death from yellow fever in early December 1900 further removed Sarah Pettey from public life. Without her husband's income, she struggled, a situation that was not helped by the reluctance of the AME Zion church leadership to provide her with several years of back pay owed to Charles Pettey. She continued her "Woman's Column" in the *Star of Zion*, but she wrote only sporadically and without her previous verve and spice. A more conservative editor replaced her in 1904. In 1906, still in mourning for her husband, Sarah Dudley Pettey fell ill and died within a few weeks, aged only thirty-seven. Her pioneering work to secure full citizenship rights for African American women was largely forgotten for nearly a century after her death. In the 1990s Pettey was rediscovered by historians who saw in her life and writings a fresh perspective on the intricacies and interconnectedness of race, gender, class, and politics in the late-nineteenth-century South.

FURTHER READING
Cecelski, David S., and Timothy B. Tyson, eds. *Democracy Betrayed: The Wilmington Race Riot of 1898 and Its Legacy* (1998).
Gilmore, Glenda Elizabeth. *Gender and Jim Crow: Women and the Politics of White Supremacy in North Carolina, 1896–1920* (1996).
Majors, Monroe A. *Noted Negro Women: Their Triumphs and Activities* (1893).

STEVEN J. NIVEN

Pettiford, Oscar (30 Sept. 1922–8 Sept. 1960), composer and musician, was born in Okmulgee, Oklahoma, the son of Harry "Doc" Pettiford, a veterinarian and amateur guitarist of African American and Cherokee descent, and Leontine Bell, a music teacher and pianist who was a full-blooded Choctaw. Pettiford's father gave up his career in the 1920s, and the family moved to Minneapolis to form what later became an outstanding regional band. All eleven children contributed, the older ones generally playing instruments and the younger singing. Ira, on the trumpet, eventually worked with EARL HINES and Benny Carter; Marjorie, on the clarinet, flute, and saxophone, went on to become a member of the Sweethearts of Rhythm; and Alonzo later performed with LIONEL HAMPTON and JAY McSHANN. Oscar began with the band at age three as a vocalist and drummer. He learned to play piano in 1933 and played trumpet and trombone as well; he also made occasional appearances with the band as a singer, dancer, and baton twirler until the age of fourteen.

In 1936 Oscar's father lent him a string bass that was in storage with the Pettifords at the time. Pettiford immediately began to play the instrument, and when the bass was reclaimed, his father purchased one. After an absence from the band for several months, Pettiford returned, as a bassist, to performing. He was able to finish high school, although his ambition to study medicine remained unfulfilled. He began to enjoy the band, which worked steadily in Minneapolis and toured the Midwest and South, performing primarily new material, and he was even auditioned by DUKE ELLINGTON. Brief mention of the band in the November 1938 issue of *Down Beat* acknowledged the band's popularity.

Pettiford and other family members would attend jam sessions in Minneapolis after finishing the evening's work. It was there that he first heard of JIMMY BLANTON, bassist with Ellington and the father of modern bass playing. Pettiford's style evolved much in the manner of Blanton's, featuring florid, facile, hornlike solo passages. Other bass players who influenced Pettiford are Milt Hinton (with CAB CALLOWAY), Billy Taylor (with Duke Ellington), Moses Allen (with JIMMIE LUNCEFORD), and Israel Crosby (with FLETCHER HENDERSON). The Minneapolis bassist Adolphus Alsbrook, who performed with both Ellington and COUNT BASIE, suggested that Pettiford consider moving to New York as a freelance musician.

In 1941 the family band, down to five pieces and unsuccessful in locating work, finally split up. Pettiford played with several local groups during that time, but by 1942 he'd abandoned the bass and worked for five months as a tailor in a war plant. When Milt Hinton, during a visit to Minneapolis with Calloway's band, discovered that Pettiford was no longer playing, he urged him to return.

In January 1943 Pettiford auditioned for Charlie Barnet, who was looking to replace the bassist Chubby Jackson. Pettiford was hired and soon after composed a "Concerto for Two Basses," which made Jackson and Pettiford a two-bass team until May 1943, when the group reorganized in New York. Pettiford still attended jam sessions while playing with Barnet and once even carried his bass two miles in subzero weather to join a jam session in a Chicago hotel with CHARLIE PARKER and DIZZY GILLESPIE.

In 1943 Pettiford worked Minton's Playhouse with THELONIOUS MONK for four months. Later that year he played with ROY ELDRIDGE for sixteen weeks at the Onyx. In December Pettiford recorded for the first time with Leonard Feather's All-Stars, which included the saxophonist COLEMAN HAWKINS and the pianist ART TATUM. Other early recordings were "The Man I Love" and "Crazy Rhythm" with Coleman Hawkins. Pettiford won top honors as bassist in the 1943 *Esquire* magazine Critics' Poll, the 1944 *Metronome* and *Esquire* polls, and the 1945 *Esquire* poll.

On 18 January 1944 Pettiford performed in a Metropolitan Opera House jam session. Listed in the band were BILLIE HOLIDAY, vocals; LOUIS ARMSTRONG, trumpet and vocals; Jack Teagarden, trombone and vocals; BARNEY BIGARD, clarinet; Coleman Hawkins, saxophone; Roy Eldridge, trumpet; Art Tatum, piano; Al Casey, guitar; Lionel Hampton, vibraphone and drums; SIDNEY CATLETT, drums; and Pettiford on double bass.

In the winter of 1943–1944 Pettiford formed a group, along with Gillespie, that was considered the first bop combo on Fifty-second Street and included DON BYAS on tenor saxophone, George Wallington on piano, and MAX ROACH on drums. This group played in a bop style inspired by Pettiford in which the horns (usually trumpet and tenor) play lines in unison rather than a single line accompanied by a horn playing whole notes. Pettiford composed several charts about this time, including "Max Is Making Wax / Something for You" for Max Roach, which Pettiford recorded in January 1945 with a big band called Oscar Pettiford and His 18 All-Stars, which included Gillespie, and "Bass Face," which became the standard "One Bass Hit," recorded in 1946 by Gillespie and the bassist Ray Brown. After only four months, however, Pettiford and Gillespie had artistic differences and Pettiford left the group in 1944.

For the rest of the year Pettiford continued to work along Fifty-second Street, leading groups at the Onyx, Spotlite, Yacht Club, and Three Deuces. During this time Pettiford met Harriet Noren, who later became his wife. They had a son.

In January 1945 Pettiford recorded "Interlude (A Night in Tunisia)" and "March of the Boyds" with the Boyd Raeburn band. Later that year he had a long stint at Billy Berg's in Hollywood, California, with Coleman Hawkins's band, which included HOWARD MCGHEE, Sir Charles Thompson on piano, DENZIL BEST on drums, Hawkins, and Pettiford; they recorded "Stuffy" and "Hollywood Stampede." In October 1945 Pettiford headed his own trio, working California and Nevada for five months.

Pettiford joined Duke Ellington on 10 November 1945, remaining with the band until 11 March 1948. Pettiford became disillusioned with Ellington's band; most of the players he wished to perform alongside had already quit, and the dance book proved too repetitive.

After he left Ellington, Pettiford joined ERROLL GARNER on piano and J. C. HEARD on drums in a trio and subsequently gigged around New York City with Lucky Thompson on saxophone, JOHN LEWIS on piano, BENNIE HARRIS on trumpet, and Denzil Best. Later, the pianist George Shearing, Pettiford, and KENNY CLARKE played the Clique. After turning the trio over to Shearing, Pettiford put together a short-lived all-star group that included MILES DAVIS and FATS NAVARRO on trumpet, Kai Winding on trombone, Lucky Thompson and DEXTER GORDON on tenor sax, MILT JACKSON on vibes, BUD POWELL on piano, and Kenny Clarke.

Pettiford joined Woody Herman's orchestra in February 1949, which at the time included Stan Getz, Serge Chaloff, and Zoot Sims on saxophone, Ernie Royal on trumpet, Terry Gibbs on vibes, and Red Rodney. Pettiford performed with them for five months before he broke his arm pitching softball on Herman's team. The next eighteen months of recovery allowed Pettiford to reorient his playing approach toward increased tone production and projection. He also began to play the cello, pizzicato style, similar to how he played bass.

After his recovery Pettiford toured with a group led by Louis Bellson and CHARLIE SHAVERS. Late in 1951 he led his own group on a USO tour through Korea and Japan and throughout the Pacific. After an altercation at Okinawa, Pettiford was ordered home on 7 January 1952.

From 1952 to 1958 Pettiford was active in New York City with his own small group and big band. Kenny Clarke, the pianist Dick Katz, the trumpeter Art Farmer, the alto saxophonist GIGI GRYCE, the reed player Jerome Richardson, and the pianist HORACE SILVER were just a few of the members of Oscar's bands. Among the works Pettiford wrote during that time were "Bohemia after Dark," "Swingin' till the Girls Come Home," "The Pendulum at Falcon's Lair," "Now See How You Are," and "Blues in the Closet (Collard Greens and Black-Eyed Peas)."

Pettiford left the United States for England in September 1958, never to return. He worked throughout France, Austria, and Germany before finally settling in Copenhagen in June 1959. In 1958 he was hospitalized in Vienna after an automobile accident; he had multiple injuries, including a skull fracture, a concussion, and severe face and mouth lacerations. Pettiford worked with Stan Getz at the Café Montmartre from the summer of 1959 to early 1960 and then led his own group of Scandinavian musicians. He made his last recording in July 1960.

On 4 September 1960 Pettiford entered Fiedfrederiksberg Hospital in Copenhagen after playing at an art exhibition, complaining of a sore throat similar to a strep infection. By 7 September Pettiford was completely paralyzed, and he died the next day. The fatal virus was apparently not polio, but its exact identity was never determined.

Pettiford was the foremost bassist of the late 1940s and 1950s. As a composer he was responsible for many standards of the bop repertoire; as a performer his innovations with the horn line led to one of bebop's significant style characteristics. In addition, his performing style helped change the role of the bass in the rhythm section. Pettiford's innovative melodic style on bass, similar to CHARLIE CHRISTIAN's approach to the electric guitar, presented long eighth-note passages that featured frequent turning around of meter, rhythmic patterns, and melodic figures, with a clarity and power not unlike Charlie Parker's on alto saxophone.

FURTHER READING

Gitler, Ira. "Oscar Pettiford and the Bassists," in *Jazz Masters of the 40's* (1966).

Lyons, Len, and Don Perlo. *Jazz Portraits: The Lives and Music of the Jazz Masters* (1989).

Southern, Eileen. *Biographical Dictionary of Afro-American and African Musicians* (1982).

This entry is taken from the *American National Biography* and is published here with the permission of the American Council of Learned Societies.

DAVID SPIES

Pettiford, William Reuben (20 Jan. 1847–21 Sept. 1914), pastor, banker, and race leader, was born in Granville County, North Carolina, the son of William Pettiford and Matilda (maiden name unknown), farmers. Pettiford, a free black, spent his early years laboring on the family farm. He received a rudimentary education at home and then attended Marion Normal School; he was employed from 1877 to 1880 as a teacher and financial agent at Selma Institute (later Selma University). In 1869 he married Mary Jane Farley, who died that same year. In 1873 he married Jennie Powell, who died in September 1874. In 1880 he married Della Boyd, with whom he had three children.

Pettiford's most remarkable accomplishments were achieved after he accepted in 1883 the pastorate at the Sixteenth Street Baptist Church in Birmingham, Alabama. Birmingham was a booming city of the "New South," where blacks migrated in search of employment, primarily in the steel mills and coal mines. Pettiford recognized the need for black institutions to assist the black community members' adjustment and to educate them in the value of thrift and self help. Pettiford translated his observations as a pastor into practical business. He responded to the economic and social needs of the black community when he and other prominent local blacks organized a bank with the assistance of the Negro Progressive Association. The Alabama Penny Savings and Loan Company (later the Alabama Penny Savings Bank) opened its doors in 1890 with Pettiford as president, becoming the fourth black-owned bank in the United States.

The bank's reputation was built on the character of its president and its commitment to the black community. Early on it gained credibility when it weathered the economic crisis of 1893, during which 110 banks across the country closed their doors and some of Birmingham's white-owned banks failed. Although many depositors withdrew their savings from the Penny Savings Bank, the directors maintained their commitment to the black community. The community's confidence was ultimately restored, and the bank thrived. During the institution's precarious first decade Pettiford preached the value of education and home ownership; he resigned his position at the church to devote his time entirely to the bank.

To assist blacks in their pursuit of owning their own homes Pettiford and the bank's directors, acting on the bank's behalf, purchased real estate in large quantities. They then subdivided this property and sold it in small parcels both to facilitate home ownership and to produce additional profit. The Alabama Penny Savings Bank financed numerous homes, scattered throughout Birmingham and its environs, that blacks purchased in the late nineteenth and early twentieth centuries. In 1905 at a National Negro Business League meeting Pettiford boasted, "One of the main features of our work has been and is, to teach the art of saving money and of purchasing homes, so that out of the 8,000 depositors who have been with us more than a thousand have purchased their homes."

The bank's success prompted Pettiford to pursue a more far-reaching banking system, but his attempt to operate branches beyond those in Anniston, Montgomery, and Selma were squelched when the Alabama state legislature passed a law prohibiting additional branches of any banks. Nevertheless, Pettiford's influence reached beyond the state. In 1906 he played a pivotal role as president and cofounder of the National Negro Bankers' Association, an organization designed to encourage the establishment of other black-owned banks. The *Reformer* reported in 1908 that Pettiford had "started the ball to rolling" in Atlanta, Georgia, for the organization of the first African American bank in that state. And by 1914 there were approximately "63 black-owned banks in sound, healthy condition." Undoubtedly the speeches that Pettiford delivered at the Business League meetings and also at the 1903 Hampton Conference sessions served to inspire other entrepreneurially spirited blacks.

Pettiford's philosophy of self-help, racial pride, and economic development mirrored that of BOOKER T. WASHINGTON. They held mutual respect and shared a commitment to the concept of establishing an economic foundation on which to uplift the entire race. Furthermore, Pettiford stressed the need to patronize black-owned businesses. He stated that "in this way the money of our people is kept constantly in circulation in our immediate community." In Birmingham during this time numerous black-owned businesses were cropping up in what became the black business district (BBD). The Alabama Penny Savings Bank building—constructed in 1913—lay on the edge of the thriving BBD. The black architect Wallace Rayfield designed the edifice, and T. C. Windham, a black contractor, built it. The building stood as a testament to black achievement and symbolized black pride.

Pettiford was a moving force in the business community; he supported the creation of new businesses and participated in the founding of others. The Reverend T. W. Walker, another ambitious entrepreneur, established numerous diverse businesses in Birmingham. He and Pettiford, along with several other black businessmen, joined forces to establish the Birmingham Grate Coal Mining Company. Pettiford also founded the Alabama Orphans and Old Folks Home, was president of the Negro American Publishing Company, and was a director in the National Economic League. He was also instrumental in gaining approval for Industrial High School (later Parker High School), the first black high school in Birmingham.

Although Pettiford devoted much attention to economic advancement, he never lost sight of his religious role. He considered his business affairs an extension of his "missionary work." Through his roles as entrepreneur and pastor, Pettiford's philosophy reached many blacks, who embraced his ideals and worked toward economic and social betterment. By the time of Pettiford's death in Birmingham the bank he founded had become the country's largest and most solid black-owned banking institution, with one hundred thousand dollars in capitalization and more than five hundred thousand dollars a year in business. Despite the directors' efforts to maintain the bank's financial position, without the leadership of William Pettiford and his valuable connections with affluent whites the Alabama Penny Savings Bank could not survive. During what was a period of high unemployment, borrowers were unable to meet their financial obligations and depositors were withdrawing their funds. The bank was closed on 23 December 1915, just fifteen months after Pettiford's death.

FURTHER READING

Numerous letters of correspondence between Washington and Pettiford appear in the Booker T. Washington Papers held at the Library of Congress.

Boothe, Charles O. *The Cyclopedia of the Colored Baptists of Alabama* (1895).

Ingham, John N., and Lynne B. Feldman. *African-American Business Leaders: A Biographical Dictionary* (1994).

Simmons, William J. *Men of Mark* (1887).
This entry is taken from the *American National Biography* and is published here with the permission of the American Council of Learned Societies.

LYNNE B. FELDMAN

Peyton, Dave (c. 1885–May 1955), bandleader, pianist, and columnist, was born in Louisiana. Details of his birth and family life are unknown. Peyton was a member of the clarinetist Wilbur Sweatman's trio in Chicago from about 1908 to 1912, when he became the music director at the Grand Theater. In 1914 he founded his own symphony orchestra of about fifty instrumentalists; they gave monthly concerts. On 29 October 1924 he opened the Plantation Cafe as the leader of the Symphonic Syncopators. They played for dancing and for musical revues, the latter including the show *Plantation Follie*. Peyton wrote the music for some of these shows. The reed player Darnell Howard played with Peyton's fifteen-piece Symphonic Syncopators, and in November the cornetist KING OLIVER joined. Oliver's purpose may have been to ingratiate himself with the management and take over Peyton's job. If so, he succeeded; this episode might account for some of the bitterness that Peyton later felt toward New Orleans jazz musicians.

When Oliver formed his Dixie Syncopators for a two-year engagement at the Plantation beginning in late February 1925, Peyton moved to the Persian Palace. He bought partial ownership of the Peerless Theater in April 1926 and installed a fourteen-piece orchestra there, but the venture soon failed. Beginning in November he led a twelve-piece group at the Café De Paris (formerly Lincoln Gardens). The singer ETHEL WATERS was the star of a show there during the first three months of 1927. Early in June 1927 Peyton concurrently led a ten-piece band at the Plantation, which had reopened after a recent bombing and problems with licensing. By month's end the Plantation was closed again, and the Café de Paris was bombed; both orchestras lost their jobs. Such disruptions were a normal element of Chicago nightlife during the Prohibition era as gangsters competed for turf. In September Peyton led an orchestra for the Plantation revue at the Grand Theater. He worked at the Club Baghdad from late 1927 to January 1928, and then at the Pershing Palace (presumably a different venue from the Persian Palace). Throughout the mid-1920s Peyton also worked as a band contractor, operating additional bands under his own name and supplying musicians for other engagements. "It looked like he wanted to corral the whole damn business," said the clarinetist BARNEY BIGARD (Bigard, 28).

From 10 October 1925 to 24 August 1929 Peyton was an influential weekly musical columnist for the *Chicago Defender*. In these columns, which circulated nationally, Peyton preached his belief in the superiority of European classical music, and he advocated a behavior associated with performers and listeners within that concert tradition. This sort of advocacy extended beyond music, and before the Depression struck he urged fellow musicians to take up a financially cautious and responsible lifestyle—a prescient but largely unheeded piece of advice. Most important, in accounts and categorizations of the music scene Peyton supplied information on local ensembles and the activities of local musicians that is now invaluable.

When the Regal Theater opened for movies in February 1928, Peyton established an orchestra there, raiding the violinist Erskine Tate's Vendome Theater orchestra for talented musicians. Peyton's most distinguished sidemen in the late 1920s were the trombonist KID ORY and the drummer BABY DODDS. In 1930 the orchestra included the trombonist Preston Jackson, the reed player Jerome Don Pasquall, and Howard. In addition to playing music for the silent films, they played for stage shows that presented top-quality artists and the theater's own chorus girls, the Regalettes. The elaborate shows, which included many different kinds of music, were sometimes conducted by Fess Williams rather than Peyton. The writer Dempsey Travis gives the flavor of one of Peyton's performances early in April 1930:

He turned to face the twenty-two men in the symphony orchestra who sat in the pit with their eyes fixed attentively upon him. Peyton raised the baton in his right hand and slowly lowered it as the drummer gave a long roll on the timpani, and the trumpeters lifted their instruments to begin the *William Tell* Overture. On the stage was a magnificent replica of a lush green meadow. While the overture was playing, Clarence Tidale, a singing shepherd, led fifty live sheep onto the stage where Tidale was joined by Mame Moon, a graceful and charming contralto. The show included a dramatic thunderstorm, complete with lightning, and the overture ended with the stage lights illuminating a brilliant rainbow, as the singers completed their duet and led the sheep offstage. Peyton's orchestra and Moon received a standing ovation (Travis, 148, 150).

Peyton's group also worked as a dance band, and in May 1930 he engaged in a battle of the bands with Tate at Chicago's Savoy Ballroom. Peyton was fired from the Regal in January 1931, but he continued leading groups, of which the trumpeters Guy Kelly and Zilner T. Randolph were members in 1934. Soon thereafter he switched to a career as a soloist. In September 1935 he made his one and only recording, "Baby o' Mine," as pianist in Richard M. Jones's orchestra. He was still working as a soloist in the late 1940s when he held an engagement at the Spot O' Fun. Peyton ran a dry cleaning business until his death in Chicago.

From 1924 to 1931 Peyton was one of the most prominent bandleaders in Chicago. Orchestras such as his satisfied the popular tastes of the day, and he performed steadily in the city's major theaters while the great recorded jazz bands held lesser jobs or found little or no work outside of the studio—as was the case most notably with LOUIS ARMSTRONG's Hot Five and Hot Seven and JELLY ROLL MORTON's Red Hot Peppers. But Peyton's interpretation of the European repertory, his stage shows, and his polite brand of dance music yielded nothing of lasting consequence. Within a few years his approach had been overwhelmed by the vitality of jazz and pop as they were being played by countless numbers of now better-known musicians. Instead, his significance lies in his writings for the *Chicago Defender*. He is considered by some as having been the leading publicist for the city's African American jazz establishment, aiming to gain acceptance by the white middle class.

FURTHER READING

Bigard, Barney. *With Louis and the Duke: The Autobiography of a Jazz Clarinetist*, ed. Barry Martyn (1985).

Kenney, William Howland. *Chicago Jazz: A Cultural History, 1904–1930* (1994).

Travis, Dempsey J. *An Autobiography of Black Jazz* (1983).

This entry is taken from the *American National Biography* and is published here with the permission of the American Council of Learned Societies.

BARRY KERNFELD

Peyton, Thomas Roy (1897–3 Aug. 1968), proctologist and author, was born in Brooklyn, New York, the grandson of a former slave from North Carolina, and the son of Thomas Henry Peyton, one of the first black policemen in New York City, and Louisa Jones, of African American and Mohawk Indian ancestry. Peyton attended a manual training high school in Brooklyn and continued his studies at the Long Island College of Medicine from where he graduated as the only black student of his class in 1921. In 1923 he married Gladys (maiden name unknown) and the couple had three children, Roy (b. 1925), Carter (b. 1928), and Joyce (b. 1935). Peyton lived during a time when black doctors experienced severe professional discrimination in training and practice. Yet, like Peyton, their commitment to medicine and civil rights bound them together in a ceaseless effort to advance scientific knowledge, provide better educational opportunities for the next generation of black doctors, and end discriminatory healthcare practices.

Though Peyton encountered little prejudice as a student—even winning the 1921 Ford Prize at Long Island College of Medicine for the best dissection in anatomy—after graduation in 1921 everything changed. Barred from membership in most medical societies, from attendance to professional meetings, and from hospital facilities and medical libraries, Peyton was forced to keep up with the latest scientific developments by maintaining his own subscriptions to journals and reading independently. He started his medical practice in the black neighborhood of Jamaica, a Long Island suburb. Aside from blacks, many of his patients were European immigrants who consulted him only for minor illnesses and openly worried about his medical competence. Despite their concerns, he became the first black doctor appointed to Jamaica Hospital and Mary Immaculate Hospital in 1925, both white institutions, and his general practice gradually became more prosperous. Even so, Peyton grew increasingly dissatisfied.

In the 1920s, when physicians increasingly had access to vaccines and scientific breakthroughs in diagnostic and therapeutic capabilities, black doctors continued to experience severe professional limitations. Moved by the suffering of his patients with terminal rectal cancer, Peyton eventually decided to specialize in proctology. Many of his patients had experienced rectal bleeding for years, but other physicians refused to examine them and thereby missed any chance of early detection and cure. Few whites chose proctology and Peyton became the first black doctor trained in that area. In 1929 Peyton secured an appointment at Harlem Hospital, where his daily contact with mostly black patients made him realize the need for further training. He applied at a large downtown hospital for training but his application was denied because it would not allow black doctors to attend bedside instruction. In 1933, unable to receive training as a proctologist in the United States, Peyton left for Canada to study six months at the Royal Victoria Hospital in Montreal, and then moved to Europe, where he obtained postgraduate medical training in France and England, under internationally acclaimed physicians. Peyton wrote that this training—and his interactions with professors, students, and surgeons—was free of racial prejudice. Throughout his stay abroad he supported both his education and family by playing piano in bars, bands, and concert halls throughout Europe, thereby encountering many expatriate African American musicians and artists who enjoyed the success they could not have had in America. On at least one occasion he joined JOSEPHINE BAKER for a dinner party at her home in Paris.

In 1936, after mastering advanced surgical procedures, he returned to the United States and continued his appointment at Harlem Hospital. But racism again manifested itself. Asked to train a young white doctor as proctologist, Peyton obliged and shared his knowledge and experience. However, at the next clinical promotion, Peyton was passed over while his young protégé advanced to a far superior position. Discouraged, he decided to establish a private practice for those black patients who could afford a specialist. He endured great financial sacrifices and eventually succeeded in building a steady patient base. However, in 1937, his precarious financial situation and continued discrimination at Harlem Hospital sent him to Europe a second time. He studied with proctologists in England and Scandinavia, but was forced to depart when war in Europe became imminent.

Upon his return, Peyton contacted all black hospitals in the United States, eager to share his research in proctology. None had any specialized clinic for treating such cases. The medical director of Mercy Hospital in Philadelphia expressed interest and Peyton consequently developed a clinic there. He remained in Philadelphia, establishing a private practice and gaining surgical experience at Mercy and Douglass Hospital. In 1942 he attained a United States patent for an ano-rectal dilator and became a member of the chartered Institute of American Inventors. These opportunities notwithstanding, Peyton continued to feel intellectually isolated. If a specialist wanted to remain informed about the advances in his area, he needed a chance to exchange ideas with other competent representatives of the profession. But all his attempts to be placed on the staff at white hospitals with proctologists failed. Some white medical professionals befriended and advised him. Dr. Collier Martin, dean of proctology at Pennsylvania Graduate School of Medicine, for instance, arranged for Peyton to observe operative clinics, but after several visits the invitation was recalled. Yet, regardless of how many times he had been offended and rejected, he continued to fight on. He attempted to attend the National Conference of Proctologists in Norfolk, Virginia, but to no avail. In later years, he attended the National Meeting of Proctologists in Atlantic City and Chicago. In order to obtain full membership in the American Proctologic Society, a physician had to visit three meetings and receive a recommendation from another member. He fulfilled both requirements and also published several articles in both white and black medical journals of national circulation, contributing greatly to the understanding of *lymphogranuloma venereum*, a venereal disease that required a colostomy if misdiagnosed and left untreated. Nevertheless his membership was not acknowledged. He learned that the unwritten but most important requirement was to be white.

At the invitation of Dr. CHARLES DREW, he taught proctology at Howard University in Washington, D.C., from 1941 until 1944, but resigned his position, unwilling to accept the segregated conditions in the South. He moved to Los Angeles, California, and tried to establish a practice there. Forced to buy a house, because no landlord was willing to rent space to a black doctor in that particular section of Los Angeles, he faced eviction after the builder found out that he was black. He began to fight racism on more than a personal level, joining the Catholic Inter-Racial Council of Los Angeles, crusading for improved rights for blacks, Mexicans, Japanese-Americans, and Filipino-Americans, and giving talks at various colleges in Los Angeles to specifically address the difficulties of aspiring black doctors.

His autobiography, *Quest for Dignity* (1950), which won a Freedom Foundation Gold Medal Award, charts his medical career, his travels to Europe for professional opportunities, and his struggle against racism. After retiring in 1964 he continued to dedicate his time to fight discrimination, publishing articles and editorials on civil rights issues such as school desegregation, black leadership, and the persistence of the black mammy image. In the year before his death at age seventy, he called upon all Americans to support a "Boycott on Racism" (Peyton, "Racism Boycott," *Los Angeles Times*, 25 Dec. 1967, B4).

FURTHER READING
Many of the medical papers by Dr. Peyton can be found in the *Medical Record*, the *Journal of the National Medical Association*, the *American Journal of Syphilis, Gonorrhea and Venereal Diseases*, and the *Journal of the American Medical Association*.

Peyton, Thomas R. *Quest for Dignity: An Autobiography of a Negro Doctor* (1950).

Morais, Herbert M. *History of the Negro in Medicine* (1967).

Obituaries: *New York Times*, 8 Aug. 1967; *Los Angeles Times*, 7 Aug. 1967.

ANDREA PATTERSON

Phillips, Carl (23 July 1959–), poet and professor, was born Carl Phillips Jr. in Everett, Washington, the oldest child of Helen Elizabeth Savage, a white British painter and homemaker, and Carl Phillips Sr., an African American U.S. Air Force master sergeant. His parents met in 1955 while his father was stationed at South Ruislip Air Station outside London; they married in England in 1957, a time when interracial marriages were still illegal in many American states. Phillips's family, including sisters Tracy and Susan, moved continually to different air force bases, something that contributed to the young man's retreat into a private world of writing.

Phillips attended school in Oregon, Michigan, Massachusetts, and Germany, but experienced isolation due to the constant uprooting and the intimidation from the racism prevalent on air force bases. The family returned from Germany to Massachusetts, where Phillips attended Falmouth High School from 1973 until 1977 and excelled in languages, eventually gaining admission to Harvard University. After one semester there, however, he gave up his dream of becoming a veterinarian and received his B.A. in Latin and Greek in 1981, then his master's degree in Latin and classical humanities from the University of Massachusetts Amherst. In 1983, the same year he received his graduate degree, he married Joanna Luczak; they remained married for ten years. The couple had no children. Phillips taught Latin at area high schools for three years, until returning to Falmouth, his alma mater, where he taught Latin for four years in the same room where he had learned the language.

A decision to teach at the college level brought Phillips back to Harvard to study classical philology. He began in the Ph.D. program in 1991, but soon left to pursue an M.A. in Creative Writing, which he received from Boston University in 1993. The catalyst for the dramatic life changes, both personally and professionally, occurred when he met his partner Douglas Macomber, a landscape photographer, which allowed Phillips to embrace his sexuality. His first volume of poetry, *In the Blood* (1992), had just been published and had won the Samuel French Morse Poetry Prize, heralding the emergence of the serious poet who would explore identity, sexuality, morality, and life's contradictions. The poet laureate Robert Pinsky offered him a place in the creative writing program at Boston University after Phillips, at Macomber's urging, appeared at Pinsky's door with a manuscript in hand. Pinsky would later be instrumental in helping Phillips to secure an academic home, informing him of the poet-in-residence position at Washington University in St. Louis, Missouri, which Phillips took up in 1993, the year of his divorce. Phillips returned to teach at Harvard from 1995 to 1996, and while there his second book of poems, *Cortège*, came out and was a finalist for the National Book Critics Circle Award. He was granted tenure at Washington University and was later promoted to full professor in 2000. Meanwhile his poetry won a Pushcart Prize in 1994, appeared in the *Nation* and the *Yale Review*, and was recognized in *The Best American Poetry* (1994, 1995, 1996, 2000, 2001, 2002, 2004) and *The Best of the Best of American Poetry* 1988–1997. In 1997 he received the $12,500 Witter Bynner Foundation Fellowship from the Library of Congress, followed by an Academy of American Poets prize, an Award in Literature from the American Academy of Arts and Letters, and a Guggenheim Foundation Fellowship.

Phillips resisted allowing his multifaceted identities to be reductively characterized by critics and believed that good poems transcend historical time and supersede the poet's identity and experience. In poems such as "In the Blood Winnowing" from *In the Blood*, he addressed what it is like physically to inhabit a human body, rather than allowing his work to be limited by people's expectations of the stereotypical African American or gay male experience:

there was this morning now,
in the shower, when you know
you are dying,
you are dying and your body—
a lozenge or a prayer, whatever goes

slim and unimportant when the tongue
has grown overly zealous—
contracts under the steam (71).

Devotion, trust, risk, and both reaching for
and retreating from desire—these are some of the
themes he explored in his work. The erotic charge
in his poems illustrates the burden of temptation
that the five senses present to humans. In *From
the Devotions* (1998), which was a finalist for the
National Book Award, he wrote: "*Because*, you
thought, *what else can it be, so much wanting, except
wrong?*" ("The Gods" 46), displaying the physical
and emotional temptations with which human
beings struggle.

In *Pastoral*, winner of the Lambda Literary
Award in 2000, his poems show a fascination with
the problems created by human reason, a motif that
runs thematically throughout his work:

To be animal means
never to court, once
recognized, what's dangerous.
To be human: the recognition,
the coming closer, to think
surely a way will
open up, by which we
shall outswerve what could
undo us ("Animal," 58–59).

As he pondered such philosophical issues
Phillips also directed the creative writing program
at Washington University and continued to receive
accolades for his poetry. By the time *The Tether*
won the esteemed Kingsley Tufts Award and the
Society of Midland Authors Award in 2002, he had
won another Pushcart Prize.

Spiritual longing is addressed in his 2002 book
Rock Harbor: "If the world is godless, then / an
absence I am / always with, and / it with me. Or /
else the / world is stitched with gods / and unavoid-
ably I am / with them, / they with me" ("The
Threshing," 39).

Not surprisingly, the Sophocles play *Philoctetes*
that he translated in 2003 also grappled with many
of the conundrums that concerned him—the
human capacity to cope with isolation, endure
physical suffering, trust others, and bear betrayal.
In *Coin of the Realm: Essays on the Life and Art
of Poetry* (2004), which was runner-up for the
Society of Midland Authors Award, Phillips discussed, among other topics, his favorite poet, the
seventeenth-century British metaphysical poet
George Herbert. Phillips states, "What is required

to be an authentically original artist is an inability
to think conventionally" (233), something Phillips
managed to realize in his literary career. In the same
year, he published *The Rest of Love*, which won the
Theodore Roethke Memorial Poetry Award and the
Thom Gunn Award for Gay Men's Poetry and was a
finalist for the 2004 National Book Award. He recognized: "I am no less grateful for / the berries than
for the thorns that are / meant, I think, to help."
("All It Takes," 21). He was elected to the American
Academy of Arts and Sciences in the same year.
Riding Westward was published in 2006; the poem
"Sea Glass" declares "I've / loved this life. If it's one
thing to have missed / the constellations for/ the
stars themselves, / it's another, entirely, / to have
never looked up" (7). *Quiver of Arrows: Selected
Poems 1986–2006*, published in 2007, showcases
twenty years of stellar poetry.

FURTHER READING
Hennessy, Christopher. *Outside the Lines: Talking with
    Contemporary Gay Poets* (2005).

ZISCA ISABEL BURTON

Phillips, Channing E. (23 Mar. 1928–11 Nov.
1987), minister and civil rights activist, was born
Channing Emery Phillips in Brooklyn, New York,
the son of Porter Phillips, a Baptist minister, and
Dorothy Fletcher. He attended public schools in
Brooklyn and Pittsburgh, Pennsylvania, where the
family moved in 1939 and where his father pastored a church. He earned a scholarship in painting
and sculpture to Carnegie Technical School (now
Carnegie Mellon University) but elected instead
to serve in the U.S. Army Air Force from 1945 to
1947, attaining the rank of sergeant. In 1950 he
completed his bachelor's degree in Sociology at the
predominantly black Virginia Union University in
Richmond, where he played center on the basketball team. He received his first divinity degree at the
Colgate-Rochester School of Divinity in Rochester,
New York, in 1953. After graduate training from
1953 to 1956 at Drew University in Madison, New
Jersey, from which he received the LDH and the
DD, he lectured in New Testament studies in and
around Washington, D.C., at American University,
the Virginia Episcopal Seminary, and Howard
University. In 1956 he married Jane Nabors; they
had five children. By 1958 he was assistant minister at Grace Congregational Church in Harlem
then he was minister at Haynes Congregational
Church in Jamaica, New York, beginning in 1959.
In 1961 he returned to Washington, D.C., as senior

minister of Lincoln Temple Church of Christ, and later that year he became senior minister at the United Church of Christ in Washington, where he remained until 1970.

An early advocate of home rule for the District of Columbia, Phillips also marched with MARTIN LUTHER KING JR. in Selma, Alabama, in 1965 in support of voting rights for blacks. A vocal critic of the United States' effort in Vietnam, he was chosen by Senator Robert Kennedy of New York to run his 1968 campaign in the city for the Democratic Party nomination for president. Following Kennedy's assassination, Phillips led a mostly black delegation to the Democratic National Convention in Chicago. A "black caucus" meeting that Phillips attended agreed that, in order to demonstrate the importance of the black vote to the party and to afford black delegates more leverage at the convention, supporting Phillips's nomination as a favorite-son candidate from Washington for U.S. president would be a bold and potentially rewarding political move. Phillips's name was placed in nomination by codelegate Phillips Stern, a writer, then seconded by Gary, Indiana, mayor Richard Hatcher and Michigan congressman JOHN CONYERS. Thus, Phillips became the first African American ever nominated for president at a major political party convention, and he garnered 67.5 votes from eighteen states on the first ballot. His seventeen votes from California delegates were three votes greater than those received by Vice President Hubert H. Humphrey, the ultimate victor at the convention. Between 1968 and 1972 Phillips remained active in the party as a member of the executive committee and of the rules commission. In 1971 he came in third, losing to Walter Fauntroy, in an election to become Washington's first nonvoting member of the U.S. House of Representatives.

Returning to Washington after the 1968 convention, Phillips, who the year before had helped launch the city's first Head Start program, headed the non-profit Housing Development Corporation, directing its acquisition, rehabilitation, management, and property sales until 1974, at which time he resigned abruptly in protest of the city's failure to subsidize low-income housing. He served a brief stint as vice president for university relations at Virginia Union University, where he was fired in a dispute with the school's administration in 1975. By 1978 Phillips was back in Washington working as a congressional liaison for the National Endowment for the Humanities. He left this post in 1982 to relocate to

New York City with his family. He was employed as an assistant minister for planning and coordination at the interdenominational Riverside Church of New York. Still a feisty, outspoken man, he delivered a controversial sermon on 9 May 1985 condemning homosexuality that brought him into conflict with the church's senior minister, the Reverend William Sloane Coffin Jr., a cleric long noted for his antiwar activism and liberal social views.

By 1987 Phillips's supporters in the congregation were accusing Coffin of ageism and racism in attempting to force Phillips, who was suffering from lung cancer, to resign. Phillips succumbed to the disease at Columbia-Presbyterian Hospital in New York City. Considered by his detractors to be obstinate and aloof and by his allies to be sharp-witted, articulate, and persuasive, Phillips was a complex, determined man of conviction but also one who had limited ambition and who too often lacked the inclination to be conciliatory. He refused to subordinate his political activities to his religious calling, and conversely, as when he declared homosexuality a sin, he was not apt to do what was convenient or politically expedient when he felt moral principles based on religious teachings were at stake. Though Phillips's brief moment in the spotlight at the 1968 Democratic National Convention did not translate into a more prominent national leadership role, he nevertheless remained an influential figure in local politics until the early 1970s. Toward the end of his career he expressed cynicism about the political process and downplayed attempts to effect meaningful reform through it. "I thought I could make some social changes," he told the *Washington Post* in 1982, "but in fact, politics is designed to maintain the status quo, not change it."

FURTHER READING

Asher, Robert L. "Rev. Phillips Is Nominated as Champion of 'Voiceless,'" *Washington Post*, 29 Aug. 1968.

Schlein, Alan M. "Whatever Happened to Channing Phillips?" *Washington Post*, 4 Feb. 1982.

Obituaries: *Washington Post*, 12 Nov. 1987; *Los Angeles Times* and *New York Times*, 13 Nov. 1987.

This entry is taken from the *American National Biography* and is published here with the permission of the American Council of Learned Societies.

ROBERT FIKES

Phillips, Esther (23 Dec. 1935–7 Aug. 1984), singer, was born Esther Mae Jones in Galveston, Texas. Her parents, Lucille Green and Arthur

Washington, had divorced, and she migrated between her father in Galveston and her mother in Los Angeles, but moved full time to that city in 1949. Esther Phillips had no formal musical training and her only musical experience prior to entering a talent contest at the Largo Theatre in Watts, California, in 1949 was singing in church as a child.

When Phillips was only thirteen years old, an older sister induced her to sing DINAH WASHINGTON's "Baby Get Lost" (Washington remained her idol and a chief influence throughout her career). As though magically, the bandleader, writer, producer, and performer Johnny Otis was in the audience. He took her on as a protégée. Otis worked for the Savoy label, and Phillips tagged along to a session for the singing group the Robins, whom he produced. At the end of the job, she begged Otis to let her take a turn, and, in less than twenty minutes, cut an impromptu track with Bobby Nunn of the Robins. The DJ "Broadway Bill" Cook heard the tape, and began to play it on his show. He initiated a contest to name the track, and "Double Crossing Blues" won. The release hit number 1 on the *Billboard* R&B charts, and initiated Phillips's career. The hits "Cupid Boogie" and "Mistreatin' Blues" followed, and she joined Otis's California Rhythm and Blues Caravan under the name Little Esther, without a surname.

Life on the road proved traumatic for the young girl. Not only were her school studies truncated, but also she fell prey to some of the worst impulses of adults, drinking and drug taking, including heroin. Her relationship with Savoy and Otis became fractious, and she quit the label over a dispute about royalties. She signed with Federal, a subsidiary of the Cincinnati-based King label, but remained only a year or so before an equally short arrangement with Decca. The label-hopping continued, as she moved back to Savoy, then to the independent concern Warwick. The effect of her drug abuse further complicated her private life, and she relocated to Houston, where she lived with her father in an attempt to recoup her composure.

Another fortuitous occurrence resurrected Phillips's career. The then-unknown Kenny Rogers heard her perform in 1962 at Rick's Sidewalk Café. He recommended Phillips to his brother, Lelan, who signed her and started Lenox Records. No longer a child, she changed her professional name to Esther Phillips, taking the surname from the façade of a Phillips 66 gas station. Now twenty-seven, she took on a new genre and recorded fourteen country and

western songs in Nashville. This was just shortly after RAY CHARLES released his influential *Modern Sounds in Country and Western Music* album and the single, "I Can't Stop Loving You." Phillips most memorably tore into a version of "Release Me," already a hit for Ray Price and Kitty Wells. The record hit number 1 on the R&B charts and rose to the Top Ten of the Pop charts, too. Phillips had achieved artistic resurrection.

The Lenox label was shortly thereafter bought by Atlantic Records, along with Phillips's contract. The company wished to widen her repertoire and therefore cut an album of standards, including "People" and "Making Whoopee." The last track in the session was John Lennon and Paul McCartney's "And I Love Her." Couched in her trademark emotional style and re-titled "And I Love Him," it was a Top Ten R&B hit and ascended the Pop charts, too. However, success proved short-lived and her association with Atlantic soured. The label dropped her in 1968, due to poor sales and a professional reputation clouded by her drug use.

Phillips tackled the addiction by joining the therapeutic community Synanon and left in 1969, a changed woman. She resettled in Los Angeles and began a professional association with the bandleader and saxophonist KING CURTIS. This led to her resignation from Atlantic and a spectacular live recording, *Burnin'*, cut at Freddie Jett's Pied Piper Club. The album resulted in television exposure and a growing public reputation. Eager once again to try a new format, Atlantic had Phillips record in Miami with the session musicians known as the Dixie Flyers. The experiment proved unsuccessful and produced yet another break with the label.

Subsequently, like a kind of commercial phoenix, Phillips rose again, and had some of the greatest commercial and critical successes of her career with the Kudu label, started in 1971 by the jazz producer Creed Taylor. Her first album, *From a Whisper to a Scream*, remains one of her best, and her rendition of GIL SCOTT-HERON's "Home Is Where the Hatred Is" possesses a chilling degree of conviction. Four more albums for Kudu followed, while her 1975 cover of Dinah Washington's "What A Difference A Day Makes," sung to a disco beat, came to be one of Phillips's most successful releases, reaching the top of the R&B and Pop charts.

Once again, however, Phillips's career took a tailspin, and for the remainder of her life, prominence proved elusive, though her skills continued to be top drawer. She signed with Mercury in 1977, but left in 1981 after four albums. She worked for an independent label, Winning, and cut some jazz sides for Muse, which appeared posthumously. Her sense of-humor and high spirits remained, however, as attested by a duet with the underrated performer Swamp Dog, "Our Love Ain't Worth Two Dead Flies."

Little is known of Phillips's personal life. Married more than once, she had no children. Esther Phillips died of liver and kidney failure in 1984. Her career may have been brief, but her skills can well be attested by the fact that in 1972 ARETHA FRANKLIN, who had won a Grammy for *Young, Gifted & Black*, gave the award to Phillips, feeling that Phillips's recording *From a Whisper to a Scream* to be the more deserving.

FURTHER READING

Nathan, David. *The Soulful Divas* (1999).

Oliver, Paul, ed. *The Blackwell Guide to Recorded Blues* (1991).

Shaw, Arnold. *Honkers and Shouters: The Golden Years of Rhythm & Blues* (1979).

Wexler, Jerry, and David Ritz. *Rhythm and the Blues: A Life in American Music* (1993).

DAVID SANJEK

Phinazee, Alethia Annette Lewis Hoage (25 July 1920–17 Sept. 1983), library educator and administrator, author and developer of special collections, was born Alethia Annette Lewis in Orangeburg, South Carolina, on the campus of South Carolina State College, the first of two children of William Charles Lewis II and Alethia Minnie Lightner Lewis. Her parents were both educators and church and civic leaders. W. C. "Dad" Lewis was a professor and coach at South Carolina State College. Alethia Lightner Lewis taught in a one-room rural schoolhouse for all the African American children in the county for many years before accepting a position teaching first grade in town during the early 1950s. Her brother, William Charles "Pap" Lewis III, coach and educator, was the only African American to retain his head coaching position at a high school in the state of South Carolina after desegregation.

Annette Lewis completed her primary and secondary education in Orangeburg at age sixteen and earned a B.A. in Modern Foreign Languages with a minor in music from Fisk University in 1939. The tutelage, example, and mentorship of John Cottin and John W. Work, and exposure to James Weldon and Rosamond Johnson, Charles S. Johnson, Aaron Douglas and Arna Bontemps during her years at Fisk left an indelible brand of excellence and commitment to service and uplift of the race upon her.

After waiting for her fiancé's tour of duty in World War II to end, Annette Lewis married George Lafayette Hoage on 22 April 1944, only to be widowed on 22 August 1945, when he was killed in a traffic accident in downtown Los Angeles two weeks before her only child, Ramona Hoage Edelin, was born on 4 September 1945. Her marriage to Joseph Phinazee on 14 July 1962 lasted the rest of her life. Joseph Phinazee, the foster child of John Wesley Dobbs, was a veteran of the Korean conflict, a printer, and a bookkeeper for the Masonic order until his retirement in 1970.

Phinazee completed her bachelor and master of library science degrees from the University of Illinois in 1941 and 1948, and she became the first woman and the first African American to earn the doctorate in library science from Columbia University in 1961. Her dissertation, "The Library of Congress Classification in the United States," was considered a seminal and authoritative work in the field.

Phinazee was a teacher and librarian at the Caswell County Training School in North Carolina from 1939 to 1940, and a cataloger in the Talladega (Alabama) College library from 1941 to 1942. She was journalism librarian at Lincoln University in Jefferson City, Missouri, from 1942 until 1944. At Atlanta University, she was the teacher of cataloging and classification from 1946 to 1957, and she was head of special services from 1962 to 1967. This position included the management of the Trevor Arnett Library's Negro Collection, an internationally recognized resource for the study of African American life. Phinazee accepted a position as cataloger at Southern Illinois University in Carbondale from 1957 to 1962, becoming the first African American on that faculty. These were the only years during which her service was not at an African American institution in her forty-four-year career. In 1969 she worked as assistant director of the Cooperative College Library Center of the United Board for College Development, whose charge was to establish or upgrade libraries throughout historically black colleges and universities. In these roles she was teacher, counselor, and inspiration to generations of African American librarians.

In 1970, Phinazee accepted the call from President Albert Whiting to come to North Carolina Central University in Durham as dean of its School of Library Science, which had been unaccredited since its founding in 1939. Under Dean Phinazee's leadership, the American Library Association accredited the program in 1975 and again in 1982. One of the innovations she instituted, the Early Childhood Learning Center, was unique in the nation. It expanded the utility and competitiveness of library and information services and brought the work of the university to the community at an important time. Phinazee was a proactive and highly regarded member of the American Library Association for more than three decades. She called the association to task for its racist practices at the 1961 annual conference, resulting in the passing of strong resolutions permitting freedom of access to libraries and ending the ALA's imprimatur upon segregated professional library associations in the South. The most noteworthy of her contributions to the many committees and subdivisions on which she served are her leadership as chair of the Classification Committee of the ALA (1962–1967), her role as co-chair of the Institute on the Use of the Library of Congress Classification in 1966, considered a marker among meetings in the history of the subject, and her service as the first chairperson of the ALA's Standing Committee on Library Education.

Phinazee became the first African American chair of the North Carolina Library Association. As a member of the Citizen's Advisory Committee to the Governor's Conference on Library and Information Services, she became a delegate to the conference and ultimately headed the North Carolina delegation to the White House Conference on Library and Information Services. Governors Sanford and Hunt appointed her to the North Carolina Public Librarian Certification Commission, the State Library Committee, and the State Advisory Council on Libraries.

Phinazee was passionate about retaining bibliographic documents and the personal papers of important African Americans for posterity. She moderated the Institute on Materials By and About Negroes in 1965, and she edited its proceedings. From 1971 to 1974 she led the African American Materials Project, examining and creating a census of black library resources at historically black colleges and universities in Virginia, North and South Carolina, Georgia, Tennessee, and Alabama. The Southeastern Black Press Institute of the University of North Carolina at Chapel Hill, on whose board she served, was transferred to North Carolina Central University under her direction, in 1979.

A third-generation Presbyterian, Annette Phinazee was elected a ruling elder in her Atlanta and Durham churches, and she often served as a leader of the church school and as pianist. Her civic leadership included the second vice-presidency of the Atlanta-Fulton County League of Women Voters, a position as chair of the Citizen's Advisory Committee for the Durham City Council, and membership on the North Carolina Assembly on Women and the Economy. She was an active member of Delta Sigma Theta Sorority, Inc., Order of Eastern Star, Golden Circle, and Daughters of Isis.

Phinazee's high standards and her devotion to scholarship, her students and her colleagues, as well as her integrity in public representations of African American advancement were legendary within and beyond the borders of the United States. Her passing symbolized the end of an era when African American women willed themselves from the relegated status of domestic worker to that of teacher. She and many other African American women like her taught excellence, service, duty, and uplift, as well as their specialized fields, and laid the perfect foundation, or template, for the next evolution of the race in the United States.

FURTHER READING

Phinazee, Annette L., ed. *The Black Librarian in the Southeast: Reminiscences, Activities, Challenges*, papers presented for an 8–9 October 1975 colloquium (1980).

Phinazee, Annette L. *Report to the Alumni*. North Carolina Central University. School of Library Science (1983).

Black Caucus of Librarians, eds. *Lift Ev'ry Voice and Sing*, Proceedings of the Institute for Training Librarians for Special Black Collections and Archives (1974).

Jordan, Casper LeRoy. "Annette L. Phinazee," in Jessie Carney Smith, ed. *Notable Black American Women* (1992).

Who's Who in Library and Information Services (1981).

Obituary: American Library Association. *Yearbook of Library & Information Science* (1985).

RAMONA HOAGE EDELIN

Pickens, William (15 Jan. 1881–6 Apr. 1954), activist, was born in Anderson County, South Carolina, the sixth of ten children of Jacob and Fannie Pickens, both of whom were former slaves. The family of sharecroppers moved frequently—some twenty times by Pickens's estimate—and relocated to Arkansas in 1887. Pickens was raised in a household in which learning was revered, and he became valedictorian of his graduating class at Union High School in Little Rock in 1899. Following a summer working with his father in railroad construction in Arkansas, Pickens entered Talladega College, a missionary institution in Alabama, where he majored in foreign languages, and earned a B.A. in 1902. Pickens earned a second bachelor's degree, in Linguistics, from Yale University, in New Haven, Connecticut, where he received the Phi Beta Kappa key in 1904. He later earned an M.A. degree from Fisk University, in Nashville, Tennessee, a doctorate in Literature from Selma University (Alabama), and an LLD from Wiley University (now Wiley College) in Marshall, Texas.

In 1905 Pickens married Minnie Cooper McAlpine, a graduate of Tougaloo College, with whom he had three children: William, Harriet, and Ruby. Pickens possessed diverse talents and authored two autobiographies, *Heir of Slaves* (1911) and *Bursting Bonds* (1923), as well as a short-story collection, *Vengeance of the Gods* (1922), and a collection of essays, *The New Negro* (1916). Between 1904 and 1914 Pickens taught foreign languages at his alma mater, Talladega, before moving to Wiley University to head its Greek and sociology departments. The following year he accepted a position as dean of Morgan College (now Morgan State University) in Baltimore, Maryland.

Although he initially supported BOOKER T. WASHINGTON's more pragmatic approach to race relations, Pickens evolved into a civil rights militant fairly early in his intellectual career. He supported W. E. B. DuBois's radical Niagara Movement and was a charter member of the National Association for the Advancement of Colored People (NAACP) and the American Civil Liberties Union. He was also ecumenical in his organization affiliations, working to some degree with the League for Industrial Democracy, the YMCA, and the Council for Pan American Democracy. Given his broad education and training, Pickens was something of a maverick. He proposed to the businesswoman MADAME C. J. WALKER that he accompany her on a trip around the world and write a book about her travels, and in the early 1920s he flirted briefly with MARCUS GARVEY's Universal Negro Improvement Association (UNIA) while he was still an NAACP employee. Pickens was later a fierce critic of the UNIA, however, and even demanded that Garvey be imprisoned.

In 1919 Pickens left Morgan College—where he had risen to the vice presidency—to take a position as assistant to JAMES WELDON JOHNSON of the NAACP. As a founding member of the association, Pickens was well connected with its leadership and had also tirelessly recruited members at Talladega,

Wiley, and Morgan College. In 1915 he had accompanied the NAACP chairman Joel E. Spingarn on a dangerous fact-finding mission to Oklahoma, to gather information for a test case challenging Jim Crow on the railroads. In 1920 Johnson was appointed the first black executive secretary of the NAACP, and Pickens was subsequently appointed to the post of field secretary.

During his tenure as field secretary, Pickens shepherded the NAACP through a period of fluctuating membership during the 1920s and the Depression, and he helped lay the groundwork for the association's massive increase in resources and membership in the 1940s. His relations within the NAACP, however, were often rocky, especially with WALTER WHITE, who succeeded Johnson as executive secretary in 1930. Mary White Ovington, chair of the NAACP board, also reprimanded Pickens in 1931 for praising the Communist Party's work in support of the SCOTTSBORO BOYS in the midst of open hostility between the Communists and the NAACP. Pickens subsequently adopted the NAACP party line and even traveled to Scottsboro, Alabama, where he tried, unsuccessfully, to persuade the nine imprisoned youths to abandon their Communist backers. Pickens's decision to accept a position with the U.S. Department of the Treasury in 1942 probably was motivated, at least in part, by his deteriorating relations with White. He was succeeded as field secretary by the radical grassroots organizer ELLA BAKER.

In 1942 Pickens was cited as a subversive by the House Un-American Activities Committee (HUAC) and its conservative chairman, Martin Dies. In a gesture that eerily presaged Senator Joseph McCarthy's allegations in Wheeling, West Virginia, almost a decade later, Dies, a conservative Texas Democrat, presented the House of Representatives with a list of thirty-nine "subversives" who should be removed from the federal payroll. Of those people, William Pickens was the only one in federal employ at the time. As a director of the War Savings Staff, Pickens was charged with increasing the number of African Americans purchasing war bonds. In short order, a-measure was introduced that held up the federal budget until such time as Pickens's allegiances could be ascertained. Wary of provoking conservative southern Democrats who had perpetually threatened to hobble Franklin Roosevelt's presidency, Pickens gave a politic response to the charges. "I do not know Mr. Dies," he remarked, "but feel sure from the position he holds that he would not want to speak anything but the truth.

Therefore, I conclude that somebody has misled Mr. Dies" (press release, 18 Sept. 1942, Associated Negro Press Papers, Library of Congress).

With the budget hanging in the balance, some members of the HUAC were surprised at Pickens's appearance—not knowing that he was African American. Pickens's appearance thus gave the arch-segregationist Dies an opportunity to link subversion and civil rights. Northern Democrats, mindful of the Great Migration and the swelling numbers of black Democratic voters, however, were less than thrilled with the prospect of questioning Pickens. WILLIAM DAWSON, the black freshman congressman from Chicago, devoted his maiden speech to Pickens's defense, and Walter White sent a series of letters to members of the House of Representatives protesting the charges against Pickens. Those charges were ultimately dismissed, and Pickens remained in his position at the Treasury Department.

After World War II, Pickens attempted to return to the NAACP but was blocked by Walter White. Shut out of the organization where he had worked for twenty-three years, Pickens remained with the Treasury Department until 1951, when he retired. Pickens's political radicalism diminished somewhat during this period, and strains of his youthful admiration for Booker T. Washington might be seen in his Treasury Department campaigns to educate blacks on economic matters, savings bonds, and thrift. Pickens traveled extensively after his retirement and died during a cruise aboard SS *Mauritania*, on 6 April 1954, just one month before the U.S. Supreme Court issued its landmark school desegregation ruling in *Brown v. Board of Education*.

Pickens played a significant role in the development of the NAACP. Between 1920 and 1940 he recruited more members and organized more branches than any other officer in the association, and his efforts helped transform the organization from a small civil rights lobby to a mass organization with nationwide influence.

FURTHER READING

The primary archival collection of William Pickens's papers is housed at the Schomburg Center for Research in Black Culture of New York City. Substantial information regarding his public career, however, can be found in the NAACP collection at the Library of Congress.

Pickens, William. *Bursting Bonds* (1923, 1991).

Pickens, William. *Heir of Slaves* (1911).

Avery, Sheldon. *Up from Washington: William Pickens and the Negro Struggle for Equality, 1900–1954* (1989).

Obituary: *New York Times*, 7 Apr. 1954.

WILLIAM J. COBB

Pickett, Bill (5 Dec. 1871–2 Apr. 1932), rodeo entertainer, was born in Jenks-Branch community in Travis County, Texas, the son of Thomas Jefferson Pickett, a former slave, and Mary "Janie" Virginia Elizabeth Gilbert. The second of thirteen children, Pickett reportedly grew to be five feet seven inches tall and approximately 145 pounds. Little is known about his early childhood, except that he attended school through the fifth grade. Afterward he took up ranch work and soon developed the skills, such as roping and riding, that would serve him well in rodeo. On 2 December 1890 Pickett married Maggie Turner of Palestine, Texas, the daughter of a white southern plantation owner and his former slave. They had nine children. The Picketts joined the Taylor Baptist Church, where Pickett served as deacon for many years.

Sometime prior to 1900 Pickett and his brothers organized the Pickett Brothers Bronco Busters and Rough Riders Association, operating out of Taylor, Texas. Benny was president, Bill was vice president, Jessie was treasurer, Berry was secretary, and Charles was general manager. They proudly advertised in their handbills: "We ride and break all wild horses with much care. Good treatment to all animals. Perfect satisfaction guaranteed. Catching and taming wild cattle a specialty." The association operated for several years and boasted of an excellent reputation among the residents of Taylor.

By this time Pickett had originated the tactic of "bulldogging," for which he would become internationally known. A skilled steer-wrestling maneuver, bulldogging involved the performer's riding alongside a steer, throwing himself on its back, gripping the horns, and twisting the animal's neck and head upward, causing the beast to fall over. The rider and the steer would skid to a stop in a cloud of dust. Pickett would then sink his teeth into the steer's upper lip or nose and release both his hands. It is believed that Pickett developed his technique as a result of having witnessed a cattle dog holding a "cow critter" with its teeth. According to the author Colonel Bailey C. Hanes, Pickett perfected the maneuver when working with cattle in the brush country of Texas, where direct interaction with the steer was required to bring the animal under control. Pickett soon began displaying his bulldogging

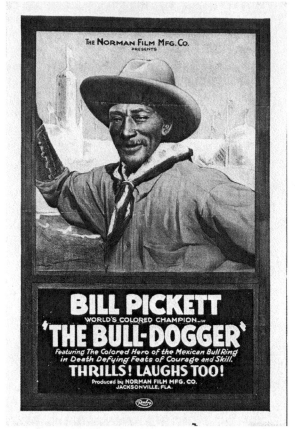

Bill Pickett. A promotional poster for "The Bull-Dogger."
(Library of Congress.)

technique before audiences, first at stockyards and later at county fairs. These audiences would watch in amazement as Pickett restrained a steer only by his viselike teething grip on the animal's lip or nose. This unique approach to steer wrestling immortalized Pickett, as it became the first original rodeo technique that can be traced to one individual.

In 1904 Pickett became an instant celebrity at the Cheyenne Frontier Days in Wyoming. The *Wyoming Tribune* reported in part:

> The event par excellence of the celebration this year is the great feat of Will Pickett, a Negro who hails from Taylor, Texas….Pickett is not a big man but is built like an athlete and his feat will undoubtedly be one of the great features of this year's celebration. It is difficult to conceive how a man could throw a powerful steer with his hands unaided by rope or a contrivance of some kind and yet Pickett accomplishes this seemingly impossible task with only his teeth.

New York's *Harper's Weekly* had sent John Dicks Howe, a special reporter, to cover the event. He reported:

> "20,000 people watched with wonder and admiration a mere man, unarmed and without a device or appliance of any kind, attack a fiery, wild-eyed and powerful steer and throw it by his teeth….The crowd was speechless with horror, many believing that the Negro had been crushed…Pickett arose uninjured, bowing and smiling. So great was the applause that the darkey again attacked the steer…and again threw it after a desperate struggle."

On 10 August 1905 Pickett was honored with national attention in *Leslie's Illustrated Weekly* tabloid as "a man who outdoes the fiercest dog in utter brutality." Capitalizing on his popularity, he signed a contract in 1907 with the Miller Brothers, owners of the famous 101 Ranch Wild West Show based along Oklahoma's Cherokee Strip. Becoming the show's headline performer, Pickett made appearances across the United States as well as in Canada, Mexico, Argentina, and England. Colonel Zack T. Miller described Pickett as "the greatest sweat and dirt cowhand that ever lived—bar none." His style of bulldogging gave him many nicknames, including the "Dusky Demon," "The Modern Ursus," and the "Wonderful Colored Cowboy." The wiry performer was also acclaimed for his bronco riding and steer-and calf-roping talents. Around 1914 he starred in a silent film called *The Bull-Dogger*, produced by the Norman Film Manufacturing Company. The film advertised the techniques of his steer-wrestling artistry, but no copies of the film have ever been located.

Pickett retired as a rodeo performer in 1916 and worked on the 101 Ranch until 1920, before settling on a 160-acre homestead near Chandler, Oklahoma. After Maggie's death in 1929, he returned to the 101 Ranch as a ranch hand to overcome personal financial difficulties brought on by the Great Depression. While attempting to cut horses out of a herd, Pickett was roping a chestnut stallion on foot when the horse suddenly turned on him and fractured his skull. Never regaining consciousness, Pickett died eleven days later at a hospital in Ponca City, Oklahoma. The Cherokee Strip Cowpunchers Association erected a marker in honor of him, with a hand inscription of "Bill Pickett, C.S.C.P.A.," on the 101 Ranch that he made famous, near the monument to the Ponca Indian chief White Eagle.

FURTHER READING

Hanes, Colonel Bailey C. *Bill Pickett, Bulldogger* (1977).

Katz, William Loren. *Black Indians: A Hidden Heritage* (1986).

This entry is taken from the *American National Biography* and is published here with the permission of the American Council of Learned Societies.

LARRY LESTER

Pickett, Tidye (3 Nov. 1914–17 Nov. 1986), track and field athlete, Olympian, and educator, was born Tidye Anne Pickett in Chicago, Illinois, the younger of two children of Sarah Elizabeth Patton, homemaker and active member of the War Mothers, and Louis Alfred Pickett, who worked for the International Harvester Corporation. Tidye's parents doted on her and her elder brother Charles, raised them to love family, God, and country, and were diligent in protecting and guiding them through the sometimes harsh realities of American racism in the first half of the twentieth century.

Sarah Pickett was involved in local community affairs, and politics eventually led her to several leadership positions as chaplain, historian, and president of a local chapter of the American War Mothers, which was founded in 1917 by mothers whose children were in the armed services, and was incorporated by an Act of Congress of 24 February 1925. The organization's mission is to assist in any way in their power men and women who served and were wounded or incapacitated in World War I or World War II or conflicts of the United States and to promote camaraderie and understanding between America and the Allies. Louis Pickett, a stoic and industrious man, committed forty-four years of service to the International Harvester Corporation, in Chicago. During World War II, Tidye Pickett's brother Charles served in the U.S. Army and had a distinguished military career; he rose to the rank of major and received numerous citations, including the Victory Metal, the Occupational Medal, and the Cross of Merit.

The Picketts lived in the 5600 block of Prairie Avenue close to Washington Park, where Tidye Pickett began to participate in various Chicago Park District athletic programs open to black youths. She also took part in the Carter School playground under the Chicago Board of Education Playground Programs. At that time, Pearl Green, director of the girl's athletic program, impressed with Tidye's natural talent, entered her in various athletic competitions. Outstanding in track and field events, Pickett also began to run for other athletic organizations. She entered various races sponsored by the *Chicago Daily News*, church organizations such as the Union Church Athletic Association and the YMCA, and she joined the Chicago Park District's South Park track team.

Pieroth states that "at barely 5'3" and 100 pounds, Pickett could run faster than all of her competitors at these events. At an invitation meet in the Armory on Cottage Grove Avenue she met John Brooks, who went on to qualify for the 1936 Olympic team himself as a long jumper. Working with Brooks, Pickett became an outstanding hurdler and broad jumper as well as a sprinter; she soon began running in citywide meets and traveling to competitions across the country and in Canada, winning everything she entered" (Pieroth, 32).

As a seventeen-year-old student at Chicago's Englewood High, Pickett qualified as a member of the Olympic Team in July of 1932, becoming one of the first African American women, as well as the youngest African American woman, named to the 1932 U.S. Olympics squad. Another black woman, Louise Stokes of Massachusetts, also made the team.

Pickett's experiences as part of the 1932 Olympic track and field team were bittersweet. With much hoopla, the team members boarded a train to Los Angeles. They had a stopover in Denver, Colorado, where the girls stayed in a lovely dormitory. That evening a banquet was held in their honor, but both Pickett and Stokes were prevented from joining the celebration. Instead they were given a room in the attic, where they ate dinner together. This was a painful slight that Pickett would never forget. Once they arrived at the games in Los Angeles, both women witnessed the open bigotry of numerous officials. Although Pickett qualified to compete in the eighty-meter hurdles, broad jump, and the 100-meter and eighty-yard sprints, neither she nor Stokes were selected to participate in any event at the 1932 Olympic Games. Pickett believed that racism and politics killed their opportunity to display their talent.

Between 1931 and 1936 Pickett received countless medals and won many competitions around the country and in Canada. She won medals at numerous city and state championships for the fifty-yard dash and the low hurdles. As her skills developed, she earned recognition as an accomplished athlete in the 100-meter sprint, the running broad jump, and the eighty-meter low hurdles. At one time during her athletic career, she held the women's world record for the forty-yard dash and the Canadian world record for the running broad jump in 1934. In 1936 she won the gold medal for the fifty-yard hurdles at the U.S. National indoor championships.

Pickett attended the 1936 Olympics in Berlin, Germany, and was expected to bring home the gold; however, she broke her foot in the eighty-meter hurdle semifinals, causing her to forfeit any further participation. Louise Stokes was not chosen for the relay; thus neither of the African American women was able to successfully achieve a medal at those games.

Pickett recalled of the 1936 Olympics that Adolf Hitler had bragged so much about what his athletes could do but when JESSE OWENS got there, he ran right through them. She also believed that while she and Louise Stokes suffered from discrimination as pioneering black female Olympians, they also opened the door for other African American women athletes.

Following the 1936 Olympics, Pickett hoped to earn a spot on the 1940 team, but those games and the 1944 Olympiad were cancelled because of World War II. Although greatly disappointed, she then refocused her energy on her personal life.

Pickett remained involved with the Chicago Park District, married Gail Eldridge in 1948, and had one child, Sara Elizabeth, born in 1942. Several years later the Pickett family, including her brother Charles and his wife, moved to Aurora, Illinois (forty miles west of Chicago). In 1947 she gave birth to another daughter, Lugenia Faye. After her marriage ended in 1948, she became a single parent. With family close by to look after her daughters, she found work as a secretary at the Boy's Home in St. Charles, Illinois, where she met and married Frank Phillips, an English teacher also working at the Boys' School, in 1949.

In 1952, the couple built a new house in Aurora and moved in with their young family. In June 1953 Tidye Pickett earned a bachelor's degree from Pestalozzi Froebel Teachers College (Chicago). She then taught science at the Boys' School and commuted between Aurora and St. Charles to work, and between St. Charles and DeKalb, Illinois, several evenings a week. Though the long journeys meant that she did not return to Aurora until late at night, she persevered and earned a master's of science degree in Education from Northern Illinois University in August 1956.

In September 1957 she was hired as a teacher at Cottage Grove Elementary School in East Chicago Heights (Illinois) School District 169. She taught at Cottage Grove for one year before being appointed principal of Woodlawn School, in the same district. In 1962 Pickett adopted a six-year-old girl named Bernita Denise. In later years she moved her family back to Chicago and then to East Chicago Heights due to demands of her principalship and weariness from years of commuting. She served as principal for twenty-three years, and retired in 1980. At her retirement ceremony the school district paid tribute to her by renaming the school the Tidye A. Phillips School.

Tidye passed away at the age of seventy-two. She serves as an excellent role model not just for African American women but also for all women of all ages everywhere. She helped pave the way for women following in her footsteps as athletes, and as proof every person can "reach the impossible dream"; as she often told her daughters, first one must dare to dream.

FURTHER READING
"Ex-track Star Recalls Racism at '32 Games." *Chicago Sun-Times* (5 Aug. 1984).
Pieroth, Doris H. *Their Day in the Sun: Women of the 1932 Olympics* (1996).

BERNITA D. LUCAS

Pickett, Wilson, Jr. (18 Mar. 1941–19 Jan. 2006), singer and songwriter, was born in Prattville, Alabama, in 1941, one of eleven children born to Wilson and Lena Pickett. The family's eleven children were immersed in gospel music by their grandfather, a minister. He refused to allow any other music to be played in the house, and Wilson sang in the chorus at his local Baptist church. When Pickett was fourteen, his mother moved him to Detroit to live with his father in 1955. There he sang lead vocals in a regionally popular gospel group called the Violinaires while attending Northwestern High School.

In 1959 Pickett joined the Falcons, a popular vocal group at the time, and sang harmonies with Sir Mack Rice and Eddie Floyd, who already had a hit with "You're So Fine." The Falcons, part of the nationally popular Detroit R&B scene of the early 1960s, often performed with the Primettes, later known as the Supremes. The group once toured with singer Sam Cooke. "I Found a Love," the Falcons' biggest hit, was written by Pickett and released in 1962. This led to Pickett's signing as a solo artist at Correctone Records. The single he released there was not a hit; however, Lloyd Price's Double L Records signed Pickett and moved him to New York City in 1963. He had several hits at Double L, including "If You Love Me" and "It's Too Late." Atlantic's singer SOLOMON BURKE released "It's Too Late" the same year, and it eclipsed Pickett's recording.

Pickett signed with Atlantic Records in 1964, and it was there that he would make R&B history. His first single, "Come Home, Baby," flopped, and the label had some trouble finding the right production setting for Pickett. Atlantic record executive Jerry Wexler hit on the idea of setting up sessions for Pickett in 1965 at Stax (Volt) Studios in Memphis. Some R&B historians claimed that it was there that he picked up the nickname "Wicked Pickett" for his raw interpretation of the music, but Wilson claimed the nickname came from a studio secretary remarking on his smooth-talking seductiveness. Pickett collaborated with Booker T. and the M.G.s, a studio band assembled by BOOKER T. JONES that included Donald "Duck" Dunn and Steve Cropper, to create the hit "In the Midnight Hour." It became an R&B standard, despite reaching only number twenty-one on the pop charts. A second single from the Stax sessions, "634-5789," reached number thirteen in 1965. Pickett recorded a string of hits, including "The Land of 1000 Dances," which hit number six on the pop charts in 1966, and "Mustang Sally," which rose to number twenty-three on the singles charts. Pickett's Fame recordings, "She's So Good to Me" and "Ninety-Nine and a Half (Won't Do)," continued to chart in 1967.

In 1970 Stax studios announced that it would no longer record artists for outside labels, and Wexler, seeking to maintain Pickett's raw southern sound, moved the singer to Fame Studios in Muscle Shoals. That same year, Pickett began working at American Studios in Memphis, where he recorded several early BOBBY WOMACK tunes. He continued to collaborate on songwriting with Womack periodically throughout his career. Womack had played guitar on Pickett's 1968 album, *The Midnight Mover*.

Pickett was among the few soul singers of his generation who successfully not only moved from the polished Detroit sound to the grittier style of southern soul but also scored hits with the lush predisco of the Philadelphia sound. Pickett's albums had always been on the cutting edge because of the quality of the studios he recorded in and the superior musicianship of the session players he used— for example, the late guitar virtuoso Duane Allman plays on Pickett's rendition of "Hey Jude" recorded during the Muscle Shoals period. Pickett was also unique among early R&B artists in that he wrote, or cowrote, most of the songs he recorded.

In 1970 Pickett arrived at Kenny Gamble and LEON HUFF's Sigma Sound Studios to record an album he hoped would revitalize his mildly sagging chart fortunes. The album, *Wilson Pickett in Philadelphia*, featured the sophisticated arrangements and funky grooves that typified Gamble and Huff's production. The album produced two crossover mainstream pop hits, "Engine Number Nine" and "Don't Let the Green Grass Fool You." In spite of the success, Wexler, unhappy with the sound of the record, and Pickett, unhappy with the cost of recording, returned to Muscle Shoals for what would be Pickett's last Atlantic sessions. The resulting album, *Don't Knock My Love*, produced a few hits in 1971 but marked the end of Pickett's most productive period. After recording several lackluster albums for RCA, he was dropped by the label in 1975, and recorded only sparingly thereafter. He released a set of new Muscle Shoals sessions on *Funky Situation* in 1978 on his own label, Wicked, and he put out a few studio albums for EMI and Motown, but thereafter he would focus on touring rather than recording. Soul singers were a hot ticket with European audiences in the 1980s and 1990s, and Pickett played on the Continent to large crowds with fellow soul legends Solomon Burke, BEN E. KING, JOE TEX, and Don Covay as part of the Blues Clan Touring Show.

Pickett was honored with induction into the Rock and Roll Hall of Fame in 1991 and the Alabama Music Hall of Fame in 1999. Also that year, he released *It's Harder Now*, his first studio album in nearly twelve years. Though some anticipated a disappointing reworking of old material, the album achieved significant critical acclaim. Pickett captured soul/blues male artist of the year at the W. C. HANDY Awards given by the Blues Foundation and *It's Harder Now* won comeback blues album and soul/blues album of 1999 at the Handy Awards. He was also nominated for a Grammy Award that year for best traditional R&B vocal performance.

Pickett's legend continued to new generations with the movie *The Commitments*, where the lead characters are obsessed with R&B music including Pickett's song stylings. His biography was included in *Only the Strong Survive*, a documentary on the soul music. Pickett had struggled throughout his career with addictions and had been arrested and jailed for various offenses over the last decade of his life, including driving under the influence and driving while in possession of a loaded shotgun in 1991. Known for having a volatile temper, Pickett was also arrested for assault and disorderly conduct in a misunderstanding during a tour with the Isley Brothers in May 1991 after he shot the lock on a motel room in order to gain entry. The most notorious arrest happened in 1996 after driving his car on the lawn of a public official's home. Pickett died of a heart attack on 19 January 2006, near his home in Reston, Virginia, after experiencing declining health for a year. He was survived by his former wife, Jean, fiancée, Gail Webb, and four children: sons Michael Wilson and Lynderrick and daughters Veda and Saphan. Pickett was buried in a grave next to his mother in Louisville, Kentucky. His legacy is seen in the number of solo artists and groups releasing Pickett's songs, including the Rolling Stones, singers Jojo and Ani DeFranco, Echo and the Bunnymen, Hootie and the Blowfish, and Los Lobos.

FURTHER READING
Garofalo, Reebee. *Rockin' Out: Popular Music in the USA* (2005).
Ramsey, Guthrie P. *Race Music: Black Cultures from Bebop to Hip-Hop* (2003).
Obituaries: *Billboard*, 19 Jan. 2006; *Washington Post*, 20 Jan. 2006.

PAMELA LEE GRAY

Pico, Andrés (1810–14 Feb. 1876), soldier, ranchero, and politician, was born at the Presidio of San Diego, one of the twelve children of María Eustaquia Gutierrez and José María Pico. His father, like many immigrant men, was a soldier at the Presidio or fort, and he died when Andrés was nine. After his death, the Presidio helped support his widow and children. Andrés Pico's maternal and paternal grandparents had arrived in California in 1776 with two hundred immigrants in an expedition led by Lieutenant Colonel Juan Bautista de la Anza. Like most families who journeyed from New Spain (Mexico), they were poor and of mixed race: African, Indian, and possibly Spanish. Census records classified Andrés Pico's grandmother and uncles as "mulatos."

After working as a customs official and managing his brother's ranch, Pico chose a military career in the 1830s and rose through the ranks, becoming a captain in 1844. Andrés Pico and his brother Pío were involved in politics as well, for which they were occasionally arrested and at other times awarded with land grants for their efforts. These activities took place at a time when California was part of Mexico.

During the Mexican-American War of 1846 to 1848, U.S. forces occupied parts of California, imposing curfews and restrictions; in response the Mexican army organized a resistance to the invasion. Pico was an experienced soldier; he had fought in rebellions for and against unpopular governors, and in 1846 he commanded forces under José María Flores in Southern California. Violent mobs pushed the Americans out of Los Angeles, and the Mexican soldiers watched the U.S. soldiers in San Diego carefully.

On 6 December 1846, in what is known as the Battle of San Pascual, Pico and his men were attacked by eighty Americans at San Pascual, a town near the modern city of Escondido. Armed mainly with lances and muskets, the Californios (as the Mexican citizens of California were called) fought back and killed twenty-one Americans and wounded nearly as many, while suffering few casualties of their own. The Americans, who were part of a larger force led by Brigadier General Stephen Kearney, retreated to a hilltop. Pico hesitated to attack, because the U.S. Army had cannons and rifles, and reinforcements would soon arrive from San Diego. Pico led his victorious Californios back to Los Angeles.

Mexican forces led by Flores were less successful, and they lost engagements with the U.S. Army near Los Angeles and La Mesa. As a result, Flores abandoned the fighting and returned to Mexico, after which Pico became first in command, and it fell to him to negotiate the peace. On 13 January 1847 Pico signed the Cahuenga Capitulation with Lieutenant Colonel John Frémont of the United States. Because of his courage in battle and in peace, Pico was esteemed by both Americans and Mexicans for most of his life.

After gold was discovered in California, Pico and other ranchers made tremendous profits by selling beef to the entrepreneurs coming into the state. Pico also recruited and outfitted Mexican laborers to mine for gold and set them to digging south of Sutter's Fort near Sacramento, California.

By 1850 California law excluded anyone who had an eighth or more Negro or Indian blood from giving testimony against white men in court cases. Even while it was well known that Pico fell into this category, he was elected, twice, to the State Assembly for one-year terms, in 1851 and 1852. If race was mentioned, Pico was referred to as a Spaniard. In subsequent years Pico served as a presidential elector, the vice president of the Democratic convention, and the brigadier general of the militia. He also safeguarded funds from the Federal Land Office. He served again in the State Assembly, in 1858 and 1859, and in the state senate for a two-year term, from 1859 to 1861, becoming a Republican halfway through his term. Pico never fully mastered English, but the majority of voters in Los Angeles were Mexican. When Pico switched his allegiance to the Republican Party and supported Abraham Lincoln for president, it cost him votes, and he lost his bid for sheriff of Los Angeles County, where sympathy for the Confederacy was strong. Pico's position as head of the militia in Southern California was also terminated.

In late July or August 1856 a small criminal group of Mexicans threatened (according to rumor) to lynch a white constable who had panicked and shot a Mexican in a dispute. Pico was one of several Los Angeles leaders who held a public meeting and, over several months, organized volunteer vigilance committees to go after the mob of outlaws. Pico himself led a group of twenty Californios to arrest the outlaws, calming the small American population that feared violence. While there were certainly dangerous lawbreakers in the area, the large, organized, pillaging mobs of Mexicans that most Americans feared simply did not exist. Working with Americans, Pico attacked, captured, and hung a horse thief and a second outlaw named Juan Silvas (Silvas's crime was not recorded). The citizens of Los Angeles hailed Pico as a hero.

Pico lived well in a twenty-two-room building that had once been the seminary and residence for priests at the Mission (later Rancho) San Fernando. He also owned sixty-two thousand acres of land surrounding it. Like most wealthy Californios, Pico entertained generously, hosting dances, fiestas, and formal dinners. An excellent horseman, he participated in bullfights and gambled huge amounts of money on horse races. But when cattle prices declined after the mid-1850s, Pico fell deeply in debt. Instead of amending his extravagant lifestyle, he began borrowing money, and in 1862 his cattle were seized by creditors. He put his property into his brother's name, though he continued to manage it, but a drought in the 1860s ruined the cattle industry, and in 1869 the Rancho San Fernando was sold. Among other properties, Pico and his brother Pío owned the Rancho Santa Margarita y Las Flores. With creditors hounding them, the brothers transferred ownership of the ranch to their brother-in-law, John Forster. A bitter, and unsuccessful, lawsuit resulted when they later claimed that Forster defrauded them. The Rancho Santa Margarita remained intact until 1942, when it became the U.S. Marines' Camp Pendleton.

Andrés Pico never married, but he lived for many years with Catalina Moreno. After his death, Pico was identified as the father of at least one son, Rómulo, by a married woman. Pico had adopted the infant daughter of a friend who left California during the Civil War; she later married his natural son, Rómulo Pico.

Pico died under mysterious circumstances. His family claimed he was beaten, left on his own doorstep in Los Angeles, and lingered in a coma for several weeks. His attackers were never caught. Pío and Rómulo Pico fought for seven years over the nine hundred acres of property he left; the land ended up as the property of the attorney handling the probate.

FURTHER READING
Gray, Paul Bryan. *Forster vs. Pico: The Struggle for the Rancho Santa Margarita* (1998).
Pitt, Leonard. *The Decline of the Californios: A Social History of the Spanish-Speaking Californians, 1846–1890* (1971, 1998).

VICKEY KALAMBAKAL

Píco, Pío (5 May 1801–11 Sept. 1894), revolutionary, governor, city councilman, landowner, and businessman, was born Pío de Jesus Píco at the San Gabriel Mission in California, the fourth of the ten children of José María Píco, founder of the Píco family in Southern California, and a native of Fuerte, Sinaloa, Mexico, and María Eustaquia Gutiérrez, from San Miguel de Horcasitas, Sonora, Mexico. Pío's ancestry was a combination of African, Hispanic, Native American, and European. José Píco migrated to California in 1801 with the Anza Expedition, which was authorized in 1775 by the viceroy of Spain. Soldiers and their families were recruited from Sonora to occupy and settle the port of San Francisco. A successful overland emigration and supply route was established between Sonora and Alta California. Among the positions he held were sergeant and corporal. Many members of the Píco family served in the military, including Pío Píco's maternal and paternal uncles. The military career of José Píco perhaps set the tone and example for his sons' military and political involvement.

After the death of his father in 1819, Píco and his family moved south to San Diego. Their financial circumstances were grim—they had no funds or property. Píco ran a general store of sorts that carried liquors, provisions, chairs, and shoes; he also traded and sold cattle, sugar, and other goods. His mother and sisters worked at fine needlework. Little is known of Píco's early formal education except that he learned to read and write from Don José Carrillo, a military leader, rancher, and politician, as well as a teacher, and his wife, Matilde. Although Don Carrillo had a school at the presidio of San Diego, it is unlikely that Píco ever attended. There is no indication that Píco received any formal institutional learning. At a relatively early

Pío Píco, the last Mexican Governor of Alta California, c. 1897. (Library of Congress.)

during California's Mexican period. They were also the means for political advancement. Píco was integrally involved in the unrest and was a major figure in the unsuccessful attempt in 1828 to establish Los Angeles as the seat of the Mexican territory. In 1831 he was one of the leaders of a revolt against the despotic policies of Governor Manuel Victoria. Victoria surrendered after the famous (First) Battle of Cahuenga Pass, and Píco was installed as provisional governor for just twenty days. Píco married María Ygnacia Amador, the daughter of another career soldier, in February of 1834 in Los Angeles. In April of that same year Píco was named administrator of the Mission de San Luís Rey.

In 1845, after the Second Battle of Cahuenga Pass, against Governor Manuel Micheltorena, Píco was installed in the gubernatorial office, which he kept until 1846. During his tenure as governor he would be responsible for the secularization of the California mission system. As he told Thomas Savage in 1877:

> My principal objective in respect to these establishments was to abolish completely the regime of the missions, and to establish pueblos in their place, reserving the necessary buildings for worship and the needs of their ministers, while suitable buildings would be assigned for ayuntamientos [city halls] and public schools (Píco, 121).

age—somewhere in his early-to-mid-twenties—he would begin gambling, a habit that would plague him throughout his life.

The Píco family was intimately involved in the politics of the day; patriarch José María remained in the active Mexican military until his death. When the Pícos lived in California it was a part of Spain and subsequently Mexico, which gained its independence in 1821. (The state became a part of the United States in 1848 with the signing of the Treaty of Guadalupe Hidalgo, which ceded California to the United States.) Píco was politically aware but would not become actually involved until 1827–1828 when he was named scribe or secretary to Attorney General Captain Don Pablo de la Portilla.

Píco's political opinions were forming, influenced by his late father and other military officials. His feeling that California was a nation over which the military had no sovereignty formed the core of his political views and his role as a revolutionary when the state was still a part of Mexico. Revolutions and counter-revolutions were the order of the day

This meant that the vast land holdings of the Catholic Church were sold to private parties. The administration of the missions was passed from the missionaries to secular clergy. Píco was accused of recklessly redistributing mission property to friends and allies of the Mexican government—as well as himself—as the American takeover of California neared. The missions of San Gábriel, San Luís Rey, San Fernando, San Diego, San Juan Capistrano, and San Buenaventura were sold off. He personally amassed vast acreages of land, including Rancho Santa Margarita y Las Flores in what is now Orange County and Rancho Paso de Bartolo in what is now the city of Whittier. Píco was successful this time in relocating the capital of California from Monterey to Los Angeles. One of his great concerns was the unchecked immigration of Americans into the state. In a foreshadowing of later sentiments he lamented:

> What are we to do then? Shall we remain supine, while these daring strangers are overrunning our fertile plains, and gradually

outnumbering and displacing us? Shall these incursions go on unchecked, until we shall become strangers in our own land (Píco, 1973)?

The impending threat of an American takeover of California was very real. There was a lack of financial resources and none were forthcoming from the Mexican government. Given that fact, Pico also considered whether the state should not be an independent protectorate of either the British Empire or France. Mexican general Andres Píco, the brother of Pío, surrendered California to American forces under General John Fremont at Campo de Cahuenga on 13 January 1847. Fearing reprisals from the American forces, Pico fled to Sonora, Mexico. The Treaty of Guadalupe Hidalgo in 1848, which ceded the state and much of the Southwest to the Americans, signaled the end of the Mexican period in California. Pico would be the last Mexican governor of California before American statehood.

Pico returned to Los Angeles in 1848 after the Treaty of Guadalupe Hidalgo was signed and was elected to the Los Angeles Common Council, but did not assume office. He did, however, use that position, as well as his wealth and influence, to foster education, banking, and town development. In 1870, he was responsible for building the Píco House hotel, which still stands today, on Main Street. In its day this hotel was the city's largest and most luxurious hotel as well as its social nexus. Píco was an early pioneer in California's first oil venture, which would eventually become Standard Oil Company of California.

Píco was disadvantaged by his illiteracy in English, and near the end of his life he was swindled out of his vast land holdings. In a financial bind, he entered into a questionable transaction with a man named Bernard Cohn in the form of the title to all of his properties masquerading as a mortgage. Pico appealed to the California Supreme Court to reestablish title in a seven-year court case. In *Píco v. Cohn* (California, 1891) the court ruled against him. The ruin of Píco typified the demise of the landowning dons in California when the region became a part of the United States. Their vast wealth was either reduced or completely lost. Penniless and ill, Pío Píco died in 1894 at the age of ninety-three in Los Angeles, at the home of his daughter Joaquína Moreno.

The name Pío Píco is prominent in Southern California history as evidenced today by Californian place names, which include Pico Boulevard and the city of Pico Rivera, as well as the many businesses that bear the name. Little known is the fact that the Pícos were one of many African Mexican families, including the Cameros, the Reyeses, the Tápias, and the Valdezes, who played key roles in California state and city government and were landowners in the nineteenth century. Shortcomings aside, Pío Píco was an early champion of the rights of the state of California spanning the Spanish, Mexican, and American periods.

FURTHER READING
Píco dictated his memory of the revolutionary years in California history to Thomas Savage in 1877. This was translated from the original Spanish by Arthur P. Botello as *Don Pio Pico's Historical Narrative* (1973).

Bromilow, Jessie Elizabeth. *Pío de Jesús Píco: His Biography and Place in History* (1931).

"Pío Píco Mansion: Fact, Fiction and Supposition," *The Journal of the West*, vol. 2, no. 3 (July 1963).

Rice, Hallie Evelyn. *Pío Píco: Last Mexican Governor of California* (1932).

Smith, Marian Elizabeth. *Pío Píco, Ranchero and Politician* (1971).

ALVA MOORE STEVENSON

Picou, Alphonse (19 Oct. 1878–4 Feb. 1961), jazz clarinetist, was born Alphonse Floristan Picou in New Orleans, Louisiana. His parents' names are unknown; his father was a cigar maker. From age fourteen until he was established in music, Alphonse worked as a sheet metal worker by day. Around 1894 he took up guitar, but performances at the French Opera House inspired him to switch to clarinet, which he studied under a Professor Marand, a member of the opera orchestra. Picou played professionally from age sixteen as a member of brass bands, dance bands using written music, and dance bands playing by ear, these last perhaps helping to develop what later was called jazz. At the turn of the century he traveled to Texas and Oklahoma with a carnival show. He was married in New Orleans on 28 October 1901; his wife's name is unknown.

Picou's musical scope expanded in 1903 when he joined the twenty-two-piece Bloom Philharmonic Orchestra, while continuing to work in dance and brass bands, including jobs with the legendary cornetist BUDDY BOLDEN. Having played with the Excelsior Brass Band in the late 1890s, he became a regular member in 1904 and remained through the mid-1920s. He worked with the cornetist FREDDIE KEPPARD's dance band, the Olympia Orchestra, from 1907 until 1910, and it was around this time that he claimed to have given clarinet lessons to

SIDNEY BECHET. In 1909 Picou also joined Louis Keppard's Magnolia Orchestra, which included KING OLIVER and POPS FOSTER; Foster reported that Picou played soprano saxophone in addition to clarinet. Picou worked regularly with the cornetist MANUEL PEREZ for three years from 1910, and he was a founding member of PAPA CELESTIN's Tuxedo Orchestra in 1910 and Tuxedo Brass Band in 1911. He also led his own band from 1912 until 1915. During this period the common repertory of New Orleans bands included Porter Steele's composition "High Society" (1901) in Robert Recker's arrangement, which featured a florid written solo for piccolo. Picou's adaptation of this solo became a fixture of New Orleans clarinet playing; his opening phrase also was inserted into diverse jazz improvisations.

Picou performed in Chicago briefly in 1915, then returned home to work with John Robichaux (from 1915 until 1927), ARMAND JOHN PIRON, Celestin (from 1915 into the mid-1920s), the cornetist Wooden Joe Nicholas's Camelia Brass Band and Dance Orchestra (from 1917 until the 1920s), Perez, Buddy Petit (in 1918), and Lee Collins (in 1923–1924). Collins related a story of Petit's band outplaying KID ORY's group in 1918. Picou was generally soft-spoken (except when drinking) and friendly, but evidently he never hesitated to outperform a rival when the opportunity arose.

His dashing back and forth among bands included another brief foray to Chicago in 1923, at which time Oliver recorded two of his compositions, "Olympia Rag" and "Onzaga," which were retitled, respectively, "Chattanooga Stomp" and "New Orleans Stomp." Picou also claimed to be the clarinetist on a version of "High Society" that CLARENCE WILLIAMS recorded in New York in 1929 or 1930, but no evidence supports this claim. Around this time he was given a distinctive old French clarinet with a curved bell at the end, which he played for the rest of his life.

Opportunities for musical work in New Orleans declined severely during the Depression, and Picou worked regularly as a tinsmith, although he continued to perform whenever possible. Eventually he became financially independent, having invested in many successful properties in New Orleans and Los Angeles. In 1940, as a part of the emerging revival of New Orleans jazz, he recorded for the first time. The session was led by the trumpeter Kid Rena, with whom Picou worked for several years. On "High Society Rag" he performs his famous melody twice, as a solo and again at the end of the piece in a duet with fellow clarinetist Big Eye Louis

Nelson. (Unusually, Rena's recording group had two clarinetists.)

After leading his own group, Picou joined Papa Celestin's new Original Tuxedo Orchestra, which first recorded in 1947. Its success brought Picou considerable local fame, and at age sixty-nine, "serene and merry, he displayed the naive and dignified self-absorption that often marks an original man," according to musicologist Alan Lomax. In 1949 the Tuxedo band began several engagements at the Paddock Lounge, with Picou remaining into 1954 as leadership passed from Celestin to the bassist Richard Alexis to the pianist Octave Crosby. At age seventy-five Picou retired from playing full time to manage his properties and to help his daughter run Picou's Bar and Restaurant, where he performed on Sunday nights. He remained active in brass bands, and although "retired" he marched four miles with the Eureka Brass Band as it was being recorded in 1956.

Picou died in New Orleans. His funeral was held during Mardi Gras, and nearly ten thousand people are said to have paid him tribute on the march to his grave, with the Eureka Brass Band performing at his graveside. He is remembered for his solo on "High Society," which became a test piece for clarinetists aspiring to work in the New Orleans style.

FURTHER READING

Foster, Pops. *Pops Foster: The Autobiography of a New Orleans Jazzman* (1971).

Haby, Peter R. "Alphonse Picou: New Orleans Creole," *Footnote* 11, no. 5 (1980).

Lomax, Alan, ed. *Mister Jelly Roll: The Fortunes of Jelly Roll Morton, New Orleans Creole and "Inventor of Jazz"* (1950).

Obituary: *New York Times*, 5 Feb. 1961.

This entry is taken from the *American National Biography* and is published here with the permission of the American Council of Learned Societies.

BARRY KERNFELD

Picquet, Louisa (1828?–?), former slave, abolitionist, and memoirist, was born in Columbia, South Carolina, to an enslaved, biracial seamstress and cook, Elizabeth Ramsey. Her mother's white master, John Randolph, was Louisa's father. From infancy through age thirteen, Picquet, along with her mother and her younger brother John, were owned by a former cotton planter from Monticello, Georgia, named Cook. To pay for losses at the gaming tables, Cook fled to Mobile, Alabama, where he "hired out" or leased Picquet, a child herself, to "nurse" or look after the children of slaveholders.

When Picquet was almost fourteen, in order to settle Cook's remaining debts, a sheriff from Georgia sold her to a Mr. Williams, a middle-aged New Orleans "gentleman" (Picquet, 16). Her other family members were auctioned to A. C. Horton of Warton, Texas. Picquet was forced to become Williams's mistress, and she bore him four sons before he died. With funds from his brother, she traveled to Cincinnati in 1849 with two surviving sons, and then raised nine hundred dollars by the fall of 1860 to purchase her mother's freedom.

What is known about Picquet is derived from her narrative *Louisa Picquet, The Octoroon: Or Inside Views of Southern Domestic Life* (1861). Much like HARRIET JACOBS's memoir, *Incidents in the Life of a Slave Girl*, published the same year, Picquet reveals how enslaved African American women were frequently vulnerable to rape and sexual violence, even though many owners insisted that they enjoyed a degree of protection and security that they would not acquire in freedom. Her interviewer, the Methodist minister and abolitionist Hiram Mattison, wrote, "There is not a family mentioned, from first to last, that does not reek with fornication and adultery" (51). The Reverend Mattison brought out Picquet's narrative as part of her campaign to raise funds to purchase her mother's freedom. It underscored how slavery really divided girls from the protection of their parents and made them easy targets of sexual abuse. The white complexions of Picquet, her mother, and her sons by Mr. Williams, in addition to her brother John who was "as white as one in a hundred of our fellow citizens" (46), bore witness to the hypocrisy that existed in slave-owning families who would piously attend Sunday service and read the Bible at meals and prayers, ignoring stories of masters who raped or whipped young girls like Picquet at their pleasure, and mistresses who dared not rebuke their husbands. In Picquet's case, Williams, her third master, had separated from his wife, making it easy for him to sequester her as his concubine away from the prying eyes of neighbors or spousal accusations. She complained that he refused to allow her to "darken a church door from the time he bought me till after he died" (19). He ignored her pleas to permit her to "get religion" and join a church because of her sinful relationship with him (22).

Picquet's contrast of the slave's piety to the slave-owner's immorality was a rhetorical strategy customarily employed among former slaves writing (or, as in her case, dictating) their memoirs. One of the justifications of slavery was that the system exposed them to the redemptive benefits of Christian instruction. Domestic horror stories, in which masters like Picquet's so openly defied Christian teachings, could enlighten Northern readers, "the Christian citizen, especially," with evidence of how far from the mark slavery really had strayed (52).

Pre–Civil War American society expected women in general and mothers in particular to serve as Christian role models for family members. At the auction block, amid the terror and tears, Picquet's mother Elizabeth dropped to her knees and prayed for her daughter's safety. If a slave mother could demonstrate such religious faith, only to be mocked and abused by the whites who purported to be her moral superiors, then slavery could not be such a Christianizing influence after all. Nearly two-thirds of Picquet's memoir, sixteen of her book's twenty-seven chapters, focused on her life in Cincinnati and her efforts there to locate and redeem her mother from southern bondage. Three years after she arrived in the city, she married Henry Picquet, a mulatto ex-slave from Georgia who had been emancipated by his master. Her description of marriage and motherhood in Ohio intended to undermine readers' uncertainties of "whether or not slaves have any proper affection for their offspring," even as it underscored the difficulties African Americans encountered keeping their families together in slavery or freedom (33).

Picquet reprinted correspondence between herself and her mother (once she discovered her location in Texas), dictated to trusted friends and posted by a secret method, since neither were literate and both were fearful that they might jeopardize the safety of friends and family still in bondage. Their affection and hopes for reunion commingled with the blunt language of financial transaction—"One Thousand Dollars for me, & Fifteen Hundred for your Brother"—as if to demonstrate to abolitionist readers how the unity of black families was inconsequential to slaveholders' accumulation of wealth and property (33–34). Picquet was able to purchase her mother from A. C. Horton for one hundred dollars less than the original asking price, but he was not willing to part with her brother for any sum. Just as slavery dismembered individual families, so too did it disrupt collective racial solidarity. Picquet, for example, who could pass for white, was accused by a minister of not really being the black woman she said she was. On another occasion, she ran into an old friend from slavery who was passing for white, and had concealed his identity as a black man in order to marry a white woman.

When, where, and how Picquet died is unknown. The incomplete elements of her life story that she shared in print reflected the direction and focus of the Reverend Mattison's questions and his interests in specific themes, in particular the complicity of his fellow Methodists in slavery, and the violence and sadism of slaveholders.

FURTHER READING

Picquet, Louisa. *Louisa Picquet, The Octoroon: Or Inside Views of Southern Domestic Life* (1861)

Foreman, P. Gabrielle. "Who's Your Mama?: 'White' Mulatta Genealogies, Early Photography, and Anti-Passing Narratives of Slavery and Freedom," in *American Literary History* 14.3 (Fall 2002).

Fulton, DoVeanna S. *Speaking Power: Black Feminist Orality in Women's Narratives of Slavery* (2006).

Moody, Joycelyn K. "Enslaved Women as Autobiographical Narrators: The Case of Louisa Picquet," in *Rhetoric and Ethnicity*, ed. Keith Gilyard and Vorris Nunley (2004).

BARBARA MCCASKILL

Pierce, Billy (14 June 1890–11 Apr. 1933), choreographer, dance studio owner, and journalist, was born William Joseph Pierce in Purcellville, Virginia, the only child of Dennis Pierce and Nellie Shorter, who spent their childhoods enslaved and later became truck farmers. After attending the public schools in Loudoun County, Virginia, Pierce attended two colleges, Storer College in Harpers Ferry, West Virginia, and Howard University in Washington, D.C. During World War I he served with the Eighth Illinois Regiment in the United States Army.

Pierce was a journalist, an often overlooked aspect of his life and work. He was a reporter and editor for the *Chicago Defender*, the (Washington, D.C.) *Dispatcher*, and the *Washington Eagle*, adding to the stature of these newspapers in the area of arts coverage. But Pierce's heart belonged to show business. He made his dancing debut in the early 1920s at the Pekin Theater in Chicago. During this time Pierce worked as a vaudeville dancer, a trombonist, a ticket-taker in a minstrel show, and the banjo player in Dr. Diamond Dick's Kickapoo Indian Medicine Show on what was commonly called the "TOBA" (Tough on Black Actors) circuit before heading to New York City.

Shortly after arriving in New York, Pierce realized his dream of owning a dance studio. He rented a fourteen-by-sixteen-foot room in a building on Forty-sixth Street where he worked as an elevator operator. There was no shortage of dance studios on Broadway, but Pierce's reputation grew, and he was able to expand the Billy Pierce Dance Studio to two whole floors in the same building and devote himself full-time to choreography. Established performers and would-be dancers from all over the country sought classes at his studio.

During the Harlem Renaissance theater critics began to acknowledge the influence of African American dance in Broadway shows and revues. BUDDY BRADLEY, a behind-the-scenes choreographer for many productions, taught Broadway stars at the Billy Pierce Dance Studio. The space provided inspiration to artists working outside of the performing arts as well. BEAUFORD DELANEY, for example, launched his painting career with a series of Degas-like sketches and portraits created there.

Pierce was noted for creating original routines, and he encouraged whole-body dancing. He perfected the "exchanging steps" and "milking applause" routines. He taught Norma Tarria, who "took the show" in *Show Boat*; wrote the "Sugar Foot Strut" for *Rio Rita*; and conceived "Moaning Low," the signature number by the famed dance team of Cliff Webb and Libby Holman. He was also a pioneer in the movement to send African American artists abroad, where their chances of achieving fame were greater than in the United States. In 1924 he trained and sent Tea for Two, the first African American group of dancing girls, to the Moulin Rouge in Paris.

In July 1927 Pierce staged the dances for *Half a Widow*, a musical. That same year he married Nona Stovall. They became the parents of two children, Billy Jr., born in 1928, and Denise, born in 1930. In 1930 Pierce spent eleven months working in Europe with the directors and producers Charles Cochran, Joseph Stern, and Max Reinhardt. He staged productions in London, Moscow, Rome, and Paris. Although rarely credited on theater programs, he was mentioned in newspaper articles, and autographed photographs of stars acknowledging his work covered the walls of his studio. He received full credit for the Broadway show *Walk a Little Faster*, which was staged in 1932.

Throughout his life Pierce retained a deep interest in civil rights. In 1931 he was active in rallying support among New Yorkers for the defense of the SCOTTSBORO BOYS, a group of young men who had been falsely accused of rape in Alabama. He was a founder and lifelong member of the Dennis Pierce Lodge No. 795, Northern Virginia Council, Order of Elks, which was named in honor of his father. A year before his death Pierce followed in his father's footsteps and was elected to the board of directors of the Loudoun County Emancipation Association, Inc., in Purcellville, Virginia.

Pierce's career was cut short by his untimely death due to complications from mastoiditis. After funeral services in New York City and Washington, D.C., Pierce, hailed as the master of dance, the maker of Broadway stars, and choreographer extraordinaire, was returned to his native Virginia for burial.

FURTHER READING

Carter, Elmer A. "He Smashed the Color Line: A Sketch of Billy Pierce," *Opportunity: A Journal of Negro Life* 8:5 (May 1930).

Cohen-Stratyner, Barbara N., ed. "Billy Pierce," in *Biographical Dictionary of Dance* (1982).

Hamilton, Kendra Y. *The Essence of a People II: African Americans Who Made Their World Anew in Loudoun County, Virginia, and Beyond* (2002).

Yenser, Thomas, ed. *Who's Who in Colored America* (1933).

Obituaries: *New York Times*, 12 Apr. 1933; *Washington Tribune*, 21 Apr. 1933.

ELAINE E. THOMPSON

Pierce, De De and Billie Pierce (18 Feb. 1904–23 Nov. 1973) and (8 June 1907–29 Sept. 1974), jazz musicians, were born, respectively, in New Orleans, Louisiana, and Marianna, Florida.

De De Pierce was born Joseph De Lacrois Pierce, the son of LaCroix Murine Pierce, a brickmason. His mother's name is unknown. His father, who had a well-established business, expected his son to follow in the masonry trade, but De De was attracted to music. A cousin gave him a trumpet, which he began to learn on his own, following by instruction from Kid Rena and Paul Chaligny, the leader of the Onward Brass Band. Before long, Pierce was being given work by the more established Rena and by Buddy Petit, and he was in demand for brass band jobs, dances, parties, Fair Grounds extravaganzas, jobs on advertising wagons, and appearances at Heinemann Park athletic events. He also worked at honky-tonks on the riverfront. In these early years he played with the Young Tuxedo Brass Band, the Olympia Brass Band, and the Happy Pals Brass Band, as well as with bands led by Rena and by Arnold DuPas. But because his father was opposed to his horn playing, he refused most out-of-town jobs.

Billie Pierce was born Wilhelmina Goodson, the daughter of Madison H. Goodson and Sarah Jenkins. She was the younger sister of the popular New Orleans pianist Sadie Goodson. Billie, who also played piano, went to New Orleans in 1929 to temporarily replace her sister. She settled there in 1930 and was soon leading a four-piece group at the Kingfish (also known as the Pig Pen). At the time, De De Pierce was playing trumpet with a band led by Billie's sister at Mama's and Papa's, a nearby club.

Stories vary about how the couple first met. Regardless of which anecdote may be accurate, De De and Billie briefly courted and were married in March 1935. The jazz clarinetist GEORGE LEWIS acted as best man. From that time on, the couple worked together, except when De De accepted an occasional brass band job and Billie played piano for several months at the Absinthe House with ARMAND JOHN PIRON. By then, De De was spending more time with his music and less time laying bricks. The Pierces worked at obscure dance halls and clubs, and they accompanied the blues singer IDA COX on a tour of the South, probably in the early and mid-1920s. Returning to Louisiana, they played for a while at the Club Playtime in Bunkie, and for some twenty years they performed off and on at Luthjens, a weekend dance hall called the "old folks' home" because of its elderly patrons.

In the early 1950s ill health plagued the couple. De De suffered from glaucoma, and Billie was struck by a debilitating stroke. When De De became blind, he was forced to give up bricklaying; Billie regained her strength, as she said, "to care for De De." Together, they revived themselves musically.

In the early 1960s Allen Jaffe (with the assistance of the jazz historian William Russell) opened Preservation Hall in the French Quarter of New Orleans. Although the Pierces were far from successful in the past, with Preservation Hall as a showcase and a steady stream of tourists as customers, their future success was assured. By the end of the decade their band was a Preservation Hall fixture. Over that span the band's varying personnel included such veteran jazz players as the clarinetists Lewis and Willie Humphrey, the trombonists JIM ROBINSON and Louis Nelson, and the bassist Chester Zardis. With the Pierces' singing featured, the group performed "Just a Closer Walk with Thee," "Bill Bailey," "When the Saints Go Marching In," De De's "Eh la Bas" and "Sallie Dame," and other staples. The *New York Times* jazz critic John S. Wilson described De De's singing as "husky." Other listeners referred to his voice as "gravelly" in the style of LOUIS ARMSTRONG. De De Pierce was the first recipient of the George Lewis Memorial Award for "courageously dealing with his handicap and continuing to contribute to jazz."

The Pierce band traveled extensively, touring Europe, Japan, and the Soviet Union as well as playing at colleges and jazz festivals in the United States. A novelty with younger audiences of the time, the group appeared at concerts with the Grateful Dead, Jefferson Airplane, and other rock performers. The Woody Allen film *Sleeper* (1973) featured the band on its soundtrack, and the Pierces, with their sidemen, recorded for the American Music, Atlantic, Riverside, and Preservation Hall labels. During the summer of 1973 more than twenty thousand listeners heard them at Stern Grove near San Francisco.

De De died in New Orleans. Four bands played traditional jazz and hymn tunes in the funeral procession of several thousand mourners. Within a year, Billie died in New Orleans.

FURTHER READING

Berry, Jason, Jonathan Foose, and Tad Jones. *Up from the Cradle of Jazz: New Orleans Music since World War II* (1992).

Carter, William. *Preservation Hall: Music from the Heart* (1991).

Obituaries: For De De Pierce: *New Orleans Times-Picayune*, 24 Nov. 1973; *New York Times*, 24 and 27 Nov. 1973; *Variety*, 28 Nov. 1973. For Billie Pierce: *New Orleans Times-Picayune*, 2 Oct. 1974.

This entry is taken from the *American National Biography* and is published here with the permission of the American Council of Learned Societies.

ANTOINETTE HANDY

Pierce, Elijah (5 Mar. 1892–7 May 1984), a self-taught folk artist, was born with a veil as the second youngest of nine children in Baldwyn, Mississippi, to the farmers Richard Pierce, a former slave, and Nellie Wallace Pierce. Among African Americans, a baby born with a veil, a thin membrane covering the child's head, is blessed with the ability to prophesy and is viewed as being chosen by God to be religious.

By the age of eight, Pierce was already carving. Having a favorite uncle who carved and getting some rudimentary knowledge of carpentry from growing up on a farm undoubtedly had a great deal to do with Pierce's avocation. By his teenage years, Pierce had already decided that he would not be a farmer. He laid track for the railroad but sought a trade that would give him independence. Accordingly, he apprenticed with a local

barber. On 26 September 1920, Pierce became an ordained preacher at the Mt. Zion Baptist Church in Baldwyn. He married Zetta Palm. When she died suddenly after a year of marriage, sometime in the 1920s, Pierce saw no reason to remain in Mississippi. He landed first in Champaign, Illinois, where he met his second wife, Cornelia Houeston, before eventually settling in Cornelia's hometown of Columbus, Ohio. He opened a barbershop in the black section of the city. Pierce married Cornelia on 8 September 1923, and the marriage lasted until her death in 1948.

Pierce's oldest surviving carving, *The Little Elephant*, is believed to date from the mid-1920s. He carved and painted between haircuts. Works from this early period exhibit the characteristic flatness that is clearly the mark of an artist learning how to translate flat drawings into three dimensions. This tentativeness did not last long. Pierce began to carve deeper and more confidently into the wood as heads, arms, and shoulders are stacked in front of and behind each other. At this point, Pierce discovered undercutting as a technique for making his figures float above a background. Pierce, like many other woodcarvers, saw wood as possessing personality. He once told an interviewer that most of his carvings came when he saw a picture in the wood or heard a sermon come from the wood. He usually prayed over a piece of wood for inspiration before he sunk his knife in it with a flaking knife stroke.

In the 1930s, Pierce began to combine cutouts and small reliefs into large assemblages. Some of these assemblages, including *Monday Morning Gossip* (1934), were mounted on paper and cardboard then framed as large wall pieces. Meanwhile, Pierce served as associate pastor at the Gay Tabernacle Baptist Church (formerly Gay Street Baptist Church). Often, after delivering a sermonette, he would conclude the service by surprising a member of the church with a recently completed woodcarving, frequently of a religious subject. In 1947 Pierce joined Master Lodge 62 of the Ancient Free and Accepted Masons. This black Masonic lodge would hold a large place in his heart.

As he gained confidence, Pierce began adding nuances and decorations to his art. His relief compositions became more active and complex, playing flat and round forms against each other. Pierce's work also became increasingly secular. He carved the biblical figures of Noah, Jonah, Samson, and Job, but he also portrayed notable African Americans such as the boxer JOE LOUIS, singer

MARIAN ANDERSON, and track star JESSE OWENS. Pierce's art began to draw from the comic strips and popular advertising of the 1930s and 1940s as well as illustrated Bibles and Sunday school books. As he would do for the remainder of his career, Pierce recycled visual elements of popular culture, making his works into an art of the familiar.

For reasons that remain unclear, Pierce stopped carving after the mid-1950s. Married to Estelle Greene in 1952, Pierce may have simply decided to focus more on his church and lodge. He picked up his knife again in the 1960s. Pierce's art works were discovered by the world of museums and collectors about 1970. By 1974 Pierce carved small animals and ambitious large panels as well as John F. Kennedy and MARTIN LUTHER KING JR. He used enamel paints after 1970 rather than the house paint that had sufficed for his earlier works. Other black artists, notably AMINAH BRENDA LYNN ROBINSON and Leroy Almon, came to Pierce for guidance and support. Pierce continued to carve until a few days before his death from a sudden illness.

FURTHER READING

Maciejunes, Nannett V. et al. *Elijah Pierce: Woodcarver* (1992).

Wertkin, Gerard C. et al. *Self-Taught Artists of the 20th Century* (1998).

CARYN E. NEUMANN

Pierce, Joseph Alphonso (10 Aug. 1902–18 Sept. 1969), mathematician and educator, was born in Waycross, Georgia, the son of William Arthur Pierce, a Methodist minister, and Fannie McGraw. Orphaned at an early age, Pierce was raised by his maternal uncle, Joseph McGraw, in Waycross. Following studies in sociology and business and participation in varsity football, Pierce in 1925 received a B.A. degree from Atlanta University. He accepted an assignment as assistant coach at Texas College in Tyler, Texas, but upon arrival he learned that he would also be required to teach mathematics. Four years of teaching mathematics proved so agreeable that Pierce adopted it as his profession. He returned to school at the University of Michigan to earn an M.S. in Mathematics in 1930, and he became professor of mathematics at Wiley College in Marshall, Texas. Pierce married Juanita George in 1933; they had one child.

In 1938 Pierce earned a Ph.D. in Mathematics at the University of Michigan with a dissertation on statistical sampling. In that work and subsequent publications, he generalized previous sampling theory for grouped data to show that a single formula could be applied to both finite and infinite populations, and he made contributions to the theory of time series analysis as well. Pierce was appointed professor of mathematics at Atlanta University in 1938; the following year he served as project supervisor for the National Youth Administration in Georgia while carrying his normal teaching load at the university.

Pierce was the research director for a massive study of black businesses and opportunities from 1944 to 1946. This cooperative effort, sponsored by the National Urban League and Atlanta University, was supported by twenty black universities and colleges throughout the South. Pierce published the results of this study in *Negro Business and Business Education* (1947). In his introduction to a 1995 reprinting of this book, John Butler identified Pierce as a prescient leader who foresaw the need for cooperation between the educational and business communities in an effort to create jobs and wealth for the black community. The concepts were not new, nor were they unique to the black community; however, Pierce saw that segregation and white attitudes about blacks in the 1940s created an opportunity for blacks to advance their own interests through the formation of small business communities dedicated to serving black needs. Pierce linked blacks' opportunity to do so to their ability to acquire necessary theoretical and practical skills, thus connecting business education to the success of business enterprise. The principles outlined in *Negro Business and Business Education* remained applicable years later, providing a model for similar analyses of immigrant communities. Butler argues strongly for the historical as well as the theoretical importance of *Negro Business and Business Education* and positions it in the continuum of leading information on that topic that had its origin around the turn of the century in the work of W. E. B. DuBois.

Pierce was active in promoting solidarity among black scientists as a member of the National Institute of Science, serving as its president in 1947–1948. He remained active in numerous other professional and fraternal organizations throughout his life. He was elected to membership in Sigma Xi and Beta Kappa Chi honorary organizations.

In 1948 Pierce returned to Texas as professor and chairman of the mathematics department at Texas State College for Negroes, which was reorganized as Texas Southern University (TSU) in 1951. Pierce accepted added responsibility as chairman of the division of natural physical sciences in 1950 and was named dean of graduate studies in 1952. He continued teaching mathematics in addition to these duties until 1963.

Admission to graduate programs had been denied to blacks at southern universities until 1948, when Texas State College for Negroes was granted authority to confer the master's degree. Thus there was a pent-up demand for graduate degrees, particularly in education, and when Pierce took over as dean of graduate studies, he faced burgeoning enrollment and faculty overloads. He was particularly effective in recruiting senior professors from nearby universities to assist with this demand for graduate faculty. Master's degrees conferred by TSU rose dramatically, from 95 in 1948 to a peak of 304 in 1955. In the first 10 years of Pierce's tenure as dean, TSU conferred a total of 2,287 master's degrees and 3,663 bachelor's degrees. In 1963, when the Manned Spacecraft Center was established near Houston, Pierce and B. A. Turner, TSU dean of technology, were released from teaching duties for eighteen months to recruit minority engineers for the National Aeronautics and Space Administration (NASA).

Although his health was poor and he was planning retirement, in 1966 Pierce was appointed interim president and later president of TSU. The decade of the 1960s was a period of intense unrest among blacks and on college campuses, and the one academic year in which Pierce served as president was marred by that general turmoil. After retiring from TSU in 1967, Pierce served as a consultant to NASA. Two years after his retirement, however, he died in San Antonio, Texas.

As a hardworking and effective administrator, Pierce served his institutions and his community well over a long career. His greatest love, however, was working with students as a teacher. A patient, careful listener, he counseled and cajoled his students to work, as he did, to the limits of their abilities. Pierce was committed to the concept that blacks are no less able than any other race to learn mathematics, and it was in teaching them to be successful mathematicians that he found his greatest satisfaction. Although his assumption of the role of university president was the fulfillment of a life's dream, it came too late in life and at a time of campus turmoil as well as diminished personal capacity, leaving him with less than complete satisfaction as he retired. Pierce will be remembered for his advocacy of black mathematical skills by the many students who benefited from his wise counsel as well as by all who study the relationship between business success and business education in minority communities.

FURTHER READING

The Robert W. Woodruff Library, Special Collections Department, at Atlanta University Center has a collection of Pierce's papers related to the studies of black business.

Sammons, Vivian Ovelton. *Blacks in Science and Medicine* (1990).

Troup, Cornelius V. *Distinguished Negro Georgians* (1962).

This entry is taken from the *American National Biography* and is published here with the permission of the American Council of Learned Societies.

THOMAS R. WILLIAMS

Pierce, Ponchitta (5 Aug. 1942–), journalist, television host, producer, writer, and editor, was born Ponchitta Marie Ann Vincent Pierce in Chicago, Illinois, the daughter of Alfred Leonard Pierce, a plasterer and contractor, and Nora Vincent Pierce, a teacher. She was educated through elementary school in New Orleans. From her mother Pierce inherited "a desire to reach out to people and work to improve the life of others" (Smith, 526). Her father imparted to her a "healthy dose of realism in terms of how to conduct a business" (Smith, 526). Through four years of schooling in a Catholic all-girl high school in Los Angeles, California, Pierce fell in love with books and writing. As a University of Southern California student, Pierce wrote for the student newspaper. She also spent a summer of studying at England's Cambridge University in 1962. She received a B.A. degree cum laude in Journalism from the University of Southern California in 1964.

In the same year, Pierce received a letter of invitation from the John Johnson Publishing Company to work as an assistant editor for *Ebony* and *Jet* magazines. In the following year, she was promoted to associate editor of *Ebony*. Two years later, Pierce became New York editor for *Ebony* and New York bureau chief for Johnson Publishing Company. Pierce was a contributing editor at *McCall's* magazine from 1971 to 1977. From 1976 until 1981, she wrote for *Reader's Digest*.

Modern Maturity, *Family Circle*, *Newsday*, and *Ladies Home Journal* are some of the national publications to which Pierce contributed. Her subjects have covered various topics, including politics, social issues, health, and finance. One of the Pierce's articles, "Leading in a Constantly Changing World," was published in *The Leader of the Future 2: Vision, Strategies, and Practices for The New Era* (2006). In this article, Pierce discussed the serious challenges of the day, including "natural disasters, the rising tide of globalization, the constant threat of terrorism, and nuclear war" and concluded that in a "constantly changing world we need strong, secure men and women…leaders, who are able to provide world peace, economic progress, and social development" (114). In another article, "We're Not Going to Be Afraid" (*Parade*, Nov. 1993), Pierce described the involvement of U.S. citizens in the prevention of crime by joining police forces, forming neighborhood watches, and videotaping criminals. In "How Would You Raise a Brilliant Child" (*Parade*, Apr. 1997), Pierce concluded that gifted children should be allowed to enjoy their childhoods and talents. They need to be loved as individuals. Another article by Pierce, "Blazing New Paths in Corporate America" (*Ebony*, July 1997), described the goals of Kenneth Chenault, president and chief operating officer of American Express.

Pierce met, interviewed, and wrote about a wide range of people throughout her career. In 2004, some of Pierce's interviews appeared in Juan Williams's *My Soul Looks Back in Wonder: Voices of the Civil Rights Movement*. The book is a compilation of memories from diverse groups of people who believed that the struggle for equality and civil rights must continue. In the introduction of his book, Williams writes that Pierce "performed a critical job of getting the right people to talk" (xiii). In addition to the racial divide, Pierce concerned herself with political and social issues such as terrorism, the rise of the Taliban, the loss of the art of writing in the Internet age, and heath care reform.

In addition to writing and editing for magazines, Pierce served as a television correspondent, host, reporter, interviewer, producer, and moderator. In 1968, she was a special correspondent for CBS News. She also served as a reporter and interviewer for CBS *Morning News* and *Evening News*, respectively. In 1973 she was on the staff of WNBC television in New York and co-hosted *The Sunday Morning Show* on New York's channel four, WNBC. From 1982 to 1987, she hosted and co-produced NBC TV's *Today in New York*. Cathleen Schine, writer and journalist, described her as an amazing host for *Today in New York* and a great "white-gloved killer interviewer" (*Vogue*, Apr.1986). Pierce also hosted for New York WNET programs, channel 13.

Pierce received a number of awards throughout her life. In 1967, she was the recipient of the Penney Missouri Magazine One Thousand Dollar Award for her article "The Mission of Marian Wright," which was published in the June 1966 issue of *Ebony*. The award was to "honor excellence in woman's interest journalism in a national magazine" (*Ebony*, Nov. 1967). She also received the New York Urban League's John Russwurm Award for excellent interpretation, analysis, and reporting of the news as well as the Headliner Award for "outstanding work in the field of broadcasting" by the National Theta Sigma Phi Sorority. In 1974, the American-Italian Women of Achievement (AMITA) Award honored Pierce for "distinguished achievement in the field of communications arts." Later, she received two more awards from the National Women's Political Caucus—an Exceptional Merit Media Award, for her position as an NBC-TV host, and the American Women in Radio and Television Commendation Award.

Pierce took part in a number of professional associations and nonprofit organizations, including the board of directors of the Foreign Policy Association (New York, NY), the International Women's Forum (Washington, D.C.), and the Inner-City Scholarship Fund of Catholic Archdioceses of New York (Smith, 526). In addition she was a member of several associations, such as the American Federation of Television and Radio Artists, the Council on Foreign Relations, and Columbia Presbyterian Health Sciences Advisory. She also served on the board of the directors of the Xavier University in New Orleans.

Of her contribution to *My Soul Looks Back in Wonder: Voices of the Civil Rights Movement*, Pierce wrote: "It was an inspiration to capture the voice of those who challenged this nation to overcome racism.…Their optimism and commitment obligates the rest of us to continue the fight for a color blind America" (xiii).

FURTHER READING

Pierce, Ponchitta. "Blazing New Paths in Corporate America," *Ebony* (July 1997).

Pierce, Ponchitta. "We're Not Going to Be Afraid," *Parade* (Nov. 1993).

Hesselbein, Frances, and Marshall Goldsmith, eds. *The Leader of the Future 2: Vision, Strategies, and Practices for New Era* (2006).

Schine, Cathleen. "Thinking Heads Charlie Rose and Ponchitta Pierce: Under Cover of Night, TV Gets Smart," *Vogue* (Apr. 1986).

Smith, Jessica Carney. "Ponchitta Pierce," in *Notable Black American Women* (1992).

Williams, Juan. *My Soul Looks Back in Wonder: Voices of the Civil Rights Movement* (2004).

FIROUZEH DIANAT

Pierce, Samuel (8 Sept. 1922–2 Nov. 2000), lawyer and politician, was born Samuel Riley Pierce, Jr. in Glen Cove, New York, to businessman Samuel Riley and Hattie Eleanor Pierce. The oldest of three boys, Pierce was influenced by his father's belief in the values of Republicanism as the party of Abraham Lincoln, Reconstruction, and a commitment to civil rights. A star athlete, Pierce earned a football scholarship to Cornell University, graduating with honors in 1947. Pierce's time at Cornell was briefly interrupted by a three-year military stint during World War II, where he earned the rank of First Lieutenant and was the only black member of the Army's criminal investigation division. Upon his return, Pierce married his childhood friend Barbara Penn Wright, a physician, and had one daughter, Victoria. Pierce continued his studies at Cornell, graduating from the School of Law in 1949; he also earned a LLM from New York Law School in 1952, and conducted post-graduate work as a Ford Foundation Fellow at the Yale University School of Law in 1957. His substantial training and interest in legal education would help him to become one of the most prominent African American lawyers of the twentieth century.

Pierce's life was marked by a dedication to black equality and a desire to excel in the legal field. In 1949, after graduating from law school, Pierce worked briefly as a New York public defender before serving as Assistant United States Attorney for the Southern District of New York in 1953. Pierce made a smooth transition into politics in 1955 when he was appointed the first black Assistant Under Secretary of Labor under the Eisenhower Administration. His political ascent was enhanced by his work on Kenneth Keating's 1958 Senate campaign, where he served as campaign treasurer. Impressed by Pierce's commitment to black uplift, Republican Party officials often asked his advice on issues of minority concern. Governor Nelson Rockefeller was so taken by this insight that he appointed Pierce to fill vacancies on the New York County's Court of General Sessions in 1959 and 1960. Although Pierce attempted to win long-term appointments to the court, he was unsuccessful, a fact he attributed to the strong Democratic leanings of New York voters.

Undeterred, Pierce continued to balance his political ambitions with his private work, becoming the first African American to be named partner at the major New York firm Battle, Fowler, Stokes, & Kheel in 1961. Pierce's partnership was especially significant given the racial climate of New York; he had joined the firm in 1957 after being racially discriminated against at other major New York law firms. Pierce's experience with inequality motivated him to use his legal skills to fight for equality, and in 1961, he successfully defended civil rights leader Dr. MARTIN LUTHER KING JR. and the *New York Times* in front of the United States Supreme Court, over the course of a three-year period. *New York Times Co. v. Sullivan*—a case that pitted King and the *New York Times* against racist Alabama officials—played a pivotal role in the civil rights revolution, defending freedom of speech and activity. Pierce's involvement in the case also reinforced his interest in positive African American initiatives, and he dedicated much energy to helping minorities advance in the business world. In 1964, Pierce and other prominent black businessmen (including baseball star JACKIE ROBINSON), founded Freedom National Bank, the first black owned and operated bank in New York. In the same year, Pierce became first African American to sit on the board of a Fortune 500 company, when he was appointed to the U.S. Industries board. These events of the 1960s pushed Pierce into the national spotlight and cemented his role as one of the nation's most powerful black lawyers.

Pierce's prestige was still of interest to the Republican Party, and in 1968, after serving on the Committee of Black Americans for [Richard] Nixon–[Spiro] Agnew, he was offered a position as director of the Civil Service Commission. Pierce declined, but in 1970 accepted the sub-cabinet post of head general counsel for the Department of the Treasury—yet another African American "first." Pierce worked in government until 1973 when he returned to his old law firm—Battle, Fowler, Stokes, Pierce, & Kheel—revamped to include his name in the masthead. In 1980, Republican President Ronald Reagan approached Pierce about a new opportunity, nominating him for Secretary of Housing and Urban Development (HUD) in December. The black community received Pierce's nomination with mixed emotions. While the nomination was historic and made Pierce the highest-ranking (and only) African American in Reagan's Cabinet, most were distrustful of the conservative Republican initiatives. Pierce himself questioned the nomination, wondering if he was better suited for a labor or treasury position. Nonetheless, Pierce immediately jumped into his role by promoting business-oriented initiatives. During his eight-year tenure at HUD, Pierce generated a number of minority initiatives including lobbying the Reagan Administration for a Voting Rights Act extension and awarding over two million dollars in financial aid to minority groups and colleges in 1983.

Continuing to promote his beliefs in self-advancement, and hoping to inspire future generations, Pierce told 1986 Baruch College graduating class, "For each of you, whatever your background, your race your faith or your ethnic heritage, the road with the sign marked 'Tomorrow' is wide open."

However, Pierce's tenure was controversial and earned him the nickname "Silent Sam," due to his quiet demeanor—even Reagan was guilty of not recognizing Pierce, mistakenly addressing Pierce as "Mr. Mayor" during a June 1981 luncheon. Many also attributed the nickname to Pierce's acceptance of the administration's economic policies—severely reduced, HUD annual spending on housing programs dropped from $26 billion to $8 billion between 1980 and 1984. Privately, Pierce disagreed with many of the cuts and considered quitting in 1984.

His decision to remain at HUD until 1989 proved disastrous, as criminal accusations of government mismanagement erupted in 1990, and subsequently tarnished Pierce's legal and civic reputation. Although he was never charged, investigators found that under Pierce's leadership, millions of dollars in federal money was given to Republican consultants throughout the 1980s. The corruption made national headlines, further enraging the public when it was disclosed that the corruption occurred while HUD was severely reducing its budget. By the conclusion of the five-year investigation, most of Pierce's aides had been convicted of felony charges. Pierce lamented his own wrongdoing in 1995, stating, "My own conduct failed to set the proper standard." Pierce never fully recovered from the public embarrassment and scandal, and retreated to private life. He died on 2 November 2000 in Washington, D.C., after suffering a stroke. Despite the turmoil toward the end of his career, Samuel Pierce's life was remarkable for its commitment to black uplift and civic engagement.

FURTHER READING

Schaller, Michael. "Prophets (Profits) of De-Regulation," in Michael Schaller. *Reckoning with Reagan: America and its President in the 1980s* (1992).
"Samuel Pierce." *Current Biography Magazine* pp. 318–322 (1982).
"Samuel R. Pierce Speeches, 1981–1987," *Archives* (The National Press Club Washington, D.C.).
Obituary: *New York Times*, 3 Nov. 2000.

LEAH M. WRIGHT

Pigee, Vera Mae (2 Sept. 1924–18 Aug. 2007), beautician and civil rights activist, was born Vera Mae Berry in Leflore County, near Glendora, Mississippi, the home of her maternal great grandmother. She was the daughter of Wilder Berry, a barber and tailor, and Lucy Wright Berry. Her father walked away from his livelihood and his young family, leaving her mother to raise Vera and her brother, W. C., in Tutwiler, Tallahatchie County.

Lucy Berry's influence left its mark on her daughter. With only an eighth-grade education, she raised livestock and a garden while also working in the fields and as a domestic, so her children never felt the hunger of poverty, unlike the sharecroppers around them in the Delta. As an adult, Vera Pigee remembered her mother's resistance to white racism, a tenacious and dangerous stance in the Mississippi Delta during the years of Jim Crow. Her good work and diligence made her a valuable employee who further instructed her children to become active churchgoers.

Raised in a religious and hardworking household, fourteen-year-old Vera Berry took her mother's lessons with her when she left her childhood home to marry eighteen-year-old Paul Pigee, who worked at a grocery store in Glendora, helping to support his mother and seven siblings. A day before her sixteenth birthday, a daughter, Mary Jane, was born. The Pigees' marriage remained strong, withstanding the loss of their second child in infancy, and the increasingly physical and economic pressures as Pigee's civil rights activism drew the attention of white supremacists. They made plans together for their life, setting out concrete goals that included homeownership, careers, and sending Mary Jane to college. They were successful on all counts. When Pigee was twenty years old, the family moved into their first home. Pigee studied cosmetology at an integrated beauty school in Chicago, returning to Clarksdale, the seat of Coahoma County, to manage Pigee's Beauty Salon in the early 1950s and later sending Mary Jane to study music in Ohio.

Before she left for Chicago, Pigee began her NAACP career. Following the 1951 unpunished rape of two young black women in Clarksdale, a small group in the black community, including AARON HENRY, who remained a prominent and vocal civil rights activist in Mississippi until his death in 1997, established a local NAACP branch by September 1953. Pigee returned to Clarksdale in the fall of 1955. In her absence, white racists in the Delta had reacted to the passage of the Supreme Court decision, *Brown v. Board of Education* with the foundation of the White Citizens' Councils in nearby Indianola. The local NAACP started to collect affidavits and testimonies of black citizens who had suffered economic pressure or physical violence at the hands of those seeking to dissuade any activity to desegregate the state school system. Under this cloud, Roy Bryant and J. W. Milam murdered the fourteen-year-old Chicagoan EMMETT TILL while he visited Money, Mississippi. Pigee quickly took part in supporting the NAACP's attempt to find witnesses, meeting the Detroit congressman Charles Diggs, who attended the trial.

That fall, Pigee was elected secretary of the Clarksdale branch, and she attended her first NAACP Mississippi State Conference in Jackson. There she accepted the role as a Youth Council State Advisor, admitting that the Clarksdale branch had yet to establish a Youth Council. In the midst of the violence in the Delta that suppressed the activities of the NAACP in the late 1950s, Pigee persistently campaigned to enlarge the Youth Councils, traveling around the state dispensing advice to chapters regarding campaigns and activities. Her hard work paid off. In October 1959, the national NAACP chartered Clarksdale's Youth Council with thirty-one members, Mary Jane Pigee serving as vice president.

During the early 1960s Pigee's Youth Council became the most active in the state. While the Student Nonviolent Coordinating Committee (SNCC) attracted members in other states, the Youth Councils had provided the only safe outlet for youthful black activist energy in the Delta, despite claims by other organizations, including SNCC, that the NAACP's tactics were too accommodating and slow for the pressing struggles. Pigee played a huge role in preparing local youth for non-violent protest. She mediated between youthful wishes to employ direct action and the national NAACP office's reluctance. In the spring of 1960 members of the Youth Council engaged in direct action to test the local waters. As she said, "We kept the youth busy" (Interview, 12 Oct. 2001).

Pigee put her own body on the line. For example, in fall 1961 she and another branch officer walked into the Greyhound Bus Terminal's white entrance, booked a ticket, and stopped to quench their thirst at the drinking fountain before departing. Black citizens regularly continued this nonviolent defiance so that by Christmas, the segregation signs duly disappeared from both the bus and train terminals. On 7 December 1961 she and eight other local leaders, including Aaron Henry, were arrested in Clarksdale for conspiring to organize a boycott of downtown business after the Chamber of Commerce refused the participation of two black school bands in the annual Christmas parade. She said to the arresting officer, "I am *Mrs.* Vera Pigee, a wife, mother, political prisoner, business and professional woman. Wherever I go, even if I am brought in handcuffs, my name is still *Mrs.* Vera Pigee" (Pigee, 55). Unafraid, she responded to a probable verbal insult on the part of the officer, insisting on the use of her full titled name, as one of the NAACP campaigns to change racial attitudes and practices. On 23 April 1963 a gas station attendant physically attacked her, yet she was charged with assault when she struck back in self-defense. Later, on the night of 8 June, her home, which often housed visiting civil rights leaders, was shot into by unknown assailants, narrowly missing the sleeping couple inside. No arrests were ever made. Throughout her tribulations, her faith strengthened her fearlessness.

Aside from her responsibilities as secretary of the local NAACP, Pigee assumed roles in the Council of Federated Organizations, the umbrella organization for the major civil rights groups in the state. With David Dennis, she co-chaired the Emergency Welfare and Relief Committee at the end of 1961, dedicated to collecting money and goods to aid those suffering economic reprisals for their efforts to attain equal rights. Always in the center of civil rights activity in Clarksdale, Pigee's position as a self-employed beautician meant she could take risks others could not. Recognizing her ability to organize, the activist SEPTIMA CLARK came to Clarksdale in 1961 to seek Pigee to participate in training programs in Dorchester, Georgia, and at the Highlander Folk School in Tennessee. As a result, citizenship schools began after-hours in the salon. Through her trade during the day, she could disseminate information rapidly and effectively, as she reiterated, "I think freedom and talk freedom with my customers" (Pigee, "God Has Always Had a Time"). The building stood in the heart of black Clarksdale with a degree of protection, despite the intermittent searches and harassment by local police.

Pigee continued organizing the youth councils and directing voter registration drives into the late 1960s, until she fulfilled her desire to finish school. Leaving Clarksdale, she spent more and more time in Detroit, Michigan, where she completed her degree in Journalism and Sociology at Wayne State University. Her family permanently moved by the mid-1970s. Writing her autobiography, *Struggle of Struggles*, she recorded her personal story for prosperity. It was self-published in 1975 and speaks to her strong self-awareness and the recognition of competing and overbearing voices in the retelling of civil rights history. Indeed much of her book acknowledges the deep rifts that undercut between and within civil rights organizations, both locally and nationally. Indeed, much of Pigee's contribution to the civil rights movement has been left out of subsequent narratives and remembrances, despite her indispensable role at the local level. Her story mirrors that of many women in the civil rights movement who worked close to home and away from the media spotlight, but whose labors ensured the success of local campaigns and struggles.

FURTHER READING

Quotes from interview with author, 12 October 2001. Another oral history is housed at Ralphe Bunch Oral History Collection, Howard University, Washington, D.C.

Pigee, Vera Mae. *Struggle of Struggles: Part One* and *Part Two* (1975).

Hamlin, Françoise N. " 'The Book Hasn't Closed, the Story Isn't Finished': Continuing Histories of the Civil Rights Movement" (PhD diss., Yale University, 2004).

Hamlin, Françoise N. "Vera Mae Pigee (1925–): Mothering the Movement." *Proteus: A Journal of Ideas* 22:1 (Spring 2005).

FRANÇOISE N. HAMLIN

Pigfoot Mary. *See* Dean, Lillian Harris "Pig Foot Mary."

Pigmeat. *See* Markham, Dewey "Pigmeat."

Pinchback, P. B. S. (10 May 1837–21 Dec. 1921), politician, editor, and entrepreneur, was born Pinckney Benton Stewart Pinchback in Macon, Georgia, the son of William Pinchback, a Mississippi plantation owner, and Eliza Stewart, a former slave of mixed

P. B. S. Pinchback, Union army officer, politician, and attorney, became the first African American governor in the United States and the only African American to hold a governorship during Reconstruction. (Library of Congress/Brady-Handy Photograph Collection.)

ancestry. Because William Pinchback had taken Eliza to Philadelphia, Pennsylvania, to obtain her emancipation, Pinckney was free upon birth.

In 1847 young Pinckney and his older brother Napoleon Pinchback were sent to Cincinnati to be educated. When his father died the following year, Eliza and the rest of the children fled Georgia to escape the possibility of reenslavement and joined Pinckney and Napoleon in Cincinnati. Because the family was denied any share of William Pinchback's estate, they soon found themselves in financial straits. To help support his family, Pinckney worked as a cabin boy on canal boats in Ohio and later as a steward on several Mississippi riverboats. In 1860 he married Nina Emily Hawthorne. Four of their six children survived infancy.

When the Civil War started, Pinchback made his way back to the South. In May 1862 he jumped ship at Yazoo City, Mississippi, and managed to reach New Orleans, already in Union hands. There he enlisted in a white Union regiment as a private, but within a few months he was assigned to recruit black soldiers. He rose in rank to captain in the Second Louisiana Native Guards, later renamed the Seventy-fourth U.S. Colored Infantry. In September 1863 Pinchback resigned from the army, citing discriminatory treatment by white officers and voicing opposition to the army's practice of better compensating white soldiers. He reentered the army as a recruiter when General Nathaniel P. Banks, commander of the New Orleans Union forces, decided to expand the participation of African American troops in the defense of New Orleans. When Banks refused Pinchback a commission as captain, he resigned again.

Pinchback's advocacy of African American rights started during the Civil War. As early as November 1863 he spoke in New Orleans at a rally for political rights, asserting that if black Americans were not allowed to vote, they should not be drafted into the Union army. He then spent two years in Alabama speaking out publicly in support of African American education. On his return to Louisiana in 1867, he became involved in state politics. He was elected to the constitutional convention of 1868, where he worked to create a state-supported public school system and wrote the provision guaranteeing racial equality in public transportation and licensed businesses.

In 1868 Pinchback was elected to the Louisiana state senate and, as a delegate, attended the Republican National Convention in Chicago. In 1871 he became president pro tempore of the senate and, because of this position, advanced to lieutenant governor upon the death of the incumbent OSCAR J. DUNN late that year. Pinchback clashed politically with Governor Henry C. Warmoth, a carpetbagger who had previously vetoed a civil rights bill that Pinchback sponsored. When Warmoth was impeached in 1872, Pinchback served briefly as acting governor, from 9 December 1872 to 13 January 1873. He was the only African American to hold a governorship during Reconstruction.

Although Pinchback, a Republican, was an important figure in state politics, he was unable to hold any other major political office. Earlier in 1872 radicals in the state's Republican Party had sought to nominate him for governor, but he declined the nomination in the interest of preserving party unity. As a reward for his withdrawal, he was nominated for the position of U.S. congressman at large,

and he apparently won the election. While the outcome was being contested by the Democrats, during Pinchback's tenure as acting governor, he was also elected by the state legislature to the U.S. Senate, again drawing protests from the Democrats. Eventually their allegations that Pinchback was guilty of bribery and election irregularities led to his being denied both the seat in the U.S. House of Representatives and the one in the Senate. This was not Pinchback's first brush with corruption. In 1870, when he was serving as a state senator, he acted on inside information to purchase a tract of land that he quickly sold to the city of New Orleans for a tidy profit.

In 1877 Pinchback left the Republican Party to support the newly elected Democratic governor, F. T. Nicholls. In return, Governor Nicholls appointed him to the state board of education. In 1879 Pinchback served as a delegate to the state constitutional convention, where he drafted a plan to create Southern University. He was a trustee of that school in the 1880s.

Pinchback was active in the New Orleans business community while he was engaged in politics. He was a co-owner of the city's *Louisianian* newspaper, which not only gave Pinchback a forum to articulate his political views but also helped shape the political and social opinions of the local African American community. In addition, he operated a brokerage and commission house and from 1882 to 1886 was surveyor of customs for the port of New Orleans.

In 1887 Pinchback entered Straight University Law School and passed the state bar exam. After working as a U.S. marshal in New York City in the early to mid-1890s, he practiced law in Washington, D.C., and became part of the city's black elite, entertaining often. He continued to profit from worthwhile business ventures as part owner of a cotton mill and sole owner of the Mississippi River Packet Company. His political activities shifted to support of BOOKER T. WASHINGTON, after whose death, however, Pinchback's clout was sapped. Pinchback died in Washington, D.C.

FURTHER READING

Collections of Pinchback's papers are in the Moorland-Spingarn Research Center at Howard University and the Howard-Tilton Memorial Library at Tulane University. Also worth consulting is the correspondence between Pinchback and Booker T. Washington in the Booker T. Washington Papers at the Library of Congress.

Haskins, James. *Pinckney Benton Stewart Pinchback* (1973).

Ingham, John N., and Lynne B. Feldman. *African American Business Leaders* (1994).

Simmons, W. J. *Men of Mark: Eminent, Progressive and Rising* (1887).

Obituaries: New Orleans *Times-Picayune* and *Washington Post*, 22 Dec. 1921; *Baltimore Afro-American*, 30 Dec. 1921.

This entry is taken from the *American National Biography* and is published here with the permission of the American Council of Learned Societies.

ERIC R. JACKSON

Pinckney, William (27 Apr. 1915–21 July 1976), World War II Navy Cross honoree, was born in Dale, South Carolina, to Renty and Jenny Pinckney. His father was a carpenter working on shrimp boats in the Beaufort area; his mother died when he was young. William Pinckney was subsequently raised by his older sister Ethel, and attended school through the seventh grade. Times were rough during the Depression, so Pinckney followed in his father's footsteps, working as a carpenter on the Beaufort waterfront, and became a partner in his own business. However, the navy beckoned with the offer of free housing, food, and a steady paycheck. William Pinckney joined the U.S. Navy on 6 July 1938 at Raleigh, North Carolina, and was sent to the Unit K West training camp for African American recruits at Norfolk, Virginia.

Growing up in the segregated South, Pinckney likely had no delusions about the place of African Americans in the navy hierarchy. Indeed, black men occupied the lowest position in the navy's pecking order at this time. They were strictly limited to service in the Steward's Branch and their sole job was to serve the officer corps as mess attendants. Duty for men such as Pinckney, LEONARD ROY HARMON, and DORIE MILLER included keeping the officer's staterooms clean and tidy, helping to prepare and serve their meals, and a number of other personal chores that were often disagreeable. Trained in segregated facilities, and seldom viewed as real sailors by their officers or white crewman, the men of the Steward's Branch nonetheless would soon prove their effectiveness as fighting men in World War II.

William Pinckney completed his training at Norfolk on 13 October 1938 and was subsequently assigned to Bomber Squadron 6 aboard the aircraft carrier *Enterprise* (CV-6) on 8 November 1938. He would remain on the *Enterprise* for the next four and a half years, serving in the Caribbean before the carrier was ordered to the Pacific in April 1939. Stationed first at San Diego, and then Pearl Harbor, Pinckney and his ship were en route to Hawaii from Wake Island when the Japanese attacked Pearl Harbor. Following the United States' entry into World War II, William Pinckney would continue to serve on the *Enterprise*, taking part in the Battle of Midway and the epic battles off Guadalcanal. Even though Pinckney had a young woman named Henrietta waiting to marry him back home, he was committed to serving his country. When his first four-year term of enlistment expired on 23 June 1942, he immediately reenlisted.

By late 1942 William Pinckney and the men of *Enterprise* were battle-tested veterans. However, they would be tested yet again during the Battle of Santa Cruz. It was during this battle that William Pinckney would demonstrate the extraordinary capability of America's fighting mess attendants. The battle began when the carriers *Enterprise* and *Hornet* were stationed off the Santa Cruz Islands in order to provide protection for American troops fighting on Guadalcanal. The men of the *Enterprise* struck first when her scout planes spotted formidable enemy navy forces, and scrambled fighters to attack the Japanese carrier *Zuiho*. However, the Japanese carrier planes struck back with a vengeance, sinking *Hornet* after two air strikes.

Enterprise too would feel the brunt of the Japanese attack. When battle was imminent and the call to General Quarters sounded, William Pinckney was assigned to an ammunition handling room deep below the main deck. This General Quarters station was a traditional one for African Americans. Here, it was the job of Pinckney and his fellow mess attendants to sling the heavy shells and powder onto the hoists that would carry them above to the gun-tubs working to defend the carrier. Not only was it physically demanding work but it could also be deadly; if the ship were struck and in danger of sinking, the mess attendants deep inside the ship would be amongst those least likely to survive. On the morning of 26 October 1942 the *Enterprise* was attacked by forty-three Japanese bombers and the ship took three bomb hits that killed seventy-four men and wounded ninety-five. One of the hardest hit areas was that where William Pinckney was stationed. Four men around him were killed when a five-inch shell exploded and knocked Pinckney unconscious. When he came to, the area was afire and filled with smoke. While attempting to escape, he came across a shipmate, James Bagwell, who was too weak to escape. Without regard for his own safety, the smaller but sturdy Pinckney threw Bagwell over his shoulder and worked to save him. Encountering loose electrical lines while climbing upward, Pinckney was again knocked down unconscious. Upon regaining consciousness yet again, Pinckney grabbed Bagwell once more and carried him upward to the hangar deck and safety. Despite burns on his hands, back, and leg, William Pinckney returned below to see if he could save any of his other shipmates. Sadly, all left below were dead, and Pinckney returned topside, collapsing with third degree burns over much of his body. For his heroics that day William Pinckney, on 6 February 1943, was awarded the Navy Cross, the navy's second-highest award for bravery. He was one of only three African Americans to be accorded this honor during the war, and the only one that would survive to fight another day.

Following this achievement, William Pinckney recovered from his wounds and continued aboard the *Enterprise* for eight months before being sent stateside. He married his fiancée, Henrietta, months later on 6 November 1943 and remained with her for the rest of his life. At war's end, Pinckney's service was over and he left the navy on 25 June 1946. However, he was not yet done with being a sailor. He and his wife moved to Brooklyn, New York, and here Pinckney joined the merchant marine, serving on several ships for some years as a cook. Upon retiring, he and Henrietta moved back to Beaufort, South Carolina, where he died of cancer. Quiet and modest to the end, William Pinckney is perhaps the least well known of those African American sailors who earned decorations in World War II. However, it was by his actions, and those of his fellow mess attendants—part of the broader struggle for black equality—that African American in the navy would eventually gain true acceptance and equality. The navy, too, has recognized the achievements of William Pinckney; in 2004 a guided missile destroyer, USS *Pinckney* (DDG-91), was commissioned in his honor.

FURTHER READING

Information regarding Pinckney's military service stations and specific assignment dates are taken from his official military records at the National Personnel Records Center in St. Louis, Missouri, and were obtained under the Freedom of Information Act.

Knoblock, Glenn A. *Forgotten Sacrifice: African American Casualties in the Navy, Coast Guard, and Merchant Marine in World War II* (2008).
Miller, Richard E. *The Messman Chronicles; African Americans in the United States Navy 1932–1943* (2004).
Stafford, Edward P. *The Big E: The Story of the USS Enterprise in World War II* (1962).
United States Navy. William Pinckney's Biography. Available at http://www.pinckney.navy.mil (2004).
GLENN ALLEN KNOBLOCK

Pindell, Howardena (14 May 1943–), artist, curator, art historian, filmmaker, writer, and activist, was born in Philadelphia, Pennsylvania, the only child of Howard Pindell and Mildred, both educators. By the age of eight Pindell already aspired to be an artist, and she attended Saturday drawing classes at the Fleischer Art Memorial.

Pindell graduated cum laude with a BFA from Boston University and earned an MFA from Yale University's School of Art and Architecture in 1967. She moved to New York City in 1967, after graduating from Yale, and she worked primarily as a painter of nonobjective and figurative works during the early years of her career. That year she landed a job at the Museum of Modern Art (MoMA) as an exhibition assistant in the department of national and international circulating exhibitions. At MoMA she rose through the ranks from curatorial assistant to associate curator in the Department of Prints and Illustrated Books by the time she left the institution in 1979—a major achievement for a woman of color trying to establish herself in the exclusive and exclusionary New York art world.

During the winter of 1979, Pindell was involved in a serious car accident and suffered temporary memory loss. It was at this point that she turned away from figuration, and her work took conceptual, autobiographical turns. According to the critic Halima Taha, Pindell "began to assemble small dots of paper pasted onto paper or canvas, creating subtly textured and delicate images that attached her to other movements of the period, including Process art and Conceptual art." While recovering in the summer of 1980, Pindell made the bitingly satirical film *Free, White, and 21*, in which she performed in a blonde wig, sunglasses, and white pancake makeup to expose and attack white skin privilege and racism in the United States. That same year she wrote the article "Art World Racism: A Documentation" to address the institutional racism in major New

York museums and galleries; she presented it as a lecture at the Agencies of Survival Conference in New York City in June 1987. In the article she explained that she had "experienced all of its paradoxes and double-speak perspectives about issues of 'quality.'" Pindell's study highlighted the paucity of artists of color participating in mainstream exhibitions and cultural events.

In 1979 Pindell became an associate professor in the Art Department at the State University of New York (SUNY) at Stony Brook, where she later became a full professor as well as director of the MFA program. She began teaching in the summer of 1980 as a visiting artist faculty member at the renowned Skowhegan School of Painting and Sculpture in Maine. Subsequently she was a visiting professor at Yale University's School of Art.

Pindell's works are in both public and private collections and in museums and galleries throughout the United States and Europe, such as the Metropolitan Museum of Art, the MoMA, the Schomburg Center for Research in Black Culture, Zurich Kunsthalle (Zurich, Switzerland), the Afro-American Museum (Los Angeles), and the Chase Bank Collection (New York and Tokyo). Continuing with her social activism, she presented a conference paper at the Johannesburg Biennale in Johannesburg, South Africa, in October 1997 that argued for the equal representation and presence of artists of color in a "postcolonial world." That same year Pindell's book, *The Heart of the Question: The Writings and Paintings of Howardena Pindell*, was published.

Pindell received honorary doctorates from the Massachusetts College of Art (1997), the New School for Social Research, and Parsons School of Design (1999). Her awards included the Stony Brook University Service Award for Twenty-five Years of Service (2005), the Anonymous Was a Woman grant (2006), and the Pen and Brush Organization and Brandywine Workshop Van Der Zee Artist Award in Printmaking. In February 2007 the Louisiana Art and Science Museum mounted her exhibition Howardena Pindell: Hidden Histories.

FURTHER READING
Pindell, Howardena. *The Heart of the Question: The Writings and Paintings of Howardena Pindell* (1997).
Taha, Halima, *Collecting African American Art: Works on Paper and Canvas* (2000).

C. M. WINSTON

Pinn, Petra Fitzalieu (9 Feb. 1881–21 Feb. 1958), nursing administrator, was born in Zanesville, Ohio, the daughter of William H. Pinn and Lizzie Hicks. She attended the John Andrews Memorial School of Nursing at Tuskegee Institute in Alabama and graduated on 24 May 1906. She later organized an alumni association, of which she served as president for many years. She returned to Tuskegee every April to participate in the Free Clinic, a community health fair. After graduation Pinn went to Montgomery, Alabama, as head nurse of the Hale Infirmary; she remained in this position for three years.

In 1908 Pinn joined the National Association of Colored Graduate Nurses (NACGN), newly organized by MARTHA FRANKLIN to eradicate segregation and the discriminatory practices against black nurses, who faced differences in pay, lack of respect, and exclusion from local, state, and national nursing organizations. The new organization published its meeting and member activities in the *Journal of the National Medical Association*, the publication of the black physicians' association, which was supportive of the NACGN.

On 1 June 1909 Pinn became superintendent of nurses and matron of the Red Cross Sanitarium and Nurse Training School in Louisville, Kentucky, a position that combined administration and teaching. In April 1911 she left to work as a private-duty nurse for two years. She left nursing briefly and may have married around 1913, since a 1913 NACGN report refers to "Mrs. Petra Pinn Walker"; after 1913 she was known as Petra Pinn.

On 1 August 1915 Pinn returned to nursing as relief nurse for the District Nurses Association in Louisville, Kentucky. The NACGN noted, "Miss Petra Pinn is making good as the only colored visiting nurse on the white staff in Louisville" (*Journal of the National Medical Association* 7, no. 4 [1915]: 327). This position, however, was short-lived, and on 24 February 1916 Pinn went to La Grange, Georgia, where she worked as a private-duty nurse.

In March 1916 Pinn was called to Palm Beach, Florida, to help open a hospital. She had written to John Kenny, medical director at Tuskegee Hospital, of her interest in returning to hospital work, and Kenny facilitated this appointment.

Pinn did most of the work at the Pine Ridge Hospital. Built with funding from philanthropists in the North, this small hospital served a racially diverse patient population during an era in which segregation was the national norm. Most patients suffered from tuberculosis and other contagious diseases. Pinn made many friends who supported the hospital as she sought contributions. She remained in this position for ten years, after which she resigned to rest for one year.

Pinn declined many offers from larger hospitals in various parts of the United States in order to continue her work in small southern hospitals. In 1927 she accepted an eighteen-month appointment as manager of a small Miami hospital. In 1929 she became manager and superintendent of the Working Benevolent Society Hospital in Greenville, South Carolina. Over the years she maintained and opened hospitals in Alabama, Florida, Kentucky, South Carolina, and Virginia.

In 1919 Pinn was elected corresponding secretary of the NACGN. She worked closely with the other officers of the association, among them MARY ELIZA MAHONEY, America's first trained black nurse and national chaplain of the NACGN, and its president, ADAH BELLE SAMUELS THOMS, who had fought to have black nurses accepted into the American Red Cross.

In April 1920 Pinn attended the American Nurses Association (ANA) biennial convention in Atlanta, Georgia. She reported to the NACGN that, although some ANA members were prejudiced against black nurses, this attitude was not universal.

At the 1923 NACGN convention in Chicago, Pinn, a charter member and consistent supporter, was elected president. Her 1924 presidential address focused on the importance of establishing a national headquarters to coordinate the activities of the organization. During her presidency the annual conventions were well attended and the membership grew. Pinn was elected treasurer of the NACGN in 1929 and served in that position until 1946. In 1936 the national headquarters was established in New York City, housed in the office of the National Health Circle for Colored People.

Pinn moved to New York City, in part to support the NACGN effort, and worked at Seaview Hospital in Staten Island. She also helped to establish a national registry to secure jobs for black nurses. A reflection of the NACGN motto, "Not for ourselves but for humanity," Pinn was continuously involved in community service.

In 1939 the NACGN awarded Pinn the Mary Mahoney Medal, given to a nurse who made significant contributions to intergroup relations. Fiorello La Guardia, mayor of New York City, also gave Pinn an award for meritorious service.

In 1946 Pinn retired and returned to Wilberforce, Ohio, to live with her sister. Her legacy of nursing leadership and providing access to health care for the black population continued to flourish. The Nurses Club of Dayton, Ohio, was named in her honor. Pinn suffered a stroke and died in Wilberforce.

FURTHER READING

Carnegie, Mary Elizabeth. *The Path We Tread: Blacks in Nursing, 1854–1994*, 3d ed. (1995).

Staupers, Mabel K. *No Time for Prejudice: A Story of the Integration of Negroes in Nursing in the United States* (1961).

Thoms, Adah B. *Pathfinders: A History of the Progress of Colored Graduate Nurses* (1929; repr. 1985).

Obituary: *Xenia (Ohio) Daily Gazette*, 21 Feb. 1958.

This entry is taken from the *American National Biography* and is published here with the permission of the American Council of Learned Societies.

ALTHEA T. DAVIS

Pinn, Robert (1 Mar. 1843–5 Jan. 1911), Civil War soldier and Medal of Honor recipient, was born in Stark County, Ohio. His father was a native of Virginia, while his mother was from Pennsylvania. Federal Census records of 1870 classify Robert Pinn as a "Mulatto," an indicator that one of his parents was probably white, or perhaps that he was fair in complexion. Little is known about Pinn's early life, but he was most likely raised in Massillon, Canton, or the surrounding area in Stark County. The early years of the Civil War found Pinn a resident of Massilon, Ohio, making a living as a farmer. At the age of twenty, on 15 September 1863, Pinn set aside his farming tools and traveled the eighty-odd miles westward to the town of Delaware to enlist in the 127th Ohio Regiment, the state's first regiment of black soldiers raised to fight in the Civil War.

Little prior thought had been given in the state to enlisting an all-black regiment to help fill Ohio's quota of men for the Union army, though earlier precedents had been set; well known in historical lore was the regiment of black troops, the 1st Rhode Island Regiment, raised in a similar time of need during the American Revolution. In Ohio itself, a precedent of sorts had been set in Cincinnati in the fall of 1862, when the city was threatened by a Confederate Force led by General Henry Heth. In response to a possible siege, civilian militia groups were formed, though the city's blacks were excluded from joining. However, when in early September

Robert Pinn, c. 1900. (Library of Congress/Daniel Murray Collection.)

battle seemed imminent, hundreds of Cincinnati's African American citizens were forcibly conscripted and employed in constructing fortifications around the city for several weeks. Though sometimes ill-treated by early commanders, this group of men, referred to as the Black Brigade, later came under Federal control and may have been the first formally organized black military unit raised by a Northern state in the war.

Perhaps an even greater impetus for the establishment of a black regiment in Ohio was the example set by Massachusetts; in February 1863 the state became the first in the North to enlist blacks as soldiers when it formed the Fifty-fourth Massachusetts Regiment. Many free blacks from other states flocked to Massachusetts to serve in the Fifty-fourth Massachusetts, including many from Ohio. Faced with the prospects of even more Ohio fighting men, blacks though they were, enlisting in the regiments of (and being credited to the quotas for) other states, Governor David Tod authorized the formation of an all-black unit, the 127th Ohio

Regiment, in August 1863. Command of the newly formed regiment was offered to Oberlin college graduate Giles Shurtleff, an ardent abolitionist, but he passed on the opportunity; captured in fighting earlier in the war, he was simply too worn out to assume full command. He did, however, accept a subordinate role as lieutenant colonel, and assumed the task of training the men of the 127th Ohio at Camp Delaware. Blacks from all over the state, as well as neighboring Pennsylvania, soon arrived to enlist as word of the regiment's formation spread; Pinn came from Massillon, while others came from more distant locales. No matter what their origin, all were eager to join the fight against slavery. That ideal, indeed, was what the Civil War had evolved into—a fight to end slavery. Though Governor Tod was known as the "soldier's friend" and worked tirelessly to raise Ohio regiments for the Union army, his reluctance to accept this ideal, perhaps manifested in the state's tardiness to raise a black regiment, would later cost him the governorship.

Once Robert Pinn and his fellow soldiers arrived at Camp Delaware, they were formed into companies and began their training as privates. Those who showed exceptional ability, men who commanded the respect of their peers, were selected to serve as sergeants in their company within a month. Among these men was Robert Pinn, the six-foot-tall farmer turned soldier, chosen as sergeant in Company I, as well as MILTON HOLLAND. Fully trained and equipped, now re-designated as the Fifth U.S. Colored Troop (USCT) Regiment, Pinn and his fellow soldiers headed for the war on 18 November 1863. At first, the regiment saw little action as it was shuffled between duty in North Carolina and Virginia. The boredom was somewhat relieved in late May 1864 when the Fifth USCT was assigned to Major General Benjamin Butler's Army of the James and was assigned to the trenches opposite Richmond. The regiment had its true baptism under fire when it played a supporting role in the epic Battle of the Crater following the mine explosion at Petersburg Heights on 15 June 1864 and suffered a number of casualties. With the stalemate and trench warfare continuing around Richmond, Union General Ulysses S. Grant decided to make his move to capture the key city in late September 1864. Devising a multi-pronged assault above and below the James River to capture four key forts, Butler and the USCT regiments were assigned the difficult task of assaulting the Confederate works at New Market Heights south of the city. After a short but poignant speech by their new commanding officer, Col. Giles Shurtleff, the men of the Fifth awaited their orders and began the assault on New Market Heights in the early morning hours of 29 September 1864. The fire that day from Confederate troops well-entrenched at Fort Harrison was deadly and mowed down a large number of the Fifth's company and regimental officers, Shurtleff included. However the regiment never faltered and continued the assault, led by sergeants Robert Pinn, JAMES BRONSON, POWHATAN BEATY, and Milton Holland, and captured their objective, achieving the only real success in the two-day battle. In an incredible display of courage and leadership, "these gallant colored soldiers were left in command" and led their companies "gallantly and meritoriously through the day" (*The War of the Rebellion*, 168). The sergeants of the Fifth USCT were not the only black soldiers to thrive under fire at New Market Heights; men from other USCT regiments, including JAMES DANIEL GARDNER, EDWARD RATCLIFF, MILES JAMES, SAMUEL GILCHRIST, and WILLIAM BARNES, were also noted for their heroism that day. Robert Pinn, promoted to first sergeant just weeks before the battle, saw additional fighting in the battle and was later wounded at Fort Gilmer in an unsuccessful attempt to capture that fort.

The fighting at New Market finally and forever earned the black troops of the Union army the respect as fighting men that that they well deserved and had so dearly paid for with their own blood; before the war was over, 178,000 such soldiers would serve the Union cause. The gallantry of Robert Pinn and his fellow sergeants in the Fifth USCT at New Market was such that they directly inspired General Butler to commission a special medal for the men of the USCT, later known as Butler's Medal. More importantly, of the eighteen black army Medal of Honor winners in the Civil War, sixteen achieved this distinction at New Market Heights.

Following this epic battle, resulting in 5,000 casualties for the Union, a wounded Robert Pinn was confined to a hospital bed at Portsmouth, Virginia, and was subsequently mustered out of the service with the rest of his regiment in North Carolina on 20 September 1865. Pinn returned to Massillon, Ohio, where he would live the remainder of his life. He soon attended Oberlin College, likely influenced by his old regimental commander turned professor at Oberlin, Giles Shurtleff. Graduating with a law degree, Robert Pinn returned to Massillon and resided there with his wife, Emily, working as an attorney. Upon his death in 1911 he was buried with full honors at the Massillon City Cemetery.

FURTHER READING

Medal of Honor Citation. "Civil War Medal of Honor Recipients—Robert Pinn." Available at http://www.army.mil/CMH_pg/mohciv2.htm.

Mercer, John. "Giles Waldo Shurtleff: Leadership in the Cause of Freedom." Available at http://www.oberlin.edu/external/EOG/ShurtleffBio-Mercer.htm

United States Government Printing Office. *The War of the Rebellion: A Compilation of the Official Records of the Union and Confederate Armies* (1893, volume 42, series I, part III).

GLENN ALLEN KNOBLOCK

Piper, Adrian Margaret Smith (20 Sept. 1948–), multimedia artist, philosopher, and educator, was born in Harlem, New York, the only child of Daniel Robert, a lawyer, and Olive Xavier Smith Piper, an administrator. Belonging to a light-skinned African American family, she was confronted early on by challenges that ultimately gave her work some of its unique characteristics, namely the firm assertion of her black identity, her unremitting fleshing out of racial stereotypes, and her commitment to cross-cultural bridge-building. Her involvement with the arts began in childhood: a piano prodigy and ballet dancer, she also took classes at the Museum of Modern Art in 1957. Her political consciousness was first shaped in the Student Nonviolent Coordinating Committee (SNCC), which she joined in 1962, and by the events surrounding the March on Washington in 1963, commemorated in her 1983 poster *Think about It*. She graduated from New Lincoln School in 1965 and worked as a freelance fashion model and discotheque dancer, keeping abreast of the avant-garde happenings, both in New York and worldwide.

In 1966 she entered the School of Visual Arts, and was also initiated into Indian philosophy. Influenced by the conceptual art movement (1966–1978) and, more specifically, Sol LeWitt, for whom the concept behind an artistic piece takes precedence over its finished form, Piper's artistic output began in earnest with the publication of some of her works in Vito Acconci's *0 to 9* magazine in 1968, and her subsequent participation in New York art shows, at venues such as the Paula Cooper Gallery and the Museum of Modern Art, as well as in various French, German, and Swiss art exhibitions. In 1970 she withdrew her piece *Hypothesis* from the "Conceptual Art and Conceptual Aspects" show at the New York Cultural Center, in protest against President Nixon's invasion of Cambodia and the Kent State massacre. Indeed, her art work began engaging racial, social and gender issues, while remaining attached to the tenets of conceptualism.

After graduating from the School of Visual Arts (1969) and City College of New York summa cum laude (1974), she moved on to Harvard University for her doctoral work in philosophy, which she completed in 1981. During this prolific period of her life, she inaugurated two series of performances: *Catalysis* (1970) in which she transformed into an odd passer-by and *Mythic Being* (1972–1981), an investigation of her male alter ego, were staged in public places as a strategy to elicit spontaneous responses from the unsuspecting crowd. *I Embody Everything You Most Hate and Fear* illustrates her work in that era. She also exhibited works at the Museum of Modern Art (1970) and at the Whitney Museum of American Art (1976). A Harvard Sheldon Traveling Fellowship, granted in 1977, enabled her to travel to Germany and further her studies in philosophy, in particular Immanuel Kant's meta-ethics. For Piper, Kant's propositions in *The Critique of Pure Reason*—that our experiences are filtered to fit our pre-existing categories, and that, consequently, we know of things only what we input into them—were essential in representing and interpreting contemporary race and gender dynamics. Art is then, according to Piper, the most potent remedy for xenophobia and political discrimination.

In 1979 Piper received an NEA Fellowship and was the recipient of a second in 1982, along with a Mellon Post-Doctoral Fellowship to do research in philosophy at Stanford University. She continued challenging aesthetic borders by incorporating new media in her work such as photographs, videos, maps, written texts, and herself at times (*It's Just Art*, 1981; *Cornered*, 1989). In 1982, she married Jeffrey Evans; they had no children and divorced in 1987. She also began a prodigious series of publications and a teaching career in philosophy that led her successively to Harvard, the University of Michigan (1979–1985), Georgetown (1986–1988), the University of California at San Diego (1988–1990), and Wellesley College (1990–). Piper's performance work, most notably *Funk Lessons* (1983–2003) and the *Calling Cards Series* (1986), represents another application of her concept of the "indexical present," a system of signs that apostrophizes viewers ("You," "here," and so forth) and urges them to question their biases about Otherness. In *Funk Lessons*, for instance, participants reflected on their preconceived notions on black popular culture while learning Funk dance steps. *My Calling (Card)*

Number 1, subtitled *Reactive Guerilla Performance for Dinners and Cocktail Parties*, was a business card designed to privately inform the author of a racist statement, at a social gathering, of the nature of his or her utterance: "Dear friend: I am black…. I regret any discomfort my presence is causing you just as I am sure you regret the discomfort your racism is causing me." *Calling (Card) Number 2* confronts misogynistic attitudes on the same principle. In 1986 Piper prepared another thought-provoking series entitled *The Vanilla Nightmares* that mimics subconscious racial obsessions hidden in the pages of the *New York Times*. A Guggenheim Fellowship in conceptual art crowned this decade of achievements in 1989.

In spite of physical exhaustion and a spine condition, Piper did not curtail her production in the 1990s. Among the new works she exhibited, *Decide Who You Are*, an image-text composition, served as a model for many of her later works. In 1995 she was awarded the Skowhegan Medal for Structural Installation and the Bessie Award for new genres in Dance Performance. In 1999 her third major retrospective, "Adrian Piper Since 1965," began touring with much acclaim, both in the United States and abroad. Meanwhile, her art criticism and discussions of her own work were compiled in the two volumes of *Out of Sight, Out of Order* (1996). She also reorganized a manuscript that became *Rationality and the Structure of Self*, volumes I and II, and she outlined two additional philosophical treatises. She continued probing identity politics, analyzing the conflicts within her own family, most notably with her essay "Passing for White, Passing for Black," first published in *Transition* in 1991 and reprinted in *Out of Sight, Out of Order*.

In the same decade, Piper's commitment to yoga increased. A lifelong student of Hindu philosophy, she embarked on teaching the Vedas and the philosophy of Yoga at Wellesley. Her *Color Wheel* series (2000) and videos such as *You/ Stop/Watch/ a Shiva Japam* and *Shiva Dances* (2002), brought together Kantian metaphysics and the Hindu notion that self-knowledge is attained by peeling away sensorial illusions that superimpose arbitrary qualities on to perceived objects. Thus in these pieces, Shiva, god of yoga dance and destroyer of illusions, occupies a prominent place.

Adrian Piper, the recipient of several major awards and grants in the humanities and in the arts, was immensely successful in both fields. Upon joining the faculty at Georgetown University, she became the first tenured African American woman professor of philosophy. Her multifaceted multimedia work was the object of several national and international retrospectives, numerous solo exhibits and countless pieces of criticism. Pinpointing Piper's location in the art theory landscape is, however, a complicated matter. As a conceptual artist, she focused, against the grain, on color and gender issues in a deliberate, incisive, yet humorous manner, and both locally and transnationally. Passionately attracted to abstractions, Piper explored, through art, broad metaphysical questions revolving around self-definition and perception of the Other, adding, at the turn of the new millennium, a spiritual dimension to her quest. Piper's work represents a pioneering contribution to the ongoing debate on hybridity, gender roles and aesthetic borders.

FURTHER READING

Berger, Maurice, ed. *Adrian Piper: A Retrospective, 1965–2000* (1999).

Smith, Cherise. "Re-member the Audience: Adrian Piper's Mythic Being Advertisements," *Art Journal* 66, 1 (Spring 2007).

SYLVIE KANDÉ

Piper, Rose (1917–11 May 2005), artist, illustrator, and textile designer, was born in the Bronx, New York. Her father was a public school teacher of Latin and Greek from Augusta, Georgia, while her mother was from Roanoke, Virginia. Piper was raised and spent most of her life in New York City. Her interest in painting began when she was in high school. Although she was offered a four-year scholarship to the Pratt Institute, a New York art school, in 1936 she instead enrolled in Hunter College with the intention of becoming a teacher. In 1940 she graduated, receiving a B.A. in Fine Arts, with a minor in geometry. From 1943 to 1946 she continued her art education at the Art Students League in New York City, where her most influential teachers were painters Yasuo Kuniyoshi and Vaclav Vytlacil.

Piper was awarded a fellowship from the Rosenwald Foundation in 1946, allowing her to travel throughout the American South and to study in Paris. The following year, she returned to New York and, after winning a second Rosenwald Fellowship, moved into a studio on West 11th Street, next to the White Horse Tavern in Greenwich Village. Here she prepared for her first solo exhibition, which opened in the fall of 1947 at Michael Freilich's Roko Gallery. This show, Blues and Negro Folk Songs, featured fourteen oil paintings on this musical theme, such as *Slow Down Freight Train* (1946). The abstracted planes of striking colors in this painting displayed a strong grounding in modern art, particularly synthetic cubism, but also recalled a geometric, expressionist realism employed by other artists interested in the black folk experience, such as CHARLES ALSTON and WILLIAM H. JOHNSON. The title of this work referred to Trixie Smith's 1924 recording of "Freight Train Blues." Before embarking on this series of paintings, Piper contacted STERLING BROWN, a professor at Howard University, who referred her to "race records," 1920s musical recordings whose target audience was black America. These lyrics of race records often addressed the Great Migration, providing rich material that inspired Piper's interpretations of African American experiences.

Also in 1947 she was the only woman to exhibit in a group show at the Roko Gallery that also included the work of Alston, Claude Clark, BEAUFORD DELANEY, Norman Lewis, and CHARLES WHITE. In 1948 Piper's painting *Grievin' Hearted* (1947) won $300, the highest prize from the Seventh Annual Exhibition of Contemporary Negro Art, a national competition sponsored by Atlanta University that attracted entries from many well-known artists, such as Alston, ROMARE BEARDEN, and JACOB LAWRENCE (who won second prize that year). During this time, Piper also exhibited at the ACA Gallery and the Jane Street Gallery. In the late 1940s Piper's painting career was interrupted by family and financial obligations. Caring for two children, elderly parents, and a disabled husband, she provided for a growing family by starting her own greeting card design business in 1949. Piper had studied with the illustrator Arthur Lidov in New York, and oversaw everything from design to writing and printing until 1953.

In 1952 Piper (then known as Rose Ransier; she worked under the name of her second husband, perhaps to distinguish her fine art career from that of her design career) began creating knit patterns in the garment business, which would become her occupation for the next twenty-eight years. Her first position was designing silks for Fred Levi Studios, and by the 1960s Piper was well known in the industry for her innovative designs. Because of her background in mathematics at Hunter College and her fine arts training, she was able to produce exact geometric drawings that were easily adaptable to the knitwear machines. As she later recalled, "When knit fabrics became high fashion in the early 1960s, I was the only designer who could design directly for the machines; others handed over sketches and seemed surprised when they were altered for production" (Kirkham, 130). During this period, her most popular designs sold more than two million yards each. Because of her enormous success in this field, Piper worked her way up from designer to managerial positions in various companies, eventually becoming a senior vice president in what had traditionally been a male-dominated industry.

After retiring from textile design in 1980, Piper returned to painting. As in her work from the 1940s, Piper's later paintings drew upon folk music and African American history and experiences; she also painted small-scale still lifes. Her technical experience as an illustrator and designer of minute patterns on graph paper inspired an interest in figural realism, as opposed to the abstracted forms of her earlier work.

Despite her early success during the 1940s, like many women artists Piper was obliged to make difficult choices that delayed her taking her rightful place in the history of American art until fairly late in her life. In the late twentieth and early twenty-first centuries her work came to be included in several public collections, including the Ackland Art Museum in North Carolina and the High Museum of Art in Atlanta, and her name began to appear in critical studies and textbooks on African American art as an important figure in the New York art scene of the 1940s. Finally, despite the inherent anonymity of textile production, Piper is now recognized as a noted designer and one of the few black women to achieve a highly respected place in the largely male world of the garment industry.

FURTHER READING

"The Annual Art Exhibit." *Atlanta University Bulletin* (July 1948).

Gibson, Ann Eden. *Abstract Expressionism and Other Politics* (1997).

King-Hammond, Lesley, ed. *Gumbo Ya-Ya: Anthology of Contemporary African-American Women Artists* (1995).

Kirkham, Pat, ed. *Women Designers in the USA, 1900–2000: Diversity and Difference* (2000).

Powell, Richard J. *Black Art in the 20th Century* (1997).

SARAH POWERS

Pippin, Horace (22 Feb. 1888–6 July 1946), painter, was born in West Chester, Pennsylvania, the son of Horace Pippin. On a biographical questionnaire Pippin listed his mother as Harriet Johnson Pippin, but Harriet may actually have been his grandmother; she was the mother of Christine, a domestic servant, who may have been Pippin's birth mother. When Pippin was quite young the family moved to Goshen, New York, so that his mother could find work, and it was there that Pippin attended a one-room school through the eighth grade. He showed an ability for and love of drawing while in school, but because he had to help support his family, he began a series of menial jobs at the age of fourteen. In 1905 he took a job as a porter in a hotel, and he worked there until his mother's death in 1911. He then moved to New Jersey, where he worked at a number of manual labor jobs in industry until April 1917, when the United States declared war on Germany. Pippin enlisted in the army in July 1917 and was trained at Camp Dix, New Jersey, achieving the rank of corporal before leaving basic training.

Pippin continued to sketch, but soon he was sent abroad to France, where he became a part of the famous 369th Infantry, an all-volunteer black regiment (except for the white officers) whose bravery was so extraordinary that the entire regiment was awarded the Croix de Guerre by the French government. In the fall of 1918 Pippin was shot in the right shoulder, and the bullet destroyed muscle, nerves, and bone. His arm hung uselessly from his side, and after five months in army hospitals he was discharged, returning emotionally and physically exhausted to his mother's relatives in West Chester.

Pippin was unable to make a living through physical labor and attempted to survive simply on his small soldier's pension. He met Jennie Ora Featherstone, a widow with a young son, and they were married in 1920. She took in laundry to help support him, but Pippin was psychologically devastated by his disability, and his memories of the war lingered. He found some relief in local American Legion meetings, and ultimately he began to make art again. He began with some decorated cigar boxes and then turned to burning his drawings into wooden panels. He strengthened his arm enough to draw and paint, and he began to create powerful images based on his memories of the war. Making art helped to heal him and gave him a sense of purpose. He soon expanded to oil paints, but because of his injury he rarely painted anything larger than 25 by 30 inches.

Pippin was an unschooled artist, called a "primitive" in the 1930s. However, he had a tremendous ability to relay a narrative using simple, flat forms that moved rhythmically and dramatically across the composition. His works are quite sophisticated in their constructions, even though Pippin stated quite emphatically that he simply painted what he saw. In spite of his talent, viewers of that time often connected his purity of vision with a certain naïveté and believed him to be only an instinctual artist, even linking that quality to the primitivism of Africa.

One of the most powerful images among his early works is *The End of the War: Starting Home* (1931), which depicts the grim reality of trench warfare. During this time painting was still an extremely slow process for Pippin, and his production was limited. As time went on he became more prolific, moving to images based on calendar art and then to portraits. He also turned to religious themes, images of African American life, interiors, and still life paintings.

In 1937 Pippin began to sell his paintings in local shops, and it was quite possibly in this way that the famous American illustrator N. C. Wyeth and the art critic Christian Brinton saw one of his important works, *Cabin in the Cotton I* (1935). Pippin's paintings may also have come to Brinton's attention through friends of the artist who alerted this connoisseur of new talent. *Cabin in the Cotton I* was the first of a series of paintings based on what the artist imagined was the African American's life in the South, and it was the first work to deal with the life of his people, a subject that would soon make up a large part of Pippin's oeuvre.

Brinton soon championed his new discovery and decided to hang two works by Pippin in the Chester County Art Association's Sixth Annual Exhibition, which attracted 2,550 people. Pippin's *Cabin in the Cotton I* captivated the public, encouraging Brinton to give his full support to his new "discovery," thus helping connect Pippin to several important figures in the New York art scene, including Holger Cahill, then acting director of the Museum of Modern Art and a tremendous supporter of American folk art. Cahill included Pippin's work in an important exhibition, Masters of Popular Painting—Artists of the People, at the Museum of Modern Art; Pippin was the only black artist to be included.

During this period ten of Pippin's paintings and seven burnt-wood panels were also exhibited at the West Chester Community Center, a focus of black cultural activity. Pippin's work also came to the attention of a Philadelphia dealer, Robert Carlen, and it was while the work was at Carlen's gallery that Dr. Albert C. Barnes saw it. Barnes, an important collector, was very early interested in art by African Americans, and he immediately purchased several works, as did his assistant, Violet de Mazia. Barnes wrote a new essay for Pippin's show with Carlen in which he commented on the artist's ability to tell a story simply and directly with his own language. Both Brinton and Barnes tried on several occasions to "educate" Pippin about modern art and painting, but, fortunately, Pippin ignored them both and continued on his own individual path. However, Carlen and Pippin formed an enduring business relationship. Pippin later exhibited with the New York gallery of Edith Halpert, while still exhibiting with Carlen in Philadelphia.

Pippin's African American heritage continued to offer subjects for the artist, ranging from images of Abraham Lincoln to portraits of the famous soprano MARIAN ANDERSON to scenes of everyday life. He created a series on the abolitionist John Brown, in addition to painting a number of images with religious themes, which reflected both his own devout nature and the importance of the church in black American life. Pippin was opposed to war and depicted the "peaceable kingdom" in a number of works titled *Holy Mountain*. He loved nature and continued to paint floral images as well as interiors remembered from his childhood. His originality attracted a wide audience, and his work became increasingly sophisticated over time, drawing admiration from a number of critics of modern art.

Unfortunately his last years, while financially secure, were personally unhappy. His stepson left to join the armed forces, and his wife was institutionalized because she suffered from emotional problems. Having grown more and more lonely, Pippin died in West Chester from a stroke in his sleep; his wife, who was confined to a state mental hospital, died two weeks later, never learning of her husband's death.

FURTHER READING
Bearden, Romare, and Harry Henderson. *A History of African-American Artists* (1993).
Stein, Judith E. *I Tell My Heart: The Art of Horace Pippin* (1993).
This entry is taken from the *American National Biography* and is published here with the permission of the American Council of Learned Societies.

J. SUSAN ISAACS

Piron, Armand John (16 Aug. 1888–17 Feb. 1943), jazz and popular violinist, composer, and bandleader, was born in New Orleans, Louisiana, the son of "Professor" Piron, a music teacher and band-leader. His mother's name is unknown. Armand broke his hip at age seven and was unable to walk for five years, during which time he studied violin. Sometime after 1900 he joined his father's dance orchestra. He became a member of the Bloom Philharmonic Orchestra in 1903 and the Peerless Orchestra around 1910.

Piron married in 1912, but the details are unknown. When the cornetist FREDDIE KEPPARD left for California in the spring of 1914, Piron took his place as leader of the Olympia Orchestra. Its members included CLARENCE WILLIAMS, with whom Piron formed a publishing company in 1915, when he wrote "I Wish I Could Shimmy like My Sister Kate." Piron also wrote "Brown Skin (Who You For)" in collaboration with Williams.

In 1918 Piron established a society dance band, the Piron Orchestra, to play at Tranchina's restaurant at Spanish Fort on Lake Pontchartrain. Its members included the cornetist Peter Bocage, with whom Piron composed "Mama Gone, Goodbye"; the clarinetists LORENZO TIO JR. and Louis Warnicke; the pianist Steve Lewis, with whom Piron composed "The Purple Rose of Cairo"; and the drummer Louis Cottrell.

Late in 1923 Piron brought the band to New York City for an engagement at the Cotton Club, and he made his first recordings, including "Bouncing Around," "New Orleans Wiggle," "Mama's Gone, Goodbye," and "Sud Bustin' Blues." After performing at the Roseland Ballroom early in 1924, the group returned to New Orleans to play at Tranchina's, until Piron dissolved the group in 1928. He led his Moonlight Serenaders on the SS *Pelican* and continued playing on river steamers for the remainder of his career. Suffering from a brain abscess and delirious, he nonetheless continued rehearsing his band nearly up to the time of his death in New Orleans.

Recollections of the decade when jazz emerged, probably from around 1905 or 1910 onward, occasionally include reports of New Orleans dance bands led by violinists, but Piron's orchestra was evidently the only one to survive for a further decade and to make recordings. For this reason it holds a special place, offering provocative insights into how an early blend of ragtime, jazz, and dance music might have sounded. According to the writer Edmond Souchon, the recordings made in New York "do not represent in the faintest, the real Piron greatness" (7), and indeed the leader sounds nearly incompetent on "Lou'siana

Swing" (recorded early in 1924), where he seems unable to follow the beat. Nonetheless, the musicologist Gunther Schuller characterizes the band's "vocal melodic style...[and] polyphonic ensemble conception...with its inflexible assignment of functional roles (and even register)," and its "flowing and unfrantic...country-style playing" as representing "fine examples of the politer branch of the New Orleans style as practiced by the 'society orchestras' in the twenties....They lack the extraordinary cohesiveness of Oliver's [KING OLIVER] best Chicago recordings, but retain a most important element: the joyous, relaxed feeling that was the essence of New Orleans playing" (255).

FURTHER READING
Schuller, Gunther. *Early Jazz: Its Roots and Musical Development* (1968).
Souchon, Edmond. "Armand J. Piron," *Second Line* 3 (Jan.–Feb. 1952).
This entry is taken from the *American National Biography* and is published here with the permission of the American Council of Learned Societies.

BARRY KERNFELD

Pittman, William Sidney (1875 14 Mar. 1958), architect, was born in Montgomery, Alabama, the son of Sarah Pittman, a laundress. The identity of his father is unknown. Raised by his widowed mother and educated in the black public schools of Montgomery, William enrolled in 1892 at Tuskegee Normal and Industrial Institute in Alabama, completing his studies in mechanical and architectural drawing in 1897. With financial support from Tuskegee's principal, BOOKER T. WASHINGTON, Pittman continued his education at Drexel Institute in Philadelphia, Pennsylvania, earning a diploma in architectural drawing in 1900. Returning to Tuskegee as an instructor, he assisted in the planning and measured drawing of several of the buildings on the campus.

In May 1905, dissatisfied with his faculty status and unable to get along with his supervisor, Pittman left Tuskegee for Washington, D.C., and began work as a draftsman in the office of architect John A. Lankford. Within a year he opened his own office of architecture in the capital. In November 1906 Pittman won the competition for the design of the Negro Building at the Jamestown (Virginia) Ter-Centennial Exposition. The exposition was partially supported by appropriations from the U.S. Congress, under the supervision of the secretary of the treasury. Pittman's contract to supervise construction of his design was the first U.S. government contract with a black architect. The Negro Building was a large (213 feet by 129 feet) exposition building of stuccoed wood, executed in Second Renaissance Revival style, with a large exhibition area on the first story and an auditorium on the second. Open for six months in 1907, the building was a significant success and launched the career of its architect.

In 1907 Pittman married Portia Marshall Washington, daughter of Booker T. Washington; she was a professional musician who had been educated in Europe and who taught music for much of her adult life. The Pittmans had three children. In the following years Pittman was commissioned to design several important buildings in Washington, D.C., including the Garfield School, built in 1909, and the Twelfth Street Young Men's Christian Association Building, begun in 1908 and completed in 1912. During the same period he designed institutional buildings in several southern states: at Kentucky State Normal School (later Kentucky State University) in Frankfort; at the National Religious Training School in Durham, North Carolina; and at the Colored State Normal School in Montgomery, Alabama. At the same time Pittman was greatly involved in the planning of Fairmount Heights, Maryland, a black community on the outskirts of Washington, D.C., where he designed his family's home, the town meeting hall, and the first elementary school. He was also active in the Washington chapter of the Negro Business League, serving as its president in 1908.

In 1912 Pittman received several commissions to design buildings in Texas, and at the end of the year he moved his family to Dallas, where he continued to design churches and institutional buildings, notably the Knights of Pythias Temple in 1912. His architectural career began to wane in the 1920s as blacks who could afford to contract with white architects increasingly did so. Embittered by this situation, Pittman began in 1931 to publish *Brotherhood Eyes*, a local tabloid that railed against the "evil doers within the race"—particularly the greed of some black pastors, and the employment of whites by some blacks who had earlier proclaimed their commitment to black civil rights. In later years Pittman supported himself by doing carpentry work.

Portia Pittman left her husband in 1928 and returned to Tuskegee; they were never divorced. Pittman died in near poverty in Dallas. He was buried in an unmarked grave in south Dallas by friends who operated a funeral home. In 1985, through the Dallas Historical Society and several architects and admirers of his work, a granite memorial stone was erected at his grave site.

The design and construction of the Negro Building at the Jamestown Exposition was the springboard for the architectural career of William Sidney Pittman. His career, though illustrious, was relatively brief. It was hampered by a combination of eccentricity, arrogance, and personal frustration that caused Booker T. Washington to point out (in a letter of 26 Aug. 1904) that Pittman had "strong points" but was "a curious and troublesome individual." He was, however, imaginative and industrious, and in the early years of his career, R. W. Thompson described him as "an idealist and a practical man of affairs—a dreamer,…a hard-headed pusher for results. Following not the beaten paths trodden by the masses, he has wooed fortune as an architect—a builder of everlasting temples. A self-made man…he has struggled upward through the morasses of poverty and prejudice, until today he stands at the head of his chosen profession" (*Washington Bee*, 12 Oct. 1907). Though for many years nearly forgotten, Pittman's work has been rediscovered and appreciated anew. Because of his talent, ambition, and industry, Pittman made a place for himself at the beginning of a field just opening to African Americans.

FURTHER READING

Davis, Daniel Webster. *The Industrial History of the Negro Race of the United States* (1908).
Kliment, Stephen A. *America's Black Architects and Builders* (2002).
Stewart, Ruth A. *Portia: The Life of Portia Washington Pittman, the Daughter of Booker T. Washington* (1977).
Wilson, Dreck Spurlock. *African-American Architects: A Biographical Dictionary, 1865–1945* (2004).
This entry is taken from the *American National Biography* and is published here with the permission of the American Council of Learned Societies.

SUSAN G. PEARL

Pitts, Riley Leroy (15 Oct. 1937–31 Oct. 1967), Vietnam War soldier and Medal of Honor recipient, was born in Fallis, Oklahoma, the son of Theodore and Dorothy (Rainger) Pitts. At a young age, the Pitts family moved to Oklahoma City, where Riley attended public schools. After graduating from

Douglas High School in Oklahoma City, Riley Pitts attended the University of Wichita (now Wichita State University) in Wichita, Kansas. He was encouraged to attend college there because he had relatives in Wichita, and lived with an aunt while attending school. During his four years at the University of Wichita, Pitts worked for the Boeing Company and also joined the Reserve Officer Training Corps (ROTC), committing to three years service in the army upon graduating. He also met his future wife, Eula Tolson, during his time in Wichita. Riley Pitts subsequently graduated with a degree in Political Science in 1960 and married his sweetheart in Yuma, Arizona, on 6 August 1960, shortly after joining the U.S. Army.

On 5 June 1960 Riley Pitts enlisted in the U.S. Army at Wichita, Kansas, and received a commission as an officer. Pitts future with the army was very bright. He was intelligent, multilingual, and had dreams of becoming a general, which few doubted he would achieve. His mother, Dorothy, later recalled that "he was always reaching for the sky," while his wife, Eula, recognized him as "a soldier through and through" (Murphy). After going through basic training at Fort Benning, Georgia, Pitts subsequently served at Fort Sill, Oklahoma, where his daughter Stacie was born (1961) and then for three years in Orléans, France, where his son Mark was born (1963). Riley Pitts subsequently received the orders sending him directly from France to Vietnam in late 1966. Both he and his wife thought the Vietnam War would soon be over. He left for Vietnam on 27 December 1966 and would not see his family again until the following September.

The fact that Riley Pitts had attained the rank of captain by 1966 clearly indicates that even at an early date he had the leadership skills to be a successful career officer. Indeed, the service of African American officers during the Vietnam War, men such as Riley Pitts, CHARLES ROGERS, JOHN WARREN, and RUPPERT SARGENT, was an important indicator that the army had entered a new era in terms of opportunities for black servicemen. While African Americans had served as junior officers in World War II and the Korean War, it was usually under restricted circumstances, often in segregated units with little or no chance for further promotion. However, by the time of the Vietnam War, the army had become fully integrated, and African American officers were an important part of the command structure, now promoted on the basis of their soldiering skills and leadership abilities, not held back by the color of their skin.

Once in Vietnam, Captain Riley Pitts first served as an information officer and was generally away from the scene of direct combat, though he was close enough to hear gunfire in the distance. However, he soon transferred to a combat unit and in less than eight months he had proven himself an excellent officer in combat, earning the Bronze Star and the Silver Star medals. On 31 October 1967 he was in command of Company C, 2nd Battalion, 27th Infantry, 25th "Tropic Lightning" Infantry Division during an airmobile assault at Ap Dong, Republic of Vietnam, when Viet Cong elements opened fire just after American forces landed. Captain Pitts led his company in an assault on the enemy position, and then went to the assistance of another company to the north. While moving forward, Pitts and his men endured heavy fire from three directions in the dense jungle terrain. When rifle fire proved ineffective, Pitts used a rocket-propelled grenade launcher, and also hurled a grenade at an enemy bunker. However, due to the heavy jungle, the grenade bounced back into Company C's position. Pitts quickly threw himself on the grenade to protect his men, but luckily it was defective and did not explode. Continuing to lead his men toward the enemy positions, killing at least one enemy soldier while advancing, Pitts kept up a heavy fire and continuously exposed himself to enemy fire until he was subsequently mortally wounded. His tour of duty in Vietnam nearly complete, Pitts had been scheduled to return home in just days, but it was not to be. One of his men, Roger Cates, would later say about Pitts "He truly cared for his men who he led into battle…on the battlefield he was a true warrior and fearless leader" (Cates).

Survived by his wife Eula, and two children, Riley Pitts was buried at Hillcrest Memory Gardens in Spencer, Oklahoma. He was posthumously awarded the Medal of Honor, the second of just four African American officers to earn the medal during the war, and the first black officer ever to receive the Medal of Honor up to that time. The medal, our nation's highest award for valor, was presented to his wife Eula, with her children Stacie and Mark by her side, by President Lyndon Johnson during a White House ceremony on 10 December 1968. A number of army facilities were later named in honor of Captain Pitts and the ultimate sacrifice he made, including Pitts Hall at the Headquarters, U.S. Theater Army Support Command, Europe, in Worms, Germany, and the Captain Riley L. Pitts Weapons Range at Fort Sill, Oklahoma. Riley Pitts also has a public park named after him in Oklahoma

City, and he was posthumously inducted into the Oklahoma Military Hall of Fame in 2000.

FURTHER READING

The author kindly acknowledges the help of Mrs. Eula Pitts, Captain Riley Pitts's widow, in the preparation of this article.

Cates, Roger B. "Riley Leroy Pitts-Charlie Co. 2/27th Inf Regiment." *The Virtual Wall.* Available at http://www.virtualwall.org/dp/PittsRL01a.htm.

Hanna, Charles W. *African American Recipients of the Medal of Honor* (2002).

Murphy, Lynette. "1997 Achievement Award-Profile in Courage." *Wichita State University Alumni News* 6, no. 1 (Jan.–Feb. 1998).

GLENN ALLEN KNOBLOCK

Planciancois, Anselmas (?–27 May 1863), soldier and regimental color bearer of the First Regiment of the Louisiana Native Guards, is a person about whom little early information is available. The date and location of Planciancois's birth is not known, but his infantry company was made up of individuals who were descended from free African Americans and Creoles living in New Orleans, Louisiana. According to postwar accounts, the spelling of Planciancois's first name could also be "Anselino."

One of the first African American regiments raised for service in the Civil War, the First Louisiana Native Guards was mustered into service on 27 September 1862. The entire regiment was native to Louisiana. Roughly 11 percent of the unit was made up of educated free African Americans of mixed Creole ancestry from New Orleans. Contrabands, slaves liberated by the Union occupation of New Orleans, and fugitive slaves made up of the rest of the infantry companies of the unit. Planciancois was a member of Company E of the First Regiment of the Native Guards. His company commander was ANDRE CAILLOUX, who was one of the leaders of the free community of African Americans within New Orleans. Cailloux was a cigar maker by profession and was fluent in both English and French.

Cailloux and other black officers recruited their fellow African Americans to fill out the non-commissioned ranks within their companies. As a result, Captain Cailloux selected Planciancois to serve as a sergeant with his infantry company in 1862. Within regiments serving during the American Civil War, one infantry company was selected to carry the regimental colors in combat.

This company, known as the Color Company, would be the best-drilled and best-led company within the regiment. In addition, the best sergeant or non-commissioned officer in that infantry company was selected to bear the colors in battle. Colonel Spencer Stafford presented the colors to Sergeant Planciancois, and told him to "protect, defend, die for, but do not surrender these flags." Color Sergeant Planciancois responded "Colonel, I will bring these colors to you with honor or report to God the reason why" (Glathaar, 128).

On 8 November 1862, Union Major General Nathaniel P. Banks took command of the U.S. Department of the Gulf, and received orders to prepare an advance up the Mississippi River. His orders were to open the Mississippi to Union control by advancing north from New Orleans. By December 1862 General Banks's Federal forces were in Baton Rouge, Louisiana, and preparing to move north to Port Hudson to cooperate with Major General Ulysses S. Grant's campaign against Vicksburg, Mississippi. General Banks's forces, which included the three regiments of Louisiana Native Guards, had completely surrounded the river port of Port Hudson by 25 May 1863. General Banks believed that his four-to-one advantage in manpower would ensure his rapid entry into Port Hudson, and he set the date of his massive assault for the 27 May 1863.

Color Sergeant Planciancois and the rest of the First Louisiana Native Guards were deployed north of Port Hudson next to the Mississippi River. They were deployed to guard the left of the Federal line, and General Banks had no plans to use them in the assault. At 5:30 A.M., Union artillery and naval shellfire rained down on the Confederate defenders with Port Hudson. At 6 A.M., 6,000 Union soldiers moved forward to attack the prepared earthworks surrounding the Confederate-held river town. In several hours, the massive Union assault was a complete failure. Assaulting columns suffered horrendous losses attempting to reach the Confederate works through swampy terrain and obstacles. To relieve the Federal units pinned down along the lines, Brigadier General William Dwight Jr. was ordered to send in the Native Guards to capture the Confederate works along Telegraph Road and draw attention from the other Federal units. Dwight was drunk on the morning of the 27th, and did not conduct a reconnaissance of the area in front of the Union lines. The Native Guards were to move across a pontoon bridge, and then charge through a low swampy field flanked with

Confederate works on a bluff and Confederate artillery positioned on a water battery in the Mississippi River.

After crossing the bridge, six companies of the First Native Guards formed the front rank, and nine companies of the Second Native Guards composed the second rank. As Color Company, Captain Cailloux and Color Sergeant Planciancois were positioned in the center of the formation. At 10 A.M., the Native Guards started for the Confederate works at a run. Immediately, Confederate infantry opened fire on their left flank, as artillery fire rained down from the water battery. Color Sergeant Planciancois was hit and killed instantly when a shell ripped his head in two. Two corporals attempted to remove the regimental colors from his hands, but his hands would not release the flagstaff. After one of the corporals was killed, the other corporal was able to free the flag. Captain Cailloux was killed leading his company forward to the works, after being wounded in the arm. After three attempts, the Native Guards were forced to retreat back to their defensive works. After the engagement, the Confederate forces did not allow the Federals to bury the dead from the charge. It was not until three days later that Confederate soldiers buried Planciancois's and Cailloux's bodies. Roughly 540 Native Guardsmen participated in the assault, and 373 were casualties by the end of the day on 27 May 1863.

After the American Civil War, the survivors of the three Louisiana Native Guards regiments gathered in New Orleans to start their own chapters of the Grand Army of the Republic (GAR), a National Union army veterans organization. One chapter was named for the gallant Captain Andre Cailloux, who died so close to the Confederate works at Post Hudson. Another post was named for Planciancois in honor of his bravery on 27 May 1863.

FURTHER READING

Cornish, Dudley T. *The Sable Arm: Negro Troops in the Union Army, 1861–1865* (1956).

Glathaar, Joseph T. *Forged in Battle: The Civil War Alliance of Black Soldiers and White Officers* (1998).

Hewitt, Lawrence L. *Port Hudson: Confederate Bastion on the Mississippi* (1987).

Hollandsworth, James G., Jr. *The Louisiana Native Guards: The Black Military Experience during the Civil War* (1995).

Williams, George W. *A History of the Negro Troops in the War of the Rebellion 1861–1865* (1880).

WILLIAM H. BROWN

Plato, Ann (1820–?), poet, biographer, and essayist, was a member of one of Hartford, Connecticut's noted African American families, and an active member of REV. JAMES W. C. PENNINGTON's Talcott Street Colored Congregational Church, where at thirteen she professed her faith in Christ. Plato began teaching at age fifteen in the Hartford area, and she devoted some of her poetry to the subject of teaching—topics included teacher training and examination, her end-of-the-school-year hope that students would retain knowledge gained through the year, and her class of very young children. Little is known of her life, but her poetry suggested that piety, morality, and spiritual devotion were central to her outlook.

Plato's *Essays; Including Biographies and Miscellaneous Pieces, in Prose and Poetry* (1841) was a self-published work containing sixteen essays, four biographies, and twenty poems. The Reverend Pennington, an abolitionist leader, cast the book as a pious text intended especially for young women, and he believed that it was promising in its articulation of religious ideas and that it was a demonstration of the author's growing literary talent. In his introduction to the book, Pennington wrote that "she is willing to be judged by the candid, and even to run the hazards of being dealt with by the critics, in order to accomplish something for the credit of her people." Although her poetry and prose may not readily suggest it, Plato believed she was able to contribute to the progress of her race. Her goal was to gain African American patronage through publication of *Essays* and thereby continue her literary work.

"Lessons from Nature," a five-page essay, set forth what seems to be Plato's sensibility about race and her egalitarian message. The story is told by a youngster who is led to knowledge of divine order among human populations by a much-admired older man, perhaps a pious grandfather. Together the youngster and the man review pastoral scenes of hatchlings with their mother, young students with their teacher, and mourning children with their grieving mother at an open grave. After observing these things, the older man draws a conclusion that feels inevitable in Plato's text: "We are all God's family, and he provides for all. Although there are many nations, and many stations in life, yet he watches over us, he has given us immortal souls. Some have white complexions, some are red, like our wandering natives, others have sable or olive complexions….'But God hath made of one blood all who dwell upon the face of the earth.'"

The tale normalizes racial and cultural difference while making it all a part of God's intentional creation. The elder articulates what the youngster has observed in nature. Nature speaks, in this short text, with a divine voice about human unity.

Plato's biographies (Louisa Seabury, Julia Ann Pell, Eliza Loomis Sherman, Elizabeth Low) highlight the lives of four pious women held in high regard by adults and religious leaders in their communities. It is intriguing that each of the four women died when they were quite young, under thirty-five years of age. Plato seems to have been struck by the notion that their youthful piety could not be sustained in a world that did not celebrate their devotion to the Sabbath. Concentration on the lives of the departed was a theme in her poetry as well. A number of her poems eulogize the lives of departed friends, and they touch on the pain of the open grave and the certainty of death. Particularly poignant is the poem "I Have No Brother." Probably recounting the actual loss of an only brother named Henry in his infancy, the poem speaks to her continuing and unresolved grief over his passing.

While Plato clearly identified herself with African Americans, her poem "The Natives of America" may suggest that she had identifiable American Indian ancestors whose stories were passed through generations. Plato's vision of her Indian past was pastoral; she imagined nonviolent, cooperative relations among Indian communities, and a culture in which trade, language, and habits of dress were fully adapted to the needs of the people. Christopher Columbus is a villain in the poem, bringing with him "cruel oppression" and wars. With dismay, the poem notes that the rich American Indian culture has been lost, and the people have been diminished and destroyed. The poem admonishes readers to recall the history of the natives of America. Scholars have likened Plato's poetry to Puritan poetry in its vocabulary and religious themes, but this poem particularly undermines that impression of her poetry, and it is perhaps the most strident of her texts in its discussion of history, identity, and the obligation of youth to "seal [their history] upon thy memory." While this poem marks cultural loss, it is political as few other of her poems seem to be, save "To the First of August," which is about the end of slavery in the British West Indies in 1838.

Ann Plato was born beyond the reach of slavery, and she apparently lived comfortably in Hartford's prosperous black middle-class community during a period when this type of life was rare among African Americans. Yet, she devoted herself to a life of piety, teaching, and literary arts. She is notable and rare among early to mid-nineteenth-century African American women for having had her work published.

FURTHER READING

Plato, Ann. *Essays; Including Biographies and Miscellaneous Pieces, in Prose and Poetry* (1988).

Bassard, Katherine Clay. *Spiritual Interrogations: Culture, Gender, and Community in Early African American Women's Writing* (1998).

Foster, Frances Smith. *Written by Herself: Literary Production by African American Women, 1746–1892* (1993).

Sherman, Joan R. *Invisible Poets: Afro-Americans of the Nineteenth Century* (1974).

MARTHA L. WHARTON

Player, Willa Beatrice (9 Aug. 1909–27 Aug. 2003), educator and college president, was born in Jackson, Mississippi, the youngest of three children born to Clarence Player, a plasterer and contractor, and Beatrice Day. Devout members of the Methodist faith, the Players involved Willa in Sunday school, the youth choir, and other church organizations. When the family relocated to Akron, Ohio, in 1916, she completed her elementary and high school education in the Akron public schools. After briefly attending Akron University, she followed her sister to Ohio Wesleyan University, in Delaware, Ohio, where she earned a B.A. in Latin and French in 1929. She was the first black student teacher in the Akron public schools in 1929. She received her M.A. in French from Oberlin College in Ohio in 1930. Awarded a Fulbright Fellowship in 1935, she continued her studies in French at the University of Grenoble, France, and was awarded the Certificat d'Etudes, a general degree usually issued at the end of primary schooling. Player furthered her graduate education at the University of Chicago and the University of Wisconsin-Madison, eventually earning a doctorate of education at Columbia University in New York City in 1948. As was often the case for well-educated blacks prior to school integration, Player's options for professional employment were largely limited to historically black institutions. In 1930 she was hired to teach Latin and French at Bennett College in Greensboro, North Carolina. Bennett College was founded in 1926 as a college for women by the board of education of the Methodist Episcopal Church and the Woman's Home Missionary Society. Player served the institution

Willa Beatrice Player, poet, novelist, and professor. (University of Massachusetts, Amherst.)

as professor, director of admissions, coordinator of instruction, and vice president, and from 1955 to 1966 she served as president of the college, becoming the first black woman president of a four-year women's college. Despite the fact that Player's work ethic and competence were well known to the Bennett College community, the board of trustees' decision to appoint her president was not without controversy in the surrounding community. When questioned about this precedent-setting decision, Player responded, "All I was thinking about was that I had a job to do" (Guy-Sheftall, 17).

In recognition of her contribution to the institution, Bennett College designated her president emerita and endowed a chair in the humanities in her honor in 1988. It was a fitting tribute; under her leadership, Bennett became one of the first historically black schools to be accredited by the Southern Association of Colleges and Schools.

Her contributions were not, however, confined to the campus. During the early days of the civil rights movement, Player organized a campus appearance by MARTIN LUTHER KING JR. in 1958. King's speech at Bennett contributed to making central North Carolina a focal point for the movement. In 1960 students at nearby North Carolina A&T State University organized a sit-in aimed at desegregating a downtown Greensboro Woolworth's lunch counter. Bennett students joined in the protest. Although not overtly urged on to this action by Player, it was well known that she supported student participation in nonviolent protests. When asked by city leaders to order the Bennett students back to campus, Player refused. It is estimated that as many as 40 percent of Bennett's students were jailed at various times during the civil rights movement. Player visited the students in jail and on protest picket lines. Because of her race, Player had been denied the opportunity to live in a campus dormitory while a student at Ohio Wesleyan University; she was not only well aware of the educative and civic value offered by participation in the movement but also of the power of education to change society.

After her retirement from Bennett College, Player became the director of the Division of Institutional Development for the Bureau of Postsecondary Education in Washington, D.C., a position she held until 1977. Under her leadership, federal support for historically black colleges and universities increased significantly under Title III, the Strengthening Developing Institutions program. Among the numerous awards and honors she received were the Superior Service Award and the Distinguished Service Award from the U.S. Department of Health, Education, and Welfare, in 1970 and 1972, respectively. In 1984 she was inducted into the Ohio Women's Hall of Fame. For many years she was affiliated with the United Negro College Fund and United Methodist Women. Player died in Greensboro, North Carolina, at the age of ninety-four.

While serving as the registrar at Bennett College, Player expressed her goal for women's education and commented on the role of women's colleges for black women: "Somewhere in her college experience [a black woman] must have an opportunity to develop poise, to increase her self-esteem and to establish a sense of her worth and dignity as an individual" (Player, "The Negro College and Women's Education," *Association of American Colleges Bulletin* 33.2 [May 1947]: 364–365). It was her firm belief that college-educated black women would be relied upon to provide leadership for the community. Player herself exemplified the expanding role of educated black women in the post-1945 period.

FURTHER READING

Information on Willa B. Player is included in the Bennett College Archives, Greensboro, North Carolina.

Guy-Sheftall, Beverly. "A Conversation with Willa B. Player," *SAGE: A Scholarly Journal on Black Women* 1 (Spring 1984).

Hood, Stafford. *Legislative Intent, Program Implementation, and Higher Education Policy: The Case of Title III of the 1965 Higher Education Act.* Ph.D. diss., University of Illinois, Urbana, Illinois (1984).

Lumpkins, Barbara. "Black Women: Special Challenges, Rewards," *Akron Beacon Journal*, 4 Feb. 1985.

JAYNE R. BEILKE

Pleasant, Mary Ellen (1812?–1904), legendary woman of influence and political power in Gold Rush and Gilded Age San Francisco, was born, according to some sources, a slave in Georgia; other sources claim that her mother was a Louisiana slave and her father was Asian or Native American. Many sources agree that she lived in Boston, as a free woman, the wife of James W. Smith, a Cuban abolitionist. When he died in 1844 he left her his estate, valued at approximately forty-five thousand dollars.

Mary Ellen next married a man whose last name was Pleasant or Pleasants and made her way to California, arriving in San Francisco in 1849. Her husband's whereabouts after this time have never been made clear. She started life in San Francisco as a cook for wealthy clients, then opened her own boardinghouse. Her guests were said to be men of influence, and it was rumored that her places were also houses of prostitution.

Many sources state that Pleasant was a very active abolitionist, helping escaped slaves find jobs around the city. When she heard of John Brown's desire to incite slave rebellions, she supposedly met with him in Canada in 1858, handing him thirty thousand dollars of her own money to further his cause. When Brown's attempt to seize the arsenal at Harpers Ferry failed, authorities began searching for her, though she was able to disguise herself and find her way back to San Francisco under the name of Mrs. Ellen Smith. When Brown was captured, he supposedly had a note in his pocket that said: "The ax is laid at the root of the tree. When the first blow is struck, there will be more money to help." It was signed with the initials W.E.P., though some conjecture that Pleasant signed the note and deliberately made her "M" look like a "W."

Back in San Francisco, Pleasant fought racism by suing a streetcar company for not allowing her to ride. She sued twice, once in 1866 and again in 1868. She finally received damages in the latter suit, but she had to have a white man witness the streetcar conductor refusing her a seat in order to win her case. During the 1860s she supposedly found wives for wealthy men as well as homes for their illegitimate children. She placed former slaves as servants in homes all over the city, creating a communication network for the receipt of gossip and information, in much the same way that her contemporary, the voodoo priestess MARIE LAVEAUX, built a power base in New Orleans.

Pleasant is best known for being the housekeeper of the banker Thomas Bell, who married Teresa Percy, one of Pleasant's protégés. By this time Pleasant was known to white San Franciscans as "Mammy" and was said to have some sort of power over the Bells. It was even rumored that voodoo rituals were held in the Bell home on Octavia Street, and the mansion soon became known as the "House of Mystery." Pleasant was considered a woman of mystery herself and was described in newspaper articles and in the memoirs of native San Franciscans as "strange," "mesmeric," and "picturesque."

In 1883 and 1884 Pleasant's name was again in local newspapers because of her involvement in the court case of *Sarah Althea Hill v. William Sharon.* Sharon, a millionaire, former Nevada senator, and owner of the opulent Palace Hotel, was being sued by Hill for support under the terms of a secret marriage contract. The contract later proved to be a forgery and supposedly had been arranged by Pleasant. Pleasant's access to and seeming power over the rich men of San Francisco made this a believable story to most of the city's citizens. During the trial, Hill claimed to be "controlled" by Pleasant, and Pleasant's appearance in court always caused a stir, as recorded on 6 May 1884 in the *San Francisco Call*: "Mammy Pleasant, as the plaintiff calls her colored companion, shows herself in court only as a bird of passage, so to say. She bustles in, converses pleasantly with the young men attached to the defendant's counsel…and like a wind from the south astray in northern climes departs and leaves but chill behind."

One of the few established facts in the life of Mary Ellen Pleasant is that Thomas Bell died in 1892 after a fall from the second-story landing of the House of Mystery. Many thought Pleasant had murdered him; if so, and if the murder was for gain, it was fruitless, for when his wife inherited Bell's money, she eventually forced Pleasant out of the house and into a small flat in the city's African American district. Living in poverty, Pleasant was taken in by the Sherwood family, to whom she had rendered assistance at one time. When Pleasant died in San Francisco, she was placed in the Sherwood family plot in the Tucolay Cemetery in Napa, California. At her request, her gravestone contained the words: "She Was a Friend of John Brown." After her death the *San Francisco Call* (12 Jan. 1904) reported a mysterious matter that pertained to her association with John Brown: "Among her effects are letters and documents bearing upon the historical event in which she played an important part. The Brown family raided her flat when Mrs. Sherwood took her home. After her death, the Sherwoods found Mrs. Pleasant's trunks in her Webster Street flat to be all but empty."

Pleasant seems to have wielded power over influential people, yet because she was African American and female, her activities did not reflect her racial and social status, which possibly led to the rumors that she engaged in voodoo and even murder. She moved freely through the highest levels of society, yet she dressed always like a servant. She left nothing in writing, and surviving diaries and newspaper articles paint her as a mysterious and sinister figure. At the same time, some recalled Pleasant as "generous," claiming that she used her own money to aid African American railroad strikers and assisted with other black causes. A few San Franciscans who were children during Pleasant's lifetime remembered her as a churchgoing "lovely old lady" and said that they never believed the voodoo stories.

Historians have rediscovered Mary Ellen Pleasant, and perhaps new materials will come to light to reveal more about this woman whose presence haunts the annals of nineteenth-century San Francisco.

FURTHER READING

Few primary materials on Mary Ellen Pleasant have survived or been discovered. A photograph, generally agreed to be that of Pleasant, is in the Schomburg Center for Research in Black Culture of the New York Public Library. Pleasant's biographer, Helen Holdredge, has placed notes and transcripts of interviews in the San Francisco Public Library.

Holdredge, Helen. *Mammy Pleasant* (1953).

Hudson, Lynn. *The Making of "Mammy" Pleasant: A Black Entrepreneur in Nineteenth-Century San Francisco* (2003).

Wheeler, B. Gordon. *Black California: The History of African-Americans in the Golden State* (1993).

This entry is taken from the *American National Biography* and is published here with the permission of the American Council of Learned Societies.

LYNN DOWNEY

Pledger, William Anderson (1852–8 Jan. 1904), editor, Republican Party leader, and civil rights activist, was born near Jonesboro, Georgia, the son of a slave mother and a white planter father whose names are unknown. He received limited formal education as a child but attended Atlanta University as an adult and finally gained entrance to the Georgia bar as a self-taught lawyer in 1894. Little is known of his childhood, though Pledger himself related his early interest in politics to a contemporary journalist. According to a 1902 biographical account by Cyrus Field Adams, brother of JOHN QUINCY ADAMS (1848–1922), one of Pledger's "most pleasant recollections of his youth" was informing his mother in 1856 that presidential candidate John C. Frémont was "for the Negro" (Adams, 147).

After the Civil War Pledger moved to Atlanta and worked in city hotels and on the railroad. In the early 1870s he moved to Athens, Georgia, where he taught school for five years and began publishing the *Athens Blade*. About this time Pledger married, though information about his wife is unknown. The couple had two children. In 1872 Pledger began stumping for the Republican Party in Georgia. Four years later he became a delegate to the Republican National Convention. By the time he was thirty Pledger had become one of the leading black Republicans in Georgia.

In the late 1870s and early 1880s, when Pledger entered Republican Party affairs, the state party was deeply divided along racial lines. Pledger became one of the major leaders of the Black and Tan faction, a biracial coalition that aimed to maintain the Republican Party's Reconstruction-era commitment to black civil rights. His opponents, the "lily white" faction, wanted to make the Republicans an all-white party in the South. In 1880 Pledger led a revolt of black party members to elect a new state committee that was three-quarters black.

In the same year he was elected chairman of the Republican state committee, the first black man to serve in that office. In 1882 Pledger was ousted and replaced by a white Republican. Pledger's removal was supported by President Chester A. Arthur, who favored the lily white faction over Pledger's Black and Tans. Hoping to aid the lily whites and assuage Pledger, Arthur appointed Pledger surveyor of customs in Atlanta in 1882.

In 1888 Pledger ran for office as a Republican candidate for state legislature from Clarke County. He was defeated, according to the historian Donald L. Grant, because white intimidation prevented half of the eligible black voters in Clarke County from going to the polls. Although poll taxes and residency requirements legally disenfranchised many black voters, the absence of a secret ballot effectively disenfranchised many more by exposing black voters to the reprisals of whites who watched them mark their ballots. White Democrats seemed to view Pledger as particularly dangerous, and he was regularly attacked in the white press for his involvement in civil rights organizations. The Democratic *Augusta Evening News* once warned Pledger, "Some of these days Pledger's smartness will lead him to take a step that will bring him to the end of his career very suddenly" (Grant, 134).

In an era when violence against blacks escalated but remained virtually unpunished in the South, Pledger was an outspoken advocate of civil rights and a fearless opponent of lynching. In 1882 he led an armed group of Athens blacks and successfully forestalled a mob of whites determined to lynch two prisoners. He also assumed leadership roles at two major late nineteenth-century black civil rights conventions, at Louisville in 1883 and at Macon in 1888. In 1890 Pledger helped organize the Afro-American League in Chicago, which combated lynching, defended black voting rights, and sought an end to discrimination in public accommodations and transportation. In 1898, when the league reemerged as the Afro-American Council, Pledger served as vice president. In 1902 Pledger testified to a congressional committee on lynching in the South.

Pledger also enjoyed a career as one of the nation's leading African American journalists. He frequently used his position as editor to promote black civil rights. As his contemporary white counterpart, Henry Grady, promoted the idea of the "New South" through the *Atlanta Constitution*, Pledger used his position as an editor to expose the violence and atrocities of the post-Reconstruction South. In addition to the *Athens Blade*, Pledger founded the *Atlanta Weekly Defiance* and the *Atlanta Age*. He served for several years as vice president of the National Afro-American Press Association.

Although Pledger occasionally declined to support Republican candidates, he remained active in the party his whole life, serving as a delegate to the national convention from 1876 to 1900. In the 1890s he opposed Republican efforts to fuse with Populists and supported a Democratic candidate over the Populist Tom Watson. In the 1890s party membership won him an appointment as immigrant inspector in Savannah. Pledger was reelected Republican state party chairman in 1902, but the party's weakness in twentieth-century Georgia rendered this a less influential position.

Like BOOKER T. WASHINGTON, Pledger often emphasized material success as a means to uplift the race, but his courageous efforts against lynching, disenfranchisement, and segregation suggest that he was also a committed advocate of protest. Pledger remained active until his final days, working with the Afro-American Council, lobbying within the Republican Party, and practicing law in Atlanta. Though many of Pledger's efforts went unrewarded in his lifetime, his leadership was critical in sustaining the ideals and organizational foundation of black activism through one of the darkest periods in the history of civil rights in the South.

FURTHER READING
Adams, Cyrus Field. "Col. William A. Pledger, the Forceful Orator and Fearless Editor," *Colored American Magazine* 5 (1902).
Grant, Donald L., and Jonathan Grant. *The Way It Was in the South: The Black Experience in Georgia* (1993).
McDaniel, Ruth Currie. "Black Power in Georgia: William A. Pledger and the Takeover of the Republican Party," *Georgia Historical Quarterly* 62 (1978).
Shadgett, Olive Hall. *The Republican Party in Georgia from Reconstruction through 1900* (1964).
This entry is taken from the *American National Biography* and is published here with the permission of the American Council of Learned Societies.

MICHELLE BRATTAIN

Plessy, Homer Adolph (1858?–1925), plaintiff in the 1896 landmark U.S. Supreme Court case *Plessy v. Ferguson*, was born probably in New Orleans. Beyond the case, very little is known about Plessy. He was said to be thirty-four years old at the time of his arrest in 1892, which places his birth around 1858; yet his tombstone lists his age as sixty-three years old when he died in 1925, which places his birth around 1862. Described as a "Creole of Color," Plessy was white in appearance but known to have had a black great-grandmother. He worked as a carpenter.

On 7 June 1892, on a sixty-mile train trip from New Orleans to Covington, Louisiana, Plessy, defined as black by Louisiana law because of his mixed-race heritage, sat in the coach designated for white passengers. Railroad officials were aware that he had boarded the train in order to test the 1890 Louisiana statute requiring all railroad companies to provide and enforce separate-but-equal accommodations for black and white passengers. Thus, although Plessy had no discernible black features, he was asked to move to the car reserved for black passengers. When Plessy refused, he was arrested.

Through his attorneys, Albion Tourgée and S. F. Phillips, and with the aid of the Citizens Committee to Test the Constitutionality of the Separate Car Law (*Comité des Citoyens*), an organization of blacks in New Orleans, Plessy filed a suit questioning the constitutionality of the state statute. After the suit was overruled by the lower court, Plessy petitioned the Louisiana Supreme Court for writs of prohibition and certiorari against the lower court judge, John Ferguson, prohibiting him from holding Plessy's trial. The request was denied, but the court allowed his case to go before the U.S. Supreme Court on a writ of error.

The argument in *Plessy v. Ferguson* revolved around the constitutionality of the Louisiana statute and whether it violated the Fourteenth Amendment's equal protection clause. The question of equal accommodation was not discussed. As for race, Plessy did not admit to any court that he had African blood. Tourgée argued that because Plessy had no distinguishable black features he was entitled to all the privileges and immunities of white people, and, further, that the Louisiana law gave railroad officials the power to determine racial identity arbitrarily and assign coaches accordingly.

The Supreme Court rejected Tourgée's arguments. With Justice Henry Billings Brown delivering the majority opinion, the Court ruled against Plessy. A compelling aspect of the decision was the opinion of Justice John Marshall Harlan, the lone dissenter. Whereas Brown, employing nineteenth-century Darwinian reasoning, argued that blacks *perceived* "a badge of inferiority"

because of the law enforcing segregation, Harlan argued that "our constitution is color blind, and neither knows nor tolerates classes among citizens. In respect to civil rights, all citizens are equal before the law." However, the Court established the doctrine of separate but equal, which would not be revisited until well into the twentieth century when it was unanimously overturned in another landmark case, *Brown v. Board of Education* (1954).

Homer Plessy's trial was held on 11 January 1897, four and a half years after his arrest. He pleaded guilty and paid a twenty-five-dollar fine. Plessy died in New Orleans.

FURTHER READING

Higginbotham, A. Leon. *Shades of Freedom* (1996), chapter 9.

Lofgren, Charles A. *The Plessy Case: A Legal-Historical Interpretation* (1987).

Thomas, Brook, ed. *Plessy v. Ferguson: A Brief History with Documents* (1998).

Woodward, C. Vann. "The Case of the Louisiana Traveler," in *Quarrels That Have Shaped the Constitution*, ed. John A. Garraty (1964).

This entry is taken from the *American National Biography* and is published here with the permission of the American Council of Learned Societies.

MAMIE E. LOCKE

Plinton, James O., Jr. (22 July 1914–4 July 1996), World War II pilot, entrepreneur, and airline executive, was born in Westfield, New Jersey, the son of a Jamaican dental technician. His parents' names are unknown. A driven and determined student at Lincoln University in Pennsylvania, where he graduated with a bachelor of arts in 1935, Plinton was a solid student-athlete who participated on the varsity soccer, wrestling, tennis, and track teams. He was also a member of the dramatic society and the glee club and was president of the German society. An accomplished musician, he played the piano and organ well and one summer played the organ at Tuskegee Institute. With the encouragement and unbending rearing of his father, it was evident that the black college experience was critical to his development as a future leader and visionary who would defy the odds against systematic racial injustice. In a 1973 interview Plinton revealed: "Going to Lincoln was the best thing that ever happened to me. It proved that being Black was a privilege—a new awakening I'll be proud of the rest of my life" (Wilkerson, 22). After his graduation from Lincoln, Plinton attended the University of Newark in New

Jersey, where he studied aeronautics, navigation, and meteorology and earned his commercial pilot's license. Although he was accepted and excelled in his program, the field of aeronautics proved to be a difficult barrier to break within a racially charged interwar period. Between 1936 and 1940 he worked odds jobs to make ends meet—as a ditchdigger, a floor sweeper, a seaman in South America, a postal worker, a biology and chemistry teacher in West Virginia, and a fencing teacher at an all-white country club in Plainfield, New Jersey.

Between 1940 and 1942, the early years of World War II, Plinton was awarded three federal scholarships to become a commercial flight instructor. However, during this period the U.S. War Department excluded blacks from the air corps. Confronted with a racist institution that believed blacks were ill equipped to engage in combat or to make contributions in mechanics or aviation, Plinton endured discriminatory comments from white training officers who believed that "Negroes…are too uncoordinated to fly" (Wilkerson, 22). Plinton's confident retort to those officers illustrated his love for flying and his motivation to become a pilot at all costs: "I have been a Negro all my life, and I'm coordinated towards obstacles" (Wilkerson, 22).

Among the select few blacks who earned their positions in the civilian flight program and who were inevitably relegated to the rank of flight officer, Plinton believed the only way to escape this "racist deep freeze" was to commit himself to military duty abroad. Indeed Plinton's military commitment in World War II demonstrated an unfortunate tradition of black Americans and colonial subjects who offered their bodies in warfare to prove themselves worthy of full citizenship in an unequal society.

In 1942, after a year of duty, Plinton became a flight instructor for the first African American army air corps unit, the Ninety-ninth Pursuit Squadron, in Tuskegee, Alabama. This unit was a highly trained class of pilots who at first were perceived as unqualified to engage in combat, but soon they contributed remarkably to the war effort in Europe. Throughout World War II Plinton served in a number of upper-management and teaching positions in aviation. In 1943–1944 he managed Tuskegee Airport #1 and worked as the assistant director of the Tuskegee Division of Aeronautics. From 1944 to 1946 he taught primary, basic, and advanced aeronautical courses in Tuskegee, which helped produce DANIEL JAMES JR., the first African American four-star general.

These administrative, teaching, and flying experiences at Tuskegee and in World War II were foundational for Plinton's international business ventures during the postwar period. African American leadership in particular increasingly participated in the politics within the black international arena, often finding connections with the racial and freedom struggle they experienced on the domestic front. From 1945 through the mid-1950s Plinton established himself as a formidable entrepreneur and aviation visionary by directing a transnational airline in Latin America and a modern laundry service in Haiti. Influenced by his Jamaican father, who told him to "be somebody, regardless of your color" (Wilkerson, 22), and his earlier employment as a seaman in South America, Plinton realized the potential of transnational business ventures, particularly in the Caribbean and Latin America. In 1945 he and a partner from the Virgin Islands organized and franchised Latin American Airways, Inc., with the help of the African American millionaire Major RICHARD ROBERT WRIGHT SR. Plinton acquired full control of daily airline operations in Ecuador, where the government recruited him to reorganize its "shaky commercial airline industry" (Wilkerson, 22). Unfortunately his time in Ecuador was short-lived because of, in Plinton's words, "politics and race." He accepted an offer from the Haitian president Dumarsais Estimé to help organize and operate Haitian National Airways. The Haitian National Airways never materialized, but from 1947 to 1949 Plinton overcame adversity and started another small airline, Quisqueya, which carried passengers, mail, and cargo to a number of Caribbean islands. He is credited with being the first person to land a plane on Grand Turks Island.

By 1949 the pilot believed it was essential to seek his fortune "on the ground" as well as in the air. The Caribbean became a trendy destination for middle- and upper-middle-class Americans and Europeans because of Europe's postwar troubles and slow reconstruction efforts. Like many other African American entrepreneurs, intellectuals, and artists, Plinton maintained a strong connection to Haiti, the Caribbean's only independent black nation. He wanted to capitalize on the emerging tourist industry in Haiti—due to its growing popularity in the cultural arts (Haitian folkloric dance and painting) and well-publicized Bicentennial Exposition (1949)—and contribute to the modernization of the country. In 1949 he installed and operated the first modern laundry service in Haiti. He owned five branches in the country, employed more than fifty of its citizens,

PLUMMER, HENRY VINTON 151

and often piloted his plane to its various coasts to handle the laundry of incoming cruise ships.

Plinton became an integral part of Haitian business society and culture. He represented the Republic of Haiti three consecutive years at the U.S. Department of Commerce Conference of Negro Business and received the highest award from Haiti's Department of Labor and the government's highest honor, *L'Ordre National Honneur et Merité*.

By the middle 1950s Plinton's entrepreneurial ventures grew beyond laundries and commercial flying. He introduced an orange beverage to the Schrafft restaurant chain in New York City, which probably facilitated his move back to the United States. Haiti's declining economy, waning tourist industry, and political instability were also potential factors for his return. By 1957 Plinton had received an offer from Trans World Airlines (TWA) to serve as its executive assistant to the director of personnel and industrial relations. In 1971 Eastern Airlines proposed that he become its vice president of marketing affairs, a position that made him the first African American high-ranking executive at a major airline.

Plinton clearly understood the importance of creating tangible linkages with the African diaspora. During the 1970s he served as a lecturer, board member, and consultant to a number of organizations with a global focus, including East African Airlines and the International Management Development Institute, which lobbied for structural development on the African continent. Furthermore, Plinton was president of the national YMCA and instrumental in the revitalization of Liberty City, a Miami neighborhood, after riots in 1980. From the local to the international, he was a businessman with the foresight and determination to succeed in spite of prevailing discriminatory practices in order to create opportunities for himself and the larger black community. Plinton was married to Kathryn Hancock; they had two children, James O. Norman Plinton and Kathryn Plinton-Roman. He died of cancer at Lake Wales Medical Center in Lake Wales, Florida.

FURTHER READING

Information on Plinton is in the James O. Plinton Photograph Collection, Schomburg Center for Research in Black Culture, New York City, and the Claude Barnett Papers, Chicago Historical Society, Chicago.

Allman, Christian. "Black Pioneers in Mainstream Corporate America," *Black Collegian* (April 1996).

Polyné, Millery. "Modernizing the Race: Political and Cultural Engagements between Haitians and African Americans, 1930–1964," Ph.D. diss., University of Michigan (2003).

Wilkerson, Owen T. "Eastern's Flying Black Exec," *Encore* (Nov. 1973).

Obituaries: *New York Times*, 14 July 1996; *Westfield Leader*, 18 July 1996.

MILLERY POLYNÉ

Plummer, Henry Vinton (31 July 1844–8 Feb. 1906), Baptist clergyman and U.S. Army chaplain, was born in Prince George's County, Maryland, the son of Adam Francis Plummer and Emily Saunders. His parents were slaves on "Goodwood," the plantation of George H. Calvert, a direct descendant of Lord Baltimore. When he was still young, Henry was sold to people living in Washington, D.C., and then to Colonel Thompson in Howard County, Maryland.

After the outbreak of the Civil War in the spring of 1861, Maryland, although a slave state, remained in the Union. Exercising extralegal powers, President Abraham Lincoln placed parts of Maryland under martial law and suspended the writ of habeas corpus, arguing that the Constitution did not provide for procedures to address a rebellion and secession and thus necessitated extraordinary measures. With tensions high and rebels making incursions into Maryland, in the spring of 1862 Plummer managed to escape from the Thompson plantation and went to live with his aunt, Margaret Tyler. Late in 1864 he entered the Union navy and served for the duration of the war, mostly on the gunboat *Cordelion*, which patrolled the Potomac River. During this time he learned to read. At the end of the war he took a job as coachman and gardener for B. F. Guy of Hyattsville, Maryland. The following year he made a trip to New Orleans to find a sister who had been sold some years before to an owner in Louisiana. He found his sister Miranda and brought her back to the family home near Bladensburg, Maryland.

Plummer was baptized at the Second Baptist Church in Washington in May 1867. That summer he married Julia Lomax; they had nine children. Recognizing that freed blacks needed financial assistance in burying their dead, in June 1870 he formed the Bladensburg Union and served for fourteen years as its first president and treasurer. Feeling called to preach, he ministered to small Baptist congregations in Charles and Prince George's counties in Maryland.

In 1871 Plummer left his job with the Guy family and worked as a night watchman at the U.S. post office in Washington. There he started taking courses at Wayland Seminary, which had opened in 1865 under the auspices of the American Baptist Home Missionary Society of New York City. He and his family lived in a three-room house near Bladensburg and then moved to Hyattsville, where they had a thirteen-acre farm and grew fruit trees. He graduated from Wayland in 1878 and was ordained. He served as pastor at St. Paul's in Bladensburg (1876–1881) and then at Mount Carmel Church in Washington (1882–1884), and under his leadership both congregations grew and prospered.

At the urging of FREDERICK DOUGLASS, who then was U.S. marshal of the District of Columbia, and several prominent Republicans, President Chester A. Arthur in July 1884 named Plummer chaplain of the Ninth Calvary, making him, as far as what can be determined, the first African American chaplain in the U.S. Army following the Civil War. In August Plummer went to Fort Riley, Kansas; he later was stationed in Wyoming and at Fort Robinson, Nebraska (1893).

As an army chaplain, Plummer promoted temperance. With slavery no longer an issue, the two great social issues in late-nineteenth-century America were women's rights and temperance, the latter claiming Frances Willard as its most vocal and visible spokesperson. Plummer's advocacy challenged the military's rationing system, which included a daily allowance of alcohol. Through the Loyal Temperance Legion, which he formed for the children of the black troops at Fort Robinson, Plummer became very popular with the troops; however, the commanding officers, who were white, considered him a nuisance and reacted negatively. He was also interested in the repatriation of American blacks to Africa and became more and more involved in colonization schemes. One of the best-known advocates of African colonization was HENRY MCNEAL TURNER, who was a bishop of the African Methodist Episcopal Church and vice president of the African Colonization Society. He believed that blacks would not do well in the American culture and society, which was dominated and controlled by whites. Moreover, after Reconstruction much of the civil rights legislation of that period was rolled back or declared unconstitutional.

Apparently influenced greatly by Turner's beliefs, Plummer submitted a proposal to the U.S. War Department that he be given command of an expedition, including between fifty and one hundred black soldiers, to establish settlements in central Africa. He argued that the emigration of blacks to Africa would eliminate racial tensions in America while at the same time providing the United States with opportunities in Africa, which was being dismembered by several European powers, including France, Britain, Belgium, Italy, and Germany. Turner supported Plummer's plan wholeheartedly.

The War Department never seriously entertained his extravagant idea. Shortly thereafter the army charged Plummer with drunkenness and court-martialed him. Bishop Turner and others intervened but to no avail. The only witness to the alleged incident was Sergeant Robert Benjamin, who admitted to having had a grudge against Plummer from their Fort Riley days. At the trial, in the fall of 1894, Plummer was convicted and lost his commission.

Returning to Kansas in 1895, Plummer was pastor of the Second Baptist Church in Wichita; he then became pastor of Rose Hill Baptist Church in Kansas City, Kansas. In the summer of 1899 he visited friends and family in Maryland, where he preached on the occasion of the twenty-eighth anniversary of the founding of the Bladensburg Union. In 1902 he was elected to the executive board of the Kansas Baptist Convention. He died in Kansas City.

Plummer's sister Nellie Arnold Plummer remembered her brother in a family memoir as energetic and a man of action. "Religion to him was helping the poor and needy, as well as praising God in church," she wrote. In February 2005 the U.S. Army reversed Plummer's dishonorable discharge.

FURTHER READING

Information on Plummer's military career and court-martial is in the Records of the Adjutant General and Judge Advocate General in the National Archives. Material pertaining to Kansas Baptists is in the Kansas State Historical Society.
Harvey, Paul. *Redeeming the South: Religious Cultures and Racial Identities among Southern Baptists, 1865–1925* (1997).
Plummer, Nellie Arnold. *Out of the Depths* (1927).
This entry is taken from the *American National Biography* and is published here with the permission of the American Council of Learned Societies.

GEOFFREY GNEUHS

Plumpp, Sterling (30 Jan. 1940–), poet, author, and university professor, was born Sterling Dominic Plumpp near Clinton, Mississippi, to Cyrus Hampton, a laborer, and Mary Emmanuel Plumpp. He lived with his grandparents on a sharecropper's cotton plantation until he was fourteen years old, at which time he moved to Jackson following the death of his grandfather. The years that followed his time in Clinton were fraught with a constant sense of displacement and relocation—both spiritually and physically. The harsh early years of the sharecropper's life, coupled with an itinerant adolescent home life led the young Plumpp early on to distrust the institutions that he felt were destructive forces to himself and the black community. His high school education in Mississippi church schools led him to move away from the black church and to his conversion to Catholicism, and he graduated with honors and accepted a full scholarship to St. Benedict's College (later Benedictine College) in Atchinson, Kansas, in the fall of 1960.

It was at St. Benedict's that Plumpp's early education into the ways of institutional confinement began to take intellectual shape, but it was also where he found the study of literature that would sustain him. "It was here amid these monks and farmers from Nebraska, Kansas, Missouri, and Iowa that I walked through the portals of Western literature and my life was changed forever," he said (Plumpp, 169). After two years at St. Benedict's Plumpp left for the big city, and took a job at the Chicago Main Post Office in the fall of 1962. During the "nightmarish" years of 1964 and 1965 he served in the army at the Aberdeen Proving Ground in Maryland, and followed that with another stint at the post office in Chicago from 1966 to 1969. During his time at the post office, Plumpp was enrolled at Roosevelt College in Chicago, and there earned a bachelor's degree under the tutelage of James Cunningham. It was also at this time that Plumpp began his study of blues and jazz music. Toward the end of his undergraduate education at Roosevelt, Plumpp married Falvia Delgrazia Jackson (a registered nurse) on 21 December 1968; they had one daughter.

In the years following his undergraduate degree from Roosevelt Plumpp worked as a counselor for North Park College while earning a graduate degree in psychology from Roosevelt University; he also honed his skills in poetry, formulating what would become his master's thesis and first book of prose, *Black Rituals*. In *Black Rituals* (1972) Plumpp found the political voice that would be much of the source for his early books of poetry—*Portable Soul* (1969), *Half Black, Half Blacker* (1970), and *Steps to Break the Circle* (1974). During this time he started working as an instructor at the University of Illinois at Chicago, a job that would eventually turn into a full professorship in the Department of Black Studies in the 1980s. With the publication of the pamphlet-length poem *Clinton* (1976), Plumpp was hitting his aesthetic stride. The poem is a densely imagistic chronological telling of the autobiographical and mythical journey from the plantation cotton fields of Mississippi to the trappings of the northern metropolis, where "the traveler could very well exchange Paradise for Hell." "*Clinton* is a blow-by-blow account of the battering my sensibilities underwent from birth through childhood and adolescence in Mississippi to manhood in Chicago and the United States Army" (Plumpp). Many of this period's major poems were later collected in *The Mojo Hands Call, I Must Go* (1982), which earned Plumpp an Illinois Arts Council Award (1981) and a Carl Sandburg Literary Award for Poetry (1983). The mid-1980s then became a personally and artistically transitional period for Plumpp. His marriage was breaking up, and his voice was finding new direction. The publication of *Blues: The Story Always Untold* (1989) finds Plumpp abandoning the epic quest poems collected in *Mojo Hands* in favor of an immersion in the language of the blues lyric, and more open forms.

Though Plumpp's poetry was first published by the two most important publishing houses of the Black Arts Movement of the 1960s and 1970s (Broadside Press and Third World Press), his work is generally thought to be, as DUDLEY RANDALL has said, that of "a poet's poet" and slightly outside of the BAM aesthetic. Though his subject matter almost always had to do with locating a personal history within the mythical and real ethos of the African and African American experience, his early poetics more resemble Anglo modernists and postmodernists in his use of abstraction and experimentation. Increasingly, though, his work uses the jazz line and the blues lyric to create "music poems" and convey what was often dense imagery about personal and shared folklore. Beginning with *Blues: The Story Always Untold*, continuing with *From Johannesburg* (1993), *Ornate with Smoke* (1997), and *Velvet Be-Bop Kente Cloth* (2003), his poetry is more and more made to be as much experienced as song as poetry. His book *Blues Narratives* (1999) continues his examination of the personal past by addressing his mother and grandfather directly.

Plumpp became so identified with the music aspects of his work that he was picked to be honored by a River Road Lifetime Achievement Award from the Mississippi Valley Blues Society—something that in the past was given only to blues musicians, and he performed his poetry with musical accompaniment. In 2001 he won a lottery jackpot in the Illinois State Lottery and subsequently retired from teaching at the University of Illinois at Chicago in order to write, perform, and give workshops in poetry and music.

FURTHER READING

Correspondence, ephemera, handwritten and typed manuscripts, galleys, proofs, and photographs are housed at the University of Mississippi Libraries, Department of Archives and Special Collections.

Plumpp, Sterling. "Sterling Plumpp," *Contemporary Authors Autobiography Series, Volume* 21 (1995).

Cunningham, James. "Baldwinian Aesthetics in Sterling Plumpp's Mojo Poems," *Black American Literature Forum,* Vol. 23, No. 3, *Poetry Issue* (Autumn 1989).

MICHAEL RODRIGUEZ

Poage, George Coleman (6 Nov. 1880–11 Apr. 1962), athlete and teacher, was born in Hannibal, Missouri, to James Poage, a tanner, and Annie Coleman Poage, a domestic worker. In 1884 they moved to La Crosse, Wisconsin, but Poage's father soon died. The family then moved in with an affluent white financier who employed Annie Poage as a "stewardess" and who encouraged the education of her two children. George Poage excelled at La Crosse High School, where he was the institution's first black student. He was salutatorian of his twenty-five-member graduating class in 1899 and was the school's best athlete, representing La Crosse in regional track meets.

After graduating, he enrolled at the University of Wisconsin, which, like most schools outside of the South, accepted African Americans and permitted them to take part in campus activities. Poage was an active member of his class, frequently representing his peers in public speaking competitions, and he was a three-year member of Philomathia, a literary and oratorical society.

It was in athletics that Poage enjoyed his greatest success. He competed with the freshman track team, and in 1901 he made the varsity squad. Poage's best events were the short dashes and hurdle races, and he was a frequent point winner for the Badgers as an undergraduate. At the Western Conference

(later the Big Ten) track championships in 1901, he captured third place in the 440-yard run. Two years later he repeated his third-place finish and added a second-place finish in the 220-yard hurdles. A respected member of the squad, he often ran practices when the coach was away.

Poage graduated in 1903 with a major in the civic-historical course, penning a senior thesis entitled "An Investigation Into the Economic Condition of the Negro in the State of Georgia During the Period from 1860 to 1900." He was a popular member of his class, and the yearbook editors described him as being "Of matchless swiftness, but of silent pace" (*Badger Yearbook* [1904], 109). Poage's career at the University of Wisconsin, however, was not finished. The school's athletic department hired him as a "rubber"—or trainer—and he enrolled in graduate history classes.

His extra year began on a high note when he wore the colors of the Milwaukee Athletic Club (MAC) in the Junior Amateur Athletic Union championships in September 1903. The first African American to represent the MAC, he captured first place in the 220-yard hurdles and second place in the 100-yard dash to help lead the MAC to the national title. Poage's success continued in intercollegiate contests. The following spring he became the first black champion in the Western Conference when he finished first in the 440-yard dash and the 220-yard hurdles during the annual championship meet.

That summer Poage made history again when he represented the Milwaukee Athletic Club at the 1904 Olympics in St. Louis. A sidelight to the Louisiana Purchase Exposition and World's Fair, the Olympics were disorganized and not well attended, and the athletes competed not for their countries but as individuals or as members of athletic clubs. The event's local organizers built Jim Crow accommodations for attendees, and, accordingly, some prominent African Americans called for a boycott. Poage opted not to heed the boycott, and the St. Louis organizers were powerless to stop him from competing. At least one other African American, Cleveland's Joseph Stadler, participated in the 1904 Olympics. On 31 August both Poage and Stadler became the first African Americans to earn Olympic medals, Poage winning bronze in the 400-meter hurdles and Stadler capturing silver in the standing high jump. Poage would later add another bronze medal in the 200-meter hurdles.

Poage's career in organized athletics ended after the Olympics. He soon returned to St. Louis to teach in that city's segregated public schools. He headed the English department at Sumner High School and helped coach the school's sports teams. He left St. Louis about 1915 and his subsequent career is unclear. He worked as a farmer in the rural Midwest around World War I before moving to Chicago, where he again taught in public schools and eventually worked as a clerk for the U.S. Postal Service. He retired from the post office in the 1950s and died about ten years later. Poage never married and had no children. Although he lived most of his life in obscurity, his pioneering accomplishments have been rediscovered, and he was inducted into both the Wisconsin State Athletic Hall of Fame and the University of Wisconsin Athletics Hall of Fame in the 1990s.

FURTHER READING
Chalk, Ocania. *Black College Sport* (1976).
Dorn, Pat. "Alumni and the Olympics," *Wisconsin Alumnus* (July 1988).
Mouser, Bruce L. *Black La Crosse, Wisconsin, 1850–1906* (2002).
Mouser, Bruce L. "George Coleman Poage," *Newsletter of the La Crosse County Historical Society* (Jan.–Feb. 1998).
Press, Pat. "First Over the Hurdles," *Washington Post*, 9 Aug. 1984.

GREGORY BOND

Poe, L. Marian (13 Aug. 1890–20 Mar. 1974), lawyer, was born Lavinia Marian Fleming in Warwick County, Virginia, the daughter of Archer R. Fleming, a blacksmith and former slave, and Florence M. Carter. She grew up in Newport News, Virginia, with her parents and her brothers.

In the early 1910s she worked in Newport News as a stenographer for a black banker, notary, and real estate agent, E. C. Brown, president of the Crown Savings Bank. In 1910 she married Abram James Poe, a waiter; they had two children. For a time around 1920 Marian Poe worked in the office of JOSEPH THOMAS NEWSOME, a black attorney. The experience convinced Poe to become a lawyer.

Success would not come easy. The law schools in Virginia—Washington and Lee University, the University of Virginia, and the University of Richmond—excluded black applicants. Few black men in Virginia had become lawyers, and Virginia law before 1920 did not permit women to be licensed to practice the profession. Poe moved with her two young children to Washington, D.C.,

where she worked as a bank teller while studying law at Howard University. She earned her law degree from Howard University in 1925 and later that year passed the Virginia bar examination. She was the first black woman lawyer in Virginia and one of the first black women lawyers in the South.

Poe's professional activities stretched far beyond Newport News. A charter member of the predominantly black Old Dominion Bar Association, she served throughout the 1940s as its secretary, and she served for a time as an assistant secretary of the predominantly black National Bar Association. In addition, Poe served once at mid-century and twice in the 1960s as the Virginia delegate to the national convention of the National Association of Women Lawyers. Thus she participated in the support systems that promoted the work of black lawyers, particularly in Virginia, and of female lawyers across the nation.

Poe also worked on behalf of the Newport News African American community. For nearly a half century she served as a general practitioner, one of only a handful of black attorneys in Newport News. The focal point of her life remained the building where she lived and worked. Poe owned the property, which was located in the center of the black business district in Newport News, and which for a time also housed Alice's Beauty Shop, which her daughter ran, and her son-in-law's enterprise, Webb's Grill and Guesthouse. She was active in civic organizations, and at the First Baptist Church of Newport News, where she taught Sunday school, sang in the choir, and became the first woman on the board of trustees. Following her own advice, she kept busy to the end of her life.

By the time Poe died in Newport News, the number of black female lawyers in Virginia had risen into the double digits, and both African American men and women could be admitted to any law school in the state.

FURTHER READING
Dark, Okianer Christian, and Allen R. Moye, "L. Marian Poe: A Model of Public Service," *Virginia Lawyer* 38 (Mar. 1990).
Smith, J. Clay, Jr. *Emancipation: The Making of the Black Lawyer, 1844–1944* (1993).
Smith, J. Clay, Jr. *Rebels in Law: Voices in History of Black Women Lawyers* (1998).
Obituaries: *Richmond News Leader*, 23 Mar. 1974; *Norfolk Journal and Guide*, 30 Mar. 1974.

This entry is taken from the *American National Biography* and is published here with the permission of the American Council of Learned Societies.

PETER WALLENSTEIN

Pogue, Stephanie (27 Sept. 1944–12 Nov. 2002), professor, printmaker, artist, and curator, was born Stephanie Elaine Pogue in Shelby, North Carolina, to Elbert Hugo Pogue, a doctor, and Mildred Wallace. She was raised in Elizabeth, New Jersey.

In 1962 Pogue enrolled in Syracuse University, but transferred to Howard University one year later. She earned a bachelor of fine arts degree in painting from Howard in 1966 and a master of fine arts degree from Cranbrook Academy in Michigan in 1968. Her art historical expertise included the sculptural art of the Bamana people of Mali, reliquary art of the Bakota people in Gabon, and the sacred Hindu art of India. In 1968 she joined the fine arts faculty as an assistant professor for Tennessee's Fisk University, one of the first Historically Black Colleges and Universities (HBCUs) and the alma mater of W. E. B. DuBois. During her tenure at Fisk, she advanced to the positions of associate professor, chair of the fine arts department, and director of the university's gallery. In 1981 Pogue joined the Department of Art at the University of Maryland as a full professor of printmaking and drawing and a member of the graduate faculty. She also developed the department's first papermaking facility.

Also in 1981 Pogue was awarded a Fulbright-Hays Cross-cultural Fellowship to study Hindu art in India. As an abstract expressionist, she had formerly painted in a linear and figurative style. In India she began to consider the creative ideas formed in the human subconscious, and this was the basis for a "concept of the universal." Pogue investigated three-dimensional forms, new media, and uses for traditional media. For example, she reconstructed her monoprints as sculptures, and she "painted" with translucent paper to create highly textured and colorfully layered mosaics. The signature piece of this period was *India Pattern-Pattern of India*, her rendering of afternoon sunrays crossing the lotus pattern of a temple floor. In 1986 Pogue was awarded a second Fulbright fellowship to study traditional arts and crafts in Pakistan. The University of Maryland granted her a travel award so that she could mount her one-woman exhibition in Warsaw, Poland. Her solo exhibition of color etchings traveled throughout Poland for four years. Between 1991 and 1993 she served as the acting assistant dean of equity affairs for the College of Arts and Humanities. In 1993 she

became the department chair, a position she held for five years.

In 1996 Pogue was one of twenty-five artists included in the landmark group exhibition, "Bearing Witness: Contemporary Works by African American Women Artists," curated by Jontyle Theresa Robinson, associate professor of Art History at Spelman College. "Bearing Witness" bore a three-fold purpose. First, it recognized the historically, culturally, and politically influential work of African American women artists from nearly four generations. Second, it was the inaugural exhibition for the newly opened Spelman College Museum of Fine Art, which emphasized art by and about women of the African diaspora. Third, it marked the 115th anniversary of Spelman College as the first institute of higher learning for African American women. Pogue created two monoprints, *Woman on a Pedestal* and *Self-Portrait: Vulnerable*, which operated as self-portraits and addressed the complexity of issues faced by black women artists.

Pogue exhibited extensively throughout the world. In addition to "Bearing Witness" and her solo show in Poland, she had major exhibitions at Colombia's El Museo de Arte Moderna La Tertulia (1976), New York's Cinque Gallery (1977), Taiwan's City Museum of Fine Arts (1983), Belgium's Centre d'Art de Rouge-Cloitre (1988), Brazil's Museo do Gravura (1991), and Howard University's James V. Herring Art Gallery (1992). Her work was posthumously exhibited in "ASCENSION: Works by African American Artists of North Carolina," a yearlong exhibit at Winston-Salem State University's Diggs Gallery from June 2004 to April 2005. Pogue's work was included in several permanent collections, including that of the Whitney Museum, which houses one of the most comprehensive collections of twentieth-century American art; Fisk University's Carl Van Vechten Gallery, which is named for the prominent photographer and documentarian of the Harlem Renaissance; and the University of Maryland's David C. Driskell Collection, named for one of the world's leading authorities and historians of African American art and former director of University of Maryland's Department of Art.

Pogue died of cardiac arrest at the age of fifty-six. Through her work, Pogue sought to forge connections between people and the world around them. During the course of her thirty-six year career, she succeeded in creating a sense of universal, multicultural understanding not only visually but educationally as well. Teaching art and providing opportunities for other artists, particularly young artists, to learn and exhibit was her primary mission. Pogue also took tremendous pride in her cultural and artistic background, as is evidenced by her personal collection of African American art. She continued to teach at the University of Maryland until her death. In honor of Pogue's contributions, a departmental award was established in her name.

FURTHER READING

Angelou, Maya, et al. *Bearing Witness: Contemporary Works by African American Women Artists* (1996).

Bontemps, Arna Alexander. *Forever Free: Art by African-American Women* (1980).

Farrington, Lisa E. *Creating Their Own Image: The History of African-American Women Artists* (2005).

CRYSTAL AM NELSON

Poindexter, Hildrus Augustus (10 May 1901–20 Apr. 1987), physician, microbiologist, and public health specialist, was born on a farm near Memphis, Tennessee, the son of Fred Poindexter and Luvenia Gilberta Clarke, tenant farmers. After attending the normal (teacher training) department of Swift Memorial College, a Presbyterian school for blacks in Rogersville, Tennessee (1916–1920), he entered Lincoln University in Pennsylvania and graduated with an A.B. cum laude in 1924. Also in 1924 he married Ruth Viola Grier, with whom he would have one child, a daughter. He attended Dartmouth Medical School for two years before earning an M.D. at Harvard University in 1929, an AM in Bacteriology at Columbia University in 1930, a Ph.D. in Bacteriology and Parasitology at Columbia in 1932, and an MPH from Columbia in 1937.

Poindexter had hoped to proceed directly into public health fieldwork in 1929, following his graduation from Harvard, but his application for a laboratory post in a U.S. government laboratory in the Philippines was declined because of his race. Instead, he served an internship at the John A. Andrew Hospital at Tuskegee Institute in Alabama, one of the few facilities open to African Americans seeking postgraduate training. In addition to his regular duties at the hospital, he began an epidemiological survey and implemented a health education program in Union Springs, Bullock County, a poor, predominantly black settlement. He left after ten weeks to accept a two-year fellowship offered by the General Education Board. This Rockefeller-funded fellowship for graduate study at Columbia University was part of a larger plan of

Hildrus Augustus Poindexter, physician, microbiologist, and public health specialist. He graduated from Harvard University with an M.D. in 1929, and received a Ph.D. from Columbia University in Bacteriology and Parasitology in 1932. (University of Massachusetts, Amherst.)

the administration at Howard University to provide advanced training for several promising young black medical scientists, who, after earning their Ph.Ds, would assume faculty positions at the medical school and help to upgrade the curriculum and research program.

Poindexter served at Howard University as assistant professor of bacteriology, preventive medicine, and public health (1931–1934), associate professor (1934–1936), and professor and department head (1936–1943). He also held posts at Freedmen's Hospital as bacteriologist, immunologist, and assistant director of the allergy clinic. Despite the pressure of administrative, teaching, and clinical duties, he resumed the research he had begun as an intern in Alabama. For three years (1934–1937), he returned periodically to the South and worked, with Rockefeller support, as an epidemiologist for the states of Alabama and Mississippi. The information he had gathered earlier, along with new data, provided him with an opportunity to draw some general conclusions about the state of African American health in the rural South. Poindexter identified malnutrition, syphilis, insect-borne diseases such as malaria, and hookworm infestation as the four most important health problems confronting rural southern blacks. He distributed blame for these conditions almost equally among blacks and whites. Blacks, he felt, were overly swayed by an "illiterate religious leadership" and a "mania for cotton and corn crops," while he believed whites tolerated an "apathetic county health service" and an "inequitable system of education." His solution called for joint "practical education" efforts by state boards of health, black churches, and the schools.

In 1943 Poindexter was appointed a tropical medicine specialist in the U.S. Army, serving in the racially segregated hospital at Fort Huachuca, Arizona, and later as a malariologist, parasitologist, and epidemiologist (with rank of major) at Guadalcanal and elsewhere in the Pacific. In recognition of his military service, he was awarded the Bronze Star and four combat stars. He retired from the army (with the rank of lieutenant colonel) effective 26 March 1947.

Poindexter's role during World War II laid the groundwork for nearly two decades of federal public health service. On 13 January 1947 he received a commission as senior surgeon with the United States Public Health Service (USPHS). His first post was with the USPHS Mission in Liberia (MIL) as chief of laboratory and medical research in West Africa. This post he held until his appointment a year later as medical director and chief of mission for MIL and as medical and health attaché to the American Embassy in Monrovia. In 1953 he was transferred to Indochina and served (1955–1956) as chief of health and sanitation, U.S. Operation Missions (OM) in Vietnam, Cambodia, and Laos. Other OM appointments followed in Suriname (1956–1958), Iraq (1958–1959), Libya (1959–1961), and Sierra Leone (1962–1964). While in Iraq he also served as a professor of preventive medicine at the Royal Baghdad Medical College. Poindexter was a consulting malariologist in Jamaica (1961–1962) and undertook several assignments under USPHS's international section during the early 1960s. He retired from USPHS in 1965.

Poindexter's work in Liberia included the training of indigenous health care personnel, conducting epidemiological surveys and other research projects, antibiotics assay and evaluation, implementing preventive programs, initiating immunization and epidemic control, improving nutrition, and orchestrating demonstration projects in health education. MIL was one of the programs that had emerged from a 1943 agreement between the U.S. and Liberian presidents for increased U.S. assistance in health, economics, agriculture, and other fields. Poindexter's predecessor, John B. West, had begun the program in 1946. While their work focused on technical assistance, the doctors were interested in larger cultural factors as well. Poindexter, for example, wrote about the need not just to correct "social and economic handicaps" but also to develop—for the mutual benefit of Africans and non-Africans alike—"a clearer picture of the people as they live and breathe." His approach to subsequent assignments in Indochina, South America, the Caribbean, and elsewhere in Africa was similar.

Poindexter was a certified specialist of both the American Board of Preventive Medicine and Public Health and the American Board of Microbiology. In 1949 he became the first black member of the American Society of Tropical Medicine and subsequently served as a vice president of the Washington, D.C., chapter and as a trustee of the national body. He had been denied admission to the society in 1934 because of his race.

Following his retirement from USPHS, Poindexter returned briefly to Howard University as a professor of community health practice. He remained active in teaching and research for the next fifteen years. He trained Peace Corps workers; served as a special consultant to the U.S. Department of State and the Agency for International Development, including a six-month tour of duty in 1965 with the relief and rehabilitation unit in Nigeria; and published several articles on public health issues, notably on malaria, sexually transmitted diseases, and medical problems of the elderly. He died at his home in Clinton, Maryland.

FURTHER READING

Correspondence, manuscripts, and other papers of Hildrus Augustus Poindexter are preserved in the Moorland-Spingarn Research Center, Howard University.

Poindexter, Hildrus Augustus. *My World of Reality* (1973).

Cobb, W. Montague. "Hildrus Augustus Poindexter, M.D., M.P.H., Ph.D., D.Sc., 1901–," *Journal of the National Medical Association* 65 (May 1973): 243–47.

Miller, Carroll L. "Hildrus Augustus Poindexter (1901–)," Howard University *Profiles* (Feb. 1980): 1–15.

Obituary: *Washington Post*, 25 Apr. 1987.

This entry is taken from the *American National Biography* and is published here with the permission of the American Council of Learned Societies.

KENNETH R. MANNING

Poindexter, James Preston (25 Sept. 1819–7 Feb. 1907), minister, educator, civil servant, and social activist, was born in Richmond, Virginia, to Evelina Atkinson, of both African American and Cherokee descent, and Joseph Poindexter, a white newspaperman. Little is known about the circumstances surrounding his birth or of the nature of his parents' relationship, only that his mother passed away when he was four. At the age of ten he became an apprentice barber and practiced the trade for the next twenty-eight years.

Poindexter left Virginia at the age of eighteen, having already married his wife, Adelia (maiden name unknown), and moved to Dublin, Ohio, and soon thereafter settled in Columbus, which then had the state's largest population of African Americans. Because of his mixed blood and light complexion, Poindexter, although it was known that he was African American, was allowed to actively participate in the political process and even to vote a right not accorded his fellow African Americans until 1869.

Once in Ohio, Poindexter became active in both the antislavery and black rights movements. He was a member of the Columbus Second Baptist Church for most of his life. Between 1847 and 1858, however, he led a breakaway congregation, known as the Anti-Slavery Baptist Church, a body he formed following an internal division in his home church over the membership of blacks who were former slave owners. He initially served the Second Baptist Church as a lay preacher, and later, following his return from the breakaway congregation, he became the church's regular pastor, serving from 1858 until his retirement in 1898. His ministry was favorably regarded among both whites and blacks and led to his membership and subsequent leadership of the citywide Columbus Pastor's Union Association, the only black person accorded such a privilege. He was both a gifted orator and author of sermons. The latter often focused on the religious foundations of social equality and the need for patient activism.

In 1847, the same year he founded the Anti-Slavery Baptist Church, he helped found the Anti-Slavery Baptist Association, dedicated to eradicating the practice among all Baptists. He and his wife also formed the Colored Soldiers Relief Society in Columbus during the Civil War and later participated in the Sons of Protection, an African American burial and benefit association. In private letters he also claimed active participation in the Underground Railroad, but exact details of his involvement, either as a conductor or someone who sheltered runaway slaves, are unknown.

As a leading community figure, Poindexter also served in local and statewide political positions, some elected and some appointed. He was one of the leading figures of the celebratory events after the first election, held in 1869, in which African Americans could freely vote, taking the dais alongside men such as Rutherford Hayes, then governor of Ohio. A staunch Republican, he served as a leader among his fellow citizens during the Colored Republican Convention of 1871, supporting the candidacy of Grant for reelection. He was so revered that calls were made for him in 1873 to make a run for the Senate—calls that eventually led to his selection as a candidate for the state legislature that same year. He was subsequently defeated in that election and in the election that followed in 1876, when he once again stood for the Ohio House of Representatives. Although he never held a nationally or statewide-elected office, Poindexter remained influential. He served as the state's first black delegate to the Republican National Convention in 1876, even strategizing with Rutherford Hayes and Frederick Douglass while Hayes's election was still in doubt. As a result of his close connections with Hayes, Poindexter was, for a time, considered as a possible ambassador to Haiti (following in the footsteps of Ebenezer D. Bassett, who in 1869 became the minister-resident ambassador to Haiti).

Although he was sometimes disaffected by the policies and practices of the Republicans, he held his ground, believing the only way he could influence the party was by remaining a member. Thus, he led both state and national efforts to oppose calls for blacks to leave the party. His efforts led to his election to the Columbus City Council in 1880, and he served two terms, one of them as the council's vice president. In his later years he also continued to serve the state and people of Ohio through gubernatorial appointments to the Ohio State Forestry Board and the National Forestry Congress.

Poindexter's role in education was one of substantial influence—he served several terms on the Columbus Board of Education. Ohio's population of free blacks numbered nearly 25,000 in 1850, placing sixth among all states; and by the time of Poindexter's death, the state's black population was just over 111,000, comprising just 2.3 percent of the state's entire population. But these numbers were substantial enough to contribute to an overall progressive educational perspective, making Ohio home to the all-black Wilberforce University and the integrated Oberlin College, as well as desegregated public schools. But these efforts did not come without controversy, opposition, or cost. Poindexter was appointed to the school board in 1884 and reelected for four more terms for a total of ten years, during which time he served in a variety of offices and capacities. His most important contributions resulted from his ongoing quest for integration of both teachers and students. As early as the 1870s Poindexter had begun to lobby for integrated schools, citing the need to assure all of the state's children of a quality education, granting them access to the state's vast educational resources. He demanded an education in line with the morals and values of the era's leading liberal thinkers, including William Lloyd Garrison and Wendell Phillips.

Poindexter's views earned him a reputation for being a visionary but also a demagogue, leading to his rejected nomination as a trustee of Ohio State University in 1885, but successful appointments to the boards of the State School for the Blind in 1880 and Wilberforce University in 1896. Although he lacked a formal education, his efforts were constantly directed toward bettering the future of the state's young African Americans; and for his efforts, he was awarded an honorary Doctor of Divinity by Kentucky State University in Louisville.

Poindexter died in 1907 following a career in education, the church, and civic affairs of more than sixty years. He survived his wife, who had died in 1876, by thirty-one years, but was buried beside her in Columbus's Green Lawn Cemetery. He was eulogized by the Reverend Washington Gladden whose published sermon in the *Columbus Dispatch* of 11 February 1907 (11) noted, "To him more than any other belongs this country." Following his death, the Second Baptist Church became known as the James Preston Poindexter Baptist Church, in his honor.

FURTHER READING

Minor, Richard Clyde. "James Preston Poindexter, Elder Statesman of Columbus," *The Ohio State Archeological and Historical Quarterly* (July 1947).

Rodabaugh, James H. "The Negro in Ohio," *Journal of Negro History* (Jan. 1946).

White, Luella, et al. "Distinguished Negroes in Ohio," *Negro History Bulletin* (May 1942).

Wittke, Carl, ed. *History of the State of Ohio* (1944).

J. D. BOWERS

Poitier, Sidney (20 Feb. 1927–), actor, director, and producer, was born in Miami, Florida, the youngest of the seven children of Reginald Poitier, a tomato farmer, and Evelyn Outten. The family lived on Cat Island in the Bahamas, but when the tomato business no longer proved lucrative, they moved to Nassau, where Poitier attended Western Senior High School and Governor's High School. But even in the more prosperous urban center of Nassau, the Poitier family remained impoverished, and he was forced to leave school during the Depression in order to help his father.

Despite their financial difficulties, Reginald instilled a sense of pride in his family, and Poitier learned never to indulge in self-pity but rather to make the best out of every situation. With the urban landscape arrived the difficulties of adolescence and the influence of wayward youth, and when Poitier fell into some trouble his parents sent him to Miami to live with relatives. Working as a delivery boy, Poitier encountered racism in the form of police hostility and the Ku Klux Klan. Such experiences were jarring for a young teenager accustomed to the all-black environment of his native Bahamas, and, stifled by the oppressive racism, Poitier headed for New York. He quickly found a job as a dishwasher and struggled to make ends meet. In 1944, lying about his age, he joined the army, and after serving two years in a medical unit during World War II, he returned to Harlem in 1945.

While scouring local newspapers in search of a job, Poitier stumbled upon an advertisement for "actors wanted" and decided to audition at the American Negro Theater (ANT). His first audition ended rather dismally, when he was interrupted and told to stop wasting the director's time. That director, FREDERICK DOUGLASS O'NEAL, was not impressed with Poitier's halting, accented English as he struggled through the dialogue. Poitier was undaunted and left the theater even more determined to act. During the next six months he

Sidney Poitier with his Oscar statuette at the 36th Annual Academy Awards in Santa Monica, Ca., on 13 Apr. 1964. (AP Images.)

listened to the radio and improved his English, and by imitating the voices he heard, he managed to strip himself of his Bahamian accent. In addition, he devoured any available written text, knowing that reading extensively would help him accomplish his goal. Initially driven simply by a desire to show O'Neal that he could indeed act, Poitier soon began to take the theater seriously. His efforts paid off, and at his next audition O'Neal agreed to give him acting lessons in exchange for janitorial work.

Cast as HARRY BELAFONTE's understudy in *Days of Our Youth*, Poitier got his first break when Belafonte was unable to perform the night the Broadway director James Light came to see the play. Light was impressed by Poitier and offered him a role in his 1946 production of *Lysistrata*. Unfortunately, what should have been a promising debut performance was tarnished by an attack of nervousness that caused Poitier to flub most of his lines. But the critics were gentle, noting particularly Poitier's gift for comedy. Following this production, Poitier appeared at the ANT in *On Strivers Row* (1946) and then as Lester in *Anna Lucasta*. In 1950 he was cast in the leading role as a doctor struggling to do his job well during the tense racial climate after World War II in Joseph Mankiewicz's drama *No Way Out*. Also in 1950 Poitier married

the dancer Juanita Hardy, with whom he would have four children before the couple's divorce in 1965.

The success of *No Way Out* led to roles in *Cry, the Beloved Country* (1951), *Red Ball Express* (1952), *Go, Man, Go!* (1954), and *The Blackboard Jungle* (1955). With these films under his belt, Poitier gained access to more of what Hollywood had to offer, and he worked consistently during the 1950s and 1960s, appearing in *Edge of the City* (1957), *Something of Value* (1957), *The Defiant Ones* (1958), and *Porgy and Bess* (1959). In each case he portrayed polite, well-spoken African Americans, defying the stereotype of the singing, dancing, and joking black man that had prevailed in American film. With his performance in *The Defiant Ones* he became the first African American to be nominated for an Academy Award as Best Actor.

With his reputation established as a Hollywood star, Poitier returned to the stage in 1959, originating the role of Walter Lee Younger in LORRAINE HANSBERRY's *A Raisin in the Sun*, produced by Lloyd Richards. Poitier won a Best Actor Tony for this role before returning to film in *All the Young Men* (1960) and again as Younger in the film version of *A Raisin in the Sun* (1961). These two roles led up to his part in *Lilies of the Field* (1963), the story of a construction worker who comes to the aid of a group of German-speaking nuns. With this performance Poitier became the first African American to win the Academy Award for Best Actor in 1964. Thereafter Poitier was even more sought after as an actor, and in 1967 alone he appeared in three films for which he earned enormous success: he starred in *To Sir with Love* and then played Virgil Tibbs, a northern police detective struggling with a racist sheriff in a southern town in *In the Heat of the Night*. He then played a successful young doctor who is engaged to a young white woman in *Guess Who's Coming to Dinner?*, which was nominated for ten Academy awards.

With each role, Poitier was highly conscious of representing his family and his race, and he accepted only those roles that he believed portrayed African Americans in a positive light. For all of his efforts, he still received criticism from other black actors who believed Poitier was doing a disservice to his race by embodying the "good Negro" stereotype—the noble and magnanimous black man who never steps out of the mainstream perception of what a "proper" black man ought to be and do.

In 1970 Poitier reprised his role as Virgil Tibbs in *They Call Me Mister Tibbs*, and in 1972 he appeared as Buck, opposite Harry Belafonte, in *Buck and the Preacher*, a role that marked a departure from the generally distinguished characters he had previously portrayed. The latter was also his directorial debut. Two years later he collaborated with BILL COSBY in *Uptown Saturday Night* (1974). In 1974 Poitier married the actress Joanna Shimkus; they had two children. He also worked with Paul Newman and Barbra Streisand, among others, to form First Artists, an independent production company. He subsequently filmed two sequels to *Uptown Saturday Night*, titled *Let's Do It Again* (1975) and *A Piece of the Action* (1977).

In 1980 Poitier published an autobiography, *This Life*, and gave up acting in favor of directing such movies as *Stir Crazy* (1980), *Hanky Panky* (1982), and *Fast Forward* (1985). He collaborated with Bill Cosby once again in 1990 and directed *Ghost Dad*. Poitier returned to acting with *Shoot to Kill* (1988), *Little Nikita* (1988), *Sneakers* (1992), and television films such as *Separate but Equal* (1991), *Children of the Dust* (1995), *To Sir with Love II* (1996), *Mandela and de Klerk* (1997), and *The Simple Life of Noah Dearborn* (1999).

In 1997 Poitier served briefly as the Bahamian ambassador to Japan. He published a second autobiography, *The Measure of a Man: A Spiritual Autobiography*, in 2000. He has received numerous honors, including two Emmy awards, five NAACP Image awards, Lifetime Achievement awards from the American Film Institute and the Screen Actors Guild, and a knighthood from Queen Elizabeth of England. In 2002 Poitier was awarded an Honorary Academy Award. That same night HALLE BERRY became the first black woman to win a Best Actress Oscar and DENZEL WASHINGTON became the first African American actor to win a Best Actor Oscar since Poitier broke that color line in 1964. In 2009 President BARACK OBAMA awarded Poitier the Presidential Medal of Freedom, one of the nation's two highest civilian awards. Poitier received another major honor in 2011 when he was the recipient of a Gala Tribute by the Film Society of Lincoln Center. Previous winners included John Ford, Billy Wilder, and Jane Fonda. Poitier was the first person of color to be honored by this award.

FURTHER READING

Poitier, Sidney. *The Measure of a Man: A Spiritual Autobiography* (2000).

Poitier, Sydney. *This Life* (1980).

Ewers, Carolyn H. *Sidney Poitier: The Long Journey, a Biography* (1969).

Keyser, Lester J., and André H. Ruszkowski. *The Cinema of Sidney Poitier: The Black Man's Changing Role on the American Screen* (1980).

RÉGINE MICHELLE JEAN-CHARLES

Poles, Spottswood (9 Dec. 1887–12 Sept. 1962), Negro League baseball player, was born in Winchester, Virginia, the son of French Poles, a laborer, and Matilda (maiden name unknown). "I played baseball since I was six years old, using a broomstick and a tennis ball," Poles once reminisced. At age fifteen he was playing for the Hello Bill boys' club, graduating to the Springdale Athletic Club. In 1906 he joined the Harrisburg, Pennsylvania, Colored Giants. "I looked like my name," he said, "a bean pole."

He joined the illustrious New York Lincoln Giants as an outfielder in 1909. With the Hall of Fame shortstop JOHN HENRY LLOYD, the pitchers Joe Williams and DICK REDDING, the catcher LOUIS SANTOP, and Poles, the team was one of the best in black baseball history. They claimed a record of 105 wins and only seventeen losses in 1909. Although most of their opponents were semiprofessional teams, they split a doubleheader with the Jersey City Skeeters of the Eastern (later International) League. The 1912 team was good enough to once beat the New York Yankees 6–0 and the National League champion New York Giants by the same score, although Poles did not play in either game. He did play in four games against the National League Philadelphia Phillies in 1913, getting ten hits and stealing four bases. Three of his hits and two stolen bases came against the pitching great Grover Cleveland Alexander. The Lincoln Giants' record for the year was 101–6. In later seasons Poles made three hits in two games against Chief Bender of the Philadelphia Athletics and against Pol Perritt of the New York Giants in 1915; in 1917 he had four more hits in two games against the A's Bullet Joe Bush.

Poles's best years were achieved before World War I, when Negro League statistics were sketchy. But as center fielder for the Lincoln Giants, he was credited with averages of .440, .398, and .487 against semiprofessional opponents in 1911, 1912, and 1914. He put together an outstanding record against white major league barnstormers: a .607 batting average in seven games. Stolen bases were reported for only four games; in them, Poles stole five times.

In 1917 Poles enlisted in the 369th Infantry Regiment, which was later attached to the French army. He earned five battle stars and a Purple Heart. Mustered out in 1919, he returned to the Lincolns for five more years. Only his 1922 statistics, when he batted .286, are available. One young semiprofessional pitcher, Waite Hoyt, who went on to star with the Yankees, recalled that Poles leaned forward on fly balls and caught them behind his back.

Sometimes called the "black Ty Cobb," Poles was one of the fastest men in black baseball—some old-timers considered him faster than the illustrious COOL PAPA BELL. Pitcher Sam Streeter of the Negro League Atlantic City, New Jersey, Bacharach Giants had heard of Poles's reputation, but he still was not prepared for Poles's speed at age thirty-six. "He hit that ball on one hop back to me," Streeter said. "I turned to throw to first, and he crossed the base before the ball got there! I said, 'Well, I won't play around with *you* anymore!'"

In 1923 Poles retired from baseball. He could still hit, he said, but "got tired of all the train travel and carrying those bags around all the time." He worked at Olmstead Air Force Base in Harrisburg until 1945, the year that JACKIE ROBINSON signed with the Brooklyn Dodgers. "Old Poles grew too soon old," he said. "But I came close." John McGraw, manager of the New York Giants, reportedly indicated that had black players been allowed in the major leagues, he would have wanted Lloyd, Williams, Redding, and Poles on his team. Poles later coached a young black pitcher, Brooks Lawrence, who played in the major leagues. Whether Poles was ever married is not known. He died in Harrisburg and is buried in Arlington National Cemetery.

FURTHER READING

Lantot, Neil. *Negro League Baseball: The Rise and Ruin of a Black Institution* (2004).

Heaphy, Leslie A. *The Negro Leagues, 1869–1960* (2002).

Holway, John B. "Spottswood Poles," *Baseball Research Journal* 4 (1975).

McNeil, William F. *Cool Papas and Double Duties: The All-Time Greats of the Negro Leagues* (2001).

This entry is taken from the *American National Biography* and is published here with the permission of the American Council of Learned Societies.

JOHN B. HOLWAY

Polite, Carlene Hatcher

Polite, Carlene Hatcher (28 Aug. 1932–7 Dec. 2009), author, dancer, and activist, was born Carlene Hatcher in Detroit, Michigan, the daughter of Lillian Cook and John Hatcher, international representatives of the United Automobile Workers–Congress of Industrial Organizations (UAW–CIO). By age twelve she was already exhibiting an interest in creative writing, completing several poems while attending public schools in Detroit. After her high school graduation, she attended Sarah Lawrence College, a coeducational liberal arts school outside New York City.

While attending Sarah Lawrence she decided to pursue dance at the prestigious Martha Graham School of Contemporary Dance, one of the nation's oldest dance schools. From 1955 to 1963 Polite enjoyed a career as a professional dancer, appearing on stage with the Concert Dance Theatre of New York City from 1955 to 1959, the Vanguard Playhouse in Detroit from 1960 to 1962, and as a dancer and organizer at the Equity Theater in Detroit from 1962 to 1964. In the early 1960s, she appeared as a specialty dancer in *The King and I*, *The Boy Friend*, and *Dark of the Moon*. Polite taught modern dance in the Martha Graham technique as a guest instructor at the Detroit Young Women's Christian Association (YWCA) from 1960 to 1962, the Detroit Young Men's Christian Association (YMCA) from 1962 to 1963, and at Wayne State University. She married Allen Polite, a librarian for the United Nations; the couple had two daughters, Glynda and Lila, before they divorced.

During the 1960s, while maintaining a career in dance, Polite also became involved in politics and civil rights as her parents had been. Her mother, who worked with Eleanor Roosevelt, was instrumental in the creation of the Fair Employment Practices Commission. Polite worked as a staff worker for the Michigan Democratic Party in Detroit and was later elected to the Michigan State Central Committee, where she served from 1962 to 1963. While working for the Detroit Council for Human Rights in 1963, she served as special assistant and coordinator for the Walk to Freedom on 23 June, which served to commemorate the Detroit riot of 1943 and to shed light on the social ills of the time. Some say Dr. MARTIN LUTHER KING JR. first gave his "I Have a Dream" speech to a crowd of more than 125,000 people at the Walk to Freedom. In November 1963 Polite helped coordinate the Freedom Now rally and served as an organizer of the Northern Negro Leadership Conference. She was also active in the NAACP throughout the early 1960s.

When Polite met the French editor Dominique de Roux in Detroit, he encouraged her to move to Paris, where she might be able to focus on her writing exclusively. Before leaving for Paris in 1964, where she would reside for seven years, Polite worked as a special assistant to Rev. C. L. FRANKLIN, civil rights leader and father of ARETHA FRANKLIN, organizing a freedom march. Once in Paris, Polite began to publish essays in journals and magazines. In 1968 "Speak, Brother!," an essay concerned with civil rights, appeared in *Mademoiselle*. She was in Paris when she wrote and published her first novel, *Les Flagellents*, in 1966. *Les Flagellents* was the first publication released by Christian Bourgois Editeur. A year after its French debut, Farrar, Straus and Giroux published *The Flagellants* in the United States. Praised by critics in France for its experimental prose, *The Flagellants* was translated into several languages, including Dutch, Italian, and German. The novel consisted of interior monologues, speeches, and exchanges by the main characters, Ideal and Jimson, an interracial couple living in New York in the midst of a relationship collapsing under the burden of presumed gender roles and racial stereotypes.

Shortly after *The Flagellants* was published in English and received a Pulitzer Prize nomination, Polite was honored with the National Foundation on the Arts and Humanities fellowship and the Rockefeller Foundation fellowship in 1968. Her second book, *Sister X and the Victims of Foul Play*, was published in 1975. In the novel, an ex-convict and a seamstress reminisce about the life of a mutual friend named Sister X. As in *The Flagellants*, Polite used a nontraditional approach including flashbacks, rich African American vernacular, and folklore.

During the 1970s, Polite returned to the United States and took an associate professorship at the State University of New York at Buffalo, where she worked in numerous capacities, including as a creative writing and African American literature professor and as the chair of the African Studies department.

In 1995 Polite was still committed to politics, particularly women's issues. She attended the International Conference on Women in China as part of a 500-member delegation of the Majority People's Fund for the 21st Century. While there, she sat on panels discussing art, spirituality, religion, culture, and education. In 2004 Polite contributed a short story to *Black Satin: Contemporary Erotic Fiction by Writers of African Origin*, edited by J. H. Blair. She died in Cheektowaga, New York, at the age of 77.

FURTHER READING

Dobson, Frank E., Jr. "Carlene Hatcher Polite," in *Contemporary African American Novelists: A Bio-Bibliographical Critical Sourcebook*, ed. Emmanuel S. Nelson (1999).

Donald, Kalenda C. Eaton. "Carlene Hatcher Polite," in *An Encyclopedia of African American Literature*, eds. J. David Macey and Hans Ostrom (2005).

Mallory, Devona. "Carlene Hatcher Polite," in *Writing African American Women: An Encyclopedia of Literature by and about Women of Color*, ed. Elizabeth Ann Beaulieu (2006).

Palazzetti, Agnes. "UB Professor En Route to Women's Conference in China Activist Works to Attain Equality for Everyone," *Buffalo News* (29 Aug. 1995).

Worthington-Smith, Hammett. "Carlene Hatcher Polite," in *Dictionary of Literary Biography: Afro-American Fiction Writers after 1955*, vol. 33, eds. Thadious M. Davis and Trudier Harris (1984).

KAAVONIA HINTON

Polk, Prentice Herman (P. H.) (25 Nov. 1898–29 Dec. 1984), photographer, was born Herman Polk in Bessemer, Alabama, the son of Jacob Prentice Polk, a laborer and mineworker, and Christine Romelia Ward, a laborer and seamstress. He grew up with three older sisters, Mayme, Freddie, and Georgia, and was eleven when his father died of black-lung disease in 1909. He enrolled in the Hard School (junior high) and later attended the Tuggle Institute, a boarding school for African American boys in Birmingham. He returned to Bessemer in 1913 to help support his family financially, working as a presser for William A. Freeman, a local African American tailor.

In 1916 Polk assumed his father's name Prentice. Inspired by the work of the painter Vincent Van Gogh, Polk entered Tuskegee Normal and Industrial Institute (Tuskegee University) as an evening student intent on studying painting but was enrolled by the dean in a house-painting course, the founder BOOKER T. WASHINGTON having emphasized teacher training and instruction in "practical skills," such as farming, carpentry, brick making, shoemaking, cabinetmaking, and printing at the school. The following term Polk became a full-time day student. Learning about a newly formed photography division headed by the school photographer CORNELIUS M. BATTEY, Polk was the first to sign up.

Polk studied with Battey for three years, leaving in 1920 with hopes of attending photography school. At the same time his mother and sister relocated to Chicago to seek better employment opportunities. Unable to get into photography school, Polk moved briefly to Mobile and worked for a power plant before relocating to nearby Chickasaw to work in the shipyards. There he responded to a magazine advertisement for a photography correspondence course and saved the $150 needed for materials. The packet included an article on the Dutch painter Rembrandt that discussed the artist's use of deep shadow to define form. Polk was intrigued by Rembrandt's compositional approach and incorporated a shadow-based technique in his photography.

Polk completed the course and in 1922 joined his mother and sisters in Chicago, where he became a painter for the Pullman Company and began dating Margaret Blanche Thompson from Brunswick, Georgia. The couple married on 12 January 1926, the month Polk met the commercial photographer Fred A. Jensen, who was known for his darkroom skills. Polk became Jensen's apprentice and took a second painting job to defray the cost of supplies. When his wife became pregnant that year with the first of their nine children, Polk solicited photography jobs door-to-door, earning more money than he made from the painting jobs combined. But the approaching winter began to limit the amount of time he could tolerate the outdoors, and he returned to Alabama.

In Tuskegee by October 1927 with his wife, their five-month-old son Prentice H. Polk Jr., and less than $100, Polk secured a free photography space and opened Polk's Studio. During the first year he photographed *The Spinning Wheel* for *Prince's Magazine* and made initial portraits of Tuskegee students and local rural subjects. In 1928 he began teaching photography at Tuskegee and assisting Leonard G. Hyman, Battey's successor. His portraits of rural figures, such as *Pipe Smoker* (1932), *George Moore* (1930), and *The Boss* (1932), along with official work and commissioned assignments were examples of his propensity for "working from the dark side." In 1933 he became the official photographer and head of the photography division. Except for 1938, when he tried unsuccessfully to establish a studio in Atlanta, Georgia, Polk was affiliated with the institute for the remainder of his life.

In addition to images of campus dignitaries, distinguished guests, and campus events, Polk created more than five hundred photographs of GEORGE WASHINGTON CARVER between 1927 and 1942, over one hundred images of the more than one thousand men who served as Tuskegee Airmen from 1940 to 1946, and a portfolio of figures and events related to the 1960s civil rights movement in the United States, including portraits of ROY WILKINS, THURGOOD MARSHALL, WHITNEY YOUNG, MARTIN LUTHER KING JR., JULIAN BOND, DICK GREGORY, STOKELY CARMICHAEL (KWAME TOURE), MALCOLM X, FANNIE LOU HAMER, LOUIS FARRAKHAN, ADAM CLAYTON POWELL, and MUHAMMAD ALI. Polk captured Carver with the automobile mogul Henry Ford, President Franklin Delano Roosevelt, and numerous other leaders. He also documented CHARLES ALFRED "CHIEF" ANDERSON seconds before the renowned African American pilot took Eleanor Roosevelt on a demonstration flight that played a significant role in diffusing congressional efforts to terminate the flight program. The photograph was on view at NASA in 1983 during the launching of the space shuttle *Challenger* when GUION S. BLUFORD became the first African American astronaut in space and Polk was a special guest.

Polk received the National Conference of Artists' Award in 1979, the Black Photographers' Annual Testimonial Award in 1980, and a National Endowment for the Arts Fellowship in 1981. His photographs were exhibited overseas in Italy, Russia, and Nigeria and domestically at the Studio Museum in Harlem, the Corcoran Gallery of Art, the Smithsonian Institution, the High Museum of Art, and the Rhode Island School of Design. The Photographs of P. H. Polk, organized for the Southern Arts Federation in 1996, became the longest running exhibition of work by an African American artist in history as of 2007. His work is in the permanent collections of the Corcoran Museum of Art, the High Museum of Art, the Paul R. Jones Collection, the Birmingham Museum of Art, and the Carver Museum at Tuskegee University.

Polk died in Tallahassee, Alabama, in 1984 from complications related to diabetes and was buried in the Tuskegee University Cemetery. In 2002 he was the subject of a simulcast television and radio documentary titled *Moments of Destiny* produced by the University of Alabama Center for Public Television and Radio.

FURTHER READING

Amaki, Amalia K., ed. "Flash from the Past: Hidden Messages in the Photographs of P. H. Polk," in *A Century of African American Art: The Paul R. Jones Collection* (2004).

Chapp, Belena S., et al. *Through These Eyes: The Photographs of P. H. Polk* (1997).

AMALIA K. AMAKI

Pollard, Auburey (1947–26 July 1967), killed by police during racial disturbances in Detroit, Michigan, in July 1967, was the second of five children born in that city to Auburey Pollard Sr., a janitor and laborer for the Detroit Department of Public Works, and his wife Rebecca, a laundress, whose maiden name is unknown.

Rebecca Pollard had arrived in Detroit from Tennessee in 1943, the year of the city's first major race riot, in which wartime racial tensions over housing and jobs left thirty-four people dead, twenty-five of them black, and most of them shot by the police. Economic opportunities had improved somewhat by the time she and her husband Auburey began raising their family in the economic boom years after World War II. With both parents working extra jobs the Pollards achieved their goal of buying their own home and car by 1955. Auburey was a sickly child, troubled by stomach and hernia problems, but by the time he reached his early teens his health had improved. A keen swimmer, he was a lifeguard at his local YMCA and, like thousands of boys in the city of JOE LOUIS, he also dreamed of becoming a champion boxer. Pollard showed some promise in art, but did not perform well academically at Detroit's Northwestern High School, where he took special education classes. Shortly before leaving high school in early 1965, he got in a fight with a special education teacher who had allegedly taunted him in front of his classmates. Pollard responded by assaulting the teacher, for which he was sentenced to fifteen days in the Detroit House of Correction.

On leaving high school, Pollard enrolled in October 1965 at Detroit's McNamara Skills Center, one of the nation's first employment training programs established as part of President Lyndon Johnson's War on Poverty. Despite his dream of becoming a commercial artist, Auburey Jr. followed his father's advice by training to be an arc welder, an extremely practical vocation in a city dominated by the automobile industry. In October 1966 he began working as a welder at a local Ford plant.

Pollard's personal life became increasingly fraught, however. Shortly after beginning work at Ford, and while still only seventeen, he began living with a woman older than his own mother. Despite the attention Pollard showed the woman's children, she later arranged for two male friends to attack him and force him to leave. When Pollard beat the men up instead, the Wayne County Prosecutor's Office cautioned him. He began drinking and hanging out with several childhood friends, all of whom had spent time in juvenile detention centers as he had. Together they engaged in petty crime and fights, and had several run-ins with Detroit's notoriously racist police force, who assaulted them on at least one occasion. Pollard's economic prospects also diminished. In early 1967 he was transferred from welding to simple laboring at the Ford plant, at tasks that caused him sinus problems. Ford terminated his contract in April 1967. Unemployed and angry at his father for allegedly stealing money he had given him to make down payments on a car, Auburey Jr. spent less time with his family and more time with his friends, who spent their time at Detroit's Algiers Motel, which was frequented mainly by prostitutes, pimps, drug pushers, and other petty criminals.

In the early hours of 23 July 1967 a police raid on a "blind-pig," an illegal drinking den, in the heart of black Detroit precipitated a full-scale riot involving clashes between African American youths and the heavily white Detroit police force. Later that day, along with his friends and thousands of others, Auburey Pollard joined in looting on the main black thoroughfare, Twelfth Street, stealing a couple of radios. As the violence escalated over the next two days, however, leaving more than twenty Detroiters dead, Pollard sought safety indoors as civil rights leaders and local, state, and federal officials bickered about how best to quell the riot. Despite the addition of federal troops on 25 July, the violence continued, with reports of sniper attacks on law enforcement officials in several neighborhoods.

In the early hours of 26 July, local police, national guardsmen and a federal paratrooper were called to the Algiers Motel because of reported sniper fire in that vicinity. No weapons were ever found in the motel, however, and police ballistic experts later testified in court that no shots had been fired from that building. The journalist John Hersey later uncovered evidence that a motel guest fired a starter pistol shortly before the authorities arrived. The precise sequence of events at the motel may never be fully known, given the changing and conflicting statements provided by both law enforcement officers and motel guests. It quickly became apparent, however, that police officers had shot and killed Auburey Pollard and two other black teenagers who were with him at the motel that evening, Carl Cooper and Fred Temple. Evidence provided at several trials between 1969 and 1972 and in Hersey's best-selling investigation of the incident suggests that young, inexperienced officers probably shot and killed Cooper and Temple immediately upon entering the motel. Pollard, six other black men, and two white female prostitutes who were with them in the motel were then rounded up by three police officers, who struck them with rifle butts and lined them up against a lobby wall. The officers then continued to assault and verbally abuse each of the guests, including the women, who were called "nigger lovers," and whose clothing they ripped. One officer held a shotgun between the legs of one of the men and threatened to blow his testicles off. Although the survivors offered slightly different versions of what happened next, it appears that the officers then played a "death game," in which they brought each of the men to separate rooms for questioning about the alleged sniper, and then fired shots so as to force those in the other rooms to confess their guilt for fear of being the next one killed. Sometime during this "game," police officer Ronald August shot and killed Auburey Pollard, who had already been severely beaten. Although August made no report about the incident at the time, he confessed five days later to having shot Pollard in self-defense during a struggle in which Pollard had allegedly reached for the officer's weapon.

Patrolman August's confession came two days after JOHN CONYERS, other civil rights leaders, and the press had been alerted to the suspicious nature of the deaths at the Algiers Motel. A pathologist found that the three men had all been shot at close range, while in "non-aggressive postures" (Fine, 282). In all, forty-three people were killed during the 1967 Detroit riots, all but ten of them African Americans; two thousand people were injured and seven thousand arrested. By August of that year, however, the deaths of Temple, Cooper, and Pollard had become the most significant aspect of the riot for many whites and African Americans in Detroit. Doubting that white police officers would ever be found guilty of killing young black men, the Student Nonviolent Coordinating Committee (SNCC) activist H. RAP BROWN called for a "people's tribunal," to call the police to account. Although the officers did not attend the tribunal held at the Reverend ALBERT CLEAGE's church in late August 1967, between 700 and 2,000 Detroiters did attend the mock trial. The jury, which included two whites and ROSA PARKS, found the police officers guilty, although no one followed Rap Brown's suggestion that a guilty verdict required that "the people…carry out an execution" (Fine, 285).

The state trial took much longer and in 1969 was controversially moved from Detroit, a city with a predominantly black jury pool to Mason, a small Michigan town where MALCOLM X's father had been killed and that was 99 percent white. None of the police officers were ever convicted of the killings, although the City of Detroit later paid the Pollard, Cooper, and Temple families $62,500 each after they promised to withdraw civil damage suits. The state senator and future Detroit mayor COLEMAN YOUNG summed up the prevailing mood of African Americans in his city when he stated in 1971 that the exoneration of the police officers in the Algiers Motel killings, "demonstrates once and again that…there is no law and order where black people are involved, especially when they are involved with the police" (Fine, 290).

FURTHER READING

Fine, Sidney. *Violence in the Model City: The Cavanagh Administration, Race Relations, and the Detroit Race Riot of 1967* (1989).

Hersey, John. *The Algiers Motel Incident* (1968).

STEVEN J. NIVEN

Pollard, Charlie Wesley (13 Apr. 1906–29 Apr. 2000), farmer, civil rights activist, and lead plaintiff in the lawsuit against the government in the Tuskegee Syphilis Study, was born in Notasulga, Alabama, the third child of six children of Lucius and Alma Pollard. The Pollard family owned and farmed their land in the Notasulga area, just outside of Tuskegee, for generations after the Civil War. As with many farmers, they often needed to secure liens, with their animals as the collateral, in order to complete their crop. In the early 1900s the family began to buy more acreage, and by 1908 Pollard's father was farming 160 acres and was the first black man in the county to own a mechanical cotton picker. Pollard learned early how to horse and cattle trade, and to build upon his family's farming skills. He was educated in the Shiloh School, one of the earliest Rosenwald schools built in the South for African Americans, in the 1910s. He married Georgia Momon in 1924 and had one daughter, Ralphine. After his wife died in childbirth, he had two more daughters Louise Randall and Drucilla Shealey. He later married Luiza Woods, but had no children in this marriage.

Charlie Pollard became active in the Tuskegee Civil Association, serving as the precinct captain for Notasulga, and contributing to protecting voting rights in the area. He was a stalwart in his church, remembered for always sitting in the second row of pews and making sure that every child in the congregation received a little something on his or her birthday. In 1932 he was recruited at the Shiloh Missionary Baptist Church, next to the school, to be in what became known as the Tuskegee Syphilis Study. Pollard was told he was being treated for his "bad blood," a euphemism for syphilis, even though the study participants were not offered treatment after the first few months. The study continued for the next forty years. During that time, Pollard never knew that he was not getting treated. His father, uncle, and cousins were also in the Tuskegee Study.

Pollard realized he was part of the infamous study through a discussion with a newspaper reporter in a stockyard in nearby Montgomery, days after the story of the study broke in the newspapers in 1972. Almost immediately, he went to see Fred D. Gray, a well-known civil rights activist/attorney in Tuskegee. Pollard became the lead plaintiff in *Pollard v. United States of America*, the class action suit against the federal and state government and others involved in the study. The case was heard in federal court—despite the difficulties of bringing this kind of case against the government—and settled out of court for $10 million in 1974. It brought some compensation to the families of the 632 men who had been unwittingly included in the study. Pollard appeared before the Senate committee investigating the study, was interviewed by numerous newspaper and television reporters, and was one of the six survivors of the study in the East Room of the White House on 16 May 1997, when President Bill Clinton offered a formal apology for the study. Charlie Pollard is buried next to his wife, Luiza (who died in 1989), in the Shiloh church graveyard along with more than two dozen other men from the study, and is remembered for the important role he played in bringing voice and closure to the survivors and families of the syphilis study and for his civil rights activism.

FURTHER READING

Gray, Fred D. *The Tuskegee Syphilis Study* (1998).

Reverby, Susan M., ed. *Tuskegee's Truths: Rethinking the Tuskegee Syphilis Study* (2000).

SUSAN M. REVERBY
ELIZABETH SIMS

Pollard, Fritz (27 Jan. 1894–11 May 1986), football player and coach, was born Frederick Douglass Pollard in Chicago, Illinois, the son of John William Pollard, a barber, and Catherine Amanda Hughes, a seamstress. Pollard grew up in the all-white Rogers Park section of Chicago, where his family

Fritz Pollard reminisces at his home in New Rochelle, N.Y. on 12 Feb. 1975. A native of Chicago, he became player-coach of the Akron Pros in 1920. (AP Images.)

was grudgingly accepted. He was nicknamed Fritz by the neighborhood's many German-speaking residents.

Following the example set by his father, who had gained a boxing reputation in the Union army, and by his older brothers and sisters, who were superb high school athletes, Pollard became a standout athlete in football, baseball, and track. During his senior year at Lane Technical High School (1911–1912) he was named to all-Cook County teams in track and football. Despite his small stature (5' 8", 150 pounds), he used his speed and agility to score touchdowns, establishing himself as one of the Chicago area's best high school football players.

After high school, Pollard looked for a college where he might showcase his football talent. In the process he became a "tramp athlete," briefly attending five different schools from 1912 until 1914. In June 1914 he married Ada Parker Laing; they had four children. The oldest child, Fritz Pollard Jr., went on to become a Little All-American football player and a bronze medal winner in the 110-meter hurdles at the 1936 Olympic Games. After attending Springfield (Massachusetts) High School in 1914–1915 to earn needed foreign language credits, Pollard entered Brown University in 1915.

At Brown, Pollard was at first harassed and ostracized by the other members of the football team, all of them white, but he ultimately won acceptance through superior play and perseverance. By making a number of long spectacular runs, he won national acclaim in Brown's 3–0 upset victory over Yale in 1915. To play in that game at the Yale Bowl, however, Pollard had to be escorted onto the field just before the opening kickoff to avoid insults or possible physical injury by Yale fans. When he ran with the ball, Yale fans taunted him by singing verses of "Bye, Bye, Blackbird." Pollard later recalled how he had been "niggerized" during Brown's games with Yale, Harvard, and other schools. At the end of the season Brown was invited to play in the Tournament of Roses game in Pasadena, California, against Washington State College. Although his performance was subpar on a muddy field in Brown's 14–0 loss, Pollard became the first African American to compete in what would soon be known as the Rose Bowl game.

During the 1916 season Pollard led Brown to one of its most successful records: eight wins and one defeat. His efforts were particularly notable in Brown's victories over Yale and Harvard, both premier college teams. Walter Camp, a former Yale player and college football innovator, named Pollard to a backfield position on his prestigious All-American team. Camp remarked that Pollard was "one of the greatest runners I have ever seen." Pollard was only the second African American selected to the first team by Camp (the first was WILLIAM HENRY LEWIS, a center rush from Harvard, in 1892–1893) and the first selected as a back. During the spring semester Pollard neglected his studies and became ineligible for the 1917 season. Failing to improve his academic standing by the end of the year, he accepted a position as physical director in the army's Young Men's Christian Association unit at Camp Meade, Maryland, in February 1918. In the late summer of 1918 he became head football coach at Lincoln University in Pennsylvania, a position he held through 1920.

While at Lincoln, Pollard was recruited to play professional football for the Akron Indians in 1919. By the following year he and Jim Thorpe became leading players and gate attractions in the American Professional Football Association, which was renamed the National Football League (NFL) in 1922. Pollard led Akron (renamed the Pros) to a world championship in 1920. During the 1921 season he became the team's head coach, making him the first black head coach of a team in a major sport and the first in NFL history. He coached the Milwaukee Badgers in 1922 and the Hammond Pros in 1923.

Pollard's professional playing career lasted from 1919 through 1926, including all or parts of seven years in the NFL and parts of two seasons and all of one (1924) with Gilberton in the Pennsylvania Anthracite League. After he retired as a player, Pollard coached two independent all-black teams: the Chicago Black Hawks (1928–1932) and the New York Brown Bombers (1935–1937). His expressed intention in coaching these teams was to show that many African American athletes had the ability to play in the NFL. Despite his efforts, NFL teams did not include any African American players from 1934 through 1945.

Early in his playing career Pollard became an active businessman. In 1922 he founded an investment firm in Chicago that served the black community. The firm prospered during the 1920s but went bankrupt in 1931. Heavily in debt, he moved to New York in 1932, where he ran a coal company for several years. In 1933 he was a casting agent for his friend and former Akron teammate PAUL ROBESON in the filming of *The Emperor Jones*. While remaining active as an entertainment agent, Pollard founded the first black tabloid newspaper, the *New York Independent News*, in 1935. He owned the paper until 1942. The following year he took control of Suntan Studios in Harlem, where he reviewed talent he employed through his booking agency. At the same time he became New York manager of Soundies Distributing Company, a business that produced an early form of music videos, which involved a projected film image synchronized with sound, that were played in hotels, bars, and restaurants. Pollard produced all the soundies that featured prominent black artists until the company was bought out by white interests at the end of World War II. After securing a divorce, he married Mary Ella Austin in 1947. They had no children.

In the postwar years Pollard continued to book talent in nightclubs and on radio and television. He produced a feature film, *Rockin' the Blues* (1955), showcasing new black artists. From the early 1950s until his retirement in 1975, he devoted much of his time to his successful tax consulting firm. Learning the business on his own, he became relatively prosperous in what he called "the income tax racket." Among his many honors, he was the first African American elected to the National Collegiate Football Hall of Fame in 1954, and he received the National Urban League's Whitney M. Young Jr. Memorial Award, honoring outstanding African Americans, in 1978. He died in Silver Spring, Maryland.

FURTHER READING
Carroll, John M. *Fritz Pollard: Pioneer in Racial Advancement* (1992).
Nesfield, Carl. "Pride against Prejudice: Fritz Pollard, Brown's All-American Pre-World War I Vintage," *Black Sports*, Nov. 1971 and Dec. 1971.
This entry is taken from the *American National Biography* and is published here with the permission of the American Council of Learned Societies.

JOHN M. CARROLL

Pomp (c. 1762–6 Aug. 1795), enslaved man and farmer, was probably born in West Africa. He worked as a farmhand and slave in Massachusetts. A transcript of Pomp's dying confession, which survives as a one-page broadside, is the only source of information about his life, but one that provides rare insight into the life of an African American in New England in the days of the early republic.

How exactly Pomp came to America, and specifically Boston, is unclear, but he arrived as a baby along with both his parents. His father died soon after his arrival in Boston and Pomp was put into the service of a Mr. Abbot of Andover (whether in slavery or indenture is not known). Pomp remained with Mr. Abbot until the age of sixteen, at which time he was passed on to his master's son (also referred to as Mr. Abbot). It was at this point that Pomp apparently began to question the nature of his servitude and his lack of appropriate compensation and attempted to assert his freedom. The American Revolution and the rhetoric surrounding it may have affected him, though unlike David Walker and other black nationalists he does not explicitly refer to the Declaration of Independence or the war. Pomp's confession does not indicate if he was influenced by the lawsuits filed by others enslaved in Massachusetts in response to the 1780 state constitution. People such as Elizabeth Freeman (Mum Bett) in 1781 and Quok Walker in 1783 successfully challenged the legality of slavery under the constitution of Massachusetts and gained their immediate freedom. After appealing to the selectmen of Andover for clarification of his status as slave or free, and not being freed from his service, Pomp briefly remained with the second Mr. Abbot and then became the servant of Captain Charles Furbush. While slavery was no longer legal in Massachusetts after 1783, the status of some servants continued as perpetual servitude and not as limited time indenture.

In his confession Pomp described his life on the Furbush farm as a time of unjustly difficult work with little aid from his master. Pomp tended to large numbers of cattle and horses as well as growing grain crops. The main grievances that Pomp recounted were lack of time to go to church on Sundays, no time off for public holidays such as Election Day, virtually no compensation for his labor, and the lack of other laborers to assist him in his tasks. As with many other black New Englanders, Pomp had no community of fellow servants or fellow African Americans with which to interact. His society was composed almost entirely of Europeans of alien culture and customs from those he brought to the New World. Like many other slaves and servants in the new American republic, Pomp chose to resist his master by running away. His confession illustrates that escape and harsh response to escape were not the sole prerogative of the southern plantation. Treatment could be as harsh in Massachusetts as in Charleston, and without recourse to a community of those similarly treated. Had Pomp lived in Boston, his lot might have been different and his options for an independent life greater, but Andover was a town with a minuscule African population.

Pomp's escape was short-lived. He was recaptured and whipped severely in punishment. Despite the harsh treatment, Pomp again ran away. Again recaptured, he continued to work on the Furbush farm for more than ten years. Finally, sometime around 1795, Pomp attempted escape one more time, and while able to maintain his freedom for a week was again recaptured and, in his words, "I was again brought back by my master, stripped naked, tied up by both hands, and unmercifully flogged. This was in the evening, and though it was late in the fall, and cold, frosty, icy weather, my master left me thus naked and tied up, till the morning." This indignity, on top of the years of bondage, caused Pomp to resist his captivity in the most direct way possible: "I took an axe and went softly into the bed room of my master, and the moon shining bright distinguished him from my mistress." Pomp killed Captain Furbush, but not Mrs. Furbush, and was soon arrested without resistance. As he explained it, he thought by eliminating his master he would obtain his freedom and, oddly enough, the right to his master's house and wife, as well. On 6 August 1795 Pomp was tried, convicted, and hanged in Ipswich, Massachusetts, for the murder of Captain Furbush.

Pomp's demise at the gallows was not an uncommon end among black New Englanders. Unlike in the plantation South, where the body of the slave was a valuable object, and the enslaved person was intrinsically valuable as a piece of property that could be rented, sold, or foreclosed upon—and not just as a source of labor, a condition that conferred protection from execution except in the most egregious circumstances—in New England there were no financial barriers to executing black people, and in fact execution was seen as a tool to control what was considered a dangerous population. Indeed, the criminalization of African and Native American behavior often served the dual purpose of upholding the law and carrying out an object lesson for outsiders within New England's mostly white society. From Maria Negro in Charlestown to Tituba in Salem and then to Pomp in Andover one can read a history of control of non-white individuals through the legal process. It is likely that this is why Jonathan Plummer (1795) chose to record and publish the life and death of Pomp and to add about him that "[T]o crown his ignorance, he lost his life by not knowing that murder was a sin, he expecting that he should immediately rise to good estate and great felicity whenever he should be fortunate enough to kill his master."

FURTHER READING

Plummer, Jonathan. *Dying Confession of Pomp, A Negro Man, Who Was Executed at Ipswich, on the 6th August, 1795, for Murdering Capt. Charles Furbush, of Andover, Taken from the Mouth of the Prisoner, and Penned by Jonathan Plummer, Jun.* (1795).

Piersen, William. *Black Yankees: The Development of an Afro-American Subculture in Eighteenth-Century New England* (1988).

TIMOTHY J. MCMILLAN

Poole, Cecil F. (14 July 1914–12 Nov. 1997), circuit court judge, was born in Birmingham, Alabama, the third of four children born to William and Eva Poole. In 1918 the family moved to Pittsburgh, Pennsylvania, when Poole was four years old.

In 1932 Poole entered the University of Michigan, graduating in 1936 and earning a law degree in 1938. A year later Poole went on to earn a master of law degree from Harvard University. In 1940 Poole passed the Pennsylvania bar, and in 1941 he obtained a job as an attorney for the National Labor Relations Board (NLRB), which investigates unfair labor practices. Poole studied federal laws covering labor and labor relations and advised the NLRB board members on cases.

Poole was drafted into the army in 1942 and married Charlotte Crump that same year. Poole's experiences in the segregated army were harsh. From Poole's experience, the duties of black soldiers seemed restricted to menial work or hard labor. Still, Poole's leadership skills led to his promotion to staff sergeant. After his honorable discharge in 1946 the Pooles relocated to California, where he obtained employment with the West Coast Office of Price Administration as a research attorney. He studied for and passed the California bar on the first attempt. In 1949 Poole was appointed as an assistant district attorney and prosecuted minor cases.

Between 1958 and 1961 Poole served as Clemency Secretary to Governor Edmund "Pat" Brown of California, a Democrat. In 1961 President John F. Kennedy appointed Poole as the U.S. attorney for the Northern District of California, making him the first black U.S. attorney appointed in the United States. Poole's office handled several cases involving civil rights and the Vietnam War. Poole would not prosecute cases involving draft dodgers and worked to have charges dismissed. Poole remained in this position until 1969, at which time he returned to private practice after the Senate failed to confirm his nomination by President Lyndon B. Johnson to the U.S. District Court for Northern California. Senator George Murphy, a Republican from California, objected that Poole was too liberal.

In 1976 President Gerald Ford appointed Poole to the U.S. District Court for the Northern District of California. In 1979 President Jimmy Carter appointed Poole to the U.S. Court of Appeals for the Ninth Circuit, and in 1996 he assumed senior judge status. Poole was the second black judge to serve in the federal circuit.

Poole was director of the NAACP Legal Defense and Educational Reform Fund from 1971 to 1976. During his tenure he was instrumental in raising money and advising the NAACP on legal matters. He was also an adjunct professor at the University of California at Berkley between 1970 and 1976 and a member of the National Urban League and American Bar Association. Judge Poole died after a long illness.

FURTHER READING

Haskins, James. *Cecil Poole: A Life in the Law* (2002).

DONNAMARIA CULBRETH

Poole, Robert. *See* Muhammad, Elijah.

Poor, Salem (c. 30 Oct. 1742–after 20 Mar. 1780), Revolutionary War veteran, credited with causing the death of the British lieutenant colonel James Abercrombie at the Battle of Bunker Hill on 17 June 1775. Folklore has it that a teenage Lydia Abbott and her father purchased an African American male infant at a Salem, Massachusetts, slave auction block. The Abbotts lived in nearby Andover and were traveling by horseback. According to tradition, the baby rode either on the "bow" of the saddle or in the saddlebag of Lydia's horse. However he got to Andover, Lydia's family owned him, and had him baptized in the Congregational Church in 1747. In later years, Lydia Abbott gave Poor to her daughter, Chloe. As a child this African American male slave became known as "Salem Pony." At approximately twenty-seven years of age, Salem purchased himself for twenty-seven pounds. The date was 10 July 1769, and the other party to the transaction was John Poor III, then his owner. Perhaps John was the same John Poor that Chloe would later marry in 1776, or one of his relatives. Salem married the former Nancy Parker, a free woman of mixed heritage in Andover, Massachusetts, on 4 November 1771. Salem and Nancy had at least one child, a son, Jonas, baptized 29 September 1776.

In 1775 Salem answered the call to fight in the Revolutionary War. Perhaps Nancy had family in the area, or the Andover African American community—free and enslaved—took care of Nancy and Jonas. Whatever the reason, Salem left his family behind to serve, although occasionally wives and children accompanied their men on their campaigns. History does not record when and where he enlisted; however, under General George Washington's command, Poor served as one of the minutemen present at the battles of Bunker Hill, Massachusetts (17 June 1775); White Plains, New York (16 September 1776); and Valley Forge, Pennsylvania (winter of 1777–1778). At Bunker Hill, Poor was assigned pioneer duty, constructing a fort and fortifications on 16 June 1775, a common duty for African American servicemen. There were at least 103 other African Americans at Bunker Hill with Poor. Among them were Seasor, Pharaoh, Barzillai Lew, and Cuff Whittemore. Seasor and Pharaoh, of Colonel James Scamman's

York County Regiment of Foot (Infantry), were among the troops who received the now legendary order, "Don't fire until you see the whites of their eyes!" Lew worked as a cooper (barrel maker) in Chelmsford, Massachusetts, before the fighting began. He became a fifer during the Revolution, and had previously seen service in the French and Indian War. Cuff Whittemore survived a musket ball shot through his hat and went on to scavenge the sword of a British officer. On 13 December 1775, his minuteman company issued an order to give Poor a wool bounty coat. It was an award of distinction.

Poor enlisted in the Continental army on 11 May 1777 for three years' service under Captain Nathaniel Alexander's Company of Colonel Edward Wigglesworth's Massachusetts Regiment. When General Burgoyne surrendered to American forces, Colonel Wigglesworth's Regiment was sent to Valley Forge. With Poor at Valley Forge was the First Rhode Island Regiment, which included 150 to 300 men of color (Native Americans or African Americans). Poor was still at Valley Forge in May 1778 but did not arrive at White Plains until June 1778. One fourth of the troops at the Battle of White Plains were African American.

On 5 December 1775, fourteen of the officers under whom Poor served petitioned the Massachusetts General Court to recognize Poor for his bravery in the Battle of Bunker Hill. The petition reads in part: "Wee declare that a Negro Man Called Salem Poor…behaved like an Experienced officer, as Well as an Excellent Soldier…in the Person of this said Negro centers a brave & gallant Soldier" (Moebs, *Black Soldiers, Black Sailors, Black Ink*, 232–233). Of the two to four thousand patriots present at Bunker Hill, no one else (white or African American) received this honor. Unfortunately, no record exists that he ever received the commendation. Neither does history record Poor's motives for serving in the first place. Did he enlist for the meager salary that soldiers received? Was he recruited as a substitute for some unnamed white man? Did he have patriotic feelings for a colony where he was not free? Or did he aspire to a hope for true and equal freedom? Poor did receive several accolades posthumously. A century later, on 4 July 1876, in a speech for America's Centennial, the pioneering African American historian GEORGE WASHINGTON WILLIAMS remembered all the African American troops at Bunker Hill, including Salem Poor and PETER SALEM. Then a call went out from the National Equal Rights League, published in the

Chicago Defender, that 17 July 1927 be declared "Peter Salem Day," to observe the anniversary of the Battle of Bunker Hill, and to honor both Peter Salem and Salem Poor for their valor that day. America again invoked the name of Salem Poor when the United States Postal Service honored him with a postage stamp on 25 May 1975. The stamp was part of the "Contributors to the Cause" series minted for the nation's Bicentennial in 1976. Even though court officials of the period ignored his service, modern day federal workers recognized this "brave and gallant" soldier.

FURTHER READING

Moebs, Thomas Truxton. *Black Soldiers, Black Sailors, Black Ink: Research Guide on African Americans in U.S. Military History, 1526–1900* (1994).

Quarles, Benjamin. *The Negro in the American Revolution* (1996).

Quintal, George, Jr., and Alfred E. Young. *Patriots of Color: 'A Peculiar Beauty and Merit,' African Americans and Native Americans at Battle Road & Bunker Hill* (2003).

KAREN E. SUTTON

Pope, Manassa Thomas (24 Aug. 1858–13 Nov. 1934), physician, businessman, and political activist, was born near Rich Square, Northampton County, North Carolina, the son of free black parents who were Quakers. His father, Jonas Elias Pope, freed from slavery in 1851, was a prosperous carpenter and landowner; his mother's name was Permelia. A younger half brother, Jonas Elias Pope II, born to his father's second wife in 1898, was his only known sibling.

A gifted student, Pope was educated first in the common schools of Northampton County, before enrolling in 1874 at the Baptist-affiliated Shaw University in Raleigh, where he received his bachelor's degree in 1879. In 1880 he worked as a schoolteacher in Halifax County, near his birthplace, and boarded at the Brinkleyville home of Hilliard J. Hewlin, a farmer and aspiring Republican legislator. In 1882 Pope entered the first class at Shaw University's new Leonard Medical School, from which he received his medical degree in 1886.

He established his first medical practice in the Vance County seat of Henderson, North Carolina, and in 1887 was married to his first wife, Lydia Walden. The young couple moved in 1890 to Charlotte, North Carolina, where Dr. Pope soon branched out into other business activities, establishing the Queen City Drug Company and helping found an insurance firm, the People's Benevolent and Relief Association.

After the United States declared war on Spain in 1898, Dr. Pope answered his country's call for volunteers by enlisting in North Carolina's Third Regiment, a military unit of African American volunteers being organized by the Republican governor Daniel L. Russell. Pope became that regiment's first lieutenant and first assistant surgeon, serving under the command of Colonel JAMES HUNTER YOUNG of Raleigh, his Shaw classmate from two decades earlier.

The Third Regiment was not sent abroad during the war, but was instead stationed as a reserve garrison unit in three successive domestic locations: Fort Macon, on North Carolina's Outer Banks; Camp Poland, near Knoxville, Tennessee; and Camp Haskell, near Macon, Georgia. Lieutenant Pope had hoped to continue military service after the war, and in December 1898 wrote to the nation's only black congressman—GEORGE HENRY WHITE of North Carolina—in hopes of prolonging the Third Regiment's service. Representative White intervened with the McKinley administration, but without success; the Third Regiment was duly mustered out in February 1899, and Dr. Pope returned home as a civilian, resuming private practice as a physician.

Probably at the suggestion of James Hunter Young, a leading citizen in Raleigh's African American community and editor of the city's African American weekly newspaper, the *Gazette*, the Popes then moved to Raleigh. Pope's new medical practice in Raleigh thrived, and he became an advisor to the Leonard Medical School, which remained in operation until 1918. He also became an active member of the National Medical Association, established in the 1890s, and of Raleigh's First Baptist Church. In 1901 he built an impressive brick residence near the State Capitol in downtown Raleigh, where Lydia Pope died in September 1906.

After Lydia's death, Pope married Delia Haywood Phillips, a Raleigh schoolteacher. Their two daughters, Evelyn Bennett Pope and Ruth Permelia Pope, both became schoolteachers, after attending Shaw University and receiving master's degrees from Columbia University.

Despite the new era of Jim Crow segregation and black disfranchisement in North Carolina, a determined Pope remained politically active after 1900. By producing his father's emancipation certificate from 1851, Dr. Pope was able to demand the right to vote under the amended state constitution's "grandfather clause," and was one of just seven black men allowed to register to vote in Raleigh in 1902. In the April 1919 primary, he ran for mayor of Raleigh on a nonpartisan black slate of candidates that included Calvin Lightner, father of Raleigh's future black mayor, Clarence Lightner.

After Dr. Pope's death at age seventy-six, his widow applied for and received a veteran's pension from his Spanish-American war service. She died in Raleigh in 1955. The Pope sisters continued to live in the family home in downtown Raleigh until their own deaths at the end of the twentieth century.

The Pope home, now listed on the National Register of Historic Places, has since been converted into a museum by the Pope House Museum Foundation. An extensive collection of his family's papers was donated to the Southern Historical Collection at the University of North Carolina at Chapel Hill in 2002.

FURTHER READING

The Pope Family Papers, 1851–1983, Southern Historical Collection, Wilson Library, University of North Carolina at Chapel Hill.

Gatewood, Willard B., Jr., "North Carolina's Negro Regiment in the Spanish-American War." *North Carolina Historical Review* 48, no. 4 (October 1971): 370–387.

BENJAMIN R. JUSTESEN

Pope.L, William (28 June 1955–), artist, was born in Newark, New Jersey, to Lucille Lancaster and William Pope II. His mother worked as a reporter, an office worker, nurse, and housewife, and his father was a factory worker and clothes presser.

Self-proclaimed the "Friendliest Black Artist in America," Pope.L is a multidisciplinary artist whose broad-based conceptual performances aggressively address consumerism, racism, class, and gender. The unusual name, Pope.L, was given to him at birth by his mother, the L representing her maiden name, Lancaster. Pope.L would later recall, "As mum would say, she only got one letter" (interview with the author, July 2004).

Pope.L didn't really "commit to a life of art" until he was a junior in high school, although he remembers a female art teacher in grammar school encouraging him. His grandmother, he tells me, was very much for his becoming an artist. "No one in my family had much of an idea what that meant except that it might be a way for me to escape the typical life of crime and violence that attracted most young black men my age" (interview with the author, July 2004).

There was a period of "breaking and entering" from age ten to sixteen, he recalls, an experience that contributed to his work in a big way. Much of his art derives from "have-not-ness," a condition entirely familiar to him. Other significant life events include: "a deep depression at Montclair at 19; working in a band, John Wayne, from 21 to 26; participant in Mabou Mines' ReCherChez weekly critiques at 25 to 30, and moving to Maine and working at Bates College."

Pope.L studied at Pratt Institute and the Whitney Museum of American Art Independent Study Program, and received a B.A. from Montclair State University (1978), and an M.F.A. from Mason Gross School of the Arts at Rutgers University (1981). He was selected as one of the United States Arts Fellows in 2006, is a Guggenheim Fellow, has held residencies at Yaddo and Skowhegan artist colonies, and has exhibited widely, including New York, Chicago, Los Angeles, Montreal, London, Vienna, Berlin, Zurich, and Tokyo.

In 1990 he moved to Lewiston, Maine, where he taught Theater and Rhetoric at Bates College until 2010, leaving that post when offered a faculty position at the University of Chicago. While at Bates, Pope.L directed a performance of LORRAINE HANSBERRY's *A Raisin in the Sun* in which he cast African American and Caucasian actors as members of the same family.

In the late 1970s, Pope.L began eRacism, a project that included more than forty strenuous performance pieces he calls "crawls," in which he gets down on all fours and literally inches his way across the streets of busy cities. He talks about this in light of the homeless and otherwise underempowered, how a typical vertical carriage conveys power, but when you crawl, you are not standing tall. You are vulnerable. And crawling is physically challenging and exhausting, as are the situations faced by the disenfranchised. In one of these crawls, called "The Great White Way," Pope.L wore a superman outfit with a skateboard strapped to his back. Performed in segments, this public piece took five years to complete, and covered 22 miles across Broadway, from the Statue of Liberty to the Bronx. Documentation of this crawl was included in the 2002 Whitney Biennial.

Other confrontational performances include his tying himself to the door of a bank in Manhattan with an eight-foot length of sausage links, wearing only a skirt of dollar bills, which he offered to passersby and seating himself prominently on a "throne" of *Wall Street Journals* in Boston's financial district while eating and regurgitating the newspaper, which he referred to as the "rag of the rich."

In 2001 Pope.L suffered a severe, but short-lived blow, when the National Education Association (NEA) declined a $42,000 grant request for the twenty-five-year retrospective exhibit "William Pope.L: eRacism," scheduled to open in 2002 at the Institute of Contemporary Art at Maine College of Art. The proposal had been recommended by the National Council on the Arts, and by the NEA's own advisory grant review panel. The Andy Warhol Foundation for the Visual Arts, alarmed at what it considered to be "an attack on freedom of expression" and a potential loss of "an important exhibition of art" (*New York Times,* 21 Dec. 2001) immediately announced a grant of $50,000 toward the exhibition's budget, and the MIT Press agreed to publish a catalog for the exhibit.

In 2004 Pope.L initiated The Black Factory, displayed at the Massachusetts Museum of Contemporary Art (Mass MOCA) as part of "The Interventionists" show. This traveling art performance installation, consisting of a 22-foot-long van equipped with a gift shop, web kiosk, sound system, a pulverization workshop, and inflatable igloo housing a library of actual black objects donated by participants, seeks to promote discussion about "difference" throughout America's heartland.

Speaking of his art and directions, Pope.L reflects: "I hope to convey a stubbornness and fragility, a stupidity at being in the world; I look to make my viewers sad, upset, curious, hopeful and perplexed" (interview with the author, July 2004).

FURTHER READING

Bessire, Mark H. C. *William Pope.L: The Friendliest Black Artist in America* (2002).

Cotter, Holland. "Art in Review; William Pope. L." *New York Times,* 8 June 2001.

Cotter, Holland. "The Topic is Race; the Art Is Fearless," *New York Times,* 20 Mar. 2008.

Wilson, Martha. "William Pope.L." *Bomb Magazine* (Spring 1996).

DIANE HUDSON

Popel, Esther (16 July 1896–28 Jan. 1958), poet, was born in Harrisburg, Pennsylvania, where her family had lived since 1826 when her paternal grandfather had been taken there by his free-born parents. Popel was of mixed heritage (African American, Native American, and German) on her paternal side. Little is known of her maternal side. Popel attended Central High School in Harrisburg and then commuted to Dickinson College in Carlisle, Pennsylvania. She was, according to Dickinson College Archives, a day student and the first African American woman to attend the school, where she graduated Phi Beta Kappa after majoring in modern languages. The description accompanying her yearbook picture (*The Microcosm* [1919]) is indicative of her life at the college: "We see her but we seldom hear her....[Y]et her recitations and marks prove her to be a scholar and we feel sure that she will make good practical use of her vast knowledge and ability."

Racism prevented Popel from making full use of this knowledge at her first job, the War Risk Insurance Department. She was, however, able to use her language skills successfully as a teacher. For more than thirty-nine years she taught French and Spanish (she also knew German and Latin) at junior high schools in Baltimore and Washington, D.C. In addition to teaching, she wrote six plays (seemingly lost) for junior high school students and published a collection of her students' works from Francis Junior High in *The Franthology: A Collection of Verse* (1949).

Popel was married in 1925 to William A. Shaw, an African American, who died in 1946. The couple had one child. Shortly after her marriage, Popel moved to Washington, D.C., where she became a member of the Lincoln Memorial Congregational Temple. She gave talks to women's clubs, often speaking on race relations, several of which were published in *The Journal of the National Association of College Women.* One series of addresses given at the Women's Club in Lawrenceville, New Jersey, was published by the Women's Press of the YMCA as *Personal Adventures in Race Relations* (1946). These talks, leavened with a cautious optimism, present a poignant picture, of "[t]he unlovely story of race relations in the United States" (3).

Though little remembered today, Popel published several poems in *The Crisis* and *Opportunity* between 1925 and 1934 as well as a privately printed collection, *A Forest Pool* (1934). In addition, Popel was active in GEORGIA DOUGLAS JOHNSON's famous Saturday Night reading groups in Washington. Her lack of recognition today may be because of the perceived raceless nature of her poetry, which was in the genteel tradition. However, as recent feminist critics have demonstrated, the poetry of these pioneering women often contained a thinly disguised subversive element. Popel's poetry seems conventional, with themes frequently about nature, death, and lost love, yet these commonplace subjects often masked a deeper agenda.

Her nature poems link nature with the condition of women. Such a view of nature as a nurturing figure, one that protects women from the everyday oppression in their lives from men and white women, is typical in women's poetry of the time (Honey, 8). In "Theft" (*Opportunity*, Apr. 1925), the moon is personified as an old woman in search of her children. The blinding white snow mocks the misery of the woman. "Popel's central figure is ambiguous in that she evokes pity, modifying the image of the moon as dangerous. At the same time, she represents weakness, debility, and devastating loss" (Honey, 11).

Popel's poetry reveals conflicting views of death. One of her finest poems about death is an elegy, likely to the poet's mother, "Reach Down, Sweet Grass," in which the speaker hopes that the beauty of spring will provide comfort to the deceased. In "October Prayer," death is seen as a suitor, in some ways reminiscent of Emily Dickinson's "Because I could not Stop for Death." But here, death is not like the courteous caller in Dickinson's poem: Death will strip off her clothes and she will "stand / Before him, proud and naked, / Unashamed, uncaring."

Lost love and unfulfilled desires are recurrent in Popel's poetry. In "A Forest Pool," reminiscent of Georgia Douglas Johnson's "Heart of a Woman," we are told: "A woman's heart, / A forest pool / Are one!" Though seemingly calm, in reality, it contains just beneath the surface "...hidden things / Imprisoned in its dark and secret depths." Sexual frustration burns in "Storage," where the fancy linen, left unused, rots. This sexual tension is further reflected in "The Pilferer," where Time with "a pass-key" boldly opens "the strong box / Hidden in my heart."

Popel also wrote several poems with a highly political message, most notably the chilling "Flag Salute" (*The Crisis* [Aug. 1934]) and "Blasphemy— American Style" (*Opportunity* [Dec. 1934]) both based on actual lynchings. In the former poem, the pledge of allegiance is intertwined with the report of a lynching. In the latter poem, a mob lynches a black man, mocking him for praying as he is about to be killed. These poems, like the talks she gave on race relations, indicate that Popel had a clear commitment to social justice.

Popel's writings accurately reflect the hopes and ambitions of many middle class African American women of the 1920s and 1930s. Although she is a minor poet, her best work, including "Flag Salute,"

"Blasphemy—American Style," "Reach Down, Sweet Grass," "A Forest Pool," "October Prayer," and "Storage," resonates in a voice still worth hearing.

FURTHER READING
Material on Esther Popel is held in the Dickinson College Archives, Carlisle, Pennsylvania.
Honey, Maureen, ed. and intro. *Shadowed Dreams: Women's Poetry of the Harlem Renaissance* (1989).
Roses, Lorraine Elena, and Ruth Elizabeth Randolph. *Harlem Renaissance and Beyond: Literary Biographies of 100 Black Women Writers 1900–1945* (1990).

LOUIS J. PARASCANDOLA

Populus, Vincent (fl. 1814), shoemaker, soldier, and officer in the First New Orleans Battalion of Free Men of Color, was the first African American recognized by the U.S. government as an officer of field grade status. He was also known as "Vass Populus," and little is known about his life apart from the fact that he worked as a shoemaker before embarking on a military career.

New Orleans in the eighteenth century was already a vibrantly multiracial and multicultural city, with fully a quarter of its black population being free, variously composed of Africans, African Americans, and mixed-race Creoles. The French created a small black militia, consisting of free and enslaved volunteers, to augment the army in repelling Indian attacks in the early 1730s, and which performed admirably against the British and their native allies during King George's War (1739–1747). Those who had been slaves were eventually granted their freedom in reward for their service, thus increasing the free black population in the city. By the time of the American War for Independence, the free black community had become a permanent feature of New Orleans life and culture recognized and respected by the Spanish since they took over administration of Louisiana in 1762. As part of their war effort against the British as allies of the United States, Spanish Louisiana organized a *milicias de color* under the command of Bernardo de Gálvez, originally consisting of 169 black and mulatto soldiers, which he augmented with larger numbers of whites, other mixed-race Creoles, and Indians to a peak of 1,430 men. This small force conducted successful raids against British outposts along the Mississippi River and the Gulf Coast during the American Revolutionary War, and became the nucleus for a permanent Battalion of Free Men of Color (BFMC) based in New Orleans that saw action in area conflicts spawned by the French Revolution in 1792–1793.

The purchase of the Louisiana Territory by President Thomas Jefferson in 1803 created an uncomfortable situation for William C. C. Claiborne, provisional governor of the newly acquired territory. He could hardly refuse to disband a trained military unit that would be badly needed to maintain security in New Orleans and ease transition from Spanish to U.S. authority, but the idea of the BFMC flew in the face of established American racial attitudes, especially in the South. While in the previous century southern colonial governments had countenanced the idea of arming slaves and free blacks in moments of extreme emergency, by the early 1800s it had become conventional wisdom that to do so at any time was too dangerous and would set bad precedents. Claiborne thus faced pressure to dissolve the BFMC, yet knew that "to disband them would be to raise an armed enemy in the very heart of the country and to disarm them would savor too strongly of that desperate system of government which seldom succeeds" (McConnell, 33). However, the existence of commissioned black troops and officers was expressly forbidden by federal policy, so he wrote to his superiors in Washington, D.C., to ask for advice. Others, such as Benjamin Morgan, wondered what might become of the free black and mixed African American population of the Territory now that it was under U.S. jurisdiction, whether they would "be entitled to the rights of citizens or not" (McConnell, 34). For their part, the majority of New Orleans's free black community celebrated the Louisiana Purchase and made various expressions of loyalty to the United States, members of the BFMC submitting a petition to Claiborne offering its services to him, of which Populus and his brother, Maurice, were signers. These and other pragmatic considerations led Claiborne, the State Department, and Secretary of War Henry Dearborn to make an exception for the BFMC, which was maintained and placed under the command of General James Wilkinson. Opposition from New Orleans's white population was evident, however, especially from newly arriving immigrants from the emerging Deep South states. Rumors that the BFMC represented a militant wing of a black insurrectionist movement against the territorial government persisted among Louisiana's growing white community, which successfully pressured the legislature to rescind its recognition in 1806. Such insurrectionist fears in New Orleans seemed to have been confirmed by the outbreak of a slave revolt in

1811, though former members of the BFMC distinguished themselves for their efforts to suppress the revolt and to maintain public order. This and the outbreak of war with Great Britain in 1812, which nearly coincided with Louisiana's admission to statehood, led Claiborne to convince the legislature to organize new provincial militia units, of which a reformed BFMC was a part.

By 1814 the BFMC had grown to include four distinct companies, which, along with the regular army, were under the command of General Andrew Jackson, who had been public in his praise for the black troops' patriotism and professionalism. The BFMC played a key role in the Battle of New Orleans during the War of 1812. Captain Vincent Populus of the First Battalion of Free Men of Color was promoted to second major on 1 December 1814, second in command only to Major Pierre Lacoste, and it was Populus who assembled the First BFMC for action on 16–17 December 1814, taking up a position at Chef Menteur River, where they dug redoubts and awaited the enemy. Lacoste, however, in response to British incendiary tactics, ordered a retreat of his units from Chef Menteur, which earned him a reprimand from Jackson, though he later accepted Lacoste's explanation. Lacoste and Populus promptly advanced back to their original positions on 22 December, which provoked a firefight with the British. During the confusion Jackson was able to pin the main British ground forces against the river and force them to abandon their plan to take New Orleans. This victory is widely recognized as rescuing the Louisiana Territory from a potential British conquest, as well as being the single greatest American victory in the War of 1812. Jackson singled out the BFMC for valorous service, as did Baltimore's *Niles Weekly Register*, which commended the black troops who "fought like desperadoes and deserved distinguished praise" (McConnell, 91).

In spite of the applause, free blacks in Louisiana inherited the low status accorded to their counterparts throughout the rest of the United States.

FURTHER READING
Greene, Robert Ewell. *Black Defenders of America, 1775–1973: A Reference and Pictorial History* (1974).
Ingersoll, Thomas N. "Free Blacks in a Slave Society: New Orleans, 1718–1812," *The William and Mary Quarterly*, 3.48 (1991).
McConnell, Roland C. *Negro Troops of Antebellum Louisiana: A History of the Battalion of Free Men of Color* (1968).

Morazon, Ronald R. *Biographical Sketches of the Veterans of the Battle of Orleans, 1814–1815* (1979).

JOHN HOWARD SMITH

Porter, David (21 May 1941–), songwriter, singer, producer, and record executive, was born in Memphis, Tennessee. Details on Porter's early life are not available, but it is known that his father died when he was two years old, and that he and his family lived in Memphis all of his life. Porter attended the all-black BOOKER T. WASHINGTON High School, an institution perhaps most famous for one of its history teachers, Nat D. Williams, an enterprising visionary who helped transform Memphis radio station WDIA into the nation's first black-owned-and-operated radio outlet. During the late 1950s and early 1960s a group of Washington High students helped provide the foundation for a fledgling record label called Satellite—later Stax—Records. Beginning as a record shop on McLemore Avenue, across the street from the grocery store where Porter worked for several years, the company soon became, thanks to the talents of local Memphis musicians and producers, one of the nation's most prominent labels, crafting an immensely successful brand of intense, funky soul music over the next fifteen years.

One of the company's first hires was David Porter. In 1962 he became Stax's first salaried songwriter and its first full-time black employee. Porter recorded singles for Stax and (under an alias) other Memphis labels, but these efforts did not prove entirely satisfying, either commercially or artistically. It was instead as a songwriter that Porter became an integral part of the Stax organization, particularly when, in 1964, he began a collaboration with ISAAC HAYES. Over the next several years, the Hayes-Porter team became arguably Stax's most successful songwriting and producing partnership. They crafted hits for Stax artists like Johnnie Taylor, Carla Thomas, and—unquestionably most importantly—Sam and Dave, an energetic Florida-based duo whose string of 1960s hits were all written and produced by Hayes-Porter. (Their first minor hit, "Goodnight Baby," was penned by the Porter and Stax studio guitarist Steve Cropper.) Tracks like "Hold On, I'm Comin'," "When Something Is Wrong with My Baby," and "Soul Man" are classic examples of the "Stax sound," based in gospel performance styles combined with horn-driven rhythms and driving beats, courtesy of the studio drummer AL JACKSON JR. (Porter also expressed affection for the lush productions of the Holland-Dozier-Holland team at Motown Records.) These Sam and Dave hits, written and produced by Isaac Hayes and David Porter, were central to the company's legacy.

Porter participated in many facets of the creation of Stax recordings. Apart from his work with Hayes (which made the duo the company's top songwriters in the mid-1960s), Porter continued writing and producing for other artists, recorded occasionally himself, and provided background vocals (most famously, perhaps, his harmony on Eddie Floyd's 1967 hit "Knock On Wood"). For his contributions, Porter became—along with Hayes and the four members of the Stax house band (and hit artists in their own right) BOOKER T. and the MGs—one of "the Big 6," originally a collaborative production pool that for a time became essentially Stax's board of directors.

Stax underwent a near-complete transformation in 1968 and 1969, changing on every level from ownership to the day-to-day workings of the studio. Although both Hayes and Porter remained at Stax, with Hayes becoming its top star in the early 1970s, their songwriting partnership was no longer dominant in the company. Hayes and Porter continued to produce, mainly for new signings the Soul Children and the Emotions; while both of these groups would be successful, neither propelled Hayes-Porter back to the heights they had scaled with Sam and Dave. Early in the 1970s, the partnership fell apart. Stax historian Rob Bowman asserts that this, combined with the death of his mother in 1970, sank Porter into a depression that he battled throughout the decade (Bowman, 191).

During this period, Porter devoted more time to a solo career, releasing four albums on Stax between 1970 and 1973. While these albums are of variable quality, one of note is Porter's ambitious 1971 "soul opera" *Victim of the Joke?*, in which Porter mixed original songs and cover versions with spoken meditations on the nature of love. While he did score a couple of minor R&B hits, Porter's solo work never brought him much fame. At 1972's "Wattstax" festival, a triumphant moment for Stax Records and its roster, Porter's performance was limited to one song. His production work and songwriting contributions slowed, and it appeared that one of Stax's longest-serving stars was fading from relevance.

As Stax Records fell apart in 1974 and 1975, Porter rose out of his depression. Beginning in 1974 he once again began producing and writing for Stax performers (often with his new collaborator Ronnie

Williams). In 1975 Stax chief Al Bell put Porter in charge of the Stax recording studio, an important role that was nonetheless diminished by the deteriorating state of the label. Thanks to the songwriting royalties he had accumulated in his 1960s heyday, Porter was one of the few Stax employees who were financially comfortable; many others in the organization were strapped, and Porter lent money to his friends and associates throughout the period. Stax folded in December of 1975.

In 1977 Fantasy Records purchased the Stax name and catalog and made David Porter the head of the relaunch. Porter succeeded in resigning Stax artists, but his new signings to the label did not prove as impressive. After a brief run of middling success, Fantasy dropped the Stax imprint, although the Porter-led series of Stax reissues were better received. Porter and his family continued to live in Memphis, where he owned a variety of music-oriented businesses and—like many of his contemporaries from Washington High and Stax Records—is celebrated as an important figure in the city's, and country's, cultural history.

FURTHER READING

Bowman, Rob. *Soulsville, U.S.A.: The Story of Stax Records* (1997).

Guralnick, Peter. *Sweet Soul Music: Rhythm and Blues and the Southern Dream of Freedom* (1986).

Unterberger, Richie. "David Porter," in *All Music Guide To Soul*, ed. Vladimir Bogdanov (2003).

CHARLES L. HUGHES

Porter, Gilbert Lawrence (6 Jan. 1909–8 July 1995), educator and scholar, was born in Baldwin City, Kansas. Little is known about his parents; his mother died when he was nine and he was raised by his three maternal uncles, Elbert, Giles, and Theodore Wright, and his grandparents. In 1928 Porter enrolled at Talladega College in Alabama with a major in chemistry and a minor in biology. Upon graduation, he became a teacher at Booker High School in Sarasota, Florida. After only four months at his teaching position, the institution closed due to financial woes, so Porter returned to college. He enrolled at Florida Agricultural and Mechanical University (FAMU). Upon graduation, he became principal of Tivoli Junior High School in Defuniak Springs, Florida.

Porter moved to New York during the 1930s and worked as a redcap at the New York Central Railroad Station. He later moved to Michigan to pursue a master's degree in educational administration at the University of Michigan. Upon graduation, he returned to Defuniak Springs as principal of Tivoli High School for four years.

In the late 1930s Porter secured a position as principal of Lincoln High School in Tallahassee, Florida. He married Willie Pearl Kelker in 1939, and the couple had two children, son Albert Wesley and daughter Laurestine Eleanor. Porter played a significant leadership role in the faculty preparation and publishing of the manuscript entitled *The Evolution of Susan Prim* in 1944, which became a standard text for curriculum development at Lincoln High School. The manuscript was a tool for improving teaching skills and student management.

During the 1920s he also became active in the Florida State Teachers' Association (FSTA), an association of African American teachers throughout the state of Florida organized in 1890. Porter played a major role in teacher salary equalization cases throughout the state of Florida from 1937 until 1944. He communicated with local attorneys representing African American plaintiffs throughout the state and engaged in fund-raising activities to help pay attorney fees and court costs.

He also helped to compensate and supplement the incomes of African American teachers and families adversely affected by the lawsuits. Porter was active in the NAACP and assisted with the organization's state mobilizing efforts. He received a Rockefeller Foundation Scholarship to pursue a doctoral degree at Ohio State University and earned a Ph.D. in Curriculum Development in 1950.

As president of the FSTA, Porter presided over the group's fifty-sixth annual convention in 1949. He sought to address persistent problems and issues facing African American educators throughout the state of Florida. He played a principal role in the publication of the FSTA *Bulletin*, the organ of Florida teachers, which addressed fundamental educational issues and concerns. In 1949–1950 Porter directed the course of the organization in addressing statewide bond issues, tax levies, building, and athletics programs.

As president of the FSTA, he worked with educator C. C. Walker Sr. to increase the number of African American institutions accredited by the Southern Association of Colleges and Schools. On 28 October 1950 Porter and organization officers made notable changes to the FSTA constitution by redistricting the sixty-seven counties within which the organization operated into ten districts governed by a vice president. He also assisted with the official chartering the FSTA as a nonprofit organization in 1951 and incorporated county teacher associations into the group.

Porter participated in the issuance and sale of building bonds and school tags to secure financing and construction of new headquarters for FSTA. In 1954 Porter and his executive board negotiated acquisition of a permanent structure for the group. It was dedicated in 1962 and served as the central headquarters of the FSTA in Tallahassee, Florida.

As the FSTA first salaried executive secretary (1954–1965), Porter strengthened the ties between the National Education Association (NEA) and the FSTA to better utilize educational resources throughout Florida's state and local districts. During the 1950s and 1960s he served on the FSTA teacher education and professional standards commission (TEPS), which advanced professional education standards and affirmed rights and privileges of local and state educators. Porter secured appointments of organization members to state and nationwide education committees and formalized uniform membership dues throughout the state of Florida. From 1954 to 1962, he also assisted with the reinstatement of over three hundred African American teachers to their positions following the Supreme Court decisions in the *Brown v. Board of Education* decisions in 1954 and 1955. When the Florida legislature mandated that all teachers take the National Teachers Examination (NTE) in 1961, Porter played a substantive role in employing institutional, local, and organizational resources to assist African American teachers. In 1964 Porter was among three hundred educators invited to meet with President Lyndon B. Johnson in the White House.

Porter resigned from the FSTA on 1 July 1965 to accept a position with Miami Dade County, Florida, as special assistant to the superintendent of public schools and as a special assistant deputy superintendent of public schools (1965–1973). His immediate task was to enforce integration of more than two hundred public schools in Miami-Dade County. He resigned in 1973. Porter wrote several articles concerning educational, social, political, and economic inequities. In 1977 he coauthored *The History of the Florida State Teachers Association* with the historian Leedell Neyland.

Porter received numerous distinguished awards throughout his lifetime, including the Distinguished Black Floridian Award from the 1987 Black Economic Conference and the WHITNEY YOUNG JR. Memorial Humanitarian Award in Education from the Urban League of Miami in 1990. On 11 March 1991, the Miami-Dade County school board named the Dr. Gilbert L. Porter Elementary in his honor. The Miami Dade school board also designated Gilbert L. Porter Elementary a "School of Discovery"—a learning environment where children explore their full potential—in Miami, in his honor.

In 1993 Porter received the Distinguished Alumni Award from FAMU and the Samuel H. Johnson Award of Excellence from Alphi Phi Alpha Fraternity Inc. He was also an active member of several organizations, including the Family Christian Association of America, Inc., Alpha Rho Boule, Sigma Pi Phi, and Beta Beta Lambda Chapter of Alpha Phi Alpha Fraternity, Inc. He served on various educational and civic boards and was the director of development of Florida Memorial College (later Florida Memorial University) and served on the Black Archives History and Research Foundation of South Florida, Inc.

FURTHER READING

Lincoln High and Elementary School Faculties. *The Evolution of Susan Prim* (1944).

Porter, Gilbert L., and Leedell W. Neyland. *History Of The Florida State Teachers Association* (1977).

ROSE C. THEVENIN

Porter, James Amos (22 Dec. 1905–28 Feb. 1970), painter, art historian, and writer, was born in Baltimore, Maryland, the son of John Porter, a Methodist minister, and Lydia Peck, a schoolteacher. The youngest of seven siblings, he attended the public schools in Baltimore and Washington, D.C., and graduated cum laude from Howard University in 1927 with a bachelor of science in Art. That same year Howard appointed him instructor in art in the School of Applied Sciences. In December 1929 he married Dorothy Louise Burnett of Montclair, New Jersey; they had one daughter.

In 1929 Porter studied at the Art Students League of New York under Dimitri Romanovsky and George Bridgeman. In August 1935 he received the *certificat de présence* from the Institut d'Art et Archéologie, University of Paris, and in 1937 he received a master of arts in Art History from New York University, Fine Arts Graduate Center.

Porter first exhibited with the Harmon Foundation in 1928 and in 1933 was awarded the ARTHUR SCHOMBURG Portrait Prize during the Harmon Foundation Exhibition of Negro Artists for his painting *Woman Holding a Jug* (Fisk University, Carl Van Vechten Collection).

Other early exhibitions in which he participated included the Thirty-second Annual Exhibition of the Washington Water Color Club (Gallery Room, National Gallery of Art, Smithsonian Institution, Washington, D.C., 1928), Exhibition of Paintings and Sculpture of American Negro Artists at the National Gallery of Art (Smithsonian Institution, 1929), Exhibition of Paintings and Drawings by James A. Porter and Block Prints by JAMES LESESNE WELLS (Young Women's Christian Association, Montclair, New Jersey, 1930), and Exhibition of Paintings by American Negro Artists at the United States National Museum (Smithsonian Institution, 1930). His first one-man show was Exhibition of Paintings and Drawings by James A. Porter (Howard University Gallery of Art, 1930).

Porter began writing about art in the late 1920s. One of his earliest articles, "Versatile Interests of the Early Negro Artist," appeared in *Art in America* in 1931. One of his most important and still-discussed articles, "Four Problems in the History of Negro Art," published in the *Journal of Negro History* in 1942, mentions numerous artists and analyzes the following four problems: documenting and locating the earliest art by blacks—or the reality of handicrafts and fine arts by blacks before 1820; discovering when racial subject matter takes vital hold on the black artist—or the black artist's relation to the mainstream of American society; investigating the decline of productivity among black artists between 1870 and 1890 (a process that coincided with the end of an era, especially of neo-classicism and portraiture), concentrating on the period of Reconstruction; and determining the role of visual artists in the New Negro movement of 1900–1920, the period of self-expression for the African American.

Porter's classic book, *Modern Negro Art* (1943), has proved to be one of the most informative sources on the productivity of the African American artist in the United States since the eighteenth century. Its placement of African American artists in the context of modern art history was both novel and profound. "For some, *Modern Negro Art* was considered presumptuous and certainly premature. But Porter's bold and perceptive scholarship helped those who subsequently focused their attention on African American expression in the visual arts to see the wealth of work that had been produced in the United States for over two centuries" (*James A. Porter Inaugural Colloquium on African American Art*, brochure, 31 Mar. 1990, Howard University).

First reprinted in 1963 for use as a standard reference work on black art in America, the book was reprinted again in 1992 and is considered by many to be the fundamental book on black art history. As Lowery S. Sims of the Metropolitan Museum of Art has noted in the 1992 edition, *Modern Negro Art* "is still an indispensable reference work fifty years after its initial publication"; and, in the view of the art historian Richard J. Powell, it "continues to provide today's scholars with early source information, core bibliographic material, and other essential research tools for African American art history" (*Modern Negro Art* [1992]).

Porter also wrote about many artists, including HENRY OSSAWA TANNER, ROBERT S. DUNCANSON, Malvin Gray Johnson, and LAURA WHEELER WARING. His other writings included monographs, book reviews, introductions to books, including CHARLES WHITE's *Dignity of Images* and LOÏS MAILOU JONES's *Peintures, 1937–1951*, introductions and forewords to exhibition catalogs, and newspaper and periodical articles.

In 1953 Porter was appointed head of the department of art and director of the Gallery of Art at Howard University. This dual position enabled him to organize exhibitions featuring artists of many races from many countries who previously had not been recognized. He is credited with enlarging the permanent art collection of Howard University and strengthening the art department's collection of works by black artists as well as its art curriculum. Porter's leadership led the Kress Foundation to include Howard among the roughly two dozen American universities selected in 1961 to receive the Kress Study Collection of Renaissance paintings and sculpture as a stimulus to the study of art history.

In 1955 Porter received the Achievement in Art Award from the Pyramid Club of Philadelphia, Pennsylvania, and also was appointed a fellow of the Belgium-American Art Seminar studying Flemish and Dutch art of the sixteenth to eighteenth centuries. In 1961 he was a delegate at the UNESCO Conference on Africa, held in Boston, and he served as a member of the Arts Council of Washington, D.C. (1961–1963), and as a member of the conference Symposium on Art and Public Education (1962). In August 1962 he was a delegate-member of the International Congress on African Art and Culture, sponsored by the Rhodes National Gallery, in Salisbury, Southern Rhodesia.

In 1963–1964, having been awarded a Washington *Evening Star* faculty-research grant to gather materials for a projected book on West African art and architecture, Porter took a sabbatical leave to West Africa, including Nigeria and Egypt. From September 1963 to July 1964 he collected various pieces of African art throughout West Africa and Egypt and participated in a USIA exhibition. Also in this period he lectured on African and African American art for the radio broadcast *Voice of America*. In August 1964 he traveled to Brazil in search of documentation of the African influence on and contribution to Brazilian colonial and modern art and to Latin American art and culture. Porter thought a worldview was needed to explore the transcontinental, historical, and cultural perspectives of blacks, and he wanted the quantitative and qualitative factors examined that affected the African's experience outside Africa. Only through comparative research of this kind, Porter argued, would it become possible to relate and reconstruct the dissimilar experiences and cultural expression of the transplanted African. Upon returning to the United States in the fall with twenty-five of his own paintings that he had completed while in Lagos, Nigeria, Porter said that he hoped "my paintings reflect the enthusiasm and the understanding [and] admiration which I have felt for Africa and the Africans, even though, admittedly the most skillful expatriate artist may utterly fail to capture those ineffable traits in the African people which we believe are made visible to us in their arts" ("Professor Porter Paints in Nigeria," *Howard University Magazine* 7, no. 4 [July 1965]: 12–16).

In March 1965 Porter and twenty-six other teachers in the United States were named "America's most outstanding men of the arts." They received the first National Gallery of Art Medals and Honoraria for Distinguished Achievement in Art Education, which were presented at a White House ceremony by First Lady Lady Bird Johnson. These medals were specially designed as part of a daylong celebration commemorating the twenty-fifth anniversary of the founding of the National Gallery of Art.

Since Porter's death in Washington, D.C., his legacy has been honored in various ways. The James A. Porter Gallery of African American Art was dedicated at the Howard University Gallery of Art on 4 December 1970. Aesthetic Dynamics organized in Wilmington, Delaware, Afro-American Images (1971), an exhibition dedicated, according to the catalog, to "a man ahead of his time. Unique in the sense that he was totally involved in the creative expression which characterizes the Black life-style in African, Latin American and African American art as an historian and was an accomplished practicing artist as well." In March 1990 the department of art at Howard University organized the James A. Porter Inaugural Colloquium on African American Art. This annual event seeks to continue Porter's efforts to bring previously invisible artists to the attention of the American mainstream and to define and assess the enduring artistic values that are meaningful for African Americans. In *James A. Porter, Artist and Art Historian: The Memory of the Legacy*, the catalog for a retrospective exhibition held at the Howard University Gallery of Art in 1992–1993, ROMARE BEARDEN wrote that, because of Porter's efforts, college art programs, in particular art programs in traditionally black colleges, are no longer considered secondary to the other disciplines.

FURTHER READING

Porter's papers are in the Dorothy Porter Wesley Archives, Wesport Foundation and Gallery, Washington, D.C.

Bearden, Romare. *A History of African-American Artists from 1792 to the Present* (1993).

Davis, Donald F. "James Porter of Howard: Artist, Writer," *Journal of Negro History* 70 (1985): 89–91.

Powell, Richard. *Black Art: A Cultural History* (2003).

Obituaries: *Evening Star* (Washington, D.C.), 3–4 Mar. 1970; *International Herald Tribune*, 5 Mar. 1970; *Washington Post*, 14 Mar. 1970; *Jet* (19 Mar. 1970); *Art Journal* 29 (1970).

This entry is taken from the *American National Biography* and is published here with the permission of the American Council of Learned Societies.

CONSTANCE PORTER UZELAC

Porter, Marion Anthony (c.1924–25 June 2000), World War II sailor and Silver Star recipient, was born in Spartanburg, South Carolina, the son of Berkley and Bessie Porter. The Porter family was well off for the times, according to the 1930 Federal Census. Berkley Porter owned his home, valued at $600, and supported his family working as a chauffeur. Bessie Porter remained at home to take care of her children, including daughter Louise and sons Marion and Clarence. Nothing else is known about Marion Porter's life before joining the navy.

Like many young African Americans, Marion Porter voluntarily enlisted in the military after the attack on Pearl Harbor, joining the navy on 6 February 1942 at Columbia, South Carolina. He was subsequently sent to the navy's segregated training facility, Unit K West–Unit B East, at Norfolk, Virginia. Here he learned to perform the only duties that were open to African American enlisted men serving in the navy early in the war, that of a mess attendant (later in the war changed to "steward"). The duties of mess attendants were many and varied, but all involved serving white officers, either in shore-based facilities or at sea. The tasks performed by these mess attendants, men like Porter, LEONARD HARMON, and CARL KIMMONS, included preparing and/or serving meals to officers, taking care of the officer's quarters, and similar duties. In addition, for those men serving aboard a ship at sea, everyone had a "general quarters" or battle-station position during those times when a vessel was operating under combat conditions. It was when black sailors were serving in these battle station positions that they achieved, if only briefly, some measure of equality with their white shipmates, serving as members of a gun crew, ammunition handlers, aiding the wounded, or performing damage control duties. Despite their minimal, often nonexistent, training in weapon's handling, black mess attendants early on in the war, as demonstrated by the heroics of DORIE MILLER, soon demonstrated their fighting capabilities to a very high degree.

After completing his mess attendant training at Norfolk on 31 March 1942, Mess Attendant 3rd Class Marion Porter was immediately assigned to the destroyer USS Lansdale (DD-426), then based on the East Coast performing convoy escort duties all the way from Iceland to the Caribbean. Porter would stay aboard Lansdale during the rest of its service during the war, making convoy runs to the United Kingdom, North Africa, and the Caribbean from 1942 to 1944. During these two years of service, Marion Porter excelled at his duties, receiving high marks for job proficiency, and even higher marks for his personal conduct, rising to the petty-officer rating of steward third class. As future events would show, however, Porter was not just a good steward; with an assigned battle-station position manning one of the destroyer's antiaircraft guns, he proved to be an equally effective gunner.

On the night of 20 April 1944, Marion Porter and the crew of Lansdale were performing convoy duty off Cape Bengut, Algeria, in the Mediterranean Sea when they came under heavy air attack from German bombers. The third wave of German dive and torpedo bombers to hit the convoy pounced on Lansdale, which was silhouetted by a burning merchant ship hit in the first wave. Jumped by five

aircraft at once, the destroyer's gunners shot down one attacker, but others got through and were able to drop their torpedoes. One of these torpedoes subsequently struck Lansdale and almost cut the ship in two. Though badly damaged, the destroyer stayed afloat, and its gunners, including Marion Porter, continued to defend the crippled ship. One more attacker was subsequently shot down, but Lansdale was doomed; continuing to take on water, the destroyer took on a heavy list, and damage control efforts proved difficult. In less than a half an hour after being struck, Lansdale's captain ordered its crew to abandon ship. The destroyer subsequently broke in half, with one part sinking immediately, while the other soon followed. As for Marion Porter, he was seriously wounded when the destroyer was first hit, but continued to man his antiaircraft gun station, "directing accurate, effective fire against attacking planes until the seriousness and intense pain of his injuries made it impossible for him to carry out his duties" (Knoblock, p. 183). Relieved by an officer, Porter dragged himself clear of the gun position so as not to interfere with its operations. When the order to abandon ship came, Porter made it off Lansdale and stayed afloat for three hours before he was finally rescued.

A month after the loss of Lansdale, her captain, Lieutenant Commander D. M. Swift, recommended Steward 3rd Class Marion Porter for the Silver Star Medal on 26 June 1944, which award was subsequently approved on 24 July 1944. Porter received the medal stateside while he was recovering at the U.S. Naval Hospital at St. Albans, New York. Marion Porter's naval service during World War II was significant for several reasons. He was one of just a small group of African American sailors to become the recipient of a high level combat award; no African Americans in the navy during the war were awarded the Medal of Honor, fewer than ten were awarded the next highest naval decoration, the Navy Cross, while fewer than ten men have been identified as Silver Star recipients. Even more important, however, is the fact that Porter's distinguished naval career is truly indicative of the fine service rendered by black stewards at sea, often accomplished under difficult conditions of racial segregation and limited opportunities. For the most part, the service of these men in every combat theater of the war from the beginning of the war and throughout its entire duration remains largely unknown to this day.

After being awarded the Silver Star, Marion Porter remained at the St. Albans Naval Hospital until his final discharge from the navy on 29 March 1946. Nothing is known of his subsequent civilian life.

FURTHER READING

Knoblock, Glenn A. *African American World War II Casualties and Decorations in the Navy, Coast Guard, and Merchant Marine: A Comprehensive Record* (2009).

Miller, Richard. *The Messmen Chronicles: African Americans in the U.S. Navy, 1932–1943* (2004).

GLENN ALLEN KNOBLOCK

Posey, Cum (20 June 1890–28 Mar. 1946), baseball player and team owner, was born Cumberland Willis Posey Jr. in Homestead, Pennsylvania, the son of Cumberland Willis Posey, a businessman, and Anna Stephens, a teacher. The man who made people think about the river town of Homestead for something other than its steel mills and the epic labor confrontation of 1892 was the son of one of black Pittsburgh's most prominent and wealthy men. Captain Cumberland Posey Sr. was a riverboat engineer who turned to shipbuilding and later coal mining and real estate. The president of the *Pittsburgh Courier* newspaper, the prestigious Loendi Club, and the Warren Methodist Episcopal Church, the elder Posey bequeathed to his son access to "respectable" black Pittsburgh.

But young Cum gravitated to the sporting scene in the Hill, Pittsburgh's black section, where he often played for "roughneck" teams against those representing black Pittsburgh's upper crust. After graduating from Homestead High School, where he starred in basketball, Cum played at both Holy Ghost College (later renamed Duquesne University) and Pennsylvania State University. His acceptance was made easier by his light complexion and athletic prowess. At Holy Ghost, he enrolled as Charles W. Cumbert and passed for a white student.

After leaving college in 1911, Posey joined the Homestead Grays as an outfielder and also promoted and starred for the Monticellos and the Loendi Club semipro basketball teams. Playing against both white and black teams from across the nation, Posey's basketball clubs were considered the informal national champions by the black press. The *Courier* sportswriter Wendell Smith called Posey, who was five feet nine inches and 140 pounds, "the outstanding athlete of the Negro race" during the late 1920s, "perhaps the most colorful figure who has ever raced down the sundown sports trail."

Posey, who married Ethel Truman in 1913 and had five daughters with her, worked as a clerk for the Railway Mail Service until 1920. He divided his time between work and sport, finally opting to focus on sports. By 1917 he was managing and promoting the Homestead Grays. He and Charles Walker were the club's co-owners by the early 1920s, and while Walker handled gate receipts and concessions, Posey selected players and booked games. Together they made the club into a profitable business venture by the mid-1920s. Posey recruited some of the best black players in the Americas, including SMOKEY JOE WILLIAMS, MARTIN DIHIGO, Sam Streeter, and VIC HARRIS, to play alongside the Grays' core of local talent. Posey played for the Grays until 1928 and managed the squad until 1935. Although considered a valuable player, he drew the most praise for his managerial and promotional expertise. Eddie Gottlieb, who owned the Philadelphia Stars of the Negro National League, said, "As a manager and promoter, Cum Posey was one of the greatest baseball men I ever met."

During the 1925 and 1926 seasons, the Grays' record was 232 wins, 29 losses, and 11 ties, with a stretch of 43 consecutive victories. Although most of their games were against white and black semipro teams, the Grays defeated Negro National League clubs as well as white major leaguers in postseason exhibitions.

By 1930, with the addition of the future Hall of Famers OSCAR CHARLESTON, JUDY JOHNSON, and JOSH GIBSON, the Grays were considered black baseball's best team. They beat the Lincoln Giants for the Negro championship that fall. But Posey soon lost Gibson, Charleston, Johnson, and other key players to his crosstown rival GUS GREENLEE, who had made a pro team out of the sandlot Crawfords. The Grays suffered both on the field and at the gate, and Posey turned to Homestead numbers banker Rufus "Sonnyman" Jackson, who helped keep the club afloat financially. The numbers, a lottery in which bettors wager that the three-digit number they select will be the one that "hits" that day, was the largest black-controlled business in the country at that time, and many a Negro League team depended on its revenues to remain solvent.

Posey joined the Negro National League in 1935 and rebuilt the Grays after the Pittsburgh Crawfords' collapse in 1937. With the return of Gibson and the emergence of the first baseman BUCK LEONARD, the Grays had the black equivalents of Babe Ruth and Lou Gehrig. The Grays won an unprecedented nine straight National Negro League pennants from 1937 through 1945 as well as the 1948 Negro World Series, the last ever played.

Posey was widely respected in the sporting world. His players usually accepted a handshake as confirmation of a deal. Former Pittsburgh Steelers' owner Art Rooney, who played against Posey on the sandlots, said that Posey had "a knack of persuasion…he always knew when to be hard and when to be compassionate. He was one of the smartest men I knew."

During the late 1930s and World War II, Posey booked three games a week for his team at Griffith Stadium in Washington, D.C., where the Grays frequently outdrew the hapless Senators. Black baseball had become the nation's second largest legal black-owned enterprise, behind only the black insurance companies. While not the wealthiest black owner, Posey was a key figure in league decisions.

Posey wrote a weekly column, "The Sportive Realm," for the *Pittsburgh Courier* in the 1930s and 1940s and used it to critique league policies and attack the influence of white booking agents over black baseball. He also served as the Negro National League secretary and was a member of the Homestead school board.

Although black baseball's prospects seemed bright in the mid-1940s, the postwar integration of the major leagues brought an end to the Negro Leagues. Posey protested that major league teams were signing his best players, usually without compensation, but he did not live to witness JACKIE ROBINSON's 1947 debut. He died of lung cancer.

The *Courier* writer John L. Clark wrote, "In his death, the race lost one of its most dynamic citizens, baseball lost its best mind…Homestead lost its most loyal booster." The Grays played a few more seasons but folded in 1950.

FURTHER READING

Ruck, Rob. *Sandlot Seasons: Sport in Black Pittsburgh* (1987).

Snyder, Brad. *Beyond the Shadow of the Senators: The Untold Story of the Homestead Grays and the Integration of Baseball* (2003).

This entry is taken from the *American National Biography* and is published here with the permission of the American Council of Learned Societies.

ROB RUCK

Poston, Ted (4 July 1906–11 Jan. 1974), journalist, was born Theodore Roosevelt Augustus Major Poston, in Hopkinsville, Kentucky, the youngest of eight children of Ephraim Poston and Mollie Cox, who were both teachers. In the short stories later collected in *The Dark Side of Hopkinsville* (1991), Poston provided a folksy, sometimes fictionalized account of his small-town southern childhood. Poston's father, for example, was elevated in one story to the position of dean of male students at the Kentucky State Industrial College for Negroes in Frankfort, when he was, in fact, an instructor in that school's preparatory department. Yet the stories accurately reflected the importance of education and intellectual debate in the Poston household. Ted's older siblings also pursued careers in writing and journalism. In 1918 his brothers Robert and Ulysses helped their father establish a newspaper, the *Hopkinsville Contender*, which gave Ted his first experience in journalism. Ted's elder brothers later moved to Detroit, Michigan, where they worked on MARCUS GARVEY's newspaper, the *Negro World*. Poston wrote short stories about his childhood because he believed that "someone should put down the not-always-depressing experiences of a segregated society like the one I grew up in" (*Dark Side*, xv). His stories celebrated the simplicity of rural life, of lazy summer afternoons spent fishing and poaching. They also highlighted the importance of the black church and of extended family networks in helping African American children not only to survive in an unequal society but also to flourish.

Yet for all of the Postons' relative wealth and security—they were one of the few black families in Hopkinsville to own their own home—Poston's childhood was not without its indignities and suffering. As his short story "The Revolt of the Evil Faeries" makes clear, he deeply resented the prejudice within his own community against dark-skinned blacks like himself. During his late childhood years Poston also mourned the loss of several close family members in quick succession: his brother Ephraim Jr. in 1914, his mother three years later, his sister Roberta in 1919, and his brother Robert—who had married the sculptor AUGUSTA SAVAGE—who died of pneumonia in 1924, on his return from a Garveyite mission to Liberia.

Despite these tragedies, Poston graduated from high school in 1924 and set off—on foot—for Nashville, where he enrolled in the Tennessee Agricultural and Industrial Normal College (later Tennessee State University). He supported himself by working a series of laboring jobs, including stints as a tobacco stemmer and as a Pullman porter, and he graduated with a degree in English and Journalism in 1928. He then moved to New York City to work with his brother Ulysses, who had established the *Contender* as a Democratic Party news sheet in that city and who was working on the New York governor Al Smith's 1928 presidential campaign. Poston soon joined A. PHILIP RANDOLPH's efforts to unionize black railroad workers, and he began penning a column about Harlem for the *Pittsburgh Courier*. In 1931, under the byline T. R. Poston, he launched his full-time journalistic career as a reporter for the New York *Amsterdam News*, the city's leading African American newspaper.

Poston quickly became one of the leading lights of the Harlem intelligentsia. He began lifelong friendships with the poet LANGSTON HUGHES and the NAACP political strategist HENRY LEE MOON, whom he accompanied in 1932 on a trip to the Soviet Union to make a movie about American racism. After two months, however, the Soviet leader Joseph Stalin cancelled the movie—in which Poston was to play a lynching victim—so as not to offend the United States, which was then close to reopening diplomatic ties with the Soviet Union. Closer to home, Poston earned plaudits for his sympathetic coverage of the trials of the SCOTTSBORO BOYS, who were accused of raping two white women in Alabama, and of the tribulations of their Communist Party defenders in the 1930s. He also, in 1935, helped lead efforts to unionize the *Amsterdam News*, for which he was rewarded with the sack. That year he married Miriam Rivers, a young and glamorous Harlemite, whom he had met during the *Amsterdam News* strike; they divorced in 1940. All three of Poston's marriages were childless.

Following a spell with the Federal Writers' Project, Poston joined the *New York Post* in 1936, where he adopted the new byline Ted Poston. Though he was not the first black writer for a major white-owned daily, over the span of three decades he became the best-known African American in the ranks of the nation's journalists. In addition to his journalistic efforts for the *Post*, Poston began to publish some of his short stories in the *New Republic*, among other outlets. His fame was aided not only by his journalistic skill but also by his continuing interest in politics. Along with Moon, ROBERT WEAVER, and MARY McLEOD BETHUNE, he became a member of President Roosevelt's "Black Cabinet" in the New Deal years of the 1930s and 1940s. Such contacts undoubtedly helped provide Poston with the connections needed for his exclusive and well-regarded interviews with white

political leaders such as Huey Long, Louisiana's populist and controversial governor, and Wendell Wilkie, the Republican presidential candidate in 1940. During World War II Poston worked at the Negro News Desk of the Office of War Information and later in the White House, where he helped to monitor the often tense racial situation of the war years. While in Washington in December 1941, he married Marie Byrd Tancil, an ambitious young socialite and assistant on Weaver's staff. They divorced in 1956.

Poston returned full-time to the *New York Post* in 1945. Over the next two decades he emerged as one of the leading commentators on the civil rights movement. During those years the *Post* earned a reputation as one of the most racially liberal northern newspapers, in large part because of Poston's pioneering role in translating the hopes and fears of southern African Americans to a white northern audience. In several of his finest pieces, Poston's role as a black northern journalist covering racial tensions in the South became part of the story. His 1949 series on the "Little Scottsboro" trial of three black youths accused of raping a white woman in Tavares, Florida, for example, resulted in a lynch mob chasing Poston down a deserted Florida road. The series earned Poston the George Polk Journalism Award and a nomination for the Pulitzer Prize for journalism. Poston's biographer Kathleen Hauke has suggested that he might have also become the first African American to win the Pulitzer, but his nomination was sabotaged by some of his colleagues on the *Post*. Among other stories, Poston covered the career of the first black baseball star in the major leagues, the Brooklyn Dodgers' JACKIE ROBINSON, the *Brown v. Board of Education* school desegregation decision, the Montgomery bus boycott, and the Little Rock school integration crisis. While covering the opening of the integrated Little Rock schools in 1959, Poston and CARL ROWAN were shot at by a carload of whites while standing outside the home of DAISY BATES, a fellow journalist and a mentor to the nine black students who faced white violence as they integrated the schools.

Poston covered many of the great victories of the civil rights movement in the 1960s; one memorable piece he wrote in 1966 was about an Alabama man named Jeff Hamilton, who cast his first-ever ballot that year at the age of seventy-seven. Poston was by then widely regarded as the "dean of black journalists," but his relationship with the *New York Post* had become increasingly fraught. Management at the

Post began to view his journalistic style as dated and began to look for new reporters who they believed might better capture the new black nationalist phase of the civil rights movement. Poston, in return, criticized management for failing to understand the complexity of its African American readership and believed that the paper's reputation in the African American community had been tarnished. By the late 1960s Poston was drinking and smoking heavily, and his drinking, especially, began to interfere with his once tireless workload. Sent to cover the assassination of MARTIN LUTHER KING JR. in Memphis in 1968, Poston got drunk—a not altogether unnatural reaction to a senseless killing and the seeming end of a civil rights dream—and missed his deadline with the *Post*.

Poston's family life was also troubled. He had married Ersa Hines Clinton, a personnel manager, in 1957, but the couple barely saw each other because of their hectic work schedules. They separated sometime before Poston's retirement from the *Post* in 1972, the same year that the city of New York awarded Poston its distinguished service medal. In retirement Poston was unable to muster the energy to complete his planned collection of short stories, *The Dark Side of Hopkinsville*, though they were published posthumously.

Ted Poston often said that his three loves were writing, whiskey, and women. But his three marriages were tempestuous, and he spent his final years alone. His love of whiskey—and of tobacco, another homegrown Kentucky vice—undoubtedly hastened his physical demise and his relatively early death at age sixty-seven in Brooklyn. But his writing, especially his trailblazing civil rights reportage for the *New York Post*, is a fitting legacy. Poston created for the *Post*'s primarily white urban readership an understanding of the nature of the apartheid system that flourished within its own nation and of the need for racial change in both the South and the North.

FURTHER READING

Poston, Ted. *The Dark Side of Hopkinsville: Stories by Ted Poston*, ed. Kathleen A. Hauke (1991).

Poston, Ted. *A First Draft of History*, ed. Kathleen A. Hauke (2000).

Hauke, Kathleen A. *Ted Poston: Pioneer American Journalist* (1998).

Reporting Civil Rights: Part One, American Journalism 1941–1963, comp. Clayborne Carson, David J. Garrow, Bill Kovach, and Carol Polsgrove (2003).

Obituary: *New York Times*, 12 Jan. 1974.

STEVEN J. NIVEN

Potter, Eliza (1820–?), lady's maid, hairdresser, and author, was presumably born free in Cincinnati or New York. Little is known about her childhood and personal life in general. She was raised in New York but her parents' names are unknown. One biographer lists her maiden name as Johnson and another states that she was the former Mrs. Johnson but neither provides a source. As a child she apparently did not obtain extensive education and began working as a domestic while young.

Most information about Potter stems from the anonymously published *A Hairdresser's Experience in High Life* (1859). At the time of publication it was universally attributed to her; however, within her work, she masked most of her private life and instead described her clientele. According to the autobiography Potter moved to Buffalo, "committed a weakness" and married (Potter, 12). Ever private, she neglects to mention to whom she married, whether they had children, or the length of time they stayed together. After some time she abandoned her husband and began her life traveling as an independent woman. She sailed to Canada, where she stayed with family for a short duration. Deciding to "leave pleasure for something more important," she returned to Buffalo and then traveled to Pittsburgh (Potter, 14). Soon afterward she was hired as a lady's maid in Cincinnati, Ohio.

In the early 1840s Potter sailed to France to care for a judge's family in Paris. There she had a dispute with her employer and found other families for which to work in that city. Wanting to travel, she followed a family to England and remained there for about a year, learning how to dress hair, cook, and sew. She witnessed the baptisms of the Prince of Wales and the Count of Paris and attended many balls and social receptions. During this time she acquired the nickname "Iangy."

Upon returning to the United States, Potter traveled with wealthy families of Ohio and Kentucky to various national retreats. She vividly described the Creoles that she met while in New Orleans. She also visited Natchez, where she taught hairdressing. Eventually Potter settled in Cincinnati, having decided it had grown more cosmopolitan and could provide her with a sufficient number of clients interested in her French styles. The home of 3,237 African Americans in 1850, Cincinnati, like many antebellum cities, was fairly integrated rather than containing distinct black neighborhoods. She lived on Six Home Street near the Colored Asylum.

Primary sources contain contradictory information about Potter's life during the late 1840s. Potter's autobiography does not mention children, but an Eliza Potter was allotted in the 1860 Federal Census for Hamilton County, Ohio, with Kate, aged eleven, and James, aged nine. *A Hairdresser's Experience* neglects to mention a second marriage. Potter remained in Cincinnati until at least 1861, according to *Williams' Directory*.

The Potter children's birth dates found in the census indicate that they resided in Pennsylvania in 1849 to 1851. However, Potter herself doesn't mention having lived in Pennsylvania. In February 1850 two advertisements for a "good husband for a widow lady" appeared in the Cincinnati *Daily Commercial*. Although the advertisements name the widow by only "Mrs. Eliza C.," the biographer Susan Graber believes this to be Potter. This widow is described as being of brunette skin, auburn hair, and good form. The advertisements state that she was a member of the Episcopal Church and had "a family to train up." One supporting piece of evidence given is Eliza C. Potter's inclusion as a communicant in the St. Paul's Episcopal Church records.

In 1859 Potter decided to "tell her story in simpler language" (Potter, iv). Self-published in Cincinnati, *A Hairdresser's Experience In High Life* was described as "bold, if not very polished" (Harlow, 171). Through her work, the life of a hairdresser may be slightly reconstructed.

Potter's workday consisted of traveling to the homes of ladies to dress their hair. On an ordinary day she worked from 8:00 A.M. to 6:00 P.M. On ball nights she could expect to work for twenty-four ladies between 7:00 A.M. and 11:30 P.M. A popular hairdresser, Potter refused dozens of other clients on the day of each ball. She tactfully relayed some women's interest in attending balls by assisting many ladies with the construction of invitation lists. "Continuously backstage in the social melodrama," Harlow states, "she seems to have become a sort of social arbiter and fixer" (173). Further Harlow states that "Potter was writing of a society in a state of flux," with upwardly mobile families intruding into the social sphere of the entrenched aristocracy (172).

Potter also focused on her wealthy clientele's social lives. The autobiography is filled with accolades for her young charges, minute details of feminine clothing, genteel descriptions of disagreements with former employers, and criticisms of the women who confided in Potter. In one instance she describes "a lady in Cincinnati who makes herself notorious for visiting milliners, dress-makers, confectioners....I will give her name as Mrs. Envy; because she is envious of every one from the leaders of fashion down to the tradesman" (196–197). Because she omits the names of the individuals about whom she wrote, social historians can not confirm her facts against primary sources. But Potter's vivid descriptions and boldly offered opinion of the Cincinnati elite provides a great deal of insight into high society.

Despite her visits to slave states, long-term residence near slaveholding Kentucky, and her own mixed racial background, Potter says little about the institution of slavery. Early in her memoir she mentions that she gave the directions to Canada to a runaway slave of a harsh mistress and later went to court to defend her actions. Although she was critical of people's treatment of slaves, she did not criticize the institution. While in New Orleans, she petitioned "to prevent the colored people from owning slaves" after meeting a particularly cruel creole (Potter, 191).

Potter's opinion about slavery and the abolition movement may have been disguised to protect her business. As she describes it, she had contact with slaves, runaways, and abolitionists. Certainly, the fervor surrounding the 1852 publication of *Uncle Tom's Cabin* by Cincinnati resident Harriet Beecher Stowe would have been a common topic among Potter's clientele and companions. Yet Potter's position as a free person of color was tenuous despite living in Ohio, the home of many antislavery Quakers and other abolitionists.

It appears that there is no record of Potter in the 1870 census. Although she may have died or married, her wandering nature might have led her to a new town instead. HARRIET WILSON's *Our Nig*, a contemporary book by a northern free woman of color, has been reissued and studied within academia. Harlow wrote in 1950 that "naturally, [*A Hairdresser's Experience In High Life*] was a bestseller" (171). However, possibly due to Potter's concentration on her white clients to the neglect of her own opinions, her full importance has yet to be realized. *A Hairdresser's Experience In High Life* is included in the Schomburg Library of Nineteenth-Century Black Women Writers.

FURTHER READING

Potter, Eliza. *A Hairdresser's Experience In High Life* (1859).

Blassingame, John W. *Black New Orleans, 1860–1880* (1973).

Graber, Susan P. "A *Hairdresser's Experience in High Life* by Mrs. Eliza Potter: Cincinnati in the Mid-Nineteenth Century," in *Bulletin of the Historical and Philosophical Society of Ohio* 25.3 (1967).

Harlow, Alvin F. *The Serene Cincinnatians* (1950).

Huot, Nikolas. "Eliza C. Potter," in *African American Autobiographers: A Sourcebook* (2002).

Ryan, Barbara T. *"Uneasy Relation": Servants' Place in the Nineteenth-Century American Home* (1994).

Santamarina, Xiomara A. *Belabored Professions: Narratives of African American Working Womanhood* (2005)

Williams' Directory (1857, 1858, 1860, 1861).

KATHRYN L. STALEY

Potter, Richard (1783?–20 Sept. 1835), ventriloquist and magician, was born in Hopkinton, Massachusetts, the son of Dinah Swain (often called Black Dinah), a slave. Potter's mother was kidnapped by Dutch slave traders during her childhood, sold at an auction, and taken to Boston as a slave by Sir Charles Henry Frankland, a tax collector for the Port of Boston. She had five children while serving in Frankland's household. The identity of Potter's biological father remains a mystery. According to speculation, Potter's father was Frankland. Early church records indicate that Potter's father was a white man by the name of George Simpson. The origin of Potter's name is another mystery.

Potter spent his early years on the Frankland estate in Hopkinton, Massachusetts. At the age of ten, in 1793, he took work on a ship as a cabin boy. His travels took him to England, where he came across a Scottish magician and ventriloquist by the name of John Rannie. After watching Rannie perform, Potter became interested in the arts of ventriloquism and magic. He joined Rannie, and for the next six years he learned from this mentor. Potter and Rannie moved to the United States in 1800, where they worked with a traveling circus. In 1801, at the age of eighteen, Potter performed his ventriloquism and magic with the traveling circus for the first time. In 1806 Rannie, who considered himself more a ventriloquist than a magician, began to focus on plays, in which he used more magic. Potter performed in several theatrical plays with Rannie, who often hired local performers to help in his productions.

In 1807 Rannie and Potter secured a booking in Boston. It was in this year that Potter met the twenty-year-old Sally Harris, a dancer from Roxbury, Massachusetts. Rannie was staging a play called *The Provoked Husband*, and he needed a female lead. The part went to Sally. Over the course of the production, Potter and Sally became close, and they married on 25 March 1808. The following year their first son, Henry M. Potter, was born.

In 1811 Rannie performed his last show at the Exchange Coffee House in Boston, Massachusetts, and Potter inherited all of his equipment. That same year Potter, who was now twenty-eight years old, began a solo career, performing in Boston at the Exchange Coffee House. He became a member of the first African Masonic Lodge in Boston and occasionally displayed the Masonic symbol on his broadside advertisements. In 1813 the Potters purchased land in Andover, New Hampshire, and they settled there in 1814, the same year that their son Richard Potter Jr. was born. A daughter, Anganet Potter, was born in 1815.

Between 1818 and 1831 Potter performed in New York City, Raleigh, North Carolina, and Boston. By 1833 he began to focus solely on ventriloquism and removed magic from his performances.

Potter died at the age of fifty-two and was followed the next year by Sally, who died at the age of forty-nine. After Potter's death, Richard Jr. lived in his father's house for a few years and sold the property shortly afterward. While the family was no longer located in New Hampshire in the early twenty-first century, Potter's legacy remained. In 1871 the section of Andover where Potter lived became known as Potter's Place.

FURTHER READING

Burns, Stanley. *Other Voices: Ventriloquism from B.C. to T.V.* (2000).

Charles, Mary Grant. "America's First Negro Magician," *Negro Digest* (Dec. 1949).

Haskins, Jim, and Kathleen Benson. *Conjure Times: Black Magicians in America* (2001).

Magus, Jim. *Magical Heroes: The Lives and Legends of Great African American Magicians* (1995).

CHARLIE T. TOMLINSON

Poussaint, Alvin (15 May 1934–), psychiatrist, author, and educator, was born in the East Harlem section of New York City, the seventh of eight children of Christopher Poussaint, a typographer and printer, and Harriet Johnston Poussaint, a homemaker. At the age of nine, Poussaint was stricken with rheumatic fever. A lengthy convalescence forced him to take up reading and avoid most of the physical activities that other children his age would normally participate in. But it was his love of reading that flourished during this time and fueled his academic prowess. His thirst for knowledge carried into extracurricular activities, where he taught himself how to play the clarinet, the saxophone, and flute.

Poussaint graduated from Stuyvesant High School in 1952. He immediately went on to attend Columbia University as a premedical student with a concentration in French, and he graduated in 1956. In medical school Poussaint chose to specialize in psychiatry and earned an M.D. from Cornell University in 1960. In 1964 he completed his residency in postgraduate training at the UCLA Neuropsychiatric Institute. Simultaneously, he received an M.S. in Research Methodology in Psychiatry from UCLA.

In 1965, soon after completing his training in psychiatry, Poussaint joined the civil rights movement instead of seeking an academic appointment. He felt racism was at the root of the mental health crisis in the black community. He accepted the position of southern field director of the Medical Committee for Human Rights in Jackson, Mississippi. Poussaint concluded that helping to put an end to segregation was a better means of serving the community than individual counseling. He and his staff provided a medical presence for civil rights workers and local citizens. They also worked to desegregate hospitals and health facilities in the South. His quest for equality continued after leaving Mississippi in 1967 to become a member of the Tufts University School of Medicine faculty in Boston, Massachusetts. Poussaint was also director of psychiatry at a community health center at Columbia Point housing project in Dorchester. Poussaint fought for blacks' professional equality as well. He played a key role in forming the first Black Caucus of the American Psychiatric Association in 1969. He roundly criticized studies and treatments he found to be slanted by racial bias.

While still in Boston, Poussaint met Spelman graduate Ann Ashmore. A Simmons College psychiatric social work major and later a psychologist, Ashmore had participated in the first sit-in held in Atlanta. In 1969 Poussaint joined Harvard Medical School as associate dean of students and associate professor of psychiatry. He was one of the founding members of Operation PUSH (People United to Serve Humanity), which was established in 1971. Poussaint published the little-known volume *Why Blacks Kill Blacks* in 1972. He and Ashmore married in 1973. Three years later, along with fellow psychiatrist James P. Comer, Poussaint coauthored *Black Child Care: How to Bring Up a Healthy Black Child in America*. From 1975 to 1978 he served as Director of Student Affairs at Harvard Medical School. The Poussaints' only child, Alan, was born in 1979.

Poussaint took on one of his most famous projects as script consultant to NBC's award-winning *The Cosby Show* from 1984 to 1992. He served in the same capacity for the spin-off show, *A Different World*, from 1987 to 1993. While guiding the shows to more realistic portrayals of cohesive, stable black families, Poussaint and his wife divorced in 1988. In addition to becoming a consultant to the media concerning responsible programming, in 1992 Poussaint revised and reissued *Black Child Care* as *Raising Black Children: Two Leading Psychiatrists Confront the Educational, Social, and Emotional Problems Facing Black Children*. That year he married pediatric neuroradiologist Tina Inez Young; in 1999, they had a daughter, Alison.

As a culmination of Poussaint's reputation as an expert on race and mental health issues, in 2000 he coauthored, with Amy Alexander, the book *Lay My Burden Down: Unraveling Suicide and the Mental Health Crisis among African-Americans*. This study explored suicide in the context of general mental health issues affecting African Americans. Poussaint was a noted proponent of nonviolent parenting and violence prevention programs, and he continued his work into the new millennium at Harvard and as director of the media center at Boston's Judge Baker Children's Center.

FURTHER READING
Poussaint, A. F. "Black Children: Coping in a Racist Society" in *Voices of Multicultural America: Notable Speeches Delivered by African, Asian, Hispanic and Native Americans, 1790–1995* (1996).
Poussaint, A. F. *Black Suicide* (1975).
Poussaint, A. F. "Interracial Relations and Prejudice" in *Comprehensive Textbook of Psychiatry/III* (1980).
Poussaint, A. F. "Racial Issues in Medicine: A Psychosocial Perspective" in *Humane Medicine: A New Paradigm in Medical Education and Health Care Delivery* (2001).
Metcalf, George R. *Up from Within: Today's New Black Leaders* (1971).

WILLIE HOBBS

Poussaint, Renee Francine (12 Aug. 1944–), journalist, news anchor, writer, documentary producer, and activist, was born in New York City to Christopher Poussaint, a printer, and Bobbie Vance Poussaint, a social worker who would eventually become New York City's human resources administration commissioner. Poussaint was born into a nurturing family in East Harlem, surrounded by her aunts and uncles. One of them, ALVIN POUSSAINT, later became a well-known psychiatrist, writer, and civil rights activist.

Initially Poussaint attended a neighborhood Catholic school in Harlem, but in 1953 she, her parents, and her younger brother moved to Queens, New York. Three years later her parents divorced. In Queens, she attended public schools. She had a deep curiosity about the varied cultures of the world and a passion for literature, writing, and African dance—she performed briefly with a professional company. In 1962 Poussaint graduated as salutatorian of her class at one of New York's largest high schools, Andrew Jackson.

Poussaint's grades and community service record got her a scholarship to Sarah Lawrence College in Bronxville, New York. She was among only a handful of African Americans in a school of some five hundred students. Although she had to work several part-time jobs to make ends meet, the educational opportunities she was exposed to were well worth it. A turning point came when she was able to spend a year studying in Paris as part of the college's junior year abroad program. That exposure fueled her longtime interest in different cultures and ethnicities. She would later spend significant periods living and working in Africa.

Poussaint graduated from college when the civil rights movement was in full swing. Although she had participated in demonstrations and worked periodically for the Congress of Racial Equality (CORE) and the NAACP Legal Defense Fund, she wanted to bring useful, concrete skills to the struggle. In 1966 she entered Yale Law School, and although it was a good academic fit, it was less so when it came to temperament. After a year she took a leave of absence and went to live and work in Malawi, East Africa, joining her future husband, Henry Richardson, who was under contract to handle international legal affairs for the Malawi government. Although she managed to find a minimum-wage job working for the Malawi radio station, job possibilities for foreign women were extremely difficult to come by.

After a year Poussaint returned to New York and got a job as program director of an international exchange organization for graduate business students. Eventually, she moved to Los Angeles to complete a master's degree in African studies at UCLA.

She also worked as associate editor of the highly respected *African Arts* magazine. After finishing her M.A. she became a doctoral student in comparative literature (African and African American) at Indiana University in Bloomington, Indiana.

While working as a teaching assistant for a course on African American writers, Poussaint was stunned to discover that a number of the freshmen in the class were functionally illiterate. They could barely read and write and had been what was then called "socially promoted" through various high schools. They had little interest in reading the works of the authors she loved, and they told her that they got whatever information and entertainment they needed from watching television. Realizing that to reach these students she had to learn how to use the medium they responded to, Poussaint changed her doctoral major to mass communications and took a leave to attend the Michelle Clarke Fellowship Program for Minority Journalists at Columbia University. In 1972, at the end of that program, she was placed as a news writer at WBBM-TV, the CBS affiliate in Chicago. A year later, despite her preference for staying behind the camera, Poussaint moved into general-assignment reporting. She covered all kinds of stories, but she felt particularly drawn to stories that gave voice to children and the disenfranchised.

After only a year as a local reporter, CBS offered her a promotion to network reporter operating out of New York. In what she was later told was an unprecedented move, Poussaint turned the offer down. She understood that with so few blacks on network television, whether she liked it or not, she would be representing not only herself but also her race. She felt that she had to gain more experience and hone her skills as a journalist to reach the level at which she felt she could do her job as well as or even better than her professional peers.

A year later CBS came back with another offer that gave Poussaint the kind of reporting opportunities she had hoped for. Rather than starting her network career in the crowded CBS bureau in New York, Poussaint was assigned to work from the smaller Midwest bureau, where five reporters covered eleven states. She was constantly on the road and appeared frequently on the *CBS Evening News with Walter Cronkite*.

Poussaint moved to Washington, D.C., in 1977 and married Henry Richardson, who was then handling African affairs for the National Security Council during the Carter administration. She continued to report for CBS out of the Washington bureau, working primarily at the White House and on Capitol Hill.

In 1978 she accepted an offer to leave CBS to become the 6:00 P.M. and 11:00 P.M. co-anchor for the ABC station in Washington, WJLA-TV. She remained there for thirteen years, winning seven local Emmy awards for her reporting and anchoring. She also worked energetically with various community groups, and she was consistently recognized for her commitment to the community. Poussaint was awarded honorary doctorate degrees from Georgetown University and Mount Vernon College, both in Washington, D.C.

Poussaint accepted an offer in 1992 to join ABC network news as a correspondent for the newsmagazine show *Primetime Live*. She remained with ABC for three years and won three national Emmy awards for her reporting. She also regularly substituted for the lead anchor Peter Jennings on the ABC evening news.

Eventually Poussaint decided that it was time to move out on her own and do the kinds of social-issue video projects she felt so passionate about. She left commercial television and started her own independent, nonprofit documentary production company, Wisdom Works. One of her most celebrated and successful documentaries was *Tutu and Franklin: A Journey Towards Peace*, a meeting between Archbishop Desmond Tutu, the noted historian Dr. JOHN HOPE FRANKLIN, and a multiethnic, international group of twenty-one high school students. Poussaint filmed them together on the island of Gorée, Senegal, an infamous former slave port, as they worked together to find new approaches to race and reconciliation in the twenty-first century. The two-hour film aired on PBS, and it was used by schools and community groups to encourage intergenerational discussions of race. She also made a compelling ninety-minute video biography, *The Life and Surprising Times of* DR. DOROTHY HEIGHT, and participated in independent productions for various cable networks, including Discovery, Lifetime, TLC, and A&E.

Over the course of her career, Poussaint reported from virtually every state and from dozens of foreign countries. She reported in the midst of riots in Haiti, the widespread famine in Africa, and the growing plague of AIDS in the United States. Poussaint interviewed presidents, entertainment legends, representatives of the Ku Klux Klan, prisoners, priests, and ordinary folk. She found the ultimate home for her communication skills and lifelong commitment to teaching in the creation of a nonprofit organization, the National Visionary Leadership Project (NVLP).

Poussaint cofounded NVLP with Dr. CAMILLE COSBY in 2001. Their mission was to conduct and preserve extensive videotaped interviews with extraordinary African American elders and to teach young people to do the same in their own communities. The material was distributed through various media, including NVLP's Web site, to schools and to the general public. In 2004 the two coedited a popular book of excerpts from these elders' interviews called *A Wealth of Wisdom: Legendary African American Elders Speak*, which reached number twenty-one on the *New York Times* bestseller list.

FURTHER READING
Much of the information for this article was obtained through interviews with its subject.

LUTHER BROWN JR.

Powell, Adam Clayton, Jr. (29 Nov. 1908–4 Apr. 1972), minister and congressman, was born in New Haven, Connecticut, the son of the Reverend ADAM CLAYTON POWELL SR. and Mattie Fletcher Shaffer. The family moved to New York City in 1909 after the senior Powell became minister of the Abyssinian Baptist Church, then located at Fortieth Street between Seventh and Eighth avenues. In 1923, at the elder Powell's urging, the church and the family joined the surge of black migration uptown to Harlem, with the church moving to 138th Street between Seventh and Lenox avenues.

Adam Powell Jr. earned an AB at Colgate University in 1930 and an AM in Religious Education at Columbia University in 1932. So light-skinned that he could pass for white, and did so for a time at Colgate, he came to identify himself as black, and, although from a comfortable background, he advocated the rights of workers.

Powell's rise to power, and his adoption of various leadership roles in civil rights, dated from the 1930s. His power base throughout his career was the Abyssinian Baptist Church, where his father ministered to his flock's social and economic as well as spiritual needs. There, during the Great Depression, young Powell directed a soup kitchen and relief operation that supplied thousands of destitute Harlemites with food and clothing. In 1930 he became the church's business manager and director of its community center. In 1937 he succeeded his father as pastor. He married the Cotton Club

Adam Clayton Powell, Jr., congressman from Harlem, minister, and lifelong warrior for civil rights. (Library of Congress.)

dancer Isabel Washington in 1933 and adopted her son from a previous marriage.

Beginning in 1936 Powell published a column, "The Soap Box," in the black weekly *Amsterdam News*. Active in a campaign for equal employment opportunities for black residents of Harlem, his first major social campaign involved efforts to improve blacks' employment opportunities and working conditions at Harlem Hospital. By the mid-1930s, "Don't buy where you can't work" became a slogan in Harlem, as it already had become in Chicago and some other cities. Powell became a leader of organized picketing of offending stores. By 1938 he led the Greater New York Coordinating Committee for Employment, which pushed successfully in the next few years for jobs for blacks not only in stores but also with the electric and telephone companies, as workers at the 1939 New York World's Fair, as drivers and mechanics on city buses, and as faculty at the city's colleges.

During World War II Powell continued proselytizing from old platforms, and he found new ones. He preached at Abyssinian Baptist, which had the largest Protestant congregation in the United States; led the militant Harlem People's Committee;

published the *People's Voice*, a Harlem weekly; and wrote *Marching Blacks: An Interpretive History of the Rise of the Black Common Man* (1945). Divorcing his first wife, he married the pianist and singer HAZEL SCOTT in 1945, and they had a son. Powell's prominence in Harlem resulted in his election in 1941 to the New York City Council, where he continued to hone his combination of political and protest skills. From this political base he ran for Congress in 1944 when a new congressional district was formed for Harlem. Winning, he became New York City's first black congressman; WILLIAM L. DAWSON of Chicago was the only other African American then in Congress.

For many years an often lonely voice in Congress, Powell called for a permanent Fair Employment Practices Commission, an end to the poll tax in federal elections, and an end to racial segregation in the military. Finding that House rules banned him because of his race from such facilities as dining rooms, steam baths, and barbershops, he nonetheless proceeded to make use of all such facilities, and he insisted that his staff follow his lead. He brought an end to the exclusion of black journalists from the press gallery in the House of Representatives. As early as the 1940s he was characteristically offering what became known as the "Powell Amendment" to spending legislation. The proviso, supported by the National Association for the Advancement of Colored People, would have banned federal funds from any project that supported racial segregation, and though it failed to pass, it made him known as "Mr. Civil Rights."

A New Deal Democrat, Powell nonetheless maintained political independence, whether from his father or from the Democratic Party's leadership. Charting his own way, though his father remained a Republican, Powell campaigned in 1932 for the Democratic presidential nominee Franklin D. Roosevelt. In 1944 he ran for Congress as the nominee of the Republican and American Labor parties as well as the Democratic Party. In 1956 he broke with the Democrats over the party's temporizing stance on civil rights issues to support Dwight Eisenhower's reelection campaign. Throughout his years in Congress he saw his main mission as thwarting the southern wing of his own party in Congress. He demonstrated no patience with liberal Democrats who trimmed sails or pulled punches when civil rights legislation was at stake.

One of Powell's chief roles, often behind the scenes, was to monitor the behavior of organized labor and the federal government on the racial front. He believed apprenticeship programs in the labor market should be open to blacks, progressive legislation should be enacted, and no federal agency should practice or foster racial segregation or discrimination. During the 1960s he tried to ensure that blacks would hold leadership positions in the Peace Corps, the Poverty Corps, and federal regulatory agencies. Ambassadorships, cabinet positions, and the Supreme Court, he urged, should have black representation. His relations with the Eisenhower administration enabled him to arrange in 1954 for the Ethiopian emperor Haile Selassie, while on a visit to the United States, to visit Abyssinian Baptist Church. There the emperor presented Powell with a large gold medallion, which he proudly wore on a chain around his neck for the rest of his life.

Powell divorced his second wife and married Yvette Flores in 1960, and they had a son. As a result of the seniority system in Congress, Powell's peak in power came in the 1960s, the years of the New Frontier and the Great Society. For three terms, from 1961 to 1967, he chaired the House Committee on Education and Labor. From his committee came such landmark legislation as the 1961 Minimum Wage Bill, the Vocational Education Act, the Manpower Development and Training Act, various antipoverty bills, and the Elementary and Secondary Education Act. When the National Defense Education Act of 1958, with its promotion of education in science, mathematics, and foreign languages, came up for renewal in 1964, Powell steered through an expansion of coverage to the humanities and social sciences. And when the Civil Rights Act of 1964 became law, Title VI, which authorized all federal agencies to withhold aid from institutions that practiced racial segregation or discrimination, embodied the "Powell Amendment." His time had come; he pushed ahead to challenge school segregation in the North.

Powell's fall from power came at the height of his national prominence. Always flamboyant and controversial, he displayed moral behavior anything but ascetic, spent tax dollars merrily on pleasure trips, and often missed important votes in Congress. In a television interview in March 1960 Powell referred to a Harlem widow, Esther James, as a "bag woman," someone who collected graft for corrupt police. She sued and won. Powell refused to apologize or pay, or even respond to subpoenas to appear in court to explain his failure to comply. After he was cited for contempt of court in November 1966, a Select Committee of the House investigated Powell's affairs, partly because of the James case and partly because of an alleged misuse of public funds. Powell remained convinced that the real purpose was a racist attempt to silence a key proponent of civil rights. In March 1967 the Select Committee recommended Powell's public censure and his loss of seniority. The full House went farther and voted to exclude Powell from the Ninetieth Congress. In a special election to fill the vacant seat, Powell trounced his opponents. Then, after a successful fund-raising effort, he paid James her award. An agreement was worked out that ended the threat of jail for contempt of court so—after spending much of 1967 in an idyllic exile on Bimini—he could return to New York whenever he wished. In January 1969 the House voted to seat him in the Ninety-first Congress, though it stripped him of his seniority and fined him for misuse of payroll and travel funds. Later that year, in *Powell v. McCormack*, the Supreme Court ruled against the House's exclusion of him in 1967.

After being out of Congress from 1967 to 1969, Powell retrieved his seat. But he was no longer committee chairman, and his power had evaporated. Worse, in 1969 Powell was hospitalized with cancer. Weakened physically and politically he nonetheless entered the Democratic primary in 1970 but was narrowly defeated by State Assemblyman CHARLES RANGEL. Powell's time in Congress was over. He wrote an autobiography and retired in 1971 from Abyssinian Baptist.

Powell liked one characterization of him as "arrogant, but with style." His legacy is a mixed one, for his personal presumptions clouded his political accomplishments. Yet during the 1940s and 1950s he ranked with A. PHILIP RANDOLPH among the great leaders of African Americans. He proved a resourceful and effective leader in America's largest city from the 1930s through World War II. From the mid-1940s through the mid-1960s he combined his political position as a congressman with a commitment to progressive politics that far outstripped his few black congressional predecessors of the 1930s or his few black colleagues of the 1940s and 1950s. In the 1960s he had greater power to get things done, but he was also less irreplaceable, for American politics had begun to catch up with his positions on matters of race and class. He died in Miami, Florida.

FURTHER READING

No large collection of Powell papers exists, but
    scattered materials by or about him are at the

Schomburg Center for Research in Black Culture of the New York Public Library and the Lyndon B. Johnson Presidential Library in Austin, Texas.

Powell, Adam Clayton, Jr. *Adam by Adam: The Autobiography of Adam Clayton Powell Jr.* (1971).

Hamilton, Charles V. *Adam Clayton Powell Jr.: The Political Biography of an American Dilemma* (1991).

Haygood, Wil. *King of the Cats: The Life and Times of Adam Clayton Powell Jr.* (1993).

Reeves, Andrée E. *Congressional Committee Chairmen: Three Who Made an Evolution* (1993).

Obituaries: *New York Times* and *Washington Post*, 5 Apr. 1972.

This entry is taken from the *American National Biography* and is published here with the permission of the American Council of Learned Societies.

PETER WALLENSTEIN

Powell, Adam Clayton, Sr. (5 May 1865–12 June 1953), pastor, was born in Martins Mill, Virginia, the son of a German planter he knew only as "Powell" and a woman of African American and Indian heritage named Sally. Powell's father was killed during the Civil War before his son's birth, and shortly before Powell was born his recently freed mother moved into the cabin of the tenant farmer Anthony Dunn, a former slave of Powell's father. His family migrated to West Virginia in 1875 to work on a farm and the next year settled at Paint Creek. There Powell attended school for two years, which, combined with one year of schooling at Martins Mill, constituted his entire formal primary education. Powell later described his eight years in West Virginia as "a mental and moral disaster" (13). Often involved in fights, he was forced to leave the state in 1884 to avoid being lynched or murdered because of his role in the shooting of an influential white resident of Paint Creek while Powell was guarding a melon patch.

Powell then took a job at the W. P. Rend coal mines in Rendville, Ohio. Most months he lost all his pay gambling. In 1885 a revival swept through Rendville, shutting down the coal mine and all the town's businesses for a week. Along with many residents of the community, Powell was "born again" and then attended the Rendville Academy, supporting himself by working as a school janitor. Inspired by reading about the lives of FREDERICK DOUGLASS and other prominent black leaders, Powell decided to prepare for a career in law and politics, with the hope of someday serving in Congress.

Powell moved to Washington, D.C., in 1887 to attend Howard University School of Law. When both his inadequate academic preparation and his lack of funds prevented him from studying at the university, Powell took a job at Howard House, a hotel in Washington. While reading the Bible, he "was seized with an unquenchable desire to preach" (Powell, 20) and in 1888 began classes in both the academic and theological departments of Wayland Seminary (later Virginia Union University) in Washington, graduating from both programs in 1892. In 1889 Powell married Mattie Fletcher Shaffer, whom he had met while living in West Virginia. They had a daughter and a son.

After short pastorates in Baptist congregations in St. Paul and Philadelphia, Pennsylvania, in 1893 Powell became the minister of the Immanuel Baptist Church of New Haven, Connecticut. During his fifteen-year tenure in New Haven, his congregation grew from 135 to 600 members, and the church building was remodeled for $10,000. Powell participated in interdenominational and interracial endeavors to improve the quality of life in New Haven. For some of these years he earned more money by lecturing on racial issues and holding evangelistic services throughout the country than he did by serving his church. According to one of his contemporaries, the key to Powell's successful ministry in New Haven was his winsome personality, his eloquent, enthusiastic preaching, his continuous quest to broaden his knowledge, and his passion for serving others. To become a more effective minister, Powell attended classes at Yale Divinity School in 1895–1996. He also served as a delegate to the World's Christian Endeavor Convention in 1900.

In 1908 Powell accepted a call to pastor the century-old Abyssinian Baptist Church in New York City, then located in the neighborhood surrounding West Fortieth Street between Seventh and Eighth avenues, one of the city's most notorious red-light districts. Shortly after his arrival he led a successful campaign to close down houses of prostitution in the area around his church. A talented organizer, an inspiring orator, and a shrewd publicist, Powell during a twenty-nine-year ministry built the Abyssinian Baptist Church, composed primarily of middle-class New Yorkers, into the largest black congregation in the world. After threatening to resign to become a full-time evangelist, Powell convinced the congregation to move uptown to a new facility on 138th Street in Harlem that was dedicated in 1923. Because the area between 125th and 145th streets was becoming heavily populated with African Americans, the church gained tremendous potential for both growth and ministry by moving there.

In its new location the congregation became a center during the 1920s and 1930s for programs designed to help community residents. Like many other institutional churches in major American cities, the Abyssinian Baptist Church sponsored a wide array of religious, educational, and social programs, including a free food kitchen, job counseling, a home for the aged, and a clothing ministry. When Powell retired in 1937, the membership of the church had grown to more than 10,000 (from 1,600 in 1908), and its budget had increased to $135,000 (from $6,000 in 1908). Its staff numbered three ministers and nineteen other paid workers. Powell claimed that his church hosted the nation's largest adult education school, which held classes in physical education, English, political science, dressmaking, nursing, typewriting, and many other subjects, and a large teacher training school (operated in conjunction with Columbia University). He also insisted that under his leadership the congregation had made great strides toward achieving its four main objectives: providing a model church for African Americans, teaching blacks the value of punctuality, helping to improve race relations, and working to promote social justice. These accomplishments brought many visitors from around the world to Harlem to study the church's programs.

While serving his church, Powell conducted evangelistic crusades throughout the country and became active in politics. A captivating and persuasive speaker, he inspired thousands of blacks in Baltimore, Indianapolis, Toronto, Los Angeles, and dozens of other cities to repent of their sins, profess their faith in Christ, and join local congregations. In 1937 he delivered one of the main addresses, "The Negro's Enrichment of the Church Today," at the Northern Baptist Convention's annual meeting in Philadelphia. Deeply involved in Republican politics in New York, Powell was chosen in 1932 by the Republican State Committee to represent the state in the electoral college. Like many other blacks, he shifted his allegiance to Franklin Roosevelt in 1936 but thereafter primarily supported the American Labor Party (ALP). Organized by key labor leaders in 1936, the ALP had strong ties with labor unions and supported candidates, Democratic or Republican, who endorsed liberal social legislation.

As one of the most prominent black clergymen in the United States, Powell had a significant influence on black attitudes and strategies toward racism and discrimination. He was a founder of the Urban League in 1910 and served on the first board of directors of the National Association for the Advancement of Colored People and as a vice president of the organization. Powell was influenced by the ideas of both W. E. B. DuBois and Booker T. Washington. While he held leadership positions in several black protest organizations, he generally favored a conciliatory approach to white-black relations and the philosophy of self-help advocated by Washington. He wrote in his autobiography that in his lectures to whites during the past twenty-five years he had asked only for one right for his race—"the right of equal opportunity with all other American people" (Powell, 180). This included, he argued, the same educational opportunities, equal pay for equal work, and equivalent living conditions, but it did not include the "pernicious doctrine" of social equality or integration. He praised whites for their support of black colleges, churches, and social agencies, denounced racial prejudice among both blacks and whites, and insisted that in the United States the destiny of the races was "inextricably intertwisted." Each had a contribution to make to the other. While blacks needed whites' "courage, initiative, punctuality, business acumen and aggressiveness," whites needed blacks' "meekness, love, forgiving spirit, and emotional religion" (Powell, 187).

Although Powell was an advocate of the premillennial view that held that the world would grow worse and worse until Christ's Second Coming, he worked energetically to reform social conditions. During his ministry Powell trumpeted many of the themes proclaimed by fundamentalists during the 1920s and 1930s: that a new birth experience was paramount, that Christ's Second Coming was imminent, and that Christians should seek to develop a deep spirituality and abstain from alcohol. He was also a political conservative and supported the Republican Party's commitment to limited government. However, he recognized that people's social environments formed them, and he strove to help blacks find jobs, gain education, improve their living conditions, and advance socially. When Powell retired from the active ministry, three thousand friends and admirers jammed his church to honor him. One speaker attributed Powell's great success to five factors: his executive ability, vision, courage, honesty, and faith in God. Powell was replaced as the senior minister of the Abyssinian Baptist Church by his son, Adam Clayton Powell Jr., who during the 1940s used the congregation as a base to launch a campaign that made him the first African American from New York to be elected to Congress.

After his retirement, the elder Powell continued to lecture and preach throughout the nation, wrote five books, and took an active part in community affairs. *Against the Tide* (1938) told the story of his life, ministry, and philosophy. In *Riots and Ruins* (1945) he analyzed the causes and effects of the Harlem riots of 1943 and suggested ways to improve race relations. During this racial conflict Powell co-chaired the citywide Citizens' Committee on Harlem that sought to discover and remedy the conditions that provoked the riots. Powell's first wife died in 1945, and in 1946 he married Inez Means Cottrell, a nurse. He died in New York City.

FURTHER READING

The Schomburg Center for Research in Black Culture in New York City contains several accounts of Powell's work with the Abyssinian Baptist Church.

Powell, A. Clayton. *Against the Tide* (1938; repr. 1980).

Hickey, Neil, and Ed Edwin. *Adam Clayton Powell and the Politics of Race* (1965).

Obituaries: *New York Times*, 13 June and 17 June 1953; *Amsterdam News*, 20 June 1953.

This entry is taken from the *American National Biography* and is published here with the permission of the American Council of Learned Societies.

GARY SCOTT SMITH

Powell, Bud (27 Sept. 1924–1 Aug. 1966), jazz pianist, was born Earl Powell in New York City, the son of Pearl (maiden name unknown) and William Powell Sr. His father, a building superintendent who spent his evenings as a pianist and bandleader, started teaching Bud to play the piano at age three. Powell began formal lessons at six, studying the classical repertoire with W. F. Rawlins. His father exposed him to jazz, recalling that "by the time he was ten he could play everything he'd heard by FATS WALLER and ART TATUM" (Groves and Shipton, 2). TEDDY WILSON and Billy Kyle were also early influences. Nevertheless, Powell continued classical instruction into his midteens and started playing the organ at Harlem's St. Charles Catholic Church.

Jazz beckoned, however, and by age fourteen Powell was working in a dance band led by his older brother William Powell Jr. Bud quit DeWitt Clinton High School at age fifteen and in 1940 was appearing at clubs in Harlem and Greenwich Village. With

THELONIOUS MONK, who became another important influence, he began frequenting after-hours sessions at clubs such as Minton's Playhouse, where younger musicians were developing the more intellectual form of jazz that became known as bebop or bop. Powell later lamented that the new music had not "been given a name more in keeping with the seriousness of purpose" (Groves and Shipton, 1).

After a brief time in the trumpeter-vocalist VALAIDA SNOW's Sunset Royal Entertainers, Powell got his first job of note in mid-1943, when he joined the big band led by the trumpeter CHARLES "COOTIE" WILLIAMS, formerly a featured soloist with the DUKE ELLINGTON Orchestra. During his two-year tenure with Williams, Powell made his first recordings. He also began having problems that would affect him for the rest of his-life.

At twenty, Powell was already drinking heavily and showing early signs of mental illness, conditions that may have contributed to his disorderly conduct arrest in Philadelphia, in January 1945. He reportedly suffered a severe beating at the hands of the police, an incident that many blamed for Powell's subsequent mental instability. Fined and released, he was sent—apparently by his mother—for a ten-week stint at Pilgrim State Hospital on Long Island.

Powell emerged to find bebop beginning to flourish in the clubs along New York's Fifty-second Street. By the fall of 1945 he was playing with the saxophonist CHARLIE PARKER and the drummer MAX ROACH in a group led by the trumpeter DIZZY GILLESPIE. Their success at the Three Deuces marked the emergence of bebop as a commercially viable form of jazz and gave Powell status within the movement. This short-lived combo never recorded, but its members became the most influential jazzmen of the next decade. Powell himself learned much from the legendary Parker, relating to another pianist that the alto player showed him "the way to a means of expression."

"Super erratic" behavior, as Gillespie described it, cost Powell many jobs, but his talent and reputation allowed him to continue working steadily, including a brief stay with Gillespie's second big band. He recorded sporadically, notably with the saxophonists DEXTER GORDON in January 1946 and Parker in May 1947 and for the first time as a leader in January 1947.

That November Powell suffered a mental breakdown and was committed to Creedmoor State Hospital in Queens, where he remained for eleven months. Electroshock therapy and sedatives turned the formerly confrontational pianist introspective and somewhat incoherent. Yet the period just after his release proved to be the most inspired of his career.

Most of Powell's studio recordings from 1949 to 1951 are collected in two sets, *The Genius of Bud Powell* (1988) and *The Amazing Bud Powell* (1989). These small-group albums represent his creative peak and showcase his best-known compositions, including "Bouncin' with Bud," "Dance of the Infidels," and "*Un Poco Loco*." His style, with melodic, hornlike figures of great speed and intricacy in the right hand accompanied by dissonant, irregular left-hand chording, reached full flower. His personal life, however, remained in disarray.

With his problems intensified by drug use, Powell was arrested in June 1952, was taken from prison to Bellevue, and in September was taken back to Pilgrim State Hospital, where he remained until the following February. He would be hospitalized again in 1954, 1955, and 1959. Powell married Audrey Hill in March 1953 and had one child with her, but by 1954 he was living with Altevia "Buttercup" Edwards, who became his manager and common-law wife. His fragile psyche was not helped when his younger brother Richie (also a pianist), Richie's wife, and the trumpeter CLIFFORD BROWN were killed in a 1956 auto accident.

When not institutionalized, Powell continued to work, with widely varying results. His best-known recording from these years is of a May 1953 concert in Toronto featuring Parker, Gillespie, Roach, and the bassist CHARLES MINGUS. Two years later he walked off the stage in New York during what proved to be Parker's final public appearance. Powell recorded irregularly during the mid- to late 1950s, almost always in a trio setting. His musicianship was as precarious as his mental state, and while there were flashes of the earlier brilliance, he never managed to sustain it. *The Amazing Bud Powell* (1989) collects some of his better work from this period.

After traveling to Paris for a March 1959 engagement, Powell decided to take up residence there. That summer he was befriended by Francis Paudras, a young fan who eventually took the pianist into his home. Edwards had been using the drug Largactyl to keep Powell under her control, and its interaction with the alcohol he regularly sought had a debilitating effect. Paudras weaned him off Largactyl and tried to reduce his alcohol consumption, and by 1963 Powell was showing signs of a resurgence. Then he contracted tuberculosis. Doctors found a seven-centimeter hole in his lung, and Powell remained hospitalized for four months.

Powell spent the early part of 1964 recovering, was performing by summer, and in August recorded two of his better European albums with the saxophonist Johnny Griffin. Against Paudras's judgment, Powell accepted a job in New York later that month. The return was initially triumphant (preserved on two good recordings, *Return to Birdland* and *Award at Birdland*), but within two months he had succumbed to his old habits. Paudras went back to Paris, and Powell deteriorated rapidly, playing poorly in his few 1965–1966 appearances. After his death in New York, officially attributed to tuberculosis, malnutrition, and alcoholism, an estimated five thousand people turned out for the funeral procession through Harlem.

Despite his tortured existence, Powell was regularly described as a "genius" at the keyboard, a creative force who influenced practically every jazz pianist who came after him. "Have you ever heard of Bud Powell?" Charlie Parker asked an aspiring pianist in the early 1950s. "Go out and get yourself a Bud Powell record" (Gitler, 270–271).

FURTHER READING

Gitler, Ira. *Swing to Bop: An Oral History of the Transition in Jazz in the 1940s* (1985).

Groves, Alan, and Alyn Shipton. *The Glass Enclosure: The Life of Bud Powell* (1993).

Paudras, Francis. *Dance of the Infidels: A Portrait of Bud Powell* (1986; repr. 1998).

DISCOGRAPHY

Schlouch, Claude. *Bud Powell: A Discography* (1993).

This entry is taken from the *American National Biography* and is published here with the permission of the American Council of Learned Societies.

KENNETH H. WILLIAMS

Powell, Colin (5 Apr. 1937–), U.S. Army general and secretary of state, was born in Harlem in New York City to the Jamaican immigrants Luther Powell, a shipping clerk, and Maud Ariel McKoy, a seamstress, both of whom worked in New York City's garment district. When he was six years old, Powell moved with his family to Hunts Point, an ethnically diverse neighborhood in the South Bronx. Powell's autobiography portrays Hunts Point as a community of stable families and a certain roughhewn racial tolerance, but it does not ignore the neighborhood's upsurge in drug- and gang-related crime, particularly after World War II. The Powells escaped the crumbling South Bronx tenements in the mid-1950s, however, a testament to his parents' unstinting work ethic and shrewd housekeeping. But luck also played a part. Luther Powell, a regular numbers player, placed a twenty-five-dollar bet on a number that he had dreamed about and then saw again on a hymn board in church. That number hit and netted the Powells ten thousand dollars, a sum three times Luther's annual salary and more than enough for a down payment on a three-bedroom home in the borough of Queens.

By the time his family moved to Queens, Powell had already enrolled in the City College of New York (CCNY). He was a competent, though not stellar, student, and his parents worried about their son's apparent aimlessness. But in his first semester at CCNY, Powell found the structure and order that he had previously known only as an acolyte in the Episcopal Church. "Something had caught my eye," Powell recalls in his autobiography, "young guys on campus in uniform" (Powell, 25). On joining the college ROTC and receiving his own uniform, he began, for the first time in his life, to feel a sense of purpose. Thereafter, Powell's college career revolved around the Pershing Rifles, an ROTC fraternity, in which he enjoyed the camaraderie of his fellow cadets and excelled as a drill leader. Such drills proved invaluable in strengthening his self-confidence, particularly in teaching him that "being responsible sometimes means pissing people off" (Powell, 35). Powell earned his degree from CCNY in June 1958 but found the ceremony anti-climactic after graduating first in his ROTC class with the rank of cadet colonel. He also received a commission as a second lieutenant in the army.

Powell's first military assignment was in Fort Benning, Georgia. He resented the racism and indignities that he encountered, particularly in the segregated communities surrounding the camp, but he refused to let his anger dictate his actions. He vowed then to answer racist critics of blacks in the military by striving to be the consummate professional soldier. This he did at Fort Benning and on later assignments in West Germany, at Fort Owens, Massachusetts, and at the Unconventional Warfare Center at Fort Bragg, North Carolina, where he trained as one of sixteen thousand military advisers who were to be sent by President John F. Kennedy to assist the anti-communist South Vietnamese government of Ngo Dinh Diem. Powell arrived in Saigon on Christmas Day 1962, leaving behind his wife of just four months, Alma Johnson, a speech pathologist from Birmingham, Alabama, whom

he had met in Boston while he was serving at Fort Owens. The Powells had three children: Annemarie, Linda, and Michael.

Powell's first tour of duty in Vietnam was relatively uneventful, though he returned to Fort Benning in November 1963 with a Purple Heart, after being wounded by a Vietcong booby trap. In 1967 he attended the highly selective U.S. Army Command and General Staff College at Fort Leavenworth, Kansas, and graduated second in a class of 1,244. Powell's military reputation was further enhanced when he returned to Vietnam in 1968 and received a second Purple Heart, the Legion of Merit, and the Soldier's Medal for rescuing two crewmen from the burning wreckage of a helicopter.

On his first Vietnam tour, Powell had believed that the American presence in Indochina was justified by the goal of defeating communism, but by 1969 he had begun to question—in private, at least—the course of that war. He later came to believe that the expansion of the U.S. military draft after 1965 resulted in a breakdown in morale and in the deployment of too many poorly trained officers and noncommissioned personnel. The inexperience of these soldiers, he argues in his 1995 autobiography, led to atrocities such as that at My Lai in the Batangan peninsula in March 1968, in which 347 unarmed Vietnamese civilians, mostly old men, women, and children, were tortured and killed by troops of the Americal Division. Powell, a major in the same division, arrived in Vietnam after that incident, but has been criticized for not thoroughly investigating subsequent reports of a massacre at My Lai.

Powell left Vietnam in July 1969 to study for an MBA at George Washington University in Washington, D.C. He graduated in 1971, was promoted to the rank of lieutenant colonel, and began working in the Pentagon as an operations research analyst. While that position marked Powell's ascent on the military career ladder, his selection for a White House Fellowship in 1972–1973 brought him into the quite different milieu of Washington politics. Powell chose to work in the Office of Management and Budget (OMB), an unglamorous but powerful department, where he worked with Frank Carlucci, the deputy to the OMB's director, Caspar Weinberger. On completing his fellowship, Powell served for a year as a battalion commander in South Korea before returning to Washington to attend the National War College. He graduated in 1976, was given a brigade command with the 101st

Airborne Division at Fort Campbell, Kentucky, and then served as a Pentagon aide in the administration of President Jimmy Carter, an appointment that resulted in Powell's promotion to brigadier general at the age of only forty-two. Powell did not, however, support his commander in chief's reelection and voted for Carter's Republican challenger Ronald Reagan, in 1980.

Reagan's victory enabled Powell to work again with his former bosses Weinberger and Carlucci, who became secretary and deputy secretary, respectively, at the Defense Department. Both men valued Powell highly and did much to further his career, alternatively recommending him for military promotions and recalling him to Washington to serve in various political posts. In 1981 they encouraged his return to a military posting by appointing him assistant division commander in Fort Carson, Colorado. Powell's next assignment, at Fort Leavenworth, Kansas, further broadened his résumé, acquainted him with the army's newest weaponry and technology, and gained him a second star and promotion to the rank of major general.

Powell was reluctant to leave the Kansas base, where he had helped establish a memorial honoring the Buffalo Soldiers, black cavalry and infantrymen who had served on America's western frontier after the Civil War. In 1983, however, he returned to Washington to serve as Weinberger's military assistant, a post that made him the chief gatekeeper of information to and from the defense secretary. By all accounts, Powell excelled at this role. His direct, even blunt approach ruffled some feathers, but most Pentagon insiders found his honesty, humor, and apparent lack of political guile refreshing. Above all, he earned high marks in Washington for his consummate people-handling skills. One Pentagon veteran remarked of Powell that he had "never seen anyone who could run a meeting more effectively with senior people and cut through the crap and get a decision" (Means, 206).

Although he was Weinberger's chief aide from 1983 to 1986, Powell was not tainted by the Iran-Contra affair that resulted in Weinberger's indictments in 1992 for perjury and for misleading Congress. A full accounting of Powell's role in the scandal may never be known, however, since President George H. W. Bush pardoned Weinberger in 1992, just weeks before his trial for perjury. Powell, for his part, denies any complicity in Iran-Contra and notes in his autobiography that he and Weinberger opposed the arms-for-hostages deal hatched by the national security adviser Admiral John Poindexter. Independent Counsel Lawrence Walsh's investigation into the affair found, though, that Weinberger and his closest aides had greater knowledge of the illegal arms sales than they had admitted. Nonetheless, Iran-Contra advanced Powell's career. At the time the scandal broke, he was in command of the Fifth U.S. Corps in Frankfurt, West Germany, but returned to Washington in January 1987 as deputy to Frank Carlucci, whom Reagan had appointed to replace the disgraced Poindexter as national security adviser. Ten months later, when Carlucci replaced Weinberger as secretary of defense, the president appointed Powell, by then a lieutenant general, as the nation's first African American national security adviser.

Powell took that post at a time of rapid change in global affairs. By the late 1980s the radical reforms instituted by the Soviet leader Mikhail Gorbachev had set in motion the breakup of the Eastern bloc, although at that time neither the Soviets nor the Americans predicted that it would happen so rapidly. At the same time, the Reagan administration came to portray Islamic fundamentalism as an even greater threat to the American national interest than the Soviets. On most matters, Powell shared the basic foreign policy philosophy of the Reaganites—increased military spending, support for anticommunist regimes, and unswerving loyalty to Israel. Powell's genius lay, however, in quickly summarizing and analyzing a complex and rapidly changing world to President Reagan, a man he viewed as a "visionary" but who, as Iran-Contra made abundantly clear, had only a vague grasp of the details and constitutionality of foreign policy. Capitol Hill veterans, military professionals, and television pundits were likewise impressed by the professionalism and clarity of Powell's briefings on national security affairs.

Although Reagan's successor, George H. W. Bush, offered Powell a number of high-ranking cabinet posts, he chose to return to the military. Powell's time as commander in chief of Forces Command at Fort McPherson, Georgia, lasted only four months, long enough to earn him a fourth star and the service record required for the military's top post, chairman of the Joint Chiefs of Staff. In August 1989 Bush duly nominated Powell to that post, making him the youngest soldier and the first African American to lead the nation's military. The implosion of the Soviet empire in that year left the United States as the world's largest superpower and set the stage for an era of unprecedented American military engagement across the globe. As chairman, Powell oversaw the most significant deployments of American military force since Vietnam.

Powell initially advised Bush against the use of force in Panama in 1989, but he earned plaudits for his deft handling of both the military and media campaigns once the president decided to remove from power the Panamanian dictator Manuel Noriega. Many in the international community condemned the death of nearly one thousand Panamanian civilians, but the war proved highly popular in the United States, primarily because the military had used a strategy that became known as the "Powell doctrine." According to this doctrine, the United States in Vietnam had fought a halfhearted war "for half-hearted reasons that the American people could not understand or support" (Powell, 144–145). Powell's strategy for future American wars, therefore, was to "have a clear political objective and stick to it." He advocated that the United States "use all the force necessary," and that it should not "apologize for going in big if that is what it takes. Decisive force ends wars quickly and in the long run saves lives" (Powell, 420–421).

As with Panama, Powell initially advised President Bush to act cautiously in August 1990, when Iraq invaded Kuwait. Once Bush had decided on a military campaign to remove Iraqi forces, however, Powell again proved highly effective. He oversaw the logistics of a massive American military buildup in Saudi Arabia and proved adept at handling the unprecedented demands of the emerging twenty-four-hour global news media. Most famously, Powell informed the watching billions of his "very, very simple" strategy for defeating Iraq: "First we are going to cut it off, and then we are going to kill it" (Means, 278). With strong international support, the Allied forces did just that in 1991, suffering only 246 combat deaths—60 percent of them American—in the 45-day air- and ground-war campaign.

By contrast, Iraqi losses were devastating. According to U.S. Census Bureau estimates, 158,000 Iraqis died as a result of the war and its immediate aftermath, three-quarters of them civilians. Such figures make it all the more remarkable that Powell was subsequently attacked in some quarters for advocating a cease-fire once Kuwait was liberated and Iraqi forces crushed. He answered those critics in his 1995 autobiography by arguing that occupying Iraq would have eroded the powerful international coalition that had made victory possible. Assassinating the Iraqi president Saddam Hussein, Powell added, would have destabilized the entire Middle East by fragmenting Iraq into separate Sunni, Shia, and Kurdish enclaves. Shortly after the end of the conflict, the NAACP honored Powell with the Springarn Medal, its annual award for achievement by an African American.

Powell emerged from the Gulf War as the most popular American soldier since Dwight Eisenhower, and commentators speculated that President Bush might replace his widely ridiculed vice president, Dan Quayle, with the charismatic Powell for the 1992 presidential race. Bush, perhaps fatally for his re-election chances, remained loyal to Quayle. Powell likewise remained loyal to Bush, spurning the advances of Bill Clinton, who approached him regarding the Democratic vice presidential nomination through their mutual friend VERNON JORDAN. Powell's retirement as chairman of the Joint Chiefs of Staff in 1993 prompted further rumors about his presidential ambitions, speculation that was fueled by the enthusiastic reception that met Powell's 1995 autobiography, *My American Journey*, and the vastly popular book tour that followed. Powell ultimately resisted strong pressure to challenge Clinton as either an independent or a Republican candidate, even though opinion polls suggested that he would have received support from Americans of both parties and all races. Republicans, mostly white, identified with Powell's military record, while Democrats, who were disproportionately African American, applauded the general's support for affirmative action and abortion rights. Powell chose instead to establish American Promise, an organization that advocates volunteerism and mentoring to help disadvantaged children. He did not entirely abandon politics, however, and campaigned for the Republican Party in both 1996 and 2000.

Powell returned to Washington in 2001, when President George W. Bush appointed him secretary of state in a foreign policy team that included CONDOLEEZZA RICE as national security adviser. Early reviews of the Bush presidency highlighted tensions between Powell, who believed that the United States should seek international cooperation in solving global crises, and others, such as Rice and Defense Secretary Donald Rumsfeld, who argued for a more unilateralist approach. Those distinctions blurred significantly in the aftermath of the 11 September 2001 terrorist attacks on the

World Trade Center and the Pentagon. Powell joined with a united Bush cabinet to advocate the removal from power in Afghanistan of the Taliban, a fundamentalist Muslim sect suspected of financing the al-Qaeda terrorist network that had carried out the terrorist attacks.

In 2002 Rumsfeld, Rice, and others advised President Bush to launch a preemptive strike on Iraq to destroy an alleged, though as yet unproven, link between that nation and al-Qaeda. Others in the Bush administration advocated a military invasion of Iraq to remove weapons of mass destruction, allegedly held by Iraq in defiance of U.N. Security Council resolutions. Powell initially urged Bush to work toward those goals in association with the United Nations, but he apparently abandoned that strategy in early 2003, when France, Russia, and China made clear that they would use their Security Council veto powers against any preemptive strike by the United States. As a consequence, the United States launched a military invasion of Iraq in March 2003 without U.N. sanction, but with the support of about thirty allies described by Powell as a "coalition of the willing." Since only Britain and Australia provided significant support to the American cause, some war critics contrasted Powell's diplomatic efforts unfavorably with his predecessor during the first Gulf War, James Baker, who had enlisted financial and military support from France, Japan, Germany, and even some of Iraq's Arab neighbors.

American military success in both Iraq conflicts owed much to Colin Powell. For three decades as a career soldier and Washington insider, he lobbied vigorously for the technologically advanced, state-of-the-art weaponry that ensured an overwhelming advantage to the U.S. military. Both military victories secured another of Powell's career goals: restoring public support for and trust of the U.S. military that had eroded after Vietnam. Powell's diplomatic legacy is less clear, however. In 2002–2003, he could not bridge the divide between an increasingly nationalistic Bush administration and members of the United Nations fearful of American military and economic supremacy. In the uncertain new world order that emerged after the second Iraq war, Secretary of State Powell tried to draw upon his much vaunted charisma and powers of persuasion to reconcile two potentially antagonistic objectives: maintaining American military hegemony while ensuring international cooperation and stability. However, shortly after George Bush won election to his second presidential term, Powell resigned his position as secretary of state, ending a disappointing four years. Once a rising star in the Republican Party, Powell saw his influence and power slowly erode as time and again he lost political battles against Donald Rumsfeld and the Department of Defense, the vice president's office, and the national security adviser Condoleezza Rice (who replaced Powell at the State Department, becoming the first black woman to hold the position).

But perhaps Powell's lowest moment was the February 2003 speech he gave to the United Nations, in which he presented a case for war against Iraq using what turned out to be false evidence of Iraq's possession and continuing development of weapons of mass destruction; it remains uncertain whether Powell knew of the falsity of the evidence before presenting it to the world, though it is generally understood that those above him and others responsible for providing the evidence were aware of the dubiousness of their claims. In 2005 he admitted in a television interview that his presentation to the U.N. constituted a "blot" on his record. Powell returned to private life after his resignation.

In the years after leaving political office, Powell devoted much of his time to charitable work, notably with his wife Alma, in their America's Promise charity. In 2005 he joined Kleiner Perkins Caufield & Byers, Silicon Valley's most prestigious venture capital firm, as a part-time partner. Despite some inevitable speculation again that he might seek the Republican nomination, attempt a third party run, or serve as a vice-presidential candidate, Powell remained on the sidelines for most of the 2008 election campaign. He was, however, critical of President Bush's slow response to Hurricane Katrina on the Gulf Coast in 2005, and indicated that he might support a Democrat as early as February 2008, before BARACK OBAMA had won that party's nomination, and before his friend and onetime ally John McCain had won the Republican nomination. Obama courted Powell for a year, and eventually persuaded the former Secretary of State to endorse him for President. Although Powell made clear that he remained a Republican, he announced in mid October 2008 that, "Senator Obama has demonstrated the kind of calm, patient, intellectual, steady approach to problem-solving that I think we need in this country." (Halperin, Mark. "How the Powell Endorsement Boosts Obama" Time Oct. 19, 2008 http://www.time.com/time/nation/article/0,8599,1851832,00.html#ixzz1c0WfPaAm). Powell was also critical of McCain's choice of the inexperienced Alaskan Governor, Sarah Palin, and the GOP's campaign to depict Obama as a creature of the far left. Not only did Obama benefit from Powell's gravitas, and his appeal to independents and moderate Republicans, but the timing of the announcement, just two weeks before polling day, was politically astute.

Powell sought no role in the Obama campaign, and sought no office once Obama was elected. He did, however, consult frequently with the president throughout his first term. In the summer of 2011, Powell returned to the Iraq controversy, following the publication of former Vice-President Dick Cheney's memoirs, which were strongly critical of Powell's role as Secretary of State. Cheney accused Powell of going behind President Bush's back to undermine his Iraq policy, a claim Powell strenuously denied. Shortly after Cheney's book hit the shelves. Powell announced the publication of his own new book in 2012, *It Worked for Me: Lessons in Leadership and Life*, which led many to speculate that he would use the book to refute Cheney's attacks more forcefully. Powell's publisher, Harper Collins announced that the book would include "revealing personal stories" and Powell's 13 rules of leadership, one of which is, "Get mad, then get over it."

FURTHER READING

Powell, Colin. *My American Journey* (1995).
DeYoung, Karen. *Soldier: The Life of Colin Powell* (2006).
Means, Howard. *Colin Powell* (1992).
Woodward, Bob. *The Commanders* (1991).

STEVEN J. NIVEN

powell, john a. (27 May 1947–), civil rights and antipoverty activist, was born John Anthony Powell in Detroit, Michigan, the sixth of nine children born to Marshall Powell, an autoworker and minister, and Florcie Mae Rimpson, a nurse. Both parents were former sharecroppers. From a young age powell had exceptional abilities and unconventional ways of thinking that challenged his deeply religious family.

At age eleven he decided to leave the church where his father was minister. At issue was the church's teaching that all non-Christians would go to hell; Powell was concerned about what this meant for the millions of people who were non-Christian. Around this same time, his great-grandmother, with whom he had a special bond, died as a result of poor medical care. Powell's grief was amplified by the sense of exclusion he already felt in his family because of having left the church, and his anger at the injustice of racially biased medical treatment. At a time of feeling deeply alone in the world he had a profound spiritual experience, and this event gave him a sense of direction for his life's work. In high school he decided to write his name in all lowercase letters, a choice that reflected his characteristic "both/neither" logic: he simultaneously rejected the vestiges of a slave name while also honoring his mother who had named him after her father.

Despite Powell's superior academic abilities, school authorities refused to admit him to the segregated college preparatory classes, and he had to persuade his parents to advocate on his behalf. Although they had concerns about how academic pursuits might detract from a spiritually based life and were unused to challenging white authorities, they supported their son. Powell went on to graduate as valedictorian of his high school class with a 4.0 average and was pursued by prestigious schools, including Harvard. He rejected Harvard's offer, not wanting to associate himself with a school that did not accept women. Powell enrolled at Stanford University in 1965 and earned a degree in psychology in 1969. Inspired by the civil rights struggles of the times, he enrolled at Yale Law School but left during his first year because he found the students and faculty unwilling to confront difficult issues in the world. He went on to receive a law degree from the University of California at Berkeley in 1973, intending to use the language and tools of the law to achieve social justice.

Powell's lifelong effort to challenge injustice continued in 1973 when he took a job with the Seattle public defender's office. In 1977 he received an International Human Rights Fellowship to work and study in southern Africa in collaboration with Bill Sutherland, the nonviolent peace activist who played an important role in developing connections between U.S. civil rights activists and African liberation movements, and who became a significant father figure in Powell's life. The next year, while working and studying in India, powell had a life-changing experience precipitated by an encounter with a spiritual teacher. The anger that had previously fueled his social justice work disappeared, and he found himself motivated instead by a deep sense of love and compassion, a force that has stayed with him throughout his life.

After returning to the United States, Powell served as staff attorney at Evergreen Legal Services in Washington State, where his innovative problem-solving resulted in an affordable housing production that became a national model. Later, as the first African American national legal director of the American Civil Liberties Union (ACLU), from 1987 to 1993, Powell again brought original thinking to bear on difficult legal dilemmas, most notably in the areas of poverty and education. He was instrumental in developing an antipoverty docket, but his major contribution may have been his groundbreaking approach to educational civil rights cases, which were repeatedly being lost in federal courts. Powell's idea was to turn to state constitutions, which guaranteed students a right to an adequate education, but previously had not been used as the basis for legal arguments. Along with several collaborators Powell developed a theory of "educational adequacy," which suggested that schools should receive resources based on the needs of students. While prior efforts had been directed at schools receiving equal resources, adequacy theory suggested instead that ensuring the outcome of an adequate education was the goal, and this required differing inputs, depending on students' needs. Since then, adequacy education suits in state courts have been the most frequently used approach to educational civil rights cases. As he litigated disputes involving education, housing, homelessness, immigration, and other issues, powell became aware that research data to support social justice work was often inadequate and not well linked to policy initiatives. As a result he helped create the Poverty & Race Research Action Council (PRRAC) and went on to found and direct the Institute on Race and Poverty at the University of Minnesota from 1993 to 2003.

Powell was pivotal in developing an understanding of "spatial racism" by looking at how land-use policies related to issues such as taxation, zoning, and urban sprawl were racialized, denying people of color access to opportunity and reproducing disparities along racial lines. Believing that solutions to the problems of segregation and concentrated poverty required a more equitable distribution of resources and opportunities, he introduced the concept of opportunity-based housing, an idea that has been widely adopted throughout the United States. In 2003 powell assumed the position of executive director of the Kirwan Institute for Race and Ethnicity at Ohio State University. Since that time he has extended his work to focus on globalization, on challenging the false dichotomy between social justice and spirituality, and on structural racism, which he named a key civil rights challenge for the twenty-first century.

Powell has written extensively on numerous issues, including the relationship between social justice and spirituality, opportunity-based housing, the multiple self, white privilege and the nature of the white self, concentrated poverty and urban sprawl, racial justice and regionalism, the link between housing and school segregation, disparities in the criminal justice system, voting rights, and affirmative action. In addition to his scholarly articles, Powell's contribution includes using this knowledge in numerous ongoing partnerships with foundations and community- and faith-based organizations. Known for his ability to translate complex conceptual and legal ideas into everyday language and practical applications, Powell frequently has helped organizations not only to "think bigger," but also to think differently. He has described his life's work as being a social justice worker who makes the invisible visible.

Powell's interest in the inseparable relationship between the institutional and the individual has been a defining theme in his life, personally as well as professionally. His choice to have never married reflects, among other personal convictions, a stand against participating in the legal institution of marriage when that right is denied to others. In addition to his own two children, Fon and Saneta, Powell has been a parent to a number of other children.

John powell's life has been defined by his efforts to transform the structures that create suffering and by his care and compassion for those who suffer. Known for his gentle humor and playfulness, powell has been described as a "visionary" and as an "original and progressive thinker." He has inspired policy makers, foundations, government agencies, social activists, and students to challenge paradigms and to imagine and create social arrangements that support Dr. MARTIN LUTHER KING JR.'s dream of "the beloved community."

FURTHER READING

Powell, J. A. "Addressing Regional Dilemmas for Minority Communities." In B. Katz (ed.), *Reflections on Regionalism* (2000).

Powell, J. A. "Living and Learning: Linking Housing and Education. In J. A. powell, G. Kearney, and V. Kay (Eds.), *In Pursuit of a Dream Deferred: Linking Housing & Education Policy* (2001).

Powell, J. A., and K. M. Graham. "Urban Fragmentation as a Barrier to Equal Opportunity." In D. M. Piche, W. L. Taylor, and R. A. Reed (Eds.), *Rights at Risk: Equality in an Age of Terrorism* (2002).

TERRI A. KARIS

Powell, Michael Anthony (Mike) (10 Nov. 1963–), track-and-field athlete, was born in Philadelphia, Pennsylvania. Powell and his family moved to California when he was eleven years old. During his high school career, Powell high-jumped seven feet and long jumped twenty-three feet, eight inches while at Edgewood High School in West Covina, California.

Powell began his collegiate career at UC Irvine. Powell never scored in an NCAA meet at UC-Irvine and was nicknamed "Mike Foul" for frequently hitting the boards during his long-jump attempts. Powell finished sixth at the Olympic Trials in 1984, his last year at UC Irvine. Powell transferred to University of California at Los Angeles (UCLA) in 1985, and soon he was ranked number ten in the world as a redshirt freshman. Powell's collegiate career came to an abrupt end in 1986 after suffering a hamstring injury.

Powell underwent an emergency appendectomy six weeks before the 1988 U.S. Olympic Trials. He qualified for the U.S. team with his final long jump, along with Larry Myricks and rival CARL LEWIS, but had to settle for a silver medal behind Lewis. His constant observations of Lewis's style resulted in Powell altering his airborne pedaling stance; this helped Powell to jump twenty-eight feet and three-quarter inches at the Bruce Jenner Classic in 1989. He lost this event to Carl Lewis twice in 1990.

In 1991 Powell won twelve meets without having to compete against Lewis. The two finally squared off at the National Championships in New York City. Powell cleared twenty-eight feet, seven and three-fourths inches, but Lewis edged out Powell by half an inch. On 30 August 1991 Powell soared twenty-nine feet, four inches with a legal wind to win the event and break Bob Beamon's previous mark of twenty-nine feet, two and a half inches. Powell's jump not only broke a twenty-three-year-old record, but it also ended Lewis ten-year streak of consecutive victories. Later that year, Powell received numerous endorsements, and he won the prestigious Sullivan Award.

In 1992 Powell jumped twenty-eight feet, seven and three-fourths inches at the Modesto Relays, dispelling the cynics who believed his record-breaking jump was a fluke; but once again, he placed second to Carl Lewis, this time at the 1992 Summer Olympics in Barcelona, Spain. In 1993 Powell was undefeated in twenty-five meets and reached jumps of twenty-seven feet close to twenty-three times.

He won the World Championships in Stuttgart, Germany, that year with a jump of twenty-eight feet, two inches.

Powell's attempt to win a gold medal at the 1996 Olympic Games in Atlanta, Georgia, ended in defeat. He entered the competition with a frayed groin muscle that was badly torn during his last attempt during the final. He came in fifth place.

After Powell retired from track-and-field competition in 1996, he returned to win the long-jump competition at the Modesto Relays in 2001 with a jump of twenty-six feet, five and one-fourth inches. He went on to become the men's and women's long-jump coach at his alma mater, UCLA. He was inducted into the National Track-and-Field Hall of Fame in 2005.

FURTHER READING

People (Sept. 1991).

"Sports Briefing: Track and Field," *New York Times* (Dec. 2005).

Sports Illustrated, September 9, 1991, 14–19; September 16, 1991, 36–39.

Track and Field News, November, 1991, 31; November, 1993, 30; January, 1994, 13, 37.

LISA DANIELS

Powell, William Frank (1848–23 Jan. 1920), educator and diplomat, was born in Troy, New York, to William and Julian (Crawford) Powell. He was educated in Brooklyn and Jersey City, New Jersey, and graduated from the New Jersey Collegiate Institute, the New York College of Pharmacy, and the Ashmun Institute (named for Jehudi Ashmun, a white American administrator in 1820s Liberia, and later renamed Lincoln University) in Chester County, Pennsylvania.

In 1869 Powell was teaching freedmen at the Presbyterian Board of Home Mission, in Leesburg, Virginia. The following year he opened what is believed to be Virginia's first state school for black children in Alexandria, and he served as its director from 1870 to 1875. With few exceptions the rest of his career centered on education in New Jersey. He served as the principal of a school in Bordentown, New Jersey, from 1875 to 1881, and in 1881 he obtained a position as a bookkeeper for the U.S. Treasury Department, fourth auditor's office, in Washington, D.C. Also in 1881 he was offered an appointment as consul at Cap Haïtien, Haiti, but he declined the position.

In 1884 Powell was elected district superintendent of schools of the fourth district of Camden,

New Jersey. In that capacity, he introduced manual training to the curriculum, as well as advanced industrial training and teacher training. He was also responsible for the construction of a building for industrial training. Two years later he began teaching at Camden High and Training School, a predominantly white institution, and taught there from 1886 to 1894. By this time he had gained a reputation as an articulate spokesman for the Camden and New Jersey public school systems.

After President William McKinley was inaugurated on 4 March 1897, there was a brief wave of appointments of African Americans to various diplomatic posts. Among those, Powell received an appointment on 17 June 1897 as minister plenipotentiary to Haiti and chargé d'affaires to the Dominican Republic. He served in those positions, which were typically held by one individual, until 1905 and 1904, respectively.

The political situation in Haiti during these years was volatile, and Haitian-American relations were tense, so Powell confronted numerous difficult challenges throughout his tenure. In an early controversy the Haitian government attempted to impose a tax on American merchants and clerks working in Haiti. Powell, with the backing of U.S. Secretary of State John Sherman, over the period from October 1897 through May 1898 was able to convince Haitian leaders to retreat from the tax. At almost the same time Powell had to grapple with the complex and long-standing issue of asylum. In a series of exchanges between Powell and the State Department, the American minister argued that "humanitarian" factors should serve as a yardstick to differentiate between asylum-seekers charged with "political crimes" and those charged with capital or civil crimes. Although the State Department ultimately instructed Powell that humanitarian issues should not play a role in asylum decisions, the exchange of dispatches laid the groundwork for future policy making.

Powell's eight years in Port-au-Prince were filled with political and diplomatic crises, negotiations with Haitian leaders, and correspondence with Washington. In most instances he successfully resolved disputes in favor of the United States. In 1900, for example, he argued against the legitimacy of special courts established in Haiti by foreign governments, maintaining, instead, the U.S. position that American citizens had the right to use Haitian courts according to an 1864 treaty and that courts established by foreign governments violated Haitian sovereignty. By 1902, with civil war imminent, Powell maintained a delicate balance in dealing with the competing factions. The remaining two years of his appointment were similarly trying and turbulent, and for the most part Powell followed State Department policies and came to decisions that were endorsed by Washington. It was mainly over the application of humanitarian criteria and a concern for those treated unjustly in Haiti that Powell and Washington parted company—with the U.S. government tending to emphasize legalistic responses to events. After eight years Powell resigned on 12 October 1905 and reestablished his residence in Camden, New Jersey.

Powell continued to be prominent within African American Republican circles. Even while he was serving in Port-au-Prince, he had been viewed as a potential force in the 1904 Republican National Convention, when it was likely that President Theodore Roosevelt would face competition for the nomination from Ohio Senator Marcus A. Hanna (the issue became moot as Hanna died of typhoid fever before the convention). Powell received an honorary LLD from Lincoln University in 1907, and in 1909 he became an editorial writer for the Philadelphia *Tribune*. At the same time he was active with Prince Hall Masonry. Powell had been married twice: in 1868 to Elizabeth M. Hughes of Burlington, New Jersey, and in 1899 to Jane B. Shepard of Camden, New Jersey.

An educational leader who believed in practical vocational training for African Americans, Powell proved that he possessed diplomatic skills even though he had received no prior formal or extensive experience in the complex world of foreign diplomacy. During his career he left his mark on New Jersey education and ably implemented American foreign policy in Haiti through difficult years in U.S.–Haitian relations.

FURTHER READING

Powell's dispatches from Haiti, and the instructions to him, are available in the Records of the United States Department of State, Record Group 59, National Archives, Washington, D.C.

Crew, Spencer. "Making Their Own Way: Black Social and Institutional Life in Camden, New Jersey 1860–1920," in *The Black Experience in Southern New Jersey. Papers Presented at a Symposium February 11 & 12, 1984, Camden County Historical Society* (1984).

Justesen, Benjamin R. "African-American Consuls Abroad, 1897–1909," *Foreign Service Journal* vol. 81, no. 9 (September 2004).

KENNETH J. BLUME

Powell, William Peter (1807–c. 1879), abolitionist and activist, was born in New York City, the son of Edward Powell, a slave. His mother's name is unknown. A passport application later described Powell as "of mulatto colour but of Indian extraction." He apparently received some education before becoming an apprentice sailor and spending several years at sea in the 1820s. By the early 1830s he had settled in New Bedford, Massachusetts, an active whaling port, and established a boardinghouse for sailors. He married Mercy O. Haskins of Plymouth, Massachusetts, in 1832; they had seven children.

Powell readily embraced the immediate abolitionism of William Lloyd Garrison and participated in the immediatist movement from its beginnings in the early 1830s. He signed the constitution of the American Anti-Slavery Society and joined the New England Anti-Slavery Society. Powell's abolitionism emanated from a deeply held religious conviction that slavery was a sin and required a moral, not a political, remedy. Although he remained a steadfast Garrisonian and refused to ally with any antislavery political party, he supported efforts to protect and expand black voting rights. Literate, thoughtful, and possessing a lively wit, Powell assumed a position of leadership among New Bedford blacks. He helped establish in his community an antislavery auxiliary affiliated with the American Anti-Slavery Society, served on a committee to scrutinize local political candidates, and led local protests against racial discrimination and against the colonization of freed blacks in Africa. He also participated in the black national convention movement in the 1830s and represented New Bedford at the 1835 convention in Philadelphia, Pennsylvania.

Powell returned to New York City in 1839 and opened a boardinghouse for black sailors with support from the American Seamen's Friend Society, a Protestant missionary group. The Colored Seamen's Home accommodated several hundred sailors annually, and Powell made his establishment a center of antislavery and reform activity. He offered an employment service for the lodgers, sheltered fugitive slaves, promoted temperance, provided a library of reform literature, and sponsored antislavery meetings. Powell brought the public's attention to the discrimination and exploitation suffered by black sailors, focusing particularly on the "negro seaman's acts"—laws passed by several southern states that subjected all black sailors to temporary imprisonment and possible enslavement whenever their ships docked in a southern port.

Powell served as secretary of the Manhattan Anti-Slavery Society, a Garrisonian organization. He helped establish the Committee of Thirteen, a group of prominent New York City blacks who coordinated the local opposition to the Fugitive Slave Law and other racial discrimination. Powell despaired of any improvement in American race relations, however, and he was further discouraged by the dismal prospects for educating his seven children. He visited England late in 1850 to investigate the possibility of a permanent move and returned there early in 1852 to establish his residence in Liverpool. Powell found employment as a clerk in a customhouse, and during almost ten years in England he remained active in the antislavery movement. He addressed antislavery gatherings and challenged pro-slavery opinion in the British press. Powell aided fugitive slaves and hosted American abolitionists during their lecture tours in the British Isles. He served as a contact between American and British antislavery groups, collected subscriptions for American antislavery newspapers, and helped arrange the shipment of British goods for sale at the annual Boston Anti-Slavery Bazaar.

Powell returned to the United States in 1861, drawn home by the secession crisis and the prospect of an end to slavery. He reestablished his sailors' boardinghouse in New York City in 1862, and the following year he received a commission to serve in the Union navy. His son William Jr., who had trained as a physician in England, accepted a surgeon's commission in the Union army. During the July 1863 draft riots in New York City, a white mob looted and destroyed Powell's boardinghouse. He and his family avoided physical harm by making a dramatic escape, but Powell suffered almost five thousand dollars in property damage as a result of the riots. In 1865 Powell became the first African American appointed as a notary public by the governor of New York.

Powell took an active role in the labor movement, particularly those organizations that promoted the rights of black workers and sailors. He helped organize the American League of Colored Laborers in 1850, cofounded the American Seamen's Protective Union Association in 1863, and represented black sailors at the Colored National Labor Union Convention in Washington, D.C., in 1869. These organizations helped improve working conditions for African American sailors by, for example, serving as a clearinghouse for sailors seeking employment or shelter during layovers, thus protecting sailors from unscrupulous employment agents, landlords, and lodge keepers.

Powell spent his last years in California. He arrived in San Francisco in 1874 and later gained public notice through his involvement with PHILIP ALEXANDER BELL's weekly newspaper, the *Elevator*. As assistant editor of the *Elevator*, Powell contributed political and social commentary, as well as recollections of the early years of the antislavery movement. Powell probably died in San Francisco. His dedication on behalf of thousands of African American sailors distinguishes him as a civil rights and labor leader.

FURTHER READING

Foner, Philip S. *Essays in Afro-American History* (1978).

Grover, Kathryn. *The Fugitive's Gibraltar: Escaping Slaves and Abolitionism in New Bedford, Massachusetts* (2001).

Ripley, C. Peter, and George E. Carter, eds. *Black Abolitionist Papers, 1830–1865: A Guide to the Microfilm Edition* (1981).

This entry is taken from the *American National Biography* and is published here with the permission of the American Council of Learned Societies.

MICHAEL F. HEMBREE

Powers, Georgia Davis (23 Oct. 1923–), politician, was born Georgia Montgomery, the second of nine children and the only girl to Frances (Walker), a homemaker, and Ben Montgomery, a farmer. She was always determined to rise above the discrimination her gender and interracial heritage weighed upon her. Beginning life in Springfield, Kentucky, she grew up to be the first female (and first African American) state senator in Kentucky history. In 1925 the Montgomery family moved to Louisville, Kentucky, where Georgia received most of her education. She attended Virginia Avenue Elementary School (1929–1934), Madison Junior High School (1934–1937), Central High School (1937–1940), and Louisville Municipal College, which she attended until 1942. She earned certificates from the Central Business School and the U.S. Government IBM Supervisory School. A year after she left the Louisville Municipal College, she married Norman F. Davis in 1943, and the two had one son, William F. Davis.

She began her political career in 1962, training volunteers for Wilson Wyatt's U.S. senatorial campaign. Powers pursued her political calling, leading campaigns for senatorial candidates, the governor of Kentucky, the mayor of Louisville, Congressional candidates, and presidential candidates within the next five years.

Powers was also involved in many civil rights activities throughout the 1960s. As one of the organizers of the Allied Organizations for Civil Rights, a group that worked toward the enactment of fair employment and public accommodations laws, she helped organize the 1964 march on Frankfort, Kentucky, that reportedly encompassed more than ten thousand participants. The keynote speaker for the Frankfort march was MARTIN LUTHER KING JR., with baseball great JACKIE ROBINSON also addressing the crowd. Through these efforts, the Kentucky Civil Rights Act was passed in 1965. That same year Powers helped organize the Kentucky Christian Leadership Conference and attended the historic march in Selma, Alabama, supporting the National Voting Rights Act. She also marched with King in the 1968 Memphis Sanitation Strike. Other important civil rights activities that she participated in included the St. Petersburg, Florida, Sanitation Strike, the Washington, D.C., Poor People's Campaign, and organized marches in Louisville for open housing.

Powers eventually realized she could make more of a political impact by holding political office. She ran as a Democrat for a seat in the Kentucky State Senate in 1967. Her campaign included endorsements from the AFL-CIO, Kentucky Medical Association, Kentucky and Louisville education associations, and the Louisville Chamber of Commerce. She won the seat easily. Once she had a voice in the legislature, her first bill for statewide housing soon passed. Powers collaborated with fellow members of Congress MAE STREET KIDD and Hughes E. McGill in introducing the first open housing law in the South, which was passed in 1968. Other legislation that she either sponsored or cosponsored were bills for low-cost housing, the Displaced Homemakers Law, a bill to increase the Kentucky minimum wage, an amendment to the Kentucky Civil Rights Act (that would eliminate discrimination on the basis of gender, age, or race), the Equal Rights Amendment Resolution, and a bill to omit "race" from Kentucky driver's licenses. She was also secretary for the Kentucky Democratic Caucus during her entire career in the Senate. She and her husband divorced in 1968.

In 1968 she attended her first Democratic National Convention, which was in Chicago that year; she spoke before the assembly in support of Hubert Humphrey. That year, she also received the Kennedy/King Award by Kentucky Young Democrats. And in 1973 Georgia married James F. Powers.

While serving in the Kentucky Senate for twenty-one years, Powers chaired the Health and Welfare Committee (1970–1976) and served as a member of the Rules Committee (1976–1978). In 1978 she received the Woman of the Year Award by the Women's Coalition, and the next year she won the Kentucky Chapter NAACP Award of Recognition. In 1981 Senator Powers would cultivate special ties to Kentucky State University, when there was a movement afoot to change the black institution into a two-year school under the community college system. Powers championed the institution and obtained 103 signatures from the 138 legislators to retain the university's status.

She also served as chair on the Labor and Industry Committee for ten years (1987–1988). She would also attend the 1984 and 1988 Democratic National Conventions in San Francisco and Atlanta, respectively, serving as the Kentucky chairperson for the JESSE JACKSON presidential campaigns.

During the course of her illustrious career, Senator Powers received countless other awards and honors, including the University of Louisville Board of Appreciation Award and the Kentucky State University Distinguished Service Award.

Following her retirement in 1988, she was awarded an honorary Doctor of Laws degree from the University of Kentucky (7 May 1989) and the honorary Doctor of Human Letters from the University of Louisville (21 May 1989).

In 1995 Senator Powers published her memoir, *I Shared the Dream: The Pride, Passion and Politics of the First Black Woman Senator from Kentucky*. This work offers a firsthand account of her life and career as a champion for blacks, poor people, the handicapped, women, and children. In 1996 Senator Powers was inducted into the Kentucky Commission on Women's Kentucky Women Remembered Hall of Fame by Governor Brereton Jones, and her portrait was hung in the State Capitol Building. She was also given an honorary Doctor of Human Letters from Kentucky State University (8 May 1999), which was the state's public historically black institution.

Powers also published *The Adventures of the Book of Revelation* in 1998 and *Celia's Land, a Historical Novel* in 2004. Surviving her husband James Powers, Powers spent her retirement years in Louisville, Kentucky.

FURTHER READING
The primary repository for Senator Georgia Powers's papers and memorabilia is Special Collections, Paul G. Blazer Library, Kentucky State University in Frankfort, Kentucky.

"Georgia M. Powers, Mrs.," *Who's Who Among African Americans*, 17th ed. (2004).

Powers, Georgia Davis. *I Shared the Dream: The Pride, Passion and Politics of the First Black Woman Senator from Kentucky* (1995).

Smith, Jessie Carney. "Georgia Powers," *Notable Black American Women, Book 1* (1992).

KAREN COTTON MCDANIEL

Powers, Harriet (29 Oct. 1837–1 Jan. 1910), quilt maker, was born a slave, probably in Georgia. Her maiden name is unknown, as are the names and occupations of her parents. As is often the case with little-known historical figures, most of the details of Powers's life have been gleaned from tax and census records. Before the Civil War, Harriet married Armstead Powers, a farmer who lived in Clarke County, Georgia. The date of their marriage is unknown, but it appears that two of the couple's children were born into slavery (Amanda in 1856 and Leon Joe in 1860) and several more were born after Emancipation (including Alonzo in 1865, Nancy in 1866, Lizzie in 1868, and Marshall in 1872). The Powerses, neither of whom could read nor write, found moderate success as farmers, and the 1870 census lists Armstead as a "farmhand" and Harriet as "keeping house." Sometime in the 1800s the Powerses bought four acres of land near Sandy Creek, a black settlement north of Athens, Georgia. The family worked their small farm until economic hardship forced them to sell two of their acres in 1891. By 1894 they were unable to pay their taxes. In 1894 or 1895 it seems that Armstead left Harriet and moved to another farm a few miles away. Records show that Harriet managed quite well on her own, paying her yearly taxes and, in 1897, displaying keen business acumen by mortgaging an acre of land so that she could buy a buggy for $16.89.

In 1886 Powers exhibited an unusual quilt at the Athens Cotton Fair. It was there that Oneita Virginia "Jennie" Smith, a trained artist and teacher at the Lucy Cobb Institute, a school for girls in Athens, first offered to buy the quilt; Powers refused. But five years later, having encountered financial difficulties, Powers sold Smith the quilt for five dollars, although she had initially asked for ten dollars. According to Smith's documentation of her conversations with Powers, it was very difficult for Powers to part with her quilt. Taking Smith up on her offer, Powers returned on several occasions to "visit" with her unique creation. When Smith died in 1945, the executor of her estate donated the quilt to the Smithsonian's National Museum of American History (NMAH).

The NMAH quilt is the first of two narrative, or story, quilts that brought Powers posthumous fame. They are her only surviving works. Story quilts themselves were less popular than the purely geometric and color field designs preferred by most American quilters (both black and white), and Powers's quilts were even more unusual than most story quilts, with no surviving prototypes. Neither of her quilts conforms to the standard sizes for use as bedcovers, indicating that they were intended for display or instruction or both. The two quilts are similar in construction and design, featuring flat, simplified figures and emblems made of colored fabric (orange, red, polka dot, blue) attached to a background fabric. Powers used a sewing machine to affix the appliquéd pieces and hand-sewed the three layers of each quilt. Using colorful thread, she hand-sewed additional pictorial details (hair, stigmata) directly onto the quilts after their assembly.

Appliqué, used to embellish linens, hats, and clothing, flourished in the American South between 1775 and 1875. Powers's quilts, however, in their technique and iconography, reached even farther, to a tradition of appliqué popular in Africa, particularly among the cloth workers of Benin (formerly Dahomey), West Africa. Illustrating stories from history and folklore through the use of symbolic figures, especially animals, rendered in vibrant, even fantastical, colors attached to a solid-color background, the Benin tapestries employ many of the same pictorial elements and strategies as Powers's quilts. Powers's quilts are also rich in celestial images of suns, moon, and stars. Powers took special care in incorporating these emblems, hand-sewing each piece into openings cut into the quilts rather than appliquéing the pieces.

Unlike the single-panel design of Benin tapestries, Powers's quilts are organized into a series of separate panels, each square illustrating an entire story or scene. The NMAH quilt (seventy-three inches by eighty-eight inches) consists of eleven panels laid out in three horizontal rows. The width of each panel is different, providing a tidy but varied series of squares and rectangles that—unlike traditional story quilts, which are read up and

down—progress horizontally, left to right. Each panel is framed by a sashing one and a half inches wide, which was originally bright green and now appears light brown. Small orange squares mark the intersections of the sashing. The quilt's original rose-colored background fabric (now faded to a cream color) ties together a series of biblical stories from the Garden of Eden to the nativity, all heavily populated with animals and symbolic elements.

Although she is not identified by name, Powers was interviewed about the quilt by Lucine Finch for an article eventually published in 1914 in the *Outlook*, a YMCA publication. Powers's detailed and impassioned explanation of the quilt's narrative and imagery, as well as her earlier conversations with Smith, illustrate that she was well aware of her artistic choices and the symbolic function of her work. Powers told Finch that her intention in creating the quilt was "to preach a sermon in patchwork." "Dis heah quilt," she continued, "gwin show where sin originated, outen de beginnin' uv things." Of the quilt's eleven panels, five are drawn from Genesis: two panels depicting Adam and Eve, Cain murdering Abel, Cain and his wife in Nod, and Jacob dreaming of an angel on a heavenly ladder. The remaining six panels refer to the New Testament: Satan among the seven stars, the baptism of Christ, and, in reverse chronological order, the crucifixion, Judas with thirty pieces of silver, the last supper, and the holy family of Joseph, Mary, and Jesus.

In 1895 Smith exhibited Powers's quilt at the Cotton States and International Exposition in Atlanta, where it was displayed with 122 other needlework pieces in the largest exhibit in the Negro Building. It is possible that a group of faculty wives from Atlanta University saw Powers's handiwork in Atlanta and commissioned a second quilt. Other sources claim that the women were not introduced to Powers's work until 1898 at the Nashville Exposition, at which time they bought her second, completed quilt. In any event, in 1898 Powers's second surviving quilt was presented as a gift to the Reverend Charles Hall, chairman of the board of Atlanta University, by a group of faculty wives. Upon his death Hall left the quilt to his son, who later sold it to the folk art collector Maxim Karolik, who donated his collection to the Museum of Fine Arts (MFA) in Boston, in 1964.

Larger in size (60 inches by 105 inches) than her first quilt, the MFA quilt features fifteen, rather than eleven, panels in a gridlike (five by three) arrangement of equal-sized squares. The quilt is similar in style, technique, and color to her first quilt but introduces a wider variety of colors and fabric, including polka dot sashing. Instead of using a single, contiguous background, Powers (with one exception) alternated light and dark squares, giving the design more visual interest.

Wholly unique, and considerably more complex in its composition and iconography than her first work, the quilt includes biblical scenes, local legends, and meteorological events. To Adam and Eve and Christ's baptism and crucifixion, Powers added Moses, Job, Jonah, and Noah. Interspersed among the biblical scenes are four unexpected panels, each depicting actual events that had become, either before of during Powers's lifetime, legendary stories.

In describing the quilt, Powers gave specific dates for these events, all of which have been found to match records of remarkable natural phenomena. "Dark Day of May 19 1780" refers to an event sometimes called Black Friday, when the skies over New England grew dark as a result of severe pollution from Canadian forest fires. Similarly, the "Falling of The Stars on November 13 1833" and the "Red Light Night of 1846" correspond to the Leonid meteor storm of November 1833 and the meteor showers of August 1846, respectively. Records show that the "Cold Thursday of February 1895" was indeed an unseasonably and dangerously cold day. The inclusion—and accuracy—of these events illustrates the strength of oral tradition, as well as documentation, of a Christian ideology infused with local folklore and cautionary tales appropriated from natural phenomena.

By 1900, two years after her second quilt was given to Atlanta University's Reverend Hall, only three of Powers's children were still alive: Lizzie lived at home, Marshall was a bricklayer, and Alonzo was a farmer and Baptist preacher. In 1901 Armstead must have returned to Sandy Creek long enough for the couple to sell the remaining two acres of their land, after which Harriet remained in the area for another nine years. With her resources depleted, she moved to neighboring Buck Branch. She died in 1910, leaving a total inheritance of seventy dollars.

In the mid-1970s the folklorist Gladys-Marie Fry brought Powers and her distinctive quilts to the attention of scholars with an essay in *Missing Pieces: Georgia Folk Art*. The quilts are now recognized as sites of history. Objects made and used as part of daily life, quilts are literally made out of the scraps of everyday material culture. Unable to leave written records, many women left quilts. For Powers, her quilts served as a means of artistic and spiritual expression, astonishingly personal in their interpretation of religious and historical events. Arguably the most important and unquestionably the best-known quilts in America, Powers's two quilts have become icons for those interested in the history of art and craft, slavery, women, and African Americans.

FURTHER READING

Fry, Gladys-Marie. "'A Sermon in Patchwork': New Light on Harriet Powers," in *Singular Women: Writing the Artist*, eds. Kristen Frederickson and Sarah E. Webb (2003).

Fry, Gladys-Marie. *Stitched from the Soul: Slave Quilts from the Antebellum South* (2002).

Lyons, Mary E. *Stitching Stars: The Story Quilts of Harriet Powers* (1993).

Hicks, Kyra E. *This I Accomplish: Harriet Powers' Bible Quilt and Other Pieces* (2009).

Perry, Regenia A. *Harriet Powers's Bible Quilts* (1994).

LISA E. RIVO

Pozo, Chano (7 Jan. 1915–2 Dec. 1948), percussionist, was born Luciano Pozo y Gonzalez in Havana, Cuba. The names and occupations of his parents are unknown. Pozo grew up in Solar el Africá, a slum neighborhood of former slave quarters in Havana. He began drumming as a young child in ceremonies conducted by the Abakwa, a West African secret religious society that was brought to Cuba by slaves. Pozo became a celebrity in Havana for his drumming and dancing in the annual Carnival celebration. He won several prizes for his songs at Carnival in the 1930s and developed a reputation among musicians in the Caribbean and the United States. Pozo recorded several of his winning songs, including "El Pin Pin" and "Nague," which made him relatively wealthy.

In 1937 Pozo moved to Harlem, New York, where his fame among jazz musicians spread. He played regular gigs in nightclubs and bars in East Harlem and in the El Barrio section of Manhattan's Upper West Side. In 1947 Pozo was hired by DIZZY GILLESPIE, who wanted to add a conga player to his big band. Pozo premiered with the band in winter 1947 at the Town Hall auditorium in New York City. For his solo he crouched in the middle of the stage for thirty minutes as he chanted and pounded out intricate polyrhythms. His performance made him the first Latin percussionist to perform with an American jazz band and also made him an

Chano Pozo, Afro-Cuban conga drummer who helped create Afro-Latin jazz during the 1940s. (Library of Congress.)

overnight sensation in the jazz world. After the concert Gillespie said that Pozo was "the greatest drummer I ever heard."

Pozo was soon prominently featured in Gillespie's band, both as a performer and as a composer. His best-known composition, "Manteca," greatly broadened the appeal of Afro-Cuban music in the jazz world. Pozo helped make Gillespie's band the winner of *Metronome* magazine's Band of the Year Award for 1947. Soon scores of jazz bands added Latin percussionists and began experimenting with Afro-Cuban rhythms.

For a year following the Town Hall concert Pozo toured with the Gillespie band, teaching the bandleader and his sidemen Afro-Cuban chants and rhythms. Gillespie fused Pozo's teachings with American jazz styles, creating what came to be known as "Latin jazz." The group's recordings of "Manteca" and "Cubana Be, Cubana Bop" in 1947 established the genre within the jazz world.

In February 1948, only one year after joining Gillespie's band, Pozo was shot and killed at a bar in Harlem. The murderer was caught and convicted, but the motive remained unknown. Considered by many jazz authorities as the greatest conga player of all time, Pozo can also be credited with playing a pivotal role in the fusion of Caribbean music and American jazz.

FURTHER READING

Fernández, Raúl A. *Latin Jazz: The Perfect Combination* (2002).

Roberts, John Storm. *Latin Jazz: The First of the Fusions, 1880s to Today* (1999).

Roberts, John Storm. *The Latin Tinge: The Impact of Latin American Music on the United States* (1979, 1998).

Stearns, Marshall. *The Story of Jazz* (1956).

This entry is taken from the *American National Biography* and is published here with the permission of the American Council of Learned Societies.

THADDEUS RUSSELL

Prater, David (9 May 1937–9 Apr. 1988), singer and member of Sam and Dave, was born in Ocilla, Georgia, the son of working-class parents. Like his future partner Sam Moore, Prater began singing in church. At an early age, he and his brother J. T. joined The Sensational Hummingbirds, a gospel quartet. Prater's gospel career led him to Miami, Florida, where in 1961 he met Moore at Miami's King Of Hearts Club. Entering a weekly amateur night contest emceed by Moore, a nervous Prater immediately ran into difficulties. The house band was unable to play his chosen song, and his anxiety made him unsure of the lyrics of his impromptu second choice. Moore knew the words, assisted Prater, and—impressed with the performance—offered to join Prater as a performing duo. The pair's high-energy, gospel-soaked performances clicked, triggering an interest with two Miami-based record labels. The two eventually signed with Roulette Records.

The Roulette tracks, along with the duo's growing reputation as live performers, piqued the interest of Jerry Wexler, the powerful Atlantic Records executive who had built his company's reputation as a prominent distributor of African American music. In Miami for a convention in 1965, Wexler visited the King of Hearts Club, where Sam and Dave were performing. Their talent convinced him that they belonged with Atlantic. Wexler signed them and sent them to record at Memphis's Stax Records, a regional label that Atlantic distributed nationally. Wexler anticipated that Stax's sound, anchored by the gritty playing of the interracial house band Booker T. and the MGs (SEE BOOKER T. JONES), would serve as a perfect complement to the potential he heard in the interlocking harmonies and energetic call-and-response of Moore and Prater.

Upon their arrival in Memphis, Sam and Dave began recording a series of now-legendary singles that forever linked them with Stax. Vital to their success was the young songwriting and production team of ISAAC HAYES and DAVID PORTER. The two were a consistent source of hit material for Sam and Dave, who, within the year, emerged (along with OTIS REDDING) as the studio's most successful client. The pulsing "Hold On, I'm Comin'," a number one R&B smash, established their signature interplay in which Moore's soaring tenor was firmly grounded by Prater's husky baritone; Prater both provided necessary foundation for Moore's intensity and delivered intense performances of his own. Sam and Dave's stage show bowed only to JAMES BROWN's in its legendary reputation. In performance, Moore and Prater extended and intensified the gospel textures of

their recordings, and used their training as nightclub entertainers to craft movements, dances and crowd-engaging techniques to bring audiences to a fever pitch of excitement and response. When Stax took its roster to Europe in 1967 for a celebrated series of shows, Sam and Dave routinely stole the show.

Sam and Dave propelled themselves to the top of the R&B ladder with up-tempo numbers such as "You Don't Know Like I Know," slow-burning groovers such as "I Thank You," and aching ballads such as "When Something Is Wrong with My Baby." One entry in their storied run deserves special mention. Hayes and Porter wrote "Soul Man" after Hayes saw footage of black business owners in rioting Watts painting the word "SOUL" on their storefronts for protection. Hayes and Porter subsequently wrote one of the genre's greatest anthems. After the MGs and Memphis Horns added funky backing, and Moore and Prater delivered superior performances, a true classic was born. In 1967 "Soul Man" became a chart-topping R&B hit, perhaps the defining example of the "Memphis sound."

Sam and Dave's career suffered greatly when Jerry Wexler severed ties with Stax in 1968. The last hit they recorded at the unusually hospitable Memphis movie theater–turned-recording studio was the uplifting love song "Soul Sister, Brown Sugar." Following Atlantic's break with Stax, Sam and Dave attempted to work their magic at a series of lesser-known R&B recording studios with much less success. Although their post-Stax recorded work was generally inferior, other factors also contributed to their artistic and commercial downfall. In 1968 Prater became a leading suspect, though he was never prosecuted, for the shooting of his first wife, with whom he had had five children. In addition, the relationship between Prater and Moore grew increasingly rocky. As their music's combustible energy began to dissipate, their personal rapport turned volatile. The mutual animosity reached such high levels that in the end they spoke to one another only while on stage. In 1970 Sam and Dave parted ways.

Despite the ill will, Moore and Prater reunited several times during the 1970s, recording material that drew little fanfare (beyond a minor R&B hit in 1974) and performing to adoring, though dwindling crowds. As their career stalled, both men endured battles with drug addictions and assorted personal demons. The duo made a comeback of sorts, with the surprising popularity of the Blues Brothers, an affectionate R&B pastiche performed by the comedians Dan Aykroyd and John Belushi. Suddenly there was a newfound interest in Sam and Dave. Not only did the Blues Brothers repeatedly express love for their R&B influences, they also used (backed, in part, by former MGs) "Soul Man" as their signature song. Buoyed by the attention, Sam and Dave performed a series of shows throughout 1980 (the year of the Blues Brothers film), but old hostilities reemerged, and they dissolved their musical partnership following a show on New Year's Eve in 1981. Prater hired Sam Daniels as a new partner, and they briefly, if disingenuously, billed themselves as "Sam and Dave." Moore successfully sued to prohibit the unauthorized use of a moniker so closely attached to his own celebrity.

In the meantime, Prater's problems continued, most notably with a 1987 arrest for selling crack cocaine. Less than a year later, on 9 April 1988, Prater died in a car crash as he drove to his mother's home, leaving five children and widow, Rosemary. His death, and the unsavory circumstances surrounding the group's demise, however, did not dull the public appreciation for Sam and Dave's body of work. The group was elected to the Rock and Roll Hall of Fame in 1992, and their songs have proven popular source material for covers by artists in rock, pop, and rhythm and blues. Moore's profile grew throughout the 1990s and early years of the new millennium. Particularly gratifying was his association with Bruce Springsteen, a self-professed Sam and Dave fan who emphasized that the duo's high-energy gospel style served as a creative touchstone for his own career. Without doubt, Moore and Prater were two of the most significant performers in 1960s soul, whose creative example and commercial success greatly influenced those who came after them.

FURTHER READING

Bogdanov, Vladimir, et al., eds. *All Music Guide* (2001).

Bowman, Rob. *Soulsville, U.S.A.: The Story of Stax Records* (1997).

Marsh, Dave. *Sam and Dave: An Oral History* (1998).

CHARLES L. HUGHES

Pratt, Awadagin (6 Mar. 1966–), pianist, was born to Theodore Pratt, a physics professor, and Mildred Sirls Pratt, a professor of social work, in Pittsburgh, Pennsylvania. Pratt spent his youth in Normal, Illinois, where his father, originally from Sierra Leone, and his mother, a native Texan, were both professors at Illinois State University. His parents had a deep appreciation for classical music, so young Pratt heard a great deal of music during his formative years.

Pratt took his first piano lesson at age six. By the time he was nine, he was taking violin lessons. Unlike many serious musicians, Pratt never considered himself to be a prodigy. He liked music, but did not spend every waking moment in practice, and had a great love for tennis.

While he may not have considered himself a prodigy, Pratt became an accomplished pianist and violinist during his youth. When he was sixteen, he was offered a violin scholarship from the University of Illinois School of Music. He also was offered a tennis scholarship at Kalamazoo College, but he accepted the University of Illinois award.

After two years at the University of Illinois, Pratt transferred to the Peabody Conservatory in Baltimore. He earned piano and violin diplomas in 1989 and a graduate conducting diploma in 1992, becoming the first student at Peabody to have earned two performer's degrees and a conducting degree.

Pratt's big break came in 1992, when he won the Naumburg prize as part of the Walter F. Naumburg Foundation Competition. Previous winners included performers considered to be music legends of the twentieth century: the pianist Jorge Bolet, the violinist Joseph Silverstein, the soprano Dawn Upshaw, the and cellist Nathaniel Rosen. Pratt considered his winning of the Naumburg prize to be the beginning of his professional career. The acclaim he received landed him an EMI recording contract. At this time, Robert Mann, president of the Naumburg Foundation and an accomplished violinist of the Juilliard String Quartet, singled out Pratt as one of the world's outstanding musicians. The compliment remained one of Pratt favorite career highlights.

Pratt's performance record was extremely varied. He played concertos with orchestras throughout the United States and abroad. He played in prestigious venues such as the Dorothy Chandler Pavilion, the Kennedy Center, the White House, and the Lincoln Center. He also performed on such unlikely venues as *Sesame Street*, the *Today Show*, and *Good Morning America*. He played Beethoven sonatas most frequently, but his repertoire ranged from J. S. Bach to John Harbison and Carlos Sanchez Gutierrez.

Pratt's "unusual" appearance and demeanor attracted the attention of audiences and critics alike. His dreadlocks—unremarkable in society-at-large, perhaps, but a rare sight in a classical music venue—were his trademark. He rejected the standard "tux and tails," often opting instead for a collarless, long-sleeve, open-neck sports shirt and black pants. He sat on a very low piano bench and appeared to slouch while playing, hunched over the keys in the manner of one of his idols, the late Canadian pianist Glenn Gould.

By the first years of the twenty-first century, Pratt's discography included six compact discs. His first, *A Long Way from Normal*, included works by Liszt, Franck, Brahms, and Bach. He also recorded four Beethoven piano sonatas for EMI/Classics; *Live from South Africa*; and *The Caveman's Valentine*, Terence Blanchard's soundtrack from the film of the same name.

In 1998 Pratt started the Pratt Foundation, in memory of his father. The foundation funded lessons and scholarships for gifted, disadvantaged children from the Bloomington-Normal, Illinois, community, his hometown. The recipients took lessons at Illinois Wesleyan University Preparatory School of Music in Bloomington. Pratt supported the foundation through benefit concerts and by sponsoring individual students himself. In 2002–2003 there were sixteen students receiving scholarships for lessons.

When not traveling or teaching, Pratt resided in Albuquerque, New Mexico. In the summers he directed the Next Generation Festival, which took place at venues around the Lancaster, Pennsylvania, area. He enjoyed chess and continued to play tennis. Pratt was an exciting, innovative performer, characterized by his youthful energy, enthusiasm, and unconventional approach to music.

FURTHER READING

Barron, James. "On Tour with: Awadagin Pratt; Knowing What It Means to Solo," *New York Times*, 16 Feb. 1995.

"Prize-Winning Pianist Awadagin Pratt Is Classical—but Not Conventional; Now He's a Player." *People* (17 Aug. 1992): 71.

Rhein, John von. "Triple Threat: Awadagin Pratt Masters the Piano, Violin and Baton," *Chicago Tribune*, 5 July 1992.

MATTHEW A. HAFAR

Pratt, Geronimo (13 Sept. 1947–2 June 2011), activist, was born Elmer Gerard Pratt in Morgan City, Louisiana, the youngest of eight children of Enoch "Jack" Pratt Sr., a junkman, and Eunice Petty Pratt. When Pratt was twelve, his father suffered a severe stroke. Though he survived, he was never able to

Geronimo Pratt leader of the Black Panther Party in Los Angeles awaiting a jury's verdict on 15 Dec. 1971. (AP Images.)

work again. In order to help support his family, Pratt hunted and sold the meat for money.

Pratt attended Morgan City Colored High School, where he was a star quarterback on the football team. The day before his graduation in 1965, the town's black elders instructed him to join the military in order to acquire skills that would help African Americans combat racism in his community. These elders were members of the Deacons for Defense and Justice, a clandestine black organization in Louisiana that advocated armed self-defense. Pratt deeply respected the town elders, so the following day he joined the U.S. Army.

Pratt completed paratrooper training at Fort Benning, Georgia, and was sent to Vietnam with the Eighty-second Airborne Division. After only six months he was promoted to squad leader and awarded the Soldier's Medal for rescuing soldiers from a burning helicopter. By the end of his tour, Pratt had also earned the Purple Heart and the Air Medal. After a second tour he returned to Morgan City with an honorable discharge in the summer of 1968.

In August 1968 one of Morgan City's town elders informed Pratt that he was going to put him in touch with a distant relative from Louisiana, Alprentice "Bunchy" Carter, who was the leader of the Los Angeles branch of the Black Panther Party for Self-Defense (BPP). Pratt drove to Los Angeles with his sister Emelda and met Bunchy Carter three days after they arrived. Pratt and Carter quickly became close friends. Carter bestowed on Pratt the name Geronimo ji Jaga. The name literally means "Geronimo of the Jaga"; Geronimo was the name of the famous Apache chief, and the Jaga were an African warrior tribe. Through his friendship with Carter, Pratt became immersed in the Black Panther Party. He soon participated in a variety of the party's community service programs, including sickle-cell anemia testing and serving free breakfast to children. Pratt enrolled in the High Potential Program at the University of California, Los Angeles, an advanced course of study limited to fifty students, in which Carter was also enrolled. Pratt majored in black studies and political science, which enabled him to teach political education classes to his fellow Panthers.

Pratt joined the Panthers at precisely the moment when the party came under attack by the FBI. In September 1968 the director of the FBI J. Edgar Hoover described the party as the greatest threat to national security. The FBI immediately directed COINTELPRO, a secret counterintelligence program, to undermine the party by creating divisions within the organization and between the party and other groups. The tension created by the FBI between the Panthers and US, a black nationalist organization in Los Angeles, turned deadly on 17 January 1969 when members of US shot and killed Carter and a Panther co-leader, John Huggins, after a meeting of UCLA's Black Student Union. Three months after Carter's death, Pratt was named as his successor by the Central Committee, the party's decision-making body. Pratt was also named deputy minister of defense of the entire party. Soon after Pratt's promotion he met a Panther named Saundra Lee, who became his common-law wife. In November 1971 Lee, who was pregnant with Pratt's first child, was found shot to death.

As deputy minister of defense, Pratt utilized his military experience to train party members to better defend themselves against the increasingly violent attacks by police departments and the FBI. In the summer of 1970 Pratt visited party chapters around the country and instructed them on building fortifications. While in New Orleans, Pratt was instructed to go to Dallas, Texas, by an FBI informant who had infiltrated the party. When Pratt arrived in Dallas he was immediately arrested. The next day it was announced that Pratt had been expelled from the party. After two months Pratt was extradited to Los Angeles, where he was charged with the murder of Caroline Olsen, a twenty-seven-year-old teacher who had been robbed and shot to death on a tennis court in Santa Monica, California, on 18 December 1968.

Pratt maintained that he was in Oakland for a meeting of the Black Panther Party's Central Committee on the day of Olsen's murder. Pratt was defended in court by JOHNNIE COCHRAN JR. The trial largely revolved around the testimony of Julius Butler, whom Pratt had expelled from the party in August 1969. Cochran and Pratt did not know that Butler was also an FBI informant. As a result of Butler's testimony Pratt was convicted in July 1972 and sentenced to life in prison. For the first eight years of his incarceration Pratt was kept in solitary confinement. He was released from solitary after his attorney Stuart Hanlon proved that Pratt's treatment was unfair and unnecessary.

As a legal strategy, Pratt married Linda Session in 1976. Though it was initially a marriage of convenience, the couple developed a genuine affection for each other. Session soon changed her name to Ashaki Pratt. She gave birth to Pratt's daughter Shona and son Hiroji while Pratt was incarcerated. The strain of separation proved to be too much, however, and the Pratts divorced in 1995.

In 1976 COINTELPRO was made public by a Senate investigation. Through the Freedom of Information Act, Pratt's lawyers requested and received FBI documents that revealed that Pratt had been targeted by the FBI beginning in 1969. The FBI's stated goal was to neutralize his effectiveness as a Panther leader. It was also shown that the FBI had Pratt under surveillance at the time of Caroline Olsen's murder. The revelation of the FBI's involvement turned Pratt's case into a cause célèbre, garnering support from progressive activists, celebrities, and politicians. Pratt's legal team filed numerous petitions and briefs in hopes of getting Pratt's sentence overturned.

On 29 May 1997 Orange County Superior Court Judge Everett Dickey reversed Pratt's 1972 conviction on the grounds that the prosecution in the original trial had acted improperly by not providing the defense with the information that Butler was an informant. Pratt was released from prison on 10 June 1997. In April 2000 Pratt settled a suit against the city of Los Angeles and the FBI for false imprisonment and violation of civil rights. The city of Los Angeles paid Pratt $2.75 million, and the FBI paid $1.75 million.

Following his release Pratt returned to his hometown of Morgan City, Louisiana, with his ex-wife Ashaki and son Hiroji, and he subsequently began traveling the country speaking on behalf of political prisoners. In 1999 Pratt, along with the attorney Ed Jones, founded the Kuji Foundation, a nonprofit organization that promoted cooperative economic development in Morgan City and East and West Africa. Despite being internationally famous for serving twenty-seven years in prison for a murder he did not commit, Pratt shied away from celebrity and insisted that his work as an activist on behalf of the oppressed was far from complete.

Pratt died in Tanzania at the age of 63.

FURTHER READING

Amnesty International. *United States of America: The Case of Elmer "Geronimo" Pratt* (1988).

Olsen, Jack. *Last Man Standing: The Tragedy and Triumph of Geronimo Pratt* (2000).

Obituary: *CNN.com*, 3 June 2011.

LAUREN ARAIZA

Prattis, Percival Leroy (27 Apr. 1895–29 Feb. 1980), editor of the Pittsburgh *Courier* and the first black journalist accredited to the press office of the U.S. Congress, was born in Philadelphia, Pennsylvania, the only child of Alexander and Ella Spraggins Prattis. Alexander Prattis, probably born in 1856, was absent for most or all of his son's childhood, but came from a line of Prattises well established in Caroline County, Maryland, many of whom had been free since the early 19th century, some owning their own land. Percival Prattis was sometimes sent to spend summers with relatives in Maryland, or near Smyrna, Delaware. During his first 13 years, he had perhaps two years of school, and associated with African American, Irish and Polish children on the streets of the Germantown neighborhood.

Prattis attended Christiansburg Industrial Institute in Virginia (1908-1912) and graduated from Hampton Normal and Agricultural Institute in 1915. For a year after graduation, he was in charge of the institute's poultry department at Shellbanks. He then entered the Ferris Institute, Big Rapids, Michigan, in the fall of 1916, and in 1917 registered for the World War I draft. He claimed exemption as the sole support of his mother, listing his home address as 1726 Kater Street, in Philadelphia. He reported to Camp Sherman, Ohio, in 1918; according to *The Southern Workman*, this interrupted

plans to enter the University of Michigan Law School. He was promoted to the rank of sergeant-major while serving in France. Mustered out at Fort Dix, New Jersey, in July 1919, he returned to Grand Rapids, considering it the closest thing to home he had.

Returning to work in the restaurant of the Pantlind Hotel, Prattis boarded with Samuel and Harriett Pinkney, a married couple in their forties registered as "black." Their neighbors were mostly first- or second-generation immigrant families of Italian, Swedish, Irish, and German descent. He soon began work as editor and writer for the *Michigan State News*. He found himself in Chicago in January, 1921, after thirty waiters at the Pantlind threatened to quit if a checking girl who referred to a waiter as "Nigger" was not dismissed; only three, Prattis among them, actually quit when the management refused to take action. Working temp jobs at different hotels, he was recommended by his landlady to Robert S. Abbott, owner and editor of the *Chicago Defender*. He started work April 9, first as a reporter, then as city editor. In 1923 he began writing for the Associated Negro Press in Chicago.

In 1928, on the orders of his boss at Associated Negro Press, Claude Barnett, Prattis abandoned his allegiance to Republican presidential candidate Herbert Hoover, accepting an assignment with R. Irving Johnson to campaign for Al Smith, the Democratic nominee. Hoover's supervision of flood relief in the Mississippi River valley in 1927 had alienated many, in states where the black vote was significant, and his campaign ignored Barnett's advice to shore up support in those communities. Instead, inspired by the fact that Smith was a Roman Catholic, despised by the Ku Klux Klan, Hoover aimed to secure his nomination with black support and then become competitive among southern "white" voters in the general election for the first time ever.

In 1930 Prattis, now news editor for the press agency, was lodging in Chicago at 4910 Vincennes Avenue in the 4th ward, an African American neighborhood, with a married couple his own age, George and Pauline Moore, and their thirteen-year-old son, George Jr. In 1932, he married Lillian Sherman, a friend of eleven years, who left him in 1934, moving to New York. Prattis, who had been reporting for the Pittsburgh Courier and handling Courier circulation in Chicago, followed his wife to New York, with a stop in Pittsburgh to negotiate a possible permanent position with the Courier. At the recommendation of William Pickens, an old friend and NAACP field secretary, Prattis accepted work as editor, managing editor, and city editor of the *Amsterdam News*during a strike by members of the Newspaper Guild. He had to cross a picket line, on which Rev. Adam Clayton Powell was supporting the strike. Prattis moved to Pittsburgh, working as city editor of the Pittsburgh *Courier*, owned by ROBERT L. VANN. He also served as a correspondent for *Our World* magazine. He married the Pittsburgh native Helen Marie Sands, a *Courier* employee with a teaching certificate from Cheney State University. Their only daughter, Patricia, born 16 July 1941, became a widely acclaimed symphony keyboardist (Patricia Prattis Jennings).

With the United States engaged in a vast military mobilization, Vann advocated a separate Negro division in the army, protested demeaning duties assigned to blacks in the services, and supported the Committee on Participation of Negroes in the National Defense Program. When Vann died in 1940, Ira F. Lewis succeeded him as president, promoting Prattis to executive editor. While Prattis editorialized that, "We must stop asking for more segregation," he also highlighted that as long as the armed forces remained racially segregated, a Negro division would ensure that the front-line fighting duties, as well as the service and support duties, were filled with soldiers of African descent.

Earlier that year, the *Courier* received a letter from thirteen black sailors serving on the U.S.S. *Philadelphia* concerning the navy's treatment of sailors not considered "white." The navy, learning about the complaint, had them arrested and scheduled for a court-martial. After the story was printed in the 5 October 1940 issue, letters of protest poured in to the *Courier*, and Prattis interceded with the navy, which canceled the court-martial, but released the sailors with undesirable or bad-conduct discharges (Simmons, p. 73).

The *Courier* launched and spearheaded a nationwide war mobilization "Double V" campaign, calling for victory over the fascist enemy without and the racist enemy within the United States. The idea arose from a letter by James G. Thompson, a twenty-six-year-old cafeteria worker at the Cessna airplane factory in Wichita, Kansas. The campaign featured placards and signs and emblazoned every issue for a year, with a selection of photos showing people giving the "Double V" sign, and even women with "Double V" woven into their hair style. At the same time, Prattis proposed organization of War Bond Savings Clubs, which was widely advocated by the Negro Business League in 1943.

On 5 February 1944, Prattis read a statement on behalf of thirteen editors and publishers of African American newspapers, who had been invited to meet with President Franklin Roosevelt at a time when no African American reporter had been admitted to the White House press gallery (except to cover a visit by the president of Liberia in May 1943). Three days later, Harry S. McAlpin was admitted to a White House press conference as a representative of the National Negro Publishers Association and the *Atlanta Daily World*. The same year, Prattis received an honorary doctorate from Wiley College. Three years later, on 3 May 1947, Prattis became the first black newsman accredited to press galleries of the House and Senate. That month, *Courier* circulation reached an all-time high of 357,212 and was widely recognized as the most influential black newspaper in America, distributed far beyond the Pittsburgh area. In 1948, the writer JAMES BALDWIN called the *Courier* "a high class paper" and "the best of the lot." It had fourteen editions, including a national edition, the local Pittsburgh edition, and editions specific to twelve other cities or regions across the United States.

The *Courier* under Prattis's leadership stood out for its refusal to bend to cold war anticommunist propaganda. At a time when WALTER WHITE refused NAACP support for W. E. B. DuBois, indicted for refusing to register the Peace Information Center (PIC) as an agent of a foreign government, Prattis boldly editorialized: "Handcuffs on Dr. DuBois Is Evidence of the Terror Used to Victimize Us" (Prattis Papers, Reel 67). While White repeated statements that the PIC had been paid for by "soviet money," Prattis observed that the indictment had been designed to intimidate black leadership into silence, and given the NAACP's behavior, had succeeded in doing so (Anderson, pp. 172–174).

Prattis was dubious of pan-African philosophies and movements, observing that peoples of color had divergent interests, leadership, cultures, and alliances. At the time of the founding conference of the United Nations, he wrote "The zealous advocacy of the American Negro of the causes of other colored peoples throughout the world is not repaid in kind." Finding in particular the delegations from Ethiopia, Liberia, and Haiti to be "disinterested," he suggested African Americans could find "bigger dividends in the long run…on a plan to increase the number of fair-minded white Americans" (Plummer, p. 139).

By 1950, *Courier* circulation had fallen to 280,000. In 1954 Prattis wrote a favorable series of articles about Israel after an extended visit to the new nation, while cultivating good relations with the Nation of Islam (NOI). He allowed *Courier* columnists J. A. ROGERS and GEORGE SCHUYLER to suggest that imperialist nations were using Israel and that this was not in the best interest of Jews there or anywhere in the world. Prattis became editor-in-chief of the *Courier* in 1956. In 1957 the *Courier* began to publish extensive accounts of NOI events and theology, while NOI distributed and sold the paper aggressively. Pettis also began a feature series on Muslim countries, hoping to obtain financing for a larger publication project (Plummer, pp. 263, 265–266).

Circulation fell to just over 100,000 in 1960. Prattis later observed that as qualified black journalists began to find jobs in major daily papers, information formerly found only in black newspapers would be "in the white papers before Negro reporters get to it," leading to a decline in circulation (Washburn, p. 203). In 1961 Prattis became associate publisher and treasurer. He resigned 31 Aug 1962, disenchanted with changes at the paper after Chicago cosmetics manufacturer S.B. Fuller became Chairman of the Board in 1959, then Publisher, while the financially ailing paper became dependent on Fuller's investment of additional cash. He was prevailed upon to return in May 1963 to try to save the paper but resigned 26 April 1965, one day before his seventieth birthday. He was increasingly unhappy with Robert L. Vann's widow, Jessie Vann, being forced out in 1963, William Nunn in 1964, and the interference of Fuller and his representatives. In 1966, Fuller sold the Courier to his Chicago business associate, John Sengstacke, owner of the *Chicago Defender* and other newspapers. After bankruptcy, the paper's assets were sold to a separately incorporated New Pittsburgh Courier Publishing Co. Prattis died at the age of eighty-five at the Veterans Administration hospital in Aspinwall, Pennsylvania.

FURTHER READING

The Percival L. Prattis Collection, including his personal and professional papers, is housed at the Moorland Spingarn Research Center, Howard University, Washington, DC.

Anderson, Carol. *Eyes off the Prize: The United Nations and the African American Struggle for Human Rights, 1944–1945* (2003).

Plummer, Brenda Gayle. *Rising Wind: Black Americans and U.S. Foreign Affairs, 1935–1960* (1996).

Simmons, Charles A. *The African American Press: A History of News Coverage during National Crises, with Special Reference to Four Black Newspapers, 1827–1965* (1998).

Washburn, Patrick Scott. *The African American Newspaper: Voice of Freedom* (2006). Evanston, IL.

Obituaries: *New York Times.* "Percival L. Prattis, 85." 3 Mar. 1980.

Pittsburgh Post Gazette. 3 Mar., 1980.

CHARLES ROSENBERG

Preer, Evelyn (16 July 1896–17 Nov. 1932), actress and singer, was born Evelyn Jarvis in Vicksburg, Mississippi, to Blanche and Frank Jarvis. While Preer was still a young child, her father passed away, and she and her mother migrated north to Chicago. There she completed grammar school and high school, and she eventually persuaded her strict Pentecostal mother to allow her to pursue an acting career. Initially Preer's opportunities were limited to performing with minor traveling musical and minstrel shows. However, while still in her early twenties she met the pioneering African American filmmaker OSCAR MICHEAUX and began her film career in his 1919 film *The Homesteader.*

Preer would owe the lion's share of her exposure in cinema to Micheaux, who featured her in a number of his subsequent films, including *Within Our Gates* (1920), *The Brute* (1920), *The Gunsaulus Mystery* (1921), *Deceit* (1923), *Birthright* (1924), *The Devil's Disciple* (1925), and *The Conjure Woman* (1926). Her role in *Within Our Gates* is particularly noteworthy because of the film's reputation among film scholars as having been Micheaux's "answer" to the racist history presented in D. W. Griffith's 1915 blockbuster *The Birth of a Nation.* Micheaux sought to unveil the brutal southern tradition of white-on-black violence ignored in Griffith's film by explicitly portraying a white mob's lynching of a helpless African American family. *Within Our Gates* also depicted Preer's character, Sylvia Landry, as the victim of an attempted rape by a white man who is discovered to be her biological father.

Preer's prominence in so many of Micheaux's films draws attention to the important history of "race movies," films made by independent African American directors like Micheaux during the silent era, when Hollywood studios were disinclined to produce movies targeting black audiences. Preer became acquainted with many race movie actors through her membership in the Harlem-based

Lafayette Players, a professional black stock acting company founded by Anita Bush in 1915. The company's members regularly appeared both in stage dramas and in the screen works of race filmmakers. Many accomplished black actors and actresses got their training and professional experience through their association with the Lafayette Players. Preer first joined the Players in 1920, as the troupe was enjoying a run at Chicago's Lincoln Theater. Among their members was the actor Edward Thompson, the son of the black composer DeKoven Thompson and who would himself appear in race films like Micheaux's *The Spider's Web* (1927). Preer and Thompson acted together in a number of the Lafayette Players' 1920s stage productions. The pair fell in love and was married during a Players tour in 1924, just outside of Nashville, Tennessee.

Preer was also an accomplished singer and recorded a number of jazz tunes over her lifetime. She performed and recorded with the jazz legend DUKE ELLINGTON songs such as "If You Can't Hold the Man You Love," and "Baby Won't You Please Come Home." Sometimes appearing in her singing career as Evelyn Thompson, Preer also performed with accomplished entertainers like ETHEL WATERS and JOSH WHITE. Her singing landed her roles in stage musicals like *Rang Tang* (1927), as well as a lead role in her first sound film, *Georgia Rose* (1930), a race musical produced by Aristo Films.

Preer was, however, an actress first and foremost. In addition to her appearances in race films, Preer acted in small roles in Hollywood productions. She appeared as a prisoner in the 1931 Paramount film *Ladies of the Big House*, which starred Sylvia Sidney. In the following year Preer was cast in another Paramount film, *Blonde Venus* (1932), starring Marlene Dietrich. Also appearing with her in this film were HATTIE McDANIEL and her fellow Lafayette Player CLARENCE MUSE. Paramount distributed a series of comedy shorts produced by the Christie Film Company, and some of these, like *The Framing of the Shrew* (1929) and *Oft in the Silly Night* (1929) also featured Preer. For some of the Christie Company roles, Preer's light skin was darkened with makeup, illustrating the endurance of the minstrel idiom and, moreover, the deep anxiety around the representation of race in Hollywood during this era. Such "blackface" appearances in mainstream comedies provided an odd visual counterpoint to Preer's appearances in uplift-oriented race movies with predominantly light-skinned black casts, many of whom could "pass" for white.

Indeed, for African American actresses like Preer, color was a highly significant and highly complex indicator of their prospects on screen in the early decades of American cinema. Darker-skinned actresses like Hattie McDaniel and LOUISE BEAVERS worked fairly steadily in Hollywood films, but they appeared overwhelmingly in predictable comic or tragic maid roles. Among whites and blacks, they would become associated with the stereotyping of the black image. Lighter-skinned actresses like Preer, NINA MAE McKINNEY, and FREDI WASHINGTON (who was also darkened with makeup for Hollywood films) had a more difficult time getting Hollywood roles, presumably because their light skin signified "beauty" and suggested sexuality, concepts that white audiences were often uncomfortable perceiving with respect to black characters. They also threatened to upset the simple visual opposition of race as black and white that Hollywood studios relied upon for their audiences' comfort and recognition.

Preer's professional endeavors generally met with substantial acclaim, with critics both black and white giving her performances high marks. The *Pittsburgh Courier* reporter Floyd Calvin treated her in a 1927 article entitled "Evelyn Preer Ranks First as Stage and Movie Star." Citing the variety of Preer's accomplishments, Calvin called her "a pioneer in the cinema world for colored actresses" (Thompson, 29). Though Preer and her husband, Edward Thompson, enjoyed considerable professional success, their personal dreams of beginning a family were more difficult. In the years after they married, they were told by a number of doctors that Preer would never be able to bear children. Thus it was with great joy and satisfaction that in April 1932, the couple announced the birth of their daughter, Edeve (Sister Francesca) Thompson.

Tragically, the family's joy was short-lived. Preer grew ill after delivering the child, and she died of double pneumonia only seven months after Edeve was born. Her Los Angeles funeral was lavish, attended by throngs of her fans and fellow actors. Preer was movingly eulogized by Clarence Muse, who honored the quality of her work as an actress, concluding that "the world has been uplifted" (Thompson, 32). Her obituary in the Hollywood trade magazine *Variety* proclaimed that she was "considered the foremost dramatic actress of the colored race."

FURTHER READING

Cripps, Thomas. *Slow Fade to Black: The Negro in American Film, 1900–1942* (1977).

Musser, Charles, et al. "An Oscar Micheaux Filmography: From the Silents through His Transition to Sound, 1919–1931," in *Oscar Micheaux and His Circle: African-American Filmmaking and Race Cinema of the Silent Era*, eds. Pearl Bowser, Jane Gaines, and Charles Musser (2001).

Thompson, Sister Francesca. "From Shadows 'n Shufflin' to Spotlights and Cinema: The Lafayette Players, 1915–1932," in *Oscar Micheaux and His Circle: African-American Filmmaking and Race Cinema of the Silent Era*, eds. Pearl Bowser, Jane Gaines, and Charles Musser (2001).

Obituary: *Variety* (22 Nov. 1932).

MIRIAM J. PETTY

Premice, Josephine (21 July 1926–13 Apr. 2001), actress, dancer, and singer, was born in Brooklyn, New York, the daughter of Lucas Premice, a furrier, and Theloumene Thomas Premice. Josephine and her older sister Adele spent summers in Haiti, in an attempt by their parents to keep them in touch with the family's roots. As a child Premice was sickly, and an affliction with rickets left her bowlegged.

Premice was educated in Brooklyn public schools. At home her parents, whose origins were in the Haitian aristocracy, schooled her and her sister in the art of being ladies. Although it may seem ironic that a black girl who attended a Brooklyn public school was educated in upper class etiquette, Premice's schooling in the social graces paid off later when she was a part of the society circles in which she would travel the United States and abroad.

Despite her parents' attempts to dissuade her, Premice always wanted to perform. At an early age she had a love of dance and studied ballet, jazz, and tap. Her sense of these dance forms was influenced by the rhythms of the Caribbean. She went on to study with such greats as Martha Graham, KATHERINE DUNHAM, and Charles Weidman. By the time Premice reached the age of fourteen, it became clear to her family that she was destined for a career on the stage.

Known primarily for her talents as a singer, dancer, and stage actress, Premice launched her professional career in 1945 with her Broadway debut in *Blue Holiday*. She performed calypso in the 1940s, when she recorded her first single, and in the 1950s, when she toured France, England,

Italy, and Spain as a soloist. In the United States she performed in nightclubs, including the Village Vanguard and the Blue Angel, and she recorded two calypso albums, *Josephine in Paris* and *Calypso*. In 1947 Premice performed in the calypso musical *Caribbean Carnival*.

Throughout her acting career, which spanned nearly fifty years, Premice shared the stage with such greats as LENA HORNE (*Jamaica*), PEARL BAILEY (*House of Flowers*), and ETHEL WATERS (*Blue Holiday*). Her stage acting credits include *Blue Holiday*, *Caribbean Carnival*, *Mister Johnson*, *Bubbling Brown Sugar*, *House of Flowers* (a musical comedy by Truman Capote, choreographed by George Balanchine), *Electra*, *The Cherry Orchard*, and *Glass Menagerie*, her last stage performance. She was nominated for Tony awards for her performances in *Jamaica* (1958, Best Featured Performer) and *A Hand Is on the Gate* (1966, Best Supporting Actress). Premice began her career on television with several spots on *The Merv Griffin Show* (1966–1968) and a role in the TV movie *The Autobiography of Miss Jane Pittman* (1974). She followed these with appearances on many shows, including *The Jeffersons* (1979), *The Cosby Show* (1986), and *A Different World* (1991–1993).

Premice met Timothy Fales, a white businessman, in 1958. On 14 November of that year they were married by the U.S. congressman and civil rights activist Reverend ADAM CLAYTON POWELL JR. Fales, a descendent of an old Anglo-Saxon Protestant family whose paternal ancestors included the first governor of the Massachusetts Bay Colony, was expelled from the Social Register upon his marriage to Premice. After their marriage, Premice and Fales lived in Rome for six years, after which time a business venture of Fales's brought them back to the States. The couple had two children, Susan Fales-Hill, who became an author and television producer, and Enrico Fales.

While Premice enjoyed some degree of success in her early career, she worked less in the 1960s and 1970s, and it appears that she spent some of these years traveling with her husband and raising a family. Known for her effervescence, liveliness, and sense of style as well as her talent, it was said that the very slender Premice could fill up a room with her presence. Her keen fashion sense, glamour, and attitude sent a message to the world that she was important. A quintessential hostess, her domestic side was expressed through her love of entertaining, expert cooking, and the bountiful tables that she set. Her salons were celebrated and well attended. Her circle of friends and acquaintances was composed of all the greats of the arts—writers, actors, producers, directors, composers, and choreographers—black, white, and other. Special among them were her "sister friends," DIAHANN CARROLL, Lena Horne, and DIANA SANDS.

Premice dazzled the world with her talents as a dancer, actress, and singer, as well as with her elegance and personal style. She lived in many worlds—among her Haitian relatives in Brooklyn, her white in-laws, the legends of show business in theater, dance, and television—in the United States and abroad. Perhaps her greatest contribution to the world of performing arts lay in her introduction of and raising to prominence calypso music and dance in the United States. She died in her Manhattan home of emphysema at the age of seventy-four.

FURTHER READING
Fales-Hill, Susan. *Always Wear Joy: My Mother Bold and Beautiful*. (2003).
Obituary: *New York Times*, 17 Apr. 2001.

SUSAN D. TOLIVER

Preston, Richard (1791?–4 July 1861), slave, minister, and community leader, was born in Virginia in the early 1790s. Almost nothing is known about his childhood or young adulthood except that he had been a slave preacher. Preston's life changed during the War of 1812 when his mother and approximately four thousand black American refugees escaped to the safety of British ships that had conducted raids along the American eastern seaboard. About half of these former slaves migrated, via the British Royal Navy, to Nova Scotia. Admiral Alexander Cochrane had offered freedom to African Americans in an effort to disrupt the economy and terrorize local whites. Preston did not escape with his family, but he purchased his freedom after the conclusion of the war. Preston left the United States and traveled to British North America in search of his relatives. Eventually he found his mother in Nova Scotia at Preston, a small settlement of former American slaves outside of the local population center Halifax. The happy reunion of mother and son marked the beginning of a long religious and political career for the former slave preacher.

During his first years in Nova Scotia, Preston hoped to continue serving God by conducting religious services for the black community. Before his arrival the black American refugees had been ministered to by an Englishman named John Burton, the head of the Baptist church in Halifax. Burton had always welcomed people of African descent to his church and attempted to provide social and economic support to the recent migrants while shielding them from pervasive racial hostility in Nova Scotia. After meeting Preston, Burton supported the younger man's career by securing his appointment to the Nova Scotia Baptist Association in 1821, and in 1823 he convinced the religious authorities to formally license Preston as a preacher.

After establishing himself as a licensed preacher, Preston focused his attention on spreading the gospel throughout Nova Scotia's black population, which resided in various areas ranging from Tracadie in the north to Yarmouth in the southern part of the colony. As Preston traveled throughout the colony he converted several blacks to the Baptist faith and encouraged them to connect with people of African descent from other towns. His outstanding rhetorical abilities and personal familiarity with slavery made him an impressive figure who enjoyed a large popular following. As increasing numbers of African Americans and people of African descent attended Preston's religious gatherings, Burton's influence waned. By the end of the 1820s Preston and other leaders in the black community decided that separate African congregations were needed to meet the religious desires of the community. Around the same time, in 1828, Preston found time within his busy schedule to marry a woman named Mary, but the union would not produce any children.

Preston decided to create separate African congregations because, as he stated in a petition to the colonial government in the early 1830s, "circumstances of an unpleasant nature…existed between the white and colored members of the Baptist church" (The Humble Petition of the Undersigned Trustees for and on Behalf of the Congregation of the Baptist African Chapel Established at Halifax, 25 Feb. 1833, RG 5 P, vol. 42, doc. 51, Nova Scotia Archives and Record Management [NSARM].) These "unpleasant" circumstances were not necessarily related to a falling-out between Burton and Preston but were the result of the resentment of certain white Baptists against the inclusion of people of African descent in fellowship. Preston and his supporters realized that to create a church they needed an ordained minister to conduct functions such as marriages and funerals, so the black community in Halifax collected money to send Preston to England for ministerial training. Preston also hoped to obtain money from wealthy philanthropists for the construction of a church.

Preston arrived in England in January 1831 and studied under the West London Association of Baptist Ministers. In London, Preston found time to travel to several local churches and give speeches about slavery. At a time when interest in emancipation in the British colonies had been increasing, Preston struck an important chord for Britons. His stories of the cruelties of American slavery and the life of former slaves in the British colonies found a ready audience, and local newspapers complimented his "pleasing" manner of speech (*Novascotian* [Halifax], 27 June 1832). In traveling to London and discussing the situation of African Americans he predated the experience of FREDERICK DOUGLASS by nearly fifteen years. In the spring of 1832 the West London Association ordained Preston, and he returned to Nova Scotia with enough money to begin construction of a church for the black community in Halifax.

The African congregation was founded in Halifax on 14 April 1832 with smaller branch meeting houses in the surrounding rural black communities of Preston, Hammonds Plains, Dartmouth, and Beech Hill. Yet the actual building structure of the mother church on Cornwallis Street in Halifax was not completed until the spring of 1833. The church became a symbol of African American freedom in the heart of an important colony in British North America. The African congregation in Halifax served as the spiritual center of the local black community, but it also became a meeting place for several community organizations that served social and political purposes as well.

During the 1840s Preston established the Anglo-African Mutual Improvement and Aid Association and the African Abolition Society. His status as the leader of the major black church in Halifax (there was also an African Methodist church) offered a sturdy foundation for these organizations to pursue more secular goals, including racial improvement and the abolition of slavery. The Anglo-African Mutual Improvement and Aid Association had been founded to offer political and economic advice to black people in Halifax. In contrast, the African Abolition Society had a more international focus. Although slavery had been illegal in Nova Scotia and British North America for several years, as a former slave Preston wanted to advocate for the abolition of slavery in the United States. The society held parades to commemorate emancipation in the British West Indies, conducted public discussions about the Fugitive Slave Law, and aided fugitive slaves from the United States by resettling them in Nova Scotia. The creation and development of institutions that were common to nearly every free black community in the United States, such as separate churches, social organizations, and abolitionism, demonstrated the linkages and similarities between black expatriates in Nova Scotia and their people in the United States.

In 1854, after years of preaching to various black enclaves throughout Nova Scotia, Preston established the African Baptist Association. This union of twelve black Baptist churches throughout the colony gave a sense of common purpose to widely scattered communities. Preston spent the last years of his life conducting services, marriages, and funerals. Perhaps the most important event of Preston's later life occurred when he traveled to Canada West to be reunited with a daughter he had not seen since the end of the War of 1812. No information is available about the daughter or her mother. Preston's vigorous life came to an end during the summer of 1861, shortly after the beginning of the war that would free several relatives that he had left behind more than forty years earlier.

FURTHER READING

Several documents relating to Richard Preston are available at the Nova Scotia Archives and Records Management, Halifax, Nova Scotia; the Baptist collection is also important and can be accessed at the Acadia University Library Archives, Wolfville, Nova Scotia.

McKerrow, Peter Evander. *A Brief History of the Coloured Baptists of Nova Scotia, 1783–1895*, ed. Frank Stanley Boyd Jr. (1976).

Whitfield, Harvey Amani. *Blacks on the Border: The Black Refugees in British North America, 1815–1860* (2006).

HARVEY AMANI WHITFIELD

Preston, William Everett "Billy" (2 Sept. 1946– 6 June 2006), rhythm and blues and rock musician, was born in Houston, Texas. As a youngster he relocated to Los Angeles, California, in 1949, when his mother, Robbie Preston Williams, assumed the position of organist for the Victory Baptist Church. His family included one sister, Gwen Gooden, and two half sisters, Lettie Preston and Rodena Williams. Information about his father is unavailable. Preston attended Athens

Elementary School, John Muir Junior High School, and Dorsey High School in Los Angeles. His earliest musical efforts were at preschool age, sitting on his mother's lap playing the organ, and by age ten he was playing organ for MAHALIA JACKSON. He played a young W. C. HANDY in the 1958 film *St. Louis Blues*. In the early 1960s Preston played organ for the famed tent revivalist A. A. Allen, but he soon moved into secular music, meeting and touring with SAM COOKE, LITTLE RICHARD, and RAY CHARLES. Preston also appeared on the 1960s television show *Shindig!*

Preston began playing organ and electric piano with other stars of popular music in addition to releasing his own solo albums. His signature instruments were the Hammond B-3 organ and later the ARP synthesizer. His solo recordings included dozens of singles and albums, either in collaborations or under his own name, beginning with *Sixteen Year Old Soul* (1963), *The Most Exciting Organ Ever* (1965), and *The Wildest Organ in Town!* (1966). A momentous encounter with the Beatles (John Lennon, Paul McCartney, George Harrison, and Ringo Starr) in 1963 in Germany transformed Preston's life and launched him into international stardom (and probably also led to his self-destructive habits later on). A religious man, Preston wrote in the liner notes to his 1968 album *That's the Way God Planned It*, "You don't know how glad I am that God laid his hands on me." Other notes provided for the album claimed that Preston was "young and beautiful and kind and he sings and plays like the son of God" (Billy Preston, *That's the Way God Planned It*, liner notes, 1968).

Preston was commonly known as "the fifth Beatle," and as a friend of both Harrison and Lennon, he seems to have helped hold that band together as relations among the four principal Beatles became strained. He played keyboards on their later albums, 1968's *The Beatles* (also known as the *White Album*), 1969's *Abbey Road*, and 1970's *Let It Be*. Fans of 1960s and 1970s music also remember him for "That's the Way God Planned It" (previously number 62 on the 1969 Billboard Pop Singles chart), which he performed in 1971 at Madison Square Garden in New York City during Harrison's Concert for Bangladesh. The resulting album, *The Concert for Bangladesh* (1971), contains Preston's stirring performance and was followed by a concert film of the same name in 1972. Preston was immortalized for moviegoing fans of rock music in the dance he performed in the middle of his song. The benefit performances raised about $243,500 for relief in Bangladesh, which was plagued by political turmoil and dangerous weather.

During the early 1970s Preston also played keyboards for the Rolling Stones on some of the group's most popular albums, *Sticky Fingers* (1971), *Exile on Main Street* (1972), and *Goat's Head Soup* (1973). He also toured with the group several times. It seems likely that being in an environment in which substance abuse was common contributed to Preston's problems with alcohol, drugs, and miscellaneous illegal activities.

Several of Preston's solo hits, such as "Outa-Space" (1972), "Will It Go Round in Circles" (1973), and "Nothing from Nothing" (1974), had enduring crossover appeal in funk, soul, and popular music, loved by adults and children alike. A list of the most notable musicians with whom Preston played in the 1960s and 1970s includes the Everly Brothers, the Beatles, the Rolling Stones, ARETHA FRANKLIN, Eric Clapton, Merry Clayton, Stephen Stills, Delaney and Bonnie, Martha Reeves, SLY STONE, GLADYS KNIGHT, LUTHER VANDROSS, and Joe Cocker. Cocker scored one of the biggest hits of his career in 1975 with "You Are So Beautiful," a song that Preston co-wrote in 1973 with his longtime collaborator Bruce Fischer. In Preston's solo efforts, his own backup band included luminaries such as Harrison, Keith Richards (of the Rolling Stones), and Clapton and Ginger Baker (of Cream). Preston also performed the title track in the soundtrack of the 1972 Jim Brown film *Slaughter*. In 1975 Preston was a musical guest in the first episode of the classic television show *Saturday Night Live*. Image was important in the popular culture of the 1960s and 1970s, and Preston stepped up memorably with a huge Afro and sequined outfits. In later years he sported a more subdued fade or "short" cut.

But Preston's joy and great accomplishments were intermingled with sadness and troubles. In the early 1980s, as his life began to unravel, he performed with Syreeta Wright, the former wife of STEVIE WONDER. The duo charted with several songs, most notably in 1980 "With You I'm Born Again." Around this time Preston was using both cocaine and alcohol, and he was widely considered an addict in the 1980s. He was accused of sexual transgressions, such as showing a teenaged boy pornographic images and leading the youngster into obscene acts. He was charged with assault with a deadly weapon in the early 1990s. The court sentenced him to rehabilitation and probation in 1992, but he tested positive for cocaine, which was a violation of the terms of his probation, in 1997. He was then sentenced to serve three years in prison. An additional sentence of one year was added in 1998 after he admitted to insurance fraud involving a number of fires, burglaries, and automobile accidents.

In the early twenty-first century Preston conducted the choir at Los Angeles's Brookins African Methodist Episcopal Community Church and lived with his elderly mother and other family members. He moved to Arizona several years before his death. The conditions that led to his demise are generally believed to have been caused by years of substance abuse. After his death, his legacy and memory were guarded by his manager and friend, Joyce Moore, the wife of the rhythm and blues singer Samuel Moore ("Sam" of Sam and Dave). Preston's last collaborations were with Neil Diamond and the Red Hot Chili Peppers. Even if Preston himself abandoned purely spiritual music, his influence was still felt in early twenty-first-century religious music, particularly in Pentecostal gospel performances, in which survive his energetic style of keyboard playing and his style of singing that combined elements of hymns, soul, and rock.

Preston died in Scottsdale, Arizona, four years after receiving a kidney transplant in an effort to stave off kidney failure. The immediate cause of his death was pericarditis. His grave is in Inglewood Park Cemetery, Inglewood, California.

FURTHER READING

Preston, Billy. *Billy Preston in Concert (That's the Way God Planned It)* (1973).

"Billy Preston About His Touring with the Rolling Stones," *Jet* (11 Sept. 1975).

Harrington, Richard. "'Fifth Beatle' Billy Preston Made the Greats Even Greater," *Washington Post* (8 June 2006).

JOHN DANIEL SAILLANT

Price, Florence B. (9 Apr. 1887–3 June 1953), composer and instrumentalist, was born Florence Beatrice Smith in Little Rock, Arkansas, the daughter of James H. Smith, a dentist, and Florence Gulliver. Besides working as a dentist, her father was also an amateur novelist, painter, and inventor. Her mother, who had been an elementary school teacher in Indianapolis, had been trained in music and provided her daughter's earliest musical instruction. Price attended the black schools of Little Rock, where she was a classmate of WILLIAM GRANT STILL, who would later become the leading black American composer of the twentieth century.

Florence B. Price was one of the first African American women composers to achieve widespread recognition. (Moorland-Spingarn Research Center.)

Price graduated high school at the age of fourteen and enrolled in the New England Conservatory of Music in Boston. Whereas racial tensions were increasing in Little Rock, the climate at the conservatory was favorable to black students, and George W. Chadwick, the director of the school and a composer of note, had a considerable interest in black musical materials. In 1906 Price graduated with a degree in Piano Pedagogy and Organ Performance. She then returned to Arkansas and taught at the Cotton Plant-Arkadelphia Academy for a year and then at Shorter College in North Little Rock for the next three years.

In 1910 Price began a promising academic career at Clark University in Atlanta as head of the music department, but she left the post in 1912 to marry Thomas J. Price, a rising Little Rock attorney; they had three children. While raising the children, Price taught music privately and composed, twice submitting prize-winning works to *Opportunity* magazine's Holstein competition.

Increasing racial tensions in Little Rock, climaxed by a lynching in a black middle-class neighborhood, led the Price family to move to Chicago in 1927. There Price continued her composition studies at a number of schools, among them the Chicago Musical College, the American Conservatory of Music, and the University of Chicago. She also continued to give organ and piano performances and instruction and to compose. By 1928 her works were being published by G. Schirmer and the McKinley Company, and her pieces for beginning piano students were in great demand.

During the 1930s Price's reputation as a composer and performer grew rapidly in the Chicago area. In 1932 she was awarded the first-place prize in the Wanamaker competition for her Symphony in E Minor, having won three other Wanamaker awards that year, plus an honorable mention the year before. In addition, one of her composition students, MARGARET BONDS, also received a prize in 1932.

At Chicago's Century of Progress Exposition in 1933, Price's Symphony in E Minor was performed by Frederick A. Stock, leading the Chicago Symphony Orchestra. Later her symphonic compositions were played by orchestras in Detroit, Pittsburgh, and New York. In 1934 she appeared as a piano soloist with the Chicago Women's Symphony, playing her own Concerto in F Minor.

Price remained an active organist in Chicago, and her organ compositions were published by Lorenz, Summy, and Galaxy. She also continued to publish piano pieces and began to add choral works, spiritual arrangements, and songs to her catalog. Several well-known black concert singers performed Price's songs, notably MARIAN ANDERSON, who was especially fond of "My Soul's Been Anchored in the Lord" and a setting of LANGSTON HUGHES's poem "Songs to a Dark Virgin." In later years her songs were her best-known compositions and were included in anthologies such as *Art Songs by Black American Composers* (1977) and *Art Songs by American Women Composers* (1994).

After her husband's death in the early 1940s, Price continued her active career as a teacher, performer, and composer for another decade. She wrote the Second Violin Concerto in 1952 and the Suite of Negro Dances in 1953, which was performed on a television Pops concert by Chicago Symphony members. She died in Chicago. In 1964 a Chicago elementary school was named in her honor.

For many years Florence Price was primarily known as the first black woman to compose a work performed by a major symphony orchestra. A full appreciation of her work was hampered during this period by the fact that many of her compositions remained unpublished. In addition, a number of the larger works had been lost. Until the early 1970s Price was almost unknown outside of Chicago, but with the increasing emphasis on women's and multicultural studies, she has begun to receive recognition as one of the major African American women composers. Price's compositional style combines black folk idioms with late nineteenth-century emphasis on lyricism and chromatically altered tonality. During the avant-garde 1950s and 1960s her music fell out of fashion, but then attracted more interest in the neo-Romantic climate of the following decades. Her songs and spiritual arrangements came to be particularly favored by performers for the compelling rhythmic, melodic, and harmonic aspects of her text setting.

FURTHER READING

Price's papers are held by the University of Arkansas at Fayetteville.

Jackson, Barbara Garvey. "Florence Price, Composer," *The Black Perspective in Music* 5 (Spring 1977).

Walker-Hill, Helen. *From Spirituals to Symphonies: African-American Women Composers and Their Music* (2002).

This entry is taken from the *American National Biography* and is published here with the permission of the American Council of Learned Societies.

RUTH C. FRIEDBERG

Price, George Washington, Jr. (Mar. 1845?–22 Oct. 1901), businessman, public official, and state legislator, was born in North Carolina, the oldest of at least six children born to Rev. George W. Price, Sr., and Eliza Price. The exact date and location of his birth are not certain, nor is his birth status as free or enslaved. Little is known of his early life or education before the Civil War, although unconfirmed accounts list him as a sailor in the Union navy during the conflict.

Price's father was a popular Methodist clergyman in Wilmington, North Carolina, a presiding elder in the African Methodist Episcopal Zion (AMEZ) Church who abruptly left that denomination in 1871 for the newly formed Colored Methodist Episcopal (CME) Church, taking his Wilmington congregation and several other churches with him. As early as 1865, the younger Price had also moved to Wilmington, where he served as an organizer of the state's Colored Convention of 1865 and was employed as a speaker by the Republican Congressional Committee in 1867. He quickly became active in Republican politics in New Hanover County, and was elected in 1868 to the Wilmington city board of aldermen while serving as both a justice of the peace and a county assessor.

In March 1868 Price was elected as one of three Republican members representing the predominantly black county in the North Carolina House of Representatives. Price served as a House member in two sessions of the General Assembly, from 1868 to 1869, and again from 1869 to 1870, appointed to the Committee on Military Affairs during both sessions. Like his colleague John Leary of Fayetteville, Price took the unpopular position of favoring, albeit unsuccessfully, the immediate restoration of political rights to former Confederate sympathizers. Now that his race's political rights were safe, he professed to believe in equity, not punishment.

In 1870 Price was elected as one of two state senators from the Thirteenth District (New Hanover County), along with Charles W. McClammy. During the new General Assembly, which met from 1870 to 1871 and again, in extra session, from 1871 to 1872, Price served on the Senate Committee on Education. But his earlier belief that African American political rights were safe was now severely tested, as Democrats impeached and removed Republican governor William W. Holden from office and began rolling back gains made by African American voters by such means as shifting county boundaries and amending city charters.

After House Republicans openly proposed the expulsion of three Ku Klux Klan members from both houses of the General Assembly in November 1871, the House defeated the resolution. But when Senator. Price rose to read a similar request on the floor of the Senate, he was ordered to halt by the Senate leadership, on grounds that the memorial's language was deemed disrespectful and libelous. Subsequent attempts to offer official rewards for the murderers of three African American activists were also rejected.

Price left the legislature in 1872, and never sought statewide office again, although he held a number of posts in New Hanover County, including membership in the local school committee for Federal Point Township, city marshal, and justice of the peace. During the 1870s he served as president of the Fourth Ward Republican Club in Wilmington.

A gifted orator, Price frequently lectured on the subject of education, both in Wilmington and other cities, and he attended an 1877 statewide convention of black politicians and educators. He retained strong interest in his race's political rights and in the Republican Party, serving as a delegate from the Third Congressional District to the Republican National Convention in Chicago in 1880, at which James A. Garfield was nominated for president. Following Garfield's inauguration, Price led an African American delegation to Washington, D.C., in March 1881 to ask the new president to appoint James H. Harris as Raleigh's new postmaster, succeeding former Governor Holden after eight years in the position.

The delegation failed to secure its goal, but Price persisted in his efforts, and he was soon prominent in his support for a statewide convention in May of African Americans interested in securing federal appointments under the new administration. He even proposed that a second delegation visit the White House in June, but Garfield's assassination in July and subsequent death ended the drive. Price turned his attention to elective offices, and a year later he was among the featured speakers at a Goldsboro, North Carolina, convention intended to spur interest among African American candidates for state and local office in the 1882 election.

In 1885, he was invited by the General Assembly to address a Raleigh audience on "The Negro of the South—-His Future Status as a Political Factor on the Body Politic of the Country," following the election of Democrat Grover Cleveland to the U. S. presidency. During Cleveland's first administration, Price was appointed in 1887 as a special U. S. customs inspector in Wilmington, his final public office.

Having worked for years as a contractor, builder, and plasterer, he now devoted most of his energies to a series of business ventures, including a real estate firm and a secondhand furniture and appliance store, and eventually worked as an auctioneer in the 1890s. Like his father, Price was also active in fraternal affairs, serving as a member of the Giblem Masonic Lodge, Grand Lodge of Colored Masons in North Carolina, and as an officer in the Zeruabel Royal Arch Chapter No. 14.

Price was married twice. His first wife, Amelia Nelson (b. 1846), died sometime after 1870. His second wife was Sophie A. Sadgwar (b. 1847) of Wilmington, a daughter of David E. Sadgwar. By his second marriage, Price had at least two children, including a daughter, Fanny, and a son, William, both of whom appear to have died young. Sophie Price died of natural causes in 1898.

Three years later, George Price died in a mysterious train accident in Wilmington, an apparent victim of his own haste. He attempted to cross the tracks between two cars of a shifting freight train, which began to move before Price could exit the coupling, and he fell beneath the train's wheels. A conductor heard Price's screams, but was unable to save him. Price's funeral, held days later in Wilmington's Chestnut Street Presbyterian Church, attracted a large crowd of mourners.

FURTHER READING

Foner, Eric. *Freedom's Lawmakers: A Directory of Black Officeholders During Reconstruction* (1993).

Reaves, William M. *"Strength Through Struggle": The Chronological and Historical Record of the African-American Community in Wilmington, North Carolina, 1865–1950* (1998).

Obituary: Wilmington *Morning Star*, 24 Oct. 1901.

BENJAMIN R. JUSTESEN

Price, Hugh Bernard (22 Nov. 1941–), lawyer, journalist, philanthropist, and activist, was born in Washington, D.C., the son of Charlotte Schuster and Kline Price, a physician. Dr. Kline Price raised his middle-class family in close relationship to Howard University where he practiced medicine. Hugh began his primary schooling at Blanche K. Bruce Elementary School during segregation, later to finish in the desegregated Coolidge High School. Price received his bachelor's degree in 1963 from Amherst College, where he was a member of Alpha Phi Alpha fraternity. Also in 1963, Price married Marilyn Lloyd, Washington, D.C., resident and daughter of Ruth Lloyd and Dr. Sterling Lloyd, a professor of anatomy at Howard University's medical school. Price and his wife had three daughters—Lauren, Janeen, and Traer. The couple moved to New Haven, Connecticut, where Price attended law school at Yale University until his graduation in 1966. During his years in law school at Yale, Price became involved with urban issues in the New Haven community.

In 1966 he served as an attorney with the New Haven Legal Assistance Association providing services to low-income clients. In 1968 Price led the Black Coalition of New Haven as its first executive director. Although he did not become an activist in the organized civil rights movement of the 1960s, he did focus his attention on issues related to urban poverty. In 1970 Price continued his work with issues of inner-city poverty as an attorney with Cogen, Holt, & Associates, an urban-affairs law firm in New Haven. During this time he cooperated with the New Haven governmental agencies and learned the intricacies of public affairs as he advocated for his clients. This knowledge prepared him to serve as the City of New Haven's human resources administrator in 1977.

A year later, in 1978, Price and his family moved to New York City, where he served as an editorial writer for the *New York Times*. Price wrote primarily on issues of domestic policy, such as zoning regulations, education, and other civil issues specifically affecting the urban poor. In 1982 Price moved from newspaper journalism to television at New York City's WNET-TV. During his six-year stint with WNET-TV Price served as senior vice president and director of WNET's production center. In 1988 Price shifted to a more overtly philanthropic position as vice president of the Rockefeller Foundation, a global, knowledge-based organization that funds projects and research devoted to the well-being of mankind, especially the poor and those traditionally excluded from opportunities. Price worked specifically with the Special Initiatives and Explorations grant fund and led the foundation in providing opportunities for minorities through urban school reform and equal opportunity projects. His six-year tenure with the Rockefeller Foundation provided the bedrock for his most notable accomplishment—presidency of the National Urban League.

The National Urban League formed officially in 1910 as the Committee on Urban Conditions among Negroes. Focused on mobilizing African Americans into the economic and social mainstream of America, it is the oldest and largest civil rights organization of its kind. In 1994 Price was chosen to assume leadership of the National Urban League as the organization's president and chief executive officer. The 1990s were a turbulent period for African Americans; e-globalization affected the United States and international economies, and a national political conservative backlash threatened the gains of the civil rights movement. As a result, the National Urban League's popularity and financial stability waned. Price's selection as president of the organization was met with some resistance because of his low-profile in the civil rights movement. However, his experience with law, community development, advocacy, and financial structuring equipped Price to be the most capable leader for the challenges faced by the National Urban League in 1994.

Price's leadership of the National Urban League centered on three policy areas: education and youth development, economic empowerment, and inclusionary programs such as affirmative action.

He believed that to gain equal access to society's benefits, those traditionally denied such access must gain economic power and pursue quality education advocated three ingredients for attaining equal access: He believed, too, that society had a responsibility to show compassion for the most oppressed. In 1997 he instituted the "Campaign for African American Achievement," a network of churches, fraternities, sororities, civic associations, and professional organizations that offered support for the educational growth of African American youth. The Campaign targeted the infrastructures in communities, which affected youth and sought to ensure the health of those infrastructures for developing youth physically, mentally, spiritually, and emotionally. Price developed the National Achiever's Society, Doing the Right Thing recognition, and the National Urban League's Scholarship Program under the umbrella of the Campaign for African American Achievement. During this time, Price also published *Achievement Matters: Getting Your Child the Best Education Possible*, which outlined the tenets and strategies of the Campaign for African American Achievement. Price also established the Institute of Opportunity and Equality, which conducted research on the state of urban social and civic services. He also resurrected publication of *Opportunity*, the journal of the National Urban League. Price notably stabilized and advanced the financial status of the National Urban League by tripling its endowment and restoring its strength as an organization. His time as president ended in 2003. Price maintained affiliation with many other organizations and corporations. He served on the boards of Metropolitan Life Insurance Company, Bell Atlantic, Sears Roebuck & Company, Educational Testing Service, and the Urban Institute. Price retired in 2005.

FURTHER READING

Parris, Guichard. *Blacks in the City: A History of the National Urban League* (1971).

Price, Hugh Bernard. *Achievement Matters: Getting Your Child the Best Education Possible* (2002).

Price, Hugh Bernard. *Destination: The American Dream* (2001).

SARA BAGBY

Price, Joseph Charles (10 Feb. 1854–25 Oct. 1893), public orator, college president, philosopher, and clergyman, was born Joseph Charles Dozier in Elizabeth City, North Carolina, to Emily Pailin, a freeborn woman, and Charles Dozier, a former slave and ship carpenter. While Joseph was a young boy, Dozier moved away to find work in Baltimore, Maryland, at a shipyard. Joseph's mother later married David Price, and Price adopted Joseph as his own son. In 1863 the Price family moved to New Bern, North Carolina, which was controlled by federal troops at the time. While in New Bern, Joseph attended St. Andrews Chapel, a parochial school, and he attended the Lowell Normal School of New Bern in 1866. Beginning in 1871 he began teaching in Wilson, North Carolina, where he stayed for the next four years. He attended Shaw University in Raleigh in 1873 for a brief period. In 1875 he transferred to Lincoln University in Pennsylvania. While at Lincoln, he became acquainted with the oratory of FREDERICK DOUGLASS and others. Price won oratorical prizes in his freshman and junior years and was valedictorian of his class in 1879.

That year Congressman JOHN A. HYMAN, who represented New Bern, offered Price a clerkship in the Department of the Treasury in Washington, D.C., with an annual salary of $1,200. Price rejected the offer, preferring to complete his college studies. By 1880 he had been ordained as an elder in the African Methodist Episcopal Zion (AMEZ) Church. During his senior year in college Price studied theology, and he graduated from the Theology Department in 1881.

In 1881 the AMEZ Church chose Price to serve as a delegate to the Ecumenical Conference of Methodism held in London, England. There he was introduced to the great leaders of all branches of Methodism, and he earned renown as one of the premier orators of African American Methodism. He lectured throughout Europe and the British Isles on the condition of the American Negro and black Methodism, perfecting his signature style of oration, called the "Pricean" method. His popularity was such that the *London Times* named Price one of the seven greatest orators in the world.

In 1882 the board of trustees of the AMEZ-affiliated Livingstone College in Salisbury, North Carolina, elected Price president. That fall the school opened with five students in a two-story building and forty acres of land; by the end of the year it had one new building and ninety-three students. Under Price's leadership, Livingstone College excelled in educating its students in liberal arts, theology, scientific training, political science, and social responsibility. Students not only learned in the classroom but also through practical experience, working in road building, millinery, printing, carpentry, shoemaking, dressmaking, agricultural management, broom making, brick masonry, and the domestic sciences. Although he was only twenty-eight years old when he became president of Livingstone College, Price rapidly attained regional and national prominence as a leader. His contemporary, W. E. B. DuBois, remarked, "The star of achievement to which Joseph Charles Price a black boy of those days hitched his wagon was the founding of a school for colored youth a sort of black Harvard" (DuBois, 224).

Price traveled widely. In Europe he raised more than $10,000 for Livingstone College, and he returned repeatedly to New England and California to interest philanthropists in his life's work. In 1882 he married Jennie Smallwood of Beaufort, North Carolina. The couple had five children, William, Louise, Alma, Joseph, and Josephine

Price took full advantage of meeting the leading African American leaders of the day to help gain more exposure for Livingstone College. In 1883 the Bethel Literary Society of Washington, D.C., arranged a symposium that included Douglass, JOHN MERCER LANGSTON, FANNY JACKSON COPPIN, and Isaiah C. Wears, as well as Price. At that time Price was unknown except to a few personal friends from North Carolina and some former students of Lincoln University. However, as the historian JOHN W. CROMWELL noted, Price's more illustrious fellow speakers soon came to appreciate his gifts as an orator. "When he arose and uttered his first sentence," Cromwell noted, "the effect was electrical" (Cromwell, 174). Many of Price's speeches were in support of the temperance movement, a religious effort to support laws against liquor consumption and encourage the prevention of alcoholism in the community.

In 1885 Price visited the West Coast and succeeded in raising nearly $9,000 for Livingstone College, which helped establish two dormitories on the college campus. These donors that Price brought to the aid of Livingstone College—Collis P. Huntington, William E. Dodge, and Leland Stanford—were among the greatest businessmen and philanthropists of the nineteenth century. Price was also involved in politics and in 1885 became a widely acknowledged leader, holding the offices of president of the Afro-American League and the North Carolina State Teachers Association and chairman of the African Methodist Episcopal and AMEZ Church Commission, and he was appointed commissioner general of the Grand Southern Exposition at the World's Columbian Exposition in Chicago in 1893, which marked the four hundredth anniversary of the exploration of the New World by Christopher Columbus and the promotion of humans, science, industry, culture, and history since that historic event.

Although most African Americans in North Carolina supported the Republican Party, Price urged African Americans to pursue independence in politics. He encouraged blacks to forge better links with the Democratic Party, and he supported the presidential candidacy of the Democrat Grover Cleveland. In 1888 Cleveland offered Price the post of minister resident and consul general of the United States to Liberia, but he declined in order to focus his attention on Livingstone College. At a time when many southern states were developing a range of methods to disfranchise African Americans, Price supported literacy tests in 1890 to ensure that voters of both races were qualified.

On 25 October 1893, at the age of thirty-nine, Price died of Bright's disease in Salisbury, North Carolina. He was given the largest funeral Salisbury had ever seen, attended by a crowd of over one thousand people, both blacks and whites. In attendance were the mayor of Salisbury, prominent educators, businesspeople, and church leaders from all over the world. In addition to the Price Administration Building and his tomb on the Livingstone College campus, two facilities were built in Salisbury honoring him, Price High School (1932) and the Price American Legion Post (1949).

FURTHER READING
A significant amount of information on Price is in the Special Collections and Archives at Livingstone College in Salisbury, North Carolina, and the North Carolina State Archives in Raleigh.

Cromwell, John W. *The Negro in American History* (1914).

Crow, Jeffrey J. *A History of African Americans in North Carolina* (2002).

DuBois, W. E. B. "The Ruling Passion: An Estimate of Joseph C. Price," *The Crisis* (Mar. 1922).

Meier, August. *Negro Thought in America, 1880–1915: Racial Ideologies in the Age of Booker T. Washington* (1963).

Walls, William J. *The African Methodist Episcopal Zion Church: Reality of the Black Church* (1974).

Walls, William J. *Joseph Charles Price, Educator and Race Leader* (1943).

JOY G. KINARD

Price, Leontyne (10 Feb. 1927–), opera singer, was born Mary Violet Leontine Price in Laurel, Mississippi, one of two children of James Anthony

Leontyne Price in costume for her leading role in Samuel Barber's *Antony and Cleopatra* at the Metropolitan Opera in New York in 1966.

Price, who worked in the local sawmills, and Katherine Baker, a popular Laurel midwife. Katherine nurtured her daughter's talent by enrolling her in piano lessons at age three and by encouraging her to sing in church and community events. Listening to recordings at home and attending concerts, including a memorable performance by MARIAN ANDERSON, enlarged Price's passion for music. In 1944 she graduated from Oak Park Vocational High School and received a scholarship to Wilberforce College in Ohio. Although she had planned a career in music education, Price's vocal gifts attracted such attention that she changed her major to voice, graduating with a B.A. in 1948.

After graduating, Price enrolled at the Juilliard School of Music in New York City, which she attended on a four-year scholarship. While in her senior year at Wilberforce, she had performed on the same program as PAUL ROBESON. Wanting to help the young singer, Robeson helped her pay for Juilliard by giving a fund-raising concert for the Leontyne Price Fund, established by her professors. Living in New York enabled the young singer to attend the Metropolitan Opera, exposing her to the world's finest operatic productions. When she sang the part of Mistress Ford in Verdi's *Falstaff* in a Juilliard opera workshop, her talent so impressed the composer Virgil Thomson that he cast her in the revival of his all-black American classic, *Four Saints in Three Acts* (1934), which was staged in New York and Paris in 1952.

Price made her triumphant international debut as Bess in Robert Breen's revival of George Gershwin's dramatic masterpiece *Porgy and Bess*. Abandoning plans to study in Europe on a Fulbright Fellowship, Price accepted the starring role in the touring production which opened in Dallas in June 1952 and continued in Chicago, Pittsburgh, and Washington, D.C., where President Truman attended the performance, and on to several major European cities. In March 1953 the show opened at New York's Ziegfeld Theatre, where it continued for 304 performances. For a young singer in her mid-twenties, the applause and accolades were stunning. She was "a Bess of vocal glory" (Hollis Alpert, *The Life and Times of* Porgy and Bess [1990], 155), and critics praised her imaginative interpretation and her focused soprano voice. As her repertoire expanded to include the operas of Mozart, Orff, Massenet, Verdi, and others, Price's glamorous demeanor came to the fore. As one observer noted, she "literally spilled charm over the footlight" (Harrison).

Price made history when in 1955 she became the first black prima donna to appear in a major production of opera on television. Despite some strenuous objections and cancellations by several local affiliates, Price sang the lead in Puccini's *Tosca* on NBC. The following year, she appeared on the air as Pamina in Mozart's *Die Zauberflöte*. In September 1957 she thoroughly enchanted audiences at the San Francisco Opera and won high acclaim for her first appearance in a staged opera with a major company when she performed as the devout Madame Lidoine in Poulenc's *Dialogues of the Carmelites*. When she sang Verdi's *Aïda* under Herbert von Karajan at the Vienna State Opera in 1958, a felicitous association with the noted conductor brought her engagements in such important European venues as the Verona Arena, the Salzburg Festival, and London's Covent Garden.

The Ethiopian princess in *Aïda* has long been a signature role for Price. When she sang *Aïda* at La Scala in 1960, she was hailed as the quintessential Verdi soprano: "Our great Verdi would have found her the ideal" (Walsh, 67). Indeed, the monumental *Requiem* and other works by Verdi that Price has sung with the Metropolitan Opera, such as *Aïda, La Forza del Destino, Ernani*, and *Un Ballo in Maschera*, are among the soprano's most compelling showpieces. As Amelia in *Un Ballo in Maschera*, her lush *lyrico spinto* (a lyric soprano with dramatic power) dazzled audiences in the standing-room-only house. By the time Price left the Metropolitan Opera in *Aïda* in 1985, she had sung the role at the Met more than forty-two times.

Price made her debut with the Metropolitan Opera in Verdi's *Il Trovatore* on 27 January 1961, receiving a forty-five-minute standing ovation. "As Leonora," wrote Ronald Eyer, "Leontyne Price was a sensational success….The lovely fast vibrato which is characteristic of her voice gave liquidity and warmth to the soaring line; her coloratura was of extraordinary flexibility and lightness of touch for so large a voice" (*New York Herald Tribune*, 28 Jan. 1961). Price's other Metropolitan Opera roles have included Anna in Mozart's *Don Giovanni*, Cio-Cio-San in Puccini's *Madama Butterfly*, and the Prima Donna/Ariadne in Strauss's *Ariadne auf Naxos*. Few, however, will forget her luminous tones and beautifully shaped phrases when she sang her last *Il Trovatore* at the Met in 1982, at age fifty-five.

Perhaps the strongest character Price ever played was that of Cleopatra in Samuel Barber's *Antony and Cleopatra*. The opera, commissioned by the Metropolitan Opera for the opening of its new $50 million house at Lincoln Center, was given its premiere on 16 September 1966 with Thomas Schippers conducting. Although her interpretation of the character was spellbinding and her vocal powers in finest form, Price had to rise to the challenges of Franco Zeffirelli's overeffulgent staging and an electrical upset that forced Cleopatra to make her entrance in total darkness. "I was locked in the pyramid at the first aria," Price recounted. "There was no way in the world I could make that cue. I was to be dressed in the pyramid for the next scene, and I simply said 'Zip this one back up, whether it fits or not. I'll keep singing and just go out'" (Leontyne Price in an interview with Peter Dickinson, BBC broadcast, "Samuel Barber Retrospective," 23 Jan. 1982). And so she did.

Few artists have received so many distinguished honors from U.S. presidents as Price. On 4 July 1964 Lyndon Johnson awarded the Presidential Medal of Freedom to both Price and the American composer Aaron Copland. They became the first musicians to receive the distinguished award, created by John F. Kennedy shortly before he died. Price also made history when she performed in the first nationally televised concert series from the White House, initiated by President Carter in 1978. On 26 March 1979 the soprano's majestic interpretation of "Pace, pace, mio Dio," from *La Forza del Destino*, for the signing of the Israeli–Egyptian peace treaty at the White House moved all who heard her. She also sang for the White House ceremonies welcoming Pope John Paul II, and in 1980 she was a recipient of the Kennedy Center Honors for a lifetime achievement in the arts. Price received the NAACP's Spingarn Medal in 1965.

Price was one of the first African American prima donnas to appear regularly on the world's great opera stages. In her later years she sang less in opera and more in recitals, focusing on spirituals, Broadway tunes, hymns, and art songs. For her many fine recordings she received at least eighteen Grammy Awards. Married on 31 August 1952 to the baritone WILLIAM WARFIELD (her costar in *Porgy and Bess*), Price was divorced in 1973. She has long lived in Greenwich Village in Manhattan, giving master classes and enjoying the picturesque charm of her federal-style home. With her vocal powers and distinguished presence, Leontyne Price has drawn international acclaim. Her fortitude and achievements have become models not only for young black singers but also for aspiring artists everywhere.

FURTHER READING

Lyon, Hugh Lee. *Leontyne Price: Highlights of a Prima Donna* (1973).

Steane, J. B. *Divas of the Century, Vol. III* (2000).

Story, Rosalyn M. *And So I Sing: African-American Divas of Opera and Concert* (1990).

DISCOGRAPHY

The Essential Leontyne Price (BMG Classics).

ELISE K. KIRK

Price, Lloyd (9 Mar 1933–), rhythm and blues singer and songwriter, was born Lloyd Price in Kenner, Louisiana, a suburb of New Orleans, the eighth of eleven children of Louis Price and Beatrice Price. His parents owned and operated a "fish fry" restaurant with a jukebox that young Price enjoyed dancing to for patrons. Price sang gospel in his church choir and sang lead vocals in the high school quintet formed with his younger brother Leo. He played the trumpet and later took interest in the piano. Price became know for writing commercials and jingles for the New Orleans radio station WBOK.

Upon graduating he assumed a position at Moisant Field; now Louis Armstrong International Airport, earning twenty-six dollars a week. One evening Price was plucking eight-bar blues at the piano in a bar his brother owned. He was improvising a song using an expression, "Lawdy Miss Clawdy," made popular by the New Orleans disc jockey Okey Dokey Smith, similar to exclaiming "Oh my goodness!" David Bartholomew, who had produced albums for the artists Roy Brown and FATS DOMINO, was impressed and asked Price if he would be interested in making a record. Early 1952 Price performed for the Specialty Records producer

Art Rupe and on 13 March 1952 Price recorded "Lawdy Miss Clawdy" with a band that included Fats Domino on the piano; the single remained number one on the R&B charts for seven weeks; Elvis Presley later covered the song but did not receive the same acclaim for his rendition. Having received documents drafting him into the Korean War together with his band, Price improvised a song for the B-side of the record entitled "Mailman Blues." He was hired at the Dew Drop Inn in New Orleans to perform for $50 dollars a day, a salary that grew as his record got bigger, ranking number one on the R&B charts, eventually reaching $2,500 a day. Price soon recorded four more songs for Specialty that topped the R&B charts; including, "Oooh, Oooh, Oooh," "Ain't It a Shame," "Tell Me Pretty Baby," and "Restless Heart." Although Rupe hired a lawyer to keep Price out of the army, eventually Price served twenty-three months and eleven days on assignments in Korea and the Far East and finally as a valet to entertainers performing for the military.

Price returned to the United States from the armed forces in 1954 and in 1956 recorded "What's the Matter Now?" for Specialty Records. His contract was not renewed so he moved to Washington, D.C., and formed Kent Record Company with the promoter Hal Logan and Bill Boskent, a friend from New Orleans. Through KRC he retained control of his distribution rights and leased his material to ABC-Paramount. He recorded the ballad "Just Because," which was released on ABC-Paramount. In 1959, ABC-Paramount released three Price hits that went straight to number one on the R&B and Pop charts in the United States and ranked high in the U.K: "Stagger Lee,"—about the legendary folk hero, STAGOLEE—"Personality," and "I'm Gonna Get Married."

Price also helped introduce the flamboyant rock and roller LITTLE RICHARD into the recording industry in the 1950s; Little Richard also cowrote a song with Price's brother Leo. He continued to record hit records for ABC-Paramount until 1962, when he again partnered with Logan to form Double L Records and signed artist WILSON PICKETT. Price covered the song "Misty" for his new label, his first single in three years to reach the top 100. In 1964 Price became the first African American to sign to white singer Roy Orbison's Monument label, and his song, "Billie Baby" ranked low at number eighty-four on the Pop charts. At the same time he was establishing a college scholarship foundation for African American youth. After Hal Logan was murdered in 1969, Price started a new label, Turntable, and opened a club by the same name in New York City. The same year he released "Bad Conditions," his final hit, which ranked at number twenty-one on the R&B charts.

In 1974 Lloyd partnered with the promoter DON KING for a three-day musical festival in Zaire (now the Democratic Republic of the Congo) featuring artists including ETTA JAMES, JAMES BROWN, and B. B. KING. The concert had initially been scheduled as a prelude to the famous "Rumble in The Jungle" boxing match between MUHAMMAD ALI and the heavyweight World Champion GEORGE FOREMAN, but an injury to Foreman delayed that bout for several weeks. Price had befriended the boxer MUHAMMAD ALI in the late 1950s, and in the early '70s introduced him to Don King, who was also an old friend of Price's

During the 1970s and 80s Price primarily made cameo appearances at clubs and on television, including *Midnight Special* on NBC. His major return to performing did not happen until 1993, when he toured with Jerry Lee Lewis, LITTLE RICHARD, and Gary "U.S." Bonds. Price invested in Icon Food Brands, which specializes in Southern-style food, or "soul food," which includes Lawdy Miss Clawdy food products.

In 1995 Lloyd Price Avenue was named for the artist in his hometown, Kenner, Louisiana, where they also hold an annual celebration, Lloyd Price Day. Also in 1998, he received the Pioneer Award from the Rhythm and Blues Foundation. Price was inducted into the Rock and Roll hall of Fame in 1998.

FURTHER READING

"Lloyd Price and Allen Toussaint among Recent Inductees into the Rock and Roll Hall of Fame." *Jet*, 2 Feb. 1998, 10.

Hauser, Thomas. *Muhammad Ali: His Life and Times* (1992).

Marcus, Greil. *Mystery Train: Images of America in Rock 'n' Roll*, 4th edition (1997).

SAFIYA DALILAH HOSKINS

Price, Nelly (fl. 1780–1790), free woman of color, property holder, and trader in Natchez, Mississippi, was most likely born in the mid-eighteenth century. Very little is known about the early life of Eleanor, or Nelly, as she was often called. She testified in a court document in 1786 that she had been in America for twenty years, although her country of origin is unclear. In the same petition, she was identified as an "English mulatto woman," suggesting perhaps she was born in the British-held West Indies or in the American colonies. As the Natchez District was under British rule from 1763 until 1779, it is possible that she was the daughter of an enslaved woman and a British man who subsequently manumitted his daughter and furnished her with property.

Most of the biographical details concerning her life surface in court documents from the Natchez District, which was controlled by the Spanish from 1779 to 1795. Eleanor used the courts to protect her liberties as a propertied free woman of color on at least seven different occasions spanning the period of eight years. Kimberly Hanger noted in her research of New Orleans's free women of color during the Spanish period that "many slave and free black women did not hesitate to use the legal system, along with kinship and patronage networks, to improve their status and material circumstances" (Hanger, 172–173). The majority of the cases she brought to the court's attention involved the recovery of money or property, usually from white individuals in Natchez.

In approximately 1782, Eleanor moved to a plantation in the Grand Gulf area in the Natchez District where she occupied herself in a great many pursuits. In addition to farming, she operated a trading network with settlers and local Native Americans. A few suits she initiated before the courts involved the repayment of goods or services. For instance, in 1782, she brought a suit against James Barfield and his wife for failing to recompense her for provisioning the couple with food while he was imprisoned for forty-eight days at the expense of $38. The court responded in Eleanor's favor and the Barfields were ordered to reimburse her. Another case she initiated was against John Stowers who owed her $4 in "sundries" and $2 for a plow she furnished him with.

Eleanor was also a healer of sorts as well as a midwife. In the Stowers case, in addition to merchandise, he owed her $8 for delivering an enslaved woman's baby. In that same year of 1783, she brought suit against another man, John Stanley, who did not fulfill his obligation to repay her for attending to a wounded Indian. He promised to pay her with a cow for her services. She sent a hired man to collect the cow, but he was only able to bring Eleanor three quarters of the meat, which she then sold to the local garrison.

Thus, she brought suit for the remainder of the value of the meat as well as the hire of the man that Stanley owed her.

As with many free women of color, Eleanor formed a partnership with a white man, Spaniard Miguel Lopez. This relationship commenced at approximately the time that she moved to Grand Gulf in 1782 and continued until Lopez's death in 1788. She lived with him as his housekeeper while remaining engaged in the abovementioned activities. As a woman of color, Eleanor was vulnerable to some challenges, such as physical abuse. Indeed, she used one act of violence committed against her to her advantage.

In 1788, she brought a claim against the estate of Lopez, who was then deceased. She petitioned the court to allow her to claim the house that she had constructed at her expense on a lot given to her by Lopez. She additionally requested to be paid out of the estate wages that she had accrued over the years, at $10 a month, and money that she had spent on her own to settle Lopez's accounts, all totaling $967.

Witnesses testified for her that in June of 1782 while Nelly and Miguel lived together they had quarreled and that Lopez beat her. One of the witnesses, Patrick Murphy, recounted that he encountered Eleanor crying and when pressed for an explanation as to why, she informed him that Lopez had beaten her. Eleanor subsequently moved out of his house and resided at another domicile in the city and refused to return even after Lopez entreated her to come back. She eventually did, but only on the promise that he would recompense her for her trouble at $10 a month. In spite of the fact that she endured a beating, she was able to recover from it and turned it to her gain.

During the course of this litigation, Eleanor produced five witnesses, all white men, who corroborated her story and agreed that Eleanor had been held in Lopez's employment for wages. Three of them confirmed that they heard Lopez say that her monthly wage was $10. William Irwin related that Lopez told him that a part of the house belonged to Nelly. It was not enough, however, as a few weeks after these proceedings took place the house was put up for sale by the court. On every Monday for three weeks, the house was exposed to sale, but no one bid on it. On 14 February 1789, five months after the house had initially been offered to the public, Nelly outbid Robert Abrams by a few dollars and purchased the house for $335. Unfortunately, she lost the house by June 1789 when she was not able to produce funds for it, and it defaulted to Abrams. Evidently, she had not been successful in her bid to be rewarded the wages and accounts from Lopez's estate. Eleanor disappears from the records after this case.

FURTHER READING

Hanger, Kimberly. "'The Fortunes of Women in America: Spanish New Orleans' Free Women of African Descent and Their Relations," in *Discovering the Women in Slavery: Emancipating Perspectives on the American Past*, ed. Patricia Morton (1996).

McBee, May Wilson. *Natchez Court Records 1767–1805*, in the May Wilson McBee Collection (1953).

NICOLE S. RIBIANSZKY

Pride, Charley (18 Mar. 1938–), country music singer, was born Charl Frank Pride to Mack Pride and Tessie B. Stewart, sharecroppers in Sledge, Mississippi, a small community in the Mississippi Delta county of Quitman. The fourth of eleven children, Charl's name was mistakenly changed to Charley on his birth certificate, and the name stuck. His upbringing in Sledge was in many ways similar to that of his parents and to the vast majority of African Americans who had labored in the cotton-growing Delta region since it had been cleared of its forests, hanging vines, and canebrakes and settled in the late nineteenth century. Young Charley grew up in a three-room, tin-and-wood shotgun shack, where the children slept four to a bed and picked cotton from an early age. Charley admired and loved, but as a child did not particularly like, his father, a deacon in the Baptist Church and a stern disciplinarian who frequently used a leather strap to punish his children. Charley's mother was more openly affectionate toward her son and tried to assure him that, though poor, he had much to be thankful for, notably that he was not blind and that he had all of his fingers.

Because he was a black child growing up in the Delta during the Depression, Charley's fingers were needed primarily to pick cotton, but he hated the drudgery of the work and soon found other uses for his hands: picking guitars and pitching baseballs. Modernity, in the form of the radio, came to the Delta in the 1940s, ending the region's relative isolation from the outside world. From the age of six Charley began listening to broadcasts of the *Grand Ole Opry* from WSM, the Nashville radio station that popularized what had been known as hillbilly music and was in the process of becoming

Charley Pride with a gold album he received from RCA records, in London, England, on 15 Feb. 1975. (AP Images.)

country music. He began by imitating the white country stars of the day, notably Hank Williams, Ernest Tubb, and Roy Acuff, and saved what little money he earned from picking cotton to purchase a guitar when he was fourteen. When his guitar was destroyed by a summer Delta thunderstorm, the young musician improvised by crafting instruments with cotton bailing wire until he had saved up enough money for another.

Several accounts of Pride's early affinity with country music suggest that such tastes were unusual for a young man growing up in the Delta, the home of the blues, and that his siblings and friends criticized him for playing "white music." But since there was relatively little in the way of black music programming on radio stations in the rural South before the late 1950s, many black vocalists, including Ike Turner from the Delta town of Clarksdale, Mississippi, drew upon the country and hillbilly performers they heard on WSM, as well as the blues performers they heard at local juke joints.

The suggestion that Pride's love of country music was somehow at odds with his racial background also ignores the deep-rooted connections and borrowings between African American and white American music and culture. The harmonica player DeFord Bailey had been a fixture on the early *Grand Ole Opry* of the 1920s and 1930s. Hank Williams, whose vocal stylings Pride faithfully copied, was himself deeply influenced by Rufus "Tee Tot" Payne, a street musician in his hometown of Greenville, Alabama, and at the beginning of his career in the 1940s Ray Charles was often billed as a "colored singing cowboy." Indeed, the color line was more sharply drawn in Pride's other childhood love, baseball, than in music. When that color line was broken by Jackie Robinson signing for the Brooklyn Dodgers in 1947, Pride, then nine years old, determined that he would get out of the Delta by becoming a professional baseball player.

To a considerable extent, however, Pride's decision to leave the cotton fields behind did not lie in his own hands. By the early 1950s the Delta had been transformed by the large-scale mechanization of cotton production and by generous federal subsidies to the region's already wealthy planters, who no longer needed a large African American labor force. Thousands of black Mississippians left the state after World War II in search of employment. Between 1950 and 1970 Quitman County experienced the largest out-migration of any county in Mississippi. Many headed to Chicago; others, like Charley Pride in 1955, traveled the much shorter distance—sixty miles—to Memphis, Tennessee. There Pride briefly played semiprofessional baseball as a pitcher for the Memphis Red Sox, a Negro American League team, and in 1956 he played in Alabama with another Negro League team, the Birmingham Brown Barons. He played in several exhibition games against major league stars including Willie Mays and Hank Aaron.

One month after being drafted into the U.S. Army in November 1956, Pride married Rozen Cohran, a cosmetologist from Oxford, Mississippi. The couple had three children, Kraig, Dion, and Angela. Upon being discharged from the army in 1958, Pride returned to the Memphis Red Sox but was again unsuccessful in his efforts to attract attention from major league teams or to secure a living wage in the minors. In 1960 Pride secured a berth with the semiprofessional Pioneer League Montana Timberjacks in Great Falls, Montana, a position that required him to supplement his income by working at a local tin smelter.

In Montana Pride began to play again the country music that he had loved in childhood. He entertained both the fans at various minor league baseball stadiums and his fellow workers at the smelter, where he was the only African American worker. He continued to dream of playing in the majors but failed in tryouts for the Los Angeles Angels in 1961 and the New York Mets in 1964. In 1963, however, his country music performance at a Great Falls, Montana, nightclub impressed two visiting country music performers and producers, Red Sovine and Red Foley. Foley, who had grown up near an all-black community in Middletown, Kentucky, and who had attended black church services as a child, encouraged Pride to audition for the Nashville manager-promoter Jack D. Johnson in early 1964. Pride recorded a demonstration tape later that year; upon hearing that tape Chet Atkins, the country performer who headed RCA Victor in Nashville, signed Pride to his label.

Pride's first single, "Snakes Crawl at Night" (1964), received extensive radio play in Nashville and on other country music stations throughout the United States. His second, "Just between You and Me" (1965), was nominated for a Grammy Award for Best Country and Western Vocal Performance. Afraid that Pride's color might discourage the overwhelmingly white and, at that time, largely southern audience for country music, however, RCA Victor decided to include no biographical material or photographs on Pride's records. It was only in 1966 when Pride's record sales were such that RCA Victor could no longer keep their artist's race a secret that Pride embarked on a major tour.

The selection of Detroit for Pride's debut concert in 1966 was not propitious; Pride's management may have thought that he would receive a warmer reception in a northern city than a southern one, but as the Detroit riot the following year would show, racial hostility was no longer peculiar to Dixie. The cheers that accompanied Pride's introduction in Detroit soon gave way to a stony silence when the audience discovered that he was black. Race was clearly in the ear of the beholder. Gradually, however, Pride won over the audiences by performing the same songs in the same rich baritone voice that his fans had loved when they thought he was white and by telling self-deprecating jokes about his "permanent tan." Support from established and racially progressive country music stars, notably Willie Nelson and Johnny Cash, eased Pride's acceptance among white audiences in the late 1960s. Even strict segregationists like the Grand Wizard of the Texarkana Ku Klux Klan came up to shake his hand after one performance. Indeed, Pride increasingly found more opposition among African Americans, notably on a United Services Organization (USO) tour in Germany in 1968 when black soldiers heckled him for not singing a song for "the brothers."

Pride was adamant, however, that his was no novelty act and that his music was neither black nor white, but simply American. He resisted suggestions by his management to change his name to George Washington Carver III, among others, though he did initially conform to their insistence that he avoid performing the popular "Green, Green Grass of Home." It was still taboo in the late 1960s for a black man to sing of his love for a woman "with hair of gold and lips like cherries." In 1967 Pride became the first African American to perform at the Grand Ole Opry since DeFord Bailey. By the end of the decade Pride had achieved the first of thirty-six number 1 singles on the country charts, "All I Have to Offer You (Is Me)." He also recorded several best-selling albums for RCA Victor, notably *Country Charley Pride* (1967), *Songs of Pride…Charley, That Is* (1968), and *The Best of Charley Pride* (1969).

Pride's heyday was the 1970s, especially the first half of the decade, when he emerged as the nation's most popular concert and television performer and recording artist. Among artists on the RCA Victor label, only Pride's fellow Mississippian Elvis Presley has sold more records. In 1971 Pride was named the Country Music Association entertainer of the year and male vocalist of the year. That same year he also won two Grammys, Best Sacred Performance for his album "Did You Think to Pray" and Best Gospel Performance for his single "Let Me Live." In 1980 *Cash Box* magazine named Pride its top male country artist of the 1970s.

Pride continued to record and sell out concert tours in North America, Europe, and Asia in the 1980s, though he did not reach the dizzying heights of the previous decade. He invested in several businesses, including his own production company, Cecca Productions, a sausage factory, a cattle ranch in Texas, and the Charley Pride Theater in Branson, Missouri, where he performed regularly beginning in the early 1990s. He was also a major stockholder in the First Texas Bank, one of the nation's leading black-owned corporations.

In 2000 Charley Pride became the first African American inducted into the Country Music Hall of Fame. What is perhaps most remarkable about Pride's career, however, is that despite his dramatic success at breaking down racial barriers within the country music scene, virtually no African American performers have followed him. Certainly none has come close to approaching Pride's fame and ubiquity in the country music charts. Although the national audience for country music soared in the 1980s and 1990s, the African American share of that audience remained minuscule. Indeed, it can be argued that country music has actually become more disconnected from the African American since Charley Pride's breakthrough in the late 1960s than it was in the era of legalized segregation.

FURTHER READING

Pride, Charley, with Jim Henderson. *Pride: The Charley Pride Story* (1995).

Harrington, Richard. "Pride in His Country: The Black Singer Who Crossed Over," *Washington Post*, 6 July 1984.

Malone, Bill C. *Country Music, USA: A Fifty Year History* (1985).

Malone, Bill C., and Judith McCullough. *Stars of Country Music: Uncle Dave Macon to Johnny Rodriguez* (1975).

Ward, Brian. *Just My Soul Responding: Rhythm and Blues, Black Consciousness, and Race Relations* (1998).

STEVEN J. NIVEN

Pride, Curtis (17 Dec. 1968–), baseball player, was born in Washington, D.C., to Sally Pride, a nurse, and John Pride, a government employee. His mother suffered a bout of rubella during her pregnancy leading to Curtis being born deaf.

His parents decided early in Pride's life that he would have all the opportunities available to a hearing child. They had to battle, threatening the Silver Springs Boys Club with legal action to force it to allow him to play baseball. Placed into classes and activities with hearing students by the seventh grade, he started to show tremendous athletic ability. He made the sixteen-and-under national soccer team, and played before a crowd of 60,000 in Beijing, China. He received numerous college basketball scholarship offers, and also graduated from high school with a 3.6/4.0 grade point average.

Pride chose to attend the College of William and Mary and made an unusual arrangement to pursue multiple sports. Taken in the tenth round of the 1986 draft by the New York Mets, the team agreed to sign him at the beginning of each baseball season and unconditionally release him at its end, thus allowing him to play college basketball during baseball's off season. For William and Mary, Pride became a four-year starting point guard, earning Colonial Athletic Association All-Defensive Team honors twice. He also earned a degree in finance in 1990.

His baseball career languished, however, perhaps hindered by his missing spring training to attend class. After batting .227 for Class AA Binghamton in 1992, he was released by the Mets and considered quitting. His parents convinced him to stay with baseball and he signed with the Montreal Expos. He flourished in the Expos' farm system, batting .356 at AA Harrisburg and .392 at AAA Ottawa.

This earned him a chance at the majors, and he made the most of it. On 17 September 1993 he collected his first major league hit, a pinch-hit two-run double that allowed the Expos to overcome a three-run deficit and beat the Phillies. The 45,757 fans at Montreal's Olympic Stadium responded with a thundering standing ovation that Pride could not hear; he did not acknowledge the ovation until a base coach pointed out the cheering to him. By joining the Expos Curtis Pride became the first-ever African American deaf major league baseball player, and the first deaf player since Danny Lynch played seven games for the Chicago Cubs in 1948.

After this brief taste of stardom, though, it was back to the minors for the 1994 season, then a short forty-eight game stint for the Expos in 1995, where he batted .175. In 1996 he went to the Detroit Tigers and had the best season of his career, batting .300 in ninety-five games. Pride asserted he would have always played that well in the majors if he had been given the chance, an early oblique reference to the discrimination he endured as a deaf ballplayer.

Pride started the 1997 season with Detroit, then moved to the Boston Red Sox, where he hit a home run in his first Fenway Park at bat. In 1998 he was on the playoff-bound Atlanta Braves, but controversy over deaf discrimination erupted again when manager Bobby Cox inexplicably left Pride off the post-season roster, going instead with Danny Bautista, who posted offensive numbers inferior to Pride's.

Pride tore a tendon in his right wrist and missed the 1999 season, then resurfaced in the majors with the Boston Red Sox in 2000. Almost immediately the issue of deaf discrimination came to the fore. In a game on 25 June 2000 between the Red Sox and the Toronto Blue Jays, Pride was blamed for an error that broke open a tie game in the thirteenth inning, leading to a Red Sox loss. Pride, playing left field at the time, and center fielder Carl Everett both ran after a routine fly ball in left center field. Everett waved off Pride, who kept running

after the ball. The ball bounced off Everett's glove for a three-base error.

"I should have backed off earlier," explained Pride, claiming responsibility for the error. Everett, who was given an error by the official scorer, said it was his fault. Pride was released by the Red Sox a few days later, and it was widely suspected that manager Jimy Williams believed Pride did not hear Everett call him off, and blamed him for the loss. Except for brief appearances with the Montreal Expos and the New York Yankees, Pride would spend the next three seasons in the minor leagues. For a period he was even out of organized baseball, playing for the independent Nashua (New Hampshire) Pride.

The issue of deaf discrimination continued to dog his career. A stint with the New York Yankees in 2003 started with Pride hitting a home run in his first Yankee at bat (earning him inevitable "Pride of the Yankees" headlines in New York newspapers) and ended eighteen days later when he was removed in favor of forty-six-year-old Jesse Orosco (who quickly proved he no longer had major league skills and was released).

In the spring of 2004 Curtis Pride was back with the Nashua Pride. He soon signed with the Anaheim Angels farm system, and on 17 July returned to the major leagues with the Angels. After batting .250 in a utility role for the Division-winning Angels he was named to the postseason roster. When he appeared as a pinch-hitter in the Angels' Division Series loss to the Boston Red Sox, he became the first deaf player ever to appear in the major league postseason.

The year 2005 opened with Curtis Pride entering his twentieth season of professional baseball. He has been in eleven major league organizations, and played in the majors on six different teams. Speaking of his career, Pride said only that "I never quit. I never give up," and refused to discuss how discrimination affected it. But clearly it did. Journeymen players usually do not have twenty-year professional careers, and players with twenty-year careers usually have much more major league playing time than did Pride.

In 1998 Pride married Lisa Matejcik, and in December 2004 they had a child. Pride received numerous honors in his career. In 1995 he was named one of ten "Outstanding Young Americans" by the U.S. Junior Chamber of Commerce, and in 1997 was given the Tony Conigliaro award for persevering through adversity. In 2001 he formed the Together with Pride Foundation, whose purpose was to help hearing-impaired young people reach their educational goals.

FURTHER READING

Articles relating to Curtis Pride's life and career are maintained in the Curtis Pride major league player file, National Baseball Hall of Fame Library, Cooperstown, New York.

Eschenbach, Stephen. "It's All about Pride," *William and Mary Alumni Magazine* (Fall 2003).

Jordan, Pat, and Mark Newman. "Baseball's Pride and Joy," *The Sporting News* (2 May 1994).

Lupica, Mike. "Listen Hard for Baseball Pride," *New York Newsday*, 17 Feb. 1995.

STEPHEN ESCHENBACH

Primus, Holdridge (1817–22 Apr. 1884), porter, clerk, and civic leader in Hartford, Connecticut, was born in Guilford, Connecticut, the son of Ham Primus, a sailor, and Temperance Asher. His grandfather, named simply Primus, is recognized in one local history as a servant and apprentice to a Dr. Wolcott in East Windsor, Connecticut, in the mid-eighteenth century. Later on, inspired by Dr. Wolcott's work, this Primus became a doctor himself, setting up his own office. We know little about Holdridge Primus's early life, but we do know he was earning a living by age twelve. In his early teenage years, he made his way to Hartford, Connecticut, where he worked and apprenticed for William Ellsworth, (later governor of Connecticut from 1838 to 1842). When Ellsworth served in Congress around 1848, he chose to take Primus with him based on his merit, intelligence, and dedicated service. Primus was employed in a variety of trades and gained valuable experience.

In 1849, Primus took a job with a Hartford-based mining and trading company during the California Gold Rush. In that same year, the mining company sent him on a trip to California, where he experienced the state's gold fever, negotiated mining prospects, and arranged trade between Connecticut and California. He accompanied a Mr. Humphrey, whose father owned the grocery firm Humphrey and Seyms. The elder Humphrey had told his son that he could only join the mining expedition if Primus went along, which he did, as a cook. Primus worked diligently, proving to be an outstanding asset to the company. While in California, Primus took up a job in Sacramento working at the Adams Express Company, where he was noted for his powers of persuasion and business skills. Adams Express, in

return, awarded Primus for three years of service with a gold watch, chain, and a medal of honor. Primus and Humphrey supposedly had "struck a modest sum," in California and returned after three years, but the "sum" was lost on the voyage back. Primus returned to his normal life working as a porter, refusing an offer to start a restaurant business in Sacramento.

As an adult, Primus enjoyed great respect within his community for his efforts at self-education, and for his faith. He was the head of his family, and earned the esteem of others by acting as a dependable friend, and a pillar of strength to the Talcott Street Congregational Church, where he was a preacher. It was there that he met his future wife Mehitable Jacobs, a dressmaker and a stalwart of the congregation. Together the Primuses ensured that the church was a place where community and faith were interconnected. They also provided an informal, nonprofit employment service, matching employers with African American women who needed a reliable and safe means of work to provide for their children and families. Holdridge Primus was also prominent in Hartford's black freemasons.

The Primuses had four children, Rebecca, Nelson, Isabelle, and Henrietta. With a family to support, Holdridge was known as a man constantly looking for work, whether it was a temporary job or a permanent position. He spent about forty-seven years, the majority of his life, as a porter at the grocery firm Humphrey and Seyms, later known as Seyms & Co. He gained trust in the business community throughout his lifetime, and expanded his network across the country. The Primus children, like their parents, played in an important role in their community. REBECCA PRIMUS educated freedmen in the South during Reconstruction. NELSON A. PRIMUS was an artist who designed and painted carriages and sleighs. Henrietta Primus was a domestic servant and a seamstress. Isabelle Primus, the youngest, known as Bell, was a baker.

After a few years of marriage, Holdridge and Mehitable were able to afford a comfortable two-story home on 20 Wadsworth Street. It was a fully furnished, tastefully decorated middle-class home, complete with a carpeted parlor, a grand piano, and many books. In the sitting room, there was an array of different kinds of chairs, a stove, more books, a grandfather clock, and a rich carpet. The house also contained a sewing room for the women in the house, and a kitchen supplied with silverware and porcelain dishes. The Primus property holdings also included a lot in Branford, Connecticut, which the family rented out, but ultimately sold to Holdridge's nephew and son-in-law.

On 22 April 1884, Holdridge suffered a severe paralytic stroke and died. Hartford's most noted African American citizen, he left an estate valued at $3,924. His life's achievements include the successes of his family, his church, and his good name, which became synonymous with dignity and initiative in the black community in Connecticut.

FURTHER READING

Biographical information found in US Federal Census *Hartford, Connecticut*; Roll T9_97; Family History Film: *1254097*; Page: *191.4000*; Enumeration District: *10*; Image: *0622, 1880*.

n.a "Article 6," *Hartford Daily Courant*, 16 May 1859.

Beeching, Barbara Jean. "The Primus Papers: An Introduction to Hartford's 19th Century Black Community," Ph D. dissertation, Trinity College, (CT) 1995.

Brown, Haines. "Citizens of Color, 1863–1890: The Black Elite: The 'Talented Tenth'" *Citizens of Color, 1863–1890: The "Talented Tenth"* 08 Dec. 1997. Web. 14 Oct. 2010. <http://www.hartford-hwp.com/HBHP/exhibit/05/3.html>.

Obituary: "Holdridge Primus," *Hartford Daily Courant*, 23 April 1884.

CHAITALI KORGAONKAR AND ROBERT SMIEJA

Primus, Nelson A. (24 March 1843–29 May 1916), painter, was born in Hartford, Connecticut, the son of Holdridge Primus, a porter at a grocery store and an active member of the Talcott Street Congregational Church, and Mehitable Jacobs, a dressmaker. The Primuses, one of the few African American families in the state to own property, consisted of the parents, Nelson, and his siblings Rebecca, Isabelle, and Henrietta, and their home was located on Wadsworth Street in Hartford. During Reconstruction, REBECCA PRIMUS was active in efforts to educate the southern freedmen. Nelson Primus discovered his artistic talent at an early age. At the Hartford County Fair, he was recognized twice: in 1851, when he was only nine years old, he received a diploma for his sketches, and in 1859 he received a medal for his drawings.

Nelson Primus wanted to pursue that talent by painting professionally. His father likely thought that this would be a financially insecure career and was probably the person who suggested that Nelson seek a more practical career by apprenticing with George Francis, the owner of a local carriage making business. In 1858, Primus followed his father's advice and learned to design and paint the decorations on sleighs and carriages. Fortunately, Francis supported Primus's dream to be a painter and gave him lessons in painting landscapes and portraits. From 1860 to 1862, Primus also received informal art instruction from Elizabeth Gilbert Jerone, a local artist.

On 15 June 1864, Primus married Amoretta Prince and later that year moved to Boston, Massachusetts, where he hoped to be the pupil of EDWARD MITCHELL BANNISTER, an older, established black artist. In April 1865, Primus wrote of his satisfaction with Bannister, but this was short lived. According to Primus, Bannister soon realized how talented his pupil was and began to see him as competition. In July he wrote, "Mr. Banister i think is a little Jealous of me he says that i have got good tast in art. But does not try very hard to get me any work. The Colored people here think he could get me work if he was a mind to …"Primus felt betrayed by his mentor, but this conflict proves how difficult it was to make a living as an artist. If Primus's speculations were true, Bannister probably didn't personally dislike Primus; he just couldn't afford to share any of his precious clients.

From the beginning of his painting career, Primus's dream was to study abroad in Europe where, as other artists found, he might have faced less racial discrimination than in the United States. Primus didn't have the money nor did he make the connections necessary to ensure his admission into an art institute, but his dream was not an impossible one. Indeed, Charles Ethan Porter, also an African American painter from Hartford, had a background similar to Primus, but fulfilled Primus's dream. The famous writer Mark Twain, a Hartford resident, noticed Porter's paintings and wrote him recommendations that resulted in his enrollment of several art institutes, including one in Paris. Eventually, Porter was able to support himself with his art as his sole source of income. Porter was not necessarily a better painter than Primus; he was simply luckier. He attracted the attention of an influential white man and that was what a nineteenth-century black painter needed to do to succeed. However, as time passed and people forgot about Twain's recommendations, Porter faced many of the same problems as Primus; few would buy paintings from a black man. In addition to the problems that all painters face, Primus faced racial discrimination while struggling to support himself and his family.

In 1865, Primus's daughter Leila was born. But with such an unsteady and unpredictable income,

Primus had to send her to Hartford to stay with his family from March to September of 1867. This ensured her comfort and it allowed his wife more time to work outside the house. This desperate action was the result of a period of time in which Primus tried to rely on his painting as his family's sole source of income. When he failed to meet his goal, he was forced to borrow money from his parents in January of 1867 and again later that year. But he never stopped painting. That year, he painted *Sunset, Italian Scene, Boston Boot Blacks*, and *the Madonna*, and sent them to Hartford for sale. On 3 October 1867, the *Hartford Daily Courant*, now known as the *Hartford Courant*, praised four of Primus's paintings. But, dejected by his financial failure, he wrote to his family, "I am wirking at my old traid again carriage painting....i have given portrait painting up for a while." This hiatus lasted for a few months before he wrote a letter describing his latest project.

In 1872, Primus moved his family to Somerville, Massachusetts, where he remained listed in the Boston city directory until 1889. On 18 July 1876 Primus's wife, Amoretta, died. In 1886 Primus saw *Christ Before Pilate*, by the Hungarian painter Mihály Munkácsy and was inspired to reproduce it. On 30 December 1888 Primus's copy of *Christ Before Pilate* was on exhibition at Boston's Horticultural Hall when an accidental fire spread through the building and destroyed the painting. Primus painted a second copy and after Leila died in 1894, he toured the copy around the country with Mary, his second wife. In 1896, he and his wife settled down in San Francisco, California, where he found work at a delicatessen. On 29 May 1916, Primus died from pulmonary tuberculosis at age seventy-four with laborer listed as the occupation on his death certificate.

Primus never saved enough money to fulfill his dream to study abroad in Europe nor did he ever manage to support his family with his painting career, but he never stopped painting. Today he is remembered as a talented black painter. That was the core of his being, and that was how he identified himself, but the tragedy of his life, and of many African Americans seeking a career in the arts in the nineteenth century, was that he was never given the chance to fulfill his potential.

FURTHER READING

Nelson Primus's correspondence is located in the Primus Family Papers, Connecticut Historical Society, Manuscript Collection, Hartford, Connecticut.

"Citizens of Color, 1863–1890: The 'Talented Tenth,'" *The Hartford Black History Project*. Web site available at http://www.hartford-hwp.com/HBHP/exhibit/05/3.html

Beeching, Barbara J. "Reading the Numbers: Census Returns as Key to the Nineteenth Century Black Community in Hartford, Connecticut," *Connecticut History* 44.2 pp. 224–247 (2005).

———. "The Primus Papers: An Introduction to Hartford's Nineteenth Century Black Community," dissertation, Trinity College, 1995.

Holland, Juanita Marie. "Co-workers in the Kingdom of Culture: Edward Mitchell Bannister and the Boston Community of African-American artists, 1848–1901," dissertation, Columbia University, 1998.

"Work of a Bungler," *New York Times* p. 1, 31 (December 1888).

JENNIFER KY

Primus, Pearl (29 Nov. 1919–29 Oct. 1994), dance pioneer, anthropologist, and choreographer, was born in Trinidad, the daughter of Edward Primus and Emily Jackson, and migrated with her family to New York City when she was two years old. She majored in biology and premedicine at Hunter College of the City University of New York and graduated in 1940. Seeking support for graduate studies, she solicited help from the National Youth Administration (NYA). Under the auspices of the NYA she was enrolled in a dance group, subsequently auditioned for the New Dance Group in New York, and earned a scholarship with that institution.

During Primus's tenure at the New Dance Group, she began to do research on African culture. She visited museums and consulted books, articles, and pictures for months to produce on 14 February 1943 her first significant dance work, *African Ceremonial*, which she had asked continental Africans to judge on its authenticity. *African Ceremonial*, a regal depiction of African heritage and tradition, had its premiere performance at the Ninety-second Street Young Men's Hebrew Association in New York. On that program she also presented her earlier works *Strange Fruit* and *Hard Time Blues*.

During the summer of 1944 Primus spent an extended period in the South visiting churches as well as living and working with sharecroppers. This experience served as a springboard for dance works and scholarly articles. She was concerned not only with African heritage but also with African retentions in the religious ceremonies of southern blacks. When Primus was rehearsing *Strange Fruit* with Michelle Simmons in Los Angeles fifty years

Pearl Primus on 11 Oct. 1943. (Library of Congress/ Photographed by Carl Van Vechten.)

later, she said, "I didn't create *Strange Fruit* for a dancer, I created it to make a statement within our society, within our world." A telling indictment of the horrors of humanity, *Strange Fruit* comments on the widespread practice of lynching African Americans in the southern United States during the 1940s. *Hard Time Blues* was a result of Primus's observations of sharecroppers in whose work she found strength and power.

In October 1944 Primus debuted on Broadway at the Belasco Theatre, where she performed her dances depicting African culture as well as works representing African American experiences. *African Ceremonial* and *Yanvaloo*, based on a snakelike dance characteristic of some Caribbean cultures, depicted African traditions, while *Strange Fruit*, *The Negro Speaks of Rivers*, and *Slave Market* were based on African American experiences. Primus's ballets drew attention to social conditions and challenged racism in American society; at the same time they demonstrated that African American motifs were powerful vehicles for concert dance. Like ASADATA DAFORA, who brought authentic African dance patterns to the American stage, Primus showed that accurate portraits of Africans were possible using the language of dance.

Edith Segal of the *Daily Worker* praised Primus's 1944 concert as a "historic evening in the theatre." Other critics agreed that her "dances of protest" were "message" works to draw attention to the harsh realities of injustice toward citizens of color in the United States. *The Negro Speaks of Rivers* (1943), based on LANGSTON HUGHES's poem of the same name, figuratively addressed the deep mesh of African and African American heritage. That Primus presented the African with dignity is one of the major contributions of her work to world arts and culture.

In 1948 Primus received a fellowship from the Rosenwald Foundation to study in Africa. Her first trip to West Africa in December 1948 expanded her understanding of the culture, which enabled her to enhance her dance works and added to her knowledge of "people little understood" in American society. Primus visited Nigeria, Angola, Cameroon, the Ivory Coast, Liberia, Senegal, and the Belgian Congo (later Zaire, later still the Democratic Republic of Congo). There for eighteen months, she performed for dignitaries and villagers. All were overwhelmed by the incredible physical power and grace of her movement. Although short in stature, Primus had the ability to leap like a gazelle, hover in the air, and then land delicately. Her energetic performance style, at times playful, as in *Haitian Play Dance* (1947), at other times serious, as demonstrated in her dances of social protest, powerfully influenced mainstream modern dance.

Primus's African journey laid the foundation for her teaching. The more she learned about the function and meaning of dance in African life and culture, the more she was able to pass on the African dance tradition to her American students. She developed a system of notation that helped preserve extant traditional dances and not only studied indigenous dances but also wrote about dance history as it evolved within the culture. Her articles include "Spiritual and Shout Songs of America" (*Dance Encyclopedia*, ed. Anatole Chujoy [1949]), "Out of Africa" (*The Dance Has Many Faces*, ed. Walter Sorell [1951]), and "Earth Theater" (*Theatre Arts* [Dec. 1950]). Known for her meticulous discipline and precise execution of patterns, Primus was a demanding teacher. She stressed the importance of preserving the original intent and focus of traditional dances. Primus's awareness of life in Africa as a dance through which one learns how to be in the world and as the vehicle that teaches life skills and affirms identity made her a treasure among African people. Her extraordinary personal aura, courage, and open heart reminded African elders of their own children, and she was given the name "Omowale" (Child Come Home).

Primus made it a personal mission to preserve traditional dance and at the same time provide a framework for the study of African people throughout the diaspora. In the dances she created before her sojourn to Africa, like *African Ceremonial*, Primus sought the advice of the master drummers Alphonse Cimber and Norman Coker. She relied on their knowledge of specific rhythmic patterns as communicators of particular messages. Primus's visit to Africa affirmed the accuracy and appropriateness of her well-researched interpretations of indigenous African rhythms, rituals, and gestural nuances.

Dances that Primus choreographed after her return from Africa included *Prayer for Thanksgiving* (1949), in which a traditional priestess pays homage to the gods for peace and fertility; *Excerpts from an African Journey* (1951), a dance in four parts, *War Dance* (1946), *Fanga* (1949), *Egbo Eskapede* (1950), *Everybody Loves Saturday Night* (1950), and *Impinyuza* (1951), based on material from the Belgian Congo. The lively *Fanga*, a Nigerian dance of welcome, went on to become a staple in the repertory of many African American dance companies, including the African American Dance Ensemble in North Carolina (formerly the Chuck Davis Dance Company in New York) and Dinizulu Dancers and Drummers in New York. *Impinyuza* was re-created by the ALVIN AILEY AMERICAN DANCE THEATER in 1990, and in 1993 Primus passed on the legacy of *The Negro Speaks of Rivers* to Kim Bears of the Philadelphia Dance Company.

Primus's anthropological skills coupled with her creative abilities provided a venue for appreciating, exploring, and using traditional African dance to study African people. She became a world-renowned teacher. In 1953, while she was studying dance in the Caribbean, noting its links to African dance, she met the dancer-musician PERCIVAL BORDE. Their marriage in 1954, which produced one child, was the beginning of an artistic union that proved important in building cultural bridges. When Primus performed as a guest artist with Borde's troupe in a 1958 performance of *Fanga*, the *New York Times* critic John Martin wrote, "This is an unusually well unified and atmospheric presentation, unpretentious in manner but with a wealth of knowledge behind it and both skill and taste in its execution."

Primus's leadership in the preservation of African dance is significant. As early as 1959, the year she received an M.A. in Education from New York University (NYU), she was named director of Liberia's Performing Arts Center. Her job as archivist of the dance—restoring, reviving, and expanding African dance and related arts—helped maintain a rich heritage. After two years in Liberia, she and her husband returned to the United States and opened the Primus-Borde School of Primal Dance in New York City. There Primus taught anthropology and sociology as well as dance. The school opened and closed several times while Primus and Borde journeyed back and forth to Africa, gathering information. Ever conscious of the value of looking at dance in a cultural context, they created a blueprint for the contemporary study of African dance and culture. Having received a Ph.D. in Anthropology in 1977 from NYU, Primus also served as a professor of ethnic studies from 1984 to 1990 at the Five Colleges (Amherst, Smith, Hampshire, Mount Holyoke, and the University of Massachusetts) in Massachusetts and served as the first chair of the Five Colleges Dance Consortium in 1990. She also founded the Pearl Primus Dance Language Institute in 1978, but the project never came to fruition.

Primus was the recipient of numerous awards and honors, among them the National Medal of Arts, presented to her by President George H. W. Bush in 1991; the first Balasaraswati–Joy Ann Dewey Beinecke Chair for Distinguished Teaching at the American Dance Festival in 1991; the Star of Africa from the Liberian government; the National Council of Negro Women's Scroll of Honor as Woman of the Year; and the Distinguished Service Award from the Association of American Anthropologists. She died in New Rochelle, New York. The cultural originality of Primus's choreography is the legacy she left to African people in particular, to American society and to world culture generally.

FURTHER READING

Allen, Zita. "An Interview with Pearl Primus," *New York Amsterdam News*, 21 June 1980.

Estrada, Ric. "Three Leading Negro Artists and How They Feel about Dance in the Community: Eleo Pomare, Pearl Primus, and Arthur Mitchell," *Dance Magazine*, Nov. 1968.

Martin, John. "The Dance: In Liberia," *New York Times*, 31 July 1960.

"Pearl Primus, Foremost Dancer to Unveil New Exciting Work Based on Long Study of African People," *Ebony*, Jan. 1951.

Obituary: *New York Times*, 31 Oct. 1994.

This entry is taken from the *American National Biography* and is published here with the permission of the American Council of Learned Societies.

C. S'THEMBILE WEST

Primus, Rebecca (1836–24 Feb. 1932), Reconstruction-era schoolteacher, was born in Hartford, Connecticut, the daughter of Holdridge Primus, a porter and later clerk, and Mehitable Jacobs, a seamstress. The Primuses were a prominent family in Connecticut's African American community, and her younger brother, Nelson Primus, achieved some success as an artist. They were one of the only thirty-five African American families in Hartford who owned property, and because of this they lived in a predominantly white neighborhood. This did not prevent them from forging strong ties with fellow blacks in Hartford. The family attended the Talcott Street Congregational Church, and their home doubled as an employment agency for young African American women. Rebecca attended the school located in the church, taught by Pastor JAMES W. PENNINGTON, a former runaway slave, a nationally known abolitionist, and the author of one of the earliest histories of African Americans.

Rebecca's social standing, the influences of her well-known father and abolitionist pastor, and her own observation of her community, gave her a strong idea of the qualities and assets needed by African Americans to advance socially and economically. She believed that the greatest of these was an education. This spawned her desire to become a teacher. At age twenty-five she officially become a teacher, although it is not known where or how she accomplished it. She taught Sunday school at Talcott Street Congregational Church, and she may have also taught in one of Hartford's African Schools, possibly the one she attended as a child between 1861 and the end of the Civil War in 1865, when Hartford's Freedmen's Aid Society was founded. This society was dedicated to the support of the newly freed slaves, and its president was Calvin Stowe, the husband of Harriet Beecher Stowe, author of *Uncle Tom's Cabin*.

In 1865 the Freedman's Society selected five teachers to head to the south and start schools. Rebecca Primus was the only black teacher selected, departing for Baltimore, Maryland, by 7 November 1865. Sometime before her departure to Maryland, Primus came into contact with ADDIE BROWN, a black domestic servant who worked in several different places in New York and Connecticut. During her stay in Royal Oak, Maryland she kept consistent correspondence with Addie, sharing with her occurrences, thoughts, and challenges while teaching the newly freed slaves. The letters also reveal an intimate romantic relationship between the two women, one that often left Addie depressed when they were apart. Scholars have noted that the letters between Primus and Brown provide a rare insight on same sex love between two African American women in the nineteenth Century.

Rebecca Primus lived and taught in Royal Oak, Maryland, boarding with Charles Thomas, a well-respected, free black landowner, and his wife. Rebecca taught in the basement of a church, teaching children in the morning and adults at night, a total of approximately seventy-five students. She also taught Sunday school at the church and kept a regular correspondence with those she left behind in Connecticut.

While teaching in Royal Oak, Rebecca often wrote home about experiences she had, such as dealing with sickness, retelling accounts of racism and harassment suffered by her African American students and friends, and her general surprise and delight about the number of African Americans in the area, especially in Baltimore. Hartford's population of African Americans at the time was 716, only two percent of the city's total population, while Maryland was experiencing an influx of newly emancipated slaves seeking work and escaping from the prejudice and violence of the rural south.

The school year ran from October to July, much like the school year in the twenty-first century, and teachers were allowed to return to Connecticut during the break. Teachers were given ninety dollars as an initial payment, then approximately thirty dollars a month for each following month. Rebecca felt the need for her own schoolhouse from the first day she began teaching. In order to raise funds for the school she organized fairs in Maryland and through her family and friends back home, campaigned for free lumber, and got her students to donate what they could. In September of 1867 The Primus Institute of Royal Oak was completed.

In June of 1869, the Hartford Freedmen's Aid Society formally dissolved. Although Rebecca's school was partially funded by the local residents, there was not enough money for her to continue her school alone, forcing her to return to Hartford with the other five teachers. Hartford wasn't welcoming to Rebecca Primus after her return, even through she had proved her will and talent through her teaching in Maryland. There are no records of employment outside of teaching in the Sunday school at the Talcott Street Congregational Church. In 1873, Rebecca married Charles Thomas, her former landlord from Royal Oak. Upon Charles's death in 1891, Rebecca moved in with her mother in her childhood home, at 20 Wadsworth Street, and died in Hartford's Municipal Hospital after a long illness. She was the last surviving member of the Primus family.

FURTHER READING

The Primus Family Papers are held at the Connecticut Historical Society and the Connecticut State Library.

Beeching, Barbara. *Twain's World: Essays on Hartford's Cultural Heritage* (1998).

Griffin, Farah Jasmine. *Beloved Sisters and Loving Friends: Letters from Rebecca Primus of Royal Oak, Maryland and Addie Brown of Hartford, Connecticut, 1854–1868* (1999).

JOSHUA V. P. SIBBLIES

Prince (7 June 1958–), rock and pop musician, songwriter, producer, and actor, was born Prince Rogers Nelson in Minneapolis, Minnesota. He was named after his father's jazz band, the Prince Rogers Trio. Both parents were well known local musicians: his father, John Nelson, worked as a plastic molder at Honeywell Electronics and was a pianist; his mother, Mattie Shaw, a homemaker, sang. They had a daughter, Tyka, in 1960 (there were four older stepsiblings from other marriages), but divorced when Prince was ten. Around age twelve Prince moved in with his father, who gave his son his first guitar (Prince began playing piano while his parents were still married). Prince did not remain long with his father. He lived briefly with various relatives before finally moving in with the family of his high school friend André Anderson (who later performed as André Cymone).

Already largely self-taught on guitar, piano, and drums, Prince began studying music in high school. With Anderson, he started the band Grand Central, later changing the name to Champagne. Recording at a studio in early 1976, he came to the attention of the studio's proprietor, Chris Moon. A songwriter, Moon offered Prince the chance to put

Prince performed in Cincinnati, Oh., on 21 Jan. 1985. (AP Images.)

music to Moon's lyrics. Not quite out of high school (he would graduate in late spring 1976), Prince dissolved Champagne to work with Moon.

Prince spent virtually all his free time working on compositions for Moon's lyrics and learning how to operate studio equipment. With Moon's help, he put together a fourteen-song demo of original material, on which he played all the instruments. With a new manager, Owen Husney, he landed a three-album deal at Warner Bros., just weeks after turning nineteen. The contract gave Prince unprecedented autonomy and control for such an untested and young musician.

Written, performed, and produced by Prince, his first album, *For You* (1978), made a splash on the R&B charts with the single "Soft and Wet," but was otherwise unremarkable. *Prince* (1979), which featured songs moving into a pop vein, with strong melodies, complicated harmonies, and sparing production, resulted in a number 1 hit on the Soul Singles Chart, "I Wanna Be Your Lover." By

1980 Prince had put together a backing band that included his longtime friend André Cymone on bass, Matt Fink on keyboards, Bobby Z on drums, and Dez Dickerson on guitar. A second keyboardist, Gayle Chapman, was replaced by Lisa Coleman, who quickly became a close and briefly intimate friend with Prince. His third album, *Dirty Mind* (1980), however, was still a solo project. Prince's new songs were sexually explicit in ways that his previous material had not been. Sex had always played a role in his music, but the graphic treatment of it along with his exploration of deviant sexuality and taboos like incest pushed the boundaries of acceptability. The album was full of musical experimentation, too, including New Wave and rock. Though not a commercial success, it received excellent reviews in *Rolling Stone* and *New Musical Express* and helped launch Prince's reputation as one of the most talented musicians of his generation.

For his fourth album, *Controversy* (1981), Prince continued to experiment with New Wave influences, employing electronic textures and cold synthesizer-based rhythms combined with rock guitar, funk bass-lines, and multi-voice harmonies. In addition to explicit tracks like "Sexuality," and slow seduction songs like "Do Me, Baby," he also exhibited the beginnings of a political sensibility on "Controversy" and "Annie Christian." At the same time, Prince was managing his first protégé band, the Time, writing and recording their self-titled first album, which became a surprise hit. While *Controversy* sold well, going gold, it didn't produce the breakthrough hit he was looking for.

Prince began work on another protégé group, Vanity 6, fronted by a woman he had christened Vanity, one of a long line of beautiful and variously talented women with whom he would become romantically and professionally involved. Their self-titled debut released in August 1982. He wrote and recorded most of the Time's second album against the wishes of the band member, who were interested in performing their own music; nonetheless, the 1982 release was another hit, going gold. Prince was quickly becoming a driving force in American popular music and was the recognized architect of "the Minneapolis Sound," which combined elements of funk, R&B, soul, rock, punk, and New Wave. Prince's reputation was enhanced in October 1982 with the release of *1999*, another almost entirely solo effort that represented his finest work to date. The album sold more than 3 million copies in its first year and included his first Top Ten single, "Little Red Corvette," and the hits "1999" and "Delirious." The video for "1999" went into regular rotation at the new music-video channel MTV, introducing Prince to a large new audience who liked his mix of funk and rock, and the rebellious androgyny and hypersexuality of his image. The success of the *1999* album and tour made Prince one of the most popular black artists of the 1980s. By the end of the tour only MICHAEL JACKSON, whose album *Thriller* was released three months after *1999*, surpassed him in terms of both critical success and popularity.

Wendy Melvoin replaced Dez Dickerson on guitar in 1983, completing what was probably Prince's most dynamic and collaborative band, the Revolution. Prince's next venture, the semi-autobiographical film *Purple Rain* (1984), despite mixed reviews from critics, earned nearly $8 million its first weekend and grossed more than $68 million domestically. The soundtrack received rave reviews and spent twenty-four weeks at number 1 on the *Billboard* chart. Ostensibly providing a window into Prince's private world, the film was actually a glamorized and mythologized version of his life that ended up revealing not much more than was already known. Also in 1984 Prince released two more hit albums by protégé projects—the Time (their third) and Sheila E. (her first)—and also wrote the song "Sugar Walls," a raunchy departure for the formerly family-friendly Scottish pop singer Sheena Easton that went to number 3 on the pop charts. In 1985 Prince received an Academy Award for best soundtrack and won three Grammy Awards—two for *Purple Rain* and one as songwriter for Chaka Khan's "I Feel for You."

By the mid-1980s Prince had become an international superstar, with Michael Jackson, Bruce Springsteen, and Madonna his only peers. Becoming a pop icon, though, meant that his music and image were now subject to a new and much higher level of scrutiny, forcing him to become less challenging musically and less subversive culturally. An intensely private individual and artist, Prince did not enjoy the many intrusions into his life and personal relationships that came with stardom; for someone who had always been driven by his work and by a need to control every aspect of his music and career, compromising his image and art to any degree was difficult to accept.

Around the World in a Day (1985) followed *Purple Rain* in reaching number 1 on the album charts. Awash with pseudo-psychedelia and 1960s flower-generation optimism, the album marked a step forward in his development as a songwriter and composer, but spent only three weeks at number 1. His next project, the film *Under the Cherry Moon* (1986), failed to match the box office success of *Purple Rain* and was savaged by critics. The soundtrack, *Parade*, however, yielded Prince's third number 1 hit, "Kiss." While considered inconsistent by some critics, the album was generally praised as more evidence of his steady artistic development and seemingly boundless talent. Also in 1986 Prince encountered his first failure with a protégé band, the Family, whose debut album sold poorly (the one success from the album was the song "Nothing Compares 2 U," which Sinead O'Connor would make into a number 1 hit in 1990). Though he would never stop working with bands or developing new artists, almost none of his protégés' releases would achieve the prominence of his early efforts.

Prince disbanded the Revolution in October 1986 and began recording the material that became the double album *Sign O' the Times*. His new band retained Matt Fink on keyboards, featured Sheila E. on drums, Levi Seacer Jr. on bass, Miko Weaver on guitar, and Boni Boyer, a vocalist who also played keyboards. Released to universal acclaim, the album has since become recognized as his finest work. It went to number 6 on the *Billboard* chart and yielded three Top Ten hits. The album combines the elements of every musical style with which Prince had ever experimented and the entire gamut of themes he had explored—from the drug-dystopia and violence of the title track to the androgynous sexuality of "If I Was Your Girlfriend" to the religious yearning of "The Cross" to the pure celebration of "It's Gonna Be a Beautiful Night."

Prince's next record, *The Black Album*, was cancelled at the last minute, after he decided it was too focused on negative themes, violence, and dark sexuality. Only the love song "When 2 R in Love" was retained for the record that Prince released instead. An attempt to make a profound statement about love, both sexual and religious, *Lovesexy* was one of the most personal of his career, full of music that retained much of the energy and excellence of *Sign O' the Times*, but which continued to experiment with new ideas and sounds. However, reviewers and fans were largely disappointed with the album and it was his first in many years that did not go platinum in the United States. After *Lovesexy* and the 1989 movie soundtrack *Batman* (a commercial success that earned him another platinum album), Prince's output began to suffer in terms of

consistency, artistic development, and boundary-pushing experimentation. While the soundtrack for the film *Graffiti Bridge* (1990) featured some good songwriting and ensemble work, it was otherwise a weak album, largely a retread of past efforts. The film itself was a critical and popular disaster that effectively ended Prince's film career.

Working with yet another new band, the New Power Generation, in 1991 Prince released *Diamonds and Pearls*. Though it broke virtually no new ground, the album was hailed by critics as a return to form. It sold nearly 3 million copies (more than any other Prince record save *Purple Rain*) and included his fifth number 1 hit, "Cream." Still, though his output was as steady as ever, his popularity was in evident decline. His twelfth album, named for a combination of symbols for male and female, was a Top Ten record, but it was another critical disappointment that sold well below expectations.

Though he signed a new deal in 1992 with Warner, a six-record contract potentially worth $100 million, the company's refusal to release new records as soon as and as often as Prince produced them set off a war between the two. Prince changed his name to the symbol from his album, forcing the media to resort to various tortured ways of referring to him, most settling on "the Artist Formerly Known as Prince." He performed with the word "slave" written on his face and announced that he would complete the terms of his contract using previously recorded songs stored in his "vault." Prince's last album for Warner was released in 1996, after which he disbanded the New Power Generation, "retiring" to spend time with his new wife, Mayté Garcia, pregnant with their first child, and to record the work that would announce his love and commitment to his family and his freedom from corporate oppression, *Emancipation*. The baby was born 16 October 1996 with severe physical defects. After a week of operations, the child was removed from life support and died. Prince refused to acknowledge any problems with the child and went to great lengths to hide its tragic death from the public and media, which led to police investigations that found he was only trying to protect his family's privacy and cleared the couple of any wrongdoing, but which added to the public's view of Prince as an increasingly odd and erratic personality.

Released in November 1996, *Emancipation* was Prince's most consistent and focused work in years, its many strengths reminding fans and critics of the songwriting skills and musicianship he had displayed throughout the 1980s. Still, the work added virtually nothing new to his sound and exhibited little experimentation. Incredibly, Prince followed the three-disk *Emancipation* with a four-disk effort titled *Crystal Ball* (1998). Cobbled together from old material and recently recorded acoustic and classically influenced instrumental music, the set was poorly received by critics and further eroded his fan base. In 2000 he reclaimed the name Prince when his publishing deal with Warner ended. Prince and Mayté divorced that year; he married Manuela Testolini in 2001 (she filed for divorce in 2006). He became a Jehovah's Witness after making a promise to his dying mother.

Between 1998 and 2002 Prince released nine more records, though none sold especially well or were critically acclaimed. Yet as his stature as a songwriter and recording artist declined after the early 1990s, Prince's reputation as a performer grew. By 2007, when he performed a stunning set in the rain during half-time at the Super Bowl, many critics and even music historians were calling Prince "the greatest living performer in the pop tradition" (Frere-Jones). Known throughout his career as a dynamic and almost preternaturally gifted live performer, his stage performances as he neared the age of fifty became the place for him to showcase his still-virtuosic skills, to experiment and once again test the boundaries of his art as he constantly refashioned and reinterpreted older material, then melded it with newer ideas and songs. Defined more than almost any other pop and rock musician by his art, Prince's life story is often the story of his writing, recording, producing, and performing a catalog of songs that dwarfs most artists active in the twentieth and twenty-first centuries. The series of albums stretching from *Dirty Mind* (1980) to *Lovesexy* (1988) rival the consecutive output of legends like JAMES BROWN, MILES DAVIS, JIMI HENDRIX, the Beatles, Bob Dylan, and the Rolling Stones—albums that despite his diminished popularity and music-making abilities and his sometimes odd decisions and erratic behavior have ensured Prince's place in music history.

FURTHER READING

Frere-Jones, Sasha. "Dorian Purple," *The New Yorker* (9 Apr. 2007).

Hill, Dave. *Prince: A Pop Life* (1989).

Hahn, Alex. *Possessed: The Rise and Fall of Prince* (2003).

Jones, Liz. *Purple Reign: The Artist Formerly Known as Prince* (1998).

Nilson, Per. *Prince: The First Decade* (1999).

Starr, Larry, and Christopher Warren. *American Popular Music: From Minstrelsy to MTV* (2003).

ANTHONY AIELLO

Prince, Abijah (c. 1706–19 Jan. 1794), freed black slave, New England property owner, and husband of LUCY TERRY, is thought to have been born in or near Wallingford, Connecticut, near New Haven. He was the slave of the Reverend Benjamin Doolittle, and accompanied Doolittle and his wife, Lydia Todd, from Connecticut to Northfield, Massachusetts, in early 1718, when Doolittle, after graduating from Yale, was named minister of that town. Based on what is known of other nearby towns, the nature of Prince's years in Northfield can be surmised. Northfield, in the Connecticut River Valley just south of the modern Vermont border, was then a small frontier town. Originally settled in 1673, it was abandoned soon afterward, following strife with the native population during King Philip's War. Resettlement began around 1685, but in 1718 it held perhaps only a dozen households, none of which owned slaves. Although slaveholding was common among New England ministers, it was unusual for Northfield residents. Prince seems to have lived for decades as the only black occupant of the town.

Prince would have been employed by his master in all aspects of daily life as required by Doolittle's growing landholdings: hunting, farming, husbandry, carpentry, and masonry. It was likely that he participated in the town's and family's defense during periods of Indian warfare, even accompanying Doolittle as he made his rounds ministering to and doctoring soldiers in nearby forts, including Fort Dummer in what is now southern Vermont. He may have been allowed to work in small ways, by his own account, for other townspeople. By early adulthood, Prince would have learned the basic skills providing him overall self-sufficiency. Beginning in March 1747, during King George's War, Prince served in the Massachusetts provincial army as a soldier in a Deerfield company. (Deerfield was a more established and populated town some fifteen miles south of Northfield.) Although it was rare for enslaved men to serve in the Massachusetts military, Prince was among those who did. After his service period ended in October 1747, though still enslaved, he gained some measure of independence. Not returning to Northfield, he instead worked in Enfield, Massachusetts, for Elijah Williams, a prominent

Deerfield merchant and politician, under whom he had served in the war.

In the early 1740s, some of the more prominent members of the Northfield congregation raised objections to Doolittle's ministerial conduct. Their complaints were partly doctrinal, but also stemmed from his increasing activity as a physician (both to the army, for which he was paid by the province, and to private citizenry), and his slave ownership. Thus, sometime before his death in 1749 Doolittle sold Prince to Northfield merchant Aaron Burt. In 1751 the town of Northfield decided to distribute unowned land within its boundaries. In order to be eligible to receive land, one needed to be included in the town's taxpayers roll of 1751, and of course needed to be a freeman. The recipient would receive land, and also become, if he were not one already, a Northfield proprietor. Proprietorship of New England towns can be thought of as ownership of corporations. The proprietors jointly owned the land underlying the town and formed the town's governing body. Subject to Provincial Law, they made their own rules and decided how and when to divide up the jointly held town property and distribute it to themselves as individual owners.

Prince, who wanted the benefits of land ownership, would have to become free and get himself on the tax rolls before this could be accomplished. Astoundingly, he managed to achieve both. Burt manumitted Prince in May 1751; the circumstances surrounding his attainment of freedom are uncertain. However, the salary he had earned during his military service in 1747 was considerable for a slave, and it seems likely he purchased his freedom. Prince then returned to Northfield, where he remained only long enough to attain residency as a free man, establish himself as a taxpaying citizen, and thus become the black proprietor of a New England town—at the time, a remarkable achievement. Northfield's land distribution did not occur immediately. Thus, when Prince left Northfield sometime in 1752, although he did not have deeds for specific lots of land, he believed he had the rights and privileges associated with proprietorship, including land ownership when distributions were made. For the next four years he lived and worked in several towns near Deerfield.

On 17 May 1756, in Deerfield, Abijah Prince married Lucy Terry, slave to Deerfield's Ebenezer Wells, a merchant and tavern holder. Terry today is known as the first African American poet. It is not known how Terry was freed, but it is likely that Prince purchased her freedom. They had six children. Later in 1756, Prince seems to have served in the French and Indian War, although it is unclear whether it was as part of a local militia, or a provincial force. They lived in Deerfield for about twenty years. Prince supported them by his farming and husbandry, by working for others providing common and semi-skilled labor, and with small entrepreneurial ventures, similar to whites of the same economic class.

Beginning in the 1750s the Province of New Hampshire sought to establish towns in the unpopulated (at least by non-Indians) lands now known as Vermont. Governor Benning Wentworth approved the location of the township, and the list of its initial owners or proprietors. In 1761 Prince became one of the original proprietors of Sunderland, a town in today's southwestern Vermont. As such, he could expect to receive some 300 acres, when all the town lands eventually were divided between him and his fellow proprietors. Among his peer proprietors were prominent New England politicians, ministers and notables, including the Massachusetts governor Francis Bernard, and the Yale president Thomas Clap. Similarly, the town of Guilford was established in southeastern Vermont. Although not an original proprietor, Prince ultimately acquired 100 acres from his military superior and former employer, Elijah Williams, and became one of Guilford's earliest settlers. Between the years 1760 and 1775, the Prince family divided their time between Deerfield and Guilford, spending summers in Guilford clearing the land for their farm and building a home, and winters in Deerfield, after which they settled permanently on their Guilford land.

Their years in Guilford were troubled by harassment instigated by one of their immediate neighbors, John Noyes, a man of some means and political influence. Two Prince children were beaten, their crops were set afire, and their house was broken into. By now in his eighties, Prince was not cowed, and he initiated a series of court cases to protect his family and property. His wife, Lucy Terry, traveled to appear before Vermont's governor and Council seeking protection, ultimately affording them peaceful possession of their homestead. Also during this period, apparently unknown to Prince, his Sunderland and Northfield properties ownership became clouded. In Northfield, for reasons undocumented, his name was dropped from the list of proprietors, thus preventing the distribution of land to him. Prince argued his case before the Northfield Proprietors and successfully redressed this, receiving compensation for the property to which he was entitled, and receiving future land as it would be distributed. In Sunderland, a fellow proprietor engaged in self-aggrandizing, but questionable land transactions, which stripped Prince of his property.

Following Prince's death in Guilford in 1794, Lucy Terry Prince and sons Caesar and Festus initiated a series of ultimately successful legal actions before the Vermont courts and Sunderland town government to regain family property. Prince's story provides remarkable insights into early New England slavery. After forty-five years of enslavement, Abijah Prince managed not only to secure his own freedom and that of his wife, but also to establish proprietorship in two towns and land ownership in a third. He ably used the legal systems to defend his rights as a freeman, and inculcated his determination and strength of character in his children.

FURTHER READING

Gerzina, Gretchen Holbrook. *Mr. and Mrs. Prince: How an Extraordinary Eighteenth-Century Family Moved Out of Slavery and into Legend* (2008).

Minkema, Kenneth P. "Jonathan Edwards's Defense of Slavery," in *Massachusetts Historical Review* 4 (2002).

ANTHONY GERZINA

Prince, Mary (1788?–?), the first woman to publish a slave narrative, was born in Brackish-Pond, Bermuda, the daughter of slave parents. The name of her mother, a household slave, is unknown. The surname of her father, a sawyer, was Prince; his first name is unknown. Mary Prince grew up in her mother's care among five younger brothers and sisters. She later described her first mistress as extremely kind and her early years as carefree. When she was twelve her owners were either unable or unwilling to support her, and she was hired out to a nearby family as a nursemaid. She was treated kindly and permitted to maintain contact with her family and her owners; still, even as a girl Mary sensed the injustice of her circumstances and chafed against them.

Within a year her mistress died, and she and her two sisters were sold at auction to different owners. Prince's new owners, the Inghams, gave her her first taste of the brutality of slavery, which she described with pointed detail: "[My mistress] caused me to know the exact difference between the smart of the rope, the cart-whip, and the cow-skin, when applied to my naked body by her own cruel hand."

In addition to being given continual beatings, Prince was worked to the point of exhaustion and often forced to labor through the night. Finally she ran away to her mother for protection. Eventually her father intervened, returning her to her master with a plea for better treatment, and Prince herself spoke up on her own behalf. Her willingness to stand up to cruel owners even as a young teenager demonstrates the determination that eventually led to her escape from slavery.

After five years with the Inghams, Prince was sold to a Mr. D____ and taken to Turk's Island, a remote salt-mining island in the Bermudas. Prince's description of the savage treatment of slaves in the salt ponds illustrates the factory mentality of slavery, where human labor was exploited to its utmost with no regard whatever for the health of the laborers. Poor nutrition, dangerous working conditions, and frequent beatings were a matter of course. Even under those dehumanizing circumstances Prince exhibited a spirit of resistance, maintaining family ties when her mother and a young sister arrived on the island; Prince also spoke of the slaves' persistent efforts to form a religious community.

Prince returned to Bermuda with Mr. D____ and his family about ten years later, rejoicing to be closer to her family and to be away from the harsh labor of Turk's Island. Her situation soon proved difficult, however, and she again made efforts to change masters. Her narrative hints at sexual abuse by Mr. D____: "He had an ugly habit of stripping himself quite naked and ordering me then to wash him in a tub of water." Scholars of Prince's narrative point out the impossibility for slave women to reveal the truth about their sexuality and sexual abuse, because abolitionist texts were designed to support the notion of a morally upright victim of the corrupt institution of slavery. In her 1997 introduction to Prince's narrative, Moira Ferguson refers to a "pattern of omissions," including any references to Prince's sexuality, as well as stories of Bermudan slave resistance that she likely heard from family members that may have emboldened her in her own interactions with cruel masters.

Prince was determined to leave Mr. D____ and succeeded in getting herself sold to John Wood, and she moved with the Wood family to Antigua. She soon fell ill, probably as a result of her ten years of hard labor in the salt mines, and describes her slow recovery in "a little old out-house, that was swarming with bugs and other vermin," nearly abandoned by her new owners. Once she was well enough to work she clashed frequently with her mistress, who verbally and physically abused her. She tried several times to find new owners, but the Woods refused to sell her. Prince set about earning her own money by taking in washing and trading provisions from incoming ships; she also probably engaged in a form of sexual barter in exchange for both money and protection with at least one white man, Captain Abbot. She refers to Abbot only as a "gentleman" who "lent me [money] to help buy my freedom" in the narrative; in a later court case she admits to having lived with Abbot for several years and to fighting over his attentions with another woman.

During her years in Antigua, Prince joined the Moravian Church, where she learned to read the Bible. In 1826 she married Daniel James, a former slave who had purchased his freedom and hoped to purchase hers. The Woods were outraged at Prince's marriage and still refused to sell her. After three years of marriage Prince agreed to go with the Woods to England, where she hoped to cure her rheumatism and attain her freedom before returning to Antigua and her husband. Instead, Prince's rheumatism grew worse than ever, and her inability to perform all her assigned duties resulted in continual conflict with the Woods. Though technically free in England, Prince hesitated to claim her freedom without any means of support, but after several months she sought out Moravian missionaries for assistance. The Moravians took her in and introduced her to members of the Anti-Slavery Society, who approached the Woods several times with offers to buy Prince's freedom, to no avail. In 1829 with the help of the society, Prince submitted a petition to the British Parliament in an attempt to gain her freedom so that she could return to the West Indies without being reenslaved, but English law did not accommodate such legal maneuvers.

Prince ultimately attained a position as a servant in the household of Thomas Pringle, a prominent member of the Anti-Slavery Society, and it was there that she dictated her story to a family friend. Pringle edited and published the narrative, *The History of Mary Prince, a West Indian Slave, Related by Herself*, in London in 1831 to great controversy. The narrative went through three editions in a matter of months. In 1833 two libel cases involving *The History of Mary Prince* were argued in the English courts. The first was brought by Thomas Pringle against the publisher of *Blackwood's Magazine* regarding a response to the *History* written by James Macqueen. Macqueen had attacked Prince's character, presenting her as a sexually depraved woman and drawing on common stereotypes of black women's sexuality. What Pringle sued over, however, was Macqueen's attack on the ladies of his own family and the intimation that Pringle himself had taken Prince as a concubine. Pringle won the suit but received damages of only three pounds.

The second case was brought by John Wood against Pringle as the publisher of Prince's narrative. Prince testified on behalf of Pringle, repeating much of the story of the Woods' treatment of her as portrayed in the *History* and answering additional questions about her relationship with Captain Abbot. Wood produced several witnesses from Antigua to attest to his kindness as a slaveholder. Pringle, unable to refute this testimony with witnesses other than Prince herself, lost the case and was forced to pay damages of twenty-five pounds.

The History of Mary Prince and the controversy that it inspired played an important role in British abolitionist debates. Though Prince disappears from history in 1833, one year before the abolition of slavery in the British colonies, her life provides a crucial perspective on the role of slaves, particularly female slaves, in attaining freedom and autonomy.

FURTHER READING

Prince, Mary. *The History of Mary Prince, a West Indian Slave, Related by Herself*, ed. Moira Ferguson (1997).

Sharpe, Jenny. *Ghosts of Slavery: A Literary Archaeology of Black Women's Lives* (2003).

Temple, Kathryn. *Scandal Nation: Law and Authorship in Britain, 1750–1832* (2003).

Whitlock, Gillian. "Volatile Subjects: *The History of Mary Prince*," in *Genius in Bondage: Literature of the Early Black Atlantic*, eds. Vincent Carretta and Philip Gould (2001).

ALICE KNOX EATON

Prince, Nancy (15 Sept. 1799–c. 1856?), abolitionist, writer, lecturer, women's rights activist, and social critic, was born Nancy Gardner in Newburyport, Massachusetts, the daughter of an African American and Indian mother and an African American father, Thomas Gardner, who was born in Nantucket, Massachusetts, and died within three months of Nancy's birth. What is known about her is drawn primarily from her 1850 memoir, *A Narrative of the Life and Travels of Mrs. Nancy Prince*. While Prince does not name her mother in her narrative, she provides descriptions of both parents that highlight their African descent, and she recounts her grandfather's violent removal to America, along with his memories of a proud life in Africa. She briefly notes the capture of her Indian grandmother by local English colonials. Her narrative speaks clearly to issues of race, gender, slavery, and morality in the United States and the Caribbean.

Prince's childhood in Gloucester, Massachusetts, was marked by poverty, homelessness, hard labor, and profound concern for her own survival and that of her more than seven siblings still living at home. Her mother married three times; each of her husbands died from illness or overwork, and her second and third husbands were hostile toward Prince and the other children they did not father. By the time they reached adolescence, Prince, her brother George, and her oldest sister, Silvia, had become responsible for their younger siblings and their mother. They collected fruits and fish to sell and ran errands in order to provide food and resources to support the struggling family. George, overwhelmed by the enduring poverty, soon signed on to a ship sailing from the local harbor, and Silvia hired out as a domestic with a family that lived seventy miles from their family home in Gloucester. Prince took a service position in a home in Salem, Massachusetts, where she worked until she became ill from hard labor and poor treatment. Her employers were pious, and she had hoped to receive religious instruction while among them. But although they observed family prayers twice daily, their cruelty to fourteen-year-old Prince provided her with an early opportunity to question the morality of white Christians.

The experiences of her sister and mother undoubtedly shaped Prince's adult choices. Silvia, who by 1815 had moved to Boston to secure better wages, became a prostitute. In the winter of 1816, with the help of friends, Prince rescued her sister from a brothel. Never stable or comfortable among her family again, Silvia died in 1827. In her narrative, Prince briefly eulogizes her sister, calling her "precious" and "very dear" and revealing that she had often protected Silvia from their stepfather's abuse. Silvia's fall and death were not the result of a flawed character, Prince argues, but rather a consequence of the limited choices available to poor women, especially poor African American women.

Thrice widowed and the mother of at least ten children who had been either hired out or placed for care with local families, Prince's mother became financially and emotionally dependent on her father, Tobias Wornton, called Backus, the only constant male presence in her life. When he died, about the same time as her third husband, she lost all reliable means of support. Unable to work because of her poor health, she eventually suffered a mental collapse and took to wandering miles from home until she died without ceremony in 1827, the same year as her daughter Silvia died. "My mother wandered about like a Jew," Prince wrote about her mother (17).

In her narrative, Prince casts her childhood and adolescence as determined by her race, gender, and class. If her mother's life was to be any model, Prince saw her own life as proceeding toward misfortune and disease of the body, mind, and spirit. The chain of predetermination was broken for Prince on 6 May 1819, however, when she was baptized by the Reverend THOMAS PAUL of Cambridge, Massachusetts, a religious and political leader known for his abolition work. Within three years, Prince left employment as a domestic, learned a trade, and developed a "determination to do something for myself" (20). By 1822 she decided to leave the country. In September 1823 she met Nero Prince, who had recently arrived from Russia, where he served as one of twenty "colored" men in the court of the emperor Alexander. They married on 15 February 1824 and sailed for Russia on 14 April.

The Russian experience is at the heart of Prince's narrative and at the core of her development as a political advocate, activist, and social critic. She was accepted as a member of her local St. Petersburg community quite easily, and during the flood of 1824 her home became a place of refuge for flood victims. In her narrative, Prince comments in travelogue style on the Russian folk, community life, holiday and funeral celebrations, religious and family life, the flood of 1824, high-court culture, and the life and pastimes of the empress Elizabeth. She also details political assassination, violent regime change, and war between Russia and Turkey. She comments as well on the apparent lack of race prejudice in the empire and the fact that serfs were treated better in Russia than slaves were treated in America. The contrast she draws between American and Russian laboring classes formed the basis of her antislavery activism upon her return to the United States.

By late 1833, troubled by the harsh winter climate, Prince returned to the United States, while her husband remained in Russia, apparently in the court's service under the new emperor. Nero Prince, intending to return to his wife in New

England after two years of accumulating property, died before reaching home. Taking up the cause of children, Nancy Prince continued the work she had begun during the 1824 Russian flood, establishing an asylum for orphaned children. When the project failed financially after three months, Prince deepened her interest in antislavery causes, aligning her philosophy with that of William Lloyd Garrison's. Impassioned statements in her narrative indict American immorality and sin and warn that the sins are not hidden from God's notice.

After attending a lecture about the lives of former slaves in Jamaica and their need for spiritual, social, and financial support, Prince was persuaded to volunteer with a missionary contingent, and on 16 November 1840 she sailed from Charlestown, Massachusetts, to St. Ann's Bay, Jamaica. Her goal in Jamaica was to "raise up and encourage the emancipated inhabitants, and teach the young children to read and work, to fear God, and put their trust in the Saviour" (45). Her good intentions notwithstanding, Prince had considerable difficulty accepting the cultural and religious habits of local Jamaicans. In her narrative she complains of lax standards among religious leaders and the women's societies within the church, and she opines that "the meeting house is more like a play house than a place of worship" (47).

In 1841 she published *The West Indies: Being a Description of the Islands*, a pamphlet which exposes and explains the destructive effects of slavery on the culture and character of the Jamaican people. The pamphlet reveals and derides corrup tion among black and white church–sponsored missionaries, who were colluding, in Prince's view, to take advantage of the recently emancipated population. In addition, *The West Indies* provided American readers with a thorough topographical description of the islands and information about the islands' black, white, and "mulatto" inhabitants. Prince reports on the British colony's violent internal civil conflict, turmoil in the church in the period immediately after emancipation, and extracolonial efforts to aid the newly freed, industrious, often illiterate, and proud former slaves. The pamphlet is reprinted for the most part, though in slightly different order, in Prince's narrative.

A life of labor on behalf of others placed Nancy Prince in the company of prostitutes, in the czarist court in St. Petersburg, and among missionaries selling Bibles in Jamaica. Through all these experiences, Prince remained self-sufficient, committed to her labors and her faith, and humble. Hard labor,

extreme weather, and limited medical attention over her lifetime eventually left her infirm. In 1850 Prince published *A Narrative of the Life and Travels of Mrs. Nancy Prince*. "My object is not a vain desire to appear before the public," Prince wrote in her introduction, "but, by the sale, I hope to obtain the means to supply my necessities" (3). A second edition of Prince's eighty-nine-page book was published in 1853. Although it is seldom anthologized, Prince's narrative is a rare combination of faith story, travelogue, and political chronicle. The date and place of Prince's death remain unknown.

FURTHER READING

Prince, Nancy. *A Narrative of the Life and Travels of Mrs. Nancy Prince* (1850, 2d ed. 1853).

Peterson, Carla L. *"Doers of the Word": African-American Women Speakers and Writers in the North, 1830–1880* (1995).

MARTHA L. WHARTON

Prioleau, George Washington (1856–15 July 1927), Buffalo Soldier, U.S. Army chaplain, and African Methodist Episcopal (AME) pastor, was born a slave in Charleston, South Carolina, to L. S. and Susan Prioleau. After the Civil War he was educated at Charleston's public schools and Avery Institute. He then entered Claflin College in Orangeburg, South Carolina, and in the winter months taught school at the Lyons Township in Orangeburg County. During the same period he joined the AME Church at St. Matthews, South Carolina, where his father served as pastor. Young Prioleau assisted his father and was eventually ordained.

After completing his education at Claflin in 1875, Prioleau served as pastor of the Double Springs Mission in Laurens County, South Carolina. In 1880 he entered Wilberforce University in Ohio, where he pursued the bachelor of divinity degree. He helped pay for his studies by working as a farmhand in nearby Green and Clark counties and serving at an AME mission in Selma, Ohio.

After graduation from Wilberforce in June 1884 Prioleau continued pastoring various churches and teaching school in Selma, Ohio. He also met and married Anna L. Scovell, an 1885 graduate of Wilberforce, on 23 September 1885. In addition he was also an active Mason, eventually rising to the 33rd degree.

In September 1889 Prioleau was called to serve as professor of ecclesiastical history and homiletics at Wilberforce. The theology department soon became Payne Theological Seminary and Prioleau served as the chair of historical and pastoral theology from 1890 until 1894. He also maintained positions in the AME Church as presiding elder and conference chair, as well as associate editor of the AME *Lesson Leaf*, one of the denomination's leading publications.

Prioleau had been interested in becoming a U.S. Army chaplain for some time, and when a position came open with the Ninth U.S. Cavalry he applied and was approved for service. President Grover Cleveland signed his commission on 25 April 1895 and he became one of only five Buffalo Soldier chaplains. The Buffalo Soldiers were the black soldiers who served in the American West during this era and they were given that name out of respect by their Native American foes. The rough and tumble world of the Buffalo Soldiers of Fort Robinson, Nebraska, presented quite a shock to someone who had grown accustomed to the refined world of the black elite of Ohio. The gambling, drunkenness, and prostitution the men engaged in led Prioleau to conclude that the army was an "atmosphere pregnated with evil and sin" (Prioleau, 28). In a chapter he wrote entitled "Is the Chaplain's Work a Necessity?" in *Theophilus G. Steward's Active Service or Gospel Work among the U.S. Soldiers* (1897), Prioleau maintained that army chaplains served as a shield to protect the men from the temptations and trouble found in the towns located just outside military posts. Prioleau worked diligently to combat those influences at Fort Robinson by counseling the men, setting an example, performing his pastoral duties, and maintaining the post Sunday school. On occasion he was even invited to preach at the local Congregational Church in the nearby town of Crawford.

In 1898 the United States declared war on Spain and the men of the Ninth Cavalry prepared to deploy to Cuba. Just before their departure Prioleau led four hundred people in a memorial service for those who had died aboard USS *Maine*. The *Maine* was the American battleship that mysteriously blew up in the Havana, Cuba, harbor that helped provoke the United States into declaring war on Spain. As Prioleau and the Ninth made their way by train from Nebraska to the rallying point at Tampa, Florida, he was shocked to see well-wishers who came out to greet white troops, but who then confronted the Buffalo Soldiers only with coolness. He wrote of the hurt he and the men felt in letters published in the *Cleveland Gazette*.

Living conditions in overcrowded army camps in Tampa were appalling and Prioleau contracted malaria just before the Ninth Cavalry was deployed to Cuba. Forced to stay in Florida while his regiment went on without him, Prioleau eventually recovered and was sent on recruiting duty throughout the South. Everywhere he went he was confronted by racism, even though he was wearing the uniform of a U.S. Army officer. The experience was a new one for a Buffalo Soldier, for in the American West troopers of the Ninth were appreciated for the protection they brought to the frontier. But in the Jim Crow South, Prioleau found himself forced to sit in the gallery of a white church in Tuskegee, Alabama, threatened with lynching at one point, and even treated viciously in Orangeburg, South Carolina, the home of his alma mater. Prioleau concluded that whites hated him even more than common blacks precisely because he was an educated black man and an army officer—in other words, a black man who did not know his place.

Chaplain Prioleau continued his service with the Ninth Cavalry and was sent to the Philippines on two tours of duty during the Philippine War from 1899 to 1905. His first wife, Anna, died in February 1903 at Fort Walla Walla, Washington, at the age of forty. Two years later, on 20 February 1905, Prioleau married Ethel C. Stafford of Emporia, Kansas. The couple eventually had four children.

Prioleau stayed with the Ninth Cavalry for over twenty years until he was transferred to the Tenth Cavalry, another Buffalo Soldier regiment, on 15 November 1915, and served with that unit along the Mexican border. In 1917 he was promoted to major and was transferred to the all-black Twenty-fifth Infantry Regiment stationed at Schofield Barracks, Hawaii. Chaplain Prioleau was a strong advocate for African American causes and helped to raise $3,200 for the NAACP and African American victims of the East St. Louis race riot in 1917. This riot had broken out in February 1917, after 470 black workers were hired to replace striking white workers from the American Federation of Labor union. Angry whites killed and mutilated 35 blacks and burned the homes of hundreds of other blacks, leaving them homeless.

Prioleau retired from the army in 1920 but did not retire from the ministry. In October 1921 he helped to organize the Bethel AME mission in Los Angeles, California. He worked tirelessly, receiving no pay during his first three years. His wife, Ethel, served as Sunday school superintendent. Through their efforts Bethel quickly became a full-fledged church and by 1927 was preparing to build a new church building. Prioleau never lived to see it completed, however, for he fell off a ladder and suffered internal injuries that were slow to heal. He died at the age of seventy-one.

FURTHER READING

Prioleau, George W. "Is the Chaplain's Work in the Army a Necessity?" in *Active Service or Gospel Work Among U.S. Soldiers*, edited by Theophilus G. Steward (1897).

Beasley, Delilah. *The Negro Trail Blazers of California* (1919).

Cashin, Hershel V. *Under Fire with the Tenth U.S. Cavalry* (1899; reprint 1969).

Fowler, Arlen L. *The Black Infantry in the West, 1869–1891* (1971).

Gatewood, William B., ed. *"Smoked Yankees" and the Struggle for Empire: Letters from Negro Soldiers, 1898–1902* (1971).

Lamm, Alan K. *Five Black Preachers in Army Blue, 1884–1901: The Buffalo Soldier Chaplains* (1998).

Schubert, Frank N. *Buffalo Soldiers, Braves and the Brass: The Story of Fort Robinson, Nebraska* (1993).

Schubert, Frank N. *Voices of the Buffalo Soldier* (2003).

ALAN K. LAMM

Pritchard, "Gullah" Jack (?–12 July 1822), conjurer and slave rebel, was born in East Africa during the final quarter of the eighteenth century. He was a native of the country of "M'Choolay Morcema" (possibly modern Mozambique), from which he was captured, taken to Zanzibar, and sold to Zephaniah Kingsley in 1805. At the time of his enslavement, he possessed a bag of conjuring implements and had been a "priest" in his homeland. Jack may have initially gone to Kingsley's plantation in East Florida but was purchased by the wealthy Charleston shipbuilder, Paul Pritchard, in April 1806 and worked on the docks as a joiner and caulker.

Jack's position as an urban and skilled slave allowed him a number of relative luxuries in a city and society that were dominated by slavery. Jack, who was single, lived by himself off of his master's property and received permission to hire out his time and move about the city with little interference from whites, who saw him as nothing more than an "industrious 'little man with large black whiskers'" (Edgerton, p. 119). But to the city's black residents, Jack was an African priest "of great power and magic" (his wild whiskers was one sign of his power) and an important member of the African Church, as both blacks and whites called it, in the Hampstead neighborhood of the city. Jack exerted immense sway over the black population because of his role as a "magician," "conjurer," or "doctor." His spiritual authority was firmly rooted in his manipulation of recognizably African tools and ceremonies of divination, healing, and supernatural control. Many African villages had at least one man or woman who acted as a healer, guide, or interpreter of the supernatural. Few blacks doubted his ability to heal or control people and events, a vivid example of the transplantation of African religious practices to America.

By 1817, Jack had befriended the fiery and revolutionary self-emancipated black carpenter Denmark Vesey. Each man saw in the other a powerful and complementary ally in their struggle against slavery. Vesey was free, wealthy, and a respected pillar of the black community; he had also developed a stinging antislavery message that was based on the Old Testament, ideas of the Age of Revolution, and abusive white control over sacred black religious life, especially an armed intrusion and arrest of black congregants in June 1818. Jack was a powerful and feared conjurer who provided a direct link to African spirituality that appealed to many blacks in Charleston. Together, these two men would allegedly spearhead the largest slave conspiracy in North American history.

If we believe the confessions—many extracted by torture—gathered by white interrogators in the summer of 1822, in late 1821 Vesey initially approached Jack to help organize a slave revolt in Charleston. Over the course of early 1822, Jack played a number of invaluable roles in the conspiracy and proved an active and effective recruiter holding regular secret meetings with slaves in and around Charleston. At these meetings, Jack made great use of his magical powers and apparently performed elaborate initiation rituals that were meant to assure loyalty and success. A number of the conspirators would later claim that Jack had taken control of them through the use of magic. His role as African shaman was an essential ingredient in the recruitment and retention of slave rebels who gained immeasurable confidence from his supernatural powers.

Jack played such a vital role in organizing the rebellion that by the spring of 1822 he had stopped hiring out his time so he could devote all of his energies to plotting the insurrection. According to the confessions, he intended to poison the water supply of Charleston to weaken the white population. Jack also helped to acquire a powder keg and arranged to have a number of pikes made. When the date of the revolt arrived, Jack was to lead a detachment of armed rebels that who charged with the responsibility of seizing and distributing weapons from various stores and militias in Charleston.

Despite the careful planning, Vesey and Jack's rebellion was betrayed by a number of black informers. White authorities began to round up alleged conspirators on Monday, 17 June, but Vesey and Jack remained at large even as a hysterical Charleston began to try the first conspirators on 19 June. On 22 June, Vesey was captured. Jack continued to lead a group of devoted revolutionaries and allegedly devised a plan to rescue Vesey and his followers from the city's jail, but he gave up the plan and Vesey was hung on 2 July. Still, Jack sought to sustain the revolt by spreading the word among trustworthy slaves that the revolution would begin on 6 July. On 5 July, however, whites captured him, putting an end to the conspiracy.

Jack's trial quickly got underway and he was afforded no legal representation. A steady stream of slave witnesses testified to Jack's role in the conspiracy and to the fact that he had used his considerable magical powers to shape events and control participants. Jack's owner, Paul Pritchard, offered little defense of his property and Jack simply denied any role in the conspiracy or possessing any magical powers. On 9 July, white authorities unanimously sentenced him to death in a decision that invoked the strongest possible language, portraying him as a conniving and bloodthirsty master of the black arts.

> In the prosecution of your wicked designs, you were not satisfied with resorting to natural and ordinary means, but endeavored to enlist on your behalf, all the powers of darkness, and employed for that purpose the most disgusting mummery and superstition. You represented yourself as invulnerable ....Your boasted charms have not protected yourself ....Your alters [sic] and your Gods have sunk together in the dust (Edgerton, p. 192).

Although Jack never provided evidence against any other enslaved African Americans and he was probably tortured, his response to the death sentence was to plead desperately for one more week of life. He spent his remaining days in physical and mental anguish, locked in the top floor of the city' sweltering Poor House. On 12 July, Jack was taken beyond the central city to face the scaffold. He resisted, but his executioners dragged him up the steps and hung him, a stark testimony to other slaves that his magical powers were no more.

FURTHER READING

Egerton, Douglas. *He Shall Go Free: The Lives of Denmark Vesey*, rev. ed. (2004).

Robertson, David. *Denmark Vesey* (1999).

Silverman, Susan, and Lois Walker. *A Documented History of Gullah Jack Pritchard and the Denmark Vesey Slave Insurrection of 1822* (2000).

NATHANIEL MILLETT

Pritchard, Robert Starling, II (13 June 1927–), concert pianist, composer, humanitarian, educator, and advocate of Black History Month, was one of three children born to R. Starling Pritchard Sr. and Lucille Pickard Pritchard in Winston-Salem, North Carolina. His parents adopted two children. Lucille had a vision, before Robert's birth, that he would be the first viable African American classical pianist. She would place a hand-wound Victrola record player close to her stomach so that the baby would be saturated with jazz, spirituals, and the blues as well as the classical European music of Beethoven, Chopin, and Mozart. Due to Robert Sr.'s inability to find work and their experience with racism in North Carolina, the family moved to Buffalo, New York, shortly after Robert's birth. They soon found out that racism also existed in Buffalo. Moreover, Pritchard's father could not find work in that city, so he moved the family, again, to Syracuse, New York, where he obtained a job in a steel mill.

Robert's parents were not satisfied with the public education their children received in Syracuse because it excluded African American history. Conversations at the dinner table often included the lives and contributions of great African Americans. International visitors were invited into their home so that the children could get a view of what was happening outside of Syracuse. Robert was introduced to the piano early in life by his father, who played jazz improvisations on the piano and music from the Victrola. Robert was also encouraged to listen to classical music. Robert Pritchard II received a B.A. from Syracuse University in 1948, and an M.A. from the same institution in 1950. He earned honorary doctorates from the University of Haiti and from Claflin University in Orangeburg, South Carolina.

At the age of fifteen, he made his debut with the Syracuse Symphony Orchestra. He studied piano with Edwin Fischer, Arturo Benedetti Michelangeli, Carl Friedberg, Hans Neuman, and Robert

Goldsand from 1948 to 1959 and began touring as a concert pianist in 1951. Dr. Pritchard was the first and only African American who was sponsored by the United States Cultural and Exchange Program to perform in the United States and overseas in 1957, touring Europe, the Middle East, and North Africa as a solo performer.

In 1958 he was artist-in-residence at the Conservatoire Nationale D'Haiti, Port-au-Prince, and helped revitalize the department. In 1959 Pritchard established the first music department at the University of Liberia. In 1961 he made his debut at Town Hall in New York City and received rave reviews from music critics. In the early 1960s, Dr. Pritchard was a visiting humanities lecturer at the New School for Social Research and Barnard College of Columbia University. Rosario said, "Dr. Pritchard performed at the grand opening of Lincoln Center in 1962 at the behest of the Rockefeller Family." After his performance, he collapsed and was rushed to the hospital via ambulance. The doctor who treated him said that Dr. Pritchard would make him famous. Dr. Pritchard was curious. The doctor explained that Dr. Pritchard was a rarity in medical history because there had to his knowledge been no other recorded documentation of an African American with the rare disease of porphyria, a genetic blood disorder.

He was chairman of the American Festival of Negro Arts in 1964 and wrote the foreword to the inaugural publication of 30 African American Choral Spirituals collected and arranged by EDWARD HAMMOND BOATNER of Hammond Music Company. In 1965 Dr. Pritchard was also one of the first advocates of expanding on Negro History Week, founded by Dr. CARTER G. WOODSON in February 1926, to a full Black History Month. In 1976 the Association for the Study of African American Life and History (ASALH), the leading promoter of Negro History Week, followed Pritchard's lead by establishing February as a full month's celebration of African American history.

In 1965 he also founded the Panamerican-Panafrican Association, Inc., a nongovernmental organization (NGO) in consultative status (Category II) with the Economic and Social Council of the United Nations. One of the main programs of the Panamerican-Panafrican Association is the National International Black History Month Founder's Commission. In 1976 he was musical director and pianist for the United Nations Symphonic and Choral Concert Gala celebrating the thirteenth anniversary of the founding of the Organization of African Unity. In 1991 he was selected as the American Cultural Advisor to the Ethiopian Royal Family.

Since 2007 he has lived in Dumfries, Virginia. Dr. Pritchard never married. His adopted son, Tyrone Shardel Pritchard, lives in San Diego, California.

FURTHER READING
The Capitol Spotlight 45, no. 17 (26 Feb. 1998).
New York Times, 23 September 1962.
Panamerican-Panafrican Association www. PaPaUSA.org
Pritchard, Robert Starling II. *Who's Who among African Americans,* 23rd ed., edited by Kristen B. Mallegg in celebration of the 100th anniversary of the NAACP (2009).

DISCOGRAPHY
Smithsonian Folkways Special Series, CDMP3, Catalog SFS60002 released 29 March 2011 remastered and reissued album released previously as an album by Spoken Arts, Inc., 1962.

LOIS BELLAMY

Procope, Russell (11 Aug. 1908–21 Jan. 1981), jazz alto saxophonist and clarinetist, was born in New York City's San Juan Hill, the son of William A. Procope, a violinist, and Mary E. Levy, a pianist. Raised in a musical environment, Procope started violin at age six and later played first chair in his junior high school orchestra. At age fourteen he began clarinet studies with Bobby Stark's teacher, Lieutenant Eugene Mikell, and played in the 369th Infantry Cadet Band.

His first major influence in jazz was the FLETCHER HENDERSON Orchestra of 1924, which featured LOUIS ARMSTRONG, COLEMAN HAWKINS, and BUSTER BAILEY, his initial model on clarinet. After noting the remarkable progress that Benny Carter was making on alto sax, he prevailed upon his mother to buy him one, and by 1926 he was playing all three instruments in the bands of Willie Freeman and Jimmy Campbell. Procope also worked for a year and a half at a dime-a-dance hall and in Henri Saparo's band in Harlem. In 1927 he joined the pianist Charlie Skeete's group at the Rose Danceland and remained there through JELLY ROLL MORTON's takeover in the summer of 1928. One of the first changes Morton made in the band was to send for OMER SIMEON, his favorite clarinetist and one from whom Procope learned much about New Orleans style. After Simeon returned to Chicago, Procope made his first records on 6 December 1928 with Morton, playing clarinet solos on "Red Hot Pepper" and "Deep Creek" in the style he had learned not only from Simeon but also from the records of JOHNNY DODDS, SIDNEY BECHET, ALBERT NICHOLAS, and BARNEY BIGARD. After the recording session Procope toured with Morton from December 1928 through April 1929.

After a brief association with Benny Carter's band at the end of 1929, Procope joined CHICK WEBB's band, in which he played alongside the alto saxist Hilton Jefferson, another strong influence on his own sax style. In March 1931 Webb and Fletcher Henderson decided to trade a few key sidemen, with the result that Procope took Benny Carter's place as Henderson's lead alto and clarinetist. Along with such other prominent sidemen as REX STEWART, Bobby Stark, Claude Jones, J. C. HIGGINBOTHAM, and Coleman Hawkins, from the beginning Procope was featured in solo, and his Simeon-based clarinet and Carteresque alto can be heard on "Clarinet Marmalade," the Melotone recording of "Sugar Foot Stomp," "Radio Rhythm," "My Sweet Tooth Says 'I Wanna' (But My Wisdom Tooth Says 'No')," "Malinda's Wedding Day," and "Blue Rhythm." On subsequent records, though, the alto solos were taken by Hilton Jefferson, who entered the band around October 1932. When Henderson disbanded in November 1934, Procope went with TINY BRADSHAW's band briefly before joining Teddy Hill's group at the Savoy Ballroom in early 1935. Procope remained with Hill through the fall of 1937, playing alongside ROY ELDRIDGE, FRANKIE NEWTON, DICKY WELLS, CHU BERRY, Cecil Scott, and DIZZY GILLESPIE, and recording solos on "At the Rug Cutters' Ball" and both versions of "Blue Rhythm Fantasy." After touring in Europe with Hill in mid-1937 Procope returned home and worked briefly in Willie Bryant's orchestra. Also that year he married Helen (maiden name unknown); they had no children. In addition to his recordings with Henderson and Hill, during the 1930s Procope also appeared on sessions with Benny Carter, LIONEL HAMPTON, HORACE W. HENDERSON, Bob Howard, Frankie Newton, Timme Rosenkrantz, and CLARENCE WILLIAMS.

Procope's widest exposure as a soloist began in May 1938 when he joined the former Henderson bassist JOHN KIRBY's sextet, a tightly arranged, innovative group, which also included the trumpeter CHARLIE SHAVERS, the clarinetist Buster Bailey, the pianist Billy Kyle, and the drummer O'Neill Spencer. By this time Procope had become a highly polished, pure-toned saxophonist, whose fleet technique and genteel, cerebral approach not only matched Shavers's and Bailey's own styles but were also perfectly suited to the swing arrangements of classical and folk themes, operatic arias, exotic mood pieces, and jazz standards that were the group's specialties. The Kirby sextet opened at the Onyx Club playing opposite STUFF SMITH's popular combo until Smith's contract expired, at which time they became the featured attraction. At first, the group used no written arrangements, basing their performances on "talk over" rehearsals and on-the-job practice, but after their popularity was secured, Shavers and Kyle became the group's primary arrangers. During their residencies at the Onyx Club, Famous Door, Hickory House, Café Society Uptown, and the Zombie Club at the World's Fair, the sextet also broadcast several times weekly on CBS and NBC and recorded widely for both radio transcription and the major commercial labels. Besides recording two sessions under the name of Buster Bailey, the sextet also accompanied the violinist Eddie South and the singers Mildred Bailey, UNA MAE CARLISLE, MAXINE SULLIVAN, and Midge Williams, and worked nine months at the Ambassador Hotel in Chicago and at various venues in Los Angeles. Though an integral member of the group, Procope left Kirby in 1943 to enlist in the army, and after two years' service stationed in New York, as a musician, he rejoined the band at the Copacabana.

On 20 October 1945, probably while he was working with Kirby, Procope appeared on a DUKE ELLINGTON broadcast as a guest soloist on "Honeysuckle Rose" and "Perdido." Although he had never played with Ellington before, his performance was so impressive that Ellington called on him the following spring to substitute for the lead altoman Otto Hardwick. After the show he was asked to stay for the next night's engagement, and by April he had become Hardwick's permanent replacement. With the exception of two brief absences—in 1961 when he played with WILBUR DE PARIS, and 1971 when he was ill—Procope remained with Ellington until the leader's death in May 1974. While with Ellington, Procope and his colleagues JOHNNY HODGES, Jimmy Hamilton, Paul Gonsalves, and HARRY HOWELL CARNEY were members of the longest-lasting sax section in jazz history. Hodges had been the principal alto soloist since 1928, so Procope's duties were at first limited to the sectional role that his predecessor had performed from the band's inception. Ellington, though, wanted a New Orleans–style clarinetist to carry on the tradition that Barney Bigard had begun in 1928 and that was sorely missed in the orchestral palette since his 1942 departure. Although Hamilton was a brilliant clarinetist, his Benny Goodman–influenced style was entirely different from Bigard's, so in order to provide that missing tonal color Ellington encouraged Procope to concentrate on clarinet again.

In 1950 Ellington recorded an extended version of his 1930 masterpiece, "Mood Indigo," and Procope's two solos and a scored duet passage with Hamilton were important new additions to the arrangement. The contrast between the two clarinet styles was further emphasized in 1952 with "The Mooche," which counterpoised Procope's somber, low-register, melodic exposition with Hamilton's delicate, higher-pitched, filigree obbligato. Other featured solos followed in 1956 with "Creole Love Call" and "Blues to Be There," the second movement of the specially composed "Newport Jazz Festival Suite." Ellington's 1959 score for the film *Anatomy of a Murder* incorporated a section called "Way Early Subtone," which again highlighted Procope's broad low register, and he is similarly showcased on 1968's "Swamp Goo," "Almighty God," and "4:30 Blues." In addition to his many broadcasts, concerts, and recordings with Ellington from April 1946, Procope also appeared on sessions led by Chris Barber, CAT ANDERSON, LAWRENCE BROWN, EARL HINES, Hodges, Butch Miles, Ernie Royal, BILLY STRAYHORN, and CLARK TERRY. However, he recorded only two leader dates in his entire career, one in late 1946 and the other in early 1956. From the mid-1970s Procope worked in New York City in a trio with the pianist Brooks Kerr, a young Ellington disciple, and the drummer SONNY GREER, who had been with Ellington from early 1920 through March 1951. Procope also played in the show *Ain't Misbehavin'* and led a group called Ellingtonia. He died in New York City.

Although not an original jazz stylist, Procope always had a readily identifiable tone on both saxophone and clarinet, the latter being more in evidence during his tenure with Ellington, with whom he assumed the role formerly played by Bigard.

FURTHER READING

Allen, Walter C. *Hendersonia: The Music of Fletcher Henderson and His Musicians* (1973).

Dance, Stanley. *The World of Duke Ellington* (1970).

Ellington, Duke. *Music Is My Mistress* (1973).

Wright, Laurie. *Mr. Jelly Lord* (1980).

Obituary: *Jazz Journal*, Apr. 1981.

This entry is taken from the *American National Biography* and is published here with the permission of the American Council of Learned Societies.

JACK SOHMER

Proctor, Henry Hugh (8 Dec. 1868–12 May 1933), Congregational clergyman, was born and grew up on a farm near Fayetteville, Tennessee, the son of former slaves, Richard Proctor and Hannah Wetherley (or Murray). He studied at rural schools outside of Fayetteville and the public schools of Fayetteville. Before continuing his education, Proctor taught school at Pea Ridge and Fayetteville. In 1884 he entered Central Tennessee College at Nashville, but he transferred to Fisk University in Nashville, Tennessee, after one term. Proctor completed preparatory studies at Fisk and graduated with an AB degree in 1891 and then studied at Yale Divinity School, where he graduated with a BD degree in 1894. In 1893 he married a Fisk student, Adeline L. Davis, of Nashville; they became the parents of six children.

On 1 July 1894 Proctor was ordained and became pastor of Atlanta's First Congregational Church. The first African American pastor of this biracial mission, which was founded by white missionaries during Reconstruction and remained closely affiliated with Atlanta University, he increased its membership from 100 to 400 within four years and put it on a self-supporting financial basis. On a trip south, the *Outlook*'s Ernest Hamlin Abbott declared that "without exception, white or black," Proctor's "was the most progressive and best organized church I saw in the South" (Abbott, *Religious Life in America: A Record of Personal Observation* [1902]). It was more influential than some congregations five or six times its size. In 1901 Proctor helped defeat efforts to disfranchise black Georgians. A year later the *Atlanta Constitution* took note of his sermons, which crusaded against crime and vice along Decatur Street. By 1904 Proctor's work was winning him wider recognition; Clark University awarded him an honorary doctor of divinity degree, and he was elected as assistant moderator of the National Council of Congregational Churches.

In September 1906, stirred by the racist rhetoric of a bitter political campaign, white mobs swept from Decatur Street across Atlanta, indiscriminately attacking black people wherever they were found. During a lull in the rioting, white leaders of the city, including attorney Charles Hopkins, conferred about how to contain the violence. As it subsided, they contacted Proctor, who helped to arrange a meeting of twenty leading white men and twenty leading black men at the courthouse. Their committee to restore order in the city led to continued discussions between leaders of both races. Hopkins

Henry Hugh Proctor, pastor of the First Congregational Church in Atlanta, Ga., c. 1900. (Library of Congress.)

school rooms, library, model kitchen, gymnasium, showers, lavatories, auditorium, offices, ladies' parlor, and galleries. The church offered a counseling service, an employment bureau, a home for working women, a kindergarten, a prison mission, and a music festival. Northern white pastors, including Washington Gladden and Russell Conwell, and popular novelist Bruce Barton praised its potential. First Congregational Church was, said Barton, "The Church That Saved a City." By 1920, when Proctor left Atlanta, First Congregational Church comprised 1,000 African American members who worshipped in the handsome new building.

During the spring and summer of 1919 Proctor toured France for the War Work Council, addressing more than 100,000 African American soldiers. In 1920 he became pastor of Brooklyn, New York's Nazarene Congregational Church. In his thirteen years there he increased church membership from 160 to more than 1,000 and established another institutional church. In 1926 he was elected moderator of the New York City Congregational Association. He also served as vice president of the Brooklyn Urban League and the Lincoln Settlement Association. He died in Brooklyn of blood poisoning and was buried in Atlanta's Southview Cemetery.

A lifelong Republican and an ardent advocate of the civil rights of African Americans, Proctor was nonetheless instinctively a conservative who supported the suppression of vice and believed in law and order. Within the African American community he valued the friendship and the wisdom of both W. E. B. DuBois and Booker T. Washington. Proctor was "a magnificent specimen of a man, six feet two or three inches, and finely proportioned, with the dignity and self-command of the true orator; it is easy to understand the hold he maintains over [his] large congregation," said Washington Gladden. "At a glance, I should have thought him a Methodist," Lura Beam wrote. "He lacked entirely the Congregational austerity, the Emersonian residue. He came singing transcendentalism, and the vigor of his natural endowment gave him social acceptance from both races" (*He Called Them by the Lightning: A Teacher's Odyssey in the South, 1908–1919*).

organized the Atlanta Civic League of two thousand white members, while Proctor secured fifteen hundred members for a parallel Coloured Cooperative Civic League. Executive committees of the two leagues met regularly to discuss and plan concerted action on issues that irritated local race relations. Black radicals, such as W. E. B. DuBois, dismissed the effort as "gotten up primarily for advertizing purposes," but Atlanta's plan for dialogue between parallel structures of racial leadership was a model for southern racial liberalism's idea of "interracial cooperation" in the first half of the twentieth century.

Impelled by the crisis created by the Atlanta riot, Proctor mounted a campaign to build an institutional church, one that would be equipped to meet the community's broader social needs. He raised money for it from the local black and white communities before turning to northern philanthropists to finish paying for it. BOOKER T. WASHINGTON spoke at the ground breaking for the new building in January 1908. Theodore Roosevelt and William Howard Taft inspected its Sunday

FURTHER READING
Proctor's papers are at the Amistad Research Center, Tulane University, New Orleans, Louisiana.
Proctor, Henry Hugh. *Between Black and White: Autobiographical Sketches* (1925).

Crowe, Charles. "Racial Massacre in Atlanta, September 22, 1906," *Journal of Negro History* 54 (Apr. 1969).

Dittmer, John. *Black Georgia in the Progressive Era, 1900–1920* (1977).

Luker, Ralph E. *The Social Gospel in Black and White* (1991).

This entry is taken from the *American National Biography* and is published here with the permission of the American Council of Learned Societies.

RALPH E. LUKER

Proctor, Samuel DeWitt (13 Jul. 1921–22 May 1997), minister, educator, and humanitarian, was born in Norfolk, Virginia, the son of Hughes Proctor, who worked at the Norfolk Navy Yard, and Velma Gladys. His parents had met as students at Norfolk Mission College, the same college attended by Velma's parents; Hughes's mother had attended Hampton Institute during Reconstruction. It was unusual for a black family to have such educated parents and grandparents so soon after slavery, and Samuel and his six siblings were raised to believe that educational attainment was natural and expected. Music and religious devotion also helped shape Samuel's childhood. His father played the violin, he played the clarinet, and the other children were each encouraged to learn an instrument. They entertained themselves at home, and they all sang in the choir of the Baptist church founded by his great-grandfather Zechariah Hughes.

As a boy Samuel shined shoes at local barbershops; one of these was a front for a small-time bootlegging operation, while another used a rear room for card games so patrons could gamble after closing. Thus Samuel was exposed to two sides of the world in which he lived: the saintly and the sinful. Early on he saw life as a series of choices, and he chose to excel in school and skipped three grades as a result, which allowed him to start college at the same time as his older sister. However, he also saw that even principled choices can have costly consequences when in 1935 a popular biology teacher at his segregated school was fired for participating in a lawsuit sponsored by the NAACP that demanded equal pay for black teachers. In 1937 Samuel graduated from high school as president of his senior class. The summer before he enrolled at Virginia State College, he worked as a busboy and bellhop at a beach hotel.

As a young man Proctor desired to become a lawyer—although he attended Virginia State College on a music scholarship and while there played the saxophone in a jazz band called the Trojans, which included the legendary pianist Billy Taylor. During his sophomore year Proctor decided to join a fraternity. The hazing ritual that he endured involved beatings so brutal that Proctor threatened to report the group if they used such sadistic practices against other recruits. When the beatings continued, he reported this to the administration, even though it meant being ostracized. In 1939 Proctor joined the U.S. Naval Apprentice School and began training to become a shipfitter, though he did not want to fight in World War II. After only a year, he abandoned that career path and enrolled at Virginia Union University, thinking that he might become a minister. As a youth, despite his religious upbringing, he had declined to be baptized; but after consultation with a professor, Proctor visited a Baptist church some distance from campus, heard the minister preach a fiery sermon about God and Joshua, and decided to take that first step toward a life of Christian service.

In 1942 Proctor received an AB degree from Virginia Union University, then studied for a year at the University of Pennsylvania before enrolling as the only black student at Crozer Theological Seminary in Upland, Pennsylvania. While working as an elevator operator in Norfolk, Proctor met a white trustee of Crozer who offered him a scholarship when he learned that Proctor wished to study theology. While at Crozer, Proctor married Bessie Tate, a classmate from Virginia Union University. Eventually the couple would have four children, but at Crozer they lived in the home of the college president, performing household duties in exchange for room and board. But the hardest adjustment for Proctor to make at Crozer was not racial; it was intellectual. For the first time he encountered professors of religion who did not interpret the Bible literally as God's unaltered truth. As he put it, "[M]y Bible had been ripped apart by historical and literary criticism." In 1945 Proctor was awarded a bachelor of divinity degree. He accepted both of the offers he received upon graduation: one was to pastor the Pond Street Church in Providence, Rhode Island, the other was the John P. Crozer Fellowship and two thousand dollars to study ethics at Yale University in New Haven, Connecticut.

Proctor's commitment to social action was evident at his first congregation as he fought for the Fair Employment Practices Act in Rhode Island, yet the pressures of dividing his time between two states while awaiting the birth of his first child proved to be too much. He transferred to Boston University, where he received a Ph.D. in Theology in 1950. That year he was invited back to Crozer to give an address, and he befriended a new black student there, MARTIN LUTHER KING JR. He told King that the works of Reinhold Niebuhr and Harry E. Fosdick, particularly Fosdick's *The Modern Use of the Bible* (1924), had enabled him to keep his faith intact. Their relationship remained close over the years, and following the arrest of ROSA PARKS in December 1955, King invited Proctor to Montgomery, Alabama, to give a "Spring Lecture Series" during the ensuing bus boycott. Proctor would later entertain audiences by recalling how he and King were followed by Alabama state troopers as they drove to Tuskegee, Alabama, to buy gas to fuel the cars used in the boycott, pointing out the irony that the road on which they had risked their lives had since been renamed Martin Luther King Jr. Boulevard

In 1955 Proctor was appointed president of his alma mater, Virginia Union University. He was only thirty-three years old. His meteoric rise from dean to vice president to president reflects his excellence as an administrator and as an inspiring leader. These qualities brought a steady deluge of offers and opportunities during his tenure (1955–1960). President Dwight D. Eisenhower invited Proctor and other black leaders to the White House to ask them to "ease up" on the demands for equality in the wake of the 1954 *Brown v. Board of Education* school desegregation decision. They respectfully refused. Proctor also began to travel internationally. His speaking and studies brought him to the Soviet Union; he visited the concentration camp at Auschwitz, toured biblical sites in Israel, attended meetings in Scandinavia and the South Pacific, and began a long and deep commitment to the African continent. In 1960 Proctor accepted the presidency of the Agricultural and Technical College of North Carolina (now North Carolina Agricultural and Technical College). JESSE JACKSON JR., who was the quarterback of the school's football team and the president of the student body, would both challenge and admire Proctor's style of leadership, which was diplomatic rather than confrontational. While Proctor did not publicly condone the student-led sit-ins of lunch counters begun shortly before his arrival in 1960, he and other administrators worked behind the scenes to raise bail money and secure legal representation for students arrested in these actions.

Proctor worked closely with the Kennedy administration, taking a leave of absence from 1963 to 1964 to become associate director of the first Peace Corps chapter in Africa, and he also served in Washington, D.C., during the historic 1963 March on Washington. He then moved his family to Nigeria, where his children integrated a school that had previously barred black students. After returning to the United States, he served as associate general secretary for the National Council of Churches from 1964 to 1965 and played an active role in President Lyndon B. Johnson's War on Poverty program by serving in the Office of Economic Opportunity as a special assistant to the director of the Northeast region. Always concerned about issues that affected youth, Proctor became president of the Institute for Service to Education, and in 1966 he published *The Young Negro in America, 1960–1980*. In 1968 Proctor accompanied Vice President Hubert Humphrey and Supreme Court Justice THURGOOD MARSHALL to Africa. When he returned he spoke out against the decadence and corruption he witnessed, and he testified before Jacob Javits's U.S. Senate committee on education in favor of such programs as student loans, Head Start, Upward Bound, and work-study programs. During the Carter Administration, Proctor served as an ethics adviser on a committee to oversee recombinant DNA research.

While considering an offer to become a dean at Harvard University, Proctor spoke at Rutgers University on the first anniversary of King's death following his assassination in 1968. Many of the college's administrators were there, and they soon offered him the newly created Martin Luther King Distinguished Professorship in Education. He held this position from 1969 until he retired in 1984. During this period he wrote four of his eight books and preached and lectured widely to diverse audiences. In 1972 he also assumed leadership of the Abyssinian Baptist Church in Harlem from Rev. ADAM CLAYTON POWELL JR. With eighteen thousand members, this was one of the largest Baptist churches in the world, as well as one of the oldest black Baptist churches in America. With the Reverend CALVIN O. BUTTS III as his protégé, Proctor provided needed stability to the congregation at a pivotal time in its history. He also convinced the church to join the American Baptist Churches, USA, and the National Baptist Convention. Through the Abyssinian Housing Development Program, the congregation built fifty housing units for needy families. During Proctor's tenure, the church's revenues grew from $146 thousand to more than $1 million.

During his final years Proctor held teaching positions at Vanderbilt University (1990–1991), United Theological Seminary (1991–1993), and Duke University (1993–1995). He received forty-five honorary degrees before he died of a heart attack while speaking to students at Cornell College in Mount Vernon, Iowa. Following his death the Samuel DeWitt Proctor School of Theology was created at Virginia Union University and a chair endowed in his honor at Rutgers University.

FURTHER READING

The main body of extant papers pertaining to Samuel DeWitt Proctor's ministerial career can be found at the Abyssinian Baptist Church in Harlem, New York; the Schomburg Center for Research in Black Culture, New York City Public Library; and at the Virginia Union University. His work with government agencies can be found in the Library of Congress and in various presidential papers

Proctor, Samuel. *My Moral Odyssey* (1989).

Proctor, Samuel. *The Substance of Things Hoped For: A Memoir of African-American Faith* (1995).

Obituaries: *New York Times*, 26 May 1997; New York *Daily News*, 25 May 1997, and *New York Amsterdam News*, 6 June 1997.

SHOLOMO B. LEVY

Professor Longhair (19 Dec. 1918–30 Jan. 1980), blues pianist and singer, also known as Roy Byrd, was born Henry Roland Byrd in Bogalusa, Louisiana, the son of James Lucius Byrd, a clothes cleaner and presser, and Ella Mae Rhodes, a housekeeper. His parents, both natives of Mississippi, separated in 1919, and he and his mother moved to New Orleans, where Byrd absorbed the city's musical styles. Byrd's mother, his first major musical influence, played popular songs such as "Tiger Rag" on the piano and also taught him to play guitar and drums. Byrd attended elementary school but dropped out around the third grade after being lured away by the New Orleans street life. By his early teens Byrd had mastered the rudiments of the drums, guitar, and piano, performed regularly in neighborhood bands, and tap-danced on street corners.

There were dozens of saloons and nightclubs on South Rampart Street in downtown New Orleans where itinerant African American blues pianists practiced their trade. Byrd continued to perform as a dancer and worked with his neighbor, an aspiring piano player who was later known as Champion Jack Dupree. Lured by Dupree's raucous music, Byrd also heard the music of elder players like Robert Bertrand, Isidore "Tuts" Washington, Kid Stormy Weather, and Sullivan Rock, and he gradually learned the local piano tradition. "Come here boy," Rock shouted to Byrd. "Let me show you the 'Pine Top Boogie Woogie' so you'll have something to play." Washington recalled that Byrd "jumped up and learned how to play a few blues. At that time I didn't play nothin' but blues. In the speakeasies in them days that's all the women wanted."

During the 1930s New Orleans suffered from the economic devastation of the nationwide depression. In 1936 Byrd joined the Civilian Conservation Corps, a work-training program administered by the U.S. Army, where he labored outdoors, attended school, drilled in military fashion, and entertained the troops during his free time. Inspired by film performances of the Nicholas Brothers and BILL "BOJANGLES" ROBINSON, Byrd formed a dance team for performances at the Ritz, Lincoln, and Palace theaters and at the Cotton Club on South Rampart Street. Around 1940 Byrd entered a common-law marriage with Alice Walton, with whom he had two children. The couple drifted apart after Byrd enlisted in the army in 1942.

Byrd was discharged from the army in early 1944 because of a burst appendix and a hernia. Upon his discharge he returned to New Orleans, where entertainment work was not always steady. He therefore worked for several years as a cab driver, short-order cook, bartender, laborer on the riverfront, and gambler.

In 1948 Byrd took the professional moniker "Professor Longhair"—"professor" being a traditional title given to piano players of that time. All of the members of Byrd's band, the Four Hairs Combo, wore their hair long, an uncommon style in the late 1940s, hence the name "Longhair." Byrd recalled, "We were playing at the Caledonia Inn. We had Big Slick on drums, Apeman Black on sax, and Walter Nelson on guitar. We had long hair in those days and it was [so long that it was] almost against the law."

Longhair's first recordings, a unique mixture of rumba and boogie, were made in 1949 for the small, poorly distributed Texas-based Star Talent label. The following year Longhair recorded for Mercury Records, producing the only hit song of his career, "Baldhead" (formerly called "She Ain't Got No Hair"), which climbed to number five in the *Billboard* rhythm and blues charts in August

Professor Longhair performed at the New Orleans Jazz and Heritage Festival in New Orleans, La., on 13 Apr. 1973. (AP Images.)

1950. The success of "Baldhead" led to a series of recordings with Atlantic Records that produced the classic regional blues piece "Mardi Gras in New Orleans" (1949), later known as "Go to the Mardi Gras." The Atlantic Records executive Jerry Wexler, who produced the recordings, wrote of Longhair, "He belongs in that rare company with LOUIS ARMSTRONG, SIDNEY BECHET, and JELLY ROLL MORTON, Crescent City innovators whose contributions to our musical culture are immeasurable.... Longhair is the Picasso of Keyboard funk."

What emerged from these early Longhair recordings was a piano style shaped and inspired by boogie-woogie but fundamentally rooted in the late nineteenth-century New Orleans piano vernacular. Longhair's compositions were constructed within the eight- and twelve-bar blues format but contained a tone and rhythmic dimension reflective of the city's rich music heritage. With his left hand he played powerful octave rumba bass patterns that worked against a syncopated right hand, a rhythmic form that Morton called the "Spanish tinge," a reference to New Orleans's Afro-Caribbean influence.

After recording for various labels in 1950 and 1951, Longhair jumped back to Atlantic in 1953, producing another regional hit, "Tipitina," which became one of his theme songs. In 1954 his career was interrupted by a serious but undiagnosed illness that left him bedridden for more than a year. Even after returning to the music business he remained worried about his health and refused to tour to promote himself or his records. He did not record again until 1957. In that year Longhair got back in touch with Alice Walton after seeing her sister in a local club. The couple resumed their common-law relationship, raising four children from Alice's second marriage as well as a third child of their own. They remained together for life, cementing their union in a formal marriage ceremony in 1975.

From 1957 to 1964 Longhair recorded for such local labels as Ebb, Ron, Rip, and Watch. Though two of his recordings, "Go to the Mardi Gras" and "Big Chief," had become synonymous with New Orleans's yearly Mardi Gras celebration, Longhair had all but disappeared from the music scene. In fifteen years of recording he earned little more than session fees. His health was failing, and to get by he swept out the One Stop record shop on South Rampart Street and returned to gambling as a source of income. It was not until 1970, when a young college student, Quint Davis, rediscovered his music and became his promoter, that Longhair's career was reborn. His appearance at the 1971 New Orleans Jazz and Heritage Festival marked his formal return to the stage.

Longhair's comeback in the 1970s was accelerated by rock and jazz critics in the United States, and Europe and Japan viewed him as the long-awaited undiscovered guru of New Orleans rock and roll. Atlantic Records reissued his 1949 and 1953 sessions as collectors clamored for old discs. New recording offers came from diverse sources, and demands by festival promoters led to appearances across the United States and throughout Europe, as well as a yearly spot in the New Orleans Jazz and Heritage Festival. In 1977 he became part owner of a New Orleans club, Tipitina's, and became its featured artist.

The final triumph of Longhair's recording career came with the release of the *Crawfish Fiesta* album for Alligator Records, considered by many critics to be his finest work. Sadly, he did not live to see it released. He died at home in New Orleans in his sleep. A continuing legacy saw his induction into the Blues Foundation Hall of Fame in 1991 and into the Rock and Roll Hall of Fame in 1992, and a Grammy Award in 1991. In 1996, with funds raised by the Professor Longhair Foundation, "Longhair Square," a long-awaited park built across from Tipitina, was designated by New Orleans officials.

Although Longhair achieved both national and international fame toward the end of his life, he is best described as a hometown artist. His music—a gumbo of blues, boogie, rock, calypso, rumba, and mambo, all mingled with the pluralistic sounds and rhythms of Mardi Gras—embodied the history and spirit of New Orleans and has had a profound influence on much of the popular music produced there since the 1950s. As a pianist, his style seemed to reiterate the rhythms that he learned as a dancer and percussionist, giving him a sound that was truly singular. Though he had few hits, he was a musician's musician, a creative force who influenced other New Orleans piano players, including JAMES BOOKER, Huey Smith, FATS DOMINO, ALLEN TOUSSAINT, and Dr. John (Mac Rebennack).

FURTHER READING
Berry, Jason, et al. *Up from the Cradle of Jazz: New Orleans Music since World War II* (1986).

Broven, John. *Rhythm and Blues in New Orleans* (1978).
Hannusch, Jeff. *I Hear You Knockin: The Sound of New Orleans Rhythm and Blues* (1984).
Wexler, Jerry, and David Ritz. *Rhythm and the Blues: A Life in American Music* (1993).
Obituary: *Living Blues* 45/46 (Spring, 1980).
This entry is taken from the *American National Biography* and is published here with the permission of the American Council of Learned Societies.

TAD JONES,
BILL MCCULLOCH, AND
BARRY LEE PEARSON

Prophet, Elizabeth (19 Mar. 1890–18 Dec. 1960), sculptor, was born Nancy Elizabeth Prophet in Warwick, Rhode Island, the daughter of William H. Prophet, an employee of the Providence Parks Department, and Rosa E. Walker. Her paternal grandmother was a Narragansett-Pequod who had bought her husband out of slavery. Prophet was always ambivalent about her mixed ethnicity, alternately accepting and spurning her African heritage. She implored Cedric Dover not to include her work in his book, *American Negro Art*, declaring that he "must certainly know" that "I am not a negro" and "I, too, have my race pride" (Dover, 56).

Coming from a modest household, Prophet partially paid for her education by working as a housekeeper. She earned a BFA in Painting and Drawing with a specific interest in portraiture at the Rhode Island School of Design (1914–1918). At the age of twenty-four, a student, she married Francis Ford, then thirty-four, but she told few people about the relationship.

In August 1922, after trying to make a living as a portraitist for four years, Prophet left her husband and traveled to Paris, France, where she lived until 1934. She was forced to stay in bed in Montparnasse for the first two months because she was suffering from nervous exhaustion. Prophet's life abroad was characterized by poverty and hunger, which forced her to move often in search of inexpensive housing. Despite her deprivation and initial trouble communicating in French, she produced at least two sculptures in 1923, both busts. One untitled wooden piece was exhibited at the Salon d'Automne the following year.

Prophet made a living by peddling batik items in 1924. Given two thousand francs by a sympathetic female patron, she began work on her first life-size statue, *Volonté* (which means "will" or "wish"). At the end of April 1926, frustrated by what she perceived as her lack of progress, she destroyed the work.

Prophet lived in what she described as a "filthy shack" outside Paris. Although she grew and ate her own vegetables, she was admitted to the American Hospital for malnutrition in the summer of 1925; medical practitioners there suspected her of drug addiction because she was so thin. Prophet was back at work within three weeks, even though doctors urged her to do no physical labor for a year.

In December 1925 Prophet's husband visited her drunk and remained with her. By April 1926 she had decided to leave him. It was not until three years later, however, that he quit his job as a waiter and returned to the United States with the sale of one of Prophet's sculptures. To indicate the death of the relationship, Prophet began calling herself a widow. In June 1932 she received a legal affidavit that allowed her to use her maiden name again. She disinherited Ford in 1946 with a notary statement, but it is unclear whether she ever formally divorced him.

In June 1926 Prophet moved into a tiny studio at 147 rue Broca, where she lived for seven years. In this studio she created an androgynous figure, *Poverty*. She kept it and her other pieces draped with black cloths so she would not be haunted by their mediocrity. Yet one bust, *Tête de jeune fille*, was accepted by the Salon d'Automne in 1927. Prophet preferred to work from life and modeled pieces after people she met in cafés. More often, however, she could not afford sitters and so worked from imagination. Some of her pieces—*Discontent*, *Bitter Laughter*, *Silence*, and *Prayer* (also called *Poverty*)—reflected her physical and emotional pain. Others, such as *Poise*, *Peace*, *Confidence*, and *Le pélerin*, expressed her longing for what she called the "abstract qualities" of poise and courage she sought to attain in her life and work. These meditative heads and figures (all difficult to date more precisely than c.-1924–1933) have an androgynous quality, featuring close-cropped or covered hair, heavy-lidded eyes, broad foreheads, enigmatic smiles, and small breasts and hips. They bear a stylistic resemblance to the work of Antoine Bourdelle, a student of Auguste Rodin. Prophet sculpted in marble, wood, bronze, alabaster, granite, terracotta, and clay. Occasionally she painted basreliefs with gold highlights. She had every work photographed in black and white; many of these images seem to be all that remain of much of her sculpture. Fewer than ten pieces are in known institutions; the rest, which total perhaps not even two dozen, were destroyed or are in private collections.

Prophet exhibited both in France and in the United States; her work appeared in the Rhode Island School of Design Museum and the Boston Independent Exposition in 1928. Despite her success, she sold few works and continued to battle destitution with the help of friends. Mabel Gardner, an American sculptor in Paris, wrote to the actress Louise Brooks on Prophet's behalf. Through Brooks, the Students Fund of Boston provided Prophet thirty dollars a month for two years, which began in July 1927. After discovering that Prophet was nearly starving in 1928, the painter HENRY OSSAWA TANNER recommended her to the Harmon Foundation in New York. The Harmon Foundation was a philanthropic organization that supported African American artists. Prophet's application was denied, however, because she stated her high school as "the College of serious thought and bitter experience, situated on the Campus of Poverty & Ambition." Nevertheless, they awarded her the $250 Otto Kahn Prize for *Head of a Negro* the following year. She also exhibited the marble *Buste d'homme* at the Société des Artistes Français in April 1929.

In October 1929 Prophet returned to the United States for a visit, staying nearly a year with the W. E. B. DuBois family in New York and with friends in Providence the following summer. During that time her work was exhibited at the Salons of America, the American-Anderson Galleries, and the Boston Society of Independent Artists (to which Prophet was elected a member). Ellen D. Sharpe and Eleanor Green, wealthy white women, bought *Discontent*, then donated the piece to the Rhode Island School of Design Museum Despite their support and the many efforts of DuBois to secure aid for Prophet in the wake of the Great Depression, Prophet realized only five hundred dollars in profits.

Back in Paris, Julia and Edouard Champion (an author) became Prophet's patrons. Prophet's work subsequently was shown at the Société des Artistes Français (a marble bust, 1931, and *Violence* and *Buste ébène*, 1932) and was praised in the periodical *Le Rayonnement Intellectuel*.

In May 1932 Prophet came to the United States again to promote her art, again staying for nearly a year. Her work was exhibited at the Robert C. Vose Jr. Galleries in Boston and at the

Boston Society of Independent Artists. In June Prophet was elected to the Art Association of Newport, and her sculpture was included in the Twenty-first Annual Exhibition by the group shortly thereafter. *Discontent* won the Richard B. Greenough grand prize of seventy-five dollars, and *Congolais* (c. 1930), a cherrywood head of an African with a Masai warrior's headdress, was purchased by the Whitney Museum of American Art.

In Paris from February 1933 to the summer of 1934, Prophet suffered severe financial setbacks. After police harassed her for avoiding import taxes, she appealed to the minister of fine arts and received a grant of three hundred dollars from the minister of finance. However, by mid-1934 Prophet was nearly ten thousand francs in debt. With the encouragement of DuBois and at the request of JOHN HOPE, president of Atlanta University, Prophet accepted a teaching position at Spelman College, her salary sponsored by the Harmon Foundation.

Prophet taught sculpture and the history of art and architecture at Spelman from 1934 to 1944. She exhibited in the Whitney Sculpture Biennials of 1935 and 1937 and the Philadelphia Museum of Art's Sculpture International of 1940. In 1939 she was featured in *Who's Who among American Women*. Yet, frustrated with the limitations of a southern town, Prophet retreated from social engagements and became increasingly eccentric, often dressing in a dramatic black cape and felt hat, and reputedly on occasion carrying a live rooster. After ten years of teaching, Prophet felt that she had given enough to society and went to live with friends in Providence, Rhode Island, where she worked odd jobs, including a brief stint in a ceramics factory. She apparently had an exhibition at the Providence Public Library in 1945, but she never displayed her work again.

In 1951 Prophet became Catholic, believing that the church offered the last hope for sculpture; in Paris she had been enthusiastically encouraged by a Catholic abbé. Still, there is no suggestion that she received any religious-sponsored patronage. After Prophet passed away in Providence intestate, Edward J. Carley, for whom she had been employed as a housekeeper, raised the money to cover her funeral expenses.

However, Prophet continues to be a significant figure in African American art history, and her sculpture is frequently reproduced in survey texts and exhibition catalogs.

FURTHER READING

Prophet's art is in the collections of the Rhode Island Black Heritage Society; Rhode Island College, Adams Library; Rhode Island School of Design; Rhode Island Urban League; Schomburg Center for Research in Black Culture, New York Public Library; and Whitney Museum of American Art, New York.

Dover, Cedric. *American Negro Art* (1960).

This entry is taken from the *American National Biography* and is published here with the permission of the American Council of Learned Societies.

THERESA LEININGER-MILLER

Prosser, Gabriel. *See* Gabriel.

Prosser, Inez Beverly (30 Dec. 1895–7 Sept. 1934), educator and psychologist, was born in San Marcos, Texas, one of eleven children to Samuel Andrew Beverly, a waiter, and Veola Hamilton, a homemaker. Her exact birth year is not known, though 1895 has been reported with greatest frequency. The family was poor, but education was valued, and many of the Beverly children went on to earn high school and college degrees. Money, though, was hard to come by, and the family was itinerant through much of Prosser's childhood. She eventually attended Yoakum Colored School in tiny Yoakum, Texas, graduating in 1910 as valedictorian. There was little money for college, but Prosser was allowed to continue her education when an older brother chose marriage over a college degree. She matriculated to Prairie View State Normal and Industrial College (later Prairie View A&M University) and in 1912 graduated from the normal school with a two-year degree and teaching certificate.

Prosser soon found work teaching around Austin, Texas, including at Anderson High School, where she was an English and spelling instructor. She met Allen Rufus Prosser, an elevator operator at a local department store, and the two were married in 1916. In the meantime, she was determined to continue her education. In 1924 she received a bachelor's of education from Austin's Samuel Huston College (later Huston-Tillotson University). At the time, African Americans were not allowed to seek advanced degrees in the state of Texas, so Prosser took part in both summer and correspondence programs offered by the University of Colorado and in 1927 received a master's degree in Educational Psychology.

That same year, Prosser joined the faculty of Tillotson College, where she would remain for three years. In 1930 she transferred to Tougaloo College in Jackson, Mississippi, where, remarkably, she also served as the principal of the local high school. Meanwhile, she was writing about and studying various aspects of educational psychology, including important research on the effects of inequality and segregation among children of color, though her conclusion was that segregated environments often offered black students a more balanced and supportive education. In later years, her work would figure prominently in the national conversation on race and public education and the debate leading up to *Brown v. Board of Education* (1954).

In 1931 Prosser enrolled in a doctoral program at the University of Cincinnati. She completed her dissertation, *The Non-Academic Development of Negro Children in Mixed and Segregated Schools*, in 1933 having returned to Tougaloo College. Whether she is the first or second African American woman to receive the Ph.D. in Psychology (rather than RUTH WINIFRED HOWARD) is a matter of some debate. Prosser's degree was granted by the university's education department, whereas Howard's, awarded a year later in 1934, was bestowed by the psychology department. Whatever the case, she was without doubt one of the key voices at the heart of one of the most momentous and controversial debates of the day.

She was at the very beginning of what would have no doubt been an important and revelatory career when her life was cut short. On 28 August 1934, she was returning from a family visit and was on her way back to Mississippi with her husband and a sister when their car was involved in a catastrophic accident in Louisiana. Prosser was thrown clear of the vehicle. She was taken to a hospital in Shreveport and died there several days later.

She was buried in San Antonio. In 2008 the University of Cincinnati's Department of Psychology and College of Education, Human Services, and Criminal Justice founded the Inez Beverly Prosser Memorial Symposium on Black Women in Psychology in honor of its too-often unheralded graduate.

FURTHER READING

Guthrie, Robert V. *Even the Rat Was White: A Historical View of Psychology* (2004).
O'Connell, Agnes N., and Nancy F. Russo, eds. *Models of Achievement: Reflections of Eminent Women in Psychology* (1983).
Warren, Wini. *Black Women Scientists in the United States* (1999).

JASON PHILIP MILLER

Prosser, Nancy (c. 1773–?), slave, participant, and co-conspirator in an attempted slave revolt in 1800. There is a scant historical record of the life of Nancy Prosser. She is best known for her role in the 1800 aborted slave revolt led by her husband, GABRIEL, and his two brothers, Solomon and Martin. Nancy, who went by the nickname Nanny, was born a slave in Henrico County, Virginia. She married Gabriel sometime around 1799. There is no record of any children born of the union. Gabriel was the slave of Thomas Henry Prosser; the couple has often been called Prosser, but there is no evidence that they used their owner's surname. After the two were married, it is not certain if Nancy lived with Gabriel on the Prosser plantation, Brookfield, located approximately six miles from Richmond. Whether the two lived together or not, they probably influenced each other and shared a commitment to liberty, freedom, and dignity.

Nancy Prosser was most likely illiterate and had very little contact outside of the plantation where she lived. However, Gabriel's worldview was expanded because he was literate. He was a skilled blacksmith, and Thomas Prosser often hired him out to work in Richmond. He also hired himself out, which allowed him more freedom and autonomy as well as a view of how unjust and undemocratic the slave system was. Gabriel's experience in an urban environment at the center of Virginia's economy in the early republic exposed him to various ideas. Nancy, like most slaves, knew from day-to-day experiences that the institution of slavery was brutal, degrading, and dehumanizing, and that people should not be the property of others. In addition, she probably thought that her husband should have the right to earnings acquired from contract labor. She also witnessed how her husband was treated after he got into a fight with a white slave owner who accused him of stealing a pig. In the altercation he bit off part of the white man's ear. For this he was jailed and later branded (Egerton, 1993).

The fact that Nancy knew about the insurrection and played a role at all is significant because men dominated the activity of slave conspiracies. Men and women, whether slave or free, often occupied separate spaces that would have prevented women from knowing about plans for an insurrection. Men in urban areas were recruited to participate because they had more mobility and autonomy than women, who were often confined to the plantation because of child and family responsibilities. Urban men who had the ability to disseminate information were highly valued for such an operation; some of these men included mail carriers and boatmen. In addition, men were recruited in public spaces both in urban and rural areas that women did not often frequent, such as drinking establishments, docks, and picnics and barbecues. Moreover, the leaders and planners of the rebellion may not have wanted women to participate because they did not want to endanger women's and girls' lives if the plan failed, or the men simply did not trust women and girls to keep the plans secret.

Regardless of how men felt, Nancy was aware of the plans, and she attempted to recruit others to join. She must have known that if such a daring plan failed it would result in certain death for those who participated. It is estimated that approximately one thousand slaves were recruited from the urban areas of Richmond, Norfolk, Petersburg, and Charlottesville and from plantations in the surrounding counties. The "guerrillas" were to meet at Brookfield, Thomas Prosser's plantation, where Prosser was to be killed. Some rebels would continue on to Richmond while others stood guard at Brook Bridge, which controlled traffic in and out of Richmond. Once they reached Richmond they would take Governor James Monroe hostage, kill some whites, and capture arms and ammunition. When word of the successful siege reached other slaves, they would march there and join the insurrection. The end result would be freedom.

However, on Saturday, 30 August 1800, there was a terrible thunderstorm that washed out roads and bridges. Those conspirators who lived in the countryside were unable to reach Richmond, and those who lived in Richmond could not reach Prosser's plantation or Brook Bridge. There were no means to communicate whether the plan was postponed or not, so people were left in a quandary. Nancy attempted to alert the participants that they should meet the following day at the Prosser plantation. However, two slaves revealed the plans. The governor, other government officials, and slave owners were eager to capture and try the main leaders of the conspiracy. Nancy did not escape with her husband after the plot was revealed. She was not implicated in the insurrection, and she was not charged for her role, so her life was spared. Gabriel and several others were hanged. After the revolt there is no record of her life.

FURTHER READING

Egerton, Douglas. *Gabriel's Rebellion: The Virginia Slave Conspiracies of 1800 and 1802* (1993).

Giddings, Paula. *When and Where I Enter: The Impact of Black Women on Race and Sex in America* (1984).

Sidbury, James. *Ploughshares into Swords: Race, Rebellion, and Identity in Gabriel's Virginia, 1730–1810* (1997).

CASSANDRA VENEY

Prout, Mary Ann (14 Feb 1801?–c. 1884), educator, activist, and philanthropist, was born free in Baltimore, Maryland. Prout received at least a basic education, though no record remains of where or how she did so. Little is known of the Prout family, though they are known to have been heavily involved in the American Colonization Society of Maryland. Both of her older brothers emigrated to Liberia, where William A. Prout served as governor of the Independent State of Maryland in Liberia from 8 June 1854 to April 1856. The state was established by the Maryland State Colonization Society and incorporated into Liberia on 18 March 1857. Jacob W. Prout served as secretary to the 1847 Constitutional Convention, which drafted the Declaration of Independence and Constitution for the newly formed Republic of Liberia.

At the age of twelve Prout joined the Bethel African Methodist Episcopal (AME) Church on Saratoga Street in Baltimore. From this time on she devoted her life to religious activities. She was an active member of the Daughters of Conference at Bethel AME. According to Bishop James Handy, "During the early days of Bethel, when it was poor and in debt, Prout was constantly devising ways and means of relieving it" (Dannett, 141). Prout founded a day school in 1830 and taught there until 1867, at which time the school closed. Active in her church and in education, Prout was also involved in other areas of her local community. When the Gregory Aged Women's Home opened in Baltimore on 21 July 1867, Prout was one of two black trustees. She also served as president of the association in charge of the home.

In 1867, following the closure of her school, Prout founded the Grand United Order of St. Luke, an African American fraternal society and cooperative insurance organization. The order was named after the Luke of the Gospels, and initiates vowed to "be true and faithful to the Christian religion" and to devote leisure time to "searching the Holy Scriptures, so that [he or she] may become useful and true to all mankind." The Grand United Order of St. Luke was originally established to provide insurance for the sick and financial aid for funeral costs—services that were generally unavailable through white agencies. Initially the society catered solely to women, but it soon admitted men and expanded to New York and Virginia.

In 1869, following a factional dispute, dissenting members in Richmond split off to form the Independent Order of St. Luke, with William M. T. Forrester as grand secretary. This is said to have been because the dissenters objected to turning over to Prout the fifty cents each "degree" (that is, level of advancement within the order) cost. There is evidence that a few chapters remained loyal to what became known as the Independent Order of St. Luke of Maryland and continued to send 25 percent of their net proceeds to Prout until her death in 1885. Thereafter her niece, Miss Vincent, as heiress of the "works," or rituals, became grand supreme chief of the order. The Virginia chapters of this order broke away at the end of the 1890s and formed still another St. Luke Order. By 1899 there were at least three Maryland and five Virginia chapters in existence.

There were elaborate rituals associated with membership and advancement in the order. Initiates were "members of the same family" who pledged to "stand by one another at all hazards." They specified that what they "lack[ed] by the sacred ties of blood we make up by a solemn oath-bound obligation, declaring ourselves sisters and brothers, children of the same Father" (Independent Order of Saint Luke, *Degree Ritual of the Independent Order of Saint Luke* [1924]: 8). The centerpiece of the initiation ceremony of the Independent Order of St. Luke featured a symbolic journey to Jerusalem. To foster humility, candidates were required to wear a torn white robe. Prior to the journey a guide foretold what lay ahead: "You may find the road rough and rugged, and you may meet with disappointment and mistrust....You will find no friendly hand extended, or kind advice given you on which to lean....You must seek to find the emblem of the cross, with patience and unceasing energy as it is claimed Helena possessed in searching for the cross of Calvary" (Independent Order of Saint Luke, 19).

In 1899 MAGGIE LENA WALKER replaced Forrester as grand secretary, and under her leadership the order expanded rapidly—at its peak having 2,010 local chapters and more than one hundred thousand members in twenty-eight states. The Independent Order of St. Luke became one of the largest and most successful of the many mutual benefit societies of the time. In addition to its early program of sickness insurance and death benefits, the society became heavily involved in economic development—it founded the St. Luke Penny Savings Bank in 1903—and in social and political activism. It was "[to] promote the general welfare of society by uniting fraternally Negro persons of good moral character who are physically, morally, and socially acceptable, to educate and assist its members in thrift, to create and maintain funds out of which members...may receive benefits for themselves or their beneficiaries, [and] to provide death benefit protection to members" (*Rules and Regulations*, 1933). The society also established a printing plant, a newspaper called the *St. Luke Herald*, and, for a brief time, a department store— the St. Luke Emporium. The society disbanded in the 1930s because of the Great Depression as well as increased competition from commercial insurance agencies, the lure of competing forms of entertainment, such as radio and movies, and the expansion of government social welfare—including mothers' pensions and workers' compensation.

Prout never married, devoting her entire life to her church, her educational endeavors, and to her extensive community service. Her life is exemplified by the motto of the order she founded, which was to promote "love, purity, and charity." Prout died in Baltimore.

FURTHER READING

Information on Prout can be found in the Daniel Murray Papers in the Beulah Davis Special Collections, Morris A. Soper Library, Morgan State University, Baltimore. A collection of documents relating to the Independent Order of St. Luke (MS 1988–121) can be found in the Special Collections, Carol M. Newman Library, Virginia Tech., Blacksburg. The *Baltimore Afro-American Ledger*, 24 Aug. 1901, contains a photograph of Prout.

Beito, David T. "To Advance the 'Practice of Thrift and Economy': Fraternal Societies and Social Capital, 1890–1920," *Journal of Interdisciplinary History* 29.4 (1999).

Dannett, Sylvia G. L. *Profiles of Negro Womanhood. Vol. 1, 1619–1900* (1964).

Fiftieth Anniversary—Golden Jubilee Historical Report of the R. W.G. Council, I.O. Saint Luke, 1867–1917 (1917).

JEFF CROCOMBE

Pryor, Richard (1 Dec. 1940–10 Dec. 2005), comedian and actor, was born Richard Franklin Lenox Thomas Pryor in Peoria, Illinois, the son of LeRoy "Buck Carter" Pryor Jr. and Gertrude Thomas. Carter managed the family bar, the Famous Door, while Thomas and her mother-in-law—whom Pryor called Mama—managed a handful of mixed-clientele brothels in Peoria's black neighborhood. Between spying on the couples (which occasionally included his mother) and frequenting the Famous Door, Pryor lived a childhood of inconsistency and emotional turbulence; he did, however, credit Mama and his parents for the relative affluence that accompanied their professions. Prompted by Thomas's severe alcoholism and subsequent disappearances, sometimes for as long as six months, Carter divorced her in 1950. Thomas moved to her family farm in Springfield, Missouri, and Pryor would later identify his visits there as the most peaceful moments of his life.

When Pryor was six years old, a local teenager sexually molested him; at about the same age he also discovered he could make his family laugh with pratfalls off the front porch or by slipping on dog feces. He earned high marks at a Catholic grade school but was expelled at the age of ten when the school's administration learned of his family's businesses. In junior high his teacher bribed him to do homework by promising him a few minutes every week to tell jokes at the front of the classroom. Gaining confidence and enjoying the attention, Pryor continued his class shenanigans until a couple of years later, when another teacher requested that he stop. Pryor responded by jokingly—so he claimed—swinging at the teacher. He was expelled instantly and left to work odd jobs in Peoria for four years until he joined the army at age eighteen. Pryor was stationed in Idar-Oberstein in West Germany, but his tour ended in 1960 when he aided a fellow black soldier in a bar fight by stabbing the white opponent.

Narrowly escaping jail, Pryor was discharged and allowed to return home, where he flitted about for a couple of months before conning the manager of a local "black and tan" nightclub (that is, one catering to blacks and whites) into letting him play the piano and sing. Pryor could do neither. But his onstage charisma and likability rescued him, and he became the regular MC. He began working other such clubs and was soon introduced to marijuana and amphetamines. Also in 1960 Pryor married his girlfriend, who was pregnant with his first son, but he left Peoria almost immediately

Richard Pryor in 1977. (AP Images.)

after Richard Jr.'s birth, accompanying some local comedians and singers on a tour of the Midwest and Canada.

After a year of touring, Pryor, along with many black comedians of the time, was particularly affected in 1963 by seeing BILL COSBY on the cover of *Newsweek*, and he thought: "Goddamn it, this nigger's doing what I'm fixing to do. I want to be the only nigger. Ain't no room for two niggers" (Pryor, 68). He left immediately for New York, and although he "only had $10" in his pocket, he swore he looked at least "like $50" (Pryor, 69).

Pryor's contemporaries in the Greenwich Village comedy scene included Cosby, Woody Allen, George Carlin, DICK GREGORY, FLIP WILSON, and Joan Rivers. Under pressure to avoid a resemblance to every club owner's bête noire, the raunchy and unpredictable Lenny Bruce, Pryor emulated Cosby as closely as possible. Moving quickly from small jazz clubs to larger venues, such as the Apollo Theater in Harlem, Pryor made his first television appearance on 31 August 1964 on Rudy Vallee's *On*

Broadway Tonight; appearances on *The Merv Griffin Show* and *The Ed Sullivan Show* soon followed. By this time Pryor, at the urgings of a prostitute he was dating, had also begun using cocaine. Except for a purported seven-month period of sobriety more than a decade later, Pryor fought cocaine addiction until he reached a degenerative state of illness in the early 1990s.

The increasing turmoil of Pryor's personal life provided a body of subject matter that he expertly wove into his performances, but the success that accompanied his newly emerging comedic style only worsened his addictions and increased his philandering. The late 1960s sped by in a whirlwind that included his first movie appearance—a bit role in Sid Caesar's film *The Busy Body* (1967)—the birth of two more children, another failed marriage, and his father's death. Finally, Pryor had a nervous breakdown in Las Vegas, when he walked onstage, froze, and spoke only one sentence before walking off: "What the fuck am I doing here?"

In 1969, with the help of friends, Pryor attempted to write, produce, and star in an innovative yet poorly executed racial satire titled *The Trial*, in which one white man is tried for every racial crime in American history. But Pryor destroyed the only copy of the script in a domestic dispute. His career brought to a standstill by unarticulated frustrations, Pryor moved to Berkeley, California, in 1970 and lived eccentrically, walking the streets in a kimono and getting high for days at a time. Still, he managed to stumble upon a sympathetic and like-minded emerging set of African American intellectuals and activists, namely ISHMAEL REED, ANGELA DAVIS, and CLAUDE BROWN. Pryor shut himself in and compulsively read a collection of MALCOLM X's speeches and listened to MARVIN GAYE's song "What's Goin' On?" Determined to find his voice, he began delivering increasingly experimental performances in small clubs. He would typically speak a curse word, such as "bitch" or "motherfucker," dozens of times, attempting to hit a different inflection for every one. Eventually he tried "nigger." Speaking the one word that every club owner had hitherto prohibited provided the breakthrough he needed.

In 1971 Pryor returned to the Improv in New York City to record new material for his first concert film, *Smokin'*, and his second stand-up album, *Craps after Hours*. Mel Brooks then solicited him to help pen the ribald comedy *Blazing Saddles*, for which it was understood that Pryor would play the lead, a black sheriff in the Old West. The studio,

however, apparently feared Pryor's controversial edge and cast Cleavon Little instead. But Pryor demonstrated his commitment to acting by playing Piano Man in DIANA ROSS's vehicle *Lady Sings the Blues* (1972), for which he earned an Academy Award nomination.

Television opportunities soon presented themselves: Pryor most enjoyed collaborating on Lily Tomlin's variety show, but he also hosted NBC's new skit series, *Saturday Night Live*, and the network quickly offered him his own show. He locked horns with the censors, however, and *The Richard Pryor Show* ran for only four episodes. Otherwise, Pryor continued to experience a creative boon in comedy and film. Three consecutive albums won Grammys: *That Nigger's Crazy* (1974), *Is It Something I Said?* (1975), and *Bicentennial Nigger* (1976). He played his first dramatic film lead in *Greased Lightning* (1976), in which he portrayed the race-car legend WENDELL SCOTT. Pryor teamed with Gene Wilder in *Silver Streak* that same year, and delivered in *Blue Collar* (1978) what some critics consider his most accomplished performance. His cocaine use dangerously increased as well, and he suffered the first of two heart attacks. A recovered Pryor then divorced his third wife, Deboragh McGuire, and began dating Jennifer Lee, with whom he traveled to Africa at decade's end and later married.

In perhaps his most rounded concert film, *Live on the Sunset Strip* (1982), Pryor explains the revelatory experience of waiting in a Kenyan hotel lobby after a three-week sojourn: "A voice said, 'What do you see? Look around.' And I looked around, and I looked around, and I saw people of all colors and shapes, and the voice said, 'You see any niggers?' I said, 'No.' It said, 'You know why? 'Cause there aren't any'" (Pryor, 175). In three weeks Pryor had not used the word once; he vowed never to use it again, a vow he faithfully kept for some time. Many black entertainers, however, chastised him for "selling out" and rejecting what they believed was a reclaimed term of black empowerment. More important than such shifting semantics, however, was Pryor's unique take on American racial dynamics, prompting one critic to observe that if Pryor "played the race card, it was only to show how funny he looked when he tried to shuffle the deck" (Als, 385).

In *Sunset Strip*, Pryor also speaks of the notorious self-immolation he had suffered a year earlier while freebasing cocaine, a tremendously dangerous method of using the drug that involves inhaling the fumes of a melted clump of cocaine laced with ether. Although accounts differ, a strung-out Pryor apparently poured cognac or rum over his body and flicked a lighter, then ran out of his Los Angeles house and down the street, where the fire extinguished itself by burning his clothes into his skin. In shock, Pryor continued walking alongside police officers who were asking him to stop for an ambulance. Pryor responded, "If I stop, I'll die."

Pryor's work in subsequent years became uneven. Lee divorced him after six months, and his directorial debut, the autobiographical *Jo Jo Dancer, Your Life Is Calling* (1986) teetered indecisively between comedy and drama. He fired his confidant and business partner, the former football star JIM BROWN, from his film production company, a decision that further strained his relationship with the black entertainment community, and he repeatedly agreed to appear in lifeless but high-paying movies like *The Toy* (1982), *Superman III* (1983), and *Brewster's Millions* (1985). It was on the set of *Critical Condition* in 1986, however, that Pryor first felt the symptoms of multiple sclerosis; he was officially diagnosed at the Mayo Clinic later that year. Keeping the affliction secret, Pryor made another movie with Gene Wilder in 1986 and teamed with REDD FOXX and EDDIE MURPHY in 1989's *Harlem Nights*. The multiple sclerosis, compounded with decades of heavy drug use, contributed to another heart attack and subsequent quadruple bypass surgery in 1991.

Pryor logged one final "stand up" performance in 1992 at the Circle House Theater in San Francisco, sitting in a leather chair onstage with a cane by his side. Buoyed by positive reviews, he briefly attempted a tour, which exhaustion brought to a close in early 1993. He reunited with Jennifer Lee in 1994, who assumed caretaking duties. In 1998 Pryor was awarded the Kennedy Center's inaugural Mark Twain Prize, a significant tribute for which he was feted by lifelong friends and fellow comedians. After suffering for years with multiple sclerosis, Richard Pryor died of a heart attack just days after his sixty-fifth birthday.

FURTHER READING

Pryor, Richard, with Todd Gold. *Pryor Convictions and Other Life Sentences* (1995).
Als, Hilton. "A Pryor Love," in *Life Stories: Profiles from The New Yorker*, ed. David Remnick (2001).
Haskins, Jim. *Richard Pryor: A Man and His Madness* (1984).
Robbins, Fred, and David Ragan. *Richard Pryor: This Cat's Got Nine Lives!* (1982).
Williams, John A., and Dennis A. Williams. *If I Stop I'll Die: The Comedy and Tragedy of Richard Pryor* (1991).

DAVID F. SMYDRA JR.

Puckett, Kirby (14 Mar. 1960–6 Mar. 2006), baseball player, was born and raised in the South Side of Chicago, Illinois, the youngest of nine children of William Puckett, a department store and postal worker, and Catherine Puckett, a homemaker. Growing up in the crime-ridden Robert Taylor Homes projects, Puckett taught himself baseball fundamentals at an early age, throwing sock balls at a chalk strike zone on building walls. As a third baseman at Calumet High, he lifted weights to compensate for his diminutive (five-foot, eight-inch) stature.

After receiving little collegiate attention his senior year, Puckett worked on a Ford assembly line following graduation in 1979, at the age of 19. Noticed by a college coach at a free-agent tryout, Puckett was offered a scholarship to Bradley University. Though small and round—the atypical body for a centerfielder, let alone leading base stealer—the speedy Puckett moved to center field, and led the team in home runs and stolen bases his freshman year. Having transferred to Triton College following his father's death, he played for a semi-professional league during the summer, and caught the eye of a Minnesota Twins scout. After he was named the regional Junior College Player of the Year, he signed with the Twins, who selected him in the 1982 winter draft. Assigned to rookie ball, Puckett led the 1982 Appalachian League in batting average, runs, stolen bases, and outfield assists; along with earning All-Star honors, Puckett was named the league's Player of the Year by *Baseball America*. He continued to progress in the Twins' Single-A affiliate in Visalia, California, in 1983, and though he started the 1984 season in Triple-A, Puckett advanced to the majors after twenty-one games. Puckett made an immediate impression with the Twins when he became the ninth player in history to collect four hits in his first starting game. Along with leading the league in outfield assists, his .296 batting average and fourteen stolen bases were good enough to earn him a third-place finish for Rookie-of-the-Year balloting.

Puckett worked with Twins' batting coach Tony Oliva during the spring of 1986 to add more muscle to his frame, and exploded for thirty-one home runs

Kirby Puckett in the batting cage as the All-Star team worked out at Dodger Stadium in Los Angeles on 1 Nov. 1988. (AP Images.)

while pacing the team in almost every offensive category. He was voted to his first All-Star Game, won his first Gold Glove, and finished third in the league in batting. Off the field, Puckett cemented his relationship with his team's state, when he married Minnesota native Tonya Hudson in November 1986. In 1987 he finished third in MVP voting and led the franchise to a World Series victory over the St. Louis Cardinals. His .356 mark in 1988 was the highest by a right-handed hitter since Joe DiMaggio in 1941.

While becoming a leader in the clubhouse, Puckett also became one in the community. As Major League Baseball dealt with widespread cocaine abuse in the mid-1980s, Puckett joined Minnesota's drug education program, drawing on his own background in the projects for speeches in public schools. During his early career with the Twins, Puckett noticed the scarcity of black representation on the team. A year before he made his major league debut, a minority advocacy group charged racial bias when the Twins started a white shortstop over a black one. Though Puckett expressed no discomfort with the organization, he did state his desire to see more black fans in the stands.

Over his twelve-year career, Puckett hit .318, averaging ninety-nine RBIs and nineteen homers a season, was named to ten All-Star teams, won six Gold Gloves, and finished in the top ten of MVP voting seven times. His crowning baseball moment came during the 1991 World Series against the Atlanta Braves. Facing elimination in the sixth game, Puckett announced in the clubhouse that he would carry the team that evening. He did just that, making a leaping catch against the outfield wall in the third inning and hitting an eleventh-inning game-ending home run. The series was sent to a seventh game and an ultimate Twins' victory.

The gregarious outfielder nicknamed "Puck" became a Minnesota favorite. With an infectious smile and work ethic, Puckett became one of the most respected players in baseball. He and his wife became involved with a number of charitable organizations, and in 1991 established the Kirby Puckett Eight-Ball Invitational Pool Tournament to raise money for Children's HeartLink. For his community involvement he was a recipient of the 1993 Branch Rickey Award and the 1996 Roberto Clemente Award, and was inducted into the World Sports Humanitarian Hall of Fame in 2000. Puckett and his wife also became notable foster parents when they adopted two children, Catherine Margaret (in 1991) and Kirby Jr. (in 1993).

Puckett's last regular-season game came on 28 September 1995, when a fastball from Cleveland Indians pitcher Dennis Martinez struck Puckett in the face, breaking his jaw. Though he recovered and hit well in spring training, Puckett awoke with blurred vision on the final day of exhibition games. He underwent four surgeries but, nearly blind in his right eye from glaucoma, announced his retirement from baseball in July 1996. Reluctant to part ways with the face of its franchise, the Twins gave Puckett a nominal job as vice president that same year, with an office overlooking a street renamed Kirby Puckett Place.

The Twins retired Puckett's uniform number in 1997, and in 2001 he became the third-youngest player elected to the Baseball Hall of Fame. At his induction ceremony Puckett recalled his early days growing up in the projects near drug dealers, thanking his late mother for his success.

Within a year of his enshrinement in Cooperstown, Puckett's image was tarnished as reports leaked out about lewd behind-the-scenes behavior. The Twins settled out of court with a former employee who accused him of sexual harassment; Puckett's wife filed for divorce, citing past violent episodes; a mistress of eighteen years came forward, revealing their affair; and a woman alleged that he sexually assaulted her in a bar bathroom. Though Puckett was acquitted of this final charge and denied other accusations, he shrank away from the public spotlight. Despite the Twins' attempts to hire him as a coach, Puckett moved to Scottsdale, Arizona, in October 2004.

In the years following his retirement and Hall of Fame induction, Puckett saw his weight climb out of control. Three months before his planned wedding to fiancée Jodi Olson, Puckett suffered a major stroke caused by hypertension and died on 6 March 2006. Six days later, fans and former baseball players packed the Metrodome (the Twins' stadium) for a public ceremony honoring the late ballplayer on what the city of Minneapolis would call "Kirby Puckett Day."

Puckett's late indiscretions aside, his journey from a kid in the projects to one of the best and well-paid athletes in the baseball remained an inspiration for many, especially as he continued with non-profit work. Furthermore, as Major League Baseball began to draw fewer and fewer black fans to the games, evidenced by a 1987 *New York Times Magazine* article "Where Are the Black Fans?" Puckett had voiced his concern, while remaining one of the most popular figures in the game.

FURTHER READING

Puckett, Kirby. *I Love this Game! My Life in Baseball* (1993).

Deford, Frank. "The Rise and Fall of Kirby Puckett," *Sports Illustrated* (17 Mar. 2003).

ADAM W. GREEN

Puff Daddy. *See* Combs, Sean.

Puffy. *See* Combs, Sean.

Pugh, Charles (3 Aug. 1971–), radio broadcaster, television journalist, and politician, was born Charles Pugh in Detroit, Michigan, the only child of Marcia and George Pugh. His mother was murdered when he was three, and his father, an employee of Ford Motor Company, remarried when he was six. One year later, George Pugh lost his job and committed suicide; from his bedroom across the hall seven-year-old Charles heard the gun shots and rushed to call 911. Pugh was raised by his grandmother and grew up on the west side of Detroit; his stepmother continued to be active in his life. In 1989 he graduated from Murray Wright High School with a scholarship to attend the University of Missouri. Having had early aspirations of someday becoming a news reporter in his hometown; he enrolled in the School of Journalism. In 1993 Pugh earned a Bachelor's Degree in Journalism from the University of Missouri and began work as a television journalist for KOMU-TV in Columbia, Missouri. Additionally, he worked in Topeka, Kansas, for WIBW-TV; at WKJG-TV in Fort Wayne, Indiana; and in Norfolk, Virginia, for WAVY-TV. Despite his successes, Pugh held on to his dream of being an anchor and reporter in Detroit.

In 1999, ten years after completing high school and a progressive career in television journalism, he finally returned home, two months before his ten-year class reunion, to the city he loved as reporter and anchor on WJBK-Fox 2 Detroit. Moreover, Pugh began to coanchor a three-hour news show on Saturday and Sunday mornings. Five years into his tenure with Fox 2 he joined WJLB-FM 98, Detroit's top urban radio station, as a commentator and news director. Pugh reported the news, traffic, and sports, and gained a lofty following for his commentary on the popular "Pugh's Perspective" segment on the weekday morning show with Coco, Foolish, and Mr. Chase. In addition, he hosted a Sunday evening talk show. After ten years with Fox 2 and five years with WJLB, in August 2008 Pugh entered the primary election for Detroit City Council. He won the primary election with 59,560 votes or 8.9 percent; 10,000 votes over President Kenneth Cockrel Jr., placing him in first place for the council seat he desired. In March 2009 Pugh resigned from radio and television; he then submitted his name as a candidate for president of Detroit's City Council, a position he felt would allow him the privilege of serving the people and the city he loved, that much more. On 3 May 2009 he formally announced his candidacy.

When Detroit citizens went to the polls in November 2009 Pugh faced five incumbents and twelve challengers for only nine available council seats. Pugh assured Detroit that his participation on the council would mean ethical, competent, and transparent leadership in a city that had been troubled by scandal involving the former Mayor Kwame Kilpatrick. In January 2004, Detroit media

Charles Pugh waves during a parade in Mexicantown in Detroit on 4 June 2009. (AP Images.)

had confirmed Pugh as being homosexual after he had presided over a conference at Detroit's Charles H. Wright Museum of African American History addressing homophobia. Undaunted by the media's discovery, Pugh continued to serve the city he loved; after all, his friends, family and colleagues were aware of his sexuality. Despite disputes in Detroit's African American community regarding homosexuality in general, and his in particular, Pugh was supported by Christian ministers who perceived him as the best man for the job, above anything else. Opposition attempted to question his ability to govern the city council due to a discovery that his three-story home near downtown Detroit was facing foreclosure. Pugh maintained that his personal financial situation had nothing to do with serving on the city council and remained confident that this would not sway voters decisions at the polls. On 4 November 2009 Pugh was elected by 88,704 votes to the Detroit City Council as president, becoming the first openly gay person in the political history of Detroit to win a major election. He easily defeated his closest rival ex-Detroit Deputy Police Chief Gary Brown, who won only 80,698 votes.

Passionate about education, Pugh has served as a mentor, speaks at Detroit schools, volunteers at Bethune/Fitzgerald Pre-K School, and performs outreach at the Wayne County Juvenile Detention Center. Pugh is a member of several boards and commissions; among them the Detroit Riverfront Conservancy, Southeast Michigan Council of Governments, and Democratic Municipal Officials.

FURTHER READING

Gray, Steven. "Can Detroit's First Openly Gay Pol Save the City?" *Time*, 2 Nov. 2009.

Riley, Rochelle. "Charles Pugh: Let City, Not Mayor Run Schools." *Detroit Free Press*, 9 July 2010.

SAFIYA DALILAH HOSKINS

Pullen, Don (25 Dec. 1944–22 Apr. 1995), jazz pianist and composer, was born Don Gabriel Pullen in Roanoke, Virginia. His parents' names are unknown, but his father worked professionally as a singer, guitarist, and dancer. He attended public schools in Roanoke and as a youngster took up the piano. One likely guide in his studies was a cousin,

Clyde "Fats" Wright, later cited by Pullen as a core influence. In addition to piano, Pullen became adept on the organ accompanying gospel singers at local church services. He soon was working with groups in-area nightclubs, mainly backing rhythm and blues vocalists.

While Pullen attended Johnson C. Smith University in Charlotte, North Carolina, he first became interested in jazz through listening to recordings of the pianist ART TATUM. During that period dramatic changes were occurring in jazz, the music moving well beyond the overriding bebop, postbop, and soul styles of the postwar years. Pullen immersed himself in the new sounds. He was especially affected by the expressive playing of the reedman ERIC DOLPHY and the pioneering efforts of ORNETTE COLEMAN as saxophonist and composer. CECIL TAYLOR's astonishing technical skills and confident blending of classical, blues, and jazz elements in his compositions and piano improvisations deeply impressed him as well.

By 1964 Pullen was in Chicago, working with MUHAL RICHARD ABRAMS's Experimental Band. That same year he played and recorded with the reedman Giuseppi Logan's quartet. Also with Logan was the drummer Milford Graves. A key percussionist in the "free jazz" movement, Graves had a drumming style that was fluidly proficient, incorporating African and Asian rhythms. He and Pullen formed a close-knit duet in which they experimented, performed, and recorded together. Two albums featuring their intuitive interplay were made at Yale University in 1966, an event that one jazz critic called "a major performance."

The exigencies of making a living caused Pullen to shift musical direction over the next half dozen years. Whenever possible he continued to perform in jazz clubs with his own groups. But away from jazz he found jobs more plentiful as an accompanist for such rhythm and blues vocalists as RUTH BROWN, Arthur Prysock, and Big Maybelle. During "the lean times," as Pullen called them, he also played jazz, soul, and funk with organ-dominated duos and trios in northern New Jersey nightspots.

In 1972 Pullen became music director for the jazz and pop vocalist NINA SIMONE. Within less than a year, however, he was back full-time on keyboards with the drummer ART BLAKEY's Jazz Messengers. Pullen then took a major career step in 1973 when he joined bassist-composer CHARLES MINGUS's quintet. Two other musicians in the group became Pullen's long-term associates, the tenor saxophonist GEORGE ADAMS and the drummer DANNIE RICHMOND.

During 1974 and 1975 the Mingus group worked regularly as part of the Newport Jazz Festival's U.S. tour, at the Umbria and Montreux jazz festivals, and at many concerts in Scandinavia. Although the quintet made few recordings, two of its three albums are considered essential modern jazz entries in many collections. *Charles Mingus: Changes One* and *Changes Two* explore several of the leader's finest compositions, including "Orange Was the Color of Her Dress, Then Silk Blue," "Sue's Changes," and "DUKE ELLINGTON's Sound of Love." Always aware of each piece's intentions, Pullen and Adams were free to "solo any way they want[ed] to," according to Mingus. Pullen's improvisations, ranging from the gently reflective to the percussively turbulent, anticipate the playing of his most mature years.

After leaving Mingus late in 1975 Pullen recorded his first solo album. He then collaborated on studio recordings with such free jazz players as the saxophonists SAM RIVERS, in 1975, and Hamiet Bluiett, in 1977, and the percussionist Famoudou Art Moye of the Art Ensemble of Chicago in a duet setting, *Milano Strut* (1978). With the tenorist David Murray, Pullen played a "smoky organ" (in one reviewer's words) on a 1977 album session. In October 1978 he performed solo at New York's Public Theater. In 1979 he joined Mingus Dynasty, an ensemble formed after Mingus's death to perpetuate his music and spirit. Pullen also performed several times as co-leader with the drummer Beaver Harris of the 360 Degree Music Experience, once in June 1980 at Town Hall in New York.

Throughout this period Pullen maintained his musical empathy with former Mingus colleagues Adams and Richmond. By 1979 they formed a quartet that harked back to their earlier association. Among the ten albums that the group recorded over the next eight years, critics cite *City Gates* (1983) as the most readily accessible and rewarding.

The quartet disbanded in 1986, and for the next several years Pullen performed and recorded in piano-bass-drums formats. Perhaps his two most fully achieved albums come from this time, *New Beginnings* (1988) and *Random Thoughts* (1990). More than in any other setting Pullen's stylistic individuality came to the fore in his solo and trio recordings. He said of his performances of that time, "I don't play any different than I did before, except in terms of growth and understanding....I know how to use the same tools and techniques in a more natural way."

To many listeners, the most identifiable "tools and techniques" of Pullen's improvisations were cleanly executed, extremely rapid fingerings, a percussive keyboard approach that elicited a spectrum of sounds, conventional harmonic progressions that were continually punctuated by unexpected clusters of notes; and swirling sonic splashes and thunderous eruptions achieved by the dexterity of his wrists and the backs of his hands. At their brightest and darkest Pullen's solos attained joyous exuberance or brooding cries of age-old pain.

In 1990 Pullen again took a new path when he formed the African Brazilian Connection, whose instrumentation included alto saxophone, bass, and Brazilian and African percussion. In four recordings on the Blue Note label the group created infectious ethnic musical elements over an explicitly declared jazz foundation. Early in 1994 Pullen was diagnosed with lymphoma. He underwent chemotherapy but continued to perform, compose, and record with the Connection. With only six weeks left to him he completed recording his most ambitious composition, which was released on his final album, *Sacred Common Ground*.

Pullen died in Orange, New Jersey. His marital status is unknown, but he fathered four children, and he was with a longtime companion, Jana Halmsohn, at his death. By 1980 many serious critics agreed that Pullen was one of the most original and gifted pianists in jazz, and he remained so for the rest of his life.

FURTHER READING

Feather, Leonard, and Ira Gitler. *The Encyclopedia of Jazz in the Seventies* (1976).
Kernfeld, Barry, ed. *The New Grove Dictionary of Jazz* (1994).
Wynn, Ron, ed. *All Music Guide to Jazz* (1994).
Obituary: *New York Times*, 24 Apr. 1995.
This entry is taken from the *American National Biography* and is published here with the permission of the American Council of Learned Societies.

ROBERT MIRANDON

Purvis, Charles Burleigh (14 Apr. 1842–14 Dec. 1929), physician and medical educator, was born in Philadelphia, Pennsylvania, the son of ROBERT PURVIS SR., a well-to-do abolitionist, and HARRIET FORTEN PURVIS, daughter of JAMES FORTEN, a prosperous sailmaker and civic leader. Purvis received his early education in Quaker-administered public schools and then at Oberlin College, which he attended from 1860 to 1863. For his medical studies he attended Wooster Medical College, which later was incorporated into Western Reserve University Medical School, in Cleveland, Ohio, graduating with an M.D. in 1865. During the summer of 1864 Purvis served as a military nurse, based at Camp Barker, a contraband hospital in Washington, D.C., which later formed the foundation of Freedmen's Hospital.

Upon graduating he petitioned to and was accepted by the U.S. Volunteers as an assistant surgeon for the Union army, one of only eight African Americans accepted as surgeons during the war. He held the rank of first lieutenant from 1865 to 1869 and was posted in the Washington, D.C., area. Following the Civil War the War Department relinquished its control of medical services for African Americans to the Bureau of Refugees, Freedmen, and Abandoned Lands, and like many of the other African American army surgeons, Purvis had his services contracted. The African American population in the capital city had more than doubled between the years of 1860 and 1867, with only six physicians to minister to their needs. With the bureau Purvis served as an assistant surgeon attending patients at an outdoor clinic in Washington, D.C.

In 1869 Purvis was appointed to the medical faculty of Howard University, making him only the second African American to hold such a position at an American university (the first was ALEXANDER T. AUGUSTA). From 1869 to 1873 he lectured on subjects such as materia medica, therapeutics, botany, and medical jurisprudence; during 1871 and 1872 he held the Thaddeus Stevens Chair; and from 1873 until 1906 he was professor of obstetrics, gynecology, and diseases of women and children. In 1871 the board of Howard University conferred on him an honorary M.A, and in 1914 he was the recipient of an LLD for his service. In 1871 Purvis married Ann Hathaway; they had two children.

In 1873 the nation faced a fiscal crisis that prompted the Howard University trustees to ask for the resignations of the entire medical staff. However, the staff was given the option of being reappointed to the faculty on a pro bono basis, a condition that lasted until 1907, when the medical faculty was awarded partial remuneration for its services. Only doctors Charles Purvis, Alexander Augusta, and Gideon Palmer chose to remain on a "self-supporting" basis, probably because they had income from other sources, including private practices. In an 1873 letter to General O. O. Howard, the university president for whom the institution is named, Purvis wrote, "While I regret the university will not be able to pay me for my services, I feel the importance of every effort being made to carry forward the institution and to make it a success" (Winston, Howard University Archives).

That same year Purvis assumed the position of secretary pro tempore of the medical department, a position he held until 1896. His leadership and innovative restructuring of the department was instrumental in saving the medical department from demise. Purvis was said to be a hard taskmaster and intolerant of those who failed to keep themselves apprised of the latest medical developments. His determination ensured that all students, and in particular African American and female candidates, continued to be trained as physicians. From 1899 to 1900 he served as president of the faculty and in 1900 was elected to the post of dean, which he declined.

When President James Garfield was wounded in an assassination attempt in 1881 Purvis was one of the consulting physicians, making him the only African American to attend a president of the United States. In acknowledgment of his service, newly elected president Chester A. Arthur appointed him surgeon in chief of Freedmen's Hospital, the teaching facility affiliated with Howard University's medical department. At this time the hospital was administered by the Department of the Interior rather than the War Department, making Purvis the first African American civilian to head a hospital under civilian auspices. He retained the position until 1894. Under his administration the number of patients attended increased greatly, and the care was substantially upgraded.

Purvis, a firm believer in professional development, in 1869 had his name, along with Augusta and later A. W. Tucker, all black physicians, forwarded for membership in the Medical Society of the District of Columbia, a branch of the American Medical Association (AMA). Membership in the AMA accorded a physician the latest medical information at lectures and workshops in addition to a level of prestige that could result in increased financial compensation. All three doctors had their applications denied strictly on the basis of race. Despite efforts from a group of local white physicians including Robert Reyburn, Joseph Burrows, and Silas Loomis, and a resolution Senator Charles Sumner of Massachusetts introduced before the U.S. Senate, the drive to have the racist entrance policies of medical societies abolished was defeated.

While residing in Washington, Purvis was also active in civic matters, serving on the board of education and the board of health for the district; the board of medical examiners from 1897 to 1904; and the board of trade for Washington.

In 1905 he relocated to Boston, Massachusetts, where he spent the remainder of his life and established a general practice. He was admitted to the Massachusetts Medical Society in 1904. However, his affiliation with Howard University continued. He resigned his teaching position in 1907 but was elected in 1908 to the board of trustees, a position he held until 1926. Purvis died in Los Angeles, California.

FURTHER READING

Cobb, W. Montague. "Original Communications: A Short History of Freedmen's Hospital," *Journal of the National Medical Association* 54, no. 3 (May 1962).

Logan, Rayford W. *Howard University: The First Hundred Years 1867–1967* (1969).

Morais, Herbert M. *The History of the Negro in Medicine* (1967).

Simmons, William J. "Charles B. Purvis, A.M., M.D.," in *Men of Mark: Eminent, Progressive and Rising* (1887, 1968).

This entry is taken from the *American National Biography* and is published here with the permission of the American Council of Learned Societies.

DALYCE NEWBY

Purvis, Harriet Davy Forten (1 Feb. 1810–30 October 1884), a Philadelphia abolitionist, was the daughter of JAMES FORTEN, a sailmaker and landlord, and Charlotte Forten, a homemaker. The senior Fortens had a total of nine children, and they used each birth to honor personal or financial benefactors. Harriet Davy, their third daughter, was no exception; her first and middle names came from two of her father's sail-making contacts. Weaving family matters with outside interests such as abolition and social reform became a recurring theme in Forten's life. She was directly involved in the abolition movement, created women's anti-slavery groups, and helped finance the vigilance committees—the informal organizations that provided food, shelter, and safe transport to slaves escaping southern masters and northern deputies.

However, to define Forten's activities simply in terms of abolition overlooks a key part of her personal history and that of the antebellum community of free northern blacks. Forten, her sisters, and other women in the families of African American artisans living in Philadelphia at the time engaged in both typical and atypical public behavior, with the support of their families. These women were traditional caregivers as well as activists who used legal and extralegal means to overturn slavery and prejudice. Forten's affiliation with the non-political, moral suasion branch of abolition did not prevent her from using her personal residence as a hideaway for fugitives. Additionally, she used her membership in the Philadelphia Female Anti-Slavery Society to direct money to groups that aimed to aggressively defy the Fugitive Slave Act of 1850. Forten represented a female culture that both trained her in a conventional role and prepared her to oppose the laws and customs that supported slavery. The Philadelphia of Forten's time consisted of an assortment of groups dedicated to improving the moral and economic well-being of the black community. The desire for progress—mental, spiritual, and financial—came from churches, reading groups, and mutual aid societies.

Forten's education came from a private tutor and later from a school created by her father and others who were dissatisfied with the public instruction offered to black youths. Nearly every aspect of Forten's life was intimately bound with reformers and reform movements. Her father supported temperance and industrial training to improve employment opportunities, and he proved an important ally of Boston's famed abolitionist William Lloyd Garrison. Forten and her immediate family were members of a small group of highly educated and financially independent African Americans whose extensive social networks protected them from the worst aspects of antebellum life: poverty, harsh physical labor, and illiteracy. The family's material wealth came from James Forten's earnings from his sail-making operation, and income from rental properties. Unlike the majority of black Philadelphians, Forten and her siblings were not compelled to enter the workforce at a young age. As a matter of course, her education included learning how to run a household, but she and each of her siblings mastered skills that were practical and highly useful for various reform causes. For example, one sister's poetry developed into social commentary and a brother's drawings were marketed at antislavery fairs. Forten became a charter member of the Philadelphia Female Anti-Slavery Society (PFASS), which she joined with her mother and her sisters, Sarah and Margaretta. Forten was a

seamstress and one of her assignments within the PFASS was the organization of a sewing class for poor women.

When Forten married in 1831, she wed a man whose economic and civic visibility surpassed her father's. Her husband, ROBERT PURVIS, was the son of a free woman of color and a white planter who had relocated to Philadelphia. Together, Harriet and Purvis, a founding member of the American Anti-Slavery Society, created a family and sustained commitments to abolition and other types of reform. Harriet was a delegate to the Anti-Slavery Convention of American Women in 1839. By 1845, Robert was president of the eastern branch of the Pennsylvania Anti-Slavery Society. Harriet co-chaired antislavery fairs for PFASS and ran a household that eventually included eight children and stowaway space for fugitive slaves. The money Harriet raised selling fancy goods during antislavery fairs made its way to the local vigilance committee responsible for spiriting slaves from the sheriff and other legal officers.

Harriet Purvis represented a small but notable group of antebellum black women activists. The bulk of her public service occurred amid debates about the appropriate role of women. Although she worked within the traditional role of mother and wife, her actions eventually sparked an expanded definition of women's social role. The ultimate goal of Harriet's reform was full citizenship for blacks that included educational opportunity, industrial training, and personal liberty. Her later affiliation with voting rights reflected a dual push for racial and gender equity. As a daughter of a Revolutionary War veteran, Harriet claimed a fundamental American citizenship. But because she was a daughter of a man of color she could expect exclusion from the benefits of government.

Harriet was married to a wealthy man, but racial prejudice denied her children access to public schools. Neither her valor nor her wealth could displace her race. After the Civil War, Harriet protested segregation on Philadelphia streetcars. Some of her children entered public service: her son CHARLES BURLEIGH PURVIS became a doctor and became an assistant surgeon at the Freedman's Hospital in Washington, D.C. Later, in 1873, he became chair of obstetrics and diseases of women and children at Howard University. Another son, Henry, moved to South Carolina and in 1868 won a seat in the South Carolina House of Representatives. Her daughter Hetty was a member of the National American

Woman Suffrage Association and attended the International Council of Women in 1899.

FURTHER READING
Microfilm copies of annual reports of the Philadelphia Female Anti-Slavery Society contain information about Harriet's leadership of the antislavery fairs. For details about social and civic relationships among blacks in Philadelphia, see the following:

Forten, Charlotte L., ed. Brenda Stevenson. *The Journals of Charlotte Forten Grimke* (1988).

Willson, Joseph., and Julie Winch, eds. *The Elite of Our People: Joseph Willson's Sketches of Black Upper-Class Life in Antebellum Philadelphia* (2000).

Winch, Julie. *A Gentleman of Color: The Life of James Forten* (2002).

ALFREDA JAMES

Purvis, Robert (4 Aug. 1810–15 Apr. 1898), abolitionist and reformer, was born in Charleston, South Carolina, the son of William Purvis, a naturalized British cotton broker, and Harriet Judah, the free daughter of a German Jewish flour merchant and an emancipated slave of Moorish extraction. In 1819 the family settled in Philadelphia, Pennsylvania, and at William's death in 1826 Harriet and her three sons came into a substantial fortune. After private schooling, Robert attended Pittsfield and Amherst academies in Massachusetts, decamping from the latter in 1829 following a Fourth of July prank. At age seventeen, inspired by his father's opposition to slavery, he spoke at an antislavery convention. But in 1830, upon meeting the abolitionist Benjamin Lundy, whom he revered all the rest of his life, Purvis resolved on a career as a reformer.

An intimate of JAMES FORTEN, the wealthy black sailmaker, Purvis threw himself into anticolonization activities, denouncing the design to deport free blacks to colonies outside the United States. Purvis married Forten's daughter, Harriet (HARRIET FORTEN PURVIS), in 1831; they had eight children. After Harriet's death in 1875, Purvis married Tacy Townsend, a white Quaker. When Lundy's associate, William Lloyd Garrison, looked to publish the *Liberator* (1831) and his hostile *Thoughts on African Colonization* (1832), Purvis and Forten aided him by gathering subscriptions and raising funds. Both were charter members of the American Anti-Slavery Society formed in Philadelphia in 1833. Following the first annual meeting of the society, Purvis, having obtained a U.S. passport through the intervention of President Andrew Jackson, sailed in 1834 to Britain, where for three months he promoted the American antislavery cause and visited relatives. His return voyage provided him with a tale that he delighted to tell for the remainder of his life: he had been showered with social courtesies by fellow passengers, notably the racial purist Arthur Peronneau Hayne of South Carolina, all of them miscued by his light complexion, until he disclosed, shortly before landing, that he belonged "to the degraded tribe of Africans."

Back in Philadelphia, Purvis moved his family to a house on Ninth and Lombard, in the heart of the city's black community. He embraced the free produce movement, which eschewed products of slave labor, such as rice and sugar; joined the black-led American Moral Reform Society, founded to promote "Education, Temperance, Economy, and Universal Liberty," as its corresponding secretary; and journeyed to Harrisburg as a delegate of the Philadelphia City Anti-Slavery Society to launch the Pennsylvania Anti-Slavery Society in 1837. That year, concerned at the abduction of increasing numbers of free blacks by agents sent to apprehend fugitive slaves, Purvis set up the Vigilant Association and, upon its restructuring in 1839 as the Vigilant Committee, was elected president of, in his words, "the first organized society of the Underground Railroad" (Smedley, 355). Purvis's home served as a haven for fugitive slaves on their way to freedom. He also became prominent as the drafter of *The Appeal of Forty Thousand Citizens, Threatened with Disfranchisement, to the People of Pennsylvania* (1838), a vain attempt to persuade the state electorate not to adopt a new constitution that would wipe away forty-seven years of black voting rights.

In 1842 Philadelphia suffered a race riot, and as in an 1838 riot, Purvis's residence was besieged. This time, abandoning the principle of nonresistance, he was prepared to shoot any intruder. Shaken and indignant, Purvis moved his family to two farms of 140 acres that he had bought in Byberry, about fifteen miles away. There he led the life of a gentleman farmer, proud of his prized cattle and horses, blue-ribbon poultry, and orchards. He continued to serve the American Anti-Slavery Society—he was vice president from 1841 to 1865, and thereafter he was on the executive committee—and to uphold radical Garrisonian doctrines, including the dissolution of the political union of the North and South. He was an energetic affiliate of the Bucks County Anti-Slavery Society, the Pennsylvania Anti-Slavery Society (president, 1845–1850), and the Pennsylvania Abolition Society (he was the only nonwhite member from 1840 to 1859). He gave money to the Repeal movement in Ireland—which agitated against the 1800 union of Great Britain and Ireland that provided for a single parliament—championed prison reform as well as temperance (while privately abstaining from liquor and smoking), and advocated women's rights.

The "damnable" Fugitive Slave Act of 1850, with its sweeping and stringent provisions for the restitution of runaway slaves to their masters, galvanized Purvis into publicly advocating violence. Barely one month after the passage of the act, declining reelection as president of the Pennsylvania Abolition Society, which shied away from use of "weapons of death," Purvis declared to its members, "Should any wretch enter my dwelling to execute this…law, I'll seek his life. I'll shed his blood, though my own life and that of my family should be sacrificed in consequence" (*Liberator*, 1 Nov. 1850). Avoiding active participation in the newly formed Philadelphia Vigilance Committee of 1852 because of delicate health, Purvis redoubled his fugitive rescue efforts, his farm having a secret room to hide fugitive slaves until they could be safely spirited away. Although he praised Harriet Beecher Stowe's *Uncle Tom's Cabin* (1852) for its condemnation of "the infernal system" of slavery, he openly deplored its favorable view of black resettlement in Liberia, which the Pennsylvania state legislature considered endorsing in April.

In 1853 Purvis found himself embroiled in a series of public controversies. In an August issue of his weekly journal, the black abolitionist FREDERICK DOUGLASS wounded Purvis deeply by referring to his "blood stained riches," implying that the riches had originated in the production of cotton by slaves. The two men later reconciled in 1886. In October Purvis was outraged after his son and two women were asked to leave an exhibition at the Franklin Institute in Philadelphia because of their color and after the Poultry Society Fair at the Philadelphia Museum excluded his fowl. The following month he publicized his refusal to pay Byberry's school tax because his children were barred from being pupils because of their race. Although he contemplated moving to England or Canada, Purvis persevered in his commitments. Eventually the Byberry officials, well aware that Purvis was the township's second largest taxpayer, opened school doors to all children. In 1855 the fugitive slave and reformer WILLIAM WELLS BROWN asserted, "There is no colored man in this country to whom the Anti-slavery cause is more indebted than Mr. Purvis" (*The American Fugitive…with a Memoir*, 312).

The *Dred Scott* decision of March 1857, declaring that Americans of African descent were not U.S. citizens, stirred Purvis's powers of excoriation and hyperbole to increasing frequency. He declared in a fiery speech of 12 May that the decision meant that blacks had "no rights which white men are bound to respect." In December 1859 he pronounced John Brown, the radical white abolitionist who had attempted to incite a slave insurrection at Harpers Ferry that October, the "Jesus Christ of the Nineteenth Century." He claimed in May 1860 that in "this cursed land" with its "hellish laws and precedents" he expected nothing from the new Republican Party because it favored colonization and supported slavery where it already existed. Five months later, while lambasting slaveholders, Purvis labeled Thomas Jefferson a "scoundrel," although better judgment moved him to omit that epithet in a printed version of his remarks.

Purvis welcomed armed conflict to end slavery, but after the Civil War began he criticized the race-related policies of President Abraham Lincoln, particularly Lincoln's proposal to deport and colonize freed slaves. He grew to trust the Lincoln administration, however, and took heart from Attorney General Edward Bates's declaration that he believed that blacks were citizens, the *Dred Scott* decision notwithstanding. After the official release of the Emancipation Proclamation in 1863, Purvis admitted freely that he was "proud to be an American citizen." When the government began recruiting black troops in 1863, Purvis urged black volunteers to enlist at Camp William Penn near Philadelphia. Joining with others to organize the Pennsylvania Equal Rights League in 1864, he rejoiced at the passage of the Fourteenth and Fifteenth amendments, although he remained a disappointed yet steadfast proponent of women's suffrage.

Greatly respected in the postwar era, Purvis refused an 1867 bid to head the Freedmen's Bureau but served as a commissioner in Washington, D.C., of the Republican-sponsored Freedmen's Savings Bank (1874–1880). After returning to Philadelphia he dedicated himself, as an elder statesman of abolitionism, to the defeat of slavery's "twin relic of barbarism, prejudice against color." He supported municipal reform and independent political action to battle race discrimination in city employment, to ameliorate the economic plight of black workers, and to shore up civil rights. In 1881 he backed for mayor the reform Democrat Samuel G. King, who after his election appointed four black policemen. In 1884, ignoring mounting Republican displeasure that he did not adhere to the party that had freed the slaves, Purvis flirted with the Greenback Party. Dissatisfied with the 1887 state civil rights law, he lobbied for more inclusive legislation.

Although increasingly enfeebled by the weight of years in later life, Purvis was honored by being named to the Pennsylvania World's Fair Board in 1891. He graciously granted interviews on the early days of slave rescues—his last interview being in December 1897—and he enrolled as a founder of the American Negro Historical Society in 1897. He died in Philadelphia, the last survivor of the American Anti-Slavery Society, at his home at 16th and Mount Vernon. After his death, books from Purvis's large private library, including two bound volumes of the *Liberator* bearing his autograph, were donated to the University of Pennsylvania. The oil portrait of CINQUÉ that he had commissioned from the painter Nathaniel Jocelyn to honor the hero of the 1839 *Amistad* slave ship mutiny was donated to the New Haven Colony Historical Society.

FURTHER READING

Boromé, Joseph A. "Robert Purvis and His Early Challenge to American Racism," *Negro History Bulletin* 30 (1967).

Boromé, Joseph A. "The Vigilant Committee of Philadelphia," *Pennsylvania Magazine of History and Biography* 92 (1968).

Brown, William Wells. *The Black Man: His Antecedents, His Genius, and His Achievements* (1863).

Quarles, Benjamin. *Black Abolitionists* (1969).

Smedley, Robert C. *History of the Underground Railroad in Chester and the Neighboring Counties of Pennsylvania* (1883; rpt. 2005).

Winch, Julie. *Philadelphia's Black Elite: Activism, Accommodation, and the Struggle for Autonomy, 1787–1848* (1988).

Obituary: *New York Times*, 16 Apr. 1898.

This entry is taken from the *American National Biography* and is published here with the permission of the American Council of Learned Societies.

JOSEPH A. BOROMÉ

Purvis, Sarah Louisa Forten (1814–30 Oct. 1883), poet and abolitionist, was born Sarah Louisa Forten in Philadelphia, Pennsylvania, to JAMES FORTEN, a sailmaker, and Charlotte Vandine, both of whom were active social reformers. Sarah was the fifth of eight surviving children. Her siblings included MARGARETTA FORTEN, HARRIET FORTEN PURVIS, ROBERT BRIDGES FORTEN, and James Jr., who were all active in the antislavery movement. A year before Sarah's birth, James Forten wrote a series of public letters objecting to proposed legislation that would have prohibited the migration of blacks into the state of Pennsylvania. Forten's poetry mirrored her father's dissatisfaction and disappointment with the evolving American society of the 1830s. Both father and daughter used the public forum of print to remind white Americans of broken promises and to define a growing race consciousness among free African Americans. Unfortunately for Forten, gender proscriptions and family obligations stymied the production of her written work.

Like her older sisters Forten received an education from a private tutor. The Forten family had the resources to strive for the most refined aspects of nineteenth-century culture. Forten and her siblings assembled an arsenal of skills like drawing, foreign languages, and calligraphy that firmly placed them among the educated classes. As Americans of African descent, however, they faced exclusion from public institutions and cultural activities. To combat routine discrimination, the Fortens and other like-minded families of color developed a self-contained microcosm of private tutors, reading groups, mutual aid associations, and eventually abolition societies. Forten was born into a community that, while not totally isolated from whites, contained independent organizations, including Philadelphia's Bethel African Methodist Episcopal (AME) Church and St. Thomas African Episcopal Church. The Fortens were members of St. Thomas and were active in its governance structure.

Writing under the names Ada or Magawisca, Forten submitted more than a dozen poems and essays to the *Liberator*, William Lloyd Garrison's antislavery newspaper, from 1831 to 1837. Forten's choice of the nom de plume Magawisca would have held special significance for readers of the *Liberator*. Magawisca was an important figure in *Hope Leslie*, a popular nineteenth-century novel by Catherine Sedgwick. Sedgwick's Magawisca was a Pequot Indian who rejected Puritans and the authority of whites.

Following the custom of the time Forten's work appeared either anonymously or under a nom de plume. Not even her father was initially aware of her identity as a poet. In an 1831 letter to Garrison, James Forten remarked that he had only recently learned that the poet "Ada" was his daughter. Forten's decision to work under a pseudonym spoke volumes about the status of women even in a household dedicated to abolition and racial and gender equality. Despite the self-actualized and progressive nature of black Philadelphia in general and the Forten family in particular, there were limitations. Had Forten been a man she might have developed into a public speaker. She began sending her poems to the *Liberator* without her father's knowledge because it was not appropriate for a young woman to engage in public discourse. In disguising her identity Forten was following a well-established nineteenth-century practice of anonymous public commentary. When William Lloyd Garrison printed extracts of correspondence from James Forten in the *Liberator*, the editor closed the letter by identifying its author as "an intelligent colored gentleman in Philadelphia."

Along with her mother and sisters Forten was a founding member of the Philadelphia Female Anti-Slavery Society (PFASS) in 1833. She collected signatures for petitions to the U.S. Congress to end slavery in Washington, D.C., and helped to organize an annual antislavery fair. Forten's 1834 poem "An Appeal to Woman" challenged white female abolitionists to fulfill their "Christian's part" and lay aside their antagonism toward women of color. Later ANGELINA WELD GRIMKÉ adapted the title of Forten's poem to the pamphlet *An Appeal to the Christian Women of the South*. Forten's "An Appeal to Woman" was circulated among the delegates during the inaugural national meeting of female abolition societies in New York City in 1837.

Surviving correspondence between Forten and Grimké and between Forten and the abolitionist Elizabeth Whittier reveals interracial tension within the ranks of the antislavery movement and the extent of the Forten family's influence among white abolitionists. In her poems and correspondence Forten described an antebellum community that was anything but open, full of mobility, or democratic—a society that claimed to value merit while it ignored the accomplishments and civic contributions of African Americans. For modern readers her work is important because she depicted racial hostility and discrimination as routine features of life in a Northern state, where the absence of legal slavery did not guarantee economic or social liberty.

Sarah Forten's literary production appears to have ended with her 1838 marriage to Joseph Purvis and the birth of their eight children. Joseph Purvis was the younger brother of ROBERT PURVIS, who had married another Forten sister, Harriet. The Purvis brothers were born in South Carolina and had inherited wealth from their father, William Purvis, who was born in England but made his fortune as a South Carolina cotton broker. His common-law wife was Harriet Judah, a free woman of color. Robert and Joseph used their inheritance to buy real estate, and they earned income from property rentals and farming. Joseph and Sarah Purvis settled on a farm in Bucks County, Pennsylvania, after their marriage. Joseph Purvis died without a will in 1857, and his death swept his immediate family into economic chaos. The children were all underage, and Sarah Purvis had to sell off pieces of property to generate income and pay debts.

After her marriage Sarah Purvis remained a member of the PFASS, but her distinct identity as a writer was over. The economic and personal stability that was critical to her ability to write and publish dissolved in her efforts to sustain her household. She remortgaged her remaining property and borrowed money from family friends. Her children were unable to match the accomplishments of their cousins in the area of public service. The offspring of Robert and Harriet Purvis continued the family legacy of reform by participating in government and education. Another cousin, CHARLOTTE FORTEN GRIMKÉ, published essays on her observations of the newly liberated slaves and later married a prominent minister, FRANCIS GRIMKÉ. Sarah Purvis eventually returned to her father's house in Philadelphia, where she died at the age of sixty-nine.

FURTHER READING

Gernes, Todd S. "Poetic Justice: Sarah Forten, Eliza Earle, and the Paradox of Intellectual Property," *New England Quarterly* 71.2 (June 1998).

Sterling, Dorothy. *We Are Your Sisters* (1984).

Winch, Julie. *A Gentleman of Color* (2002).

Yellin Jean Fagan, and Cynthia D. Bond. *The Pen Is Ours* (1991).

ALFREDA S. JAMES

Puryear, Martin (23 May 1941–), sculptor, was born in Washington, D.C., the eldest of seven children of Reginald Puryear, a postal worker, and Martina Morse, a schoolteacher. Puryear was an avid reader and an illustrator of detailed drawings of insects and birds. After graduating from Archbishop Carroll High School in 1959, he entered the Catholic University of America, switching his major from biology to art in his junior year. He also began working in wood, designing and building furniture, canoes, and a collapsible guitar. After receiving a B.A. in Art in 1963, Puryear joined the

Peace Corps, serving from 1964 to 1966 in Sierra Leone, West Africa. He taught French, English, and biology and studied the work of local carpenters and artisans, whose work, he discovered, combined beauty with utility. The vernacular architecture of the area and the centrality of simple man-made objects in West African daily life would serve as contributing forces in his later work.

An admiration for Scandinavian design and woodworking brought Puryear to Sweden after his service in Africa ended. While studying printmaking and wood sculpture at the Swedish Royal Academy of Art in Stockholm, he fell further in love with objects and their construction. As he had been in Sierra Leone, he was drawn to sculptural work born of wood construction rather than wood carving, and he augmented his formal studies with a brief apprenticeship under the renowned furniture maker James Krenov. Puryear's return to the United States in 1969 coincided with seismic and fast-moving developments in the history of modern sculpture, including minimalism, postminimalism, and earthworks—all profound influences on his work. Puryear began graduate training at Yale University in 1969, and, under the tutelage of Al Held, Richard Serra, Robert Morris, and Salvatore Scarpitta, he earned an MFA in Sculpture in 1971. From 1971 to 1973 he taught at Fisk University in Nashville, Tennessee, after which he moved to Brooklyn, New York, where he produced his first mature pieces, including *Rawhide Cone* (1974, artist's collection), *Bask* (1976, Guggenheim Museum), and *Circumbent* (1976, artist's collection). He also continued teaching, commuting to the University of Maryland from 1974 to 1978.

In February 1977 a fire destroyed Puryear's studio. "The fire," he later reflected, "was followed by a period of grieving and then by an incredible lightness, freedom, and mobility" (Benezra, 24). Having lost most of his work and possessions, Puryear responded with *Cedar Lodge* (1977) and *Where the Heart Is (Sleeping Mews)* (1977), two temporary installations inspired, respectively, by a tepee and a yurt (a portable hut used by Mongol and Afghan nomads), and several pieces dedicated to the mountain man JIM BECKWOURTH. In 1978 Puryear accepted a teaching position at the University of Illinois and relocated to Chicago, where he remained until 1990.

By the late 1970s Puryear's work began attracting critical attention. In 1977 he received both a National Endowment for the Arts Individual Artist Fellowship and a Robert Rauschenberg Foundation Grant, as well as his first solo museum exhibition, held at the Corcoran Gallery of Art in Washington, D.C. His sculptures appeared in exhibitions across the country, including the 1979 and 1981 Whitney Museum Biennials. One-person shows followed, culminating in a large traveling exhibition organized by the University of Massachusetts. Puryear's studio works of the late 1970s and early 1980s, dominated by a series of wall-mounted, circlelike wood sculptures, mostly untitled, gave way to larger, freestanding wood sculptures, such as *Old Mole* (1985, Philadelphia Museum of Art, Pennsylvania) and *Cask Cascade* (1985, private collection). He introduced wire in works like *Keeper* (1984, private collection) and wire mesh combined with tar in such pieces as *Sanctum* (1985, Whitney Museum) and *Maroon* (1987–1988, Milwaukee Art Museum). In the late 1980s and 1990s Puryear experimented further with new materials and delivered a variety of intriguing new compositions with the unique *Lever Series* (1988–1989) and such beguiling pieces as *Horsefly* (1996–2000, private collection)

After receiving a MacArthur Foundation Fellowship in 1989, Puryear represented the United States at the Twentieth São Paulo Biennial in Brazil with a suite of eight large sculptures that won the grand prize. The following year he moved to upstate New York with his wife of four years, Jeanne Gordon, a classical pianist and artist. By then he was the father of a young daughter and no longer teaching full-time, and his production and visibility increased. Puryear was the subject of a number of exhibitions, including a major traveling retrospective organized by the Art Institute of Chicago in 1991. In 1992, at the invitation of the French government, he served as artist-in-residence at the Calder Atelier in Sache, and from 1997 to 1998 he was an artist-in-residence at the American Academy in Rome. A major retrospective, charting the evolution of Puryear's career and featuring more than forty sculptures, was organized by the Museum of Modern Art in New York City in 2007.

A self-described outsider who "never felt like signing up and joining and being part of a coherent cadre of anything, ideologically, or esthetically, or attitudinally" (*New York Times*, 1 Nov. 1987), Puryear remained somewhat outside the shifting fashions and politics of the art world. Drawing from a diverse range of artists and styles, including Constantin Brancusi, Isamu Noguchi, Jan Arp, Louise Bourgeois, dadaism, modernism, and Russian constructivism, Puryear's work rejects pigeonholing. Inspired by the landscapes and artistic production of other cultures, he traveled worldwide, including to Japan, where he studied landscape design and architecture in 1983 on a Guggenheim Fellowship. Perhaps his outsider status and journeyman's spirit account for Puryear's admiration for MATTHEW HENSON, JEAN BAPTISTE POINTE DU SABLE, and Jim Beckwourth, historic black men who transcended racial and social as well as spatial boundaries.

The surfaces and construction of Puryear's wood and mixed-media sculptures are labor intensive, and they look it, revealing forms and methods borrowed from the folk technology, art, and architecture of nonindustrial cultures. Employing accumulative building processes such as wrapping, weaving, tying, and joinery associated with furniture making and shipbuilding, Puryear bridges the divide between art and craft. He celebrates traditional wood-bending techniques with *Alien Huddle* (1993–1995, private collection) and *Plenty's Boast* (1994–1995, Nelson-Atkins Museum of Art), basket weaving with *The Spell* (1985, artist's collection) and *Charm of Substance* (1989, St. Louis Art Museum), and architectural construction with *Thicket* (1990, Seattle Art Museum). "At bottom it's a class issue really," he argues. "'Art' means thought; 'craft' means manual work. In Japan you'll never see that kind of snobbery; potters and carpenters are honored there as living national treasures" (*Time*, 9 July 2001).

In their geometric abstraction, economy of form, and clarity of shape, Puryear's sculptures draw upon a minimalist sensibility, but he never considered himself a minimalist: "I tasted Minimalism. It had no taste. So I spat it out" (*Washington Post*, 25 Mar. 1988). Minimalism's rejection of craft, its insistence on industrial materials and fabrication, and its denial of metaphor did not appeal to Puryear, whose work succeeds by its subjectivity, reverence for materials, and evocation of narrative through form. "I value the referential quality of work, the fact that it has the capacity to allude to things" (*Chicago Tribune*, 3 Nov. 1991). Enigmatic and mysterious, Puryear's sculptures encourage interpretation. "I do not start with a particular thing and abstract from it. I have more a recombinant strategy. It's like combining from many sources into something that has clarity and unity. I like a flickering quality, when you can't say exactly what the reference is" (*Chicago Tribune*, 3 Nov. 1991). The results are complex and elegant abstractions—distilled essential forms—suggesting humans, animals, and objects, often in states of metamorphosis and transformation.

Evoking containers, boats, shelters, birds, tools, heads and profiles, cocoons, and amoebas, his sculptures suggest man-made and biomorphic elements without mimicking them. Some might see a bird's beak, falcon's talon, shark's tooth, or birdcage in *Seer* (1984, Guggenheim Museum). At twelve feet high, *Untitled* (1997–2001, Donald Young Gallery) is simultaneously a children's game, dinosaur, construction crane, and sea monster. "If you believe strongly," Puryear contends, "you can pump life into materials" (*Washington Post*, 25 Mar. 1988).

Puryear plays with notions of inside and outside, size, volume, and perspective, challenging the audience's sensual, emotional, and intellectual expectations. The basketlike *Brunhilde* (1998–2000, artist's collection), for example, was laboriously constructed to look like weaving, though its pieces are not interlaced. *Self* (1978, Joslyn Art Museum), *Confessional* (1996–2000, artist's collection), and *Untitled* (1997, Museum of Modern Art) appear solid but are actually hollow. Narrowing from two feet to one inch, *Ladder for* BOOKER T. WASHINGTON (1996, artist's collection) teases the eye while meting out social commentary. Another poignant experimentation with perspective and transformation, *This Mortal Coil* (1998–1999) features an eighty-five-foot-high spiral staircase, its massive red cedar steps becoming lighter with its ascension, eventually turning into muslin. Aided by materials like wire mesh and tinted glass, Puryear achieves both solidity and transparency with massive pieces that are, in fact, quite fragile.

In addition to his studio work, Puryear created a number of significant outdoor sculptures, beginning with *Box and Pole* (1977, Artpark, Lewiston, New York), a dramatic juxtaposition of a 100-foot-tall pole and a 4.5-foot wooden cube. Other major outdoor installations include *Bodark Arc* (1982, Nathan Manilow Sculpture Park, Governor's State University, Illinois), *Knoll* (1983, National Oceanographic and Atmospheric Administration, Seattle, Washington), *Ampersand* (1987–1988, Walker Art Center, Minneapolis, Minnesota), *North Cove Pylons* (1994, Battery Park, New York City), *Bearing Witness* (1995, Ronald Reagan Building Plaza, Washington, D.C.), and *That Profile* (1999, Getty Museum, Los Angeles), which Puryear conceived as "a drawing in space that would change as you walk around it."

"This isn't showoff sculpture," explained the critic Peter Plagens. "It's just old-fashioned lyricism whose tires you can kick" (*Newsweek*, 11 Nov. 1991). Encountering a Puryear sculpture is like discovering a vestigial artifact or relic, mysterious in its anachronism but rich in history.

FURTHER READING

Benezra, Neal, and the Art Institute of Chicago. *Martin Puryear* (1991).

Crutchfield, Margo A., and the Virginia Museum of Fine Arts. *Martin Puryear* (2001).

Davies, Hugh Marlais, Helaine Posner, and the University of Massachusetts. *Martin Puryear* (1984).

LISA E. RIVO

Putney, Martha (9 Nov. 1916–11 Dec. 2008), military officer and historian, was born Martha Settle, the fifth of eight children born to Ida Baily, a homemaker and Oliver Settle, a laborer, in Norristown, Pennsylvania. Martha Settle attended Norristown public school in an integrated school system, where she excelled in Latin. Graduating from high school in 1935, she attended Howard University in Washington, D.C., on a scholarship. There she majored in history and education earning a bachelors degree in 1939 and a masters degree in history the following year.

After graduation Putney went to work for the U.S. Civil Service Commission and then the War Manpower Commission, before joining the Women's Army Auxiliary Corps (WAAC) on 1 February 1943. Her decision to join the WAAC was met with family approval. Like many of the early African American WAAC recruits, she took her basic training at Fort Des Moines in Iowa. While at basic training Putney applied for Officer Candidate School (OCS). Owing to her high level of education and other qualifications, Putney was admitted to OCS training and received her commission as a second lieutenant on 7 July 1943. African American WAACs were often limited to where they could be assigned for duty. All WAACs were deployed based on request by commanders who needed the use of women to free men for combat related duties; however, African American WAACs often faced discrimination in assignments which limited their assignments and promotions. After OCS, lacking an immediate assignment, Putney attended Intermediate Officer School (IOS); she subsequently remained at Fort Des Moines, where she became a platoon and supply officer. During her tenure at Fort Des Moines, Putney was instrumental in ending segregation in recreation facilities used by WAACs.

The opportunity to leave Fort Des Moines came when she received an assignment to attend Adjutant General School (AG) at Fort Sam Houston, Texas. It was in Texas that Putney experienced her first intense encounters with segregation. At times her military uniform shielded her from overt racism while serving in the South, but not always. After AG school, she was assigned to a special training unit of the plans and training office. In this capacity, Putney helped to prepare recruits for the general classification test and basic training. She was also responsible for the plans and training of this integrated unit.

Between 1945 and 1946 she was assigned as the commanding officer of a company at Gardiner General Hospital in Chicago, where she was responsible for black WAACs working in the hospital, and in particular to ensure there were no "racial incidents" since the presence of the women had been protested by the white locals in the community. By 31 December 1946 Putney had decided to leave the army to pursue other goals.

Using the G.I. Bill's education benefits, Putney attended the University of Pennsylvania where she earned a Ph.D. in European History in 1955. While in graduate school, she married William Putney and gave birth to a son, William Putney Jr. Upon graduation she taught one semester at Prairie View, Texas, before returning to Washington, D.C., where she went to work at Morgan State University (Maryland) for two years after which she took a position at Bowie State (Maryland), where she spent the next nineteen years before retiring in 1974. She did not stay retired for long, taking a part-time position at Howard University where she taught until 1983.

Among Putney's publications was her autobiographical account of her time as a WAAC, *When the Nation Was in Need: Blacks in the Women's Army Corps During WWII* (1992). The book won the 1992 Outstanding Book Award from the Gustavus Myers Center for the Study of Human Rights in the United States. She also wrote *Black Sailors: Afro American Merchant Seaman and Whale Men prior to the Civil War* (1983). In addition to numerous articles, Putney also spoke publicly about her experience in the military during World War II. She was also featured in the journalist Tom Brokaw's *The Greatest Generation* television special (1999) and in the follow-up publication *The Greatest Generation Speaks: Letters and Reflections* (1999). After an unparalleled career as participant in and observer of the military's racial evolution, Putney died in Washington, D.C., 2008, at the age of 92.

FURTHER READING

Putney, Martha. *When the Nation Was in Need: Blacks in the Women's Army Corps during WWII* (1992).

Sims-Wood, Janet. "We Served America Too!: Personal Recollections of African Americans in the Women's Army Corps during World War II." M.A. Thesis, Cincinnati, Ohio: Union Institute (1994).

Obituary: *New York Times*, 18 Dec. 2008.

KELLI CARDENAS WALSH

Pyles, Charlotta Gordon (c. 1806–19 Jan. 1880), lecturer and abolitionist, was born a slave to parents whose names remain unknown. Family lore maintains that her father was of mixed black and German ancestry and her mother was a full-blooded Seminole. She was initially owned by Hugh Gordon, a Scot who had settled in Virginia, had a large family, and moved in 1797 to Washington County, Kentucky, where he owned about four hundred acres of land. While still a teenager, Charlotta married John McElroy, and the couple had a daughter named Julia Ann (sometimes listed as Julian); McElroy is otherwise absent from the historical record. She married again, probably in the late 1820s, to Henry (Harry) MacHenry Pyles, the light-skinned son of Scot William MacHenry and a woman who one of the Pyles's granddaughters (Grace Morris Jones) referred to as "a light colored maid, who worked in the home" (Brown, p. 34). Henry and Charlotta Pyles would have ten children.

When Hugh Gordon died around 1834, his estate was parceled out among his several children. His daughter Frances Gordon, already approaching fifty years of age and still unmarried, received Charlotta and her children; all are listed—without names—in the 1850 Slave Schedule of the Federal Census of Washington County (p. 48). The Gordons were Wesleyan Methodists, and Grace Jones's account claims that Frances Gordon "promised her father on his death bed that she would free" Pyles and her children (p. 35). Apparently, Gordon began the process of manumitting Pyles and her family in 1853, but her siblings—especially Baptist minister and farmer Joel Gordon, who lived next to her—objected. Some of the Gordon brothers kidnapped Charlotta's third child, Benjamin, and sold him to a trader from Mississippi. Incensed, Gordon briefly jailed Charlotta and her children in Springfield, Kentucky, to keep them safe from her brothers while she legally established her ownership, and then, with the aid of an Ohio minister, began a journey north with Henry and Charlotta Pyles,

their remaining children, and several of Charlotta's grandchildren by daughters Julia Ann and Emily. They traveled first to Louisville, then to Cincinnati, and then to Saint Louis, with the goal of settling in Minnesota. Winter hit hard, though, soon after the party crossed the Des Moines River, and they settled in Keokuk, Iowa.

Henry Pyles and the eldest son, Barney, soon found work—Henry as a carpenter and Barney as a teamster—and Henry built a brick house on Johnson Street in Keokuk. In addition to caring for the several children in the home, Charlotta turned her energies toward securing the freedom of Julia Ann and Emily's husbands, Catiline (or Thomas) Walker and Joseph (or Joel) Kendricks, who were enslaved by neighbors of the Gordon family who were willing to free them for fifteen hundred dollars each. At the same time, in early 1855, she apparently heard from her son Benjamin; however, according to Jones, she made the difficult choice to work for the freedom of her sons-in-law rather than Benjamin's because she "felt that as her son Benjamin was not married and had not little ones to care for it would be easier for him to liberate himself" (p. 40). Jones claims that she "secured good letters of recommendation from prominent white citizens"—though Jones lists Hiram Scofield, later a Union general among them even though Scofield would not move to Iowa until 1858). Pyles then traveled east, lecturing and attempting to raise money to purchase her sons-in-law. The 14 December 1855 issue of *Frederick Douglass's Paper* included an unsigned poem datelined "Providence, Sept. 1855" that was dedicated to "Charlotte Piles. A noble woman, now travelling [sic] in the free States, soliciting aid for the redemption of part of her family from REPUBLICAN Slavery," that praised the biblical Mary and Martha and linked Pyles to these figures. Jones reports that Pyles was befriended by FREDERICK DOUGLASS, Lucretia Mott, and Susan B. Anthony and that she lectured in Philadelphia's Old Penn Hall—"a difficult task for a poor ignorant woman, who had never had a day's schooling in her life, to travel thousands of miles in a strange country and stand up night after night, day after day before crowds of men and women, pleading for those men back in slavery and for the union of their wives and children" (Brown, p. 41). Apparently, though, she was successful and able to return briefly to Kentucky to purchase the men: Joel Kendricks was in Keokuk by 1856, as Joel and Julia Ann's daughter Charlotte was born there in 1857 and all are listed in the 1860 Federal Census; Emily Walker is similarly listed with Kentucky-born husband Thomas (p. 213, p. 190). The late 1850s and early 1860s seem to have been a period of relative prosperity and celebration for the family: in the midst of the marriages of several of the Pyles daughters, Henry and Charlotta made their marriage official on 2 April 1857. They would remain together in Lee County, Iowa, until Henry's death in the mid-1870s, and by the 1870 Federal Census had accumulated fifteen hundred dollars in real estate (p. 341).

The large Pyles family reportedly became active in working to aid fugitive slaves passing through Iowa. They also maintained close ties to Frances Gordon, who apparently lived with the family at some points. Charlotta seems to have especially encouraged her children to educate themselves: daughter Mary Ellen, who boarded with a Quaker family in Salem, Iowa, in order to gain schooling, would see her daughter Grace Morris marry Laurence C. Jones and help found Mississippi's well-known Piney Woods School; daughter Charlotte's son Geroid (or Gerard) Smith was involved in court cases in the 1870s that led to Keokuk's high school being briefly desegregated. Charlotta Pyles died of heart disease in Keokuk.

FURTHER READING

Jones, Mrs. L. C. [Grace Morris Jones.] "Charlotta Gordon MacHenry Pyles," in *Homespun Heroine and Other Women of Distinction*, ed. Hallie Q. Brown (1926).

Jones, Mrs. Laurence C. [Grace Morris Jones.] "The Desire for Freedom." *Palimpsest*, May 1927.

ERIC GARDNER

Quamino, Duchess (c. 1739–29 June 1804), slave, renowned pastry maker, and entrepreneur, also referred to as "Charity," was born on the Gold Coast of Africa to a minor royal family. In the middle of the eighteenth century she was taken captive, sold into slavery, and transported to Newport, Rhode Island, where she became a domestic slave in the home of William Channing, a prominent attorney.

Like many of that port town's female slaves, Quamino would have been responsible for a variety of activities that maintained the household. One job in which she excelled early was baking, a skill that would hold her in good stead in later years. The historical record does not indicate what kind of personal relationship Quamino had with her master, but it is significant that she converted to Christianity while working and living with the Channing family. Her exact motives for doing so are not certain; she may have perceived Christianity as a way to mitigate the harshness of slavery, as a possible tool with which to gain her freedom, or as a spiritual response to her experience with slavery. She attended Ezra Stiles's Second Congregational Church with the Channings but, like most blacks in white churches, was probably relegated to the back or balcony of the church. By 1769 Quamino had married JOHN QUAMINO, an African slave owned by Captain Benjamin Church. John Quamino later purchased his freedom with the earnings from a winning lottery ticket and volunteered for an African evangelical mission (which never took place because of the American Revolution). The couple had at least three children—Charles (born in 1772), Violet (1776), and Katharine Church (1779), though it is not certain whether the couple ever cohabitated.

The American Revolution disrupted Quamino's life in many ways. Indeed, no period was more bittersweet for her than between 1779 and 1780. In the early autumn of 1779 she learned of her husband's death. He had enlisted as a privateer, presumably in an effort to earn enough money to purchase his wife's freedom, and had died in battle with the British in August. Now suddenly alone, Quamino might have been comforted somewhat by the birth of their new child, whom she named Katharine Church and baptized in October. In addition, Quamino apparently had secured her own freedom, and probably her children's, by 1780.

It is still not entirely clear whether she was manumitted, but local folklore suggests that she baked her way to freedom, using the Channings' oven to make pastries that she sold to local Newporters. Like many newly freed blacks, she was hired as a servant in the same household that had previously enslaved her, and she was entrusted to be caretaker to the family's newest member, William Ellery Channing. Born in 1780, the young Channing would later gain fame as a prominent Unitarian clergyman and abolitionist. Indeed, local folklore suggests that Quamino, now a free woman, had a significant influence on the impressionable Channing's attitudes toward religion and slavery as he was growing up, and Channing's well-documented antislavery sentiment may well have germinated under Quamino's care.

In addition to taking care of the Channings' children, Quamino was quite busy looking after her own and establishing an independent house-hold, which she had done by 1782. Unfortunately, in January 1792, her daughter Violet passed away at the age of fifteen. Quamino would have been quite familiar with the funerary practices of Newport's black community, as she was at that time a member of the Pall and Biers Society, a branch of Newport's African Union Society, which subsidized funeral expenses for free blacks in need.

As Quamino was forming an independent household and becoming a more active member in the community, she was also gaining local fame as "the most celebrated cake-maker in Rhode Island" (Channing, 171). She was known for her frosted plum cakes, and she apparently both delivered cakes to her clients and catered popular events like the subscription assemblies that took place in Newport during the winter. Local folk-lore has it that Quamino still used the Channings' large oven to bake for these events, and she often expressed her gratitude by inviting members of that family over to her home for tea. Though she left no records in her own words, baking probably fulfilled several financial, social, and emotional needs. First, it had the obvious consequence of granting her a niche in the food market that she could exploit to her own financial advantage. Her culinary creativity also offered her prestige and recognition in a society where most whites denied it to blacks. Finally, baking might have served a therapeutic purpose for Quamino because she could be alone with her work, contemplate the loss of her husband and the fate of her children, and reflect on both the trials and blessings that characterized her life.

Though the reason for Quamino's death near the age of sixty-five is still unclear, Newporters long recalled the large funeral the community gave her. Fittingly, it was William Ellery Channing who wrote the effusive epitaph on the Quamino's grave, which still stands in Newport's Common Burial Ground. The epitaph praised Quamino for her "dis-tinguished excellence" and "Exemplary Piety." The stone obituary also described her as "Intelligent, Industrious, Affectionate," and "Honest." While blacks and whites usually had separate funerals in Newport, her death offered the community an opportunity to join together to reflect on Quamino's life and influence.

FURTHER READING
Channing, George Gibbs. *Early Recollections of Newport, R.I., from the Year 1793 to 1811* (1868).

Melish, Joanne Pope. *Disowning Slavery: Gradual Emancipation and "Race" in New England, 1780–1860* (1998).
Sweet, John Wood. *Bodies Politic: Negotiating Race in the American North, 1730–1830* (2003).
Youngken, Richard C. *African Americans in Newport: An Introduction to the Heritage of African Americans in Newport, Rhode Island, 1700–1945* (1995).

EDWARD E. ANDREWS

Quamino, John (c. 1744/45–Aug. 1779), also referred to as "Quaum" or John Quamine, slave, African missionary in-training, possibly the first African to attend college in the American colonies, and Revolutionary privateer, was born near Annamoboe, on the Gold Coast of Africa. He came from a wealthy family, and in the mid- to late 1750s he was sent by his father to receive a Western edu-cation. However, the captain who agreed to take him reneged on this agreement and sold him into slavery.

By the mid-1760s Quamino had become a slave to Captain Benjamin Church of Newport, Rhode Island. The historical record does not detail exactly what Quamino did under Church's ownership, but he converted to Christianity after his arrival in Newport. Quamino attended the First Congregational Church, which was taken over by Jonathan Edwards's avid protégé, Samuel Hopkins, in 1769. In that same year Quamino mar-ried DUCHESS QUAMINO, then a slave of Newport's prominent Channing family. Duchess would later become a successful entrepreneur as one of the region's most renowned pastry makers. Though it is unclear whether the couple ever lived together, they had at least three children—Charles (born in 1772), Violet (1776), and Katharine Church (1779).

The year 1773 was a watershed year for John Quamino. Early in that year, he and Bristol Yamma (a friend he most likely knew from their mutual attendance at Newport's First Congregational Church) collaborated to purchase a lottery ticket, and they subsequently won the prize. The winnings covered most of the cost for Quamino to buy his freedom (Yamma was not able to purchase his free-dom until later), but it is not clear whether he left the Church household, joined the Channings (with his wife and new child), or rented his own house. In addition, this was the year that ministers Samuel Hopkins and Ezra Stiles formulated a plan to send black missionaries to preach the gospel in Africa. This was not necessarily a novel scheme, as both the

Moravians and the Church of England had already sent black missionaries to Africa's west coast by this time. Though the two ministers predicted that they may have eventually been able to send thirty or forty black missionaries to Africa, the project began with an inauspicious core of two: the same John Quamino and Bristol Yamma who shared the fortune of purchasing a winning lottery ticket.

Stiles and Hopkins immediately began soliciting funds for the African missionary plan, and in a 1773 circular letter they offered a vivid description of why Quamino and Yamma were chosen to serve as the vanguard of this experiment. They claimed that both candidates had sincerely converted to Christianity and "have from that time sustained a good character as christians, and have made good proficiency in christian knowledge" (Ezra Stiles, *To the Public*, [1776], 1). Most importantly, Yamma and Quamino could still speak African dialects, an advantage that even the most learned academics and divines usually lacked. Nevertheless, they were still in need of training in reading, writing, and scriptural study, and the circular requested donations for a college fund for the further education of these two candidates. The plan generated considerable support from religious leaders as far away as London and Africa and cultural figures like Boston's famous poet PHILLIS WHEATLEY. While there is no reason to doubt the sincere conversion of Yamma and Quamino, their desire to return to Africa and see their families must have also been a strong motivation for attempting to embark on such an ambitious and adventurous mission. Indeed, one black missionary working out of London had found Quamino's mother (his father was dead), and through the correspondence of this missionary she expressed her sincere desire to see her son return to his family in Africa.

In November 1774 the two African missionaries set sail in stormy waters for New York, where they disembarked and traveled overland to the College of New Jersey to study under President John Witherspoon. Quamino and Yamma thus became possibly the first two blacks educated at an American college (though they never graduated and were not officially enrolled as students). They spent a few months studying under Witherspoon, a Scottish Presbyterian who would later gain even more fame as a signer of the Declaration of Independence. Witherspoon was respected throughout the Atlantic world for his scriptural scholarship, so Quamino and Yamma could have found no better teacher. Yet the actual content of their education is still unclear. While others were learning Hebrew, divinity, mathematics, and oration, Quamino and Yamma were probably sharpening their language skills and fine-tuning their understanding of the many complexities of Christian theology.

However, the American Revolution forced the college to suspend its normal routine, hastened the evacuation of Newport, and caused the abandonment of this missionary enterprise altogether. While the war disrupted Quamino's plans to evangelize Africa and, perhaps most importantly, return to his original family, Quamino attempted to use wartime opportunities to better the prospects of his own family in Newport by enlisting as a privateer. Unfortunately, Quamino died while fighting the British in August of 1779. (Yamma would live until 1793, by which time he was a community leader in Providence.)

John Quamino's story is both exceptional and familiar. His frequent reversals of fortune signify the tumultuous life that blacks experienced in the eighteenth century. Yet it also appears that his missionary experiment, devotion to Christianity, and marriage to Duchess Quamino offered him some semblance of stability in an unstable world. Though John Quamino would eventually lose his life in the Revolutionary War, the idea of sending educated, Christianized blacks to preach the gospel in their "homeland" continued and became a central justification for both British and American colonial experiments in Liberia and Sierra Leone.

FURTHER READING

Melish, Joanne Pope. *Disowning Slavery: Gradual Emancipation and "Race" in New England, 1780–1860* (1998).

Sweet, John Wood. *Bodies Politic: Negotiating Race in the American North, 1730–1830* (2003).

Youngken, Richard C. *African Americans in Newport: An Introduction to the Heritage of African Americans in Newport, Rhode Island, 1700–1945* (1995).

EDWARD E. ANDREWS

Quarles, Benjamin Arthur (23 Jan. 1904–16 Nov. 1996), historian, was the eldest of five children born in Boston, Massachusetts, to Arthur Quarles, a subway porter, and Margaret O'Brien. Although he grew up in a poor neighborhood and, like his siblings, had to work menial jobs, Quarles graduated from English High School in 1922. Later, he and his brothers worked as waiters in Florida and as seamen on ships sailing from Boston to Bar Harbor,

Maine. Both of these jobs were typical of the forms of employment available to African American men in New England from the late eighteenth century into the twentieth century.

In 1927 Benjamin Quarles enrolled at Shaw University in Raleigh, North Carolina, where he became a debater and a student leader, graduating in 1931 as valedictorian of his class. Following commencement he enrolled at the University of Wisconsin, Madison, after being awarded a Social Science Research Council Fellowship for graduate study in history. After studying there for four years and earning his master's degree, Quarles returned to Shaw University to teach history. Two years later he married Vera Bullock of Greensboro, North Carolina. Their daughter, Roberta, was born in 1938. Still writing his dissertation in 1939, Quarles moved with his family to another black institution, Dillard University in New Orleans. After teaching at Dillard for two years, he became head of the social sciences division and, later, dean of the college.

While still a graduate student, Quarles began publishing in the *Journal of Negro History*. His 1940 article, "FREDERICK DOUGLASS and the Woman's Rights Movement," became a classic, marking the beginning of his focus on gender in his discussions of black life in U.S. history. In the meantime, he completed his dissertation on Frederick Douglass, earning his Ph.D. in History from the University of Wisconsin in 1940. Quarles's reputation as a young scholar began to grow, enabling him to earn five fellowships between 1931 and 1945, including one from the Rosenwald Fund.

By 1948 Quarles had expanded his dissertation into a full-length scholarly biography of Frederick Douglass, published by the Associated Publishers, Inc., an affiliate of the Association for the Study of Negro Life and History, which CARTER G. WOODSON had cofounded in 1915. *Frederick Douglass*, the first definitive study of the nineteenth-century civil rights giant, was reprinted several times over the next five decades. According to the recollections of colleagues and family members, no white publishers had been interested in the manuscript, but the book was well received among black academics and intellectuals. Members of the Frederick Douglass Cultural Society, for example, held a book party, sponsored by the Frederick Douglass Book Center in Harlem, New York, to honor the publication. More than fifty years later Douglass's biographer William S. McFeely described Quarles's biography as an excellent study, still relevant to twenty-first-century readers interested in Douglass.

Although he was committed to academic publishing and research, Quarles, like many of his black cohorts in higher education, also served his community. While teaching and living in New Orleans during the 1940s, Quarles was secretary of the New Orleans Urban League and served on the New Orleans Council of Social Services. Always the scholar, during the 1950–1951 academic year Quarles went on sabbatical leave from Dillard to research his second book, *The Negro in the Civil War* (1953), a work that highlighted his expertise in black military history.

While he was away, his wife, Vera, died suddenly, leaving Quarles and their daughter, Roberta, alone and devastated. In December 1952, however, he married Dr. Ruth Brett, dean of students at Fisk University. The following academic year they left for Morgan State College in Baltimore, Maryland, an historically black institution, where Quarles became chair of the history department; he remained in that position until the mid-1960s. Their daughter, Pamela, was born in 1954. By 1956 Ruth Brett Quarles was developing the Counseling Center at Morgan, of which she became coordinator; both she and her husband continued to work at the college (which became a university in 1974) until their retirement. While teaching and writing at Morgan, Quarles earned more fellowships, including a prestigious Guggenheim in 1959.

In his professional prime as a renowned historian, Quarles thrived at Morgan, where he became known as an outstanding mentor and popular professor and, in 1963, was selected as the college's first Teacher of the Year. During the 1950s and 1960s he continued to serve the community and his profession as vice president of the Urban League and as vice president of the Association for the Study of Negro Life and History. As a mentor and scholar during this period, the self-effacing Quarles never acknowledged that he was special. Others, however, always praised his willingness to help and promote them. Despite his claims of being unworthy of special awards, several were forthcoming. In 1967 Maryland's U.S. senator Daniel Brewster attended the Morgan State College celebration of Frederick Douglass's birth and introduced Benjamin Quarles as the speaker. The senator was so impressed with Quarles's lecture that he entered it into the *Congressional Record* (23 Feb. 1967).

When Morgan's president, Martin D. Jenkins, recommended Quarles to the governor of Maryland for a newly established honor, Distinguished Professor, Quarles became the first to receive such an award. Outside the state of Maryland, he continued to be honored for scholarship and mentoring. Between 1966 and 1996 Quarles received twelve honorary doctorate degrees. In addition, he received the American Historical Association's Senior Historian Scholarly Distinction Award and the Smithsonian Institution's National Museum of American History Lifetime Achievement Award (1996).

Retiring from active teaching in 1974 did not slow down Quarles's scholarly work. He continued serving on the editorial boards of the *Journal of Negro History* and the *Maryland Historical Magazine*. Throughout the 1970s Quarles served on several community committees and boards, including the Joint Center for Political Studies' Project Advisory Committee on Black Congress Members. He was also a member of the Committee of Advisers of the National Humanities Center Fellowships and the Department of Army Historical Advisory Committee. A prolific writer, Quarles continued to research and write into his mid-eighties, at which time he published the revised and expanded edition of his popular textbook *The Negro in the Making of America* (1987).

Although Quarles is best known for his biography of Frederick Douglass and his textbooks, scholars have also praised his influential and pathbreaking volume *The Negro in the American Revolution* (1961) and *Black Abolitionists* (1969). He has been revered as a major pioneer in writing about the African American experience before the Civil War, publishing a total of fourteen books from 1948 to 1988. In 1996 the historian V. P. Franklin wrote that Quarles was successful not only in writing about black troops in U.S. wars but also in examining the broad cultural contributions of African Americans to American society. Franklin described Quarles as one of the most distinguished scholars of African American history.

Quarles's reputation as a mentor to the younger generation of African American scholars included his support in 1979 for black women historians seeking to organize their own professional association. As an adviser to the Association of Black Women Historians, he helped secure a National Endowment for the Humanities grant for a research conference funded in 1983.

When Ruth Brett Quarles retired in 1980, the couple continued to reside in Baltimore. By 1988 they decided to donate Quarles's papers and awards to the Morgan State University Soper Library and moved to the Collington Episcopal Life Care Community in Mitchellville, Maryland. They were living in this community when Quarles began to experience poor health. He died in Mitchellville of heart failure at the age of ninety-two.

The views of colleagues in his field may best speak to the impact that Benjamin Quarles had on his profession for more than fifty years. In assessing his scholarship and historiographical development, the historian August Meier found that, in his work, Quarles, like his contemporary JOHN HOPE FRANKLIN, brought attention to the diversity of black life in U.S. history.

FURTHER READING

Franklin, V. P. "Introduction," Benjamin Quarles, *The Negro in the Making of America* (3d ed., 1996).

McConnell, Roland C., and Daniel B. Brewster. "Introduction," Benjamin Quarles, *Frederick Douglass: Challenge and Response* (1987).

McFeely, William S. "Introduction," Benjamin Quarles, *Allies for Freedom and Blacks on John Brown* (repr., 2001).

Meier, August. "Introduction," Benjamin Quarles, *Black Mosaic: Essays in Afro-American History and Historiography* (1988).

Quarles: Memorial Convocation; Celebrating the Life and Legacy of Dr. Benjamin Quarles (1996).

Turner, W. Burghardt, and Joyce Moore Turner, eds. *Richard B. Moore: Caribbean Militant in Harlem* (1988).

Obituary: *Baltimore Sun,* 19 Nov. 1996.

ROSALYN TERBORG-PENN

Quarles, Norma (11 Nov. 1936–), television newscaster, was born Norma Field in New York City to Dorothy and Lincoln Field, Trinidadian immigrants whose collective heritage was African, Scottish, Portuguese, British, and Chinese. She had one brother, Arthur, who later served as a Port Authority Police Officer and died in 1996. Their parents came to the United States as teenagers, Dorothy at sixteen and Lincoln at nineteen, settling in a diverse neighborhood in the South Bronx. Quarles's mother was a seamstress, and her father worked at Macy's Herald Square for fifty years (from 1926 to 1976), in the restaurant kitchen and later as an elevator operator. Quarles and her father appeared as extras in the film *Miracle on 34th Street* (1947).

Quarles attended P.S. 39, P.S. 63, and P.S. 89. She was selected to attend the National Conference of Christians and Jews at age thirteen and was an honors student and Junior Arista member at Evander

Childs High School, where she also lettered three times in athletics and graduated at the age of sixteen in 1953. After entering Hunter College in the Bronx with plans to become a physical therapist, she soon changed course, taking evening business classes at Bernard Baruch City College while working as an assistant buyer at Roaman's department store.

On 17 September 1955, eighteen-year-old Norma Field married Lawrence Quarles, an insurance executive of African American, Native American, and British heritage. Four days later the couple moved to Chicago. Norma Quarles went to real estate school, was licensed as a real estate broker in 1957, and joined the Katherine King Real Estate and Insurance Company (owned and operated by her mother-in-law). The Quarleses had two children, Lawrence II, born in 1957, and Susan, born in 1961. Concluding that real estate would not be her long-term career, Quarles answered an open call for auditions at jazz radio station WSDM. She impressed station executives with her on-air voice—honed in part during public speeches at PTA meetings—and was then trained to assemble newscasts. During her eight-hour days at the station she also played music and operated the sound board.

In 1966 Quarles separated from her husband—they would divorce one year later—and she returned to New York with her children. After looking for jobs in real estate and advertising, she went to NBC in search of radio work and learned about the network's training program. Quarles was one of just three applicants chosen in 1966 for NBC's one-year paid training program, where she worked with legends of broadcasting including Barbara Walters, Chet Huntley, David Brinkley, Gabe Pressman, and Edwin Newman. She accepted a job offer from WKYC-TV in Cleveland, one of several NBC-owned stations around the country. There she anchored weekend newscasts, did a five-minute daily network news show, and reported stories ranging from riots in Cleveland's Glenville neighborhood to an interview with astronaut Neil Armstrong's parents in Wapakoneta, Ohio, during Armstrong's moon mission.

As the civil rights movement gathered strength, Quarles, who viewed her multiracial heritage as a broadening influence, was criticized by some for not being militant enough. In 1960s Chicago she sensed much more racism and discrimination than she had felt growing up in New York, and her identification with African Americans was strengthened in that decade's milieu of social change.

In 1970 Quarles returned to New York to work at WNBC, reporting local stories and anchoring the morning news breaks during the *Today Show*. She won several awards for her work, including the Sigma Delta Chi Award and the Front Page Award. She was the first woman and the first African American to win either award. Quarles's strong performance as a guest host for three weeks on Barbara Walters's *Not For Women Only* led to the offer of a 6:00 pm co-anchor position on WNBC, the first such post ever offered to a black woman in New York City. During these years, putting motherhood first, she did not accept assignments that involved extensive travel.

Since starting at NBC, Quarles had been considered a local reporter even when her reports were carried by the national network. She served a four-year stint from 1977 to 1981 at Chicago's WMAQ-TV, where she won a local Emmy Award, and in 1978 she was promoted to network correspondent with reports airing only on network programs such as the *Today Show* or *NBC Nightly News*. In 1981 Quarles returned again to New York as an NBC correspondent, covering important stories such as the Bernhard Goetz ("Subway Vigilante") shooting of four youths in 1984 in Manhattan, which aroused controversy over the limits of what could be considered self-defense, and the Baby M case (1986–1988) in New Jersey, which drew national attention to the custody rights of surrogate mothers. Quarles also anchored the *NBC News Nightly Digest*. She was chosen by the League of Women Voters to be a panel member on the 1984 vice presidential debate between George Herbert Walker Bush and Geraldine Ferraro.

After twenty-one years with NBC, Quarles accepted an offer in 1988 to join CNN's New York bureau, where she continued to win awards for her work as a reporter and daytime anchor, including the CINE Golden Eagle Award for Excellence in Film and Video in 1993. In 1990 she was one of seven pioneers inducted as charter members of the National Association of Black Journalists Hall of Fame. In 1996 Quarles was diagnosed with acoustic neuroma, a potentially life-threatening type of brain tumor. Surgery, while successful, left her with vertigo and partial hearing loss in one ear; months of physical therapy were required to restore her to health. She retired from full-time news broadcasting in 1998 and from freelance reporting in late 2001.

Quarles taught a graduate course on television writing at the New School in 1977 and mentored younger colleagues and students. One of these was Renee Chenault-Fattah, evening anchor at Philadelphia's WCAU–TV, whom Quarles recommended to NBC executives. Her son-in-law Geoff Stephens was a producer with NBC for nineteen years, and her daughter Susan interned with NBC during three national political conventions and worked at the network for four years, before beginning a career in law.

Norma Quarles remained an active photographer and enjoyed the visual arts. Her lifelong love of movies served as inspiration in editing film and video footage for her reports, and she was also a frequent advocate of increased news coverage of the arts. As of 2007 she continued to be a member of the National Academy of Television Arts and Sciences.

FURTHER READING
Gelfman, Judith S. *Women in Television News* (1976).
"Upsurge in TV News Girls," *Ebony* 26 (June 1971).

DAVID BORSVOLD

Quebec, Ike (17 Aug. 1918–16 Jan. 1963), musician, was born Ike Abrams Quebec in Newark, New Jersey. The names of his parents are unknown. Nothing is known about his musical background prior to 1940. As a teen in the late 1930s he worked as a dancer with a traveling show titled Harlem on Parade.

The point at which Quebec entered the musical establishment would prove to be a pivotal time in the history of jazz. Big band swing, with its regular phrasing and predictable dance beat, along with the lively piano blues affectionately known as boogie-woogie for its rapidly oscillating bass ostinato, were the reigning popular forms of jazz during the 1930s. They were challenged in the early 1940s by musicians who promoted a new genre featuring greater harmonic and rhythmic complexity. Bebop, a name derived from the syllabic vocal improvisation of a jazz melody more commonly known as scat singing, altered and extended the harmonic vocabulary inherent in swing and combined it with a conceptually different form of rhythmic activity designed to highlight harmonic progressions often found in blues. Within this context Quebec's career would serve as a transition between bebop and its immediate precursors.

During the early 1940s Quebec distinguished himself as a worthy jazz musician, performing right away with many of swing's and bebop's legendary performers. Pianist with the Barons of Rhythm from 1940 to 1941, he switched to tenor saxophone in 1942, playing at many Harlem jam sites where he met THELONIOUS MONK, BUD POWELL, and other developing bebop musicians. Quebec worked briefly with the scat legend ELLA FITZGERALD's orchestra in 1942 and toured regularly with the swing bands of ROY ELDRIDGE and FRANKIE NEWTON in 1943. Quebec worked with Benny Carter from 1942 to 1944 and performed alongside the bop forerunner COLEMAN HAWKINS during the same period. Other musicians Quebec performed and recorded with during 1944 include Sammy Price's Texas Blusicians, HOT LIPS PAGE—a leading figure in the Kansas City jazz style who started in Texas blues—and the swing trombonist TRUMMY YOUNG. One notable club performance by Quebec took place at the Yacht Club on Fifty-second Street in New York City. The triple bill included the swing-oriented Trummy Young Sextet and BILLY ECKSTINE's orchestra along with Coleman Hawkins' sextet, which included the bop musicians DON BYAS and THELONIOUS MONK.

Early in his musical career Quebec had been exposed to traditional jazz, blues, and swing, which, in turn, influenced his unique musical approach. He counted the trumpeter LOUIS ARMSTRONG and the pianist EARL HINES, who were both traditionalists, among the major influences on his musical life, with Coleman Hawkins and BEN WEBSTER, both swing musicians who anticipated the newer bop style, as particular models for his tenor saxophone playing. Other models included the pianist and bop precursor Clyde Hart and the tenor saxophonist Stan Getz—who was known for his innovations in cool jazz, a subsequent movement—as well as the blues-oriented arranger Buster Harding. Steeped in the styles of blues and swing, Quebec's maturing style mirrored a change in orientation toward bebop in jazz. A hard-swinging tenorman, he often contrasted a smooth legato melody with a strong sense of rhythmic intensity. He possessed a full, round tone with big, fast vibrato that was clear and powerful. Quebec had a special propensity for the blues, especially slow blues, that emphasized his musical and emotional directness most often in ballads. His up-tempo blues and standards reflected his influences from southwestern blues, particularly those of Texas and Kansas City, with their frenetic driving energy.

In the summer of 1944 Quebec joined CAB CALLOWAY's orchestra, where he found employment in touring, radio broadcasts, and Columbia recording sessions. While with Calloway, Quebec recorded with a smaller spin-off group known as the Cab Jivers. He left Calloway in 1947 or 1948 to form his own band, but he rejoined Calloway occasionally for tours and record dates until 1951.

He made an association with Blue Note records during the mid-to-late 1940s that would effectively transform the label and mark his recording heyday as a tenor saxophonist. Quebec's recording debut as a leader with the label in July 1944 produced the hit "Blue Harlem." Quebec experimented with large combos, generally septets of three horns and four rhythm pieces, in his sessions of the 1940s, which framed the period that Blue Note recorded "swingtets." The flexible instrumentation that allowed swing groups to incorporate newer stylistic developments instigated a transition phase for the label from traditional jazz and boogie-woogie to modern swing, and provided an instrumental basis for many bebop combos. In the late 1940s Quebec worked as an artists and repertoire (A&R) man for the label and was directly responsible for recruiting bebop musicians such as Thelonious Monk, Bud Powell, TADD DAMERON, and other bop talent that allowed Blue Note to emerge as a leading jazz label. Quebec even contributed two tunes for Monk's first session with Blue Note.

The slowdown in jazz that followed the postwar economic boom created tough economic times for Quebec. He continued to lead a band during the 1950s, but recording and club dates diminished. Quebec recorded as a sideman with LUCKY MILLINDER and Bob Merrill in 1949. He led a quartet with Mal Waldron from 1950 to 1952. With the exception of a session for Hi-Lo in 1952 and a brief record date for Secco in 1953, he gradually faded from public view, partially because of his acknowledged battle with heroin. From 1954 to 1959 Quebec performed most often as a solo act, even playing in Canadian cabaret shows. Ira Gitler, noted jazz critic, spotted him briefly at the Cafe Bohemia in 1955. He was able to get through this tough time by maintaining his contacts from Calloway's band. He traveled somewhat during this period, performing at small venues in Canada, Manhattan, and the British West Indies when he wasn't serving short sentences at Riker's Island prison.

The remaining years of Quebec's life saw a renewed level of musical and business activity. He returned to the jazz scene from July 1959 to late 1962 as both leader and sideman, recording with Jimmy Smith, DUKE PEARSON, SONNY CLARK, GRANT GREEN, and Dodo Greene. Eight tunes recorded by Blue Note in July 1959 were released as singles. These tunes, in addition to the output from several other sessions in September 1960 and September 1962 are included in a 1984 release by Mosaic records. In 1961 Quebec recorded *Heavy Soul* and *Blue and Sentimental* and played on Sonny Clark's *Leapin' and Lopin'*. He recorded prolifically in 1962, including five albums as leader—*It Might as Well Be Spring, Soul Samba, With a Song in My Heart, Congo Lament*, and *Easy Living*—and Grant Green's *Born To Be Blue*. He also returned to Blue Note as a businessman, serving as an A&R man and coproducer. He was responsible for signing new talent such as Freddie Roach as well as older artists like DEXTER KEITH GORDON and Leo Parker. It is believed that Quebec never married or had children. Quebec became seriously ill late in 1962 and died of lung cancer in New York City.

Quebec's distinctive playing style, firmly grounded in southwestern blues and modern swing coupled with constant contact with the leading figures of swing and bebop, created his unique niche within the jazz community of the middle twentieth century. His affiliation with Blue Note both as a player and a businessman directly influenced the label's rise to eminence as a jazz icon.

FURTHER READING

Ramsey, Douglas K. *Jazz Matters: Reflections on the Music & Some of Its Makers* (1989).

Schuller, Gunther. *The Swing Era: The Development of Jazz, 1930–1945* (1989).

Obituary: *Down Beat*, 28 Feb. 1963.

DISCOGRAPHY

Cuscuna, Michael. *The Complete Blue Note 45 Sessions of Ike Quebec* (1987).

This entry is taken from the *American National Biography* and is published here with the permission of the American Council of Learned Societies.

DAVID E. SPIES

Queen Latifah (18 Mar. 1970–), singer, rapper, and actress, was born Dana Elaine Owens in Newark, New Jersey, to Lancelot Owens, a police officer, and Rita Owens, a high school art teacher. When Dana was eight years old her mother and father divorced, and that same year a cousin nicknamed her Latifah (which means "delicate, sensitive" in Arabic). She played for her school basketball team, sang in the choir of her local Baptist church, and rapped and beat-boxed with the group Ladies Fresh while in high school.

Queen Latifah performs on ABC's "Good Morning America" summer concert series in Bryant Park, New York, 15 July 2005. (AP Images.)

In 1988 Latifah's friend and fellow hip-hop artist DJ Mark the 45 King helped her work up a demo and passed it on to *Yo! MTV Raps* host Fab Five Freddy, who facilitated her signing to Tommy Boy Records. She released her first single, "The Wrath of My Madness/Princess of the Posse," that year, and by the time she graduated from high school, the single had already sold more than 40,000 copies. Latifah invested her money in a few local businesses and enrolled in the Borough of Manhattan Community College, where she joined up with Afrika Bambaataa's Native Tongues collective, a group that sought to project positive Afrocentric messages while maintaining hip hop's coarse edge. The influence of that philosophy was evident on her first album, *All Hail the Queen* (1989), which featured performances with De La Soul, KRS One, and Daddy-O and combined politically and socially aware lyrics with hard beats and reggae influences. The album broke into the top ten of the R&B charts and its most popular and memorable single, "Ladies First," became a hip-hop classic.

In 1991 Latifah used the profits from her first record to start the management company Flavor Unit Entertainment, which managed acts like Naughty by Nature, and later LL Cool J and Outkast. That year

she also released her second album, *Nature of a Sista*. Less intense than the first album, *Sista* nevertheless showcased Latifah's ability to rap to various styles, including R&B, jazz, and hip hop, but it was not as well received as her freshman effort and was her last for Tommy Boy. Just as she was working through her sophomore slump, she was personally devastated by the death of her brother Lance when he was riding a motorcycle she had bought him. She lurched into a period of depression and drug abuse.

In spite of the loss, her 1993 album *Black Reign* turned out to be one of her best, and was regarded by some critics as a seminal hip-hop work, offering frank commentary on youth violence, the inner city, misogyny, and the perils of stardom. The album was certified a gold record and its standout track, "U.N.I.T.Y.," earned Latifah a Grammy Award for Best Rap Solo Performance.

By the time *Black Reign* was released, Latifah had already embarked on an acting career, which would absorb much of her energy for the next decade. In 1991 she appeared in her first roles in the movies *House Party 2* and Spike Lee's *Jungle Fever*. In 1993 she wrote the theme song for, and co-starred in, the television comedy series *Living Single*. In 1996 she acted in the movies *Juice* and *Set It Off*. Her role as a lesbian in *Set It Off* and her position as an advocate for same-sex marriage and gay rights contributed to the rumor that she was a lesbian. In 1998 she acted in the films *Sphere* and *Living Out Loud*, where she performed a number of jazz classics. In 1999, she began hosting her own daytime talk show called *The Queen Latifah Show*, which ran in syndication until 2001.

Latifah did not release another album until 1998 with *Order in the Court*, by which time she had expanded her style to include more R&B and urban contemporary influences, in keeping with the direction of developments in hip hop more generally. The album featured duets with Pras of the Fugees and Faith Evans, singer, songwriter, and wife of the Notorious B.I.G., and marked what became a move away from the hard-edged rap of her early career. After another extended hiatus, she released *The Dana Owens Album* (2004), a collection of soul, jazz, and pop standards that reached number sixteen on the *Billboard* Top 200 and featured legends such as Al Green and Herbie Hancock.

In 2002 Latifah appeared in her most prominent and acclaimed role to that time as Matron Mama Morton in the Oscar-winning film version of the musical *Chicago*, for which she earned Golden Globe and Oscar nominations as best supporting actress. She continued to appear mostly in comedies, from *Bringing Down the House* and *Scary Movie 3* (2003), *Barbershop 2* and *Taxi* (2004), to *Beauty Shop* (2005), and the 2007 remake of *Hairspray*. She played a lead role in the early 2006 release *Last Holiday*, and also provided a voiced performance within the computer generated (CG) film *Ice Age 2*. She appeared in the 2006 movie *Stranger Than Fiction* and in *Life Support* the following year.

In spite of occasional run-ins with the police—she pleaded guilty to marijuana and gun possession in 1996, and to driving under the influence in 2002—Latifah worked to provide a model of female self-empowerment and determination not only through her music but also through books and entrepreneurship. Her 2000 autobiography, *Ladies First: Revelations of a Strong Woman*, was equal parts memoir and inspirational tract, and she followed this with *Stay Strong: Simple Life Lessons for Teens*, co-written with Terrie Williams. In 2006 she published her first children's book, *Queen of the Scene*, about a supremely self-assured elementary schoolgirl. Even her career as an entrepreneur and celebrity endorser incorporated her feminist philosophy. Both as a spokesperson for Cover Girl and developer of her own line of cosmetics for women of color, and as a model for Curvacion, a lingerie and apparel line for full-figured women, she encouraged women to appreciate their own beauty, regardless of conventional standards.

Known as the First Lady of Hip Hop, Queen Latifah became the first iconic female rapper, paving the way for later artists such as Missy Elliott. In 2006 she became the first hip-hop artist ever to receive a star on the Hollywood Walk of Fame. With long and successful careers in music, acting, and business, and with a commitment to social justice, Latifah has served as both a role model and an advocate for women in hip hop.

Latifah continued to make music—her 2007 album of jazz and soul covers, *Trav'lin' Light*, went platinum, but 2009's *Persona*, a return to hip hop, did less well. In 2007 she received a Golden Globe Award, a Screen Actors Guild Award, and an NAACP Image Award for her portrayal of an HIV positive woman in the HBO movie *Life Support*. In film, she starred in the comedy, *Mad Money* and the drama *The Secret Life of Bees* (both 2008), winning another NAACP Image Award for the latter. She also appeared in the 2010 romantic comedies *Just Wright* and *Valentine's Day*.

FURTHER READING
Light, Alan. *The Vibe History of Hip Hop* (1999).
Hip Hop Divas, by the editors of *Vibe Magazine* (2001).

Tracy, Kathleen. *Queen Latifah (Blue Banner Biographies)* (2004).

CURWEN BEST

Quinichette, Paul (17 May 1916–25 May 1983), jazz tenor saxophonist, was born in Denver, Colorado, the son of a French surgeon and an African American businesswoman whose full names are unknown. His father, whose surname was originally "Quinichet," died in 1929; in spite of adopting the altered spelling, the family retained the French pronunciation ("Quinishay") of its name. Paul's mother worked her way from head of the stenographic department to the chair of the board of American Woodman, a prosperous African American insurance company. With his parents' encouragement to excel in music, Paul was given his first clarinet around the age of seven. Under the supervision of a local German teacher, he acquired a strong foundation in the classical tradition. Later he studied the alto saxophone. He studied music briefly at the University of Denver in 1942 and at Tennessee State University in Nashville, where he was a scholarship student for two years. His claim to have graduated from the University of Denver with a music major cannot be documented by institutional records.

His involvement with jazz came early—he played along with recordings on his family's manual Victrola and credited the "oldtimers" with helping him learn to improvise. His first professional opportunities, taken without his mother's blessing, occurred in local nightspots in his native Denver. Around 1938 he began to devote his summer vacations to on-the-job training as a sideman in the so-called "territory bands" of Lloyd Hunter and Nat Towles (out of Omaha) and Ernie Fields (out of Tulsa) and played a relentless series of one-night stands throughout the upper Midwest. For a time, with the Fields ensemble, he backed up the stage shows of the dancer BILL "BOJANGLES" ROBINSON, but he grew dissatisfied with the nature of the production as well as the star's personal antics. He worked briefly with Shorty Sherock's quintet in Chicago and played in a band led by LUCKY MILLINDER. During this period he stopped playing the clarinet because of its waning popularity in jazz circles.

In 1941 his dissatisfaction with Robinson's show led to his joining JAY MCSHANN's band in Kansas City as a tenor saxophonist and the opportunity to work alongside a young CHARLIE PARKER. He stayed with McShann for less than a year but identified with the blues-based repertory of that ensemble. Later he characterized himself as "a Kansas City type, a 4-Beat swinger" (Rusch, 33). He followed this association with memberships in the bands of the rhythm and blues drummer Johnny Otis and the jazz saxophonist Benny Carter and in the quartet of SID CATLETT. A move to New York City in the late 1940s enabled him to play and record with a variety of ensembles, including those led by LOUIS JORDAN, Millinder, JOE THOMAS, Eddie Wilcox, J. C. HEARD, RED ALLEN, DINAH WASHINGTON, and HOT LIPS PAGE. His maturity as an improviser and his prominence as an artist occurred after the heyday of big-band jazz when, between 1951 and 1953, he worked in the smaller ensembles (with five, seven, or nine players) constituted by COUNT BASIE in response to evolving economic conditions and tastes.

During the Basie years Quinichette acquired the nickname "Vice Pres" because of affinities between his personal style and that of jazz immortal LESTER YOUNG, known to his intimates as "Pres." Significantly, the two saxophonists were longtime acquaintances, having known each other and practiced together before Young left Denver to join FLETCHER HENDERSON's band. As a fledgling performer, Quinichette had the benefit of Young's counsel and advocacy on numerous occasions. Yet Quinichette resisted his reputation as an illustrious disciple or follower of Young or, in the view of harsher critics, as an outright copycat, contending that he did not emulate Young as others did. Much admired for his sense of swing, Quinichette believed that his own sound and concept developed "parallel" to that of Young and that stylistic similarities had been present from the beginning. He proudly acknowledged his debt to Young and to the pioneering jazz saxophonist Frankie Trumbauer, who had likewise profoundly influenced Young and others of their generation. Young, moreover, held Quinichette in high personal and professional esteem.

In the course of his career Quinichette's talents as an improviser became even more apparent and his solos demonstrated greater originality, while still echoing his southwestern roots. The critic Whitney Balliett, in response to a live performance in New York in January 1974, contrasted Quinichette's seasoned playing with that of Young: "The skin is Young but the stuffing is Herschel Evans and Buddy Tate.... His tone was somber, and there were blue notes, low-register booms, and abrupt high exclamations. It was the sort of naked lyrical performance that Young could never have lowered his cool for" (Balliett, 130).

In early 1953 Quinichette left Basie's band to lead his own combo; he had made five recordings for Mercury as a combo leader in 1952. These endeavors, however, occurred under Basie's guidance; Basie

himself participated as pianist in one recording session. Quinichette also performed with the Benny Goodman octet in 1955, the Nat Pierce big band in 1955, collaborated with JOHN COLTRANE in 1957, and toured with BILLIE HOLIDAY for almost a year.

Reduced opportunities for freelance jazz musicians caused by the emerging popularity of rock and roll forced Quinichette to seek an alternate trade. He studied electronics in a three-year course at an RCA-sponsored school in the 1960s and worked as a technician in New York City. After some experiences gigging on weekends, he resurfaced in the New York jazz scene as a regular player in clubs beginning in early 1973. In 1974 he was featured in a Saturday and Sunday series at the West End Cafe in a group called Two Tenor Boogie, which involved the pianist Sammy Price and at different times tenor players Buddy Tate, George Kelly, and Harold Ashby. He was also reunited briefly with McShann. Among his last performances was a tribute to Count Basie in January 1975. He died in New York City.

While Quinichette did not succeed in earning a place in the highest tier of jazz artists, the length of his career, the variety of performance contexts, the stature of his associates, and the quality of his improvisations all suggest the quality and durability of his contributions. His recorded legacy is found on both 78-rpm recordings and long-playing records: the former includes as sideman four titles with Johnny Otis and five titles with Count Basie and as leader fourteen titles. His long playing records include, as sideman, *Kansas City Memories*, with Jay McShann; *The Herd Rides Again ... in Stereo*, with Woody Herman; *Borderline*, with Mel Powell; *The Big Sound*, with Gene Ammons; *Big Band at the Savoy Ballroom*, with Nat Pierce; and *Basie Jazz* and *Wheelin' and Dealin'*, with Basie. As leader he recorded *The Vice Pres*, *Moods*, *The Kid from Denver*, and *Cattin' with Coltrane and Quinichette* (coleader). He performed in three films: *Look out Sister* (1948), an all-black musical featuring Louis Jordan's ensemble, and two retrospective documentaries, *The Subject Is Jazz* (segment 5, 1958) and *The Last of the Blue Devils* (1979), a celebration of Kansas City jazz. He was the composer of at least three jazz tunes: "Prevue," "Crossfire," and "Sandstone."

FURTHER READING

Balliett, Whitney. *New York Notes: A Journal of Jazz in the Seventies* (1977).
Dance, Stanley. *The World of Count Basie* (1980).
Horricks, Raymond. *Count Basie and His Orchestra: Its Music and Its Musicians* (1971).

Rusch, Robert D. *Jazztalk: The Cadence Interviews* (1984).

This entry is taken from the *American National Biography* and is published here with the permission of the American Council of Learned Societies.

MICHAEL J. BUDDS

Quinn, William Paul (10 Apr. 1788–21 Feb. 1873), fourth bishop and first authorized missionary of the African Methodist Episcopal (AME) Church, was born either in India, as he claimed definitively in the 1870 census, or in British Honduras (now Belize), which he never claimed directly. An 1851 affidavit attesting to Quinn's birth in Honduras may have been executed to provide protection against detainment or kidnapping during the turbulence following the passage of the 1850 Fugitive Slave Act. His father appears to have been a mahogany dealer of either Spanish or Indian (Asian) descent. The Honduran version of his birth indicates that his mother was from what was then Anglo-Egyptian Sudan.

The India version of Quinn's birth states that he was born in Hindustan, near Calcutta. Quinn appears to have been interviewed for an 1865 Richmond, Indiana, city directory, where he claimed Hindustan as his birthplace. His birth into an English-speaking environment seems indisputable, however, because he was well educated, apparently in a colonial school, and he spoke excellent English.

According to both versions of his early life, Quinn had a life-altering encounter with Quakerism when he was about seventeen. Both versions highlight his reaction to the persecution of a Quaker woman missionary, Elizabeth Walker. According to the India version, Walker outraged Hindus with her teachings. Quinn defended her right to preach, and his actions angered his family, who banished him. He migrated to England for an unknown period. While Quinn was living in England he came under the influence of Samuel Hicks, a merchant in Sheffield. At that time Hicks's cousin, a Quaker evangelist and abolitionist named Elias Hicks, was living in Jericho, Long Island, New York. Reportedly Samuel Hicks sent Quinn to live with Elias, but no evidence has been discovered pertaining to Quinn's purported stay with Elias Hicks.

The alternate version, in which Quinn is said to have been born in Honduras, states that Quinn defended Elizabeth Walker, a Quaker woman missionary whose teachings had angered the local Catholic community. Mrs. Walker reportedly returned to New York and related the story to the Quaker community. Supposedly, the Quakers brought Quinn to New York, and he was "placed under the care of Elias Hicks, the world-known friend of the impressed" (*Richmond Palladium-Item*, 36). At the start of the nineteenth century Quinn's movements become easier to track. Between 1806 and 1807 he was affiliated with the Methodist Episcopal Church at New Hope, Bucks County, Pennsylvania, until he became dissatisfied with the racial prejudice exhibited by the church. Seeking greater opportunities in the newly organizing AME Church, he converted to AME in Bucks County, Pennsylvania, in 1808 and received his license to preach in 1812.

During this time, Quinn was strongly influenced by Reverend Samuel Collins, with whom he began living in 1809. Reverend Collins took Quinn with him to Philadelphia in 1816 when RICHARD ALLEN formed the AME conference. Despite the fact that Quinn was merely an observer at the conference, in eight months he had risen sufficiently in Allen's estimation to be appointed one of the first seven AME itinerant preachers. He traveled widely in Pennsylvania, Maryland, Delaware, and possibly elsewhere.

By 1822 he was appointed to head the Pittsburgh Circuit. He pastored Macedonia AME in Flushing, New York, between 1824 and 1826. He was transferred to East Point, Bucks County, Pennsylvania, where he came into conflict with Bishop Allen between 1826 and 1827. The conflict developed over financial and other issues of independence. Subsequently Quinn went to New York City and established a church with one hundred and fifty members, who were apparently outside the AME Connection. During this time he also became a Prince Hall Mason in a New York lodge. He was popular and active in the New York community. Allen apparently saw him as a threat and excommunicated him from the AME in 1828.

Between 1828 and Allen's death in 1831 Quinn ventured as far west as Illinois and Indiana and possibly Michigan. With the death of Allen, Quinn petitioned for readmission to the AME Connection. Bishop Morris Brown presided at the 1833 annual conference in New York at which Reverend Quinn was readmitted and assigned to missionary duties in the West and Midwest. He was immediately transferred to the Ohio Conference and departed for Pittsburgh.

In 1835, Bishop Brown gave official sanction to Quinn's proselytizing by naming him as general missionary to the West. He had great success in this role. By 1844 Quinn was able to aggressively seek nomination and election as bishop. At the General Conference that year, Quinn reported that he had traveled from Pittsburgh to three hundred miles beyond Missouri and had established seventy-two new congregations, organized forty-seven churches and forty temperance societies, and had started many schools and Sunday schools. He accomplished much of this work on foot or horseback. The church leaders received his report with acclamation, and he was elevated to bishop. His sphere of influence encompassed New York, Western Pennsylvania, Ohio, Indiana, Illinois, Michigan, Kansas, California, and the slave states of Maryland, Missouri, Kentucky, and Louisiana.

Shortly after Quinn was elevated to the rank of bishop in 1844, Bishop MORRIS BROWN suffered an incapacitating stroke. The rugged Quinn managed his own responsibilities and shouldered Brown's as well. In 1846 Quinn led the standard range of USA AME Conferences such as the Baltimore, Philadelphia, New York City, New England, Ohio, and Indiana Conferences, as well as the Canada Conference. In addition to being active in the Underground Railroad, he led the westward and southern expansion of AME and was responsible for its early international expansions. Quinn's broad influence touched Richard Robinson, missionary to Haiti and the first pastor of Saint Peter's AME in Port-au-Prince.

After Bishop Brown's death in 1849 Quinn became senior bishop and continued to move the church in new directions. With passage of the Fugitive Slave Law in 1850 many AME members migrated to Canada and the church took a public stance against slavery, designating the last Friday in June as a day of fasting and prayer for the abolition of slavery. Quinn assigned Reverend T. M. D. WARD, a trailblazer of African Methodism in California, as one of the first ordained ministers on the Pacific Coast. By the time Ward arrived at the close of 1852, the AME had already established churches in San Francisco and Sacramento. Bishop Quinn also sent Elder JOHN MIFFLIN BROWN to New Orleans to reinvigorate AME work there. That same year Quinn took the radical position of supporting a motion to license women preachers, which was defeated by the AME Council of Bishops.

Quinn's political views and his work toward abolition also focused his energies. He appropriated portions of DAVID WALKER'S 1828 manifesto, "Walker's Appeal" (1830), to express his own radical views in an 1834 pamphlet that was a passionate attack on slavery and slave owners. By 1854 Quinn was associating with emigrationists such as MARTIN DELANY. Quinn, along with Mary Bibb, served as vice president of Delany's 1854 First National Emigration Convention in Cleveland.

Two years later Quinn and bishops DANIEL ALEXANDER PAYNE and Willis Nazrey were present at the Chatham Conference of the Canadian AME. In view of the persistence of slavery in the United States, Quinn was elated by the Canadian church's desire for independence. The British Methodist Episcopal Church (BME) resulted from these efforts.

Quinn was rugged, dashing, and strong, stood over six feet tall, and weighed about 250 pounds. His skin was reddish brown in color, and he had black piercing eyes and flowing, curly black hair. By all accounts he was dramatic, charismatic, down to earth, and pragmatic. Despite his physical prowess Quinn faced danger during his years of evangelizing. In 1858 a stabbing rendered him unable to fulfill his speaking commitments and left him incapacitated for the first time. Because of the extent of Quinn's injuries, Bishop Payne replaced him for this event.

According to accounts in the *Christian Recorder*, Quinn travelled relatively widely during the Civil War years. Bishop Arnett's eulogy stated also that Quinn spent the war years providing relief to freedmen in the West, particularly in Kansas. He gathered freed slaves as they came across Union lines. According to Arnett, he was captured several times by rebel forces but managed to escape.

During the time he was preaching in the East Coast circuit, Quinn endured the death of his wife and two children and remained a bachelor throughout most of his missionary career. By war's end, Quinn's life settled sufficiently for him to remarry. He married Mary Jane Symnes [Sims] of Hamilton, Ohio, in 1866. She was a forty-year-old widow with four children. No further information exists on the deaths of the first wife and two children.

Quinn was active as late as 1869 when he visited Wisconsin, although his health began to fail between 1869 and 1871 because of cancer of the stomach. By 1872 he could no longer work effectively and was superannuated. He died on 21 February 1873 at Richmond, Indiana, his home since 1840. *The Richmond Telegraph* (28 February 1873) reported extensively on his death, funeral, and burial at Earlham College.

Quinn oversaw the growth of AME membership from 3,000 to 250,000 and from 7 itinerant preachers to 1,260 pastors. He played a monumental role in the development of independent black churches consisting of freed and enslaved congregants in northern and southern states before the Civil War. In addition to his powerful religious legacy, Quinn's work in the secular realm was also extraordinary. He exerted significant influence on black urban development, on supporting Payne's insistence on educational aspirations for the black community, on promotion of women in the church, on helping to mobilize the black middle class through Prince Hall and similar organizations, and on many other aspects of his multifaceted career. Laying the foundations for financial stability and governance of the church were also high among his achievements. Quinn was able to secure the legacy of the church through the careful selection of the bishops who would succeed him. Starting with bishops Daniel A. Payne and Willis Nazrey (1852), Alexander W. Wayman and Jabez P. Campbell (1864), and James A. Shorter, Thomas H.D. Ward and John M. Brown (1868), these men came to power with decades of pastoral experience and remained in office until the eve of the twentieth century. They inherited a great legacy of leadership and by their actions added to it, broadening and deepening AME's impact throughout the nineteenth century. Mirroring the leadership of Richard Allen, Quinn exerted overarching influence on the national and international growth of the church and on the spread of African Methodism into the twentieth century.

FURTHER READING

Quinn, William Paul, "The Origin, Horrors and Results of Slavery, Faithfully and Minutely Described in a Series of Facts, and its Advocates Pathetically Addressed," in *Early Negro Writing, 1760–1837*, ed. Dorothy Porter Wesley (1971).

Arnett, Reverend Benjamin W. *In Memoriam. Funeral Services in Respect to the Memory of Reverend William Paul Quinn Late Senior Bishop of the African M.E. Church* (9 March 1873). This pamphlet is available from the Ohio State Library.

Richmond Palladium-Item (1 Aug. 1976).

Watkins, Ralph C. "Complexity in Search for Security and the Establishment of the A.M.E. Church, 1860–1872, Part 1," in *The A.M.E. Church Review*, CXXII (2006).

Welch, Elaine. *William Paul Quinn: A Militant Churchman, 1799–1872, A Biographical Sketch* (1933).

Obituary: *Richmond Telegram*, 28 Feb. 1873

CHERYL JANIFER LAROCHE AND
RONALD D. PALMER

Quinton, Cyril, Jr. *See* Gans, Panama Joe.

Quivers, William Wyatt, Sr. (14 Sept. 1919–18 Mar. 2011), pediatric cardiologist and Tuskegee Airmen supply officer, was born in Phoebus, Virginia, the second child of Robert and Irma Quivers. His father worked as stable hand and his mother as a schoolteacher. When his mother fell ill with typhoid, William helped the public health nurse who looked after her. His interest in medicine was piqued.

With the encouragement of his family, Quivers went to nearby Hampton Institute as a physical education major in 1937, lettering in both tennis and football. After World War II broke out he was drafted in 1942 but convinced the medical officers to let him finish college and to stay on for several months to train in medical technology. He entered the Army Air Corps in 1942 and then was sent to Officer's Candidate School in 1944. The same year he was detailed to Tuskegee to become a post-processing and supply officer for the Tuskegee Airmen. He implemented the protocols that simplified the Airmen's deployment. While in the air corps he met Evelyn C. Seace, a WAC and Spelman College graduate. They married in Tuskegee in 1945, and had three children.

Quivers found race relations around the airbase outside of Tuskegee startling, even though he was from rural Virginia. He was told not to leave the base very often after an airman got into an altercation in town and was followed back to the base by armed white men. Because the airmen had weapons, there was fear that the violence might go both ways. Eventually, only the military police were allowed to carry sidearms and the airmen were kept closer on base.

After the war in 1948, Quivers went to medical school at Meharry in Nashville, Tennessee, while his wife Evelyn earned her master's in library science from Atlanta University. After his graduation in 1953 and except for one or two years of private practice in Charlotte, North Carolina, Quivers worked in numerous black medical schools and hospitals, moving his family to Winston-Salem, Nashville, and Baltimore. He was board certified in pediatrics in 1967. From 1963 until 1965 he took a fellowship at UCLA to become a pediatric cardiologist, just two years after the field became the first pediatric subspecialty. He returned to practice at Meharry and then became the chief of pediatrics at Kate B. Reynolds Hospital in Winston-Salem from 1969 to 1972, and then at Provident Hospital in Baltimore from 1972 to 1985. He retired from active practice in 1985 and his wife Evelyn died in 2005.

In 1992 the Quivers family was named an "Outstanding Family" by his alma mater, Hampton University. Other honors include election into the Royal Society of Health in 1971, selection as one of the Personalities of the South in 1973, and a People to People Ambassador to China in 1983. Quivers was an active participant in the National Medical Association and the Association for Black Cardiologists. He died in Plum, Pennsylvania, at the age of 91.

FURTHER READING

Scott, Lawrence P., and William M. Womack Sr. *Double V: The Civil Rights Struggle of the Tuskegee Airmen* (1998).

Ward, Thomas J., Jr. *Black Physicians in the Jim Crow South* (2003).

WILLIAM W. QUIVERS JR.

SUSAN M. REVERBY

Quy, Libbeus (30 Aug. 1741–5 Oct. 1822), Revolutionary War soldier, was born in Norwich, Connecticut, to unknown parents. On 19 August 1753 he was baptized in the Norwich First Congregational Church. Quy was an enslaved African American. Until the Revolutionary War, his master was Daniel Brewster of Norwich.

Libbeus Quy was recruited into General Israel Putnam's Third Regiment, probably between May and April of 1775. He was one of a few African Americans who served in the Patriot cause in the Revolutionary War before 1777. It is not known whether Quy served in place of his master, a common practice in the Revolutionary War. But it is known that Daniel Brewster did not enlist in the military. Quy served under Colonel John Durkee in the Third Company, and in May 1775, the Third Company marched to and camped around Boston, Massachusetts. Quy was stationed in Cambridge, Massachusetts, until December 1775, when the regiment was terminated. Later, in 1776, the Third Regiment was adopted as the 20th Continental Regiment, and command was assumed by Colonel Durkee. In April 1776, Quy marched from Boston to New York and was stationed in Bergen Heights, now Jersey City, until 15 September 1776. When General

George Washington ordered his regiment to retreat through New Jersey, Quy saw his first action at the Battle of Trenton on 25 December 1776.

On 10 June 1777, Daniel Brewster freed Quy, who promised to enlist for the remainder of the Revolutionary War. Quy was one of the many African Americans emancipated in exchange for service. It is possible, but not confirmed, that Libbeus Quy served during the war as a surrogate for Daniel Brewster in exchange for his freedom. Serving again under the command of Colonel John Durkee in the Fourth Regiment of the Connecticut Line, he was camped in Peekskill, New York. In September 1777 he marched to Pennsylvania to join with General Washington's army. He fought in the Battle of Germantown on 4 October 1777 on the left flank of Washington's army. Quy wintered with his regiment at Valley Forge during the winter of 1777–1778. On 28 June 1778, he fought at the Battle of Monmouth and was afterward camped at White Plains, New York.

Quy was then camped in the area around New York, New York, until his assignment to the First Regiment in 1781, where he finished his last years of service under the command of Colonel Zebulon Butler. Serving in Captain Reverend Moot's company at West Point, New York, he was honorably discharged in June 1783. By the end of the Revolutionary War, Quy had served eight years with the Connecticut Line.

According to Quy's pension request, he received a pay of eight dollars a month while under the six-year command of Colonel John Durkee. After the war, he took advantage of his new status as a freedman and became a paid farmer and laborer. Other blacks in the Nutmeg state were not so fortunate. While the state enacted gradual emancipation in 1784, 15 percent of the state's black population remained enslaved in 1800. On 26 September 1782, he married Lucina, whose maiden name is unknown, at Bozrah Church in Bozrah, Connecticut. Libbeus fathered three children with Lucina: Lucina, Eber, and Joseph. Eber Quy became a mariner and married Catherine Fitch on 3 October 1819; they had six children. Joseph Quy married his wife Julia and had five children, both brothers are buried next to each other in Norwich City Cemetery.

Libbeus Quy died in Franklin, Connecticut, on 5 October 1822. His pension request from 29 June 1820 states that Quy owned an estimated $8.85 of belongings while supporting his ill wife for more two years. He is also the only listed African American pensioner of Norwich, Connecticut, and while he was serving with the Connecticut Line, his family received state aid.

Libbeus Quy's life may not have been as dramatic as that of his fellow black Connecticutian, VENTURE SMITH (BROTEER), born an African prince in Guinea and later enslaved in New England. But it nonetheless sheds important light on the experiences of many African Americans in Connecticut during the Revolutionary War era.

FURTHER READING
Brown, Barbara. *Black Roots in Southeastern Connecticut, 1650–1900* (2001).

Information on Libbeus Quy's Revolutionary War service and his life thereafter can be found in his Pension File Number 36249. Volume 3, Page 335. Arrangement of 1870.

Johnston, Henry Phelps. *Record of Service of Connecticut Men in the I. War of the Revolution, II. War of 1812, III. Mexican* (1889).

New London County Connecticut Revolutionary Pensions.

Norwich Land Records, XXII, 216.

JACOB BENJAMIN DOERFLER

Rachell, James "Yank" (16 Mar. 1910–10 Apr. 1997), blues musician, was born in Brownsville, Tennessee, to George Rachell and Lula Taylor, farmers. One of the few blues mandolinists, Rachell first began to play at age eight after a neighbor traded him a mandolin in exchange for a pig. His uncle, Daniel Taylor, taught him basic chords and soon Rachell began making music at home with his two brothers. In the early 1920s he met local mandolin player Hambone Willie Newbern, who gave him additional instruction, and the two subsequently performed at several parties in the Brownsville area. At one of these performances Rachell met SLEEPY JOHN ESTES, a blues guitarist with whom he would intermittently collaborate over the next fifty years. Rachell and Estes briefly teamed up with jug player Hammie Nixon and the trio toured as a jug band throughout Tennessee, playing primarily for white farmers who often paid the group up to four dollars a day. By 1928 Rachell and Estes had settled in Memphis, where they formed a group with the pianist Jab Jones. Known as the Three J's Jug band, they became a popular attraction in the clubs of Memphis's Beale Street during the brief heyday of jug band music.

In early 1929 Rachell and the Three J's cut their first record, "Broken-Hearted, Ragged and Dirty Too," for the Victor label. The record sold moderately well, and the group recorded five more numbers later that fall. The most popular of these songs, "Divin' Duck Blues," garnered them more recording work as well as the attention of harmonica ace Noah Lewis, who asked them to accompany him on what became his final recording sessions.

The onset of the Great Depression ended the recording careers of many blues musicians, as record companies either folded or released fewer "race" records. Accordingly, Rachell moved back to Brownsville while Estes settled in Chicago (continuing to record for the Decca and Bluebird labels). After working on a dairy farm for several years Rachell landed a job with the L&N Railroad. However, he earned extra money playing the blues at private parties in Brownsville and Jackson, Tennessee. In 1937 he married Ella May Johnson and started a family, eventually raising four children.

After a party in Jackson, Rachell met fellow blues musician John Lee "Sonny Boy" Williamson, who quickly became a friend and collaborator. The two began playing together at local gatherings and in 1938 they traveled to Chicago to record for the Bluebird label. Each accompanied the other on their respective recordings. Rachell provided steady mandolin and guitar work over which Williamson added his plaintive harmonica solos. The duo remained friends and musical partners, performing and recording frequently throughout the 1940s, until Williamson's death in 1948.

Still largely unknown, especially outside of the South, Rachell briefly settled in St. Louis in the early 1950s, where he found occasional work performing in clubs. However, he was still largely unknown outside of the South. After moving to Indianapolis, Indiana, in 1958, he performed less frequently as his wife's health began to decline. After she died in 1961, Rachell resumed his performing career, primarily playing in Indianapolis. In 1962 Estes was rediscovered by a documentary filmmaker, who brought him to Chicago to record new material. Estes contacted Rachell and Hammie Nixon and the trio mounted a tour of coffeehouses and college campuses. In the mid-1960s Rachell also cut several solo records for labels such as Blue Goose and Delmark.

Throughout the 1960s and 1970s Rachell enjoyed the resurgence in popularity of the blues, and he gained a small but devoted following in Europe, where he occasionally toured, both as a solo performer and accompanying Estes. However, in 1977 Estes died, and Rachell cut his schedule back considerably. He continued to play club dates in Indianapolis, becoming a fixture in the city's local blues scene—he was a regular at the Slippery Noodle Club—through the mid-1990s. Beginning in 1986 Delmark began re-releasing some of his recordings from the early 1960s, and in the mid-1990s he recorded new material for his final album, *Too Hot for the Devil*.

Rachell died in Indianapolis. His contribution to the history of the blues has often been overlooked, but as one of the genre's only mandolin players, Rachell offered a unique sound that gave the music of more celebrated performers such as Sleepy John Estes and Sonny Boy Williamson a nimble delicacy that meshed with their often rudimentary guitar and harmonica work. A musician and devoted father of four, Rachell was known for his gregarious personality, which Estes credited with helping the pair land their early recording sessions. Although his best work often appeared as accompaniment to other artists, James "Yank" Rachell's career spanned more than sixty-five years, and occupies a noteworthy place among the greats of blues music history.

FURTHER READING
Bastin, Bruce. *Red River Blues: The Blues Tradition of the Southeast* (1986).
Charters, Samuel B. *The Country Blues* (1975).
Congress, Richard. *Blues Mandolin Man: The Life and Music of Yank Rachell* (2001).

BRENTON E. RIFFEL

Radcliffe, Alec (26 July 1905–18 July 1983), Negro League baseball player, was born Alexander Radcliffe in Mobile, Alabama, the eighth and youngest son of the ten children of James Radcliffe, a carpenter from Alabama, and Mary Marsh, also from Alabama. The South in the early 1900s was an intolerable place for blacks, and when the chance arose many of them headed to the North for a better life. In 1919 Alec and his brother TED "DOUBLE DUTY" RADCLIFFE moved to Chicago to live with one of their older brothers already living in the city. The rest of the Radcliffe family soon followed. In Chicago the Radcliffes lived in the shadow of old White Sox Park, where the Chicago American Giants, the Negro League team managed by RUBE FOSTER, played. Alec Radcliffe was a batboy for the Giants and perfected his baseball skills on the sandlots of Chicago.

In 1927 Radcliffe began his baseball career playing third base for the Chicago American Giants of the Negro National League. The team, which nearly won the 1928 pennant race, disbanded in 1931 because of financial difficulties. But baseball was not his primary love for long. In 1927 Radcliffe married his first wife, Marlean. They had three children and lived a few blocks away from his parents and siblings on Wentworth Avenue. Radcliffe spent much of his time settling into family life and providing for his young family. Later Radcliffe reportedly had a second wife, Gladys, and they had four children.

Like many players in the Negro Leagues, Radcliffe was a journeyman going wherever a baseball game was being played. The players' wages were low, and the teams would travel all night to the next game hoping to find rooming houses that had space for them. From 1932 to 1935 Radcliffe played for Cole's American Giants. As an important part of the pennant-winning 1932 team, Radcliffe batted .283. During that season the Giants were members of the short-lived Negro Southern League. In 1933 and 1934 the Giants claimed two more pennants as part of the Negro National League II. Also in 1932, in a game against Double Duty Radcliffe and the Pittsburgh Crawfords, Alec Radcliffe ended his brother's no-hitter in the ninth inning with a solo home run. As a part of the Giants, Alec Radcliffe was an East–West All-Star from 1933, when he was elected with more than thirty-six thousand votes, to 1939. From 1933 to 1936 he maintained a .330 batting average.

Radcliffe briefly played in 1936 for the New York Cubans in the National Negro League II but returned to Chicago to play for the Chicago American Giants, which was by then part of the Negro American League, from 1936 to 1939. The 1937 All-Star game was the first game to have siblings—the Radcliffe brothers—playing simultaneously. In the winter of 1939 Radcliffe played ball in Cuba, and in 1940 he returned to Chicago to play briefly for the Palmer House All-Stars, an independent club. From 1941 to 1944 he played once again for the Chicago American Giants, then under the management of his brother, who suspended his younger brother in 1942 for disputing a called strike with an umpire and again in 1943 for insubordination.

During the 1944–1945 season Radcliffe played with the Cincinnati-Indianapolis Clowns, a team known as much for the comedy they provided as for their baseball talent—a fact that was unsettling to many. He batted .325 with the Clowns and, again, enjoyed all-star status both years. In the 1944 All-Star game Alec hit a two-run triple but was outdone by his brother, who hit a two-run home run. Radcliffe batted .500 in the West's 7–4 victory, and he and his brother delighted the crowd with their dazzling performances. Wendell Smith of the *Pittsburgh Courier* wrote, "as I write this high above the thousands now leaving this big ballpark … the names of Ted and Alex [Alec] Radcliffe are becoming household words … their exploits will be told and retold here in Chicago" (Lester and Black, 233). Radcliffe was also the Negro American League home run leader in 1944 and 1945. His last All-Star appearance was in 1946 at the age of forty-one as a member of the Memphis Red Sox. Radcliffe played in both East–West games that year, although he went hitless in both.

Although his baseball career has often overshadowed by that of his charismatic older brother, Alec is considered by many baseball historians one of the best third basemen ever to play in the Negro Leagues. He was elected to and played in every East–West All-Star game from 1933 to 1946, excluding the years 1940 to 1942. He is the lifetime Negro League All-Star leader in at bats (forty-four), hits (with a .341 average), and most consecutive games with a hit. The All-Star statistics show Radcliffe tied for second place for the most RBIs in a game and bases stolen in a game, fourth in career stolen bases, second in career RBIs behind BUCK LEONARD, and tied for first place, with Buck Leonard, in most games played. Radcliffe has the distinction of playing on more winning All-Star teams than any other Negro League player.

Radcliffe played third base, shortstop, pitcher, and outfield, but he is best known as a third baseman. Swinging a forty-ounce bat, the six-foot, two-hundred-pound right-hander was a power hitter and a good fielder. "GENTLEMAN DAVE" MALARCHER, his manager and Chicago American Giants teammate, once said, "Radcliffe, in my estimation, became one of the truly great third baseman in baseball history; a fast man, a powerful hitter and one who possessed the mind that enabled him to fit into [our system]" (Shatzkin, 890).

But in spite of his great baseball numbers, Alec Radcliffe is often eclipsed not only by his brother

but also by other players of the era. Radcliffe ended his career with the semipro Detroit Senators in 1947 under the management of COOL PAPA BELL. He retired from baseball in the early 1950s and became a bouncer at his brother's club in Chicago. Radcliffe lived in Chicago until his death.

FURTHER READING

Lester, Larry, and Joe Black. *Black Baseball's National Showcase: The East–West All-Star Game, 1933–1953* (2001).

McNary, Kyle P. *Ted "Double Duty" Radcliffe: 36 Years of Pitching and Catching in Baseball's Negro Leagues* (1994).

Shatzkin, Mike. *The Ballplayers: Baseball's Ultimate Biographical Reference* (1990).

GERA SMITH

Radcliffe, Ted "Double Duty" (7 July 1902–11 Aug. 2005), Negro League baseball player, was born Theodore Roosevelt Radcliffe in Mobile, Alabama, the seventh of the ten children of James Radcliffe, a carpenter from Alabama, and Mary Marsh, also from Alabama. Roosevelt, as he was called at the time, grew up in Mobile helping his father with carpenter jobs and playing baseball with childhood friends including LEROY "SATCHEL" PAIGE and Bobby Robinson. His obvious natural baseball talent eventually led to Roosevelt's getting a spot on the Mobile Black Bears baseball team. Although he was not paid, he used the opportunity as practice for his future in the big leagues.

In his younger years Roosevelt Radcliffe worked as many as ten hours to earn only one dollar. In 1919 Roosevelt and his younger brother ALEC RADCLIFFE, looking for better economic opportunities, hopped a train for Chicago, where their older bother was living. Their trip was financed with money that Roosevelt had won shooting dice. Being only a few blocks away from where the Chicago American Giants played, the two Radcliffe brothers had the opportunity to practice with the team and dream of being professional ballplayers. Before beginning his professional baseball career, Roosevelt, now using the name Ted, pitched batting practice for the Giants. In 1920 he signed with the Illinois Giants, a black semiprofessional traveling team, and soon learned that the North was not as accommodating to African Americans as many had thought. He would sometimes travel for days without a shower because no hotel would rent rooms to the black players and the team would sleep in railroad stations when no rooming houses could be found. After six seasons with the Giants, Ted Radcliffe played for Gilkerson's Union Giants, another semipro team.

Radcliffe's professional Negro League baseball career began in 1928 with the Detroit Stars of the Negro National League. He played the positions of pitcher and catcher with equal skill. It was this distinction that earned him the nickname "Double Duty." The New York sports writer Damon Runyon attributed the name to Radcliffe after seeing him play in a doubleheader during the 1932 Negro League World Series at Yankee Stadium. While a member of the Pittsburgh Crawfords, Radcliffe pitched a shut out in one game and caught for his childhood friend Satchel Paige in the other. The nickname Double Duty stuck, especially since Radcliffe was never fond of being named after a president.

Throughout his baseball career Double Duty Radcliffe enjoyed the freedom to go wherever the money was best. The teams he played for in his career included the St. Louis Stars, in 1930; the Pittsburgh Crawfords, in 1932; the Homestead Grays, in 1931, 1933, 1936, and 1946; the Columbus Bluebirds, the Cleveland Giants, and the New York Black Yankees, a team co-owned by BILL "BOJANGLES" ROBINSON, all in 1933; a team in Bismarck, North Dakota, with Paige and Quincy Trouppe, from 1934 to 1935; the Chicago American Giants, in 1934, from 1941 to 1943, and from 1949 to 1950; the Brooklyn Eagles, in 1935; the Cincinnati Tigers, from 1936 to 1937; the Memphis Red Sox, from 1938 to 1939 and in 1941; the Kansas City Monarchs, in 1945; the Harlem Globetrotters, in 1947; and the Louisville Buckeyes, in 1949. He was a player and manager for the Jamestown (North Dakota) Red Sox, in 1934; the Cincinnati Tigers, from 1936 to 1937; the Memphis Red Sox, from 1938 to 1939 and in 1941; the Chicago American Giants, in 1943 and 1950; and the Elmwood Giants of the Manitoba-Dakota League, in 1951.

Radcliffe played for three teams that were arguably the greatest Negro League teams ever: the 1931 Homestead Grays with OSCAR McKINLEY CHARLESTON, JOSH GIBSON, SMOKEY JOE WILLIAMS, and Jud Wilson; the 1932 Pittsburgh Crawfords; and the 1930 St. Louis Stars.

In 1943 Radcliffe won the Negro American League Most Valuable Player Award and followed the honor with a special appearance in the 1944 All-Star game. He was a teammate with his brother Alec, and their mother was in the stands to watch them play. Ted Radcliffe did not disappoint. He hit a home run that contributed to a 7–4 victory for the West in front of more than forty thousand fans.

Although he had a reputation as a ladies' man, Radcliffe was married to Alberta Robinson for more than fifty years. They had five children: Ted Jr., James, Robert, Louis, and Debra. At the age of forty-nine, while with the Elmwood Giants, Radcliffe had a batting average of .459 and a 3–0 pitching record. As a manager during the late 1940s he integrated the semipro leagues of Southern Minnesota and Michigan-Indiana. Radcliffe is also credited with integrating the Chicago American Giants when as the team's manager he signed three white players in 1950 in an attempt to remain competitive with the newly integrated Major League.

Radcliffe and his wife, Alberta, made news in 1989 when their plight of living in Chicago's Ida B. Wells Housing Project got attention. The two had moved there twenty-six years before and had watched the area become dangerous and infested with gangs. They had been mugged twice, and the Radcliffes' car had been stolen and crashed. As a result they and other senior citizens had become housebound. With assistance from the mayor, a local newspaper columnist, and Major League Baseball, the Radcliffes moved to a safer senior community.

Double Duty Radcliffe had a remarkable career that spanned thirty years playing with or managing or both more than thirty teams. In 1999 he became the oldest player to appear in a professional game when he threw one pitch for the Schaumburg (Illinois) Flyers. He was received at the White House by presidents Jimmy Carter, Ronald Reagan, and Bill Clinton.

It is said that in his career Radcliffe had five hundred wins, four thousand hits, four hundred home runs, and seven hundred doubles. He was a six-time Negro League all-star, with three appearances as a catcher and three as a pitcher. Reportedly, in twenty-two exhibition games played against major league players he had a batting average of .406 and a pitching record of 3–0. He is not a member of the Major League Baseball Hall of Fame, however, possibly because of the lack of complete statistics on the Negro Leagues. When he died at 103 years old he was the oldest Negro League player and had become an ambassador of baseball's past, telling the stories of the Negro Leagues from firsthand knowledge.

FURTHER READING

McNary, Kyle P. *Ted "Double Duty" Radcliffe: 36 Years of Pitching and Catching in Baseball's Negro Leagues* (1994).

GERA SMITH

Railroad Bill (?–7 Mar. 1896), thief and folk hero, was the nickname of a man of such obscure origins that his real name is in question. Most writers have believed him to be Morris Slater, but a rival candidate for the honor is an equally obscure man named Bill McCoy. But in song and story, where he has long had a place, the question is of small interest and Railroad Bill is name enough. A ballad regaling his exploits began circulating among field hands, turpentine camp workers, prisoners, and other groups from the black underclass of the Deep South several years before it first found its way into print in 1911. A version of this blues ballad was first recorded in 1924 by Gid Tanner and Riley Puckett, and THOMAS A. DORSEY, who sang blues under the name Railroad Bill. The ballad got a second wind during the folk music vogue of the 1950s and 1960s, and in 1981 the musical play *Railroad Bill* by C. R. Portz was produced for the Labor Theater in New York City. It subsequently toured thirty-five cities.

The name Railroad Bill, or often simply "Railroad," was given to him by trainmen and derived from his penchant for riding the cars as an anonymous nonpaying passenger of the Louisville and Nashville Railroad (L&N). Thus he might appear to be no more than a common tramp or hobo, as the large floating population of migratory workers who more or less surreptitiously rode the cars of all the nation's railroads were labeled. But Railroad Bill limited his riding to two adjoining South Alabama counties, Escambia and Baldwin. Sometime in the winter of 1895 he began to be noticed by trainmen often enough that he soon acquired some notoriety and a nickname. It did not make him less worthy of remark that he was always armed with a rifle and one or more pistols. He was, as it turned out, quite prepared to offer resistance to the rough treatment normally meted out to tramps.

An attitude of armed resistance from a black man was bound inevitably to bring him into conflict with the civil authorities, who were in any case inclined to be solicitous of the L&N, the dominant economic power in South Alabama. The conflict began on 6 March 1895, only a month or two after trainmen first became aware of Railroad Bill. L&N employees discovered him asleep on the platform of a water tank in Baldwin County, on the Flomaton-to-Mobile run, and tried to take him into custody. He drove them off with gunfire and forced them to take shelter in a nearby shack. When a freight train pulled up to take on water he hijacked it and, after firing additional rounds into the shack, forced the engineer to take him farther up the road, whereupon he left the train

and disappeared into the woods. After that, pursuit of Railroad Bill was relentless. A month to the day later he was cornered at Bay Minette by a posse led by a railroad detective. A deputy, James H. Stewart, was killed in the ensuing gunfight, but once again the fugitive slipped away. The railroad provided a "special" to transport Sheriff E. S. McMillan from Brewton, the county seat of Escambia, to the scene with a pack of bloodhounds, but a heavy rainfall washed away the scent.

In mid-April a reward was posted by the L&N and the state of Alabama totaling five hundred dollars. The lure of this reward and a rumored sighting of the fugitive led Sheriff McMillan out of his jurisdiction to Bluff Springs, Florida, where he found Railroad Bill and met with death at his hands. The reward climbed to $1,250, and the manhunt intensified. A small army with packs of dogs picked up his scent near Brewton in August, but he dove into Murder Swamp near Castelberry and disappeared. During this period, from March to August, the legend of Railroad Bill took shape among poor blacks in the region. He was viewed as a "conjure man," one who could change his shape and slip away from pursuers. He was clever and outwitted his enemies; he was a trickster who laid traps for the trapper and a fighter who refused to bend his neck and submit to the oppressor. He demanded respect, and in time some whites grudgingly gave it: Brewton's *Pine Belt News* reported after Railroad Bill's escape into Murder Swamp that he had "outwitted and outgeneraled at least one hundred men armed to the teeth." During this period a Robin Hood–style Railroad Bill emerged, who, it was said, stole canned goods from boxcars and distributed them to poor illiterate blacks like himself. Carl Carmer, a white writer in the 1930s, claimed that Railroad Bill forced poor blacks at gunpoint to buy the goods from him, but Carmer never explained how it was possible to get money out of people who rarely if ever saw any. Railroad Bill staved off death and capture for an entire year, a virtual impossibility had he not had supporters among the poor black population of the region.

Sightings became infrequent after Murder Swamp, and some concluded Railroad Bill had left the area. The "wanted" poster with its reward was more widely circulated. The result was something like open season on vagrant blacks in the lower South. The *Montgomery Advertiser* reported that "several were shot in Florida, Georgia, Mississippi and even in Texas," adding with unconscious grisly humor, "only one was brought here to be identified."

That one arrived at Union Station in a pine box in August, escorted by the two men from Chipley, Florida, who had shot him in hopes of collecting the reward. Doubts about whether he remained in the area were answered on 7 March 1896, exactly a year and a day after the affair at the water tower when determined pursuit began. Railroad Bill was shot without warning, from ambush, by a private citizen seeking the reward, which by now included a lifetime pass on the L&N Railroad. Bill had been sitting on a barrel eating cheese and crackers in a small Atmore, Alabama, grocery. Perhaps he was tired as well as hungry.

Railroad Bill's real name probably will never be known. At the time of the water-tower incident and up to the killing of Deputy Stewart he had only the nickname, but in mid-April the first "wanted" posters went up in Mobile identifying Railroad Bill as Morris Slater, who, though the notice did not state it, had been a worker in a turpentine camp near Bluff Springs, Florida. These camps were often little more than penal colonies. They employed convict labor and were heavily into debt peonage. People were not supposed to leave, but Slater did, after killing the marshal of Bluff Springs. When railroad detectives stumbled on this story their interest was primarily in Slater's nickname. He had been called "Railroad Time," and "Railroad" for short, because of his quick, efficient work. The detectives quickly concluded, because of the similarities in nicknames, that Slater was their man. The problem, of course, is that the trainmen called their rider Railroad Bill precisely because they had no idea who he was and well before railroad authorities heard about Slater. If the detectives were right, then it follows that the same man independently won strangely similar nicknames in two different settings, once because he was a good worker, and again because he was a freeloader.

No one from the turpentine camp who had known Slater identified the body, but neither the railroad detectives nor the civil authorities involved questioned the identification. The body was taken to Brewton, on its way to Montgomery, where it would go on display for the public's gratification, but it was also displayed for a time in Brewton and recognized. The *Pine Belt News* reported that residents recognized the body as that of Bill McCoy, a man who would have been about forty, the approximate age of the corpse, since he had been brought to the area from Coldwater, Florida, as a young man eighteen years earlier. McCoy was remembered as a town troublemaker who two years earlier had threatened T. R. Miller, the richest man in town, when he worked

in Miller's sawmill and lumberyard. He had fled the scene hastily, not to be seen again until his corpse went on display as Railroad Bill. But, apart from the local newspaper stories, no one disputed the Slater identification, and the local Brewton people seem to have concluded that Morris Slater must have been a name used by Bill McCoy after he fled the town. The problem with that conclusion is that when the incident at Miller's sawmill occurred, Morris Slater had already earned the nickname "Railroad Time" in a Florida turpentine camp.

FURTHER READING

The Brewton newspapers *Pine Belt News* and *Standard Gauge* are the best places to follow the story of Railroad Bill.

Penick, James L. "Railroad Bill," *Gulf Coast Historical Review* 10 (1994): 85–92.

Wright, A. J., comp. *Criminal Activity in the Deep South, 1700–1933* (1989).

This entry is taken from the *American National Biography* and is published here with the permission of the American Council of Learned Societies.

JAMES L. PENICK

Raines, Franklin Delano (14 Jan. 1949–), corporate executive and government official, was born Franklin Delano Raines in Seattle, Washington, the fourth of seven children of Delno Thomas Raines, a custodian, and Ida Mae Raines, a cleaning woman. He was named after his uncle Frank and his father, but the hospital misspelled his middle name as "Delano."

The Raines family eventually moved into a house that Delno Raines had built himself over the course of five years. The household was constantly fighting economic challenges. When Raines was a young boy, his father was hospitalized for an illness and lost his job. As a result, the family received welfare for two years. Eventually, Delno Raines got full-time work as a custodian for the city of Seattle. Ida Raines added to their income by working as a cleaning woman for the aircraft company Boeing. But Raines would always remember the lessons of being on the brink of financial ruin. He later recalled that the experience of living with nothing to fall back on made him "quite sensitive to issues of personal and financial security. That probably made me very conservative in my own financial dealings and also made me worry a lot about people" (Stevenson, *New York Times*, 17 May 1998). Very early in his life it was clear that Raines was an achiever and destined for great things. When he was in high school, the *Seattle Times* called him "Mr. Everything" (Karen Tumulty, *Time*, 10 Feb. 1997). He was state debate champion, captain of the high school football team, and student president of his high school. His academic excellence (reflected in his 4.0 average) earned Raines a four-year scholarship to Harvard University, which he entered in 1967. He worked toward a B.A. in Government and impressed many, including Professor Daniel Patrick Moynihan, the future U.S. senator. In 1969 Raines was asked to intern at the White House in the Urban Affairs Department headed by Moynihan. At age twenty Raines was making a presentation to President Nixon.

After graduating in 1971 Raines went to Magdalen College at the University of Oxford as a Rhodes scholar. After that, in 1974, he entered Harvard Law School, from which he graduated cum laude in 1976. After a seven-month stint at the law firm Preston, Gates, and Ellis, Raines's impressive résumé earned him a position as assistant director for economics and government in the Office of Management and Budget in President Jimmy Carter's administration. This was the beginning of a career that would marry his political savvy and his financial acumen. In 1979 he moved to Wall Street and became an investment banker for the prestigious firm Lazard Frères.

Raines worked in the municipal finance department and advised cities and states about their finances and ability to raise money for government projects, such as bridges and buildings. The political skills that he had developed over his career continued to help him in his new position. Raines landed accounts with major cities like Washington, D.C., Chicago, and Detroit. He also worked on statewide accounts for Texas and Iowa, among others. With his help these municipalities, many of which were in dire financial trouble, were able to strengthen their finances. The most dramatic example of his work came in Washington, D.C. He helped reorganize the city's finances with such success that Wall Street allowed Washington to borrow money for the first time in a century.

Raines's success was rewarded in 1985 when he was named a partner at Lazard Frères. This appointment had broader implications. He had already been one of a handful of African American investment bankers in the clubby world of Wall Street. Now he was the first African American partner at a major investment bank. Raines once reflected about the importance of his achievement in the securities industry by saying: "I felt it was significant because for years, people would be wowed by

Franklin Raines, Fannie Mae Chairman and CEO. Raines defends his agency before the House Financial Services Committee on Capitol Hill, 6 Oct. 2004, following a auditor's report critical of accounting practices and management policies. (AP Images.)

the fact that you were black and a vice president. Now partner or managing director became the new standard" (Bell, 143).

During this period things were also blossoming in Raines's personal life. He married Wendy Farrow in 1982, and the couple went on to have three daughters. His commitment to his family persuaded Raines to make a career-altering decision. In 1991, after twelve years of working in municipal finance, he decided to leave Lazard. Tired of the extensive traveling that was necessary in his work with municipalities around the country, a workload that had him on a plane as many as five days a week, he decided that he would quit his lucrative career on Wall Street to spend more time with his family.

Raines, with his impeccable reputation, was not out of work for long. Later that year he was asked to join Fannie Mae, a huge mortgage corporation located only minutes from his house. Fannie Mae, formerly known as the Federal National Mortgage Association, was created in 1938 as a government agency. In the 1960s it was turned into a corporation owned by shareholders. It purchases mortgages from lending institutions and resells them to the secondary market. As vice chairman, Raines had the main responsibility to improve Fannie Mae's technology. He was also in charge of the firm's credit policy and legal issues, along with sundry other functions.

Raines continued in this position until 1996, when President Bill Clinton called to ask him to head the Office of Management and Budget. He reentered public service and led the country to its first balanced budget since 1969. After years of success in this position, Fannie Mae came calling again, and in January 1999 Raines made history. He became the first African American to lead a Fortune 500 company, and soon other black executives like STANLEY O'NEAL, RICHARD DEAN PARSONS, and KENNETH CHENAULT would also head major corporations.

Under his leadership, Fannie Mae earned record profits, helped maintain low interest rates, and encouraged minority homeownership. However, in December 2004, Raines parted company with Fannie Mae in controversial circumstances. Investigations by the Securities and Exchanges Committee, and the Office of Federal Housing Enterprise Oversight (OFHEO) charged Raines with abetting accounting malpractices, which in turn augmented his bonus structure, deceived investors, and left Fannie Mae illequipped to deal with a slump in the housing market. In December 2006 OFHEO sued Raines for approximately $84.6 million of the $91.1 million he made in bonuses during his tenure. In a 2008 settlement with the federal government, Raines agreed to pay $24.7 million, including a $2 million fine, and also gave up company stock options valued at $15.6 million, but did not admit any wrongdoing. The government had been seeking $100 million in fines and $115 million in restitution from Raines, and two colleagues. His colleagues ended up paying under $7 million between them. In 2011 it emerged that U.S. taxpayers had paid over $132 million in legal fees for Raines and other Fannie Mae executives since 2004.

Despite this controversy, Frank Raines has come a long way from his old neighborhood in Seattle. He has conquered prestigious universities, Wall Street, and government and headed one of the biggest corporations in the world. In addition to his business sense, he also recognizes the responsibility of being a "first." As he once said: "It's part of my job to insure that the path I've been able to follow can be followed by other black kids. There are a lot of shoulders I get to stand on. I need to provide a hand and shoulders for others to follow" (Stevenson, *New York Times*, 17 May 1998).

FURTHER READING

Bell, Gregory S. *In the Black: A History of African Americans on Wall Street* (2001).

Cose, Ellis. *The Envy of the World: On Being a Black Man in America* (2002).

O'Brien, Timothy L., and Lee, Jennifer. "A Seismic Shift under the House of Fannie Mae," *New York Times*, 3 Oct. 2004.

Stevenson, Richard W. "A Homecoming at Fannie Mae," *New York Times*, 17 May 1998.

GREGORY S. BELL

Raines, Timothy, Sr. (16 Sept. 1959–), baseball player, was born in Sanford, Florida, one of six children of Ned Raines Sr., a heavy machine operator, and Florence (Reynolds) Raines, a day-care worker. Though he excelled early on at baseball—he and his four brothers all played semipro ball for the Sanford All-Stars—Raines also played football and basketball at Seminole High School. Despite being offered numerous football scholarships, Raines opted for baseball, and was selected by the Montreal Expos in the fifth round of the 1977 amateur draft.

Raines enjoyed a breakout season for Memphis of the Double-A Southern League in 1979, and the following year led his Triple-A league in batting average and steals, and was *The Sporting News*' Minor League Player of the Year. After brief call-ups in the major leagues in 1979 and 1980, Raines made the team for good out of spring training in 1981.

Though Raines was initially a second baseman, even by his own estimation he was more suited as an outfielder: "There was no way I could catch a ground ball hit right at me. I guess that's how I got the nickname 'Rock,'" said Raines in a *Sports Illustrated* interview in June 1984, referring to his hands. The outfielder's moniker was also attributed to his muscular physique.

Even though the 1981 baseball season was shortened by a players' strike, Raines still set the record for most steals by a rookie, swiping seventy-one bases in just eighty-eight games, while hitting .304, and finishing second in Rookie of the Year voting to the Mexican pitcher Fernando Valenzuela. Though he was on pace to break LOU BROCK's single-season stolen base mark before the strike, the following year it was broken—not by Raines, but rather by RICKEY HENDERSON, to whom he would often be compared. They were considered two of the best leadoff hitters in history; while Henderson would become the career leader in steals, Raines would retire fifth all-time, with 808 stolen bases.

In the middle of a bumpy 1982 season, Raines admitted that he had developed a cocaine addiction, and estimated that he had spent a thousand dollars a week on the habit, often keeping gram bottles of it in his batting gloves and back pocket. In October 1982, he was admitted to a California rehabilitation center, famous for treating athletes and celebrities. Three years later, Raines appeared before a Pittsburgh grand jury as Major League Baseball and its commissioner, Peter Ueberroth, sought to confront a cocaine scandal that embroiled numerous players.

Raines attributed much of his recovery to the good friendship of fellow Expos outfielder ANDRE DAWSON, for whom his second son, born in 1983, was named. Raines also had an older son, Tim Jr., born 31 August 1979, two months before he married his high school girlfriend, Virginia Hilton.

Raines returned to the Expos clean in 1983 and stole a career-high ninety bases while batting .298. Raines would make the All-Star Game in seven consecutive seasons with Montreal, earning MVP votes in six of them. Despite leading the league in batting with a .336 average in 1986, Raines was offered only a slim raise by Montreal, and drew no serious offers from other teams as a free agent. He resigned with the Expos in May 1987 for a small salary increase and a signing bonus; later that month, an arbitrator ruled that MLB owners had colluded against dozens of players in an attempt to keep salaries in check. Five years later, Raines was retroactively awarded more than $868,000 in damages.

In his first game back with the Expos in 1987, Raines went 4-for-5 with a game-winning grand slam. Despite missing a month of the season, he set a personal high in home runs that year, and led the league in runs scored. Over his career, Raines mixed his trademark enthusiasm with a high on-base percentage and stolen base success rate; he retired with a career stolen base percentage of 84.7%, better than both Henderson and Brock.

Raines was traded to the Chicago White Sox in December 1990, and then to the New York Yankees five years later, where he quickly became one of the most popular players. Yankee pitcher Andy Pettitte said that "when he walks into a locker room, everybody just lights up. The guy always came to work with a smile on his face."

After winning two World Series rings with the Yankees, Raines signed with the Oakland Athletics as a free agent in January 1999. He was diagnosed with lupus that July, and underwent treatment immediately. After an aborted comeback the following spring with the Yankees, Raines tried out for the 2000 Olympics team, but failed to make the cut.

The Expos brought him back from retirement for the 2001 season for a part-time role. Playing in the minors while rehabbing from arm surgery that August, he and his son, Tim Jr., who was in the Baltimore Orioles' farm system, became the first father–son duo to play against one another in a regular-season game. Raines was traded to the Orioles at the end of the season, forming the second father–son pair of teammates in baseball history. After part of one more season with the Florida Marlins as a pinch hitter, Raines announced his retirement in September 2002.

Raines spent the next five years in various coach and manager positions for the Expos/Washington Nationals' and Chicago White Sox teams and affiliates. In 2009 he became the manager of the independent Atlantic League's Newark Bears. After divorcing his first wife, Raines married Shannon Watson in 2007.

FURTHER READING
Farber, Michael. "Raines Beats $1,000-a-Week Habit." *The Montreal Gazette*, 11 Dec. 1982.
Fimrite, Ron. "Don't Knock the Rock." *Sports Illustrated*, 25 June 1984.
McRae, Earl. "The Thief." *The Montreal Gazette*, 14 Aug. 1982.

ADAM W. GREEN

Rainey, Joseph Hayne (21 June 1832–2 Aug. 1887), politician, was born a slave in Georgetown, South Carolina, the son of Edward L. Rainey and Gracia C. (maiden name unknown). The elder Rainey purchased his family's freedom and moved with them in about 1846 (the exact date is unknown) to Charleston, where he was employed as a barber at the exclusive Mills House hotel. He prospered and purchased two male slaves in the 1850s. Joseph Rainey received a modest education and was trained by his father as a barber. In 1859 he traveled to Philadelphia and married Susan E. (maiden name unknown). As a result of the intervention of several friends, the couple managed to circumvent the state prohibition against free people of color entering or returning to South Carolina, and they moved to Charleston. After the Civil War began,

Rainey was conscripted to serve as a steward on a Confederate blockade runner. He was later compelled to work in the construction of Confederate fortifications around Charleston. He escaped with his wife to Bermuda on a blockade runner. They settled first in St. George and then in Hamilton. He resumed barbering, and his wife worked as a dressmaker. They returned to Charleston in 1865, shortly after the war ended.

Rainey and his older brother Edward participated in the 1865 Colored Peoples' Convention in Charleston, and Joseph served as a vice president. The convention endorsed legal and political rights for black men and condemned the recently passed black code, which largely restricted black men and women to agricultural and domestic work, defined a master and servant relationship between white employers and black employees, and severely limited the legal and civil rights of black people. In 1867 Congress passed Reconstruction legislation that divided the South into five military districts, authorized the reestablishment of southern state governments, provided for universal manhood suffrage and black office holding, and disfranchised those who had supported the Confederacy. In 1867 Rainey and his wife relocated to Georgetown, where he was elected to the constitutional convention in 1868. Later that year he was elected as a Republican to represent Georgetown County in the state senate, and in 1870 he was elected to the U.S. House of Representatives. He filled the unexpired term of the white Republican Benjamin F. Whittemore, whose seat had been declared vacant by the House after allegations were made that Whittemore sold appointments to the U.S. Military Academy and the U.S. Naval Academy.

Rainey was the first black man to serve in the U.S. Congress. He was reelected four times, serving from 1870 to 1879. In 1878, as white Democrats regained political power in South Carolina, he lost his bid for a sixth term. He was a cautious, conservative, and conciliatory political leader. In the constitutional convention he supported an unsuccessful measure to permit creditors to collect debts owed for the purchase of slaves before the Civil War. He was among the minority who favored the imposition of a one-dollar poll tax with the stipulation that the proceeds be devoted to public education, though the measure would disfranchise impoverished freedmen.

In Congress, Rainey supported the passage in 1872 of the Ku Klux Klan Act, legislation intended to outlaw the intimidation and violent repression

Joseph Rainey, the first African American man to serve in the United States Congress, c. 1870. (Library of Congress/ Brady-Handy Photograph Collection.)

of black people through the enforcement of the Fourteenth and Fifteenth Amendments. He also favored a general amnesty to remove remaining disabilities on former Confederates if the civil rights bill prohibiting racial discrimination in public facilities proposed by Senator Charles Sumner was passed. Rainey spoke passionately for both measures on the House floor: "It is not the disposition of my constituents that these disabilities should longer be retained. We are desirous of being magnanimous; it may be that we are so to a fault. Nevertheless we have open and frank hearts towards those who were our former oppressors and taskmasters. We foster no enmity now, and we desire to foster none…. I implore you, give support to the Civil-rights Bill." Rainey delivered one of the eulogies following Sumner's death in 1874. The amnesty bill passed immediately, but Sumner's civil rights measure was not enacted until 1875.

Though committed to equal treatment in public facilities, Rainey opposed legislation supporting social equality or interracial marriages. As a black man with a fair complexion, he was ridiculed by a black political opponent in an 1868 campaign appearance in Georgetown and was accused of having attempted to act white while attending the National Negro Laborers Convention in Washington, D.C., the previous year. Rainey won the election.

Rainey was a director of the Enterprise Railroad Company, a black-owned Charleston business created in 1870 by several prominent politicians to haul freight by horse-drawn streetcars from the city wharves on the Cooper River to the South Carolina Railroad terminal. The Enterprise did not thrive, and it was taken over by white businessmen in 1873. Rainey also owned stock in the Greenville & Columbia Railroad Company.

Rainey served as an Internal Revenue Service agent in South Carolina from 1879 to 1881. In 1881 he unsuccessfully sought appointment as clerk of the U.S. House of Representatives. His attempt to operate a brokerage and banking business in Washington failed. In poor health and with his finances depleted, he returned in 1887 to Georgetown, where he died.

Rainey pursued moderation during Reconstruction. He was determined to protect and enlarge the civil and political rights of his black constituents without alienating or offending white citizens.

FURTHER READING

There are two small collections of Rainey papers and materials in the South Caroliniana Library at the University of South Carolina and in the Duke University Library.

Christopher, Maurine. *America's Black Congressmen* (1971).

Holt, Thomas. *Black over White: Negro Political Leadership in South Carolina during Reconstruction* (1977).

Packwood, Cyril Outerbridge. *Detour—Bermuda, Destination—U.S. House of Representatives: The Life of Joseph Hayne Rainey* (1977).

Rogers, George C., Jr. *The History of Georgetown County, South Carolina* (1970).

This entry is taken from the *American National Biography* and is published here with the permission of the American Council of Learned Societies.

WILLIAM C. HINE

Rainey, Ma (26 Apr. 1886–22 Dec. 1939), vaudeville artiste and "Mother of the Blues," was born Gertrude Pridgett in Columbus, Georgia, the daughter of Ella Allen, an employee of the Georgia Central Railroad, and Thomas Pridgett, whose occupation is unknown. Around 1900, at the age of fourteen, Pridgett made her debut in the *Bunch of Blackberries* revue at the Springer Opera House in Columbus, one of the biggest theaters in Georgia and a venue that had been graced by, among others, Lillie Langtry and Oscar Wilde. Within two years she was a regular in minstrel tent shows—troupes of singers, acrobats, dancers, and novelty acts—which traveled throughout the South. At one show in Missouri in 1902 she heard a new musical form, "the blues," and incorporated it into her act. Although she did not discover or name the blues, as legend would later have it, Gertrude Pridgett was undeniably one of the pioneers of the three-line stanza, twelve-bar style now known as the "classic blues."

In 1904 the seventeen-year-old Gertrude married William Rainey, a comedian, dancer, and minstrel-show veteran. "Ma" and "Pa" Rainey soon became a fixture on the southern tent-show circuit, and they achieved their greatest success in 1914–1916 as Rainey and Rainey, Assassinators of the Blues, part of the touring Tolliver's Circus and Musical Extravaganza. Their adopted son, Danny, "the world's greatest juvenile stepper," also worked with the show. The summer tent shows took the Raineys throughout the South, where Ma was popular among both white and black audiences. Winters brought Ma, billed as Madame Gertrude Rainey, to New Orleans, where she performed with several pioneering jazz and blues musicians, including SIDNEY BECHET and KING OLIVER. Around 1914 Ma took a young blues singer from Chattanooga, Tennessee, BESSIE SMITH, under her wing—legend erroneously had it that she kidnapped her—and the two collaborated and remained friends over the next two decades. During these tent-show years, Rainey honed a flamboyant stage persona, making her entrance in a bejeweled, floor-length gown and a necklace made of twenty-dollar gold pieces. The blues composer THOMAS A. DORSEY recalled that Rainey had the audience in the palm of her hand even before she began to sing, while LANGSTON HUGHES noted that only a testifying Holiness church could match the enthusiasm of a Ma Rainey concert.

Rainey's voice was earthy and powerful, a rural Georgian contralto with a distinctive moan and lisp. One blues singer also suggested that Rainey held a dime under her tongue to prevent a stutter. Far from hindering her performance, these imperfections made Rainey's vocal style even more appealing to an audience that shared her down-to-earth philosophy, captured in "Down in the Basement": "Grand Opera and parlor junk, / I'll tell the world it's all bunk, / That's the kind of stuff I shun, / Let's get dirty and have some fun." Rainey often sang of pain and love lost or betrayed, but her songs—and her life—also celebrated the bawdy and unabashed pleasures of the flesh. Rainey joked with her audiences that she preferred her men "young and tender" (Barlow, 159), but in songs such as "Lawd Send Me a Man Blues," the preference matters less than the pleasure: "Send me a Zulu, a voodoo, any old man, / I'm not that particular, boys, I'll take what I can."

By World War I, Ma Rainey's star had eclipsed that of Pa's. (They separated in the late teens, and Pa died soon after.) In 1923 Rainey began a recording career with Chicago's Paramount Records, which brought her down-home country blues to a national audience. Over the next five years, she recorded more than a hundred songs with many of the leading instrumentalists of the day, including LOVIE AUSTIN, COLEMAN HAWKINS, and Thomas A. Dorsey, who also led Rainey's touring band. In 1924 a young LOUIS ARMSTRONG played cornet on her most famous release, "See See Rider." Though already a blues standard, Rainey's rendition was the first and, bluesologists contend, the definitive recording of the song.

Her success as a recording artist and the general popularity of the "race records" industry led to a string of headlining tours with the Theater Owners' Booking Association (TOBA). Black performers often called the organization "Tough on Black Asses" because of its low wages and grueling schedule, but Rainey's sense of fairness may have assuaged any complaints from the touring entourage of singers, dancers, and comedians. Unlike many TOBA headliners, Rainey never skipped town without paying her fellow performers. As a teenager, LIONEL HAMPTON, who knew Rainey through his bootlegger uncle in Chicago, "used to dream of joining Ma Rainey's band because she treated her musicians so wonderfully and always bought them an instrument" (Lieb, 26). Rainey's TOBA shows were even more popular than her tent shows had been, and her audience spread to midwestern cities, whose black populations had swelled during the Great Migration. The shift from tents to theaters also provided new outlets for Rainey's showmanship. She now made an even grander entrance, stepping out of the doors of a huge Victrola onto the stage, wearing her trademark spangles and sequins.

Contemporaries often contrasted Rainey's evenhanded temperament with Bessie Smith's

Ma Rainey in the touring show The *Rabbit Foot Minstrels*. Known as the "Mother of the Blues," she toured regularly in the South and Midwest. (AP Images.)

hard-drinking, fiery temper, but Rainey was not unacquainted with the wrong side of the law. Her love of jewelry once led to an arrest onstage in Cleveland, Ohio, when police from Nashville, Tennessee, arrested her for possession of stolen goods. Rainey denied knowing that the items were hot, but was detained in Nashville for a week and forced to return the jewelry. More notoriously, Rainey spent a night in jail in Chicago in 1925, when neighbors called the police to complain about a loud and drunken party that she was holding with a group of women. When the police discovered the women in various states of undress, they arrested Rainey for "running an indecent party." Her friend Bessie Smith bailed her out the next day.

That incident and several biographies of Smith have highlighted Rainey's open bisexuality and the possibility of a lesbian relationship between the two women. To be sure, Ma Rainey's life and songs rejected the prevailing puritan orthodoxy when it came to sexuality. In "Sissy Blues," written by Tom Dorsey, she bemoans the loss of her man to his male lover: "My man's got a sissy, his name is Miss

Kate, / He shook that thing like jelly on a plate." Most famously, in "Prove It on Me Blues," Rainey declares, "Went out last night with a crowd of my friends, / They must've been women, 'cause I don't like no men." Ma's bold assertion of her preference for women alternated with a coy but knowing wink to the taboo of that choice: "'Cause they say I do it, ain't nobody caught me, / Sure got to prove it on me." Paramount's advertisement for the record was somewhat less coy, depicting a hefty Ma Rainey in waistcoat, men's jacket, shirt, tie, and fedora— though still wearing a skirt—towering over two slim, femininely dressed young women while a policeman looks on.

The sexual politics of the lyrics was just one aspect of the song, however. Paramount appeared just as keen to highlight that it was "recorded by the latest electric method," all the better to hear Rainey's vocals and the "bang-up accompaniment by the Tub Jug Washboard Band." Indeed, the company saw no problem in promoting some of its most popular gospel spirituals on the same advertisement. Like Ma Rainey herself, the race records industry of the 1920s may have been less squeamish about open declarations of homosexuality than many media giants in the late twentieth century.

Paramount ended Rainey's recording contract in 1928, shortly after the release of "Prove It on Me Blues," but not because of any controversy regarding the record itself. The company argued that Rainey's "down home material had gone out of fashion," though that did not deter the label from signing male country blues performers who accepted lower fees. Ma returned to the southern tent-show circuit with TOBA, but by the early 1930s the Great Depression and the rival attractions of radio and the movies had destroyed the mass audience for the old-time country blues and black vaudeville at which Rainey excelled. Undeterred, though as much through necessity as choice, Rainey returned to her southern roots, touring the oilfield towns of East Texas with the Donald MacGregor Carnival. Gone were the gold necklaces, the touring bus, and the grand entrance out of a huge Victrola. Now MacGregor, formerly the "Scottish Giant" in the Ringling Brothers' circus, stood outside Rainey's tent and barked his introduction of the "Black Nightingale" inside. Rainey's performances were as entertaining as ever, but the uncertainty and poor wages of the tent-show circuit may have somewhat diminished her trademark good humor and generosity. A young guitarist who toured with her in those years, AARON "T-BONE" WALKER, described

Rainey as "mean as hell, but she sang nice blues and never cursed *me* out" (Lieb, 46–47).

The death of her sister Malissa in 1935 brought Ma Rainey back to Columbus to look after her mother. At some time before that Rainey had separated from her second husband, whose name is not known. Although she no longer performed, Rainey opened two theaters in Rome, Georgia, where she died of heart disease in December 1939, at age fifty-three. The obituary in Rainey's local newspaper noted that she was a housekeeper but failed to mention her musical career. In the 1980s, however, both the Blues Foundation Hall of Fame and the Rock and Roll Hall of Fame recognized Ma Rainey's significance as a consummate performer and as a pioneer of the classic blues.

FURTHER READING
Barlow, William. *"Looking Up at Down": The Emergence of Blues Culture* (1989).
Carby, Hazel. "It Jus' Be's Dat Way Sometime: The Sexual Politics of Women's Blues," in *The Jazz Cadence of American Culture*, ed. Robert G. O'Meally (1998).
Davis, Angela Y. *Blues Legacies and Black Feminism: Gertrude "Ma" Rainey, Bessie Smith, and Billie Holiday* (1998).
Lieb, Sandra. *Mother of the Blues: A Study of Ma Rainey* (1981).

DISCOGRAPHY
Complete Recorded Works in Chronological Order, 1923–1927 (vols. 1–4, Document Records DOCD 5581–5584).
Complete Recorded Works: 1928 Sessions (Document Records DOCD 5156).

STEVEN J. NIVEN

Rakim (28 Jan. 1968–), rapper, producer, and hip-hop pioneer, was born William Michael Griffin Jr. in Wyandanch, New York, the son of an artistically inclined father, William Michael Griffin Sr., and a mother (name unknown) who sang jazz and opera. His aunt, RUTH BROWN, was an award-winning rhythm and blues singer and actress. Not unlike his musically oriented family, siblings included, Griffin Jr. began studying music composition, saxophone, and drums in his youth. Using the alias Kid Wizard, he began his foray into rap as a hobby, hanging with the Love Brother Crew, deejaying and mastering production boards. Griffin Jr. was a gifted high school athlete with aspirations to play quarterback at the State University of New York at Stony Brook. At age sixteen he joined The Nation of Gods and

Earths, an organization founded by Clarence 13X, also referred to as the Five-Percent Nation, and adopted the name Rakim Allah.

Rakim set new standards for MC techniques. Most notably he pioneered the use of internal rhymes, which occur in the middle of lines as opposed to the end. Until then MCs had improvised simplistic rhymes; now Rakim demonstrated the value of composing lyrics. He was also popularized for his introduction of the use of metaphors with multiple meaning in rhymes. Rakim's smooth syncopation of lyrics is evidence of his early exposure to jazz, music studies, and poetry. In 1985 the WBLS radio disc jockey ERIC B. (ERIC BARRIER) approached Rakim to rhyme over his beats composed of sampled music. In 1986 they recorded *Eric B. Is President* and in the same year it was released on the independent Harlem-based record label Zakia with *My Melody* on the flipside. These records earned the duo, Eric B. & Rakim, a record deal with Island Records subsidiary 4th & B'way. In 1987 their album *Paid in Full* was released to critical acclaim. It certified gold in 1987 and platinum in 1995. *Paid in Full* was influential in the evolution of hip-hop and has been called a classic. In 1988 Eric B. & Rakim released the album *Follow the Leader*, which certified gold after reaching Top Ten that same year. The rap duo achieved cross-over recognition when they teamed with Jody Watley on her Top Ten Pop Single, "Friends," in 1989. In 1990 a third album, *Let the Rhythm Hit 'Em* was released and certified gold the same year. Amid legal disputes with Eric B. and their label MCA over royalties and contracts, *Don't Sweat the Technique* was released in 1992. Later that same year the duo disbanded and Rakim sought a solo career despite Eric B.'s refusal to sign a formal release.

Rakim performed sporadically and appeared as "guest" on recordings from 1992 until November 1997 when finally, *The 18th Letter*, his highly anticipated debut album was released in two versions; one included an Eric B. & Rakim greatest hits CD entitled *Book of Life*. He collaborated with DJ Premiere and Pete Rock to produce the certified gold album tracks that appealed to fans across generations and received rave reviews. Also that year, he performed with Mobb Deep on the soundtrack for *Hoodlum* and the following year contributed a song to *The Rugrats Movie*.

The Master was released in 1999, and again Rakim received praise for his solo efforts. In 2000 Rakim signed with Aftermath Entertainment, founded by the rap producer DR. DRE (Andre Young),

Rakim performs during the third annual VH1 Hip Hop Honors awards show on 7 Oct. 2006 in New York. (AP Images.)

noted for his work with N.W.A., Snoop Dogg, and Eminem, to create an album tentatively named, *Oh My God*. During his tenure with Aftermath, Rakim appeared as a guest on several Dr. Dre–produced projects including *Addictive* with Truth Hurts, *The Watcher Part 2* with JAY Z, and the soundtrack for Eminem's *8 Mile*. Creative differences with Dr. Dre stifled the progression of Rakim's hopeful third solo release; in 2003 he left the label and signed with Dream Works Records. Dream Works was soon discontinued, but that did not stop Rakim. He performed on songs with Timbaland & Magoo, Busta Rhymes, and Juelz Santana. He was featured in a commercial for All-Pro Football 2K8 and was honored by the iconic MTV with the title "Greatest Hip Hop Album of All Time" for *Paid in Full* and ranked number four on their list of "The Greatest MCs of All Time."

In November 2009 Rakim released his third solo album, *The Seventh Seal*. The album's fourteen tracks feature production by notable hip-hop artists and a guest appearance from his daughter, Destiny.

FURTHER READING

Bradley, Adam. *Book of Rhymes: The Poetics of Hip Hop* (2009).

Chang, Jeff. *Can't Stop Won't Stop: A History of the Hip-Hop Generation* (2005).

Coleman, Brian. *Check the Technique: Liner Notes for Hip-Hop Junkies* (2007).

Dyson, Michael Eric. *Know What I Mean? Reflections on Hip-Hop* (2007).

George, Nelson. *Hip Hop America* (2005).

Neal, Mark Anthony. *That's the Joint!: The Hip-Hop Studies Reader* (2004).

SAFIYA DALILAH HOSKINS

Rampersad, Arnold (13 Nov. 1941–), educator, literary critic, and biographer, was born in Port-of-Spain, Trinidad, to Jerome Rampersad, a journalist, and Evelyn De Souza Rampersad, a telephone operator at the American naval base. His parents divorced shortly after his birth, and the boy was shuffled between relatives until he began living with his father as a teenager.

Young Rampersad became interested in literature after a neighbor loaned him F. Scott Fitzgerald's *The Great Gatsby* and Thomas Wolfe's *Look Homeward, Angel.* Wolfe's novel was a particular revelation, speaking to Rampersad's sense of being a misunderstood outsider in his community. While in high school Rampersad joined the Little Carib Theater workshop of the poet-playwright DEREK WALCOTT, the future Nobel laureate, acting in Shakespearean plays and other productions.

After high school Rampersad did not consider higher education because he could not afford it. He continued acting, taught high school English, geography, and history, and worked in public relations for the office of Trinidad's prime minister before seeing an advertisement placed by the U.S. State Department offering partial scholarships to West Indian students. He won a scholarship to study journalism at Bowling Green State University in Ohio, an institution he had never heard of. As a senior Rampersad acted in a student production of Ben Jonson's *Volpone* and seriously considered becoming a professional actor.

Graduating magna cum laude in 1967, he earned an M.A. in English the following year. At Harvard University he received an AM in 1969 and a Ph.D. in English in 1973. Rampersad married Marvina White on 10 October 1985. The couple met when White invited him to speak at the City College of New York, where she taught English. Their son,

Luke, was born in 1987. Rampersad became an American citizen in 1985.

Rampersad taught at the University of Virginia in 1973–1974; Stanford University from 1974 to 1983; Rutgers University from 1983 to 1988; Columbia University, where he was the ZORA NEALE HURSTON Professor of English, from 1988 to 1990; and Princeton University, from 1990 to 1998, as the Woodrow Wilson Professor of Literature. In 1998 he returned to Stanford as the Sarah Hart Kimball Professor of the Humanities. Rampersad also served as a visiting professor in Harvard's department of Afro-American studies in 1979–1980. He received fellowships from the National Endowment for the Humanities, the Rockefeller Foundation, the Center for Advanced Studies in the Behavioral Sciences, and the Guggenheim Foundation. In 1991 he was named a MacArthur Fellow.

While a graduate student in 1969 Rampersad published *Melville's Israel Potter: A Pilgrimage and Progress,* a study of Herman Melville's 1855 novel. He saw a kinship between the American literature of Melville's age and the emerging nationalism he had experienced in the Caribbean. In 1976 he published *The Art and Imagination of W. E. B. DuBois,* about the life and writings of the civil rights activist. A major theme in this work, as well as elsewhere in Rampersad's biographies, is the duality experienced by African Americans as both Africans and Americans.

Rampersad was drawn to biographical writing because he had always been interested in the combination of literature and history and because the genre was a powerful means of grasping history. The biographer received critical acclaim for his gifts as a storyteller and his ease at creating a strong sense of time and place and delineating character. Influenced by the theories of Sigmund Freud, Rampersad approached his subjects from a psychological perspective, striving to reveal their inner lives.

As a result of his DuBois biography Rampersad was asked by GEORGE HOUSTON BASS, executor of the LANGSTON HUGHES estate, to write a life of the black poet. Rampersad's extensive research included looking at six thousand folders of Hughes's papers at Yale University. *The Life of Langston Hughes: 1902–1941: I, Too, Sing America* (1986) and *The Life of Langston Hughes: 1941–1967: I Dream a World* (1988) constitute the definitive examination of the life of a Harlem Renaissance leader and one of the major American poets of the twentieth century. Rampersad looks at the irony of how Hughes's efforts to treat the African American experience realistically resulted in his being criticized by black intellectuals for depicting black life negatively. The biographer's research included living in a cramped room in Paris, France, for six weeks to experience bohemian life as Hughes did.

Reading almost like a novel, the biography earned Rampersad the highest praise of his career. Houston A. Baker Jr. of the University of Pennsylvania, with whom Rampersad cofounded that school's Center for the Study of Black Literature and Culture, argued that Rampersad had set the standard for African American biographies. The first volume of the Hughes biography won the Anisfield-Wolf Book Award in Race Relations in 1987 and the Clarence L. Holte Prize in 1988. In 1990 the second volume received an American Book Award and was honored by the Before Columbus Foundation.

Rampersad edited a 1995 edition of Hughes's collected poems, two volumes of the works of RICHARD WRIGHT for the Library of America in 1991, and a 1995 collection of critical essays about Wright. Rampersad cowrote ARTHUR ASHE's autobiography, *Days of Grace: A Memoir* (1993), while the tennis star was dying of AIDS contracted during a blood transfusion. The book reached the top of the *New York Times* and *Publishers Weekly* best-seller lists. Rampersad followed with a 1997 biography of the baseball legend JACKIE ROBINSON, becoming the first writer with full access to Robinson's archives. *Ralph Ellison: A Biography* was published in 2007 and was praised as an honest view of the novelist who struggled after the success of *Invisible Man* (1952).

Rampersad distinguished himself as a professor by being an exponent of traditional methods of studying literature during an era when such fashionable theories as deconstruction dominated American academics.

FURTHER READING

Mandell, Gail Porter. *Life into Art: Conversations with Seven Contemporary Biographers* (1991).

"Rampersad, Arnold," in *Current Biography Yearbook*, ed. Elizabeth A. Schick (1998).

Serafin, Steven, ed. *Dictionary of Literary Biography, Volume 111: American Literary Biographers, Second Series* (1991).

Valentine, Victoria. "Biographical Notes: With Quiet Passion, Arnold Rampersad Brings History to Life," *Emerge* (Mar. 1998).

MICHAEL ADAMS

Randall, Dudley (14 Jan. 1914–5 Aug. 2000), publisher, poet, and librarian, was born Dudley Felker Randall in Washington, D.C., the son of Arthur Clyde Randall, a Congregational minister, and Ada Viola Randall, a teacher and later a full-time housewife. He was the middle son of five children.

The Randall family moved to Detroit in 1920. Arthur Randall instilled in his sons his interest in politics and would take them to hear black speakers such as W. E. B. DuBois and JAMES WELDON JOHNSON. Although Dudley Randall inherited his love of poetry from both parents, he mirrored his mother's calmer demeanor. Randall wrote his first poem when he was four years old, and his first published poem appeared in the *Detroit Free Press* when he was thirteen. He excelled in his studies, graduating from high school at sixteen. He found work at a Ford Motor Company foundry, and he later worked for the postal service as a clerk and letter carrier.

Randall met the poet ROBERT HAYDEN in 1937. Their friendship served to strengthen Randall's interest in poetry by providing him with the intellectual stimulation he found lacking in his work life. He served in the U.S. Army Air Corps in the South Pacific during World War II. He returned to his postal job following the war and began attending Wayne University, where he earned a B.A. in English in 1949. After receiving his master's degree in Library Science in 1951 from the University of Michigan, Randall began his career in librarianship. In 1956 he began work in the Detroit public library system, where he remained until he became reference librarian and poet-in-residence at the University of Detroit in 1969. He retired from the university in 1976. In 1962 Randall began participating in events at Boone House, a black cultural center founded by the poet Margaret Danner. His association with the Boone House poets helped to focus Randall's writing by welcoming him into a supportive and artistic environment. He later collaborated with Danner on the book *Poem Counterpoem* (1966), the first book published by Randall's Broadside Press.

Two events led to the founding of Broadside Press—the September 1963 bombing of a church in Birmingham, Alabama, in which four black children were killed, and the assassination of President John F. Kennedy later that year. In response to these tragedies, Randall wrote two poems, "The Ballad of Birmingham" and "Dressed All in Pink." Both poems were set to music by folk singer Jerry Moore in 1965, but in order to protect his copyright

Dudley Randall, poet, publisher, editor, and founder of Broadside Press, July 1965. He sits with Melvin B. Tolson (center) and Olivier LaGroan (right). (Library of Congress/Melvin Beaunorus Tolson Papers, 1932–1975.)

interests, Randall published each as a broadside. This marked Randall's entry into publishing and the establishment of Broadside Press, so named for the format of its initial publications.

In May of 1966 Randall attended a writers' conference at Fisk University, where he received permission from Robert Hayden, MARGARET WALKER, and MELVIN B. TOLSON to publish their poems in his broadside series. These, along with Randall's poems and one by GWENDOLYN BROOKS, formed the first six broadsides from the press, which were grouped together as *Poems of the Negro Revolt*.

From its humble beginnings, Broadside Press quickly became a small but vital outlet for black writers at a time when they often experienced difficulties in finding publishers. Randall described the press as "one of the institutions that black people are creating by trial and error and out of necessity in our reaching for self-determination and independence"

(Randall, 28). During Randall's tenure, Broadside Press published ninety broadsides and fifty-five books by authors such as ETHERIDGE KNIGHT, Don L. Lee (later Haki R. Madhubuti), SONIA SANCHEZ, NIKKI GIOVANNI, AUDRE LORDE, AMIRI BARAKA, LANGSTON HUGHES, ALICE WALKER, and others.

Broadside's authors often exhibited a fierce loyalty to the press. Some refused royalties so that proceeds from their books could be returned to the press. However, like most small presses, Broadside operated on a minute budget, and mounting debts forced Randall to sell the operation in 1977.

While involved in the busy affairs of the press, Randall continued to write poetry. *Cities Burning*, a thematic collection of poems, appeared following the 1967 rebellion in Detroit. The early 1970s were a productive period for Randall. A collection of love poems, *Love You*, appeared in 1970 and his first major collection, *More to Remember: Poems of*

Four Decades, was published the next year. In addition to his own work, Randall edited three anthologies between 1967 and 1971: *For Malcolm: Poems on the Life and Death of Malcolm X* (coedited with MARGARET G. BURROUGHS), *Black Poetry: A Supplement to Anthologies Which Exclude Black Poets* and *The Black Poets*.

After the financial difficulties of Broadside Press and its sale, Randall entered a period of depression and stopped writing for three years. He returned to poetry in 1980, and the following year saw the publication of *A Litany of Friends: New and Selected Poems*, as well as his designation as the first poet laureate of Detroit. In 1983, Randall returned as the publisher of Broadside Press; he sold the press for a final time two years later but remained as consultant.

Dudley Randall continued to write poetry until his death in 2000. The numerous awards and accolades presented to Randall throughout his life were indicative of the significant contributions he made to African American poetry, as well as to American literature in general. By publishing young black poets when outlets for their work were not readily available, as well as by writing a body of work that mirrored the struggles and triumphs of African Americans, Dudley Randall and Broadside Press left a lasting influence.

FURTHER READING

First editions of works by Dudley Randall and Broadside Press are available as part of the University of Detroit Archive Collection at the University of Detroit-Mercy. The archives of Broadside Press are housed in the Special Collections Department at the University of Michigan in Ann Arbor.

Randall, Dudley. *Broadside Memories: Poets I Have Known* (1975).

Boyd, Melba Joyce. *Wrestling with the Muse: Dudley Randall and the Broadside Press* (2003).

Miller, R. Baxter. "Dudley Randall." *Dictionary of Literary Biography*, vol. 41 (1985).

Obituary: *Detroit Free Press*, 10 August 2000.

CHRISTOPHER HARTER

Randall, William P. "Daddy Bill" (19 Sept. 1915–3 Feb. 1995), elected county official and Macon, Georgia, civil rights leader, was born in Valdosta, Georgia, the fourth of six children of Harry and Carrie Randall. He was reared in Macon, where his father, formerly the Valdosta manager for the Afro-American Life Insurance Company, had returned to work for his own mother's grocery wholesale and retail business. William P. Randall graduated from Hudson High School and Beda Etta Business College in Macon before going to work as a carpenter. He worked for a large construction company but after World War II went into business with his brother, a bricklayer. Eventually he became one of the major black contractors in the Southeast, working on large-scale commercial and residential projects.

In an era when Jim Crow custom forced African Americans to step aside when a white approached on the sidewalk, Randall's father taught him not to give way. As an adult in the early 1950s Randall experienced humiliation when he and his son went to buy ice cream after church. When he sat on a stool at a "whites only" counter, the clerk threatened to call the police. Randall quietly took his son home, but he wept bitterly. Randall later said the experience stiffened his determination to work for change. Throughout the 1950s Randall worked to organize black voters to support moderate white candidates in Macon—as Randall termed it, "the lesser of two evils." Blacks had won the right to participate in previously all-white primary elections in 1944, in the *Smith v. Allwright* U.S. Supreme Court case, and they were beginning to wield their newfound political influence in southern urban elections. Before 1944 blacks made up less than 10 percent of Bibb County voters. After the 1944 decision, that number increased to about 30 percent (Manis, 205).

In June 1960 Randall's voting activities brought him into conflict with white county officials. A Bibb County Superior Court judge called on the grand jury to investigate "Negro bloc voting," particularly the role of "dominating individuals or conspiratorial organizations" in that vote. After a month of taking testimony from at least fifty witnesses, the grand jury issued a report critical of Randall and another African American leader, Thomas B. Hooper. The panel issued no indictments but suggested that Randall had sought funds from candidates "for personal gain" and criticized his bookkeeping. The grand jury also claimed that his political organization was formed "solely for the purpose of influencing Negro voters" (Manis, 205–208). Randall issued a public reply noting the grand jury's failure to indict. He said, "What I have done politically has been done for 'personal gain' only in the sense that I have firmly believed that the candidates for who [sic] I have worked without personal compensation would give us a better government and a better community" (Manis, 209).

In the early 1960s Randall became active in the local NAACP and was a founding member of Macon's branch of the Southern Christian Leadership Conference. His Bibb County Coordinating Committee pressed for integration of a public golf course. Randall and some of the other adult African American leaders in Macon also played a supporting role for students who were staging sit-ins and marches. They helped organize and train the young people and provided bail money when demonstrators were arrested. In 1961 Randall helped organize students who staged sit-ins at five department store lunch counters in June and a group that sat down in white seats on Bibb Transit Company buses. When the bus company failed to integrate its seating and hire black drivers, Randall advocated a boycott. When he drew criticism from some conservative black ministers he said, "Don't give a preacher money who won't support you in your fight against oppression." When collections dropped, a number of Randall's critics began to offer their church sanctuaries for mass meetings. The bus boycott ended with federal court rulings in the protesters' favor. But before it was over, an anonymous opponent fired shots into a vacant house Randall owned (Manis, 222).

Randall's growing profile in the civil rights movement cost him economically. His financing for construction loans dried up, prompting him to change careers. He bought a funeral home and renamed it Randall Memorial Mortuary. It remained his primary business for the rest of his life.

Like much of Georgia, the city of Macon and Bibb County had at-large election systems that diluted black votes and hindered the election of black candidates. That changed in the late 1970s when two black state representatives—one of them Randall's son—pressed for the creation of district-based elections in the city and county. In 1980, after the county system was changed, William P. Randall and Albert Billingslea became the first African Americans elected to the county commission. Randall held the office until he died. As an elected official and chair of the personnel committee, Randall was an advocate for county employees. Black employment increased in county government, particularly in white-collar jobs. Randall also pressed successfully for the county to recognize a MARTIN LUTHER KING JR. holiday.

Randall was married for sixty-three years to Lillian Hudson Randall. His son William C. "Billy" Randall became a state representative and later the Bibb County chief magistrate and civil court judge.

His granddaughter Nikki Randall was later elected to the state house of representatives, and his grandson Lance Randall was an executive in the Greater Macon Chamber of Commerce and a 2004 candidate for Bibb County Commission chair.

Throughout the 1960s, as African Americans pressed for change in Macon and surrounding communities, Randall was at once a proponent of that change and a behind-the-scenes advocate for non-violence. The *Macon Telegraph*, which had opposed Randall in the 1960s, ultimately acknowledged his contributions: "Randall's life has been a picture of community dedication…. He has accomplished all of this without much fuss or antagonism toward whites—he just asked for what he thought was right and just" (*Macon Telegraph*, 17 June 1994).

FURTHER READING

Manis, Andrew M. *Macon Black and White: An Unutterable Separation in the American Century* (2004).

DON SCHANCHE JR.

Randolph, A. Philip (15 Apr. 1889–16 May 1979), labor organizer, editor, and activist, was born Asa Philip Randolph in Crescent City, Florida, to Elizabeth Robinson and James Randolph, an African Methodist Episcopal (AME) Church preacher. In 1891 the Randolphs moved to Jacksonville, where James had been offered the pastorship of a small church. Both Asa Philip and his older brother, James Jr., were talented students who graduated from Cookman Institute (later Bethune-Cookman College), the first high school for African Americans in Florida.

Randolph left Florida in 1911, moving to New York to pursue a career as an actor. Between 1912 and 1917 he attended City College, where he was first exposed to the ideas of Karl Marx and political radicalism. He joined the Socialist Party in 1916, attracted to the party's economic analysis of black exploitation in America. Randolph, along with W. E. B. DuBois, HUBERT HENRY HARRISON, and CHANDLER OWEN, was one of the pioneer black members of the Socialist Party—then led by Eugene Debs. Like a number of his peers, Randolph did not subscribe to a belief in a "special" racialized oppression of blacks that existed independent of class. Rather, he argued at this point that socialism would essentially "answer" the "Negro question." His faith in the socialist solution can be seen in the title of an essay he wrote on racial violence, "Lynching: Capitalism Its Cause; Socialism Its Cure" (*Messenger*,

Sept. 1921). In 1916 Randolph and Owen began working to organize the black labor force, founding the short-lived United Brotherhood of Elevator and Switchboard Operators union. Shortly thereafter, they coedited the *Hotel Messenger*, the journal of the Headwaiters and Sidewaiters Society. After being fired by the organization, they created the *Messenger* in 1917—with crucial financial support from Lucille Randolph, a beauty salon owner whom Randolph had married in 1914. The couple had no children. Lucille Randolph's success as an entrepreneur was a consistent source of stability—despite the fact that her husband's reputation as a radical scared away some of her clientele. Billing itself as "The Only Radical Negro Magazine," the boldly iconoclastic *Messenger* quickly became one of the benchmark publications of the incipient New Negro movement. A single issue contained the views of ABRAM HARRIS, KELLY MILLER, GEORGE SCHUYLER, ALICE DUNBAR-NELSON, COUNTÉE CULLEN, EMMETT JAY SCOTT, and CHARLES S. JOHNSON.

In the context of the postwar Red Scare, however, Randolph's leftist politics brought him to the attention of federal authorities determined to root out radicals, anarchists, and communists but who showed little regard for civil liberties. With the *Messenger* dubbed "the most dangerous of all Negro publications" by the Bureau of Investigation (later the FBI), Randolph and Owen were arrested under the Espionage Act in 1918 but were eventually acquitted of all charges.

When the Socialist Party split in 1919 over the issue of affiliation with the newly created socialist state in Russia, Randolph and Owen remained in the Socialist Party faction. The left wing of the party broke away, eventually coalescing into the Communist Party USA (CPUSA). Randolph's ties to the Socialist Party remained firm, and he ran as the party's candidate for New York State comptroller in 1920 and as its candidate for secretary of state in 1921. Initial relations with the black CPUSA members were warm, with the Communists LOVETT FORT-WHITEMAN and W. A. DOMINGO writing for the *Messenger*. By the late 1920s, however, Randolph had become involved in the sometime fractious politics of the black left in the New Negro era.

In the early 1920s Randolph worked for the "Garvey Must Go" campaigns directed by an adhoc collection of black leaders opposed to the charismatic—and often belligerent—black nationalist MARCUS GARVEY. Randolph and Garvey had shared a common mentor in the socialist intellectual Hubert Harrison. Randolph claimed, in fact, to

have introduced Garvey to the tradition of Harlem street-corner oratory. Randolph's opposition to Garvey appears to have been rooted in his perspective that Garvey's Universal Negro Improvement Association ignored the "class struggle nature of the Negro problem," as well as in his belief that Garvey was untrustworthy.

At the same time that W. A. Domingo charged that the *Messenger*'s attacks on Marcus Garvey had metastasized into a general anti-Caribbean bias, the magazine began devoting much less attention to radical politics in general and Russia specifically. Randolph's embryonic anticommunism was partially responsible for this shift, but the *Messenger* had also attempted to broaden its base by appealing to more upwardly mobile black strivers.

With the *Messenger* in editorial and financial decline, Randolph accepted a position as the head of the newly established Brotherhood of Sleeping Car Porters (BSCP) and spearheaded a joint drive for recognition of the union by the American Federation of Labor (AFL) and the Pullman Company. Randolph led the organization to affiliation with the AFL in 1928—a significant accomplishment in the face of the racial discrimination practiced by many of its sibling unions in the AFL. Randolph's decision to cancel a planned BSCP strike in 1928, however, resulted in a significant loss of confidence in the union and opened him up to criticism from the Communist Party, among others.

The Communist Party–affiliated American Negro Labor Congress, created in 1925, became increasingly critical of Randolph and the BSCP by the end of the decade. At the same time, Randolph's thinking and writing took a strong and persistent anticommunist turn. In the 1930s the economic upheaval of the Great Depression and the controversial treatment of the wrongfully imprisoned SCOTTSBORO BOYS brought Communists an unprecedented degree of recognition and status within black America. The era's radicalism found expression in 1935 in the creation of the National Negro Congress (NNC)—an umbrella organization with liberal, radical, and moderate black elements. Randolph was selected as the organization's first president in 1936. Given his standing as a radical socialist, labor organizer, and civil rights advocate, Randolph was one of the few prominent African Americans with ties to many of the diverse constituencies that made up the NNC.

Global politics shaped the organization from the outset. The NNC had been founded in the midst of the "Popular Front" era and, in many ways, had been

A. Philip Randolph at a meeting between Civil Rights leaders and Lyndon B. Johnson in the Oval Office, Washington, D.C., 11 Aug. 1965. (LBJ Presidential Library/Yoichi R. Okamoto, photographer.)

facilitated by the shared concern of communists, liberals, socialists, and moderates about the spread of fascism across Europe and the lack of civil rights for blacks in America. However, the Hitler-Stalin Pact of 1939 effectively ended the Popular Front, and tensions within the NNC increased. Randolph resigned in 1940, charging that Communist influence had undercut the NNC's autonomy and saying famously that "it was hard enough being black without also being red" (press release, 4 May 1940, in NAACP papers, A-444).

World War II brought Randolph a new set of challenges. With America on the verge of war in 1941, he organized the March on Washington movement, an attempt to bring ten thousand African Americans to Washington to protest discrimination in defense industries. President Franklin Roosevelt, recognizing the possible impact upon morale and public relations and the significance of the black vote in the 1932 and 1936 presidential

elections, issued Executive Order 8806, which forbade discrimination in defense industries and created the Fair Employment Practices Commission. In response, the proposed march was cancelled. Randolph, however, remained at the head of the organization until 1946.

In 1948 Randolph, along with BAYARD RUSTIN, with whom he would work closely in later years, organized the League for Nonviolent Civil Disobedience against Military Segregation. The organization's efforts led to a meeting with President Harry S. Truman in which Randolph predicted that black Americans would not fight any more wars in a Jim Crow army. As with the planned March on Washington, the 1948 efforts influenced Truman's decision to desegregate the military with Executive Order 9981.

During the 1950s Randolph became more closely aligned with mainstream civil rights organizations like the NAACP—organizations that he had fiercely criticized earlier in his career. He also became more outspokenly anticommunist, traveling internationally with the Socialist Norman Thomas to point out the shortcomings of Soviet communism. He was elected to the executive council of the newly united AFL–CIO in 1955. The high-water mark of his influence, however, had passed. Randolph did not exert as much influence with the union president George Meany as he had with the AFL president William Green, whom he had known since the BSCP's affiliation in 1928. In 1959 Randolph assumed the presidency of the Negro American Labor Council (NALC). That same year, Randolph's address on the subject of racism within the AFL–CIO elicited a stern rebuke from Meany. Wedged between the radical younger members of the NALC and his contentious relationship with Meany, Randolph resigned his position in 1964.

Randolph reemerged in the 1960s in connection with the modern civil rights movement; in 1962 Rustin and the seventy-two-year-old Randolph proposed a march on Washington to MARTIN LUTHER KING JR. and the NAACP's ROY WILKINS. Randolph was the first speaker to address the two hundred thousand marchers at the Lincoln Memorial on 28 August 1963, stating that "we are not a pressure group, an organization or a group of organizations, we are the advance guard for a massive moral revolution for jobs and freedom." The march was a decisive factor in the passage of the Civil Rights Act of 1964.

Randolph presided over the creation of the A. Philip Randolph Institute in 1964 and spearheaded the organization's efforts to extend a guaranteed income to all citizens of the United States. His anti-communist views led him to support the war in Vietnam—a stance that put him at odds with his one-time ally Martin Luther King, among others. He distrusted the evolving radicalism that characterized the decade, stating that Black Power had overtones of black racism. His public support for the United Federation of Teachers in the Ocean Hill–Brownsville conflict of 1968, in which black community organizations attempted to minimize the authority of the largely white teachers' union, further alienated Randolph from the younger generation of Black Power advocates.

By the time of his death in Manhattan in 1979 Randolph had become an icon in the struggle for black equality in the twentieth century. More than any other figure, A. Philip Randolph was responsible for articulating the concerns of black labor—particularly in the context of the civil rights movement. His organizing abilities and strategic acumen were key to the desegregation of defense contracting and the signal legislative achievement of the civil rights era: passage of the Civil Rights Act of 1964.

FURTHER READING

A. Philip Randolph's papers are housed in the Library of Congress. Microfilm versions are available at other institutions, including the Schomburg Center for Research in Black Culture of the New York Public Library.

Anderson, Jervis. *A. Philip Randolph* (1972).

Kornweibel, Theodore. *No Crystal Stair: Black Life and the "Messenger", 1917–1928* (1975).

Marable, Manning. "A. Philip Randolph, An Assessment," in *From the Grassroots* (1980).

Pfeffer, Paula. *A. Philip Randolph: Pioneer of the Civil Rights Movement* (1990).

Obituary: *New York Times*, 17 May 1979.

WILLIAM J. COBB

Randolph, Amanda (2 Sept. 1902–24 Aug. 1967), actress, singer, and comedian, was born in Louisville, Kentucky. Many sources confuse Amanda Randolph with her sister Lillian Randolph, also an entertainer but ten years her junior. In radio and onstage they stood in for each other, which makes a precise accounting of her career as a performer nearly impossible.

Randolph's father was a Methodist minister and the family moved frequently. After his death in 1920, Randolph settled in New York and began

a career as a performer in the NOBLE SISSLE and EUBIE BLAKE productions of *Shuffle Along* (1921) and *The Chocolate Dandies* (1924). From 1925 to about 1927 Randolph performed at the Alhambra Theatre in New York City, in the All-Colored Musical Burlesque vaudeville review called *Lucky Sambo*. She then spent a year in London with the Harry Clifford Scott and Eddie Peter Whaley variety act. A talented, earthy-voiced singer, in 1932 she teamed with Catherine Handy as the Dixie Nightingales. That same year she appeared on a variety bill at New York's Capitol Theatre in a solo act as the character Venus Geetch.

As the Depression took its toll on the entertainment industry, Randolph left show business for a time and, with her husband, ran an after-hours eatery called The Clam Shop. Using the moniker Mandy Randolph, she made recordings of "In the Groove: Fox Trot" (1936), "Rainbow on the River: Fox Trot" (1936), "Cryin' Blues," (1936), and "I'm Gonna Jazz My Way Right Straight thru Paradise" (1937). Billed as Amanda Randolph and her Orchestra, she also made recordings for Bluebird Records.

Randolph's career includes numerous radio credits. She performed in an unknown number of episodes of the CBS radio programs, including *Young Dr. Malone* (1939–1960), *Big Sister* (1936–1941), *The Romance of Helen Trent* (1933–1960), and *Aunt Jenny's Real Life Stories* (1937–1956). Later she was cast in the part of Lily on the program *Abie's Irish Rose* (1942–1944); she was Ellen on the show *Kitty Foyle* (1946–1947); and on Ethel Barrymore's 1945 program *Miss Hattie*, Randolph reprised her role as the comic character, Venus Geetch. In 1937 she was heard singing the song "Tain't Right, Tain't Wrong" on LOUIS ARMSTRONG's radio show. She also performed with PAUL ROBESON and EDDIE GREEN on the WABD program *All God's Chillun* (1940), and appeared in costume as the character Aunt Jemima on the audience-participation show *Lady Be Seated*. The CBS radio show *Aunt Jemima* ran from 1929 to 1945, and beginning in 1943, Randolph played the lead part at various times. She is perhaps best remembered for her performances on two particular radio programs: *Amos 'n Andy* (1926–1955), where she and her sister Lillian played the part of the character Sapphire Stevens; and *The Beulah Show*. *Beulah* ran from 1945 to 1954, and Amanda and her sister Lillian played the lead from 1950 to 1954.

During the 1940s Randolph appeared in Broadway stage plays. In 1940 she was cast as Cleota, "a comic servant girl," in the James Thurber comedy *The Male Animal*. In 1942 she was cast as the servant, Tinny, in the John Patrick play *The Willow and I*. Also in 1942, she appeared at the Ritz Theatre in the black-cast musical revue *Harlem Cavalcade*.

Randolph's extensive career in motion pictures includes appearances in full-length productions, soundies, and two-reelers, in both mainstream Hollywood films and race movies (black-cast films produced for black audiences). *Swing* (1938), *Lying Lips* (1939), and *The Notorious Elinor Lee* (1941) were produced by the pioneering filmmaker OSCAR MICHEAUX. In Hollywood pictures she was often uncredited or typecast as an unnamed household servant. Her credits included *At the Circus* (1939), *The Iron Mistress* (1952), *She's Working Her Way through College* (1952), *Bomba and the Jungle Girl* (1952), *Mister Scoutmaster* (1953), *A Man Called Peter* (1955), *Heller in Pink Tights* (1960), and *The Last Challenge* (1967). Of particular note, however, is her role as the character Gladys in the Twentieth Century–Fox production of *No Way Out* (1950). This film, which explored the Negro problem in America, is one of a cycle of Hollywood pictures released during the postwar era that portrayed the country's racial divide.

In 1948 Randolph began her long association with the new medium of television, appearing in the Dumont Network comedy *The Laytons* (1948). She also briefly had her own show, *Amanda* (1948); she was described in the *New York Times* as an "actress, singer, and genial back-fence philosopher." Randolph was the first African American woman to host her own daytime television show. Though *Amanda* lasted for only a few episodes, Randolph became associated with another show that remained on television for more than a decade, *Make Room for Daddy* (ABC from 1953 to 1957, and CBS from 1957 to 1964). Randolph appeared as the family housekeeper from 1955 to 1964.

Among other television appearances, Randolph earned the part of Grace on an episode of *Perry Mason*, appeared on the *Matinee Theatre* production of *The Serpent's Tooth* (1957) and on the police drama *The New Breed* (1961); she played Marian in the 1967 teleplay *Do Not Go Gentle into That Good Night*. Most notably, however, Randolph appeared on two of the most polarizing and contentious programs ever to air on television, *Amos 'n Andy* and *The Beulah Show*.

Amos 'n Andy, which originated on radio in 1926, featured the comic exploits of two black men: Andy, the dull-witted president of the Fresh Air Cab Company, and his friend and associate, the level-headed Amos. On radio, the lead roles were played by white actors who used so-called black vernacular and dialect. When the radio program transitioned to television, both Amanda Randolph and her sister Lillian, both of the radio cast, earned parts on the television show, with Amanda playing the role of character Mama. *Amos 'n Andy* was first broadcast on CBS television in June 1951 and lasted two years before the program was canceled in the midst of a firestorm of contention and debate. Postwar African Americans, bolstered by recent civil rights gains, looked to television as a medium that would be free of the old racial stereotypes promulgated on film and other forms of popular culture. Many considered the characters of *Amos 'n Andy* to be offensive.

Beulah was the black maid on the highly popular radio show, *Fibber McGee and Molly* (1945–1953). In early episodes, the part of Beulah was played by a white, male actor, Marlin Hurt. *The Beulah Show* (1945–1953), a spin-off of *Fibber McGee*, with HATTIE McDANIEL as Beulah, debuted in CBS radio 1945. A television sitcom was developed from the radio program, which debuted on ABC in 1950. Amanda Randolph followed ETHEL WATERS, Hattie McDaniel, and LOUISE BEAVERS as the fourth actress to play the part of Beulah. In its brief run the program was criticized for its inclusion of black "types." Actors in the male roles complained of being forced to act "Tomish," and the NAACP leveled complaints and threatened to begin a boycott of the show's sponsors. The show was canceled in 1953.

Multitalented and versatile, Amanda Randolph enjoyed a lengthy and successful career in show business as a performer, vaudevillian, singer, and radio, film, and television pioneer. She died of a stroke at Santa Teresita Hospital in Duarte, California, leaving behind her sister, Lillian; a son, Joseph; and a daughter, Evelyn.

FURTHER READING

Atkinson, Brooks. "The Play: James Thurber and Elliott Nugent's 'The Male Animal' Begins a New Theatre Year." *New York Times*, 10 Jan. 1940.

Ely, Melvin Patrick. *The Adventure of Amos 'n' Andy: A Social History of an American Phenomenon*, 2d ed. (2001).

MacDonald, J. Fred. *Blacks and White TV: Afro-Americans in Television since 1948* (1993).

Terrace, Vincent. *Radio Programs, 1924–1984: A Catalogue of Over 1800 Shows* (1999).

Obituaries: *New York Times*, 25 Aug. 1967; *Variety*, 30 Aug. 1967.

PAMALA S. DEANE

Randolph, Benjamin Franklin (1820?–Oct. 1868), Reconstruction politician, civil rights leader, and murder victim, was born free in Kentucky, the child of parents of mixed ethnicity whose names are unknown. When he was a child Randolph's family moved to Ohio, where he was educated in local schools. In 1854 he entered Oberlin College's preparatory department, before attending the college from 1857 to 1862. At Oberlin Randolph received instruction both in the liberal arts and at the college's theological seminary. Soon after graduation he was ordained as a Methodist Episcopal minister. During the Civil War Randolph served as a chaplain in the Twenty-sixth Colored Infantry, which was dispatched to Hilton Head, South Carolina, in 1864.

After the war ended in 1865 Randolph applied for a position with the Freedmen's Bureau. He was not initially given an appointment but was instead sent to South Carolina by the American Missionary Association, a northern antislavery organization founded in 1846, which was after the war the most influential and best financed northern society in South Carolina. Once in South Carolina Randolph founded, with the Reverend E. J. Adams, the Charleston *Journal* in 1866, before becoming editor of the Charleston *Advocate* in 1867. Randolph also became active in the organization of the Republican Party in South Carolina as an organizer for the Union League. In February 1867 Randolph was appointed as an agent of the education division of the Freedmen's Bureau, first as a teacher then eventually as assistant superintendent of schools for the bureau in South Carolina. In that position Randolph advocated for integrated public schooling. He argued that with the help of the bureau, "we are laying the foundation of a new structure here, and the time has come when we shall have to meet things squarely, and we must meet them now or never. The day is coming when we must decide whether the two races shall live together or not." Randolph was recognized by his contemporaries as an eloquent and persuasive speaker. In 1865 he attended the Colored Person's Convention held in Zion Church in Charleston; the secretary of the convention noted that during an evening rally Randolph delivered a speech "abounding in thought and enforced by a serious earnestness which impressed the minds and commanded the attention of the House." Randolph was "a pleasing speaker, calm and deliberate, and took the position that thought, like the ladies, 'when unadorned is adorned the most.'"

Randolph also remained active in the Methodist church and worked with the Reverend B. F. Whittmore to spark political activism in the South by the Northern Methodist church. In 1867 Randolph and Whittmore were admitted to the South Carolina Conference of the Methodist Episcopal church (Northern) on a trial basis, although he did not receive a ministerial assignment until 1868. Randolph was one of several black Northern-Methodist minister-politicians, and he went to several congregations throughout the state as a party organizer when the Republican Party began formally organizing in South Carolina in the spring of 1867.

In 1867 Randolph was made vice president of the Republican state executive committee, and the following year he was elected chairman of the committee just before the presidential campaign of 1868. Randolph was too radical even for some in his own party, and following his election as party chairman, several conservative Republicans staged a walkout during the party convention. The following year Randolph was one of 226 African American delegates to the 1868 South Carolina Constitutional Convention. Randolph was part of the influential faction of ministers at the convention who were natives of the North and who had come south as missionaries or with the Freedmen's Bureau. At the convention Democrats accused Randolph of making incendiary speeches.

In that same year Randolph was elected to the South Carolina legislature as a state senator, representing Orangeburg County. In the state senate he worked for legal equality for blacks and on 31 August 1868, during a debate on a bill that would end many types of public discrimination in South Carolina, demanded that no public accommodation be closed to him or to any other African American on the basis of their race.

In mid-October 1868, while canvassing for the Republican Party in the predominantly white upcountry districts of South Carolina, Randolph was shot and killed by "unknown parties" in Donaldsville. It was commonly believed that the Ku Klux Klan had ordered his death, almost certainly because Randolph was an outspoken black leader. A white man of questionable sanity later confessed to killing Randolph for money, but he killed himself, or perhaps was murdered, before he identified who allegedly had paid him. Randolph was one of at least twenty-six black delegates to the South Carolina Constitutional Convention who were later victims of Klan attacks, and was one of six delegates who were murdered by the Klan. Though Randolph's life was cut short, he is remembered as an early radical and influential black leader, and he is an example of the kind of African American activist elected to office in South Carolina during Reconstruction.

FURTHER READING

Foner, Eric, ed. *Freedom's Lawmakers: A Directory of Black Officeholders during Reconstruction* (1993).

Foner, Philip S., and George Walker, eds. *Proceedings of the Black State Conventions, 1840–65* (2 vols., 1980).

Holt, Thomas C. *Black over White: Negro Political Leadership in South Carolina during Reconstruction* (1977).

Litwack, Leon, and August Meier, eds. *Black Leaders of the Nineteenth Century* (1988).

Rabinowitz, Howard N., ed. *Southern Black Leaders of the Reconstruction Era* (1982).

Simkins, Francis. *South Carolina during Reconstruction* (1932).

Williamson, Joel. *After Slavery: The Negro in South Carolina during Reconstruction, 1865–1877* (1965).

Woody, Robert H. *Republican Newspapers of South Carolina* (1936).

This entry is taken from the *American National Biography* and is published here with the permission of the American Council of Learned Societies.

DANIEL W. HAMILTON

Randolph, Paschal Beverly (10 Aug. 1825–29 July 1875), visionary, spiritualist, Rosicrucian, sex magician, reformer, teacher, and novelist, was born to Flora Clark, a single mother, and grew up in the notorious Five Points section of New York City. His mother, he later claimed, was a descendent of the queen of Madagascar, and his father a scion of the Randolph family of Virginia, signers of the Declaration of Independence and descendants of Pocahontas, but the truth was probably more prosaic. His father was either William Randon or William B. Randolph, neither scions of the Randolphs nor married to his mother. When circumstances demanded it and when it suited his purposes, Randolph denied that "a drop of continental African, or pure negro blood" ran in his veins—"not that it were a disgrace," he added (Randolph, *Curious Life*, 4, 18). At the same time, however, when he was what he called "a red-hot politician" at the end of the Civil War and ran a Freedman's School in New Orleans, he gloried in his African ancestry: "We men of color were born here…. Are we to go to the lands of our African ancestors because our skins are dark?" (*New Orleans Tribune*). In the final analysis, after Randolph had experienced the open hostility of the South and the veiled, condescending bigotry of the New England reformers who had lionized

him during the Civil War but denied him a place after victory, race became largely irrelevant to him and no longer appeared in his writings—though the indignities of bigotry continued to haunt him until his death. The newspaper account of his death in the *Toledo Blade* identified him as "a Spaniard," the guise he must have adopted in the end.

Randolph never knew his father, and his mother died when he was seven. He grew up on the streets of New York, learned to write by copying the letters of bills pasted on fences, and had at most a year of formal education. Before he was twenty, he had worked as a cabin boy, cook, barber, and bootblack and might well have remained in obscurity if it were not for the appearance of spiritualism in 1848. The movement swept the United States and then Europe as people became convinced that the spirits of the dead could talk with them through "mediums." Randolph believed that he had been a seer from childhood, visited by the spirit of his mother, and he became an ardent advocate of the new movement, traveling the country as a trance medium and delivering more than three thousand of what were by all contemporary accounts extraordinarily powerful and eloquent speeches.

By the late 1850s he was famous as a spiritualist medium but had become convinced that the possession of his mind by the spirits in trance was destroying him. He tried several times to kill himself and then fled to Europe from 1857 to 1858 and then again from 1861 to 1862, at which time he traveled through the Near East from Egypt to the borders of Persia and then to Constantinople. In England he encountered and mingled with the adherents of a developed, though antiquarian, version of magic, Rosicrucianism, and occultism, which he soon mastered; in Egypt he came upon hashish and a form of sexual intercourse used to develop occult powers. These transformed Randolph, and he returned to the United States as the missionary of drug use for mystical purposes (he was the largest importer of hashish before the Civil War) and of a sweeping vision of a vast hierarchy of beings, born and never born on earth, emanating as divine sparks from the Grand Central Sun of Being and gradually returning to that source over the vast ages of the universe. He embodied the results of his experiences in his most masterful book, *Dealings with the Dead* (1861), which revolutionized the limited worldview of American spiritualists.

After trying to raise African American troops for the Union army and then teaching in a Freedmen's Bureau School in New Orleans, in 1866 Randolph settled in Boston, where he practiced as a physician specializing in sexual ailments and spread his vision of the vast hierarchies of beings surrounding man and his teachings on the possibility of participating with these entities through clairvoyance—spiritual vision developed by use of the magic mirror, drugs, and sexual magic. He continued to publish books, including several notable novels, especially *The Wonderful Story of Ravalette* (1863), but because of the intimate nature of the sexual practices he taught, his most important works were circulated in privately printed sheets or handwritten letters. He had begun to call himself a "Rosicrucian" in 1858, after the mythical fraternity of the early seventeenth century, and worked the last ten years of his life trying to establish his Rosicrucian Fraternity on a permanent basis, first in San Francisco, later in Boston, and later again in San Francisco. All of these were short-lived as organizations, but his ideas found a wider, international audience.

On 29 July 1875, after a final trip to San Francisco to establish his Rosicrucian Fraternity, Randolph shot himself in Toledo, Ohio, leaving an infant son who passed as white and became a physician in Toledo and at least one other child from a previous marriage, who deliberately embraced the African American side of his ancestry and became a member of the Brotherhood of Sleeping Car Porters organized by A. PHILLIP RANDOLPH (no relation).

Randolph was a brilliant writer and orator, and transformed occultism from a bookish, antiquarian pursuit into active practice designed to achieve personal spiritual development. Echoes of his work abound in the books of H. P. Blavatsky, the founder of Theosophy, and Randolph's explicit sexual practices formed the core of the teachings of the Hermetic Brotherhood of Luxor, an influential secret society that flourished in England and the United States in the 1880s. It was in Europe, though, that Randolph was to have his most significant successes. His novel *The Wonderful Story of Ravalette* was published in German in 1922, and his visions and drug advocacy were welcomed by the Surrealists of the 1920s and the Bohemian underground of Paris in the 1930s.

FURTHER READING

Randolph, P. B. *P. B. Randolph, the "Learned Pundit," and "Man with Two Souls," His Curious Life, Works and Career. The Great Free-Love Trial. Randolph's Grand Defence. His Address to the Jury, and Mankind. The Verdict* (1872).

Rosicrucian, The (P. B. Randolph). *Dealings With The Dead; The Human Soul, Its Migrations And Its Transmigrations* (1861).

Deveney, John Patrick. *Paschal Beverly Randolph: A Nineteenth Century Black American Spiritualist, Rosicrucian and Sex Magician* (1996).

Godwin, J., J. P. Deveney, and C. Chanel. *The Hermetic Brotherhood of Luxor: Initiatic and Historical Documents of an Order of Practical Occultism* (1995).

New Orleans Tribune (2 Dec. 1864).

Toledo Blade (29 July 1875).

JOHN PATRICK DEVENEY

Randolph, Peter (c. 1825–1897), slave, minister, and author, was born at Brandon Plantation in Prince George County, Virginia, one of eighty-one slaves owned by Carter H. Edloe. The names of his parents are unknown. Randolph's father was a black slave-driver owned by George Harrison, whose plantation was adjacent to Edloe's. His mother was a slave and a devout Christian.

Randolph's father died when he was ten years old, leaving his mother with five children. Randolph's oldest brother, Benjamin, unsuccessfully tried to run away and was eventually sold to a Negro-trader, who sent him south to work on the cotton and sugar plantations. Randolph never saw him again. Randolph was a sickly child who, at the age of ten or eleven, felt he was called by God to preach to other slaves. He taught himself to read the Bible and, eventually, how to write. Edloe died in 1844, and in his will he called for the emancipation of his slaves. Randolph's ability to read and write helped him secure the execution of Edloe's wishes, despite the resistance of John A. Seldon, the executor of Edloe's estate.

With a group of sixty-six slaves, Randolph arrived in Boston on 15 September 1847. They were welcomed by a large group of prominent citizens, including the abolitionists Wendell Phillips, William Lloyd Garrison, and Samuel May, and the future governor of Massachusetts John A. Andrews.

Randolph became involved with the Anti-Slavery Society and, around 1855, published a pamphlet titled *Sketches of Slave Life: or, Illustrations of the 'Peculiar Institution,' by Reverend Peter Randolph, an Emancipated Slave*. In addition to his antislavery activities, he worked at various business firms in Boston and became licensed as a preacher for the Baptist Church.

In 1852 Randolph visited St. John, New Brunswick, as a missionary for fugitive slaves who had fled to Canada. He was surprised to discover that racial prejudice existed even on British soil. Returning to Boston, Randolph continued his religious work despite what he described as white resistance to a "negger preacher."

In 1856 Randolph was ordained as a Baptist minister and took over a small church in New Haven, Connecticut. He remained there for a year, attending lectures at Yale College and performing ministerial duties. When the church could no longer financially support a pastor, Randolph returned to Boston. In 1858 he was invited to become the pastor of a church in Newburgh, New York.

At the outbreak of the Civil War, Randolph was back in Boston, working at a small newspaper business and preaching at the Colored Old Ladies' Home. As the war continued, Randolph expressed a desire to serve as a chaplain for one of the black regiments stationed in the South. He was unable to make it to Virginia until after the war, when he was dispatched to City Point, where many newly freed slaves were quartered. It was during his journey south that President Lincoln was assassinated.

After a brief stay at City Point, Randolph made his way to Richmond, which he described as lying "in smoke and ashes." He began to preach at Schinnborazzo, a temporary camp that had been erected for refugee former slaves. He was soon appointed to the Freedmen's Bureau, and his advice was sought by state and national politicians.

In Richmond, Randolph became the first African American pastor of Ebenezer Baptist Church. He ended the church's gender-segregated seating and gave women a greater voice in church affairs. He also threw himself into the "marriage question," working to legalize slave marriages and to resolve situations in which freed slaves, attempting to reunite with their families, discovered that their spouses had remarried and established new families.

After four and a half years in Richmond, Randolph returned to Boston, where an influx of freed slaves had arrived since the war. Randolph established an Ebenezer Church in Boston, which grew to become one of the largest black churches in the city. He spent a year at the Ebenezer Church in Providence, Rhode Island, and also supplied a small church at Mashpee, Gay Head, Massachusetts, where his congregation was made up of Indian descendents. He also worked at churches in Albany, New York, and West Newton, Massachusetts. In 1893 Randolph's slave narrative, *From Slave Cabin to the Pulpit. The Autobiography of Rev. Peter Randolph: The Southern Question Illustrated and Sketches of Slave Life*, was published in Boston.

Although Randolph was born in Virginia, he felt a deep affection for Massachusetts, which he described as his "adopted mother." He was one of many northern missionaries to head South in the years during and after the Civil War to organize churches and to aid in Reconstruction. Through his efforts in converting southern blacks, he helped turn the Baptist Church into a national force; and by the end of the century, Baptists made up the largest denomination among African American Protestants.

FURTHER READING

Randolph, Peter. *Sketches of Slave Life: or, Illustrations of the 'Peculiar Institution,' by Reverend Peter Randolph, an Emancipated Slave* (1855).
Randolph, Peter. *From Slave Cabin to the Pulpit. The Autobiography of Rev. Peter Randolph: The Southern Question Illustrated and Sketches of Slave Life* (1893).
Starling, Marion Wilson. *The Slave Narrative: Its Place in American History* (1981).

JULIA LEE

Randolph, Virginia Estelle (May 1870?–16 Mar. 1958), educator, humanitarian, and the first countrywide Jeanes Supervising Industrial Teacher, was born in Richmond, Virginia, the second oldest of four daughters of Nelson Edward Randolph, a laborer from Richmond, and Sarah Carter Randolph, a native of Campbell County, Virginia. Both of Virginia's parents were former slaves. Although Randolph's date of birth is commonly given as 8 June 1874, the Bureau of Vital Statistics' Register of Births for the City of Richmond reveals the month and year of her birth as May 1870. An earlier birth year is further substantiated by the fact that she is listed by name on her father's 15 Feb 1871 application for a Freedman's Bank account. As a youngster Randolph attended Baker Elementary School, the first school built specifically for blacks after Richmond's public school system's formation. She reportedly encountered difficulty learning the alphabet but persevered to earn class honors (Jones, p. 23). Her father reportedly died when her youngest sister, Emma, born 4 June 1874, was about one month old, leaving the Randolph family in financial difficulty. Her mother continued to work outside of the home several days a week, and in addition began to take in clients' laundry. Sarah Randolph was very resourceful and instilled in her daughters the importance of cleanliness and proper hygiene. She also taught them how to sew, knit, and crochet.

According to Richmond census records and city directories, Sarah Randolph had remarried by 1880 to carpenter John Anderson; by 1890 she had again remarried, this time to day laborer Joseph Minor. The family later moved to 813 West Moore Street in Richmond, a change pivotal in exposing Virginia Randolph to industrial education. Although researchers have generally attributed her interest in industrial education to her mother, a previously overlooked influence was perhaps the Moore Street Industrial Institution, located directly across the street from the family at 814 West Moore Street. According to an 1888 school circular, the institution was incorporated in 1882 with the primary mission of fostering opportunities for destitute children by combining elementary and industrial education. Thus in addition to its academic department, the school had carpentry, printing, and sewing departments. It was organized around 1879 under the auspices of the Moore Street Missionary Baptist Church, located on the grounds at the same address. Randolph and her family would become longtime members of this church, founded in 1875 by the Reverend William Troy and several deacons of the Second (African) Baptist Church in Richmond.

The Freedmen's Bureau played an integral role in educating blacks after the Civil War. In Virginia and other Southern states primary, grammar, and normal schools were organized to aid the freedmen in successfully traversing the road from slavery to freedom. The Bureau's educational operations in Virginia formally began in June 1865. From its inception it worked in concert with several freedmen's aid societies to rent and construct buildings and to recruit and hire schoolteachers. One school central in preparing Randolph and other black Virginia educators was the Richmond Colored Normal and High School. Richmond Colored Normal (as it was commonly called) was organized in 1867 by army chaplain Robert Morse Manly, who served as Virginia's Superintendent of Schools for the Freedmen (under the auspices of the Freedmen's Bureau) for the majority of its tenure in the state. The three-year course of study provided a rigorous curriculum that included courses in physiology, botany, geography with map drawing, natural philosophy, and government. The school also combined courses in methods of teaching with practical experience teaching in its model school. Richmond Colored Normal enjoyed an extraordinary reputation that extended far beyond Virginia's borders: Its graduates were in great demand, and many went on to become leaders and pioneers in areas as diverse as business, law, government, education, medicine, and journalism. Among its most notable graduates were JOHN MITCHELL JR.,

WENDELL P. DABNEY, ROSA BOWSER, MAGGIE LENA WALKER, and SARAH GARLAND BOYD JONES, M.D. Although Randolph attended Richmond Colored Normal, unspecified circumstances necessitated her departure just prior to graduation (*Richmond Times Dispatch*, 1 June 1932).

Randolph began her teaching career in Goochland County around 1890 and received an appointment in 1892 to become the teacher for the old Mountain Road School in Henrico County. The school, located just outside of Richmond was a dilapidated, one-room structure situated on a red clay hill. Undaunted, Randolph began her tenure there with a little over a dozen students and began immediately to recruit students and initiate beautification projects for the school and grounds. With others' help she whitewashed the school and planted vines, flowers, and shrubbery, and with part of her meager earnings purchased gravel to line pathways to the school. Randolph organized Willing Worker Clubs and Patron Improvement Leagues to assist in raising the funds necessary to maintain school improvements. One of her greatest legacies was developing extraordinarily successful interracial coalitions that became models in garnering community support for fostering educational opportunities for blacks. Her patrons were a diverse group that included parents, church organizations, businesses, government officials, and affluent citizens. Their esprit de corps was due in large part to Randolph's humble nature and indefatigable dedication to bettering the entire community. In keeping with the theme of educating the head, heart, and hands, Randolph—a woman who possessed a strong and abiding faith—initiated evening year-round Sunday School. She enlisted the help of her pastor and students from Virginia Union University to carry out the services, and ardent members of her coalition donated hymnals, Bibles, and an organ. In addition to integrating manual labor instruction with an academic curriculum, Randolph sought to educate the community on preventing disease by promoting the values of cleanliness and good hygiene.

Several educational foundations founded from the Reconstruction Era through the early twentieth century greatly fostered the educational opportunities for blacks in the South. One of these, the Negro Rural School Fund, would play a profound role in propelling Randolph's work into prominence. This fund, originally known as the Jeanes Fund, was created by a $1 million endowment by Miss Anna T. Jeanes in 1907. A Quaker philanthropist and Philadelphia resident, Jeanes donated the sum for the sole purpose of "fostering rudimentary education in rural Negro schools" (Jones, p. 18). Jeanes had previously donated $200,000 to the General Education Board in 1905 for the same purpose. Jackson Davis, superintendent of Henrico County schools from 1905 to 1909, had observed the positive impact that extension and vocational education could have upon rural school communities, and as a result wrote to James Dillard, the newly appointed president of the Jeanes Fund. He inquired about funding the salary of one teacher who would travel throughout the county to supplement the work of Negro schools' teachers by initiating an industrial education component to the curriculum. Dr. Dillard and the board reacted favorably, and in October 1908 Davis's choice for the position, Virginia Randolph, became the first countywide Jeanes Supervising Industrial Teacher in the United States. Her salary was set at forty dollars per month. Randolph extended her integration of vocational skills such as basket-making, cooking, and canning to all of the county's black schools. Her total commitment to the community continued, and her patron improvement leagues were set up to assist each school. Her plan of action in integrating vocational education with the academic curriculum in all the county's black schools became known as the Henrico Plan. After completing her first session, Randolph's summary report of activities and improvements for schools under her jurisdiction was so concise and succinct that Dr. Dillard had a thousand copies printed and distributed to county superintendents throughout the South (Dillard, p. 197). The Henrico Plan would go on to serve not only as a blueprint for Jeanes teachers of the South, but for those in several African countries as well.

Randolph was vigilant in marketing both her students' work and needs. When the governor of Virginia proclaimed the state's first Arbor Day, Randolph had her patrons donate twelve sycamore trees that were planted on school grounds and named for the twelve Disciples. She then presided over the state's first known Arbor Day exercises. She exhibited students' handiwork at the Colored Industrial Exchange in Richmond, and sent samples of their work to the Negro Exhibit at the 1907 Jamestown Tercentennial Celebration. Randolph continued to work tirelessly to enhance students' health and educational experiences. To conduct cooking demonstrations at schools, Randolph was known on occasion to dismantle a warm wood stove, transport it to a school, and reassemble it. In 1915 the Virginia Randolph Training School was named in her honor on the grounds of the old Mountain Road School. When adjacent land became available, Randolph again assembled groups and raised the funds needed to purchase the acreage for farm demonstrations. She also boarded dozens of students in her home over the years.

Randolph received many honors for her dedication to education and the community. Among the most notable was the 1926 Harmon Award of first prize for her distinguished achievements in the field of education. This award carried a $400 cash prize and a gold medal. Given by the William E. Harmon Foundation, Harmon Awards acknowledged recipients' work in science, education, literature, and religion. Other 1926 Harmon Award recipients included ARTHUR SCHOMBURG, COUNTEE CULLEN, JAMES WELDON JOHNSON, and C. C. SPAULDING (*Richmond Planet*, 18 Dec. 1926). Randolph was also awarded a certificate of meritorious service from Virginia State College in 1938 for her pioneering achievements in education and her dedication to the black community. In honor of her groundbreaking work as a Jeanes teacher, in 1937 the South's Jeanes teachers organized the Virginia Randolph Fund, which merged later that year with the Peabody, Slater, and Jeanes funds to form the Southern Education Foundation.

After nearly sixty years as an educator and supervisor, Randolph, who never married, retired in the late 1940s. She later died at her home in Richmond on 16 March 1958. The Museum in Memory of Virginia E. Randolph honors her legacy and is listed as a Virginia Historic Landmark and a National Historic Landmark. Her educational philosophy is truly encapsulated in an excerpt from an essay she wrote in the early 1900s: "The world is held back today not so much by bad men as by good men who have stopped growing. The moment one stops his education he begins to lose the power to educate others. Teach the child that he must never stop trying to learn all the good he can [,] for whenever you stop you are standing in the way of progress." Her indomitable spirit, indefatigable dedication, and faith in God and her fellow humans were truly ones for the ages.

FURTHER READING

The Museum in Memory of Virginia E. Randolph houses Randolph's manuscripts, portraits, photographs, correspondence, and personal memorabilia.

Dillard, James H. "Fourteen Years of the Jeanes Fund," *South Atlantic Quarterly* (1923).

Fosdick, Raymond, with Henry Pringle and Katherine Douglas Pringle. *Adventure In Giving: The Story of the General Education Board* (1962).

Jones, Lance G. E. *The Jeanes Teacher in the United States 1908–1933: An Account of Twenty-Five Years' Experience in the Supervision of Negro Rural Schools* (1937).

Richardson, Archie G. *The Development of Negro Education in Virginia 1831–1970* (1976).

Wright, Arthur D. *The Negro Rural School Fund, Inc. (Anna T. Jeanes Foundation), 1907–1933* (1933).

Obituaries: *Richmond Afro American and Richmond Planet*, 22 March 1958; *Richmond Times-Dispatch*, 17 March 1958.

ELVATRICE PARKER BELSCHES

Range, M. Athalie (7 Nov. 1915–14 Nov. 2006), civil rights activist, first African American to serve on the Miami City Commission, and first since Reconstruction to head a state agency, was born Mary Athalie Wilkinson in Key West, Florida, to Edward L. Wilkinson, a cigar factory and loading dock foreman, and Grace Shultz.

Range's family moved to Miami around 1921. She graduated from Booker T. Washington Senior High School in Overtown, a historically black town established when blacks were not allowed to live in segregated Miami. During World War II, she worked picking up trash from railroad cars. In 1937 she married Oscar Range. A certified funeral director, he opened the Range Funeral Home in Miami in 1953. They had four children.

When her husband died of a heart attack in 1960, Athalie Range enrolled in the New England Institute of Anatomy, Sanitary Science and Embalming (Boston, Massachusetts) where she earned her funeral director's certification. She ran the funeral home herself and built a highly successful mortuary business in Liberty City. Range's activism began in 1948 when, as a member of Parent Teacher's Association (PTA) at the Liberty City Elementary School she demanded better facilities for the twelve hundred black students. The school was operating out of temporary classrooms; there were not enough toilets, and no clean drinking water or lunchroom. As president of the PTA,

Athalie M. Range, right, former member of the Miami Board of Commissioners, and Benjamin Hooks, executive director of the NAACP, appear on NBC-TV's *Meet the Press,* broadcast from Washington, 25 May 1980. The two were questioned about the riots in Miami. (AP Images.)

she led a group of over one hundred to the Dade County School Board meeting to demand hot lunches. As a result, the school board arranged for hot lunches, and built a new building.

In 1964, Range became involved in local politics by winning the primary for a seat on the Miami City Commission, but she lost the election by only one thousand votes. She accused her white male opponent of racial scare tactics for her loss (for which he later apologized). Miami Mayor Robert King High, wanting support from the black community, convinced one commissioner to resign, and appointed Range as the first black and second woman member of the commission. She was reelected twice. She negotiated with the city manager to hire the first black motorcycle policeman. In 1967, to protest sporadic pick-up of trash in the black Liberty City section of Miami, Range mobilized residents to bring their bags of trash to the commissioner's desk in protest, resulting in passage of a mandate for twice-a-week pick-up. In 1971, she protested the destruction of Overtown, citing the lack of public transportation planning that resulted in displacing residents in the 1960s.

As a respected community leader, Range delivered a speech on local television after MARTIN LUTHER KING JR. was assassinated in 1968, pleading for calm. In another first for blacks in state government, Florida Governor Reuben Askew appointed her to the cabinet position of secretary of community affairs in 1970. She served until 1973, and helped secure $8 million in state and federal aid for drought-stricken farmers.

President Jimmy Carter nominated Range to the National Railroad Passenger Corporation (AMTRAK) board in 1978, because of her knowledge of and involvement in public transportation issues. She was a member of the executive board of the NAACP. She retired from active political life in the 1990s, but remained active in local organizations. Affectionately known as "Mama" or "Mother" Range, she continued to work with her son Patrick running the funeral home. She chaired a guidance program for first-time youth offenders when a young employee of the funeral home was killed by a mob in 1994, and she worked to get guns off the streets. In 1997 she founded the Athalie Range Cultural Arts Foundation to preserve black history, especially the arts, in the Miami area. She helped save Virginia Key Beach from developers; once the only beach where blacks could swim, the beach was a historic monument to segregation.

Range received three honorary doctorates, from the University of Miami (1984), Florida International University (1998), and St. Thomas University in Miami (2003). In 1997, she was inducted into the Florida Commission on the State of Women's Hall of Fame. In 2007, Miami-Dade College established a scholarship in her name. Many parks, buildings, and a boulevard have been named for her around Miami.

From the humble beginnings of a railroad car cleaner, Range's civil rights activism preceded even those of Dr. Martin Luther King Jr.'s campaigns. She worked to improve schools and parks, provide jobs for the community, and for gun control, and, in her capacity as a mortician, was a very successful businesswoman. She had an impact not just locally, but statewide and nationally. She died of cancer.

FURTHER READING

In 1989, Range was interviewed for "Eyes on the Prize II," archived at Washington University Libraries, Film and Media Archive, Henry Hampton Collection.

Porter, Bruce D. *The Miami Riot of 1980* (1984).

Obituary: *The Miami Herald,* 14 Nov. 2006.

JANE BRODSKY FITZPATRICK

Rangel, Charles (11 June 1930–), member of the U.S. Congress, was born in Harlem, New York, the second of three children of Ralph Rangel and Blanche Wharton. When Rangel was still young, his father abandoned them; his mother worked in New York's garment industry and occasionally did housecleaning to support them. She was active in the International Ladies 'Garment Workers' Union and in Harlem's civic life. In 1948 Rangel joined the army, serving until 1952; he earned a Purple Heart and a Bronze Star for his service during the Korean War. Discharged as a staff sergeant, Rangel attended New York University on the G.I. Bill and in 1957 earned a B.A. in Business Administration. In 1960 he earned a law degree from St. John's University Law School, Brooklyn, and began the practice of law in Harlem, where he also joined the local Democratic Party club. Rangel subsequently worked in a variety of legal positions, including legal assistant to the New York district attorney, counsel to the New York City Housing and Redevelopment Board, and assistant U.S. attorney. In 1964 he married Alma Carter, a social worker, and together they had two children.

In 1966 Rangel's involvement in Harlem Democratic Party politics paid off, when he was elected to the New York State General Assembly. Rangel's rise in Harlem politics was promoted by the legendary J. Raymond Jones, the first

African American chair of the New York County (Manhattan) Democratic Party Committee. Four years later Rangel defeated another legend in Harlem politics—ADAM CLAYTON POWELL JR.—and was elected to the House of Representatives. Powell, the pastor of one of Harlem's most influential churches and the first African American elected to the U.S. Congress from New York, for years had been the best-known and most influential black politician in the United States. However, despite his iconic status in Harlem and among African Americans in general, by 1970 he was vulnerable—in 1967 he had been expelled from Congress, and though he was reelected in 1968, his power was greatly diminished. In addition, because of an outstanding civil warrant, Powell could visit Harlem only on Sundays. Rangel seized the opportunity to challenge him, narrowly defeating him in the four-person Democratic primary election. Winning by a mere 150 votes and one percentage point, Rangel was successful mainly as a result of white votes. In a development unrelated to the election, a largely white section of the Upper West Side of Manhattan had been added to Powell's district. Rangel won in these white areas by fifteen hundred votes. However, like most incumbent members of the House, once elected Rangel was easily returned to office, often running unopposed or winning by margins of victory of 80 percent or more against little-known opponents. The only serious challenge to his reelection occurred in 1994, when Adam Clayton Powell IV, a city councilman and the son of the former congressman, ran against him. Fearing the allure of the Powell name, Rangel raised nearly a million and a half dollars and easily defeated the young Powell.

Rangel came to the House the year several new black members were elected, including Bill Clay of Missouri, LOUIS STOKES of Ohio, and SHIRLEY CHISHOLM of New York, increasing the size of the black congressional delegation from six to thirteen. Younger and more activist than their senior colleagues, Rangel and these new members decided to form the Congressional Black Caucus. Many white and several of the senior black members of the House, including ROBERT C. NIX of Pennsylvania and AUGUSTUS HAWKINS of California, opposed the formation of the caucus, arguing that it was inappropriate for members of Congress to organize on the basis of race. But influenced by the ascendant Black Power philosophy, which called on blacks to establish racially separate organizations, Rangel and his colleagues argued that a caucus of blacks was necessary to advance the interest of blacks in the House, getting good committee assignments, for example, and nationally, through the development and articulation of a black legislative agenda. In 1974 Rangel was elected chair of the caucus, becoming its third chair after Congressmen CHARLES DIGGS and Louis Stokes.

In his first term Rangel was assigned to two relatively minor committees—Public Works and Science and Aeronautics—whose jurisdictions had little to do with issues of concern to Harlem or blacks. However, in his second term he was assigned to the Judiciary Committee, which has jurisdiction over civil rights legislation, and to the Committee on the District of Columbia, which oversees the largely black city of Washington, D.C. Rangel was on the Judiciary Committee in 1974 when, in nationally televised proceedings, it considered articles of impeachment against President Richard Nixon. He spoke and voted in favor of each of the three articles charging Nixon with "high crimes and misdemeanors" that merited impeachment. Nixon resigned shortly after the committee approved the articles. In 1986 Rangel was appointed to the Ways and Means Committee, the oldest, most prestigious, and most powerful House committee, with jurisdiction over taxes, international trade, Social Security, Medicare and Medicaid, and welfare. In 1995 Rangel, the first African American to serve on the committee, became the committee's ranking Democrat, meaning that he would become its first African American chair if the Democrats were to win a majority of House seats. Reflecting the concerns of his district specifically and, to some extent, the concerns of blacks nationwide, Rangel also served on the Select Committee on Crime and the Select Committee on Narcotics Abuse, chairing the latter from 1983 until it was abolished in 1993. More so than many big-city ghettos, Harlem had been plagued by problems of crime and drug trafficking. Rangel used his position of leadership on the Narcotics Committee to press for policies to interdict the flow of drugs into the country and to spend money on rehabilitation as well as incarceration. However, Rangel's position on narcotics generally has been relatively conservative. For example, he opposed the legalization of marijuana and other drugs and the provision of free needles to addicts to combat AIDS.

Rangel has several important legislative accomplishments to his credit. He was a principal author of federal empowerment zone legislation (1993) and the Targeted Jobs Tax Credit (1978), both designed to attract jobs to low-income areas like Harlem. He also sponsored the Low Income Housing Tax Credit

Charles B. Rangel chairs the House Committee hearing on Narcotics And Drug Abuse on Capitol Hill in Washington, 10 Dec. 1976. (AP Images.)

(1986) to encourage home ownership among the poor. And he was a principal author of the Africa Growth and Opportunity Act, legislation designed to encourage trade between the United States and African nations.

At the beginning of the twenty-first century, after more than thirty years in the House, Rangel was one of its most influential and widely respected members. He was also a leading player in national Democratic Party politics and a broker in New York City and New York State politics, successfully maneuvering in 2002 to obtain the Democratic Party nomination for governor for CARL MCCALL, an African American. He encouraged and helped Hillary Clinton, the wife of the former president, win a seat in the U.S. Senate, representing New York. He was also instrumental in persuading President Bill Clinton to locate his post-presidential office in Harlem. In 2003, as the United States approached war with Iraq, Rangel introduced legislation to reinstate the military draft, arguing that all social classes, rather than mainly the lower-middle class and the poor, should be represented in the military.

Like his predecessor, Rangel managed to project his representation of Harlem onto a national platform, where he has been recognized as one of the highest ranking and most influential black elected officials in the United States.

Democratic victories in the Congressional midterm elections of 2006 demonstrated the nation's dissatisfaction with George W. Bush's foreign and domestic policies, and finally enabled Rangel to become the first African American chair of the powerful House Committee on Ways and Means. Rangel chaired the committee until the 2010 midterm elections, when the Republicans took back the House. Rangel's powers as Committee chair were more limited that he might have hoped, however. He continued to face a Republican president for the first two years of his tenure, and in 2008, before the election of Democrat BARACK OBAMA, Rangel faced an ethics probe related to improper use of his office to raise money for the Rangel Center at the City College of New York. Under pressure from colleagues and the White House as well as from Republicans, Rangel stepped aside as Ways and

Means Chair in March 2010. Shortly after the 2010 midterm elections—in which Rangel was returned with 80 percent of the vote—the House Ethics Committee found him guilty on 11 counts, including failing to report rental income; improper use of a rent-stabilized apartment; and soliciting charitable donations from people with business before Congress. In December 2010, Rangel faced an official censure from the House, becoming the first Congressman to receive that condemnation since 1983, and only third since the Committee's founding in 1966. In 2007 Rangel published an autobiography, *And I Haven't Had a Bad Day Since: From the Streets of Harlem to the Halls of Congress*. In 2012 Rangel was re-elected to Congress with 91 percent of the vote in New York's 13th Congressional district.

FURTHER READING

Clay, Bill. *Just Permanent Interests: Black Americans in Congress, 1870–1991* (1992).

Jacobson, Mark. "Charlie Rangel: Chairman of the Money," *New York* (15 Jan. 2007).

Swain, Carol. *Black Faces, Black Interests: The Representation of African Americans in Congress* (1993).

ROBERT C. SMITH

Ranger, Joseph (1760?–?), Revolutionary War seaman, was born probably in Northumberland County, Virginia, to parents whose names are unknown. It is not known whether Ranger was a free black or a runaway slave. He probably worked as a seaman in Northumberland County and Elizabeth City County before the Revolutionary War. In the early eighteenth century Virginia's waters were sailed extensively by free blacks and slaves, who also worked in the colony's two shipyards. Despite long-standing concern among the elite in the South about arming even free blacks for fear of inciting slave revolts, the maritime experiences of Virginia's blacks made them prime candidates for enlistment in the state navy, just as many black seamen served in the Continental navy.

Ranger enlisted in the Virginia navy in 1776, one of many blacks who served on racially mixed naval crews. Ranger served in the Virginia navy for eleven years, the longest recorded term of service of any black sailor. The Virginia navy was composed of a motley assortment of forty vessels, from barges to ships, which were designed to support the cobbled-together navy created by the Continental Congress in 1775 and to protect the exposed Virginia coastline from British invasion. Ranger's home county

of Northumberland provided at least six black seamen to Virginia's navy.

It was usual for sailors to transfer frequently between ships, and Ranger served aboard four naval vessels, the largest recorded total number of any black sailor. Ranger first served for three months aboard the ship *Hero*, one of the ships with the largest number of black crew members. For the next four years he served aboard *Dragon* as one of five blacks in a crew of 104. Aboard *Dragon*, Ranger and the other black crew members were recorded as receiving full rations of pork, flour, and liquor.

After *Dragon* was converted into a fireship in 1780, Ranger transferred to *Jefferson*, where he served for one year, until it was blown up by the British as it sailed on the James River. After the explosion Ranger was assigned to serve aboard *Patriot*, which he did for approximately six months. Shortly before Lord Cornwallis surrendered to George Washington at Yorktown, Virginia, on 19 October 1781, Ranger was taken prisoner by the British along with the rest of *Patriot*'s crew. He was probably released soon after the surrender.

The British naval threat to Virginia did not end with the formal cessation of Revolutionary War hostilities, and the Continental Congress granted Virginia the right to maintain two armed ships, *Liberty* and *Patriot*, after the war ended. Ranger served aboard both of these ships until Virginia's navy was finally disassembled in 1787.

Ranger had been paid for his service in the navy. He was recorded in the Virginia State Auditors' records as having received two pounds, ten shillings, for one month's service in 1786 and five pounds, seven shillings, for two months' service in 1787. Not much is known of Ranger's life or of how he earned a living after the disassembly of the Virginia navy, but he may have continued to work as a sailor.

Within a few years after the end of the Revolutionary War, Ranger received a land grant from the state of Virginia as a reward for his military service. His grant of one hundred acres, located in Virginia's western Kentucky and Ohio territories, represented the usual grant received by Virginia's African American privates. Ranger probably never occupied his land; more likely he sold it to one of many land speculators who bought up soldiers' bounties for a fraction of their worth.

In addition to his land grant from the state of Virginia, Ranger also qualified for a federal Revolutionary War pension under the congressional acts of 1818, 1820, and 1832. At least twenty-one African Americans in Virginia qualified for veterans' pensions. Ranger received ninety-six dollars a year after he swore out a deposition in a local Virginia court attesting to his wartime naval service.

It is unknown when and where Joseph Ranger died. His Revolutionary War service in the Virginia navy exemplifies the importance of African Americans to American military forces, even in states such as Virginia that had extremely restrictive slave systems. Ranger's long maritime service shows how African Americans were able to capitalize on their seafaring experience to gain economic status and even freedom. Ranger, like other African American sailors, was rewarded by his state and his country for his patriotic service.

FURTHER READING

Jackson, L. P. "Virginia Negro Soldiers and Seamen in the American Revolution," *Journal of Negro History* 27 (1942).

Lanning, Michael Lee. *Defenders of Liberty: African Americans in the Revolutionary War* (2002).

Wright, Donald R. *African Americans in the Colonial Era: From African Origins through the American Revolution* (1990, 2000).

This entry is taken from the *American National Biography* and is published here with the permission of the American Council of Learned Societies.

SARAH J. PURCELL

Ransier, Alonzo Jacob (3 Jan. 1834–17 Aug. 1882), Reconstruction politician and U.S. congressman, was born in Charleston, South Carolina, to free parents, whose names are unknown. Contemporary accounts describe his education as "limited." In the 1850s he secured a position as a shipping clerk with a prominent commercial firm in Charleston. In 1856 he married Louisa Ann Carroll, and they were the parents of eleven children. Carroll died in 1875, and Ransier married Mary Louisa McKinlay in 1876.

Ransier was a leading figure in Reconstruction and Republican politics in South Carolina. He participated in the 1865 Colored Peoples' Convention in Charleston that urged the state's white leaders to enfranchise black men and abolish the black code, a series of measures designed to limit the rights of black people and to confine them to menial and agricultural labor. In 1867 Congress passed a series of Reconstruction laws that provided for the reorganization of the southern states, the enfranchisement of black men, and the disenfranchisement of southerners who had supported the Confederacy. Ransier subsequently represented Charleston in the 1868 constitutional convention. He served as vice president of the State Republican Executive Committee and then as president from 1868 to 1872, following the assassination of BENJAMIN FRANKLIN RANDOLPH. Ransier was elected to the state house of representatives in 1868 and was Charleston County auditor from 1868 to 1870. In the state house in 1870 he sponsored a measure that, while not explicitly guaranteeing civil rights for blacks, provided blacks with the same legal right to pursue judicial remedies that was available to whites. Ransier was also a director and secretary of the Enterprise Railroad Company, a corporation organized in 1870 by black political leaders to operate a horse-drawn streetcar line to haul freight between the South Carolina Railroad terminal and the Cooper River wharves. The company did not survive as a black-owned business, and by 1873 a group of white businessmen led by S. S. Solomon had taken over the railroad. Ransier joined with several other black political leaders, including Benjamin A. Boseman, ROBERT SMALLS, ROBERT BROWN ELLIOTT, and BEVERLY NASH, in forming the South Carolina Phosphate & Phosphatic River & Mining Company.

Described in 1870 by the *Charleston News and Courier* as exercising "considerable influence," Ransier reached the pinnacle of his political power in the early 1870s. In 1870 he was elected as South Carolina's first black lieutenant governor on a ticket headed by incumbent Robert K. Scott. In 1872 he was elected to represent South Carolina's Second District in the Forty-third Congress, from 1873 to 1875. From 1875 to 1877 he was the collector for the Internal Revenue Service for South Carolina's Second District.

Though Ransier was often regarded as timid and reticent, he was frequently willing to take a bold stand on controversial issues. He joined the black delegate WILLIAM WHIPPER in speaking out strongly in the constitutional convention in opposition to legalizing the collection of debts incurred in the purchase of slaves prior to the Civil War. In doing so, Ransier and Whipper opposed three formidable black leaders, FRANCIS LOUIS CARDOZO, JOSEPH HAYNE RAINEY, and William McKinlay, who favored payment. Ransier also joined two other Charleston black leaders, RICHARD HARVEY CAIN and ROBERT CARLOS DELARGE, in opposing a literacy requirement for voting, which was easily defeated. Ransier consistently supported women's suffrage and attended an 1870 women's suffrage convention in Columbia. He urged rigid safeguards to protect black voting rights, insisting that voting "is our chief means for self-defense." He opposed

Alonzo J. Ransier, South Carolina's first black lieutenant governor, c. 1865. (Library of Congress/Brady-Handy Photograph Collection.)

segregation in public education so strongly that he abstained from voting on the 1875 Civil Rights Bill in Congress because provisions prohibiting discrimination in education had been deleted from the measure.

Ransier was deeply involved in the struggles of the Republican Party. In 1872 as a delegate to the Republican National Convention and to a black convention in New Orleans, Ransier supported Ulysses S. Grant for reelection and would not join reformers who backed Horace Greeley. As a member of the "Charleston Ring"—one of the factions that thrived in a divided Republican Party in Charleston—Ransier attacked fellow Republicans for their inept leadership of the public schools. In 1871 Ransier cited the bitter conflicts over patronage among Republicans as the cause of the Democratic victory in the municipal election. Yet he was willing to embrace patronage in 1876 when his tenure as Internal Revenue Service collector was about to expire. He pleaded with Governor Daniel Chamberlain for help in securing nomination to office: "I have a large family and no means for their support and would be greatly obliged if my friends will take me into consideration in connection with such a position on the state ticket as they may think me qualified for." He was not nominated, and by 1879 he was reduced to working as a night watchman at the Charleston Customs House for $1.50 per day. He was later employed at the Pacific Guano works and as a street laborer. When he died in obscurity in Charleston, the *News and Courier* did not note his passing.

Though he was one of South Carolina's prominent political figures by the early 1870s, Alonzo Ransier's influence and reputation faded quickly. Having served as a party leader, lieutenant governor, and congressman, he was not able to sustain that leadership until Reconstruction's end in 1877 when white South Carolinians regained political power.

FURTHER READING

Christopher, Maurine. *America's Black Congressmen* (1971).

Holt, Thomas. *Black over White: Negro Political Leadership in South Carolina during Reconstruction* (1977).

Williamson, Joel. *After Slavery: The Negro in South Carolina during Reconstruction, 1861–1877* (1965).

This entry is taken from the *American National Biography* and is published here with the permission of the American Council of Learned Societies.

WILLIAM C. HINE

Ransom, Emma Sarah Connor (?1864–15 May 1943), clubwoman, and civic leader, was born to Jackson and Deatlie Connor (or Conner), former slaves. The Connors moved their ten children to Selma, Ohio, where Emma attended school. Details of her early life are sketchy, but as a young adult, Emma Connor worked as a teacher and was active in the local African Methodist Episcopal (AME) Church. In 1886 Emma met REVERDY CASSIUS RANSOM, a senior at Wilberforce University, when he was appointed student pastor at the Selma church. He and Emma were married in Selma on 27 October 1887, and she joined him in Altoona, Pennsylvania, where he was assigned a pastorate. The following year, their infant son died a few hours after he was born. A second son, named for his father, was born 2 September 1889. Reverend Ransom's son from a first marriage, Harold, moved in with them after Reverdy Jr.'s birth so Emma raised two boys while working alongside her husband in church and community activities.

Following the AME General Conference in 1890 the Ransoms were sent to Springfield, Ohio, for three years, then to Cleveland for three years. From 1890 to 1896 Emma Ransom helped her husband's congregations in Ohio evolve into dynamic churches that attended to the holistic needs of the community. In 1893 family moved to Cleveland, where Ransom organized a Sunday school for neighborhood children, established a kindergarten to care for children of black domestics, and organized a Queen Esther's Guild of young women that met for etiquette training and intellectual improvement. She also founded the Tawawa Literary Society that brought notables such as PAUL LAURENCE DUNBAR and IDA B. WELLS-BARNETT to the St. John AME congregation that Reverdy Ransom pastured at the Reverdy Ransom Church.

During this time, Emma Ransom began to acquire a global perspective as she and another pastor's wife, Lida A. Lowry, co-published a magazine called *Women's Light and Love*, which highlighted the economic and social needs of African Americans who had migrated from the South as well as the needs of people in Africa. Ransom became more actively involved in the missionary movement when the Third District Women's Parent Mite Missionary Society (WPMMS), the major women's organization within the AME Church, convened at St. John in July 1894 and she began to envision its potential for evangelization and social change. She founded local missionary societies at three other churches and organized the Ohio Conference Branch Missionary Society. An effective advocate of a broadened role for women in the church and community, Emma Ransom also encouraged her husband to organize and consecrate the first Board of Deaconesses—an organized group of women who helped with sacramental acts (such as baptism and communion) and charitable work—in the AME church during his tenure in Cleveland.

In 1896, when Reverdy Ransom became pastor of Bethel Church in Chicago, Emma Ransom organized and became president of the Women's Parent Mite Missionary Society at Bethel. She led the society to develop outreach projects to assist poor families in the Chicago community and set a new standard for mission fundraising. In 1898, Ransom's organizational skills were extended regionally as she became first vice president of the Women's Mite Missionary Society for the Iowa Conference of-the AME Church. Her resourcefulness and creativity reached a new height in July 1900 when Reverdy Ransom was released from Bethel AME Church to establish the Institutional Church and Social Settlement, an urban mission in Chicago

that provided spiritual, economic, and educational services and social support to community residents and transients.

The Ransoms' unshakeable faith and ingenuity enabled them to secure funds from leading philanthropists to refurbish and maintain the large building on Dearborn Street that he persuaded the AME Church to purchase. Contributions and proceeds from benefits helped to establish programs and services. Emma Ransom organized a free kindergarten that was attended by sixty-two children. She also helped oversee the other activities at Institutional Church, including an employment bureau; a nursery and day care center; a penny savings bank for children; a Sunday school; a department of instrumental music; a department of vocal music; a "kitchengarten" which taught scientific housekeeping and homemaking; a girls club; a boys club; and a gymnasium that opened two days a week for women and two days for men.

The Ransoms spent the next three years, 1904 to 1907, in New England, where Reverend Ransom received a new pastorate and pastored churches in New Bedford and Boston. The Ransoms left Boston for New York City in July 1907 when Reverdy Ransom assumed the pastorate of the 2,500-member Bethel Church. In New York, Emma Ransom worked with young people and the missionary society at Bethel; however, her emphasis shifted during their tenure in America's most diverse metropolis. She attained prominence in activists' circles and became a leader in the YWCA when the Colored YWCA on Fifty-third Street asked her to chair its board of management. Along with Cecelia Cabaniss Saunders, and Virginia Scott, Ransom shaped the Harlem YWCA into an institution that contributed mightily to the social and moral uplift of the black community.

In 1932 the Ransoms returned to Wilberforce, where Reverdy Ransom served as Bishop of the Third Episcopal District of the AME Church. Emma Ransom died at her home in Wilberforce, Ohio. Unlike countless spouses of pastors whose contributions are unrecorded and unacknowledged, Bishop Ransom, his ministerial contemporaries, and his biographers all identify Emma Ransom as the bishop's partner in ministry, as well as a leader of women's organizations. Calvin Morris wrote, "The success accompanying Ransom's ministry came in large measure as the result of the loyal support and work of his second wife. They were a team during the early years of his career" (113).

Emma Ransom's work with the missionary society and the periodical catapulted her into the national limelight and established a formal structure through which many women gained voice and influence in the AME church. She effectively used her considerable intellect and influence to promote her belief that both women and men were called to Christian service. Emma's work in New York City was so significant that in 1926 the Harlem YWCA named its residence hall the Emma Ransom House in her honor. Most assuredly, Emma Ransom was an inspiration to countless women whose lives intersected with hers.

FURTHER READING

Selected Ransom family documents and may be found at the Wilberforce University Library in Wilberforce, Ohio.

Gomez-Jackson, Annetta L. *The Sage of Tawawa: Reverdy Cassius Ransom, 1861–1959* (2002).

Morris, Calvin S. *Reverdy C. Ransom: Black Advocate of the Social Gospel* (1990).

Ransom, Reverdy C. *The Pilgrimage of Harriet Ransom's Son* (1950).

Weisenfeld, Judith. *African American Women and Christian Activism: New York's Black YWCA, 1905–1945* (1997).

ARTHUREE MCLAUGHLIN WRIGHT

Ransom, Leon Andrew (6 Aug. 1899–25 Aug. 1954), lawyer and educator, was born in Zanesville, Ohio, the son of Charles Andrew Ransom, a janitor who later ran a stable, and Nora Belle Lee. He attended Ohio State University for a year from 1917 to 1918, joined the army during World War I in 1918, and graduated from Wilberforce University in Ohio in 1920. After five years, from 1920 to 1925, working as a dining car waiter and in real estate in Chicago, where he served as assistant executive secretary of the Spring Street Branch of the YMCA, he decided to go to law school. His widow later recounted that he became a lawyer as "a form of protest" against the racial discrimination he saw all around him in Chicago. He earned a law degree with honors at Ohio State University in 1927. In 1924 he married Willa C. Carter; they had two children. Ransom was a practicing African Methodist Episcopalian. In politics he was an active Republican and then an Independent. "Andy" Ransom's easygoing demeanor belied his solemn commitment to racial progress.

After practicing law in Columbus, Ohio, from 1927 to 1931, Ransom moved to Washington, D.C. There he taught law at Howard University Law School as an instructor from 1931 to 1933 and then as an assistant professor from 1933 to 1934. After spending time away studying toward an advanced degree in law at Harvard University—he earned an SJD in 1935, two years after his colleague WILLIAM HENRY HASTIE—he returned to Howard, working as an associate professor from 1935 to 1939 and then as a professor from 1939 to 1946. During those years he worked with CHARLES HAMILTON HOUSTON and Hastie to make the Howard University Law School a training ground for African American civil rights lawyers and an arena for formulating successful strategies to win civil rights victories in the courts. A member of the Washington Bar Association, the National Bar Association, and the National Lawyers Guild, Ransom served on the National Legal Committee of the National Association for the Advancement of Colored People (NAACP) beginning in 1936. From 1941 to 1946 he served as assistant editor of the *Journal of Negro Education*, which was published at Howard, and he wrote a regular section called "Negroes and the Law."

Ransom played various roles in a number of civil rights cases. As early as 1933 he went to Leesburg, Virginia, as cocounsel with Houston to mount a defense of a black man, George Crawford, against charges of murdering a wealthy white woman and her white housekeeper. Nobody in the area, black or white, had ever before seen a black attorney, and Ransom and Houston caused a sensation as they demonstrated their mastery of the craft. While the jurors were all white, not all witnesses were, and the defense insisted on addressing black witnesses as "Mr." and "Mrs." The judge found himself incapable of so addressing the lawyers, but he settled on an alternative and addressed them as "Doctor Houston" and "Doctor Ransom." Though they learned, to their surprise, that Crawford was in fact guilty, upon his conviction he was given a life sentence instead of being executed. Just as Ransom's appointment at Howard University reflected Dean Houston's shift in the early 1930s to law faculty who were both full-time and African American, the Crawford trial reflected the NAACP's shift to all-black counsel in many important cases.

Over the years Ransom participated in many cases and argued a number in the courts. Some of those cases, in Maryland and Virginia, challenged racially discriminatory teachers' salary schedules in the "separate but equal" era. Others, in Tennessee and Missouri, challenged the exclusion of black students from public institutions of higher education. Ransom argued a case, *Chambers v. Florida*, in 1940 before the Supreme Court that led to a unanimous decision against coerced confessions.

In 1942 in Tennessee, where Ransom was arguing a case about the exclusion of blacks from juries, he was struck by a deputy sheriff who took exception to the kinds of litigation he and his colleagues were bringing. In April 1946 Ransom participated in a significant meeting in Atlanta, Georgia, to plan the course of litigation challenging segregation in higher education.

During and after World War II, while Hastie, the law school dean, was away on various assignments for the U.S. government, Ransom served as acting dean. When the U.S. Senate confirmed President Harry S. Truman's nomination of Hastie as governor of the Virgin Islands in 1946, Ransom aspired to be appointed permanent dean but was thwarted when the board of trustees appointed George M. Johnson to the post. The decision has been explained in terms of the politics of the post, but some people at the time whispered of Ransom's declining mental stability.

Bitterly disappointed, Ransom resigned immediately from Howard and returned to private practice. From 1946 to 1949 he served as chair of the Committee for Racial Democracy in the Nation's capital. In 1948 the Grand Chapter of Kappa Alpha Psi awarded him the Laurel Wreath for distinguished public service. He continued to live in Washington, D.C., but faded from view over the next few years. He died on vacation in Point Pleasant, New Jersey, of a cerebral vascular hemorrhage.

FURTHER READING

McNeil, Genna Rae. *Groundwork: Charles Hamilton Houston and the Struggle for Civil Rights* (1983).

Tushnet, Mark V. *Making Civil Rights Law: Thurgood Marshall and the Supreme Court, 1936–1961* (1994).

Ware, Gilbert. *William Hastie: Grace under Pressure* (1984).

Obituaries: *Washington Post*, 27 Aug. 1954; *Richmond Afro American*, 4 Sept. 1954.

This entry is taken from the *American National Biography* and is published here with the permission of the American Council of Learned Societies.

PETER WALLENSTEIN

Ransom, Reverdy Cassius (4 Jan. 1861–22 Apr. 1959), African Methodist Episcopal (AME) bishop and civil rights leader, was born in Flushing, Ohio, the son of Harriet Johnson, a domestic worker. He never knew the identity of his father. In 1865 his mother married George Ransom, gave her son Ransom's surname, and moved to Washington, Ohio. There Reverdy

began school in the local AME Church. At eight, Ransom moved with his family to Cambridge, Ohio, where he attended school with African American youth. In addition to his formal schooling, Ransom worked in a local bank and was tutored by family members of his mother's white employers. In 1881 Ransom married Leanna Watkins of Cambridge, Ohio, and entered Wilberforce University. He transferred to Oberlin College at the end of his first year, but when he challenged racial discrimination at the liberal white institution, he lost his scholarship. He returned to Wilberforce in 1883 and graduated in 1886. Despite the birth of a son, he and his first wife divorced that same year.

Licensed to preach in the AME Church in 1883, Ransom was ordained a deacon in 1886 and an elder in 1888. He married Emma Sarah Conner of Salem, Ohio, in 1886. They became the parents of one son. From 1886 to 1888 Ransom served small AME congregations in Altoona and Hollidaysburg, Pennsylvania, and from 1888 to 1890 he pastored a church in Allegheny City, Pennsylvania. Ransom then moved to Ohio, serving at North Street AME Church in Springfield from 1890 to 1893 and at St. John's AME Church in Cleveland from 1893 to 1896. In 1896 Ransom moved to Chicago, where he served as pastor of Bethel AME Church from 1896 to 1900. At Bethel he organized a men's Sunday club for the discussion of cultural, moral, and social issues. As early as 1899 Ransom ardently disagreed with BOOKER T. WASHINGTON's accommodationist approach to race relations and the Tuskegeean's forceful determination to control the Afro-American Council.

As Ransom observed the needs of black migrants from the South, he bristled at the constraints of a traditional congregation. Influenced by the work of Jane Addams at Hull House, he left Bethel in 1900 to organize the Institutional Church and Social Settlement. The building included a large auditorium, a kitchen, a dining room, a gymnasium, and eight other rooms for a nursery, a kindergarten, and boys' and girls' club meetings. It offered concerts, an employment bureau, lecture series, a print shop, and classes in cooking, music, and sewing. A year later, when Ransom attacked the policy rackets in Chicago, the building was bombed. Yet his social ministry at the Institutional Church and Social Settlement survived for another three years.

In 1904 Ransom moved to AME congregations in New Bedford and Boston, Massachusetts. As pastor of Boston's Charles Street AME Church, he paid tribute to the spirit of the abolitionists and joined

W. E. B. DuBois's Niagara Movement to demand social justice for African Americans. In 1906 Ransom addressed the movement's annual meeting at Harpers Ferry, West Virginia, speaking on "The Spirit of John Brown." Ransom moved to New York's Bethel AME Church in 1907. While there, he helped to organize the National Association for the Advancement of Colored People. In 1912 Ransom was elected editor of the *A.M.E. Church Review*, the denomination's literary and theological journal. For twelve years he directed the publication of articles on a wide range of issues. At heart, however, Ransom was a pastor on a social mission, and consequently he in 1913 established a mission to black Manhattan, the Church of Simon of Cyrene, which ministered to destitute African Americans in New York's "Black Tenderloin." In 1918 the United Civic League of New York sought to place Ransom's name on the ballot as a candidate for Congress from Manhattan's Twenty-first District. Dropped from the ballot because of a discrepancy in his filing petition, Ransom lost an uphill battle as a write-in candidate.

Ransom had represented the AME Church at conferences of world Methodism in London (1901 and 1921) and Toronto (1911), and in 1924, at the age of sixty-three, he was already an elder statesman in the AME denomination when he was elected one of its bishops. It is unclear what role his early divorce and rumors of his alcoholism, which were circulated by Booker T. Washington's associates and conservatives within his denomination, may have played in delaying Ransom's elevation to the episcopacy. As a bishop, however, he made his home at Wilberforce University and served as president of the board of trustees from 1932 to 1948. In 1934 Ransom helped organize the Fraternal Council of Negro Churches and was elected its first president. He was the first African American to serve as a commissioner of Ohio's Board of Pardon and Parole, a position he held from 1936 to 1940, and in 1941 President Franklin D. Roosevelt appointed Ransom a member of the Volunteer Participation Committee in the Office of Civil Defense. After his wife of fifty-five years died in 1941, Ransom married Georgia Myrtle Teal Hayes of Wilberforce in 1943. A graduate of Cheyney Training School (later Cheyney State University) and Cornell University, she was dean of women at Wilberforce from 1934 to 1943 and an officer of the AME Missionary Society from 1943 to 1956. In 1952 Ransom retired from the active episcopacy. He died at his home, "Tawawa Chimney Corner," at Wilberforce.

Ransom was his era's foremost advocate of the social gospel in the African American community. He developed institutional church models for urban black communities and was an important radical ally of DuBois in the struggles with Booker T. Washington that led to the founding of the NAACP. Later, as a bishop and elder statesman in his denomination, Ransom also made advances in African American ecumenism.

FURTHER READING
The papers of Reverdy Cassius Ransom are in collections at Wilberforce University and at Payne Theological Seminary near Xenia, Ohio.
Ransom, Reverdy Cassius. *The Pilgrimage of Harriet Ransom's Son* (1949).
Luker, Ralph E. *The Social Gospel in Black and White: American Racial Reform, 1885–1912* (1991).
Morris, Calvin S. *Reverdy C. Ransom: Black Advocate of the Social Gospel* (1990).
Wills, David. "Reverdy C. Ransom: The Making of an A.M.E. Bishop," in *Black Apostles: Afro-American Clergy Confront the Twentieth Century*, ed. Randall K. Burkett and Richard Newman (1978).
Wright, Richard R. *The Bishops of the African Methodist Episcopal Church* (1963).
This entry is taken from the *American National Biography* and is published here with the permission of the American Council of Learned Societies.

RALPH E. LUKER

Rapier, James Thomas (13 Nov. 1837–31 May 1883), member of Congress, was born of free parents in Florence, Alabama, the son of John H. Rapier, a barber, and Susan (maiden name unknown). As a youngster he was sent to live with his father's mother, Sally Thomas, and his father's half-brother after whom Rapier was named, James Thomas, and to attend school in Nashville, Tennessee. Sally and James Thomas, although legally slaves, hired their own time and lived autonomous lives. Young Rapier thrived under their care and learned to read and write.

At the age of nineteen Rapier was sent by his father to Buxton, Canada West, an all-black settlement, to continue his education. At a school founded by the Presbyterian minister William King, he studied Latin, Greek, mathematics, and the Bible. He also underwent a religious conversion and later taught school in the settlement. "My coming to Canada is worth all the world to me," he wrote in 1862. "I have a tolerable good education and I am at peace with my Savior."

Returning to the South in 1864, he went to Nashville, and later to Maury County, Tennessee. In 1865 he entered the political arena by delivering a keynote address at the Tennessee Negro Suffrage Convention in Nashville. When former Confederates returned to power during Tennessee's first postwar elections in 1865–1866, Rapier returned home to Florence. With the assistance of his father he rented a farm on Seven Mile Island in the Tennessee River, hired black tenant farmers, and raised a cotton crop.

Following the passage of the Congressional Reconstruction Acts in 1867, which enfranchised freedmen and provided for new state governments in the South, Rapier again turned to politics. He won a seat at Alabama's first Republican convention in Montgomery and helped draft the new party platform calling for free speech, free press, and free schools. But he knew the fragility of the new coalition of blacks and pro-Union whites and asked fellow Republicans to proceed with "calmness, moderation and intelligence." In November 1867 Rapier attended the Alabama Constitutional Convention, supporting a civil rights plank and a moderate franchise clause that would exclude from the vote only those disfranchised by acts of Congress.

Despite his advocacy of moderation, however, during the tumultuous months preceding the 1868 presidential election, Rapier was driven from his home in Lauderdale County by the Ku Klux Klan. Barely escaping with his life (several fellow blacks were hanged from a bridge near Florence), he fled to Montgomery, where he spent almost a year in seclusion. In 1869 he attended the National Negro Labor Union convention in Washington, D.C. (he also attended two subsequent conventions), and in 1871 he founded the Alabama Negro Labor Union in an effort to improve working conditions for laborers and tenant farmers.

In 1870 Rapier became his party's nominee for secretary of state. Despite a vigorous campaign and publishing a newspaper, the *Republican Sentinel*, he went down to defeat largely because of violence and opposition from white Republicans to any black candidate. But at the national level, as a reward for his party loyalty, he was appointed assessor of internal revenue for the Montgomery district in 1871, the first black to attain such a high patronage position in the state.

Using his Montgomery office, in the heart of the Black Belt, he mounted a campaign for the Second District congressional seat, received the nomination, and during a period of calm following the passage of the Enforcement Acts, which provided for federal suppression of the KKK, defeated the popular one-armed Confederate veteran William Oates by a vote of nineteen thousand to sixteen thousand. Before taking his seat in Congress he represented Alabama at the Fifth International Exhibition in Vienna, Austria, reporting on the state's exhibits. During his congressional term (1873–1875), Rapier pushed through a bill to make Montgomery a port of delivery, making federal funds available to assist in dredging the Alabama River as far inland as Montgomery. He also supported legislation to improve education in the South, arguing that federal funds be used to support public schools, and spoke on behalf of Charles Sumner's civil rights bill, which became law in 1875.

Seeking a second term Rapier launched a campaign in 1874, but renewed violence, intimidation, and voter fraud led to his defeat. Two years later, in the newly gerrymandered Fourth Congressional District, which included Lowndes County where Rapier rented several cotton plantations, he tried again, but fraud and the entry of JEREMIAH HARALSON, a black man from Selma, into the 1876 race resulted in a second defeat. The differences between himself and Haralson were hard to pinpoint: both advocated civil rights, voter protection, and leadership roles for blacks. In large measure their difference was a matter of style. Haralson was young, brash, outspoken, and rhetorical; Rapier was older, prudent, diplomatic, and his speeches, while forceful (he was an outstanding orator) and well organized, had few rhetorical flourishes.

With the "redemption" of the state by conservatives, Rapier turned his attention to the emigration movement. Appointed collector of internal revenue for the Second Alabama District in 1877, he used the office to urge former slaves to leave Alabama and settle in the West. The black man, he asserted, would never be accorded equal rights or economic opportunity in the South. He traveled several times to Kansas, purchased land for a settlement in Wabaunsee County along the route of the Kansas-Pacific Railway, gave pro-emigration speeches in Alabama, and testified in Washington, D.C., before a Senate committee on emigration.

During the early 1880s, as his health began to decline, Rapier slowed his activity. He had never married, and despite the hectic pace of his career he was a lonely man who admitted he had few real friends.

By the end of his life Rapier had come full circle. From seeking to work within the system to gain equal rights for blacks in the South, he now advocated that former slaves and their children should abandon the land of their birth. His efforts, however, were cut short. Rapier died in Lowndes County, Alabama, of pulmonary tuberculosis.

FURTHER READING

Rapier's correspondence can be found in the Rapier-Thomas Papers, Moorland-Spingarn Collection, Howard University, Washington, D.C.

Feldman, Eugene. *Black Power in Old Alabama: The Life and Stirring Times of James T. Rapier* (1968).

Foner, Eric. *Freedom's Lawmakers: A Directory of Black Office Holders during Reconstruction* (1993).

Schweninger, Loren. *James T. Rapier and Reconstruction* (1978).

This entry is taken from the *American National Biography* and is published here with the permission of the American Council of Learned Societies.

LOREN SCHWENINGER

Rashad, Phylicia Ayers-Allen (19 June 1948–   ), actress, singer, was born Phylicia Ayers-Allen in Houston, Texas, the second-oldest child of Dr. Andrew Arthur Allen, a dentist, and Dr. Vivian Elizabeth (Ayers) Allen, a poet and educator. Her father is of Cherokee descent; her mother, an African American, won a Pulitzer Prize nomination for her first published work, *Spice of Dawns*. Ayers-Allen's siblings, like their mother, embraced the arts; her older brother Andrew Arthur "Tex" Allen Jr. became a jazz musician; her younger sister DEBBIE ALLEN is an actor, choreographer, and director who won an Emmy Award for her role on the television series *Fame*; her youngest brother Hugh Allen is a real estate banker. In the 1950s Ayers-Allen moved with her family to Mexico, where she learned to speak Spanish fluently. Ayers-Allen attended Jack Yates Senior High School in her hometown and at the same time began studying at the Merry-Go-Round Theater, a youth training program, sponsored by the Alley Theater, also in Houston. Upon graduating she attended Howard University in Washington, D.C., where she joined Alpha Kappa Alpha Sorority, Incorporated, the first African American sorority in the United States. Ayers-Allen was still an undergraduate when she appeared in the off-Broadway production, *Miss Weaver* (1968); and in 1970, when she earned a Bachelor of Fine Arts degree from Howard, she relocated to New York City for a career in theater.

Ayers-Allen joined the Negro Ensemble Company, a sounding board and boot camp for many African American actors—SHERMAN HEMSLEY, ANGELA BASSETT, and DENZEL WASHINGTON among them—and successfully achieved a number of roles in New York. During this period she married William Lancelot Bowles Jr., a dentist, on 13 May 1972. Three years later, in 1975, they were divorced. Ayers-Allen continued her theater life as a Munchkin in the Tony Award winning musical production of *The Wiz*, in which she was also an understudy to the two lead actresses, the singers STEPHANIE MILLS and DEE DEE BRIDGEWATER as Dorothy and Glinda the Good Witch, respectively. Ayers-Allen married a second time on 28 April 1978, to Victor Willis, a lead singer for the Village People. During the same year she performed a disco biography of JOSEPHINE BAKER, *Josephine Superstar*, produced by her husband; they divorced two years later. In 1981 Ayers-Allen joined the original cast of another Tony Award–winning musical, *Dreamgirls*, as an understudy to Sheryl Lee Ralph, who played Deena. Ayers-Allen made her television debut in 1983 as the attorney Courtney Wright on the ABC soap opera *One Life to Live*.

In 1984 the veteran comedian and actor Bill COSBY invited Ayers-Allen to portray the role of his television wife, the attorney Clair Olivia Hanks Huxtable, on NBCs groundbreaking sitcom *The Cosby Show*. The Huxtable children were portrayed by the actors Malcolm Jamal-Warner, Lisa Bonet, Keisha Knight-Pulliam, Tempest Blesdoe, and Sabrina Lebeauf. The Huxtables presented for the world a portrait of a solidly middle-class African American family without the dysfunctions or stereotypes previously portrayed on television. Ayers-Allen was hailed as the quintessential matriarch and professional female role model for her portrayal of Clair, and received two People's Choice Awards (1985, 1989), one NAACP Image Award (1984), and two Emmy nominations.

During the period of her *Cosby Show* success, Ahmad Rashad, the former NFL wide receiver turned sportscaster, proposed to Ayers-Allen live on the pregame show for the nationally televised Thanksgiving Day football game, November 1985; unannounced, she arrived at the studio and tearfully accepted his proposal on national television. The couple was married on 14 December 1985, with Debbie Allen standing as her maid of honor and O. J. SIMPSON the former NFL running back, spokesman, and actor as the best man. Ayers-Allen adopted her third husband's last name. In 1992 *The Cosby Show*, ended its historic television run.

Rashad starred in the film *Once Upon a Time When We Were Colored*, directed by Tim Reid

Phylicia Ayers-Allen Rashad, as Clair Huxtable, talks on the telephone while other cast members of *The Cosby Show* gather around during the final episode in New York City, 6 March 1992. From left clockwise: Clarice Taylor as Anna Huxtable, Bill Cosby as Dr. Cliff Huxtable, Earl Hyman as Russel Huxtable, Malcolm Jamal Warner as Theo, Keshia Knight Pulliam as Rudy, and Raven Symone as Olivia. (AP Images.)

and also starring Al Freeman Jr. and Leon. In 1996 Cosby invited her to portray Ruth Lucas, the wife of his character on the CBS sitcom *Cosby*. For her role on *Cosby* she won an NAACP Image Award (1997), a Satellite Award (1999), and a TV Guide Award (2000). *Cosby* aired for the last time in 2000, and that same year Cosby cast Rashad on his animated television series *Little Bill*, as the voice of Bill's mother. Her marriage to Ahmad Rashad ended in 2001, and *Little Bill* ended the following year.

Theater always remained a staple in Rashad's professional career among her appearances are *Jelly's Last Jam* (1992–1993), The Pearl Cleage production of *Blues for an Alabama Sky* (1996), *The Vagina Monologues* (1999, 2003), *Helen* (2002), and from 26 April 2004 through 11 July 2004 she appeared as the matriarch Lena Younger in LORRAINE HANSBERRY's play *A Raisin in the Sun*; twenty years earlier, in the same play, she had portrayed the young, ambitious Ruth. She performed opposite the music mogul SEAN "PUFFY" COMBS in his theater debut for a fifteen-week run that earned Rashad the Drama

Desk Award and the Tony Award for Best Actress, the first African American woman to win the title. Even more, the play became the second-highest-grossing production in Broadway history. From 6 December 2004 to 6 February 2005 Rashad portrayed Aunt Ester in the AUGUST WILSON play *Gem of the Ocean*; for her performance she received a Tony Award nomination; she directed the play in 2007 for the Seattle Repertory Theater.

A Raisin in the Sun was adapted for television in 2008; Rashad portrayed Lena Younger opposite her 2004 Broadway cast including Combs, Sanna Lathan, and Audra McDonald. She earned the 2009 NAACP Image Award for Outstanding Actress in a Television Movie, Mini-Series, or Dramatic Special for her performance. In 2008 Rashad starred on Broadway in an all–African American production of *Cat on a Hot Tin Roof*, directed by her sister Debbie Allen, opposite JAMES EARL JONES; Terrance Howard, a film actor making his Broadway debut; and Anika Noni Rose, who played the role of the first African American Disney princess.

Rashad received an honorary Doctor of Fine Arts degree from Brown University in 2005 and from Carnegie Mellon University in 2009. She is on the board of directors for the largest regional theater in the southeastern Unites States, the Alliance Theater Company in Atlanta, Georgia. Rashad has narrated several children's books including *Ellington Was Not a Street* (2005) and *Sahara Special* (2006); and literature for young adults. With her sister she has a production company, D.A.D, an acronym for Doctor Allen's Daughters.

Rashad has two children, William Lancelot Bowles III, born in 1973, and Condola Phylea, born in 1986.

FURTHER READING

Lee, Felicia R. "Phylicia Rashad." *New York Times*, 26 June 2009.

"Phylicia Rashad: Wins Historic Tony Award to Become the First African American Woman to Win in Lead Actress Category." *Ebony* August 2004.

Warren, Marc. "America's Favorite Mom Phylicia Rashad." *Afro-American* [Washington], 16 June 2000.

SAFIYA DALILAH HOSKINS

Raspberry, William (12 Oct. 1935–17 July 2012), journalist and editor, was born in Okolona, Mississippi, to James Lee Raspberry, a school shop teacher, and Willie Mae Tucker, an English teacher and amateur poet. Both parents were intensely interested in education and in seeing to it that their children were the beneficiaries of good educations. They prodded their six youngsters to achieve, instilling in them a passion for reading, a positive approach to life, and a desire for logical thinking. From his mother Raspberry said that he learned to care about the rhythm and grace of words, and from his father he recalled learning that "neither tables nor arguments are worthwhile unless they stand solidly on four legs." Raspberry went north first, moving to live with an older sister in Indianapolis. In a few years the rest of the family left the South to become residents of Indianapolis, where Raspberry and the rest of his brothers and sisters attended public schools. And it was during that period that young Raspberry developed a lifelong passion for reading murder mysteries.

William Raspberry graduated from high school in 1954 and immediately enrolled at Indiana Central College (later the University of Indianapolis), where he began his studies by majoring in mathematics but subsequently switched to history and English. For a while he was also a seminary student.

While in college he began working for the *Indiana Recorder*, an all-black weekly newspaper for which he was a reporter, proofreader, and managing editor. He received his B.S in History from Indiana Central College in 1938.

In 1960 he was drafted into the U.S. Army and became a public affairs officer stationed in Virginia. Two years later when he mustered out of the army he moved to nearby Washington, D.C., and took a job on the *Washington Post* as a teletype operator, even though he had never seen one of the machines before. But his enthusiasm and abilities were quickly noticed. Joe Paull, then an assistant managing editor at the *Post*, recognized Raspberry's promise and had the young journalist assigned to writing for the obituary section. It was not long before he had landed a coveted reporting position.

In order to distinguish himself from the pack of young reporters at the *Post*, Raspberry took on the task of writing about civil rights issues, since the veteran reporters were not interested in covering the topic locally. In just a few years he became something of an authority on the subject, as well as on education, criminal justice, and drug abuse—all issues that were usually avoided by other writers.

His ascendance to assistant city editor came in 1965, the same year that he earned the Journalist of the Year Award from the all-black Capitol Press Club (the National Press Club at that time had only tentatively begun to desegregate). He also began writing his "Potomac Watch" column for the *Post*, which became a thrice-weekly endeavor and eventually was syndicated across the nation. Raspberry also began contributing articles on race relations and public education to other publications, including *Reader's Digest*. Less than ten years after he began "Potomac Watch," *Time* magazine declared Raspberry "the most respected black voice on any white U.S. paper."

In 1966, the same year that he became the *Post*'s urban affairs columnist, Raspberry married Sandra Patricia Dodson, an adjunct professor at Trinity College and a researcher at Howard University. When they got married the young Raspberrys agreed that home and children would be paramount for them; they decided that Patricia's salary would go toward buying a home and that William would support the family. Soon they owned their home, and in the ensuing years the Raspberry household grew with the addition of the children Patricia, Angela, and Mark.

In 1971 Raspberry began teaching journalism at Howard University, before becoming a lecturer on race relations and public education. In addition to the Howard job and his regular work he found time to be a television commentator for WTTG television from 1973 to 1975 and a panelist for WRC television. His first nomination for a Pulitzer Prize came in 1982 and was for his commentary. Raspberry became a member of the Pulitzer Prize board in 1976 and remained a member until 1985. He became a member of the Poynter Institute for Media Studies in 1984. In 1985 he became a member of the board of visitors for the University of Maryland's school of journalism.

Raspberry received honorary doctorate degrees from Georgetown University, the University of Maryland, the University of Indianapolis, and Virginia State University. Because of his contributions and his prominence he was a member of several prestigious organizations, including the National Association of Black Journalists (NABJ), Kappa Alpha Psi fraternity, and the Gridiron Club.

In 1994 Raspberry won a Pulitzer Prize for commentary for his columns, and in 1995 the National Society of Newspaper Columnists presented him with its Lifetime Achievement Award. The American Bar Association gave him its Liberty Bell Award. In June 2000 Raspberry was inducted into the Mississippi Press Association's hall of fame. He also became in the following year a visiting professor of journalism at Duke University. At the end of 2004 he retired from the *Post*, although he continued to contribute an occasional column, and devoted himself to lecturing and teaching.

In July 2012, Raspberry died in Washington, DC, of prostate cancer. He was 76.

FURTHER READING

Astor, David. "William Raspberry Talks about His Work," *Editor and Publisher* 124 (2 Feb. 1991).

Fibich, Linda. "The Solutionist," *American Journalism Review* 16 (May 1994).

Raspberry, William. "Crisis of Community: Making America Work for Americans," *Vital Speeches of the Day* (1 June 1995).

Raspberry, William. *Looking Backward at Us* (1991).

Obituary: *Washington Post*, 17 July 2012.

LUTHER BROWN JR.

Ratcliff, Edward (8 Feb. 1835–10 Mar. 1915), Civil War soldier and Medal of Honor recipient, was born the son of an African slave named Hannah and a white father in James City County, Virginia, on the farm of Nathaniel Hankins. Two years later, when Alexander Hankins inherited his father's 400-acre farm, he also inherited the slaves that worked it and their families, including the infant Edward. Married before the war to a woman, also a slave, named Grace, Ratcliff continued as a slave until one day in early 1864 when he "laid down his hoe in the field" and walked the distance to Yorktown to join the Union camp there as a contraband (Virginia State Senate Joint Resolution, 484). He joined the 38th U.S. Colored Troop Regiment (USCT) when it was organized in Virginia on 28 January 1864, thereby becoming a free man and hoping that soon his family would also be free.

Ratcliff quickly rose from private to the rank of a noncommissioned officer, serving as first sergeant in Company C, likely because of both his maturity and bearing. The 38th USCT spent its first months assigned to the Department of Virginia and North Carolina and was stationed in the area of Norfolk and Portsmouth, Virginia. It was here that its men gained valuable training experience while performing garrison duty. In June 1864 Ratcliff and the men of the 38th were sent to the front during the siege of Petersburg and Richmond. Here many black soldiers, Edward Ratcliff included, would earn their country's highest decoration for bravery in combat.

By 1864 the style of battle in the Civil War had evolved into a different kind of fighting; gone were the pitched battles that had occurred early in the war at Bull Run and Gettysburg. Now it was a war of attrition and the Confederacy was hanging on for dear life. Especially around the capital city of Richmond, Virginia, elaborate trenches and fortifications were built to keep the Union army at bay. However, Confederate President Jefferson Davis and his lieutenants sadly misjudged the North's resolve and the chief of the Union army, General Ulysses S. Grant, was prepared to win at all costs; Grant and his army had enough manpower to sustain heavy losses—such as the 4,000 to 7,000 casualties suffered in less than five hours at the Battle of Cold Harbor on 3 June 1864—while the Confederate army could not. Among the troops available to Grant late in the war were the soldiers of the U.S. Colored Troop regiments, often spurred on to enlist in the army by recruitment posters depicting black soldiers exhorting their fellow blacks to "Come and Join Us, Brothers." Join they did; by the end of the war, approximately 178,000 free blacks and former slaves had served in 175 black regiments, eventually constituting 10 percent of the Union army's manpower.

Late September found Edward Ratcliff and the men of the 38th USCT stationed near New Market Heights just south of Richmond, Virginia, on the James River as part of General Benjamin Butler's

Army of the James. Other black units present in the area included the 4th, 5th, and 36th USCT regiments. As the southern anchor in the Confederate chain of fortifications surrounding Richmond, and located on a large bluff, New Market Heights (also called Chaffin's Farm after a local resident) was a keystone in the Confederate defense and General Grant hoped to capture the heights and the forts surrounding it. The Battle of New Market Heights was to be a two-pronged assault against Confederate forts on both sides of the James River. The Northern attack was carried out by General Edward Ord's XVIII Corps, which included Ratcliff and the men of the 38th. The attack began on the morning of 29 September 1864 and would prove to be the Union's only success in a battle that lasted two days and cost the Union 5,000 casualties. Despite fierce hand-to-hand combat, the black troops in Butler's Army of the James prevailed and captured the heights and overwhelmed the Confederates at Fort Harrison, the only fort out of four to be captured that were the Union's objectives in the battle.

While the Union action at New Market Heights turned out be but a minor victory, the actions of the USCT men were among the highlights of the fighting; First Sergeant Edward Ratcliff distinguished himself by being the first man to enter Fort Harrison, and he was subsequently awarded the Medal of Honor on 6 April 1865 because "he gallantly led his company after the commanding officer had been killed" (Medal of Honor). Ratcliff was not the only black soldier to distinguish himself in the fighting that day, as at least six other men also earned the Medal of Honor at New Market Heights, including POWHATAN BEATY, JAMES BRONSON, MILTON HOLLAND, and ROBERT PINN of the 5th USCT, CHRISTIAN FLEETWOOD of the 4th USCT, JAMES GARDNER of the 36th USCT, and Ratcliff's fellow 38th USCT member, James Harris. Indeed, the battle at New Market Heights highlights not only the broad contributions of African American soldiers to the Union war effort but also exemplifies the individual qualities of leadership and courage present in many of the men of the USCT.

Following the Battle of New Market Heights, Edward Ratcliff continued with the 38th USCT, subsequently rising to the rank of sergeant major and serving in the trenches around Petersburg and Richmond, Virginia, and later at the battles of Deep Bottom and Fair Oaks. It is unknown, but likely, that Ratcliff continued with his regiment to the Texas Department after the war before the 38th was finally mustered out of service on 25 January 1865. Afterward, Ratcliff would return to his native Virginia and farmed in the peninsula area called the "reservation" because it was populated by Indians and former slaves. Grace and Edward Ratcliff would have seven children, including a daughter named Hannah and a son named Edward. The family name would later be changed to "Radcliffe," and a namesake grandson of Edward Ratcliff would serve in the army in World War II, while his son Edward was, in turn, a Marine corporal in 2006.

When he died at the age of eighty, Sergeant Major Edward Ratcliff, Medal of Honor winner, was buried in Cheesecake Cemetery. Once fallen to ruin, the site is now part of the grounds at the Yorktown Naval Weapons Station, Virginia. A Medal of Honor gravestone was erected for Ratcliff in 2006 and a ceremony celebrating Edward Ratcliff's service, as well as that of his family, was held in his honor and attended by his descendants.

FURTHER READING
Medal of Honor. "Edward Ratcliff, Medal of Honor." Available at http://www.homeoftheheroes.com/moh/citations_1862_cwq/ratcliff.html.
Virginia State Senate. Joint Resolution No. 484: "Celebrating Posthumously the Life and Heroism of Edward Ratcliff." Available at http://leg1.state.va.us/cgi-bin/legp504.exe?071+fuh+SJ484+405120.

GLENN ALLEN KNOBLOCK

Rawls, Lou (1 Dec. 1933–6 Jan. 2006), R&B, pop, and gospel singer and philanthropist, was born Louis Allen Rawls in Chicago, Illinois, to Virgil Rawls, a Baptist preacher and clothes presser, and Evie Rawls. Raised by his paternal grandmother, Eliza, herself a gospel singer, he started singing in the choir of the Greater Mount Olive Baptist Church in Chicago at age seven. Although Rawls supposedly had an impressive four-octave vocal range, jazz critic Ben Ratliff claims that Rawls "became best known for the unmistakable, mentholated baritone end of his vocal range" (Obituary, *New York Times*). Rawls was influenced by blues singers such as JOE WILLIAMS and crooners such as Billy Eckstine and Frank Sinatra.

In the early 1950s Rawls sang in several gospel groups, including the Teenage Kings of Harmony with SAM COOKE. In 1951 Rawls replaced Cooke in the Highway Q.C.s and went on to sing with the Chosen Gospel Singers and the Pilgrim Travelers. In 1955 Rawls joined the U.S. Army, serving in the Eighty-second Airborne Division. He was discharged at the rank of sergeant in 1958 and returned to the Pilgrims to embark on a tour with Sam Cooke. While on tour, Rawls and Cooke were in a serious car accident. Rawls nearly died on the way to the hospital, and he spent a little more than five days in a coma. He suffered from amnesia for several months and would not fully recover until a year later. But the experience gave him a new lease on life.

After the accident, Rawls followed the trail already blazed by Cooke and began performing secular music, though initially in a crooning jazz style rather than straight soul. In 1962 he released his first solo album, *I'd Rather Drink Muddy Water* (also known as *Stormy Monday*), on Capitol Records. He soon pioneered the idea of talking in songs (as he does on a number of well-known songs such as "Tobacco Road" (1963) and "Dead End Street" (1967)). According to Ben Ratliff, "He became famous for his monologues, sequences in which he would just talk over a chugging vamp, leading into and away from a song's refrain" (Obituary, *New York Times*). This distinct style was reflected in his 1966 album *Live!*, which went gold. With *Soulin'* (1966) Rawls turned his attention entirely to soul music and scored his first major hit with "Love Is a Hurtin' Thing," which reached number one on the R&B charts and nearly cracked the top ten on the pop charts. The following year, Rawls won a Grammy for Best Male R&B Vocal Performance for "Dead End Street." That year he also opened for the Beatles at Cincinnati's Crosley Field.

Rawls continued to record for Columbia for the remainder of the decade, but his sales had begun to slip by the time he moved to MGM and earned another Grammy (for "Natural Man") in 1971. His stint at MGM was brief, as was his tenure on the independent label Bell, and it was not until he joined hit factory Philadelphia International Records in 1976 that he enjoyed the peak of his commercial success. Rawls became a spokesman for Anheuser Busch that same year, appearing in ads for their most famous product, Budweiser beer. Proving to be an excellent vehicle for the songwriting prowess of Kenny Gamble and LEON HUFF, he recorded the platinum single "You'll Never Find (Another Love Like Mine)" in 1976, which reached the top five on five different *Billboard* singles charts and became one of the most popular and enduring songs of the late twentieth century. Rawls's adoption of the sleek Philadelphia sound propagated by Gamble and Huff was something of a departure from his earlier, grittier records of the 1960s; but at the same time, Gamble and Huff's elegant production qualities helped fashion his image into that of the quintessential smooth crooner. Yet some fans and critics felt that his jazz and blues roots may have been obscured by his fantastic success at the height of the 1970s disco era. Rawls figured as one of Philadelphia International's biggest stars for the remainder of the decade, earning another Grammy for best R&B album with 1977's *Unmistakably Lou* and charting with the singles "See You When I Git There," "Lady Love," and "One Life to Live."

Anheuser Busch later sponsored the *Lou Rawls Parade of Stars* telethon, which began in 1979 (and was renamed *An Evening of Stars* in 1998) to raise money for the United Negro College Fund. In 1982 he was recognized for both his artistic and philanthropic work with a star on the Hollywood Walk of Fame. From 1979 to 2004 the United Negro College Fund claimed the telethon raised over $200 million. In 1990 Rawls established the Bring It On Home Roots Festival in the city's Bronzeville neighborhood to raise funds for the Cultural Center. The fund established a Lou Rawls Lifetime Achievement Award in his honor in 2007. Rawls was also active as a philanthropist in his hometown of Chicago. He contributed substantially to the construction of the Harold Washington Cultural Center on the former site of the Regal Theater, where he had gone to see concerts by the likes of COUNT BASIE and NAT "KING" COLE as a youth.

Rawls kept very busy through the 1990s and the beginning of the twenty-first century, recording albums, appearing in concert, and appearing in film and television, particularly as an in-demand cartoon voice (in popular cartoons such as *Garfield* and *Rugrats*). He always looked up to Frank Sinatra in particular, and in 2003 he recorded the album *Rawls Sings Sinatra*.

Rawls had been one of the most prominent vocalists of his generation. During his career Rawls recorded more than sixty albums, sold forty million records, and garnered thirteen Grammy nominations. The City of Chicago renamed South Wentworth Avenue as Lou Rawls Drive in recognition of his charitable work there. Florida Memorial College's Lou Rawls Center for the Performing Arts opened in 2004, and Rawls also received an honorary doctorate from Wilberforce University. That same year, Rawls was diagnosed with brain and lung cancer in 2004 and died on 6 January 2006 at the Cedar-Sinai Medical Center in Los Angeles.

FURTHER READING

Anonymous. "Lou Rawls" United Negro College Fund Web Site. http://www.uncf.org/webfeature/Lou_Rawls_Bio.asp

Ifill, Sherrilyn. "Can We Give Lou Rawls Some Love?" Blackprof.com (2006). http://www.blackprof.com/archives/2006/01/can_we_give_lou_rawls_some_lov.html

Obituary:*New York Times*, 7 January 2006.

PAUL DEVLIN

Ray, Charles Bennett (25 Dec. 1807–15 Aug. 1886), journalist, educator, and minister, was born in Falmouth, Massachusetts, the son of Joseph Aspinwall Ray, a postal worker, and Annis Harrington, a well-read and deeply religious woman. He claimed descent from American Indians, as well as English and Africans. After schooling in Falmouth, Ray went to work for five years on his grandfather's farm in Rhode Island and then settled on Martha's Vineyard to learn the bootmaker's trade.

A profound experience of Christian conversion convinced Ray to become a Methodist minister. With financial aid from white abolitionist friends he gained entrance into the Wesleyan Academy in Wilbraham, Massachusetts. Though he was the only black in the school, the atmosphere was friendly. The principal, Wilbur Fisk, was a broad-minded and widely respected Methodist minister and educator. Chosen as the first president of Wesleyan University in Middletown, Connecticut, Fisk admitted Ray to the college in the fall of 1832. Student anger at the presence of an African American, however, forced Ray to withdraw after only six weeks.

During a visit to New York City, Ray met THEODORE S. WRIGHT, pastor of Manhattan's thriving First Colored Presbyterian Church. A close friendship developed and was a strong force in Ray's life. Now in his late twenties, Ray set up his trade as a bootmaker in the black district of lower Manhattan, only a few blocks from Wright's home and church. Ray lived in the city for over fifty years and became acquainted and influential with all segments of the city's black community.

By the mid-1830s Ray had acquired as partner in his boot and shoe business SAMUEL CORNISH, a black Presbyterian pastor who founded the first black newspaper, *Freedom's Journal*, in 1827. When some of the city's black leaders founded another paper, the *Colored American*, in 1837, Cornish was asked to be chief editor. He in turn invited Ray to be the paper's traveling reporter and promoter of subscriptions. Ray had married Henrietta Green Regulus in 1834, but in October 1836 she died in childbirth, as did her baby. Ray was ordained a Methodist minister in 1837,

but melancholic and without a family, he took to the road with little payment beyond expenses. Over a two-year period he became an effective link between the *Colored American* and individual blacks living in southern New England, upper New York State, New Jersey, Pennsylvania, and Ohio. The paper published his reports regarding black education, business, and church life in various communities. His eloquent endorsement of the *Colored American* in speeches and sermons built up subscriptions and kept the paper afloat. Its circulation probably ranged between 1,500 and 2,500.

While traveling in New York State Ray was engaged in overtly political activity, securing signatures for three petitions to the state legislature: one to recover full voting rights for black men, of which they had been deprived in the 1820s; another to end the policy allowing slaveowners to enter the state with a slave, stay for up to nine months, and leave with their ownership unchallenged; and the last to secure a jury trial for any black falsely accused of being a runaway slave. The accused were customarily taken by the "slave catcher" to a city magistrate and sworn by bribed witnesses to be runaways from a particular southern slaveowner.

By 1839 Ray had become owner and editor of the *Colored American* after Cornish had resigned and some of its early financial backers had withdrawn support. Through it, and in spite of the opposition of many white abolitionists and some black leaders fearful of a white backlash, he successfully promoted a convention of New York State blacks, during the summer of 1840, to organize a statewide petition drive and lobbying effort to recover the vote. Ray's faith in black political activism had been strengthened in May 1840 when the New York State legislature passed and Governor William Henry Seward signed a bill requiring a jury trial for blacks charged with being fugitives. Nearly 140 black delegates met for three days in Albany in August 1840. They endorsed public letters to the state's black citizens and to the white population. Ray and his fellow activist, the young Presbyterian minister HENRY HIGHLAND GARNET, spent the fall collecting thousands of petition signatures. But in spite of these efforts and the governor's public endorsement of a bill providing re-enfranchisement, the measure was defeated in the state assembly in April 1841 by a vote of forty-six to twenty-nine.

After a long battle to prevent the financial collapse of the *Colored American*, Ray closed it out at the end of 1841. However, the paper remained the most impressive black-edited and black-financed paper up to the Civil War (FREDERICK DOUGLASS's journals were financed primarily by whites).

Ray remained active after the paper's closing. He was prominent among the black supporters of the antislavery Liberty Party in the early 1840s and remained a leader in both the New York City and state vigilance committees devoted to aiding runaway slaves and preventing the kidnapping of black people by slavecatchers.

Ray was also a central figure in the most highly organized pre–Civil War black attempt to improve schooling for blacks in a large city. With two sons and five daughters borne by his second wife, Charlotte Augusta Burroughs, whom he married in 1840, Ray had a personal stake in better education. In 1847 some of Manhattan's black leaders founded the New York Society for the Promotion of Education among Colored Children, and from 1851 to 1865, Ray was the organization's president. The society's most significant achievements were the founding and efficient operation of two new elementary schools for black children, and an 1859 review of the whole system of city-run black schools, which revealed that only one-fortieth as much had been spent per black child for school sites and buildings as per white child. He urged that New York City schools be desegregated as they had been in Boston. If not, the board should at least provide better school buildings for blacks in less dismal locations. Within two years the board mandated substantial improvements.

Shortly after closing out the Colored American Ray had returned to the Christian ministry that had been his original calling. In 1844 he began what would be several decades of work as "City Missionary to the Destitute Colored Population." He did street preaching, conducted Sunday services, and held weekly worship meetings for the poor, the handicapped, and the elderly. In 1845 he was installed as minister of a small new Congregational Church, Bethesda, whose members were largely drawn from the "lost souls" he had aided on the city streets of lower Manhattan.

In the aftermath of John Brown's 1859 raid, Ray joined other black clergy in awed tributes to the "Old Man" for his commitment and courage. Once the Civil War had begun Ray strongly supported black enlistments in the Union army. In 1863, in the wake of the New York City draft riots, which had left scores of blacks dead and thousands homeless, Ray and Henry Highland Garnet teamed up once more, to visit three thousand families and ascertain the amount of relief needed.

In later years Ray delighted in the accomplishments of his three daughters. In the early 1870s, for instance, CHARLOTTE E. RAY became the first woman to graduate from the Howard University Law Department and was said to have been the first woman admitted to the practice of law in the District of Columbia. Charles B. Ray served as pastor of Bethesda Church until 1868 and as city missionary until his death in New York in 1886.

FURTHER READING

Files related to Ray and the *Colored American* can be found at the Schomburg Center for Research in Black Culture, New York Public Library.

Ray, Florence, and Henrietta Cordelia Ray. *Sketch of the Life of Rev. Charles B. Ray* (1887).

Swift, David E. *Black Prophets of Justice: Activist Clergy before the Civil War* (1989).

This entry is taken from the *American National Biography* and is published here with the permission of the American Council of Learned Societies.

DAVID E. SWIFT

Ray, Charlotte E. (13 Jan. 1850–4 Jan. 1911), lawyer, was born in New York City, the daughter of Charlotte Augusta Burroughs, a native of Savannah, Georgia, and CHARLES BENNETT RAY, a journalist, abolitionist, and minister of Indian, English, and African ancestry, who became editor of the *Colored American*, after SAMUEL CORNISH. The Rays had seven children, two of whom died in adolescence. Charlotte was the youngest of the three surviving daughters, all of whom attended college like their brothers.

As a child, Charlotte attended the Institution for the Education of Colored Youth in Washington, D.C. Founded in 1851 by the educator Myrtilla Miner, the private institution was one of the few schools that black girls could attend. By 1869 Ray was a teacher at the Howard University Normal and Preparatory Department. In the evenings she studied law at Howard University, where she specialized in commercial law. As a senior, in February 1872, she delivered a well-received paper on chancery (a court of equity in the American judicial system). Listed in school records as one of fourteen graduating seniors in the fifteen-member class of 1872, Ray was the first woman to graduate from the Howard University Law Department. (Another woman would not graduate from the department for a decade.) At her graduation—only twenty-five years after MACON BOLLING ALLEN, the first black American lawyer, was admitted to an American bar, in Maine—Ray became the first black female lawyer in the United States.

On 23 April 1872 Ray was admitted to the District of Columbia bar, which only recently had been opened to women. A month later it was announced, in the 23 May 1872 issue of the *New National Era*, a Washington, D.C., paper published by African Americans, that Ray "had been admitted to practice before the Supreme Court of the District of Columbia" (Rayford Logan, *Howard University: The First Hundred Years, 1867–1967* [1969], 50). In addition to being the first black woman graduate of any law school in the United States, the first female graduate of Howard University's law school, the first woman admitted to the District of Columbia bar, and the first woman admitted to practice in the Supreme Court of the District, Ray is also sometimes referred to as the first woman to graduate from any nonprofit university law school. As the historian Rayford Logan has noted, however, the last two "firsts" are "difficult to establish."

Challenging Ray's designation as the first female lawyer admitted to the D.C. bar is the following, which appears in an 1882 publication: "In the District of Columbia Mrs. B. A. Lockwood was admitted in 1870, and Charlotte E. Ray in 1872, on graduating from Howard University" (Phebe A. Hanaford, *Daughters of America* [1882], 643). It is not clear, however, to which bar the reference is made—the District of Columbia bar or the Supreme Court of-the District of Columbia. Complicating the issue is the fact that this same publication also quotes from the 23 May 1872 *Woman's Journal*, which grants to Ray "the honor of being the first lady lawyer in Washington" (Hanaford, 649), the latter statement seeming to contradict the preceding assertion that Lockwood was admitted to the bar in 1870 and Ray in 1872. Another source, however, indicates that Lockwood graduated from law school in 1873 and was admitted to the D.C. bar the same year (Robert McHenry, ed., *Liberty's Women* [1980], 250). Thus, the listing of Ray's traditionally acknowledged "first" seems to be in order.

Not long after she opened her own law office in Washington, D.C., presumably in 1872, Ray was forced to give up active practice because constitutional and legal segregation of the races had precluded her ability to attract sufficient business to remain open. By 1879 she had returned to New York City, where she taught in the Brooklyn public school system along with two of her sisters, one of whom, H. Cordelia Ray, was a poet whose poems were published in the *AME Review*. Cordelia, who

was fluent in French, Greek, Latin, and German, earned a master's degree from the University of the City of New York in 1891. Sometime after 1886 Ray was married to a man named Fraim, of whom nothing else is known.

After 1895 Ray seems to have been active in the National Association of Colored Women, and she also apparently supported the cause of voting rights for women because in 1876 she attended the annual convention of the National Woman Suffrage Association in New York. By 1897 she was living in Woodside, Long Island, where she died fourteen years later of acute bronchitis. She was buried in Brooklyn's Cypress Hill Cemetery in the Ray family plot, where her tombstone records her married name as "Fraim." (She is listed as "Traim" on her death report, apparently a typo.)

Despite the fact that her legal practice was short-lived, Ray earned a reputation for being one of the country's best lawyers on questions involving corporation law. As one contemporary noted, "Her eloquence is commendable for her sex in the court-room, and her legal advice is authoritative" (Monroe A. Majors, *Noted Negro Women* [1893] 184). According to the 1920 census Ray was, during the previous decade, one of two women among the 950 black lawyers in the United States.

FURTHER READING

Drachman, Virginia. *Sisters in Law: Women Lawyers in Modern American History* (1998).
Higginbotham, Leon A., Jr. *Blacks in the Law* (1983).
Smith, J. Clay. *Emancipation: The Making of the Black Lawyer, 1844–1944* (1993).
Smith, J. Clay. *Rebels in Law: Voices in History of Black Women Lawyers* (1998).

This entry is taken from the *American National Biography* and is published here with the permission of the American Council of Learned Societies.

LOIS BALDWIN MORELAND

Ray, Emma J. Smith (7 Jan. 1859–25 Nov. 1930), Christian missionary and temperance advocate, was born Emma Smith, enslaved in Springfield, Missouri. She lived with her mother, Jennie Boyd, and both her sister and her father, John Smith, lived on a neighboring plantation. There were also four older siblings living on yet another plantation near Springfield. One month after her birth in 1859, Emma was put up for auction alongside her mother and sister. Her father threatened his owners that if they did not purchase his wife and daughters he would run away. The strategy proved successful and Smith was able to have his wife and two daughters live with him.

Emma Smith was only two years old when the Civil War erupted. In 1864, as the Union army secured remaining portions of Missouri from rebel control, the white slaveholding Smith brothers (John Smith kept the name of his owners) fled south to Arkansas with Confederate forces, taking their bondpeople with them. Emma Smith's older siblings remained in Springfield, and her three brothers ran away to join the Union army. Smith's older sister was eventually reunited with the family after the war. Emma Smith's family returned to Springfield after only a few months in Arkansas. At first they resettled with their former owners before relocating to land nearby that was owned by a white man sympathetic to the North's cause.

After the war, many freedpeople began the search for missing family members. Emma's father was able to help neighbors by writing letters for them. Bondpeople were often forbidden from learning to read and write, so John Smith's literacy is notable. In 1868 Jennie Smith died after a brief illness, and Emma's father struggled to keep the family together, reluctantly hiring her out to work in the home of a white doctor. She visited her father and siblings for only a few hours on Sundays. Tormented by the separation from her family, nine-year-old Emma ran away, returning to her father's house and begging him to not return her to the doctor. The doctor's attempt to retrieve Emma failed, so he insisted on taking back the two dresses Emma had received for her labor. Emma then went to work as a nursemaid (and later a housekeeper) in the house of someone named Mrs. Timmons. Timmons's religious influence stayed with Emma for the rest of her life and proved to be a key factor in guiding her into Christian mission work. Up until the fourth grade, Smith worked for Timmons during the summer and went to school during the winter.

In 1881 Smith moved to Carthage, Missouri, where she met Lloyd P. Ray, a stonecutter and mason. They were married in Fredonia, Kansas, in 1887, and the couple then moved to Seattle, Washington, in the summer of 1889; but the marriage was already suffering from Lloyd Ray's heavy drinking. Emma Ray invested her energies in her local African Methodist Episcopal Church (AME), experiencing a Christian rebirth and eventually convincing her husband to devote himself to Christianity as well. Ray had lived through problems caused by alcohol, and she also witnessed the consequences of alcohol abuse in the Yesler-Jackson neighborhood

where she and her husband lived. Because of this, Ray decided to found the Frances Harper Colored Women's Christian Temperance Union in the early 1890s. The Women's Christian Temperance Union (WTCU), which had been created in 1873, inspired women (both black and white) to form similar groups throughout nineteenth-century America. The WCTU boasted 245,000 members by 1911. Women's clubs sought self-improvement as well as social reform. Although some African American women joined white women's clubs, black women were usually not welcomed into white women's organizations. But in 1895 when the Jones Street AME pastor demanded that the women dissolve the Frances Harper WCTU in order to focus on the church, Ray joined the white WCTU.

Emma and Lloyd Ray also brought the word of God into the Seattle City jail. The WCTU elected Emma as County Superintendent of Jail and Prison Work and named Lloyd an honorary member. The Rays also occasionally welcomed former prisoners into their homes to help them begin their lives outside of jail. In the spring of 1900 Emma Ray returned to Missouri to share her Christian rebirth with her family, hoping that they, too, would choose to dedicate themselves to Christ. Apparently Ray met with success; she reported that her family received her efforts favorably. Lloyd Ray joined Emma in Kansas City and the couple remained there for more than two years, opening a mission and continuing their Christian service by holding meetings and helping needy African Americans with food, clothing, and shelter. Unlike the couple's work in Seattle, their work in Kansas focused solely on the African American community—primarily because of Seattle's relatively small black population. In 1900 Seattle's black population numbered only 406 out of a total population of 80,671.

The Rays returned to Seattle in 1902, and the next year they purchased land in the Green Lake suburb where they built a house in preparation for Emma Ray's father and his new wife's move there (there is no information about the purchase of the land). Lloyd and Emma Ray continued their evangelical work in prisons, and Emma Ray began to work with Mrs. Ollie S. Ryther (also known as "Mother Ryther") who opened a Rescue Home for prostitutes and unwed pregnant women. Ray and Ryther held meetings in the "slums," visiting people in boardinghouses to sing and pray with them. The Rays also visited the County Hospital on a regular basis to bring prayer and flowers to patients. In 1920 the Rays decided that their advanced ages would no longer permit them to work the streets of the red light district. They did, however, continue much of their community service, including participating in revivals around the state. Ray's 1926 autobiography, *Twice Sold, Twice Ransomed*, details many of the people they met and offered to help. Emma Ray's devotion to her community is indicative of many African American women's aims to "uplift" their race. Ray also had the unusual opportunity to help both black and white people who were down and out.

FURTHER READING

Ray, Emma. *Twice Sold, Twice Ransomed* (1926).
Mumford, Esther Hall. *Seattle's Black Victorians, 1852–1901* (1980).
Taylor, Quintard. *The Forging of a Black Community: Seattle's Central District form 1870 through the Civil Rights Era* (1994).

KARLA SCLATER

Ray, Henrietta Cordelia (1850?–5 Jan. 1916), poet and educator, was born in New York City, the youngest of five surviving children born to Charlotte Augusta Burrough, from Savannah, Georgia, and CHARLES BENNETT RAY, a Congregational minister who became editor of the third black-owned newspaper in the United States, the *Colored American*. Charles Ray was a recognized activist, opening his home for safe passage to slaves along the Underground Railroad and fund-raising for numerous black causes. William Wells Brown, a well-known abolitionist, claimed Charles Ray was a steadfast figure in activist meetings held throughout the 1840s. Ray's parents could afford to educate their children: all three of their daughters graduated from college. H. Cordelia Ray, as she preferred to be called, followed her sister Florence's example and attended New York University to obtain a master's degree in Pedagogy.

Ray's life illustrates well the popular belief among black leaders after Reconstruction that well-heeled African Americans should uplift the race by attaining what they considered to be the civilized standards valued by white Americans. Setting an example for African American potential meant following the refined ways of Victorian society. Ray's life principally conformed to the mores and ambitions of genteel society: exhibiting exquisite manners and mastering music, mathematics, Latin, Greek, French, and English literature well enough to teach to others. As HALLIE QUINN BROWN describes in her biography of Ray, "She was well-born, well bred and enjoyed all the advantages accruing to her

position in a family where birth, breeding and culture were regarded as important assets" (173).

Ray's career as a teacher in New York public schools lasted about thirty years. However, she did not feel fulfilled as a teacher, and yearned to pursue her literary interests. In 1876 she achieved national literary attention when she was invited to write a poem to commemorate Abraham Lincoln on the anniversary of his death, at the unveiling of Lincoln's statue in Lincoln Park, Washington, D.C., by President Ulysses S. Grant. Ray's poem, "Lincoln: Written for the Occasion of the Unveiling of the Freedmen's Monument in Memory of Abraham Lincoln, April 14, 1876," was read by William E. Matthews and was followed by a keynote address from FREDERICK DOUGLASS. When she eventually retired from the school system, Ray devoted her time to writing. Supported by her pension and the companionship of her sister Florence with whom she lived, Ray enjoyed a reclusive life steeped in literature.

Typical during Ray's lifetime was the view that a woman's education was to "vivify and enlighten a home," as nineteenth-century author Sarah Lewis wrote (*Woman's Mission*, 1839). Far less common were women who used their training to publish. Though Ray continued to work as a tutor, she embarked on a literary career that produced two books of poems and a short biography of her father, *Sketch of the Life of Rev. Charles B. Ray* (1887), which she coauthored with Florence. Ray's sonnet "To Our Father" preceded the sketch. Ray's first book, *Sonnets*, was published in 1893. The collection of twelve poems follows a Petrarch-like structure and demonstrates her mastery of poetic form and technique. The first two poems are on the theme of motherhood, one a tribute to her mother. In four other sonnets she honors William Shakespeare, John Milton, Ludwig van Beethoven, and the Renaissance artist Raphael. She also included poems titled "Life," "Aspiration," "Incompleteness," and "Self-Mastery." The last two sonnets deal with artistic inspiration for music, "Two Musicians," and poetry, "The Poet's Ministrants."

Ray published 147 poems in her next and final book, *Poems* (1910), which she dedicated to Florence and to their household "made beautiful by the presence of those loved ones who have entered the Life Immortal." The book is arranged into ten sections: A Rosary of Fancies, Meditations, Sonnets (including those from her first book), Champions of Freedom, Ballads and Other Poems, Chansons D'Amour, Quatrains, The Procession of the Seasons, a trilogy—"The Seer," "The Singer," and "The Sage"—and the Heroic Echoes. Reception to Ray's prolific collection was positive. JESSIE REDMON FAUSET, in the August 1912 issue of *The Crisis*, commends Ray for her thematic versatility. The January 1913 *A.M.E. Church Review* admired the refreshing idealism in Ray's work. One of Ray's most vociferous advocates was Hallie Quinn Brown, who writes of Ray's life to "arouse that admiration that leads to emulation." In her book *Homespun Heroines* Brown describes *Poems* as a demonstration of Ray's "versatility, love of nature, classical knowledge, delicate fancy, an unaffected piety" (175).

Though Ray's work pays tribute to champions of freedom, she never comments on issues of racial injustice. Instead, her work falls into abstract themes acceptable in Victorian society: Christian faith, love, nature, and literature. Contemporary literary critics commonly view Ray's work as sentimental and effete, yet they mention her technical skill with poetic form as exemplary. But even her adherence to structure dulled the effect of her work to some, who hold up examples from her nontraditional ballads as her finest writing. Distinctive to Ray's writing is her contribution to an African American literary tradition that reclaims classical literature. Ray continued PHILLIS WHEATLEY's practice of retelling and reshaping classical stories. In her versions of "Antigone and Oedipus" and "Echo's Compliant," Ray casts women protagonists in what were typically male stories.

H. Cordelia Ray is relatively unknown as a poet, despite her successes. Hallie Quinn Brown claims that Ray's humility and decorum tempered her recognition: "Among a generation of brainy New York women, she was probably the most accomplished, yet outside her immediate circle the least known" (174). After her death in Brooklyn, New York, Ray's legacy was largely defined by her character, "pure, gentle, peaceable and easy to be entreated," as her obituary in *The Crisis* (April 1916) emphasized. Ray's commitment to education and ornate language stood as a challenge to theories and practices that degraded black women as uncultured. During a time when women and African Americans were decrying their lack of rights, Ray quietly wrote impeccable quatrains, sonnets, and ballads, advancing an argument for African American inclusion in the established American literary tradition.

FURTHER READING

Brown, Hallie Quinn, ed. *Homespun Heroines and Other Women of Distinction* (1926).

Knight, Denise D. and Emmanuel S. Nelson, eds. *Nineteenth-Century American Women Writers: A Bio-Bibliographical Critical Sourcebook* (1997).

Sherman, Joan R, ed. *Collected Black Women's Poetry, Vol. 3* (1988).

CALEB A. CORKERY

Ray, Henrietta Green Regulus (29 Apr. 1808–27 Oct. 1836), activist, was born in New York City to as yet unknown free parents. Little is known of her youth, although she joined the Abyssinian Baptist Church circa 1815 and had close ties with the family of *Freedom's Journal* editor SAMUEL CORNISH, with whom she lived for three years. At some point in the mid-1820s, she married Laurent (sometimes listed as Lawrence) D. Regulus, the mixed-race son of French merchant Dominique Regulus and a black Caribbean woman named Delaydo. The elder Regulus has business interests in both Saint Thomas (in the Virgin Islands) and New York, and he had his son trained as a shoemaker. Propertied and tied to the reform circles surrounding *Freedom's Journal*, Laurent and Henrietta Regulus became active in the community; Henrietta served as the assistant secretary of the African Dorcas Association, an aid society with ties to both the New York Manumission Society and the African Free Schools, beginning in early 1828.

Laurent and Henrietta Regulus do not seem to have had children, and Laurent died in November 1828. He left a combination shop and house at 153 Orange Street which Henrietta and Laurent's brother Alexandre shared for a time after his death. Henrietta Regulus may well have met the Massachusetts-born CHARLES BENNETT RAY—destined to be her second husband—soon after he settled in New York in 1832 (after being admitted to Connecticut's Wesleyan University, studying there for six weeks, and then being forced out because of his race). Friends with abolitionist minister Theodore Wright and then Samuel Cornish, Ray had settled in New York and set up (like Laurent Regulus) a shoemaker's shop.

The Rays married in 1834, the same year in which Henrietta Ray helped found the New York Female Literary Society (also referred to as the New York Colored Ladies' Literary Society), of which she as elected president. Like her work with the Dorcas Association and like her marriage to the young activist and soon-to-be minister Ray, her leadership in the literary society marked a deep commitment to New York's free blacks (especially in terms of education and elevation) as well as to abolitionism and civil rights.

The Rays had their first and only child, a daughter named Matilda, in January of 1836, but both mother and daughter contracted tuberculosis. Matilda died at six months, and Henrietta followed her in death a few months later in New York City. Charles Ray and his second wife named one of their daughters, poet and teacher HENRIETTA CORDELIA RAY, in her memory.

FURTHER READING

Boylan, Anne. *Origins of Women's Activism* (2002).

Harris, Leslie M. *In the Shadow of Slavery: African Americans in New York City, 1626–1863* (2003).

Obituary: *Colored American*, 4 Mar. 1837.

ERIC GARDNER

Rayner, John Baptis (13 Nov. 1850–14 July 1918), politician, was born in Raleigh, North Carolina, the son of Kenneth Rayner, a white planter, and Mary Ricks, a slave. His father had a long public career as a Whig congressman, Know Nothing Party leader, and, after the Civil War, a Republican federal office-holder. Kenneth Rayner acknowledged that John was his son and helped him secure a college education at Raleigh Theological Institute (today Shaw University) and Saint Augustine's Normal and Collegiate Institute.

Before he graduated, John Rayner moved in 1872 to Tarboro, North Carolina, where, as a Republican, he held the local offices of constable and magistrate during Radical Reconstruction. He married Susan Staten in 1874; they had two children. In 1880 Rayner became a labor agent for several Texas cotton planters and persuaded a number of black farm workers to move with him to Robertson County, Texas. He settled in Calvert, where he taught school and preached. Later Rayner attracted considerable attention as a prohibition speaker and political strategist in Texas's 1887 prohibition referendum campaign. Also in 1887 his wife died, and later that year he married her sister, Clarissa Staten, with whom he had three children.

Rayner joined the People's (or Populist) Party in 1892. Founded by members of the Farmers' Alliance, the party sought to inflate the currency, make credit more available for farmers, and reform a political system that Populists viewed as corrupt. In Texas and some other states, the Populists also sought black support, appealing to African Americans on the grounds that they shared a common financial plight with poor white farmers. By 1894 Rayner had become the new third party's leading black spokesman in Texas. At the Populist state convention that year, delegates elected him to the party's state executive committee and to the platform committee, where he used his influence to move the party toward stronger positions on issues of importance to African Americans. These issues included reforming the convict lease system, placing black trustees in charge of black schools, and providing for fair elections.

Rayner continued to be active in the party as a highly effective lecturer and organizer until the demise of Populism near the end of the century. Billed as the "Silver-Tongued Orator of the Colored Race" (Cantrell, *Limits of Southern Dissent*, 209), Raynor earned his living and a deserved reputation as one of the finest public speakers in Texas, often addressing racially mixed audiences. Rayner's sharp tongue and his advocacy of issues such as seating blacks on juries sometimes brought him threats of physical violence, but he worked hard not to antagonize white Populists, insisting that blacks were not seeking "social equality" with whites and reminding his audiences of the friendship between southern whites and blacks. According to the white Texas Populist leader H. S. P. "Stump" Ashby, Rayner was doing work that "no white man can do" (Cantrell, *Limits of Southern Dissent*, 226).

With the rising tide of segregation and the success of efforts to disenfranchise blacks in the early years of the twentieth century, Rayner became involved in black vocational education. Between 1904 and 1914 he served as chief fund-raiser for two schools, Conroe College and the Farmers' Improvement Society School. Leaving behind his assertive political activism of the Populist years, Rayner publicly adopted an accommodationist stance. Later he became a friend of the famed Texas lumber baron John Henry Kirby, who despite his conservative stance on most political issues contributed to Rayner's educational projects. Kirby also occasionally employed Rayner as a labor recruiter for his mill towns. Later some blacks criticized Rayner because of the extreme lengths to which he went to ingratiate himself with whites such as the politically powerful Kirby. In his private papers, however, Rayner wrote bitterly of the white man's "hallucinated idea of race superiority" (Cantrell, *Limits of Southern Dissent*, 289).

Rayner also reentered politics after the turn of the century as an operative behind the scenes. Reversing his position of 1887, when he supported prohibition, he began working against prohibition. The Texas Brewers' Association, a beer cartel, employed him between 1905 and 1912 as an organizer to help get out the antiprohibition vote in the black community. Rayner also became a frequent contributor of essays and editorials to Texas newspapers, offering blacks and whites advice on a variety of topics such as politics, education, and religion. Rayner retired from political activity around 1912, although he continued to write for newspapers. After several years of declining health he died at his home in Calvert.

Rayner's primary historical significance lies in his status as perhaps the most important black southern Populist. In that capacity he was a major figure in the Populists' attempt to build a biracial coalition in the 1890s. His failure, and the failure of the Populist movement in the South, underscores the strength of white supremacy in the era and the risks that were inherent in challenging the racial status quo. His accommodationist stance in public after the turn of the century demonstrates the degree to which even the most committed black activists were forced to compromise their principles if they hoped to survive as public figures.

FURTHER READING

Rayner's papers dating from after 1900 are on deposit at the Barker Texas History Center, University of Texas at Austin.

Abramowitz, Jack. "John B. Rayner—A Grass-Roots Leader," *Journal of Negro History* 36 (1951).

Cantrell, Gregg. *Feeding the Wolf: John B. Rayner and the Politics of Race, 1850–1918* (2001).

Cantrell, Gregg. *Kenneth and John B. Rayner and the Limits of Southern Dissent* (1993).

This entry is taken from the *American National Biography* and is published here with the permission of the American Council of Learned Societies.

GREGG CANTRELL

Razaf, Andy (15 Dec. 1895–3 Feb. 1973), song lyricist, was born Andreamentania Paul Razafkeriefo in Washington, D.C., the son of Henry Razafkeriefo, a military officer and nephew of the queen of Madagascar, and Jennie Maria Waller. His grandfather was John Louis Waller, a U.S. consul to Madagascar whose arrest in Tamatave and subsequent imprisonment in Marseilles, France, touched off an 1895 upheaval in Madagascar that resulted in his father's death there and his mother's flight home to the United States, where she gave birth. From the spring of 1896, when John Waller returned from prison, the young Razafkeriefo followed in the trail of his grandfather's ultimately unsuccessful political and entrepreneurial activities in Baltimore,

Kansas City, Cuba (for two years), Manhattan (from 1900), and Yonkers (from 1905). By 1911—after his grandfather's death in 1907 and his mother's short-lived second marriage, which brought the family to Passaic, New Jersey—he and his mother had settled in Manhattan.

Razafkeriefo dropped out of high school at the age of sixteen to work as an elevator operator, a telephone operator, a butler, a cleaner, and a custodian while endeavoring to break into the world of popular song. He had a few insignificant successes, and early on, in 1913, someone made the pragmatic suggestion that he shorten his name to Andrea Razaf. This in turn became Andy Razaf, although he did not adopt that name systematically until the mid-1920s.

Razaf married Annabelle Miller in 1915, but he was an incorrigible womanizer, and the relationship never blossomed; the couple had no children. Following World War I he developed a reputation in the African American press as a poet protesting racism, and he wrote poetry for many years. Temporarily abandoning his lyric-writing ambition, Razaf pitched in Cleveland's semiprofessional baseball league while working as a porter there in 1920, only to move back to New York City the following year with the prospect of participating in the new craze for blues and jazz. There he met FATS WALLER (no relation to John Waller). Razaf's biographer Barry Singer argues that Razaf wrote lyrics to Waller's tune "Squeeze Me" in 1923 or 1925, and that somehow Clarence Williams appropriated Razaf's credit, such appropriations being commonplace in American popular song at that time. If true, then "Squeeze Me" is by far the most important product of Razaf's first dozen years of professional songwriting.

In 1924 Razaf initiated a modest complementary career, singing on radio broadcasts under Williams's direction and, as "Anthony," forming a song-and-dance duo with Doc Straine at the Club Alabam, where FLETCHER HENDERSON's big band was based. Razaf contributed to and toured with the revue *Desires* from October 1926 through early 1927, wrote with Waller late in 1927 for the Broadway revue *Keep Shufflin'*, and collaborated with the songwriter J. C. Johnson for the revue *Brown Skin Models*, with which he toured in 1928. Having achieved modest hits with lyrics to Johnson's songs "My Special Friend," "When," and "Louisiana" (1926–1928), Razaf wrote both words and melody for the delightfully clever, humorous, and risqué song "My Handy Man" (1928).

Razaf's greatest work began in February 1929 in collaboration with Waller and songwriter Harvey Brooks (whose precise contribution is unknown) for the show *Hot Feet*, which was modified and renamed *Connie's Hot Chocolates* in June. The show ran at both Connie's Inn in Harlem and at the Hudson Theater downtown. "Ain't Misbehavin'" displays Razaf's characteristic talent for expressing an innocently suggestive outlook. By contrast, "(What Did I Do to Be So) Black and Blue?" presented separately by the singers EDITH WILSON and LOUIS ARMSTRONG in different portions of the show, is unusual and was the first significant African American protest in American popular song.

Later that same year Razaf wrote "S'posin'" with another regular collaborator, the English-born songwriter Paul Denniker; "Gee, Baby, Ain't I Good to You?" with DON REDMAN; and "Honeysuckle Rose" with Waller, this last for a new revue at Connie's Inn, *Load of Coal*. In 1930 Razaf wrote "A Porter's Love Song to a Chambermaid" with James P. Johnson for the *Kitchen Mechanic's Revue* at Smalls' Paradise in Harlem, and "Memories of You" and "My Handy Man Ain't Handy No More" with EUBIE BLAKE for Lew Leslie's *Blackbirds of 1930*. *Blackbirds* starred MINTO CATO, with whom Razaf was living, although he was still married to Annabelle. "Keepin' Out of Mischief Now," written with Waller, was a hit in 1932. From that year into the 1940s Razaf wrote for new musical comedies at Connie's Inn (which closed in 1933), at the Grand Terrace in Chicago, at the Cotton Club in Cleveland, and at the Ubangi Club (on the site of Connie's Inn), but the content of these shows grew excessively predictable and their success diminished accordingly. Nonetheless, Razaf wrote lyrics for "Christopher Columbus," "Big Chief de Sota" (two marvelously silly songs), and "Stompin' at the Savoy," all from 1936, and "The Joint Is Jumpin'" (1937). Despite all this he was in continuous financial difficulty, as unscrupulous managers, producers, and publishers, both white and African American, took advantage of him, denying him opportunities and appropriating portions of his composing royalties. No doubt racist structures contributed to this situation, particularly in his exclusion from a new and lucrative forum for lyricists, Hollywood movie musicals; however, Razaf himself exacerbated the situation time and again by shortsightedly bartering away future royalties for modest fixed fees.

Finally divorced, he married Jean Blackwell in 1939, and they settled in Englewood, New Jersey. Amid his continuing financial problems and extramarital affairs during the 1940s, and in the absence of new professional success, the relationship ended. On obtaining a second divorce he married Dorothy Carpenter in 1948 and moved to Los Angeles. Neither marriage produced children. Despite all of his naive dealings Razaf still received enough royalties as a member of ASCAP (American Society of Publishers, Authors, and Composers) to survive. In 1951 a spinal attack of tertiary syphilis made him a paraplegic. Dorothy supervised his care until, at decade's end, her infidelity led to his third divorce. In January 1963 he was reunited with Alice Wilson, whom he had renamed Alicia when at age fourteen she met him in Chicago in 1934. They married the next month, and she cared for him in his final years. He died in North Hollywood, California.

In the decade 1928–1937 Razaf was one of the most important lyricists in American popular song. His ability to create at a moment's notice a polished verse, perfectly matched to a given melody, was legendary. And however brilliantly spontaneous his-method may have been, the results epitomize popular song of the swing era, in which sentiments of joy, nostalgia, politeness, and yearning toy with sensuality.

FURTHER READING
Brackney, R. L. "The Musical Legacy of Andy Razaf," *Jazz Report* 8, no. 5 (1974).
Singer, Barry. *Black and Blue: The Life and Lyrics of Andy Razaf* (1992).
Obituaries: *New York Times* and *Los Angeles Times*, 4 Feb. 1973.
This entry is taken from the *American National Biography* and is published here with the permission of the American Council of Learned Societies.

BARRY KERNFELD

Reagan, John Walter (5 Mar. 1920–31 Aug. 1994), naval officer, was born in Marshall, Texas, one of three children of John Llwellyn, a mechanically inclined jack of all trades who at one time worked for the Buick Company in Michigan, and Bernice Bonita Ector Reagan, a domestic servant. The family left Texas when Reagan was a child. He grew up in Shreveport, Louisiana; Chicago, Illinois; and Flint, Michigan. Most of his education was in Chicago, where he graduated from Lindblom High School in 1939. A talented athlete, Reagan won city and state championships in wrestling and earned letters as well in football, track, and boxing. He also earned scholastic honors in high school. He was recruited to Montana State University in Missoula on a football scholarship. Reagan was a quarterback, running back, and blocking back on various plays. He completed five semesters of instruction there but did not return after the fall semester in 1941 because he had applied for pilot training with the U.S. Army Air Forces.

After leaving school, Reagan returned to Chicago to work while awaiting orders. However, after the nation entered World War II as an active combatant in December 1941, Reagan received pressure from his draft board, so he enlisted in the navy in July 1942 as an apprentice seaman while his Army Air Force application was still pending. Soon afterward he received orders for Army Air Forces training, but by then it was too late. Reagan underwent recruit training in the all-black Camp Robert Smalls, part of the large Great Lakes Naval Training Station complex north of Chicago. Subsequently he was ordered to the naval training school established on the grounds of Hampton Institute, a vocational school in Hampton, Virginia, for African American students. He graduated in December 1942 and was rated as an electrician's mate third class. Until June 1942 black sailors had been limited almost exclusively to being cooks and servants for white officers. With the opening of general service ratings to blacks, Reagan was among the early trainees in the electrical field. He then served in the crew of the auxiliary minesweeper *Firefly*, based at Point Loma, San Diego, California.

Reagan's first marriage, in September 1943, was to Lillian Davis. During their seventeen years together, they had four children: son John W. "Skip" Reagan, Jr., and daughters Bernida, Katherine Anne, and Penny Elizabeth. (Twenty-year-old Marine Corporal Skip Reagan was later killed by hostile fire in July 1966 while serving in Vietnam.)

In the autumn of 1943 Reagan was advanced to electrician's mate second class and in January 1944 reported to Great Lakes as one of sixteen members of a training course that would lead to the commissioning of the first black officers in the history of the U.S. Navy. The sixteen were selected from a population of some 100,000 black sailors. Included in the process were recommendations by white officers and detailed background investigations by the FBI. In two and a half months, the sixteen men went through a cram course that included training in such areas as navigation, communications, gunnery, propulsion machinery, seamanship, naval history, and the navy disciplinary system. At the conclusion of training in March 1944 Reagan was among twelve men commissioned as Naval Reserve ensigns; one other man became a warrant officer.

Years later these pioneers were retroactively titled the "Golden Thirteen." The other three men passed the course but were not commissioned.

Following his commissioning, Ensign Reagan returned to the service school at Hampton Institute. The commanding officer of the school was Commander E. Hall Downes, a naval academy graduate with a background in education. He assigned Reagan to serve as officer in charge of the electrical school; in practice, Reagan was also a role model for the hundreds of black sailors in the school. At the time black officers were not yet able to serve in combatant-type ships. Reagan was instead assigned to a submarine chaser and later to a tugboat that operated in the vicinity of New York City. At war's end he was assigned to Guam and Okinawa as part of a logistic support company made up of black enlisted personnel who worked as stevedores. These men loaded and unloaded ships as the navy geared up for the planned invasion of the Japanese home islands in late 1945. Instead, the war ended in September 1945, and Reagan, by then a lieutenant (junior grade), was released from active duty in January 1946.

Back in civilian life, Reagan resumed his education at Montana State, from which he graduated in June 1948 with a bachelor's degree in Economics and Sociology. (He later took graduate courses in public administration at the Univeristy of Southern California.) In 1948 Reagan played one season of professional football for the Winnipeg Blue Bombers of the Canadian Football League. After a few years of civilian life and holding two jobs, Reagan returned to active navy duty. Whereas the navy had reluctantly commissioned its first black officers in 1944 in response to political pressure, by the late 1940s it had changed course and was actively seeking to recruit African Americans. Reagan had maintained his Naval Reserve commission, and in 1949 the navy recalled him to active duty to take part in the recruiting effort in New York City; he was promoted to lieutenant in 1950. He went on to serve overseas and from 1953 to 1954 was executive officer of Boat Unit One in Yokosuka, Japan, before being released to inactive duty in 1954. He continued to participate in the naval reserve and in the early 1960s was promoted to lieutenant commander.

Reagan's second marriage, to Dr. Hazel P. Morse from 1960 to 1980, also ended in divorce. His third wife was the former Willita "Dede" Thompson, whom he married on Christmas Day in 1983, and who survived Reagan when he died in 1994. (Reagan did not have children after his first marriage.)

In his postnaval civilian endeavors Reagan was involved in several areas, including working for the California State Department of Employment. He also spent several years with the Los Angeles and Pasadena, California, offices of the National Urban League. Among his concerns were job training for youths, development of community housing, and restoration of the Watts section of Los Angeles in the wake of devastating riots there in 1965. Later he was active as a real estate broker and investor in San Diego, California.

FURTHER READING

"Reminiscences of John W. Reagan, Member of the Golden Thirteen." United States Naval Institute (1991). This oral history consists of a bound volume of transcripts of the oral interviews. Copies are available at the Naval Institute and Naval Academy library in Annapolis, Maryland, and at the Naval Historical Center in Washington, D.C.

Stillwell, Paul, ed. *The Golden Thirteen: Recollections of the First Black Naval Officers* (1993).

PAUL STILLWELL

Reagon, Bernice Johnson (4 Oct. 1942–), musician, social activist, songtalker, and scholar, was born Bernice Johnson in Albany, Georgia, the daughter of a Baptist minister, the Reverend Jessie Johnson, and a homemaker, Beatrice Johnson. Johnson was steeped in the traditions and culture of the southwestern Georgia community surrounding Mt. Early Baptist Church. Her home church did not have a piano for many years, so she honed her a cappella vocal skills in the school and church choir.

After graduating from high school, she auditioned for the music program at Albany State College and was accepted, enrolling in 1959 as music major. While in college, she served as the secretary of the youth division of the NAACP and became more deeply drawn into the civil rights struggle. Reagon began to attend meetings of the Student Nonviolent Coordinating Committee (SNCC) in the city and eventually formed a bond with Cordell Reagon, a field marshal for SNCC and a gifted singer. Her arrest in 1961 and her consequent expulsion from college served as a catalyst for further organizing. After attending Spelman College briefly later that year, Reagon was compelled to return to full-time work for SNCC and returned home.

In 1962 she and Rutha Harris, both minister's daughters studying voice at Albany State College, joined forces with Cordell Reagon and Charles Neblett to form the SNCC Freedom Singers, a group that sang locally and toured nationally to arouse interest and support for the growing civil rights movement. The SNCC Freedom Singers rallied support for those arrested in the movement, sang at the jails, rallies, and meetings and made an historic appearance at the 1963 March on Washington. In an interview in *Smithsonian Global Sound*, Reagon said that during this time, she saw freedom songs "pull sections of the Black community at times when other means of communication were ineffective. It was the first time that I knew the power of song to be an instrument for the articulation of our community concerns." Bernice Johnson and Cordell Reagon married in 1963. Reagon gave birth to their daughter, Toshi, in 1964, and her son, Kwan, in 1965. Although the demands of motherhood were many, she was still able to record her first album in 1964, entitled *Songs of the South*. Her demanding schedule would be exacerbated by her single motherhood status after she split with her husband in the late 1960s. In 1966 she became a founding member and director of the Harambee Singers in Atlanta, a group of black a cappella women singers who also sang at rallies, marches, and protests. She also reenrolled at Spelman College and graduated in 1970 with a B.A. in History.

Opportunities then beckoned her to Washington, D.C.; in 1972, she became the vocal director for the D.C. Black Repertory Theater and enrolled in the graduate school at Howard University. In 1973 she embarked on what would become a thirty-year journey when she founded Sweet Honey in the Rock, the widely acclaimed Grammy Award-winning a cappella singing group composed solely of black women. The name is a biblical and metaphoric reference to both the strength and sweetness of black women. She composed, arranged, and sang with the group, which continued to perform the sacred music of the African American experience, jazz, blues, and liberation songs well into the 2000s. The group benefited from Reagon's skills as a performer, artistic director, and writer. Under her artistic direction, the group produced several albums and CDs, including *Sweet Honey in the Rock, Feel Something Drawing Me On, Sacred Ground, Still on the Journey*, and *Live at Carnegie Hall*.

In 1974 Reagon began working as a folklorist, program director, and curator for the Smithsonian Institution while she continued to develop material and tour with *Sweet Honey in the Rock*. She received her Ph.D. in History from Howard University in 1975.

Dr. Reagon received the prestigious MacArthur Fellowship in 1989. She edited and contributed to

We'll Understand it Better By and By (1992), a collection of essays highlighting gospel history and performers, in addition to writing *We Who Believe in Freedom: Sweet Honey in the Rock—Still on the Journey* (1993). Also that year she joined the faculty of American University as Distinguished Professor of History; also that year she became a curator emerita at the Smithsonian Institute. She received the Peabody Award in 1994 for *Wade in the Water: African American Sacred Traditions*. In 1995 she won the Charles Frankel Award and Presidential Medal and she won the Isadora Duncan Award in 1996 for her score for the ballet titled *Rock*.

In addition to organizing her own company, Songtalk Publishing, to manage her music and other works, Reagon was a much-sought-after musician. She served as the principal composer, arranger, and consultant for many television programs and films. These endeavors included the landmark PBS history of the civil rights movement, *Eyes on the Prize*, and the Ken Burns series *The Civil War*. She served as a composer for *Beah: A Black Woman Speaks*, the film *Beloved*, and the miniseries *Africans in America: America's Journey through Slavery*, for which she received a Peabody Award in 1998.

She contributed to *Home Girls: A Black Feminist Anthology* (2000) and published articles in the *Journal of American History*, *Black Music Research Journal*, and *Black Scholar*, among others. Also that year she won the Leeway Laurel National Award for Women in the Arts. She authored a history of gospel titled *If You Don't Go, Don't Hinder Me* (2001). In 2002 she became a professor emerita at American University. She was appointed the William and Camille Cosby Endowed Professor in the Fine Arts at Spelman College from 2002 to 2004.

In 2003 she was given the Heinz Award for the Arts and Humanities. Also that year, in collaboration with dramatist Robert Wilson, she created the music and the libretto for *The Temptation of Saint Anthony*, which premiered in Germany and traveled to several European countries, with a New York premiere in 2005. In this production, she worked with her daughter Toshi—an accomplished musician in her own right—who served as the tour's musical director. Together, they produced the studio cast recording in 2006. Dr. Reagon has also been awarded honorary doctorates from Bates College, Boston College, Spelman College, the University of Michigan, Princeton University, and several other colleges and universities.

A fierce advocate for social justice and a believer in music's potential to celebrate unity in diversity, Reagon enriched the gospel tradition and black feminism through both her music and her scholarship.

FURTHER READING

A significant collection of Bernice Johnson Reagan's works can be found at the Smithsonian Folkways Recordings in Washington, D.C.

Harding, Rachel, and Vincent Harding. "Singing to Freedom," *Sojourners* (Aug. 2004).

Harrington, Richard. "Singing the Freedom Song; Bernice Johnson Reagon: Through Words and Music, the Voice of Culture," *Washington Post* (23 June 1987).

Kernan, Michael. "Conveying History Through Song," *Smithsonian* (Feb. 1999).

JOAN F. MCCARTY

Reason, Charles Lewis (21 July 1818–16 Aug. 1893), educator and reformer, was born in New York City, the son of Michel Reason and Elizabeth Melville, both from the Caribbean. Reason attended the African Free-School along with his brothers Elmer Reason and PATRICK HENRY REASON, the illustrator-engraver, as well as with the future abolitionists HENRY HIGHLAND GARNET, ALEXANDER CRUMMELL, and JAMES MCCUNE SMITH, and the future actor IRA FREDERICK ALDRIDGE. An excellent student in mathematics, Reason became an instructor at the school at the age of fourteen, receiving a salary of twenty-five dollars a year. He used some of his earnings to hire tutors to improve his knowledge. Later he decided to enter the ministry, but he was rejected because of his race by the General Theological Seminary of the Protestant Episcopal Church in New York City. Reason rejected such "sham Christianity" and resigned in protest from Saint Philip's Church, the congregation sponsoring his application. Undaunted by Episcopal racism he studied at McGrawville College in McGraw, New York.

Reason decided to pursue a career in teaching, believing strongly that education was the best means for black advancement. In the British abolitionist Julia Griffiths's *Autographs for Freedom* (1854) Reason wrote that a black industrial college would prepare free blacks, who were shut out of the "workshops of the country," to become "self-providing artizans vindicating their people from the never-ceasing charge of a fitness for servile positions." In 1847 Reason and CHARLES BENNETT RAY founded the Society for the Promotion of Education among Colored Children, a black organization authorized by the state legislature to oversee black schools in

New York City. Reason served as superintendent of P.S. 2 in 1848, and FREDERICK DOUGLASS wrote in the *North Star* of 11 May 1849 that under Reason's leadership the school had become a rigorous refutation of the calumnies of John C. Calhoun about the potentials of free blacks.

In 1849 Reason became the first African American to hold a professorship in an American college when he was hired as professor of *belles lettres*, Greek, Latin, and French and adjunct professor of mathematics at the integrated New York Central College in Cortland County. In 1852 he became the principal of the Institute for Colored Youth in Philadelphia (later Cheyney State University), where he expanded the enrollment from six students in 1852 to 118 students in 1855, improved the library, and made the school a forum for distinguished visiting speakers.

In 1855 Reason returned permanently to New York City to begin thirty-seven continuous years as a teacher and administrator in city schools. In 1873 he headed the successful movement to outlaw segregation in New York schools. In 1882 teachers, superintendents, and principals of the New York City school system honored him for fifty years of service. He was chairman of the Committee on Grammar School Work of the Teacher's Association in 1887. When Reason resigned in 1892 he held the longest tenure in the school system.

Reason was also active politically throughout his life. He was committed to the antislavery cause and worked unceasingly for improvement of black civil rights. In 1837 Reason, Henry Highland Garnet, and GEORGE THOMAS DOWNING launched a petition drive in support of full black suffrage. He was also secretary of the 1840 New York State Convention for Negro Suffrage. Reason founded and was executive secretary of the New York Political Improvement Association, which won for fugitive slaves the right to a jury trial in the state. In 1841 he lobbied successfully for the abolition of the sojourner law, which permitted slave owners to visit the state briefly with their slaves. He also lectured on behalf of the Fugitive Aid Society. An active reporter on education to the black national convention movement of the 1850s, he was secretary of the 1853 convention in Rochester, New York.

Reason spoke out against the American Colonization Society and against Garnet's African Civilization Society. In 1849 Reason, along with JAMES WILLIAM CHARLES PENNINGTON and Douglass, sponsored a mass demonstration against colonization at Shiloh Presbyterian Church in New York City. At the meeting Reason quoted a former American Colonization Society agent in Africa, who claimed that the president and secretary of the society's colony of Liberia had business dealings with European slave traders on the African coast. During the Civil War, Reason served on New York City's Citizen's Civil Rights Committee, which lobbied the New York State legislature for expanded black civil rights. After the conflict he was vice president of the New York State Labor Union. At a union meeting in 1870 he delivered a paper in which he gave statistical proof that education helped New York City blacks gain prosperity.

Reason was also a writer. He contributed verse to the *Colored American* in the 1830s and was a leader of New York City's Phoenix Society in the 1840s. He wrote the poem "Freedom," which celebrated the abolitionist Thomas Clarkson and was published in Alexander Crummell's 1849 biography of Clarkson.

Reason's personal life is obscure. He was married and widowed three times; only the identity of his third wife, Clorice Esteve, is known. He died in New York City.

FURTHER READING

Mayo, Anthony R. "Charles Lewis Reason," *Negro History Bulletin* 5 (June 1942).

Ripley, C. Peter, et al., eds. *The Black Abolitionist Papers* (5 vols., 1985–1992).

Simmons, William J. *Men of Mark: Eminent, Progressive, and Rising* (1887).

This entry is taken from the *American National Biography* and is published here with the permission of the American Council of Learned Societies.

GRAHAM R. HODGES

Reason, Joseph Paul (22 Mar. 1941–), naval officer, was born in Washington, D.C., the second child of Joseph Henry and Bernice Chism Reason. His parents, both of whom had degrees from Howard University, met when they were teaching at Florida A&M University, also a traditionally black school. They subsequently moved to Washington, where both worked in the field of education. His mother taught chemistry, physics, and biology in public high schools; his father, who had a Ph.D. in Romance Languages and a master's in Library Science, worked for many years as Director of University Libraries at Howard. Reason received his elementary and secondary education in segregated schools in Washington and graduated in 1958 from the city's newly integrated McKinley Technical

High School. He applied for a Naval Reserve Officer Training Corps scholarship and had the second highest score of the three hundred applicants who took the entrance exam; but he was turned down because of his race. Instead, in 1958 he accepted a scholarship to Swarthmore College, a liberal arts school in the Philadelphia area. Next he spent a year at Lincoln University, a traditionally black institution in Chester County, Pennsylvania, also near Philadelphia. For his third year he transferred to his parents' alma mater, Howard University, to study electrical engineering.

While Reason attended Howard, Congressman Charles Diggs was investigating charges of racial bias in Naval Academy appointments and looking for qualified black applicants. Howard's dean of men recommended Reason, whom Diggs then appointed. In 1961, with three years of college under his belt, Reason entered the Naval Academy in Annapolis, Maryland, as a plebe, the equivalent of a freshman. He received the usual hazing targeted against plebes, but none was obviously racial. In fact, only a few of his fellow midshipmen, upper classmen, expressed displeasure with his being there. Even so, there were awkward moments, such as when he showed up for mandatory dancing instruction and found that only white girls were available as partners. The dancing teacher told Reason he was dismissed from the class. The Naval Academy invited Reason's girlfriend (and future wife) Dianne Lillian Fowler to be present for subsequent lessons.

During his time at the academy, Midshipman Reason split time between academics and professional training, including summer cruises on board warships. In addition, he applied to enter the navy's nuclear power program, which was run by Admiral Hyman Rickover. As he was with all candidates, Rickover was demanding and difficult. He tried to get Reason to promise to improve his class standing. Reason promised to do well in his studies but said he couldn't guarantee improvement over his peers because that was beyond his control. Rickover accepted him into the program. At the end of his four years, Reason earned a degree in engineering and stood number 302 of the 802 graduates in the class of 1965. He was the twenty-fifth African American graduate of the Naval Academy; the first had been WESLEY A. BROWN in the class of 1949. In June 1965, three days after his graduation, Reason married Dianne Lillian Fowler. Her father, a West Point graduate, was a professor of military science at Morgan State College in Baltimore. They subsequently had two children, Rebecca L., who became an accountant, and Joseph P. Jr., who graduated from the Naval Academy in 1990 and became a naval officer.

Ensign Reason's first assignment as a commissioned officer was a brief one in the World War II-era vintage destroyer escort *J. Douglas Blackwood*, where he qualified as officer of the deck (under way) while awaiting nuclear power training in the autumn of 1965. He attended Nuclear Power School at Bainbridge, Maryland, for rigorous classroom instruction. Later he received practical experience during six months of training at a shore-based nuclear prototype plant in Ballston Spa, New York. While many of the students were slated for submarines, Reason opted to enter the program for nuclear-powered surface ships, of which the navy then had only three. His first assignment after training was to the guided missile frigate *Truxtun*, which was under construction. Reason was part of the initial crew when the ship went into commission in May 1967. The ship proceeded to the West Coast and operations out of her homeport of Long Beach, California, to the Western Pacific. During his time on board, Reason served in the engineering department as reactor training officer and qualified as officer of the deck.

The next step in his professional development was attendance at the Naval Postgraduate School in Monterey, California. In 1970 he received a master's degree in Computer Systems Management. Then it was back to sea, this time as electrical officer in the nuclear-powered aircraft carrier *Enterprise*, which deployed to the Vietnam War zone and into the Indian Ocean. During this period Admiral Elmo Zumwalt Jr., the Chief of Naval Operations, established racial sensitivity training throughout the service, and Reason added his perspective in the sessions he attended. After a course at Destroyer School in Newport, Rhode Island, Reason reported once again to the *Truxtun*, this time as combat systems officer. He was now focused on guns, missiles, submarine detection devices, radars, and computers—a departure from the engineering duty he'd had for the most part until then.

In mid-1976 Reason reported to the Bureau of Naval Personnel in Arlington, Virginia, where he was involved in the assignment of nuclear-trained surface warfare officers to various duties. Late that year, he was selected to serve as naval aide to President Jimmy Carter, a post he held until mid-1979. In that role, Lieutenant Commander Reason had an office in the White House and often accompanied the president on trips. Among his duties was to carry the "football," a briefcase that contained information reported by the media to be used in connection with possible nuclear weapons use. As a commander, Reason returned to sea later in 1979 as executive officer, second in command, of the new nuclear-powered cruiser *Mississippi*, then moved on to his first command as skipper of the oil-fueled guided missile destroyer *Coontz*. The ship operated as part of the Atlantic Fleet and made a deployment to West Africa, the Mediterranean, and the Black Sea. His next assignment was as captain of the nuclear-powered cruiser *Bainbridge*, another step up professionally. She operated out of San Diego before going to the naval shipyard in Bremerton, Washington, for a lengthy overhaul and then heading to the Atlantic. In November 1985 Reason learned that he had become the first in his Naval Academy class to be selected for the rank of rear admiral.

In 1986, after leaving the *Bainbridge*, Admiral Reason reported for duty as Commander Naval Base Seattle, responsible for naval activities in Oregon, Washington, and Alaska. His first seagoing command as a flag officer was as Commander Cruiser-Destroyer Group One. A concurrent billet was as Commander Battle Group Romeo during operations in the Pacific, Indian Ocean, and Persian Gulf. Among his flagships was the battleship *New Jersey*. In early 1991 he was promoted to the rank of three-star vice admiral. He was only the second African American to reach that rank; the first was Vice Admiral SAMUEL L. GRAVELY JR. some twenty years earlier. Reason's first three-star billet was as Commander Naval Surface Force Atlantic Fleet. His command aided in dealing with refugees from Haiti and hurricane victims in the Caribbean. He also acquired a distasteful collateral assignment as the adjudicating officer for the naval aviators who were implicated in the Tailhook scandal, which stemmed from sexual misbehavior at a convention in Las Vegas in September 1991.

His next three-star job, beginning in 1994, was as Deputy Chief of Naval Operations (Plans, Policy, and Operations), an assignment with broad responsibilities, including strategic and geopolitical considerations. It tied fleet operations in with policymaking through the developing global naval force presence policy. His responsibilities included running the Navy Command Center in the Pentagon and serving as navy operations deputy during meetings of the Joint Chiefs of Staff. He was also involved in base realignment and closure recommendations. While in the assignment, Reason was instrumental in increasing the use of computers for communication, data transmission, and decision-making.

In December 1996 Reason became Commander in Chief Atlantic Fleet, based in Norfolk, Virginia. In achieving that post, Reason became the first black four-star admiral in the history of the U.S. Navy. The navy was thus more than twenty years behind the Air Force, which in 1975 promoted DANIEL "CHAPPIE" JAMES JR. to four-star rank. The first four-star army general was Roscoe Robinson in 1982. In commanding one of the two major operating divisions of the navy, Reason was charged with the readiness of ships, aircraft, and shore installations in a wide geographic area. One particular emphasis of his tenure was in promoting relationships with foreign navies, particularly those in Latin America, and thus he traveled widely. He published a 1998 monograph titled *Sailing New Seas*, written in conjunction with David G. Freymann and consolidating the thoughts of a number of other senior naval officers. The thrust of the work was that the navy must continue to change and adapt, to be faster, more flexible, and tied together by technology—thus presaging a number of the "transformational" initiatives since made by the service in the early years of the twenty-first century. Upon his retirement from the navy in 1999, Reason became vice president for ship systems with Syntek Technologies, based in Arlington, Virginia. From 2000 to 2005 he served as president and chief operating officer of Metro Machine Corporation, a shipyard in Norfolk, Virginia, and in the year 2005–2006 he was vice chairman of that corporation. He also served on several corporate boards.

FURTHER READING

Admiral Reason's papers are in the special collections department of the Naval Academy Library, Annapolis, Maryland.

Reason, J. Paul, with David G. Freymann. *Sailing New Seas* (1998).

Massaquoi, Hans J. "The Navy's First Black Four-Star Admiral," *Ebony* (Apr. 1998).

PAUL STILLWELL

Reason, Patrick Henry (April? 1816–12 Aug. 1898), printmaker and abolitionist, was born in New York City, the son of Michel Reason of St. Anne, Guadeloupe, and Elizabeth Melville of Saint-Dominique. Reason was baptized as Patrick Rison in the Church of St. Peter on 17 April 1816. While it is not known why the spelling of his name changed, it may have been an homage to the political leader

Patrick Henry. While he was still a student at the African Free School in New York, his first engraving was published, the frontispiece to Charles C. Andrews's *The History of the New York African Free-Schools* (1830). It carried the byline "Engraved from a drawing by P. Reason, aged thirteen years." Shortly thereafter, Reason became apprenticed to a white printmaker, Stephen Henry Gimber, and then maintained his own studio at 148 Church Street in New York, where he offered a wide variety of engraving services. Reason was among the earliest and most successful of African American printmakers.

A skilled orator, Reason delivered a speech, "Philosophy of the Fine Arts," to the Phoenixonian Literary Society in New York on 4 July 1837. (It is unclear whether this association was the same as the Phoenix Society, a benevolent organization that had been founded by the Reverend PETER WILLIAMS in 1833.) The *Colored American* newspaper reported this speech to be "ably written, well delivered, and indicative of talent and research." In 1838 Reason won first premium (prize) for his India ink drawing exhibited at the Mechanics Institute Fair, and he advertised himself in the *Colored American* as a "Historical, Portrait and Landscape Engraver, Draughtsman & Lithographer" who could produce "Address, Visiting and Business Cards, Certificates, Jewelry &c., neatly engraved." He also gave evening instruction in "scientific methods of drawing," worked for Harpers Publishers preparing map plates, and did government engraving. Reason appeared as a "cold" ("colored") engraver in New York City directories from 1846 to 1866.

Perhaps Reason's best-known works are his copper engravings of chained slaves. The first, featuring a female figure and the caption "Am I Not a Woman and a Sister?" (1835), was a common letterhead of abolitionists from the mid-1830s onward and was reproduced on both British and American antislavery plaques, publications, coins, and medals. (However, while he was a staunch abolitionist, Reason did not initially support women's rights; he attended the annual meeting of the American Anti-Slavery Society in 1839 and signed a protest against extending the vote to women in the society and against their serving as officers.) A later, similar engraving (1839?) depicts a kneeling young male slave wearing tattered clothing, his wrists bound by long, thick manacles. With his head cocked to the side in a forlorn expression, he clasps his hands in prayer. This version, entitled *Am I Not a Man and a Brother?*, embellished membership certificates of Philadelphia, Pennsylvania's Vigilant Committee,

a group of young African American activists who aided escaped slaves. The committee's secretary, Jacob C. White Sr., or its president, ROBERT PURVIS, whose names are on the certificate, may have commissioned the piece. Reason's source for the imagery may have been Wedgwood relief designs or a seal (1787) bearing the same motto along with a chained, kneeling slave in a similar position and attitude, used by the English Committee for the Abolition of the Slave Trade.

As a freelance engraver and lithographer, Reason produced portraits and designs for periodicals and frontispieces in slave narratives in the mid-nineteenth century. Typically, his portraits were profile or three-quarters, bust-length images of men with stoic expressions and dressed in coats and ties, set against black backgrounds. Examples appear in Lydia Maria Child's *The Fountain for Every Day in the Year* (1836); *A Memoir of Granville Sharp* (1836), for which Reason based his work on an earlier engraving of the British abolitionist and reformer by T. B. Lord; *Narrative of James Williams, an American Slave: Who Was Several Years a Driver on a Cotton Plantation in Alabama* (1838); John Wesley's *Thoughts on Slavery Written in 1774* (reprinted in 1839); *Liberty Bell* (1839, "The Church Shall Make You Free"); and *Baptist Memorial* (members of the London Emancipation Society, the Reverend Baptist Noel and the Reverend Thomas Baldwin). Three works by Reason appeared in the *U.S. Magazine and Democratic Review*: portraits of the Ohio antislavery senator Benjamin Tappan, after a painting by Washington Blanchard (June 1840, which later appeared in the *Annual Obituary Notices* in 1857 and 1858); the lawyer and diplomat George Mifflin Dallas (February 1842); and the mathematician Robert Adrain, after a painting by Ingraham (June 1844).

Reason also completed two portraits of the antislavery lecturer HENRY BIBB, a lithograph (1840) and a copper engraving featured in *Narrative of the Life and Adventures of Henry Bibb, an American Slave* (1849). While the lithograph depicts Bibb standing rigidly before a draped window, the engraving portrays him casually holding a book in his right hand, posed against a dark background. Among Reason's other works were an engraving of a mountainous landscape after a drawing by W. H. Bartlett and a copper nameplate for Daniel Webster's coffin. Additional subjects included the slave James Williams (1838), the abolitionist PETER WILLIAMS JR., New York's governor De Witt Clinton, and the physician JAMES MCCUNE SMITH. In 1838 Reason arranged a public meeting to honor Smith on his return from a European trip. In 1840 he worked with Smith at the Albany Convention of Colored Citizens in drafting a letter to the U.S. Senate protesting racist remarks made by Secretary of State John C. Calhoun to the British minister to the United States regarding a slave revolt onboard the *Creole*.

In the 1840s and 1850s Reason was active in a number of civic groups and fraternal orders. He served as secretary of the New York Society for the Promotion of Education among Colored Children, founded in 1847. As a member of the New York Philomathean Society, organized in 1830 for literary improvement and social pleasure, he petitioned the International Order of Odd Fellows for the society to become a lodge of the association. Although the application was refused, the society received a dispensation from Victoria Lodge No. 448 in Liverpool and became Hamilton Lodge No. 710 in 1844. Reason served as grand master and permanent secretary of the group in the 1850s. His speech at the annual meeting in 1856 was declared the finest given up to that time. Reason not only developed the secret ritual of the order but also composed the Ruth degree, the first "degree to be conferred under certain conditions on Females," and in 1858 he was the first person to receive the honor.

Reason also served as grand secretary of the New York Masons from 1859 to 1860 and as grand master from 1862 to 1868, receiving the Thirty-third Degree of Masonry in 1862. Simultaneously, he was grand master of the Supreme Council for the States, Territories, and Dependencies. The printmaker created original certificates of membership for both the Grand United Order of Odd Fellows and the Masonic Fraternity.

Reason may have taught in the New York schools after 1850. Public School No. 1 was associated with the American and Foreign Anti-Slavery Society, an organization with which Reason had close ties. In 1852 MARTIN R. DELANY described Reason in *The Condition, Elevation, Emigration, and Destiny of the Colored People of the United States* as "a gentleman of ability and a fine artist" who "stands high as an engraver in the city of New York. Mr. Reason has been in business for years … and has sent out to the world, many beautiful specimens of his skilled hand." Reason also produced other artistic work. During the New York draft riots of 1863, merchants formed a committee for the relief of African American victims. The Reverend HENRY HIGHLAND GARNET wrote an address to the group that was "elaborately engrossed on parchment and tastefully framed by Patrick Reason, one of their own people."

In 1862 Reason married Esther Cunningham of Leeds, England; the couple had one son. Invited to work as an engraver with several firms in Cleveland, Reason moved to Ohio in 1869 and for the next fifteen years worked for the Sylvester Hogan jewelry firm. When Reason died in Cleveland, he left behind a large body of work that established him as one of the finest printmakers of the nineteenth century.

FURTHER READING

Brooks, Charles. *The Official History and Manual of the Grand United Order of Odd Fellows in America* (1871).

Jones, Steven Loring. "A Keen Sense of the Artistic: African American Material Culture in 19th Century Philadelphia," *International Review of African American Art* 12.2 (1995).

Porter, James A. *Modern Negro Art* (1943).

Obituary: *Cleveland Gazette*, 20 Aug. 1898.

This entry is taken from the *American National Biography* and is published here with the permission of the American Council of Learned Societies.

THERESA LEININGER-MILLER

Rector, Eddie (25 Dec. late 1890s–1962), dancer, was born in Orange, New Jersey, and moved to Philadelphia about age seven. His parents' names are unknown. He never studied dance but began performing while still a child, performing behind Mayme Remington, a former French burlesque dancer turned headliner, as one of her "picks" or "pickaninnies," a racial caricature of black children common in vaudeville and popular culture.

Rector first acquired a reputation in the stage show *The Darktown Follies* (1915). Though he joined as a chorus boy, he devised his own act in which he did a military-style tap routine—soon imitated by many others—which the producers promptly incorporated into the show. After the show closed, Rector remained in New York City, partnering with another chorus boy from *The Darktown Follies* named Toots Davis. For the remainder of the 1910s and into the 1920s Rector was one of the best of the tap-dance acts in the revues that traveled on the TOBA circuit—a circuit that was for black performers approximately what vaudeville houses were for whites, providing work for a number of black entertainers before dying out during the Depression. Though the acronym "TOBA" stood for Theatre Owners' Booking Association, performers preferred "Tough on Black Asses" because of the pitiful pay scale. A typical TOBA show started rehearsing in April, spent all summer on the road, and returned to New York City in the fall. When in New York City, Rector liked to hang out at the Hoofer's Club, next door to the Lafayette Theatre.

When he was finally able to give up the TOBA circuit, Rector appeared in such shows as *Liza* (1922) and *Dixie to Broadway* (1924). He sometimes performed with his wife Grace or his brother Harry. In 1928 Rector replaced BILL ROBINSON in Lew Leslie's *Blackbirds of 1928* when that show went on tour. By then a Broadway star, Robinson had refused to travel with the show because of the low pay. Leslie asked Rector to copy Robinson's signature stair dance, provoking a short-lived feud between the two dancers when Rector acquiesced.

The tap dancing of just a few years earlier had been done in two-to-a-bar time in a straight-up, flashy style known as buck-and-wing dancing. Rector was one of those who smoothed out this style, adding more complex rhythms and steps even as he made the dancing seem more effortless. He used the entire stage while performing, gliding across it as if he were on skates. He invented several varieties of traveling time steps for that purpose, the most famous of which was the Bambalina. He "helped perfect a new style of tap dancing (perhaps derived from the white minstrel star George Primrose) in which he traveled across the stage with superb grace and elegance, a style that transcended the stereotypes of the strutting or shuffling 'darky' and culminated in the suave 'class acts' of the 1930s and later" (Stearns and Stearns, 127). Rector was a profound influence on many younger dancers, including BUDDY BRADLEY, Pete Nugent, and Steve Condos.

Rector's signature step was the sand dance, which he claimed to have originated. A sand dancer does not use tap shoes but instead disperses sand on the floor and produces the rhythmical effect from rubbing and sliding the sand around with his feet. Rector also claimed to have originated the practice of tap dancing on a drum while performing with DUKE ELLINGTON at the Cotton Club in Harlem.

Unfortunately, Rector never appeared in a good enough musical to make him a real star and was fated to appear in mediocre shows like *Hot Rhythm* (1930). The last big show in which he appeared during his prime was the flop *Yeah Man* (1932), which closed after four performances. Soon thereafter, for circumstances that remain unclear, Rector was confined to a mental institution for several years. After his recovery and release he teamed up with Ralph Cooper in the late 1940s and early 1950s.

Though he had lost much of his fire as a performer, Rector stole the show doing the sand dance in a brief attempt to revive the musical *Shuffle Along* in 1952. In October 1954 he performed in an evening of "nostalgia" at the soon-to-be-closed Savoy Ballroom. By 1960 Rector was working as a night watchman at a theater. Though saddled with calluses, fallen arches, and a frail-looking body, he was still looking for a break in the dance world. He died in New York City.

Eddie Rector was one of the greatest of the soft-shoe artists and a key figure in the transformation of tap dancing from its early buck-and-wing style into a graceful and elegant stagecraft.

FURTHER READING

Frank, Rusty E. *Tap! The Greatest Tap Dance Stars and Their Stories, 1900–1955* (1990).

Stearns, Marshall, and Jean Stearns. *Jazz Dance: The Story of American Vernacular Dance* (1968; rpt. 1994).

This entry is taken from the *American National Biography* and is published here with the permission of the American Council of Learned Societies.

ROBERT P. CREASE

Red Thunder Cloud (30 May 1919–8 Jan. 1996) (also known as Cromwell Ashbie Hawkins West, Carlos Ashbie Hawk Westez, Ashbie Hawkins West, and Namo S. Hatirire) activist, linguist, storyteller, performer, and shaman, was born in Newport, Rhode Island. There are varying accounts of Red Thunder Cloud's parentage and upbringing. According to his own account, he was born Carlos Ashibie Hawk Westez. As a young boy, he was brought up among the Narragansett Indians of Rhode Island by his Catawba mother, Roberta Hawk Westez, and his Honduran father, Carlos Panchito Westez. He is believed to have lived among the Shinnecock Indians of Long Island in the late 1930s. His actual home during much of this time was said to be on the Catawba Reservation in South Carolina, but he traveled extensively, visiting many Indian groups. This account of his early life has been challenged by Smithsonian anthropologist and ethnologist Ives Goddard who claimed that Red Thunder Cloud was the son of Cromwell West, a black Newport, Rhode Island, druggist and Roberta (Hawkins) West. Goddard's research was based on primary documents such as the birth, death, census, and work records of Newport, Rhode Island. Despite this challenge to the accounts of Red Thunder Cloud's early life, his later accomplishments are well documented.

Red Thunder Cloud lived an active life. In addition to his ethnographic work, he was employed as a watchman and chauffeur at the Newport, Rhode Island, City Wharf from 1935 until 1937. In 1938 Red Thunder Cloud became involved in ethnographic work with various institutions. He collected ethnographic data as well as folklore from the Long Island Montauk, Shinnecock, Mashpee, and Catawba Indians. Over the years, he became more conversant in the Catawba language. Many of these years were spent documenting the language with different ethnographers. When the dog warden in Southampton, New York, put nine of Red Thunder Cloud's dogs to sleep, he sued the town for $100,000 for damages to the development of the Catawba Indian language, because the dogs understood Catawba commands. Hailed as the last living speaker of the Catawba language, he made sure this idiom would not be lost after his death by making recordings of Catawaba speech, ancient songs, and legends.

In 1986 Red Thunder Cloud moved to Grafton, Massachusetts, and then to Northbridge, Massachusetts, in 1988. He traveled to local Native American events throughout New England performing as a storyteller, singer, and dancer. Red Thunder Cloud's Accabonac Princess American Indian Teas was his own line of herbal medicines he made from herbs collected in the forest near his home. The slogan read: "Fresh from the American Forest to you." His one recorded marriage to Jean Marilyn Miller (Pretty Pony), a Blackfoot woman, is said to have been brief. Red Thunder Cloud died at the age of seventy-six at St. Vincent Hospital in Worcester, Massachusetts.

FURTHER READING

Goddard, Ives. "The Identity of Red Thunder Cloud," *Society for the Study of Indigenous Languages of the Americas Newsletter* (Apr. 2000).

Mello, Michael. "Indians Display Arts for Town Bicentennial," *Providence Journal*, July 1987.

"The Death of Catawba," *Providence Journal* (Feb. 1996).

Obituaries: "Carlos 'Red Thunder Cloud' Westez; Catawba Nation Medicine Man, at 76," *Providence Journal*, Jan. 1996; Stout, David, "Red Thunder Cloud, 76, Dies," *New York Times*, Jan. 1996.

DARSHELL SILVA

Redden, Idessa Williams (27 Nov. 1912–15 Dec. 2005), civil rights activist and community leader, was born Idessa Taylor in Montgomery, Alabama, the only child of Minnie Oliver. Other than the surname he shared with his daughter, Idessa Taylor's father's name is not recorded. Upon the early death of her mother when she was only two, Redden's maternal great grandparents, Luisa and Julius Harris, raised Redden in Montgomery until she was nine. Thereafter, her mother's brother, Robert Oliver, a railroad worker, and his wife, Dinah Beatrice Oliver, a seamstress, included Redden in their family of six children. Redden attended St. Paul's Methodist Church School, Loveless School, St. John's Catholic School, and State Normal High School in Montgomery. As an elementary student on her way to school, she had to endure the habitual taunts of young white boys. In a videotaped interview on her ninetieth birthday, Redden recounted one occasion when, in retaliation for an attack on her, she chased one of the boys up his front steps and into his house to hit him. Although she had to leave very quickly, the white family did not physically harm her. Shortly after the incident, her aunt and uncle removed her to the nearby public school for her own safety, although she has insisted that she was not afraid of white people then or ever. That same fearlessness has characterized her movement and community activities for well over half a century.

Redden's family barely managed to pay the tuition for her to attend Alabama State Normal School's private high school, the only available high school for black students at the time. A lack of funds forced her to leave school in 1928 before completing the eleventh grade. By lying about her age to get a job, at fifteen she went to work making men's shirts at the Reliance Manufacturing Company to help support the family. After working at the company for about nine years, she confronted her boss, Clarence Giesing, the plant manager, and told him she would not spy on fellow black workers on their off hours. When Giesing angrily told her that she ought to "go up North and live," she told him, "Naw, I don't need to go up there. I'm going to stay right here and help these things straighten out!" (author's interview with Idessa Williams Redden, Montgomery, Alabama, 13 April 1997). One year later, in 1938, she quit Reliance for a career in beauty culture.

That same year, in 1938, Redden married George Williams, a carpenter; they had no children and divorced in 1971. She married her second husband, John Redden Sr., in 1978 and became the stepmother to his son, John Jr. At the time of her departure from the factory, Redden was studying beauty culture, specifically hairdressing, under the direction of Mrs. Bethesda, an agent and instructor in Annie Turnbo Malone's Poro system of hair care. Malone was a contemporary of Madame C. J. Walker, noted beauty culturist and black philanthropist, who, like Walker, developed her own line of beauty products and hair-care techniques designed especially for black women. By the early 1940s, Redden had opened her own shop in the back of her house, charging her customers fifty cents for a press and one dollar and fifty cents for a press and style. Aside from the money and independence that Redden derived from her beauty trade, she benefited from and contributed to the strong women's networks that emphasized the profitability of their own businesses and support of the black community. Other black beauticians, such as Mrs. Beautie Mae Johnson, had also worked at Reliance and were among Mrs. Redden's associates within the voter registration and bus boycott network of activists.

Because Redden was self-employed as a beautician and had experience in factory work, she was able to leave Montgomery from time to time to accompany her husband on his out-of-town jobs. In the several towns where he worked, she often picked up temporary factory employment to help augment his earnings. This sort of financial independence and mobility was very useful to her during the period of the Montgomery bus boycott of 1955–1956. As an independent beautician, she did not have to fear retribution from white employers because of her political involvements.

During the late 1930s, when Redden was in her mid twenties, she joined the National Association for the Advancement of Colored People (NAACP). She had heard Roy Wilkins, at that time the editor of the NAACP's *Crisis* magazine, assistant to the executive secretary, Walter White, and eventually his successor, give an inspiring speech at a large meeting she attended and was moved by him to join the organization's youth wing. Thereafter, she became friendly with E. D. Nixon, organizer for the Brotherhood of Sleeping Car Porters and head of the local NAACP branch and, later, Rosa Parks, to whom she often submitted her annual membership dues. Throughout her participation in other organizations, she steadfastly maintained her membership in the NAACP.

In 1949, Redden registered to vote. On successive first Mondays of each month for a period of at least six months during that year, she made her trek to the registrar's office to fill out the form that would qualify her for the franchise. She became interested in voting because she had read about the Reverend S. S. Seay's campaign in the mid 1940s to assist a young black woman who had been raped by two white police officers. Redden felt that if the sheriff who was responsible for his officers' behavior were elected, she was determined to help unelect him. On her first try, when the white woman registrar asked her what she wanted there, Mrs. Redden responded with a question of her own: "Why do you think I'm here?" By the time she was able to successfully meet the registration requirements, her poll tax amounted to thirty-six dollars, a very large sum at the time, which she was forced to pay to vote. Redden was also motivated to register so that she might become a member of Rufus Lewis's Citizens' Steering Committee, which required its members to become registered voters. During subsequent elections, Redden worked the polling places for Lewis's organization on behalf of candidates supported by Montgomery blacks. She also organized groups of young people to go door to door, canvassing potential voters.

When the Montgomery bus boycott swung into action on 5 December 1955, Redden had just returned from out of town and was informed by her cousin, Consuello Crittenden, not to ride the city buses that day. Her cousin urged her to attend the mass meeting at the Holt Street Baptist Church that evening where, for the first time, she heard the young Dr. Martin Luther King Jr. speak. She was immediately drawn to King's message and his oratorical power and promptly joined the Montgomery movement, lending her full commitment and participation in the struggle to end racial oppression. She worked for Rufus Lewis, who organized the carpools, driving people to and from their work sites. She testified for the defense on behalf of Martin Luther King Jr. who, along with more than one hundred others, was indicted by the state of Alabama for conspiring to conduct an illegal boycott. She eventually became a member of the Montgomery Improvement Association's board and continued her voter registration work.

During the next several decades, Redden remained a staunch champion of civil and human rights for black people in the South and elsewhere. An ardent supporter of King, nonviolent direct action, and voter registration, Redden focused much of her activism on her home state. In May 1961, she witnessed the carnage at the Greyhound Bus Station in Montgomery and assisted the Freedom Riders—groups of black and white activists testing the enforcement of the 1960 Supreme Court decision eliminating segregated interstate bus travel, waiting room, and restaurant service—who faced some of the worst violence in that city get to safety. She helped organize in Selma and participated in the Selma to Montgomery March in 1965. She worked in difficult and dangerous Lowndes County, Alabama, when Stokely Carmichael, John Lewis, Judy Richardson, and others organized the Lowndes County Freedom Organization on behalf of voter registration in 1965. She also participated in the James Meredith March against Fear from Memphis, Tennessee, to Jackson, Mississippi, in 1966. While on the march, because of Mississippi's well-known reputation as the most violent of the Southern states, she remembered feeling mildly afraid for the first time.

After the state highway was built along a route that bisected her neighborhood, Redden's beauty shop began to experience a decline in business and she decided to take a job with the federally funded Headstart Program in 1967. In 1970, she joined the Montgomery Action Program as a social worker, where she remained until retiring in 1998 at the age of eighty-five.

FURTHER READING

A video recording made on the occasion of Idessa Williams Redden's ninetieth birthday celebration, November 19, 2002, is in the author's possession.

"Idessa Williams-Redden: Pioneer Voting Rights Activist," William Councill Trenholm State Technical College Archives, Collections Online, http://trenholmtech.cc.al.us/library/index, accessed May 31, 2007.

Robinson, Jo Ann Gibson, with David J. Garrow, ed. *The Montgomery Bus Boycott and the Women Who Started It: The Memoir of Jo Ann Gibson Robinson* (1987).

PAM BROOKS

Reddick, Lawrence Dunbar (3 Mar. 1910–2 Aug. 1995), historian, curator, writer, and educator, was born in Jacksonville, Florida. He graduated magna cum laude, probably majoring in history, from the historically black Fisk University in 1932, where he studied under African American scholars CHARLES S. JOHNSON,

HORACE MANN BOND, and with white history professor Theodore Currier, who is perhaps best known as the undergraduate mentor of historian JOHN HOPE FRANKLIN. Reddick went on to receive a M.A. in History from Fisk the following year and then pursued doctoral work at the University of Chicago, receiving his Ph.D. in History in 1939 under the direction of Avery Craven, a prominent

historian of the South. Reddick's dissertation, a study of four antebellum New Orleans newspapers and their depiction of African Americans (especially slaves), was entitled "The Negro in the New Orleans Press, 1850–1860: A Study in Attitudes and Propaganda." In 1939 Reddick wed Ella Ruth Thomas, and the couple would remain married for fifty-seven years.

Prior to the completion of his doctoral training, Reddick had already begun his career-defining work of preserving and interpreting the past. Throughout the 1930s he was a member of CARTER G. WOODSON's inner circle of young black historians, which included, among others, LUTHER P. JACKSON, RAYFORD LOGAN, and CHARLES WESLEY. In 1934 he led the task of collecting approximately 250 slave testimonies at Kentucky State College and interviewed former slaves from Kentucky and Indiana, a project for which he himself had successfully secured support from the Federal Emergency Relief Administration. This work continued in other states under the direction of the Works Progress Administration's Federal Writers' Project and provided the basis for numerous research projects. In 1936 Reddick joined the faculty of Dillard University in New Orleans, where he counted among his colleagues a bevy of rising African American scholars, including anthropologists ST. CLAIR DRAKE, ALLISON DAVIS, and fellow historian BENJAMIN QUARLES. Reddick's first major paper, based on his master's thesis, appeared in the *Journal of Negro History* in 1934, entitled "Racial Attitudes in American History Textbooks of the South." In it Reddick developed a major theme that would dominate his future scholarship: the stereotypical portrayal of African Americans in various media, including newspapers, textbooks, literature, television, radio, and film. Studying the American history textbooks of sixteen Southern states, Reddick concluded that, through a combination of misrepresentation and omission, the typical Southern textbook portrayed African Americans overwhelmingly negatively, depicting them as docile and content in slavery and unruly and unworthy of freedom following the Civil War. Two years later his well-received address before the Twenty-first Annual Meeting of the Association for the Study of Negro Life and History was later turned into an oft-cited 1937 essay for the *Journal of Negro History*. In the address, Reddick built upon his earlier 1934 essay and critiqued scholarly approaches to studying black history, noting that many historians had thus far "written under the influence of the prevailing spirit permeating the American mind" (21–22) in which "the inferential lesson has been that diligence, faithfulness and discretion on the part of individuals and the group will, in time, bring their rewards" (24). Countering this simplistic view, Reddick asserted that the study of black history ought to carry with it a progressive faith in racial advancement and, therefore, required a more sophisticated grasp of the economic forces affecting African Americans. He felt there should be a broader focus that might encompass the struggles of people of color beyond the borders of the United States, and a sensitivity to the lives, actions, and thoughts of those individuals (e.g., slaves, domestic workers, tenant farmers) frequently excluded from the historical record. In this regard, Reddick was, at once, identifying some of the positive features of contemporary scholarship, as well as suggesting the direction future historiography should take.

In 1939 Reddick left the faculty of Dillard University in order to accept the position of head curator of what was then called the Schomburg Collection of Negro Literature, a position made vacant by the death of the collection's first curator and namesake, historian and book collector Arthur A. Schomburg. During his busy tenure there, he fostered the compilation, preservation, and microfilming of archival materials related to black life, spoke out about the difficulties black scholars faced in confronting racial bias, Jim Crow restrictions on archival and library access, and inadequate or underfunded facilities; he also wrote a host of essays on race relations in America, higher education for African Americans, and the prevalent nature of racial stereotypes in American culture. In an influential 1944 essay published in the *Journal of Negro Education*, "Educational Programs for the Improvement of Race Relations: Motion Pictures, Radio, the Press, and Libraries," he assessed the treatment of African Americans in various media, finding that racial bias was largely ubiquitous and concluded that, by and large, films, radio, newspapers, and libraries served to "generate and reflect a harmfully stereotyped conception of the Negro. Their influence on the mind of the American people is overwhelming" (389). World affairs would also demand his attention. With World War II raging, Reddick became concerned with preserving the wartime experiences of black soldiers and initiated a "War Letters" campaign, in which he requested correspondence to and from soldiers as well as recollections of their experiences after the war. An outspoken critic of segregation in

Lawrence Dunbar Reddick was a vanguard interpreter and preserver of the historical past, as well as a constant critic of discrimination, Jim Crow segregation, and the historical profession's own shortcomings, misrepresentations, and omissions as they related to African American life. (University of Massachusetts at Amherst.)

the armed forces, Reddick wrote historical essays on the racially biased policies of the United States' military branches and lobbied politicians and military leaders to acknowledge the contributions and sacrifices of black veterans (Moore, 322–323). In 1948 Reddick left the Schomburg Collection and accepted a job at Atlanta University as chief librarian and professor of history, positions he would hold until leaving Atlanta in 1955.

Reddick was an ardent defender of anticolonial struggles and pan-African efforts; he was also an early advocate for scholarship that devoted attention to people of color in a global context and to the histories of Africa and Asia especially—a focus that contemporary scholars would label "diasporic" studies. Reddick was also involved in the emerging civil rights struggles of the 1950s and 1960s, becoming a close confidant of MARTIN LUTHER KING JR. and serving as a member of the board of directors of King's Southern Christian Leadership Council (SCLC). Reddick was present at the famous 5 December 1955 mass meeting of the Montgomery Improvement Association (MIA), which ignited the successful Montgomery bus boycott and propelled King to national attention. He accompanied King and his wife MARTIN LUTHER KING JR. and serving as a member of the board of directors of King's Southern Christian Leadership Council (SCLC). Reddick was present at the famous 5 December 1955 mass meeting of the Montgomery Improvement Association (MIA), which ignited the successful Montgomery bus boycott and propelled King to national attention. He accompanied King and his wife CORETTA SCOTT KING on their six-week tour of India in 1959. Prime Minister Jawaharlal Nehru had invited them so that King might further familiarize himself with Gandhi's philosophy of nonviolent resistance. That same year, Reddick published the first biography of King, *Crusader Without Violence: A Biography of Martin Luther King, Jr.* The book was an account of the young minister that focused especially on the Montgomery bus boycott and combined Reddick's own recollections and impressions as a participant-observer with more traditional historical methods. In 1960 Reddick's activism cost him his position as a history professor at Alabama State College, a position he had held since 1956, when Governor John Patterson, distraught over civil rights agitation and fearing Communist sympathies and influences, ordered college president H.C. Trenholm to fire Reddick and expel numerous students.

Reddick survived these difficulties, however, and continued to teach and write, holding academic positions at numerous universities, including Coppin State Teachers College in Baltimore from 1960 to 1967, Temple University in Philadelphia from 1967 to 1976 (where he would receive tenure as a history professor), and Harvard University, where he served as a visiting professor in the African American Studies Department during the 1977–1978 school year. He accepted his final academic position when he returned to Dillard University in 1978, almost forty years after first leaving this New Orleans institution; he taught African American history there until his retirement in 1987. Reddick died on 2 August 1995 in New Orleans. He was survived by his wife, Ella, and a brother.

Reddick had been a vanguard interpreter and preserver of the historical past, as well as a constant critic of discrimination, Jim Crow segregation, and mainstream history scholarship's own shortcomings, distortions, and omissions as they related to African American life. He doubtless stood as a representative member of that early contingent of black scholars who, following W. E. B. DuBois's lead, emerged in the early decades of the twentieth century intent on turning the tools of social scientific and historical analysis toward a greater awareness and promotion of civil rights initiatives, social justice, and a more complete appreciation of African American life, history, and culture. In following the professional path pursued by his mentor, Carter Woodson, Reddick served as a pioneer in the burgeoning field of African American historical scholarship, the scholarly arena to which he devoted a lifetime of energy and enthusiasm.

FURTHER READING

The Schomburg Center for Research in Black Culture holds the Lawrence D. Reddick Papers. The Schomburg Center additionally possesses available manuscript materials specifically related to Reddick's position as the library's head curator from 1939 to 1948. Interested readers should consult the following: Schomburg Center for Research in Black Culture Records, 1924–1979, Schomburg Center for Research in Black Culture, New York Public Library, New York, New York.

Reddick, Lawrence Dunbar. *The Autobiography of Martin Luther King, Jr.* (1998).

Reddick, Lawrence Dunbar. "Educational Programs for the Improvement of Race Relations: Motion Pictures, Radio, the Press, and Libraries," *Journal of Negro Education* (Summer 1944).

Reddick, Lawrence Dunbar. "A New Interpretation for Negro History," *Journal of Negro History* (Jan. 1937).

Meier, August, and Elliott Rudwick. *Black History and the Historical Profession, 1915–1980* (1986).

Moore, Christopher. *Fighting For America: Black Soldiers—The Unsung Heroes of World War II* (2005).

Obituary: *New York Times*, 16 August 1995.

DAVID CHRISTOPHER BRIGHOUSE

Reddick, Mary L. (31 Dec. 1914–8 Oct. 1966), professor of biology and research neuroembryologist, was born Mary Logan Reddick in Atlanta, Georgia, to Fielder Reddick, a postal clerk, and Maggie L. Reddick, a homemaker. In 1929, at the age of fifteen, Reddick graduated from the Laboratory High School of Spelman College; she received the bachelor of arts in Biology from Spelman College in 1935. She was awarded the master of science in biology at Atlanta University in 1937 and later attended Radcliffe College of Harvard University, where she received the master of arts degree in 1943 and the Ph.D. in Zoology with specialization in Neuroembryology in 1944.

In the late 1930s, before entering Radcliffe, Reddick began her career as teacher and research scientist in the Atlanta University Center, initially a consortium of Morehouse College, Spelman College, and the graduate school of Atlanta University. While studying for the M.S degree at Atlanta University, Reddick worked as a laboratory assistant at Spelman College and was later appointed instructor of biology at that institution. During the summer of 1936 she studied at the Marine Biological Laboratory in Woods Hole, Massachusetts, where she completed a six-hour course in embryology. In 1939 Reddick accepted an appointment as the first female instructor of biology at the all-male Morehouse College, where by 1952 she had advanced to professor. While at Morehouse, Reddick was awarded a Rockefeller General Education Board teacher training fellowship to pursue graduate study in zoology at Radcliffe College. There Reddick conducted research in neuroembryology with the Ph.D. dissertation entitled "The Differentiation of Embryonic Chick Medulla in Chorio-Allantoic Grafts." Her studies at Radcliffe laid the foundation for most of her research over the next two decades on embryonic nerve cell development.

Upon completion of graduate studies at Radcliffe, Reddick returned to Morehouse College where she was honored as only the tenth member of the faculty to earn a doctorate. She was also the first and only female to serve as acting chair of the Biology Department at Morehouse, where she taught graduate courses at Atlanta University and directed research projects for graduate students. In 1952 Reddick was awarded a fellowship by the Fund for the Advancement of Education of the Ford Foundation to study embryology and conduct research at the School of Anatomy, Cambridge University, England. Reddick was one of the first, if not the first, African American female scientists to receive a postdoctoral research fellowship to study abroad. During the 1940s and 1950s, when research funding was limited at historically black colleges and universities, Reddick received research grants from the Atlanta University Research Committee and through a Carnegie Grant to the institution to continue research in neuroembryology and the study of motor and sensory fibers of the embryonic medulla.

In a 1953 article in local newspapers, Rufus E. Clement, President of Atlanta University, announced the appointment of Reddick as professor of biology at that institution. Clement stated that she would work with Samuel Nabrit, whom she later succeeded as chair of the department in 1955. While chair of biology, Reddick led efforts for the construction of a biology research building—the first separate science facility built by Atlanta University. Prior to that time, Atlanta University and Morehouse College had shared both biology and chemistry buildings for instruction and research. In addition to teaching and administrative responsibilities, Reddick remained an active research investigator. In 1956, before the National Science Foundation (NSF) and the National Institutes of Health established minority research programs, Reddick received a competitive NSF grant to conduct research in neuroembryology. During the 1950s and 1960s she directed research and served as thesis advisor for more than twenty graduate students who earned the master of science degree in Biology at Atlanta University. Many of these students continued graduate studies and earned the Ph.D. in Biology and other related fields. Reddick's research studies were published in a number of scientific articles and abstracts in scholarly journals, including *Anatomical Record* (1951).

Reddick, a dedicated teacher and research scientist who never married, received numerous awards throughout her career. In 1944 she was elected to Phi Beta Kappa at Radcliffe College and was also a member of Sigma Xi and Beta Kappa Chi scientific honorary societies. In 1956 Reddick was one of twenty graduates of Radcliffe College featured in a publication by the Radcliffe Committee on Graduate Education for Women. Her career as a biologist and professor in a coeducational university was profiled in a section devoted to careers chosen by Radcliffe graduates. In 1967, she was cited by her undergraduate alma mater Spelman College as one of the "most distinguished graduates in biology" (*Spelman Messenger*, Feb. 1967). Reddick died at her home in Atlanta, leaving a legacy of many students who benefited from her unwavering and uncompromising pursuit of academic excellence.

FURTHER READING

A number of the documents used to prepare this biography are from the Robert W. Woodruff Library, Atlanta University Center Archives/Special Collections, and the Schlesinger Library, Radcliffe Institute for Advanced Study Harvard University, Radcliffe Archives.

"Biology at Spelman College." *Spelman Messenger* 83.2 (1967).

Patterson, Rosalyn Mitchell. "Black Women in the Biological Sciences," *Sage: A Scholarly Journal on Black Women* 6.2 (1989).

Warren, Wini. "Mary Logan Reddick," *Black Women Scientists in the United States* (1999).

Obituary: *Atlanta University Bulletin*, Dec. 1966.

ROSALYN MITCHELL PATTERSON

Redding, Anderson (23 Sept. 1876?–8 Nov. 1944), inventor, blacksmith, and farmer, was born Anderson Augustus Redding in Juliette, Georgia, to Anderson and Jane Darden Redding, former slaves and sharecroppers. Though his parents had been slaves on the plantation of James P. Redding—the son of a Virginia planter who fought along-side George Washington at Yorktown—the young Redding managed to acquire his own plot of land in Juliette and was relatively wealthy by the time he turned forty-five. He created a lucrative set of operations that included a syrup mill, a black-smith shop, and a series of distilleries. In addition, Redding grew a combination of sugarcane and corn on a sizable landholding. He could often be seen in a buggy pulled by his white stallion, George, in Juliette in the 1910s and 1920s—a rare sight indeed in the midst of the so-called Black Nadir.

Redding married a total of three times, but his first wife, Marilla Jane Walker, gave birth to all of his children. They married sometime before 1895 and had six children before Marilla's death in 1910. Shortly after the death of his first wife, Redding married Laura (full name unknown) in 1910 and, later, Camilla (full name unknown) by 1920. Redding had a third-grade education and fully understood the empowering nature of liter-acy. At least one of his sons, Walter Lovett, went on to attend Morehouse College—one of the many black institutions of higher learning founded in the Reconstruction era throughout the South.

Among the few educated African Americans liv-ing in Juliette at the turn of the twentieth century, Redding was both literate and highly skilled, and he used this combination of talents to his advan-tage. Among the many devices he created are a cot-tonseed distributor, a cotton chopper, and a light reflector. Though most of Redding's inventions were sold to others who patented and profited from his ideas, he did formally patent his most signifi-cant invention—a train headlight—in 1924.

Because of segregation laws and the difficul-ties that even educated African Americans had in negotiating with the patent office, Redding had to sell a half-share of his invention to a man named James T. Bray, a white railroad section foreman, for one thousand dollars. Bray did not help build the headlight and provided no intellectual input, but as an employee of the Southern Railway, he received several times more than his thousand-dollar share of the invention in patent royalties. He presented Redding's invention design to the attorney Watson E. Coleman, who in turn sent both the design for the headlight and the application materials to the U.S. Patent Office. Their patent for a "headlight" was filed on 9 May 1923 and was awarded on 2 September 1924. In the final patent, Redding describes the invention as follows: "In combination, a vertically disposed member, means for supporting the same swinging movement in a horizontal direction, an illuminating means carried by the member, an out-standing pin carried by the member, a pendulum supported for swinging movement and provided with spaced fingers between which the pin of the member extends, an outstanding magnetic member carried by the pendulum, and a stationary magnetic plate positioned adjacent to the pendulum and in close proximity to the magnetic member" (U.S. Patent No. 1,507,203). Basically the headlight was affixed to the front of trains and would swivel back and forth in order to warn cows and other livestock that wandered onto the train tracks at night. This was a significant problem because trains that were coming around turns at night could not be seen. The swiveled headlight allowed trains to produce a light that maintained "the proper relation to the path of travel of [the train] … when making a turn" (U.S. Patent No. 1,507,203).

Beginning with the Southern Railway, train companies around the country adopted the swiv-eled headlight and used variations of the design from the late 1920s to the early 1940s. Frustrated by prior failures to receive credit for his accomplish-ments, Redding reportedly destroyed many of his new inventions shortly before his death of natural causes in 1944. His grave, located at St. Peter's Rock Baptist Church in Juliette, is inscribed with the epi-taph, "He was a genius in his times." With impor-tant historical periods—Reconstruction and World War II—serving as bookends to his life, Redding's work faded into obscurity.

FURTHER READING

The papers of William Chambliss Redding, a white descendant of James P. Redding and the family's genealogist, are in the Georgia Department of

Archives and History, Atlanta. A tape recording of an interview with Louise Redding Watley, granddaughter of Anderson Redding, by the author on 15 Mar. 2001 in Atlanta is in the Auburn Avenue Research Center, Atlanta.

Obituary: *Monroe (Georgia) Advertiser,* 5 June 1969.

WALTER C. RUCKER

Redding, Dick (1891–1940?), Negro League baseball pitcher, was born in Atlanta, Georgia. His parents' names are unknown. Apparently he was unschooled and illiterate. Except for the fact that he played semiprofessional ball with the Atlanta Depins, other details of Redding's early life are sketchy. From 1911 through 1921 "Cannonball" Dick Redding and "Smokey" Joe Williams matched fastballs as teammates and opponents for the title of best pitcher in black baseball. The pitcher Jesse Hubbard, among others, insisted that "Redding and Williams were better pitchers than SATCHEL PAIGE.... Satchel didn't throw as hard as Dick Redding. You should have seen *him* turn the ball loose!"

Redding reportedly pitched against the New York Giants during spring training in 1911, and the manager John McGraw brought him north, where he joined the Philadelphia Giants. Although facts about the 1911 season are hard to verify, legends abound. Some reports claim that he won seventeen straight games that summer, while others claim twenty-nine, including five no-hitters, probably against semiprofessional opponents.

In 1912 Redding joined the New York Lincoln Giants, along with shortstop manager JOHN HENRY LLOYD and catcher LOUIS SANTOP. Unconfirmed reports about 1913 credit Redding with a 43–12 win–loss record, including a perfect game against Jersey City of the white Eastern (later International) League. It is known that in one exhibition game he struck out twenty-four players on a team gathered from the United States League, a better-than-average group.

In 1915 Redding jumped to the rival New York Lincoln Stars, where he reportedly ran up twenty straight victories. Victory number seventeen came against a white all-star club and number nineteen came against former Detroit Tiger pitcher George Mullin. In the black world series that fall, against RUBE FOSTER's Chicago American Giants, Redding won three games, including a shutout, as the two teams tied at five wins apiece.

Redding went west in 1917 to the American Giants, for whom he compiled a record of 7–1 against other black teams. His career was interrupted by World War I, which he spent with the army in France.

Redding joined the Brooklyn (New York) Royal Giants in 1918, winning three and losing three against black clubs. (Black teams played most of their games against white semiprofessional teams, and records for these games have not been compiled.) One of Redding's three losses came against the Lincoln Giants. Redding threw a two-hitter, but Williams topped him with a no-hitter. In September, Redding lost in a fourteen-inning game to Carl Mays of the New York Yankees by a score of 2–1.

In 1920, after a 6–3 season against black teams, Redding faced Williams in the first black game ever played at Ebbets Field, home of the Brooklyn Dodgers. Redding won it 5–0, and the Royals claimed the black championship of the East. Redding also faced Babe Ruth's all-stars at Shibe Park in Philadelphia, and he beat Ruth and the pitcher Mays 9–4 despite a home run by Ruth.

Redding next joined the Bacharach Giants of Atlantic City, New Jersey, and had a 17–12 record against black teams in 1921. He was 8–8 in 1922. Then it was back to the Royals in 1923 as manager. He pitched less and less, although he and Ruth met often in postseason exhibitions. At one of these the promoters told Redding that the fans had paid to see Ruth hit, "so no funny business." Ruth then hit several balls over the fence to the cheers of the crowd, and Redding went home with money in his pocket.

According to Hall of Famer JUDY JOHNSON, Redding was six feet four inches tall with hands as big as shovels. Redding turned his back on the batter before delivering the pitch, which left the hitter ready to dive for cover. Pictures usually show Redding with a broad smile. "He took everything good-natured," said one of the players he managed, Ted Page. "He didn't have a care in the world, yet he never had much money." Hall of Famer BUCK LEONARD called Redding "a nice fellow, easy-going. He never argued, never cursed, never smoked as I recall."

Redding stayed with the Royals until 1938. Statistics for most of his career are incomplete, but in confirmed games against black opponents, he finished with a mark of sixty-nine victories and fifty-four defeats. He reportedly compiled twelve no-hitters in his career, although most came against semiprofessional opposition.

Details of his death are not clear. "I know he died in a mental hospital," said Page, "down in Long Island, Islip, I think. Nobody's ever told me why, how, what happened to him."

FURTHER READING

Holway, John B. *Blackball Stars: Negro League Pioneers* (1988).

Lester, Larry. *The Ballplayers* (1990).

Riley, James A. *Biographical Encyclopedia of the Negro Baseball Leagues* (1994).

This entry is taken from the *American National Biography* and is published here with the permission of the American Council of Learned Societies.

JOHN B. HOLWAY

Redding, J. Saunders (13 Oct. 1906–2 Mar. 1988), African American educator, historian, and literary critic, was born Jay Saunders Redding in Wilmington, Delaware, the son of Lewis Alfred Redding, a schoolteacher, and Mary Ann Holmes. As graduates of Howard University, Redding's parents maintained a modest middle-class environment for their children; his father was secretary of the local Wilmington branch of the NAACP. Redding graduated from high school in 1923 and entered Lincoln University in Pennsylvania that year, with no discernible career ambitions. In 1924 he transferred to Brown University, where he received his bachelor's degree in 1928.

After graduation Redding became an instructor at Morehouse College in Atlanta, where in 1929 he married Esther Elizabeth James. The Reddings had two children. Redding felt that his liberal political beliefs, which his conservative colleagues believed were "too radical," were a major factor in the Morehouse College administration's decision to fire him in 1931. Redding returned to Brown University for graduate study and received a master's degree in 1932. He then went to Columbia University as a graduate fellow for two years, and he was an adjunct English instructor at Louisville Municipal College in Louisville, Kentucky, in 1934. From 1936 to 1938 Redding taught English at Southern University in Baton Rouge and then joined the faculty at Elizabeth City State Teachers' College in North Carolina, where he remained from 1938 until 1943 as chairman of the English department. During this period, Redding completed his first book, *To Make a Poet Black* (1939), one of the earliest works of literary criticism on African American literature.

The publication of *To Make a Poet Black* enabled him in 1939 to earn a fellowship that was funded by the Rockefeller Foundation. Redding used this fellowship to travel throughout the American South to prepare his partly autobiographical work, *No Day of Triumph*, written in 1942. *No Day of Triumph* chronicled the daily lives and aspirations of working-class African American southerners and became a critical success. In this book Redding observed that his life affirmed the importance of integrity, courage, freedom, and hope that African Americans traditionally cherished. In *No Day of Triumph* he wrote that "I set out in nearly hopeless desperation to find out, both as a Negro and as an American, certain values and validities that would hold for me as a man … to find among my people those validities that proclaimed them and me as men … the highest common denominator of mankind."

Redding joined the faculty at Hampton Institute in Hampton, Virginia, as a professor of English and creative writing in 1943; that same year he received a Guggenheim Fellowship. The National Urban League honored Redding in 1945 for outstanding achievement. Moreover, during that same year Redding became the first African American to hold a full professorship at Brown University when the university invited him to be a visiting professor of English. In 1950 Redding published his only novel, *Stranger and Alone*, which reflected his experiences as a professor in historic all-black colleges.

Redding remained best known for his monographs that document African American contributions to American history, such as *They Came in Chains: Americans from Africa* (1950), *The Lonesome Road: The Story of the Negro's Part in America* (1958), and *The Negro* (1967). These books utilized biographical vignettes and primary sources to document African American history and investigate the historical context of American race relations. Redding's fifth book, *On Being Negro in America* (1951), examined psychological dilemmas of racism in American society, while his 1954 work, *An American in India*, described his observations on Indian nationalism and anti-imperialism during a U.S. State Department–sponsored trip. In 1959 Redding received another Guggenheim Fellowship, which allowed him to continue his lecture tours. During a six-month West African lecture tour in 1963, Redding became a close friend of the Nigerian writer Wole Soyinka, who went on to receive a Nobel Prize in Literature in 1986.

In 1964 Redding became a fellow in humanities at Duke University. The following year Redding returned to Hampton Institute, and in 1966 he was the director of research and publication at the National Endowment for the Humanities in Washington, D.C. By 1969 Redding had assumed a professorship in American history and civilization at George Washington University while remaining a special consultant for the National Endowment for the Humanities. With Arthur P. Davis, he edited *Cavalcade*, an anthology of African American literature, from 1960 to 1970 at Howard University. In 1970 Redding received the Ernest I. White Professorship of American Studies and Humane Letters at Cornell University. A program of fellowships for students of color at Cornell University was established in his honor in 1986. When he retired in 1975 from Cornell University, Redding continued his writing and scholarly activities.

As a liberal Democrat, Redding worked with other progressive African American intellectuals to discuss solutions for confronting racism in American society. During the 1970s he became a member of the Haverford Group, an informal gathering of notable African American scholars who met to investigate methods to dissuade American youth from racial separatism. This group consisted of the psychologist KENNETH B. CLARK, the historian JOHN HOPE FRANKLIN, former secretary of Housing and Urban Development Robert Weaver, and federal judge WILLIAM HASTIE. Along with fellow colleagues of the Haverford Group, Redding worked with the Joint Center for Political Studies to devise political strategies for interracial cooperation.

After Redding's death at his home in Ithaca, New York, the 4 March 1988 obituary in the *Ithaca Journal* described him as the dean of African American scholars whose works influenced younger African American intellectuals, such as Henry Louis Gates, literary critic and director of Harvard University's African American Studies. The *New York Times* 5 March 1988 notice of Redding's death recalled that he was regarded as the first African American to teach at an Ivy League institution. And in an obituary in the 10 March 1988 edition of the *Cornell Chronicle*, Cornell University president Frank H. T. Rhodes commented, "J. Saunders Redding represented the essence of human dignity who often stood alone between the two worlds of white and black, contributing to an understanding of the human condition that transcends race and culture."

FURTHER READING

Redding's personal manuscripts are in the John Hay Library at Brown University.

Redding, J. Saunders. *Troubled in the Mind* (1991).

Berry, Faith, ed. *A Scholar's Conscience: Selected Writings of J. Saunders Redding, 1942–1977* (1992).

Davis, Arthur P., ed. *From the Dark Tower: Afro-American Writers, 1900 to 1960* (1974).

Emanuel, James, and Theodore Gross, eds. *Dark Symphony: Negro Literature in America* (1968).

Wagner, Jean. *Black Poets of the United States: From Paul Laurence Dunbar to Langston Hughes* (1973).

This entry is taken from the *American National Biography* and is published here with the permission of the American Council of Learned Societies.

KIMBERLY WELCH

Redding, Louis Lorenzo (25 Oct. 1901–28 Sept. 1998), attorney, civil rights activist, and public defender, was born in Alexandria, Virginia, the son of Lewis A. Alfred, a postal carrier, and Mary Ann Holmes. The Reddings moved to Wilmington, Delaware, soon after Louis's birth, and Louis later attended Howard High School. After finishing high school, Redding left Wilmington to attend Brown University in Rhode Island; he graduated in 1923. He moved to Florida to serve as assistant principal at the Fessenden Academy in Ocala, and then moved to Atlanta, Georgia, where he served as an instructor of English at Morehouse College. Redding then went back north to attend Harvard Law School, graduating in 1928 before returning to Wilmington, where he passed the bar exam in 1929, becoming the first black lawyer in Delaware history. He also had the dubious distinction of being the only black lawyer in the state for almost the next three decades.

Beginning in the 1930s Redding operated a general law practice from his small office in downtown Wilmington and handled a variety of cases ranging from mundane civil matters to criminal cases. His clients tended to be blacks and poor whites, many of whom were ignorant of the law and who, if not for Redding's generosity, would have had an even more difficult time securing legal representation. Redding had a unique style, described by those who knew him as attentive, formal, eloquent, tireless, and stoic. His Ivy League accent, propensity for Brooks Brothers and J. Press suits, Mark Cross pens, and imported English Oval cigarettes, which, the former NAACP attorney Jack Greenberg recalled, he "usually carried or let dangle from his lips … unlit and filter end outward," certainly revealed a certain aristocratic air (Greenberg, 87). But this sensibility did not come at the expense of what he viewed as his more humanitarian obligations, particularly his commitment to fighting racial discrimination and segregation. Redding was a member of the National Lawyer's Guild and the Emergency Civil Rights Committee in his early career, but his most important professional and political association was with

Louis L. Redding (left) of Wilmington, Delaware, and Thurgood Marshall, general counsel for the NAACP, conferring at the Supreme Court during a recess in the court's hearing on racial integration in the public schools, 1955. (Library of Congress/National Association for the Advancement of Colored People Records.)

the legal offices of the NAACP. His was among the first group of black attorneys appointed to the National Legal Committee of the NAACP in 1932 amid increasing criticism of the organization for its failure to integrate its legal staff. And he continued with the Legal Defense and Education Fund under the direction of THURGOOD MARSHALL when it split from the main organization in 1939. Redding was married twice, first to Ruth Albert Cook on 18 April 1944 and then, after the two had divorced, to Gwendolyn Carmen Kiah in July 1972.

Redding rose to prominence in civil rights circles through his work in a number of prominent legal cases. In 1958 he argued a case on behalf of William H. "Dutch" Burton, who was denied service at a restaurant located on property owned by the Wilmington Parking Authority. Redding's contention was that the parking authority, as a state agency, had the obligation to require its lessee, the Eagle Coffee Shoppe, to serve all customers on a nondiscriminatory basis. The Delaware Chancery Court and (after the Supreme Court of Delaware overturned the ruling) the U.S. Supreme Court agreed in 1961. This case had the effect of broadening the definition of state action that was covered under the equal protection clause of the Fourteenth Amendment. Redding also worked with LITTLETON MITCHELL, president of the Delaware Conference of the NAACP, to organize boycotts and sit-ins in the 1960s, and he participated in the March on Washington, although he resisted becoming too involved in the direct-action campaigns that later characterized the civil rights movement.

Redding's most lasting legacy, however, came in school desegregation litigation. His first big case involved a challenge to segregation at the University of Delaware, which he argued with co-counsel Jack Greenberg, on behalf of ten Delaware State College students who, citing the loss of the college's accreditation and poor learning conditions, sought admission to the university. In *Parker v. University of Delaware* (1950) the court proved sympathetic to the plaintiffs' arguments, ruled that the college was inferior to the university, and ordered the admission of the students to the university. The University of Delaware thus became the first public university to be desegregated under court order.

Redding's next big school desegregation case involved a broader challenge to segregation in the state's system of public primary and secondary schools. On behalf of a group of parents from communities in the Wilmington metropolitan area in the consolidated cases *Belton v. Gebhart* and *Bulah v. Gebhart*, Redding—again with co-counsel Greenberg—successfully argued before the Delaware Chancery Court that the black schools in question were inferior to the white schools and that segregation had a detrimental effect on the emotional development of black children. After repeated state appeals, the U.S. Supreme Court agreed to hear this case, along with four others, from South Carolina, Virginia, Kansas, and the District of Columbia, in the historic case *Brown v. Board of Education* (1954), and racially segregated schools were declared unconstitutional.

As one of his final efforts in the civil rights era, Redding, acting in conjunction with attorneys from the American Civil Liberties Union and the Center for National Policy Review, represented a group of parents challenging the racial segregation of black students in Wilmington public schools in 1971. The case, *Evans v. Buchanan*, resulted—after many appeals and over the strident opposition from white suburbanites—in the first court-ordered, interdistrict, metropolitan desegregation plan. Louis Redding was, quite literally, one of the architects of the broader movement away from accommodation and to direct challenges to institutionalized forms of racial subordination. His work, often provided at great personal sacrifice, was instrumental in extending important constitutional protections to African Americans.

FURTHER READING

Greenberg, Jack. *Crusaders in the Courts: How a Dedicated Band of Lawyers Fought for the Civil Rights Revolution* (1994).

Hays, Laurie. "Louis Redding's Fight for Dignity and Decency," *Brown Alumni Monthly* 86.38 (Feb. 1986).

Kluger, Richard. *Simple Justice: The History of "Brown v. Board of Education" and Black America's Struggle for Equality* (2004).

Ware, Leland. "Louis Redding's Civil Rights Legacy," *Delaware Law Review* 4 (2001).

Williams, Leonard L. "Louis L. Redding," *Delaware Lawyer* 16.2 (Summer 1998).

Woolard-Provine, Annette. *Integrating Delaware: The Reddings of Wilmington* (2003).

Obituary: *New York Times*, 2 Oct. 1998.

BRETT GADSDEN

Redding, Otis (9 Sept. 1941–10 Dec. 1967), singer and songwriter, was born Otis Redding Jr. in Dawson, Georgia, the son of Otis Redding Sr., a maintenance worker and minister, and Fanny Redding (maiden name unknown). In 1944, when the younger Redding was three, the family moved into the Tindall Heights Housing Project in Macon, Georgia. Redding began playing drums and piano in elementary school and sang in his church gospel choir. He was forced to drop out of high school in the tenth grade when his father contracted tuberculosis and lost his job at the local air force base. Redding then worked as a well digger and a gas station attendant and also earned money as a musician with the Upsetters, a rhythm-and-blues band led by the singer and piano player Little Richard. Redding gained fame as a rhythm-and-blues singer in the Macon area when he won several local talent show contests. By 1958 he was prominent in the Macon music scene as the singer for an R&B band called the Pinetoppers.

In 1960 Redding moved to Los Angeles to further his career and in that year recorded "She's All Right" and "Tuff Enuff" with the Shooters for the Trans World and Finer Arts labels. In 1961 Redding returned to Macon and recorded "Shout Bamalama" and "Fat Gal" with the Pinetoppers for the Confederate label. His first hit record came in 1962 with the release of "These Arms of Mine," a delicate, plaintive ballad that reached the rhythm-and-blues record sales charts. The single was released on the Volt label, which was a subsidiary of the Memphis-based Stax label, for which Redding continued to record until the end of his life.

The following year Redding reached the top of the R&B charts and established himself as a leading soul performer with another ballad, "Pain in My Heart," on which Redding's voice alternated from quavering and tentative to a hoarse gospel shout. He subsequently recorded and released several hit singles for Volt, including "Security" in 1964; "I've Been Loving You Too Long," "Respect," and "I Can't Turn You Loose" in 1965; and "Try a Little Tenderness" in 1966. Redding's simple, earnest ballads and sparse, horn-punctuated dance tracks came to be considered typical of the "Memphis sound" produced by Stax. Redding often built LPs around hit singles, including *Pain in My Heart* in 1964, *The Great Otis Redding Sings Soul Ballads* and *Otis Blue* in 1965, *The Soul Album* and *Complete and Unbelievable* in 1966, and *King and Queen* (with Carla Thomas) and *Live in Europe* in 1967.

Redding's southern "country" sensibilities and powerful, husky tenor earned him recognition as one of the most authentic, "soulful" singers in an R&B market dominated by polished Motown vocalists. But his fame grew to international proportions because he was able to appeal to white "pop" audiences. His performance tour in England in 1967 was met by huge crowds and rapturous reviews in the popular music press. Later that year Redding became one of the few black performers to be embraced by the counterculture movement when he thrilled an audience of 55,000 at the Monterey Pop Festival in California, a seminal event of the "hippie" era. Confirming his success as a crossover act, in 1967 Redding replaced Elvis Presley as the top male vocalist in the world in an annual poll conducted by *Melody Maker* magazine, the leading pop music magazine in England.

On 10 December 1967, while on a performance tour in the Midwest, Redding died when his private airplane crashed into Lake Monona, just outside Madison, Wisconsin. Recorded three days before his death and released one month later, the wistful ballad "(Sittin' on) the Dock of the Bay" rose to the top of the popular music charts and became the best-selling and most famous recording of his career. Several more hit records were released posthumously, including the singles "The Happy Song" (1968), "Hard to Handle" (1968), and "Love Man" (1969) and the albums *The Dock of the Bay* (1968), *The Immortal Otis Redding* (1968), *In Person at the Whisky a Go Go* (1968), *Love Man* (1969), and *Tell the Truth* (1970).

Though his career was cut short at its peak, within a few years Redding had composed, performed, and recorded a remarkable number of R&B hits, emerging as one of the most exciting stage performers in the history of American popular music.

FURTHER READING

Schiesel, Jane. *The Otis Redding Story* (1973).

This entry is taken from the *American National Biography* and is published here with the permission of the American Council of Learned Societies.

THADDEUS RUSSELL

Redman, Don (29 July 1900–30 Nov. 1964), composer, arranger, and alto saxophonist, was born Donald Matthew Redman in Piedmont, West Virginia, to parents whose names are unknown. What is known, however, is that Redman came from a musical family and was a child prodigy. He learned to play several instruments as a youngster, and he wrote arrangements for a visiting road band while still in his teens; he even backed up the group with his own band on occasion.

Redman graduated from Storer College in Harpers Ferry, West Virginia, at age twenty with a music degree. He worked professionally for about a year around Piedmont, then joined Billy Paige's Broadway Syncopators in Pittsburgh; he played clarinet and saxophones and wrote arrangements for the popular group. The Syncopators were invited to play in New York City in 1923, but the band broke up soon after its arrival. Redman himself, though, got a call for a recording date, and at the session he met FLETCHER HENDERSON, who led the pick-up group hired to back up the singer FLORENCE MILLS. Henderson immediately recognized Redman's talent and hired him for several more sessions, eventually asking him to join his own new orchestra. Over the next several years Redman played saxes, clarinet, and other instruments with the Henderson group, but his biggest influence lay in his revolutionary approach to arranging.

At first the Henderson band's tunes consisted mostly of unimaginative stock arrangements. Gradually, Redman completely rewrote the group's book. His August 1923 arrangement of "Dicty Blues" shows that he had already begun to employ improvised ensembles and a variety of section combinations; he separated reeds and brass, pitting the sections against each other. One would play the melodic lead, for instance, and the other would answer during pauses or punctuate the playing with brief, rhythmic figures. The band's recording of "Copenhagen" at the end of 1924 marked a significant step forward in this style, as the music moved from one section or soloist to another twenty-four times in three minutes.

Redman was undoubtedly influenced, in part at least, by the brief presence of LOUIS ARMSTRONG in the band. Armstrong was still close to the New Orleans collective style of improvisation and thus served as a bridge between it and "the newer solo-and-section style" that Redman pioneered. "Copenhagen" also employed unusual instrumental combinations, contrasting, for instance, brass with clarinet trios. By the end of 1926 Redman had also moved beyond the rhythmic stiffness that characterized even such an advanced piece as "Copenhagen," and in compositions like "Stampede," recorded in May of that year, he was writing fuller, better integrated section passages and eliciting a powerful emotional expressiveness and a richer, full-bodied sound from the band.

Redman left Henderson in March 1927 to become music director of McKinney's Cotton Pickers, a rather nondescript group that he elevated to the level of competent jazz playing. He toured and recorded extensively with the band, which became popular enough to pack Sebastian's Cotton Club in Hollywood nightly during a seven-week engagement in 1930. During this time he also played with Louis Armstrong in Chicago and with CARROLL DICKERSON's band, and he recorded with Armstrong (1928) and COLEMAN HAWKINS (1929).

In 1931 Redman left McKinney to form his own group; that same year he composed and recorded what some regard as his greatest composition, "Chant of the Weed," with its unusual, almost atonal harmonies. Don Redman and His Orchestra broadcast regularly over the radio and recorded often during the early 1930s for Brunswick Victor and other labels. Redman also used two vocalists—Harlan Lattimore and Chick Bullock—and employed the tap dancing and singing of BILL ROBINSON with particular effectiveness on a piece called "Doin' the New Low Down." However, the band was not particularly successful in musical terms, and Redman gradually decreased his activity.

Redman had two recording dates in 1934, followed by two and a half years of silence. By the time his orchestra reemerged, Benny Goodman and COUNT BASIE had forever changed the parameters of big band swing. Redman's group performed and recorded sporadically during the late 1930s, disbanding permanently in 1940. He did take JAY MCSHANN's band out under his own name a couple of times in 1942 and led another group at the Club Zanzibar on Broadway in New York City.

During the 1940s Redman composed and wrote arrangements for radio and other big bands. He opened an office on Broadway and produced arrangements for bandleaders like Fred Waring, Paul Whiteman, Harry James, Jimmy Dorsey, JIMMIE LUNCEFORD, and Basie. In 1946 he toured Europe with a group that included Tyree Glenn, DON BYAS, and the young pianist Billy Taylor.

In 1951 Redman became musical director for the singer PEARL BAILEY, a job he held for over a decade. He made a few disappointing jazz recordings at the end of the decade, including an unsuccessful reunion with Coleman Hawkins. In the early 1960s he did freelance work for CBS and for transcription and record companies while continuing his position with Bailey. He played little during his last years, writing several extended works that have never been publicly performed. Redman had one daughter with his wife, Gladys Henderson. He died in New York City.

Redman was the first master of jazz orchestration. He came up with the idea of dividing jazz bands into sections, and among later bandleaders only Basie and DUKE ELLINGTON surpassed his innovations. A gentle, kindly man whom musicians truly loved, Redman was cursed by an erratic career and self-defeating professional moves. But as unpredictable as his life was, and as uneven as even the greatest of his arrangements could be, he stands alone as the forerunner of modern jazz arranging.

FURTHER READING

Schuller, Gunther. *Early Jazz: Its Roots and Musical Development* (1968).

Schuller, Gunther. *The Swing Era: The Development of Jazz, 1930–1945* (1989).

Tirro, Frank. *Jazz: A History* (1993).

Obituary: *New York Times*, 2 Dec. 1964.

DISCOGRAPHY

Harrison, Max. *The Essential Jazz Records*, vol. 1: *Ragtime to Swing* (1984).

Allen, W. C. *Hendersonia: The Music of Fletcher Henderson and His Musicians, a Bio-Discography* (1973).

This entry is taken from the *American National Biography* and is published here with the permission of the American Council of Learned Societies.

RONALD P. DUFOUR

Redman, John (before 1763–8 Oct. 1836), veteran of the American Revolution and farmer, enlisted at Winchester, Frederick County, Virginia, served for four years in the First Regiment of Light Dragoons of the Continental Army, and was later a resident of Hardy County, Virginia (later Grant County, West Virginia). Nothing is known of John Redman's life prior to his enlistment in probably late 1778. Information about his service in the Continental Army comes from his and his widow's applications for pensions (Revolutionary War Pension Application File, roll number 2013, application number W5691).

It is not easy to estimate the number of black men who served in the Continental forces. Skin color and ethnicity were recorded in very few of the military records that survive, making it difficult to quantify their numbers. BENJAMIN ARTHUR QUARLES refers to earlier works that estimate there were a total of about 5,000 black soldiers in the Continental Army (xxix); however, Quarles does not offer his own estimate. Michael Lanning estimates that during the summer of 1778, nearly 10 percent of the Continental Army consisted of black soldiers (177), and probably about the same percentage were present in the navy. Like so many men, John Redman's service record and his pension file give no indication of his skin color.

In his 1823 application for a pension, Redman describes his enlistment and some events of his service in an affidavit given under oath before the Hardy County, Virginia, Court. Like many other black, white, and Indian men, Redman enlisted for the duration of the war. Men of color enlisted for a variety of reasons and under a variety of circumstances. John Redman does not mention serving as someone's substitute or having been drafted. He simply states that he enlisted in Winchester, Frederick County, Virginia, sometime around Christmas. He could not remember the exact year of his enlistment, but he goes on to say that he served for four years and was discharged in North Carolina sometime after Cornwallis surrendered. We know that he served at least through January 1783 from a payroll on which he appears. From studying the movements of the First Regiment of Light Dragoons (Hayes, vol. II, 50–65) in comparison with Redman's statements, it is apparent that he enlisted at Winchester at Christmas 1778.

A white man by the name of John Jenkins submitted an affidavit to support Redman's pension application. He stated that Redman served at least two years in the First Virginia Regiment of Light Dragoons as a waiter to Lieutenant Vincent Howell. The January 1783 payroll on which both Redman and Jenkins appear indicates that Redman was a private in the Fifth Troop, commanded by Captain John Hughes, First Regiment of Light Dragoons (Revolutionary War Rolls, images 10 and 11). Both Redman and Jenkins were paid as privates (eight and one third dollars for one month of service). This is the only payroll for Captain Hughes's Fifth Troop that exists in the collections of the National Archives that covers the time during Redman's service, so Redman's service cannot be tracked any further through payroll records.

The Congressional Act of 18 March 1818 for the first time allowed men who were not injured during the Revolutionary War to file for a pension (Rose, 18). By that time, though, most servicemen had long lost their discharge papers to prove their service. Consequently, the pension application affidavits often contain detailed descriptions of whom they served under and battles they took part in. John Redman states that he was in one battle "in the neighbourhood of Savannah with the Indians under their Chief, Sago." On 24 June 1782 a small group of Continental soldiers was ambushed near Savannah by the Creek Indians led by Chief Emistesigo. This could very well be the battle to which Redman refers.

According to testimony in support of Redman's widow's pension application by Richard Redman and his wife Rachel, John Redman and Sarah Days were married approximately two years after John's return from war, placing the year of their marriage at about 1785. The first record in which John Redman is found in Hardy County, Virginia, is the 1801 personal property tax list, where he is on a list of "Free Negroes and Mulattoes." It is rare to see skin color noted on the muster or payrolls of the Revolution, and rare to see it noted in a pension application for service in the Revolutionary War, so this is the first record in which his skin color is noted.

John and Sarah Redman's appearances in various documents, and as evidenced by the people associated with them, reveal that they were living in the Williamsport community of Hardy County, Virginia (later Grant County, West Virginia), after 1801 and up to the time of their deaths. John was occupied as a farmer in this rich bottom land along Patterson's Creek. According to his widow's pension application, Redman died on 8 October 1836. He left no will, but there is an inventory and appraisal of his estate and a sale bill (record of the estate auction) recorded in the Hardy County, West Virginia, will books.

John Redman and Sarah Days are the fourth great grandparents of HENRY LOUIS GATES JR. This connection was discovered during research for the PBS series *African American Lives*, which aired in February 2006. In July 2006, Gates was welcomed into the National Society of the Sons of the American Revolution on the basis of his descent from John Redman.

FURTHER READING

Berg, Fred A. *Encyclopedia of Continental Army Units: Battalions, Regiments and Independent Corps* (1972).

Hayes, John T., annotator and ed. *A Gentleman of Fortune: The Diary of Baylor Hill First Continental Light Dragoons 1777–1781.* 3 volumes (1995).

Heinegg, Paul. *Free African Americans of North Carolina, Virginia, and South Carolina: From the Colonial Period to About 1820.* 5th edition, 2 volumes (2005).

Jackson, L. P. "Virginia Negro Soldiers and Seamen in the American Revolution," *Journal of Negro History*, Vol. 27, No. 3, (Jul. 1942).

Lanning, Michael L. *African Americans in the Revolutionary War* (2000).

Quarles, Benjamin. *The Negro in the American Revolution: With a New Foreword by Thad W. Tate and a New Introduction by Gary B. Nash* (1996).

Revolutionary War Pension and Bounty-Land-Warrant Application Files. Microfilm publication M804, 2760 rolls. Washington, D.C.: National Archives and Records Administration (1985).

Revolutionary War Rolls, 1775–1783. NARA microfilm publication M246, Continental Troops, 1st Regiment Light Dragoons, folder 2. Digital images: Footnote.com (2007).

Rose, Christine, compiler. *Military Pension Laws 1776–1858 from the Journals of the Continental Congress and the United States Statutes-at-Large* (2001).

Sanchez-Saavedra, E. M., compiler. *A Guide to Virginia Military Organizations in the American Revolution, 1774–1787* (1978).

JANE AILES

Redman, Joshua (1 Feb. 1969–), jazz saxophonist, was born in Berkeley, California, the son of a former artists' model, dancer, and librarian, Renee Shedroff, and the celebrated tenor saxophonist, Dewey Redman.

Redman's mother, a single parent of Eastern European Orthodox Jewish heritage, exposed her son to the variety of music she loved, including classical, classic soul and rock, jazz, Indonesian, and Indian music. The sound of his mother's records frequently awakened him as early as 6 A.M., and although her record collection was limited, it contained the major jazz and rock artists such as the Beatles, JAMES BROWN, ORNETTE COLEMAN, Led Zeppelin, SONNY ROLLINS's *Saxophone Colossus*, JOHN COLTRANE's *A Love Supreme*, and many others. His listening skills were sharply developed in this manner and these performers strongly influenced Redman and his future eclectic style.

Redman displayed a talent for music at an early age. When he was just two, he tried to imitate the sounds he heard at a gamelan concert by arranging pots and pans according to their pitches. His mother studied Indian and Indonesian music at the Center for World Music in Berkeley, and he tagged along, gaining further exposure to an eclectic array of sounds and styles. At the center, Redman received piano lessons and by the time he was nine years old had taught himself to play the clarinet.

Redman was also self-taught on the saxophone, which he began playing at age ten. His first saxophone was acquired via the Berkeley public school system loan program, which lent musical instruments to low-income students. He was instantly drawn to the instrument's lyrical, vocal qualities and to its unlimited expressive, emotional range and communicative possibilities, but he never thought he had talent or would become a saxophonist.

Redman studied at Berkeley High School from 1982 to 1986, performing in the Berkeley High School Jazz Band conducted by Charles Hamilton. He frequently sent tapes of his playing to his father in New York, who boasted that his son sounded like Sonny Rollins. Redman continued listening to the music of key jazz figures such as DEXTER GORDON, Charles Henderson, BEN WEBSTER, Stan Getz, STANLEY TURRENTINE, and WAYNE SHORTER, who would greatly influence him. He was also fond of other performers such as Weather Report, whom he admired for fusing the jazz heritage with rock music. Despite his love of jazz and performing, he did not neglect his academic subjects and scored straight As in high school. Redman graduated valedictorian in 1986 and gained early admission and full scholarship to Harvard with plans to become a doctor. He received Harvard's L. Merrill Scholarship and two Leonard Bernstein Music scholarships.

At college, Redman played in the Harvard Jazz Band and saw such artists as HERBIE HANCOCK, McCOY TYNER, and Elvin Jones. Though his focus on his academic studies left him little time to practice the saxophone, his natural gifts allowed him to perform well at occasional gigs nonetheless. His summers in Boston were spent at the Berklee College of Music, performing in various jam sessions with other instrumentalists, and Redman made his professional debut in 1990 playing the tenor saxophone with his father at the Village Vanguard in New York City. He graduated from Harvard in 1991 with a B.A. in Social Studies, earning summa cum laude honors and induction into Phi Beta Kappa.

Despite his acceptance into Yale Law School in 1991 with a perfect score on the law school entrance exam, Redman decided to take a break from academics and survey the jazz scene in New York, where he shared an apartment with four serious musician friends. In November 1991 Redman won the $10,000 first prize in the THELONIOUS MONK International Jazz Competition in Washington, D.C. The judges included the noted jazz icons Benny Carter, JIMMY HEATH, Branford Marsalis, JACKIE MCLEAN, and Frank Weiss. They were captivated with Redman's versions of "Soul Eyes" by Mal Waldron, "Second Balcony Jump" by Jerry Valentine, and Thelonious Monk's "Evidence." This prize brought Redman recognition as a major talent and Warner Bros. Records issued him a contract.

In 1993 he released his first album, *Joshua Redman*, which brought him international acclaim. His second album in 1993, *Wish*, featured Charlie Haden, BILLY HIGGINS, and Pat Metheny, and Redman also performed on the lawn of the White House with President Bill Clinton that year. In 1994 he toured with the Lincoln Center Jazz Orchestra, and his band, the Joshua Redman Quartet, premiered on his album, *MoodSwing* (1994). Other highly popular and critically acclaimed albums followed, including *Blues for Pat: Live in San Francisco* (1995), *Spirit of the Moment Live at the Village Vanguard* (1995), *Freedom in the Groove* (1996), *Timeless Tales (for Changing Times)* (1998), *Beyond* (2000), *Passage of Time* (2001), *Elastic* (2002), *Momentum* (2005), and *Back East* (2007). Redman also played the soprano and alto saxophones in his later recordings. He performed music in the films *Blood of the Hunter* (1994), Robert Altman's *Jazz '34* and *Kansas City* (1996), *Midnight in the Garden of Good and Evil* (1997), on the PBS kids television show *Arthur* (2002), and on the PBS DVD *Music, Music, Everywhere* (2006). In 1994 he composed and performed the original score for Louis Malle's film *Vanya on 42nd Street*.

Redman married Gabrielle Armand on 15 June 1997 but their marriage ended in divorce. As of 2007 Redman was engaged and had a seventeen-month-old son.

In 2000 Redman became the artistic director and artist-in-residence of the San Francisco Jazz Festival. His trio, the Joshua Redman Elastic Band, was formed in 2002 with a focus on electric instrumentation and electric jazz. In 2002 Redman became the artistic director of the San Francisco Jazz Festival program, SFJAZZ. According to their Web site, SFJAZZ is a non-profit organization and leader in all aspects of jazz, including composition, education, history, and performance. One of their missions is to build and expand jazz audiences in the San Francisco area and around the United States and the world. In 2004 Redman, along with Randall Kline, executive director of SFJAZZ, organized the SFJAZZ Collective, a rotating and internationally acclaimed ensemble consisting of eight of the world's finest jazz artists and composers from SFJAZZ. The collective continues to issue annual CDs of their live performance tours.

Honors bestowed on Redman included several magazine readers' and critics' polls: Best New Artist in the 1992 *Jazz Times*, *Down Beat*'s Number One Tenor Saxophonist (deserving of wider recognition) and *Rolling Stone*'s Hot Jazz Artist (1993), and *Down Beat*'s Artist of the Year and Album of the Year (1994) for *Wish*. In 1994 he was nominated for a Grammy, and in 1994 and 1995 he was named Best Jazz Artist by *Rolling Stone* magazine. In 2005 *Momentum* was nominated for a Grammy.

Redman became one of the most celebrated, highly ranked, and legendary jazz artists of his time. He gave the world emotionally beautiful and electrifying jazz, which not only looked to the past but also contained his personal individual expressions and technical dexterity and precision. An eclectic composer, the impulse for his music creativity was his inner self and soul.

FURTHER READING

Giddins, Gary. "Joshua Redman: Tenor of the Times," in *Visions of Jazz: The First Century* (1998).

Lewis, Andrea. "Saxman with Chops all His Own," *Progressive* 64.10 (Oct. 2000).

Ouellette, Dan. "On the Brink," *Down Beat* (Apr. 2005).

"Redman, Joshua." *Current Biography*, ed. Elizabeth A. Schick (1997).

BARBARA BONOUS-SMIT

Redmond, Sidney Dillon (11 Oct. 1871–11 Feb. 1948), physician, attorney, and political leader, was born in Holmes County, Mississippi, near the town of Ebenezer, the son of Charles Redmond, a former slave and blacksmith, and Esther Redmond, a former slave. In 1871 large numbers of blacks were elected to state and local government positions. Less than two years earlier a new state constitution had been put into effect that promised to make democracy a reality for both black and white Mississippians. Moreover, the abolition of slavery in the United States had occurred six years before Redmond's birth. After leaving the farm near

Ebenezer along with the rest of his family, Redmond settled in Holly Springs, Mississippi, where he later attended Rust College. Upon graduation from Rust College in 1894, he entered the field of education and served both as a principal at Mississippi State Normal School in Holly Springs and as a mathematics instructor at Rust College.

He attended medical school at Meharry Medical College in Nashville, Tennessee. He graduated from the Illinois Medical College in 1897 and worked at his own medical practice in Jackson, Mississippi, for more than a dozen years. He did postgraduate study at Harvard, Massachusetts General Hospital, and Mount Sinai Hospital in Boston. He also organized and became the first president of the Mississippi Medical and Surgical Association.

Not content with treating and healing the sick, Redmond entered and completed law school at the Illinois College of Law. For the greater part of his life thereafter, the practice of law, involvement in political affairs, and his own highly successful business activities consumed his attention. Redmond was also president of the American Trust and Savings Bank, one of two black banks established in Jackson by 1904.

Politically, Redmond became an influential voice among black Mississippians. He submitted accounts about the racism encountered by black Mississippians to *Crisis* magazine, and in 1919 wrote to W. E. B. DuBois to inform him of several outrages committed against blacks. After years of involvement in state and national politics, in 1924 he became head of the Republican Party in Mississippi, a position he held until his death. One issue that Redmond championed on behalf of blacks was education. For example, in 1924 he spoke before a joint session of the Mississippi legislature that recommended the passage of legislation on behalf of African Americans in Mississippi. His fight for better schools for black youths was continuous. He called for improved reformatory schools for black boys and girls, contributing to an effort that culminated in the legislature's appropriation of $100,000 for such an institution in 1944. In 1919, years before the federal government established night schools as part of Franklin D. Roosevelt's New Deal, Redmond founded a night school at Smith Robertson School, and during the 1930s he served on the board of trustees of Jackson College.

In 1927 Redmond sought help for many Mississippians who were left in ruins after the tragedy that became known as the 1927 Flood. He investigated the situation on his own and, in turn, wrote letters to President Calvin Coolidge and the U.S. Justice Department to complain about the racist treatment to which black flood victims were subjected. Having voiced these complaints Redmond served on a special committee headed by DR. R. R. MOTEN of the Tuskegee Institute in conjunction with Red Cross relief efforts.

Redmond devoted much of his life to helping others through medicine, law, and other public services; yet as a businessman, he acquired a reputation that was not always complimentary. Some of Redmond's activities strongly suggest that he was sometimes less than fully committed to the advancement of the common good. For example, in 1915 Redmond was disbarred from the practice of law in Mississippi upon charges of "deceit, malpractice, and misbehavior," according to *Mississippi Reports*; he also retired from the practice of medicine as a result of a dispute with the State Board of Health. In 1928 Redmond faced two problems with the law: he and his son were fined for attempting to obtain money under false pretense, and Redmond was accused and arrested for participation in the selling of political office.

But Redmond was not a simple one-dimensional character, interested only in making money; he sought power, and he spoke out on black causes. Furthermore, even in some of those instances in which it appeared he was selfish, in the end it became clear that his position was justified. For example, the Mississippi Supreme Court finally ruled in his favor and permitted him to resume the practice of law. And in another case in which he was sued by a black woman who claimed he overcharged her, the court ultimately ruled in his favor.

Having lived most of his life in Mississippi, the poorest state within the United States at that time, Redmond became one of the ten wealthiest blacks in the country. He initiated Christmas Cheer Clubs in Jackson, an activity that he sponsored to assist indigent families. During World War II, when a critical shortage of doctors developed, Redmond returned to the practice of medicine to help provide much-needed health care.

Involved to the very end, Redmond died in a Jackson hospital while talking to friends about a black rally under way in the city. He left to his heirs an estate valued at $604,801.09—the equivalent of perhaps $10 million at the end of the twentieth century.

FURTHER READING
Bunche, Ralph. *The Political Status of the Negro in the Age of FDR* (1973).

Hamilton, Green P. *Beacon Lights of the Race* (1911).

Sewell, George. *Mississippi Black History Makers* (1977).

Wilson, Charles. *God! Make Me a Man* (1950).

This entry is taken from the *American National Biography* and is published here with the permission of the American Council of Learned Societies.

E. C. FOSTER

Reece, Cortez Donald (29 Jan. 1908–24 July 1974), musicologist and professor, was born in Guthrie, Oklahoma, to William (Bud) Reese and Lenora Smallwood. Reece later changed the spelling of his last name for unknown reasons. During the winter months, while his mother was teaching and completing medical school, Reece lived with his grandparents. His mother later became a practicing physician. His grandfather was a Baptist minister, and Reece described his home as "very correct but not depressingly so." He credited Guthrie as having an "excellent school system, an equally excellent public library, and a good cultural environment" and these resources helped prepare him for his studies (*Bluefieldian*, Nov. 1973, 7). In 1921 Reece was baptized and joined a local Baptist church, and in 1925 he graduated from high school.

Reece credited his decision to attend Fisk University to the inspirational Jubilee Singers and to his mother, who attended both Fisk University and Meharry Medical College, both in Nashville, Tennessee. In 1931 Reece received his associate bachelor's degree in music and became a professor at Langston University in Langston, Oklahoma, where he taught Zenobia Powell Perry, who later became a renowned pianist and composer. He left Langston University in 1935 and in 1936 received his master's degree in composition at the University of Southern California under the direction of Arnold Schoenberg.

From 1937 until 1942 Reece was acting director of the music department at Bluefield State College in Bluefield, West Virginia. In 1942 Reece left Bluefield State College and became a U.S. Army warrant officer. During his years of service Reece was a bandleader and concert pianist. He was stationed at Aberdeen, Maryland, until 1947. Reece then returned to Bluefield State College as a professor and director in the music department. During the next several years Reece worked on his two-volume doctoral thesis, "A Study of Selected Folksongs Collected Mainly in West Virginia."

From 1948 through 1953 Reece collected traditional folk songs. He recorded 240 traditional black spiritual and work-related songs from first-generation slave descendents and African American immigrants of the late 1800s and early 1900s. Reece explained that, "as with all things 'folksy,' folk music flourishes in the byways. It is untouched by the great bulk of formal education, sophistication, wealth, and social position.... We must come to recognize it as a national resource, a gem that must be dug out as part of a rich heritage and preserved for posterity" (quoted in *Work and Pray: Historic Negro Spirituals and Work Songs from West Virginia*, 6). Reece can be credited with preserving and drawing attention to black folk songs; without his work, many of the songs, and the people who sang their variations, would be lost. Reece categorized and analyzed the folk songs and how they influenced the lifestyle of West Virginia as part of his study.

Reece received his Ph.D. in Musicology from the University of Southern California in 1955. From 1955 until 1972 he was head of the division of humanities and the music department at Bluefield State College. He was a member of the Alpha Phi Fraternity, the Sigma Pi Alpha Fraternity, the Salvation Army Advisory Board, the American Musicological Society, the Music Educators National Conference, the College Music Society, West Virginia College Music Educators, and the American Choral Directors Association, and he was active in the Bluefield Community Concert Association.

During Reece's extensive career he gave lectures on the influence of the arts and sciences on the modern man, directed church choirs, and served as adjudicator and clinician for a number of choir festivals. He attended Scott Street Baptist Church in Bluefield, and he held numerous church choir clinics. At the same time, he composed many pieces, including his most famous arrangement of the African American Christmas carol "Mary Had a Baby." He composed for the piano, chorus, and orchestra and produced choral publications with Summy-Birchard and Harold Flammer, both well-known composers. During his career Reece was also featured many times on television and radio shows. He retired on 30 June 1972 because of health problems and returned to Los Angeles, California, where he died.

At a memorial concert at Bluefield State College, the well-known pianist Jasper Patton played in his honor. Six of his songs were played in tribute, including Fugue No. 3 in G Minor, Prelude ("Intimate"), Interlude ("Playful Rondo"), Scherzo, "Mary Had a Baby," and "That Man." A memorial fund was created in his honor in order to promote students in the performance arts. His students credited him with inspiring them and leaving a lasting impression on their lives. At the same time he preserved a segment in folk song history that would have been lost without his study and recordings. The West Virginia University Press released an album in 2003 of some of these work songs.

FURTHER READING

Bundy, Joseph. "The Legacy of Dr. Cortez Reece," liner notes from *Work and Pray: Historic Negro Spirituals and Work Songs from West Virginia* (2003).

Memorial Concert Program. Bluefield State College, 17 Apr. 1975.

Reece, Cortez. "Chairman Div. of Fine Arts Retires," *Bluefieldian*, Nov. 1973, p. 7.

Reece, Cortez. "Fine Arts Festival at BSC," *Bluefieldian*, 24 May 1961, p. 2.

Reece, Cortez. "Outstanding Program in Music Is Offered," *Bluefieldian*, Apr. 1969.

Obituary:*Bluefield Daily Telegraph*, 27 July 1974.

KIM MALINOWSKI

Reed, Eric (21 June 1970–), jazz pianist and composer, was born in Philadelphia, Pennsylvania, to David, who did sheet metal fabrication and design for Northrop, the aerospace company, and Jacqueline Reed, a school administrator. Reed began playing piano at the age of two. He grew up in a musical household surrounded by a vast array of musical styles. He was immersed in the musical traditions of the black church, at first in the Holiness (Pentecostal) church and later in his father's Baptist church. He especially enjoyed "funked up" versions of old hymns. Reed saw no separation or conflict between secular and religious styles of music and always tried to remain connected to his church roots. His father, who was his primary musical motivation and who taught him how to accompany, sang in a gospel quartet called the Bay State Singers. Though his parents were not avid jazz fans, Reed was exposed to many different kinds of music at home. Among his earliest influences was the RAY CHARLES and MILT JACKSON album *Soul Brothers/ Soul Meeting*.

When Reed was eleven years old he moved with his family to Los Angeles when Northrop moved his father's job there. He attended the R. D. Colburn School of the Arts, Westchester High School in Los Angeles (graduating in 1988), and California State University at Northridge. Reed was directed specifically into jazz by one of his teachers, Jeff

Lavner. His most important piano influences were HORACE SILVER and Ramsey Lewis, who reminded him of church pianists. Other major piano influences included WYNTON KELLY, AHMAD JAMAL, ERROLL GARNER, NAT COLE, OSCAR PETERSON, ART TATUM, and BUD POWELL, and he was also influenced by tap dancer Al Desio. After one year at Northridge, he went out on the road, in 1989, working with important and firmly established if not legendary musicians, at first with drummer Elvin Jones and singer BETTY CARTER. He went on to work with Jeff Clayton, Freddie Hubbard, JOE HENDERSON, GERALD WILSON, and Clara Bryant. Reed learned a great deal about music and humanity from Wilson and Bryant, in particular, who encouraged and nurtured young musicians. Reed was also no stranger to the wider world of show business early in his career, appearing on the late-night television programs of ARSENIO HALL (1990, 1994), Johnny Carson (1991), and Dave Letterman (1994).

Reed emerged onto the scene at a moment when young musicians, led both literally and figuratively by Marsalis, were embracing classic jazz. Other prominent musicians in this category include Wycliffe Gordon, Mark Whitfield, Carl Allen, and Cyrus Chestnutt. Reed maintained a sense of sartorial style on the bandstand that recalled a bygone era of jazz and also brought to mind Sunday morning church service.

Between 1989 and 2006, Reed moved back and forth from New York City to California. He became a member of the Wynton Marsalis Septet from 1990 until 1991 and 1992 until 1995. His vibrant and outgoing personality, combined with his extraordinary skill, vast musical knowledge, and early success, made him a figure similar to Marsalis, with whom he was closely identified in these early stages of his career.

In 1990 Reed released *Soldier's Hymn*, his first album as a leader, on Candid records, backed by bassist and drummer Gregory Hutchison and bassist Burno. The trio played again, accompanied occasionally by Marsalis, on a second album, 1993's *It's All Right to Swing*. The album received critical praise, but it was not until the release of *The Swing and I* the following year that Reed became a presence on the jazz charts. All three efforts were marked by Reed's characteristic blend of blues, gospel, and jazz influences.

After touring with his trio, Reed became the pianist of the Lincoln Center Jazz Orchestra from 1996 until 1998. He continued to record as a leader, releasing a dozen albums between 1995 and 2006, including *Pure Imagination* (1998), *Manhattan Melodies* (1999), and *Here* (2006). The latter figured as one of the great trio albums of the generation that came of age in the late twentieth century, featuring Reed alongside the remarkable talents of bassist Rodney Whitaker and drummer Willie Jones III. In the late 1990s, Reed also tried his hand at film scoring, composing music for *One of Us Tripped* (1997), *The Firing Squad* (1999), and *Life* (1999), and appeared as a piano player in the historical drama *Rosewood* (1997).

Reed appeared on many albums as a sideman, but some of his best work is to be heard on Marsalis's *Live at the Village Vanguard* (1999). Reed also greatly admired tenor saxophone player Stacey Dillard. Along with bassist Gerald Canon and Willie Jones III, they worked as a quartet starting in 2005. Reed recorded two albums with Wycliffe Gordon, *We* (2001) and *We Too* (2006). Reed and fellow pianist Cyrus Chestnutt, who is close to Reed in age and in knowledge of gospel and classic jazz, performed together in New York in March and April 2006.

As he entered the second decade of his career, Reed was acutely aware of the problems facing the jazz industry. While he appreciated the sound of hip hop, he feared the influence of nonswinging hip-hop rhythms on young drummers and worried about both the threat of Internet distribution of music and the closing of small, late-night venues, such as Bradley's in New York, where jazz musicians traditionally found the freedom to experiment with new sounds and collaborations.

In addition to serving as a clinician for several high school programs through the Lincoln Center Jazz Institute in the late 1990s, Reed taught in the Julliard Jazz Program in 2006. As an instructor, he believed in encouraging individuality, viewing himself as more of a "counselor" than a "teacher." At the same time, Reed also believed in making his students thoroughly familiar with the jazz canon. It was of the utmost importance to Reed that his students learn the fundamentals and history of the jazz, even if they did not always like to play it. He viewed himself as a missionary or vehicle for the promotion of the jazz tradition.

In his article "Piano Prodigy," which celebrated Reed's skill, the critic STANLEY CROUCH argued that Reed was unfairly overlooked by the jazz critical establishment. He was, of course, never overlooked by his fellow musicians. Ahmad Jamal described Reed as one of his favorite pianists, and the long list of Reed's session credits testified to his sterling reputation among his peers. He also performed a duet in a 2001 Verizon telephone commercial with the great Marian McPartland.

FURTHER READING

Crouch, Stanley. "Piano Prodigy," in *Considering Genius: Writings on Jazz* (2006).

Gladstone, Valerie. "Piano Men," *Town and Country* (July 2000).

Nocera, Joseph. "Wynton's Children," *Gentleman's Quarterly* (Aug. 1995).

Reich, Howard. "Reed's Turn on Standard's Impossible To Categorize," *Chicago Tribune*, 23 July 2004.

PAUL DEVLIN

Reed, Ishmael (22 Feb. 1938–), writer, was born Ishmael Scott Reed in Chattanooga, Tennessee, to Thelma Coleman, a saleslady. Coleman never married Reed's natural father, Henry Lenoir, a fundraiser for the YMCA, but before 1940 she married an autoworker, Bennie Reed, whose surname Ishmael received. (Ishmael has seven siblings and half siblings.) Coleman moved with her children to Buffalo, New York, in 1942, where Reed attended two different high schools before graduating in 1956; he also made his initial forays into journalism by writing a jazz column in a local black newspaper, the *Empire Star*, while still a teenager.

Reed began his college studies in evening courses at the University of Buffalo but ascended to the more rigorous daytime curriculum when an instructor read one of his short stories, in which Reed satirized the Second Coming of Christ by making him an advertising agent who is scorned by the industry because of his unique sales approach. "Something Pure," as the story was titled, gave an early indication of what would become Reed's inimitable style. Reed had read Nathanael West in high school, and West's biting social fiction and floating narrative voice were critical influences. In classes at Buffalo, Reed also absorbed the poetry of William Blake and William Butler Yeats, both of whom developed personal mythologies as an integral part of their work.

Reed's soaring intellectual life at the university was grounded by the meager prospects of a young, black male adult of the time. Low on money and discontented with academe's aloofness to social realities, he abandoned school to return as a correspondent with the *Empire Star*, moved into a Buffalo housing project in order to better assimilate the concerns of the city's underprivileged black population, and embarked on what turned out to be a discouraging attempt at activism. In one instance, he knocked on doors and registered voters on behalf of a black councilman who covertly threw the election to win favor for another job. In 1961 Reed tried his hand at moderating a radio program that was subsequently cancelled when he and another *Star* editor interviewed MALCOLM X, who was at the time the controversial spokesman for the Nation of Islam.

Compounding Reed's professional frustrations were his new responsibilities as a husband and father. In September 1960 he married Priscilla Rose, with whom he had a daughter, Timothy Brett, in 1962. Shortly after his daughter was born, however, Reed left for New York City and officially separated from his wife in 1963.

Determined to become a full-time writer, Reed immersed himself in the literary and creative cityscape of 1960s New York. He extended his literary talents to poetry through his association with the Umbra Workshop, a collective for black poets, and bolstered his journalistic expertise by working for a New Jersey weekly called the *Newark Advance*, assuming the editorship in 1965. Revamping the *Advance* inspired Reed to start his own paper, which he accomplished later that year by cofounding the *East Village Other*, taking the name from Carl Jung's theory of "Otherness." Increasingly enamored of the possibilities of cultural collision, Reed was finally beginning to enjoy an artistic career that had expanded sufficiently to satisfy his interests. This creative growth was especially marked by the release of his first novel, *The Freelance Pallbearers* (1967), a critically successful debut.

The Freelance Pallbearers grew out of Reed's attempt to parody Newark politics, but it eventually developed into a satire of the United States as a whole—in particular, the volatile social failures of the 1960s and the country's problematic participation in the Vietnam War. The novel's stand-in country for the United States is "HARRY SAM," which, as one critic points out, is a virtual homonym for "harass 'em," an attitude that Reed asserts the country takes toward its ideological opponents (Fox, 42). Reed directs his satire toward blacks as well, by drawing as his novel's protagonist Bukka Doopyduk, a black hospital worker representing African Americans who prefer assimilation over social protest. The title refers to the liberals who, in Reed's story, permit their leaders to be murdered, yet tardily appear over their corpses to praise their work and carry them away. As HENRY LOUIS GATES JR. asserts, the novel adopts the self-discovering

Ishmael Reed, novelist, essayist, and poet, in his office at his home in Oakland, California, 1 June 1998 after winning the annual MacArthur Fellowship Award. (AP Images.)

confessional prose that is the most identifiable convention of African American literature, seen most notably for Reed in RALPH ELLISON's *Invisible Man*. Through this voice, *The Freelance Pallbearers* establishes a fundamental element of Reed's writing; namely, the interrogation of artistic conventions in Western culture, both white and black and everything in between. Roused by the acclaim he received for *The Freelance Pallbearers*, Reed soon realized he needed to leave New York. His conscientious lower-class background made him suspicious of fame and the damage it would inflict upon his art. "If I had remained," he later wrote, "I would have been loved and admired to death" (*Reader*, xiv). So he left for California and eventually settled in Oakland, accepting a guest lecturing position at the University of California, Berkeley. He has held the post ever since, though not without some friction; after a few years he was encouraged to apply for tenure and was then refused, though he was allowed to continue teaching. Oakland proved to be an even more fertile environment for Reed's creativity than New York, as it cast him among a community of grassroots activist-intellectuals and cultural personalities, such as CECIL BROWN,

ANGELA DAVIS, and, for a short while in the 1970s, RICHARD PRYOR. He finally divorced Rose in 1970 and married Carla Bank, a dancer, with whom he had his second daughter, Tennessee.

In 1969 Reed released his second novel, *Yellow Back Radio Broke-Down*, which he has described as an effort to deconstruct ("break down") the yellow-back serial novels of the Old West and, by inference, the history of America. *Yellow Back* also expands upon Reed's increasing fascination with aspects of voodoo as a means of restructuring our perspective of American culture. Most telling, however, are Reed's emerging ideas concerning the novel and art generally, specifically in regard to its potential utilization by underrepresented communities. One character rages: "'No one says a novel has to be one thing. It can be anything it wants to be, a vaudeville show, the six o'clock news, the mumblings of wild men saddled by demons. All art must be for the end of liberating the masses.'"

It logically followed that Reed's next novel, *Mumbo Jumbo* (1972), would serve as a manic exploration for an authoritative African American text, an entity that, as Reed's novel powerfully points out, simply does not exist—but this nonexistence only emphasizes that the monolithic text of whiteness and homogeneous Western culture holds no true ballast either. Put differently, *Mumbo Jumbo* is an articulate defense of the dynamism of American race and culture, with particular attention to the instability of the form of the novel. Calling on his own idiosyncratic background in various media—music, radio, newspapers, magazines, and fiction—Reed infuses his novel with photographs, illustrations, charts, footnotes, copies of handbills, door signs, a bibliography, and more. The term Reed chooses for African American culture is "Jes Grew"—a rubric that lays bare the fallacy that African American traditions simply sprang out of nowhere—and in the novel it assumes the form of an epidemic whose victims uncontrollably execute a ragtime dance step, thereby preventing their assimilation in American society.

Mumbo Jumbo was nominated for a National Book Award, the second such honor of Reed's career; he had been likewise nominated for his first extensive collection of poetry, *Conjure*, the year before. Both *Conjure* and *Mumbo Jumbo* provide a name for Reed's engagement with African American religion: "Neo-Hoodoo." An integral figure in Neo-hoodoo is the trickster figure, whom Reed effectively emulates in his writing. Albeit any summation of Neo-hoodoo risks oversimplification,

it can best be understood as a politicized and religious response to Judeo-Christian and Islamic ideologies. Reed's art attempts to reconfigure the motley aggregate of beliefs that Westerners mistakenly hold as unshakable.

By the mid-1970s Reed was accepting awards from the Guggenheim Foundation (1974) and the National Institute of Arts and Letters (1975), among others. Yet with his fourth and fifth novels, as well as a growing corpus of essays that express his vitriol in a more direct manner, the controversy surrounding his work steadily increased. Reviewing Reed's fourth novel, *The Last Days of Louisiana Red* (1974), BARBARA SMITH wrote in the *New Republic* that Reed was showing a disturbing reliance on "the tired stereotypes of feminists as man-hating dykes" (23 Nov. 1974). And Reed reports that when he accepted an award for the novel, an "inebriated" Ralph Ellison—a longtime opponent of his work— shouted, "Ishmael Reed, you ain't nothin' but a gangster and a con artist" (*Reader*, xviii). With his fifth novel, *Flight to Canada* (1972), a satirical rewriting of the slave narrative that is generally considered his most accessible work, Reed enjoyed a more positive response.

While Reed would publish four more novels by 1993—*The Terrible Twos* (1982), *Reckless Eyeballing* (1986), *The Terrible Threes* (1989), and *Japanese by Spring* (1993)—the emphasis of his writing clearly shifted to essays, poetry, and drama. While all of these writings demonstrate a consummate artistry, they rarely achieved for him the renown of his early novels. In a way, Reed suffered the mishap of publishing utterly original work in the first half of his career and then being forced to explain himself in the second half—a task he has undertaken grudgingly.

Nonetheless, perhaps the most consistently positive aspect of his career in letters has been his stewardship for culturally underrepresented writers, as an editor of both magazines and anthologies. Toward this end, Reed cofounded the Yardbird Publishing Company in 1971 and the Before Columbus Foundation in 1976, both of which endeavored to gain notice, if not notoriety, for American writers of all ethnic backgrounds. Reed has edited collections of Native American literature, Asian American literature, and multicultural poetry. With the emergence of the Internet as a new literary medium, Reed also launched, in the late 1990s, a variety of online magazines, most notably *KONCH*, a forum for current events, and *VINES*, a serial collection of student writing. In 2000 Reed culled his best work from fiction, poetry, drama, and nonfiction which he collected in *The Reed Reader*.

By creating an uninhibited space in his work for play and creativity, a space that invokes seemingly every facet of American life, from religion to pop culture, Reed ranks among the country's preeminent postmodern writers. But unlike the works of Thomas Pynchon and William Gaddis, to name just two other highly esteemed postmodernists, Reed's writing is infused with a profound social concern that motivates a relentless indictment of the transgressions of modern America against minorities and the lower classes.

FURTHER READING

Reed, Ishmael. *Conversations with Ishmael Reed*, eds. Bruce Dick and Amritjit Singh (1995).

Reed, Ishmael. *The Reed Reader* (2000).

Boyer, Jay. *Ishmael Reed* (1993).

Fox, Robert Elliot. *Conscientious Sorcerers* (1987).

Gates, Henry Louis, Jr. "The Blackness of Blackness: A Critique on the Sign and the Signifying Monkey," in *The Signifying Monkey* (1988).

Gates, Henry Louis, Jr. "Ishmael Reed," in *Dictionary of Literary Biography* (1984).

McGee, Patrick. *Ishmael Reed and the Ends of Race* (1997).

DAVID F. SMYDRA JR.

Reed, Jimmy (6 Sept. 1925–29 Aug. 1976), singer, musician, and songwriter, was born Mathis James Reed in Dunleith, Mississippi, the son of Joseph Reed and Virginia Ross Reed in Dunleith, Mississippi. The Reeds were sharecroppers, moving from plantation to plantation, and Jimmy was the youngest of their ten children. Virginia sang in church, and Joseph played harmonica and encouraged his youngest son in music. Jimmy was a childhood friend of EDDIE TAYLOR, who was two and a half years older and tutored Jimmy on guitar after they worked all day in the fields. Taylor was a more advanced player and already steeped in the Delta blues, having followed master bluesmen like CHARLIE PATTON, SON HOUSE, ROBERT JOHNSON, and HOWLIN' WOLF around the area. He also knew the young MUDDY WATERS.

Jimmy Reed worked at sharecropping until he was sixteen years old, then he relocated to Chicago to live with an older brother. Mostly illiterate, he worked at various jobs until he was drafted into the navy in 1943. He was stationed in California and returned to the Delta after being discharged in 1945, and again he worked in agriculture. He married Mary Lee Davis in 1945; they had nine children. In 1948 Reed moved to Gary, Indiana. There he played harmonica with the singer John Brim and a drummer named Albert Nelson, who later switched to guitar and adopted King as his surname. Reed moved to Chicago in 1949 and played the streets for tips with the one-string guitarist Willie Joe Duncan. Reed and Taylor soon reunited when Taylor arrived later in 1949. The pair played a series of clubs on the South Side of Chicago. Reed played his harmonica in a rack and strummed guitar as Taylor laid down the shuffle rhythms that formed the foundation of their sound. Taylor's guitar style owed much to Johnson's groundbreaking use of fifths, a technique used to this day whereby the two lowest strings are played in harmony. This resulted in a full sound, propelling a driving beat. Taylor had also passed through Memphis and had met Johnny Shines, ROBERT LOCKWOOD JR., and B.B. KING.

Reed auditioned unsuccessfully for Chess Records in 1952 and was recommended to the fledgling Vee-Jay record label by ALBERT KING in 1953. Vivian Carter and Jimmy Bracken, the Vee and Jay of the new company, owned a record store in Gary, and Carter was a disc jockey at radio stations in Gary and Chicago. The pair's new label was experiencing success with the vocal group the Spaniels. Allegedly Reed was having trouble finding his sound at his first recording session, and after many hours Carter heard the now famous "da-boom da-boom da-boom da-boom" rhythm, which is a shuffle style using the aforementioned fifths technique, and directed Reed and Taylor to pursue this new sound. It became the mainstay of their many recordings. In December 1954 Reed recorded "High and Lonesome," followed by "Found My Baby," which were distributed by Chance Records in an arrangement with Vee-Jay. Reed's "You Don't Have to Go" was his first record issued on Vee-Jay. Ironically titled since Reed's earlier records generated little success and his future at Vee-Jay was doubtful, "You Don't Have to Go" slowly built momentum and became a modest hit in the spring of 1955.

Thus began the longest and best-selling run of hit recordings in that era by a blues artist. From 1955 to 1961 Reed achieved hit after hit with songs like "Honest I Do," "Hush Hush," "Baby What You Want Me to Do?" "Big Boss Man," and "Bright Lights, Big City." Many of these songs were co-written with Jimmy's wife Mary Lee "Mama" Reed. The hit formula consisted of the shuffling guitars of Taylor and Reed creating a catchy rhythm and Reed's lazy, engaging singing punctuated by his high-register harmonica playing. Reed conveyed a childlike quality in the way he put over his simple themes, even when they hinted at the risqué, that resonated with a cross section of the record buying public. He enjoyed airplay on R&B, pop, and country radio, and both blacks and whites bought his records. He has been called a genre unto himself. In 1956 Muddy Waters had two hits, while Reed had five. Chess records probably regretted passing on Reed.

Taylor was the foundation of their musical house and a much more accomplished musician than Reed; however, Reed's simple but effective singing and playing ultimately became the focus of their act. Although Taylor was a respected guitarist and vocalist in his own right and lent his seasoned experience to many recording sessions, including some by ELMORE JAMES and Muddy Waters, his greatest success and fame was from his association with Reed. Reed's sense of timing was unstable, and it fell to Taylor to provide cues and steady support both live and in the studio. The pair squabbled and broke up several times over the years but regrouped and played together until the end of the 1960s.

Reed's success led to heavy drinking, which slowly diminished his abilities to function both on and off stage. His epilepsy went unnoticed for years because of his constant drunkenness, and he was finally diagnosed in 1957. Unfortunately Reed was in no condition to capitalize on the British rock and roll invasion and R&B revival of the mid-1960s. His songs were covered by many artists, including LITTLE RICHARD, the Rolling Stones, the Byrds, Elvis Presley, and the Grateful Dead. The early Rolling Stones were particularly influenced by Reed's sound, and the founding member Brian Jones based much of his harmonica style on Reed's. Reed's piercing, high-pitched harmonica phrasings remain a mainstay for blues harmonica players and doubtless influenced folk singers like Bob Dylan. Like many blues artists, Reed was not always paid all the record royalties he was due.

In his last years Reed began to take care of himself and stopped drinking, but he was in ill health from diabetes and years of alcohol abuse. He went to Oakland, California, to help with the opening of a friend's night club. There Reed died in his sleep just before his fifty-first birthday. His son Jimmy Reed Jr. became a guitarist and his daughter Malinda Reed a singer. Though there was a huge difference between his personal life and the joy his music brought to millions of listeners, Reed's songs have become classics. He was inducted into the Rock and Roll Hall of Fame in 1991.

FURTHER READING
Fields, Kim. *Harmonicas, Harps, and Heavy Breathers* (1993).
Harris, Sheldon. *Blues Who's Who* (1981).
Leadbitter, Mike, and Neil Slaven. *Blues Records, January 1943 to December 1966* (1968).
Palmer, Robert. *Deep Blues* (1981).
Rowe, Mike. *Chicago Blues* (1981).
Slaven, Neil. *Boss Man* (1999).

DISCOGRAPHY
Boss Man (1999). SMDCD 232.

MARK S. MAULUCCI

Reed, Willis, Jr. (25 June 1942–), basketball player, coach, and executive, was born in Hico, Louisiana, the only child of Inell Ross Reed, a domestic, and Willis Reed Sr. At the time of Reed's birth, his father served in the U.S. Army, a position he held for the duration of World War II. Back in civilian life, Reed's six-foot-four-inch-tall father made his living as an agricultural worker and eventually as a warehouse foreman in the small town of Bernice in northern Louisiana.

Growing up during the Jim Crow era, Reed attended one of the segregated, underfunded rural schools of Louisiana. As a six-foot-six-inch-tall 14-year-old at Westside Consolidated School, Reed, with the guidance of his coach, practiced relentlessly on the dirt basketball courts of his neighborhood. His game improved along with his height, which reached nearly six feet ten inches during his senior year in 1960. He led his school to the Louisiana Class AA State Basketball Championship and received dozens of scholarship offers. He accepted an offer to play basketball and continue his education at nearby Grambling College. Grambling College, now Grambling State University, opened its doors in 1901 as the result of efforts on the part of many rural African Americans in northern Louisiana. Founded with the assistance of BOOKER T. WASHINGTON of the Tuskegee Institute, the school officially became a degree-granting institution specializing in training teachers by 1946.

When Reed arrived on campus in the fall of 1960 the college was known nationally for its outstanding football program, led by the legendary EDDIE ROBINSON, and its highly regarded basketball program, coached by Fred Hobdy. As a freshman Reed led his team to a National Association of Intercollegiate Athletics (NAIA) national championship. In the following three seasons Reed's team advanced to the playoffs twice more, finishing second and eighth. In 1964 Reed was drafted by the New York Knicks of the National Basketball Association (NBA) as the first pick of the second round, the tenth pick overall.

While at Grambling, Reed married Geraldine Marie Oliver in 1962. They had two children, Karl Vance, born in 1963, and Veronica Marie, born in 1965. Reed's first marriage ended in divorce. He would later marry Gale Kennedy, in 1983. His third child, Virginia Jackson, was born in 1990.

At the professional level, Reed came to the full attention of the American public and became an athletic legend. While he received individual accolades immediately—in his rookie season in 1964–1965 he won a starting position on the Knicks, was voted onto the All-Star team, and was named Rookie of the Year—his team struggled and finished last in the league. During the next four years, however, the Knicks developed into one of the NBA's premier franchises with the addition of four players: Dick Barnett in 1966, WALT FRAZIER and Bill Bradley in 1967, and Dave DeBusscherre in 1968. With Red Holzman as their coach, the Knicks went 54–28 during the 1968–1969 season but lost to the Boston Celtics in the Eastern Conference finals. With the same five starters, 1969–1970 became a magical season of basketball for the Knicks and their team captain Reed. Sporting a well-balanced offense and a spirited, aggressive defense, the Knicks went 60–22 during the regular season, a franchise record for victories. Reed was the team's rebounding star and inside scoring presence and personified the hardworking, blue-collar approach that the Knicks highlighted. In the postseason the team won the first two rounds of the playoffs and met the extraordinarily talented Los Angeles Lakers in the championship finals. That seven-game series between the Lakers and the Knicks mesmerized the American sporting world. The Lakers had three of the most talented players to ever play the game: ELGIN BAYLOR, WILT CHAMBERLAIN, and Jerry West. The two teams split the first four games. In game five Reed severely injured a thigh muscle and had to leave the game. While the Knicks eventually won that game, they handily lost game six in Los Angeles when Reed had to sit out again because of his injury. Heading into game seven at Madison Square Garden, there was one question in the mind of every fan and player: would Reed play? As the teams warmed up for the game, Reed was in the locker room receiving medical treatment, his playing status doubtful. Eventually, however, he hobbled out to the court in uniform. The sight of him electrified the crowd and stunned the Lakers. Dramatically, Reed started the game, managed to out-jump Chamberlain for the opening tip, and scored the first two baskets for the Knicks. The "Captain," as Reed was known, inspired his teammates and the home crowd. Led by Frazier, the Knicks won the championship game 113 to 99. The remarkable performance by Reed has gone down in NBA lore and was voted the greatest moment in the history of Madison Square Garden.

Reed and the Knicks won another championship in 1973, but because of another injury, Reed retired in 1974. In his professional career he averaged 18.7 points per game and 12.7 rebounds. He was a two-time Most Valuable Player, seven-time All-Star, and five-time All-NBA selection, and he was named to the NBA's Fiftieth Anniversary All-Time Team. He was voted into the Basketball Hall of Fame in 1982.

After ending his playing career, Reed continued to work in basketball. He spent twelve seasons as either assistant coach or head coach at the collegiate and professional levels and spent another sixteen years as a basketball executive for the New York Knicks and the New Jersey Nets. Under Reed's guidance the Nets reached the NBA finals in 2002 and 2003. In 2004 Reed returned to his home state of Louisiana to become vice president of basketball operations for the New Orleans Hornets. After the devastation of New Orleans following Hurricane Katrina in 2005, Reed moved with the Hornets to Oklahoma City.

Reed escaped the harsh conditions of the rural, segregated South of his childhood to become a beloved icon of American sports. He did so through his leadership, hard work, and determination, the same elements that he relied on in his most famous moment—the seventh game of the 1970 NBA finals.

FURTHER READING
Reed, Willis, with George Kalinsky. *A Will to Win: The Comeback Year* (1974).
Reed, Willis, with Phil Pepe. *A View from the Rim: Willis Reed on Basketball* (1971).
Bradley, Bill. *Life on the Run* (1976).
D'Agostino, Dennis. *Garden Glory: An Oral History of the New York Knicks* (2003).
Gutman, Bill. *Tales from the 1969–1970 New York Knicks* (2005).

KEITH WHITESCARVER

Reese, Martha L. (1900?–7 Feb. 1975), educator, mentor, and community leader, was born Martha Lucille Reese in Selma, Alabama. She was the younger of two daughters born to Bertha Wilson, a housekeeper. Very little is known of Reese's father, who died when she was a small child. As a youth in rural Alabama, Reese did not let gender, race, or social status limit her goals in life, and she spent her life helping those who were less fortunate.

Young Reese was mature well beyond her years. While helping her mother run the household, she worked odd jobs to bring in extra money. She joined community and church organizations and was an exceptional student. Reese's teachers and family recognized her intellectual ability and encouraged her to attend college. After leaving rural Selma, Reese attended Alabama Teachers College, now Alabama State University, in Montgomery, Alabama. She graduated with a bachelor's degree in Education. She went on to earn a master's degree in Education from Fisk University in Nashville, Tennessee. Reese also attended Howard University in Washington, D.C., and took additional classes in education.

After graduating from Alabama Teachers College, Reese was determined to increase the number of opportunities and improve the academic skills of blacks in rural Alabama. She began her professional career in Mobile in the early 1940s when blacks were migrating from the countryside to the city. In 1940, Mobile had a population of 70,000 people—29,000 of whom were black. By 1943, the population had grown to more than 125,000—the black population had grown to 46,000. Much of this growth was a result of the wartime economic boom, during which the city of Mobile received hundreds of millions of dollars in federal defense contracts. As the city's population grew, so did its need to improve services to the black community. Mobile's black educators, ministers, and community leaders began demanding equal access to public transportation, voting, and employment. Their quest to improve public education led them to reevaluate the conditions in Mobile County's rural schools, which were inadequately funded and whose buildings were small and oftentimes unsound.

As a result, during the early 1940s, Reese was pivotal in consolidating six small black public schools: Odom, Dawes Church, Wheelerville, Crandall, Mobile Terrace Community, and Union Church. Reese, who was principal of the Union Church School, believed that all blacks in rural Mobile would be served better if the local schools pooled their resources.

In 1948, the Mobile County School Board combined all six schools into the Dawes-Union Consolidated School. This school became the new home for hundreds of first-through-ninth-grade children who lived in rural Mobile County. Reese was the school's first and only principal. "Dawes-Union," as it was affectionately called, raised the standard of black education in rural Mobile. A new building was constructed, which vastly improved academic facilities, and more qualified teachers were hired, which led to major improvements in the school's curriculum. A caring and firm principal, Reese encouraged her students to strive to do well in their studies and her teachers to continue improving their skills in the classroom. One of her favorite sayings was "Give to the world the best that you have, and the best will come back to you," taken from a poem by Madeline Bridges entitled "Life's Mirror." She helped her students find employment before and after graduation by networking with business leaders and by teaching her students self-discipline, hygiene, and good nutrition. In addition, she offered night classes for adults, which included courses in math and reading. Reese organized the PTA, voting workshops, talent shows, movies, dances, and gospel concerts for the students, parents, and the community.

Thousands of blacks in rural West Mobile would attend Dawes-Union. As a result, Reese trained generations of teachers, ministers, engineers, college professors, doctors, and business owners, many of whom became local and national leaders. Reese, who lived in Mobile, opened her home to students who wanted to attend high school and college in the city but could not afford to pay room and board on their own. She encouraged other teachers to do the same. After Mobile County integrated its schools, Dawes-Union closed its doors at the end of the 1969–1970 academic year. Reese continued to be revered as the consummate mentor, counselor, role model and friend, even though the school was no longer in operation.

In addition to her work as a teacher and principal, Reese was a tireless community volunteer. She belonged to the Member of the Eunice, Order of the Eastern Star (OES) of Alabama, Gulf City Temple, Daughters of Elks, Optimistic Federated Club, and Household of Ruth. She was also a counselor for the Red Circle and the Young Women's Association (YWA). A deeply religious person, Reese was an active member of the Franklin Street Baptist Church, where she dedicated much of her time to youth activities, including organizing the church's children's choir, the U.J. Robinson Chorus. Reese died in Mobile, Alabama.

FURTHER READING

Personal interviews were conducted in Mobile in 2006 with family, coworkers, friends, and former students: Rosie Broughton, Dorothy Daniels, Pearlie Johnson, Jessie Robinson, Mattye J. Williams, and Margaret Yielding.

The *Mobile Beacon* and *Mobile Register* contain some personal and family background information. The Mobile County Public School Records contains information on the consolidation of schools.

TIMOTHY MARTIN BROUGHTON

Reeves, Bass (July 1838?–12 Jan. 1910), the first black deputy marshal west of the Mississippi, was born in Paris, Texas, although some historians believe he was born near Van Buren, Arkansas. The son of slaves, Reeves spent his early years on a small farm in Grayson County, Texas, owned by George Reeves, a former colonel in the Confederate army. Very little is known about Reeves's early life, and even less is known about his parents. Early on he labored in the Texas cotton fields as a water boy, where he learned stories and songs about black outlaws. He liked them so much, according to one source, that he worried his mother with his preoccupation with badmen, violence, and guns. Reeves was chosen as companion for Colonel Reeves's son and he served in this capacity until he was a young adult. The relationship came to a quick end, however, when the two argued during a card game. Reeves gave the man a severe beating, and, knowing that the penalty for striking a white man was usually death, he fled north into Indian Territory. Reeves spent the Civil War years living among the Creek and Seminoles, tribes that often had much friendlier relations with black law enforcement officials than with white lawmen. He became adept at using firearms and at hunting, and, although he never learned to read and write English, he did learn to speak several Indian languages, becoming especially adept at Creek. Living among the Indians gave him a lifelong respect for them, and living in Indian Territory, especially its wild interior, helped him learn its geography. His decision to flee into Indian Territory was soon to open up a world of possibilities. He married Nellie Jenny in 1864, and the couple had ten children, five boys and five girls. Around this time, he moved to Van Buren, Arkansas, where he became a prosperous farmer and well respected in the community.

When Isaac Parker, the well-known "Hanging Judge" of the Western Federal District Court of Fort Smith, Arkansas, was appointed in 1875, one of his first acts was to recruit two hundred deputy marshals to serve in the Indian Territory, considered to be the most dangerous place in the country. One of the men he recruited was Bass Reeves. At six foot two inches tall, weighing over two hundred pounds, with a solid reputation, and as an African American, Reeves proved a good choice for working with Native Americans. The latter quality was particularly important, because Parker considered himself to be a champion of Indian rights and was looking for someone who was not only fearless and dedicated, but who could work closely with the natives, especially those who still had a large number of freedmen and women living among them. Furthermore, blacks were not known for exploiting Indians.

Of the two hundred men Judge Parker appointed to be deputy marshal, Reeves proved to be the most successful at capturing criminals. From 1875 to 1907, he made several thousand arrests and traveled all over Indian Territory to capture outlaws. His talents were extraordinary. He could cradle a large pistol in his huge hands and was so good at drawing and shooting that he was barred from entering shooting contests. His knowledge of Indian languages made him invaluable as deputy marshal of the Indian Territory. His size—very large for that time—and physical strength allowed him to fight criminals. Reeves did not allow his illiteracy to hold him back in his work: he simply memorized the configuration of names on subpoenas, and when in doubt, would turn to someone who could read for confirmation of the names on the document.

Tales of his life represent him as a trickster who was brilliant at deception, often dressing as a cowboy, a tramp, a gunslinger, or an outlaw, and using many aliases in order to capture criminals. In one tale, he was ambushed on the Seminole Trail by three notorious brothers—men accused of murder, horse stealing, and other crimes. Forced to dismount at gunpoint, Reeves calmly showed the men the warrants for their arrest and asked for the date so he could fill them in properly. The brothers started laughing so hard that Reeves was able to shoot and kill all three of them. Another tale concerns a five-thousand-dollar reward for capturing two Indian brothers known to be holed up deep in Chickasaw Territory. He disguised himself as a tramp, wearing old shoes with removed heels and a battered hat with a floppy brim into which he shot bullet holes. Concealing a gun and some handcuffs under his ragged clothes, Reeves parked his posse wagon in the general area and walked twenty-eight miles into Chickasaw Territory. Once there, he convinced the alleged criminals' mother that he was running from the law, and during an opportune moment he arrested and handcuffed her two sons.

Several stories that became part of Indian Territory oral culture describe Reeves in heroic terms. In one case, Reeves, after watching several cowboys attempt to rescue a steer lodged in mud so deep that only its head and upper shoulders were visible, stripped off his clothes to do what several cowboys could not, and wrestled the steer out of the mud. The most popular stories illuminate Reeves's almost supernatural sharpshooter ability, such as the one in which some desperate posse men asked the deputy marshal to help them capture a desperado. It was said that Reeves was not only able to close in on the criminal but predicted he could break the outlaw's neck with his bullet and then proceeded to do just that, at a distance of a quarter mile. It is almost certain that Reeves himself circulated many of these stories. He was known as "boastful and lusty" by early Indian Territory settlers, who themselves willingly spread tales of his exploits, feeding the growing mythology of Wild West heroes. The newspapers and settlers of his time also picked up on these stories, transfiguring him into someone larger than life.

His colorful life and his reputation for killing fourteen men while in the line of duty earned him a great deal of criticism in the press. He was accused of killing out of greed, because he could make more money by killing outlaws rather than by holding them prisoner. Others in the press accused him of laziness, because he did not want to spend time chasing down men who would almost certainly resist arrest. Reeves was also accused of colluding with cattle rustlers. None of these accusations have been substantiated, however. The event that proved most controversial for his career was an accusation that he killed his cook, a black man, in 1884 during an argument after the latter allegedly threw hot grease on the deputy marshal's favorite dog. Reeves shot the cook, who fell into the campfire. He was later accused of murdering the cook and was arrested in 1886. He was relieved of his duties as deputy marshal. Reeves testified in court that his rifle misfired while he was loading it, accidentally killing the cook. Reeves was acquitted in 1887, although he lost his life savings in hiring an attorney to defend him. In fact, all of the killings he committed were investigated, according to guidelines Judge Parker set down regarding men and women killed during skirmishes with deputy marshals.

Reeves was always acquitted of all charges, more evidence of his charmed life to those who knew or heard about him, and near proof to many that he was invincible. Reeves went right back to work in the next term as a deputy marshal, but the trials by fire continued. Because an 1889 congressional act established three district courts in Indian Territory, he was transferred to Muskogee, (now Oklahoma), the seat of the Northern District Federal Court. His career continued to stir up controversy among white journalists and residents, and outright hero worship among many others, but by 1907, the year Oklahoma became a state, his years as deputy marshal were coming to an end. Local courts began to enforce federal laws, and his position of deputy marshal was phased out. He joined the Muskogee police force and served two years working a beat near the courthouse. For the two years he served on the force, no crimes occurred in that area. He was forced to leave in 1909 because of ill health. After the death of his first wife, he had married Winnie Sumter of Muskogee, Indian Territory, in 1900. Almost ten years later, on 10 January 1910, he died and was buried in the Union Agency Cemetery in Muskogee, with hundreds—black, Indian, and white—in attendance at his funeral.

FURTHER READING

Burton, Art. *Red, Black, and Deadly: Black and Indian Gunfighters of the Indian Territory, 1870–1907* (1991).

Littlefield, Daniel F., and Lonnie E. Underhill. "Negro Marshalls in the Indian Territory," *The Journal of Negro History* (April 1971).

Williams, Nudie. "Bass Reeves: Lawman in the Western Ozarks," *Negro History Bulletin* (April–June 1979).

Williams, Nudie. "United States vs. Bass Reeves: Black Lawman on Trial," *The Chronicles of Oklahoma* (Summer 1990).

Obituary: *Muskogee Phoenix*, 13 January 1910.

STEPHANIE GORDON

Reid, Ira De Augustine (2 July 1901–15 Aug. 1968), sociologist and educator, was born in Clifton Forge, Virginia, the son of Daniel Augustine Reid, a Baptist minister, and Willie Robertha James. He was raised in comfortable surroundings and was educated in integrated public schools in Harrisburg, Pennsylvania, and Germantown, a Philadelphia suburb. Reid's academic promise was as apparent as his family connections were useful. Recruited by President JOHN HOPE of Morehouse College in Atlanta, Georgia, in 1918 Reid completed the college preparatory course at Morehouse Academy and in 1922 received his B.A. from Morehouse College.

Reid taught sociology and history and directed the high school at Texas College in Tyler from 1922 to 1923. He took graduate courses in sociology at the University of Chicago the next summer. From 1923 to 1924 he taught social science at Douglas High School, Huntington, West Virginia. Reid then embarked on a model apprenticeship that GEORGE EDMUND HAYNES, cofounder of the National Urban League, had established for social welfare workers and young social scientists as part of the Urban League program. Selected as a National Urban League fellow for the year 1924–1925, Reid earned an M.A. in Social Economics at the University of Pittsburgh in 1925, and that same year he married Gladys Russell Scott. They adopted one child.

Also in 1925 Reid was appointed industrial secretary of the New York Urban League, a position he held until 1928. In this role he worked with CHARLES S. JOHNSON, director of research and investigations of the National Urban League, helping the league position itself as a source of information about the economic conditions of African Americans as well as an agency for social reform. Reid surveyed the living conditions of low-income Harlem African American families, conducted a study that was published as *The Negro Population of Albany, New York* (1928), and served as Johnson's research assistant in a National Urban League survey of blacks in the trade unions.

Reid also served as Johnson's assistant in collecting data for the National Interracial Conference of 1928 held in Washington, D.C. This conference represented a popular front of "new middle-class" social welfare activists and social scientists, white and black, who were professionally concerned with the race problem in the United States. The conference produced the landmark *Negro in American Civilization: A Study of Negro Life and Race Relations in the Light of Social Research* (1930). It was a volume that witnessed the emergence of a liberal consensus on race that would be reaffirmed by Gunnar Myrdal in 1944 in *An American Dilemma* and certified by the U.S. Supreme Court a decade later.

Reid's three-year tenure as industrial secretary completed another phase of his apprenticeship. In 1928 he succeeded Johnson as director of research for the national body, a position he held until 1934. As part of the league's procedure for establishing local branches, Reid's work included surveying seven black communities, which resulted in two important reports, *Social Conditions of the Negro in the Hill District of Pittsburgh* (1930) and *The Negro Community of Baltimore—Its Social and Economic Conditions* (1935). Drawing on earlier Urban League research, Reid also published one of the first reliable studies of blacks in the workforce, *Negro Membership in American Labor Unions* (1930).

Reid was enrolled as a graduate student in sociology at Columbia University throughout the period 1928–1934. While employed by the Urban League he began the research on West Indian immigration on which his Ph.D. dissertation would be based.

In 1934 Hope, then president of Atlanta University, encouraged W. E. B. DuBois, chair of the department of sociology, to hire Reid. DuBois complied happily. Reid, he remarked in 1937, "is the best trained young Negro in sociology today." Six feet four inches tall, confident, well dressed, and witty, Reid was an impressive figure. His biting intelligence was acknowledged—if not always appreciated—and his urbane manner made him an effective interracial diplomat in an era when black equality was an implausible hypothesis for most white Americans.

Reid worked closely with DuBois at Atlanta University until the latter's forced retirement in June 1944, at which time he ascended to chair of the department of sociology, serving from 1944 to 1946. Having served under DuBois as managing editor of *Phylon: The Atlanta University Review of Race and Culture* since 1940, the year of its founding, Reid also succeeded his senior colleague as editor in chief of the journal (1944–1948).

From 1934 until his departure from Atlanta University in 1946, Reid's work as a social scientist also had important policy implications. Under the auspices of the Office of the Adviser on Negro Affairs, Department of the Interior, Reid directed a 1936 survey of *The Urban Negro Worker in the United States, 1925–1936* (vol. 1, 1938), an undertaking financed by the Works Progress Administration. Three years later *The Negro Immigrant: His Background, Characteristics and Social Adjustment, 1899–1937* (1939) was published; it was based on the dissertation that had earned him a Ph.D. in Sociology from Columbia University that same year. In 1940 Reid published *In a Minor Key: Negro Youth in Story and Fact*, the first volume of the American Youth Commission's study of black youths. This was a cooperative endeavor of anthropologists, psychiatrists, and sociologists to study the impact of economic crisis and minority-group status on the development of youngsters in black communities. From the standpoint of the history and politics of the social sciences, the project—funded by the Laura Spelman Rockefeller Memorial—reflected the Social Science Research Council's endorsement of a "culture and personality" paradigm that would support liberal policy initiatives.

While at Atlanta, Reid also drafted "The Negro in the American Economic System" (1940), a research memorandum used by Myrdal in *An American Dilemma* four years later. In 1941, in collaboration with the sociologist Arthur Raper of the Commission on Interracial Cooperation, Reid published *Sharecroppers All*, a pioneering study of the political economy of the South. The text reflects the emerging characterization of the Depression South by social scientists and New Dealers as the country's number one economic problem; it signaled their growing impatience at the public costs of the region's class and race relations and dysfunctional labor market.

After DuBois's retirement from Atlanta University, Reid grew restless there. As a result of his desire for more congenial academic surroundings, on the one hand, and the cracks emerging in the walls of segregation, on the other, Reid became one of the first black scholars to obtain a full-time position at a northern white university (New York University, 1945).

This was again an exemplary chapter in his life. Under the racial regime of "separate but equal," job opportunities for black scholars, however well trained and qualified, were restricted to historically black institutions in the South. However, in the early 1940s, as tactical Trojan horses in a foundation-sponsored campaign to desegregate the ranks of the professoriat, a handful of accomplished black academics—among them the anthropologist ALLISON DAVIS and the historian JOHN HOPE FRANKLIN—were installed at northern institutions. Reid became visiting professor of sociology at the New York University School of Education (1945–1947) and, sponsored by the American Friends Service Committee, was visiting professor of sociology at Haverford College, Haverford, Pennsylvania (1946–1947). In 1948 Reid became professor of sociology and chair of the Haverford department of sociology and anthropology, a position he held until his retirement in 1966.

Reid and his wife joined the Society of Friends in 1950, and over the next fifteen years he was involved increasingly in the educational activities of the American Friends Service Committee. Though Reid's scholarly output decreased during this period, his important earlier contributions were gradually acknowledged. He was named assistant editor of the *American Sociological Review*

(1947–1950). Ironically, with the coming of the McCarthy era, Reid was honored for professional contributions that now earned him public suspicion. His passport was suspended from 1952 to 1953 by State Department functionaries for suspected communist sympathies. When he firmly challenged this action, the passport was soon returned. Reid served as vice president and president of the Eastern Sociological Society from 1953 to 1954 and from 1954 to 1955, respectively. He was elected second vice president of the American Sociological Association itself from 1954 to 1955.

After the milestone 1954 Supreme Court decision in *Brown v. Board of Education*, Reid was invited to edit "Racial Desegregation and Integration," a special issue of the *Annals of the American Academy of Political and Social Science* (304 [Mar. 1956]). This was another indication of his new visibility within the social science fraternity.

Reid's wife died in 1956. Two years later he married Anna "Anne" Margaret Cooke of Gary, Indiana.

Late in his career Reid enjoyed a wider public. Among other activities, he served on the Pennsylvania Governor's Commission on Higher Education and was a participant in the 1960 White House Conference on Children and Youth. In 1962 Reid was visiting director, Department of Extramural Studies, University College, Ibadan, Nigeria. From 1962 to 1963 he was Danforth Foundation Distinguished Visiting Professor, International Christian University, Tokyo, Japan. Reid retired as professor of sociology at Haverford College on 30 June 1966. He died in Bryn Mawr, Pennsylvania.

In addition to his personal achievements, Ira Reid is an important representative of the first numerically significant cohort of professional black social scientists in the United States.

FURTHER READING

No comprehensive collection of Reid manuscript materials exists. However, information about Reid, the various projects and organizations with which he was associated, as well as relevant memoranda and correspondence, may be found in the John Hope Presidential Papers and the *Phylon* Records, Editorial Correspondence (1940–1948), Special Collections/Archives, Robert W. Woodruff Library, Atlanta University; and in the Charles S. Johnson Papers and the Julius Rosenwald Fund Archives (1917–1948), Special Collections, Fisk University Library, Nashville, Tennessee. See also the Ira De A. Reid File, Office of College Relations,

Haverford College, and Ira De A. Reid File, Quaker Collection, Haverford College Library, Haverford, Pennsylvania; Ira De Augustine Reid Papers, Schomburg Center for Research in Black Culture, Rare Books, Manuscripts, and Archives Section, of the New York Public Library.

"Ira De A. Reid," in *Black Sociologists: Historical and Contemporary Perspectives*, eds. James E. Blackwell and Morris Janowitz (1974), 154–155.

Ives, Kenneth, et al. *Black Quakers: Brief Biographies* (1986).

Obituaries: *New York Times*, 17 Aug. 1968; *Philadelphia Evening Bulletin*, 19 Sept. 1968.

This entry is taken from the *American National Biography* and is published here with the permission of the American Council of Learned Societies.

PAUL JEFFERSON

Reid, Vernon (22 Aug. 1958–), guitarist, songwriter, producer, and photographer, was born in London, England, the oldest of three children, to James Reid, a postal worker, and Mary Elizabeth, a hospital worker. His parents had emigrated from the Caribbean island of Montserrat, but anti-immigrant sentiments prompted them to leave London for New York when Reid was two years old. Living in Brooklyn, Reid attended St. Gregory's Catholic School, where he demonstrated an interest in art and drawing. He also seemed fascinated with music, and his parents exposed him to a broad spectrum of their favorites—from calypso, to JAMES BROWN, to the Beatles, and the Dave Clark Five. By the time he reached Brooklyn Technical High School, focusing on industrial design, Reid enjoyed an eclectic musical mix of rock, blues, jazz, and R&B. An after-school jazz workshop intensified his interest in music and he began to play the guitar.

Reid learned from local musicians and started playing with bands at age fifteen. He was inspired by Carlos Santana and JIMI HENDRIX, as well as by the political statements that flowed through their music. His family had ensured his awareness of civil rights at home, and the images of the movement left a strong impression on him. He developed a racially inclusive perspective of rock music that differed from the attitudes of the general public—namely that rock music was associated with white males, with very little visibility for people of color.

By 1975 Reid was preparing to graduate high school. He was torn as to whether or not he should pursue a professional music career. At seventeen, he decided not to return to school. During the day he performed clerical work, and at night he attended jam sessions. In 1980 he met the producer and musician Kashif, a member of the R&B band BT Express. Kashif was starting a new group, Stepping-Stone, and invited Reid to join. It played a brand of rhythm and blues that crossed over into pop. Reid-soon discovered that the band did not meet his aspirations. Shortly after he left the group, he heard jazz drummer Ronald Shannon Jackson's group, the Decoding Society. The band played the intricate free-jazz harmonies of the saxophonist ORNETTE COLEMAN. Reid loved it. Jackson invited Reid to join the group, and in 1980 Reid began his long journey into genre-mixing. The Decoding Society's music represented avant-garde and free-form, melding different elements of jazz, rock, and blues. Reid toured the world with the group, playing with them for six years. On the side, he played with another fusion group, the jazz-punk-dance band Defunkt.

In 1984 Reid decided to form his own trio, Living Colour. The original members were Reid on guitar, Muzz Skillings on bass, and Will Calhoun on drums. At first, they played instrumental music. Eventually, Reid wrote lyrics for the melodies and the group's focus shifted. They developed into a power trio heavily influenced by the reggae-rock of the Police and the punk-pop of the Talking Heads. In 1986, the vocalist Corey Glover joined Living Colour and completed the lineup.

Following his political interests, Reid joined journalist Greg Tate to form the Black Rock Coalition, an informal group of writers and musicians who promoted freedom of expression for black musicians. Its manifesto insisted that rock and roll derived from black, not white, sources. Along with many young black musicians playing rock-oriented music at the time, such as Bad Brains, Fishbone, and Lenny Kravitz, the group challenged mainstream perceptions.

From their name to the earthy blend of blues, rock, jazz, and funk that they played, Living Colour personified the mission of the Black Rock Coalition. Still, every record label it approached rejected the group. Playing a series of gigs at the New York City rock haven CBGB's, the group caught the attention of Rolling Stones frontman Mick Jagger. The singer invited Reid to an upcoming recording session and offered to produce a song for the group. Jagger's patronage helped secure them a record deal with Epic Records in 1987.

In 1988 the group's groundbreaking debut album, *Vivid*, earned immediate critical acclaim and climbed to the Top Ten of the *Billboard* charts.

Vernon Reid in an undated publicity photograph. (Courtesy of Vernon Reid.)

Jagger produced the ska-flavored "Glamour Boys," but it was the single "Cult of Personality" that grabbed the most attention. Continuing Reid's interest in musical political statements, the song, which stayed in constant rotation on MTV, included samples of John F. Kennedy speeches and Reid's riveting guitar solo. The group won a Grammy for the song and for its next album, 1990's *Time's Up*. As a group of African American rock musicians, Living Colour found that their race, and not their music, often interested the media the most.

In 1990 Reid married Mia McCloud, but the pressures of celebrity immediately caused problems. Living Colour had opened for the Rolling Stones during the previous year and they played the first Lollapalooza festivals in 1991 and 1992 throughout North America. Incessant touring led to friction among the group's members, however, and the focus of the group shifted from music to avoiding conflict. Skillings left the group in 1992 and was replaced by Doug Wimbish, but the change did little to alleviate the discord. By the time it released its third album, *Stain*, in 1993, Living Colour's breakup seemed inevitable. So, too, did it seem for the marriage of Reid and McCloud.

Reid disbanded Living Colour in 1995 and he and McCloud, who never had any children, divorced in 1996. Reid released a solo album, *Mistaken Identity*, in 1997. The album and Masque, the subsequent group he formed, continued his usual experimentation with genres, this time with jazz and hip hop. Reid produced for the Malian superstar Salif Keita, in 1998, and the Mexican rock band Resorte, the same year.

In 2000 Reid married the choreographer Gabri Christ Stomp, and they had a daughter, Idea Viola, in 2003. Also in 2003, Reid's photography appeared in the Brooklyn Museum of Art exhibition, "Important Black Photographers of the 20th Century." (Reid had first been inspired to pick up a camera after Hurricane Hugo devastated his parents' native Montserrat in 1989.) Always absorbing various forms of creative expression from the time he was a child, Reid's ironic images often made reference to African identity.

Reid joined Living Colour for a reunion tour in 2001, and the group released *Collideoscope* in 2002. Reid continued his multigenre explorations, joining the cutting-edge turntable musician DJ Logic to form the Yohimbe Brothers in the same year. The duo released *Front and Lifter* in 2003 and *The Tao of Yo* in 2005. Reid wrote the score for the film *Paid In Full* in 2000, as well as for *The Ghost of Attica*, also in 2000.

Reid had a significant influence on American music. In forming Living Colour and the Black Rock Coalition, he helped shift society's perceptions of African American music. His fusion of different musical styles and his refusal to allow genres to limit his creativity opened the door wider for every African American musician who dared to do the unexpected.

FURTHER READING

Some of the information for this entry was gathered during an interview with Vernon Reid on 7 Feb. 2005.

Breskin, David. "Voodoo Child," *Rolling Stone* (8 July 1993).

Crazy Horse Kandia. *Rip It Up: The Black Experience in Rock 'n' Roll* (2004).

Tate, Greg. *Everything But the Burden: What White People are Taking From Black Culture* (2003).

ROSALIND CUMMINGS-YEATES

Reliford, Joe Louis (29 Nov. 1939–), baseball player, was born in Fitzgerald, Georgia, to Roscoe Reliford, a sharecropper and factory worker, and

Luronie Gillis Reliford, a homemaker. The ninth of ten children born to the couple, Reliford was named—under the advice of one of his brothers—for the world heavyweight boxing champion JOE LOUIS, who was at the pinnacle of his career. When Reliford was four, his father, who had been working at a gunpowder factory, fell ill and passed away; when his mother came down with arthritis in 1950, Reliford took a part-time job as batboy with the Fitzgerald Pioneers, a Class-D affiliate of the Cincinnati Reds.

Though Major League Baseball had been integrated five years earlier by JACKIE ROBINSON, the Georgia State League, in which the Pioneers played, and professional ball in the state of Georgia remained explicitly segregated. On 19 July 1952, the team traveled one hundred miles by bus to play the Statesboro Pilots, in front of a heavy-drinking crowd during Elks' Night. When the Pilots jumped out to a 13–0 lead, the raucous spectators started chanting for the Pioneers to put in their twelve-year-old batboy to pinch-hit. After enduring the taunts, the Fitzgerald manager Charlie Ridgeway caved in the top of the eighth inning and called for the 4'11", 68-lb. Reliford to grab a bat. As he replaced the outfielder Ray Nichting, Reliford became the first African American player in the league and state to play in an MLB-affiliated game. After letting a strike go by, Reliford hit a sharp grounder to the third baseman and was thrown out by a step. Playing right field in the bottom of the eighth, Reliford threw a runner out at third base, and made an over-the-shoulder catch to end the inning. As he ran toward the dugout, the fans stormed the field; initially terrified by the oncoming mob, the youngster was relieved to find himself the object of affection, as the elated fans congratulated him and stuffed money into his pockets for the effort.

Once the league reprimanded both the manager and the team, the Pioneers were forced to let their new star batboy go, but Reliford was offered a spot as an actual player on the local Negro League team, the Fitzgerald Lucky Stars. Reliford graduated from Monitor Elementary-High School, a segregated African American public school in 1957, and attended Florida A&M on an athletic scholarship. When he broke his collarbone in a football practice, Reliford was forced to drop athletics.

After graduating college, Reliford worked as an automatic amusement repairman, fixing jukeboxes, pinball machines, and bowling alley conveyor belts. He lived in New York City for six months, but soon moved back to Georgia, settling in the town of Douglas, where his girlfriend Gwendolyn Buchanan lived. The two wed in 1961, and had three children, Joel, Jeremy, and Jeannie.

Reliford worked in law enforcement for thirty years, as a police officer and deputy for the town of Douglas. Following his retirement in 1998, he worked as a part-time volunteer for the Board of Elections' voter registration office.

Inspired by a July 1990 *Sports Illustrated* article on his 1952 feat, and his inclusion in a minor league exhibit at the Baseball Hall of Fame, Reliford began work on his autobiography, *From Batboy to the Hall of Fame*, which was published in 1997.

FURTHER READING

Reliford, Joe Louis. *From Batboy to the Hall of Fame* (1997).

Crowe, Jerry. "For One Memorable Night, Baseball Was Child's Play," *Los Angeles Times*, 1 May 2007.

Reynolds, James E. "The Batboy Who Swung for Equality." *Sports Illustrated*, 2 July 1990.

ADAM W. GREEN

Remond, Charles Lenox (1 Feb. 1810–22 Dec. 1873), abolitionist and civil rights orator, was born in Salem, Massachusetts, the son of John Remond and Nancy Lenox, prominent members of the African American community of that town. His father, a native of Curaçao, was a successful hairdresser, caterer, and merchant. Remond attended Salem's Free African School for a time and was instructed by a private tutor in the Remond household. His parents exposed him to antislavery ideas, and abolitionists were frequent guests in their home. He crossed the paths of a number of fugitive slaves while growing up and by the age of seventeen considered himself an abolitionist. He had also developed considerable oratorical talent.

Remond was impressed by William Lloyd Garrison's antislavery views, particularly the notion of slaveholding as a sin. He heard Garrison speak in 1831 in Salem, and the two became longtime associates when in 1832 Remond became a subscription agent for Garrison's abolitionist newspaper, the *Liberator*. This move helped launch his career as a professional speaker and organizer at a time when the antislavery movement was gaining large numbers of new adherents. Remond traveled in Rhode Island, Massachusetts, and Maine in 1837, soliciting subscriptions and encouraging abolitionists to form local antislavery societies. The *Weekly Anglo-African* depicted Remond's early abolitionism: "He labored in its early movements most faithfully: he bore the brunt of the calumnies and oppression, the mobbings, the hootings, the assaults which were heaped upon that noble band in the times of 1834–7" (1 Feb. 1862).

The American Anti-Slavery Society hired Remond as its first black lecturing agent in 1838. He brought a new authenticity to the speakers' platform; his charm and eloquence aroused and impressed the predominantly white audiences. In 1842 he was joined by his younger sister, SARAH PARKER REMOND. An associate of Garrison's wing of the antislavery movement, Remond recommended immediate emancipation through moral suasion rather than political action or colonization, positions that isolated him from a growing group of black abolitionists. He opposed HENRY HIGHLAND GARNET's call at the 1843 National Convention of Colored Citizens for slave insurrection. Citing a flawed U.S. Constitution that sanctioned slavery, Remond advocated the dissolution of the Union, a view unpopular with former slaves. While Remond claimed that none of his ancestors had been slaves, he consistently declared southern slavery and northern discrimination dual violations of the Bill of Rights. He urged blacks to protest the discrimination they experienced daily. "We need more radicalism among us," he wrote to the Liberator. "We have been altogether too fearful of martyrdom—quite too indifferent in our views and sentiments—too slow in our movements" (21 May 1841).

The highlight of Remond's career came in 1840, when the American Anti-Slavery Society selected him as a delegate to the World's Anti Slavery Convention in London. Financed by female antislavery groups, Remond welcomed women's involvement in the movement and refused to take his seat at the convention when it voted to bar women's participation. In the eighteen months following the convention, he lectured to great acclaim throughout the British Isles on such topics as slavery, racial prejudice, and temperance. The antislavery press commented widely on Remond's gracious reception in England, in contrast to the discriminatory treatment he endured on his passage abroad and upon his return to Boston. His comparison between travel in the United States and Britain formed the basis of his noted 1842 address to the Massachusetts legislature, "The Rights of Colored Persons in Travelling," with which he became the first African American to speak before that body. His address is an important document of the widespread campaign to end segregated seating in railway cars in the 1840s. Throughout his career he reminded whites of the proscriptive laws and practices against blacks in northern states.

Remond was the most renowned African American orator until 1842, when FREDERICK DOUGLASS began speaking to American audiences. The two men often toured together in the 1840s, and in the fall of 1843 they sustained a heavy lecturing schedule in the Midwest, amid fears of antiabolitionist riots. On 28 October 1845 Douglass wrote Garrison of Remond's effective antislavery oratory: "His name is held in affectionate remembrance by many whose hearts were warmed into life on this question by his soul-stirring eloquence" (CARTER G. WOODSON, The Mind of the Negro as Reflected in Letters Written during the Crisis, 1800–1860 [1926]). Remond and Douglass's friendship deteriorated when Douglass publicly broke with Garrison in 1852. Contemporaries remarked that Remond felt shunned when Douglass swiftly rose to eminence in antislavery circles. Remond's corresponding decline in stature may be due to the fact that he suffered from tuberculosis, which forced him to abandon the lecture field for long periods of time.

Remond became increasingly impatient with the progress of antislavery, prompting him to reevaluate the utility of moral suasion in the antislavery struggle. The Fugitive Slave Act of 1850, which strengthened slaveholders' ability to reclaim their human property, prompted Remond to defend forcible resistance, to relax his opposition to slave insurrection, and to endorse political action. He became increasingly critical of white abolitionists for not attacking racial prejudice as vehemently as they did slavery. Though he remained ambivalent about the Republican Party, Remond welcomed the outbreak of the Civil War. When Massachusetts opened enlistment to African Americans in January 1863, Remond, Douglass, Garnet, WILLIAM WELLS BROWN, and other black leaders traveled through the northern states and Canada to recruit African Americans to the ranks of the Fifty-fourth Massachusetts Infantry Regiment. With the war's end Remond supported the continuation of antislavery societies to secure civil and political rights for blacks, a position that divided him from Garrison. He rejected the inclusion of women's rights issues in the campaign for black suffrage, arguing that their inclusion would hinder the achievement of black male enfranchisement, on which the eventual success of women's suffrage depended. Remond made his final lecture tour for a New York State black suffrage campaign in 1867. His poor health permitted him to appear only sporadically at civil rights meetings thereafter.

Remond spent most of his time lecturing rather than writing on behalf of antislavery. As one of the earliest black orators, he served as a role model, yet his ideological proximity to the predominantly white Garrisonians isolated him from other black abolitionists. Contemporaries extolled his oratory and compared his style to that of Wendell Phillips. However, as a black man who had never been a slave, his appeal and value to the antislavery movement were limited. Fellow abolitionists remarked upon his increasingly querulous demeanor, bitterness, and irascibility.

Beginning in 1865 Remond worked as a streetlight inspector and was appointed as a stamp clerk in the Boston Custom House in 1871. He died of tuberculosis at his home in Wakefield, Massachusetts. He was married twice, first to Amy Matilda Williams, who died on 15 August 1856, and then to Elizabeth Thayer Magee, who died on 3 February 1872. He and his second wife had four children.

FURTHER READING

No substantial collection of Remond's personal papers exists. Many speeches and letters can be found in the microfilm edition of C. Peter Ripley and George Carter, eds., *The Black Abolitionist Papers, 1830–1865* (1981).

Porter, Dorothy B. "The Remonds of Massachusetts: A Nineteenth-Century Family Revisited," *Proceedings of the American Antiquarian Society* 95 (Oct. 1985): 259–295.

Usrey, Miriam L. "Charles Lenox Remond: Garrison's Ebony Echo," *Essex Institute Historical Collections* 56 (Apr. 1970): 112–125.

This entry is taken from the *American National Biography* and is published here with the permission of the American Council of Learned Societies.

STACY KINLOCK SEWELL

Remond, Sarah Parker (6 June 1826–13 Dec. 1894), abolitionist, physician, and feminist, was born in Salem, Massachusetts, the daughter of John Remond and Nancy Lenox. Her father, a native of Curaçao, immigrated to the United States at age ten and became a successful merchant. Her mother was the daughter of African American Revolutionary War veteran Cornelius Lenox. Remond grew up in an antislavery household. Her father became a life member of the Massachusetts Anti-Slavery Society in 1835, and her mother was founding member of the Salem Female Anti-Slavery Society, which began as a black female organization in 1832. Sarah's brother, CHARLES LENOX REMOND, was a well-known antislavery lecturer in the United States and Great Britain.

Sarah Parker Remond attended local public schools in Salem until black students were forced out by committee vote in 1835. Determined to educate their children in a less racist environment, the Remond family moved to Newport, Rhode Island, in 1835. After the family returned to Salem in 1841, Remond's education was further developed at home with English literature and antislavery writings. She was an active member of the Salem Female Anti-Slavery Society, the Essex County Anti-Slavery Society, and the Massachusetts Anti-Slavery Society. Her experience with the Salem school committee led to early activism against racial segregation. She was awarded five hundred dollars by the First District Court of Essex after being forcibly ejected from her seat at a public place of entertainment in 1853.

In 1842 Remond began touring on the antislavery circuit with her brother Charles, who was the first black lecturing agent of the Massachusetts Anti-Slavery Society. Sarah and Charles Remond toured New York State with Wendell Phillips, Abigail Kelley Foster, Stephen Foster, and Susan B. Anthony in 1856. Remond accepted an appointment as a lecturing agent of the American Anti-Slavery Society in 1858. On 28 December 1858 she sailed to Great Britain with three goals: to work for the antislavery cause, to pursue an education, and to live for a time away from American racism. She attended the Bedford College for Ladies in London while traveling as an antislavery lecturer to more than forty-five cities in England, Scotland, and Ireland between 1859 and 1861. Her approach on the antislavery circuit was different from black male American abolitionists'. She won over the British public by drawing on her demeanor as a "lady," while recounting stories of sordid sexual exploitation forced on female slaves. She was popular in Great Britain, where lectures by women were rare. She was one of the first women to lecture in Great Britain to "mixed-sex" audiences. Because she was removed by both her race and nationality from British class politics and gender conventions, she was able to appeal to both the working class and the social elite. Perhaps her popularity as an abolitionist in London caused the American legation in London to deny her request for a visa to travel to France in November 1859. The legation claimed that because of her race she was not a citizen of the United States. Support for her included editorials in most of the major London papers. The *Morning Star* compared the "visé affair" to the DRED SCOTT decision, which had been used by the United States as a basis for its actions. Benjamin Moran, the American assistant secretary of legation, wrote on 10 December 1859 that George Dallas, the American minister to Great Britain, threatened to go home should any more attacks of the kind appear, and if he went, he would be the last American minister in England for some time. Moran believed that public opinion on this matter reached Buckingham Palace. On 25 February 1860 he wrote, "on the subject of darkies, I am reminded that the queen looked at me very [oddly] on Thursday, & I now suspect the Remond affair was dancing about in her mind, and that she wished to know what kind of person (if she thought of the matter at all) the Secretary was that refused that lady of color a visé."

Remond's manner and standing in American antislavery circles made her a great many friends in the "upper circle" of British abolitionists. She lived for a time at the home of Peter Alfred Taylor, a member of Parliament and treasurer of the London Emancipation Committee. A center for London radicals, the Taylor home was also the meeting place for many of London's early female reformers because Taylor's wife, Mentia, was active in the women's suffrage movement. Remond worked with the Taylors in establishing the first two emancipation groups in London. In June 1859 concerned individuals, including famed runaway slaves WILLIAM AND ELLEN CRAFT, formed the London Emancipation Committee. Remond was active in this group until 1 August 1859. After the committee failed to invite her to address a public meeting held in London to celebrate the twenty-fifth anniversary of the abolition of British colonial slavery, Remond stopped attending its meetings. The London Emancipation Committee concluded operations in February 1860 at a meeting attended by men only.

Four years later Remond and Mentia Taylor were founding members of the London Ladies' Emancipation Society, which claimed that slavery was a question especially and deeply interesting to women. In 1864 the society put into circulation more than twelve thousand pamphlets printed by the feminist publisher Emily Faithful. Remond's contribution was titled *The Negroes and Anglo-Africans as Freed Men and Soldiers*. After the end of the Civil War, Remond was a member of the Freedmen's Aid Association along with Ellen Craft. In 1865 she wrote a letter of protest to the *London Daily News* when the London press began attacking blacks after an insurrection in Jamaica.

Remond returned to the United States later in 1865 and worked for a short time with the American Equal Rights Association. She had served as a delegate to the National Woman's Rights Convention in 1858. In 1866 she moved to Florence, Italy, to attend a medical training program at Santa Maria Nuovo Hospital. After receiving a diploma for "professional medical practice" in 1871, she started a medical practice in Florence. On 25 April 1877 she married an Italian named Lazzaro Pintor. Sarah Parker Remond is buried in the Protestant Cemetery in Rome, Italy.

FURTHER READING

Remond, Sarah Parker. "Sarah Parker Remond," in *Our Exemplars, Poor and Rich; or, Biographical Sketches of Men and Women Who Have, by an Extraordinary Use of Their Opportunities, Benefited Their Fellow-Creatures*, ed. Matthew Davenport Hill (1861).

Midgley, Clare. *Women against Slavery: The British Campaigns, 1780–1870* (1992).

Porter, Dorothy B. "The Remonds of Salem, Massachusetts: A Nineteenth-Century Family Revisited," *Proceedings of the American Antiquarian Society* 95 (Oct. 1985): 259–295.

Ripley, C. Peter, ed. *The Black Abolitionist Papers*, vol. 1, *The British Isles, 1830–1865* (1985).

This entry is taken from the *American National Biography* and is published here with the permission of the American Council of Learned Societies.

KAREN JEAN HUNT

Renfro, Mel (30 Dec. 1941–), football player, was born Melvin Lacy Elisha Renfro in Houston, Texas. When Mel was four his family moved to Portland, Oregon. He attended Jefferson High School, where he excelled as a football player, playing offense (quarterback and running back), defense (defensive back), and special teams (kick and punt returner). Renfro led Jefferson to thirty-four consecutive victories, including three state championships. The only loss he suffered was the state championship his senior year. He graduated high school in 1960.

Renfro attended Oregon University, where he ran track and played football, becoming one of the best players in the school's history. As in high school, he played offense, defense, and special teams. For his career, he amassed 1,540 rushing yards, averaging 5.5 yards per carry, and twenty-three touchdowns. On defense he played safety and once recorded an astounding twenty-one tackles in a game against Ohio State his senior year. Renfro also excelled as a kick returner, averaging 26.7 yards per kickoff return and 12.9 yards per punt return. He possessed world-class speed and ran a leg of Oregon's world record-setting 4x100 relay team in 1962. On 14 July 1962, he married Clara Burch; they had three children before divorcing in 1976.

Renfro had a superb senior season at Oregon, rushing for 789 yards and thirteen touchdowns, and many considered him one of the finest college athletes in the nation. A bizarre injury, however, dropped his stock among professional scouts. The assassination of President John F. Kennedy left Renfro despondent, and, coupled with the pressure he felt being a married student-athlete, he lost his temper and punched a mirror, seriously injuring his hand. The injury left permanent nerve damage and made professional teams cautious. He fell to the ninth round of the 1964 American Football League draft, when he was selected by the Oakland Raiders, but he never signed. In the April 1964 National Football League (NFL) draft, the Dallas Cowboys selected him in the second round. (At the time, the two leagues held separate drafts and it was common for athletes to be selected in both drafts.)

Cowboys coach Tom Landry was concerned about Renfro's size (6 feet tall, 185 pounds) and ability to handle the halfback position, so he moved Renfro to free safety. Renfro's athleticism impressed Landry, and Renfro became the starter the first game of his rookie season. Renfro immediately became an impact player. His uncanny ability to anticipate pass routes and to run backward at a sprint made him a disruptive force to an opponent's passing game. He finished his rookie season with seven interceptions. Renfro also excelled on special teams, leading the league in kickoff returns with 1,017 yards and punt returns with 418 yards. He was named an All-Pro and runner-up for Rookie of the Year.

Renfro alternated playing free safety and cornerback over the next few seasons as he became a star defensive player, helping Dallas rise to perennial playoff contender. After the infamous Ice Bowl game in Green Bay in 1967, the coldest game in NFL history (13 degrees below zero; 40 below with wind chill), Renfro needed three weeks of treatment to recover from frostbite.

In 1969 Renfro sued a North Dallas realtor under the Fair Housing Act of 1968 for refusing to lease a duplex to his family. Renfro lived in Oak Cliff, a southern neighborhood in Dallas, far away from the team's North Dallas offices and training facilities. He received an injunction against the realtor. His was the first lawsuit in Dallas for unfair housing and opened a floodgate of subsequent lawsuits.

The Cowboys were initially concerned that the lawsuit might affect Renfro's execution on the field, but he proved their fears wrong as he led the league in interceptions with ten and was named All-Pro. At the 1970 Pro Bowl game, he returned two punts for touchdowns, earning MVP honors.

For the 1970 season Landry moved Renfro to cornerback full time. Renfro was part of Dallas's "Doomsday Defense" that led the team to its first Super Bowl, a 16–13 loss to the Baltimore Colts. Renfro was involved in one of the most controversial plays in Super Bowl history. Officials ruled that Renfro tipped a pass that allowed Colt tight-end John Mackey to score a touchdown. Replays were inconclusive and Renfro said he never touched the ball. The Cowboys returned to the Super Bowl in 1972, beating the Miami Dolphins 24–3. The Dolphins challenged Renfro early, but he shut down Miami's star receiver PAUL WARFIELD as Dallas's defense dominated the game.

Renfro played five more seasons for the Cowboys and continued to dominate games, though his statistics did not reflect this as opponents rarely threw to his side of the field. He closed out his playing career at Super Bowl XII, in a 27–10 victory over the Denver Broncos, before retiring. He finished his career with a Cowboys record of fifty-two interceptions, a 26.4 kickoff return average, and a 7.7 yard punt return average. He played in ten consecutive Pro Bowls and four Super Bowls, winning two championships.

After retiring as a player, the Cowboys hired Renfro as a scout. He quit after a year, mainly because he was angry over not being offered a coaching position. A series of bad business ventures led him to file for bankruptcy. In 1981 he was implicated in a Super Bowl ticket scalping scheme and went to jail for a few days for failure to pay child support. Renfro believed his difficulties were tied to his race, lamenting that white players did not seem to have as many problems finding jobs or securing loans. Despite his problems, the year ended on a high note for Renfro as he was inducted into the Cowboys Ring of Honor.

Renfro continued job-hopping as he tried to define his life after football. He worked as a car salesman, worked for Miller Brewing Company, and served coaching stints with the Los Angeles Express of the United States Football League (1986) and the St. Louis Cardinals (1987). He returned to Portland in 1988 to create the Bridge Center, a Christian-based community center. He returned to Dallas, where his fame as a Cowboy helped him form the Mel Renfro Foundation. He also served as public relations director for the Starfish Foundation, an organization that counseled drug addicts and their families.

Over a fourteen-year football career, Renfro became a dominant defensive player, and his athleticism allowed him to excel at two positions. His contributions on the field were finally recognized in 1996 when he was inducted into the NFL Hall of Fame in his last year of eligibility. The delay for his induction had less to do with his play on the field than with his problems off the field.

FURTHER READING

Golenbeck, Peter. *Cowboys Have Always Been My Heroes: The Definitive Oral History of America's Team* (1997).

Monk, Cody. *Legends of the Dallas Cowboys* (2004).

MICHAEL C. MILLER

Renfroe, Earl Wiley (9 Jan. 1907–14 Nov. 2000), orthodontist, educator, and U.S. Army colonel, was born in Chicago, the son of Eugene Renfroe and Bertha. A 1921 graduate of Austin O. Sexton Grammar School, Renfroe attended James H. Bowen High School, where he was the first African American student in the school's history to achieve the rank of cadet commander in the Reserve Officers Training Corp (ROTC). This was one of many "firsts" that characterized his life.

Renfroe next enrolled at Crane Junior College, then he was admitted to the University of Illinois at Chicago (UIC) College of Dentistry. While there, he became the first student to tackle a full course load while also working full-time outside of the college. Undaunted by the difficulties of such a feat, he still managed to graduate first in a class of 127 dental students in 1931.

By the time Renfroe joined the Illinois National Guard in 1932, the country's unemployment rate hovered around sixteen million people, one-third of America's population. One year later he returned to his alma mater as a faculty member and eventually performed another memorable first: abolishing the rule that required dental students to work only on patients of their same race.

In 1934 Renfroe added to his growing list of accomplishments by becoming the first African American in Illinois and the third in the United States to earn a commercial pilot's license. He later used that expertise as an inspector for the Illinois Aeronautics Commission. By 1942 he had completed an M.S in Orthodontics at the UIC College of Dentistry. This accomplishment made him the first African American orthodontist in Chicago. The advent of World War II took Renfroe to Fort Huacha, Arizona, where he worked as chief of the U.S. Army Dental Services. He continued to serve his country as a member of the U.S. Army Reserves until he retired as a colonel in 1968.

In 1950 Renfroe accomplished two milestones simultaneously by becoming the first African American dentist and professional of any kind to open an office in Chicago's downtown Loop. Meanwhile he continued to teach at the UIC College of Dentistry, where he was named associate professor in 1953. Four years later he was promoted to full professor.

In 1957 Renfroe collaborated with Thomas K. Barber, professor emeritus at the University of California at Los Angeles, on an article detailing the concepts of preventive and interceptive orthodontics. The article, "Interceptive Orthodontics for the General Practitioner," was published in the *Journal of the American Dental Association* and was eventually translated into several languages for international publication.

In the 1950s Renfroe began extensive travels to countries such as Brazil and Barbados. The Brazilians invited him back seven times, dubbing him the "father of orthodontics." In Barbados a dental facility was named for Renfroe, who visited that country more than thirty times. By 1960 his textbook *Technique Training in Orthodontics* was published, and it became required reading for dentists in the Brazilian army four years later.

In 1966 Renfroe earned another distinction when he was chosen to lead a department at the UIC College of Dentistry, another first for an African American. In 1975 he published another textbook that two years later was translated into Japanese. In 1984 he was awarded the rank of general in the Illinois National Guard.

Renfroe's interests and hobbies were as varied as his accomplishments. He enjoyed flying, amateur radio operation, gun marksmanship, and scuba diving. He was also affiliated with several civic organizations, including the Chicago Council on Foreign Relations, the Chicago Urban League, the International Oceanographic Foundation, and the National Conference of Christians and Jews. He held professional memberships in the Illinois and Chicago Dental Society, the American Dental Association, the Illinois State Society of Orthodontists, the Chicago Council of Foreign Relations, and the Chicago Association of Orthodontists, for which he served as president in 1963–1964.

Additionally, Renfroe was a member of Alpha Phi Alpha fraternity, Sigma Pi Phi, Beta Boule, and the Druids societal group. In 1971 the University of Illinois honored him with the Alumni Loyalty Award. Chicago mayor Richard Daly and the city council inducted Renfroe into the Senior Citizens Hall of Fame in 1990.

The UIC College of Dentistry established the Dr. Earl W. Renfroe Chair in his honor to allow the institution to gain the services of a world-class clinical orthodontist in the spirit of Renfroe. Additionally, the college offered the Earl W. and Hilda F. Renfroe Endowed Memorial Scholarship Fund to aid needy minority students and to honor Renfroe as the first African American department head at the college.

Renfroe died on 11 November 2000, one month after his wife Hilda died on 13 September. He is buried in Arlington National Cemetery in Arlington, Virginia.

FURTHER READING

Sammons, Vivian Ovelton. *Blacks in Science and Medicine* (1990).

Obituaries: Bike, Bill. "Dr. Earl Renfroe, Pioneer in Orthodontics and Race Relations, Dies," 16 Nov. 2000, UIC College of Dentistry, Department of Orthodontics, http://www.uic.edu/depts/dort/Renfroe.html; *Jet*, 4 Dec. 2000.

PAMELA BLACKMON

Renfroe, Everett (26 July 1903–30 Apr. 1997), amateur radio operator, engineer, inventor, and educator, was born in Chicago to Eugene Renfroe and Bertha Wiley. He confronted racism in his pursuit of his hobby and passion—ham radio—and was instrumental in encouraging a community of "hams" known as OMIK who appreciated technology and science, while combating segregationist practices.

As a young boy, Renfroe was given ham radio equipment through family friends. His interest captured, he continued to learn about not only radio operation but also other technical fields, among them architecture and electrical engineering. Renfroe graduated from James H. Bowen Technical High School in 1921, where he was a Cadet Captain, receiving training in the Army ROTC in the summers of 1918 and 1919. In 1921 he attended Armour Institute of Technology (later the Illinois Institute of Technology). It was at this time he applied for his license as an amateur radio operator. Friend

and ham radio operator Sara E. Jackson recounted this story: Everett explained that it was difficult for people of color to obtain an amateur radio license during the time that he received his. Upon entering the Chicago downtown post office with six other applicants, Everett stated that the examiner asked, "What are you doing here?" Everett said, "Sir, I came to get a license. The first paragraph in the book says that regardless of age, race, creed or color, if you pass the examination you can get a license." The examiner never asked his name, but instructed Everett to sit down with the other applicants. When the exam was completed, the examiner told the applicants they weren't any good because only two of them had passed. When the names were called, the examiner was "dumb-founded" to find that Everett was one of the two (Jackson, 1994). While in college, Renfroe was involved in the college amateur station. However, illness forced him to withdraw from school and instead he began to seek employment. He soon had a family to support. His first marriage in the 1920's to Ethel Ferguson produced five children: Everett Jr., William, Barbara, Eugene, and Luther. The couple divorced in the 1930s. Renfroe married Elliott Suzanna Burns in 1937; they adopted a daughter, Suzanne.

Renfroe's jobs stayed within the technical realm in Chicago. He worked on electrical maintenance for railroads from 1924 to 1927. He joined the Paul E. Johnson Company (which manufactured electric-therapeutical equipment), working in the research and design department as an electrical engineer for a year; he became an electrical engineer for the Beck-lee Corporation in 1928. While there he created a high-frequency surgical knife that could cut without causing bleeding. He worked there until 1932. Following this, he worked in various Chicago industries as a radio service technician. He was a projectionist at the Owl Theatre on South State in Chicago, switching the silent machines to sound projectors and working at night as the projectionist from 1938 until 1952.

A man of many talents, Renfroe was also a constant student and teacher. He taught tactical operations and electrical communications as a member of the National Guard from 1936 to 1939. During World War II he sold his radio receiver to the government, as there was a shortage of professional receivers (as opposed to homemade). He became an instructor of Dunbar Vocational High School in 1943, teaching physics, electronics, and drafting, eventually becoming assistant principal and superintendent of shops. He completed his bachelor's degree in

Education in 1949 and received a master's degree in Education in 1951 (both from DePaul University). He retired from teaching at Dunbar in 1968.

Throughout his life, Renfroe recognized and shared the importance of amateur ham radio, encouraging people of all ages to become "hams." Lecturer and broadcast consultant Donna Halper notes that creating radio ham clubs was a way to further black education and was often neglected by the public school systems: "[B]lack engineers set up their own amateur radio clubs. By joining, you could learn how to build and repair the radio, how to send Morse code, and how to follow the rules of the Department of Commerce." Such clubs initiated young people into the world of electricity and magnetism, inspiring them to expand their educational pursuits beyond what might be offered at that time.

The ability to send messages through the airwaves created a new way to combat racism. Out of the hope that hams could be a driving force in social service, OMIK was formed by in 1952. Ham operators representing Ohio, Michigan, Indiana, and Kentucky joined together and shared similar experiences of segregation. When traveling, especially in the southern states, many black families could not simply stop at a hotel to rest, or stop at a gas station for directions. Retired professor of music and ham operator Romeo Phillips explained in his history of OMIK how OMIK members began collecting and sharing names and call numbers, creating a communications organization designed to combat racism. Hams could be in communication about families traveling in the South—listing eating and sleeping places that would be safe for blacks amidst segregation.

Membership in OMIK grew as other hams joined. OMIK continued to be a source of communication that created community as well as offering service. OMIK also encouraged young people to become involved in technology through scholarships, supported and checked on its members through a newsletter, and in general was the gathering place for a network of people whose passion was ham radio. The "Street Corner" on the airwaves was a place where information, gossip, concern, jokes, good news, and bad news were shared.

In 1994 Renfroe was honored as OMIK's "Ham of the Year." Unable to attend the OMIK conference due to poor health, he was able to speak over a conference phone. Two of his sons, William and Luther, both ham radio operators, were at the conference to accept the OMIK Image Award on behalf of their father. Renfroe heard the applause of many who had not ever met him, yet for years had heard his voice over the airwaves. He became a "silent key" in 1997 (a "silent key" is a radio ham who has died; the term is derived from the use of telegraph keys typing out Morse code, the earliest of airwave communications). Renfroe spanned the years of ham radio as an agent for communication, enjoyment, and social change, reflecting African American involvement in all three.

FURTHER READING

Barlett, Richard A. *World of Ham Radio, 1901–1959: A Social History* (2007).

Drew, Jeff. "OMIK Amateur Radio Association to Hold its Convention in Birmingham in 2009," in *BirmingHAM Amateur Radio Club Newsletter* (Sept. 2006).

Halper, Donna. *African Americans and Early Radio* (2002).

Jackson, Sara E. "A Man of All Times, Everett M. Renfroe," in *OMIK Communicator* (Fall 1994).

Jackson, Sara E. "A Man of All Times, Everett M. Renfroe, W9HG," unpublished manuscript.

LWF Communications, 18 May 2006, http://www.bjmjr.com/aaradio/part1.htm, used with the permission of Donna Halper.

Phillips, Romeo. "50 Years of OMIK," in *QST Amateur Radio*, 86.11 (Nov. 2002).

ROBIN JONES

Revels, Hiram Rhoades (27 Sept. 1827?–16 Jan. 1901), clergyman, educator, and first African American senator, was born in Fayetteville, North Carolina, the son of free parents of mixed blood. Little is known of his family or early years. At eight or nine he enrolled in a private school for black children, where he was "fully and successfully instructed by our able teacher in all branches of learning." About 1842 his family moved to Lincolnton, North Carolina, where Revels became a barber. Two years later he entered Beech Grove Seminary, a Quaker institution two miles south of Liberty, Indiana. In 1845 he enrolled at another seminary in Darke County, Ohio, and during this period may also have studied theology at Miami University in Oxford, Ohio.

Revels's preaching career with the African Methodist Episcopal (AME) Church began at this time. He was ordained as a minister in the Indiana Conference at some point between 1845 and 1847 and was confirmed as an elder by the same organization in 1849. His first pastorate may have been in Richmond, Indiana, and he is known to have served the Allen Chapel Church in Terre Haute during the 1840s. In the early 1850s he married Phoeba A. Bass, with whom he had six children.

Revels traveled extensively, becoming a noted preacher in the Indiana–Ohio–Illinois area before the end of the 1840s. An urge to carry the gospel to slaves led him to expand his circles, and in the 1850s he journeyed to lecture and teach in Missouri, Kansas, Kentucky, and Tennessee. His freedom of movement suggests that Revels was not a known abolitionist, but he later recounted that he "always assisted the fugitive to make his escape" when in a free state (Thompson, 31).

In late 1853 Revels moved his ministry to an AME church in St. Louis, but because of a dispute

Hiram Rhoades Revels in 1869. Rhoades was the first African American elected to the U.S. Senate. (Library of Congress/ Brady-Handy Photograph Collection.)

with the bishop during the following year, he left both the congregation and the AME denomination, accepting the pastorate of Madison Street Presbyterian Church in Baltimore, Maryland. He stayed in that position for two years before entering Knox College in Galesburg, Illinois. In 1857 he returned to Baltimore and to his former denomination, becoming the pastor of an AME church in the city. He also was named principal of a high school for blacks, beginning his career as an education administrator.

With the outbreak of the Civil War, Revels helped organize black work battalions for the Union army. In 1863 he moved back to St. Louis to teach at a high school for blacks and there continued his efforts to aid the North, participating in the organization of the first black regiment from Missouri. Again he did not stay long, moving to Mississippi in 1864 to work with the freedmen. Based primarily in Jackson, he was instrumental in the establishment of several schools and churches in the Jackson-Vicksburg area. Some sources claim that he was also a regimental chaplain and worked with the Vicksburg provost marshal's office.

In late 1865 Revels aligned himself with the AME Church North, the denomination with which he would be associated for the rest of his career. He held pastorates in Leavenworth, Kansas, Louisville, Kentucky, and New Orleans, Louisiana, before becoming the presiding elder at a church in Natchez, Mississippi, in June 1868. That summer Adelbert Ames, the military governor of Mississippi, appointed Revels to the city board of aldermen. Although little is known about his term of service, his primary focus was apparently on improving the city educational system. As his prominence in the community grew, Revels, who was one of the most highly educated African Americans in the state, was encouraged to seek higher office, and in late 1869 he agreed to run as a Republican for the Adams County seat in the state senate. With the military Reconstruction government assuring black voting privileges, Revels won easily, as three-fourths of the people in the county were African Americans. He was one of thirty-six blacks chosen for the legislature from across the state.

Revels was invited to offer the invocation at the opening of the legislative session. One participant later recalled that the prayer "made [him] a United States Senator, because he made a deep, profound and favorable impression upon everyone who was fortunate enough to be within the sound of his voice" (*Journal of Negro History* 16:107). Two unexpired Senate terms, dating from before the Civil War, did have to be filled, and the black legislators were insistent that at least one seat be given to an African American. Their preferred candidate, JAMES LYNCH, had been appointed secretary of state, so they turned to Revels. After three days and seven ballots, Revels was elected on 20 January to fill the seat vacated by Jefferson Davis in 1861.

The nation's first African American senator arrived in Washington ten days after his election. He could not present his credentials until Mississippi was formally readmitted to the Union, which finally took place on 23 February. Three days of contentious debate over whether to seat Revels followed, with the Senate voting 48 to 8 in favor of accepting his credentials on 25 February. Revels was then sworn in and seated.

Although his brief Senate term was relatively undistinguished, Revels's skill as an orator, honed through decades in the pulpit, earned favorable attention from the national press. He introduced three bills, but only one passed—a petition for the removal of civil and political disabilities from an ex-Confederate. He favored amnesty for white southerners "just as fast as they give evidence of having become loyal men and of being loyal," a stance that drew criticism from some in the black community. Revels served briefly on the District of Columbia Committee and nominated the first African American for enrollment at West Point (the candidate failed the entrance examination).

Revels returned to Mississippi upon the completion of his term in March 1871, and Governor James L. Alcorn asked him to oversee the establishment of a college for black males. The legislature suggested that the school be named Revels University, but the former senator declined the honor, recommending that the governor's name be used. In 1872 Alcorn University opened in Claiborne County, Mississippi, with Revels as the first president. His duties were interrupted briefly in 1873, when he was named secretary of state ad interim.

The new governor, Ames, who had given Revels his start in politics, pressured Revels into resigning the Alcorn presidency in July 1874, apparently because of Revels's political ties with the former governor Alcorn. A third of the student body and a number of faculty members left in protest against the action. Revels was reappointed as president two years later, when John M. Stone became governor. In the interim he served churches in Holly Springs and New Orleans and briefly edited the *Southwestern Christian Advocate*.

Health problems and Alcorn's financial woes led Revels to resign again in 1882. He moved back to Holly Springs, where he taught theology at Rust College for a few years and assisted the pastor of the local AME North church. He died while attending a religious conference in Aberdeen, Mississippi.

FURTHER READING

Revels's papers are at the Schomburg Center for Research in Black Culture of the New York Public Library and at Alcorn State University. Revels's unpublished autobiography is in the Carter G. Woodson Collection, Library of Congress.

Gravely, William B. "Hiram Revels Protests Racial Separation in the Methodist Episcopal Church (1876)," *Methodist History* 8 (1970): 13–20.

Lawson, Elizabeth. *The Gentleman from Mississippi, Our First Negro Senator* (1960).

Thompson, Julius E. *Hiram R. Revels, 1827–1901: A Biography* (1982).

Obituaries: *Natchez (Miss.) Daily Democrat*, 18 Jan. 1901; *Southwestern Christian Advocate*, 31 Jan. 1901.

This entry is taken from the *American National Biography* and is published here with the permission of the American Council of Learned Societies.

KENNETH H. WILLIAMS

Reverend Ike (1 June 1935–28 July 2009), religious leader, was born Frederick Joseph Eikerenkoetter II in Ridgeland, South Carolina, to Frederick Joseph Eikerenkoetter Sr., a Baptist minister and architect, and Rema Estelle Matthews, a teacher. As a boy, he was exposed to the fundamentalist theology of the Bible Way Church in Ridgeland, where his father was the pastor, and he became an assistant minister at the age of fourteen. After graduating from high school in 1952, Eikerenkoetter won a scholarship to the American Bible College in New York and earned a bachelor of theology degree in 1956. He then became a chaplain in the U.S. Air Force and started what might have become a traditional and uneventful ministerial career. However, after only two years, Eikerenkoetter left the security of the chaplaincy to embark on a new vocation as an evangelist.

Back in South Carolina, he veered from his Baptist roots and began to develop an eclectic ministry, akin to Pentecostalism, that relied heavily on faith healing, the excitement of revival meetings, and the appeal of a charismatic preacher. By 1962 the United Church of Jesus Christ, which he had founded a few years earlier, had only a few members and met in a converted storefront, yet even then he anticipated building a great church empire, and, for this reason, he established the United Christian Evangelist Association, which would become the organizational and business umbrella for his future endeavors. In 1964 he married Eula Mae Dent; together they had one son, Xavier. Ultimately, his wife would become the co-pastor of his ministries, and his son would be given the title bishop coadjutor. They moved to Boston in 1965, where he founded the Miracle Temple and acquired his first radio audience.

Until Eikerenkoetter's ascendance, the Reverend C. L. FRANKLIN, with his syndicated radio programs and recording contracts, was the most popular black preacher in America. Historically, the success of most black ministers relied on how well they delivered a standard Protestant message that emphasized faith in God and hard work and that generally deprecated the desire for material pleasures. Indeed, many ministers became quite wealthy by advocating this austere doctrine. Eikerenkoetter offered a radically different theology that contrasted sharply with the old-time religion in both form and substance.

Like FATHER DIVINE at the turn of the century, who was influenced by CHARLES FILLMORE and Robert Collier, the pioneers of New Thought philosophy, Eikerenkoetter was also drawn to ideas that originated with New Thought because they placed greater power and responsibility upon the individual to affect the course of his or her life in this world, rather than praying for a better life in the hereafter. Eikerenkoetter, however, never proclaimed himself to be God or a messiah, as Father Divine and CHARLES EMMANUEL "DADDY GRACE" had strongly intimated. It is likely that Eikerenkoetter was exposed to New Thought philosophy through white ministers, such as Norman Vincent Peale, and motivational speakers, such as Dale Carnegie, who had popularized a new gospel of positive thinking. Eikerenkoetter was the first to package this concept within an African American religious ethos and successfully market it to black consumers.

In 1966 two decisions contributed greatly to Eikerenkoetter's success: he established his flagship congregation on 125th Street in Harlem, New York, and he began to use the name Reverend Ike instead of the difficult-to-pronounce Dutch name Eikerenkoetter. Not even the flamboyant Harlem minister ADAM CLAYTON POWELL JR. was as flashy or as ostentatious as Reverend Ike, who flaunted his diamond rings, fur coats, and mink-upholstered Rolls-Royce. While the mainstream press ridiculed his extravagance and considered it proof that he was a charlatan, Reverend Ike argued to his critics and to the thousands who were drawn to him that his very wealth was proof that his program worked. In contrast to a long tradition of pie-in-the-sky preaching, Ike repeatedly said, "I want my pie now, with ice cream on top" (Morris, 180). He taught that "the LACK of money is the root of all evil" (Morris, 184) and to overcome the guilt that many religious people had about desiring money, he developed the mantra "I like money. I need money. I want money.... Money is not sinful in its right place. Money is good" (Morris, 176).

The response to this theology of prosperity was so overwhelming that in 1969 the congregation purchased the historic Palace Auditorium, which occupied a full block on Broadway and 175th Street. Five thousand people attended services there each week, and the building also contained his school, the United Church and Science of Living Institute. Reverend Ike claimed that millions of people subscribed to his magazine, *Action!*, or listened to him on more than eighty-nine radio stations. In 1971 he became the first black leader since Marcus Garvey to pack Madison Square Garden, and in 1973 he became the first black preacher to acquire a television program, *Joy of Living*. Through all of these outlets he sold literature extolling his "Blessing Plan," as well as products promising to heal or enrich the purchaser—if the person had faith and contributed to his church.

At the height of his popularity in the late 1970s, Ike was prominent among a new generation of tel evangelists. He received offers to speak to diverse audiences and once even lectured on psychiatry at Harvard Medical School. In an effort to deflect criticism that his ministry was completely self-serving, his church sponsored programs to help drug addicts, and he purchased a lifetime membership with the NAACP. During the 1980s, however, his star began to fade, and the former religious icon quickly became a parody of black preachers who prey on the poor and desperate. His public image also suffered from a number of unsuccessful criminal investigations by the Internal Revenue Service and the U.S. Postal Service and by a sexual harassment suit brought by a male employee against him in 1995. Reverend Ike's ministry survived these accusations, but it never regained its former stature.

Lingering questions about Reverend Ike's motives and character obscured the theological innovations that he pioneered, and excessive attention to Ike's showmanship prevented many observers from recognizing that at its core his message appealed to African Americans who legitimately wanted a greater share of American prosperity. He died in Los Angeles at the age of 74.

FURTHER READING

The records and papers of Reverend Ike are not publicly available. The most scholarly study of his ministry is an unpublished dissertation by Martin V. Gallatin, "Rev. Ike's Ministry: A Sociological Investigation of Religious Innovation," New York University, 1979.

Baer, Hans A., and Merrill Singer. *African American Religion* (2002).

Morris, James. *The Preachers* (1973).

Riley, Clayton. "The Golden Gospel of Reverend Ike," *New York Magazine* (19 Mar. 1975).

Sanders, Charles L. "The Gospel According to Rev. Ike," *Ebony* (Dec. 1976).

SHOLOMO B. LEVY

Reverend Run (14 Nov. 1964–), was born Joseph Lloyd Simmons in Jamaica, Queens, New York, the youngest of three sons of Daniel Simmons, a teacher and public school administrator, and Evelyn Simmons, an artist. Simmons would become famous as Run of the legendary hip-hop group Run-D.M.C. Joseph Simmons grew up in the Hollis section of Queens, New York. He enjoyed listening to music on the radio at an early age, and his father supplied him with a drum set to support his interest. As a teenager, Simmons learned to be a DJ from his childhood friend Darryl "D.M.C." McDaniels. When his older brother, Russell, became the promoter and manager of Curtis Walker (also known as Kurtis Blow), Simmons began to experiment with rhymes using Walker's lyrical style as an example; he eventually had the opportunity to DJ for Kurtis Blow in 1978. Russell's friends named Joe "DJ Run" and later "DJ Run—the son of Kurtis Blow." After a successful first performance, Simmons continued to spin for Walker and to work with McDaniels, who was emceeing under the stage name of Grandmaster Get High.

McDaniels and Simmons formed a duo, which Russell named Runde-MC. After signing to Profile Records in 1981, the group became Run-D.M.C. and Simmons urged another childhood friend, Jason "Jam Master Jay" Mizzell, to join. Mizzell initially declined, but ultimately joined in 1982. Run-D.M.C.'s first single, "It's Like That/Sucka MCs" (1983), and their eponymous first album (1984) were characterized by the hard beats and classic

Reverend Run, former lead vocalist of Run-DMC, arrives at the Annual Kids' Choice Awards in Los Angeles, on 31 March 2007. (AP Images.)

rock and heavy metal samples that would establish the group as the first rap crossover to the rock and pop market. In 1984 Simmons married Valerie Vaughn, with whom he had two daughters, Vanessa and Angela, and a son, Joseph Jr.

It was not until the release of their 1986 platinum-selling third album, *Raising Hell* (featuring a hit remixed version of Aerosmith's "Walk This Way"), that the group achieved its greatest commercial success. They became the first rap act to appear on MTV and, for a time, were the biggest-selling rap act in the genre's short history. But by 1988, when the group's album *Tougher Than Leather* was released, their popularity was already on the wane, and their subsequent albums did not have the same impact or success. In 1991 Simmons and his wife Valerie divorced, shortly after a Cleveland woman brought rape charges against Simmons. Although the charges were dismissed, the experience led Simmons to reevaluate his life, and he became heavily involved with Zoë Ministries, a nondenominational church in which he became an ordained minister in 1994, changing his stage name

to "Rev Run." While awaiting a court date on the rape charge, Simmons reconnected with Justine Jones, a high school friend; they were married in 1992. The couple had two sons, Daniel and Russell II. (A daughter, Victoria Anne, died shortly after birth in 2006.)

Simmons continued to record and tour with Run-D.M.C. after his ordination, and he published his autobiography, *It's Like That … A Spiritual Memoir* (2000). However, in 2002 Jam Master Jay was murdered, and the remaining members announced the group's retirement. After a brief hiatus, Simmons released his first solo album, *Distortion*, in 2005, which was a critical but not a commercial success. He and his family also became the stars of an MTV reality show, *Run's House*, nominated in 2007 for an NAACP Image award for outstanding reality series.

FURTHER READING

Simmons, Joseph. *It's Like That … A Spiritual Memoir* (2000).

Ro, Ronin. *Raising Hell: the Reign, Ruin, and Redemption of Run-D.M.C. and Jam Master Jay* (2006).

REGINA N. BARNETT

Reynolds, Grant (29 July 1908–30 Aug. 2004), civil rights activist, army chaplain, and lawyer, was born in Delray Beach, Florida, the son of Frank Reynolds and Emma. He attended Hampton Institute (later Hampton University), an institution of higher education for blacks in Virginia.

When he graduated from Hampton in 1928, Reynolds intended to study medicine; however, because he lacked financial resources, he had to give up this dream. With the financial support of a white patron, Reynolds entered Michigan State University, but he was later expelled due to racial flare-ups. He continued his education at the Eden Theological Seminary in St. Louis, Missouri, which wanted to integrate its facility and granted Reynolds a scholarship. Graduating in 1937, he became the minister of the Mount Zion Congregational Temple in Cleveland, Ohio. Little is known about his personal life.

With the onset of World War II, Reynolds joined the army in 1941 as a chaplain with the rank of first lieutenant; he was promoted to captain in 1942. He considered the war an opportunity to improve the position of African Americans. As a black chaplain in the racist environment of the armed forces, he became an influential contact person and adviser for black soldiers. He also, however, faced discrimination and humiliation himself on a daily basis. Even as an officer he was not allowed to live, sit, or eat with the white officers.

Reynolds openly demanded equal treatment of black and white personnel and stood up for their needs. Through his outspoken commitment to the improvement of the situation of black soldiers, he became highly respected and revered among black soldiers. But because of his role as a spokesperson for racial equality, the army considered him a troublemaker. In a psychiatric evaluation ordered by the army, Reynolds was described as unwilling to submit to the rules and as suffering from paranoia. More than once he was transferred from one base to another for his relentless activism, which also caused lifelong animosity with TRUMAN K. GIBSON, the black civilian aide to the secretary of defense who was to monitor discrimination in the military. Reynolds later called Gibson a "Negro Judas Iscariot" (*Afro-American*, 10 Apr. 1948) who did not attempt to help black soldiers but only pleased whites for his own personal gain. The army subjected Reynolds to close medical scrutiny in an attempt to find a reason to discharge him. In January 1944 the army gave him an early but honorable discharge under odd circumstances. That same year Reynolds left the NAACP, expressing his disappointment in the organization's lack of progress in improving black soldiers' position and ending segregation in the military.

With the end of the war in 1945, Reynolds settled in New York City, where he entered Columbia Law School. That year Governor Thomas E. Dewey appointed Reynolds as the commissioner of corrections for New York State. In 1946 Reynolds ran as a Republican against the Democratic congressman ADAM CLAYTON POWELL JR in Harlem's Twenty-second District, but lost in a fiercely fought campaign.

Reynolds never abandoned his fight against segregation and discrimination in the military, which climaxed in the general discussion of selective service and universal military training (UMT). Reynolds focused his struggle on assuring that a bill for a draft or UMT would include an amendment assuring racial equality and the end of segregation. He joined the influential labor leader A. PHILIP RANDOLPH in founding the Committee against Jim Crow in Military Service and Training in October 1947. Due to his standing, Randolph garnered more attention from the public, but Reynolds's war experience made him a more compelling spokesperson

for the grievances of black soldiers and veterans. Randolph and Reynolds, who was the committee's chairman, initially used traditional routes of activism through petitions to and requests for meetings with the president and congress.

Disillusioned by the lack of attention their efforts achieved, Randolph and Reynolds took a more radical path. In a meeting with the president and in front of the Senate Armed Services Committee in March 1948, they urged foremost blacks but also whites to resist the draft in order to pressure the government into ending segregation in the armed forces. They initiated a nonviolent civil disobedience campaign, thereby violating the selective service act and risking imprisonment. The draft resisters were urged to nonviolently sustain and comply with any action taken against them. Most prominently led by Randolph, they nonviolently picketed the GOP and Democratic National Conventions in Philadelphia, and held public street conventions that called young men to resist the draft—representing a break from the predominant approach to activism. Their new course of action produced a debate among civil rights activists, in the black community, and in the press over military service and the appropriate forms of civil rights activism. Reynolds also faced some personal repercussions for his statement supporting draft resistance in front of the Senate Committee. The Omega Psi Phi fraternity he had been a very active part of since his time at Michigan State disassociated itself from him and his cause. The increased publicity created by Randolph and Reynolds's committee helped bring about President Harry Truman's Executive Order 9981 on 26 July 1948, calling for equal treatment and opportunity for all persons regardless of race, color, creed or national origin, and the creation of a committee to monitor these developments. These efforts eventually brought about the gradual integration of the American armed services that was proved further necessary by the Korean War.

In August 1948 Randolph and Reynolds called off the civil disobedience campaign, but they continued to publicly express their discontent with the progress of integration, especially in the army. They organized hearings across the United States in which they asked former soldiers, armed forces officials, and politicians about their experiences with and attitudes toward military segregation and integration. At these hearings Reynolds not only acted as an organizer but also appeared as a witness to tell of his and other soldiers' humiliating treatment in the armed forces. Reynolds was invited to appear before various committees, including the President's Committee on Equality of Treatment and Opportunity in the Armed Services. In the 1950s he testified before the House Armed Service Committee when it discussed the UMT bill, and he again demanded an integration amendment.

When the committee hearings were over, Reynolds continued to work as a lawyer and civil rights activist in White Plains, New York. Aside from a short falling out in 1952 over the party's civil rights policies, he remained a lifelong member of the Republican Party. In the 1960s he worked to ensure that the Republicans took a strong stand in support of civil rights measures. In 1961 he was appointed counsel to the chairman of the Republican National Committee. While in this position he attacked the civil rights record of the Democratic Party, but he also protested Barry Goldwater's nomination as the Republican presidential candidate and the influx of more conservative forces into the Republican Party. He was active in the fight for civil rights and equality as the president of the White Plains–Greenburg NAACP for ten years. He died at age ninety-six of a heart attack in Fort Lauderdale, Florida.

FURTHER READING

The NAACP records and the A. Philip Randolph Papers are important sources of information on Reynolds's activism, and can be found at the Library of Congress.

Klinkner, Philip A. "Fighting the Jim Crow Army," in *American Legacy: Celebrating African-American History and Culture* 98, no. 4 (Fall 1998).

Klinkner, Philip A., with Roger M. Smith. *The Unsteady March: The Rise and Decline of Racial Equality in America* (1999).

Pfeffer, Paula F. *A. Philip Randolph, Pioneer of the Civil Rights Movement* (1990).

CHRISTINE KNAUER

Reynolds, Melvin Jay (8 Jan. 1952–   ), politician, was born in Mound Bayou, Bolivar County, Mississippi, to the Reverend J. J. and Essie Mae (Prather) Reynolds. He had a twin brother, Marvin Jerry Reynolds. In 1960, the family moved to Chicago's West Side. When Reynolds was ten, his father died. Mel Reynolds attended John Marshall High School. In 1972, he earned an A.A. from Mayfair College (now Truman College). Although he was awarded a Ford Scholarship to Yale, he left after a short time. He achieved his B.S. in philosophy from the University of Illinois at Champaign–Urbana in 1974. In 1975, he became one of the first black

Illinois residents to win a Rhodes scholarship. He graduated from Oxford University in 1979 with an L.L.B. (law) degree. At Harvard's Kennedy School of Government, he earned his M.P.A. (master of public administration) in 1986. There he also met Marisol Concepcion, whom he wed in 1990. They had three children: Corean, Marisol Elizabeth, and Mel Jr.

Reynolds became an assistant professor of political science at Chicago's Roosevelt University, hosted a radio talk show, and became involved with community issues like drug abuse, hunger, and education. He was already gaining firsthand experience of Democratic electoral politics. During the 1980, 1984, and 1988 elections, he worked on the presidential campaigns of Senator Ted Kennedy, Reverend Jesse Jackson, and Governor Michael Dukakis. In 1987, Reynolds participated in Harold Washington's successful bid for mayor.

Reynolds set his sights on the Illinois Second Congressional District seat, occupied since 1980 by Gus Savage and consisting of Chicago's heavily Democratic, largely black far southeast side and southern suburbs. Reynolds ran unsuccessfully against Savage in 1988, coming in third and garnering only 14 percent of the Democratic primary vote. In 1990, Reynolds achieved 43 percent of the vote. Voters in the district were by then becoming increasingly discontent with the volatile Savage, who made statements offensive to whites, Jews, and gay people and was accused of attempted sexual assault on a Peace Corps worker. More and more, Reynolds appeared a bright and promising alternative.

In the 1992 primary, Reynolds finally defeated Savage with 67 percent of the vote to Savage's 37 percent. In the general election, split among him, a Republican, and an Independent, Reynolds won 78 percent of the vote. He was sworn into the One Hundred Third Congress on 3 January 1993. He also joined the Congressional Black Caucus. With the help of veteran Chicago Congressman Daniel Rostenkowski, Reynolds was appointed to the Ways and Means Committee, a rare honor for someone in his freshman term. After his election to the One Hundred Fourth Congress, Reynolds lost this appointment, because the Republicans had become the majority and were removing seats from the committee. He was appointed to another committee, Economic and Educational Opportunities. While in Congress, Reynolds worked on the passage of the North American Free Trade Agreement, the implementation of the earned income tax credit, and gun control measures. He also held a number of job fairs at home for his constituents.

Congressman Mel Reynolds, left, and his attorney Sam Adam, right, are surrounded as they walk to court in Chicago on Thursday, 17 August 1995, for the continuation of Reynold's sexual misconduct trial. (AP Images.)

However, scandal was already bringing a quick end to Reynolds's promising Congressional career. During his first term, allegations surfaced early on that he owed thousands of dollars in unpaid student loans and campaign debts. Reynolds explained that he had chosen to spend money on his campaigns rather than the student loans because he put a higher priority on public service. His reputation deteriorated even further in August 1994 when he was indicted for having sex with a sixteen-year-old female campaign volunteer. Reynolds protested that the charges were unfounded and motivated by racism. Enough voters believed him for Reynolds to win re-election, but by a smaller margin of the vote, 56 percent. Reynolds then received a twelve-count indictment for obstruction of justice, sexual assault, and solicitation of child pornography. Pressure mounted from women's rights advocates and others for his resignation, which he finally handed in on 1 October 1995. Reynolds was sentenced to five years at East Moline Correctional Center.

Reynolds served two and a half years of this sentence. In April 1997, he was given a sixteen-count conviction for bank fraud and telling lies to the Federal Election Commission. His wife, Marisol, received a nine count conviction. These charges were unrelated to those of the sex scandal. The couple was accused of usurping campaign contributions for personal use and then covering it up. Marisol received probation and Mel was sentenced to an additional seventy-eight months in prison. However, in 2001, as President Clinton was leaving the White House, he commuted Reynolds's sentence. Prominent black Chicago ministers Jesse Jackson Sr. and James Meeks lobbied for this presidential pardon.

After his release, Reynolds was hired as director of the community development center associated with Meeks's church, Salem Baptist, as well as an advisor to Jackson on prison issues. Clinton's judgment was publicly questioned, as was Jackson's and Meeks's, especially because the President and Jackson had recently been embroiled in sex scandals of their own.

Reynolds's relationship with his wife continued to draw public criticism. While he was in prison,

Marisol moved to Boston with their children, filed for divorce, and reportedly dated other men. Marisol showed photos of her bruised face as evidence that Reynolds abused her physically, as well as mentally. In August 2002, Reynolds announced his intent to sue a man Marisol had dated for emotional damages. By this time, Marisol had returned to Chicago with the children. They were living in a Salem Baptist-provided apartment with him. On 14 October 2002, the divorce case and order of protection Marisol had filed against her husband were revoked and the couple reunited.

Reynolds attempted unsuccessfully to regain the Second District seat in 2004, but received only 6 percent of the primary vote. JESSE JACKSON JR. easily defeated him. When he started out in office, a substantial number of Reynolds's constituents found it credible when he stated that racists sought the downfall of an educated, accomplished black man who achieved power. Yet his multiple convictions and reported mistreatment of his wife turned the tide of public opinion against him.

FURTHER READING

Hernández Gómez, Carlos. "Interview with Mel Reynolds," *Chicago Reporter*.

Mel Reynolds, Biographical Directory of the United States Congress, http://bioguide.congress.gov, n.d., accessed May 7, 2009.

Mel Reynolds, Black Americans in Congress, http://baic.house.gov, n.d., accessed May 7, 2009.

Smith, Eric A. "Melvin Jay 'Mel' Reynolds," in *The Black Past Remembered*, http://www.blackpast.org, accessed May 7, 2009.

"Timeline of the Mel Reynolds Case," *Chicago Sun-Times*, January 21, 2001.

MARY KRANE DERR

Rhinelander, Alice Jones (1899–1989), cause célèbre, was born Alice Beatrice Jones, the daughter of a white mother and supposedly "black" father, both of whom had emigrated from England to the United States in 1891. While the race of her mother Elizabeth Jones was familiar and recognizable enough for Americans to classify as white, the racial background of George Jones, her father, was not as clearly determined. While general references considered him to be British of West Indian descent, he was distinctly not African American according to an array of witnesses and census documentation in the United States.

Various newspapers of the period described Alice Jones as "dusky," "a tropical beauty," or of a "Spanish complexion" (Lewis and Ardizzone, 63–66, 163). Not considering herself black in the American rhetorical denotation of race, Alice Jones Rhinelander affirmed during the annulment trial of the interracial marriage to Leonard Rhinelander (1903–1936) that she "had some colored blood" (Lewis and Ardizzone, 63–64).

Jones's parents had been servants in England. George Jones was a working-class immigrant who had sought and captured the American dream. He had managed to accumulate real estate in the form of several rental properties in the suburbs of New York City. After her parents died (Elizabeth Jones died in 1938 and George Jones died in 1933), Alice Jones inherited those properties, which provided her with a lifetime income.

In 1924 Jones, a working-class woman with an eighth-grade education, married Leonard "Kip" Rhinelander, the son and heir of a white, wealthy New York real estate family. Alice and Leonard first met in 1921, when Grace Jones, Alice's older sister, introduced Leonard to Alice. Grace and Leonard had met when Leonard and an older male acquaintance were driving through the suburbs of New York City, in Westchester County, where the Jones girls lived. After several social meetings, there was a mutual attraction as well as affection, and the couple eventually fell in love and decided to marry.

Interracial marriage was legal in New York City, but the Rhinelander-Jones marriage created sensational fodder for national newspapers in the mid-1920s, when the New York City press declared that Alice Rhinelander was a "Negro" domestic who had married across racial and class lines. Because of Leonard Rhinelander's position of wealth and affluence, reporters wanted to know about the new Mrs. Leonard Rhinelander and her social background when it became known that the son of Philip Rhinelander, the real estate tycoon, had married. Thus after only a few weeks of the marriage, newspaper reporters discovered that Leonard Rhinelander had married a woman who was not white.

Coerced by his father to terminate the marriage, Leonard Rhinelander claimed that he did not know that Alice Jones was black until after the marriage. The Rhinelander case became a national obsession in the United States during the mid-1920s, when Leonard Rhinelander sued for an annulment after being married for a month, claiming that Alice Jones had knowingly committed deceit and fraud through the misrepresentation of her racial background.

During the trial proceedings, Alice Rhinelander was forced to disrobe to the waist in the presence of the all-male, all-white jury behind closed doors in order to show evidence of her "true race." The scene was humiliating for her and fueled more publicity for the already scandalized trial. After Alice's humiliation in front of the jury, the public began to sympathize with her despite deep-rooted objections toward interracial marriage. The national press afforded the trial daily gavel-to-gavel coverage steeped in ridicule, criticism, humor, and pseudoscientific analyses on behalf of the defense or prosecution, depending on the viewpoint of the particular tabloid. Leonard's father Philip Rhinelander was absent throughout the trail, but the Jones family all attended the court sessions in support of Alice. Throughout the trial the well-dressed Alice Rhinelander's comportment was a combination of sadness, stress, and dignity.

The annulment trial ended in 1925 with the jury returning a verdict that denied the annulment of the Rhinelander-Jones marriage. The jury based the verdict on evidence that Leonard Rhinelander knew that Alice Jones was black because he had visited her family home in the suburbs of New York City many times and had seen her mixed-race sisters and father and a brother-in-law who was obviously African American. Jones had not concealed her racial identity from Leonard Rhinelander and thus had not committed fraud. Moreover Leonard Rhinelander admitted that he had been sexually intimate with Jones and therefore had seen her in the nude before the marriage.

In 1929 Leonard Rhinelander filed for a divorce in the state of Nevada. The state of New York, however, did not recognize the Nevada divorce and considered the Rhinelander-Jones union still legally valid. The Rhinelander family negotiated a settlement with Alice Rhinelander, and in 1930 Alice agreed to accept a one-time payment of $32,500 and a lifetime monetary payment of $3,600 per annum. Her husband's estate continued to pay the monetary settlement after Leonard's early death at the age of thirty-four in 1936.

As a condition of the monetary settlement, Alice Rhinelander agreed never to use the Rhinelander name or to write about or publicize her marriage and relationship with Leonard Rhinelander; she also agreed to forfeit any future marital claims on the Rhinelander estate. Living in relative obscurity, Alice Rhinelander honored the agreement until her death in 1989. Either because of her burial instructions or because of someone's memory of her remarkable biographical history, the name "Alice J. Rhinelander" is inscribed on the gravestone, allowing Alice Jones Rhinelander to distinguish her final resting place and enable the living to recognize that her ultimate identity would be as the lawful wife of Leonard Rhinelander. Regardless of his subsequent public temperament and family pressure to deny her, Leonard Rhinelander had loved and married Alice Jones Rhinelander.

The majority of Americans during this time period did not condone interracial marriage. The Rhinelander case, however, did not capture the public's attention because it involved interracial marriage, love, class prejudice, and premarital sex within the lingering shadows of Victorian morality and principles. More significantly, because of the unstable yet perpetual social construction of race in the United States, the case evoked the nuanced difficulty of assigning individuals to "definitive" appellations of race across the demarcations of gender, class, and American perceptions of universal racial phenotypes.

Despite the racial ambiguity regarding Alice Rhinelander, her lawyers argued their defense on the basis of class exploitation with the intersection of race. The press ultimately portrayed how the wealthy and less-than-honorable Leonard Rhinelander took advantage of Alice Rhinelander, a poor, working-class woman. On the other hand, Leonard Rhinelander, in the opinion of southern editorials, was an embarrassment because he had not upheld the power and racial tradition of white masculinity in that he honored Alice Jones, a "Negress," with the respectability of marriage. In the words of W. E. B. DuBois, "If Rhinelander had used this girl as concubine or prostitute, white America would have raised no word of protest.... It is when he legally and decently marries the girl that all Hell breaks loose and literally tears the pair a part" (DuBois, 112).

As a first generation American—an American-born child of immigrant parents—the biracial Alice Rhinelander did not identify herself as an African American and appears to have known that it was not to her advantage to do so. Yet American society racially defined her as an "American Negro" because of the "one-drop" rule—the rule being that she had at least one parent who was black and therefore she was black. Nevertheless, many African Americans hailed the outcome of the trial as a victory for Alice and for African American women in general. Finally, overall national female sentiments overlooked the issues of interracial marriage. Working-class black and white women identified with Rhinelander's legal victory because they recognized that marriage laws often disenfranchised poor women.

Far from being the racialized and mythologized "tragic mulatta" without agency, Alice Rhinelander used the same legal system that allowed the contestation of the marriage to fight against subsequent divorce appeals and annuity suits by Leonard Rhinelander and later by the Rhinelander estate. In each instance, she won.

FURTHER READING

DuBois, W. E. B. "Rhinelander," *Crisis* (Jan. 1926).

Ehlers, Nadine. "Hidden in Plain Sight: Defying Juridical Racialization in *Rhinelander v. Rhinelander*," *Communication and Critical/Cultural Studies* 1, no. 4 (2004): 313–334.

Johnson, R. Kevin, and Kristina L. Burrows. "Struck by Lightening? Interracial Intimacy and Racial Justice," *Human Rights Quarterly* 25, no. 2 (2003): 528–562.

Lewis, Earl, and Heidi Ardizzone. *Love on Trial: An American Scandal in Black and White* (2001).

ANGELITA D. REYES

Rhodes, Eugene Washington (29 Oct. 1895–24 June 1970), editor, publisher, and lawyer, was born in Camden, South Carolina, the son of Charles Rhodes and Laura Boyd, former slaves. Rhodes moved from South Carolina to Pennsylvania, where he attended college at Lincoln University. He received a B.A. from Lincoln in 1921. Rhodes pursued legal studies at Temple University and received his LLB in 1924. In 1926 Rhodes was admitted to the Philadelphia bar.

In 1922 Rhodes became the editor of the *Philadelphia Tribune*. He served in that capacity until 1941, at which time he became the paper's publisher, a position he held until the end of his life. Also in 1922 Rhodes married Bertha Perry of Philadelphia, daughter of the paper's founder and publisher, Christopher J. Perry. A member of the small black upper class often labeled the "Old Philadelphians," Perry had started the *Tribune* in 1884 as a means of showing the white Philadelphia community how respectable the black Philadelphia community really was. With Bertha at his side as the paper's secretary-treasurer, Rhodes ran a successful weekly paper throughout the 1920s and the Depression. The *Tribune* survived its competitors and even at the beginning of the twenty-first century remained the largest black weekly in the Philadelphia region.

Taking the reins of editorship of the *Tribune* provided Rhodes with an entrée into the rather exclusive circles of the old black middle class. Ambitious, a firm believer in the Protestant work ethic (born a Baptist, he entered the Episcopal Church after his marriage), and a staunch Republican, Rhodes used the *Tribune* as a forum for his political views and as a means of inculcating middle-class manners and values to the black masses. This could be seen in his weekly "character portraits," which extolled the virtues of successful and striving black Philadelphians or caustically derided the excesses of others. Even the comic strips exuded story lines that lauded uplift and good moral behavior.

Rhodes was critical of the New Deal programs that President Franklin Delano Roosevelt put forward. He mockingly called the National Reform Act the "Negro Removal Act" because it did not provide jobs for African Americans and in many cases displaced them from what few jobs they did have. Rhodes used the *Tribune* to push the principles of hard work and threw himself into activities that encouraged African Americans to build businesses and hire other blacks. He was a founder and member of the Philadelphia Tribune Charities and was chair of the board of directors of the Downingtown Industrial School.

Rhodes kept active as a lawyer as well, serving as an assistant district attorney for the Eastern District of Pennsylvania from 1926 to 1933. In 1938 Rhodes was elected a representative in the state General Assembly for the Sixth Legislative District of Philadelphia. It was during his term that Pennsylvania passed an expansive civil rights law. From 1939 to 1944 Rhodes assumed the chair of the state Commission to Study Conditions of Urban Colored Population. Rhodes remained active in legal circles in Philadelphia for the rest of his life and earned many commendations for his services. He received honorary degrees in law from Morris College in 1948 and from his alma mater, Lincoln University, in 1952.

But the *Tribune* was Rhodes's greatest love and clearly his most distinguished achievement. Despite stepping down at times to attend to state service, he always returned to the helm as publisher. Under his stewardship the *Tribune* maintained high journalistic standards, a sound fiscal base, and the ability to inculcate race pride and middle-class values in Philadelphia's black community. The paper stands in the company of the other black papers in the nation such as the *Chicago Defender*, *Pittsburgh Courier*, *Norfolk Journal and Guide*, *Amsterdam News*, and *California Eagle*.

FURTHER READING

Banner-Haley, Charles Pete. "The *Philadelphia Tribune* and the Persistence of Black Republicanism in the Great Depression," *Pennsylvania History* (Spring 1998).

Banner-Haley, Charles Pete. *To Do Good and to Do Well: Middle Class Blacks and the Depression, Philadelphia, 1929–1941* (1992).

CHARLES PETE BANNER-HALEY

Rhodes, Ted (9 Nov. 1913–4 July 1969), professional golfer, was born in Nashville, Tennessee, the youngest of nine children. Rhodes rarely spoke of his parents, though he did mention in an interview that his father died when he was four years old. By the time he reached the fifth grade, Ted had dropped out of school to work as a caddy on area golf courses, including being a club favorite at the Belle Meade Country Club. When he was not caddying, Rhodes took other odd jobs at any golf course he could, or played golf. Nashville had no courses for blacks to use, so Rhodes and other caddies made their own courses in neighborhood parks. Rhodes also sneaked onto courses where he caddied or played on "caddy days," and became fairly well known as a golfer and hustler.

Rhodes's golf swing—the result of endless practice—soon came to be recognized as one of the best in the game. He played his first tournament in 1943, the JOE LOUIS Open, in Dayton, Ohio, where Rhodes met Louis and the two became good friends. Louis hired Rhodes to become his personal golf instructor. Rhodes stayed with Louis from 1943 to 1951, interrupted by Rhodes's three-year (1943–1946) enlistment in the navy.

His relationship with Louis allowed Rhodes to become a professional golfer and make a living at it, a reality few black golfers could expect at that time. Louis bought Rhodes his first set of clubs (before then Rhodes had always rented or borrowed them), paid for Rhodes to study with Professional Golf Association (PGA) golfer Ray Mangrum, and financed Rhodes's professional career by sponsoring him in United Golf Association (UGA) tournaments, the tour for black golfers. In his first year as a professional, 1946, Rhodes had immediate success. He won six consecutive tournaments, was the only black golfer at the Tam O'Shanter tournament in Chicago, and was the runner-up at the National Negro Championship. In 1947 the *Los Angeles Times* crowned him "America's Greatest Negro Golfer." In 1948 Rhodes played in the three PGA tournaments open to blacks—the Tam O'Shanter, the U.S. Open,

where he placed fifty-first, and the Los Angeles Open, where he placed twenty-first.

At 5 feet 11 inches and 150 pounds, Rhodes was not physically imposing, but he had a presence that people noticed. He cared about his clothes and appearance, to the point of being flashy at times. He even changed clothes once in the middle of a round of golf. Other golfers took to calling him "Rags," a nickname that likely grew out of his clothing competition with Jimmy Demaret, a white golfer known as a sharp dresser. The nickname may also have been a holdover from his caddy days when he often showed up to caddy in tattered clothes. Rhodes also possessed a calm, quiet demeanor and, as he put it, he was not interested in fighting a race war but only wanted to play golf. Some of his contemporaries accused him of Jim Crow accommodation, but Rhodes believed that fighting back only made matters worse. He hoped a low-key approach would help white golfers accept him.

Rhodes broke from his noncombative stance in 1948 when he, along with Bill Spiller and Madison Gunter, sued the PGA over its "Caucasians-only" clause in its bylaws. Rhodes' finish at the 1947 Los Angeles Open qualified him for the Richmond Open, but PGA officials told him that he could not play there. The case eventually settled out of court with the PGA promising not to discriminate, but maintaining the exclusionary clause in its bylaws. Rhodes continued to play UGA events and PGA events when he could. He had his best year in 1949, winning the Ray Robinson Open and the National Negro Championship, as well as qualifying again for the U.S. Open. In 1950 he married Claudia Oliver, a nightclub dancer from St. Louis, Missouri, and had one child. Rhodes had another child from a relationship with Nashville, Tennessee, resident Ollie Crenshaw, but the two never married.

By 1952 the PGA reached an agreement with black golfers. A committee was formed, on which Rhodes served, that maintained a list of approved black golfers that could play at PGA events, provided they were invited by sponsors and the host club. This agreement was the long-awaited promise from the PGA, but it fell far short of the hopes of black golfers. Rhodes played the first two tournaments under the arrangement, the Phoenix and Tucson Opens, before the tour moved to Texas and the invitations ceased. The deal with the PGA proved to be a poor compromise, and indeed few invitations were forthcoming, particularly as the tour moved through Southern states.

Rhodes continued on the UGA tour and played the few PGA events he could. In 1954 he signed a three-year sponsorship deal with Burke Golf Manufacturing Co. A kidney ailment slowed him in the late 1950s, but not before he won his fourth National Negro Championship in 1957. Rhodes went to Havana in 1960 as part of a contingent of golfers invited to play there, and then retired as a professional golfer. Over his career, Rhodes reportedly won over 150 tournaments (records from the UGA are incomplete), mostly UGA, including the National Negro Championship four times (1949–1951, 1957). He competed in sixty-nine PGA events with nine top-20 finishes. His best finish was fourth at the 1953 Canadian Open.

By the time the PGA dropped the "Caucasians-only" clause in 1961, Rhodes was forty-eight and too ill to play golf competitively. He stayed close to the game and made a living as an instructor. Among his clients were ROBERT LEE ELDER, CHARLIE SIFFORD, and ALTHEA GIBSON, whom he helped make the switch from tennis to golf. Rhodes died of a heart attack the day after playing nine holes at his home course, Cumberland, in Nashville.

Most black golfers, including his students Elder and Sifford as well as Tiger Woods, have called Rhodes the most respected ambassador for African Americans in golf, both for his skill on the golf course and his demeanor off the course. In 1971 Nashville renamed the Cumberland golf course after Rhodes, and in 1993 expanded the course to eighteen holes. In 1998 Rhodes was inducted into the Tennessee Golf Hall of Fame. Golfers, black and white, have long recognized that if Rhodes had been given the opportunity to compete, he had the potential to be one of the best golfers ever.

FURTHER READING

Allen, Robert Joseph. "The Odyssey of Ted Rhodes," *Golf Magazine* (Feb. 1961).

Lipsey, Rick. "Ted Rhodes," *Golf Magazine* (Nov. 1992).

McDaniel, Pete. *Uneven Lies: The Heroic Story of African Americans in Golf* (2000).

Sinnette, Calvin H. *Forbidden Fairways: African Americans and the Game of Golf* (1968).

MICHAEL C. MILLER

Ribbs, Willy T. (3 Jan. 1955–), professional race car driver, was born in San Jose, California, to William "Bunny" Theodore Ribbs, a plumber, and Geraldine Henderson, a homemaker. Bunny was also a racer, though on the amateur track. As a child Ribbs worked on his grandfather's ranch, and was being groomed to one day take over his father's plumbing business. Perhaps not surprisingly, it was his father's other passion that won his love. Ribbs attended local schools, including San Jose City College, where he was enrolled from 1975 to 1977.

Shortly after graduating high school in 1975, Ribbs began to race cars in Europe. He won the Dunlop Championship in a Ford Formula car in just his first season as a competitor and returned to the United States more certain of his future than ever. Three years later, he made a passing go at NASCAR driving, attempting to qualify for the Winston Cup, but a lapse in discipline (he skipped a handful of practices) and a run-in with local police ended that flirtation, and he was shortly replaced behind the wheel by Dale Earnhardt. The following year, 1979, he married Suzanne Hamilton. The couple would have a daughter.

The following years saw a return to driving success. In 1982 Ribbs took the pole in the Long Beach Formula Atlantic race. A year later, he switched to the Sports Car Club of America (SCAA) Trans-AM series, seized five checkered flags, and was named pro rookie of the year. He made another go at NASCAR in 1986, but his team ran out of money and didn't finish the season. Meantime, Ribbs was gaining something of a reputation as a braggart and troublemaker. His personal affect was styled after the boastful posturing of MUHAMMAD ALI, and it rubbed some sponsors and team leaders the wrong way.

It was in 1991 that Ribbs became part of racing legend, however. He'd driven Formula One racecars as early as 1986, but now he wanted to drive them in high competition. He attempted to qualify for the Indianapolis 500 in 1990 but fell short. A year later, he drove a car cosponsored by the comedian BILL COSBY and qualified for the Indy 500. He was the first black person to do so.

Auto racing is an exorbitantly expensive endeavor, however, one that relies heavily on the deep pockets of corporate sponsorship. Despite the groundbreaking nature of Ribbs's achievement—and Cosby's celebrity status—no corporations stepped up to offer backing for Ribbs and his team. Not until the day before the race, in fact, did McDonald's become a sponsor. As such, the car's health was much in doubt, and on race day it entered the field as something of a patchwork. In the end, Ribbs finished only five laps before engine troubles ended his day.

Later in 1990 Ribbs was involved in a fatal accident when he struck and killed a track marshal who had stepped in front of his car. Ribbs was held blameless in the accident. In 1993 he again qualified for the Indy

500, but the lack of corporate backing continued to be a problem. In 1995 Ribbs left the Indy circuit. He joined the CART League and had a fairly successful racing season with a number of strong finishes, including a top ten in Denver and Michigan. In 1999 he tried out for a post on an Indy Racing League team but crashed his car during the qualifying. In 2001 he drove in the NASCAR Craftsman Truck Series, as part of the Bobby Hamilton team, but his criticism of NASCAR in a newspaper interview raised eyebrows. Still, his participation in the series made Ribbs, along with legend WENDELL SCOTT, one of the few African American drivers to take part in the popular racing league.

FURTHER READING

Golenbock, Peter. *American Zoom: Stock Car Racing— From the Dirt Tracks to Daytona* (1993).

Whitlock, Jason. "Willy T. Ribbs Loves Indy, Loathes NASCAR." *Mercury News*, 26 May 2006.

JASON PHILIP MILLER

Rice, Condoleezza (14 Nov. 1954–), secretary of state, national security adviser, educator, was born in Birmingham, Alabama, the only child of John Wesley Rice Jr., an educator and minister, and Angelena Ray, a teacher. Her mother, an accomplished pianist, named her after the Italian musical direction *con dolcezza*, meaning to play "with sweetness." The Rices viewed the restrictions of Jim Crow Alabama as obstacles for their daughter to overcome. She did so effortlessly, taking early lessons in ballet, French, flute, and piano. Extra tutoring from her father enabled her to skip the first and seventh grades.

Though she enjoyed a comfortable, if by no means wealthy, childhood, Rice was not immune to the harsh realities of Birmingham under Bull Connor, the city's notoriously racist commissioner of public safety. Like everyone else in the city, she attended segregated schools, and one of her classmates was killed in the 1963 bombing of the Sixteenth Street Baptist Church by white supremacists. While her mother fostered Condi's interest in music, her father inspired a love of politics. He was an avid Republican—as were many middle-class blacks at a time when Governor George Wallace dominated the Alabama Democratic Party—and he sat with his five-year-old daughter to watch the televised Nixon-Kennedy presidential debates in 1960. Family lore has it that on a childhood trip to Washington, D.C., Rice stood in front of the White House and declared that she would one day live there.

When her family moved to Denver, Colorado, in 1968, however, Rice appeared more likely to follow a career in music than politics. At the age of fifteen she entered the University of Denver, where her father served as an administrator, to study piano. Midway through college she left the music program, believing that she could not succeed as a concert pianist. Rice focused her energies on a new love, studying the politics and policy of the Soviet Union. Her mentor, Joseph Korbel, a Czech refugee from both Nazism and Stalinism, headed the university's School of International Studies and was influential in shaping Rice's belief that the United States should adopt hard-line policies against the Soviet Union. After receiving her B.A. in 1974, Rice spent a year in Indiana at Notre Dame earning a master's degree in International Studies. By then, she had developed a passion for the Russian language and for the arcana of Soviet military strategy, and she returned to the University of Denver to complete a doctoral dissertation in 1981, later published as *Uncertain Allegiance: The Soviet Union and the Czechoslovak Army* (1984). A postdoctoral fellowship at Stanford University in 1981 helped Rice shift her interests from the more purely academic to public policy. Stanford was home to several conservative think tanks, notably the Hoover Institution, where she found much in common with a new mentor, Brent Scowcroft, a military affairs specialist who had advised presidents from Richard Nixon to Ronald Reagan, and who became national security adviser to President George H. W. Bush in 1989. Scowcroft appointed Rice, by then a tenured professor at Stanford, to the National Security Council staff that same year. Rice's time in the first Bush White House coincided with the collapse of the Soviet Union, and her expertise in that policy area greatly enhanced her personal and political standing with the president. Unlike Defense Secretary Dick Cheney and other hard-liners, Rice urged Bush to work pragmatically with the Soviet president Mikhail Gorbachev in his efforts to reform the Soviet Union and the Eastern bloc. That stance, and her moderate views on abortion and affirmative action, earned Rice the enmity of the conservative hawks who came to dominate the Republican Party after Bush's defeat by Bill Clinton in 1992.

During the Clinton years, Rice returned to academia and, with Philip Zelikow, published an award-winning examination of the end of the cold war, *Germany Unified and Europe Transformed: A Study in Statecraft* (1999). She also served from 1993 to 1999 as the provost of Stanford, and was the first

Condoleezza Rice, U.S. Secretary of State, talks to United Nations Secretary-General Kofi Annan at La Farnesina Foreign Ministry in Rome, 26 July 2006. (AP Images.)

woman and the first African American to hold that post. She succeeded in reversing Stanford's financial problems by slashing the university budget, a move that won her the admiration of the board of trustees but also the ire of many faculty, staff, and students. The U.S. Department of Labor even began an investigation into racial and gender discrimination at the university after several women complained that Rice's budget cuts had disproportionately harmed minorities. Rice later admitted that her tenure as provost had been her toughest ever job and that she may have been too much of a "hard-ass" (Lemann, 171).

Those brusque, no-nonsense qualities proved invaluable, however, when President George H. W. Bush's son, George W. Bush, was seeking a national security expert to advise him for the 2000 presidential campaign. The younger Bush, a man with little knowledge of foreign affairs, needed a clear-thinking, direct mentor to guide him through the thickets of global policy. In Rice, famed for her lucid and entertaining lectures at Stanford, he found the ideal teacher and a common spirit, as well as someone who shared his love of professional sports and physical exercise. She was also an intimate of his father's, a family connection that mattered greatly to "Team Bush." After his controversial victory in the 2000 election, George W. Bush appointed Rice as his national security adviser.

Rice's actions in the first Bush White House placed her in the "realist" foreign policy camp which advocated a pragmatic approach based on interests rather than values. This conception of foreign policy was echoed in her 2000 essay for *Foreign Affairs*, "Promoting the National Interest," where Rice criticized Clinton for pursuing ad hoc foreign adventures. Instead she argued for a more disciplined foreign policy which would serve the interests of America and the world since "the United States is the only guarantor of global peace and stability." However, after the terrorist attacks of 11 September 2001, Rice began to gravitate toward the "moralist" camp associated with Vice President Dick Cheney and Secretary of Defense Donald Rumsfeld.

As Bush's first term progressed, Rice became increasingly influential. She was his most loyal adviser and an emollient figure in the tensions between the State and Defense departments. In 2002 Rice received the NAACP's President's Award for her expertise and influence in foreign affairs. It reflected her achievement as the nation's first female national security adviser. Bush placed Rice in charge of the Iraq Stabilization Group in October 2003, thus implicitly granting her overall responsibility for the reconstruction effort. Her star continued to rise despite criticism of her role in assessing intelligence prior to the war in Iraq. Rice rebutted further criticism at her public appearance in front of the 9/11 Commission on 8 April 2004. Displaying poise and stoicism, Rice won admiration for her performance from some quarters, criticism from others. After George Bush's election to another term as president in 2004, Rice was nominated to succeed COLIN POWELL as secretary of state. Formally announcing her appointment, Bush remarked that the world would see in Rice "the strength, the grace and the decency of our country." As the first black woman to serve in this position, Rice became, arguably, the most powerful African American of her era.

Unsurprisingly, the war in Iraq dominated much of Rice's period as secretary of state. Despite increasing sectarian violence and a mounting death toll, she remained steadfastly loyal to the president's determination to "stay the course." Rice played a key role in encouraging the Iraqi political process and consistently asserted the country was "making progress." Drawing on her knowledge of European history, she often compared the difficulties faced in Iraq to those confronted by America in the period after World War II. The putative rejection of the Iraq Study Group report published on 6 December 2006 by the Baker-Hamilton Commission suggested that Rice had distanced herself from her former "realist" colleagues. Acknowledging that "tactical errors" had occurred, Rice nevertheless supported plans to increase troop levels in Iraq in the early part of 2007.

Rice traveled widely promoting American foreign policy. In her first year as secretary of state she traveled more miles than Powell did in his entire tenure. This willingness to engage in diplomacy and the knowledge that Rice spoke for the president gave renewed vigor to American statecraft. Upon acceding to the post she worked successfully to rebuild bridges with European leaders sidelined over the war in Iraq. This was essential to Rice's efforts to engage diplomatically in other areas, particularly in the Middle East. She led American efforts to further the Israeli-Palestinian peace process and in building a diplomatic coalition to attempt to quell Iranian nuclear development. Working with allies, Rice also led the way in achieving gradual progress in talks with North Korea. Although much of her diplomatic work was undermined by the war in Iraq, Rice maintained levels of popularity significantly above other members of the administration. Rice is often portrayed as the archloyalist who, despite her own realist thinking, unfailingly supported the Bush line of thinking. She admits that his moralism is not "the orientation out of which I came" but attests that, contrary to popular belief, she has learned as much from Bush's thinking as he did from his foreign policy "tutor" (Bumiller).

Rice remained as Secretary of State until the end of the Bush Presidency. Despite some speculation that she might be the running mate for Republican nominee John McCain, she played no role in that campaign. Unlike Powell, she did not endorse Obama, but nor did she endorse McCain. Rice offered support for Obama's presidency in several ways, however. She noted her great pride in his election as the first African American president, and praised his choice of Hillary Clinton as Secretary of State. Rice also criticized Republicans and others who questioned Obama's American citizenship. She also defended Obama's commitment of US logistical and financial support to the NATO bombing campaign against Muammar Qadaffi's Libyan regime in 2011. In January 2009 Rice returned to academia, both as a professor of political science at Stanford, and as the Thomas and Barbara Stephenson Senior Fellow on Public Policy at the Hoover Institution. In 2010, she joined the faculty of the Stanford Business School, as Co-Director of the Center for Global Business and the Economy.

She also released two major books. The first, *Extraordinary, Ordinary People: A Memoir of Family* (2010) received critical and popular acclaim for its depiction of life in an upper-middle-class black family in the Jim Crow South, and allowed Rice to examine the ways in which the death of her friends in the 1963 Birmingham Church bombings shaped her coming of age and personal and political development. Rice's account of her time at the center of political power, *No Higher Honor: A Memoir of My Years in Washington* (2011) allowed her to provide her own account of the Bush White House, following books by Dick Cheney and Donald Rumsfeld who had disparaged her for not fully accepting their neo-conservative agenda. Rice noted her disagreements with Cheney—notably in her disagreement with his view that America could legitimately "disappear" terrorism suspects. She also rejected Rumsfeld's criticism of her lack of experience before entering the White House, noting that she had been Provost of Stanford. And she issued a mea culpa for choosing to go shoe shopping and watching the Monty Python comedy *Spamalot* on Broadway during Hurricane Katrina. But the book also made clear her strong belief that most of the policies that she and the Bush White House pursued had been correct, and had led to a safer world.

FURTHER READING

Rice's role in the 1989 to 1993 Bush administration may be gleaned from sources at the George H. W. Bush Presidential Library and Museum in College Station, Texas, though many of those records remain classified. The Stanford University Archives, Palo Alto, California, contain materials relevant to her tenure as provost of Stanford.

Bumiller, Elisabeth. "Bush's Tutor and Disciple," *New York Times*, 17 Nov. 2004, 1.

Kessler, Glen. *The Confidante: Condoleezza Rice and the Creation of the Bush Legacy* (2007).

Lemann, Nicholas. "Without a Doubt," *New Yorker*, 14 and 21 Oct. 2002.

Mann, James. *Rise of the Vulcans: The History of Bush's War Cabinet* (2004).

STEVEN J. NIVEN
JOHN MCDERMOTT

Rice, Jerry (13 Oct. 1962–), professional football player, was born in the rural, all-black community of Crawford, Mississippi, to Joe Nathan, a bricklayer, and Eddie B. Rice (maiden name unknown). Jerry grew up in the family home his father had built, riding horses in the nearby pasture, roughhousing with his five brothers, and helping out with the family business by mixing mortar and catching the bricks his brothers would toss to him. Rice attended local Crawford High School, where he was signed up for the football team by a vice principal as punishment for an (unsuccessful) attempt at truancy. On the field he played several positions and played them well, but Crawford was somewhat off the beaten track for college football scouts, and Rice only attracted interest from Mississippi Valley State (MVS), a small Division I-AA college in Itta Benna, Mississippi. Rice was offered a scholarship and entered MVS in 1981.

At MVS he stunned the college football world, instantly becoming one of the country's best and most dynamic young wide receivers. Rice snagged fifty touchdown catches for his college career, with 301 total catches, and 4,693 yards. He did this while facing relentless double-team coverage, designed to slow down the explosive young wide-out. His teammates began calling him "World," since, they said, no football in the world was outside his reach. In 1984 Rice finished ninth in the race for the Heisman Trophy, an especially impressive feat considering MVS's small size and relatively unknown status on the college football landscape. By the time he graduated he had set (and sometimes reset) just about every offensive record at the school, achievements that brought him to the attention of the San Francisco 49ers organization. Something of a surprise among observers of the professional game—since first-round players usually came from the biggest schools with the most competitive programs—Rice was selected as the sixteenth overall pick in the first round of the 1985 NFL draft. It was as a member of the 49ers that Rice would spend most of his legendary and long-lived career. During his rookie year in 1985 he struggled to learn the speed and complexity of the professional game, snagging forty-nine catches for a little over nine-hundred total yards; but by the end of the year, he'd won over most 49ers fans and was widely considered one of the top rookies of that season. The next two years saw Rice come into his own as a professional player. He set records for touchdown receptions (twenty-two), and set an NFL record for points in a regular season with 138. In 1988 he averaged a little over twenty yards per reception, with sixty-four catches for a total of 1,306 yards, and caught nine touchdown passes. The 49ers roared through the playoffs, defeating the Chicago Bears in the NFC championship game. They faced the Cincinnati Bengals in Super Bowl XXIII, one of the closest and most thrilling contests in the history of the game. Despite an ankle injury that nearly kept him out of the contest, Rice had 220 total yards (five of them as a rusher) and a touchdown. His masterful performance was awarded with the game's Most Valuable Player (MVP) honors, and suddenly Rice was an NFL star.

Throughout the late 1980s and early 1990s the San Francisco 49ers were the NFL's glamour team—expertly coached by the legendary Bill Walsh, they were high scoring and seemingly flawless on the field—and Rice was an indispensable part of their success. The team returned to the Super Bowl in 1989, defeating the Denver Broncos in a lopsided 55–10 blowout; the 49ers went to the Super Bowl again in 1994, defeating the San Diego Chargers. In the 1994 contest, Rice set an NFL record for his three touchdown grabs in the 49–26 drubbing.

Jerry Rice, San Francisco 49ers wide receiver, catches the ball during practice before the game against the Denver Broncos, 15 December 1997 in San Francisco. (AP Images.)

Still, Rice's career was not without its bumps, especially off the field, where the star receiver felt he'd been passed over for lucrative endorsement deals because of his race. Indeed, following his MVP win in Super Bowl XXIII, the Walt Disney company took the unusual step of asking non-MVP 49ers quarterback Joe Montana to utter its famous postgame slogan, "I'm going to Disneyland!" Rice later softened his public criticism, suggesting his criticisms of Disney had stemmed from the hurt feelings of a young man. In 1987 Rice married Jackie (maiden name unknown), whom he had met and dated in college; the couple had three children.

Rice remained with San Francisco for sixteen seasons, along the way setting (and resetting) most NFL receiving records. By the time he left the team in 2000 because of what he felt was a lack of playing time, his total reception yards numbered more than nineteen thousand, and he had been elected to twelve Pro Bowls. He refused an offer from the San Francisco franchise and instead signed with the Oakland Raiders, where he was efficient and occasionally brilliant. He appeared with the team in Super Bowl XXXVII, in which the Raiders were defeated 48–21 by the Tampa Bay Buccaneers. Still, Oakland was in a rebuilding phase and Rice was

soon on his way to Seattle, where he played briefly in 2004. He then tried out for the Denver Broncos but failed to make the team (though he was offered a reserve spot, which he refused). He retired in 2005, having signed a one-day contract with the 49ers so that he could officially retire with the team that had made him an NFL superstar; he then returned with his wife to his hometown of Crawford.

The list of Jerry Rice's records at the college and professional levels is indeed a long one. He accumulated 22,895 receiving yards, more than 23,000 all-purpose yards, 208 touchdowns, and 1,549 receptions. He held nine Super Bowl records and was named to the NFL's Seventy-fifth Anniversary All-Time Team and to both the 1980s and 1990s NFL All-Decade Teams. *Sporting News* named him number two among the top one hundred professional football players of all time (behind only the great JIM BROWN). At the time of his retirement he was considered by many players, coaches, and fans as the greatest wide receiver to ever play the game. His durability was also something of legend. He played a total of 303 games, far more than any ever played by a wide receiver. Rice was inducted into the College Football Hall of Fame in 2006, and in 2000 his alma mater, Mississippi Valley, renamed its football stadium in his honor. In 2010, Rice was inducted into the Pro Football Hall of Fame in Canton, Ohio. By then, he had gained popularity with a new audience, thanks to his successful appearance on the hit television show, *Dancing with the Stars*, in which he and his partner placed second.

FURTHER READING
Rice, Jerry, and Brian Curtis. *Go Long!: My Journey Beyond the Game and the Fame* (2007).
Summerall, Pat. *Sports in America* (1996).

JASON PHILIP MILLER

Rice, Linda Johnson (22 Mar. 1958–), publishing and business executive, was born in Chicago, Illinois, and was adopted by John and Eunice Johnson in 1961 at the age of three. Not much is known about her birth family, but her adopted family changed the course of her life. Her adopted father, John Johnson, was the founder of Johnson Publishing Company, and he introduced her to the family's business at a very young age. Rice began spending much of her time in the headquarters where her adopted mother, Eunice Johnson, was the fashion editor for *Ebony* magazine and was responsible for covering high fashion all over the world. This afforded Rice opportunities to travel, especially abroad, to places such as France and Italy. Rice accompanied her mother and learned the basics of haute couture fashion and the fashion industry at large.

Upon graduating from high school, she enrolled in the University of Southern California (USC) where she studied journalism. The distance between her chosen university and her home in Chicago was great, but it did not diminish her connection to her parents' work. Rice assisted her mother, Eunice Johnson, in reviewing and selecting fashions to be presented in the *Ebony* Fashion Fair show, which traveled around the country and featured the latest clothing and accessory styles. She also spent her summers working as an intern at Johnson Publishing and became familiar with the company's internal operations.

After graduating from USC in 1980, Rice began at Johnson Publishing as a vice president and fashion coordinator. Her interest in the business grew, and, following the death of her older brother, John Johnson Jr. (who died of sickle cell anemia in 1981), she began her rise to the top. Rice recognized that to be valuable in the family business, she needed to add a solid business education to her knowledge of the family's primary business industry, so she enrolled in the J. L. Kellogg Graduate School of Management at Northwestern University. During her time studying at Northwestern, her father introduced her to S. Andre Rice, a security sales associate with Goldman, Sachs & Company. They were married in 1984. During the early years of her marriage, she conducted business during the day and studied management in the evenings, earning her MBA from Kellogg in 1987. Her daughter, Alexa, was born in 1989. The Rices divorced in 1994.

Rice expanded her knowledge of Johnson Publishing and served in a number of roles, first as vice president, followed by a stint as president, then as chief operating officer. Although she was responsible for handling everyday operations, her father continued to mentor and encourage her development as a corporate leader. Under her father's watchful eye, Rice gradually earned the trust and respect of John Johnson Sr.'s long-time business colleagues. Rice's growing profile as a leading businesswoman was also enhanced by appointments to serve on the boards of several companies, including Bausch & Lomb since 1990 and Quaker Oats since 2000.

An innovator in her own right, Rice fostered several initiatives designed to promote self-awareness, style, and social consciousness within the African American community. She helped establish a fashion catalog, *E-style* and the *Ebony/Jet Guide to Black Excellence*. The former was a fashion catalog founded in conjunction with *Essence* magazine; the latter was a video series featuring prominent African American actors and artists in an effort targeted toward empowering young black teens and preteens. The general message of the series was to inspire people that they can reach any goal with the proper desire and commitment. Designed as a teaching curriculum, the videos included guides and worksheets.

In 2002 her father called her into his office and handed her an envelope containing a letter expressing his thanks and promoting her to CEO. An impromptu announcement followed the next day at a luncheon celebrating black women in the media. After her promotion, Rice initiated a drive to increase sales of the company's Fashion Fair cosmetic line. She increased the presence of the line with television ads and marketing spaces in department stores, but she did not alter the formulas with which their loyal customers were so familiar. Additionally, she pushed sales of the company's magazines with aggressive marketing strategies and added visibility.

In the marketplace, Johnson Publishing's products were faced with competition from publications such as *Essence* and cosmetic companies such as Estee Lauder. However, under her leadership, both *Ebony* and *Jet* magazines maintained circulations of more than 950,000 annually. Fashion Fair remained the number-one, black-owned cosmetics line, and its affiliation with the *Ebony* Fashion Fair raised almost $50 million for charity and created hundreds of scholarships for minority students.

In 2004 Rice married Mel Farr, a former football star with the Detroit Lions. Rice also served on the board of trustees for her alma mater, the University of Southern California.

FURTHER READING

Bengali, Shashank. "Jetsetter," *Trojan Family Magazine* (2002).

Dingle, Derek T. *Black Enterprise Titans of the BE 100s: Black CEOs Who Redefine and Conquered American Business* (1999).

Dykes, Witt, Jr. "Farr, Mel," in *Notable Black American Men, Book II* (2007).

Newkirk, Pamela. *Within the Veil: Black Journalists, White Media* (2000).

SIBYL COLLINS WILSON

Rice, Norm (4 May 1943–), mayor, was born in Denver, Colorado, to Otha Patrick, a porter, and Irene Hazel Jackson, who held a number of jobs, caterer and domestic among them. His grandmother was an early female minister in the AME Church, and proved a role model to the young man. Rice's parents split when he was a teenager. He attended local schools and fared well both academically and, as class president, in student governance. He graduated with honors from Manual High School in Denver in 1961 and matriculated to the University of Colorado at Boulder. He found the conditions there not to his liking, however. The school had segregated facilities, including dining rooms, and, dispirited, Rice dropped out after only a few months.

Uncertain what his future might hold, Rice took on a number of jobs, including as a meter reader. During the early sixties, he visited Seattle, Washington, and fell in love with the city. In 1969 he decided to make it his home. He enrolled in Highline Community College, from which he took an associate's degree in 1970, and then matriculated to the University of Washington. In 1972 he took a B.A. in Communications. In 1974 he graduated with a master's degree in Public Administration from the same institution. In the meantime, Rice was dabbling in public relations for the Seattle Urban League, and it was through that undertaking that he met Constance Williams, herself in public relations. The couple married in early 1973. Together they would have a son.

Rice was soon to enter the world of politics, but first he held a number of jobs around Seattle. He continued his work with the Urban League and filed reports for local television and radio. In 1976 he worked as communications director for Rainier National Bank, from which position he began the soon-to-be important work of building relationships with local businesses and entrepreneurs. In 1978 he ran for a seat on the city council and defeated the incumbent. He was reelected numerous times and enjoyed an eleven-year tenure. In 1983 he was named president of the council. His political star was on the rise.

Still, there were setbacks. Rice entered the mayoral primary in 1985 against the incumbent Charles Royer and was soundly defeated. Two years later, he ran for Congress on the Democratic ticket for the Seventh Congressional District, but was again beaten by a substantial margin, this time by Jim McDermott. Again, he returned to the city council, and soon had his eye on the next mayoral race. That proved to be the turning point that Rice had begun to despair of. In 1989 Rice entered a campaign against the Republican Doug Jewett and with a controversial ballot measure to end busing in the city a key election-year issue. Rice won handily, defeating the Republican in what had long been a Democratic stronghold, and becoming Seattle's first African American mayor in a city where blacks account for around 10 percent of the total population.

Seattle was a prosperous city, but a number of problems had recently begun to dim its lights. Crime was on the rise, as was homelessness. Rice had promised in his campaign to tackle both. He rejuvenated the downtown and shored up the city's important and lucrative tourist trade. He strengthened Seattle's manufacturing industry and lured businesses from across the country and around the world to make Seattle their home or headquarters, with an emphasis on cultural and ethnic diversity. Rice ran for reelection in 1993 and won handily. In his second term, he continued his emphasis on the problems of crime (especially drug-related), homelessness, and gun violence. From 1995 to 1996 he served as president of the U.S. Conference of Mayors.

Rice left the mayoral office after his second term. In 1996 he entered Washington's Democratic gubernatorial primary, but was defeated. He served as Distinguished Practitioner-in-Residence at the University of Washington's Evans School of Public Affairs and in 2009 became CEO of the not-for-profit Seattle Foundation, a philanthropic organization. Among his numerous honors and accolades, Rice was named an outstanding public citizen by the National Association of Social Workers and was a recipient of the American Association of Community College Students Outstanding Alumni Award.

FURTHER READING

Colburn, David R., and Jeffery S. Adler, eds. *African-American Mayors: Race, Politics, and the American City* (2001).

Taylor, Quintard. *The Forging of a Black Community: Seattle's Central District from 1870 through the Civil Rights Era* (1994).

JASON PHILIP MILLER

Rice, Sarah Lucille Webb (4 Jan. 1909–23 Mar. 2006), school teacher and domestic worker, is best known for a poignant and detailed autobiography that provides a window into daily life for the Americans who were stigmatized legally and socially, during the middle of the twentieth century, by their dark complexion.

Sarah Lucille Webb was born in Clio, Alabama, to Elizabeth (Lizzie) Janet Lewis Webb, a schoolteacher, and Willis James Webb, a minister of the

African Methodist Episcopal (AME) church. In her early years she moved with her parents to Troy, Andalusia, Birmingham, Batesville, and Eufala, Alabama. As an itinerant minister ordained by a Methodist church, Reverend Webb was subject to reassignment to a new church at any annual conference, and every one to two years he had to move. The family supplemented his minister's salary by sharecropping cotton and corn and grew field peas, greens, and vegetables for their own use or for sale.

The family lived in Birmingham from 1912 to 1917—initially because Reverend Webb was assigned to a church there. The family moved into a storefront house so that Reverend Webb could open a store, but even renting part of the space out for an ice cream parlor, he lost money—too many people he extended credit to owed him and could not pay. The Webbs remained in Birmingham for a time after he had been transferred to a circuit of several churches in southern Alabama. Settled in Batesville, 1917–1920, Sarah learned how to plow from her brother Albert, although her father didn't want his daughter learning a boy's job. The family collected hickory nuts and black walnuts and wild grapes to supplement their diet, seasonally gathering birds drunk on chinaberries to roast, while Lizzie Webb took in washing and did catering. Reverend Webb brought his wife and children to Eufala in 1921, where he died in 1925 of heart failure, in his church while delivering a sermon.

The same year, Sarah Webb graduated from high school, chosen as class valedictorian, and was hired as a teacher of young children at Mount Level Baptist Church. She passed the Alabama State Teachers' Exam in 1926, obtaining her first public school teaching job in Clio. Although legally too young for a teaching license at seventeen, she later observed, "The white people just kind of look at black folks and think they all look the same, so I could pass for 21." The following year Sarah Webb married Ernest (Jim) Hayes, the first of three marriages. This one lasted two years, resulting in one child, James David Hayes, born 23 April 1928.

A handsome young veteran who had all the girls in town after him, Hayes had been raised around people used to "cussing, drinking and gambling," unlike the sedate life of the Webb family, defined by her father's status as a pastor. Although he ardently courted Sarah, he was soon playing around with other women, taking out money to spend, which included a good part of his wife's teacher pay. She divorced him in 1929.

On her own again, Webb taught for two years at a Rosenwald School in Rocky Mount, Alabama, less than twenty miles from Eurfala. Her school was one of over five thousand built across the South, a vision of BOOKER T. WASHINGTON's, applauded by W. E. B. DuBois, and funded by Sears Roebuck CEO Julius Rosenwald, as well as money painfully scraped together by sharecropping parents, to provide rural schools for African American children. At this time, state funding for segregated "black" schools was less than one-third the funding for "white" public schools. Webb knew math and geography far better than the principal, so she taught all grades in those subjects. With state revenues depleted by the Depression and Alabama paying teachers with "warrants" that merchants were increasingly reluctant to accept, she moved in 1933 to Panama City, Florida, where she worked as live-in domestic for a Dr. Wells and his wife. She returned to teaching in Westbay, Florida, moving to a rented room, then back to Panama City when the nearby community of Bayou George reopened its public school.

Moving to Jacksonville in 1937, she returned to domestic work, handling childcare, laundry, scrubbing, and windows for a Mrs. Livesy. Laundry at this time was done in tin tubs over coal pots to heat the water. She also worked for a time for a family named Thompson, but lived in her own rented room. Sarah Webb's second marriage, to James Myers in 1937, lasted less than a year. She described him as smooth and gentle, a contrast to the rough, abusive, demanding, Hayes. However, he was just as much a womanizer, and he didn't keep up his part of the family finances: they had agreed that he would move into the house where she lived in Jacksonville, pay the rent and keep up the insurance, while she took care of food and other expenses. He didn't make the payments.

Following World War II, she entered into a period of community and church leadership that lasted for the remainder of her life. Always a member of the AME church, she joined the church's Christian Endeavor League. In 1947 she was denied an apartment in a newly built low-income housing project, because her income was deemed insufficient to pay the rent. (At the time, this project offered promise of a new, clean building, with an electric stove and lights, a definite step up from much of the rental property available in Florida.) Later that year, she was able to buy a newly built "Jim Walters house." Walters, a builder in Tampa, Florida, was just beginning a rewarding career building small, sturdy homes for people of limited means.

The nearby Moncrief Elementary School in Duval County needed a PTA president, and although her own son was grown, she was asked to fill the position. "I wasn't that smart," she recalled in her autobiography, "but it looked like things just revealed themselves to me." Proving to be a dynamic leader, she organized home room mothers to assist with each class, making sure that mothers from low-income families were mixed with those she called "upper crust" in each classroom. She also organized the Triangle Club to encourage families to build up savings.

In 1953 Sarah Lucille Webb married Andrew A. Rice, whose wife had died the previous year. They remained united until Andrew Rice died of a stroke in 1983. Sarah Webb Rice, long a member of Gregg Temple AME church in Jacksonville, decided to join her husband's church, Mt. Bethel Baptist. Becoming a church mother of Mt. Bethel at age forty-four, she took up teaching Sunday School. Among her students she was long remembered by Frederick Harper, a future Howard University professor and author of two books. Sarah Rice served in district and state church offices, as a delegate to the Florida General Baptist Convention Women's Auxiliary, vice president of the Women's District Convention Auxiliary, and second vice president and president of the state auxiliary. She served as an honorary board of trustees member of Florida Memorial University (FMU Catalog, Fall 2008, Graduate Catalog, 2009–2011) and earned an honorary doctorate degree. She died peacefully in Jacksonville at the age of ninety-seven, memorialized by the *Florida Times-Union* as a well-known civic, social, and religious leader.

FURTHER READING
Rice, Sarah, and Louise Hutchings Westling. *He Included Me: The Autobiography of Sarah Rice* (1989).
Nelson, Emmanuel Sampath. *African American Autobiography: A Sourcebook* (2002).
Obituary: *Florida Times-Union*, 26 March 2006.

CHARLES ROSENBERG

Rice, Spotswood (fl. 1830s–1880s), slave and Civil War soldier, was probably born in the 1820s or early 1830s in Missouri, where he was living in the 1850s, though he may have been brought there from another slave state. What is known about him survives in two letters he wrote in September 1864 to his children and to Kitty Diggs, the Glasgow, Missouri, slaveholder who owned them and his wife, who was

perhaps named Caroline. Further information can be found in a 1937 Federal Writers' Project interview of one of Rice's daughters, MARY A. BELL.

Bell's account reveals that Rice worked as a tobacco roller and head slave on Benjamin Lewis's plantation, several miles away from the Diggs farm. She recalled that her father diligently visited his family twice a week, on Wednesdays and Saturdays, the only days Rice's owner permitted him to do so. Rice cured Lewis's tobacco once it was brought in from the fields and also made the tobacco into various twists and plugs. Mary Bell's account suggests that Benjamin Lewis thought highly of her father's work and leadership qualities, but that Lewis's black overseer or "driver" repeatedly beat Rice for insubordination. Rice also angered his master by learning to read and write—with the help of Lewis's own son—and by reading aloud the Emancipation Proclamation to his fellow slaves. The enslaved people on Lewis's farm subsequently became incorrigible and refused to work. Ironically, the president's January 1863 declaration of freedom applied only to slaves in the rebelling slaveholding states of the Confederacy. It did not apply to Rice or other slaves in Missouri, Delaware, Maryland, or Kentucky, slaveholding states that remained loyal to the Union.

Around August 1863, perhaps for reading the Proclamation or some other infraction, Lewis's driver beat Rice until the latter man bled. Despite his wife's pleas that he go back to his owner, Rice ran away and hid from the ever-present slave patrollers in nearby woods for three days. He eventually gave himself up to a slave trader and tried, unsuccessfully, to persuade the trader to buy him from Lewis. Returned to his owner, Rice stayed on his plantation for the following six months, having agreed to his master's proposal to provide him with a house and several acres of his own once the war was over and slavery abolished. In February 1864, however, Rice decided that he could not wait any longer for freedom. Along with eleven of the allegedly best slaves on Lewis's plantation, he left the Lewis farm and enlisted in the U.S. Army at Glasgow, Missouri.

Mary Bell's recollection in 1937 of her father's fighting spirit seventy-five years earlier appears to be confirmed by two letters he wrote on 3 September 1864, while recuperating from chronic rheumatism in the hospital at the Benton federal barracks near St. Louis. The first, addressed to "my children," assured them that "I have not forgot you and that I want to see you as bad as ever" (Berlin, *Remembering*, 195). Rice advised them to be content with their lot for the time being, but wrote that he would rescue them soon, "if it cost me my life" (195). He also lambasted Kitty Diggs, indignant at her claims that he had tried to "steal" his own children from her. Diggs, in Rice's view, "is the first Christian that I ever h[e]ard say that a man could steal his own child especially out of human bondage" (195). Although Rice claimed to have once had respect for some slaveholders, such sympathies were by this time "worn out," prompting him to write a second letter, specifically to Mrs. Diggs, in which he called her his enemy and claimed to be glad she had rejected his earlier attempt to buy Mary from her. He again threatened to take his children back from Diggs, this time with the help of one thousand black soldiers. Rice also warned Diggs: "Mary is my child and she is a God given rite of my own and you may hold on to her as long as you can but I want you to remember this one thing—that the longer you keep my child from me the longer you will have to burn in hell and the qwicer [quicker] you will get there." Rice left it to Diggs's own conscience whether she would voluntarily hand over his daughter to him, but he expressed "no fears about getting Mary out of your hands." (197). Like an increasing number of black Americans in late 1864, as the Union's victory grew closer, Rice was emboldened in openly criticizing slaveholders, citing the federal government's gradual, but increasing, commitment to ending slavery throughout the entire United States. "This whole Government gives cheer to me and you cannot help yourself," he taunted Diggs in the final sentence of his letter (197).

Rice's children might never have seen these letters, however, since the Glasgow postmaster, F. W. Diggs, husband of Kitty, seized them at the post office and then forwarded them to the U.S. Army command in Missouri. Diggs, a loyal slaveholding Unionist, demanded that Rice be exiled from the state to prevent him from carrying through his plans to seize his children. "To be thus insulted by such a black scoundrel is more than I can stand," Diggs wrote after intercepting Rice's letters (Lardner). While the Union army command in Missouri probably did not wish to offend prominent white slaveholders like Diggs, it also does not appear to have acted on Diggs's request. The matter was rendered moot four months later, on 11 January 1865, when Missouri's governor signed into law an Ordinance of Emancipation that abolished slavery throughout the state. By then most Missouri slaves had already freed themselves, like Rice, by running away or by joining the army.

By mid-1865 Rice was finally reunited with his wife and children at the Benton Barracks in St. Louis, where he worked for a while as a nurse. Little is known about his postwar career, other than that he became active in Missouri's Methodist Conference and traveled throughout the West on behalf of that denomination in the 1870s and early 1880s. Alexander W. Wayman's *Cyclopaedia of African Methodism* (1882) notes that Rice was once "deprived of an education," but that since joining the Methodist Conference he had "worked hard and sustained himself very creditably" (135). The date and place of Rice's death remain unknown, but it seems likely that his determination to keep his family intact and his military service in the cause of black freedom were commemorated at his funeral.

FURTHER READING

Interview of Mary A. Bell, St. Louis, Missouri, 19 Aug. 1937, WPA Slave Narrative Project, vol. 11, *Arkansas Narratives, Part 7* and *Missouri Narratives*. Available through the Library of Congress.

Berlin, Ira, et al. *Remembering Slavery: African Americans Talk about Their Personal Experiences of Slavery and Freedom* (1998).

Berlin, Ira, and Leslie S. Rowland, eds. *Families and Freedom: A Documentary History of African-American Kinship in the Civil War Era* (1997).

Lardner, James. "Liberating Lessons of War," *Washington Post*, 12 Jan. 1983.

STEVEN J. NIVEN

Richards, Fannie Moore (1 Oct. 1840–14? Feb. 1922), educator, was born in Fredericksburg, Virginia, to Adolph "Dolph" Richards, a furniture manufacturer, and Maria Louise Moore Richards. Both of her parents were freeborn. Her father was a mixed-race man from the Dutch colony of Curaçao, in the West Indies, who was highly educated and had attended school in London. Her mother was a mixed-race woman from Virginia whose middle-class parents had provided her with a basic education. Both of Fannie's parents made the education of their fourteen children a priority. In the wake of the NAT TURNER rebellion, the state had passed a law in 1831 closing the schools that were then open for free blacks. Richards's father comprised part of a group of free blacks in Fredericksburg who unsuccessfully petitioned the state legislature in 1838 to allow them to open a school for their children. The state government further prohibited free black children from obtaining an education in another state and returning to Virginia.

In her early childhood, Richards received an illegal education in the school held in the home of William De Baptiste, a member of a prominent free black family in Fredericksburg. When Dolph Richards died in 1850, Maria sold the family home and migrated to Toronto to further the education of her five children still living at home—John D., James, Dolph Jr., Billy, and Fannie. Around 1857 the family moved to Detroit, Michigan, where Richards enrolled at the Teachers Training School to complete the studies she began in Toronto. Since 1819, Detroit's black churches and private citizens had organized schools for the children of the city's minute free black population. The Board of Education founded segregated schools beginning in 1839, and in 1860 only one public school, in the city's fourth ward, existed for black children, and it had a white teacher.

Richards objected to this lack of educational facilities for black students and opened a private school in 1863. Two years later, the Board of Education arranged for her to teach in the second public school, Colored School Two, opened in the seventh ward. Also around this time, she began teaching Sunday school classes at Second Baptist Church, one of the oldest black churches in the city, which had long been active in education.

In 1867, the Republican-dominated Michigan Supreme Court ruled to integrate the public school system, but Detroit's Board of Education, controlled by Democrats, disregarded the law. When the schools continued to prevent the admittance of black students, members of the African American community began to aggressively resist the illegal exclusion. While the school board agreed that the policy led to inferior schools for black students, they refused to end de facto segregation. However, they consented to acquiring a more suitable building to house Colored School Two and other ameliorative measures. One of these measures included hiring Richards formally by presenting her with a contract (as opposed to the unofficial terms of her earlier employment with the board), but she received a lower salary than that of her white colleagues.

In 1869, Richards and her brother John D. served on the commission of well-educated blacks who petitioned the Michigan Supreme Court to end the illegal segregation of the state's public schools. In fear of legal reprisals, the school board reluctantly agreed to establish integrated schools in Detroit in 1871. Richards began teaching the city's first integrated kindergarten class at the Everett Elementary School in the fourth ward. The school, located off the riverfront on the city's lower east side, was housed in an area where working-class French, German, Irish, and African American residents lived in close proximity. The integrated kindergarten class stayed open for only one year, and the majority of Richard's students were whites throughout her long career at Everett, during which she often taught two generations of the same family.

Because of a school board stipulation that prevented married women from teaching, Richards remained single throughout her life. She empathized with the plight of elderly black women with no means of financial support, and her concern led her to help establish the PHILLIS WHEATLEY Home in 1897, an institution partially funded by Richards's unequal and insufficient wages as a teacher. The association that was created to run the home allied with the Ann Arbor Women's Club, and together they purchased a large house on Elizabeth Street in Detroit in 1901. Only men who were prominent in the black elite of the city acted as the legal directors of the home, however, in accordance with the Progressive Era gender norms in which women participated in reforms of the domestic sphere, while men attended to the practical matters of the public sphere in the reform of society. Also in reflection of the period, in 1913 the home provided space for the Preston Union, a chapter of the Women's Christian Temperance Union (WCTU) established by black women devoted to fighting alcohol consumption and prostitution, as well as to promoting women's suffrage.

Fannie Richards retired in 1915 from a teaching career that spanned the era from the Civil War to that of the Great Migration of black Southerners to the urban industrial regions of the North. Forced from the antebellum South in order to pursue an education, the dedication of the Richards family to academics produced an educator committed to instructing children for fifty years. The Detroit Board of Education recognized Fannie as the first black teacher and celebrated her lifelong professional commitment in 1970. In 1975, Second Baptist placed a plaque on the city's lower east side commemorating her devotion to the church's Sunday school.

FURTHER READING

The Burton Historical Collection of the Detroit Public Library and the Bentley Historical Library at the University of Michigan both house papers of the Second Baptist Church that relate to Fannie Richards and her family.

Hartgrove, W. B. "The Story of Maria Louise Moore and Fannie M. Richards," in *The Journal of Negro History* (1916).

Katzman, David. *Before the Ghetto: Black Detroit in the Nineteenth Century* (1973).

Leach, Nathaniel. *The Second Baptist Connection: Reaching out to Freedom; History of Second Baptist Church of Detroit* (1988).

KATHRYN L. BEARD

Richards, Michael (2 Aug. 1963–11 Sept. 2001), sculptor and installation artist, was born in New York City and raised in Kingston, Jamaica. Little is known of Richards's parents or early education, but he earned a B.A. from Queens College in 1985 and an M.A. from New York University in 1992. The following year he was one of twelve studio artists in the Independent Study Program at the Whitney Museum of American Art in New York. Richards also completed the Artist-in-the-Marketplace Program at the Bronx Museum of the Arts in 1994 and was an artist-in-residence at the Studio Museum in Harlem from 1995 to 1996, at the Socrates Sculpture Park in Long Island City, Queens, in 1997, and at the National Foundation for Advancement in the Arts in Miami, Florida, from 1997 to 1999. Richards won an Art Matters, Inc. grant and was awarded free studio space from 1994 to 1995 by the Marie Walsh Sharpe Art Foundation Space Program. His work was included in several group exhibitions, including No Doubt: African-American Art of the '90s (1996) at the Aldrich Museum of Contemporary Art, and in the traveling exhibitions Postcards from Black America (1998), organized by the De Beyerd Center for Contemporary Art in the Netherlands, and Passages: Contemporary Art in Transition (1999), organized by the Studio Museum in Harlem.

Combining figurative elements and a conceptual approach, Richards focused on themes of movement, space, and flight in conjunction with issues of African American history and identity. His sculptures and installations, most often rendered in bronze, sometimes with feathers, hair, rubber, or leather, explore both the metaphoric and literal dimensions of flying. "The idea of flight," Richards explained when his work was on display at the Bronx Museum of the Arts, "relates to my use of pilots and planes, but it also references the black church, the idea of being lifted up, enraptured, or taken up to a safe place—to a better world." Richards's strongest pieces, including *Are You Down* (1999), an outdoor sculpture of three grounded pilots created for the Franconia Sculpture Park in Shafer, Minnesota, were anchored by life-size figures that he modeled, literally, on himself by casting his body in plaster resin and later in bronze.

Richards's particular interest was the Tuskegee Airmen, the African American World War II pilots of the 332nd Fighter Group. Named for Tuskegee Institute, where they trained under BENJAMIN DAVIS JR., the pilots destroyed more than 260 German airplanes and earned 150 Distinguished Flying Crosses, 744 Air Medals, eight Purple Hearts, and fourteen Bronze Stars. While the pilots were recognized heroes abroad, they returned to racism and segregation in the United States. In works like *Escape Plan 76 (Brer Plane in the Brier Patch)* (1996), *Great Black Airmen (Tuskegee)* (1996), and *Winged* (1999), Richards honored these men while exploring the dichotomies they experienced.

In 2001 Richards's preoccupation with space and flight proved a natural fit for the Lower Manhattan Cultural Council's World Views program, which awarded rent-free art studios located in ten thousand square feet of vacant office space in the World Trade Center high above New York City and the Hudson River. At 8:45 on the morning of 11 September 2001, Richards was alone in the World Views studios on the ninety-second floor of the North Tower of the World Trade Center when hijackers flew American Airlines Flight 11 into the building, hitting its ninety-fourth through ninety-eighth floors. Its upper floors engulfed in fire and smoke, the North Tower collapsed at 10:28 A.M., twenty-seven minutes after the collapse of the South Tower, killing, among others, all 1,344 people above the ninety-first floor, including Richards.

At the time of his death Richard was an art handler at the Bronx Museum of Art. He had arrived at the studio the evening before, and after eating dinner and watching *Monday Night Football* on television he had worked through the night on a sculpture for an upcoming exhibition. World Views artists often created site-specific works inspired by the iconic status and the one-of-a-kind views afforded by the Towers. When he was killed Richards was working on a piece relating to the Tuskegee Airmen, featuring pilots falling from the sky and riding a burning meteor into the debris below.

In all, 2,823 people were killed in or around the World Trade Center on 11 September, including passengers on the two hijacked planes, 343 firefighters, and 78 other uniformed rescuers. Approximately 8 percent of the victims were black and more than 15 percent were in their late thirties, the demographic groups to which Richards belonged. He was the only person present in the World Views studios that morning and he was the only professional artist killed in the World Trade Center attacks (a freelance photographer, Bill Biggart, was killed covering the events). Unlike more than 65 percent of the victims, his remains were identified, on 17 September.

Art had been a component of the World Trade Center from its inception. One percent of the initial construction cost was set aside for public art, and the complex was home to several arts organizations, including the Lower Manhattan Cultural Council, which lost its studios (and all of its artists' work) along with its own art collection and archives. An estimated hundred million dollars of art was destroyed in the attacks, including Elyn Zimmerman's memorial to the victims of the 1993 World Trade Center bombing, public artworks commissioned specifically for the site by Joan Miró, Roy Lichtenstein, Alexander Calder, Louise Nevelson, David Hockney, and ROMARE BEARDEN, and innumerable works held by private companies. One of the surviving public sculptures, *Double Check*, by J. Seward Johnson Jr., with its seated businessman prematurely aged by falling debris and white ash from the destroyed towers, became a spontaneous memorial to the dead and the rescuers.

Adrian Dannatt Richards, a reporter for the London *Independent*, attended Richards's memorial at the Studio Museum in Harlem and wrote, "Many of the hundreds of mourners spoke of Richards's anti-Republican sentiments and how much he would have hated any exploitation of his death for the sake of American warmongering. Many more mourners spoke of his kindness, gentleness, great generosity and genuine gift for friendship, his "cheesy" smile, shimmying shoulders, soft voice, quiet grace and inner calm. His cheerfulness and soothing ability to settle disputes were repeatedly recounted, along with the fact he never seemed angry. Performances at the service of blues, Gospel and a reggae compilation mixed by DJ Language testified to his great second love after art, that of music" (24 Sept. 2001). The most poignant of the tributes offered in the wake of Richards's death came from Monika Bravo, one of the artists with whom he shared the World Trade Center studios and the last person to see him alive. Bravo had spent the evening of 10 September filming a dramatic storm from the windows of the ninety-second floor. She turned the resulting footage, now oddly prescient in its imagery, into a short film, which she dedicated to Richards.

In a statement found on his computer after his death, Richards described the Tuskegee Airmen as "only being free, really free, when they were in the air. [They] serve as symbols of failed transcendence and loss of faith … escaping the pull of gravity, but always forced back to the ground, lost navigators always seeking home." *Tar Baby vs. St. Sebastian* (1999), Richards's best-known sculpture, reworked the well-known story and iconography of Saint Sebastian, the Christian martyr shot full of arrows and left for dead. In Richards's version, however, the hero, modeled on himself, was a World War II pilot, arms by his side and palms raised; the body is pierced all over, not by arrows, but by small airplanes.

FURTHER READING
Carr, C. "Lost Horizons," *Village Voice*, 25 Sept. 2001.
Marks, Peter, and Carol Vogel. "Arts Groups at a Tragedy's Center Try to Assess Where to Begin," *New York Times*, 17 Sept. 2001.
Obituary: *New York Times*, 15 Sept. 2001.

LISA E. RIVO

Richardson, Archie Gibbs (4 Apr. 1904–Oct. 1979), educator and activist, was born in Lexington, Virginia, the son of William Richardson and Ellen Brice. Though his grandparents were slaves and freedmen, his parents were born free. At an early age William Richardson worked for hire, buying food and clothing and attending public school until third grade. After marriage the Richardsons sustained a modest living as day laborers.

Archie Richardson entered public school in Lexington at age eight, several weeks after school had begun. Initially this late entry caused him much humiliation and trepidation, but he soon became acclimated and advanced with his classmates. Doctors, however, advised his parents to withdraw him temporarily from grade five because he appeared nervous and studied "too hard." Shortly after Richardson returned to school an older bully struck him in the stomach with a baseball; the blow rendered him unconscious and caused him to shy away from baseball and other sports.

While in elementary school Richardson secured a job as a companion to the son of a professor at the Virginia Military Institute, who, aiming to shield his son from interacting with the children of the working class, employed Richardson's services in his home. Not only did this job garner him weekly wage but it also enabled him to enjoy the outdoors, including hiking, camping, and fishing. More important, this companionship gave Richardson access to "the very best literature available for children" (Archie G. Richardson Papers).

By age fifteen Richardson had completed elementary school, but since no black high school existed in Lexington, in 1919 he traveled two hundred miles to the high school at the Virginia Normal and Industrial Institute at Petersburg, completing the program in 1923. Four years later he earned a bachelor's degree in French from Virginia State College while supporting himself with jobs in the college cafeteria and bookstore.

In autumn 1927 Richardson became principal of the Mecklenburg County Training School in South Hill, Virginia. Rural, small, and desolate, the school resembled fledgling training schools across Virginia. All struggled to educate students under the constraints of *Plessy v. Ferguson* (1896) and section 140 of the Virginia Constitution (1902) codifying "separate but equal" education; all fought to secure capricious state funds; all persisted because of philanthropists such as Julius Rosenwald and Miss Anna T. Jeanes; all survived because of determined and dedicated black parents, teachers, businesspersons, and students.

Under Richardson's leadership Mecklenburg County Training School became a template for the construction of successful Negro training schools across Virginia. Richardson instituted and fostered professional development for teachers, hired more teachers, encouraged fund-raising, advocated self-help among parents and students, fought for black teachers to receive salaries comparable to whites', advocated integration and civil liberties, improved and expanded the physical plant, attended to the needs of the parents and the community, and paved the way for the development of high schools. While at Mecklenburg Richardson married Linnie Esther Ramey of Indianapolis, Indiana, on 17 June 1931; they had one son, Archie Jr.

After eight successful years at Mecklenburg, Richardson served as director of academics at St. Paul's Normal School in Lawrenceville, Virginia, for one year. In 1936 the state superintendent of public instruction appointed Richardson assistant supervisor of Negro education, making him the "first Negro to be named to the staff of the State Department of Education" (Richardson Papers).

During this period he also continued his education. In 1939 he graduated with a master's degree in education from Butler University in Indianapolis, Indiana. In addition he received a doctor of education degree from Columbia University in New York in 1946. By 1951 he had risen to associate supervisor of elementary and secondary education in Virginia. In recognition of Richardson's extraordinary contributions to the evolution of public education during its nascent years, Virginia State

College conferred upon him the honorary degree of doctor of laws in June 1957. On 1 September 1966 Richardson achieved the highest rank hitherto by a black in the Virginia Department of Education: associate director of the division of secondary education. He excelled in this position until his retirement in April 1969.

From the Department of Education, Richardson launched pioneering innovative curricula while ferreting out Jim Crow laws at all levels. To black students at myriad school functions he brought national and world news, faith in them and in God, optimism, perspectives about professions few black students were taught to aspire to (doctor, lawyer, stenographer), and news about technological advancements (computers and space travel). To educators at regional, state, and national conferences he promulgated progressive but controversial pedagogical and political ideas.

In a seventh-grade graduation address titled "There Is Work to Be Done" delivered in 1945, for instance, Richardson articulated the civic skills needed by students within the shadow of post–World War II: sense of local and national community, self-reliance, and pragmatism. He concluded by exhorting students to become "builders and designers, not merely of the future, but helpers in building and designing the present. You have active minds. You have great minds, and great minds have purposes—others have wishes" (Richardson Papers).

In one of his early conference papers, "Creative Thinking," Richardson described strategies that presaged twenty-first-century teaching and learning theory and practice. He stressed the need for active learning (children assuming the roles of characters in a story), reader-response theory (predicting the outcome of partially read materials), and problem-based learning (recognizing and defining a problem). In the dedication address "Why Dedicate This School?" he envisioned a student-centered class in which students develop learning criteria, express themselves through various media, work constructively without teacher mediation, apply knowledge in new settings, and connect "school subjects to out of school experiences" (Richardson Papers), the latter clearly prefiguring service learning. Later in the address Richardson proffered a view of critical thinking and error among beginning writers that is remarkably prophetic of *Errors and Expectations: A Guide for the Teacher of Basic Writing* (1977), Mina P. Shaughnessy's seminal and transforming analysis of student error: "While teachers must not cease to wage a vigilant warfare against errors in expression, it may well be that a vigorous consideration of the art of thinking may lead to unexpected improvement in expression" (Richardson Papers).

While at the Department of Education, Richardson courageously and untiringly positioned the spirit and the implications of *Brown v. Board of Education* before supervisors, teachers, and parents, even as the department embraced malicious and racist ploys to usurp the 1954 Supreme Court ruling for well over a decade. Richardson cautioned that the department's myopic view of integration undercut democracy for all: "In raising the issue of integration, the Negro is merely seeking the full political, economic and social rights guaranteed by the world's great documents of rights. He realizes that it is impossible to teach the virtues of democracy without democratic practice" ("Why the Issue of Integration," Richardson Papers). Richardson's book, *The Development of Negro Education in Virginia 1813–1970* (1976), recounts the long struggle by blacks to realize democracy and the Herculean efforts that he gave to the democratization of public education in Virginia.

Richardson retired on 4 April 1969 and died ten years later. The *Richmond News Leader* parsimoniously marked his passing, but the brevity of the obituary will never diminish the legacy Richardson left to education and civil rights in Virginia. Arguably he, more than any single figure, orchestrated integration and shaped the quality of education in Virginia public schools throughout most of the twentieth century.

FURTHER READING
The Archie G. Richardson Papers are housed in the Department of Special Collections and Archives, Johnston Memorial Library, Virginia State University, Petersburg, Virginia.

FLOYD OGBURN JR.

Richardson, Clifton Frederick, Sr. (31 Oct. 1891–Aug. 1939) publisher, civic and civil rights leader in Houston during the first half of the twentieth century, was born in Marshall, Texas, the third child and only son of Charlie and Betty Richardson. His father, born in Mississippi, made a living cleaning coaches. His mother, born in Texas to parents from Mississippi, mostly worked at home.

Richardson studied at Bishop College in Marshall; he graduated with honors in 1909, probably from a secondary education program, since he was eighteen years old. Many of the colleges later recognized as "historically black" maintained such programs in addition to a bachelor's degree curriculum, because students of African descent were often denied a high school education in public schools. The same year, he married Ruby Leola Rice on 13 June 1909; for a time, the newlyweds lived with her parents, John F. and Eliza J. Rice, and Ruby's younger sisters. They had three sons, Clifton F. Richardson Jr., Leon, and Robert, born between 1911 and 1917.

The family moved to Dallas around 1911, where Richardson worked as a printer and reporter for the Dallas *Express.* Moving to Houston, he worked for the *Western Star,* and the Houston *Witness.* In 1916 he cofounded the Houston *Observer* with Campbell Gilmore, R. T. Andres, and William Nickerson, becoming first manager and then editor. He left the *Observer* in 1919, starting the Houston *Informer* in May of the same year, billing it as "the South's Greatest Race Newspaper."

In 1918 Richardson was elected to the executive committee of a newly formed Houston branch of the NAACP. There was a good deal conflict within the chapter, and he resigned in 1922. The *Informer* office was ransacked by a band of men in hoods in 1920 after Richardson detailed a Houston official's Ku Klux Klan ties. His life was threatened at least three times in the next several years. When he received death threats from the Klan, around 1922, he continued the same coverage and editorials, proudly brandishing a pistol he carried for protection. In 1925 he established a New Orleans bureau of the *Informer.*

Richardson persistently demanded compliance with laws requiring that accommodations on public carriers be equal as well as separate, while still demanding an end to segregation entirely. He campaigned for improved educational facilities and teachers' pay, housing and road improvements, creation of parks open to citizens of African descent, and to end violence against citizens of dark complexion. "If Congress can appropriate large sums" to enforce Prohibition of alcoholic beverages, he wrote, "the same Congress could appropriate sufficient money to run down and punish a few of the many lynchers, mobocrats and anarchists who are making this country the most barbarous and uncivilized of all the supposed enlightened nations of the world" (Cronin, citing "America's Reign of Lynch Law," *Houston Informer,* 10 July 1920).

The *Observer* prospered during the 1920s. Beginning as an eight-page, seven-column paper, published weekly, it sold for five cents a copy. Regional and national news was obtained from

Associated Negro Press, Lincoln News Service, and Preston News Service. During the 1920s, Houston's population more than doubled, and the black population grew from 34,000 to 63,337. Competing with four existing newspapers written by and for Houston citizens of African descent, the *Informer* had a circulation of 16,500, the largest in the state, and a staff of ten, within two years of its founding. Sufficient advertising allowed expansion to ten pages in 1923. Some weeks, Richardson's staff sold more than 2,800 copies on the street and after church on Sundays.

When leaders of the tiny Republican Party in Texas attempted to increase its influence by promoting a "Lily White" membership, a statewide Independent Voters League was formed from a number of local leagues in November 1927. The League was willing to support either Democratic or Republican candidates who offered tangible benefit to the African American population. Richardson was elected as secretary, while Waco attorney R. D. Evans became president. The local organizations promoted street lighting, and improvements in local schools. Richardson wrote an article for the *Pittsburgh Courier*, published 3 September 1927, titled "Why I Stay in Texas and Fight," contrasting with the *Chicago Defender*'s (and Dallas *Express*) call for Americans of African descent to leave the South and migrate north.

Richardson merged the *Informer* into the Webster-Richardson Publishing Company, organized 6 April 1927, receiving 100 shares in the new enterprise. George H. Webster received another 100 shares for his print shop, while attorneys Carter Walker Wesley and J. Alston Atkins received 50 shares each for cash investments of $5,000. It was not a match made in heaven. Wesley insisted on a sophisticated bookkeeping system, while Richardson was more relaxed; Richardson objected to tabloid style content he found offensive, which Wesley considered good for business. Wesley was ruthlessly determined to get control, and succeeded in January 1931, merging the *Informer* with the *Texas Freeman*. Richardson immediately founded the Houston *Defender*. Both papers continued to publish into the twenty-first century.

A founder of the Progressive Voters League in 1936, Richardson was one of many working to secure a U.S. Supreme Court decision overturning the Texas Democratic Party's "whites only" primary election rule. His original contribution, working with Julius White and Dr. William M. Drake, was the 1938 case, *C.F. Richardson et al. v.*

Executive Committee of the Democratic Party for the City of Houston, Harris County, et al. He argued that the Houston city charter declared "all qualified voters of the city shall vote in all primary elections," whatever might otherwise be permitted by state or federal law. The national NAACP declined to take up the case, wary of the disastrous result of the local NAACP pursuing *Grovey v. Townsend*, against the advice of the national organization, in 1935—resulting in a Supreme Court ruling that the Democratic Party was a private organization which could set any standards it pleased for a primary election. That ruling was overturned after Richardson's death, when the Supreme Court recognized in the 1944 decision *Smith v. Allwright*, that the "white primary" violated the Fifteenth Amendment.

In 1937 Richardson was elected senior branch president of the Houston NAACP, with Lulu White appointed director of the Youth Council. The chapter was bitterly split between supporters of Richardson and Wesley. Richardson died of nephritis (Bright's disease), succeeded by White as interim president. Wesley wrote in memoriam, "Like all men who fight prolifically and on many fronts, Richardson was not always right. But he always had the courage of his convictions and the strength of will and spirit to fight, whether he were alone or whether he was on the side of the majority" (Cronin, citing Wesley, "Death Ends Militant Editor's Ceaseless Fight for Race Rights," *Houston Informer*, 2 Dec. 1939, 1). Richardson was posthumously entered in the Black Press Gallery at Howard University in 1991.

FURTHER READING

Barr, Alwyn. *Black Texans: A History of African Americans in Texas, 1528–1995* (1996).

Cronin, Mary F. "C. F. Richardson and the *Houston Informer*'s Fight for Racial Equality in the 1920s." *American Journalism*, 23, no. 3 (summer 2006): 79–103.

Hine, Darlene Clark, *Black Victory: The Rise and Fall of the White Primary in Texas* (2003).

Lavergne, Gary M. *Before Brown: Heman Marion Sweatt, Thurgood Marshall, and the Long Road to Justice* (2010).

CHARLES ROSENBERG

Richardson, Gloria St. Clair Hayes (6 May 1922–), civil rights activist, was born Gloria St. Clair Hayes in Baltimore, Maryland, the only child of John Edward Hayes, a pharmacist, and Mabel St. Clair. In 1931 her family moved to her mother's birthplace

Cambridge, a port town of about thirteen thousand people on Maryland's Eastern Shore. Gloria spent much of her youth in her maternal grandparents' house. The St. Clair family had a long tradition of leadership in Cambridge, stretching back to the years before the Civil War, when Gloria's great-grandfather, Cyrus St. Clair, a free black butcher, helped found the Cambridge Colonization movement. Gloria's grandfather, Maynadier St. Clair, was a city commissioner for nearly fifty years and a friend of many noteworthy African Americans, such as Mordecai Johnson, the president of Howard University.

In the fall of 1938 Hayes enrolled at Howard University. While majoring in sociology, she studied with RAYFORD LOGAN, E. FRANKLIN FRAZIER, STERLING BROWN, and other prominent black intellectuals. They reinforced several lessons she had learned as a youth. As she recalled, they taught that "you were as good as anybody" (Levy, 50), that blacks had a long history of achievement, and that the black middle class had a duty to serve the black community. In addition, as Annette Brock has written, she learned "how to analyze racism and the dynamics of social action" (Levy, 50). While at Howard, Hayes also participated in a number of civil rights protests against segregation in Washington, D.C.

Not long after her graduation in 1942 Hayes returned to Cambridge, where she married Harry Richardson, a teacher with whom she had two daughters, and encountered the "color line." In spite of her degree and her family's reputation, she could not obtain employment in her chosen field because blacks were not hired as social workers. She worked briefly as a civil servant in Washington, D.C., and then returned to Cambridge where she may have worked, part-time, at her family's pharmacy. After divorcing her husband in 1960, however, she was compelled to work full-time at the pharmacy while raising her two daughters. While she took note of the burgeoning civil rights movement, she found little if any time for political activism.

Meanwhile Cambridge fell into a deep economic depression precipitated by the collapse of the city's dominant business, the Phillips Packing Company. By the early 1960s unemployment ran between 7 and 11 percent for whites and upward of 20 percent for blacks. In early 1962 Freedom Riders organized by the Civic Interest Group, a civil rights organization active in Baltimore and its environs, arrived in Cambridge, where they staged a series of sit-ins at local establishments. The riders came

to Cambridge on the invitation of Frederick St. Clair, Richardson's cousin. Richardson did not play an active role in these early protests; rather, her daughter Donna Richardson drew her into the civil rights movement. In the late spring of 1962 Gloria Richardson agreed to become the adult supervisor of the Cambridge Nonviolent Action Committee (CNAC). Along with Yolanda St. Clair, Frederick St. Clair's wife, she attended a Student Nonviolent Coordinating Committee (SNCC) conference in Atlanta, where the CNAC became the only adult-led affiliate of SNCC.

After organizing a voter education project called Project Eastern Shore, which sought to raise the political consciousness of Cambridge's blacks, the CNAC initiated a series of sustained demonstrations in the spring of 1963. These demonstrations in Cambridge began before the more famous events in Birmingham, Alabama, led by MARTIN LUTHER KING JR., which are often credited with sparking the wave of uprisings that erupted across the South. During the spring of 1963, Richardson and eighty other demonstrators were arrested. Richardson helped galvanize a grassroots mass movement, one with a working-class base and a reputation for militancy. While the CNAC staged rallies at churches, it did not seek to develop a church-based movement. Rather, Richardson made clear that she wanted to reach both the "saved and the sinners," and she was not content with the gradualism practiced by her grandfather and many middle-class black leaders. More often than protesters in other communities, those in Cambridge chose jail rather than bail when arrested. In addition Cambridge's blacks displayed a willingness to defend themselves with guns when faced with violence or threats of violence by whites, with at least the tacit approval of the CNAC and Richardson. While Richardson herself never carried a gun, in late 1963 she attended a meeting in Detroit, Michigan, where MALCOLM X delivered his famous "Message to the Grassroots" address and where he called for using "any means necessary" to achieve freedom. Richardson subsequently grew closer to Malcolm X, and in 1964 they cofounded Associated Community Teams (ACT), a coalition of independent black radicals.

During the summer of 1963, Cambridge was subjected to a series of confrontations and riots. In early June, Richardson appealed to Attorney General Robert Kennedy for aid; as a result Maryland's governor, J. Millard Tawes, mobilized the National Guard and stationed them in Cambridge for months. In late July a meeting that included Robert Kennedy, Robert Weaver, Richardson, and Cambridge officials was convened in Washington. Armed with a detailed survey of the needs and desires of Cambridge's blacks, Richardson arrived at the meeting determined to win real reforms. Her efforts prompted Kennedy to hammer out an unprecedented agreement, known as the "Treaty of Cambridge," that met most of the CNAC's demands. Federal, state, and local officials pledged to construct public housing, establish an innovative job-training program, speed up the desegregation of schools, establish a bona fide biracial human relations committee, and amend the city charter to ban racial segregation in public places. Partly in recognition of her role in producing this agreement and as a sign of the nationwide attention given these events, Richardson was one of a handful of women officially recognized at the March on Washington in August 1963.

In the late fall of 1963, Richardson shocked moderates in Cambridge and nationwide when she refused to encourage blacks in Cambridge to vote in favor of a referendum on the city charter amendment because she did not believe that constitutionally mandated rights should be put to a vote. "A first-class citizen does not plead to the white power structure to give him something that the whites have no power to give or take away" (Levy, 97). Moderates, black and white, did not understand why Richardson called for blacks not to vote on the referendum when blacks in the Deep South were fighting and dying for the right to vote, and many blamed her when the referendum was defeated, even though white voters had overwhelmingly rejected this ban on racial discrimination.

In the spring of 1964 Richardson further displayed her militancy when she refused to comply with an order issued by the commander of the National Guard that she disperse demonstrators who had gathered to protest against an appearance by George Wallace in Cambridge. While the commander of the guard blamed Richardson for the violence that followed, many younger black radicals heralded her for her willingness to hold her ground. (Many of these same activists were growing disillusioned with King for his tendency to compromise at key moments.)

Richardson's views often differed from those of the mainstream civil rights movement as represented by King and the NAACP. She supported the right to armed self-defense. While she favored desegregation of public establishments, she always insisted that the main goals of the movement were social and economic, particularly jobs and housing. She was unwilling to accommodate white moderates for the sake of accommodation alone. She did not reject electoral politics, but she did not see the vote as an end in itself but rather as part of the process to gain full equality. The fact that Richardson was a woman further confounded many of her critics, who admired the "feminine" reserve of civil rights activists like ROSA PARKS while characterizing Richardson's firebrand nature as unladylike.

In September 1964 Richardson married Frank Dandridge, a freelance photographer, and moved to New York City, his home. They had no children, and after their marriage ended in divorce, she remained in New York with her younger daughter Tamara Richardson. Even though she became involved in local politics, especially labor activities, she lived in virtual anonymity. Ironically, her advocacy of armed self-defense and emphasis on the economic needs of the black community, which seemed out of place in the early 1960s, foretold the turn of the civil rights movement to Black Power. Similarly her militancy came to serve as a model to numerous young women, who could see that she fit in a long tradition of female black activists stretching back to HARRIET TUBMAN and IDA B. WELLS and forward to ANGELA DAVIS. Most importantly she should be remembered as a leader of one of the most vibrant local struggles for civil rights, one that mobilized ordinary black citizens in Cambridge, Maryland, in a struggle for full equality.

FURTHER READING

Brock, Annette K. "Gloria Richardson and the Cambridge Movement," in *Women in the Civil Rights Movement*, eds. Vicki L. Crawford, Jacqueline Anne Rouse, and Barbara Woods (1993).

Harley, Sharon. "'Chronicle of a Death Foretold': Gloria Richardson, the Cambridge Movement, and the Radical Black Activist Tradition," in *Sisters in the Struggle*, eds. Bettye Collier-Thomas and V.P. Franklin (2001).

Levy, Peter B. *Civil War on Race Street: The Civil Rights Movement in Cambridge, Maryland* (2003).

Miller, Sandra Y. "Recasting Civil Rights Leadership: Gloria Richardson and the Cambridge Movement," *Journal of Black Studies* 26, no. 6 (July 1996): 668–687.

Robnett, Belinda. *How Long? How Long: African-American Women in the Struggle for Civil Rights* (1997).

PETER B. LEVY

Richardson, Judy (c. 1944–), civil rights activist and film producer, was born in Tarrytown, in suburban Westchester County, New York, the daughter of William "Billy" Richardson, an auto worker and union activist, and Mae Louise Tucker Richardson, who was at that time a homemaker. When Judy was seven her father died at work, forcing her mother to reenter the workforce as a civil servant. Despite efforts to place Judy on a business track at her high school, Mae Louise Richardson encouraged her daughter to take college preparatory courses, in which she was the only black student.

In 1962 Richardson entered Swarthmore College in Swarthmore, Pennsylvania, on a full scholarship. She was one of eight African American freshmen, the largest group of black students at the college to that date. During her first year at Swarthmore, Richardson began working with the Cambridge Movement in Cambridge, Maryland. Led by the activist GLORIA RICHARDSON (no relation), the Cambridge Movement was one of the most dynamic and radical community organization projects working to desegregate public accommodations in the South. Judy Richardson later recalled her admiration for Gloria Richardson's "energy, no-holds barred, speaking truth to power" (Hogan, p. 122). In Maryland, she also met several like-minded young civil rights workers involved in SNCC (the Student Nonviolent Coordinating Committee). The harsh and violent white resistance to the Cambridge protestors proved cathartic to Richardson after the more subtle racism of Westchester County and Swarthmore. After such experiences, including being arrested at a sit-in, Richardson would write of Swarthmore, "It's not exciting. It's not real. The *real* thing is Cambridge" (Logan, p. 125).

Richardson left Swarthmore in the fall of 1963 to work for SNCC full-time at its national office in Atlanta. She began as a secretary for the organization's executive secretary, JAMES FORMAN. During the Mississippi Freedom Summer (1964), Richardson moved to Greenwood, Mississippi, to work on an SNCC voter registration project. In Lowndes County, Alabama, Richardson worked with STOKELY CARMICHAEL and others in the Lowndes County Freedom Organization, an effort to build an independent African American political party in the South.

After the Freedom Summer and Lowndes County, Richardson ran the SNCC communications director Julian Bond's campaign office during his historic run for a seat in the Georgia House of Representatives. The campaign was successful, ensuring that Bond and six others were the first African Americans elected to the Georgia house since 1907. Richardson also founded a "Freedom School" in Chicago during this time. The school encouraged young Northern and Southern SNCC activists (of both races) to come together and discuss how to fight oppression and racism in their respective communities.

In the 1970s Richardson worked with several former SNCC colleagues to open Drum & Spear Bookstore, which became the largest African American bookstore in the United States. As the store's buyer for children's literature, she became interested in the development of black children's literature. Her research eventually led her to write an article on that topic, "Black Children's Books: An Overview," which was published in *The Journal of Negro Education* in 1974. In 1979 Richardson began a project with HENRY HAMPTON/Blackside Productions, which would eventually become *Eyes on the Prize*, a six-hour 1987 PBS documentary series on the civil rights movement. So acclaimed was the series that in 1990 eight additional hours were broadcast through PBS. Richardson began as a researcher and content advisor, though was appointed associate producer for the second segment. Both series became widely used resources in high school and college classrooms to teach the civil rights movement.

Since the 1990s Richardson has worked at Northern Light Productions as a senior producer. The Boston-based film company has produced several documentaries on black history, including *Slave Catchers, Slave Resisters* (2005), *Malcolm X: Make It Plain* (1994), and *Scarred Justice* (2008), a one-hour documentary on the 1968 Orangeburg Massacre in South Carolina, an event dubbed "The Kent State of the South." In 2010 the University of Illinois Press published the recollections of fifty-two civil rights activists, including Richardson, in *Hands on the Freedom Plow: Personal Accounts by Women in SNCC*. Richardson was one of the six editors of the volume. She has also served as a consultant and has created documentaries for several museums. Her honors include Peabody Awards for *Eyes on the Prize* (1988) and *Malcolm X* (1995), and Emmy Awards (1987, 1991) and an Academy Award nomination (1988) for *Eyes on the Prize*.

FURTHER READING

"The HistoryMakers." *The HistoryMakers.com— African American History Archive*. The History Makers, 9 Apr. 2007. Available at http://www.

thehistorymakers.com/biography/biography. asp?bioindex=1613&category&#x00 3D;Mediamakers&occupation=Do cumentary Film Producer & Former SNCC Activist&name=Judy Richardson. Accessed 30 June 2010.

Hogan, Wesley C. *Many Minds, One Heart: SNC's Dream For A New America* (2009).

Holsaert, Faith S., Martha Prescod, Norman Noonan, Judy Richardson, Betty Garman Robinson, Jean Smith Young, and Dorothy M. Zellner, eds. *Hands on the Freedom Plow: Personal Accounts by Women in SNCC* (2010).

"Veterans of the Civil Rights Movement—Judy Richardson." Interview by Jean Wiley. *Civil Rights Movement Veterans—CORE, NAACP, SCLC, SNCC.* 15 July 2008. Available at http://www.crmvet.org/ nars/judyrich.htm. Accessed 2 July 2010.

SAMANTHA CROWELL

Richardson, Maude B. (9 Mar. 1894–26 May 1976), civic, political, and civil rights activist, was born in Arkansas and grew up in St. Louis, Missouri. She moved to New York City in 1913. Richardson attended the Pratt Institute, a vocational school, and lived in Brooklyn the rest of her life. The mother of three, Richardson was a consummate community activist, fighting for better schools and health clinics, affordable housing, and jobs in the Bedford-Stuyvesant section of Brooklyn. Richardson was vice president of the Brooklyn chapter of the NAACP, a leader in the local Parent Teacher Association and the Brooklyn Urban League, vice chair of the Negro Republicans of Kings County in the 1950s, and staff writer for the *New York Amsterdam News* and the *People's Voice*.

Richardson's commitment to eradicating racial inequality took many forms. She was a leader of the Peoples' Committee of Brooklyn, which, among other efforts, challenged negative representations of African Americans in the press. In the struggle against employment discrimination, Richardson served as the chair of the Brooklyn Council for a Permanent Fair Employment Practice Committee. When World War II ended, African Americans found it difficult to secure well-paying jobs and decent housing. New York City may not have been a formal Jim Crow city, but segregation and discrimination were pervasive nonetheless. Richardson also chaired the Brooklyn Provisional Committee for Jobs, which embraced the logic of the Fair Employment Practices Commission (FEPC) even after it expired and fought for jobs for community residents, sometimes one at a time.

Under the auspices of the Brooklyn Provisional Committee for Jobs, Richardson sponsored a political symposium that called together city council candidates. She demanded that they propose job-creation projects for African Americans. Richardson knew that most local merchants would not end racially based discrimination in their hiring practices without a great deal of pressure, so her organization staged protests and boycotts. At the same time Richardson believed that grassroots pressure would not be sufficient to secure long-term, structural change, so she sought to make the local and state levels of government allies in the fight. She forced commitments from candidates to bring improvements to the neighborhood and then worked to hold them to their word.

By the mid-1940s many African Americans had abandoned the Republican Party, but Richardson was among those who did not. Her community-based work and her engagement in the local Republican Party club led her directly into electoral politics. In 1945 Bedford-Stuyvesant residents formed a nonpartisan committee to choose the candidate they believed would get broad public support in the city council race. Richardson was their choice. During her campaign she underscored the poor state of race relations in northern cities. Claiming that New York City was "sitting on an atomic bomb of race hatred" (*Brooklyn Eagle*, 31 Oct. 1945, 19), she promised to sponsor legislation to make it illegal to advocate racial intolerance and discrimination. Despite the Bedford-Stuyvesant community's support, Richardson lost the race. But her appetite for elected politics was only whetted.

The following year Richardson was one of only two African American women who ran for elected office in New York City. They were the only black candidates from Brooklyn, and they were vying for the same state assembly seat. Richardson squared off against ADA B. JACKSON in the Republican primary. The two women had similar backgrounds— both were long-standing, highly respected citizens in Bedford-Stuyvesant, active in their churches and community. They had worked with organizations to fight for racial equality and led numerous endeavors to improve the area's quality of life. They even shared the distinction of polling in the top ten of the *New York Amsterdam News*'s "10 Leading Brooklynites" annual contest.

Richardson had some important advantages, including strong party support and the endorsement of the city's largest black newspaper, the *Amsterdam News*. She defeated Jackson in the Republican primary and faced the Democratic incumbent John Walsh in the general election. Walsh, backed by the powerful Democratic machine, thought he had little cause for concern, especially because Brooklyn's 125,000 black residents had never sent an African American to a public office, and no district in New York State had sent a black woman to office. In the November 1946 election the vote was so close that a recount was necessary. Richardson lost to the Democratic incumbent by only seventy-seven votes. In a city as heavily Democratic as New York was, her near-victory was noteworthy for the challenge it represented to the traditional political power structure, and it sounded a warning to the borough's Democrats to change their stance on running African American candidates.

In 1948 Richardson and BERTRAM L. BAKER, both African American candidates, faced off in a campaign for a seat in the New York State Assembly. With the two major parties fielding black candidates, it was certain that Brooklyn would finally have its first black elected official. Baker ran on both the Democratic Party and the American Labor Party (ALP) tickets. Richardson ran again on the Republican slate. In the presidential election year of 1948 the Seventeenth Assembly District supported the Democratic candidate, as it usually did. Baker beat Richardson by a 2-to-1 margin to become the first African American elected in Brooklyn.

Despite Richardson's work for racial equality and community betterment, the political climate in Brooklyn did not sustain this vocally pro-Republican candidate. Richardson had run and lost her last political race. Her commitment to the Republican Party remained strong, however. In 1956 she gave the nominating speech for Richard Nixon as the presidential candidate at the Republican Party National Convention. She also remained a dedicated community activist, fighting until her death for a better quality of life for Brooklyn residents and an end to discrimination. Richardson died in Brooklyn.

FURTHER READING

Newspaper clippings on Richardson's activities are in the Brooklyn Public Library and the Schomburg Center for Research in Black Culture in New York City.

Brooklyn Eagle New York Amsterdam News

Obituary: *New York Times*, 31 May 1976.

JULIE GALLAGHER

Richardson, Willis (5 Nov. 1889–17 Nov. 1977), playwright, was born in Wilmington, North Carolina, the only child of Willis Wilder, a laborer, and Agnes Ann Harper. In 1898, when Richardson was nine years old, a white mob burned down the newspaper offices of a Wilmington newspaperman named ALEXANDER MANLY and precipitated a coup d'état in North Carolina's largest city, which resulted in the deaths of at least sixteen blacks. Many African Americans left Wilmington in the months that followed, among them Richardson and his family, who moved to Washington, D.C., because of the riots and the threats made on his father's life. Richardson would live in Washington until his death in 1977.

After completing elementary school, Richardson attended the M Street School (later Dunbar High School) from 1906 until 1910. At the school, Richardson had contact with people who would later be important in his development as a dramatist. CARTER G. WOODSON, founder of *Negro History Week* and a history teacher at the school from 1909 to 1918, later hired Richardson to edit two anthologies of African American plays. MARY P. BURRILL, an English teacher and playwright, encouraged Richardson in his writing and was instrumental in having Richardson's first play read and evaluated by ALAIN LOCKE. Another M Street English teacher, ANGELINA WELD GRIMKÉ, whose own play, *Rachel*, would give Richardson the initial impetus for his career as a dramatist, reviewed Richardson's poems before he began writing plays.

In 1911, unable to afford college tuition, Richardson began working as a "skilled helper" in the wetting division of the Bureau of Engraving and Printing. In 1912 he met Mary Ellen Jones. After the couple married in 1914, Richardson converted to Roman Catholicism, his bride's religion, and by 1921 they had three daughters.

First drawn to writing poetry, Richardson enrolled in a correspondence course, entitled Poetry and Versification, in 1915. In March of 1916, however, after seeing Grimké's play *Rachel* (1916), he switched his focus from poetry to drama. Grimké and other African American playwrights of that decade and the next used racial conflict as the theme of their plays. Richardson soon developed strong opinions about African American drama, and in the fall of 1919, three years after seeing *Rachel*, Richardson's essay "The Hope of a Negro Drama," his first of six essays on the theater, was published in *Crisis* magazine. In the essay Richardson criticized plays written by African Americans, citing *Rachel* as an example, for "showing the manner in which Negroes are treated by white people in the United States." Richardson advocated that African American playwrights should focus on problems within the black community, not on racial tensions. In this manner, Richardson's plays differed from most of the nearly 400 plays written by African Americans by 1930 (many of which were never produced).

Through his publications with *Crisis*, Richardson met W. E. B. DuBois who, in December 1920, arranged for publication of Richardson's first play for children, *The King's Dilemma*, in *The Brownies' Book*, a magazine for African American children that DuBois had helped found. Over the next year Richardson wrote three more one-act children's plays for the publication: *The Gypsy's Finger-Ring* (March 1921), *The Children's Treasure* (June 1921), and *The Dragon's Tooth* (Oct. 1921). *The Deacon's Awakening*, his first play for general audiences, was published in *Crisis* in November 1920 and first produced on in January 1921 at a union hall in St. Paul, Minnesota.

Edward Christopher Williams was another early champion of Richardson's work. In 1916, Williams, then a librarian at Howard University, read Richardson's play *The Idle Head* and declared it "the best play he had seen written by a member of our race." After reading several of Richardson's other plays, Williams suggested that the playwright show his work to his former M Street teacher Mary Burrill, who arranged a reading of the play by the Howard University Players for Alain Locke and MONTGOMERY GREGORY.

Because of the scarcity of African American plays, Locke and Gregory were enthusiastic about Richardson's submission. In a December 1922 letter, Gregory wrote to Richardson: "The sun is just beginning to shine on Negro art and I am encouraged to believe that this year will see even finer things." Aside from student productions, *Mortgaged* was the first play written by an African American to be staged at the university. Over the next several years, Richardson's plays *The House of Sham*, *Compromise*, and *The Chip Woman's Fortune* were also produced at Howard University.

DuBois arranged for *The Chip Woman's Fortune* to be produced by the Ethiopian Art Theater, a theater group in Chicago. The play opened in Chicago in January 1923 and began a two-week run at the Howard Theater in April of the same year. In May 1923, the Frazee Theater in New York presented it on a triple bill with Shakespeare's *The Comedy of Errors* and Oscar Wilde's *Salome*. This would be the first time an African American play would be produced on Broadway.

In 1925, Richardson won first place for *The Broken Banjo* in the Krigwa Literary Contest, which was sponsored by *Crisis*. Eugene O'Neill, a judge of the drama entries, remarked that he was "glad the judges all agree on *The Broken Banjo*" and that "Richardson should certainly continue working in his field" (O'Neill, 17–18). The following year Richardson was awarded first place for his play *The Bootblack Lover*.

During the 1920s, through his contacts at Howard University, Richardson began joining other artists and writers at the "Saturday Nighters," an informal group that met at the home of Washington, D.C., poet and playwright GEORGIA DOUGLAS JOHNSON. Richardson was involved with the group from its formation in 1926 until it disbanded ten years later.

After the appearance of several of his plays and essays in the magazines *Crisis*, *Opportunity*, and *The Messenger* and through his involvement with the drama department at Howard University, African American schools and little-theater groups throughout the country sought his one-act plays. For example, in 1926, the Gilpin Players, a black little-theater group in Cleveland, produced Richardson's play *Compromise*, the group's first production by an African American playwright. Rowena Jelliffe, the group's founder, remarked in an interview shortly before her death in 1992 that "Richardson's play was the first bright spot on the Karamu stage" (Interview with the author, 1 Feb. 1992). Among the most popular of his plays were *Compromise*, *Mortgaged*, and *The Broken Banjo*. In addition, Locke included *Flight of the Natives* in his anthology *Plays of Negro Life* (1927).

In 1929 Carter G. Woodson contacted Richardson about gathering African American plays and preparing them for two anthologies. Published in 1930, *Plays and Pageants from the Life of the Negro*, the first collection of plays by African Americans, included Richardson's introduction and four of his plays. In response to requests for materials on African American history, *Negro History in Thirteen Plays* (1935), the second collection, included five plays by Richardson. Both anthologies were published by Associated Publishers, an African American publishing firm in Washington, D.C., for which Woodson was editor.

On retiring from the Bureau in 1954, Richardson again attempted to get his work before the public. He compiled and published the children's plays he had written over thirty years earlier for *The Brownies' Book* and added new plays. Published in 1955 by Associated Publishers, the collection was titled *The King's Dilemma*.

Near the end of his life, Richard son began falling down frequently and at times was unable to stand; he was diagnosed with Padgett's disease, a progressive deterioration of the bone. He died on 7 November 1977. Two weeks after his death, Richardson was recognized as an Outstanding Pioneer in black theater by AUDELCO, the Audience Development Committee, a New York City organization promoting black theater.

FURTHER READING

Gray, Christine Rauchfuss. *Willis Richardson: Forgotten Pioneer of African-American Drama* (1999).

O'Neill, Eugene. Letter in "Comments on the Negro Actor." *The Messenger* 7 (1925).

Sanders, Leslie Catherine. *The Development of Black Theater in America: From Shadows to Selves* (1988).

CHRISTINE RAUCHFUSS GRAY

Richie, Lionel (20 June 1949–), pop musician, singer, and songwriter, was born Lionel Brockman Richie Jr. in Tuskegee, Alabama, to Alberta Riche (née Foster), a school teacher, and Lionel Brockman Richie, a career military officer. Richie's grandmother taught him piano at a young age. As a child, he also played the clarinet and he learned to play the saxophone as a teenager. He later recalled hearing a variety of music as a child: his grandmother played classical music, his parents enjoyed big-band, blues, and country music.

In 1965 Richie's father took a civilian job in Joliet, Illinois, and the family relocated. After attending high school in Joliet, Richie returned to Tuskegee to attend college at the Tuskegee Institute. At Tuskegee, he helped form a student dance band, the Commodores. The original line-up included the guitarist Thomas McClary, the trumpeter William King, the keyboardist Milan Williams, and Richie on saxophone. Performing the songs of JAMES BROWN and other dance-friendly rhythm-and-blues material, the group played campus parties and clubs in Montgomery.

In the summer of 1968, the group moved to New York City to pursue a music career. Under the management of Benjamin Ashburn, a New York public relations executive, the group played regular gigs at Small's Paradise, a Harlem Jazz and R&B club, and at a Chetah's, a teen disco. The group began touring full-time, playing a variety of venues: they toured on the southern rhythm-and-blues circuit opening for the duo Inez and Charlie Foxx, and also played resorts on the French Rivera.

In 1971 Motown invited the group to open for the Jackson Five on its world tour. In the following year, the Commodores signed a record deal with Motown, and in 1974 released its first hit single, "Machine Gun," a synthesizer-heavy funk instrumental from the group's first album, also titled *Machine Gun*. In 1975 they recorded a second LP, *Caught in the Act*, which contained another hit single, the funk number "Caught in the Act."

Richie married Brenda Harvey in 1975. The couple had met as students at Tuskegee. They adopted one child, Nicole Richie, and divorced in 1991. As the Commodores continued to have success touring and recording, Richie began to compose ballads for the group. Their producer anticipated that each Commodores album would contain several slower songs to balance out the upbeat funk numbers that remained the group's specialty. Richie wrote ballads because he thought they would successfully find their way onto the albums. The other members focused on writing dance material. He also may have written ballads as a way to break into the mainstream pop charts. Many considered the Commodores funk numbers to be "too black" for the period's Top-40 format.

Richie wrote "Easy" in 1977, and the smooth ballad became a hit for the Commodores. In the following years, the group also scored hits with Richie's down-tempo numbers "Three Times a Lady" and "Still." In 1981, country singer Kenny Rogers had a huge hit with his recording of Richie's ballad "Lady" and Richie himself had a chart-topping duet with Diana Ross, "Endless Love."

By 1982, with his success as a songwriter and performer becoming evident, Richie opted to record a solo album. Following the huge triumph of his self-titled debut, *Lionel Richie*, he permanently left the group. Two other hit albums ensued: *Can't Slow Down* (1983) and *Dancing on the Ceiling* (1986), and a string of hit singles, including "Hello," "Say You Say Me," and "All Night Long (All Night)" solidified his status as a solo artist.

In 1984, Richie and Michael Jackson composed "We Are the World" for the famine relief effort USA for Africa. A choir of forty-five leading pop stars, including Bruce Springsteen, Bob Dylan, HARRY BELAFONTE, and STEVIE WONDER, recorded the song and released it as a single. It immediately topped the chart, eventually selling over seven and a half million copies. It raised millions of dollars for the relief effort. Richie arguably reached the height of his popularity at this moment.

After his third solo album, the singer retreated from the music business for several years. He did not record another album of new material until 1996, when he released *Louder than Words*. A series of solo albums followed, with some success, but none matched the chart success he had attained in the 1980s. His personal life also fluctuated. Following his divorce from his first wife Brenda, Richie married Diane Alexander in 1996 and had two children, Miles and Sophia. The couple divorced in 2004.

Along with PRINCE and MICHAEL JACKSON, Lionel Richie became one of a group of African American performers who attained huge "crossover" success in the 1980s. They garnered hits on both the mainstream pop as well as the R&B charts. Like Prince and Jackson, Richie was a multi-talented pop performer who performed the material he had written. He also exploited the new music video format to promote his songs. And like the others, he drew on a wide range of pop influences to craft sophisticated pop music. Despite these similarities, however, Richie did not reap nearly the critical attention that Prince and Jackson received. He lacked Jackson's magnetism and eccentricity, and Prince's obsessions, idiosyncrasies, and self-mythologizing. He was a more traditional pop professional. He wrote romantic songs featuring direct, universal sentiments set to catchy melodies.

The lack of critical attention made it easy to overlook Richie's huge success. As a songwriter, he had #1 hits on the charts for nine consecutive years in the late 1970s and 1980s, a feat only equaled by Irving Berlin. His album *Dancing on the Ceiling* was the first to be simultaneously certified gold, platinum, double platinum and triple platinum. Without doubt, his songs helped define the mainstream pop style of a generation.

FURTHER READING

Block Debbie Galante. "Lionel Richie: Flying Solo for 20 Years," *Billboard* (2 Mar. 2002).

Plutzik, Roberta. *Lionel Richie* (1985).

JACK SIMPSON

Richmond, Bill (5 Aug. 1763–28 Dec. 1829), bare-knuckle boxer, was born William Richmond in Staten Island, New York. Both Richmond's mother and his father were Georgia-born slaves whose master eventually took them north to live near New York City.

In 1777 during the early stages of the American Revolution, New York City was occupied by British forces. In a manner not entirely clear from the historical record, Richmond, then only fourteen years old, attracted the attention of Major General Earl Percy, who later became the duke of

Northumberland. Legend has it that Richmond impressed Percy by taking on and soundly beating several British soldiers in a fight at a New York tavern. After witnessing Richmond's prowess with his fists, Percy began to arrange other fights against British soldiers to entertain his fellow officers.

Percy sent his young protégé back to England, where he was apprenticed as a carpenter. After a few years of school and learning the trade of cabinetmaking, Richmond found his real calling as a prizefighter. The world of boxing that Richmond entered in the late 1700s would be virtually unrecognizable to the modern fight fan. The "manly art," which reached its height of popularity in Great Britain during the eighteenth century, was in reality a brutish and unbelievably violent sport. Cheered on by a circle of "sports" and "fancys" (as the rich and the aristocrats who organized, watched, and bet on the fights were known), the combatants were unleashed in a bare-knuckle fight in which few tactics were illegal. In earlier years eye gouging, strangling, kicking, hitting below the belt, striking a man when he was down, and even biting were featured in most bouts. There were no referees, rounds, or time limits, and fights often lasted for hours. A bout ended only when one man signaled that he had had enough. Given the ferocity of these contests, it was not uncommon for men to suffer disabling or disfiguring injuries, and deaths were not unheard of, particularly in the longer fights.

By the time that Richmond began his career a modicum of order had been enforced. In 1734 Jack Broughton, a prizefighter and boxing teacher, established what came to be known as the "London Prize Ring Rules." Gone were the most brutal aspects of the sport, such as choking, eye gouging, and hitting a fallen opponent. There would now be a referee, and rounds would end when a man fell to the ground. The next round would begin thirty seconds later when each fighter was expected to "come up to scratch" or "toe the line" (take his place at a mark scratched into the dirt of the ring). These rule changes also began subtly to alter the nature of the fighting style from one in which men basically rushed at each other like bulls to a more sophisticated sport in which blocking blows and footwork became more important.

It was this still incredibly rough-and-tumble world that Richmond entered sometime in the late 1700s. His early fights are only sketchily documented in the historical record, with even the dates unknown. An undated account of his earliest known fight comes from Pierce Egan, who became famous in England for documenting the thriving fight scene. An unfortunate soldier by the name of George "Docky" Moore made the mistake of insulting Richmond and challenging him to a fight. Moore was a well-known bully and considerably outweighed Richmond. Nevertheless, when the fight eventually took place Richmond so battered Moore that the soldier had to be carried out of the ring. Shortly thereafter Richmond fought two other soldiers on the same day, soundly beating both of them. Other fights followed, mostly of a rather impromptu nature, usually spurred by an insult or a challenge.

By the early 1800s Richmond began to fight more prominent fighters in regularly scheduled and well-publicized bouts. His first foray into higher-level action ended disastrously when he was knocked out by the much larger George Maddox in just three rounds in January 1804. Richmond came back from the defeat with two victories in 1805, against an opponent known only as "Youssop the Jew" and Jack Holmes, whom he whipped in a twenty-six-round contest. In October 1805 Richmond faced the up-and-coming Tom Cribb. Cribb, who became the British champion in 1807, was ten years younger and nearly twenty pounds heavier than Richmond, who was then forty-two years old. For one and a half hours the two men pounded away at each other, until Richmond finally succumbed. Even in this defeat, however, Richmond gained admirers for his skill, tenacity, and bravery.

The respect that Richmond earned in the Cribb fight was all the more significant because for most Englishmen, prizefighting was a white man's sport. The idea of a black man fighting, and perhaps besting, one of England's own caused a number of British sporting fans to question whether the Cribb-Richmond fight should even take place. Richmond's brave stand and his dignified attitude in defeat silenced many of these critics.

Richmond did not fight again until 1809, when he fought and defeated three successive opponents. In August that year he had a rematch with the man who had knocked him out five years earlier, George Maddox. In an epic fifty-two-round bout Richmond finally prevailed and also won a bet of one hundred guineas. Following this fight Richmond married and opened his own tavern, the Horse and Dolphin. In subsequent years the "Black Terror" fought infrequently. In 1810, 1814, and 1815 he fought one fight each year and won them all. He boxed a few exhibition fights in 1816 and 1817, and in 1818 he had his last recorded fight, easily defeating an old opponent, Jack Carter. At the time of the bout Richmond was fifty-five years old.

As his own boxing career wound down Richmond turned more and more of his attention to a small boxing academy that he opened, training the new crop of England's fighters. Undoubtedly his most famous student was another former slave, Tom Molineaux, who arrived in England in 1809 shortly after Richmond opened his tavern and boxing school. Though the reserved and serious Richmond did not always approve of his protégé's frivolous lifestyle and lack of dedication, he saw that Molineaux had the natural talent to challenge Richmond's old nemesis Tom Cribb, who by that time had become the British champion. Under Richmond's guidance Molineaux challenged Cribb in December 1810. Cribb won a controversial bout, and the two men were slated to fight again the following year. By that time Molineaux had drifted from Richmond's tutelage, spent more time drinking and carousing than training, and was battered and defeated by Cribb in eleven rounds.

Though Molineaux died broke and alone at the age of thirty-eight, Richmond, who invested his ring winnings wisely, lived on to the age of sixty-six, passing away in London on 28 December 1829. In 1999 Richmond was inducted into the International Boxing Hall of Fame.

FURTHER READING

Egan, Pierce. *Boxiana, or Sketches of Ancient and Modern Pugilism* (1976).

Gorn, Elliott J. *The Manly Art; Bare-Knuckle Prize Fighting in America* (1986).

MICHAEL L. KRENN

Richmond, Dannie (15 Dec. 1931?–16 Mar. 1988), jazz drummer, was born Charles Daniel Richmond in New York City. Details of his parents are unknown. Richmond gave his birth year as 1935, a date reproduced in nearly all sources, but the *New York Times* obituary gives 1931, which fits better with his activities before joining the bassist CHARLES MINGUS in 1956. Richmond was raised alternately in New York City and Greensboro, North Carolina. Although his memory of his upbringing was contradictory in locating important events—for example, where he took up the tenor saxophone and where he switched to drums—the essential story is clear. It was probably in Greensboro that he first played saxophone; the instrument had been given to his older brother, who had chosen football over music and consequently left it unused. He studied mainly tenor saxophone in high school, but for student ensembles he also was asked to play xylophone and timpani, and he began to acquire a command of percussion technique. As a teenager he worked professionally in rhythm and blues groups, and at one point he dropped out of high school to play with the saxophonist Paul Williams. His mother made him finish school. His graduation, which was somewhat delayed, was presumably around 1949 or 1950, if he was born in 1931.

After graduating, Richmond returned to New York. At the Music Center Conservatory in the Bronx, he studied saxophone, clarinet, flute, piano, vibraphone, and timpani with the distinguished faculty of jazz musicians, which included the drummers MAX ROACH and KENNY CLARKE and the pianist JOHN LEWIS. He also learned to maintain a simple beat on the drum set. After at least two years Richmond moved back in with his mother and continued his musical studies at the Agricultural and Technical College of North Carolina in Greensboro. In the course of jam sessions with fellow students, including the alto saxophonist JACKIE MCLEAN, Richmond took over the drum chair on a day when the regular drummer failed to appear. He played so well that his friends encouraged him to switch instruments. Richmond immediately bought a drum set and practiced incessantly at home.

About six months later, in October 1956, Richmond was back in New York. That month he sat in with Charles Mingus's Jazz Workshop band in place of the drummer Willie Jones, who was failing to keep up a furiously fast version of "Cherokee." Mingus hired Richmond immediately, and over the next decade he held a reasonably stable position in the otherwise ever-changing Jazz Workshop. Mingus said, "Dannie … gave me his complete open mind to work with as clay…. I didn't play drums so I taught Dannie bass. Dannie is me with his own sense of will" (Brian Case, "Minus Mingus," *Melody Maker*, 22 Mar. 1980). Thus his career during this period closely paralleled Mingus's own, with club work mainly in New York, occasional concerts and festivals, a European tour in 1965, and a series of monumental recordings, including *Blues and Roots and Mingus Ah Um* (both 1959), *Charles Mingus Presents Charles Mingus* (1960), *The Black Saint and the Sinner Lady* (1962), *Mingus, Mingus, Mingus, Mingus, Mingus* (1963), *Town Hall Concert* (1964), and *Mingus at Monterey* (1965).

Apart from his work with Mingus, Richmond recorded on the pianist HERBIE NICHOLS's trio album *Love, Gloom, Cash, Love* (1957), and he performed with the tenor saxophonist Zoot Sims, the trumpeter Chet Baker (on and off for about a year from 1958 to 1959), and the pianist Freddie Redd. Richmond was also away from Mingus briefly because of his arrest in Philadelphia, Pennsylvania, for possession of drugs in 1962.

By 1966 Mingus was in semiretirement, owing to severe personal problems, and Richmond moved back and forth between work in the Greensboro area and jobs with Mingus in New York. Around this time he married Juniata (maiden name unknown), a high school principal in Greensboro; they had a daughter. After Mingus stopped working altogether, Richmond formed a cooperative band, LTD, which toured with the rhythm and blues singer Johnny Taylor. Then in 1970 Mingus re-formed his band, with Richmond rejoining briefly for performances at Ronnie Scott's nightclub in London.

While at Scott's Richmond sat in with the then-drummerless folk- and jazz-rock group of the singer and guitarist Jon Mark and the multi-instrumentalist Johnny Almond. As with Mingus years before, his contribution was so useful that he was immediately asked to join the band. He toured Canada and the United States with the Mark-Almond band, made recordings, including *Mark-Almond 2* (1972), and performed in England. He also accompanied the rock singer Joe Cocker and toured with the pianist-singer Elton John.

Richmond rejoined Mingus in 1974. He remained with the band until Mingus's death in 1979, often taking over its direction as the leader's health deteriorated. His British experience made him well suited to Mingus's turn toward jazz-rock during this period, but the recorded results are consistently unsatisfying. Turning back toward the hard bop, soul jazz, and semifree jazz styles in which Mingus's music flourished, Richmond attempted to carry on in the posthumous Mingus Dynasty, but he found it frustrating to deal with frequent changes in group size and instrumentation that undermined his efforts to adhere to Mingus's conception. He left to focus on his own quintet, which he had first led in 1978 with Mingus's sidemen Jack Walrath, Ricky Ford, and Bob Neloms, and with the bassist Eddie Gomez replacing Mingus. Cameron Brown had replaced Gomez by 1980, when they made their finest album, *Dannie Richmond Plays Charles Mingus*. The group remained intact, touring Europe and the United States until 1983, when Richmond began leading a quartet.

Still more successful was Richmond's membership from 1979 onward in the quartet of the tenor saxophonist George Adams and the pianist DON PULLEN, again with Cameron Brown. Their recordings, including *Don't Lose Control* (1979) and *Earth Beams* (1980), convincingly present the stylistic amalgam that the Mingus Dynasty had attempted to capture. Richmond also recorded several albums with the tenor saxophonist Bennie Wallace, including *Bennie Wallace Plays Monk* (1981), and appeared on the tenor saxophonist Lew Tabackin's album *Angelica* (1984). Richmond died of a heart attack in New York City shortly after returning from a West Coast tour with the Adams-Pullen quartet.

After his experiences with rock music, Richmond played a number of ostentatious drum solos, but he may be heard in tasteful and lyrical settings on a variety of solos recorded earlier with Mingus, including "Better Git It in Your Soul" on *Mingus Ah Um* and "Folk Forms, No. 1" on *Charles Mingus Presents Charles Mingus*. It was, however, as an accompanist that he was most distinguished, both for his explicit and detailed manner of supporting Mingus's compositions by accenting melodies and counter-melodies and for his almost telepathic reactions to Mingus's bass playing. This involved, for example, abrupt changes in volume and tempo on pieces such as "Fables of Faubus" on *Mingus Ah Um* and the album-length suite *The Black Saint and the Sinner Lady*.

FURTHER READING

Kernfeld, Barry. *What to Listen for in Jazz* (1995).
Priestley, Brian. *Mingus: A Critical Biography* (1984).
Santoro, Gene. *Myself When I Am Real: The Life and Music of Charles Mingus* (2001).
Obituaries: *New York Times*, 18 Mar. 1988; *The Independent*, 30 Mar. 1988.

This entry is taken from the *American National Biography* and is published here with the permission of the American Council of Learned Societies.

BARRY KERNFELD

Richmond, David (20 Apr. 1941–7 Dec. 1990), civil rights activist who initiated the 1960 Greensboro sit-in, was born David Leinail Richmond in Greensboro, North Carolina, the son of Mozelle Richmond and John F. Richmond.

Richmond grew up in the East White Oak community and attended Jonesboro Elementary and Lincoln Street Junior High School. Richmond subsequently attended Dudley High School in Greensboro, where he served as student body president and was a member of the track team. In his senior year at the high school, he set the state's record for the high jump. After graduating from Dudley High, he entered North Carolina Agricultural and Technical State University in Greensboro in the fall of 1959, majoring in Business Administration and Accounting.

On 1 February 1960 David Richmond and three fellow students, FRANKLIN MCCAIN, EZELL BLAIR JR., and JOSEPH MCNEIL, entered the Woolworth store in downtown Greensboro. The four freshmen had discussed ideas of challenging segregation for some time. When they were declined service at Woolworth, they refused to leave the counter reserved for white seating by law and custom, standing their ground until the store closed at 5:30 P.M. At that time black people were allowed to order food at Woolworth but had to eat it standing away from the counter. When the store closed, the four students promised the manager they would be back the next day. News teams had arrived at the scene and reported about the incident. The story spread quickly, and that same night a committee was formed to coordinate the efforts of the coming days and weeks. By Saturday the number of students had already grown to several thousand. The sit-ins only lasted six days; Woolworth closed its store after a bomb threat. The students then decided to picket in front of the store instead and extended their protests to lunch counters all over the city. Losing $200,000 in business, Woolworth finally integrated the counter in its Greensboro affiliate on 25 July 1960. Within two months the sit-ins had spread to fifty-four cities in nine different states. The students faced physical and verbal abuse but stood by their principle of nonviolence.

According to a statement made by McCain in an article in *The Root* (*The Greensboro Four, 50 Years Later*. http://www.theroot.com/views/greensboro-four-50-years-later, accessed 23 Aug. 2010), Richmond was shy, extremely smart, and easy to be with. But he never wanted to stand out. Richmond himself confirmed in an interview he believed the focus should be on the problem of equal rights for all and not on the question of who does what to achieve that goal. While the other three protestors graduated from A&T and left Greensboro, Richmond dropped out three credits short of his degree. He had gotten married while still in school. Struggling to balance family and university, he worked at the textile manufacturer Cone Mills and later as a job counselor with a federal program under the Comprehensive Employment and Training Act (CETA). When the office closed due to financial cutbacks, he went on

David Richmond, second from left, sits with former North Carolina A&T students Joseph McNeill, Franklin McCain, and Jibreel Khazan at the F.W. Woolworth lunch counter in Greensboro, North Carolina, on 1 February 1980, as they celebrate the 20th anniversary of their historic sit-in. (AP Images.)

to work as a janitor for the Greensboro Health Care Center. It had been difficult for him to find a job after leaving school: once employers learned he was one of the students involved in the sit-ins, they feared he would cause trouble in the workplace. In 1971 Richmond left Greensboro, because of threats he received, and moved to the mountain community of Franklin, North Carolina, where he lived for nine years. He returned to Greensboro to care for his elderly parents in 1980. That same year the Greensboro Chamber of Commerce gave him the Levi Coffin Award for leadership in human rights, human relations, and human resources development in Greensboro. He made public appearances at the sit-ins' anniversary dinners and regularly visited local schools giving talks on his involvement.

Throughout most of his life, Richmond struggled with alcohol and tobacco abuse. He was frustrated that race relations had not improved as much as he had hoped, and he felt he should have been more involved in efforts to establish equality. He was married and divorced twice and had three children—a son, and two daughters. Neither

his family nor his friends realized the extent of his substance abuse until it was already too late. His last public appearance was on 1 February 1990. Ten months later, Richmond died in Greensboro of lung cancer at age forty-nine.

A&T awarded him a posthumous honorary doctorate degree. In early 2010 the International Civil Rights Center and Museum was opened in the old Woolworth building in Greensboro, marking the event's fiftieth anniversary. Other sit-ins across the South had preceded Greensboro, but this incident sparked a mass movement, which produced one of the biggest civil rights organizations of the time, the Student Nonviolent Coordinating Committee (SNCC) and inspired students to successfully challenge segregation in other facilities such as swimming pools, theaters, libraries, museums, churches, and public parks.

FURTHER READING

Oral History Interviews with David Richmond are available at the website of the University of North Carolina at Greensboro.

Chafe, William H. *Civilities and Civil Rights:
Greensboro, North Carolina, and the Black Struggle
for Freedom* (1981).
Wolff, Miles. *Lunch at the 5 & 10* (1990).
www.sitinmovement.org

GRETA KÖHLER

Rickford, John R. (16 Sept. 1949–), linguistics
professor, was born in Georgetown, Guyana, the
youngest of the ten children of Eula (nee Wade),
a homemaker, and Russell Howell Rickford, an
accountant and auditor. In 1968 he began studying
in California on a U.S. scholarship at the University
of California at Santa Cruz (UCSC). He worked
closely with anthropology Professor Roger Keesing
and Professor J. Herman Blake, an African American
sociologist who was working on the biography of
HUEY NEWTON (whom Rickford later met). It was
through a program of Blake's that Rickford first went
out to Daufuskie Island, one of the South Carolina
Sea Islands, in 1970, an experience that he described
as "life/career changing in many ways" (personal
interview with subject, 2007).

Rickford once said that as a mixed-race person his black consciousness and identity crystallized when he came to the United States. He was
elected president of the Black Students Association
at UCSC. He won a book collection contest with
a collection focused on the black experience in
America, and he wrote an honors thesis, "De Train
Dey Ridin on is Full of Dead Man's Bones: Language,
Death and Damnation on Daufuskie, S. Carolina."
Throughout his undergraduate years, Rickford was
an activist. Much of his career-long concern about
affirmative action, the need to mentor students of
color, and his work for equality and justice sprang
from his focused undergraduate activities.

In 1971 Rickford married Angela Marshall, also
a teacher, and a textbook author. They had four
children. That same year, Rickford graduated from
UCSC with a self-designed B.A. in Sociolinguistics.
He studied next at the University of Pennsylvania,
earning an M.A. in Linguistics in 1973 and a Ph.D. in
Linguistics in 1979. Between 1974 and 1980, Rickford
taught linguistics at the University of Guyana and
(for one semester) at Johns Hopkins University.
In 1980 Rickford joined the linguistics faculty of
Stanford University in Palo Alto, California. The
first course he taught was "Black English," later
renamed "African American Vernacular English,"
a course that remained one of his most popular
offerings there. Among the other courses he taught
regularly at Stanford were "Language in Society,"
"Sociolinguistic Field Methods," "Sociolinguistic
Theory and Analysis," "Language in the USA,"
"Ebonics and Other Vernaculars in Schools and
Society," and "Pidgins and Creoles." Such courses
related to Rickford's interest in and passionate concern for black people and the "down pressed" (as
described in Jamaica) everywhere.

Rickford won a Dean's Award for Distinguished
Teaching in 1984 and a Bing Fellowship for Excellence
in Teaching in 1992. He was also the recipient of
the American Book Award (2000), the Linguistics
Society of America's Language and the Public Interest
Award, the Anthropology Association of America's
Anthropology and the Media Award (2002), and a
Fulbright Teaching and Research Fellowship at the
University of the West Indies, Mona, Jamaica. He
was also elected chair of the Faculty Senate of the
Academic Council at Stanford from 2001 to 2002.
In recognition of his contributions to undergraduate education at Stanford, Rickford was appointed
as the Pritzker Fellow in Undergraduate Education
at Stanford in 2004. He was president of the
International Society for Pidgin Creole Linguistics,
a member of the Linguistics Panel of the National
Science Foundation, a member of the executive
committee of the Linguistic Society of America, and
the chair of the Stanford Faculty Senate (2001). From
1998 to 2005 he was also director of African and
African American studies at Stanford, and the holder
of the MARTIN LUTHER KING JR. Chair. During his
tenure, he initiated a series of Learning Expeditions
for students, staff, and faculty to places of historical
and cultural interest in the black world, including
Ghana, Jamaica, Belize, and the South Carolina and
Georgia Sea Islands. Subsequent expeditions have
been to Harlem and Paris Noir.

Rickford's primary academic interest was sociolinguistics, or the study of language in society,
including the relation between language variation and ethnicity, social class, and style; language
change, and the linguistic and sociohistorical forces
that shape it; pidgin and creole languages, especially
Caribbean English Creoles and the Gullah language
of the South Carolina and Georgia Sea Islands;
African American Vernacular English (AAVE); and
the application of linguistics to the understanding
and solution of educational problems, including the
teaching of reading and writing to "at risk" students.
In 2006 he began a three-year NSF-sponsored study
of grammatical variation in AAVE, Appalachian
English, Barbadian, Guyanese, and Jamaican Creole
English. His work on AAVE was equally divided
between theoretical concerns (synchronic ones

about how to describe features like the absence of the copula and negative inversion, and diachronic ones like whether AAVE was descended from or influenced by a creole variety similar to what is currently spoken in Jamaica) and applied ones (how best to use linguistic knowledge to improve the teaching of reading and writing to AAVE speakers).

Rickford was the author of numerous scholarly articles, including publications in *Language*, the premier linguistics journal in the U.S., *Language in Society*, and *Journal of Pidgin and Creole Languages*. He also contributed "Living Language Notes" and wrote an introductory essay for the fourth edition of the *American Heritage Dictionary* (2000). His books include *A Festival of Guyanese Words* (ed., 1978), *Dimensions of a Creole Continuum* (1987), *Analyzing Variation in Language* (co-ed., 1987), *Sociolinguistics and Pidgin-Creole Studies* (ed., 1988), *African American English* (co-ed., 1998), *African American Vernacular English* (1999), *Creole Genesis, Attitudes and Discourse* (co-ed., 1999), *Spoken Soul* (co-authored with his son Russell, 2000), *Style and Sociolinguistic Variation*, (co-ed., 2001), and *Language in the USA: Themes for the 21st Century* (co-ed., 2004). He was also active in many community organizations and activities, such as the Toastmasters, Early Risers Club, Boy Scouts of America, and American Youth Soccer Organization, among others. Rickford's scholarship and active participation in academic conferences were a highly motivating force for younger, aspiring linguists for many years.

FURTHER READING

Rickford, John R. *Dimensions of a Creole Continuum* (1987).

Rickford, John R., ed. *A Festival of Guyanese Words*. 2d ed (1978).

BETHANY K. DUMAS

Ricks, James Thomas "Jimmy" (6 Aug. 1924–2 July 1974), Rhythm and Blues singer, was born in Adrian, Georgia, the son of Felix Ricks and Eula Mae Cephus. Jimmy Ricks was the quintessential R&B bass, the booming lead of the Ravens for ten years, and the benchmark against which every R&B bass for the next twenty years would be measured.

James Thomas Ricks (known as "J.T." to his family and "Ricky" to the rest of the world) was born in 1924 in Adrian, Georgia, a small town of fewer than six hundred people located between Macon and Savannah. His mother (who was fourteen at the time) went to Jacksonville, Florida, to get a better job and Jimmy was raised by his father's brother, Luther, until moving to Jacksonville when he was around thirteen.

During World War II, Ricks relocated to New York City and there embarked upon his professional singing career. In 1945 he was working as a waiter at the Four Hundred Tavern in Harlem, where he met baritone Warren Suttles. The two of them found a shared interest in singing, spending lots of time harmonizing along with tunes on the jukebox (especially those of Ricks's inspiration, the Delta Rhythm Boys' Lee Gaines). This was the beginning of the Ravens. They soon added two second tenors: Leonard Puzey and Ollie Jones.

The public was first introduced to Jimmy Ricks in June 1946, when "Honey" was released on the Hub label (owned by their manager, Ben Bart). The Hub recordings were big jukebox hits, but never really sold in stores. The biggest break of their early career came on 6 December 1946 when they played a benefit show at New York's Apollo Theater. Scheduled with daunting task of following Stan Kenton and NAT KING COLE, the Ravens were, by their own admission, scared. When Ricks sang his first booming bass line of their first number, "My Sugar Is So Refined," however, he brought down the house.

Hub Records didn't last long and between 1947 and 1951 the Ravens recorded with National Records, during which the band began to showcase Ricks's voice.

Their second National record, in June 1947, was "Ol' Man River," a natural for Ricks. This became the Ravens' first formal hit, rising to number ten on the R&B charts. This was followed by "Write Me a Letter," which climbed to number five. However, chart positions alone fail to capture the Ravens' huge popularity at the time: most of their audience heard them on juke boxes and radios.

With the release of "There's No You" in February 1948, Ricks proved that he could lead a beautiful ballad. Bass singers were usually relegated to singing up-tempo tunes.

The Ravens were one of the very few black groups seen on television in the 1940s. In January 1949 they sang "My Sugar Is So Refined" on Ed Sullivan's "Toast of the Town" show. They were supposed to have received an award as the top vocal group in the country, but the show ran overtime and the award presentation wasn't made on the air.

Over the years, there were many, many personnel changes in the Ravens, but there was always one constant: Jimmy Ricks. After National, the group recorded for Columbia/Okeh, Mercury, and Jubilee.

In October 1950 famed orchestra leader Benny Goodman requested that Jimmy Ricks record some songs for Columbia Records with the Benny Goodman Sextet. One of the tunes, "Oh, Babe" (a duet with Nancy Reed), became a big hit for Goodman, and Ricks performed it on the DuMont TV network's "Startime" variety show, which featured the Benny Goodman Sextet as regulars.

The original Ravens broke up after their Columbia days. Leonard Puzey said of Ricks, "He wasn't the easiest person to get along with; he was very egotistical" (Puzey interview with author, 1995). By the time the Ravens started recording for Mercury Records in late 1951 Ricks had gathered a totally different group around him.

In May 1953 the *Pittsburgh Courier* released the results of its eighth Annual Theatrical Poll. In the category of Vocal Quartets, the Ravens placed first, beating out the Clovers and the Dominoes, despite having only two chart hits in the 1950s.

October 1955 saw the end of an era: Jimmy Ricks left the Ravens. There is probably no way to measure the effect Ricks had on R&B, other than to say that he was a yardstick; every R&B bass, from the late 1940s through the 1960s, was held up to Jimmy Ricks to be measured. There were many other R&B basses of note; none of them was Jimmy Ricks.

Ricks did mostly solo work for the rest of his career. He made many recordings, but without much success, through the end of the 1960s. Why did the founding father of R&B basses go on to relative obscurity, recording for a succession of labels, some quite small, with never another hit? Leonard Puzey blamed it on Ricky's personality: "It may be because of his attitude; he was very egotistical. A lot of people didn't like him" (Puzey interview with author, 1995). Also, a bass soloist was unusual and probably not seen as a saleable commodity. When he sang with the Ravens, the harmony acted as a fill-in, so he wasn't seen as a soloist.

In the early 1970s, Ricks worked as the vocalist for the COUNT BASIE orchestra. Jimmy Ricks, the inspiration to an entire generation of bass singers, died in New York on 2 July 1974.

FURTHER READING

Goldberg, Marv. *The Ravens*, http://home.att. net/~marvy42/Ravens/ravens01.html.

MARV GOLDBERG

Ricks, Martha Ann (c. 1817–24 July 1901), a slave who spent fifty years in a quest to see Queen Victoria and present her with a quilt, was born Martha Ann

Erskine. Her fine sewing was displayed on three continents during her lifetime. Her parents, George and Hagar Erskine, were slaves on the George Doherty plantation in Dandridge, Tennessee. Her father was a literate and religious man, purchased in 1815 by Isaac Anderson, a Presbyterian pastor of New Providence Church in Maryville, Tennessee, who tutored him in religious studies. In 1818 Erskine, at thirty-nine years old, became one of the first ordained African American Presbyterian ministers in the United States. He worked several years as a traveling preacher to buy his wife Hagar and at least seven of their children out of slavery. In 1830, with the assistance of the American Colonization Society, founded in 1816 to transport newly freed slaves to Liberia on the West African coast, George Erskine secured passage aboard the brig *Liberia* for his wife and children. Tragically, most members of the Erskine family died early from various causes—only thirteen-year-old Martha Ann, her oldest brother, Wallace, and her youngest brother, Hopkins, survived.

Erskine and at least one brother, Hopkins, remained in Liberia, where she attended school. She read accounts of Queen Victoria (r. 1837–1901) ascending the British throne in 1838, and over the years her admiration for the queen grew. Erskine felt that the queen protected black people. She learned from freed slaves arriving in Liberia about Victoria's welcoming American slaves into Canada. Erskine also witnessed British naval ships patrolling the West African coast to suppress the slave trade, outlawed in Great Britain since 1807. Erskine married Zion Harris, a former slave who was also from Tennessee and who was a missionary at the Methodist Episcopal Mission Station at Heddington, Liberia, where she taught at the mission school. She confided to her husband that she wished to meet Queen Victoria in person to thank the monarch for being such a good "friend of the slave."

The childless union ended tragically in 1854 when Zion Harris died from a lightning strike. Erskine later married a farmer and widower, Henry Ricks, of Clay-Ashland, Liberia, along the St. Paul's River. Henry had three sons, William, John Henry, and George, from his previous marriage, all of whom helped on the farm, where they grew coffee, cane sugar, ginger, and cotton. Like many African American women in Liberia, Ricks sewed her family's clothes and bedcovers. She possessed exceptional talent. A sampling of her work went on display at the Second National Fair held in December 1858 in Monrovia. The fair exhibited the finest agricultural crops, mechanical tools, and crafts of the young nation, which had declared independence the previous year. Ricks entered a pair of silk cotton socks that she had made from the fibers of the cotton silk tree, which grew wild in Liberia and could grow as tall as one hundred feet. The official report of the fair mentioned the extraordinary workmanship of her silk cotton socks.

Ricks's desire to see Queen Victoria did not waver through the years. She was quoted in the *Times* of London in 1892: "I want to go to London and see the Queen. I know I cannot speak to her, but I hope to see her passing along, and then I will return to my farm in Liberia and die contented. The Lord told me I should see the Queen, and I know I will." Ricks had stitched a quilt for the queen featuring a coffee tree in full bloom. Coffee was an important Liberian cash crop, and the *Coffea liberica* bean was indigenous to the country. Ricks wanted the queen to see the beauty of Liberia through the coffee tree. The *Coffee Tree Quilt*, about the size of a large bed, had more than three hundred pointed green leaves with stuffed red coffee berries appliquéd onto a white background.

Many of the Clay-Ashland townspeople heard of the quilt that Ricks had made for the queen. In early 1892 JANE ROBERTS, the widow of the first president of Liberia, JOSEPH JENKINS ROBERTS, visited the Ricks farm to see the quilt. Noting its extraordinary beauty, Roberts pledged to help Ricks sail to England and recruited the Liberian ambassador to Britain, EDWARD W. BLYDEN, to arrange an audience with Queen Victoria. Ricks, who had dreamed for more than fifty years of seeing the British monarch, sailed to England in July 1892. Queen Victoria did indeed extend an invitation to Ricks and her traveling companions. On 26 July 1892 the seventy-six-year-old former slave toured Windsor Castle and received refreshments before meeting Queen Victoria; Edward, the Prince of Wales; his wife, Alexandra; and three of their daughters, Louise, Victoria, and Maude. The *Coffee Tree Quilt* was presented to Queen Victoria, who greatly admired Ricks's fine needlework.

The following year the quilt was sent to Chicago, Illinois, for exhibit at the World's Columbian Exposition in the Liberian display in the Agricultural Building. The daily attendance at the Liberian display, according to fair records, ranged from one to twelve thousand. The fair lasted six months, and more than 180,000 visitors saw Ricks's quilt for Queen Victoria. Ricks is known to have made a second quilt, a duplicate of the *Coffee Tree Quilt*, which she gave to the African Methodist Episcopal (AME) bishop HENRY MCNEAL TURNER during his 1895 visit to Liberia. Bishop Turner lent several items that he collected on his Liberian trip, including the quilt by Ricks, to be displayed at the Atlanta Cotton States and International Exposition in Atlanta, Georgia. The quilt was displayed in the Negro Building, where the former slave HARRIET POWERS's pictorial *Bible Quilt*, now in the permanent collection of the Smithsonian Museum of American Art, was also exhibited.

Ricks died in 1901 on her Clay-Ashland farm, seven months after Queen Victoria died. Ricks's quilt and handcraft items were displayed on three continents—Africa, Europe, and North America—but neither of the *Coffee Tree Quilts*, which at the time were probably the two most-viewed quilts by a black woman of the nineteenth century, is known to have survived.

FURTHER READING

Brown, Hallie Q. "Mrs. Jane Roberts," in *Homespun Heroines and Other Women of Distinction* (1926).

Majors, Monroe W. *Noted Negro Women: Their Triumphs and Activities* (1893).

"Report of the Committee of Adjudication of the Second National Fair," *African Repository* (Nov. 1859).

"A Visitor for the Queen," *Times* (London), 13 July 1892.

KYRA E. HICKS

Riddle, Lesley (13 June 1905–13 July 1979), guitarist, was born in Burnsville, North Carolina. Forced at a young age to work as a laborer, Riddle had a limited formal education. While employed at a local cement plant, he had a serious accident in which he lost his right leg below the knee. Riddle spent much of the 1920s working as a shoe-shiner in the industrial city of Kingsport, Tennessee, where he also sang in churches and played guitar at house parties with other African American musicians. Nicknamed "Esley" by his relatives and friends, Riddle was a fingerstyle and slide guitar player.

Riddle learned his technique by listening to two other black guitar players based in Kingsport, Steve Tarter and Ed Martin. At a gathering in 1928 Riddle met A. P. (Alvin Pleasant) Carter, a singer and the chief songwriter and arranger for the Carter Family, the leading country music group of the late 1920s and early 1930s. (The trio was made up of A. P. and his wife, Sara, along with Sara's cousin Maybelle Carter; Maybelle was married to A. P.'s brother Ezra.) Riddle performed two guitar pieces for A. P. Carter; Carter, deeply impressed, immediately invited Riddle to the Carters' home in nearby Maces Spring, Virginia. Riddle accepted the offer and stayed at A. P. and Sara's house for a week.

During this and subsequent visits with the Carters, Riddle shared numerous songs that his hosts might not otherwise have heard; these songs included African American sacred songs (such as "I'm Working on a Building"), traditional blues compositions, and other secular songs, including one written by Riddle himself, "Lonesome for You Darling." (The Carter Family later recorded this song without crediting it to Riddle.) Additionally, Riddle strongly influenced the characteristic guitar style played by Maybelle Carter, who was the group's lead instrumentalist and who came to be regarded as one of the greatest guitar stylists in country music history. That guitar style—often termed "scratch" guitar—incorporates a fingerstyle technique in which the guitar player's right-hand thumb picks a tune's melody on the bass strings even as the right hand's other fingers strum the rhythm on the high strings, while the left hand adds to the range of notes played on the guitar strings by performing hammer-ons and pull-offs. Maybelle directly learned from Riddle the bluesy licks of "The Cannonball"—among her most acclaimed guitar parts—after he performed that composition for the Carters in 1928.

Over the next decade Riddle joined A. P. Carter on approximately fifteen song-collecting trips in southwest Virginia and northeast Tennessee. Riddle played an active role in collecting songs from the various people they met, as Riddle would memorize a song's tune (a vital skill among music collectors in those days before the availability of portable tape recorders) while Carter would write down the lyrics. Since they were of different races, their traveling together along the back roads of the Jim Crow South frequently placed both Riddle and Carter in awkward situations. Inevitably, Riddle had to stay in separate—and often inferior—accommodations in remote mountain locations. Despite the difficulties of their association, Riddle did not terminate the collaboration. Although he was well aware that Carter was interested in discovering unrecorded and uncopyrighted songs for possible recording by the Carter Family, Riddle recognized A.-P.'s considerable skill as an arranger of old songs.

Years later, when interviewed by musician and folklorist Mike Seeger, Riddle identified the inequality inherent to the relationship—that the Carters ultimately benefited financially from their interaction with Riddle: "I'd be settin' over there sometimes, you know, and pick up the guitar and play something. Four or five months from then, I'd be coming down the street and I'd be hearing it. The Carter Family would be singing it. You know, as many times as I was over at the Carter Family, I never got them together to sing for me but twice the whole time I was over there. They never sang for me. I'd have to do all the picking and singing while I was over there" (quoted in Zwonitzer, 3). Riddle admitted to Seeger that he was occasionally frustrated by his role as a music coach to the Carters because, though in many respects a superior musician to A. P., he was forced to live in obscurity because of the racial divide in the music industry. On several occasions Riddle tried unsuccessfully to teach A. P. how to play the guitar, but the latter struggled to perform even the simplest of chord sequences. Regardless, Riddle remained a loyal friend to the Carters throughout the years he knew them, frequently visiting them in Maces Spring and often helping with cooking and with the caretaking of A. P. and Sara's children. Supposedly, in appreciation for Riddle's friendship, Sara Carter bought Riddle a wooden leg to help him gain more mobility.

In 1937 Riddle married, and in 1942 he left Appalachia to find work in the North. Settling in Rochester, New York, Riddle continued to play music for a few years, performing sacred songs in local Pentecostal churches and at one point allegedly jamming with the blues musician SON HOUSE, a Mississippi native who had likewise settled in Rochester. Gradually playing less and less music, Riddle sold his guitar in 1945.

The late 1950s and early 1960s saw the rise of the urban folk revival across the United States, yet Riddle remained a pioneering figure whose significant contributions to country music history were not widely known. In 1963 Mike Seeger located Riddle in Rochester and encouraged the elder man to resume his performing. Between 1965 and 1978 Seeger made numerous home recordings of Riddle (featuring Riddle's singing of some of his favorite traditional songs, with his own guitar and piano accompaniment). Fourteen of those recordings were issued on the album *Step by Step: Lesley Riddle Meets the Carter Family: Blues, Country, and Sacred Songs* (Rounder Records, 1993) and another recording was issued on the compilation *Close to Home: Old Time Music from Mike Seeger's Collection, 1952–1967* (Smithsonian Folkways, 1997). Lesley Riddle died of lung cancer in Asheville, North Carolina.

FURTHER READING

Zwonitzer, Mark, and Charles Hirshberg.*Will You Miss Me When I'm Gone?:The Carter Family and Their Legacy in American Music* (2002).

TED OLSON

Rideau, Wilbert (13 Feb. 1942–), journalist and prisoner, was born in Lawtell, Louisiana, to Gladys a and Rideau's family moved to Lake Charles, Louisiana, when he was six years old. His parents divorced before he became a teenager. He attended the Second Ward Elementary School, followed by the W.-O. Boston Colored High School until he dropped out.

Rideau worked a series of menial jobs from age thirteen to nineteen, when he was convicted of robbery and murder. On 16 February 1961, he robbed the Gulf National Bank. During the fourteen-thousand-dollar heist, he kidnapped three of the bank's white employees and killed one of them, Julia Ferguson, a forty-nine-year-old woman. An all-white, all-male jury convicted him and sentenced him to death that same year. He would be tried again by all-white, all-male juries in 1964 and in 1970, and he would remain in the Louisiana State Penitentiary at Angola, known nationally for being one the nation's most brutal prisons, for four decades. He never denied his crimes.

In prison, Rideau expanded his horizons by doing two things: reading the books the guards would bring for him, and engaging in an informal correspondence course with a New York book editor, Clover Swann. Through his studies he became interested in journalism. After the U.S. Supreme Court found the death penalty unconstitutional in 1972 and Rideau's third death sentence was overturned by the Louisiana State Supreme Court the following year, Rideau's sentence was changed to life imprisonment. Transferred to Angola's general population in 1973, he asked to be put on staff at *The Angolite*, the prison-run magazine, which had an all-white staff. When rebuffed, Rideau began his own publication, *The Lifer*, and staffed it with black inmates. Eventually, some black newspapers in the South began to carry his column, "The Jungle."

Rideau was appointed *The Angolite*'s editor two years later, and under his leadership and that of his two co-editors, Tom Mason and Ron Wikberg, the *Angolite* became a glossy, award-winning magazine. The critically acclaimed book *Life Sentences: Rage and Survival Behind Bars*, an anthology of *The Angolite*'s work from 1978 and 1990, edited by Rideau and Wikberg, was published in 1992.

The self-educated Rideau established himself as a professional journalist and exposed standard conditions in the Angola prison. Along the way, his work became recognized in the industry and he won the Robert F. Kennedy and George Polk awards, two of the nation's highest journalism honors. His good behavior and good work earned him many privileges; for example, prison officials allowed him to make some public speaking appearances, and soon his reporting expanded beyond the prison newspaper. He began appearing on ABC's *Nightline* and other national television forums to discuss his work. He was narrator and co-producer of the 1990 documentary *Tossing Away the Keys*, which was aired nationally on public radio, and he began to appear on National Public Radio's *Fresh Air* program. Rideau was also one of the directors of *The Farm: Life Inside Angola Prison*, a 1998 Sundance Film Festival award-winning and Oscar-nominated documentary on Angola from the point of view of six inmates.

Besides his behind-bars journalism, Rideau also became known for the depth of his rehabilitation and the refusal of the state of Louisiana to parole him. Parole boards recommended his release four times during the 1980s, but the state's governors refused to grant parole. Meanwhile, more than seven hundred convicted murders were released by the state during Rideau's entire tenure in jail. The NAACP Legal Defense and Educational Fund was one of many groups that took up Rideau's case, citing the racial inequities involved.

On 15 January 2005, a jury composed of both blacks and whites convicted him of manslaughter. His time having been served more than twice over the twenty-one years he would have received in 1961, he was set free immediately.

FURTHER READING

Rideau, Wilbert, and Ron Wikberg, eds., *Life Sentences: Rage and Survival Behind Bars* (1992).

TODD STEVEN BURROUGHS

Ridenhour, Carlton Douglas. *See* Chuck D (Carlton Douglas Ridenhour).

Ridley, Florida Ruffin (29 Jan. 1861–Mar. 1943), writer, feminist, editor, teacher, social welfare administrator, and woman's club activist, was born in Boston, Massachusetts, the second child and only daughter of the women's club leader JOSEPHINE ST. PIERRE RUFFIN and GEORGE LEWIS RUFFIN, attorney, the state's first black judge, legislator, activist in the National Convention of Colored Men, and graduate of Harvard Law School. One of five children, Ridley was—through her mother—of mixed African, French, Indian, and English heritage. (Her maternal grandfather was from Martinique, and her maternal grandmother was a white woman from Cornwall, England.) Ridley benefited greatly from the home environment and example created by her two highly educated activist parents, both of whom were dedicated to the causes of African American and women's rights.

Ridley's career choices were strongly influenced by the spirit of her family's middle-class values, and the social justice advocacy, citizenship, and organizational work around which she had been raised. She trained to be a teacher and became a specialist in early childhood education. She was educated at Boston Teachers College and Boston University and taught in the Boston public schools before marrying Ulysses A. Ridley, a folklorist, during the 1880s. In 1890 they founded the Society for the Collection of Negro Folklore in Boston, a reflection of their interest in gathering and preserving the oral and folk traditions of the black community. The couple had two children, a son and a daughter.

Ridley was closely allied in work with her mother in the black woman's club movement and in social reform, and through this work was also closely connected to other leading African American feminists across the country. Along with her mother and Cambridge school principal Maria Baldwin, Ridley founded the Woman's New Era Club in Boston in the early 1890s. While her mother served as president, Ridley was active in public relations and committee work. Her expertise in teaching also proved invaluable to the association, since educating young children was one of its areas of focus. Along with other Woman's New Era leaders and women from other states, Ridley helped organize the first national conference of black women in Boston in 1895, out of which the National Federation of Afro-American Women was formed; she served as its recording secretary. The federation soon merged with the Colored Women's League to form the powerful National Association of Colored Women.

Ridley also wielded influence through the printing press and the pen. While her mother was the editor of the Woman's New Era Club publication the *Woman's Era*, which was the first monthly periodical published by African American women, Ridley also served as an editor and writer. As one of the editors for most of the 1890s, she reached a nationwide African American female readership.

The magazine offered inspiration for service and also the means for analysis of social problems. In an age of widespread racial discrimination, racial violence, and denigration of black womanhood—and in a time when middle-class women of all races were discouraged from seeking significant public roles—the *Woman's Era* provided a purposeful agenda for black femininity, one that emphasized personal and social responsibility and racial uplift. Club members were encouraged to make a difference on issues that affected the race, from poverty to education, child welfare, domestic labor, to home buying and lynching.

As corresponding secretary for the Woman's New Era Club, and as a committed member of the Unitarian Church, Ridley was particularly vocal on the moral and political aspects of equal opportunity and the antilynching cause. She addressed the limitations placed upon cultural and educational advancement for blacks because of segregation in concert halls, churches, and public gathering places, particularly in the South. She strongly defended black men against negative stereotypes, and challenged Christians, as well as white women, to recognize the truths about lynching. Ridley was also an active advocate of women's right to vote through her membership in the Brookline Equal Suffrage Association.

While best known for her work with the *Woman's Era*, Ridley also wrote for other periodicals and was the author of fiction. She was a member of the Saturday Evening Quill club, an elite Boston-based intellectual discussion group of aspiring black writers, who published their work, including poetry and fiction, in such periodicals as *Opportunity, The Messenger*, the *Saturday Evening Quill*, and in Harlem Renaissance-era literary magazines. With the growth of the fields of women's studies and the rediscovery of little-known work by black women writers, her story "He Must Think It Out," first published in the *Saturday Evening Quill* in June 1928, has received recognition in college classrooms and was reprinted in various literary anthologies. Originally published in 1928, the story is a psychological drama about the racial consciousness of an attorney, told from his point of view. The story fits into the genre of tales of passing, but with a twist. The protagonist, who for his lifetime has presumed he is white, learns that he is of black heritage, the relative of an African American attorney whom he admires but could not imagine welcoming into his home. He is forced through the revelation to confront the privileges of whiteness he and his well-to-do family enjoy, his own racism, and the content of his own character.

In the twentieth century, Ridley was especially active in reform and social service administration. With the onset of World War I she took secretarial courses at Boston University in 1916 to gain new administrative skills, and volunteered at the YWCA Hostess House at Camp Upton, New York. She soon became the executive secretary of the Soldiers Comfort Unit of New York, which evolved into the League of Women for Community Service, with Ridley at its helm until 1925. Ridley was organizer and president of the Association for Promotion of Child Training in the South and was involved in a kindergarten in Atlanta. She served on the board of directors for Boston's Robert Gould Shaw Settlement House from 1913 to 1925 and edited the settlement newsletter *Social Service News*, which reported on the activities of the Boston branch of the National Urban League, the Shaw house, and the HARRIET TUBMAN House, as well as others involved in providing social services to young working women, migrants, and the black and urban poor.

A political independent, Ridley campaigned for Democratic Party candidates in the 1920s, and was involved in the civil rights and reform work of the Urban League. Her lifelong interest in the promotion of African American history is reflected in a special exhibition she organized on Negro Achievement and Abolition at the Boston Public Library in 1923, and her presidency of the Society of Descendants of Early New England Negroes in the 1930s. She became the secretary of the Lewis Hayden Memorial Association, which honored the legacy of the former slave, abolitionist, and member of the Massachusetts state legislature, in 1929. Near the end of her life Ridley moved to Toledo, Ohio, to live with her daughter, and died there. She was honored with memorial services in both Toledo and Boston.

FURTHER READING

Papers of the Ruffin family, including limited material on Florida Ruffin Ridley, are housed at Howard University's Moorland-Spingarn Research Center.

Cash, Floris Barnett. "Florida Ruffin Ridley," in *Notable Black American Women*, ed. Jessie Carney Smith (1992).

Davis, Elizabeth Lindsay. *Lifting as They Climb* (1933).

Duster, Alfreda M. *Crusade for Justice: The Autobiography of Ida B. Wells* (1970).

Who's Who in Colored America (1933–1937).

BARBARA BAIR

Ridley, Gregory, Jr. (18 July 1925–10 Jan. 2004), artist and educator, was born Gregory David Leon Ridley Jr. in Smyrna, Tennessee, one of three children of Gregory David Leon Ridley Sr., a deacon minister, and Lucile (Elder) Ridley, a domestic worker and artist. Lucile Ridley was known for her quilts, appliqués, and crafts, which she displayed at local arts and craft shows and club exhibits as far away as Appalachia. Gregory Ridley often traveled with his mother when she exhibited her work, and he learned a lot from her. His mastery of repoussé, a metalwork technique used to create a relief design, often by working the reverse side of a metal surface, began when his mother taught him to mold the tinfoil from cigarette wrappers into various shapes. Ridley later graduated to pounding or molding brass and copper.

In 1936 the family moved to Nashville, Tennessee, where Gregory Ridley completed his education in the public school system in 1944, after which he served a year in the navy as an apprentice seaman during World War II. To further his interest in art, Ridley studied at Fisk University in Nashville, Tennessee, from 1945 to 1948. He was greatly influenced by his teacher and mentor AARON DOUGLAS, a renowned artist of the Harlem Renaissance and an innovator in the exploration of the African aesthetics. Douglas's Africanist perspective and the innovations that he brought through the use of both African and American techniques in his work helped to motivate Ridley, who went on to pursue his interest as an artist and also to become a mentor and teacher. In 1951 Ridley received a B.S in Art Education from Tennessee State University.

After teaching for several years at Alabama State University, Ridley became one of the first students admitted to the University of Louisville's new graduate program in fine arts and he entered graduate school with a full scholarship in the fall of 1954. The University of Louisville had only recently, after *Brown v. Board of Education* in 1954, integrated its facilities. At Louisville, Ridley was mentored by Ulfert Wilke, a German-born artist best known for his abstract calligraphic creations in watercolor and ink. In 1954 Ridley became the first student to receive a M.A. in Fine Arts from the University of Louisville. That same year Ridley met and married Gloria Louise and went on to have a family of two sons and five daughters. Ridley returned to Fisk, serving as an instructor of sculpture from 1967 to 1971. At the time the art department staff at Fisk boasted many of the most prominent black artists of the era, including Aaron Douglas, DAVID C. DRISKELL, Earl J. Hooks, and STEPHANIE E. POGUE.

Ridley worked in various mediums, including oil, wood, stone, and especially metal. Beginning with a sheet of cooper or brass, sometimes as large as four or five feet long, he hammered it into an image, often depicting historic events. In 1962 Ridley began his most extensive metal piece, using Egyptian iconography to depict fifteen major battles of the Civil War from the perspective of black soldiers who fought in the Union army.

Ridley continued to combine an Africanist perspective with American influences in works like his 1964 painting *African (Ashanti) Mask*. Ridley's paintings and sculptures added further dimension to the expression of the black experience. His work was included in several books on African American art, *Two Centuries of Black American Art* (1977) by David Driskell and *American Negro Art* (1961) by Cedric Dover. From 1953 to 1974 Ridley had several solo exhibitions in Europe and the United States. He was a founding member of the National Conference of Negro Artists and cofounder of the Black Artists Association in America. A committed educator, Ridley taught for more than fifty years at many institutions, including Grambling State, Medgar Evers College, Fisk University, Elizabeth City State College, and Tennessee State University.

Ridley was known for his friendly and warm nature. He was a storyteller who enjoyed sharing his craft and his philosophy with the many students and artists he taught and mentored. His paintings, sculptures, and metalwork are held in many collections. One of Ridley's most remarkable works of repoussé can be seen on the doors of the Carl Van Vechten Gallery of Fisk University. Another important work, *The Story of Nashville*, which consists of more than eighty panels depicting the history of Nashville from the Civil War to the present, graces the grand reading room of the main library in Nashville, Tennessee. In 1996 Ridley's work was exhibited as part of the 1996 Olympics in Atlanta, Georgia. Ridley died in Nashville, Tennessee, at the age of seventy-eight.

FURTHER READING

Atkins, J. Edwards. *Black Dimensions in Contemporary American Art* (1971).

Dover, Cedric. *American Negro Art* (1961).

Driskell, David. *Two Centuries of Black American Art* (1977).

Romero, Patricia W., ed. *In Black America, 1968: The Year of Awakening* (1969).

Obituary: *Tennessean*, 13 Jan. 2004.

LEAN'TIN L. BRACKS

Riggs, Marlon (3 Feb. 1957–5 Apr. 1994), filmmaker, was born Marlon Troy Riggs in Fort Worth, Texas, to Jean Williams, director of Equal Employment Opportunity and Civil Rights, a federal agency, and Alvin Riggs, who had a career in military and federal service. In the late 1960s Jean and Alvin Riggs moved Marlon and his sister, Sascha, to Augusta, Georgia, where, among other racist incidents, Marlon's school would not sponsor him in the state spelling bee even though he won the local contest. Alvin Riggs's military job took the family to Germany, where Marlon spent his high school years.

Like other African Americans who had lived abroad, Marlon was struck by the overt racism and segregation that he experienced upon his return to the United States. In addition to the ideological divides of race, Riggs's homosexuality further complicated the oversimplified determinants of identity. His experiences and observations of difference, however, served as key conditions for the creative and intellectual work that he subsequently created. On full scholarship, Riggs received his B.A. (magna cum laude) in History from Harvard University in 1978. From there he earned an M.A. in 1981 from the Graduate School of Journalism at the University of California, Berkeley. His thesis was also his first film, *Long Train Running: The Story of the Oakland Blues*. The film studied the blues in African American culture and won a Young Videomaker Award from the American Film Institute in 1982.

After graduate school Riggs settled in Oakland, California, while teaching in his former department at the University of California, Berkeley, where he received tenure in 1992. In 1987 Riggs wrote, directed, and produced the documentary *Ethnic Notions*, which was broadcast on PBS during Black History Month in February 1988 and won an Emmy. In this work Riggs explored the history of racist stereotypes and imagery. His 1991 documentary *Color Adjustment* traced the history of black images in American television and questioned "good" and "bad" images of black representation. The film won several awards, including the prestigious Peabody Award for excellence in media.

Hit with what he told *USA Today* were the "triple whammies in our society"—being black, gay, and HIV positive—Riggs undertook an increasingly urgent campaign to confront racism, homophobia, and AIDS through his work. *Tongues Untied* (1989), funded in part by a fellowship of five thousand dollars from the Western states' National Endowment for the Arts, was initially circulated in national and international art film festivals, including several gay and lesbian forums. The film won several awards and was well received in Berlin, Melbourne, London, Montreal, San Francisco, Los Angeles, and Washington, D.C. But it was not until PBS announced that it would air the work in July 1991 as part of its *P.O.V.* series that a furor began. Concerned program managers in several key urban markets felt that their audiences would be offended by the material. As a result, 174 of the 284 stations that broadcast *P.O.V.* declined to run *Tongues Untied*. Riggs declared in the *Atlanta Journal-Constitution* that even though the film was not originally intended for television, it was nonetheless important in its documentation of "the passion, the rage, all it means to be black and gay in America" (Phil Kloer, "Voices in 'Tongues' Echo Filmmaker's Experience," 16 July 1991).

The *Tongues Untied* controversy fueled the U.S. senator Jesse Helms's attack on the National Endowment for the Arts, an attack that he had begun in 1989. Pat Buchanan, Jerry Falwell, and the conservative American Family Association accused Riggs of blasphemy and perversion. Undaunted, Riggs continued to explore his "triple whammies" in the short films *Affirmations* (1990), *Anthem* (1991), and *Non, Je ne Regrette Rien* (*No Regret*, 1992). His final film, *Black Is ... Black Ain't*, scripted and directed from his hospital bed and completed posthumously in 1995, brilliantly placed Riggs himself in a discussion about what qualifies as "black" and "gay" identities. The metaphor of his grandmother's gumbo that Riggs used in the film highlights at once the pleasures and the difficulties of mixing many ingredients into one pot. Sometimes it works; sometimes it doesn't. But it is the possibilities of the mix that most interested Riggs.

Drawing upon his interests in literature and poetry, Riggs investigated the complexity of form with his documentary films. Riggs queried attempts at articulating a black aesthetic. The poetry of Walt Whitman and Richard Bruce Nugent, for example, interested Riggs, not because it fit easily into tidy racial and sexual categories but rather because it struggled in negotiating issues of identity. In interviews Riggs discussed "black men loving black men," as well as the opportunity of interracial love, in marking the range of possibilities that desire might take across identities. His views on interracial desire were certainly filtered through his relationship with his white life partner, Jack Vincent. And yet if poets such as Whitman and other white artists were key to his creative and personal sensibilities, Riggs was not blind to the cultural production

and representation of American racist imagery that some of that art ultimately facilitated.

Interracial desire, racism, and homophobia—particularly within the African American community—remained central to Riggs's work. This is why writers such as JAMES BALDWIN and later MELVIN DIXON, Joseph Beam, and the poet ESSEX HEMPHILL struck a deep aesthetic chord with Riggs. Riggs's creative work embodied his lived experiences, deftly and elegantly challenging the rigidity of the binary logic of gay or straight, white or black.

In 1991, along with the video artist Vivian Kleiman, Riggs founded Signifyin' Works "as a nonprofit corporation to research, produce and distribute educational media in all formats that examine past and present issues with a particular focus on the African-American experience." Three years later, at the age of thirty-seven, Riggs died from complications of AIDS.

FURTHER READING

Avena, Thomas, ed. *Life Sentences: Writers, Artists, and AIDS* (1994).

Becquer, Marcos. "Snap-Thology and Other Discursive Practices in *Tongues Untied*," *Wide Angle: A Quarterly Journal of Film History, Theory, and Criticism* (1991).

Berger, Maurice. "Too Shocking to Show," *Art in America* (July 1992).

Creekmur, Corey K., and Alexander Doty. *Out in Culture: Gay, Lesbian, and Queer Essays on Popular Culture* (1995).

Harper, Phillip Brian. "Marlon Riggs: The Subjective Position of Documentary Video," *Art Journal* (Winter, 1995).

Kleinhans, Chuck, and Julia Lesage. "Listening to the Heartbeat: Interview with Marlon Riggs," *Jump Cut* (1991).

Obituary: *New York Times*, 6 Apr. 1994.

DAVID A. GERSTNER

Rillieux, Norbert (17 Mar. 1806–8 Oct. 1894), inventor, chemical engineer, was born in New Orleans, Louisiana, the son of Vincent Rillieux Jr., an engineer, and Constance Vivant, who belonged to a wealthy free black family of landowners and landlords. Vincent Rillieux Jr., a businessman and inventor of a steam-operated press for baling cotton, was white, but Norbert and his mother belonged to the mainly Francophone and Catholic ethnic group of free people of color (often referred to as "Black Creoles" after the Civil War). Little is known of Norbert Rillieux's childhood from the time of his baptism in the St. Louis Cathedral of New Orleans to the time he and his brother Edmond were sent, like many other young freemen of color, to France to be educated. By 1830 Rillieux was an instructor in applied mechanics at the École Centrale in Paris and is reported to have published several papers on steam power.

The following year, in 1831, Norbert Rillieux made an extraordinary discovery that prompted his return to New Orleans and would eventually transform the sugar-refining process in Louisiana and throughout the world. The traditional manner of reducing sugarcane juice for sugar production, called the Jamaica Train, required the tedious and backbreaking labor of numerous slaves who, armed with long ladles, skimmed the boiling sugar juice from one open kettle to the next. Rillieux developed an ingenious apparatus, employing condensing coils that used the vapor from one vacuum chamber to evaporate the juice from a second chamber. The new invention—safer, more efficient, and less expensive than the open-kettle system—has been described as having been as significant for the sugar industry as Eli Whitney's cotton gin was for the processing of cotton.

Rillieux failed to interest French planters in his invention, but in 1833 he was invited back to New Orleans by the planter and banker Edmund Forstall to be chief engineer of a new sugar refinery. The appointment did not materialize, but Rillieux continued to perfect his apparatus and also made a fortune in land speculation, which he lost in the nationwide financial collapse of 1837. Some elegant architectural drawings that he produced with his brother Edmond during this period survive in the Notarial Archives in New Orleans. In 1843 two prominent planters hired Rillieux to install evaporators, Theodore Packwood at his plantation later known as Myrtle Grove, and Judah P. Benjamin at his Bellechasse plantation. Within three years Packwood won first prize and Benjamin and Packwood second prize for best sugar, the awards mentioning use of Rillieux's patent sugar-boiling apparatus. On 26 August 1843 Norbert Rillieux was awarded his first patent from the U.S. Patent Office for a double-effect evaporator in vacuum, followed by a patent in 1846 for a triple-effect evaporator with horizontal tubular heating surface. Approval for a later patent (1857) was at first denied on the erroneous assumption that Rillieux was a slave and therefore not a U.S. citizen. "Now, I was the applicant for the patent and not the slave. I am a Citizen of the United States and made oath of the fact in my affidavit," Rillieux wrote.

Judah Benjamin, the brilliant Jewish jurist who later served as Jefferson Davis's secretary of state for the Confederacy, became Rillieux's major supporter in Louisiana sugar circles. He publicized Rillieux's apparatus in a series of articles in J. D. B. De Bow's popular commercial magazine (which came to be known as *De Bow's Review*). In 1846 Benjamin described the sugar produced by Rillieux's method as the best in Louisiana, its "crystalline grain and snowy whiteness … equal to those of the best double-refined sugar of our northern refineries." For ten years at least, Rillieux was a conspicuous figure in New Orleans manufacturing. Benjamin's earliest biographer, Pierce Butler, reported that "frequently, for quite long visits, came the dried-up little chemist Rillieux, always the centre of an admiring and interested group of planters from the neighborhood as he explained this or that point in the chemistry of sugar or the working of his apparatus." Rillieux was described by one contemporary as "the most sought-after engineer in Louisiana," but he was still, by Louisiana law, a person of color, suffering under increasing legal and social restrictions as North-South tensions escalated.

It is not known exactly when Rillieux returned to France. He had many reasons, including the new restrictions imposed in 1855 on free people of color in New Orleans. Apparently Rillieux returned to France just before or during the Civil War and remained there until his death. There is no evidence that he knew his most famous relative, the Impressionist Parisian painter Edgar Degas, whose mother was Rillieux's first cousin. (This family connection was recently announced by Christopher Benfey in "Degas and the 'Black World': Art and Miscegenation in New Orleans," *New Republic* 21 [Oct. 1996].) Late in life Rillieux became interested in Egypt, and in 1880 he was found deciphering hieroglyphics in the Bibliothèque Nationale by the Louisiana planter Duncan Kenner. During his seventies he was still working on refinements to various devices for beet and cane sugar production. Norbert Rillieux was buried in Paris's Père Lachaise cemetery, survived by his wife, Emily Cuckow Rillieux, who lived in comfortable circumstances for another eighteen years.

FURTHER READING

Heitmann, John A. *The Modernization of the Louisiana Sugar Industry, 1830–1910* (1987).

Meade, George P. "A Negro Scientist of Slavery Days," *Scientific Monthly* 62 (1946): 317–326, reprinted in *Negro History Bulletin* 20, no. 7 (Apr. 1957): 159–163.

Obituary: *Louisiana Planter and Sugar Manufacturer*, 24 Nov. 1894.

This entry is taken from the *American National Biography* and is published here with the permission of the American Council of Learned Societies.

CHRISTOPHER BENFEY

Ringgold, Faith (8 Oct. 1930–), artist and writer, was born Faith Willie Jones at Harlem Hospital in New York City, the youngest of three children of Willi(e) Edell (Posey) and Andrew Louis Jones Sr., a truck driver for the city sanitation department. The Joneses separated in the early 1930s and divorced in 1942, by which time Willi Jones had begun work as a seamstress in the garment district. By the 1950s, using the name Madame Willi Posey, she had established a small dressmaking and design business in Harlem. Faith, who suffered from severe asthma and missed kindergarten and much of first grade because of her illness, enjoyed an especially close relationship with her mother, who organized creative projects to occupy her curious daughter. After graduating from Morris High School (she spent the first three years at George Washington High School) in 1948, Faith Jones began studying art at the City College of New York. Two years later she left school after eloping with (Robert) Earl Wallace, a pianist and childhood friend. They had two daughters in 1952 and separated in 1954. The marriage was officially annulled two years later. In 1966 Wallace died of a heroin overdose, just five years after the death of Faith's brother Andrew from the same cause.

Faith returned to City College after her separation, earning a B.S (1955) and an M.A. (1960) in Art. During this time Faith and her daughters lived with her mother, whom Faith helped by sewing clothes and emceeing the theatrical "Madame Willi" fashion shows, initiating a collaboration that continued until Willi's death in 1981. In 1955 Faith began an eighteen-year career teaching art in the New York City public schools. From 1970 to 1980 she taught part-time at several New York–area colleges, and from 1983 to 2002 she was an associate professor at the University of California at San Diego. As was the case with other artists, including JUNE JORDAN, LOIS JONES, and ALMA THOMAS, faith students played an essential role in her artistic evolution. In 1962 she married Burdette "Birdie" Ringgold, another childhood friend. He worked for General Motors until 1992.

By the early 1960s, after nearly a decade painting landscapes, Ringgold began painting in a more distinctive, personal style, which she dubbed "super realism." Her first major pieces, "The American People Series" (1963–1967), oil paintings exploring the subtleties of U.S. race relations, employed elements of pop and folk art as well as the flattened picture plane and exaggerated facial features of Cubism and moody colors of German Expressionism. By 1967 the quiet alienation of the sole black party guest in *The Cocktail Party* (1964) gave way to larger, mural size paintings, including *U.S. Postage Stamp Commemorating the Advent of Black Power* (1967) and *Die* (1967), which more directly challenged viewers about American racism. Referencing both Jasper Johns's American flag paintings and civil rights and antiwar activists' use of the American flag, Ringgold produced the provocative *Flag for the Moon: Die Nigger* (1969) and *The Flag Is Bleeding* (1967). Seeking a visual vocabulary for an African American aesthetic, Ringgold experimented with a palette of dark colors in her *Black Light Series*. By 1970 she was pursuing a more direct approach encouraged by the Black Power and feminist movements, producing text-heavy political posters, including "Committee to Defend the Panthers" (1970), "America Free Angela" (1971) referring to ANGELA DAVIS, and "United States of Attica" (1971). Her 1972 mural for the Women's House of Detention at Rikers Island launched Art Without Walls, an artists' group dedicated to bringing art to prisons, and signaled her nearly exclusive focus on black women as subjects. Ringgold worked as a political advocate for black and women artists, helping organize groundbreaking protests in 1968 against the Whitney Museum of American Art in New York, which had excluded black artists from an exhibition of art from the 1930s, and the Museum of Modern Art (MoMA), which neglected to include any African American artists in an exhibition honoring the slain civil rights leader MARTIN LUTHER KING JR. She agitated, unsuccessfully, for an African American wing at MoMA, explaining in a cowritten letter, "We are waiting. We cannot wait very much longer." Her work with the Ad Hoc Women's Art Group against the Whitney resulted in the inclusion of works by BARBARA CHASE-RIBOUD and BETYE SAAR in the 1971 Whitney Biennial. In an effort to create exhibition opportunities for black women artists she cofounded Women Students and Artists for Black Art Liberation and Where We At in 1970, participated in Women's Caucus for Art, Coast to Coast, and Artists Against Apartheid, and curated and juried exhibitions throughout the 1970s, 1980s, and 1990s.

In her own work Ringgold turned to non-Western art forms and, most significantly, to fabric. Her adoption of the Tibetan *tanka* (a painting

Series (1977), *Harlem '78* (1978), and *Atlanta Series* (1981). The latter was a memorial to the more than twenty African American boys murdered by the serial killer Wayne Williams.

The choice of fabric as a medium allowed Ringgold to spend time and collaborate with her family, especially her mother, who contributed fabric elements and costumes to all of the *tankas*, masks, soft sculptures, and, later, quilts. Ringgold's choice of medium, as well as the content of her work, furthered her exclusion from mainstream exhibition and sales routes, but it affirmed her allegiance to the artistic traditions and history of women and African Americans. Her work is feminist art, Ringgold explains, because it "came out of being a woman, and the use of craft." Concerned by the limitations of the art world exhibition and distribution system, she devised new themes, new materials, and new distribution methods. Creating portable works that were easier and cheaper to transport, she organized "trunk shows" of her work designed to travel to smaller venues across the country.

In 1980, building on her bold graphic paintings of late 1960s and the fabric and soft sculptures of the previous decade, Ringgold turned to narrative story quilts, the works for which she is best known. The quilts focus on storytelling, particularly the links between history and contemporary life, the personal and the political, and the familial and the universal. Ringgold learned quilting from her grandmother, who had been taught by her grandmother, a slave. Ringgold's first quilt, *Echoes of Harlem* (1980) was a direct collaboration with her mother, who died the following year, and a metaphoric collaboration with the generations of women, including the slave quilter HARRIET POWERS, who preceded her. Depicting places and people from her Harlem childhood, black heroes like SONNY ROLLINS, JOSEPHINE BAKER, and MARLON RIGGS, cotton fields and subway graffiti, the quilts typically feature a large, folk art–inspired painting, surrounded by cloth panels often inscribed with text. In *Who's Afraid of Aunt Jemima* (1983) panels emblazoned with an imagined narrative in which Jemima becomes a successful businesswoman are alternated with portraits drawn from Ringgold's life. Ten years later, in *The French Collection* quilts, she blended elements of her family history with a fictional story based on the experiences of African American expatriate artists in Paris, offering a complex discourse on the relationship of African Americans to the history of art. In one of the series' twelve quilts, *The Sunflowers Quilting Bee at Arles*,

Faith Ringgold sits before her quilt called *Tar Beach* in her New York City studio on 23 July 1993. *Tar Beach* is also the title of an autobiographical children's book by Rinngold and an exhibition based on the book at the Children's Museum. [AP Images]

painted on and framed by cloth) in 1972 marked a turning point, establishing the combination of artisanal and craft mediums with black themes and subjects that came to typify her work. Ringgold's first *tanka* pieces, the *Slave Rape Series* and *Feminist Series* (1972), celebrated and included excerpts from the writings of African American women, including MARIA STEWART, ANNA JULIA COOPER, and SHIRLEY CHISHOLM. Influenced by the design and use of West African tribal masks she produced the *Witch Mask Series* in 1973. The life-size needlepoint masks *The Family of Woman Series* (1973–1974), *The Wake and Resurrection of the Bicentennial Negro* (1974–1976), and the foam rubber *Portrait Masks (Harlem '76)* followed. The masks led to the creation of dolls, both hanging and self-standing, which Ringgold called soft sculptures. These unique, witty, and accessible pieces included satires of WILT CHAMBERLAIN, the *Woman on a Pedestal*

MADAME C.-J. WALKER, SOJOURNER TRUTH, IDA B. WELLS, FANNIE LOU HAMER, HARRIET TUBMAN, ROSA PARKS, MARY MCLEOD BETHUNE, and ELLA BAKER sew a sunflower quilt amid a field of sunflowers as Vincent Van Gogh looks on.

Since the mid-1970s Ringgold has used her artwork, first her masks, soft sculptures, and abstract paintings, and later her quilts, in performance. The interrelatedness of her different work and its intersection with her life, family, and politics lies at the heart Ringgold's creative enterprise. In 1985, after losing over one hundred pounds, she created a film documentary, quilt, and performance piece chronicling the experience and its resonance with issues of sexuality, gender, and race. In 1991 she wrote and illustrated *Tar Beach*, a children's book based on her story quilt of the same name. The book won a host of awards, including a Caldecott honor, and spurred Ringgold to write eleven more children's books, among them *Aunt Harriet's Underground Railroad in the Sky* (1992), *Dinner at Aunt Connie's House* (1993), *If a Bus Could Talk: The Story of Rosa Parks* (1999), and *Cassie's Word Quilt* (2001).

The first retrospective of Ringgold's work was organized in 1973. Eleven years later the Studio Museum in Harlem mounted a twenty-year retrospective and asked the cultural critic Michele Wallace, Ringgold's daughter, to write the catalog introduction. By the late 1980s she was exhibiting widely, particularly in exhibitions of women, African Americans, and quilt artists. In 1990 she received a twenty-five-year retrospective exhibition, followed by large solo shows in 1993, 1994, and 1998. Her public commissions include *Flying Home: Harlem Heroes and Heroines* (1996), a mosaic mural for the New York City subway based on a Lionel Hampton composition, *The Crown Heights [Brooklyn] Children's Story Quilt* for the area's local library, and a quilt honoring Eugenio Maria de Hostos for the De Hostos Community College in the Bronx.

Ringgold was the recipient of numerous awards, including a National Endowment for the Arts Award for sculpture (1978) and for painting (1989), a La Napoule Foundation Award (1990), a Guggenheim Memorial Foundation Fellowship (1987), and seventeen honorary doctorates. She exhibited throughout the United States, Europe, South America, Asia, Africa, and the Middle East, and her work is included in the permanent collection of many major museums, including the Solomon R. Guggenheim Museum, The Metropolitan Museum of Art, The Museum of Modern Art, and the Smithsonian American Art Museum.

Just as she pioneered the use of alternative materials, content, and distribution avenues in the 1970s, Ringgold launched two Internet projects in the 2000s: Racialquestions.com and the Anyone Can Fly Foundation, which sought to expand the art canon to include artists of the African Diaspora and to introduce African American art to American audiences.

FURTHER READING

Ringgold, Faith. *We Flew over the Bridge: Memoirs of Faith Ringgold* (1995).

Cameron, Dan, and the New Museum of Contemporary Art. *Dancing at the Louvre: Faith Ringgold's French Collection and Other Story Quilts* (1998).

Farrington, Lisa E. *Faith Ringgold* (2004).

LISA E. RIVO

Riperton, Minnie (8 Nov. 1947–12 July 1979), singer and songwriter, was born Minnie Julia Riperton in Chicago, the youngest of eight children of Daniel Riperton, a Pullman porter, and Thelma (maiden name unknown). At a young age, Riperton began taking music, dance, and ballet lessons at the Lincoln Center in Chicago. At the age of nine, she decided to experience a new genre of music and began taking opera lessons, something that contributed to the cultivation of her five-octave vocal range. She sang in the choir at the Sixth Presbyterian Church and at Hyde Park High School.

At the age of fourteen, while in the Hyde Park a capella choir, she was discovered by the pianist and songwriter Raynard Miner, who asked her to join the Gems, a girl group he frequently played with for Chess Records. Over the next few years, Riperton cut a series of singles with the group, including "I Can't Help Myself" and "Can't You Take a Hint." The Gems, under the name the Studio Three, sang backup for notable singers such as ETTA JAMES, the Dells, and Fontella Bass, but their own releases never rose beyond the level of regional hits and the group released their last single, under the name the Starlets, in 1968. After her graduation from high school in 1965, while still singing with the Gems, Riperton took up a position as receptionist at Chess Records. In 1966 she signed with the label as a solo act, releasing a single, "Lonely Girl," under the alias Andrea Davis, a name she adopted as an homage to her mentor and the song's writer, Bill Davis. In 1967 Riperton joined the Rotary Connection, a psychedelic rock group put together by Marshall Chess, the son of Chess Records' founder. Though she initially shared lead vocals with Sidney Barnes, she emerged on later recordings as the lead singer of the group. The group debuted that year with a self-titled record album on the Cadet Concept label, a subsidiary of Chess. Two singles from the album, "Amen" and "Lady Jane," found a home on underground FM radio, but the group failed to capture the attention of mainstream outlets. As a member of Rotary Connection, Riperton came to the attention of entertainers such as the producer and arranger Charles Stepney, who worked with both the Rotary Connection and Earth, Wind, and Fire; the pianist Ramsey Lewis; and the songwriter/producer Richard Rudolph.

In 1969 Riperton and Richard Rudolph were married. Her union with Rudolph was a strong stand for the couple during racist times, when interracial marriages were not always viewed as acceptable; she was African American and he was Jewish. Riperton and Rudolph had a strong relationship, both personally and professionally. She referred to him as her "soul mate" and the two worked collaboratively on her solo career. The couple later had a son, Marc, and a daughter, Maya, an actress who joined the cast of *Saturday Night Live* in 2000.

Together, Riperton, Rudolph, Lewis, and Stepney worked on the production of Riperton's first solo album, 1970's *Come to My Garden* on the GRT label, which received only minimal commercial success. Riperton then rejoined Rotary Connection for their last album, 1971's *Hey Love*. After Rotary Connection disbanded, she and Rudolph took a two-year sabbatical in Florida. There, Riperton caught the attention of a representative for Epic Records, who encouraged her to sign with the label and move to Los Angeles. She resumed her career, touring with STEVIE WONDER, ROBERTA FLACK, and QUINCY JONES. She sang on Wonder's *Fulfillingness' First Finale* as a member of his backup group, Wonderlove. She also sang jingles for commercials.

Wonder had agreed to work with Riperton on her second solo album and after touring with him, they began work on 1974's *Perfect Angel*. Due in part to Wonder's contributions, *Perfect Angel* proved to be a big success for Riperton, selling more than 500,000 copies and winning the Recording Industry Association of America's certification as a gold album. Out of *Perfect Angel* came the mesmerizing single "Lovin' You," which became an international success and her most popular song. As the story is told, it was a lullaby for her daughter, Maya, then two years old.

Minnie Riperton, singer, especially famous for her five-octave vocal range. (AP Images.)

In 1975 Riperton returned to the studio to produce a third solo album, *Adventures in Paradise*. While not quite as successful as *Perfect Angel*, the album was popular with rhythm and blues audiences, reaching #5 on *Billboard*'s Black Albums chart. In 1976, while working on her fourth solo album, *Stay In Love* (1977), Riperton found out that she was suffering from breast cancer, a fact she made public one night on *The Tonight Show* when Flip Wilson was co-hosting. Riperton said she couldn't stay silent because she wanted to help those women with breast cancer who didn't have the supportive family and husband that she had. In 1976, after a mastectomy and while still focusing on her singing career, she signed a new contract with Capitol Records and began working on her last album, 1979's *Minnie*. She became a spokeswoman for the American Cancer Society and was awarded the Cancer Society Medal of Courage by President Jimmy Carter in 1977. She also served as the American Cancer Society's education chairwoman in 1978. At that time, she was the youngest woman and the only African American to serve in that position.

Minnie contained two hits, "Memory Lane" and "Lover and Friend." Shortly after its release, Riperton died in the arms of her husband at the age of thirty-one in Los Angeles. The following year, Capitol released a posthumous album, *Love Lives Forever*, a collection of previously unreleased vocal tracks with new background music. *Love Lives Forever*, which featured vocals Riperton had recorded with various singers such as Peabo Bryson, MICHAEL JACKSON, and Stevie Wonder, made it into the top ten.

Known for her angelic vocal range, Riperton is regarded as one of the finest vocalists of her time. Her influence can be heard in the voices of performers such as Mariah Carey, Teena Marie, and Chante Moore, and samples of her songs were staples of the hip hop repertoire throughout the 1990s and 2000s.

FURTHER READING

Calloway, Earl. *Fans Plan Memorial for Minnie Riperton* (1999).

Coleman, Wayman E. "Minnie Riperton: The 'Perfect Angel' revisited," *Afro-American Red Star* (7 Apr. 2001).

"Minnie Riperton Remembered on Twentieth Anniversary of Her Death," *Jet* (19 July 1999): 54.

Norment, Lynn. "Minnie Riperton: 'Perfect Angel' Leaves Legacy of Love," *Ebony* 34 (Oct 1979): 95–100.

Roberts, Kimberly. "Collection Brings Beloved Minnie Riperton," *Philadelphia Tribune*, 23 Feb. 2001.

SHARON MCGEE

Rivers, Clarence Rufus Joseph (9 Sept. 1931–21 Nov. 2004), Roman Catholic priest, musician, and composer, was born Clarence Rufus Rivers Jr. in Selma, Alabama, to Clarence Rufus Rivers and Lorraine (Echols) Rivers. Rivers's early life was spent in Alabama. His family relocated to Cincinnati, Ohio, around 1940, where Clarence enrolled in St. Ann's school, attached to one of the oldest black Catholic parishes in the country. At that time the Rivers family was not Catholic, but when the parish offered to have Clarence baptized, his parents consented and eventually the entire family converted. Rivers continued his education in area Catholic schools through high school. Encouraged by Father Charles Murphy of St. Ann Church, Rivers aspired to become a priest. He entered St. Gregory Minor Seminary, Cincinnati, in 1946, in the eleventh grade and after completion of high school and two years of college, was sent to Mt. St. Mary's Seminary, also in Cincinnati, earning a bachelor's degree and later a master of arts in Philosophy.

When Rivers was ordained to the priesthood in 1956 he became Cincinnati's first black diocesan priest. His first assignment was to teach literature at Archbishop Purcell High School, while serving as associate pastor of St. Joseph's Church, a predominately white parish in a mostly black neighborhood, Cincinnati's West End. In addition to his teaching, he revived the school's drama guild, "the Queen's Men," exercising his interest in theatre. During his eight years at St. Joseph's Church, Rivers began to experiment in liturgical music inspired by African American culture. In 1963 he recorded *An American Mass Program*, the liturgical music utilized at one of the first English-language liturgies at the time of the Second Vatican Council. This recording of Mass hymns sold thousands of copies and led to international acclaim for Rivers, already dubbed the "father" of black Catholic liturgy and the "soul priest."

In the wake of the Second Vatican Council, the civil rights and Black Power movements, Rivers had ignited a "black renaissance" in Catholic worship by emphasizing the integration of African American spirituals, gospel, and jazz music, lively singing and preaching into the official worship of the church. As the first liturgist to explore the potential relationship between African culture and Catholic worship, Rivers placed new emphasis on the role of the spoken word, music, and dance in the liturgy, all derived from his African American heritage. Despite little training in the liturgical arts, Rivers began composing liturgical music influenced by his background, drafting what became one of his most famous compositions, "God is Love." It was selected for the liturgy at the August 1964 meeting of the National Liturgical Conference in St. Louis, and Rivers led the congregation in singing the hymn, visibly energizing the twenty thousand worshippers in attendance.

After a second pastoral assignment in Cincinnati at Assumption Church in 1962, Rivers was permitted by Archbishop Karl J. Alter of Cincinnati to pursue full-time graduate studies in 1963. Having already pursued graduate courses in English literature at Xavier University, Cincinnati, and Yale University, Rivers began a study of music and drama at the Catholic University of America, Washington, D.C. However, unable to obtain the stage experience that he desired because of racial bias at the university, he entered another graduate program, this time at the Centre Pastorale de Liturgie at the Institut Catholique, Paris, France. Finding the institute's methodology too narrow and unable to commence a study of Catholic liturgical aesthetics rather than liturgical music, Rivers again stopped short of completing his doctoral degree.

He returned to the United States in 1968 and began full-time work in the field of liturgy. His professional and spiritual aspirations resulted in the founding that year of Stimuli, Inc., a religious education institute with headquarters in Cincinnati, offering workshops in liturgy and music and specializing in the interaction between African American culture and religious worship. As president of Stimuli, Rivers toured the country speaking to numerous parishes and reaching countless more through his books on worship and culture, including *Celebration* (1969), *Reflections* (1970), *Soulfull Worship* (1974) and *The Spirit in Worship* (1978).

With an expanding readership and a national following, Rivers was tapped for a position of leadership within the American black Catholic community. The year after the National Office of Black Catholics in Washington, D.C., was founded, he was chosen as the first director of the department of culture and worship, serving in that capacity from 1971 to 1974. As director he edited the department's publication, *Freeing the Spirit*, a magazine of black Catholic liturgy published by the national office. Rivers presented the first national workshop on black liturgy at the University of Detroit to about one thousand participants in advance of the Black Catholic Lay Caucus held in 1971. While continuing to organize workshops, write, and advise parishes on liturgical praxis, Rivers rekindled his desire to earn a terminal academic degree. Finding an institution more suited to his individual scholarly interests, Rivers completed an interdisciplinary program in African American culture and Catholic liturgy, receiving a doctoral degree from the Union Institute of Cincinnati in 1978.

In his later years, Rivers's attention turned to developing television programs exploring black culture and liturgy and he devoted much of his energy to the creation of a school for the liturgical arts that he wished to be named "Lion of Judah Institute." The proposed school was to be geared to the formation of scholars as well as "worship professionals" and "liturgical practitioners." His institute was still in the planning stages at the time of Rivers's death in Cincinnati at the age of seventy-three and in the forty-eighth year of his priesthood. Rivers was the most significant black Catholic liturgist in America, a recipient of the Catholic Art Association's gold medal and a leadership award from the North American Academy of Liturgy. The popular African American hymnal *Lead Me, Guide Me*, used in many black Catholic parishes, is dedicated to Rivers, testifying to his enduring importance within the black Catholic community in the United States.

FURTHER READING
Rivers, Clarence-Rufus J. "Freeing the Spirit: Very Personal Reflections on One Man's Search for the Spirit in Worship," in *U.S. Catholic Historian* 19.2 (Spring 2001).
Rivers, Clarence Joseph. "Thank God We Ain't What We Was: The State of the Liturgy in the Black Catholic Community," in *U.S. Catholic Historian* 5.1 (1986).
McGann, Mary E. "Timely Wisdom, Prophetic Challenge: Rediscovering Clarence R. J. Rivers' Vision of Effective Worship," in *Worship* 76.1 (Jan. 2002).
McGann, Mary E., and Eva Marie Lumas. "The Emergence of African American Catholic Worship," in *U.S. Catholic Historian* 19.2 (Spring 2001).
Obituary: *National Catholic Reporter*, 7 Jan. 2005.

DAVID J. ENDRES

Rivers, Eugene F. (1950–), minister and social activist, was born in Boston, Massachusetts, and during his childhood lived in Chicago, Illinois, and Philadelphia, Pennsylvania. His Pentecostal mother was a nurse and his Muslim father a painter. Rivers's parents separated when he was three, and he was reared by his mother. While living in Philadelphia during his teenage years, Rivers joined a gang whose leaders constantly harassed him. In 1963 he responded to a message delivered by the Reverend Billy Graham through the *Hour of Decision* radio program. Consequently Rivers joined Deliverance Evangelistic Church, pastored by the Reverend Benjamin Smith. Smith helped Rivers get out of gang life and counseled him in many ways.

In 1968 Rivers won a scholarship to the Pennsylvania Academy of Fine Arts. College studies opened a new world for Rivers, who had by then become estranged from Smith. The young Rivers had observed the activism of the Black Panthers and was bothered by what he perceived to be the social aloofness of many black churches, especially black Pentecostal churches. He pressed Pastor Smith to take more of an interest in social reform issues like the Opportunities Industrialization Centers, an organization in Philadelphia dedicated to providing job training and vocational skills to unemployed blacks. Rivers finally left Deliverance because Smith could not relate to his interest in social reform.

In the early 1970s Rivers opened a street ministry and a Pentecostal storefront church through which he met Dr. C. Everett Koop, the future U.S. surgeon general. Koop was a board member at Eastern Baptist Theological Seminary (now Palmer Theological Seminary) and so raised funds to allow Rivers to audit courses there. Studying at Eastern was extremely influential in Rivers's theological development. There he was introduced to the writings of Edward J. Carnell and Francis Schaeffer, two major thinkers who had developed theological systems for the defense of the Christian faith.

In 1973 Rivers moved to New Haven, Connecticut, to audit classes at Yale University. There he met Schaeffer, who encouraged him to develop a theological defense of the black church's involvement in social work. Schaeffer's hope was that black ministers would be more inclined to social work if they could become convinced that it was mandated by Scriptures. Rivers moved to Boston in 1976 and entered Harvard University in 1980, where he spent the next three years. At Harvard, Rivers and other Pentecostals founded a student organization called the WILLIAM J. SEYMOUR Society, in honor of the pioneering African American Pentecostal leader. The Seymour Society was a forum that allowed Pentecostal students to nurture their intellectual and spiritual interests and their commitment to the poor.

In 1984 Rivers left Harvard and moved to Dorchester, Massachusetts, because he had undergone another intellectual transformation. He was increasingly critical of American society, the black middle class, and the black church, which he claimed had forsaken the poor. In Dorchester, Rivers founded a new church, the Azusa Christian Community, with some of the friends who had belonged to the Seymour Society.

Rivers married Jacqueline Cooke in 1986. They had two children. Rivers, now affiliated with the Church of God in Christ (COGIC), envisioned the Azusa Christian Community as a new type of church that could help the black middle class relate to the urban poor. The name "Azusa" was taken from the Azusa Mission pastored by William Seymour. Located in Los Angeles, the Azusa Mission was famous for encouraging blacks, whites, poor, and rich to worship God together. This was the kind of healing that Rivers aspired to replicate in Dorchester. The Azusa Christian Community,

whose early members were students from local elite schools, distributed food and engaged in political campaigns and intellectual discourse.

In 1988 Rivers expanded his ministry by founding the ELLA J. BAKER House to serve as the social arm of his church. The organization targeted high-risk youths and their families. Four years later, in the wake of the gang-related stabbing of a young man during a funeral service at the Morning Star Baptist Church in Mattapan, Massachusetts, local ministers banded together with laity to fight crime and gangs. With two fellow ministers, Jeffrey Brown and Raymond Hammond, Rivers organized the Ten Point Coalition, which vowed to make Boston safer by redeeming delinquent youths.

The ten points of the coalition were the following: establishing adopt-a-gang programs for churches; training advocates for black and Hispanic youths in the judicial system; forming evangelists to do one-on-one evangelism with drug traffickers; starting community-based economic development programs; networking with urban and suburban churches for mutual spiritual and material benefits; creating local crime-watch programs near existing churches; working with community health centers to prevent sexually transmitted diseases; instituting Christian brotherhood and sisterhood communities as alternatives to gangs; organizing a crisis center for abused women; and developing instructional programs with emphasis on Latino and black history. Soon thirty-seven churches and agencies endorsed the Ten Point Coalition.

Another technique of Rivers's was to walk the streets of Dorchester, praying with other ministers for divine assistance in removing the gangs from the neighborhood. According to some observers Rivers's activism accounted for the decrease in crime in the Boston area. Between 1990 and 1999 the number of murders decreased from 152 to 31.

The success of the Ten Point Coalition made Rivers a national celebrity, and he was sought by law enforcement agencies to assist in fighting crime. Eventually he left the coalition to pioneer and lead the National Ten Point Leadership Foundation (NTPLF) in the late 1990s. Since then the NTPLF has advised law enforcement organizations in more than fifty cities and has founded affiliates in other urban areas.

In April 2000 Rivers joined COGIC Bishop Charles Blake in founding the Pan-African Charismatic Evangelical Congress (PACEC), an institution that commits itself to the promotion of personal holiness and social justice. The initial impetus behind PACEC's creation was the devastating impact of the AIDS crisis in South Africa. As PACEC's general secretary, Rivers has challenged Christians of African descent all over the world to financially support this international organization that is concerned about issues of social justice affecting the entire African Diaspora. Because of his concern for the black poor, Rivers has supported the faith-based programs of President George W. Bush as a possible solution to black poverty. With his involvement in PACEC, Rivers has positioned himself as one of the few Pentecostal church leaders who is engaging both national and international issues affecting the material life of blacks everywhere.

FURTHER READING

Leland, John, "Savior of the Streets," *Newsweek* (1 Jun. 1998).

McRoberts, Omar M. *Streets of Glory: Church and Community in a Black Urban Neighborhood* (2003).

Parker, Anthony A., "In Jesus' Name: Azusa Christian Community Reclaims the Poor and Dispossessed in Boston," *Sojourners Magazine* (May 1993).

Zoba, Wendy Murray. "Separate and Equal: Martin Luther King Dreamed of an Integrated Society," *Christianity Today* (5 Feb. 1996).

DAVID MICHEL

Rivers, Francis Ellis (30 July 1893–28 July 1975), prominent New York City judge, was born in Kansas City, Kansas, the son of the Reverend David Foote Rivers, the last African American member of the Tennessee state legislature during Reconstruction, and Silene Gale Rivers. In 1898 his family moved to Washington, D.C., where he completed elementary and high school. He had considered becoming an athlete, but an attack of gout prevented this. He began studying law at Howard University, but in 1911 he entered Yale, where he graduated with Phi Beta Kappa distinction in economics and history in 1915. In 1916 he went to Harvard Law School but left to become an inspector for Winchester Firearms, a post he kept until the United States declared war on Germany in 1917. During the war he attended the segregated officer training school in Des Moines, Iowa, and served as a first lieutenant with New York's 367th Infantry Division (the "Buffaloes") and the 351st Machine Gun Battalion, seeing action in the Meuse-Argonne offensive—the last major, and ultimately decisive, allied push of the Great War. In May 1918, prior to leaving for France, he married Lucy Ellen Miller; they would divorce in the 1940s, and Rivers remarried to Alroy Spencer.

After the war ended, Rivers attended Columbia Law School, graduating in 1922; he was admitted to the New York bar in January 1923. He initially had problems finding work in law, until he was taken on by Judge Jonah J. Goldstein, for whom he worked for two years before setting up his own office in 1925. Goldstein would resign from the American Bar Association in early 1943 over its refusal to admit Rivers, although the ABA relented and Rivers became a member in 1944 (the ABA saved face by making another African American its first black member; Rivers became the second). In 1929 Rivers became the first African American member of the Association of the Bar of the City of New York (ABCNY) since its founding in 1870.

Also in that year, with the support of OSCAR DE PRIEST, the country's only African American Congressman and a Republican, Rivers, who was a Republican himself, was elected to the 19th Assembly District in Manhattan. His record as an assemblyman was good, but not good enough to get him re-elected the following year. During his time in the Assembly he introduced bills to help tenants and also to set up the Tenth Municipal Court District in Manhattan, which redrew court boundaries in a successful effort to enable African Americans to elect justices from their own community. Ironically, Rivers narrowly failed to be elected to one of the two new judgeships he had helped create, amid allegations that the Democratic machine had rigged the election. Rivers was also a member of the Negro Bar Association (NBA) and at its sixth annual meeting in 1930, he urged members "to analyze the needs of ... colored communities" by drafting legislation and promoting these laws through "educating public opinion" (Smith Jr, 560).

Rivers returned to private practice, impressing New York's gang-busting District Attorney Thomas Dewey, and in December 1937 he was appointed as an assistant district attorney, the first African American to hold such a position in New York. He was reappointed in 1942 and remained in the post until Dewey (governor by this point) appointed him to the City Court post, made vacant by the death of Justice James C. Madigan in September 1943. His formal election to the post in November was supported by a diverse range of groups, including the Republican Party and American Labor Party, enabling him to defeat his Democrat challenger by 166,499 to 143,858 votes (the Democrats had earlier rebuffed efforts to lend bi-partisan support to Rivers's candidacy). Rivers was the first African American to be nominated by a major political party in New York City for a post that had to be voted on by an entire county; furthermore, he was the first African American judge in New York to prosecute murder cases. Rivers's salary was $17,500 per annum, making him the highest-paid African American public official in the country at that time. His appointment was widely praised, both in New York and nationally, and he held the post for twenty years until his retirement in 1963.

Rivers was an active member of the Republican Party, leading the Republican National Committee's Colored Voters Division in the East in 1932, 1936, and 1940. In both 1936 and 1940 he condemned Roosevelt's treatment of African Americans, claiming, with some justification, that the New Deal discriminated widely and used African American labor where it was cheaper. In 1936 Rivers's pleas were in vain as, for the first time, a majority (70 percent) of African Americans voted for the Democratic presidential ticket. In 1940 Rivers wrote one of the most strident and articulate contemporary critiques of the New Deal's treatment of African Americans. The Republican pamphlet, entitled "An Appeal to the Common Sense of Colored Citizens," used the New Deal's own statistics to attack it. Rivers noted that African American employment in some federal agencies had actually fallen by half as a result of the New Deal, and large numbers of African Americans, particularly domestic and agricultural workers, did not benefit from many of the New Deal's provisions. Rivers observed that out of 115,000 field agents in the Agricultural Adjustment Administration (AAA), only four were African American, while there were more African Americans on relief and fewer in the workforce than ever before. Rivers was obviously partisan, but much of his criticism was valid. Nevertheless, his efforts were again futile as African Americans once more endorsed Franklin Roosevelt.

Rivers was a shrewd political observer and a close political ally of Governor Thomas Dewey, the Republican presidential candidate in both 1944 and 1948. Rivers viewed the Republican attitude to African Americans with alarm, realizing that they could hold the balance of power in a close election. In the 1948 presidential campaign he offered Dewey a strategy that could thwart Truman's efforts and draw African Americans to the GOP. He urged Dewey to take the initiative from Truman by using the controversial special session of Congress to try to push through civil rights legislation. If these efforts failed, it would, he believed, expose the insincerity of Truman on the issue. Embracing civil rights, he

argued, would have been in line with the party of Lincoln's historic principles and its current platform. Rivers warned Dewey that the "importance [of minority groups] to a Republican victory cannot be overestimated" (Rivers and Blinkoff Memorandum, 20 July 1948). It was vital that the GOP not align itself with southern Democrats and that Dewey publicly support the congressional battle for civil rights. Convinced he would win the election, Dewey ignored Rivers's advice. Ironically, it was Truman's showing in the African American wards of Illinois, California, and Ohio that gave him his slim margin of victory; had Dewey heeded Rivers, he may well have won more than a paltry 25 percent of the African American vote and become president.

Rivers was a member of the board of directors of the NAACP's Legal Defense and Education Fund, and he was its president from 1965 to 1970. He became a member of New York's State Board of Mediation after his retirement and presided successfully over a case involving eleven dismissed teachers in 1968 that led to widespread disruption of Brooklyn schools by teachers, pupils and parents. Rivers ordered seven of the teachers to be reinstated. Six months before his death, he was appointed, along with another retired judge, to head an inquiry into links between members of the Board of Education and companies doing business with the school system. Rivers also represented the last generation of African Americans who were instinctive Republicans; his political career was, however, a constant, losing battle against the ambivalence of the GOP toward African Americans and the successful appeals of the Democrats. He also represented perhaps the first generation of African Americans who began to break down the color barrier and rise to the top of their professions on merit alone.

FURTHER READING

Rivers, Francis E. "The Negro Should Support Landon," *Crisis*, 44 (October 1936).

Rivers, Francis E. "An Appeal to the Common Sense of Colored Citizens," distributed by the Republican National Committee, The Papers of the NAACP, part 18, series C, reel 29.

Rivers, Francis, and Jack Blinkoff, "Memorandum to Charles Breitel, Counsel to Governor Dewey" (20 July 1948), Thomas E. Dewey Papers, Series 5, Box 280, File 30.

"Black Game," *Time* (17 Aug. 1936).

"Res Ipsa Loquitur," *Time* (6 Sept. 1943).

Smith, Richard Norton. *Thomas E. Dewey and his Times* (1982).

Smith, J. Clay, Jr. *Emancipation: The Making of the Black Lawyer, 1844–1944* (1993).

Topping, Simon. "Never Argue with the Gallup Poll: Thomas Dewey, Civil Rights and the Election of 1948," in *Journal of American Studies* 38 (2004).

SIMON TOPPING

Rivers, Prince (1822–?), slave, soldier, and politician, was born and reared in Beaufort, South Carolina, to parents whose names are unknown. Little is known of Rivers's life other than that he was literate, was raised in the home of his master, and was working as a coachman both in Beaufort and in Edgefield, South Carolina, on the eve of the Civil War. Reputedly the finest coachman in Beaufort, he once drove the Confederate general P. G. T. Beauregard from that city to Charleston. Rivers was also a recognized leader of the slave community of Beaufort and was once chosen to present a petition to the governor of South Carolina requesting the redress of certain grievances. It is unknown whether he was successful. He was married to Rina Green, also a slave, who lived on a neighboring plantation.

In 1862, shortly after federal forces occupied Beaufort and other South Carolina coastal towns in December 1861, Rivers stole his master's horse and made his escape from well behind Confederate lines in Edgefield. His master posted notices throughout the state offering two thousand dollars for Rivers's capture. When he reached Union lines, Rivers offered his services to the army, and in April 1862 he was one of several hundred African Americans mustered into the First South Carolina Regiment of Volunteers, organized by Major General David Hunter.

Impressed by Rivers's bearing, command, and intelligence, Hunter made him first sergeant of the regiment in the summer of 1862 and brought him to New York City in an effort to increase Northern support for the enlistment of black soldiers in the Union army. Yet as became clear in New York City's deadly draft riots the following year, many Northern whites opposed not only enlisting blacks but also the Civil War and the protection of black rights in general. A mob attacked Rivers as he walked, or more likely marched, down Broadway, probably because of his Union army uniform and sergeant's stripes. Rivers held his own against his attackers before police officers intervened and dispersed the mob.

In late 1862 Rivers worked throughout coastal South Carolina as a recruiting officer and soon came to the attention of Colonel Thomas Wentworth Higginson, who was officially appointed commander of the First South Carolina Regiment in January 1863. On New Year's Day 1863 at a ceremony to celebrate President Lincoln's Emancipation Proclamation, Higginson chose Sergeant Rivers and Corporal Robert Sutton to receive the regiment's colors. The two soldiers, "jet black" and "fine looking men" in Higginson's view, also made impressive speeches.

Throughout 1863 Rivers served as provost-sergeant as well as color-sergeant and had primary charge of prisoners and the daily policing of the regiment's camp. So far as Higginson was concerned, no white officer in his regiment had "more administrative ability, or more absolute authority over the men" than Rivers had (Higginson, 57–58). The colonel was also impressed by Rivers's daily reports and believed that were Rivers to receive further training he could command the Army of the Potomac. Higginson went even further on one occasion, declaring that if South Carolina became a black monarchy, Prince Rivers would be its king.

Tellingly, Higginson also recorded that Rivers's men "do not love him," but that his "mere presence has controlling power over them" (Higginson, 56). Rivers's zeal and success in hunting down and capturing black deserters in Beaufort also did not endear him to many African Americans in his hometown. Unperturbed by those who found him overbearing, Rivers became increasingly interested in the political consequences of freedom, and he was one of several black South Carolina delegates who attended the Republican National Convention in 1864. At the end of the war he was billeted in Edgefield County and chose to pursue a political career there instead of Beaufort, perhaps because of lingering resentment of him in Beaufort. In 1867 he served as Edgefield's registrar, became active in the Union League—the forerunner of the Republican Party—and was chosen as an Edgefield County delegate to South Carolina's constitutional convention of 1868. At least nine of the black delegates to that convention had served in black regiments. Later that year Aiken County voters elected Rivers to the South Carolina House of Representatives, where he served for three terms until 1874.

Unlike HOLLAND THOMPSON and other black legislators during Reconstruction in South Carolina, Rivers strongly supported the recruitment of African Americans to the state militia, which he served for a time as a major general. He also chaired the House military affairs committee. Rivers supported the broad program of the Republican Party, including the expansion of public education and the extension of the vote to all black males. Through his close friendship with John J. Patterson, a railroad financier and future U.S. senator, he was also implicated in the graft scandals that tarnished the reputation of South Carolina's Reconstruction legislature. In late 1871 Rivers accepted a payment of two hundred dollars from Patterson to vote against the impeachment of Governor Robert K. Scott and to lobby other legislators to do likewise. An investigation of fraud in the legislature later revealed a separate payment of five hundred dollars to Rivers for persuading several members to vote for other pieces of legislation favorable to Patterson. Asked to defend his actions, Rivers told an investigating committee that he began to take bribes only after serving for a number of years and learning that other members were doing so. Though not an excuse for his deception, certainly Rivers was one of the poorer members of the legislature—yet as of 1870 his real estate worth $250 and his personal property worth $500 placed him somewhere in the middle of black legislators in terms of wealth.

Rivers also played a role in the Hamburg Riot of July 1876, which signaled the end of Reconstruction in South Carolina. As a resident magistrate for Hamburg in Edgefield County since 1868, Rivers enjoyed a mixed reputation. Though whites in the town lobbied to remove him from office, 109 African Americans successfully petitioned Governor Scott in 1869 to keep Rivers in his post and praised Rivers's evenhandedness in administering justice in a notoriously contentious and violent community.

By July 1876, however, the formation of rifle clubs by white opponents of Reconstruction and several rumored lynchings of African Americans challenged Rivers's authority as magistrate and his ability to maintain law and order. At the same time, DOCK ADAMS, a militia leader from neighboring Augusta, Georgia, had arrived in town to reorganize and drill the predominantly black state militia that Rivers had founded in 1870. Adams's skill in drilling the eighty or so armed militiamen was not unlike that of Rivers himself. On 4 July 1876, however, a skirmish between Adams's forces and two white men in Hamburg led the former Confederate general Matthew C. Butler, a leader of Edgefield's white rifle clubs, to demand that Rivers investigate the matter. Butler—who had no legal authority—demanded that Adams's troops surrender their weapons and publicly apologize to the two white men.

Fearing that an armed confrontation between the two sides would escalate, Rivers advised Adams and his men to give up their rifles and to withdraw to the safety of their armory. When Adams refused, a further clash between Butler's men and the militia resulted in the death of one white and several blacks. Five black militiamen were gunned down in cold blood after being captured. Although Rivers had largely taken Butler's side in the matter, white mobs also attacked the judge's home and threatened to kill him, but he escaped.

After 1877 Prince Rivers disappears from the historical record. Although Thomas Wentworth Higginson and others had predicted a bright future for him, the bloody end to Reconstruction decisively ended Rivers's political career. In his final years in Edgefield he once again found work as a coachman.

FURTHER READING
Higginson, Thomas Wentworth. *Army Life in a Black Regiment* (1871; 2001).
Holt, Thomas. *Black over White: Negro Political Leadership in South Carolina during Reconstruction* (1977).
Williamson, Joel. *After Slavery: The Negro in South Carolina during Reconstruction* (1965).

STEVEN J. NIVEN

Rivers, Ruben (1921–19 Nov. 1944), soldier and Medal of Honor recipient, was born in Tecumseh, Oklahoma. The son of farmers Willie and Lillian Rivers and one of eleven children, Ruben was of mixed heritage, being half native Cherokee and half African American. As a boy he worked on the family farm, but later left home to work on the railroad.

In 1942 Rivers, along with his brothers Robert and Dewey, enlisted for service in the army, inspired by the wave of patriotism and zeal for military service that swept the country in the days and months after the Japanese attack on Pearl Harbor on 7 December 1941. Like most African American army recruits, Rivers's brothers were assigned to support units and did not see combat action. However, Rivers was assigned to the 761st Tank Battalion, a newly formed segregated unit and was sent for initial training at Camp Claiborne, Louisiana, and later at Fort Hood, Texas, before his deployment overseas. One of his unit's junior officers was the star athlete JACKIE ROBINSON. While training in the deep south, the members of the 761st Tank were often harassed. In March 1943 several of its members were assaulted while on leave in Alexandria, Louisiana, and one was murdered. Jackie Robinson left the army due to a racial incident; Rivers, who stood out among the men of the self-named "Black Panther" battalion, rose to the rank of staff sergeant within a short time. His later instances of heroism under fire would demonstrate his outstanding soldier and leadership skills.

In the fall of 1944 the 761st Tank Battalion, with Sergeant Rivers serving in "A" Company, departed the United States for Europe, landing in France on 10 October 1944. The unit, consisting of a white commanding officer, thirty black junior officers, and nearly seven hundred black enlisted men, was subsequently assigned to General George Patton's Third Army. Before going into combat, Patton addressed the black tankers, telling them:

"Men, you're the first Negro tankers to ever fight in the American Army. I would never have asked for you if you weren't good. I have nothing but the best in my Army. I don't care what color you are as long as you go up there and kill those Kraut sons of bitches. Everyone has their eyes on you and is expecting great things from you. Most of all your race is looking forward to your success. Don't let them down and damn you, don't let me down" (Wilson, p. 53).

The men of the 761st Tank Battalion first went into combat on 7 November 1944, taking part in Patton's Saar Campaign in northeastern France, seeing heavy action at Vic-sur-Seille. Stationed in the lead tank, Rivers earned the Silver Star, the unit's first combat decoration, on 8 November when he dismounted from his tank under heavy enemy fire to remove a roadblock, thus allowing the 761st to keep up their advance without delay. On 16 November "A" Company, with Rivers's tank again in the lead, made an assault on German positions at Guebling. His tank hit a mine, and his leg was badly wounded. While Captain David Williams ordered Rivers to stay behind for medical treatment, Rivers refused and, after having his wound dressed, stayed with his company. Bogged down for three days by heavy German artillery fire, the 761st was on the move again on 19 November 1944 with Rivers in the lead tank, despite the fact that he was in great pain and had resisted further efforts by his officers to send him back for medical treatment. Near the town of Bougaltroff the 761st Tank Battalion encountered heavy German fire once again and Captain Williams ordered his tanks to pull back. However, Ruben Rivers had discovered the source of the German antitank fire and advanced on the area with one other tank directing fire to cover his unit's withdrawal. During the subsequent sharp exchange of fire, Rivers's tank took two direct hits in quick succession, killing him instantly and wounding his crew. While one of the 761st Tank Battalion's most accomplished and brave tankers was now gone, the unit continued on the battle lines in for another 171 days, earning high praise and, eventually, a Presidential Unit Citation.

Within a day after the death of Sergeant Rivers, Captain Williams recommended the tanker for the Medal of Honor; however, nothing came of it for over fifty years. Indeed, no African American received the Medal of Honor during World War II. Delayed recognition came only in the 1990s, after the army, at Congress's behest, commissioned a study of their wartime medal awards policies. After an exhaustive review by historians from Shaw University in Raleigh, North Carolina, a number of African American soldiers were recommended as being worthy of the Medal of Honor, Rivers among them. The recognition of the service of men like Ruben Rivers, Wiley James Jr., and EDWARD CARTER JR., albeit delayed for many years, is a reminder of the important contributions made by African American soldiers during World War II under the most difficult of racial conditions.

On 13 January 1997 Rivers's Medal of Honor was presented to his sister, Grace Woodfork, by President William Clinton at a moving White House ceremony. Among those present for the award was Rivers's unit commander, Captain Williams. Rivers is buried in the Lorraine American Cemetery at St. Avold, France.

FURTHER READING

Abdul-Jabbar, Kareem, and Anthony Walton. *Brothers in Arms: The Epic Story of the 761st Tank Battalion, WW II Forgotten Heroes* (2004).

Wilson, Joe, Jr. *The 761st "Black Panther" Tank Battalion in World War II* (1999).

GLENN ALLEN KNOBLOCK

Rivers, Sam (25 Sept. 1923–), multi-instrumentalist (tenor, soprano, and alto saxophones, piano, and flute), composer, arranger, and teacher was born Samuel Carthorne Rivers in El Reno, Oklahoma, to a family of musicians. Rivers's grandfather the Reverend Marshall Wiliam Taylor published a famous book of hymns and African American folk songs in 1882 entitled *A Collection of Revival Hymns and Plantation Melodies*. His parents, both college graduates from Chicago, played and toured with the Silvertone Quartet, a gospel group in which his father sang and his mother accompanied on piano. When he was still an infant, Rivers and his family moved to Chicago, where from the age of four Rivers sang in choirs directed by his mother. He joined his father on excursions to famous South Side venues—namely the Regal Theatre and Savoy Ballroom—to hear the top African American big bands of the day, from DUKE ELLINGTON and COUNT BASIE to EARL "FATHA" HINES. During this time Rivers also learned piano and violin, dropping the latter instrument a few years later to concentrate exclusively on piano.

After Rivers's father died in an automobile accident in 1937, his mother took a teaching position at Shorter College in Little Rock, Arkansas. Rivers continued to develop his musical talent, playing trombone in the marching band at age eleven, and two years later picking up a saxophone, which he found more to his liking and on which he then concentrated exclusively. By the time he graduated from high school in Little Rock at age fifteen, Rivers had learned the trombone, soprano saxophone, and baritone horn.

As a student at Jarvis Christian College in Texas, Rivers started improvising on the saxophone while learning the classic COLEMAN HAWKINS tenor saxophone interpretation and improvisation on "Body and Soul" from transcription. Soon Rivers was fervently studying other major saxophonists, like LESTER YOUNG and CHU BERRY. In the mid-1940s he heard the revolutionary innovations of "bebop" pioneers CHARLIE "YARDBIRD" PARKER and JOHN "DIZZY" GILLESPIE while working as a navy clerk stationed near San Francisco, California. He felt he had received his calling to become a professional musician. The 1945 Gillespie and Parker recording "Blue and Boogie" particularly intrigued Rivers. Rivers spent his off-hours moonlighting on gigs with singer Jimmy Witherspoon and participating in Bay Area jam sessions.

Inspired to further his musical training, Rivers enrolled in the Boston Conservatory of Music in 1947, studying composition and theory, and also attended Boston University. He occasionally worked with other artistically ambitious jazz musicians, including Jaki Byard, Nat Pierce, Charlie Mariano, GIGI GRYCE, Herb Pomeroy, and Alan Dawson. In 1952 Rivers dropped out of Boston University, suffering from illness for the next few years. He spent some time composing, but he remained relatively inactive as a performing musician. After his recovery Rivers moved to Florida in 1955, working in Miami with his brother, bass player Martin Rivers, and touring the South with rhythm and blues bands. A few years later, he returned to Boston, supporting himself by writing advertising jingles before rejoining the Herb Pomeroy orchestra (1960–1962) and forming a quartet in 1959 with pianist Hal Galper, bassist HENRY GRIMES, and a phenomenal thirteen-year-old drummer named TONY WILLIAMS.

Williams and Rivers would meet again in the summer of 1964 when the saxophonist, upon Williams's ardent recommendation, joined the MILES DAVIS Quintet, replacing tenor saxophonist George Coleman. Rivers toured and recorded with the quintet in Japan and as part of the World Jazz Festival. After his six-month tenure was over, he discovered that most of his musical peers in Boston were so busy teaching and performing on their own that they could no longer play with him. Undaunted, Rivers decided to move to Harlem and signed a recording contract with Blue Note, making his 1964 debut as a bandleader with the recording *Fuchsia Swing Song*, which demonstrated his movement from a post-bop conception into "free jazz" playing. The recording was well received by critics, and Rivers followed this success with another Blue Note session, *Contours*, with trumpeter Freddie Hubbard and pianist HERBIE HANCOCK, which was much closer to mainstream jazz traditions. Rivers returned to free jazz in 1966 with *Invocation*.

Rivers grew increasingly interested in teaching, eventually conducting a workshop with his big band music at a Harlem junior high school. After touring and recording with the CECIL TAYLOR Unit Ensemble in 1969 (he played with the group from 1968 to 1973), and a six-month stint with pianist McCOY TYNER's group, in 1971 Rivers and his wife, Bea, opened Studio Rivbea, a performance and loft living space in lower Manhattan, for rehearsals and performances of his own original compositions as well as those of musicians interested in new, experimental work in the jazz tradition. One of the first major New York "loft spaces" to emerge during the 1970s, the studio became a nurturing ground and a live performance outlet for numerous improvisational musicians and composers in New York.

From 1972 to 1982, after working again with Miles Davis as well as Chick Corea's avant-garde ensemble *Circle*, Rivers performed and recorded regularly in duos, trios, quartets, quintets, and big bands, and he continued to foster and promote his studio. Throughout the 1980s Rivers composed for orchestral and smaller groups for Impulse Records and many minor labels. In 1991, after concluding four years of international touring with Dizzy

Gillespie's quintet and big band, Rivers left New York to settle in Orlando, Florida, with his wife. While vacationing there, they had discovered a talented network of musicians working in theme parks and studios. Rivers formed his own record label (also called Rivbea) and wrote compositions for three Orlando-based ensembles: a sixteen-piece big band, an eleven-piece wind ensemble, and a trio, which was the orchestra's core rhythm section. He released two critically acclaimed albums for RCA, the 1999 Grammy Award–nominated *Inspiration* and 2000's *Culmination*. In the summer of 2000, Rivers released a double-CD on Rivbea, documenting his Orlando big band.

FURTHER READING

Davis, Francis. "At 75, a Maverick Has a Big Band 'Talking,'" *New York Times*, 10 Oct. 1999.

Gettelman, Parry. "Rivers Keeps It Fresh," *Orlando Sentinel Tribune*, 19 November 1999.

Hazell, Ed. "Big-band Bop: Sam Rivers's *Inspiration*," *Boston Phoenix*, 5 Aug. 1999.

Rubien, David. "Sam Rivers Jazz Original Reappears," *San Francisco Chronicle*, 7 Nov. 1993.

KOFI NATAMBU

Roach, Max (10 Jan. 1924–16 Aug. 2007), drummer and composer, was born Maxwell Roach in New Land, North Carolina; his family moved to Brooklyn in 1928. Roach's mother was a gospel singer, and Roach began to study piano at age eight with an aunt who was a church pianist and lived with his family; within a year he was performing at the summer Bible school of the Concord Baptist Church. At ten Roach began to study drums at a WPA-sponsored program in the church; he practiced constantly, and his parents eventually bought him a drum set as a reward for his commitment and for doing well in school. Over the next few years Roach played in various neighborhood groups, but much of his earliest professional experience came at the Putnam Central Club, owned by John Parish, a West Indian. Roach had studio space there, and there was a small ballroom where musicians could play.

During his teen years Roach studiously analyzed big-band arrangements—he later said that he learned his wire-brush technique under the influence of O'Neal Spencer, the drummer with the JOHN KIRBY Band—and he and friends from his neighborhood, including Cecil Payne and Randy Weston, would frequently take day trips to Manhattan to see bands at places like the Apollo. Soon Roach was playing at the jam sessions at Monroe's Uptown House, which

served as the incubator for bebop, and he was backing shows at George Jay's Taproom on West Seventy-ninth Street. At seventeen he even filled in briefly for SONNY GREER in DUKE ELLINGTON's band at the Paramount Theater. Throughout he maintained a serious approach to his academic and music studies, and he graduated from Boys High in Brooklyn with honors. In 1942 Roach became house drummer at Monroe's Uptown House, and he began to work regularly with the founders of bebop, especially THELONIOUS MONK, CHARLIE PARKER, and DIZZY GILLESPIE. Roach made his first recording in late 1943 on a session led by the saxophonist COLEMAN HAWKINS. In 1944 he was the drummer in what some scholars argue was the first true bebop group, a quintet co-led by the trumpeter Gillespie and the bassist OSCAR PETTIFORD at the Onyx Club. Roach subsequently joined Gillespie at the Yacht Club in a group that Gillespie co-led with the saxophonist BUDD JOHNSON. In 1944 and 1945 Roach toured with Benny Carter's big band and worked in various incarnations of the Gillespie/Parker quintet at the Three Deuces and at other clubs in New York. He toured with Gillespie's legendary big band in 1945 and 1946, and freelanced with various groups in clubs on Fifty-second Street. From April 1947 through mid-1949 Roach was the regular drummer with Parker's influential quintet.

Roach's drumming was clearly influenced by JO JONES, BABY DODDS, SID CATLETT, and especially CHICK WEBB, the most prominent swing drummers of the era. But he went far beyond them in extending the innovations of KENNY CLARKE that led to the rhythmic revolution of bebop. His earliest recordings with Parker, for instance, show "a highly responsive, contrapuntal style" (Korall, 2), centered on the essentials of bop drumming—time maintained on the hi-hat or top cymbals, a regular beat on the bass drum, comments or "bombs" on the snare and bass drums, and multiple polyrhythms. Roach also used space, silence, and dynamics in exploring the melodic elements of the drum kit in ways that few have since equaled, and he developed his uniquely delicate brushwork. Above all he told a story—and inevitably an interesting one. After Roach drummers no longer were mere timekeepers, but were soloists and instrumentalists as well.

Roach studied composition at the Manhattan School of Music in the late 1940s, but he also remained the bebop drummer of choice during the first decade of the bebop era. From 1948 to 1950 he made several recordings with MILES DAVIS groups. From 1951 to 1953 he played with Parker on a number

Max Roach, jazz drummer and composer, at the Three Deuces, New York City, c. October 1947. (© William P. Gottlieb; www.jazzphotos.com.)

of occasions, toured with Jazz at the Philharmonic in 1952, and was the drummer at the legendary 1953 Massey Hall, Toronto, concert with Parker, Gillespie, BUD POWELL, and CHARLES MINGUS.

In 1952 Roach also co-founded Debut Records with Mingus and Mingus's wife Celia, and he remained involved with the independent label until 1957. Roach also established himself as one of the premier ensemble leaders of the 1950s during these years. Most famously he was co-leader of the CLIFFORD BROWN–Max Roach quintet, until Brown's death in a car accident in 1956. Roach later said that only with Brown "did I feel that I was truly expressing myself." His playing acquired a new intensity in this group, with new rhythmic accents and unusual time signatures.

Roach's subsequent groups, on eleven recordings for Emarcy and Mercury Records (most notably *Max Roach Plus Four*, *Jazz in 3/4 Time*, *Max Roach Plus Four on the Chicago Scene*, and *The Many Sides of Max Roach*), pursued still more freedom, and he became increasingly interested in composition and in exploring longer forms. Roach began to compose works in unusual time signatures, such as 3/4, 5/4, and 7/4; on 1958's *Deeds Not Words*, a quintet session for Riverside Records, at one point the bass maintains a steady beat while Roach varied his meter throughout his solo. He also began

to employ younger musicians like the trumpeter Kenny Dorham and the saxophonists BOOKER LITTLE, HANK MOBLEY, and Clifford Jordan.

After leaving Mercury Records, Roach began to include more overtly political expressions in increasingly sophisticated compositions. Most notable was *We Insist! Freedom Now Suite* (Candid, 1960), a seven-part suite with Hawkins and Little on tenor saxes and Julian Priester on trombone. The track entitled "Tryptich: Prayer/Protest/Peace" is a powerful emotional statement featuring Roach accompanying his wife, the singer ABBEY LINCOLN (the two were married from 1962 to 1970), who shrieks and screams with rage; the album also includes similarly emotionally powerful statements in "Driva' Man" and "Tears for Johannesburg."

In 1960, again with Mingus, Roach organized the Cliff Walk Manor Festival at Newport in protest against the policies of the main festival, and throughout that decade he was centrally involved in the African American cultural arts movement. He recorded prolifically during the decade and produced a series of highly acclaimed albums, including *Percussion Bitter Suite* (Impulse!, 1960), *It's Time* (Impulse!, 1962), *Speak Brother, Speak* (Fantasy, 1962), and *Drums Unlimited* (Atlantic, 1966), which includes three unaccompanied solo pieces. In 1971 he recorded *Lift Every Voice* for Atlantic with the twenty-two-piece J.C. White Singers, dedicated to PAUL ROBESON, MARTIN LUTHER KING JR., MALCOLM X, MEDGAR EVERS, and Patrice Lumumba. Roach also wrote music for Broadway musicals, Hollywood films, television, and orchestras, and in 1970 he founded a multipercussionist group, "M'Boom," that toured and recorded periodically over the next two decades.

Roach did not slow down at all during the 1970s. He fed his musical growth by recording two albums with the multireedist ANTHONY BRAXTON on Hat Hut, 1978's *Birth and Rebirth* and 1979's *One in Two*, and a duet with the saxophonist ARCHIE SHEPP, also for Hat Hut, *The Long March*, that was filled, as one critic has noted, with filled with creative, powerful explorations of the drum kit's percussive potentials. Roach's encounter with the pianist CECIL TAYLOR at Columbia University in 1979, *Historic Concerts* (on Soul Note), shows Roach fully the creative equal of the percussive free-jazz pianist. Roach also recorded an album with the South African pianist Abdullah Ibrahim in 1977, *Streams of Consciousness*.

Roach continued to perform during these years with his own groups, particularly with a quartet that included the trumpeter Cecil Bridgewater, the saxophonist Odeon Pope, and the bassist Calvin Hill. The group made several recordings for the Italian Soul Note label, notably *Pictures in a Frame* (1979), *Chattahoochie Red* (1981), *In the Light* (1982), and *Scott Free* (1984). Always seeking new musical approaches, Roach also recorded albums with his own quartet and with a classical string quartet that included his daughter, Maxine; the best of these are *Easy Winners* (1985) and *Bright Moments* (1986). The duet album that he recorded with Dizzy Gillespie in 1989 includes a lengthy interview with the pair, and at the age of seventy-four Roach recorded a trio album for Asian Improv Records with Jon Jang on piano and Jiebing Chen on erhu (a two-string fiddle that sounds like a double bass), a challenging, brilliant synthesis of jazz and Asian music. Finally in 2002 Roach and CLARK TERRY, two of the most accomplished and adventurous musicians of the modern jazz era, recorded a quartet album called *Friendship* for Columbia Records that serves as an elegiac paean to the music and musicians of their era.

Roach's achievements have extended beyond jazz and have won him international recognition. He won an Obie Award for his musical collaboration with the director George Terencz on a set of three Sam Shepard plays in the mid-1980s, and he wrote the music for AMIRI BARAKA's "Bumpy, a Bopera" in 1990. He has also composed a sound track for "Body and Soul," Paul Robeson's first film. Roach appeared on the *Tonight* show in 1982, in 1986 on a television special on King's life, and in 1992 on an episode of *Jazz Backstage*. He was awarded a MacArthur Prize, the first for jazz, in 1988 and has received six honorary doctorates. He was a member of the American Academy and Institute of Arts and Letters. Roach has also been involved in jazz education throughout his career. He taught at the Lennox School of Jazz during the late 1950s, and in 1972 he was appointed to the faculty of the University of Massachusetts, Amherst. He served as mentor to generations of musicians, including the young rap artists that he worked with in the 1980s, long before the genre entered the musical mainstream.

Until his death, Max Roach remained among the most visible, widely recorded drummers in the history of jazz. He is the immediately recognizable drummer on hundreds of seminal bebop recordings, his "bombs" resonating amid some of the most subtle, swinging polyrhythms recorded in the history of jazz. His many interviews reveal him to be among the most generous, humanistic of modern artists, and he has spoken lovingly and with clear admiration of the many who assisted him in his life.

He brings to his life and to his playing a profound historical awareness of the music called jazz.

In a 1972 essay for *Black Scholar* he described his discontent with the word "jazz" that carries so many negative connotations and offered instead an extended alternative: "It is the cultural expression of Africans who are dispersed on this North American continent. It derives in a continuing line from the musical and cultural traditions of Africa. We must recognize what those traditions are, what it is we are doing musically, how we learn our music, how it pleases and has meaning, and what its significance is." Or as he said to his fellow drummer Art Taylor, "My music tries to say how I really feel, and I hope it mirrors in some way how black people feel in the United States." Roach died in Manhattan at the age of 83.

FURTHER READING

Roach, Max. "What 'Jazz' Means to Me," in *Black Scholar* (Summer 1972).

Cadence 5 (June 1979) and 22 (Dec. 1996).

Down Beat 53 (Oct. 1985), 57 (Nov. 1990), and 60 (Nov. 1993).

Giddins, Gary. *Visions of Jazz: The First Century* (1998)

Korall, Burt. "Max Roach: His Life in Rhythm," in *The Complete Mercury Max Roach Plus Four Sessions* (2000).

Taylor, Arthur. *Notes and Tones* (1977).

DISCOGRAPHY

The Complete Mercury Max Roach Plus Four Sessions (2000).

RONALD P. DUFOUR

Robbins, Parker David (5 July 1834–1 Nov. 1917), carpenter, statesman, and inventor, was born free in Bertie County, North Carolina, the eldest son of John A. Robbins, a farmer and carpenter, and Mary Robbins. Robbins hailed from a family and community of mixed-race, free black, and Chowanoke background in the counties of Bertie, Gates, and Hertford in northeastern North Carolina. The Algonquian-speaking Chowanokes lived on the west bank of the Chowan River that bears their name in northeastern North Carolina. Governor Ralph Lane was impressed by their villages in a 1585 Roanoke Island expedition. Parker's grandfather John Robbins was one of the chief men of the Chowanokes in 1790.

War and disease greatly reduced the Chowanoke population, and by 1790, during a sale of Chowanoke land, it was reported (whether falsely or not is unknown) that the Chowanoke men had all died and the remaining women had intermarried with several free black males who migrated into the region from Virginia. The children who descended from the Chowanoke–free black unions, classified as "mulatto," were landowners, farmers, and skilled artisans and were mostly literate. "The presumption of one's status, whether slave or free, often depended upon his color. In a series of cases, the Supreme Court established a set of principals that came to be accepted law throughout the State" (Franklin, 52). Since 1924 all Native Americans born within territorial limits of the United States have been considered United States citizens. Prior to 1924 Native Americans in North Carolina were generally listed as mulatto (Jones, 9).

A school for Native Americans existed briefly in Gates County, but free people of color in North Carolina were legally compelled to enter into apprenticeships beginning in 1762. While a 1741 mandatory apprentice law was directed at mulatto children born to white women, the 1762 law included all free black children. The 1762 law and subsequent apprenticeship laws placed large numbers of free black children under the control of authorities. Mandatory apprenticeship laws were enacted to ensure that their communities would not be burdened with poverty or possible criminal activities. It became the responsibility, by law, of the master or mistress of free black apprentices to make sure that apprenticed children learned to read and write. By 1800 free black children were being apprenticed in large numbers, which probably accounts for their high rate of literacy.

At the time of the first census in 1790 there were 5,041 free blacks in North Carolina. By 1800 that number had increased to 7,043, with the heaviest concentration in northeastern North Carolina. Free blacks and mulattoes numbered 27,463 by 1850, and the mostly rural group remained concentrated in the northeastern counties that bordered Virginia.

Unlike South Carolina and Virginia, North Carolina remained a state of small, independent yeoman farmers with its heaviest concentration of planters and slaves in the eastern and northeastern regions. The vast majority of settlers were encouraged to enter the region under the head right system, which allowed fifty acres of land for every person (including slaves) brought into the colony. As a result free blacks from Virginia moved into northeastern North Carolina and intermarried with various Native American groups, including the Chowanokes, Meherrins, Tuscaroras, and Nottoways. The members of this close-knit, racially mixed group became prosperous small farmers and skilled and literate artisans.

Although little is known of Parker's early life, by 1857 he owned 102 acres of land near Powellsville in Bertie County. He was listed in the 1860 census as a "mechanic" or carpenter and was married to Elizabeth Collins of neighboring Hertford County. Collins and her family were descended from free blacks, Meherrins, and Chowanokes who settled the Pleasant Plains community between present-day Winton and Ahoskie, North Carolina. Eight Pleasant Plains men served in the Continental army during the War of Independence, and by 1830 seven Pleasant Plains farmers owned a total of twelve slaves. However, northeastern North Carolina officials required that all free people of color carry a pass following the NAT TURNER rebellion in nearby Southampton County, Virginia.

Robbins's activities during the early years of the Civil War are not known, but he probably continued to manage his farm and carpentry business. In 1863 he and his younger brother Augustus Robbins (1842–1928) left Bertie County, crossed Union lines, made the sixty-seven-mile trip to Norfolk, Virginia, and joined the Union army. On 1 January 1864 Parker Robbins was enrolled as a sergeant major in the Second U.S. Colored Cavalry attached to Fort Monroe, Virginia. Augustus was enrolled a few days later as a first sergeant in the same unit. Within a few weeks of his enrollment, Parker Robbins contracted mumps, measles, and rheumatism so severely that he suffered partial but permanent impairment of his sight and hearing. Nevertheless, he remained in the cavalry until his honorable discharge at Hampton, Virginia, in March 1866 with a disability pension. Augustus was also discharged at that time.

Following the Civil War Robbins returned home to Bertie County, where he won election to the North Carolina state constitutional convention in the fall of 1867 and the North Carolina House of Representatives in April 1868. His single term in the legislature was notable for his bill, defeated by the House, to end racial discrimination on passenger steamboats. He was succeeded in office by Augustus Robbins. African Americans formed the majority in sixteen counties in eastern North Carolina, and the Republican Party was strong in that part of the state.

Around 1873 Robbins moved to Harrellsville in neighboring Hertford County, a few miles from his birthplace. He remained active in Republican politics and in 1875 was awarded the office of postmaster at Harrellsville. He was residing in Harrellsville when he patented both of his inventions. In 1874 he obtained a patent for a horse-drawn cotton cultivator in which a beveled gear operated choppers or blades underneath the frame of the machine. In 1877 he obtained a patent for a saw-sharpening machine, which consisted of a hand-cranked rotary file with grooves that pulled the saw through as the teeth were filed.

After resigning as Harrellville's postmaster in 1877, Robbins, without his wife, moved to Duplin County, North Carolina, where he lived for the next thirty-nine years in the towns of Hallsville and Magnolia. There he operated a sawmill and a cotton gin. By 1888 he also operated a steamboat (the *St. Peter*) that he built himself at Hallsville and used for regular passenger service between there and Wilmington along the northeast branch of the Cape Fear River. He was a member of the predominantly white Methodist church in Magnolia and lived successively in two handsome houses there, both of which he constructed himself.

In 1884 Robbins and Elizabeth divorced, and by 1896 Robbins had married Bettie Florence Miller of Keansville. They had one son. Parker Robbins remained a man of property and political influence until his death in Magnolia.

FURTHER READING

The Center for Urban Affairs. *Paths toward Freedom: A Biographical History of Blacks and Indians in North Carolina by Blacks and Indians* (1976).

Franklin, John Hope. *The Free Negro in North Carolina, 1790–1860* (1971).

Jones, Alice Eley. *Hertford County, North Carolina* (2002).

Rights, Douglas L. *The American Indian in North Carolina* (1947).

Smallwood, Arwin D. *Bertie County: An Eastern Carolina History* (2002).

ALICE ELEY JONES

Roberts, Benjamin Franklin (1814–6 Sept. 1881),

abolitionist, printer, journalist, and civil rights litigant, was born in the heart of Boston's black community on Beacon Hill, the second of Sarah Easton Roberts and Robert Roberts's twelve children. Both parents were active abolitionists—his mother was the daughter of James Easton, the successful black Massachusetts businessman and reformer, and his father was an author and household manager for the elite white families of Christopher Gore and Nathaniel Appleton. Roberts's father had been born in Charleston, South Carolina; he moved to Boston in 1805 and married in 1813. His second son, named for the famed Benjamin Franklin, reflected the family's commitment to the principles of the American Revolution and foretold his career as a printer.

As a young man, Roberts became a shoemaker's apprentice, but after completing his training, whites refused to hire him. They "refused, I suppose, merely on account of that well known crime of having dark skin" (Kendrick and Kendrick, 103). At around age twenty, he began publishing in the *Liberator*, the country's leading abolitionist newspaper, pillorying American racial attitudes and the plans of the American Colonization Society to transport free American blacks to Liberia. An unyielding integrationist, Roberts not only opposed any scheme that questioned the citizenship of African Americans, but he even rejected use of the word African in the names of black institutions. "WE ARE AMERICANS!" he once thundered. (Kendrick and Kendrick, 103).

Dissatisfied with the coverage given to black issues and events by the *Liberator* and other reform newspapers, Roberts began publication of the *Anti-Slavery Herald* in April 1838 (no issues of the paper survive). The *Herald* not only intended to give an unmediated voice to Boston's black community but would also serve as an apprenticeship program in printing for young blacks—on the model of James Easton's ironworks trade school. Roberts wanted to do all he could to promote black economic opportunity in a city notorious for its relentless discrimination. Not long after the *Herald* appeared, one of Roberts's white patrons, Amos A. Phelps, a prominent white member of the Massachusetts Anti-Slavery Society, withdrew his support and demanded that Roberts return his letter endorsing the paper. To Phelps, Roberts was nothing more than a bigot and a self-promoter. Roberts concluded that white abolitionists such as Phelps were hypocrites who sought to "muzzle, exterminate and put down the efforts of certain colored individuals effecting [sic] the welfare of their colored brethren" (Ripley, 269). However, Boston's black community remained loyal to William Lloyd Garrison and his allies and turned against Roberts, forcing him to abandon his paper six months later. Bitter over the experience, Roberts withdrew from the antislavery movement for the next ten years.

Sometime after the paper's demise, Roberts married a woman named Adeline and they moved to Lynn, Massachusetts, where he continued to work as a printer. In 1843 Roberts opened a print shop in Boston, specializing in pamphlets, Masonic literature, and books. In 1844 he printed R.B. Lewis's *Light and Truth*, a massive history of black and Native American peoples. In 1842 he and his wife lost a son, Thomas, to scarlet fever, and they had a daughter, Sarah, named after his wife's mother. Sarah lived up to the family's antislavery legacy and would soon become the focus of her father's challenge to Boston's racially segregated educational system.

Boston maintained the Abiel Smith School—on the back side of Beacon Hill—for all the city's black children. Roberts, however, attempted to enroll Sarah in a school just a few yards from his home. The city rejected the move and compelled Sarah to walk past about five different elementary schools just to attend the segregated one. Roberts was outraged. The state constitution and the laws of the Commonwealth, he fumed, protected the "equal rights of ALL the inhabitants" (Kendrick and Kendrick, 109). In the spring of 1848 Roberts hired Robert Morris, the city's leading black attorney, to sue the school board and the city of Boston. He could have hired any number of experienced and successful white attorneys, but Roberts wanted to place black achievements and black talent before the public: "unaided and unbiased we commenced the struggle" (Kendrick and Kendrick, 111). Under a city statute that allowed compensation to the families of those children deliberately excluded from Boston schools, Roberts and Morris sought $600 in damages. They lost the case and appealed, eventually winding up before the Commonwealth's Supreme Judicial Court. In 1850 *Roberts v. City of Boston*, a landmark decision in American constitutional history, was heard by Chief Justice Lemuel Shaw, a craggy mountain of judicial learning. By the time the case reached the state's highest court, Roberts agreed to add the charismatic young lawyer and abolitionist Charles Sumner to his legal team. Sumner argued that separate schools stigmatized "by caste or race" were inherently unequal and "could not be an equivalent" (Levy, 327). Despite enormous talent and sound logic, Morris and Sumner could not prevail. Shaw ruled that separate schools were in fact equal and that prejudice was "not created by law and probably cannot be changed by law" (Levy, 331). Although in 1855 abolitionists successfully convinced the state legislature to outlaw separate schools, the *Roberts* case became a dark chapter in American constitutional history. The U.S. Supreme Court in 1896 enshrined Shaw's "separate but equal" doctrine in *Plessy v. Ferguson*

where it remained constitutional law until *Brown v. Board of Education* in 1954.

In 1850 Roberts began touring with the escaped slave HENRY "BOX" BROWN, narrating Brown's diorama that depicted his famed escape from slavery by mailing himself in a wooden box. In 1853 he again tried to publish an antislavery paper, the *Self-Elevator*, but it also quickly died. In 1874 the *New York Times* reported that Roberts had brought a libel suit against the *Boston Herald*, which, Roberts asserted, had accused him of participating in a conspiracy to kidnap a young girl. He lost the suit. Little else is known of Roberts, who died of epilepsy in 1881.

FURTHER READING

Kendrick, Stephen, and Paul Kendrick. *Sarah's Long Walk: The Free Blacks of Boston and How Their Struggle for Equality Changed America* (2004).

Levy, Leonard, with Douglas Jones. "Jim Crow Education: Origins of the 'Separate but Equal' Doctrine," in *Judgments: Essays on American Constitutional History* (1972).

Price, George P., and James Brewer Stewart. "The Roberts Case, the Easton Family, and the Dynamics of the Abolitionist Movement in Massachusetts, 1776–1870," *Massachusetts Historical Review* (2002).

Ripley, C. Peter et al., eds. *The Black Abolitionist Papers* (1991).

DONALD YACOVONE

Roberts, Carl Glennis (15 Dec. 1886–15 Jan. 1950), surgeon, was born in Roberts Settlement, Hamilton County, Indiana, the son of John A. and Nancy E. (Simpson) Roberts. His parents, small-time farmers, owned a twenty-five acre farm. A native of Roberts Settlement, a prosperous free-black farm community in central Indiana, Carl Roberts came of age at a time when Midwestern farming prospects were on the wane: prices of farm products (and therefore, income) declined 50 percent from 1870 to 1900, and the increasing use of horse-powered technology, such as cultivators and threshers, favored large-scale farmers at the expense of smaller producers like his parents. As a teenager, Roberts rejected pleas to assume control of the family farm when his father retired. Hoping to escape rural life, he moved to Fairfield, Indiana, a nearby small town, and was raised by relatives.

In the 1930s Roberts donated the family's pioneer-era papers to the Library of Congress, thereby preserving a rare glimpse of free-black life in the rural Midwest. He was actively involved in extended-family "homecoming reunions" from the mid-1920s—part of a national trend of family reunions that gained popularity in the 1920s as urbanites tried to retain a sense of their rural past. He organized an extensive genealogical chart of the Roberts family that was included in the donation to the Library of Congress; *Ebony* described it in 1951 as "a 45-foot-long genealogical chart." Most notably, the Jonathan Roberts collection, as it is known, includes more than a dozen letters exchanged among Roberts's kin at the Indiana frontier with those in their native North Carolina in the early 1830s, along with a family account book used from 1780 through 1810.

After benefiting from a rigorous high school training at Fairfield Academy, Roberts enrolled in northern Indiana's Valparaiso University, receiving a B.A. in 1910 and a medical degree the following year. During his time at Valparaiso he married Lucille Eleanor Williams. Upon Roberts's graduation, the family moved to Chicago's South Side, where they resided for the remainder of Roberts's life. The couple had two children.

Roberts's medical training continued well after his graduation from Valparaiso. He pursued advanced coursework at seven Chicago-area institutions between 1911 and 1934, including the Illinois Post-Graduate School of Operative Surgery, the University of Chicago Medical School, and the Cook County Hospital Graduate School's Laboratory of Surgical Pathology. His education was complemented with medical practices at the German-American Hospital, Chicago General Hospital, and Provident Hospital. While primarily a clinical instructor, Roberts's specialty was gynecological surgery. One of his principle contributions to African American medicine came at Provident Hospital, one of the nation's premier African American hospitals through much of the twentieth century. Although founded in the 1890s as an integrated facility, Provident had become a predominantly black institution by the time of Roberts's arrival in 1912. Building on its growing reputation as among the nation's leading black hospitals, Provident embarked in 1917 on establishing the first postgraduate-level institution for African American doctors. Roberts, with his thorough and varied training, was chosen to coordinate the team that planned and staffed the inaugural program.

Perhaps equally significant was his role in 1935 to dramatically expand the hospital. As chairman of the Department of Surgery, he was instrumental in forging a formal alliance between Provident Hospital and the University of Chicago. During the process Roberts assumed principle responsibility for designing and placing into operation a five-year plan of surgical training supervised by the University of Chicago. The program received the official approval of two of the nation's leading medical organizations, the American Medical Association (AMA) and the American College of Surgeons.

Roberts also was a leading advocate for improving the standing of the black medical community in an age of increasing racial discrimination. He served eight years as a member of the Board of Trustees for the National Medical Association (NMA), the African American counterpart to the AMA, which had refused to accept blacks as members. In 1928 Roberts became the NMA's president and served the group in a variety of capacities, often as a contributor to the NMA's quarterly journal. Especially important was Roberts's role in pricking the consciousness of the American Medical Association—and raising the standing of all African American doctors in general—through his testimony as a member of the Giles Commission of 1938. At the behest of Roscoe Giles, the National Medical Association president in 1937, three leading black physicians, including Roberts, requested a "goodwill meeting" with the board of trustees of the AMA.

During the ensuing gathering, the Giles group questioned the AMA's practice of identifying African Americans with the marker "(col.)" (for "colored") after their names in the group's public directory of the nation's physicians. In his testimony, Roberts grippingly pointed to damage done to his own reputation and status caused by the designation, noting that he had experienced both the loss of his malpractice insurance and a lowered credit rating. While the AMA trustees deferred immediate judgment, the designation was quietly dropped in the directory's next publication. Two years later a similar appeal was made before the American Council of Surgeons, a highly selective body that had barred blacks from its ranks since the 1910s. When the group relented in its practice in 1945, it unanimously voted to admit four highly qualified African Americans. Carl Glennis Roberts was among those selected.

FURTHER READING

Fleming, G. James, and Christian E. Burckell. *Who's Who in Colored America* (1950).

Organ, Claude H., and Margaret Kosiba, eds. *A Century of Black Surgeons* (1987).

Vincent, Stephen. *Southern Seed, Northern Soil: African-American Farm Communities in the Midwest, 1765–1900* (2000).

STEPHEN VINCENT

Roberts, Frederick Madison (14 Sept. 1879–19 July 1952), mortician, publisher, and California state legislator, was born in Harris Station, Ohio, near Chillicothe, the son of Andrew Jackson Roberts and Ellen Wayles Hemmings Roberts. His mother was a granddaughter of SALLY HEMMINGS and U.S. president Thomas Jefferson; Sally Hemmings's father, who was also the father of Jefferson's wife Martha, was named Wayles.

Roberts's sister Myrtle Estelle was born in 1886 in Ohio, but by the time his brother William was born in 1889, the family had moved to Los Angeles, California. In 1894 they lived at 606 East Fifth Street. His father was cofounder and owner, and sometimes driver, of the Los Angeles Van, Truck, and Storage Company. In 1910 they lived at 1331 Wall Street, where their neighbors were a mix of skilled blue-collar workers, a teacher, a police officer, and an elevator boy, all classified by the census enumerator as "white." Roberts joined the Charles Sumner Marching Society at age seventeen, and took an active role in Republican Party politics. Los Angeles had only one high school, and he was the first student of African descent to graduate from it.

After fourteen years, Andrew Roberts left the trucking business for health reasons, opening one of the first undertaking businesses in the state. Both sons eventually joined the new business, as did a son-in-law, Izan E. Saunders, who became expert at embalming. But Roberts's path to the family business took him out of state for several years. After briefly enrolling at the University of Southern California, he went to Colorado College in Colorado Springs, where he was a star football player and graduated with honors. After prospecting for gold in Nevada, he returned to Colorado Springs, edited the *Colorado Springs Light,* and served as deputy tax assessor of El Paso County from 1907 to 1909. Then, he entered Barnes School of Mortuary Science in Chicago, Illinois, returning to Los Angeles in 1911 to join his father's growing business.

Around 1917, father and sons contracted to have a new building constructed, both as a funeral home and to house the *New Age,* a paper Roberts had purchased in 1912 and continued to edit until 1948. The building was described as "the most up-to-date of its kind owned by colored people in the State of California. The second floor is used for an auditorium and has perfect acoustics and will seat fully five hundred persons" (Beasley, p. 137). The entire family was active in the First African Methodist Episcopal (AME) Church, and in 1914 Roberts was elected secretary of the local Dumas Lyceum Bureau, with the stated mission to bind "the East and West more closely by an exchange of noted Race talent" (Flamming, p. 169).

Roberts was elected to represent the 74th District in the California state assembly in 1918. He won a 5-way Republican primary with 34 percent of the vote, 173 votes ahead of his nearest rival. There had been no significant Democratic strength in the district, which until recently had been dominated by the Socialist and Republican parties. The Democrat Frank Gayhart ran as an independent, with the undisguised campaign slogan "My opponent is a nigger," and lost, with 1,778 votes to Roberts's 2,261, while a Socialist took 550. Roberts voted in 1919 to ratify the Eighteenth Amendment to the U.S. Constitution, prohibiting the importation, manufacture, or sale of intoxicating liquors. He introduced Bill No. 693, which passed, increasing the fine for racial discrimination in public places to a minimum of $100, with no maximum. He also introduced legislation to protect citizens from arbitrary land seizures and excessive taxation, and to improve sanitation services and schools.

In 1921 Roberts married Pearl Hinds, who had studied at the Boston Conservatory of Music. Mrs. Roberts said, long after her husband's death, that he had briefly told her about his descent from Jefferson, adding, "We just don't talk about it." Mrs. Roberts related this was partly due to "the illegitimacy thing" and "then, too, people simply did not believe us" (Brodie). They had one daughter, Gloria, who became an internationally acclaimed pianist.

Roberts continued to be reelected until 1934, when he was defeated by AUGUSTUS F. HAWKINS, also of African descent, but a Democrat. Like Roberts, Hawkins brought together a biracial coalition, but black voters were moving from Republican to Democrat, while other working-class voters, who had divided partisan loyalties, were drawn to the Democratic ticket by the New Deal after 1932. One of Roberts's last legislative accomplishments was passage of a modest antilynching bill, cosponsored with Assemblyman William F. Knowland of Alameda County. The bill defined lynching as "the act of taking any person from custody of a peace officer by riot" and imposed a penalty of not more than twenty years in prison. Murder by a mob, of persons not already in custody, was thus not included. The bill passed the assembly on 31 March 1933, just as newspapers were announcing Nazi implementation of a boycott of Jews in Germany. Approved unanimously by the senate, it was sent to the governor for signature on 5 May.

Pearl Hinds Roberts later recalled that in his newspaper, her husband used the term "Americans of African descent" rather than the then-common "Negro." When other newspapers ran headlines "another Negro lynched," he would run the headline "another American lynched" (Brodie). The future diplomat RALPHE BUNCHE got his first job working at the *New Age*.

During his later years, Roberts became a close friend of California's attorney general and governor Earl Warren, who two years after Roberts's death was Chief Justice of the U.S. Supreme Court, when it decided *Brown v. Board of Education*. In 1946, running again as a Republican, with the endorsement of the prizefighter JOE LOUIS, Roberts lost an election for congress to the incumbent Democrat Helen Gahagan Douglas. He died at Los Angeles County General Hospital, of injuries from an automobile accident while backing out of his driveway the day before.

FURTHER READING

A collection of Frederick Madison Roberts's papers is housed by the African American Museum and Library in Oakland, California.

Beasley, Delilah L. *The Negro Trail Blazers of California* (1919).

Brodie, Fawn M. "Thomas Jefferson's Unknown Grandchildren: A Study in Historical Silences." *American Heritage* 27. no. 6 (Oct. 1976).

Flamming, Douglas. *Bound for Freedom: Black Los Angeles in Jim Crow America* (2006).

Obituary: *Los Angeles Times*, 29 July 1952.

CHARLES ROSENBERG

Roberts, George R. (c. 1771–Jan. 1861), War of 1812 privateer, was probably a free black living in Baltimore, Maryland, at the beginning of the War of 1812. Nothing is known of his origin or background. Because of his subsequent wartime service, it may be speculated that Roberts was plying the trade of a mariner, or worked in an allied trade around Baltimore's harbor district. He served aboard the Baltimore privateer *Sarah Ann* under Captain Richard Moon early in the war, and later on Captain Thomas Boyle's *Chasseur*. Aboard both these ships Roberts would experience some of the fiercest sea battles of the War of 1812.

The service of Roberts, JOHN DAVIS, JOHN JOHNSON, and other blacks in the War of 1812 was a major contribution in the war at sea. Often recognized in their own time for their gallant and valuable service, they have been largely forgotten by historians today. While many blacks served in the American Navy during the War of 1812, an even greater number served on privateers, privately owned vessels issued letters-of-marque authorizing them to prey on British merchant ships. Unfortunately, the crew records for many of these vessels have been lost and the historian is left with only fragmentary accounts and letters, composed by white sailors and ship's masters, to piece together the African American experience in the War of 1812. Because of this lack of records, the number of blacks that actually served in privateers can never be fully known. Regardless, that the number was in the thousands is evidenced by the fact that nearly 1,000 blacks alone were imprisoned in Britain's notorious Dartmoor Prison, many ruled with a fair but firm hand by a fellow black sailor–turned–prison leader named "King Dick," whose real name was RICHARD CRAFUS.

Countless other black seamen, however, were killed in action, captured, and later released under the cartel system, or simply vanished at sea without a trace due to storm or mishaps unknown. Though a sailor's life was difficult and the uncertainty of one's fate always hung in the balance, privateering did have its advantages. Not only was the discipline in privately armed vessels more relaxed than that in regular navy ships but the rewards were also potentially much higher; since all of the crew shared in the proceeds from the sale of a captured vessel and her cargo once it was brought into port, the smallest share allowed to even the lowliest man aboard could sometimes amount to a king's ransom in comparison to the wages paid by the American navy. The service of Roberts on several ships during the war, even though he was once captured, was very possibly influenced by the possibility of such financial rewards.

Roberts's first known sea service in the war came aboard Captain Richard Moon's *Sarah Ann*, a one-gun schooner with a fifty-man crew. Despite the diminutive size of his vessels, Moon proved a skilled sea-fighter; in October 1812 the *Sarah Ann* and her crew attacked a British merchantman armed with ten guns and, despite a stiff fight, captured her. However, in a later cruise, the *Sarah Ann* was captured by a British warship and her men imprisoned. Roberts came through this ordeal safely with the help of his captain; black sailors taken captive were often accorded less protection than white sailors and were sometimes pressed into service in the Royal Navy. However, according to the historian Christopher George, Moon intervened on Roberts's behalf, telling their captors that he was American born and had a wife back home. As a result, Roberts stayed aboard as part of a prisoner cartel and soon returned home to Baltimore.

Roberts's next maritime service is unknown but two possibilities may be speculated upon; perhaps grateful to Captain Moon for his action on his behalf, he may have followed Moon to his next command, the nine-gun schooner *Globe* in November 1813. If so, Roberts would have once again experienced heavy action when Moon engaged two British packet-brigs, one of fourteen and another of eighteen guns, off Madeira and fought them to a standstill. Although the *Globe* escaped to fight another day, the schooner lost eight and fifteen were wounded, including a black man named "Fortune." The other possibility for Roberts's interim service was aboard Captain Thomas Boyle's *Comet*, armed with fourteen guns and carrying a crew of 120 men. In light of Roberts's later service under Captain Boyle, it is possible that he too served on the *Comet*, and was perhaps aboard when she out-fought the twenty-two-gun *Hibernia* and captured a number of prizes in mid-1814.

No matter what his prior service, Roberts is known to have later served aboard Baltimore's most renowned privateer, the sixteen-gun *Chasseur*, nicknamed the "Pride of Baltimore," and manned by 100 men. Commanded by Captain Thomas Boyle, who had previously made a name for himself on the *Comet*, there can be no doubt that Boyle brought many of the faithful sailors from his previous command to *Chasseur*, perhaps including Roberts. In 1814 the *Chasseur* ravaged the seas around the British Isles and captured at least eighteen valuable merchantmen. Whether or not Roberts was aboard for this first cruise is unknown. However, he was aboard for Captain Boyle's last cruise of the war when, in February 1815, off the coast of Cuba, *Chasseur* captured the thirteen-gun British warship *St. Lawrence*, formerly the American privateer schooner *Atlas*. In a short but bloody battle the *Chasseur* and her crew, suffering the loss of five killed and eight wounded, captured the *St. Lawrence*, killing fifteen of her crew and wounding twenty-five. During the battle Roberts, serving as a gunner, "displayed the most intrepid courage and daring" and demonstrated a "brave

character" (George, website). Upon the *Chasseur's* return to Baltimore, Captain Boyle and his crew were accorded a heroes' welcome.

The details of Roberts's life after the War of 1812 are unknown, but his obituary leaves no doubt that he was respected and well-remembered by the citizens of Baltimore for his service. His obituary in the *Baltimore Sun* on 16 January 1861 states that he was a resident of nearby Canton and was "adorned by an amiable disposition." Most notably, he was further honored as "a man whose patriotism, good sense, and high moral character have won for him many friends for whom the news of his death will cause heartfelt sorrow."

FURTHER READING
George, Christopher T. "A Maritime Point of View … African-American Sailors Served in our Nation's Private Navy." Available at http://baltimoremd.com/monuments/blacksatsea.html.
Maclay, Edgar S. *A History of American Privateers* (1899).

GLENN ALLEN KNOBLOCK

Roberts, Grace (1844?–1 Nov. 1899), physician, was born in Wales in the United Kingdom. While still a young child she moved with her parents to Holland Patent, New York. As a youngster Roberts became very ill with an unspecified malady that, according to contemporary accounts, seemed "likely to promise for her only a life of invalidism." Roberts's parents arranged for her to be cared for in Utica, New York, by the white physician and homoeopathist Dr. Caroline Brown Winslow.

Brown, a native of Utica, had earned MD degrees at the Eclectic Medical College in Cincinnati, Ohio, in 1853 and at the Western College of Homeopathy in Cleveland, Ohio, in 1855 or 1856. Then unmarried, Brown practiced in Utica between 1856 and 1864, and it was during this period that she began to care for Grace Roberts. When Brown moved to Washington, D.C., in 1864 to assist in the care of wounded Union soldiers, Roberts moved with her. Brown arranged for Roberts to receive continued medical care and extensive schooling, including training in the sciences and classical languages. As her health improved, Roberts served as an apprentice in Brown's medical practice. Brown married Austin C. Winslow in Washington, D.C., in 1866, but she maintained her professional activities and medical practice. Deeply influenced by Winslow's medical knowledge, her advocacy of homeopathy, and her progressive political views on the issue of women's rights, Roberts decided to enter the practice of medicine.

In 1876 Roberts was admitted to the medical school at Howard University in Washington, D.C. While at Howard, Roberts became a board member of the Moral Education Society, a student organization devoted to the study of social reforms, including the expansion of women's civil and political rights. She graduated from Howard University with an MD degree in 1877. At the age of thirty-four, and already holding a recognized allopathic medical degree, Roberts decided to continue her medical studies in the allied field of homeopathic medicine. On 8 January 1878 she enrolled in the Homeopathic Medical College of the University of Michigan at Ann Arbor. It is possible that Caroline Winslow facilitated this decision, because while living in Ann Arbor, Roberts roomed with a white family named Winslow. In the spring of 1878 Roberts was awarded her second MD degree, this one from the University of Michigan. She was the first African American woman to earn a medical degree from the university, an accolade that is often mistakenly attributed to SOPHIA BETHENA JONES, who graduated from the university's medical school in 1885.

Roberts returned to Washington, D.C., and opened a homeopathic medical practice in October 1878. She branched out from private practice to become a staff physician at the newly opened National Homeopathic Hospital, the nation's leading homeopathic facility. Roberts was among the small number of physicians who formed the initial staff of this prestigious facility. When the Homeopathic Free Dispensary opened in Washington, D.C., in 1882, Roberts joined the medical staff there as well. The dispensary was the first facility in the capital where women physicians practiced alongside their male colleagues on an equal basis. Its board of directors included several advocates of women's rights, and it gave Roberts managerial responsibility for a special fund that was used to purchase food for indigent patients being treated at the dispensary.

During her professional career Roberts was active in numerous local societies organized to promote the political advancement of women. She was a member of Saint Mark's Protestant Episcopal Church in Washington, D.C., but bouts of poor health prevented her full involvement in the civic, social, and political affairs of the capital's large affluent African American community. Roberts died at her home at 1109 K Street in Washington, D.C., on 1 November 1899.

FURTHER READING
One letter written by Grace Roberts and an alumni questionnaire she completed are at the University of Michigan's Bentley Historical Library in the alumni association's necrology file.

Moldow, Gloria. *Women Doctors in Gilded-Age Washington* (1987).

Obituaries: *Washington Star*, 1 Nov. 1899; *Washington Post*, 2 Nov. 1899.

LAURA M. CALKINS

Roberts, Jane Rose Waring (c. 1819–10 Jan. 1914), First Lady of Liberia and one of the original African American emigrants to Liberia, was born Jane Rose Waring in Virginia to Colston M. Waring, a minister, and Harriet Graves. The Waring family, including their children Susannah, Thomas, Annetta, William, Jane, and John, emigrated to Liberia aboard the *Cyrus* in 1824. Other children were born in Liberia to the Warings, including Christinana, Ann, Harriet, and Colston. Elder Colston Waring served as pastor of the First Baptist Church in Monrovia. He was also a successful coffee planter and wealthy merchant. He served as vice agent for the American Colonization Society in Liberia and other administrative positions before his death in 1834. Jane learned to read and write in Liberia. She spoke French fluently and was "in all respects was well-bred and refined," according to HALLIE Q. BROWN, who met Jane in the early 1900s.

Jane Waring married JOSEPH JENKINS ROBERTS in Monrovia in 1836. Roberts, freeborn and from Norfolk, Virginia, emigrated with his mother and siblings to Liberia in 1829. He served as Governor of the Commonwealth of Liberia from 1842 to 1848, as the first and seventh president of Liberia (1848 to 1856 and 1872 to 1876), and as president of the College of Liberia, serving from 1856 to 1876. In 1838 Joseph and Jane had one child, Sarah Ann Roberts, who was educated in England for at least six years and later married William A. Johnson.

While in her thirties, a slim, black-haired Jane Roberts solemnly sat for what would become a somewhat historic portrait. She wore a billowing, white blouse and skirt with festive, contrasting dark lace and fringe. Jane was a handsome woman with an oval face, a long, straight nose and soulful eyes. She stared directly into the photographer's camera. This portrait would eventually be housed in the collection of the Library of Congress.

Jane Roberts and her family played a leading role in the early days of Liberian independence from the American Colonization Society in July

1847. Not only was her husband the nation's first president, her eldest sister, Susannah Waring Lewis, was one of seven women appointed to hand-stitch the first Liberian flag, which was unfurled to the public in August 1847, during a national celebration. Jane Roberts listened proudly as both her sister and husband gave patriotic speeches, and she later prepared a sumptuous feast at the Presidential home. Joseph Roberts's vice president, also elected in 1847, was Nathaniel Brander, Jane's stepfather. As a result, her mother served as Second Lady.

As First Lady, Roberts accompanied her husband on many of his official travels and was received by several heads of state. For example, in 1848 the couple sailed to Barbados in the West Indies, the United States, and Europe in an effort to gain recognition for their newly independent country. In England, Queen Victoria received the couple onboard one of her Royal ships with a seventeen-gun salute. Great Britain was the first nation to formally recognize Liberia. It also presented Liberia with the gift of a small ship, named the *Lark*. In Brussels, King Leopold of Belgium greeted the couple. In Paris, the president of France, Louis Napoleon III, received the couple and would meet them again in 1851. His visits with the Roberts family so impressed Napoleon III that he later donated military equipment and uniforms for one-thousand Liberian soldiers.

Sadly, in 1873 Jane suffered double losses. Her oldest sister, Susannah Lewis died after a lengthy illness. Then, her mother, Harriet, whom Jane cared for in the Roberts' home, died at age eighty.

When President Roberts left office in 1856 after four terms, he accepted the presidency of Liberia College and moved with his wife to a home outside Monrovia to monitor construction of the new school. He remained at the college until called back to lead Liberia again as president in 1872.

In 1876 President Roberts attended a rainy funeral of a close friend. He caught cold and weakened considerably. Jane tried unsuccessfully to nurse her gravely ill husband back to health. Roberts spoke tenderly to his "Ma" Roberts in his last hours.

As a widow, Jane Roberts continued to lead an active life and traveled widely. In 1887 she began raising money for a hospital for Liberian and American seamen in Monrovia in honor of her husband. She traveled to the United States, where, according to Dr. Monroe Majors, at that time Jane was, "the only Negro woman that has dined with President [Grover] and Mrs. Cleveland at the White House." President Cleveland donated $50 to the hospital.

Roberts also spoke at the Pennsylvania Colonization Society annual meeting in 1891, alongside other prominent Liberians, including Attorney General William M. Davis and former Attorney General Henry W. Grimes.

In 1892 Jane Roberts traveled from Monrovia to the settlement of Clay-Ashland in Liberia to see a quilt that was being made for Queen Victoria. She was astonished to learn that the quilter, MARTHA RICKS, had yearned to see the British monarch for more than fifty years and had made the quilt as a gift. Roberts thought the quilt was extraordinary and pledged to help Ricks meet the Queen, thus accompanying her to England. Both women met with Victoria in July 1892 at Windsor Castle; it was Roberts's second audience with Queen Victoria.

In 1905 Jane Roberts posed for another portrait (Brown). At age eighty-six, the plump, silver-haired former First Lady of Liberia sat comfortably with a gentle smile for the photographer, who may have been Londoner John Archer. From around 1906 to her death in 1914, Jane Roberts lived with close friends Bertha and John Archer in their home. John Archer, a successful photographer, became Britain's first black mayor, elected in the London borough of Battersea, just months before Jane's death. Jane Roberts, one of the last original Liberian emigrants to pass away, is buried in London, England's Streatham Cemetery in Garratt Lane.

FURTHER READING
Brown, Hallie Q. "Mrs. Jane Roberts," in *Homespun Heroines and Other Women of Distinctions* (1926).
Cassell, Dr. C. Abayomi. *Liberia: History of the First African Republic* (1970).
Majors, Monroe W. "Mrs. J. J. Roberts: Lecturer, Educator, Philanthropist" in *Noted Negro Women: Their Triumphs and Activities* (1983).
Shick, Tom W. *Behold the Promised Land: A History of Afro-American Settler Society in Nineteenth Century Liberia* (1977).
Obituary: *New York Times*, 11 January 1914.

KYRA E. HICKS

Roberts, Joseph Jenkins (15 Mar. 1809–24 Feb. 1876), college administrator, entrepreneur, and first and sixth president of Liberia, was born either in Norfolk, Portsmouth, or Petersburg, Virginia, the son of James Roberts and Amelia (maiden name unknown). A persistent rumor that his father was an unidentified white man remains no more than mere speculation. James Roberts and his wife were freed people and had seven surviving children. The family ran a boat and trading business that plied the James River. The Robertses probably lived for a while in Norfolk and later moved to Petersburg, where Joseph alternately worked for his father and in a barbershop owned by the Reverend William Nelson Colson, an African American minister and businessman. The Colson business was located at Wythe and Sycamore streets—an historical marker indicates the actual site.

By 1829 James Roberts had died, leaving considerable financial assets and property in Petersburg. Joseph, as the eldest child, had the primary responsibility for seeing to the welfare of his mother and siblings. Shortly thereafter the family decided to leave Virginia and settle in Liberia under the auspices of the American Colonization Society. On 9 February 1829 they sailed from Virginia onboard the *Harriet*. Unsubstantiated accounts state that Roberts was married and left a wife behind, but no concrete evidence supports this notion. By April 1829 the Robertses were established at the settlement of Monrovia (later the Liberian capital), where they opened a new business in transatlantic shipping, trade, and passenger service. Joseph and two of his brothers, John and Henry, initially partnered with Joseph's former employer Colson. Roberts, Colson, and Company prospered with Colson functioning as the U.S. agent and Joseph Roberts exporting indigenous West African comestibles and goods to America. Roberts and Colson thus developed strong commercial links with concerns in Petersburg, Philadelphia, and New York City. Roberts acquired a premier-class vessel, the *Caroline*, and a large coffee farm and became prominent in the colony's civic affairs. Roberts was elected high sheriff in 1833 and was soon called upon to assist Thomas H. Buchanan, who governed the colony at the behest of the American Colonization Society. In this position Roberts was active in cracking down on the slave trade and in increasing the efficiency of tax collection. His work became so invaluable that the administration of the Colonization Society appointed him lieutenant governor in 1838.

Roberts was often assigned the duty of commanding troops to put down rebellions in the hinterlands, which were largely prompted by sometimes-justifiable mistrust by indigenous Africans of the Americo-Liberian settlers, whom they feared would attempt to dominate and exploit them. He became known to many as "General" Roberts. Ultimately he was conferred the formal military rank of major general. Governor Buchanan became ill with fever and died on 3 September 1841.

Joseph Jenkins Roberts, photographed by Augustus Washington, c. 1851. Roberts arrived in Liberia in 1829, became its governor in 1841, and served as its first and seventh president. (Library of Congress/American Colonization Society Records, 1792–1964.)

In January 1842 Roberts was elevated to the post of governor over what had become the Liberian Commonwealth, the first African American to hold this distinction (LOTT CARY had previously served in the 1820s as acting governor). In this capacity and later as president of Liberia, Roberts energetically pursued efforts to eradicate slavery as practiced among the native Liberian peoples, efforts that did not go unnoticed in the United States and that lent Roberts a great deal of credibility as an advocate for Liberian independence. On 26 July 1847, thanks in large measure to Roberts's lobbying and diplomatic efforts, Liberia was proclaimed an independent republic. Roberts was elected its first president, defeating Samuel Benedict for the office. The leader of the True Liberian Party, Roberts was elected from 1847 to 1856 in biennial elections. He proved most effective in quelling discontent among the interior tribes—who remained leery of the potential threat posed by Americo-Liberians to their lands and independence—and in securing diplomatic recognition from, among other world powers, France, England, and Prussia. Among his more controversial measures were those he took to prohibit the teaching of Arabic in Liberian schools.

In 1855, in his bid for a fifth term, he was defeated at the polls by Stephen Allen Benson.

After his first series of presidential terms, Roberts devoted the bulk of his efforts to founding and administering Liberia College, holding the post of college president from 1856 to 1876. He returned to political prominence as a strident critic of the policies of the rival True Whig Party, especially over the Ports of Entry Law of 1864, which limited foreign business and investment. By this time Roberts's True Liberian Party had become the Republican Party, which followed a generally conservative ideology and was dominated by the mulatto settlers. (Roberts himself was light-skinned, often passed for white, and was accused of representing the interests of a "mulatto elite.") At the other end of the political spectrum, the True Whig Party (initially the Whig Party) was generally more liberal in outlook and was supported more by darker-skinned Liberians. The controversial True Whig president, Edward James Roye, was deposed by a military coup in 1871, and with the country in the midst of a financial crisis, Roberts was once again elected to the presidency.

Roberts died in Monrovia while serving his second series of terms in office (1872–1876) and was succeeded by James Spriggs Payne. Roberts bequeathed a sizable legacy from his rubber and coffee plantation holdings—as of 2006 administered through the J. J. Roberts Educational Foundation—for the development of educational infrastructure in Liberia. In 1836 Roberts married Jane Rose Waring, whose family had also immigrated to Liberia from Virginia. Her father was a missionary minister, and as first lady, JANE ROBERTS remained active in Christian charitable causes. The couple had one child. It may have been in large part through Jane's influence that the Roberts administrations consistently fostered what were for that time advanced policies regarding women's education.

FURTHER READING

Cassell, C. Abayomi. *Liberia: History of the First African Republic* (1970).

Clegg, Claude A., III. *The Price of Liberty: African Americans and the Making of Liberia* (2004).

Lynch, Hollis R., ed. *Selected Letters of Edward Wilmot Blyden* (1978).

Shick, Tom W. *Behold the Promised Land: A History of Afro-American Settler Society in Nineteenth-Century Liberia* (1980).

RAYMOND PIERRE HYLTON

Roberts, Kay George (16 Sept. 1950–), symphony orchestra conductor, was born in Nashville, Tennessee, the youngest of three daughters of Marion Pearl Taylor Roberts, a librarian at Tennessee State and Fisk universities, and Dr. Shearley Oliver Roberts, founder of the psychology department at Fisk University. In addition to being intellectually stimulating, Roberts's childhood on the Fisk campus was filled with music. When Roberts was in elementary school she started violin lessons with Robert Lee Holmes Jr., a teacher in the then-segregated Nashville public schools. Holmes was keenly aware of the lack of musical opportunities for Nashville's black children, so in 1958 he created the Cremona Strings, an all-black string orchestra. Holmes, recognizing Roberts's talent, selected her as a member of the group.

In junior high school, Roberts became a member of the recently desegregated Nashville Youth Symphony, conducted by Thor Johnson, who was also the conductor of the Nashville Symphony Orchestra. Johnson was so impressed by Roberts's playing that he invited her to join the Nashville Symphony as a member of its violin section when she was just a senior in high school. She was later chosen by Johnson to represent the Nashville Symphony in the World Symphony Orchestra, which was composed of 140 musicians from around the world and toured the United States.

After graduating from high school in 1968, Roberts enrolled in Fisk University as a mathematics major and continued to play with the Nashville Symphony. In her sophomore year she won a violin fellowship to attend the prestigious summer Tanglewood Music Festival in Massachusetts. While at Tanglewood, Roberts worked with Leonard Bernstein, who convinced her to change her major from mathematics to music. In 1972 Roberts graduated with honors from Fisk with a B.A. in Music and a minor in Psychology.

Roberts was accepted for graduate studies in violin performance at Yale University School of Music and received a master of music in Violin Performance in 1975. While at Yale, Roberts took her first conducting class with Otto-Werner Mueller. He considered her a highly gifted conductor and under his tutelage she received the master of Musical Arts in Conducting and Violin Performance from Yale in 1976. Mueller provided his best students the opportunity to work with professional orchestras by assisting him when he guest conducted, and Roberts was able to lead both the Atlanta and Nashville Symphony orchestras in rehearsal. As a result, she was immediately engaged to make her professional conducting debut with the Nashville Symphony Orchestra in 1976. She also studied with the renowned conducting teachers Gustav Meier and Margaret Hillis and worked with some of the world's greatest conductors, including Bernstein, Pierre Boulez, John-Eliot Gardiner, Seiji Ozawa, and André Previn. In 1986 Roberts became the first woman to earn a doctor of musical arts in Conducting from Yale.

Since 1978, Roberts has been a professor of music at the University of Massachusetts Lowell (UML) and in 2001 she became the founder and director of the UML String Project for public school students that fosters diversity in classical music. She received many significant grants, awards, and honors, including a Certificate of Special Congressional Recognition in 2001 from the U.S. House of Representatives for her "outstanding and invaluable service to the community." Critics have praised Roberts for her polished yet passionate and precise conducting.

Roberts served as music director and conductor of the New Hampshire Philharmonic Orchestra (1982–1987) and the Cape Ann Symphony (1986–1988). She conducted major orchestras throughout the United States, including those in Chicago, Cleveland, Dallas, Detroit, and the National Symphony Orchestra in Washington, D.C. As a U.S. Information Agency (USIA) Cultural Specialist in Thailand, she was the first woman to conduct the Bangkok Symphony Orchestra and was re-invited to conduct the 60th birthday celebration concert for the King of Thailand (1987). In Switzerland she made a highly acclaimed debut with the Orchestra della Svizzera Italiana in a concert that premiered Frederick Tillis's *Festival Journey for Percussion and Orchestra*, with the jazz drummer MAX ROACH as soloist, in 1994.

Roberts's concerts with the Black Music Repertory Ensemble in its New York City debut at Alice Tully Hall and at Chicago's Orchestra Hall drew critical as well as public acclaim. In Pittsburgh, she led this ensemble in concerts of new works that were recorded by Public Radio International for its series *The African-American Music Tree*. Roberts also conceived a special orchestral program, *Hearing Amistad*, with music by African American composers and performed by the New Haven Symphony for the homeport arrival celebration of the replica of the schooner *Amistad* in 2000. Her work with the Sphinx Symphony for its 2003 Sphinx Competition was shown in the Emmy Award–winning documentary on diversity in classical music, *Sphinx Competition: Breaking the Sound Barrier*.

Roberts is also the founder and conductor of the New England Orchestra, *NEO*, a professional chamber orchestra based in Lowell, Massachusetts. *NEO* is committed to building a vital artistic partnership with the community by linking cultures through music.

FURTHER READING

Handy, D. Antoinette. *Black Conductors* (1995).
Handy, D. Antoinette. *Black Women in American Bands and Orchestras* (1998).
Hine, Darlene Clark. *Facts On File Encyclopedia of Black Women in America: Music* (1997).
Smith, Jessie Carney. *Notable Black Women: Book II* (1996).
Smith, Jessie Carney. *Powerful Black Women* (1996).

JENNIFER LANG

Roberts, Leon Cedric (21 Mar. 1950–22 Jan. 1999), musician, composer, and liturgist, was born LeonCedric Roberts in Coatesville, Pennsylvania, the youngest of two sons of John Arthur and Thelma Bookman Roberts. His father was from Savannah, Georgia, and his mother was from Coatesville. Roberts grew up in a religious household and among an extended family diverse in religious affiliations from Baptist to Pentecostal and Methodist. At age six, he began to study piano under the tutelage of a local instructor known as Mr. Dell, his grandmother, Mrs. Mary Bookman, oversaw the religious direction of his musical development. Roberts attended First Apostolic Fire Baptized Holiness Church of Coatesville with his mother; there he assumed the role of choir director and the responsibility for congregational worship. At the same time he grew in faith and devotion to his religious beliefs. Roberts founded and directed two musical groups: Voices of Love and the Jubali Movement of Southern Pennsylvania. Roberts had developed a passion for music that was evident as a student in the Coatesville Area School District. He took part in numerous musical and theatrical productions and participated in various choral groups, including the Meistersingers.

In 1968, Roberts graduated from high school and enrolled at Howard University, a historically black university established in 1867, in Washington, DC. At Howard his passion for music flourished. Roberts was instrumental in the growth of the musical community at Howard University as cofounder, composer, and pianist of the Howard University Gospel Choir with one hundred members; the gospel singer Richard Smallwood was also a cofounder. Roberts joined Mount Zion Baptist Church near the campus of Howard University and served as director of their Young Adult Choir and he also directed the Library of Congress Gospel Choir. In 1972, Roberts completed his studies and earned a bachelor's degree in Music Education from Howard University. In addition, he earned a Liturgical Studies Certificate from Georgetown University, a Jesuit institution founded in 1789, in Washington, DC.

In 1977, Roberts was contacted by the St. Augustine Catholic Church in Northwest Washington, D.C., which traces its history back to 1858 and a group of emancipated African American Catholics. He accepted an invitation to direct the flagging church choir. Roberts embraced the church community, and the St. Augustine Catholic Church community embraced their new choir director and ushered him into the faith. He soon converted to Catholicism and enthusiastically worked to integrate the energy and spirit of African American Gospel music into the traditions and rituals of the Catholic liturgy.

Roberts served as director of music at the Saint Augustine Catholic Church from 1977 until 1994; at Saint Augustine Elementary School he was an instructor of choir and music appreciation. Expanding his participation in the Catholic community beyond Saint Augustine, Roberts directed the Mackin Catholic High School Choir from the late 1970s until 1983, and returning to his Protestant roots, he also served as music director of the Bishop McNamara Senior High School Gospel Choir. In 1982, he founded and directed the Archdiocesan Mass Choir for the archdiocese of Washington, DC. Roberts contributed to the vision that would, in 1983, become the Rejoice conferences on African American liturgy. Annually African Americans gathered for the conference to participate in workshops that addressed African American perspectives on the church, African contributions to the origins of the church, and liturgical innovations in the gospel mass. In 1989, Roberts lectured at the Rejoice conference convened in Rome, Italy, and at the Vatican on the topic of African American developments in liturgical music. The same year he wrote, "The Development of African American Liturgical Music since Vatican II."

Roberts composed and performed works that drew praise and commanded international audiences. In 1987 he contributed to the production of the first African American Catholic hymnal, *Lead Me, Guide Me*, which included twenty liturgical settings. Roberts toured throughout the United States and the world including Japan, the Caribbean Islands, and Italy, where in Rome he directed the Saint Augustine choir for a special audience with Pope John Paul II. He was well received during his 1990 tour of Japan with Roberts' Revival and from the early 1990s through 1996 he performed annually in Hawaii at the Big Island Liturgical and Arts Conference. In 1991, Roberts directed the Saint Augustine Gospel Choir on ABC *Nightline* on the Christmas Eve program, "The History of Gospel Music," he has also appeared on FOX television.

In 1987, Roberts composed psalm settings that were published in *Lift Every Voice and Sing*, an African American hymnal of the Episcopal Church. In 1995, Roberts released the album, *I Call upon You God*, featuring "The Mass of Saint Martin de Porres," on the Gia label. On the cover of the album he is pictured with his choir wearing African inspired clothing. In 1997, with DavidHaas, Roberts released the album, *God Has Done Marvelous Things*, also on Gia. Roberts had another Gia release entitled, *The Mass of Saint Augustine*, published by the Gregorian Institute of America, which he dedicated to his deceased sister Claudette Shatteen. With the Roberts Revival he recorded *The Coming*, on the Oregon Catholic Press. He worked with Sister Thea Bowman to produce *Songs of My People*, and *Round the Glory Manger*.

Roberts relocated to Brooklyn, New York, in 1994 to assume the position of Florence Van Keuren Artist In Residence at the Concord Baptist Church of Christ; where he directed both the Male Chorus and the Gospel Chorus. During a 1998 ceremony at the Saint Patrick's Cathedral of New York he was honored by the Office of Black Ministry of the Archdiocese of New York with a Special Achievement Award for his contributions to African American Catholic worship and the development of liturgical music. The award was presented to Roberts by the New York archbishop Cardinal John O'Connor.

On 22 January 1999 Roberts died from stomach cancer; his burial was on 28 January. During his lifetime numerous organizations, dioceses, and archdiocese were honored to have him as clinician and lecturer; among them the Catholic University of America Liturgical Studies program, the National Office of Black Catholics, the East Coast Conference for Religious Education, the National Pastoral Musicians Conventions and Notre Dame University. Roberts' Revival recorded a tribute album to the memory and works of Leon C. Roberts entitled, *God Placed a Rainbow*.

FURTHER READING

Davis, Cyprian. *The History of Black Catholics in the United States* (1995).

MacGregor, Morris J. *The Emergence of a Black Catholic Community: St. Augustine's in Washington* (1999).

Zanca, Kenneth J. *American Catholics and Slavery, 1789–1866* (1994).

SAFIYA DALILAH HOSKINS

Roberts, Lillian Davis (1928–), health care professional and union official, was one of five children. Her family lived in a very large tenement building, in what was an often seedy, rough neighborhood on the south Side of Chicago. She attended Chicago public schools, and then she managed to get a scholarship to the University of Illinois. After only six months, she had to return home and find a job. Her brother had been drafted into the U.S. Army, and there was no longer a source of income for the family.

During World War II, nurse's aide positions shifted from being the domain of upper-class women volunteers to poor (often black) women. As shortages and turnover became more prevalent in the hospitals, the conditions of work for these women worsened. In 1946 Roberts, became the first African American nurse's aide hired at the University of Chicago Lying-In Hospital. She felt isolated working at the hospital, since the white aides shunned her. However, she was very good at her job, so Roberts was assigned the workload of two or three nurse's aides. By the mid-1950s the complexion of the hospital had changed and the majority of nurse's aides were black. They also endured unfair work conditions and an overload of responsibilities. When her boss began piling on an ever-increasing amount of work while refusing to hire more staff, Roberts complained to her union, Local 1657 of the University of Chicago Employees Union. In the past, the union had failed to defend these workers, so Roberts took on the position of shop steward and organized the first hospital strike in Chicago's history. The strike lasted six months and involved much violence. Most of the strikers were black women, and many were single women and single mothers; Roberts saw the action as a movement for civil rights. Union organization proved the key to improving their situation because it gave them the right to collective bargaining so that their grievances could be addressed.

After her success in Chicago, Roberts moved to New York in 1965 to organize low-paid and often disrespected hospital workers for the American Federation of State, County, and Municipal Employees (AFSCME). At the time, AFSCME was competing with the Teamsters to represent the health workers, and the struggle became intense. Roberts had grown up an African American on welfare in Chicago, so she proved adept at organizing hospital workers, many of whom were poor, black women. She and AFSCME prevailed by organizing the hospital workers, paving the way for their local to become the dominant New York municipal union. "Putting women in leadership positions ensures that women are able to represent their own interests," Roberts noted, during an interview with Susan Reverby, "they know what their concerns are" (Roberts, *Signs*). What women contributed, according to Roberts in her speeches, is a concern for the small things as well as the overall picture. In 1968 Roberts became second in command of the country's largest municipal union when she was made associate director of District Council 37 of AFSCME.

In 1969 Roberts was jailed for two weeks for defying New York Governor Nelson Rockefeller and leading a strike against three mental hospitals. New York's Taylor Law said that municipal unions cannot strike. She did so anyway and went to jail for it. The public outcry was so great that the governor had to release her after three days. Between 1969 and 1981 she continued to organize workers and helped to establish a union-sponsored college education program that allowed members to take courses for a college degree at union headquarters. It became a model for other unions across the county. In 1981 she left the union and was appointed to be New York State industrial commissioner—the first black woman to hold such a high post in the state. From 1987 to 1992 she was senior vice president of the HMO, Total Health Systems. In 2002, as District Council 37 became embroiled in a major scandal. Over twenty local officials were indicted for the misuse of members' money involving a variety of criminal scams. Roberts returned as executive director. On 23 January 2007 the delegates of District Council 37 overwhelmingly reelected Roberts to a third term as executive director. She established an Affordable Housing program to allow members to achieve their dreams of home ownership. In 2007 she was named one of the 30 Most Powerful Black New Yorkers by the *New York Post*.

FURTHER READING

Baxandall, Rosalyn, et al., eds. *A Documentary History of Working Women in the United States* (1976).

Bernhardt, Debra, et al. "The Momentum Was Catching On: Lillian Roberts Describes Organizing Hospital Workers in New York City," 9 and 14 June 1999. Available at http://historymatters.gmu. edu/d/6944.

DuLong, Jessica. "Women at Work: These Labor Leaders are Changing the Face of the Movement, Reflecting the Concerns of a Changing Membership," *Newsday* (Sept. 2002).

Reverby, Susan. "Hospital Organizing in the 1950s: An Interview with Lillian Roberts," *Signs* (Summer 1976).

CLARE J. WASHINGTON

Roberts, Luckey (7 Aug. 1887?–5 Feb. 1968), ragtime, theatrical, and jazz pianist and composer, was born Charles Luckeyeth Roberts in Philadelphia, Pennsylvania, the son of William Roberts, an unaccredited veterinarian, and Elizabeth Roberts (maiden name unknown). His birth year is widely given as 1887, but the writer Henry T. Sampson gives 1893. Roberts's mother died three weeks after he was born, and he was raised with the Ringolds, a family active in African American show business. They brought him up as a Quaker, and accordingly he abstained from tobacco and alcohol throughout his subsequent career, even when running his own saloon.

In the 1890s Roberts toured in the role of a sleeping toddler with a troupe performing *Uncle Tom's Cabin*. He next appeared as a singer and dancer with Gus Selke (or Sulky) and His Pickaninnies, and the following year he joined Mayne (or Mamye, according to Sampson) Remington's Black Buster Brownies Ethiopian Prodigies, with which he remained for almost ten years, touring the United States and three times visiting Europe. In the course of his affiliation with Remington, Roberts added tumbling and juggling to his singing and dancing, and, far more significantly, at around age seven he began to teach himself to play piano. For some time he could only play in one key, F-sharp (that is, on the black keys), which served well enough to accompany the drum corps at Philadelphia's First Regiment Armory one summer but caused some complaints from girl singers he accompanied in a carnival the following summer.

Around 1905 Roberts spent the summer in Baltimore, Maryland, where he exchanged ideas with pianist EUBIE BLAKE at JOE GANS's saloon; took fighting lessons from Gans, a former lightweight champion boxer; and performed at Billy Williams's restaurant. During another vacation from annual vaudeville touring, he performed at the Green Dragon saloon in Philadelphia.

Roberts continued to tour in vaudeville, sometimes leading Luckey and His Brown and Blues and also serving as musical director and pianist in the Southern Smart Set Company of Salem Tutt Whitney and J. Homer Tutt. While touring with J. Leubrie Hill's My Friend for Dixie Company, he met singer Lena Stanford. They married late in 1911. Writer Terkild Vinding reports that Roberts raised ten children, but as the *New York Times* obituary mentions only one, it might be that Vinding conflated the daughter and the Robertses' several grandchildren and great-grandchildren.

Roberts composed "Junk Man Rag" in 1911. He could not yet notate music, but with ragtime pianist ARTIE MATTHEWS's help he published the piece in 1913. Writers Rudi Blesh and Harriet Janis speculate that Matthews's involvement accounts for this composition's Joplinesque sound, uncharacteristic of Roberts. He also wrote "Pork and Beans" (also published in 1913), "Shy and Sly" (1915), and "Music Box Rag" (1914).

As a soloist in New York City, Roberts worked informally with WILLIE "THE LION" SMITH, JAMES P. JOHNSON, and others at the Jungles Casino in midtown, and he held a job at Baron Wilkins's nightclub in Harlem. Johnson recalled, Luckey Roberts was the outstanding pianist in New York in 1913—and for years before and after…. Luckey had massive hands that could stretch a fourteenth on the keyboard, and he played tenths as easy as others played octaves. His tremolo was terrific, and he could drum on one note with two or three fingers in either hand. His style in making breaks was like a drummer's: he'd flail his hands in and out, lifting them high. A very spectacular pianist (Davin, 12). Throughout these years Roberts doubled as a pool hustler whose skills in this endeavor were as formidable as his playing.

While at Wilkins's, Roberts studied the technical aspects of music with Melville Charlton, a pianist, organist, and choir director. He became involved in musical theater, writing individual songs and full comedies in partnership with the lyricist Alex Rogers. Their work, extending into the late 1920s, was not especially lucrative or notable, apart from *My People*, which was among the first African American revues (1917). Around 1927 Rogers and Roberts also wrote for and acted in a popular weekly radio comedy, *The Two Black Crows*, on WABC.

Even more obscure are Roberts's piano rolls. He punched three titles, including "Railroad Blues" for the Vocalstyle company in 1919 and two further titles for QRS in 1923. Although he could reputedly outplay Johnson, Smith, and other jazz greats, Roberts did not participate in the first decade of jazz recordings, by one account because he did not need the money. Having earlier performed as an accompanist for the famous dance team of Irene and Vernon Castle, he gained entrance into American high society, and through the 1920s and 1930s he made huge fees leading dance orchestras in New York, Newport, Nantucket, Palm Beach, and other resort areas for America's wealthiest families and their visitors, including the Vanderbilts, the Carnegies, the Roosevelts, the Hearsts, the du Ponts, and the prince of Wales. The banjoist ELMER SNOWDEN recalled playing for millionaires as a member of Roberts's group as late as 1935 to 1939.

Roberts took a stab at a blend of African American and European orchestral music in compositions performed in concerts in New York at Carnegie Hall on 30 August 1939 and Town Hall on 28 May 1941. In the interim he was involved in a serious automobile accident, in which both his hands were severely injured.

For some time Roberts had been performing his "Ripples of the Nile," a composition so complicated that no other pianist attempted it. Around 1940 he slowed it down drastically to teach it to a student, and he realized that it sounded good as a ballad. With lyrics added by Kim Gannon and a new title, "Moonlight Cocktail," the piece was popularized by Glenn Miller's big band, which recorded it in 1941, and by Bing Crosby, who also recorded a version; members of the armed forces voted "Moonlight Cocktail" the number one hit in America in April 1942.

Roberts owned, operated, and often performed at Luckey's Rendezvous, a Harlem saloon, from 1940 to 1954. Known for his generosity, he had given out Christmas baskets anonymously during the Great Depression, and now he paid for a medical library at Harlem Hospital. He encouraged hopeful young musicians to perform at his saloon, and according to his piano-playing friend Smith, Roberts gave away so many free drinks that the business eventually failed.

On 18 January and 8 February 1946 Roberts was the pianist in an all-star traditional jazz group for the first two shows in the radio series "This Is Jazz," hosted by Blesh. That May, for Blesh's Circle label, he recorded "Railroad Blues" and his five durable compositions: "Ripples of the Nile," "Pork and Beans," "Shy and Sly," "Music Box Rag," and "Junk Man Rag."

Roberts's wife died in 1958, and that same year he suffered a stroke shortly after recording an album, *Harlem Piano Solos*. Later, a second stroke impaired his control of his left hand. In his final years he was writing a show, *Old Golden Brown*, to be presented concurrently with and without music. He did not realize this venture before his death in New York City.

Hopkins recalled that Roberts "was small, but he was a powerful man. He very seldom got angry, but when he did he was dangerous…. He was a swimming and boxing instructor at the Y.M.C.A., and I couldn't understand it when he took sick and died. He didn't look any eighty-one."

Roberts is a legendary figure in the transition from ragtime to jazz. By reputation he was potentially one of the giants of twentieth-century American music, but unfortunately he left little documentation in support of this position, owing to the absence of early recordings and the obscurity of his compositions and piano rolls.

FURTHER READING

Blesh, Rudi, and Harriet Janis. *They All Played Ragtime* (1950; rev. 4th ed., 1971).

Davin, Tom. "Conversations with James P. Johnson: 1912–1914," *Jazz Review* (July 1959): 12.

Sampson, Henry T. *Blacks in Blackface: A Source Book on Early Black Musical Shows* (1980).

Smith, Willie "the Lion," and George Hoefer. *Music on My Mind* (1964; repr. 1975).

Obituaries: *New York Times*, 7 Feb. 1968; *Down Beat*, 21 Mar. 1968.

DISCOGRAPHY

Montgomery, Mike. "Luckey Roberts Rollography," *Record Research*, no. 30 (Oct. 1960): 2.

This entry is taken from the *American National Biography* and is published here with the permission of the American Council of Learned Societies.

BARRY KERNFELD

Roberts, Meshack "Shack" R. (?–?), Reconstruction politician, minister, and a founder of Wiley College, was born a slave, probably in Arkansas. According to J. MASON BREWER in *Negro Legislators of Texas and Their Descendants* (1935), Roberts was enslaved by O. B. Roberts of Upshur County, Texas. While his master served in the Confederate army, Roberts "was left at home to take care of the place, protect the property and the master's wife and family. He shod horses for the soldiers and others, and baked ginger cakes and sold them to help finance the upkeep of his master's home" (Brewer, 65–66). Roberts the "faithful slave" is memorialized in a 1964 historical marker in Upshur County; yet what the marker omits suggests that his outward docility may have been misleading. As Brewer further reports, in 1867 Roberts "was whipped by the Ku Klux Klan and left for dead" (66). Although more recent sources indicate that it was not the Klan but one of many similar local terrorist organizations, by 1867, as Horace Greeley's *New York Tribune* reported, there was "no safety for Negroes or loyal men" in northeastern Texas (Campbell, 268–269).

Aided by his former owner, Roberts soon moved to nearby Marshall, county seat of the majority-black Harrison County. Apart from records of his legislative service, little is known of Roberts's life in freedom. He was apparently a blacksmith. Also a minister in the African Methodist Episcopal Church, an illiterate man with a passion for education, in 1873 he helped found the Methodist-affiliated Wiley College, said to be the oldest historically black university west of the Mississippi. (Civil rights leader JAMES FARMER graduated from Wiley College in 1938.)

Marshall in 1867 was in turmoil. After President Andrew Johnson's Reconstruction plan was supplanted in March by the Congressional program, voter registration in Harrison County began in earnest. A statewide election was called to determine whether a constitutional convention should proceed. In Marshall, this call was met with violence: on 30 December 1867, "[t]he pent up wrath of all rebeldom culminated and exploded" (Campbell, 283). But the convention was held all the same, and it produced the Reconstruction constitution of 1869, which in turn effectively gave control of Harrison County to its black majority. In April 1870 military Reconstruction in Texas ended, and authority was transferred to the Republican governor Edmund J. Davis. The county sent two blacks, Henry Moore and Mitchell Kendall, to the Republican-controlled twelfth legislature. But by the time Roberts took Kendall's place in the thirteenth legislature, in January 1873, the Democrats had gained control. They promptly called another election, which resulted in Governor Davis's defeat by Richard Coke. But although Coke's inauguration in January 1874 signified "redemption" at the state level, Harrison County remained a Republican stronghold. Roberts, a vice president of the 1873 Republican State Convention, was reelected to the fourteenth legislature.

High on the Democrats' agenda was another constitutional convention. Though the proposition carried handily, in Harrison County it was soundly defeated. Three of the fifteen Republicans at the convention came from Harrison County's congressional district. They were vastly outnumbered at the convention, however, a gathering that produced the conservative constitution of 1876 (still the framework of Texas law in the early twenty-first century). Nonetheless, the "redeemer" majority was content to let Harrison County remain "a Republican enclave in a Democratic state" (Campbell, 312). (This understanding established a dichotomy between state and national politics and local politics in Harrison County that persisted, though in unforeseen ways, into the 1950s.) Roberts, who had campaigned alongside the Republican delegates to the constitutional convention, was reelected to the fifteenth legislature in 1876, even as Rutherford B. Hayes defeated Samuel J. Tilden and federal Reconstruction came to an end.

In the minority, yet energized by larger events, Harrison County Democrats sought issues to exploit. By 1878 they had settled on fiscal mismanagement, especially on the question of the local railroad. From Governor Davis's twelfth legislature, counties had gained authority to subsidize railroad companies. Harrison County citizens, who hoped to establish Marshall as an eastern terminal for the first southern transcontinental railroad, authorized $300,000 in bonds. Two years later the Texas and Pacific Railroad demanded the money. The resulting debt stood at ten percent of the value of all real estate and other property in Harrison County.

Although promoters of this investment crossed ideological lines, the Democrats managed to politicize the issue for the 1878 election—not as Democrats versus Republicans, but as a new "Citizens Party" against the free-spending "Radicals." Continuing to separate local from state and national issues, the Citizens Party insisted it "did not oppose the Republican Party as such" (Campbell, 341). Some freedmen were apparently persuaded by these appeals to civility and responsible government. Roberts did not stand for reelection. Despite their efforts (legitimate and possibly fraudulent), the Citizens Party lost that November—or appeared to have, until a problem surfaced. A county precinct box had been placed within the Marshall city limits. Realizing that disqualifying these votes would shift the outcome, Citizens Party leaders obtained from a Democratic district judge an injunction against counting the ballots. The county judge, a Republican, refused to cede the point. Eventually the matter went to the state supreme court, but not before Citizens Party leaders forcibly removed sitting Republicans from their offices. The state supreme court, in *Williamson v. Lane*, tacitly confirmed the Citizens Party's position. In January 1879 the Democratic governor Oran M. Roberts dealt with the matter. Unsurprisingly he sided with the "redeemers." More surprising is a supportive letter the governor received from Shack Roberts: "Now I have talked to a great many of the party, and it is the general desire that the officers *now in office* remain there, and most of the citizens are satisfied" (Campbell, 354).

Whatever motivated Shack Roberts to lend his weight to the Citizens Party, it was not the first time he had operated in a spirit of compromise. He had supported the Democratic gubernatorial candidacies of Coke and Oran Roberts. These contradictory positions correspond with one analysis of the early Republican Party in Texas: homegrown and white, it was never dominated by freedmen or, for that matter, northern politicians. "The role of the Negro leaders and the carpetbaggers during and after Reconstruction continued to be one of collaboration rather than control of the Texas Republican party" (Baggett, 454).

After 1878 Roberts disappears from the historical record. Meanwhile the Citizens Party tightened its control over Harrison County by restricting its primary elections to white voters. Though the U.S. Supreme Court invalidated whites-only primaries in 1944 in *Smith v. Allwright*, the Citizens Party continued the practice until 1951, when the Fifth Circuit, in *Perry v. Cyphers*, specifically declared it unconstitutional.

FURTHER READING

Baggett, James Alex. "Origins of Early Texas Republican Party Leadership," in *Journal of Southern History* 40 (1974).

Brewer, John Mason. *Negro Legislators of Texas and Their Descendants* (1935).

Campbell, Randolph B. *A Southern Community in Crisis: Harrison County, Texas, 1850–1880* (1983).

Smallwood, James M. *Time of Hope, Time of Despair: Black Texans during Reconstruction* (1981).

SALLY GREENE

Roberts, Needham (28 Apr. 1901–18 Apr. 1949), soldier, was born in Trenton, New Jersey, to Norman Roberts, a janitor and preacher, and Emma. Roberts, who spelled his name both Neadom and Needham, grew up in segregated Trenton and attended the Lincoln Elementary School. He left school as a teenager to seek employment, first as a hotel bellman and then as a drugstore clerk. From an early age, he exhibited an interest in military affairs and was active in a local Boy Scout troop; in 1916 he attempted to enlist in the navy but was rejected due to his youth.

After the U.S. entry into World War I, Roberts seized his opportunity. On 15 November 1917, Boy Scout manual in hand, Roberts traveled by train to New York, where two of his brothers lived in that city's San Juan Hill neighborhood. The next day, at the Seventh Avenue recruiting station in Harlem, Roberts enlisted in the Fifteenth New York National Guard Regiment. Known as the Harlem Hell Fighters, the 15th New York was mustered into the U.S. Army on 25 July 1917 as part of the 369th U.S. Infantry Regiment of the 93rd Division. Like most of the 380,000 African Americans in military service during World War I, Roberts trained in segregated camps, served under white officers, and found himself assigned to a disproportionate share of heavy labor duties. After arriving in France in early 1918, the Harlem Hell Fighters were placed under direct control of the French Fourth Army.

Roberts won national attention for his actions on the night of 13–14 May 1918. That evening Lieutenant Seth MacClinton ordered five men of C Company to a remote listening post sixty yards into the no-man's-land between the French and German forces that faced off along the banks of the Aisne River. Private Roberts, seventeen years old, and Private Henry Johnson were on guard duty as the other soldiers slept. At approximately 2:30 A.M., Roberts heard advancing German soldiers cutting through barbed wire. He called for backup, triggering the German attack. Blasts from German grenades soon threw him against the dugout walls, leaving him unable to stand, although he did launch at least one grenade from his wounded position. Two Germans attempted to take Roberts prisoner until his comrade Johnson eventually fought off the enemy soldiers. The German squad, later estimated at twenty-four men, retreated; Roberts and Johnson had killed five and wounded as many as twelve. Rescued at daylight, Roberts was evacuated to a nearby French military hospital. There Roberts came to the attention of American reporters, including Irvin Cobb of the *Saturday Evening Post* and Lincoln Eyre of the *New York World*. Since American military censors forbade the use of soldiers' names in battle accounts, the journalists seized on the human-interest story offered by these

Needham Roberts, World War I veteran, decorated with the Croix de Guerre with palm, two service stripes, and two wound stripes, 1919. (Library of Congress.)

soldiers, technically under French command. The Harlem Hell Fighters' officers too saw an opportunity to publicize the heroism of African American soldiers. Beginning with Eyre's account in the 21 May 1918 issue of the *World*, news articles quickly followed across the United States, reshaping the wartime debate about race and citizenship.

French officials awarded Roberts and Johnson the Croix de Guerre, the first Americans ever to receive the honor. Roberts, promoted to the rank of sergeant, returned to the United States for treatment soon thereafter. Trenton honored him with a parade and public ceremony on 6 November 1918; Roberts also marched in the Harlem Hell Fighters' Victory Parade in New York City on 17 February 1919. He was mustered out a few weeks later and found himself much in demand as a speaker. Photographs of Roberts and Johnson were treasured keepsakes among black Americans. Their political import was not lost on whites either, including a group in Cordele, Georgia, who on

4 April 1919 beat a traveling salesman when he tried to sell Roberts's picture in that town.

Less is known of the rest of Roberts's life. Soon after returning from France, he married Margaret Burrell and moved to Princeton, New Jersey; their daughter Juanita was born in 1919. Although he reported his occupation as "lecturer" in "private enterprise" to a 1920 census taker, Roberts's financial and personal circumstances were troubled. He was arrested in 1924 for wearing an army uniform while out of service and again in 1928 on a sex crime charge. Roberts later moved to Newark, New Jersey, where he worked as a messenger and married a second time. Facing prosecution on a charge of molesting an eight-year-old girl, Roberts and his wife Iola, who insisted on her husband's innocence, hanged themselves. While Roberts's national prominence was short-lived, his military actions at a crucial moment early in the war made possible the continued mobilization of African American soldiers during World War I.

FURTHER READING

A single copy of *Brief Adventures of the First American Soldier Decorated in the World War, as Told by Neadom Roberts* (1933) is in the collection of the American Civil War Center at Historic Tredegar in Richmond, Virginia.

Harris, Stephen L. *Harlem's Hell Fighters: The African-American 369th Infantry in World War I* (2003).

Slotkin, Richard. *Lost Battalions: The Great War and the Crisis of American Nationality* (2005).

Washington, Jack. *The Quest for Equality: Trenton's Black Community, 1890–1965* (1993).

CHRISTOPHER CAPOZZOLA

Roberts, Richard Samuel (4 May 1880–Nov. 1936), photographer and businessman, was born in Florida. As a young man, he worked with his father as a stevedore while taking correspondence courses in photography. At the beginning of the twentieth century—the specific date is unknown—he married Wilhelmina Pearl Williams, a native of South Carolina, who helped Roberts open the Gem Studio in Fernandina, Florida. The two had four children during their time in Florida: Gerald Ermerson, Beverly Nash, Cornelius C., and Wilhelmina. In 1920, when Wilhelmina's health began to suffer from Florida's humidity, the couple moved to her hometown of Columbia, South Carolina, where their fifth child, Miriam, was born. They purchased a small house equipped with electricity and plumbing, both luxuries for southerners at the time. In the backyard were a barn and a smaller house, the latter of which the family used as storage space for Roberts's photographic equipment and work.

Despite being the capital of South Carolina, Columbia was little more than a large, rural outpost. Although African Americans made up nearly 40 percent of the city's total population, they remained under Jim Crow laws. Since they could not attend the state university, most African American Columbians were forced into menial labor. Professionals and schoolteachers were paid less than their white counterparts and, therefore, were forced to supplement their incomes with additional jobs that were typically beneath their skill level. Roberts worked as a custodian at the Columbia post office for two years before he opened another photography studio.

In 1922 Roberts rented studio space in downtown Columbia and reestablished his portraiture business, but this time as Roberts Studio. From 4 A.M. to 12 noon Roberts worked at the post office and for the rest of the day conducted photo shoots. To promote his services, he engaged in a widespread marketing campaign aimed at the African American community in Columbia and surrounding towns for the studio, producing his own leaflets and placing advertisements in newspapers, event programs, and school yearbooks. Schools, churches, and families responded to his ads. In addition to portraits, Roberts photographed such events as graduations, athletic games, and funerals. One of his major clients was the *Palmetto Leader*, Columbia's African American weekly newspaper. He was the paper's primary photographer from 1925—the year it was established—until 1935.

Roberts developed innovative techniques and equipment to accommodate the limited space and poor lighting of his downtown studio. Perhaps the most significant of his numerous improvisations was an artificial lighting cabinet on wheels. Since electricity was still uncommon in personal homes and the flash bulb system in photography did not gain popular use until the 1930s, the cabinet's continuous light source and its portability had a tremendous effect on the quality of Roberts's work. He offered enlargements upwards of 8x10 and would not accept payment for the photographs until the client was satisfied. As a result, Roberts quickly used much of his costly materials in an effort to produce the best work possible. During this time, his wife ran a boarding house for young women who had moved to Columbia to attend high school. These young women assisted Roberts and his family with operating the studio by serving as studio assistants, receptionists, and clerks. Some of the women may also have trained in photography under Roberts's guidance. Eventually his son Gerald played a more active role in the studio operations; he was more frugal than his father and operated the studio with tighter budget restrictions. Gerald was interested in increasing his father's studio's profit margin; however, Roberts refused to compromise artistry and quality for money.

For nearly fifteen years Roberts was the only African American commercial photographer in Columbia and its surrounding towns and cities. Roberts was also the sole photo documentarian for the African American community of South Carolina's capital city. With his lens he captured a largely neglected community and gave it a permanent, historical presence. He also documented Columbia's rising African American bourgeoisie and created the only known collection of photographic portraits of Columbia's African American middle class. His intention for the collection remains unknown. Roberts continued to work up to his death at the age of fifty-six.

Shortly after his death, Roberts's family closed his studio and put his more than 3,000 glass plate negatives in storage in the family home. The negatives remained there until 1977, when Thomas L. Johnson, a field archivist with the South Carolina Library at the University of South Carolina, found them during a visit with Roberts's children. Five years after their initial meeting, the children allowed Johnson to take their father's work to Phillip C. Dunn, an art professor and photography specialist at the University of South Carolina. Dunn's reprints proved that the negatives were still capable of producing viable and beautiful prints after they had gone through a cleaning and restoration process. For the next two-and-a-half years Dunn cleaned and restored the negatives and safely archived them. He and Johnson selected what they believed to be the most significant prints for an exhibit at the Columbia Museum in 1986 for Columbia's Bicentennial. Bruccoli Clark Publishers optioned a book of the exhibit for publication in the fall of 1986. Titled *A True Likeness: The Black South of Richard Samuel Roberts: 1920–1936*, the book was nominated for a Pulitzer Prize and won the Southern Regional Council's Lillian Smith Book Award, an award established in 1968 to honor authors who carry on writer and magazine publisher Smith's mission of exposing racial and social injustices.

FURTHER READING

Dunn, Phillip C., and Thomas L. Johnson, eds. *A True Likeness: The Black South of Richard Samuel Roberts: 1920–1936* (1986).

Willis, Deborah. *Reflections in Black: A History of Black Photographers, 1840 to the Present* (2000).

CRYSTAL AM NELSON

Roberts, Shearley Oliver (21 May 1910–Aug.? 1984), psychologist and educator, was born in Alexandria, Virginia, to George and Esther Ragland Roberts. In 1928 he graduated from Howard High School, Wilmington, Delaware, then the sole free high school for African Americans in the state. He pursued higher education at white-run institutions at a time when there were almost no African Americans in his chosen field, psychology. Bertha Garrett Holliday (2009) describes the "distinct and harsh barriers" that blacks faced in the profession during that era, including "restricted training opportunities, extremely limited occupational opportunities, and widely held assumptions among European American psychologists of the intellectual and social 'deficits' of African Americans, which promoted a disciplinary consensus of the impossibility, difficulty, or lack of necessity of identifying 'qualified' African American graduate students and professionals."

Roberts nevertheless completed both his B.A. (1932) and M.A. (1933) with honors at Brown University in Providence, Rhode Island. His master's thesis was entitled *A Preliminary Study of Manual Expressions.* He then taught psychology and education at Atlanta University (1933–1936). A George Davis Bivin Foundation Fellowship (1936–1937) enabled his pursuit of a doctoral program at the University of Minnesota. Among his professors there was Florence Laura Goodenough, an early critic of intelligence tests that did not take social environment into account. Roberts worked as a research assistant at the University of Minnesota's Institute of Child Welfare (1937–1938); an educational consultant (1938–1939); and associate professor of psychology and education, Arkansas Agricultural, Mechanical, & Normal College in Pine Bluff (1939–1942). On a General Education Board Fellowship (1941), he conducted special research in human development at the University of Chicago. He was next employed as acting dean, Dunbar Junior College, Little Rock (1942–1943).

In 1942 Roberts wed Marion Pearl Taylor, a librarian and pianist from Little Rock. Her father, Reverend George Collins Taylor, was president of that city's Philander Smith College. The couple had three daughters. Esther Pearl became a psychiatrist, Barbara Taylor (married surname: Stone) a clinical psychologist, and Kay George (born 1950) an orchestral conductor and violinist.

In 1944 Shearley Oliver Roberts achieved his Ph.D. in Child Welfare (child development) and Psychology from the University of Minnesota. His 1944 doctoral dissertation, *The Measurement of Adjustment of Negro College Youth,* assessed and contrasted the personality testing of African American and white college students. Roberts then spent one more year at Arkansas AM&N, as an education professor and dean of students. In 1945 he was appointed professor of psychology and education at Fisk University in Nashville, Tennessee. He simultaneously began working in the Psychiatry Department of Meharry Medical College as a general consultant, lecturer, and assistant clinical professor.

In 1950 Roberts launched Fisk's program in Child Life and Development. The next year, he founded the school's psychology department and became its first chair. Roberts was awarded a Social Science Grant-in-Aid (1953) and a Ford Faculty Fellowship (1953–1954). The 1951 *Directory of the American Psychological Association* (p. 388) lists Roberts's professional interests, the very ones he pursued his entire career: "growth and development of racial minorities, social and regional factors in adjustment and personality development, measurement of intelligence and vocational interest, [and] achievement testing."

Roberts published studies of black education and child and youth development in the summer 1947, summer 1948, and summer 1950 issues of the *Journal of Negro Education.* At that time, the *JNE* was a vehicle for black social scientists' challenges to "scientific" racism. He later published the study monographs *Negro American College Youths' (NACY) Outlook on the Future* (1957); *Effects of Task Difficulty, Race of Administrator, and Instructions on Digit-Symbol Performance of Negroes* (with Irwin Katz and James M. Robinson, 1963); and *The Development and Adjustment of Children: A Phase of a Longitudinal Study, 1964–1966* (1968). Roberts was a delegate to the Mid-Century (1950) White House Conference on Children and Youth, which focused on the issue of healthy personality development and recommended the abolition of racially segregated education. Roberts was also present at the 1954 Thayer Conference in West Point, New York, which helped to define the emerging specialty of school psychology.

Among his other achievements were the Fisk-Meharry Local Preparatory Commission Report "Negro American Youth, Mental Health, and World Citizenship" (1948), for which he was an editor. He served leadership roles with the Nashville Metropolitan Section Commission, the Mental Health Center of Middle Tennessee, the Tennessee Governor's Commissions on Training and Research, and the Council of Psychological Resources in the South. He belonged to the professional honor societies Sigma Xi and Psi Chi and was appointed a fellow of both the Society for Research in Child Development and the American Psychological Association's (APA's) Division of Developmental Psychology.

In 1971 John Wiley, a "mainstream" scientific press, published Roger Wilcox's groundbreaking *Psychological Consequences of Being a Black American: A Source Book of Research by Black Psychologists*. It included a reprint of and references to Roberts's work. According to the APA's member directory, Roberts still worked on both the Fisk and Meharry faculties as late as 1981. Before his death at seventy-four, he witnessed the end of legal segregation in education, an increase in the number and visibility of African American psychologists, and greater attention to black perspectives and values within the field. Shearley Oliver Roberts's own enduring work in historically black institutions and his scientific challenges to racism contributed to these developments.

FURTHER READING

Guthrie, Robert V. *Even the Rat Was White: A Historical View of Psychology,* 2nd ed. (2004).

Holliday, Bertha Garrett. "The History and Visions of African American Psychology." *Cultural Diversity and Ethnic Minority Psychology* 15, no. 4 (Oct. 2009): 317–337.

Oklahoma State University Department of Psychology. *African American Pioneers in Psychology: Brief Biographies.* http://psychology.okstate.edu/museum/afroam/bio.html.

Sammons, Vivian Ovelton. *Blacks in Science and Medicine* (1990).

MARY KRANE DERR

Robertson, Carole (24 Apr. 1949–15 Sept. 1963), schoolgirl and terrorist bombing victim, was born Carole Rosamond Robertson in Birmingham, Alabama, the third child of Alvin Robertson, a music instructor, and Alpha Anderson Robertson, a teacher and librarian. Both Carole's mother and her maternal grandmother, Sallie Anderson, were prominent in the civic affairs of black Birmingham. Alpha Robertson helped found the city's chapter of Jack and Jill, Inc., a black women's national organization dedicated to the educational, cultural, and recreational enrichment of African American children, in which Carole was an active participant. When their Saturday morning chores were completed Carole attended weekly dance classes at a Smithfield recreation center, where she received lessons in both tap and ballet. A dedicated Girl Scout, she was also interested in music; she sang in the choir at the Wilkerson Elementary School in Birmingham and later joined the marching band at the city's Parker High School.

Robertson's academic achievements were also notable. A straight-A student interested in history and a member of the science club at Parker High School, she was one of a small number of African American teenagers who applied to enter Birmingham's first integrated high school in 1963. Because of the white community's intense opposition to any kind of desegregation, only the most mature and academically gifted children were encouraged to seek entrance to all-white schools, where it was expected that they would face considerable hostility. In the summer of 1963, as other teenagers fought police chief Eugene "Bull" Connor's water cannons and attack dogs on the streets of Birmingham, Robertson attended a secret tutoring and counseling program at a local Unitarian church to help prepare her for the much better equipped, historically white high schools should she be admitted. Secrecy was required because of several recent white supremacist bombings of Birmingham homes, businesses, and churches that were either African American or had sponsored civil rights activities.

Robertson's promise would never be fulfilled, however, because of the tragic events on Sunday, 15 September 1963, at the Sixteenth Street Baptist Church where she and her mother worshiped. Early that morning Alvin Robertson drove Carole to Sunday school, dropped her off, and returned home to pick up his wife for the main eleven o'clock service at which Carole was to sing with the youth choir. On arriving home he received a telephone call informing him of an explosion at the church, and he rushed there with his wife to make sure their daughter was safe. At first, in the confusion caused by the massive explosion, Carole's parents were told that she was still alive. They later learned that Carole and her close friend and neighbor,

CYNTHIA WESLEY, along with ADDIE MAE COLLINS and DENISE McNAIR, had been killed by the blast, which had blown a massive hole in the wall of the women's lounge where the four girls had been getting ready to sing in the choir. Twenty other members of the congregation, several of them children, were also injured by the explosion of fifteen sticks of dynamite placed near the lounge earlier that morning. Alvin Robertson later told a reporter that white supremacists had made several earlier bomb threats against Sixteenth Baptist. "I guess we should have been uneasy about leaving the children there, but it never occurred to me anyone would bomb a church with anybody in it" (cited in Mendelsohn, 95).

Two days after the bombing, Carole Robertson's funeral service was held at Birmingham's St. John's Methodist Episcopal Church. Her parents had declined MARTIN LUTHER KING JR.'s personal request that they participate in a joint funeral service for the four girls the following day at Sixth Street Baptist. Alpha Robertson later explained her reluctance to participate in a politicized funeral. "We realize Carole lost her life because of the [civil rights] movement," she told *Jet* magazine in October 1963, "but we feel her loss was personal to us" (cited in McWhorter, 670). In his eulogy the Reverend John Cross of Sixteenth Street Baptist stated that to "question the rightness of Carole's death was to question the power, sovereignty, and majesty of God, who can bring light from darkness, good from evil, and order from disorder" (cited in Mendelsohn, 101). However, many observers, and certainly most blacks, viewed the murder of four innocent girls as a matter of secular authority. They believed that power and sovereignty responsible for their deaths resided with Alabama Governor George Wallace, who had encouraged white racist violence, and with the federal government in Washington, D.C., which had largely ignored a series of racist killings since the mid 1950s.

Those responsible for the murders had believed that retaliatory violence would halt the progress of the civil rights movement and perhaps expected that, like the murders of EMMETT TILL, George W. Lee, and MEDGAR EVERS, these deaths would be largely ignored in the broader American society. But the four girls' youth and the sacrilege of bombing a church provoked outrage both in America and abroad. The black activist and Birmingham native ANGELA DAVIS, a friend of the Robertson and Wesley families, who was a nineteen-year-old student in Paris at the time, experienced a great sense of anger and powerlessness. Others who did not know the girls also took their deaths personally. JAMES BEVEL of the Student Nonviolent Coordinating Committee (SNCC) viewed the bombing as a personal insult. His wife at the time, DIANE NASH, also of SNCC, similarly felt as if her own children had been killed. The tragedy of 15 September 1963 ultimately persuaded Bevel, Nash, and others in SNCC that the civil rights movement had only two options. According to Nash, one was to meet violence with violence; the other, which they ultimately chose, was to focus on a massive voting rights campaign that resulted in the 1965 Voting Rights Act. As Nash argued, "If blacks in Alabama had the right to vote, they could protect black children" (Hampton, 173).

None of those directly responsible for the Sixteenth Street church bombing was convicted until 1977, when the Ku Klux Klansman Robert Chambliss was convicted of the murder of Denise McNair. Fourteen years later, on 24 April 2001— what would have been Carole Robertson's fifty-first birthday—a second Klansman, Thomas Blanton, was convicted of all four murders. Had the FBI not withheld evidence (for reasons as yet unexplained), Blanton, Chambliss, and at least two other accomplices could have been tried thirty-five years earlier.

In 1976 the Carole Robertson Center was established in Chicago in honor of all four girls killed in Birmingham. Run by parents and community residents, it provided a wide range of childcare, education, and after-school programs for needy children in Chicago.

FURTHER READING

Spike Lee's 1998 documentary film, *Four Little Girls*, provides a compelling portrait of the bitter racial climate of Birmingham in 1963, the brief lives of Carole Robertson, Addie Mae Collins, Cynthia Wesley, and Denise McNair, and the courage of their families in coping with the tragic deaths of their daughters in the four decades that followed.

Hampton, Henry, and Steve Frayer. *Voices of Freedom* (1990).

McWhorter, Diane. *Carry Me Home: Birmingham, Alabama: the Climactic Battle of the Civil Rights Revolution* (2001).

Mendelsohn, Jack. *The Martyrs: Sixteen Who Gave Their Lives for Racial Justice* (1966).

STEVEN J. NIVEN

Robertson, Oscar Palmer (24 Nov. 1938–), basketball player, was born in Dickson County, Tennessee, the son of Bailey Robertson Sr., a meat cutter, and

Mazell Bell, a domestic. In 1942 the family moved to the west side of Indianapolis, Indiana, to a black ghetto called Frog Island or Naptown, where in 1952 Oscar entered Crispus Attucks High School. Though built after considerable debate in 1927 to segregate the Indianapolis high schools, Crispus Attucks High School had become a source of pride in the black community because of its academic and athletic excellence.

By the time that Oscar Robertson made the varsity basketball team as a sophomore in the fall of 1953, Crispus Attucks was an Indiana basketball powerhouse. The Crispus Attucks Tigers had never won a state championship, but neither had any other Indianapolis school. In addition to the general unfair treatment that black schools often had to face in integrated competition, Crispus Attucks had a special challenge because it did not have a home court and so played its games at other high schools or at the Butler University field house. Robertson devoted long hours to developing his basketball skills, which he tested against the best players in his neighborhood. When he tried out for the varsity in the fall of 1953, he stood a muscular six feet three inches tall. The coach of the Tigers was Ray Crowe, a strict disciplinarian and fierce competitor intent on winning a state championship. In Robertson's second varsity game Crowe made him a starter, and he soon became the team's leader. Though he set numerous individual scoring records, Robertson was a consummate team player. A skilled passer and tenacious defensive player, he soon demonstrated the poise that was a hallmark of his career.

In 1954 Crispus Attucks lost to tiny Milan High School in the regional final game. Milan proceeded to win the state tournament in a magical season that would be celebrated thirty years later in the movie *Hoosiers* (1986). But the years 1955 and 1956 belonged to the Crispus Attucks Tigers. In the 1955 regular season Robertson scored 450 points to establish a new Indianapolis scoring record, and the Tigers lost only one game before defeating Muncie Central, one of Indiana's perennial basketball powerhouses, 71–70 in the state semifinals. In the championship game Crispus Attucks trampled Gary's Roosevelt High School 97–74. This game was historic not only because it marked the first time that an Indianapolis high school won a state basketball championship but also because this was the first time that an all-black high school won the title and the first time that an Indiana state championship game matched two black high schools. The following year Crispus Attucks became the first

undefeated high school team in Indiana history as it won its second consecutive championship. In the 1956 state-final game Robertson scored thirty-nine points to set a new record for a state-championship game. He also set new Indiana records for scoring in a single regular-season game, in a regular season, and in a high school career. Robertson and Crispus Attucks were the toast of Indianapolis's black community.

Although Robertson was one of the best (if not the best) high school players in the country, the University of Indiana failed to get him after Coach Branch McCracken embarrassed him by wondering if he was going to ask for money to play for the Hoosiers. Offended by such a comment, Robertson chose the University of Cincinnati Bearcats, coached by George Smith, even though the team did not have a distinguished history. Robertson would change that as he became its first black player.

In the 1957–1958 season, Robertson, who had been nicknamed the "Big O," led Cincinnati to the Missouri Valley Conference Championship and its first NCAA invitation, which ended with a loss to Kansas State in the regionals. Robertson's season was marred by racism; he was not allowed to stay with the team in a Houston hotel, and fans threw garbage at him and yelled racist catcalls at North Texas State. Despite all this it was a banner year for Robertson, who averaged 35.1 points a game, was voted to the first-team all-American squad, and scored fifty-six points at Madison Square Garden—a new Garden record.

The following season Robertson took Cincinnati to the Final Four, where the Bearcats lost to the University of California. Although Robertson led the nation in scoring and had another all-America year, the ugly head of racism was again raised at the Dixie Classic in Raleigh, North Carolina. City hotels refused to provide rooms for the Bearcats because they had two black players, Robertson and a new black teammate, John Bryant. Instead the team stayed in a vacant fraternity house. On the basketball court fans showered Robertson with racial epithets. Fan conduct was a disgrace and left Robertson wondering why the University of Cincinnati exposed him to such hostility. In his senior year Robertson led the Bearcats to their third consecutive conference title and to a Final Four appearance in which Cincinnati once again lost to the University of California in the semifinals. Robertson ended his three years by breaking Frank Selvy's career collegiate scoring record, and then he led the United States to a gold medal in the 1960 Rome Olympics. Between graduation and the Olympics, Robertson married Yvonne Crittenden, a University of Cincinnati student; they eventually had three girls, Mari, Tia, and Shana.

In 1960 Robertson signed a contract with the Cincinnati Royals. The NBA was only a decade old, had a number of weak franchises, and had not won the media attention that professional football or baseball had. Unfortunately for Robertson, the Royals were one of those inept franchises. Nonetheless Robertson was a perennial all-pro who was named the NBA's Most Valuable Player in 1964. On the strength of his play the Royals played for the Eastern Division title in 1963 and 1964, losing both times to the Boston Celtics. Before it was fashionable for the media to call attention to the triple double (double figures in scoring, assists, and rebounds), Robertson averaged a triple double for his first five years, averaging 30.3 points per game, 10.6 rebounds, and 10.4 assists.

In 1970, with Robertson and the Royals at odds, the Royals traded the Big O to the Milwaukee Bucks, where he was teamed up with Lew Alcindor (later KAREEM ABDUL-JABBAR), the dominant NBA center for the 1970s and 1980s. With that duo and a strong supporting cast, the Bucks won an NBA title in 1971. Though the Bucks were the first team to win sixty or more games in three consecutive years, they did not return to the NBA finals until 1974, Robertson's last season, when the Bucks fell to the Boston Celtics in the seventh game. In fourteen years Robertson earned all-pro honors twelve times, was the all-time NBA assist leader, and was second to WILT CHAMBERLAIN in career scoring.

Off the court Robertson was the president of the NBA Players Association from 1965 to 1974. With the assistance of Larry Fleisher, legal counsel, and several other NBA stars, Robertson committed himself to eliminating the reserve clause (the contractual clause that made it impossible for a player to sell his services to the highest bidder) and to funding pension and disability plans, all of which goals were achieved in 1976. After 1974 Robertson and his family returned to Cincinnati, where he established himself as a successful businessman and devoted his energies to a variety of community projects. In 1979 he was inducted into the Naismith Basketball Hall of Fame.

The significance of Oscar Robertson's career was larger than his basketball skills. His twenty years of basketball competition coincided with the momentous victories of the civil rights movement.

Along with BILL RUSSELL, Wilt Chamberlain, and ELGIN BAYLOR, to name but a few, Oscar Robertson helped to open up opportunities for black athletes by challenging racial stereotypes and establishing new standards of basketball excellence.

FURTHER READING
Robertson, Oscar. *The Big O: My Life, My Times, My Game* (2003).
Roberts, Randy. *"But They Can't Beat Us": Oscar Robertson and the Crispus Attucks Tigers* (1999).
                                                  DOLPH GRUNDMAN

Robeson, Eslanda Cardozo Goode (15 Dec. 1896–13 Dec. 1965), chemist, author, and activist, was born in Washington, D.C., the daughter of John Goode, a clerk in the U.S. War Department, and Eslanda Cardoza Goode, an osteopath and beautician. Eslanda, or Essie as she was known to her friends, attended the integrated public schools in New York and finished high school in just three years, when she was sixteen years old. She won a scholarship to attend the University of Illinois. Originally encouraged to major in domestic science, she was so bored after two years that she considered leaving. An adviser asked her what classes she liked, and when she said that chemistry was her favorite subject, she was encouraged to pursue that instead. For her senior year she attended Columbia University Teachers College.

Through her adviser at Columbia, and due to the labor shortages created by World War I, Robeson secured employment as a chemist and technician in the Surgical Pathology Department at Presbyterian Hospital in New York in 1918. She was among the first African Americans to work for the hospital and the first woman to work in that capacity. Her job was to make "microscopic cross sections of tissues taken from patients in the operating rooms" (Buck, 15). While working there she graduated with a bachelor of science degree in Chemistry in June 1920.

In 1921 Essie quietly married PAUL ROBESON while he was still attending Columbia Law School. The ceremony was small and they waited to announce it to friends and family until December (for reasons unclear). They had met at a party in Harlem, and Essie recalled: "Everybody thought he was just one of those football players who wouldn't amount to anything. But, I thought he was terrific" (*New York Times*, 14 Dec. 1965, 43). Paul Robeson credited Essie with encouraging his acting career: "I never meant to [become an actor], I just said yes to get her to quit pestering me" (Whitman, 30).

Essie Robeson became his manager, a position she held for the rest of her life.

In 1925 Essie Robeson stopped working as a chemist to book tours and supervise her husband's successful international career as an actor and singer. She had several serious health problems in her life, including cancer and gallstones. Still she had a child, Paul Jr., in 1927. Her first book, *Paul Robeson, Negro*, published in 1930, is a personal account of the early life and career of her famous husband. Due to opportunities in Europe that were denied to African American entertainers in the United States, the Robeson family was based off and on in London from 1925 until 1939.

Robeson's interest in Africa prompted her to enroll in anthropology classes at the University of London and later at the London School of Economics in 1935. She traveled to Africa with Paul Jr, then eight years old, in 1936 in part to show him a "black world, he will see a black continent" (Robeson, *African Journey*, 17)—what he was missing growing up in white Europe. The diary and photos from that trip, which reflected her increased interest in colonialism, became the well-received book *African Journey* (1945). The *New York Times* wrote on 9 August 1945 that it was "an extremely attractive and natural book." She continued to write articles about Africa and Africans for years to come. She visited Spain during the Spanish civil war in 1938 to show her support for the troops fighting the fascist dictator Francisco Franco. Upon her return to the United States, Robeson resumed her education, working toward a Ph.D. in anthropology at Hartford Seminary. According to some sources, she completed her thesis in either 1944 or 1945.

The more she learned, the more Robeson came to believe that race issues in the United States were linked with Africans struggling for independence. Consequently she became a cofounder and leader of the Council on African Affairs in 1941 to lobby against colonialism in Africa. Representing that organization, she served as a delegate observer to the founding convention of the United Nations (UN) in 1945. Six years later she took a militant approach to bring attention to the issue of violence against African Americans, by disrupting the UN Genocide Conference along with her husband and William R. Patterson.

As an outspoken advocate of the goals of socialist countries like the Soviet Union and postrevolutionary China, Robeson was called to appear before Senator Joe McCarthy's Senate investigating committee on 7 July 1953. These hearings were supposed to find Communists responsible for harming the U.S. government. The questions asked were inflammatory and had the effect of permanently harming the reputation and career of the person being "investigated," no matter what the truth was about their political activities. Instead of answering the questions posed by the members of the committee, she responded by asking them about the state of civil rights for African Americans. She also invoked the Fifteenth Amendment, which granted African Americans the right to vote, to point out that as a woman of color she was a second-class citizen in front of "a very white committee" (*New York Times*, 14 Dec. 1965, 43). When McCarthy released her, he said that because she was a "lady" she was treated with "special consideration," and he wouldn't make her "answer those questions and cite you [Robeson] for contempt" (Duberman, 413).

Both Paul and Eslanda were under heavy surveillance for years by the Federal Bureau of Investigation due to their political beliefs, and although they were not formally charged, Paul had his passport taken away in 1950 (Whitman, 30). Because of the suspicious climate of the nation in regard to communism, the questioning of the Robesons caused Paul Robeson's income from performances to drop from over $100,000 in the late 1940s to several thousand dollars in the 1950s. The Robesons were forced to sell some of their assets to meet living expenses, and as soon as their U.S. passports were reissued in 1958, they returned to Europe.

In spite of these pressures, Essie Robeson continued her political work. In 1958 she attended the All-African Peoples Conference in Ghana as a representative of the Council on African Affairs. She was one of only seven other women delegates at the conference. In the late 1950s and early 1960s the Robesons spent considerable time in both London and the Soviet Union, where they were well received and Paul Robeson was in high demand. Essie Robeson returned to the United States during the height of the Vietnam War and actively spoke out against the war. She was awarded both the German Peace Medal and the Clara Zetkin Medal in 1963 from East Germany in recognition of her work to bring peace and justice to the world. In her acceptance speech, she told a crowd of over twenty thousand that African Americans were fighting fascism by working against discrimination and for their civil rights. Two years later, in 1965, Essie Robeson lost her battle with cancer and died in Beth Israel Hospital in New York City.

While she began her career as a scientist, breaking gender and color barriers, Robeson was widely known as a prolific writer, journalist, and correspondent who was actively engaged in social justice causes. She was largely responsible for recording and promoting Paul Robeson's formidable career. While proud to be Mrs. Paul Robeson, she worked hard to be independent. A prolific writer and correspondent, her analysis was international in scope, and she worked to make important connections among race, class, and gender.

FURTHER READING

The Robeson Family Archives are in the Moorland-Springarn Research Center, Howard University, Washington, D.C.

Robeson, Eslanda Goode. *African Journey* (1945).

Buck, Pearl S., with Eslanda Goode Robeson. *American Argument* (1949).

Duberman, Martin. *Paul Robeson: A Biography* (2005).

Hackett, Francis. "Books of the Times," *New York Times*, 9 Aug. 1945.

Ransby, Barbara. "Eslanda Goode Robeson, Pan-Africanist," *Sage* 3, no. 2 (1986).

Whitman, Alden. "Paul Robeson Dead at 77; Singer, Actor, and Activist," *New York Times*, 24 Jan. 1976.

Obituary: *New York Times*, 14 Dec. 1965.

ANN ZEIDMAN-KARPINSKI

Robeson, Paul (9 Apr. 1898–23 Jan. 1976), actor, singer, and civil rights activist, was born Paul Leroy Robeson in Princeton, New Jersey, the son of William Drew Robeson, a Protestant minister, and Maria Louisa Bustill, a schoolteacher. Robeson's mother died when he was six years old, and he grew up under the influence of a perfectionist father, a former runaway slave who fought in the Union army. During his senior year at the Somerville, New Jersey, high school, he achieved the highest score in a statewide scholarship examination to attend Rutgers College (later Rutgers University). The lone black at Rutgers as a freshman in 1915 and only the third African American to attend the institution, Robeson was an outstanding student and athlete. A varsity debater, he won class prizes for oratory all four years, was elected to Phi Beta Kappa as a junior, was one of four seniors chosen for membership in the Cap and Skull honorary society, and was named class valedictorian. The six-foot three-inch, 215-pound Robeson earned twelve varsity letters in four sports (baseball, basketball, football, and track) and was twice named football All-America (1917 and 1918). According to the former Yale coach Walter Camp, "There never has been a more serviceable end, both in attack and defense, than Robeson." Despite his popularity with fellow students, a series of social slights and racial incidents in football brought to the fore long-standing concerns about race. Robeson's senior thesis predicted the eventual use of the Fourteenth Amendment to advance civil rights, and his commencement address boldly combined the accommodationist philosophy of BOOKER T. WASHINGTON with the more militant views of W. E. B. DuBois. Robeson received the B.A. degree in 1919 and moved to Harlem preparatory to entering the Columbia University Law School in 1920. He helped finance his legal education by playing professional football for three seasons (1920–1922) with the Akron Pros and the Milwaukee Badgers. In 1921 he married Eslanda "Essie" Cardozo Goode (ESLANDA CARDOZO GOODE ROBESON) a member of a prominent Washington, D.C., black family, who worked as a laboratory pathologist at Columbia's medical school; they had one child. Recognizing Robeson's lack of enthusiasm for the law and football, his wife urged him to take up acting. After playing the lead in a Harlem YMCA production of *Simon the Cyrenian* in 1920, he appeared in several other local productions and became acquainted with the Provincetown Players, a Greenwich Village theatrical group that included Eugene O'Neill. He debuted professionally in a short-run Broadway play, *Taboo*, in 1922. Robeson, meanwhile, finished his legal studies, received the LLB degree in February 1923, and joined a New York City law firm headed by a Rutgers alumnus. But discouraged by discrimination within the firm and the legal profession generally, he quit a few months later, before taking the bar exam, to pursue an acting career.

Robeson launched his stage career in 1924 in the lead roles in two O'Neill plays, *The Emperor Jones* and *All God's Chillun Got Wings*, the latter a daring drama about interracial marriage. He achieved a spectacular triumph in London in 1930 when he not only became one of the first black actors to play Othello but also rendered the finest portrayal of the character yet seen. Robeson was also an accomplished singer, and at his wife's urging he performed at Carnegie Hall in 1925. The first soloist to devote an entire concert to Negro spirituals, Robeson both enthralled the sold-out audience and boosted the popularity of the musical genre. Robeson steadfastly refused to sing operatic and classical music, preferring to emphasize Negro spirituals and international folk songs. In time his rich basso-baritone voice was familiar to millions through national and international concert tours, radio performances, and more than three hundred recordings. He combined singing and acting in several musicals and was best known for his rendition of "Ol' Man River" in *Show Boat* (London, 1928; New York, 1932; Los Angeles, 1940). Robeson also appeared in eleven motion pictures, including film versions of *The Emperor Jones* (1933) and *Show Boat* (1936) and Hollywood extravaganzas such as *King Solomon's Mines* (1937). Robeson chafed at the stereotyping and racial slights suffered by blacks in the movie industry and demanded positive leading roles; he was most proud of his work in *Song of Freedom* (1936) and *The Proud Valley* (1940). Robeson's legacy, as actor-director SIDNEY POITIER noted, was profound: "Before him, no black man or woman had been portrayed in American movies as anything but a racist stereotype" (quoted in *Current Biography* [1976], 345–46).

Robeson's political ideas took shape after George Bernard Shaw introduced him to socialism in 1928. To escape American racism, he lived during most of the 1930s in Europe, returning to the United States only for movie and concert appearances. Impressed by the absence of racial and class discrimination in the Soviet Union during a concert tour in 1934, Robeson subsequently spent extended periods in Moscow, learned Russian, and enrolled his son in Soviet schools. He became politically active in opposing fascism, imperialism, and racism. He gave benefit performances in England for refugees from fascist countries, associated with British left-wing political groups, became acquainted with key figures in the West African Political Union, including Jomo Kenyatta and Kwame Nkrumah, and in 1938 traveled to Spain to support the republican troops engaged in the civil war against Francisco Franco's fascists.

When forced by the outbreak of World War II to return to the United States in 1939, Robeson was as well known as a critic of American racism and champion of the Soviet Union as an entertainer. He protested the segregation of organized baseball, appeared frequently at union and labor meetings, delivered antiracist lectures during concerts, joined the Pan-Africanist Council on African Affairs, and quit Hollywood because "the industry is not prepared to permit me to portray the life or express the living interests, hopes, and aspirations of the struggling people from whom I come." Robeson's political activism drew criticism but did not hurt his career, primarily because of the U.S.–Soviet military alliance. Indeed, he enjoyed his greatest hour

as a performer in October 1943 when he became the first black actor to play Othello in the United States. Following a then record-setting 296 performances for a Shakespearean drama on Broadway, the company undertook a nationwide tour and Robeson received the Donaldson Award as the best actor of the year. In 1945 the National Association for the Advancement of Colored People (NAACP) awarded him the prestigious Spingarn Medal.

However, when Robeson continued to use the Soviet Union as a hammer to pound against racism in the United States, he suffered the fate of other political leftists during the anticommunist hysteria of the cold war. In 1946 he denied under oath to a California state legislative committee that he was a member of the Communist Party but thereafter refused as a matter of conscience and constitutional right to comment on his political beliefs or affiliation. Instead, he continued to speak out against American racism and to praise the Soviet "experiment in socialism," associated openly with Marxist organizations, and, as a founder and chairman of the Progressive Party, campaigned for Henry Wallace in the 1948 presidential election. While addressing the World Peace Congress in Paris in 1949, he said, "It is unthinkable that American Negroes could go to war on behalf of those who have oppressed us for generations against a country [the Soviet Union] which in one generation has raised our people to the full dignity of mankind." He was immediately denounced by the black and white press, repudiated by most black civil rights organizations, and attacked by government agencies and congressional committees. The U.S. House of Representatives Committee on Un-American Activities labeled him a "Communist" and a "Communist sympathizer" and enlisted JACKIE ROBINSON, who in 1947 had integrated organized baseball, to "give the lie" to Robeson's statement. He was hounded by the Federal Bureau of Investigation, and in 1950 the State Department took away his passport, refusing to issue a new one until he signed a noncommunist oath and pledged not to give political speeches abroad. He refused, and his persistent use of the Fifth Amendment during House and Senate hearings and the Soviet Union's awarding him the International Stalin Peace Prize in 1952 only exacerbated the public's perception of him as a subversive. Outraged Rutgers alumni demanded that his name be excised from the school's athletic records and that the honorary master of arts degree awarded to him in 1930 be rescinded. He was blacklisted as an entertainer, and his recordings were removed from

Paul Robeson as Othello, Theatre Guild Production, Broadway, 1943–1944. (Library of Congress/Farm Security Administration—Office of War Information Photograph Collection.)

stores. His income fell from more than $100,000 in 1947 to $6,000 in 1952. Unable to travel abroad to earn money, Robeson was forced to sell his estate, The Beeches, in Enfield, Connecticut.

By the late 1950s the burgeoning civil rights movement along with the lessening of cold war paranoia and the demise of McCarthyism led to a rehabilitation of Robeson's reputation, particularly among African Americans. Critical was *Here I Stand* (1958), a brief autobiography as manifesto in which Robeson reaffirmed his admiration for the Soviet Union and in which he stated, "I am not and never have been involved in any international conspiracy." He also declared his "belief in the principles of scientific Socialism" as the basis for a society "economically, socially, culturally, and ethically superior to a system based upon production for private profit." Although essentially a recitation of the stands he had taken all along, as the first sentence of the foreword—"I am a Negro"—made clear, the book was primarily a declaration of allegiance to

the black community. Here Robeson presaged the Black Power politics of the 1960s by rejecting gradualism in civil rights, insisting that "the Negro people's movement must be led by Negroes," and advocating change through the "mass action" of "aroused and militant" black masses. He performed several concerts, recorded an album, and after being reissued a passport in 1958 (following a Supreme Court decision in a related case that confirmed his contention that the right to travel was independent of political views), left for Europe to revitalize his career.

But fifteen years of persistent harassment and political attacks had taken its toll, destroying not only his career but also his health and, ultimately, his sanity. Despite a tumultuous welcome, his sojourn in the Soviet Union was bleak. He was frequently hospitalized for exhaustion and a circulatory ailment as well as emotional instability. He attempted suicide; excessive drug and electric shock therapy likely caused permanent brain damage. He returned to the United States in 1963 and went into seclusion. His wife's death in 1965 ended their long marriage of convenience. Robeson's numerous infidelities had led to several separations, but Essie Goode Robeson, who obtained a Ph.D. in Anthropology and wrote *African Journey* (1945), resignedly managed his career in exchange for economic and social status. Robeson then moved to Philadelphia, Pennsylvania, where he lived with a sister. Virtually an invalid and suffering from acute depression, he refused interviews and was seen only by family and close friends. Too ill to attend the 75th Birthday Salute to Paul Robeson staged at Carnegie Hall in April 1973 by leaders in the entertainment and civil rights fields, he sent a recorded message: "I want you to know that I am still the same Paul, dedicated as ever to the worldwide cause of humanity for freedom, peace and brotherhood." Three years later he died in Philadelphia.

Paul Robeson is an American tragedy. He was an enormously talented black man whose imposing personality and uncompromising political ideals were more than a racist and anticommunist United States could appreciate or tolerate. One of the major performing artists of the twentieth century, his achievements as a stage actor, movie star, and singer are individually outstanding but collectively astounding. He was easily the most influential black entertainer of his day. Because he spent so much time abroad, Robeson never established close political associations in black America and thus served the African American community more as a symbol of black consciousness and pride than as a spokesperson. A victim of character assassination during the cold war, Robeson—unlike many black (and white) entertainers who maintained silence to protect or advance their careers—courageously combined art and politics. If he was politically naive and oblivious to the realities of Stalinist Russia, he astutely connected American racism and the international oppression of colored peoples. And Robeson proved to be ahead of his time in rejecting both the black nationalism of separation and repatriation as well as the assimilationism of the NAACP in favor of a cultural pluralism in which ethnic integrity was maintained amid international solidarity. For all his achievements, Robeson's pro-Soviet stance continues to preclude just recognition. He remains the only two-time All-American not in the College Football Hall of Fame.

FURTHER READING

By far the largest and most important collection of manuscript materials pertaining to Paul Robeson's life and career is the Robeson Family Archives, featuring the writings of his wife, in the Moorland-Spingarn Research Center, Howard University, Washington, D.C.

Robeson, Paul. *Here I Stand* (1958).

Davis, Lenwood G., comp. *A Paul Robeson Research Guide: A Selected Annotated Bibliography* (1982).

Duberman, Martin Bauml. *Paul Robeson* (1988).

Foner, Philip S., ed. *Paul Robeson Speaks: Writings, Speeches, Interviews, 1918–1974* (1978).

Gilliam, Dorothy Butler. *Paul Robeson: All-American* (1976).

Robeson, Eslanda Cardozo. *Paul Robeson, Negro* (1930).

Robeson, Paul, Jr. *The Undiscovered Paul Robeson: An Artist's Journey, 1898–1939* (2001).

Seton, Marie. *Paul Robeson* (1958).

Obituaries: *New York Times*, 24 Jan. 1976; *New York Amsterdam News*, 31 Jan. 1976.

This entry is taken from the *American National Biography* and is published here with the permission of the American Council of Learned Societies.

LARRY R. GERLACH

Robey, Don D. (1 Nov. 1903–16 June 1975), entrepreneur and record label owner, was born Don Deadric Robey in Houston, Texas, the son of Zeb Robey and Gertrude (maiden name unknown). Little is known of his childhood. Don dropped out of high school in the eleventh grade, reportedly to become a professional gambler in Houston nightspots frequented by African Americans; later he was suspected of being involved in the city's numbers operation. He also entered the taxi business prior to World War II and established a business in entertainment promotion, bringing name bands and celebrity attractions into segregated sections of the Houston area.

Though Robey opened his first nightclub in 1937, it was the postwar Bronze Peacock Dinner Club, opened in 1946, that he parlayed into an interconnected set of entertainment and music businesses that made him, according to the *Houston Informer*, one of the city's "foremost black business wizards." Robey's skill as a promoter in booking talent for the Bronze Peacock led to his activity first in the talent management business and eventually into records and music publishing. He established Peacock Records in 1949 to launch the blues career of Clarence "Gatemouth" Brown, a relatively unknown guitarist from San Antonio, and soon signed other secular and gospel acts.

Robey's first big record was released in 1950, when the religious song "Our Father" by the Original Five Blind Boys became a national jukebox hit. Robey once claimed that it was he who "put the beat" in gospel music. Eventually he had so many religious groups under contract that he established an additional gospel label, Song Bird.

In 1952 Robey became a partner, then owner, of Duke Records of Memphis, Tennessee, moving its operation to Houston and establishing the ballad singer JOHNNY ACE as a crooner and a nationally known rhythm and blues performer. Robey carefully cultivated the polished, uptown image that BERRY GORDY later emulated at Motown. The next year WILLIE MAE THORNTON's "Hound Dog" made her famous in the national blues community and established Peacock Records as a major independent label in black secular music. Robey is also credited with discovering Bobby Bland, Little Junior Parker, and the Dixie Hummingbirds.

With Evelyn Johnson, his business partner and common-law wife from 1953 to 1960, Robey helped establish the Buffalo Booking Agency in Houston to arrange personal appearances for his recording artists. Eventually Buffalo Booking was able to send Duke and Peacock acts to California and large cities in the East and Midwest.

After Johnny Ace shot himself playing Russian roulette on Christmas night 1954, his new record, "Pledging My Love," became the most played rhythm and blues record of 1955. It was a crossover hit on the popular music charts as well, the first ballad by a black male performer signed to an independent label to attract a white audience in the postwar era. "Pledging My Love" established Duke Records as an important cultural force in the transition between rhythm and blues and rock and roll.

In 1957 Robey developed a new label, Back Beat, and signed young white performers in an attempt to court the white teenage market. In 1963 he added the Sure-Shot label to his operation, but in the mid-1960s, as rhythm and blues became more popular, Robey's importance as an independent entrepreneur in the field of black secular music began to diminish. In addition, his hold on black gospel was threatened by an eleven-year lawsuit with Chess Records of Chicago.

When the courts ruled against him, Robey sold all his music business interests to ABC/Dunhill in 1973 for a reported $1,000,000. By this time Robey's Lion and Don publishing companies controlled some 2,700 copyrights, and his various record labels had one hundred contracted artists ($250,000 of unrecouped advanced royalties on active contracts), with approximately 2,000 unreleased masters. Robey, who had been able to acquire writer credit on many of the songs he recorded, ended up as the author of 1,200 published songs.

It is alleged that Robey was a "black godfather," "a czar of the Negro underworld," and "a character out of *Guys and Dolls*." Evelyn Johnson admitted that while he did everything his way, "he did far more good than he did bad." Robey was a pioneer in the history of black music in the United States. Galen Gart called him "the first successful black entrepreneur to emerge in the music business after World War II."

Robey married for the first time in 1921 or 1922, to Beatrice Sherman; the couple had one child. He married for the last time in 1960, to Murphy Louise Moore, with whom he had three children. In between, he married, divorced, and remarried Sadie Malone and entered into common-law marriages with Naomi Parks, with whom he had two children, and Evelyn Johnson. He was an avid sportsman and hunter who raised thoroughbred horses and promoted, and sometimes participated in, rodeos. He helped establish the first golf course for blacks in Houston, and in his later years he became a community leader in the United Negro College Fund Drive. Robey continued to work as a consultant to ABC/Dunhill (later MCA) until his death in Houston.

FURTHER READING

Gart, Galen, and Roy C. Ames. *Duke/Peacock Records: An Illustrated History with Discography* (1990).

Govenar, Alan. *The Early Years of Rhythm & Blues: Focus on Houston* (1990).

Salem, James M. "Death and the Rhythm-and-Bluesman: The Life and Recordings of Johnny Ace," *American Music* (Fall 1993).

Obituaries: *Rolling Stone*, 31 July 1975; *Variety*, 9 July 1975; *Living Blues*, Sept.-Oct. 1975; *Houston Forward Times*, 21 June 1975; *Houston Informer*, 21 June 1975.

This entry is taken from the *American National Biography* and is published here with the permission of the American Council of Learned Societies.

JAMES M. SALEM

Robinson, Aminah Brenda Lynn (18 Feb. 1940–), a visual artist, was born Brenda Lynn Robinson in Columbus, Ohio, as the middle daughter of Leroy Edward Robinson, a custodian, and Helen Elizabeth Zimmerman Robinson, a homemaker. Shortly after Robinson's birth, her family moved to a federal housing project, Poindexter Village. Much of Robinson's art derives from childhood influences. Poindexter Village and the neighborhood that preceded it, the Blackberry Patch, would become recurring themes in Robinson's art. She chronicles the lives of her former neighbors, such as the Sockman, Chickenfoot Woman, and Ragman, who peddled their wares on the streets.

Robinson's father did not identify as an artist but he spent his spare time creating beautiful objects from wood, leather, and cloth. He also taught his daughter to make art, including "hogmawg," a mixture of mud, sticks, glue, dyes, and lime that is the basis for her three-dimensional sculptures and the objects that appear in her pop-up books. Robinson's mother taught her the button and needlework that she uses in quilts. The budding young artist also grew up listening to older relatives relate tales of the African American past, such as the experience of being a slave in Sapelo Island, Georgia, and of living through the emancipation era. These historical themes appear throughout Robinson's work.

Robinson was raised as a Catholic but, since her church lacked a Sunday school, she often attended the one at Union Grove Baptist Church and listened to spirituals. Music boxes that play spirituals often appear in her mixed-media works and in sculptures such as *Spinning Wheel and Three-Legged Dog* (1968–1989) and *My Lord What a Morning* (1994). Robinson attended public schools in Columbus. While still a high school junior, she began taking Saturday classes at the Columbus College of Art and Design (CCAD). Robinson continued at CCAD after her 1957 high school graduation and began to combine text and visual images. She paid the bills by working at the Columbus Public Library.

In 1964 Robinson left her library job when she married Clarence Robinson, a Korean War veteran. Her husband's Air Force assignments took Robinson and their son, Sydney (b. 1967) to Boise, Idaho; Omaha, Nebraska; and Biloxi, Mississippi. In 1968, when Clarence went to Vietnam, Robinson and her son stayed with her parents in Columbus. Robinson met the Columbus woodcarver Elijah Pierce at this time. The older artist encouraged the young woman to develop her talents. Robinson sketched in Pierce's barbershop and the two often took long walks together through the neighborhood. When Clarence returned, the family moved to Puerto Rico on another military assignment, and Robinson spent much of her time sketching the neighborhoods of San Juan. In 1971 the Robinsons separated, largely because of the frequent moves and Clarence's drinking. They would later divorce.

After briefly living with her son on welfare, Robinson accepted a job as an art instructor with the Columbus Recreation and Parks Department. She continued to develop her art and participated in a study tour of Africa in 1979. The trip crystallized her understanding of the interconnectedness of the African past and the African American present. In accord with her desire to link the eras, Robinson legally added "Aminah" to her given names in 1980 after learning that it was traditionally used for women in the Robinson family and meant "faithful."

By the 1980s, Robinson finally began to gain artistic notice. In 1983, the Cincinnati gallery owner Carl Solway saw Robinson's art at the Contemporary Arts Center in the city. He began to exhibit her work while promoting her to galleries and museums in Chicago, New York, and St. Louis. Meanwhile, Robinson began to gather honors such as the Ohio Governor's Award for the Visual Arts in 1984 and a 1989 fellowship from the Institute for Contemporary Art in New York. A 1990 commission to create a piece for the atrium staircase of the Columbus Metropolitan Library allowed Robinson to leave her job and devote herself full-time to art. Four years later, her son committed suicide after struggling with depression. Robinson paid tribute to him in a button-beaded rag painting, *Sydney's Memorial* (1994–present). Like much of Robinson's work, she refuses to see it as finished and keeps adding to it, in accord with looking forward and backward. Robinson's art can be found in many major museums, including the National Underground Railroad Freedom Center, and she has exhibited in such places as the Wexner Center for the Arts.

FURTHER READING
Genshaft, Carole Miller, et al. *Symphonic Poem: The Art of Aminah Brenda Lynn Robinson* (2002).

CARYN E. NEUMANN

Robinson, Bill (25 May 1878–25 Nov. 1949), tap dancer, known as "Bojangles," was born Luther Robinson in Richmond, Virginia, the son of Maxwell Robinson, a machinist, and Maria (maiden name unknown), a choir director. After both parents died in an accident around 1885, Luther and his brother William lived with their grandmother, Bedilia Robinson, a former slave who sought salvation through faith and disavowed dancing of any kind in her house. Too old and infirm to care for the boys, she entrusted them to a local judge, John Crutchfield.

Robinson appropriated his brother's name, calling himself Bill, and took to the streets to earn nickels and dimes by dancing and scat-singing. In Richmond he got the nickname "Bojangles," from "jangler," meaning contentious, and he invented the famous phrase "everything's copasetic," meaning everything's tip-top or first-rate. Robinson ran away to Washington, D.C., picking up odd jobs dancing in beer gardens around town. He got his first professional break in 1892 as a pickaninny in the chorus line of Whallen and Martel's *South before the War*, a touring show that featured Mayme Remington, a former French burlesque dancer who became a top headliner in the 1890s. Shortly after arriving in New York in 1900, Robinson challenged the *In Old Kentucky* star dancer Harry Swinton to a Friday night buck-and-wing dance contest and won. With a gold medal and the valuable publicity attendant on winning, he was quickly targeted as the man to challenge.

Robinson worked wherever and whenever he could, and with a variety of partners, including Theodore Miller, Lula Brown, and Johnny Juniper. Bound by the "two-colored" rule in vaudeville, which restricted blacks to performing in pairs, he teamed with George W. Cooper from 1902 to 1914. They played the classiest tours in white vaudeville, the Keith and Orpheum circuits, without the blackface makeup expected of African American performers at the time. They also toured London with great success. Robinson married Lena Chase in 1907, although touring and professional activities kept them apart and forced them to separate around 1915 and divorce in 1922.

Robinson was a staunch professional, adamant about punctuality and a perfectionist with his routines. He was also known to anger quickly, gamble, and carry a gold-plated revolver. After an assault charge in 1908 that split up his act with Cooper, Robinson decided to launch his solo career and became one of the few blacks to perform as a soloist on the Keith circuit. He was a headliner at New York's Palace Theatre, the undisputed crown jewel of vaudeville theaters. At one point in his career, he made $6,500 a week in vaudeville and was billed as the "World's Greatest Tap Dancer." Being billed as a champion dancer meant winning dance competitions of the toughest kind to stay on top. Contests were audited by a panel of judges who sat under the stage, in the wings, and in the house, judging the dancer on the tempo and execution of steps. Robinson was challenged to dozens of contests and won, and according to tap dance lore competed against dancers such as James Barton, Will Mahoney, Jack Donahue, Fred Astaire, and Ray Bolger. Robinson's stair dance, first performed in 1918, was distinguished by its showmanship and sound, each step emitting a different pitch and rhythm. Onstage his open face, twinkling eyes, and infectious smile were irresistible, as was his tapping, which was delicate and clear. Buck or time steps were inserted with skating steps or crossover steps on the balls of the feet that looked like a jig, all while he chatted and joked with the audience. Robinson danced in split clog shoes, ordinary shoes with a wooden half-sole and raised wooden heel. The wooden sole was attached from the toe to the ball of the foot and left loose, which allowed for greater flexibility and tonality.

In 1922 Robinson married Fannie Clay, who became his business manager, secretary, and partner in efforts to fight the barriers of racial prejudice. He was a founding member of the Negro Actors Guild of America. Hailed as the "Dark Cloud of Joy" on the Orpheum circuit, Robinson performed in vaudeville from 1914 to 1927 without a single season's layoff. Yet Broadway fame did not come until he was fifty years old, with the all-black revue *Blackbirds of 1928*, in which he sang and danced "Doin' the New Low Down." Success was instantaneous, and he was saluted as the greatest of all dancers by at least seven New York newspapers. Broadway shows that followed included *Brown Buddies* (1930), *Blackbirds of 1933*, *All in Fun* (1940), and *Memphis Bound* (1945). The opening of *The Hot Mikado* (1939) marked Robinson's sixty-first birthday, and he celebrated by dancing down Broadway, from Sixty-first Street to the Broadhurst Theatre at Forty-fourth Street.

In the 1930s Robinson also performed in Hollywood films, a venue that had hitherto restricted African American performers. His first film, *Dixiana* (1930), had a predominantly white cast, but *Harlem Is Heaven* (1933) was one of the first all-black films ever made. Other films included *Hooray for Love* (1935), *In Old Kentucky* (1935), *The Big Broadcast of 1937* (1935), *One Mile from Heaven* (1937), *By an Old Southern River* (1941), and *Let's Shuffle* (1941). The well-known all-black film *Stormy Weather* (1943) featured Robinson, LENA HORNE, CAB CALLOWAY, and KATHERINE DUNHAM and her dance troupe. Robinson and Shirley Temple teamed up in *The Little Colonel* (1935), *The Littlest Rebel* (1935), *Just around the Corner* (1938), and *Rebecca of Sunnybrook Farm* (1938), in which he taught the child superstar to tap dance.

In 1936 Robinson opened the downtown Cotton Club in New York (south of the more famous uptown Harlem Cotton Club) and introduced a new dance, the Suzi-Q; he was later featured in several Cotton Club shows. Claiming to have taught tap dancing to Eleanor Powell, FLORENCE MILLS, FAYARD and HAROLD NICHOLAS, and Astaire, Robinson profoundly influenced the next generation of dancers at the Hoofers Club in Harlem, where he also gambled and shot pool. Throughout his lifetime, he was a member of many clubs and civic organizations and an honorary member of police departments in cities across the United States. Robinson was named "Mayor of Harlem" in 1933. His participation in benefits is legendary, and it is estimated that he gave away well over $1 million in loans and charities. During his long career he never refused to play a benefit, regardless of race, creed, or color of those who were to profit by his performance. In 1943 he divorced Fannie Clay and married the young dancer Elaine Plaines.

"To his own people," Marshall Stearns wrote in *Jazz Dance*, "Robinson became a modern JOHN HENRY, who instead of driving steel, laid down iron taps." Although he was uneducated, Robinson was accepted in high places that were previously beyond the reach of most African Americans. He commanded the respect due to a gifted artist and became the most famous tap dancer of the twentieth century. Robinson's exacting yet light footwork was said to have brought tap "up on its toes" from an earlier flat-footed shuffling style. Although he invented few new steps, he presented those he used with technical ease and a sparkling personality, turning relatively simple tap dancing into an exciting art.

When Robinson died in New York City, newspapers claimed that almost one hundred thousand people witnessed the passing of the funeral procession, a testament to the esteem in which he was held by members of his community. The founding of the Copasetics, a fraternity of male tap dancers formed the year Robinson died, ensured that his excellence would not be forgotten.

FURTHER READING

Fletcher, Tom. *One Hundred Years of the Negro in Show Business* (1954).

Frank, Rusty. *Tap!: The Greatest Tap Dance Stars and Their Stories, 1900–1955* (1990).

Haskins, Jim, and N. R. Mitgang. *Mr. Bojangles: The Biography of Bill Robinson* (1999).

Stearns, Marshall, and Jean Stearns. *Jazz Dance: The Story of American Vernacular Dance* (1968).

This entry is taken from the *American National Biography* and is published here with the permission of the American Council of Learned Societies.

CONSTANCE VALIS HILL

Robinson, David (6 Aug. 1965–   ), basketball player, was born David Maurice Robinson in Key West, Florida, the second child of Ambrose and Freda Robinson. His father was a naval officer and his mother was a nurse. Robinson's father was required to travel frequently. The family moved to Virginia Beach, Virginia, when he was young, and when his father retired from the navy they finally settled in Woodbridge, Virginia. Robinson was an excellent student and from the age of six attended schools for gifted children. In junior high school he continued his exceptional scholarship and standing 5 feet 9 inches tall demonstrated extraordinary athleticism in many sports, with the exception of basketball. It was not until his senior year at Osbourn Park High School in Manassas, Virginia, that the then 6-foot-7-inch-tall Robinson joined the basketball team. He earned area and district honors in his first season. Robinson achieved high scores on the SAT and upon graduating from high school enrolled at the United States Naval Academy in Annapolis, Maryland. He was 6 feet 9 inches tall when he began his basketball career with the Navy Midshipmen, wearing number 50 on his jersey in honor of his idol, Ralph Sampson of the University of Virginia Cavaliers. During his tenure with the Midshipmen he grew to 7 feet 1 inch tall, and in his final two seasons gained the USBWA College Player of the Year, All-American title and claimed the prestigious Naismith College Player of the Year (1987) and John R. Wooden (1987) awards. He is often referred to as the best basketball player in the history of the Naval Academy. In 1987 Robinson graduated with a bachelor's degree in Mathematics and was subsequently eligible for the 1987 NBA draft. He was the first overall NBA draft pick, selected by the San Antonio Spurs; however, he had two years mandatory years of service to the United States Navy to perform. Upon fulfilling his obligation to the navy, where he earned the nickname "Admiral," in 1989 Robinson joined the San Antonio Spurs in Texas for his first professional basketball season.

During his first season with the Spurs, 1989–1990, Robinson propelled the team to what was then the largest comeback in NBA history for an unprecedented thirty-five-game advancement. Consequently, he was awarded NBA Rookie of the Year, and the video game company SEGA produced *David Robinson's Supreme Court*. In 1992 Robinson was a member of the 1992 United States Olympic Dream Team alongside the talented MICHAEL JORDAN, MAGIC JOHNSON, Charles Barkley, and others, winning the gold medal in Barcelona. He joined an elite cadre of players to score above seventy points in a season, 1993–1994, including WILT CHAMBERLAIN, and Kobe Bryant. Robinson won the NBA MVP award in 1995 and was designated among the 50 Greatest Players in NBA History in 1996. In 1997 he suffered a back injury and a broken foot, which took him off the court and led to a 20–62 losing season for the Spurs. The following year the Spurs won the first draft pick and selected Tim Duncan of Wake Forest University. Robinson and Duncan complimented each other on the court and became known as "The Twin Towers." In the 1999 playoff games against the New York Knicks, they led the Spurs to their first NBA Championship. Robinson announced he would retire after the 2002–2003 season; on 15 June 2003, the Spurs won another NBA Championship, against the New Jersey Nets.

In 1991 Robinson pledged $2,000 to each fifth grader at Gates Elementary School in San Antonio who graduated and enrolled in college. In 1998 he awarded $8,000 to each student who had accomplished this goal. Robinson and his wife Valerie have given over $11 million to Carver Academy in San Antonio, a school they founded in 2001. Significant charitable contributions are recognized by the NBA with an award renamed for Robinson in March 2003, the *David Robinson Plaque*, given to recipients of the NBA Community Assist Award. Robinson formed "Admiral Capital Group" in 2008 to invest in ventures that provide social and financial benefits; the Admiral Center is a nonprofit organization to support the charitable initiatives of athletes and entertainers.

Robinson and his wife have three sons, David Maurice, Corey Matthew, and Justin Michael. On 11 September 2009 Robinson was inducted into the Basketball Hall of Fame along with the basketball legends Michael Jordan, C. Vivian Stringer, Jerry Sloan, and John Stockton.

FURTHER READING

Kingsbury, Alex. "David Robinson: Former NBA Player Turns to Education." *U.S. News and World Report*, 22 October 2009.

Wilbon, Michael. "A Hall of Fame Class Like No Other." *Washington Post*, 11 September 2009.

Thompson, Keith. *Heroes of the Hardcourt: Ranking Pro Basketball's 100 Greatest Players* (2005).

SAFIYA DALILAH HOSKINS

Robinson, Eddie (13 Feb. 1919–3 Apr. 2007), college football coach, was born Edward Gay Robinson in Jackson, Louisiana, the son of Frank Robinson, then a sharecropper, and Lydia Stewart, a domestic worker. His parents separated when he was six years old, and he lived in a two-room house with his grandparents. Both parents and grandparents were hard-working, industrious people and strict disciplinarians. Looking to break the cycle of sharecropping, Frank Robinson moved in 1925 to Baton Rouge, Louisiana, to work for Standard Oil and later separated from Lydia Stewart and married Ann Floyd, a schoolteacher. Young Eddie marveled at the respect and special status that Floyd enjoyed in the community, reflecting the high esteem that African Americans conferred on education and teachers. While Robinson was attending Scott Street Elementary School in Baton Rouge, one of his teachers invited football players dressed in full uniform to class for a project. Robinson was quite taken with the coach, Julius Kraft, and was greatly impressed by the respect his players gave him. Although he was only ten years old, he knew then that he wanted to be a football coach. Football became an obsession for him. Robinson was the first in his family to finish elementary school, and he later graduated from McKinley High School. Although he initially wanted to attend Southern University in Baton Rouge, he was not offered a scholarship, so he chose to attend Leland College in nearby Baker, Louisiana.

Robinson was raised in a segregated community with little contact with whites. He worked at several jobs to make ends meet, including one at an icehouse, where he loaded fifty-pound blocks. He also worked at a fish market after school and during the summers, making only four dollars per week. Upon graduation from Leland College, he married Doris Mott, his childhood sweetheart, in June 1941. They had two children, Lillian Rose and Eddie Jr. That same year Robinson was hired to coach football at the Louisiana Negro Normal and Industrial Institute, a two-year college with fewer than one hundred male students. The school, later renamed Grambling State University, offered Robinson a starting salary of $63.75 a month.

Robinson coached at Grambling State University for fifty-six years (1941–1997). His tenure lasted through eleven presidents and four major American wars, and he retired as the winningest coach in the history of college football, with a record of 408 wins, 165 losses, and 15 ties. That mark bettered the winning records of such coaching greats as Amos Alonzo Stagg, Pop Warner, and even Alabama's legendary Paul "Bear" Bryant. During Robinson's tenure, the Grambling Tigers won eight national black college titles and seventeen conference championships. In 1942, his second season, Robinson fielded a team that went undefeated and was not scored against, a feat that has been repeated only once in the history of college football.

Under Robinson's leadership, Grambling also became one of professional football's most productive training grounds. All told, he sent more than two hundred Grambling players to the National Football League, including the Pro Football Hall of Fame inductees Willie Davis, JUNIOUS "BUCK" BUCHANAN, and WILLIE BROWN. The first African American drafted (in 1949) from a historically black college, Tank Younger, was from Grambling, while the Tiger defensive standout Junious "Buck" Buchanan was the first African American to be selected in the first round of the NFL's draft (1963). Another Grambling favorite, James Harris, signed for the Los Angeles Rams, and in 1969 became the first black quarterback to start an NFL play-off game in 1969. Perhaps the most successful of Eddie Robinson's protégés, however, was DOUG WILLIAMS, who starred for Grambling in the late 1970s and in 1988 became the first African American quarterback to start in a Super Bowl. Williams, who led the Washington Redskins to victory, was selected the Most Valuable Player of Super Bowl XXII.

Although desegregation sapped much of the talent from historically black colleges like Grambling,

Eddie Robinson, Grambling University football coach, talks with players during the game against Mississippi Valley in Grambling, Louisiana, 8 November 1971. (AP Images.)

of America through sports for more than six decades. Penn State's coach, Joe Paterno, summed up the Grambling legend's legacy: "Nobody has ever done or will do what Eddie Robinson has done for this game. Our profession will never be able to repay Eddie Robinson for what he has done for the country and the profession of football" (Lapchick). Diagnosed with Alzheimer's disease in 2004, Robinson died on 3 April 2007 in Ruston, Louisiana.

FURTHER READING

Davis, O. K. *Grambling's Gridiron Glory* (1985).

Lapchick, Richard E. *Never Before, Never Again: The Autobiography of Eddie Robinson* (1999).

Lee, Aaron. *Quotable Eddie Robinson: 408 Memorable Quotes about Football, Life and Success by and about College Football's All-time Winningest Coach* (2003).

Wash, A., and P. Webb, eds. *Reflections of a Legend: Coach Eddie G. Robinson* (1997).

Obituary: "Eddie Robinson, College Coach, Dies," *New York Times*, 4 Apr. 2007.

FRITZ G. POLITE

Robinson continued to recruit talented student-athletes. Recognizing that historically white schools were now competing for the best and brightest black student-athletes, Robinson formed a strategy to ensure that Grambling remained attractive to African American athletes. He created and promoted a series of national games for Grambling against other Historically Black Colleges and Universities (HBCUs) that drew network coverage and large audiences. The most significant of them, the annual Bayou Classic between Grambling and Southern, attracts an annual attendance of more than sixty-five thousand spectators. Following the assassination of MARTIN LUTHER KING JR. in 1968, Robinson also established the Urban League Classic at New York's Yankee Stadium. The game was later renamed the Whitney Young Classic, after the death of the National Urban League's former executive director WHITNEY YOUNG. The success of the first of these "classics" led to three other national games that embodied Robinson's philosophy of linking sport and the civil rights movement.

Coach Eddie Robinson won more games than any coach in the history of college football. His fifty-six-year tenure at the same institution may never be repeated, and he observed the social transformation

Robinson, Frank (31 Aug. 1935–), baseball player, manager, and executive, was born in Beaumont, Texas, the youngest of ten children. His mother, Ruth Robinson, moved the family briefly to Alameda, California, before settling in West Oakland. It was here that Robinson spent his formative years and learned the game that made him famous.

Robinson has described the West Oakland of his youth as a diverse neighborhood of African Americans, Chicanos, and Asian Americans, "all getting along, few getting ahead." "We were poor," he recalled, "but I didn't know it" (*Extra Innings*, 23). His skill at baseball was obvious early on, and he spent much of his youth playing with older and more experienced boys. Robinson proved a quick study and rapidly advanced through the youth baseball ranks. In 1953 at age seventeen he signed with the Cincinnati Reds of the National League.

"I didn't know anything about racism or bigotry until I went into professional baseball in 1953," Robinson later wrote (*Extra Innings*, 23). Race was simply not a topic of conversation in his household, and poor, multiracial West Oakland was in many ways a sheltered environment. This changed abruptly when he reported for his first professional baseball assignment in Ogden, Utah, joining a low-level farm team for the Reds. While the other players stayed in private homes, Robinson and his only other black teammate shared a hotel room.

Robinson, who loved to spend his free time watching films, found that the only movie theater in town refused to admit African Americans.

Despite the rude awakening to the realities of racial discrimination that he received in his first year of professional baseball, Robinson played well enough to move up the following year to an A-level team for the Reds in Columbia, South Carolina. Robinson and his single black teammate were the first African Americans to play for the Columbia team. Again he was treated to a harsh education in racial discrimination, although this time in the heart of the Jim Crow South. Racial epithets and the daily humiliations of segregation were commonplace for the young ballplayer during his two seasons in Columbia. In 1956 at age twenty he became the regular left fielder for the Reds.

Robinson's rookie season in the majors was remarkable. He followed in a distinguished line of black stars who quickly established themselves at the top of Major League Baseball. In the National League, which was quicker to integrate than the American League, African American ballplayers dominated rookie of the year and most valuable player honors from the late 1940s through the 1950s. Robinson was the youngest starter in the all-star game, hit thirty-eight home runs (tying the rookie record), and won the National League rookie of the year award.

Robinson continued to excel on the field in the following years, combining defensive skills, baserunning speed, and power at the plate. He earned a reputation as a hard-nosed player and a fierce competitor. He slid hard into infielders attempting to turn double plays, and at bat he never feared to crowd the plate to protect the outside corner (he often led the league in getting hit by pitches). In 1961 he was named the most valuable player in the National League.

Early in his career Robinson generally tried to shelter himself from the political upheavals going on around him. He resisted entreaties by JACKIE ROBINSON to involve himself with civil rights issues. Yet inevitably he continued to feel the stings of racism. When he first arrived in Cincinnati the black players stayed in a segregated hotel. As Robinson's salary grew and he and his wife Barbara, whom he married in 1961, looked to move into more affluent neighborhoods, they ran into the barrier of residential segregation. Yet he did not translate these frustrations into social activism.

In 1965, after relations between Robinson and the team's management became strained, the Reds traded their star player to the Baltimore Orioles of the American League. Robinson quickly picked up where he had left off in Cincinnati. In his second season in Baltimore he achieved the rare triple crown, leading the league in batting average, home runs, and runs batted in. This performance won him the American League most valuable player award, making him the only player to win this award in both leagues. In that same season he led the Orioles to a World Series title, the first of two during his time in Baltimore. Robinson began to assume more leadership qualities in the clubhouse, often acting as an intermediary for players and management. In 1968 he got his first taste of managing, in a winter league in Puerto Rico. His managerial debut proved so successful that he was named league manager of the year in his first season.

Toward the end of his playing career Robinson moved frequently from team to team, making stops with the Los Angeles Dodgers (1972), California Angels (1973–1974), and Cleveland Indians (1974–1976). Robinson finished his playing career with statistics matched by few in the history of the game. He hit 582 home runs, had 1,812 runs batted in, compiled a lifetime .294 batting average, finished in the top 10 in most valuable player voting ten times, and played in twelve all-star games. In 1982, his first year of eligibility, he was easily voted into the baseball hall of fame.

Yet these accomplishments are only part of the Robinson legacy. During his final assignment as a player with the Indians he was named the team's manager, becoming the first African American to manage a major league team. If the integration of Major League Baseball in the years following Jackie Robinson's dramatic 1947 breakthrough was a slow process on the field—it was not until 1959 that the Boston Red Sox, the last team to integrate, included a black ballplayer on their roster—it was practically nonexistent within the ranks of coaches and managers. It was not until 1961 that a minor league team hired a black manager, and it was not until Frank Robinson took over the Cleveland Indians in 1975 that a black man ran a major league club.

Following his three-year stint as manager of the Indians, Robinson went on to manage three different teams: the San Francisco Giants (1981–1984), thereby becoming the first black manager in the National League as well as in the American League; the Baltimore Orioles (1988–1991); and the Montreal Expos (2002–2004). He was named the league manager of the year in 1982 and 1989. Robinson also worked in various front-office positions within baseball. Although he never gained the general manager role that he desired, from 1991 to 1995 he served as assistant general manager for the Orioles, and from 2000 to 2002 he was Major League Baseball's vice president for on-field operations.

During his second career as a manager and baseball executive, Robinson became more involved in the civil rights issues that Jackie Robinson had unsuccessfully encouraged him to confront as a young player. In reaction to the comments of the Los Angeles Dodgers general manager Al Campanis in the spring of 1987, who said that there was a shortage of black managers in baseball only because blacks "lack the necessities," Robinson became a leading advocate for baseball to address its failures to bring minorities into baseball's managerial levels. He joined a group of minority former players in creating Baseball Network, an organization designed to offer minorities the necessary connections and encouragement that would lead to coaching and managerial careers. Robinson also wrote his autobiography, which included a stinging indictment of the systematic exclusion of African Americans from coaching, managing, and administrative positions in professional baseball. He condemned the current situation as "absolutely disgraceful," noting that entering the 1987 season none of the major league teams had black managers and only 9 of the 154 professional minor league teams were managed by blacks (*Extra Innings*, 8).

Many students of baseball believe Robinson to be one of the most underappreciated greats of the game. Considering what Robinson accomplished not only as a player but also as pioneering manager, he certainly belongs alongside Jackie Robinson and HANK AARON as one of the most historically significant African American baseball figures of the modern era.

FURTHER READING

Robinson, Frank, with Berry Stainback. *Extra Innings* (1988).

Robinson, Frank, with Dave Anderson. *Frank: The First Year* (1976).

Tygiel, Jules. *Baseball's Great Experiment: Jackie Robinson and His Legacy* (1997).

CHRISTOPHER W. SCHMIDT

Robinson, Hilyard Robert (1899–2 July 1986), architect, was born in Washington, D.C., to parents whose names and professions are unknown. As a child, he spent time with his grandfather, a bootblack who worked near the U.S. capitol building.

Robinson would listen to the congressmen exchange banter while they had their shoes shined. In 1916 Robinson graduated from the M Street High School and began studying at the Pennsylvania Museum and School of Industrial Design in Philadelphia. One year later, as the United States was entering World War I, Robinson left school to enlist in the U.S. Army Field Artillery Corps, 167th Brigade. He served in France and was in Paris for the Armistice in 1918. The city's grand buildings and expert urban planning made such an impression on Robinson that he decided to pursue the study of architecture upon his return to the United States.

In 1919 Robinson returned to Philadelphia and entered the architecture program at the University of Pennsylvania. After two summers spent working in the offices of architect Vertner Woodson Tandy in Harlem, Robinson followed the advice of Tandy and his associate Paul B. LaVelle and transferred to Columbia University. He received his bachelor's degree in Architecture in 1924. Even before completing his undergraduate degree, Robinson began teaching at the School of Architecture at Howard University in Washington, D.C. Through his connections at Howard, Robinson received minor commissions to remodel residential spaces, which led him into some of Washington's poorest black neighborhoods. His experience amid the squalor and unsanitary conditions of the slums trained Robinson's focus on the need to provide better subsidized housing for the poor. Robinson was not the only architect in the 1920s to turn his attention to the need for better public housing. Following World War I architects began actively discussing how architecture could be used as an agent of social change. When he returned to Columbia for his master's degree an Architecture in 1931 he decided to make public housing his focus of study. That same year he married Helena Rooks; they had a daughter who died during childhood.

After completing his master's degree in 1931 Robinson received a postgraduate Kinne Fellowship from Columbia and returned to Europe to study recent developments in architecture. Robinson traveled through France, Germany, the Netherlands, and Russia, studying buildings designed by students of the Bauhaus, which was a German design and architecture school founded by Walter Gropius and popular in Germany from 1919 to 1933. During his travels Robinson observed how his European peers responded to the needs of the poor by designing architecture intended to elevate them and better their conditions. During his travels Robinson observed how his European peers responded to the needs of the poor through in the design of their public housing. By maintaining a very human sense of scale in large housing developments, the architects of the Bauhaus sought to imbue the residents with a sense of community and better their social condition. In particular, Robinson was much taken with the massive public housing projects built in Rotterdam after World War I.

Impressed by his firsthand experience with innovative European answers to housing for the poor, Robinson returned to his teaching post at Howard University in 1932. In 1935 he left again, this time to become the chief architect on a Public Works Administration project. During the Depression, the federal government invested heavily in building programs meant to lift the spirits of the American people. Robinson's new project, the Langston Terrace Dwellings, named for John Mercer Langston, in Washington, D.C., was a segregated public housing project for African Americans. The first federal housing project of its kind in Washington, D.C., Langston Terrace was also one of the first built in U.S. history.

Langston Terrace was a low-lying complex of apartments and townhouses, with no building standing more than four stories high. Acutely aware of current social theories, Robinson knew smaller walk-up buildings forced neighbors to interact with one another while tall elevator buildings provided anonymity that undermined community and safety. Robinson's housing design was a softer version of the modern architecture he had studied in Europe. Built in clean lines with warm-colored bricks, his buildings allowed residents to move easily from indoors to out, and from apartment to garden. From the earliest stages of the design, Robinson integrated visual art into the complex. A frieze appeared along a prominent outside wall, one that celebrated the African Americans for whom the housing was built. A large inner court contained enormous, whimsical statues of frogs and animals that children often played among.

After the success of Langston Terrace, Robinson continued to work for the federal government. Following the United States' entry into World War II, Robinson designed the training school for the Tuskegee Airmen, a segregated unit of African American military pilots. Previous to the United States' entry into World War II, the U.S. military prohibited African Americans from flying its planes. In 1940, however, the military bowed to pressure from civil rights groups and built a new facility at Tennessee's Tuskegee Institute to train a segregated unit of African American pilots and mechanics, who came to be known as the Tuskegee Airmen. Robinson moved to Tennessee in June 1941 to oversee the design and construction of the airfield, which opened in December of that year. Eventually Robinson served on the National Capital Planning Commission from 1950 to 1955. During the years following World War II he also maintained a thriving private practice, designing dormitories and academic buildings for the Howard University campus. Robinson also designed private homes, the best known being the RALPH JOHNSON BUNCHE House, built in Washington, D.C., in 1941. Bunche, a diplomat and eventual Nobel Prize winner, taught at Howard University from 1929 until 1941.

Robinson retired from active practice in the 1960s. He died in 1986 in Washington, D.C. While many other public housing projects were built only to quickly be reviled by those they were meant to shelter, Robinson's design for Langston Terrace succeeded in creating both a home and a community for some of Washington's poorest black residents. In the years following Robinson's death, the National Park Service placed both Langston Terrace and the Ralph Bunche House on the national register of historic sites.

FURTHER READING

Hilyard Robinson's papers are housed in the Moorland-Spingarn Research Center, Howard University.

Bond, Max. "Still Here: Three Architects of Afro-America: Julian Francis Abele, Hilyard Robinson, and Paul R. Williams," *Harvard Design Magazine* (1997).

Leiner, Glen B. "Hilyard Robert Robinson (1899–1986)," in *African American Architects: a Biographical Dictionary 1865–1945* (2004).

ANGELA R. SIDMAN

Robinson, Ida Bell (3 Aug. 1891–20 Apr. 1946), denominational founder and religious leader, was born in Hazelhurst, Georgia, to Robert and Annie Bell. The family later moved to Pensacola, Florida. In Pensacola Bell was "saved" at a street revival and in 1908 she joined the Church of God, a local Pentecostal group. Pentecostalism was a new religious movement claiming the restoration of apostolic gifts such as speaking in tongues and faith healing. Bell received a limited education and worked as a cook on the tugboat Silver Queen that toured around Miami. In 1910 she married Oliver

Robinson, who also worked on the Silver Queen. The Robinsons' marriage did not produce any children and so they adopted a girl, also called Ida. Looking for better opportunities, the Robinsons followed the black migration north to Philadelphia in 1917.

Once settled, Ida Robinson started evangelizing through preaching "read-on" sermons. She would ask a more literate person to read a biblical passage and then she would expound on the scripture. Robinson was one of the hundreds of women that Pentecostalism welcomed to preaching and to the ordained ministry. From the beginning Pentecostals, like their holiness forebears, argued that the Spirit of God could empower both men and women to preach according to their interpretation of Acts 2:16–18 (AV): "And it shall come to pass in the last days, saith God, I will pour out of my Spirit upon all flesh: and your sons and your daughters shall prophesy, and your young men shall see visions, and your old men shall dream dreams." Another Pentecostal claim was that the call to preach should not be measured by one's education. Poor and ambitious women of all races welcomed this opportunity that came before American women were given the right to vote in 1920. It is estimated that three thousand American women were serving as clergy at the beginning of the twentieth century. Nevertheless CARTER GODWIN WOODSON, a contemporary black historian, failed to highlight the presence of women in ministry in the two editions of his *History of the Negro Church* (1921; 2nd ed., 1945). It should be noted, however, that although most Pentecostal organizations welcomed women as evangelists, some denied them the right to pastor. The Church of God in Christ, for example, licensed women as evangelists but did not ordain them; fortunately Robinson gravitated to circles that gave much freedom to women. She worked in a Pentecostal mission pastored by Benjamin Smith. There, however, her success as an evangelist created tensions and difficulties, and Ida left Smith's mission in 1919.

In 1919 Robinson took over a small congregation located at 505 South Eleventh Street in Philadelphia and affiliated it with the United Holy Church (UHC), a denomination that ordained female preachers. Robinson pastored this congregation, Mt. Olive Church, until her death. Robinson quickly became a rising star in the denomination through her itinerant preaching and powerful pulpit delivery. She spoke widely, shared pulpits with male preachers, and was ordained as an elder by Bishop Henry L. Fisher. But in the early 1920s women's progress began to be impeded in the UHC when some started to question the biblical foundation for female ordination; soon women were being ordained in private ceremonies. Until then no woman had been ordained as bishop, the highest ministerial rank. It is reasonable to believe that Robinson's vigorous preaching and the large following she drew were partially responsible for this change in attitude. In fact, many women decided to enter the ministry because of her. Sometime during this period Robinson started a ten-day fast, and while in this pious environment she claimed that God told her to "come out on Mount Sinai and loose the women." This divine word was understood as an injunction to found not a denomination but a religious movement where women could exercise leadership. She invited local UHC congregations to join her movement, which she named "The Mt. Sinai Holy Church." Her idea was that UHC churches could share dual affiliation with Mt. Sinai. Seventeen congregations, including some from the UHC, were represented at Mt. Sinai's organizational meeting. Ultimately Robinson formed an independent entity, with herself as presiding bishop, that was incorporated in the state of Pennsylvania in 1924 as Mt. Sinai Holy Church of America Inc. Mt. Sinai was one of the few Pentecostal or black denominations that allowed female bishops.

In later historiography two conflicting accounts surfaced about why she founded a new denomination. One view argues that it was because of the restrictions imposed on women. Another maintains that she only obeyed the voice of God. Robinson left the UHC on good terms and was allowed to retain Mt. Olive's building. UHC officials who admired her preaching power continued to invite her to speak at their convocations.

As leader of a new denomination, Robinson was concerned with church growth. In 1925 she bought an Assembly of God building. This facility hosted the first annual convocation of Mt. Sinai Holy Church of America. Twenty years later Mt. Olive moved to another building that seated two thousand. In her quest to establish new congregations, Robinson traveled widely, often with her supportive husband. To facilitate church planting, she would loan money to new missions that paid her back in increments. For example, the Mt. Sinai congregation in Fruitland, Maryland, borrowed $700 that it returned in amounts ranging from $10 to $179. Once loaned funds were returned they were loaned again to new church plants. Many churches were supported through this scheme. In addition to giving money, she founded many new churches herself. According to Felton O. Best, "Between 1924 and 1932 Bishop Robinson assisted in establishing every church in the organization by conducting revivals" (159).

Robinson also stressed the importance of holiness, as the name of her denomination reflected. Holiness meant that believers should live in accordance with the definite experience of sanctification and avoid activities such as dancing, smoking, drinking, and attending movies. Women were taught to dress modestly and avoid exposure of the body. They often wore long black dresses with heads covered. They could neither wear jewelry nor braid their hair. Robinson later ruled that men should not wear ties. A distinctive belief of Mt. Sinai was that holy living and acceptance of the equality of women were signs of the presence of the Holy Spirit. Robinson's theology of equality was based on her reading of Genesis 1:27 (AV), "So God created man in his own image, in the image of God created he him; male and female created he them." She argued that this passage asserts that the essence of women is the same matter out of which God made Adam, thus all the promises (dominion over the earth, etc.) made to Adam also apply to Eve. To further promote holiness among the young people, Robinson opened Mt. Sinai Holy School, which provided elementary and secondary education. Mt. Sinai also sponsored a 140-acre farm cooperative in New Jersey that employed people and raised income for the denomination. This was another indication of the self-help philosophy that was widespread among African Americans.

It should also be noted that Mt. Sinai ordained men as well as women. Put another way, African American men were willing to be ordained or pastored by women. This male submission to, or cooperation with, women could be explained by the impact of African culture and antebellum social conditions. Many African cults allowed women to function in the role of priests, and Africans brought to the New World were aware of this. Furthermore, some African groups even allowed for the existence of a queen mother who co-ruled with the king. Studies such as Cheryl Townsend Gilkes's *If It Wasn't for the Women: Black Women's Experience and Womanist Culture in Church and Community* (2001) have revealed that the prominent role of the Church Mother, a respected figure in the Black Church, derived from the African origins of the slaves. At the same time, it is important to note that Mt. Sinai was an interracial congregation.

Robinson endorsed the interracial impulse of early Pentecostalism that encouraged people from all races to worship God together. Like Bishop Charles H. Mason of the Church of God in Christ, she ordained white ministers.

Mt. Sinai, like many Pentecostal churches, adopted a pacifist position during World War II; members were encouraged to work in noncombatant positions as conscientious objectors. This won Robinson the attention of the Federal Bureau of Investigation (FBI). FBI files on Robinson indicate that she was put "on a list of agitators in Philadelphia for statements she made" (DuPree and DuPree, 37). She stated publicly that she had "nothing against the Japanese" (Goff and Wacker, 317). FBI files also alleged that in various [Mt. Sinai] meetings blacks "expressed pleasure at Japanese victories over whites in Asia and [the] Pacific, considering it good that whites have suffered humiliation" (DuPree and DuPree, 37–38). FBI suspicion was further fueled by the fact that Robinson's secretary was a German woman married to an Italian.

Robinson died in Winter Haven, Florida, before this political persecution could affect her greatly. She had given so much attention to promoting female ministry that by her death in 1946 women accounted for 125 of the 163 elders she ordained during her lifetime. Her successor was another woman, Elmira Jeffries, whom Robinson had previously ordained as a bishop. By 2007 Mt. Sinai had grown to about one hundred churches located in thirteen states and the District of Columbia. The denomination was particularly strong in Virginia, Pennsylvania, and New Jersey, with a missions program reaching Guyana, Cuba, Japan, and India.

FURTHER READING

Best, Felton O. *Black Religious Leadership from the Slave Community to the Million Man March: Flames of Fire* (1998).

Collier-Thomas, Bettye. *Daughters of Thunder: Black Women Preachers and Their Sermons, 1850–1979* (1998).

DuPree, Sherry Sherrod, and Herbert C. DuPree, comps. *Exposed!!! Federal Bureau of Investigation (FBI) Unclassified Reports on Churches and Church Leaders* (1993).

Goff, James R., Jr., and Grant Wacker. *Portraits of A Generation: Early Pentecostal Leaders* (1994).

Owens, Rosalie. "Bishop Ida Bell Robinson," *Yes Lord Now!* (Jan.–Feb. 2002).

DAVID MICHEL

Robinson, Jackie (31 Jan. 1919–24 Oct. 1972), baseball player, was born Jack Roosevelt Robinson in Cairo, Georgia, the son of Jerry Robinson, a farmworker and sharecropper, and Mallie McGriff, a domestic worker. Six months after Robinson's birth, his father deserted the family. Faced with severe financial difficulties, Robinson's mother moved her family to Pasadena, California, in pursuit of a better life. The Robinsons settled in a white Pasadena neighborhood—where they received a chilly reception—and Robinson's mother supported her family in modest fashion as a domestic worker.

Robinson demonstrated his athletic prowess from an early age. After graduating from high school in Pasadena in 1937 as one of the city's most celebrated athletes, he entered Pasadena Junior College. He established himself as an exceptional multi-sport athlete at Pasadena and won junior college All-American honors in football. By the time of his graduation from Pasadena in 1939, he was one of the most widely recruited athletes on the West Coast. Robinson eventually decided to enter the University of California, Los Angeles (UCLA), which he attended from 1939 to 1941. Playing four sports at UCLA, Robinson continued to display extraordinary athletic ability, causing one sportswriter to label him "the Jim Thorpe of his race" (Tygiel, 60). He twice led the Southern Division of the Pacific Coast Conference in basketball scoring, averaged eleven yards per carry as an All-American running back during his junior year on the football team, and won the National Collegiate Athletic Association (NCAA) broad-jump championship in track and field. Ironically, Robinson's weakest performance came in baseball; he played only one season at UCLA and had minimal success, batting only .097. Robinson was not the only athlete in his family; his older brother Mack finished second to JESSE OWENS in the 200-meter sprint at the 1936 Berlin Olympics. Robinson dropped out of college during his senior year at UCLA to help support his family. After brief stints as an assistant athletic director at a National Youth Administration camp in California and as a player with two semiprofessional football teams—the Los Angeles Bulldogs and the Honolulu Bears—Robinson was drafted into the U.S. Army in the spring of 1942.

The U.S. Army of the 1940s was a thoroughly segregated institution. Although initially denied entry into the army's Officers Candidate School because of his race, Robinson, with the assistance of the boxer JOE LOUIS, successfully challenged his exclusion and was eventually commissioned a second

lieutenant. Robinson spent two years in the service at army bases in Kansas, Texas, and Kentucky. During this time Robinson confronted the army's discriminatory racial practices; on one occasion he faced court-martial charges for insubordination arising from an incident in which he refused to move to the back of a segregated military bus in Texas. A military jury acquitted Robinson, and shortly thereafter, in November 1944, he received his honorable discharge from the army.

Following his discharge, Robinson—who continued to enjoy a reputation as an extraordinarily gifted athlete—spent the spring and summer of 1945 playing shortstop with the Kansas City Monarchs in the Negro Leagues. Robinson proved to be a highly effective player, batting about .345 for the year. At this time Major League Baseball did not permit black players to play on either minor-league or major-league teams, pursuant to an unwritten agreement among the owners that dated back to the nineteenth century. Pressure to integrate baseball, however, had steadily increased. Many critics complained of the hypocrisy of requiring black men to fight and die in a war against European racism but denying them the opportunity to play "the national pastime." During the early 1940s a few major-league teams offered tryouts to black players—Robinson had received a tryout with the Boston Red Sox in 1945—but no team actually signed a black player.

In the meantime, however, Branch Rickey, president of the Brooklyn Dodgers baseball team, had secretly decided to use African Americans on his team. Rickey was convinced of the ability of black ballplayers, their potential gate attraction, and the injustice of their exclusion from Major League Baseball. Using the ruse that he wanted to develop a new league for black players, Rickey deployed his scouts to scour the Negro Leagues and the Caribbean for the most talented black ballplayers during the spring and summer of 1945. In particular Rickey sought one player who would break the color line and establish a path for several others to follow; he eventually settled on Robinson. Although Robinson was not the best black baseball player, his college education, experience competing in interracial settings at UCLA, and competitive fire attracted Rickey. In August 1945 Rickey offered Robinson a chance to play in the Dodgers organization but cautioned him that he would experience tremendous pressure and abuse. Rickey extracted from Robinson a promise not to respond to the abuse for his first three years.

Robinson spent the 1946 baseball season with the top Dodgers minor-league club located in

Jackie Robinson at bat for the Brooklyn Dodgers, 1954. (Library of Congress.)

Montreal. After leading the Montreal Royals to the International League championship and winning the league batting championship with a .349 average, he joined the Dodgers the following spring. Several of the Dodgers' players objected to Robinson's presence and circulated a petition in which they threatened not to play with him. Rickey thwarted the boycott efforts by making clear that such players would be traded or released if they refused to play.

Robinson opened the 1947 season as the Dodgers' starting first baseman, thereby breaking the long-standing ban on black players in the major leagues. During his first year he was subjected to extraordinary verbal and physical abuse from opposing teams and spectators. Pitchers threw the ball at his head, opposing base runners cut him with their spikes, and disgruntled fans sent death threats that triggered an FBI investigation on at least one occasion. Although Robinson possessed a fiery temper and enormous pride, he honored his agreement with Rickey not to retaliate to the constant stream of abuse. At the same time he suffered the indignities of substandard segregated accommodations while traveling with the Dodgers.

Robinson's aggressive style of play won games for the Dodgers, earning him the loyalty of his teammates and the Brooklyn fans. Despite the enormous pressure that year, he led the Dodgers to their first National League championship in six years and a berth in the World Series. Robinson, who led the league in stolen bases and batted .297, was named Rookie of the Year. Overnight, he captured the hearts of black America. In time he became one of the biggest gate attractions in baseball since Babe Ruth, bringing thousands of African American spectators to major-league games. Five major-league teams set new attendance records in 1947. By the end of the season, two other major-league teams—the Cleveland Indians and the St. Louis Browns—had added black players to their rosters for brief appearances. By the early 1950s most other major-league teams had hired black ballplayers.

In the spring of 1949, having fulfilled his three-year pledge of silence, Robinson began to speak his mind and angrily confronted opposing players who taunted him. He also enjoyed his finest year, leading the Dodgers to another National League pennant and capturing the league batting championship, with a .342 mark, and the Most Valuable Player award. Off the field, Robinson received considerable attention for his testimony in July 1949 before the House Committee on Un-American Activities in opposition to PAUL ROBESON's statement that African Americans would not fight in a war against the Soviet Union. During the next few years Robinson, unlike many other black ballplayers, became outspoken in his criticism of segregation both inside and outside of baseball.

Robinson ultimately played ten years for the Dodgers, primarily as a second baseman. During this time his team won six National League pennants and the 1955 World Series. Robinson possessed an array of skills, but he was known particularly as an aggressive and daring base runner, stealing home nineteen times in his career and five times in one season. In one of the more memorable moments in World Series history, Robinson stole home against the New York Yankees in the first game of the 1955 series. Robinson's baserunning exploits helped to revolutionize the game and to pave the way for a new generation of successful base stealers, particularly MAURY WILLS and LOU BROCK. Robinson batted .311 for his career and in 1962 became the first black player to win election to the National Baseball Hall of Fame. On 15 April 1997, the fiftieth anniversary of Robinson's first major-league game, Major League Baseball, in an unprecedented action, retired Robinson's number 42 in perpetuity.

After the 1956 season, the Dodgers traded Robinson to the New York Giants, their crosstown rivals. Robinson declined to accept the trade and instead announced his retirement from baseball. Thereafter, Robinson worked for seven years as a vice president of the Chock Full O'Nuts food company, handling personnel matters. An important advocate of black-owned businesses in America, Robinson helped establish several of them, including the Freedom National Bank in Harlem. He also used his celebrity status as a spokesman for civil rights issues for the remainder of his life. Robinson served as an active and highly successful fund-raiser for the National Association for the Advancement of Colored People and conducted frequent fundraising events of his own to support civil rights causes and organizations. He wrote a regular newspaper column throughout the 1960s in which he criticized the persistence of racial injustice in American society, including the refusal of baseball owners to employ blacks in management. Shortly before his death, Robinson wrote in his autobiography *I Never Had It Made* that he remained "a black man in a white world." Although a supporter of Richard Nixon in the 1960 presidential campaign, Robinson eventually became involved with the liberal wing of the Republican Party, primarily as a close adviser of the New York governor Nelson Rockefeller.

Robinson had married Rachel Isum in 1946, and the couple had three children. Robinson suffered from diabetes and heart disease in his later years and died of a heart attack in Stamford, Connecticut.

Probably no other athlete has had a greater sociological impact on American sport than did Robinson. His success on the baseball field opened the door to black baseball players and thereby transformed the game. He also helped to facilitate the acceptance of black athletes in other professional sports, particularly basketball and football. His influence spread beyond the realm of sport, as he emerged in the late 1940s and 1950s as an important national symbol of the virtue of racial integration in all aspects of American life.

FURTHER READING

The National Baseball Library and Archive in Cooperstown, New York, contains extensive material on Robinson. The Arthur Mann and Branch Rickey papers, both located in the Library of Congress, also contain documentary material on Robinson.

Robinson, Jackie. *Baseball Has Done It* (1964).

Robinson, Jackie, with Alfred Duckett. *I Never Had It Made* (1972).

Robinson, Jackie, with Carl Rowan. *Wait Till Next Year* (1960).

Robinson, Jackie, with Wendell Smith. *Jackie Robinson: My Own Story* (1948).

Falkner, David. *Great Time Coming: The Life of Jackie Robinson, from Baseball to Birmingham* (1995).

Frommer, Harvey. *Rickey and Robinson: The Men Who Broke Baseball's Color Barrier* (1982).

Robinson, Rachel. *Jackie Robinson: An Intimate Portrait* (1996).

Tygiel, Jules. *Baseball's Great Experiment: Jackie Robinson and His Legacy* (1983).

Obituary: *New York Times*, 25 Oct. 1972.

This entry is taken from the *American National Biography* and is published here with the permission of the American Council of Learned Societies.

DAVISON M. DOUGLAS

Robinson, James Herman (24 Jan. 1907–6 Nov. 1972), minister and founder of Operation Crossroads Africa, was born in Knoxville, Tennessee, one of six children of Henry John Robinson, a slaughterhouse laborer, and Willie Bell Banks, a washerwoman. Robinson grew up in abject poverty in a section of town called the Bottoms, where poor blacks and whites lived. Because of his father's frequent periods of unemployment and his mother's failing health, the Robinson family could not escape the reality of poverty and segregation in the Jim Crow South. Those already at the bottom of the economic pile were also denied access to the educational opportunities that might otherwise have helped them to escape poverty. Given the dire circumstances in which the family lived, Robinson had a difficult time accepting the strong religious convictions of his father, who was a member of a sanctified church and spent much of his free time there. As his family's economic conditions remained unchanged, Robinson began to view religion as a waste of time, and questioned his father's and his own faith in God.

In 1917 the Robinson family moved to Cleveland, Ohio, to escape poverty and segregation, but the greater opportunities they had anticipated remained elusive. Robinson attended an integrated school for the first time and found the experience unsettling because of the discrimination he faced from white teachers and students. His father did find work, in another slaughterhouse, but the family continued to live in poverty and in overcrowded housing. Because of these economic hardships, Robinson was not encouraged to remain in school. After his mother died, he moved to Youngstown,

Ohio, to live with his grandparents, but was forced to return to Cleveland after the death of his grandmother. Henry Robinson, who had since remarried, had little interest in furthering his son's desire to get an education. Robinson, nevertheless, found various jobs to support himself and, without his father's knowledge, attended Fairmont Junior High School and East Technical High School.

Even as a child, Robinson understood that racism was nefarious and contradictory to Christian teaching. His thoughts and feelings on this issue intensified after he moved north to the "Promised Land," because, although there were no "white" and "colored" signs to dictate where and how one lived, invisible racial boundaries continued to restrict his mobility and opportunities. Robinson's early life had been marked by many negative experiences, but there were also positive ones, most notably at the Cedar Branch Hi-Y Club, a high school chapter of the YMCA. Before coming to Hi-Y, Robinson was discouraged and distraught, but his experiences at the club expanded his worldview through interaction with middle- and upper-middle-class African Americans. He joined the debate club and through its outings he learned more of himself, the state of race relations, and the role and importance of religion. Ernest Escoe, the debate club's adviser, and Escoe's wife, Sally, supported Robinson and encouraged him to attend St. James African Methodist Church. It was there that he found his calling in life: "to be a servant of the people" (*Road without Turning*, 132). Robinson graduated from East Technical High School in 1929 at the age of twenty-two, but money problems continued to hinder him. He would have been homeless if it were not for Percy and Daisy Kelley. Percy, a waiter in a coffee shop, befriended Robinson, and the Kelleys allowed him to share their home.

Robinson continued his education at Western Reserve University in Cleveland, but dropped out because of financial problems. He then approached the minister of Mount Zion Congregational Church with a plan for a sports program to keep young men out of trouble; after Robinson had established several more clubs, a Presbyterian minister noticed his hard work and informed him that the church would fund his education. He enrolled at Lincoln University in Pennsylvania, but because the church did not provide enough funding to support him completely, Robinson spent his summers serving as pastor of a church in Beardon, Tennessee, near Knoxville. He described the social and economic conditions in Beardon as worse than the Bottoms, and used the pulpit to speak out against racial injustice and for civil rights. Robinson's experiences at Beardon, along with those at Lincoln, further expanded his understanding of race relations and the plight of the less fortunate. Because he was older than most of his classmates, Robinson found the practice of freshmen and fraternity hazing immature and self-defeating. Even more perplexing to him was the fact that, although Lincoln was a historically black college, most of the faculty and administration were white. Robinson spoke out against this glaring inequality throughout his time at Lincoln, where he graduated in 1935 at the top of his class.

After graduating from Lincoln, Robinson attended New York City's Union Theological Seminary (1935–1938), where he was president of his senior class, and director of the Morningside Community Center (1938–1961). In spite of those successes, his time at Union Seminary was troubled. He tried to uphold Christian values while enduring discrimination from his white classmates. But he also found it difficult to befriend other African American students, as he found them aloof and indifferent to the racism and discrimination they faced. Robinson's seminary experiences encouraged him to propose greater multiracial cooperation within the ministry.

The year 1938 proved to be a turning point in Robinson's life: he graduated from Union, was ordained as a minister, became head of the Church of the Master Presbyterian Church in Harlem, and married Helen Brodie. They had no children. He also worked as a youth director for the NAACP from 1938 to 1940.

For the rest of his career and life, Robinson saw his mission as being a servant of the people. He believed that his ministry and church could improve communities by providing people with the economic and social resources that they need to empower themselves. Believing that interracial cooperation was central to this goal, he recruited mainly white students from colleges in New York City to work on projects near his church in Harlem. These projects were very successful, and in 1948 land was donated in New Hampshire to establish Camp Rabbit Hollow, a rural setting in which black children from Harlem and white college students could interact and work together, fostering mutual understanding, cooperation, and respect.

The success of these interracial programs, and his experiences touring Africa, Asia, and Europe in the 1950s, encouraged Robinson to found Operation Crossroads Africa in 1958. Believing that "men will lose consciousness of their differences and divisions when they interest themselves in the common problems of one another" (*Jet* obituary, 48), Robinson encouraged American students and other volunteers to work on community development projects in Africa. In its first twenty years, more than five thousand American volunteers of all races traveled to Africa and the Caribbean to help build and repair housing, roads, health clinics, and schools. Civil rights activists figure prominently among Operation Crossroads alumni, including ELEANOR HOLMES NORTON, later chair of the Equal Employment Opportunity Commission and a U.S. congresswoman, who helped build a school in Gabon in the early 1960s. That experience, Norton recalled in 1977, "made me think about myself as a black person and as an American more profoundly than at any point since" (Rule, 58).

Robinson continued to focus on African affairs throughout the 1960s. His development efforts gained worldwide admiration and spurred other transnational volunteer programs, including Canadian Crossroads International and the U.S. Peace Corps, which John F. Kennedy founded in 1961. President Kennedy recognized his debt to Robinson by calling Operation Crossroads Africa "the progenitor of the Peace Corps" (Rule, 58). During the 1950s Robinson published four books: *Tomorrow Is Today* (1954), *Adventurous Preaching, Love of This Land*, and *Christianity and Revolution in Africa* (all 1956). Following his divorce from Helen Brodie in 1954, he married Gertrude Cotter in 1958. The couple had no children. In 1962 he resigned from Church of the Master to be a minister-at-large and to direct Operation Crossroads Africa on a full-time basis. That same year, he published *Africa at the Crossroads*.

James Robinson died in New York City in 1972, having dedicated his life to fostering a better understanding among people throughout the world. His greatest achievement lay in forging links between Africans and African Americans and between Africa and the United States. "The darkest thing about Africa," Robinson once remarked, "is America's ignorance of it" (Rule, 58). Since 1958 Operation Crossroads Africa has worked diligently to remove that veil of ignorance.

FURTHER READING

James Robinson's papers are housed in the Amistad Research Center at Tulane University in New Orleans.

Robinson, James Herman. *Road without Turning: The Story of Reverend James H. Robinson* (1950).

Robinson, James Herman. *Tomorrow Is Today* (1954).

Lee, Amy. *Throbbing Drums: The Story of James H. Robinson* (1968).

Plimpton, Ruth. *Operation Crossroads Africa* (1962)

Rule, Sheila. "A Peace Corps Precursor Observes 20th Anniversary of Its Founding," *New York Times*, 4 Dec. 1977, 58.

Obituary: *Jet* (30 Nov. 1972).

CASSANDRA VENEY

Robinson, Jim (25 Dec. 1892–4 May 1976), jazz trombonist, was born Nathan Robinson in Deer Range, Louisiana, the son of a church deacon. The names of his parents are unknown. Robinson gave one biographer his year of birth as 1890, but often in interviews he moved events forward a few years. In Deer Range he played blues guitar, and three of his brothers were musicians. He moved to New Orleans in 1914 to work as a longshoreman for the Southern Pacific Steamship Company. There he acquired the nickname "Jim Crow," a reference to his Indian features, not to southern racism. Drafted into the U.S. Army in 1917, he served in France, where a brother of the bassist POPS FOSTER quickly taught him to play trombone, to avoid his having to dig ditches.

On returning to New Orleans in 1919, Robinson worked for many years as a longshoreman for the Southern Pacific Railroad. At first he performed music only occasionally, but after filling in for Kid Rena's trombonist he began performing regularly at night and on weekends. After playing with the banjoist Jesse Jackson's Golden Leaf Orchestra and PAPA CELESTIN's Tuxedo Band, he joined Isiah Morgan's band in 1923. Three years later SAM MORGAN took over the band's leadership. The group made celebrated recordings in 1927, including "Boogalusa Strut." Sam Morgan was unable to march, and on Sundays Robinson played in brass bands under other leaders. Morgan's group toured mostly in the vicinity of New Orleans, but it held an engagement in Chicago for one week in 1929.

Robinson played for seven years at the La Vida dance hall in New Orleans with different bands, including those of Captain John Handy and Kid Howard, and one under his own leadership. Eventually the effects of the Depression and the popularity of the swing style forced him to return to work as a longshoreman, but in 1940 he played trombone at Kid Rena's recording session, a landmark in the revival of New Orleans jazz. As a consequence of this session Robinson began playing regularly with BUNK JOHNSON and Johnson's clarinetist GEORGE LEWIS. By this time his nickname had become

"Big Jim," to distinguish him from "Little Jim," his nephew Sidney Brown, a bassist; together in Lewis's band they recorded "Two Jim Blues" in 1943. Other recordings from this period include "Panama" and "Weary Blues," under Johnson's leadership in 1942; "Climax Rag" and "Just a Closer Walk with Thee," under Lewis in 1943; a jazzed-up and joyous version of "Ice Cream" ("I scream, you scream, we all scream for ice cream"), when Robinson nominally led the trumpeter "Kid Shots" Madison's band (including Lewis as a sideman) for a few titles in 1944; and "Far Away Blues" with the Eclipse Alley Five, again including Lewis, in 1946. Robinson was with Johnson at the Stuyvesant Casino in New York in 1945 and 1946, although Johnson would have preferred a swing-style orientation and tried, unsuccessfully, to replace Robinson with Sandy Williams. After Johnson's death, Robinson remained with Lewis, touring the United States and Europe into the 1960s and making recordings, including the album *George Lewis at San Jacinto Hall* (1964). He also recorded the album *Blues and Spirituals* as a leader in 1961, and perhaps he married around this time. Although the date of the marriage is unknown, his wife's name was Pearl, and a child was born when Robinson was about seventy-one years old.

From 1961 into the 1970s Robinson played at Preservation Hall in New Orleans with DE DE PIERCE and BILLIE PIERCE, Percy Humphrey, his own bands, and with others. He remained active until the age of eighty-three, having played concerts at Lincoln Center and in Boston at Symphony Hall with the Preservation Hall Jazz Band only a few weeks before his death in New Orleans. Throughout his life he took great pleasure in his music and was known to burst out laughing on finishing a passage that he felt had pleased the audience.

Robinson was, after KID ORY, one of the best of the jazz trombonists in the New Orleans "tailgate" style. He played with a powerful, rough sound, a hefty dose of sliding pitches, and an unselfish approach that complemented the trumpet and clarinet while driving the rhythm forward. He rarely played solos, but when he did he was likely to use the same stuttering, punching, spurting style that made his work in collective improvisations so effective.

FURTHER READING

Robinson, Jim. "New Orleans Trombone," in *Selections from the Gutter: Jazz Portraits from "The Jazz Record,"* eds. Art Hodes and Chadwick Hansen (1977).

Carter, William. *Preservation Hall: Music from the Heart* (1991)

Turner, Frederick. *Remembering Song: Encounters with the New Orleans Tradition* (1982)

Obituaries: *Down Beat*, 15 July 1976; *Footnote 7*, no. 5 (1976); *Jazz Journal* 29 (Aug. 1976).

This entry is taken from the *American National Biography* and is published here with the permission of the American Council of Learned Societies.

BARRY KERNFELD

Robinson, Jo Ann (17 Apr. 1912–29 Aug. 1992), civil rights activist, was born Jo Ann Gibson on a farm in Crawford County, Georgia, the youngest of twelve children of Owen B. Gibson and Dollie Webb. After the death of her father in 1918, her mother struggled to operate the farm. In 1926, however, her mother sold out and moved the family to the nearby city of Macon, to live with a son who was a postman. Robinson attended high school in Macon, graduating in 1929 as the valedictorian of her class. She then began teaching in the Macon public schools, continuing to do so while also attending Fort Valley State College. She received a B.S degree from Fort Valley in 1936. In 1943 she married Wilbur Robinson, a soldier in the U.S. Army, and in 1944 they had a child. But the child died in infancy, and in 1946 the Robinsons divorced. Robinson then resigned her position with the Macon school system and entered graduate school at Atlanta University, from which she received an M.A. in 1948. In the school year 1948–1949 she taught English at Mary Allen College in Crockett, Texas, and in the fall of 1949 she joined the faculty of Alabama State College for Negroes in Montgomery.

Almost as soon as she arrived in Montgomery, she became an active member of the Women's Political Council, which had been formed the preceding spring by female Alabama State College faculty as a black analogue of the all-white League of Women Voters. Robinson became the council's president in 1952 and registered to vote for the first time on 6 January 1953. As early as October 1952 the council had begun pressing the Montgomery bus company and the Montgomery City Commission to adopt the pattern of bus segregation in use in the Alabama city of Mobile, under which drivers could not unseat black passengers to make room for boarding whites. Robinson became the principal black spokesperson in meetings with city authorities during 1953 and 1954 about racial problems on the city buses. These meetings rectified one significant black complaint, that buses would stop at every corner in white neighborhoods but only at every other corner in black areas. But no progress was made on the problem of the unseating of black passengers.

On 21 May 1954, just after the U.S. Supreme Court's *Brown v. Board of Education* decision forbidding racial segregation in public schools, Robinson sent Mayor William A. Gayle a letter warning him that unless concessions on the bus-seating question were made, Montgomery's blacks might undertake a boycott of the busses. The arrest and conviction of a black high school student, Claudette Colvin, in March 1955 for failing to obey a driver's order to yield her seat, further exacerbated the tensions surrounding this issue. Thus, when the black attorney FRED D. GRAY called Robinson on the evening of 1 December 1955 to tell her of the arrest of ROSA PARKS under exactly the same circumstances, Robinson was primed for action. Early the next morning she went to her office at Alabama State College and mimeographed a leaflet calling for a one-day boycott of the buses on the day Parks's trial was to be held, 5 December. She and her council associates spent the rest of the day distributing the leaflets throughout the black sections of the city. The result was that when Montgomery's black leaders met that evening at the Dexter Avenue Baptist Church, at the call of EDGAR D. NIXON, president of the local of the Pullman porters' union, to discuss the possibility of a boycott, they found themselves faced with a fait accompli because of Robinson's actions, and so they voted to support the boycott proposal.

The boycott on 5 December proved to be a complete success. When Parks was convicted and fined ten dollars and costs, black leaders at a meeting that afternoon decided to continue the boycott until the bus company adopted the Mobile pattern of segregation. They formed an organization to run the protest, the Montgomery Improvement Association (MIA), and chose Robinson's pastor, the Reverend MARTIN LUTHER KING JR., to head it. During the boycott, which lasted for more than a year, Robinson continued to play a crucial role. She was one of the black negotiators who met with a white mediation committee appointed by the mayor, and she insisted that the two racial delegations be equal in numbers. She was also a member of the MIA's executive board and its strategy committee. In this role, she was a central figure in persuading these bodies in January 1956 to agree to file suit in federal court challenging the constitutionality of bus segregation, even though doing so meant abandoning the demand for the adoption of the Mobile pattern of seating. Both during and after the boycott, she edited the MIA's newsletter, which assisted in raising contributions for the organization from throughout the country.

She had promised the president of Alabama State College, H. Councill Trenholm, that she would keep secret her part in initiating the boycott, to protect the college from state legislative reprisal, and her contributions did not become publicly known until 1980, when historical investigation finally revealed them. Nevertheless, she found herself caught up in Governor John M. Patterson's furious attacks on the college when its students organized sit-ins at segregated Montgomery facilities in the spring of 1960, and she was compelled to resign from the faculty in May of that year. She taught at Grambling College in Louisiana during the academic year 1960–1961 and then became a public school teacher in Los Angeles, California. She taught in Los Angeles until her retirement in 1976. In 1987 the University of Tennessee Press published her memoir, *The Montgomery Bus Boycott and the Women Who Started It*.

FURTHER READING

Robinson, Jo Ann Gibson. *The Montgomery Bus Boycott and the Women Who Started It: The Memoir of Jo Ann Gibson Robinson* (1987).

King, Martin Luther, Jr. *Stride toward Freedom: The Montgomery Story* (1958).

Thornton, J. Mills, III. *Dividing Lines: Municipal Politics and the Struggle for Civil Rights in Montgomery, Birmingham, and Selma* (2002).

J. MILLS THORNTON III

Robinson, John C. (26 Nov. 1903–27 Mar. 1954), aviator who promoted flight training for African Americans but gained his greatest fame as a pilot for Ethiopian emperor Haile Selassie, was born in Carabelle, Florida. His father's name is unknown; his mother, Celest Robinson, may have been born in Ethiopia. Raised by his mother and stepfather in Gulfport, Mississippi, Robinson graduated from Tuskegee Institute in Alabama in 1924. For the following six years he was a truck driver in Gulfport. Then he moved to Chicago, where he and his wife, Earnize Robinson, operated a garage. In 1931 he graduated from the Curtiss-Wright Technical Institute in Chicago. He taught at Curtiss-Wright Institute and organized African American men and women pilots in the Chicago area into the Challenger Air Pilots Association.

Early in 1935 Tuskegee Institute invited Robinson to organize the first course in aviation entirely for

African Americans. By that time, he held a transport flying license and had piled up 1,200 hours of flight time, much of it as an instructor at South Side Chicago airports. At about the same time as the Tuskegee offer, a nephew of Emperor Haile Selassie invited Robinson to come to Ethiopia. Benito Mussolini's Italian legions were threatening, and Ethiopia needed experienced aviators, even though some press reports at the time said that none of the emperor's twenty-five airplanes was flyable. Robinson appeared to have selfless motives, in contrast with the many intriguers and opportunists who flocked into Addis Ababa during Ethiopia's futile attempts to repel the Italians. He "had come to Ethiopia to testify to the solidarity of the colored peoples" (Del Boca, 86).

Soon after arriving, Robinson displayed what would become a familiar penchant for prickly behavior toward others. He clashed with the only other African American pilot on the scene, Colonel HUBERT JULIAN, a Harlem native who had renounced his U.S. citizenship to serve in the Ethiopian air force. Julian, known as the "Black Eagle," apparently lost the contest, because he was banished to a far-off province to drill infantry recruits. That left Robinson, the "Brown Condor," in charge of the ragtag air force. Now a colonel, he had to deal with an Italian air force that controlled the skies over Ethiopia during the invasion in 1935 and 1936. In an unarmed monoplane, he repeatedly flew courier missions between the front lines and Addis Ababa. Robinson escaped from Ethiopia on 4 May 1936, the day before the country capitulated. Returning to the United States, he toured the country on behalf of United Aid for Ethiopia. That fall he returned to Tuskegee Institute to teach the aviation course he had given up before he left for Ethiopia.

When World War II ended, Robinson returned to Ethiopia, where Selassie granted him his old rank of colonel. Within a year, however, he was at odds with a group of Swedish technicians who were in Ethiopia to work with equipment sent by Swedish munitions makers. In August 1947 the conflict exploded into violence. Robinson was arrested and jailed for an assault on the Swedish count Carl Gustav von Rosen, who was then commander in chief of the Ethiopian air force. Robinson was found guilty by a jury, lost his appeal, and spent an undetermined amount of time in prison.

In 1951 *Ebony* magazine reported that Robinson—still the best-known African American in Ethiopia—had become disillusioned by his conviction and was thinking of returning to the United States. "But," said *Ebony*'s reporter, "despite Selassie's apparent indifference to him, he remains something of a national hero to the Ethiopian people."

Robinson died as a result of severe burns sustained on 13 March 1954, when the training plane he was flying crashed and burned at the Addis Ababa airport, after narrowly missing a nurses' home. The apparent cause of the accident was engine failure. Also killed in the accident was Bruno Bianci, an Italian engineer.

Although Robinson was a glamorous figure in Ethiopia's highly publicized resistance to Mussolini, his greatest legacy may have been his attempt to increase African American interest in aviation in the United States. Had he remained in his native country after World War II, he would have witnessed the integration of the armed forces—perhaps by some of the pilots he helped train.

FURTHER READING

Del Boca, Angelo. *The Ethiopian War, 1935–1941* (1965, Eng. trans. 1969).

Gubert, Betty Kaplan. *Invisible Wings: An Annotated Bibliography on Blacks in Aviation, 1916–1993* (1994).

Scott, William R. *The Sons of Sheba's Race: African Americans and the Italo-Ethiopian War, 1935–1941* (1993), 69–80.

Obituaries: *Chicago Tribune* and *New York Times*, 28 Mar. 1954.

This entry is taken from the *American National Biography* and is published here with the permission of the American Council of Learned Societies.

DAVID R. GRIFFITHS

Robinson, LaVaughn (9 Feb. 1927–22 Jan. 2008), dancer and educator, was born and raised in Philadelphia, Pennsylvania, one of fourteen children of David Robinson, a construction worker, and Katherine Griffin, a homemaker. Robinson's South Philadelphia neighborhood pulsed with percussive street dancing, an example of vernacular culture that became the springboard for his distinguished career. When he was seven years old, his mother took a break from preparing supper to teach him his first tap step, which he practiced on the wooden floorboards of the family's kitchen. He expanded his repertoire by watching and imitating rhythm dancers who entertained themselves and challenged each other on street corners along Philadelphia's South Street corridor, where, according to Robinson, tap dancing was a common pastime for men, women, and children.

By his early teens Robinson was a street dancer himself, "busking" (dancing for money) in Philadelphia's downtown. He and two or three other youngsters became what was commonly called a "tramp band"; they affixed metal plates to the bottoms of their shoes and danced and played homemade instruments, such as washboards and thimbles, a tin tub, a one-stringed bass, and paper-wrapped combs. During the Great Depression, Robinson's earnings from street performing were enough to make him an important breadwinner for the large Robinson household.

Lawrence Patterson was among the local street dancers who gave advice and encouragement to young Robinson and his friends. When Robinson was between twelve and thirteen, Patterson drove him to the Cotton Club, a nightclub in Lawnside, New Jersey (a popular entertainment hub for African Americans), promising the young boy that he would see a great tap dancer. Robinson never imagined that the great tap dancer would be a woman, Louise Madison, who, Robinson recalled, hit the stage with a salvo of rhythm and was decked out in white tails, top hat, and cane (Interview with the author). (Robinson encountered Madison again after he became a professional dancer when they both performed on a show at Harlem's Apollo Theater.)

Stage shows were Robinson's primary vehicle for studying the distinctive styles of professional tap dancers. Tap performances by Bill Bailey (brother of the singer and actress PEARL BAILEY), Derby Wilson, the team of Pete, Peaches, and Duke, and the dance and comedy duo of Stump and Stumpy (Eddie Hartman and James Cross) were as instructive as they were entertaining. Robinson's appreciation and imagination for tap dance was further ignited by the swing band revues of CAB CALLOWAY, JIMMY LUNCEFORD, COUNT BASIE, Charlie Barnett, and other bandleaders whose stage shows traveled the country in the 1930s and 1940s. Philadelphia's Lincoln and Earl Theaters were venues for black musical productions that included singers, chorus line dancers, comedy and novelty acts, and tap dancers such as Honi Coles, Cholly Atkins, Bunny Briggs, Baby Laurence, Buster Brown, and Leon Collins.

Drawn to the stage, Robinson left high school at age sixteen and went on the road with Howard Blow, one of his tramp band buddies. However, it was not long before Robinson was drafted into the army and stationed in Kentucky, where he was trained to operate tanks and other heavy vehicles.

With encouragement from his commanding officers, he continued to dance, finding performance outlets in United Service Organizations (USO) shows. While on a weekend furlough, Robinson was introduced to a dance technique that became the defining element of his style. Strolling one night in downtown Philadelphia, Robinson encountered a fellow tap dancer, Henry Meadows, who was also in the army. Meadows showed him a step known as the "paddle": a fast, close-to-the-ground alternation of heels and toes. That brief introduction was enough to launch Robinson on a career-long exploration of ways paddles could be used to create percussive dance and music.

When Robinson was discharged from the army in 1947, he had already decided to make his living by tap-dancing. He teamed up again with Blow, and they performed steadily throughout southeastern Pennsylvania using the stage name the Howard Brothers. The partnership was characterized by devotion to the "Philadelphia style" of tap, which involved intricate rhythmic patterns, close-to-the-ground footwork, and an attention to musicality. Over the next decade Robinson performed extensively with Blow as well as in duos and trios that at various times included Meadows, Eddie Sledge, and Earl Scoggins. They danced under such names as the Dancing Jets, the Dancing Dictators, and Vaughn and Maximillian in local nightclubs, burlesque shows, and the top forums for live entertainment. Robinson especially delighted in traveling and performing with big bands, including those led by Tommy Dorsey and Maynard Ferguson.

In the 1960s Robinson and his partners, like tap dancers in general, struggled to find work as the number of places for live entertainment declined dramatically. Tap dancing also suffered due to its association with traditions thought to perpetuate negative stereotypes of African Americans and its replacement by modern and jazz dance in American musical theater productions. By the late 1960s Robinson's dancing career was on hiatus, and by the late 1970s he was making his living by operating icing equipment at a university skating rink. The early 1980s, however, ushered in renewed interest in tap. Veteran African American hoofers were invited to perform, teach, and share their stories at festivals across the United States, and video documentaries featuring black tap masters helped to popularize tap-dancing with new audiences in the United States and across the world. Robinson seized this opportunity to reactivate his dance career. He became a popular and respected teaching artist at dance festivals in the United States, Europe, and Israel. In 1980 Robinson joined the dance faculty of Philadelphia's University of the Arts, where he taught for twenty-three years, trained thousands of dance and theater majors, and was conferred the title of distinguished professor in 2005.

In addition to his active teaching schedule, Robinson performed regularly, often with his long-time protégé and dance partner Germaine Ingram, on university concert stages and major dance performance venues. He traveled the country with *Echoes of Africa*, a production showcasing African-rooted performance traditions, and performed in Africa and the Soviet Union with U.S.-sponsored tours designed to present the best in African American performance art. Robinson and Ingram performed for the award-winning public television special "Great Performances: Gregory Hines' Tap Dance in America." He contributed to several documentation projects, including interviews archived at the Dance Collection at Temple University, *Plenty of Good Women Dancers* (2004, DVD), a video documentary produced by the Philadelphia Folklore Project, and *Dancing History* (2003), an autobiographical documentary coproduced with the filmmakers Barry Dornfeld and Carole Boughter.

Robinson referred to himself as "the last of the street dancers," expressing pride in the fact that he never had a formal dance lesson. However, on panels and in interviews he spoke often about the dancers who influenced his personal style and artistic development. His collaborations with Meadows and Blow and the mentoring he received from the older Philadelphia hoofer Jerry "Tapps" Sealey helped shape his rhythmic inventiveness and musicality. But no dancer inspired Robinson more than Teddy Hale, whom he considered the perfect combination of technical virtuosity, musical prowess, and polished stage presence.

Robinson received numerous awards for his excellence and contributions as a performing artist, teacher, and preserver of vernacular and traditional arts. He received several grants and fellowships from the National Endowment for the Arts (NEA) and the Pennsylvania Council on the Arts. In 1989 the NEA recognized him for lifetime achievement with a National Heritage Fellowship. He received a Pew Fellowship in the Arts in 1992 and the Pennsylvania Governor's Award for Artist of the Year in 2000. *Dance Teacher Magazine* presented him its highest honor, a Lifetime Achievement Award, in 2005 and featured him in its September 2005 issue. Due to illness, Robinson took an indefinite sabbatical from performing and teaching in 2005. He was married to Edna Martin, with whom he raised two sons. He died in Philadelphia at the age of 80.

FURTHER READING

Malone, Jacqui. *Steppin' on the Blues: The Visible Rhythms of African American Dance* (1996).

Philadelphia Center for Arts and Heritage. Dance Advance, 2007. http://www.danceadvance. org/03archives/lrobinson/page2.html.

Philadelphia Folklore Project. *Works in Progress: The Magazine of the Philadelphia Folklore Project* 9, no. 2 (1994). http://www.folkloreproject.org.

Stearns, Marshall, and Jean Stearns. *Jazz Dance: The Story of American Vernacular Dance* (1994).

GERMAINE INGRAM

Robinson, Lizzie (5 Apr. 1860–13 Dec. 1945), church leader and organizer, was born Lizzie Smith in Phillips County, Arkansas, one of five children of enslaved parents, Lizzie Jackson and Mose Smith. Her father died shortly after her birth, leaving her illiterate mother to raise their children alone. Nevertheless, after the Civil War all five attended school, and by age eight, Lizzie had learned to read. When Lizzie was fifteen her mother died, forcing her to quit school and work as a washerwoman to support herself. In 1880, while living in Helena, Arkansas, she married William Henry Holt and gave birth to a daughter, Ida Florence. When Holt died, she married William H. Woods, who also died soon after they were married. In 1892 Robinson settled in Pine Bluff, Arkansas, where she joined a Baptist church and where she and Ida lived together and worked as laundresses until Ida married Archie Baker. In 1901 she was introduced to *Christian Hope Magazine* which she used in her church's Bible Band class. Published by Joanna P. Moore, the first woman appointed by the American Baptist Home Mission Society (ABHMS), *Hope* promoted what was then called a deeper religious life of holiness or sanctification. A native of Pennsylvania, Moore had moved to the South to work among the formerly enslaved. Because Moore was teaching African American children to read, white supremacists forced her to leave New Orleans. In 1891 she settled in Arkansas and later met Robinson, who said she was sanctified as a result of reading *Hope*. Urged by Moore to give up work as a washerwoman to complete her education, Robinson studied at the Baptist Training Academy in Dermott, Arkansas, where she ultimately served as matron, taking in boarders to supplement her income.

In 1911 Robinson launched her career as a religious leader and organizer when she met Charles Harrison Mason, founder of the Church of God in Christ (COGIC). Mason had founded COGIC in 1897 as a holiness denomination, but after experiencing Holy Ghost Baptism at the Azusa Street Revival in Los Angeles, he had reconstituted COGIC in 1907 as a Pentecostal church. While preaching in Dermott, Mason met and persuaded Robinson that a Christian should seek the Baptism of the Holy Ghost with speaking in an unknown tongue or language as initial evidence. When Robinson proclaimed publicly that she had received the Baptism of the Holy Ghost, with the evidence of speaking in tongues, she lost her position as matron of the Baptist Academy since most Baptist leaders at that time rejected speaking in tongues or *glossolalia* as a legitimate experience for contemporary Christians. Robinson immediately joined COGIC and spent several months helping Elder R.E. Hart organize new churches in Tennessee. Before the year ended, C.H. Mason appointed her the first overseer of women's work, a title later changed to general supervisor. Mason asked Robinson to organize the large number of women who were joining COGIC and harness their energies for service and to make sure that every church in COGIC adhered to the same doctrinal precepts.

During her initial travels to COGIC churches in the Arkansas, Mississippi, and Tennessee area Lizzie met and married the COGIC Elder Edward D. Robinson. In 1916 the couple moved to Omaha, Nebraska, to live near her daughter, Ida. The newcomers joined the African American migrants to Nebraska who had come to work in the meat packing industry. Soon after their arrival, a nationwide wave of violence against African Americans called the Red Summer of 1919 swept through Omaha when a white mob lynched a black man, riddled his body with bullets, and tied his carcass to a crosslike structure and burned it in an open pit. In addition to a climate of virulent racism, the small band of Pentecostal adherents endured ridicule and abuse from those who opposed their interpretation of biblical holiness and speaking in tongues. In this often hostile environment Elder Robinson led the new COGIC congregation in the purchase of a church building. By 1922 there were enough COGIC churches in Nebraska to hold a state convocation.

While her husband remained in Omaha, Robinson maintained a daunting schedule. In 1925, traveling mainly by railroad, she visited churches in forty cities in eighteen states, going from Nebraska to Arizona and California, then north to Minnesota and east through Ohio to New York before returning to Memphis for the church's annual national convocation.

As a church organizer Robinson created the Prayer and Bible Band, which maintained doctrinal consistency for the church and sustained regular bible teaching in all COGIC congregations. She also organized the Women's Department, the Home and Foreign Mission Board, Sunshine Band and Purity Classes for children and youth, and the Sewing Circle for women. Through Robinson's efforts, Church Mother became an official position, second in authority only to the pastor. Since men were then a distinct minority in COGIC congregations, this arrangement allowed one man to be the pastor of several churches, leaving the Church Mother in charge during his absence. At each organizational level, from the local church to the state or jurisdictional level, Robinson appointed a Church Mother who served under the authority and with the consent of the pastor. At the state level she appointed State Mothers, who later became State or Jurisdictional Supervisors and served under authority of male State Overseers, later called Jurisdictional Bishops. Through the Women's Department, women became licensed missionaries and evangelists, starting new congregations until Mason appointed a pastor. This arrangement permitted women to exercise their spiritual gifts but preserved the pastorate for men.

Robinson devoted her final years to raising funds through the state Women's Department to help build a national headquarters in Memphis. During the annual international convocation held at the newly completed church building in 1945, Robinson retired to a private room where she died of heart failure. Because of Robinson's work, her successor and former assistant, Lillian Brooks Coffey, inherited a firmly established organization of women who would play a major role in the denomination's growth from about five hundred thousand members in the early 1960s to over five million by the end of the twentieth century.

FURTHER READING

Butler, Anthea D. *Making a Sanctified World: Women in the Church of God in Christ* (2006).

Hill, Elijah L. *Women Come Alive* (2005).

Israel, Adrienne. "Mothers Roberson and Coffey—Pioneers of Women's Work: 1911–1964," in *Bishop C.H. Mason and the Roots of the Church of God in Christ*, ed. Bishop Ithiel C. Clemmons (1996).

Pleas, Charles H. *Fifty Years Achievement from 1906–1956: A Period in the History of the Church of God in Christ* (1991)

Yearbook of the Church of God in Christ for the Year 1926 (1991).

ADRIENNE M. ISRAEL

Robinson, Max Cleveland (1 May 1939–20 Dec. 1988), television newscaster, was born in Richmond, Virginia, the son of Maxie Cleveland Robinson and Doris Griffin, schoolteachers. Robinson attended Oberlin College in 1957–1958 and Virginia Union University, his father's alma mater, briefly in 1959.

That year Robinson made his first venture into broadcast journalism, responding to a newspaper advertisement for a newsreading job in Portsmouth, Virginia. The ad was for whites only, but Robinson answered it anyway. He was allowed to audition along with four white candidates. He was hired, but when he read the news his face was not shown; instead a slide with the station's logo appeared. One day, wanting his family and friends to see him read the news, Robinson told the crew to remove the slide, which they did. The next day Robinson was fired after the station received a myriad of negative telephone calls.

Robinson joined the U.S. Air Force in 1959, hoping to become a pilot. Poor vision ended that dream, and the air force sent him to Indiana University to learn Russian in 1959–1960. In 1965 Robinson resumed his journalism career as a cameraman and correspondent for WTOP-TV in Washington, D.C. He learned early that the life of a black news journalist would not be an easy one: at WTOP he earned fifty dollars per week, twenty-five dollars less than his white counterparts.

Seeking advancement, Robinson left WTOP and became a news correspondent for rival station WRC-TV from 1965 to 1969. While at WRC he won six journalism awards, including two regional Emmys for a documentary on black life in Anacostia (one of Washington's predominantly black neighborhoods) titled *The Other Washington*, and an award for his coverage of the 1968 riots after civil rights leader MARTIN LUTHER KING JR. was assassinated. Despite the many accolades bestowed upon Robinson while at WRC, the news director told him that he did not think Washington was ready for a black news anchor.

Robinson returned to WTOP in 1969 in search of an anchor position. He became the first black anchor in Washington, D.C., co-anchoring the midday newscast. In 1971 he was promoted to co-anchor of the prestigious 6:00 P.M. and 11:00 P.M. news. He helped make WTOP's the top-rated newscast in Washington.

In 1977 Robinson received international attention when Hanafi Muslims seized three federal buildings and the B'nai B'rith headquarters in Washington. One of the sect leaders' first telephone calls was to Robinson, who helped negotiate the release of the hostages. Impressed with seeing Robinson so calm under fire, ABC-TV approached him about a network anchor position.

In 1978 Robinson moved to Chicago to become a prime-time co-anchor at ABC, breaking the color barrier for the most prestigious job at the major networks. He served as a national desk anchor of ABC's *World News Tonight*. While at ABC he reported on major events such as the American space laboratory, Skylab, falling to earth and the accident at the Three Mile Island nuclear plant, both in 1979. In 1981 he won an Emmy Award for his coverage of the 1980 national election.

Robinson's career at ABC was mired in controversy. In a 1981 speech at Smith College in Massachusetts, he verbally attacked the networks (ABC in particular). He was upset at the networks for not including black journalists in the coverage of Ronald Reagan's inauguration and the simultaneous release of U.S. hostages in Iran. Robinson claimed that the network officials were racist and said they promoted racially biased news coverage. He went on to say that the news media was a "crooked mirror" through which "white America views itself."

Robinson further embarrassed ABC by failing to appear at the 1983 funeral of colleague Frank Reynolds (one of the anchors of *World News Tonight*). He was supposed to have sat with First Lady Nancy Reagan. After he missed the funeral, Robinson was demoted, and Peter Jennings was made the sole anchor of *World News Tonight*. Frustrated about his demotion, Robinson became deeply depressed, grew bitter, and drank heavily. He left ABC in 1983.

In 1984 Robinson joined WMAQ-TV in Chicago as an anchor. While at WMAQ he voluntarily hospitalized himself for depression and alcoholism; after his frequent absences from the air, the station bought out his contract in 1987. This marked the end of Robinson's career as a television news anchor, even though he did some freelance journalism from 1985 to 1988.

Robinson was married three times. His first wife was Eleanor Booker; they had three children. His second wife was Beverly Hamilton; they had one child. This 1973 marriage was annulled after two months. His last marriage was to Hazel O'Leary, later an energy secretary in the Clinton administration; they had no children.

Robinson died of AIDS at Howard University Hospital in Washington, D.C. The Reverend Jesse Jackson eulogized him, telling the audience of Robinson's dying request: that everyone know he contracted AIDS through sexual promiscuity. Robinson had hoped that his death would energize the efforts to educate black Americans about the disease.

FURTHER READING
Boyer, Peter J. "The Light Goes Out." *Vanity Fair* (June 1989).
Zeigler, Dhyana. "Max Robinson, Jr.: Turbulent Life of a Media Prophet." *Journal of Black Studies* (Sept. 1989).
Obituaries: *Chicago Tribune* and *Los Angeles Times*, 21 Dec. 1988; *Jet*, 9 Jan. 1989.
This entry is taken from the *American National Biography* and is published here with the permission of the American Council of Learned Societies.

DARREN RHYM

Robinson, Prince (7 June 1902–23 July 1960), jazz clarinetist and tenor saxophonist, was born in Portsmouth, Virginia. The names of his parents are unknown. Largely self-taught, he began playing clarinet at age fourteen and, while in high school in Norfolk, worked with the Ben Jones band. Between 1919 and 1921 he played with Lillian Jones's Jazz Hounds in Norfolk and in 1922 went to Atlantic City, New Jersey, as a member of the pianist Quentin Redd's band.

In 1923 he moved to New York City, where he worked with Lionel Howard's Musical Aces and then with the banjoist ELMER SNOWDEN's highly regarded Nest Club band, which included the cornetist REX STEWART, the trombonist Te Roy Williams, the alto and baritone saxophonist Joe Garland, the pianist Freddy Johnson, the bassist Bob Ysaguirre, and the drummer Walter Johnson. In 1924 he also worked with the cornetist June Clark and along with Garland and the trumpeter Harry Cooper, made his first records with a small group called the Seminole Syncopators. In the spring of 1925 Robinson joined DUKE ELLINGTON's Washingtonians at the Kentucky Club, and in September, on "I'm Gonna Hang around My Sugar" and "Trombone Blues" from this fledgling band's

second recording session, Robinson displayed equal ability on the clarinet and tenor sax. In November on a freelance date with a group called the Gulf Coast Seven, led by WILLIE "THE LION" SMITH, he shared reed responsibilities with the formidable BUSTER BAILEY on "Santa Claus Blues" and "Keep Your Temper." In March and June 1926 Robinson appeared on four more titles with Ellington and may also be present on the eight successive sessions recorded through April 1927. During the summer of 1926 Robinson worked in the saxophonist Billy Fowler's band, and in May 1927, after a recording date with Te Roy Williams, he joined Leon Abbey's orchestra for a South American tour.

In late 1927, possibly at the urging of his childhood friend and trumpeter-arranger John Nesbitt, Robinson joined the Detroit-based McKinney's Cotton Pickers, then a major attraction at Jean Goldkette's Graystone Ballroom in Detroit. With two bandstands and a capacity of two thousand, the Graystone was also home to Goldkette's other orchestras, including the "Number One" band that featured Bix Beiderbecke, Frank Trumbauer, Don Murray, and other highly rated white jazzmen. Although Goldkette forbade drinking on the job and discouraged fraternization between the members of his racially segregated orchestras, the musicians themselves enjoyed each others' styles and often found opportunities for informal camaraderie after work.

As he did with the other bands his agency handled, Goldkette also booked the Cotton Pickers on far-ranging tours. In the fall of 1927 they substituted for the FLETCHER HENDERSON orchestra at New York City's Roseland Ballroom, playing opposite the popular white dance band of Sam Lanin. The Cotton Pickers also did battle with the redoubtable Henderson crew at the Graystone, as well as performing at private campus clubs for Princeton's house-party weekend in May 1929, where, with jazzmen from many other bands also in evidence, Robinson must certainly have had ample occasion for spirited after-hours jamming. With the harmonically advanced, challenging arrangements of DON REDMAN and Nesbitt, coupled with the group's excellent ensemble skills and a nucleus of inventive soloists, the Cotton Pickers invariably made a good impression wherever they appeared. However, despite their musical successes, both on record and off, dissension grew within the ranks over their treatment by the Goldkette office. Following a May to July 1931 booking at Frank Sebastian's Cotton Club in Culver City, California, the band broke up in late 1931, with Robinson returning in 1932 to a McKinney contingent led by the drummer Cuba Austin.

It was on the many bright-tempo, richly intoned records that the Cotton Pickers made between July 1928 and September 1931 that Robinson earned a reputation as a jazz tenorman second only to his idol COLEMAN HAWKINS, at the time Fletcher Henderson's star soloist and the universally acclaimed master of his instrument. Sharing improvised jazz solos equally with the trumpeters Nesbitt and JOE SMITH, the trombonists Claude Jones and Ed Cuffee, and the pianist Todd Rhodes, Robinson was a competent clarinetist, but because of his powerful attack, heated timbre, urgent rhythmic sense, and fluent technical command on tenor sax he enjoyed the respect and admiration of virtually all who heard him. His artistry is especially apparent on "Crying and Sighing," "Cherry," "Some Sweet Day," "Shim-Me-Sha-Wabble," "Birmingham Breakdown," "It's a Precious Little Thing Called Love," "I've Found a New Baby," "Okay Baby," "I Want a Little Girl," "Hello," and "Do You Believe in Love at First Sight?" In 1929 and 1930 and once again in 1937 Robinson participated as a freelance sideman on several recording sessions organized by the pianist CLARENCE WILLIAMS, but it was his work on the Cotton Pickers records that marked his greatest achievement.

After leaving the Cotton Pickers in Boston in early 1935 Robinson joined the singer BLANCHE CALLOWAY's orchestra in the summer and remained with her through early 1937. Along with the trumpeter Shirley Clay and the clarinetist BUSTER BAILEY, in July 1937 Robinson recorded a freelance session with the vocalist LIL ARMSTRONG during which he played tenor in a style somewhat influenced by CHU BERRY, Hawkins's then most advanced disciple. Reverting to clarinet for another freelance session in November with TEDDY WILSON and BILLIE HOLIDAY, Robinson appeared in a rather subdued role, but he acquitted himself well despite his limited opportunities for expression. Between April 1937 and November 1938 Robinson worked with the entertainer Willie Bryant, recording one session with his band in April 1938. In November 1938 Robinson began an extended engagement with ROY ELDRIDGE's orchestra at New York City's Arcadia Ballroom, and while there recorded two studio sessions with the band in October and December 1939. Broadcast performances from the preceding August and September have also been issued on record. In 1940 Robinson replaced Bingie Madison in LOUIS ARMSTRONG's orchestra and

was present at the three sessions recorded between March 1941 and April 1942. He was the sole reedman on the first date by the septet and can be heard in solo on clarinet on "Leap Frog" from November 1941. In this band the tenor sax solos were the domain of Joe Garland, Armstrong's musical director and chief arranger.

After a brief turn with LUCKY MILLINDER's orchestra in 1942–1943 Robinson spent the remainder of his career as a freelancer in and around New York City. In the fall of 1944 he played in the trombonist BENNY MORTON's sextet at Café Society Downtown and recorded a session with the group in 1945. Between 1945 and 1953 Robinson worked both casual jobs and residencies in New York City with such swing band veterans as the pianist CLAUDE HOPKINS and the tenor saxophonist Sam "the Man" Taylor, and in 1954 he went on tour with the trumpeter RED ALLEN. Between 1955 and 1959 Robinson worked in Queens with FREDI WASHINGTON's Dixiecrats, taking time out in July 1958 for an appearance with the Fletcher Henderson Reunion Band. Robinson's last recorded performance was as a clarinet soloist on arranger Andy Gibson's 1959 LP-length "Blue Print." He died of cancer in New York City.

Despite Robinson's early promise and the high plateau he reached as a soloist in the late 1920s and early 1930s he does not seem to have been able to keep up with the competition offered by younger jazz saxophonists during the swing era. By the mid- and late 1930s, with the advent of such distinctive stylists as Chu Berry, Herschel Evans, Dick Gibson, BEN WEBSTER, and LESTER YOUNG, it was clear that Robinson had fallen behind. Two years older than Hawkins, at his peak he had been a brilliant improviser in the "stomp" style, but as with some others of his generation, he found it difficult to make the transition to modern swing. As an alternative, he could have concentrated on clarinet, particularly after the mid-1940s revival of interest in earlier jazz styles. But then he would have had to compete with such specialists as OMER SIMEON, BARNEY BIGARD, ALBERT NICHOLAS, EDMOND BLAINEY HALL, and BUSTER BAILEY. Although highly regarded by his contemporaries for his early jazz work and his continuing ability as a big-band section man, Robinson spent the last two decades of his life in obscurity.

FURTHER READING

Allen, Walter C. *Hendersonia: The Music of Fletcher Henderson and His Musicians* (1973).

Chilton, John. *McKinney's Music: A Bio-Discography of McKinney's Cotton Pickers* (1978).

Dance, Stanley. *The World of Swing* (1974).

Schuller, Gunther. *The Swing Era: The Development of Jazz, 1930–1945* (1989).

This entry is taken from the *American National Biography* and is published here with the permission of the American Council of Learned Societies.

JACK SOHMER

Robinson, Randall (6 July 1941–), lawyer, human rights activist, and founder and president of TransAfrica and TransAfrica Forum, was born in Richmond, Virginia, one of four children of Maxie Cleveland Robinson Sr., a high school history teacher, and Doris Alma Jones, an elementary school teacher. His sister Jewell was the first African American admitted to Goucher College in Maryland, and his brother MAX ROBINSON was the first African American to anchor a national news program. Although both his parents attended college, the family experienced poverty early on, like most African American families living in Richmond at the time. Robinson attended public schools and felt the effects of racism and discrimination as he negotiated his way within the confines of a segregated society.

Following graduation from high school in 1959, Robinson attended Norfolk State College in Virginia on a basketball scholarship, but he left the university during his junior year. He married Brenda Randolph, a librarian, in 1965. They had two children, Anike and Jabari, before divorcing in 1982. Robinson served in the army, and, following his discharge, attended Virginia Union University, graduating in 1967. Robinson then entered Harvard University Law School but soon discovered that his life's work would not include practicing law. "After my first year of law school, I all but knew that I would never practice law…. I knew early that I simply couldn't endure the tedium of practice. I couldn't make myself enjoy the numbing task of drafting coma-inducing legal briefs and then plodding through the even more deadly labyrinthine and dreary passageways of legal procedure (Robinson, 1998, 68). Nonetheless, he graduated in 1970. His experiences at Harvard and living in the predominantly African American community of Roxbury, Massachussetts, had a profound effect on him. As a southerner, he had endured segregation, and knew what to expect from the whites he encountered, but Boston was in the North, and he had anticipated an integrated city. The racial strife that polarized the city in the 1960s and 1970s and its accompanying violence surprised and perplexed him.

Robinson became increasingly fascinated by Africa as he began to read more about the continent. He became interested in the liberation struggles of Angola, Mozambique, and Guinea-Bissau, and in 1970 he established the Southern Africa Relief Fund to provide military assistance to those who were struggling to end colonial and white-minority rule, raising four thousand dollars. In addition, he became interested in U.S. foreign policy in Africa and its relationship to American multinational corporations. Robinson recalls in his autobiography that "at the age of twenty-nine, I knew only that I wanted to apply my career energies to the empowerment and liberation of the African world" (Robinson, 69). He realized that black people throughout the world were in a similar situation; they suffered from the same legacies of slavery, colonialism, and racism. In Robinson's view it was essential that the peoples of the black diaspora had a voice in the decisions that affected their daily lives.

Robinson's sense of mission about the African continent was fulfilled in 1970 when he was given a Ford Foundation grant that allowed him to spend six months in Tanzania. Again, he could not escape racism and discrimination, and he achieved a broader understanding of the effects of colonialism. When he attempted to rent a car he was informed by an East Indian clerk that he would have to pay a deposit and that no cars were available. He returned to his hotel room and telephoned the same business. This time, when the clerk heard an American accent, but did not see Robinson's skin color, he was told that a car was available and that the deposit was much lower. Even in Tanzania he could not escape his skin color, and he realized the economic impact of the East Indian community brought to that nation by the British, who dominated the private retail sector.

Upon his return to the United States in 1971, he practiced law for the Boston Legal Assistance Project and then worked as community organizer for the Roxbury Multi-Service Center. Robinson's interest in Africa continued, and he organized the Pan African Liberation Committee to bring attention to American investment on the continent and its role in colonial liberation struggles. He devoted particular attention to the roles of his alma mater, Harvard University, and Gulf Oil in sustaining corrupt regimes in Africa and other parts of the Third World. In 1975 Robinson moved to Washington, D.C., serving first as a staff assistant for Congressman William Clay and then as an administrative assistant for Congressman CHARLES DIGGS. While working on Diggs's staff, he visited South Africa in 1976 and gained a deeper understanding of the pernicious nature of that country's apartheid system.

Two years later TransAfrica was established under Robinson's leadership. The organization soon emerged as the leading African American advocacy group on issues affecting people of African descent: white-minority rule in southern Africa, ethnic strife and war throughout the African continent, human rights violations, the plight of Haitian refugees, and the lack of economic, social, and political resources available to black people throughout the diaspora. Through Robinson's leadership, people from various religious, ethnic, social, and economic backgrounds attempted to shape American foreign policy in Africa through a series of protests, marches, and demonstrations. Robinson believed that civil disobedience was important to draw national attention to the conditions of blacks living under apartheid. It was a mechanism to galvanize students, workers, intellectuals, politicians, celebrities, the young and old, blacks, whites, and others around a common issue. His ultimate goal was to convince Congress to pass economic sanctions against South Africa's apartheid government. Others inspired by TransAfrica constructed shantytowns on college campuses to protest their universities' investment in apartheid South Africa. Though TransAfrica's methods were much more confrontational, Robinson's antiapartheid efforts paralleled those of LEON SULLIVAN, who worked closely with American corporations to end investment in South Africa.

Robinson thought that it was important for college students to understand the role that university investments played in maintaining apartheid. He also believed that people should be conscious of how their governments and companies invested their money in South Africa, and he encouraged them to push for divestment. Robinson appeared on national television, before congressional committees, and wherever else he could to encourage the U.S. government to change its policy toward South Africa by enforcing economic sanctions against the apartheid regime and to call for the end of white-minority rule in Namibia. To further debate on such matters, he established the TransAfrica Forum in 1981, an organization that engages in outreach work for the African American community and the broader public by providing seminars and conferences to inform people about the impact of U.S. foreign policy on Africa and its diaspora.

In 1986 Robinson's hard work with the Congressional Black Caucus and other members of Congress resulted in the passage—over President Ronald Reagan's veto—of the Comprehensive Anti-Apartheid Act, which served to strengthen existing sanctions and urged a transition to democratic rule in South Africa. (Some Reagan administration officials felt a closer affinity to the anticommunist regime in Pretoria than to Nelson Mandela's African National Congress, which included communists like Joe Slovo in leadership positions.)

Robinson married Hazel Ross, who worked with him at TransAfrica, in 1987. They had one daughter, Khalea.

Although ending white-minority rule in southern Africa was at the forefront of Robinson's work, he continued to push for improved economic conditions in the Caribbean, better treatment of Haitian refugees by the U.S. government, and the removal of dictators in Africa. In addition, he spoke out against the human rights violations committed by Sani Abacha's dictatorship in Nigeria and democratic failures in other African countries. He also called for reparations for blacks in the United States and was a vocal critic of the African Growth and Opportunity Act, passed by Congress in 2000 in an effort to move Africa–U.S. policy from aid to trade. His books include *Defending the Spirit: A Black Life in America* (1998), *The Debt: What America Owes Blacks* (2001), and *The Reckoning: What Blacks Owe to Each Other* (2002). In 2001 Robinson resigned as head of TransAfrica and emigrated to live in his wife's home country of St. Kitts in the Caribbean, citing a need to escape an American society he viewed as racist and arrogant. He contrasted America with the tranquility and community of St. Kitts in his book *Quitting America: The Departure of a Black Man from His Native Land* (2004). Despite his departure, Robinson has continued to advocate that American foreign policy makers address the issues, concerns, and needs of the African diaspora.

FURTHER READING

Robinson, Randall. *Defending the Spirit: A Black Life in America* (1998).

Robinson, Randall. *Quitting America: The Departure of a Black Man from His Native Land* (2004).

CASSANDRA VENEY

Robinson, Ruby Doris Smith (25 Apr. 1942–7 Oct. 1967), civil rights leader, was born in Atlanta, Georgia, the daughter of John Thomas Smith, a furniture mover and Baptist minister, and Alice Banks, a beautician. She did well in high school and in 1959 entered Spelman College. Halfway through her freshman year, Smith was deeply stirred by news of the restaurant sit-in organized by black college students in Greensboro, North Carolina. When Atlanta's college students formed a civil rights organization, Smith joined. She experienced her first arrest soon after, while trying to desegregate the state capitol building's cafeteria. A few months later she went to Shaw University in Raleigh to attend the conference at which the Student Nonviolent Coordinating Committee (SNCC) was founded. In February 1961 she and three others from SNCC joined a sit-in in Rock Hill, South Carolina, using a new tactic: "jail, no bail," which made them the first civil rights protesters to serve their full sentences. She spent thirty days in jail, acquiring a stomach ailment that remained with her the rest of her life.

In May 1961 the Congress on Racial Equality (CORE) began its Freedom Rides, testing the recent court decision outlawing segregation in interstate bus terminals. When violence in Alabama forced CORE to end the ride in Birmingham, Smith and SNCC members flew there determined to carry it on. After several days of intimidation and violence, the riders were arrested in Jackson, Mississippi. Refusing bail, they served forty-five days in Parchman State Prison. Smith remained in Mississippi after her release, working on SNCC's voter registration project. At a seminar for student activists that summer, she argued in defense of several blacks who had thrown rocks at their assailants during a demonstration.

Throughout the spring of her freshman year and all of her sophomore year, Smith spent more time on SNCC than her school work. She was arrested a dozen times and spent many weeks in various jails. Spelman College authorities were sympathetic, but in the fall 1961 they asked her to reapply for admission. Smith acknowledged the disruptive effects of her past activities but affirmed her intention to concentrate on college in the future. Granted readmission, she remained in school for two more years. She was still active in SNCC, however, serving on its executive committee, working in Cairo, Illinois, during summer 1962, and helping to organize demonstrations in Albany, Georgia, that December. In 1963 she withdrew from Spelman to work for SNCC full time.

Serving primarily in SNCC's Atlanta office, Smith spent most of her early years as administrative assistant to the executive secretary, JAMES FORMAN, though she also managed personnel, kept the accounts, and maintained SNCC's fleet of 100 cars in eight states. Developing into what one observer called "the administrative and logistical center of SNCC," Smith experienced continual stress in seeking to impose discipline and structure on a loosely organized, independent-minded staff. Both her dedication and her rages over unsatisfactory staff work were legendary. "You could feel her power on a daily basis," recalled one colleague. Said another, "Ruby just stood up to *anybody*." White volunteers were terrified of her, yet as one of them said, "Ruby was a woman I had the greatest respect for, and in a way, loved."

By 1964 Smith had begun to feel that SNCC was ignoring the fundamental economic questions that concerned most black Americans. In addition, the organization was becoming increasingly dependent on financial and political support from whites, and it was recruiting hundreds of white volunteers. This troubled Smith, who argued that blacks must continue to dominate SNCC. According to one colleague, she "had been anti-white for years." She also spoke out on the subordination of women within SNCC, though her willingness to protest this issue diminished as the organization became more polarized racially. In fall 1964 her commitment to black nationalism was intensified when she joined a SNCC delegation to Guinea's independence celebrations. Meanwhile, her personal life was placing new demands on her. She reentered Spelman in 1964 and graduated with a bachelor of science degree in physical education in 1965. She had married Clifford Robinson, an SNCC employee, in November 1964 and gave birth to a son, Kenneth Touré (named for the president of Guinea), two months after graduation.

During this period the South's continuing intransigence and the bitter disappointments of Freedom Summer led many SNCC members, like Ruby Robinson, to question the value of white liberal allies, nonviolence, and integration itself; by the spring of 1965 few whites still felt welcome in the organization. In spring 1966 Robinson was chosen to succeed Forman, becoming SNCC's first female executive secretary. Her election was perceived as an affirmation of separatism, particularly because black nationalist STOKELY CARMICHAEL was elected chair at the same time. Robinson's election was also seen as a victory for tighter administration because she and Forman had fought to hold staff more accountable. Nevertheless, her administrative efforts drew what Forman called "vicious attacks from the SNCC leadership." Some of her opponents had long fought any centralization of authority, while others explicitly objected to having a woman assert such power. Robinson's racial views also caused dissension; just as many of her colleagues were hardening their views on race, she was easing hers. Though she supported the goals enunciated by Black Power spokesmen, she told her staff that she had gone through a period of hating whites and "there's nothing to it." She insisted that they all had more important things to do than, she said, "sit around talking about white people."

By the time she was elected executive secretary, Robinson had little more than a year to live. Hospitalized in January 1967, she was diagnosed with cancer in April and died in Atlanta that fall. So contested had her administration been that some SNCC members believed she was murdered. Her friend KATHLEEN CLEAVER, who disagreed, said, "It wasn't necessary to assassinate her. What killed Ruby was work, work, work, with being married, having a child, the constant conflicts, the constant struggles that she was subjected to because she was a woman.... She was destroyed by the movement." Yet if Cleaver was right, Robinson made her sacrifice with passion and conviction, and her dedication inspired hundreds of people who worked with her. ALICE WALKER based her novel *Meridian* in part on Robinson's life. Forman described her as "one of the few genuine revolutionaries in the Black liberation movement." Stanley Wise, her successor at SNCC, called her "the nearest thing I ever met to a free person."

FURTHER READING

Paper that shed light on Robinson's career can be found at the archives of both Spelman College and SNCC (Martin Luther King Center for Nonviolent Social Change, Atlanta).

Carson, Clayborne. *In Struggle: SNCC and the Black Awakening of the 1960s* (1981).

Forman, James. *The Making of Black Revolutionaries* (1972).

Giddings, Paula. *When and Where I Enter: The Impact of Black Women on Race and Sex in America* (1984).

Sellers, Cleveland. *The River of No Return* (1973).

Zinn, Howard. *SNCC: The New Abolitionists* (1964).

Obituary: *New York Times*, 10 Oct. 1967.

This entry is taken from the *American National Biography* and is published here with the permission of the American Council of Learned Societies.

SANDRA OPDYCKE

Robinson, Spottswood William, III (26 July 1916–11 Oct. 1998), civil rights lawyer and federal judge, was born in Richmond, Virginia, the oldest of the three children of Spottswood W. Robinson Jr. and Inez Clements Robinson.

Robinson's father was a prosperous real estate broker, lawyer, and professor in the legal program at Virginia Union University from 1926 until it closed in 1931.

His father's example no doubt influenced the younger Robinson in both his choice of profession and in his work habits. In a biographical sketch of his father, Robinson wrote how juggling his varied professional roles taxed his father's energies. "The days were long—even nights and weekends largely were preempted—and the struggle against time was intense," Robinson wrote. "Nonetheless, he persevered through what for many would have been an ordeal, without a waning of interest in any of his endeavors and without complaint or expectation of praise" (Bryson, 555). As an adult Robinson worked much as his father did, spending countless hours preparing legal briefs and, later, his judicial decisions. His strong work ethic, combined with his keen intellect, earned Robinson the reputation of being one of the brightest legal minds of his generation.

Robinson graduated from Armstrong High School and attended Virginia Union University, both in Richmond. He left Union after his third year, at age twenty, to enter Howard University Law School in Washington, D.C. In the early 1930s Dean CHARLES HAMILTON HOUSTON was intent upon training young lawyers like Robinson to use their skills to help African Americans fight for their first-class citizenship rights. Robinson would soon join the cadre of black lawyers trained by Houston, including THURGOOD MARSHALL and OLIVER WHITE HILL, who led the fight against inequality and segregation in the South over the next two decades.

In 1936 Robinson married Marian B. Wilkerson. The couple had two children, Spottswood IV and Nina. In 1939 Robinson graduated magna cum laude from Howard University Law School, achieving the highest grade point average in the school's history. After graduation he taught at Howard Law School, focusing on property law.

In 1942 Robinson agreed to join Oliver White Hill in private practice in Richmond and was admitted to the Virginia bar the following year. They, along with Martin A. Martin, would form the law firm of Hill, Robinson, and Martin. These three lawyers also

Spottswood W. Robinson III (left) with Thurgood Marshall in Washington, D.C., to ask the Supreme Court to end school segregation, 1955. (Library of Congress/AP Photograph.)

comprised the core of the legal staff of the Virginia State Conference of the National Association for the Advancement of Colored People (NAACP). Founded in 1935, the Virginia State Conference served as the governing body for NAACP branches around the state and worked closely with the NAACP National Office to coordinate legal challenges. Because of the legal expertise and energy of Hill, Martin, and Robinson, Virginia emerged as one of the premier places where the NAACP challenged segregation.

In the mid-1940s Robinson guided through the state courts the case of *Morgan v. Virginia*, the 1946 ruling in which the Supreme Court declared segregation in interstate transportation unconstitutional. Robinson also helped prepare the NAACP's case in *Shelley v. Kraemer* that challenged residential restrictive covenants, agreements that forbid homeowners from selling their homes to blacks or other minorities. In its 1948 decision the Supreme

Court ruled that restrictive covenants, although private acts of discrimination, were unenforceable in a court of law.

Robinson also played a strategic role in challenging segregation in public education. In 1947 Thurgood Marshall chose Virginia as the site of a sustained legal campaign to equalize black and white public schools on a county-by-county basis. Robinson, who took leave from teaching at Howard Law School, and Virginia NAACP Executive Secretary W. Lester Banks shared responsibility for much of the work of the campaign. Robinson met with local black communities frustrated by their inadequate schools and spent much of his time investigating school facilities, petitioning school boards, and initiating court action. Some of these legal documents Robinson typed while sitting in Banks's car. By 1948 the Virginia NAACP had actions pending in seventy-five localities. In spring 1948 the Virginia NAACP won favorable decisions that required the school boards in four counties to equalize school facilities and teacher's salaries. In 1950 Robinson was named southeastern regional counsel for the NAACP, as the association shifted its legal strategy to challenge directly the constitutionality of segregation in public education. It was on this basis that Robinson and Hill agreed to sue the school board in Prince Edward County, Virginia, in April 1951. A high school junior named BARBARA JOHNS had led her fellow students at ROBERT RUSSA MOTON High School in a strike in protest of their poor, overcrowded school facilities and had called the attorneys for help. Hill and Robinson did not intend to litigate a case in rural, southern Virginia but after meeting with the students and parents agreed to take the case on the condition that they would sue to desegregate the schools, rather than to equalize facilities. *Davis v. County School Board of Prince Edward County* became one of the five cases that comprised the 1954 *Brown v. Board of Education* decision, in which the Supreme Court declared segregated education unconstitutional. Robinson was an invaluable member of the legal team that prepared *Brown* for the Supreme Court, and he also argued the *Davis* case before the Supreme Court.

In the wake of the *Brown* decision, Robinson continued to initiate school desegregation suits and fought against "Massive Resistance," the efforts of southern whites to circumvent or delay the implementation of *Brown*. Along with Thurgood Marshall, Robinson initiated the challenge to a series of Virginia laws that sought to undermine the work of the NAACP lawyers. By the time the Supreme Court held these laws unconstitutional in the case of *NAACP v. Button* in 1963, Robinson had served as dean of the Howard University Law School for three years. He also served on the U.S. Commission on Civil Rights from 1961 to 1963.

Beginning in the mid-1960s Robinson began his pioneering career on the federal bench, where he was the first African American to serve on both the U.S. District Court for the District of Columbia and the U.S. Court of Appeals for the District of Columbia Circuit. President Lyndon B. Johnson gave Robinson a recess appointment to the U.S. District Court on 6 January 1964, and the Senate confirmed his appointment on 1 July 1964. President Johnson nominated him to serve on the U.S. Court of Appeals for the District of Columbia Circuit on 6 October 1966 and the Senate confirmed him on 20 October.

The U.S. Court of Appeals is widely considered one of the most influential courts in the nation because it frequently rules on the constitutionality of federal laws. Robinson joined Chief Judge David L. Bazelon and Judge J. Skelly Wright to form a liberal bloc on the court. During Robinson's tenure the court heard important cases involving the rights of criminal defendants; the right of environmental and consumer groups to sue the federal government; the publication of the Pentagon Papers; and the release of the Nixon tapes during the Watergate scandal. In its rulings the court became one of the most active and progressive in the nation.

As a judge Robinson earned a reputation for his intellectual capacities and his meticulous legal craftsmanship. In his twenty-five years on the court he authored 411 decisions, each one carefully written and supported with case law. In one decision, which earned him gentle teasing from his colleagues, Robinson used 676 footnotes to support his position. Robinson inculcated these habits of precise writing, exhaustive research, and attention to detail in a generation of male and female lawyers who clerked for him during the 1970s and 1980s.

Robinson was elevated to chief judge of the Court of Appeals in 1981. In 1986, at the age of seventy, he was required by law to retire from the position of chief judge, although he remained on the court until 1 September 1989. In that year he assumed senior status on the court.

As both a lawyer and a jurist, Robinson fulfilled Charles Hamilton Houston's charge to use the law to create social change and to advance justice. In 1986 Robinson received an honorary degree from the New York Law School for his efforts "to achieve true equality under the law for all Americans" and thereby address "the conscience of the nation" (*New York Times*, 9 June 1986). He died of a heart attack in Richmond in 1998.

FURTHER READING

Spottswood Robinson's work with the NAACP can be found in the legal files as well as the Virginia State Conference files of the Papers of the National Association for the Advancement of Colored People in the Manuscripts Division, Library of Congress, Washington, D.C.

Bryson, W. Hamilton. *Legal Education in Virginia, 1779–1979: A Biographical Approach* (1982).

Kluger, Richard. *Simple Justice: The History of Brown v. Board of Education and Black America's Struggle for Equality* (1975).

"Spottswood W. Robinson, III: In Memoriam." *Harvard Blackletter Law Journal* 15 (Spring 1999).

Tushnet, Mark V. *Making Civil Rights Law: Thurgood Marshall and the Supreme Court, 1936–1961* (1994).

Tushnet, Mark V. *The NAACP's Legal Strategy against Segregated Education, 1925–1950* (1987).

"U.S. Court's Liberal Era Ending; Reagan Nominees Seen Giving Conservatives a Majority," *Washington Post*, 27 Jan. 1985.

Obituary: *New York Times*, 13 Oct. 1998.

LARISSA M. SMITH

Robinson, Sugar Ray (3 May 1920?–12 Apr. 1988), world boxing champion, was born Walker Smith Jr. in Detroit, Michigan, the third child of Walker Smith, a laborer, and Leila Hurst, a seamstress. Robinson divided his youth between Detroit and Georgia and later moved to New York City. It was in Detroit that he was first exposed to boxing. As he recalls in his biography, *Sugar Ray*, he carried the bag of the future heavyweight champion of the world, Joe Louis Barrow, soon to be JOE LOUIS, to the local Brewster Street Gymnasium.

Smith adopted the name Ray Robinson quite unintentionally. When his manager, George Gainford, needed a flyweight to fill a slot in a boxing tournament in Kingston, New York, young Walker Smith was available. In order to box, however, he needed an Amateur Athletic Union identity card. The AAU card verified that participating boxers were not professionals. Gainford had a stack of cards and pulled one out with the name "Ray Robinson" on it. The real Ray Robinson no longer boxed for Gainford's team, but the name stuck. The "Sugar" moniker was added later after Gainford, or perhaps a reporter or bystander (reports vary), declared that Ray was "as sweet as sugar."

Robinson turned professional on 4 October 1940, after great success as an amateur, including winning the Golden Gloves featherweight title. He was also briefly married at this time to a woman named Marjorie. That marriage was annulled after a short period, though they had a son together named Ronnie. Robinson had two other marriages. The second, in 1943, was to Edna Mae Holly. They had a son named Ray Robinson Jr., born on 13 November 1949. Ray Sr.'s final marriage was to Millie Bruce.

In 1943 Robinson joined the U.S. Army, where he spent most of his time fighting in boxing exhibitions and renewed his relationship with Joe Louis. The two men were arrested on one occasion at a military camp in Alabama for refusing to use a segregated waiting area, but were later released.

Robinson held the world welterweight title from 1946 to 1951 and was then middleweight champion five times between 1951 and 1960. At his peak his record was 128–1–2 with 84 knockouts. He never took a ten-count in his 202 fights, though he once suffered a TKO. In Robinson's day a boxer typically fought only eighty to one hundred bouts; today's boxers fight far fewer contests. Such a punishing schedule and his advancing years finally took their toll; thirteen of his nineteen defeats occurred between 1960 and 1965, when he was in his forties and well past his prime. One of the most poignant bouts in Robinson's career was his 24 June 1947, fight with Jimmy Doyle in Cleveland, Ohio. A week before the fight Robinson dreamed that he had killed Doyle in the ring. He told his manager, "the kid dropped dead at my feet, George." Robinson informed all who listened that he did not want to fight, fearing that the premonition would come true. In the end it did. Robinson knocked Doyle out in the eighth round of this fight, and Doyle never awakened.

Robinson's most notable bouts were those against Jake LaMotta in the mid-1940s and early 1950s, when they battled each other a total of six times. Those fights and LaMotta's life were intertwined with Robinson's. With the exception of their first encounter, Robinson won all of these bouts, including his first world middleweight title on 14 February 1951. LaMotta's life was memorialized in the Academy Award–winning motion picture *Raging Bull* (1980).

Perhaps Robinson's greatest boxing accomplishment was his success at a wide range of fighting weights. As an amateur he had been a featherweight, a division restricted to those weighing between 122 and 130 pounds, and began his professional career as a lightweight, where the fighting limit was 140 pounds. His first world championship victory came at the welterweight division (140–147 pounds) in December 1946, when he defeated Tommy Bell after fifteen bruising rounds in New York. In 1950 Robinson moved up to the middleweight division, where a fighter can weigh up to 160 pounds. It was at that weight that he defeated Jake LaMotta to win the world championship in 1951. In the late 1950s Robinson even contemplated a bout with the then heavyweight champion of the world, FLOYD PATTERSON. Though that bout never took place, press reports claimed that Robinson was offered $1 million to take on a boxer who outweighed him by dozens of pounds.

Robinson did, however, challenge the light heavyweight champion Joey Maxim. That bout was held in Madison Square Garden on 25 June 1952, which turned out to be one of the hottest nights in fifty-three years. The temperature at ringside

Sugar Ray Robinson, boxer, welterweight and middleweight champion. (AP Images.)

was 104 degrees. Although most of the scorers had Robinson ahead on points at the end of the bout, he lost when he passed out from exhaustion in the thirteenth round. In the tenth round the referee had to be relieved of his duties, as he was also on the verge of passing out from the heat.

Six months after the Maxim fight, Robinson announced his retirement and his intention of becoming a full-time entertainer. He developed a stage show that included tap dancing, singing, and telling jokes. He performed at venues including the French Casino in New York City as well as clubs on the French Riviera. For a variety of reasons, including the need for cash, Robinson reentered the ring three years later.

Beyond the ring and his boxing records, Robinson was responsible for a number of firsts. One of his little-mentioned contributions to sports is that Robinson was the first to have an official "entourage," the precursor of the modern athlete's posse. He first heard the word as he was disembarking from the cruise ship *Liberté* on a trip to France. When one of the porters asked whose trunks and suitcases were being unloaded, he was told that it was for Robinson's "entourage." Robinson used that term from then on. Perhaps because so many other

boxers, notably Joe Louis, suffered financially at the hands of unscrupulous managers and agents, Robinson was deeply involved in the management of his boxing career, as well as his investments outside of the ring. Those outside investments included the ownership of a bar, a dry cleaning store, a barbershop, and a lingerie store in Harlem. He often negotiated his own boxing deals and was known for pulling out of agreements when he did not feel that promoters were adhering to the negotiated terms.

Robinson's final moment of glory in the ring came on 10 December 1965. That night he formally retired from boxing before a crowd of 12,146 fans at Madison Square Garden. Four of his key lifetime opponents entered the ring before him. As Robinson entered to a standing ovation, he was lifted by his competitors and former challengers, Carmen Basilio, Gene Fullmer, Randy Turpin, and Carl "Bobo" Olson. Jake LaMotta, Robinson's best-known opponent, was not invited, as he had thrown a fight in that very venue in 1957. Robinson closed out that evening with a speech where he said: "I'm not going to say goodbye. As they say in France, it's *a tout à l'heure*—I'll see you later."

Following his second retirement from the ring, Robinson focused again on his entertainment career. He appeared in a number of motion pictures, notably *The Detective* (1968), starring Frank Sinatra, and *Candy* (1968), with Richard Burton and Marlon Brando. He was a regular on television, appearing on *The* FLIP WILSON *Show*, among other variety programs, and on *Mission Impossible, The Mod Squad*, and *Fantasy Island*. He also focused much of his time and efforts on his Sugar Ray Youth Foundation, founded in 1969 and based in Los Angeles, California, and which provided the means for tens of thousands of children to participate in sports and other programs. One of its most distinguished alumni was the Olympian and 100-meter dash world-record holder FLORENCE GRIFFITH-JOYNER.

In his final years Robinson suffered from Alzheimer's disease and curtailed almost all of his public appearances. His third wife, Millie, was constantly by his side at this stage. He died as a consequence of diabetes and Alzheimer's in Culver City, California. The mourners at his funeral included the boxers ARCHIE MOORE and MIKE TYSON, as well as Elizabeth Taylor and Red Buttons. The Reverend JESSE JACKSON delivered the eulogy. Robinson is buried, in the company of numerous other celebrities, at Inglewood Cemetery in Inglewood, California.

Sugar Ray Robinson is best known as the greatest boxer, pound for pound, of all time, according to *Ring* magazine. During his life his presence extended beyond his boxing skills to showmanship, class, and grace. In 1999 the Associated Press named him both the greatest welterweight and greatest middleweight boxer of all time and ultimately named him the fighter of the century, just ahead of MUHAMMAD ALI.

FURTHER READING

Robinson, Sugar Ray, with Dave Anderson. *Sugar Ray* (1970).

Mylar, Thomas. *Sugar Ray Robinson* (1996).

Schoor, Gene. *Sugar Ray Robinson* (1951).

Obituary: *New York Times*, 13 Apr. 1989.

KENNETH L. SHROPSHIRE

Robinson, William "Smokey" (19 Feb. 1940–), singer, songwriter, producer, and record executive, was born in Detroit, Michigan. From his youth, Robinson—nicknamed "Smokey" by an uncle due to his love of westerns—was surrounded by music and musically minded people. While attending Northern High School, Robinson formed a vocal group called the Five Chimes (later the Matadors) with his best friend, Ronnie White. As the group toured local venues, Robinson met a young BERRY GORDY JR., who was so taken with the Matadors, soon renamed the Miracles, that he and Robinson co-wrote the group's debut single, "Got A Job," an answer to the Silhouettes' R&B hit "Get A Job," which was released on Chess Records. Gordy also became the group's manager.

Gordy opened Tamla/Motown Records in 1959, and the Miracles were one of his first signed acts. Robinson quickly became Gordy's closest associate, starting a thirty-year association with Motown that included involvement as singer, songwriter, producer, and even the company's vice president, a position he held from 1961 to 1988. The Miracles' propulsive single "Shop Around," released in 1960, gave the Tamla label its first major hit, and the track's characteristic rhythmic drive, memorable melody, and romantic lyrics helped establish the incredibly successful "Motown sound" that took the Detroit-based imprint, and its predominantly African American personnel, to the top of American pop music by the middle of the decade. The rising energies of postwar industrial prosperity, assertive African American politics, and expanding teenage culture found a perfect soundtrack in Motown's rich grooves and sweetly poignant lyrics. Gordy's stated mission to create "The Sound of Young America" was fulfilled, as Motown produced countless hits and successful artists during this period.

Smokey Robinson stood at the center of this ascendancy. His aching, tremulous falsetto become one of the label's signature voices, as well as a defining element in the romantic, ballad-heavy genre of "romantic soul" that perhaps was the genre's most consistently popular element. He also produced recordings for most of the label's premier acts. Still, his most significant contribution came as a songwriter. Robinson crafted material for Mary Wells ("My Guy") and the Temptations ("My Girl," "The Way You Do The Things You Do"), among many others, and wrote or co-wrote nearly all of his own group's hits. Robinson's lyrics could be direct, like the pure-gospel pleas of "Ooo, Baby Baby" or "You Really Got a Hold On Me," or metaphorical, such as in "The Way You Do the Things You Do" or "The Love I Saw In You Was Just A Mirage." Musically, particularly when writing for his own voice, Robinson blended R&B, pop and rock, gospel, and even jazz influences with a talent reminiscent of SAM COOKE, whose musical and business vision set the model for Motown's self-sufficient crossover; Bob Dylan reportedly called Robinson "America's greatest living poet."

The Miracles scored consistent hits throughout the 1960s, from dance numbers like "Mickey's Monkey" to the epic balladry of "Tracks of My Tears." In 1967 the Miracles became Smokey Robinson & the Miracles, a billing reflecting their frontman's creative leadership. The group's career slowed somewhat during these years, due in no small part to Robinson's growing commitment to family—he and his wife and former bandmate, Claudette (née Rogers), had two children, Berry and Tamla—in addition to his vice-presidential duties. The Miracles continued to record and tour, and in 1970 their 1966 recording of "Tears of a Clown," co-written by Robinson and STEVIE WONDER, became a surprise number-one hit. Although Robinson remained with his rejuvenated group a while longer, he and Claudette stopped performing with the Miracles in 1972; the group remained active, recording another number-one hit, "Love Machine," in 1976.

Robinson quickly launched a solo career, including a number-one R&B hit ("Baby That's Backatcha") in 1975, but he still gave priority to his duties as a Motown executive. When his single "Quiet Storm" became a smash in 1976, however, Robinson found himself once again at the forefront of Motown's artist roster. The record proved a significant moment for both Robinson and pop music: its lush textures and Robinson's breathy style helped give rise to a new, adult-oriented R&B sub-genre that became known, appropriately, as quiet storm. Once again, Smokey Robinson's talents helped reshape the black musical landscape. Robinson recorded several major hits in this sub-genre, including "Cruisin'" in 1979, and a 1983 duet with Motown star Rick James, "Ebony Eyes." Now a respected elder statesman, Robinson's ongoing popularity with a wide audience remained a pivotal factor in his label's continuing success.

Robinson battled drug addiction in the 1980s, and his marriage to Claudette Robinson ended in 1986. Despite these setbacks, he returned, sober, to the charts twice in 1987 and the same year was inducted into the Rock and Roll Hall Of Fame. After Gordy sold Motown to MCA Records in 1988, Robinson left the executive position he held since the label's birth, and began recording elsewhere. Although he went more than a decade without scoring any significant hits after his 1987 comeback, Robinson's albums from the period, including a 2004 gospel effort, *Food For The Spirit*, were well received among critics and fans. He also launched SGFL Foods, which marketed specialty food items, some of which were named after the company's famous founder.

Robinson continued to record and tour into the 2000s, both in the U.S. and internationally. His shows were filled with the many hits that Robinson had been responsible for, in one way or another, over his forty years in the music business. Including all relevant chart listings, Robinson helped create seventy Top 40 hits. His distinctive singing and masterful songwriting also made him a frequently cited influence among performers and songwriters across genres. A foundation of the pivotal "Motown sound" on both sides of the microphone, Smokey Robinson figured among the most talented and important individuals in American music.

FURTHER READING

Robinson, Smokey, and David Ritz. *Smokey: Inside My Life* (1989).
Erlewine, Stephen Thomas. "Smokey Robinson and the Miracles," in *All Music Guide*, eds. Bogdanov, et al. (2001).
George, Nelson. *Where Did Our Love Go? The Rise And Fall Of The Motown Sound* (1986).
Gordy, Berry, Jr. *To Be Loved: The Music, The Magic, The Memories Of Motown: An Autobiography* (1994).

CHARLES L. HUGHES

Rock, Chris (7 Feb. 1965–), comedian and actor, was born in Andrews, South Carolina, the first son of Julius Rock, a truck driver, and Rosalie Tingman, a teacher. Chris Rock grew up in Brooklyn, New York. As a child he was bused to a majority-white school along with his siblings. This experience provided Rock with a particular perspective on the relationship between African Americans and whites. Rock dropped out of high school, but he later received his General Education Degree, or GED, which he later described as a "Good Enough Diploma." Growing up in a predominantly black and Caribbean immigrant neighborhood had a profound influence on his ideas of race and power and subsequently influenced his comedy and writing.

Rock began his career in the 1980s as a stand-up comedian. While touring the country he was noticed by EDDIE MURPHY, who became a mentor figure and assisted his career. During this period he joined the cast of the late-night comedy show *Saturday Night Live*. Despite receiving limited screen time during his three-year run on the show (1990–1993), Rock developed a popular character, a militant black nationalist named Nat X. He took advantage of his popularity by releasing his first live comedy album, *Born Suspect*, in 1991. He subsequently had a series of comedy specials including *Chris Rock: Big Ass Jokes* in 1993 and the Emmy-winning *Bring the Pain* in 1996. This one-hour special included controversial commentaries on race and politics, as well as a few jabs at Washington, D.C., mayor MARION BARRY, whose 1990 arrest on drug charges did not end his long political career; O. J. SIMPSON, one of the most contentious public figures of 1994–1995; and the leading black Republican of the moment, COLIN POWELL. Though controversial, Rock's yells and near rants found an appreciative audience among a broad cross section of America. In 1996 Rock served as a political commentator for Comedy Central during the network's coverage of the presidential election.

In 1997 Rock published his first book, *Rock This*, a *New York Times* and *Wall Street Journal* best-seller. Two comedy specials followed after 1996: *Bigger & Blacker* (which included a music CD as well) in 1999 and *Never Scared* in 2004. In both Rock used contemporary news and culture to address larger issues of race and politics. A joint collaboration with the hip-hop producer Prince Paul, the *Bigger & Blacker* CD had a hit with the single "No Sex in the Champagne Room." The song satirized gender relations by using situations found in a strip club. The CD served as an extension of the stand-up

HBO special of the same name. In that performance Rock unsettled the common understanding of race and racism. He shocked his audience by stating that the most racist people are "old black men" because they went through "real racism. He didn't go through that 'I can't get a cab' shit. He was the cab." Rock's satire was both a reflection of the past and a comment on the 1999 DANNY GLOVER cab controversy in which Glover argued that he was denied cab service in New York City because of racial discrimination.

Never Scared similarly followed Rock's popular culture commentary as he discussed car rims and the extravagant spending of black communities, MICHAEL JACKSON's child molestation charges, and Janet Jackson's notorious "wardrobe malfunction" at the 2004 Super Bowl. His deft use of popular culture as a medium for political commentary led to his being named the number five comedian of all time on the Comedy Central top one hundred.

Similar to his mentor Eddie Murphy, Rock successfully moved from the comedy club to the big and small screens. His long acting career included supporting roles in films such as *Beverly Hills Cop II* (1988), *New Jack City* (1991), *Boomerang* (1992), *Lethal Weapon 4* (1998), *Dogma* (1999), and *The Longest Yard* (2005). He also was the lead in *Down to Earth* (2001), *Head of State* (2003)—which he also directed—and the animated *Madagascar* (2005). On television, besides *Saturday Night Live*, he appeared on the last season of *In Living Color* (1993–1994).

In 1997 his HBO program, *The Chris Rock Show*, debuted. A combination of sketch comedy, interviews, and musical performances, the show hosted important figures, including the Democratic presidential candidates JESSE JACKSON and the Reverend AL SHARPTON, as well as the former president of the NAACP, KWEISI MFUME. The show lasted four seasons and was nominated for an Emmy Award in 1998. In 2005 Rock created *Everybody Hates Chris*, a television sitcom inspired by his childhood. Rock served as the show's narrator, executive producer, and occasional director. In that same year Rock hosted the 77th Annual Academy Awards show, becoming the first black man in history to lead the program.

In 1996 Rock married Malaak Compton, the founder and executive director of the New York nonprofit StyleWorks, which catered to women making the transition from the welfare system to the workforce. The couple had two daughters: Lola Simone, born in 2002, and Zahra Savannah, born in 2004.

Rock was one of several African Americans featured in HENRY LOUIS GATES's *African American Lives 2* (2008). The PBS documentary revealed that Rock's maternal great-great-grandfather, Julius Caesar Tingman, was a black Civil War veteran who was twice elected to the South Carolina State Legislature. In 2011 Rock made his Broadway debut in the play, *The Motherfucker With the Hat*.

FURTHER READING
Rock, Chris. *Rock This!* (2000).
Handy, Bruce. "Chris Rock," *Time* (9 July 2001).
Pearlman, Cindy. "Rolling Rock: Chris Rock Hits His Hollywood Stride," *Rolling Stone* (29 Jan. 2001).

SHANA L. REDMOND

Rock, John Stewart (16 Oct. 1826–3 Dec. 1866), activist, lawyer, doctor, and dentist, was born to free parents in Salem County, New Jersey. The majority of secondary sources list his middle name as "Swett" or "Sweat," although his biographer J. Harlan Buzby asserts that it was "Stewart." His father, also named John Rock, lived for more than three decades in Elsinboro, Salem County, New Jersey, and married Maria Willet on 8 June 1820. The elder John Rock was a laborer, and though the family was poor, John and Maria Rock did their best to see that young Rock was educated.

By 1844 Rock was teaching at an all-black school in Salem, a position he held until 1848. While teaching he read extensively and began studying medicine with two white doctors in the area, Quinton Gibbon and Jacob Sharpe. He attempted to gain admission to medical colleges in the area but was denied on racial grounds. After reading Samuel C. Harbert's *A Practical Treatise on the Operations of Dental Surgery and Mechanical Dentistry*, he sought out Harbert and studied further with him. By 1849 Rock was a practicing dentist, based in Philadelphia, Pennsylvania, but serving African Americans throughout the region. The 1850 census actually lists him twice: once boarding in the Spruce Ward of Philadelphia and again, on a different day, staying with the family of the black teacher Ishmael Locke in Camden, New Jersey. Rock continued to strive toward his goal of becoming a doctor and attended the short-lived American Medical College in Philadelphia, earning an MD in 1852.

Rock's time in Philadelphia shaped the rest of both his personal and his public life. He met Catherine Bowers (sometimes spelled Bowen) while boarding at the home of her widowed mother (sometimes listed as Henrietta and sometimes listed as Mary), and the two were married in 1852. Rock also became active in Philadelphia's lively free black community and in the broader abolitionist movement and was a featured speaker at the twelfth annual meeting of the Pennsylvania Anti-Slavery Society.

The young couple moved to Boston in 1853. Rock's reputation as a powerful intellect and caring activist preceded him, and when he set up a combined medical and dental practice at 83 Phillips Street he was already building a network with Boston's black elite—including LEWIS HAYDEN and LEONARD GRIMES. After the passage in 1850 of the Fugitive Slave Law, Boston, already an abolitionist center, had become a hotbed of resistance, and the Rocks became actively involved. Rock joined the Boston Vigilance Committee and offered free medical care to escaping slaves. Undoubtedly energized by the cases of fugitives like ANTHONY BURNS and SHADRACH MINKINS, Rock threw himself even further into reform. He aided the campaign to desegregate Boston's schools (working with WILLIAM COOPER NELL); he served as a delegate to the 1855 Colored National Convention in Philadelphia; he fought actively against colonization efforts; and he petitioned Massachusetts to remove the word "colored" from voter lists and tax bills. Rock lectured and wrote, and he tirelessly provided the area's black families with much needed medical care. His lecture at the dedication of a Masonic temple in Philadelphia in 1857, "The Light and Shadows of Ancient and Modern Tribes of Africa," marked one of the high points of his consistent, public advocacy of black racial pride—a pride emboldened by the birth of a son, also named John, that same year.

Perhaps the culmination of this period—and the clearest articulation of racial pride—came when Rock spoke in March 1858 at Faneuil Hall at the Boston black community's annual commemoration of CRISPUS ATTUCKS and challenged Theodore Parker's suggestion that blacks lacked courage. According to the 12 March 1858 Liberator, after praising armed slave resistance and attacking the recent Supreme Court decision against DRED SCOTT, Rock contrasted "the fine tough muscular system, the beautiful, rich color, the full broad features, and the gracefully frizzled hair of the Negro" with "the delicate physical organization, wan color, sharp features and lank hair of the Caucasian." The audience reportedly jumped to their feet, mingling applause and laughter, and Rock became one of the first to be associated with the language, "black is beautiful" (Buzby, 42).

But exhaustion and a throat condition had taken its toll on Rock, and in a difficult decision he left the United States to seek treatment in France in May 1858. Even here his race played a part: the secretary of state, Lewis Cass, had refused to give African Americans passports, arguing that they were not citizens—so Rock had to secure (with the aid of Charles Sumner) a rare state passport from the Massachusetts legislature. Rock underwent surgery in Paris—performed by August Nelaton, a member of the Académie Française—and during eight months of recovery studied the French language and culture. When he returned to the United States he followed Nelaton's advice to limit his medical practice but disregarded similar advice to limit his public speaking and activism. In 1860 he unsuccessfully petitioned the Massachusetts House of Representatives to remove the word "white" from the state's militia laws.

Always seeking new ways to aid the African American cause—and new intellectual challenges—Rock began reading law and was admitted to the Massachusetts bar on 14 September 1861; that same year he opened his own law practice and was commissioned as a justice of the peace by Massachusetts governor John Andrew. He gave major addresses at the 1862 Massachusetts Anti-Slavery Society annual meeting and at the 1 January 1863 Tremont Temple meeting where Bostonians came together to wait for confirmation of Lincoln's Emancipation Proclamation.

When it began to appear that abolitionist efforts were bearing fruit, Rock turned his energies fully toward gaining civil rights for both Northern free blacks and the thousands of newly freed slaves. Active in recruiting for Massachusetts's famous Fifty-fourth and Fifty-fifth Infantry regiments, Rock was a compelling speaker in favor of giving black soldiers both equal treatment and equal pay. His speech to the 1864 National Convention of Colored Men, at which he was elected one of the convention vice presidents, forcefully articulated this call and built from it to argue for more universal civil rights. These public successes, though, were marked by private tragedy: Rock's young wife died on 2 February 1864.

As the war drew to a close Rock traveled between Boston and Washington, D.C., where he furthered his friendship with the powerful clergyman HENRY HIGHLAND GARNET. In Washington, in addition to working for civil rights, Rock lobbied to be admitted to practice before the Supreme Court; his speeches after 1857 had regularly included attacks on the

Dred Scott decision and its citizenship implications for blacks. He achieved this goal in February 1865—and in so doing he became the first black lawyer so recognized. Following this he was received on the floor of the U.S. House of Representatives.

But even these honors were clouded by the racism that Rock had fought throughout his life. As he attempted to return to Boston he was arrested in a Washington, D.C., railroad station as a free black without a pass (an event that led Representative—and later U.S. President—James A. Garfield to introduce a bill outlawing such requirements). Already ill with a cold that would develop into a long and painful bout with tuberculosis, Rock never got the chance to practice in the Supreme Court, but he was able to return to the embrace of the Boston community, where he died the next year. His orphaned son was taken in by one of the son's maternal uncles in Philadelphia.

One of only a handful of people for whom the cliché "Renaissance man" might actually be appropriate, Rock spent his life fighting against racial barriers, often with great success. As a doctor, dentist, and attorney he was responsible for several black firsts, and as a civil rights activist he offered an articulate, powerful voice to his and succeeding generations.

FURTHER READING

Brown, William Wells. *The Black Man, His Antecedents, His Genius, and His Achievements* (1863).

Buzby, J. Harlan. *John Stewart Rock: Teacher, Healer, Counselor* (2002).

Horton, James, and Lois Horton. *Black Bostonians: Family Life and Community Struggle in the Antebellum North* (1979).

Jacobs, Donald M., ed. *Courage and Conscience: Black and White Abolitionists in Boston* (1993).

Quarles, Benjamin. *Black Abolitionists* (1969).

Teed, Paul E. "Racial Nationalism and Its Challengers: Theodore Parker, John Rock, and the Antislavery Movement," *Civil War History* 41.2 (1995).

ERIC GARDNER

Rodgers, Carolyn M. (14 Dec. 1942–2 Apr. 2010), poet, writer, and educator, was born Carolyn Marie Rodgers in Chicago, Illinois, the youngest child of Clarence Rodgers, welder, and Bazella Cato Colding Rodgers, homemaker. Rodgers was one of four children, including two sisters and a brother. The family had migrated from Little Rock, Arkansas, and settled in Bronzeville neighborhood on Chicago's South Side. Rodgers's parents

encouraged their children to read and involved them in the local African Methodist Episcopal Church. After graduating from Hyde Park High School, Rodgers attended Roosevelt University in Chicago, but left around 1965, one course short of her B.A. She earned her B.A. in English from Chicago State University in 1981 and her M.A. in the same subject from the same institution in 1984.

Rodgers found her literary voice through the Black Arts Movement of the 1960s and early 1970s. She was an original member of the Organization of Black American Culture Writers Workshop, directed by the *Negro Digest* editor HOYT WILLIAM FULLER. In the writing classes taught by the poet GWENDOLYN BROOKS, Rodgers met JOHARI AMINI and HAKI R. MADHUBUTI, with whom she cofounded Third World Press, one of black America's most influential and enduring literary publishers, in 1967. Rodgers received the Conrad Kent Rivers Memorial Fund Award for her first published poetry collection, *Paper Soul* (1968). Here as in later volumes, Rodgers explored themes of Afrocentric values and politics, revolutionary Christianity, and women's dignity, identity formation, and self-esteem, all in the vernacular speech preferred by Black Arts Movement writers.

Rodgers met with intense criticism from some men in the black liberation movement. Because she challenged male mistreatment of women and liberally used the "f word," her voice was rejected as "unladylike." Her tone softened somewhat throughout the years; however, Rodgers continued to express the black feminist consciousness later termed womanism. In 1969 Rodgers authored the poetry volumes *Two Love Raps* and *Songs of a Blackbird*, which brought awards from the Society of Midland Authors and the National Endowment for the Arts in 1970. Other collections include the National Book Award nominee *how I got ovah: New and Selected Poems* (1975), *The Heart as Ever Green* (1978), *Eden and Other Poems* (1983), *Finite Forms* (1985), *Morning Glory* (1989), and *We're Only Human* (1994). Rodgers also published several short stories, including "Blackbird in a Cage" (1967), "A Statistic, Trying to Make It Home" (1969), and "One Time" (1975).

In addition to her poetry, Rodgers contributed literary criticism and columns to publications including the *Chicago Daily News*, *Chicago Sun-Times*, *Milwaukee Courier*, and *Negro World*. During the 1960s she was a social worker and language arts teacher at the YMCA, and an instructor and/or writer-in-residence at Columbia College

Chicago (1969), University of Washington (summer 1970), Malcolm X City College (1971), Albany State College (1971), Indiana University (summer 1973), and Roosevelt University (1983). In 1989 she returned to Columbia College, and would continue to teach there for many years. She was also active as an informal writing mentor.

In 2009 Rodgers was inducted into the International Literary Hall of Fame for Writers of African Descent at the Gwendolyn Brooks Center for Black Literature and Creative Writing, Chicago State University. Only a year later, she died of cancer at age sixty-nine in the hospice at Mercy Hospital on Chicago's South Side. She was survived by one sister, Gloria, and their ninety-nine-year-old mother. Rodgers's memorial service took place on 6 May 2010 at the eta Creative Arts Foundation, a South Side nonprofit organization.

Rodgers never became as nationally well known as some other womanist Black Arts poets such as SONIA SANCHEZ and NIKKI GIOVANNI. She has, however, been cited by other writers as an important influence, both during her lifetime and after her death: Haki R. Madhubuti credited Rogers with "waking up" men in the black liberation movement about women's rights and called her a "public intellectual" before the term came into use (Kalsnes). As of 2011, Rodgers's books all remained out of print. At the same time, such widely read collections as the *Norton Anthology of African American Literature* and the Poetry Foundation's website featured her poems, introducing her to audiences born long after the heyday of the Black Arts Movement.

FURTHER READING
Rodgers, Carolyn M., "Black Poetry—Where It's At," *Black Digest/Negro World* (Sept. 1969).
Kalsnes, Lynette. "Learn More about the Late Poet Carolyn Rodgers." Interview with Haki R. Madhubuti. 14 Apr. 2010. Accessed at http://www.wbez.org/story/unfiltered-learn-more-about-late-poet-carolyn-rodgers#.
Smith, Jessie Carney. *Notable Black American Women, Book II* (1996).
University of Illinois: Modern American Poetry: Carolyn M. Rodgers. http://www.english.illinois.edu/maps/poets/m_r/rodgers/rodgers.htm.
University of Minnesota: Voices from the Gaps: Carolyn M. Rodgers. http://voices.cla.umn.edu/artistpages/rodgers_carolyn.php.
Obituary: *Chicago Tribune*, 13 Apr. 2010.

MARY KRANE DERR

Rodgers, Nile, Jr. (19 Sept. 1952–), guitarist, producer, and recording artist, was born in New York City to Beverley Goodman, a high school student, and Nile Rodgers, a professional musician. Made a ward of the court, Rodgers attended a variety of schools in New York and California. Influenced by the Beatles, Rodgers learned to play guitar, occasionally performing in New York City with his band New World Rising. In 1968 he joined and soon became a subsection leader of the short-lived lower Manhattan branch of the Black Panther Party while also attending classes at Juilliard and the Manhattan School of Music. After New World Rising split, Rodgers briefly performed with the touring band from Sesame Street before landing regular employment at the Harlem Apollo, where he played for a variety of acts including ARETHA FRANKLIN, Funkadelic, and BEN E. KING. Upon a chance meeting at a pick-up gig, Rodgers established a life-long friendship and songwriting partnership with the bassist Bernard Edwards. They shortly formed the Big Apple Band and began performing around New York.

By 1977 the Big Apple Band, which included Tony Thompson on drums, had mutated into Chic. In that year they produced and shopped around a demo, "Dance, Dance, Dance (Yowsah, Yowsah, Yowsah)," with little success. Atlantic Records, however, was intrigued and signed the group and released the song as a single. It eventually sold over one million copies and was nominated for a Grammy Award. An ironic commentary on the exploitation of endurance dancers inspired by the 1969 film *They Shoot Horses Don't They?*, "Dance, Dance, Dance" inspired listeners to focus instead on other elements of the song that in time became Chic trademarks: orchestrated strings, closely harmonized vocals from the Chic Choir (LUTHER VANDROSS, Norma Jean Wright, Alfa Anderson, Diva Gray, and David Lasley) and most notably, Edwards's bass playing which combined with Rodgers's choppy rhythm guitar to produce a unique and irresistible groove. After the exodus of several members, Chic's personnel stabilized with Rodgers, Edwards, Thompson, Anderson, and the vocalist Luci Martin. This core was augmented by numerous other vocalists, keyboard players, percussionists, and a string section dubbed the Chic Strings. Chic's next five singles—"Everybody Dance" (1977) "Le Freak" (1978; the best-selling single in Atlantic Records history), "I Want Your Love" (1979) and "Good Times" (1979)—cemented Chic's reputation as the finest pop band of the late 1970s.

The *C'est Chic* (1978) and *Risque* (1979) albums were also critical and commercial successes. At a time when many considered disco to be a transient and superficial phenomenon, Chic was a critical success whose music incorporated serious themes and made important artistic statements.

Though four additional albums—*Real People* (1980), *Take It Off* (1981), *Tongue In Chic* (1982), and *Believer* (1983)—met with decreasing critical and commercial success, declining fortunes combined with internal tensions led to the breakup of the band. Chic, however, was more than just a band. Rodgers and Edwards's skill in the studio put them in demand as producers. Chic Organization productions for Sister Sledge (*We Are Family*—the sisters' most successful album and a Chic album in all but name) and DIANA ROSS (*Diana* also replicated the band) were hugely successful. After the split Rodgers produced David Bowie's *Let's Dance* (Bowie's biggest-selling album) and Madonna's *Like A Virgin* (her breakthrough album). He also provided guitar for countless projects and released two albums on his own. By the 1990s, critics and music historians were reevaluating Chic's reputation. This renaissance of sorts enabled Rodgers to reunite with Edwards, although their ensuring album, *Chic-ism* (1992), did not attain commercial success. Further collaborations never took place. Edwards died in 1996, following a triumphant concert in Japan.

In 1998 Rodgers established Sumthing Distribution which became the largest African American–owned music label distribution company in the United States. Four years later he founded the *We Are Family* Foundation, a charity to promote multiculturalism and support victims of intolerance. He received a lifetime achievement award from the National Association of Recording Arts and Sciences, and continued into the new century to record and produce, and occasionally perform as Chic on the revival circuit.

Chic's crossover success and association with disco did not sit well with many pop music critics, and led to the denigration of its legacy. Rodgers's readiness to work within the white establishment also alienated writers of rhythm and blues. Yet he represented one half of the most successful and influential African American songwriting and producing partnership of the post-soul era. Chic emerged at a time when the great funk bands of the 1970s were collapsing under their own weight, and offered a sleek and regimented contrast to the multiple personalities of groups such as Parliament-Funkadelic. Many contemporaries associated the production sheen that Rodgers and Edwards placed over their tracks with the sterility and superficiality of commercial disco, ignoring the similarities between Rodgers's guitar and that of Motown's guitarists or JB's guitarists such as Jimmy "Chank" Nolen. Tired of repeated soloing and improvisation that marked much of the period's rhythm-and-blues, Rodgers kept his sound focused on the melody and groove, ceding the spotlight to Edwards's bass. Chic's spartan rhythms were often interpreted as a sanitized version of the funk, but such an interpretation underestimated Rodgers and Edwards's influence on the sparse sound of 1980s funk that highlighted the work of Cameo, RICK JAMES, and PRINCE. Critics who condemned Chic's sharp, cosmopolitan image as a throwback to the conformist look of early soul groups and singers similarly missed Chic's prediction of future tastes.

During the 1990s, house music's reliance on disco for inspiration and occasional melody resulted in the frequent sampling of old Chic grooves. Perhaps more significantly, the rhythm track from "Good Times" was rerecorded as the backing track for the Sugarhill Gang's "Rapper's Delight" (1979). The first worldwide rap smash hit, and the record which introduced hip hop to a wide audience, would not have existed without Chic. Most of all, Chic's sound retained a vitality and a sophistication which far outlasted disco. Its best work deserved comparison with that of Motown, Stax, and P-Funk, and Rodgers surely ranked as one of African American music's great producers and guitarists.

FURTHER READING

Easlea, Daryl. *Everybody Dance: Chic and the Politics of Disco* (2004).

JOE STREET

Rodrigues, Jan (Juan) (c. 1580–c. 1630), sailor and trader, was born in Santo Domingo (Dominican Republic), probably the son of an Afro-Caribbean mother and a European father. Like other Atlantic Creoles—persons of African descent whose names suggest that they had long experience in the western Atlantic world—Rodrigues was among those navigators, traders, pirates, and fishermen who traversed the Atlantic as free men, before and during the slavery era of the Americas. Knowledgeable in the many languages, laws, religions, and trading etiquettes of the larger Atlantic world, their presence suggests the porous character of racial lines in the sixteenth and seventeenth centuries, which allowed people of African descent to be employed and even rise to positions of authority in a world suffused with African slavery. Rodrigues arrived in the northeastern territory of North America following the arrival of at least two other free black men, including Esteban Gomez and MATHIEU DA COSTA.

In April 1525 the explorer Gomez sailed a Spanish ship into the deep bay that secluded Manhattan Island from the Atlantic, which Giovanni da Verrazano had claimed for France in the year before. Gomez sailed several miles upriver before satisfying himself that he had not discovered the fabled Northwest Passage to the "spice islands" of Asia. Completing the voyage, Gomez returned to Spain with thirty-seven natives who were sold as slaves. Further north, in what is now the Lake Champlain region in upstate New York, Da Costa arrived with French explorers in 1603. Da Costa came to know the region well enough to serve as both a guide and French-Indian translator. Soon after Da Costa's arrival, freeman Rodrigues became associated with Dutch exploration of the region.

After Henry Hudson's 1609 exploration of the river that now bears his name, Dutch ships began to frequent the region to trade with the indigenous peoples. In 1613 Dutch sea captain Thijs Volchertz Mossel sailed the *Jonge Tobias* from the West Indies to Hudson's Bay, anchoring off Manhattan Island. There he left Jan Rodrigues to trade with Native Americans.

What happened thereafter—and what we know most about Rodrigues—is conveyed mainly through a series of lawsuits between Mossel and Dutch traders, including captains Adrian Block and Hendrick Christiaensen, both of whom had encountered Rodrigues. When Block, who was mapping Long Island Sound and trading with Native Americans, returned to Holland, he found himself being sued by Mossel, who claimed Block violated his exclusive trading rights. Key to the suit was the freedom status of Rodrigues. Was he a slave, owned by Mossel, or residing on Manhattan Island as a free man doing business on his own?

Block asserted that Rodrigues was a free man, and not a servant or an employee as Mossel claimed. Block insisted that Mossel did not enjoy a trade monopoly on the island, pointing to the presence of Rodrigues, who lived alone and traded independently. Block's defense rested on the argument that Rodrigues was a "free man," who was acting on his own authority and not on behalf of Mossel's alleged monopoly.

Christiaensen supported Block. He declared that Rodrigues had boarded his vessel and presented himself as a free man. Rodrigues even offered to work for Christiaensen, who hired him as a translator to facilitate trade with the Natives.

In April 1614 Mossel returned to North America. Sailing his new ship, the *Nachtegael*, into the Hudson, the truth of the relationship between Mossel and Rodrigues became apparent, along with evidence that Rodrigues was Manhattan's first non-Native American merchant. Sighting the *Nachtegael*, Rodrigues fired his musket at the ship, and its crew returned fire. Brandishing torches, muskets, and swords, Mossel's crew chased the "black rascal" and briefly apprehended him. Though wounded, Rodrigues took a sword away from one of his pursuers and escaped. Later he found refuge with Christiaensen's crew, who took him aboard their boat and sheltered him.

Mossel claimed that Rodrigues's actions proved that he was a renegade servant or employee, and not free. However, the court ruled against Mossel, thus finding implicitly that Rodrigues was a free man.

The written record of Rodrigues, who did not travel to Amsterdam for the proceedings, apparently ended in the Dutch court. Though it is clear that Rodrigues was the sole nonnative resident of Manhattan for several months, and possibly for long stretches of time during the second decade of the seventeenth century, documentation of Rodrigues's entire length of stay is wanting.

By some accounts Rodrigues fathered children with one or more Native American women. His trading post did well, as his inventory, bolstered with axes, kettles, and beads from Christiaensen's supply, was enticing to the natives who valued highly the sturdier metalware for hunting or warfare. Early traders like Rodrigues had learned the profitability of trading with the Indians their own currency, *sewan*. Made from a dark purple or black shell found along the coast of Long Island, the Dutch purchased sewan (and the lesser valued white shells known as *wampum*) at advantageous prices and then used it as currency to trade with the natives. But, perhaps most striking or relevant about the Rodrigues saga was his proclamation of himself as a free man, and its acceptance by Europeans.

Rodrigues may have been in the colony when the Dutch West Indies Company (DWIC) arrived in Manhattan in 1625. The DWIC, whose profits were chiefly from commerce derived from slave labor and the slave trade in the Atlantic colonies, was then pursuing its interest in the fur trade, which had been cultivated by early traders like Rodrigues.

FURTHER READING

Berlin, Ira, and Leslie Harris, eds. *Slavery In New York* (2005).

Burrows, Edwin G., and Mike Wallace. *Gotham: A History of New York City to 1898* (1999).

Hart, Simon. *The Prehistory of the New Netherland Company* (1959).

Hodges, Graham Russell. *Root and Branch: African Americans in New York and East New Jersey, 1613–1863* (1999).

CHRISTOPHER PAUL MOORE

Rodríguez, Arsenio (30 Aug. 1911–30 Dec. 1970), composer, bandleader, and musician, was born Ignacio Arsenio Travieso Scull in Güira de Macuriges, Cuba, son of Dorotea Rodríguez Scull and Bonifacio Travieso. By the time Rodríguez was four years old his family had moved to Güines in the south of Cuba. Several years after moving to Güines, he lost his eyesight after being kicked in the head by a mule. Having no access to a formal education after his accident, Rodríguez immersed himself in the music of rural central Cuba, particularly African-derived secular and sacred traditions. He learned to play the *tres*, a Cuban folk guitar which would become his main instrument, in addition to percussion and, later, the double bass. He began his professional music career soon after 1926 when his family moved to Havana.

While playing and leading local *son* groups, Arsenio also began to compose his earliest songs, many of which were set in the *afrocubano* style. His most famous *afrocubano* from this period is "Bruca maniguá" which was first recorded in 1937 by Miguelito Valdés who was accompanied by the internationally-popular Orquesta Casino de la Playa. It was later recorded by Xavier Cugat. In these songs Rodríguez used conventional black character types of the Cuban popular theater of the late nineteenth and early twentieth centuries and set the texts in "Africanized" Spanish, commonly referred to as *bozal* speech. In many instances the songs' black protagonists criticized and confronted their oppressors, thereby breaking with the stereotyped and racist character types more familiar to Cuban audiences. He also inserted Congolese words and proverbs from the Palo religion into these characters' *bozal* speech, reflecting a more accurate representation of nineteenth-century African speech in Cuba than its strictly parodied form in the Cuban popular theater.

Rodríguez began his own recording career in 1940 with his group Arsenio Rodríguez y Su Conjunto. By 1942 he popularized the new *conjunto* ensemble by adding a second trumpet, piano, and conga drums to what had been the conventional Cuban *son* septet (tres, guitar, bongos, two vocalists doubling on clave and maracas, bass, and one trumpet). He also established a transformational style of Cuban *son* music known as "son montuno," which emphasized the more syncopated elements of rural *son* dance music but arranged for his new *conjunto* format. Rodríguez's *conjunto* and *son montuno* style would play a key role in the subsequent developments of mambo, *pachanga, boogaloo*, and salsa. His *conjunto's* popularity reached its apex throughout Cuba by the mid-1940s, but especially among the black working class of Havana. The crystallization of his style was directly tied to a broader flowering of black working-class social clubs whose social events were organized around the performance of music and dance. Between 1950 and 1952 Rodríguez made frequent trips to New York City, where he organized another *conjunto*, Arsenio Rodríguez y Su Conjunto de Estrellas, which was made up of mostly Cuban and Puerto Rican musicians of color. This group recorded for RCA Victor as well as local independent record companies, including Spanish Music Center and Seeco. As in Havana Rodríguez composed and recorded songs dedicated to specific neighborhoods (barrios) where he lived and performed in New York City. This included "Como se goza en el Barrio" (El Barrio Is a Lot of Fun) and "La gente del Bronx" (The People of the Bronx). He decided to stay in New York City for personal reasons—his brother, conga player, and life-time guide Israel "Kiki" had served a prison sentence in Havana for manslaughter and feared reprisals from the victim's family—and because of deteriorating social and political conditions in Cuba.

Through the first half of the 1950s he continued to compose, record, and lead his *conjunto*, which performed regularly in New York City's most prominent Latin music dance halls alongside internationally popular mambo big bands such as those led by Dámaso Pérez Prado, Ernesto "Tito" Puente, Pablo "Tito" Rodríguez, and Frank "Machito" Grillo. However, Rodríguez found international recognition for his role in the development of the mambo elusive. Nevertheless, as in Havana, his *conjunto* remained active and had a significant impact upon the local musical life of the Puerto Rican and Cuban communities in East Harlem and the South Bronx. In 1960 his *conjunto* toured extensively throughout Puerto Rico and performed in Curaçao and Aruba, where his *conjunto* and *son montuno* style had been extremely popular since the 1940s.

By the early 1960s a younger generation of musicians and entrepreneurs emerged in New York City's Latin dance music milieu to popularize *pachanga* and, later, salsa. Many of these musicians drew extensively from Rodríguez's recorded repertoire and *son montuno* style. Yet his *conjunto*, most of whose members were now middle-aged, performed sparingly. In late 1964 he moved to Los Angeles, where he attempted to create a niche for himself with a new *conjunto*, which consisted of mostly Cuban, Puerto Rican, and Mexican musicians. But once again his performances were largely relegated to peripheral locales, especially East Los Angeles. In 1966 he returned to New York City and reformed his *conjunto* as the nascent salsa industry was set to recast much of the Cuban *conjunto* music of the 1940s and 1950s, including Rodríguez's recordings, into new instrumental formations. However, he continued to be conspicuously overlooked by early salsa promoters and record producers. His alienation from the large community of Cuban political exiles in Miami and the Northeast—owing to existing racial tensions and his own suspicion of all Cuban political orientations—accounted in part for his career's demise. In July 1969 BERNICE REAGON, founding member of the Freedom Singers and Sweet Honey in the Rock, invited Rodríguez to perform at the Festival of American Folklife in Washington, D.C., in a program titled "Black Music through Languages of the New World." He then returned to Los Angeles, where he continued to perform until his death the following year.

Throughout his career Rodríguez expressed in his lyrics an Afro-diasporic perspective on issues of race and black identity. He celebrated the independence movements from colonial rule in Africa and decried the persistence of racism throughout the Americas. For instance, while living in New York City in the early 1960s, he composed and recorded "La democracia" ("Democracy") and "Vaya pa'l monte" ("Go to the Mountain"), in which he reflected on the continued injustices that blacks throughout the Americas suffered. He made no distinctions in the plight of black people based on cultural, national, or historical boundaries, as he eloquently stated in "Aquí como allá" ("It's the Same Here As It Is Over There"). In "Yo nací del África" ("I Was Born of Africa") he rejected his Spanish surnames while speculating about his true African name and ethnicity. He also expressed pride in his Cuban identity as well as his desire for peace and national reconciliation in Cuba. Like Rodríguez, Cuba's national poet Nicolás Guillén and other black Cuban intellectuals of the 1930s and 1940s were pro-Cuban and anti-imperialist. They also condemned racism as experienced among blacks everywhere. But while Guillén, in particular, became an ardent communist, ultimately attributing the suffering of blacks to capitalism, Rodríguez remained nonpartisan in Cuban politics. In effect Rodríguez affirmed his African heritage and Cuban identity as coexistent yet distinct, rather than as a *mestizaje* or synthesis as, for example, Guillén expressed in many of his poems. In short, Rodríguez projected an empowered sense of double consciousness that was antagonistic to the tenets of *mestizaje* and Latin America's myth of racial brotherhood and equality.

FURTHER READING
García, David F. *Arsenio Rodríguez and the Transnational Flows of Latin Popular Music* (2006)
DAVID F. GARCÍA

Rogan, Bullet (28 July 1889–4 Mar. 1967), Negro League baseball player and manager, known also as "Bullet Joe," was born Wilber Rogan in Oklahoma City, Oklahoma, the son of Richard Rogan and Mary (maiden name unknown). While Wilber (whose first name is often misspelled as "Wilbur") was in his teens, the Rogan family moved to Kansas City, Kansas, where Wilber dropped out of high school to play for the semiprofessional Kansas City Giants, who won fifty-four consecutive games against local and semiprofessional competition in 1909. Two years later Rogan enlisted in the U.S. Army.

The army encouraged its four segregated black regiments (the Ninth and Tenth Cavalry and the Twenty-fourth and Twenty-fifth Infantry) to make up successful athletic teams to bolster morale. Superior black athletes were diligently recruited to form some of the strongest baseball teams in the service, winning many tournaments that included white regimental teams. Rogan played three years for the Twenty-fourth Infantry Regiment in the Philippines, then reenlisted in the Twenty-fifth Infantry Regiment, where he played at Honolulu's Schofield Barracks. In 1918 the Twenty-fifth was transferred to Camp Stephen D. Little in Nogales, Arizona, on the Mexican border, where Rogan completed his military career.

Rogan, who was called "Cap" in the army, was the most storied player on the great Twenty-fifth Infantry team known as the "Wreckers." Occasionally they played white civilian teams, even major leaguers. When John J. McGraw's New York Giants played the Twenty-fifth in Hawaii during a world tour, he praised Rogan as a pitcher with major league ability. Casey Stengel was so impressed after facing Rogan in Arizona during a barnstorming tour that when Stengel returned to Kansas City he notified J. L. Wilkinson, who was then forming the Monarchs. In July 1920 Rogan and five teammates left the army and joined the nascent Negro National League (NNL). With so many veterans of the Twenty-fifth Infantry, the Monarchs in their early years were often called "the army team."

Rogan became the heart and soul of the Kansas City Monarchs—a perennial powerhouse of the Negro leagues in the 1920s and 1930s—their predominant pitcher, their most powerful hitter, and (for seven years) their manager. His imposing career is even more remarkable considering that when he joined the Monarchs in 1920 he was already thirty-one years old, having spent ten prime years playing in the obscurity of military outposts.

The Monarchs won NNL championships in 1923, 1924, 1925, and 1929 and lost a play-off to the Chicago American Giants in 1926, which was Rogan's first year as manager. Rogan's brilliance as a pitcher obscures his talent as an all-around player. He was the finest fielding pitcher in the Negro leagues, and when not pitching he skillfully played center field. His offensive accomplishments alone were remarkable during the Monarchs' glory years. At five feet nine inches tall and 175 pounds, Rogan, who hit and threw right-handed, batted fourth. Standing deep in the batter's box and wielding an uncommonly heavy bat, he was productive in key situations. His regular-season batting average through the 1920s was .340, while in championship play he hit a remarkable .410. In twenty-five recorded exhibition games against major league pitching he hit .329.

But it was on the mound that Rogan attained status as a legend. He was called "Bullet" and later "Bullet Joe" because of a blazing fastball, which he threw from a side-winding, short-arm delivery. Teammate Chet Brewer recalled that Rogan's curveball was faster than most pitchers' fastballs. And he was an innovator. His off-speed pitch was a palm ball, which Brewer credited him with inventing. He threw without a wind-up, a then-unusual technique that Stengel later taught pitchers when he managed the New York Yankees. From 1920 to 1930 Rogan won 106 and lost 44 regular season games against Negro League competition, and he had an 8–3 record in championship play. Many contemporaries

regarded him as the greatest pitcher they ever saw, and in overall versatility MARTIN DIHIGO was his only equal in Negro League ball.

Rogan's military bearing as manager probably caused him to be disliked by some of his players. Yet others regarded him as easygoing and an effective instructor. He retired from baseball in 1938 and worked for the U.S. Postal Service for twenty years, occasionally umpiring Monarchs' games until 1946. He spent his last years on a farm near a lake with his wife, Kathryn, whom he married in 1922. He died in Kansas City, Missouri, survived by a son, Wilbur, and a daughter, Jean.

FURTHER READING

Bruce, Janet. *The Kansas City Monarchs: Champions of Black Baseball* (1985).
Holway, John. *Bullet Joe and the Monarchs* (1984).
Peterson, Robert. *Only the Ball Was White* (1970).
Riley, James A. *The All-Time All-Stars of Black Baseball* (1983).

This entry is taken from the *American National Biography* and is published here with the permission of the American Council of Learned Societies.

JERRY MALLOY

Rogers, Charles Calvin (6 Sept. 1929–21 Sept. 1990), Korean and Vietnam War army officer and Medal of Honor recipient, was born in Claremont, West Virginia, the son of West Virginia natives Clyde Rogers Sr. and his wife Helen. While Charles Rogers's father supported his family by working as a coal miner, his son would have the opportunity to rise further. After graduating from high school, Rogers attended West Virginia State College, earning a B.A. in Mathematics. Interestingly, this hard working and practical young man also had a spiritual side and, despite his studies, had a desire to be a minister. However, his ministering career was soon put on hold and would not become a reality until years later after his retirement from the army.

While attending college, Charles Rogers was a member of the Reserve Officer Training Corps (ROTC), and upon graduating he subsequently gained an officer's commission when he joined the army at Institute, West Virginia, in June 1951. Rogers subsequently served during the Korean War, though the details of his early career are unknown. During the course of his thirty-year-plus military career, Rogers graduated from the Army Command and General Staff College and the Army War College. He would also gain an M.S. in Vocational and Educational Guidance from Shippensburg State

College in Pennsylvania. By 1968 Charles Rogers had risen to the rank of Lieutenant Colonel and was in command of 1st Battalion, 5th Artillery, 1st Infantry Division.

The service of African American officers in the Vietnam War, men like Rogers, RILEY PITTS, and RUPPERT SARGENT, was a true milestone in the history of the U.S. Army. While black officers had served in the army since the days of the Spanish American War, their numbers were always small and until the Korean War they served solely in segregated units and only commanded soldiers of color. Indeed, the issue of black officers giving commands to white soldiers was something that the army, and all branches of the U.S. military, had a hard time accepting for many years; this attitude was reflective of the overall racial conditions then prevailing throughout the country. Capable and brave black officers serving during World War II, men such as JOHN FOX and CHARLES THOMAS, helped pave the way for change, but it was not until the Vietnam War that these changes became effective in full force. To be sure, racial issues in the U.S. military establishment would not disappear almost completely until after the end of the Vietnam War, but the one thing that was no longer in question was the competence and bravery of African American soldiers, whether officer or enlisted man.

On the morning of 1 November 1968 Lieutenant Colonel Charles Rogers's 1st Battalion, 5th Artillery was serving in defense of a forward fire support base at the Fishhook in Vietnam, near the Cambodian border, when it came under attack from heavy mortar, rocket, and rocket-propelled grenade fire, as well as enemy soldiers that succeeded in penetrating the bases' outer perimeter with Bangalore torpedoes. Rogers quickly moved to the area under assault and rallied his soldiers to man their field pieces and subsequently directed their artillery fire on the enemy. Though wounded by an incoming round, Rogers quickly recovered and led a small counterattack against enemy units that had breached their positions. He was wounded again during this action, but refused medical attention and continued to lead his men by reforming and organizing their defensive positions. When another enemy ground attack was launched, Rogers directed artillery fire and led yet another counterattack that rallied his men. During this time, Lieutenant Colonel Rogers darted from position to position amid a hail of fire and directed and encouraged his men. When another enemy assault was launched, Rogers moved his men to the area

under fire and directed artillery fire; when one gun fell silent due to heavy casualties among its crew, Rogers joined the crew and brought the gun back into action. He was then badly wounded by fragments from a mortar round that exploded near his position. Even though Rogers was out of the fight physically, he still gave encouragement and direction to his men, and his actions ultimately led his men to successfully defend their base in the face of a superior enemy force. For his actions, Lieutenant Colonel Charles Rogers was subsequently awarded the Medal of Honor, which was presented to him by President Richard Nixon at a White House ceremony on 14 May 1970. Rogers has the distinction of being the highest-ranking African American to ever win the Medal of Honor.

After recovering from his wounds, Charles Rogers would continue to serve his country, earning many honors, including the Legion of Merit, the Distinguished Flying Cross, the Bronze Star, the Air Medal with nine oak leaf clusters, the Army Commendation Medal with two oak leaf clusters, and a number of others. He eventually rose to the rank of major general and retired from the service on 1 January 1984. A resident of Munich, Germany, Charles Rogers soon went on to become an ordained Baptist minister, serving American soldiers that were stationed in Europe. After just a few short years of retirement, Rogers died of cancer; his remains were interred at Arlington National Cemetery, Arlington, Virginia.

FURTHER READING

Hanna, Charles W. *African American Recipients of the Medal of Honor* (2002).

GLENN ALLEN KNOBLOCK

Rogers, Elymas Payson (10 Feb. 1815–20 Jan. 1861), clergyman, poet, and missionary, was born in Madison, Connecticut, the son of Abel Rogers and Chloe Ladue, farmers. His father, the son of an African slave who had survived a shipwreck off the coast of Connecticut, was raised as family by the Reverend Jonathan Todd, from whom he eventually inherited the farmland on which he made his living. In the early 1830s Rogers left for Hartford, Connecticut, where he attended school and worked for his board in the home of a Major Caldwell. His first formal church affiliation was established in 1833 as a communicant of the Hartford Talcott Street congregation.

In 1835 Rogers went to Peterboro, New York, to study for the ministry at a school established by the philanthropist-reformer Gerrit Smith. The following year, to pay for his studies, he began teaching at the recommendation of Smith in a public school for black children in Rochester, New York, where he continued for five years. In the spring of 1837 he enrolled at Oneida Institute in Whitesboro, New York, while continuing to teach. JERMAIN WESLEY LOGUEN, one of Rogers's students, who also went on to study at Oneida, became a prominent abolitionist and African Methodist Episcopal (AME) bishop. Rogers later wrote a poem, "Loguen's Position," to denounce the evils of slavery and affirm the legitimacy of Loguen's angry abolitionist stance.

Immediately after his graduation from Oneida in 1841 Rogers became principal of the Trenton, New Jersey, public school for black children. That same year he married Harriet E. Sherman, and they settled in Trenton where Rogers pursued his career by teaching and studying theology. On 7 February 1844 he was licensed by the New Brunswick Presbytery and received full ordination to the ministry one year later. His first ministerial position was as pastor of the Witherspoon Street Church in Princeton, New Jersey, where he served for two years.

Rogers sought and obtained membership in the Newark Presbytery on 20 October 1846, when he accepted the pastorate at the Plane Street Church in Newark, New Jersey. The next fourteen years were among the most fruitful of his career. By 1857 the church had grown from 23 to 140 communicants and 130 Sabbath scholars. It was one of only two churches described as "prosperous" in the *Minutes* of the 1857 denominational meeting. Rogers served as moderator of the 1856 Presbyterian and Congregational Convention; the following year in Philadelphia, he delivered the opening sermon of the denominational meeting in Philadelphia, which passed a resolution denouncing the U.S. Supreme Court's decision in the DRED SCOTT case and praising the two dissenting justices.

Rogers's abolitionist fervor is reflected in two published satires: "A Poem on the Fugitive Slave Law" (1855) and "The Repeal of the Missouri Compromise Considered" (1856). The former is an erudite exposition on law written in octosyllabic couplets. It argues that a higher law should take precedence over man-made rules advocated by such men as Blackstone, Witherspoon, and Cicero, when such rules violate human rights. The latter, a longer 925-line poem, also in octosyllabic couplets, is a dialogue between "Freedom" and "Slavery." In it he argues that national greed and expedience

had motivated both legislation and popular opinion regarding slavery. Rogers's satires are unusual in antebellum black poetry for their erudition, wit, and courageous expression of moral indignation.

Rogers's active membership in the African Civilization Society led eventually to the fulfillment, albeit brief, of his dream to be a missionary in Africa. On 5 November 1860 he sailed from New York to Freetown, Sierra Leone. He visited Monrovia, Bassa, Sinoe, and Cape Palmas, where he died of fever and heart disease. His early death cut short a career that he had hoped would extend both the gospel of Christ and civilized life to much of Africa.

FURTHER READING
Rogers's letters are held in the American Missionary Association Archives, Amistad Research Center, New Orleans, Louisiana.
Brown, William Wells. *The Black Man, His Antecedents, His Genius, and His Achievements* (1863).
Sherman, Joan R. *Afro-Americans of the Nineteenth Century* (1974).
Wilson, Joseph M. *The Presbyterian Historical Almanac ... for 1862*, vol. 4 (1862).
This entry is taken from the *American National Biography* and is published here with the permission of the American Council of Learned Societies.

MARILYN DEMAREST BUTTON

Rogers, Jimmy (3 June 1924–19 Dec. 1997), blues singer, musician, and songwriter, was born James A. Lane to Grozie Lane in Ruleville, Mississippi. His stepfather, Henry Rogers, was killed in Atlanta shortly after moving his family there in 1926. His mother moved the family back to the Delta where Jimmy was taken in by his maternal grandmother, Leanna Jackson. The family moved frequently over the years and lived in Memphis and West Memphis, Tennessee, and Helena, Arkansas, and back to Mississippi in the mid-1930s to the town of Vance.

Jimmy was strongly attracted to music although there were no musicians in his family. He built himself a diddley bow, which is a length of wire nailed to the side of a barn and fretted with a bottle or can. He became rather accomplished on harmonica, which was both inexpensive and portable, and sometimes played with three or four other harmonica players including Snooky Pryor. He learned guitar from Arthur Johnson near Greenwood, Mississippi, and met HOUND DOG TAYLOR, who played slide guitar. He was also influenced by solo artist Houston Stackhouse. Jimmy's grandmother was a devout Christian woman who frowned on his playing music. He practiced on other people's guitars and at around eighteen years of age his grandmother relented when he obtained his own instrument, deciding to devote himself to music.

Jimmy's family lived in St. Louis for a few years and moved back to Mississippi in 1938. Jimmy would rush home every day to listen to the King Biscuit Hour broadcast on KFFA where RICE MILLER (SONNY BOY WILLIAMSON II) and his band would play at noon. Many younger musicians gravitated to Helena, Arkansas, because of KFFA's influence, and a strong music scene developed there. Jimmy was profoundly influenced and inspired by Miller and his accompanists, especially guitarists JOE WILLIE WILKINS and ROBERT LOCKWOOD JR. Jimmy would follow Miller and his band to their engagements, hoping to sit in. He did eventually get his chance. He also met and accompanied ROBERT NIGHTHAWK, who was one of the most accomplished slide guitarists in the Delta and influenced the young MUDDY WATERS. In addition, Jimmy first met harmonica player LITTLE WALTER JACOBS in Helena. Jacobs was fourteen years old and he too was following Rice Miller. Jacobs would also sit in with the band, usually when Miller gambled.

Jimmy's family had visited Chicago several times before he settled there in the mid-1940s. After briefly living with his uncle, he got his own apartment on the West Side near Maxwell Street. He turned professional in Chicago and had already adopted his stepfather's surname.

Rogers had been playing parties with guitarist Blue Smitty (Claude Smith from Arkansas) while working at the Sonora Radio and Cabinet Co. A fellow employee introduced them to Muddy Waters. Jimmy's experience backing Robert Nighthawk and Rice Miller served him in good stead. He understood Waters's music and Waters found a musical soul mate in Rogers. They started spending hours together, jamming and rehearsing. At first, Rogers played harmonica with Smith and Waters on guitars.

The original first wave of Chicago blues artists like JOHN LEE (SONNY BOY) WILLIAMSON, TAMPA RED, and BIG BILL BROONZY were in the autumn of their years. The young Delta migrants were issuing forth a harsher, more modern style. They put DeArmond pickups on their acoustic guitars and used amplifiers not only to be heard but for the resulting distortion from driving the amps so hard. This set the stage for rock and roll several years later.

Waters had a car and John Lee (Sonny Boy) Williamson would invite him, Rogers, and Smith to back him up on gigs in Gary, Indiana. Invariably, Williamson would get drunk and Rogers would pick up the harmonica. Smith eventually moved on and with the help of pianist Sunnyland Slim, Waters recorded a string of singles for Aristocrat Records, which soon became Chess Records. He was accompanied by Big Crawford on bass, and the records were an immediate sensation. By this time, Waters, Rogers, and guitarist and drummer Baby Face Leroy Foster were tearing it up in blues clubs all over Chicago.

Maxwell Street was an open bazaar on Sundays and many bluesmen would play for change along the marketplace. Rogers was awakened one morning by the harmonica voicings of Little Walter Jacobs and went down to see who it was. Rogers knew brilliance when he heard it and after introducing Jacobs to Waters, turned over the harp chores to Jacobs and took over second guitar. Together, Rogers and Waters helped Jacobs mature his style, which would change the way blues harp was played. This unit became the core of Waters's band for years and changed music as we know it. They became unofficially known as the Headhunters and would go from club to club and humble any blues act in their path.

Rogers's second guitar weaved in, out, and around the songs creating a foundation that allowed Waters's resonant voice and slide guitar to shine and Jacobs's innovative amplified harmonica to fairly crackle and explode. The importance of Rogers's supporting guitar, alternating between bass lines, sophisticated chording, and tasteful single-note leads cannot be overstated. Having lived in so many cities, Rogers could handle whatever style came his way. The power of Waters's voice and Jacobs's saxophone-like harmonica most likely would not have been fully harnessed were it not for Jimmy Rogers's sympathetic, almost telepathic, accompaniment.

In 1950 the group supported Rogers on his first single "That's Alright," backed with "Ludella." Rogers's voice was smoother and his words more articulate than in Waters's style of singing. Ironically, it was the first time Waters's performing band was captured on record. Because of his previous success, Leonard Chess, the company's president, stubbornly insisted that Waters stick with the spare sound of only Big Crawford on bass. After Waters surreptitiously recorded his band on another label, Chess finally allowed the band to accompany Waters in the studio. This all-star unit, which came to include OTIS SPANN on piano and a few different drummers, recorded together from 1951 to 1956. "Long Distance Call," "I Just Want to Make Love to You," "Hoochie Coochie Man," "I'm Ready," and "Got My Mojo Working" are just some of the classics this band recorded that helped define Chicago blues and served as an archetype for modern blues and rock bands.

Rogers continued to record other compositions, such as "Money, Marbles and Chalk" and "Chicago Bound," but grew increasingly frustrated with Chess Records because many of his recordings would languish unreleased for years. In 1956 he recorded "Walkin' by Myself," his biggest hit ever, charting nationally in the R&B category. The song featured a strong harmonica solo from BIG WALTER HORTON. Rogers left Waters's band that same year. Rock and roll had captured the nation's fancy and two of Rogers's label mates, BO DIDDLEY and CHUCK BERRY, were adding to the fray. Blues musicians found it difficult to sell records and get gigs the way they had before the onset of rock and roll.

Rogers played with his own group around Chicago and was in demand as a session player, having recorded with MEMPHIS MINNIE, T-BONE WALKER, Sonny Boy Williamson (Rice Miller), and HOWLIN' WOLF. He became disenchanted with the music business and retired in 1961 to better support his family. Rogers and his wife Dorothy purchased a clothing store that was successful until it burned down in the riots after the assassination of MARTIN LUTHER KING JR. in 1968.

After that financial setback, and at the urging of Muddy Waters and Howlin' Wolf, Rogers got back into the music business and began playing again. In 1972 he recorded his first album, *Gold Tailed Bird* for the Shelter record label. He toured extensively on the blues circuit as well as in Europe. His recordings for the Antone's and Blind Pig record labels were nominated for Grammy Awards and won a W. C. HANDY Award. His son Jimmy D. Lane accompanied his father on guitar and continued a blues career. In the early 1990s Rogers played with both Eric Clapton and the Rolling Stones in London. He played and recorded right until his death from cancer in 1997, at last receiving the recognition he was due for his contribution to the way blues are played.

FURTHER READING
Gordon, Robert. *Can't Be Satisfied, The Life and Times of Muddy Waters* (2002).
"The Jimmy Rogers Interview," *Living Blues Magazine* #14 (Autumn 1973).

Palmer, Robert. *Deep Blues* (1981).
Rowe, Mike. *Chicago Blues* (1981).

DISCOGRAPHY
Chicago Bound (MCA Records).
Chicago's Jimmy Rogers Sings the Blues (Shelter Records).
Leadbetter, Mike, and Neil Slaven. *Blues Records 1943–1970* (1970).
Ludella (Antone's).
Muddy Waters Box Set (MCA Records).
MARK STEVEN MAULUCCI

Rogers, Joel Augustus (6 Sept. 1880–26 Mar. 1966), writer, historian, novelist, photo-anthropologist, and journalist, was born in Negril, Jamaica, to Samuel Rogers and Emily Johnstone. As a child growing up in Jamaica, the British ruling class told Rogers that "black people were inherently inferior and that their sole reason for being was to be servants to white people and the lighter colored-mulattoes" (Rogers, *World's Great Men*, 1). Rogers, a light-skinned black Jamaican, found it very hard to believe such sentiments. Before emigrating to the United States, Rogers served in the British army with the Royal Garrison Artillery at Port Royal, but he was discharged because of a heart murmur.

Shortly after arriving in New York on 23 July 1906, Rogers first experienced American racial discrimination at a small restaurant in Times Square, something he would never forget. He stayed briefly in New York, Boston, and Canada before relocating to Chicago on 4 July 1908. In 1909 he enrolled in the Chicago Art Institute, where he studied commercial art and worked as a Pullman porter during the summers from 1909 to 1919. Rogers tried to enroll at the University of Chicago to take a sociology course, but was denied entry because he did not possess a high school diploma. The irony of Rogers's being denied entry to this prestigious institution is that the distinguished Chicago professors Zonia Baber and George B. Foster were using Rogers's self-published race novel *From "Superman" to Man* (1917) in their classes. In fact, after learning of Rogers's rejection, Foster invited Rogers to lecture in one of his classes.

While living in Chicago, Rogers officially became a naturalized U.S. citizen on 21 February 1918. In 1921 he relocated to Harlem, where he met and befriended HUBERT HARRISON, the Caribbean black radical, and his lifetime friend GEORGE SCHUYLER, a journalist and novelist. During the late 1920s and various times afterward throughout the rest of his life, New

York and later Paris became the two places where Rogers lived while he conducted research at important libraries, art galleries, museums, and cathedrals in America, Europe, and Africa. Although Rogers never received an academic degree, he was respected for his historical and anthropological scholarship in France. In 1930 he was elected to membership in the Paris Society of Anthropology, the oldest anthropological society in the world. During that same year Rogers also gave a paper on "Race Mixing" at the International Congress of Anthropology, which was attended by President Paul Doumer of the French Third Republic. To Rogers's surprise his paper was later published in several French newspapers and in the London *Times*. Rogers was also a member of the American Geographical Society (1945), the Academy of Political Science, the American Association for the Advancement of Science, and the Association Populaire des Amis des Musées of France.

Rogers is mostly known for his writings about history and race, but he is rarely given credit for being an exceptional journalist. He contributed many columns and articles to various African American, Caribbean, and European newspapers and periodicals. His first job as a newspaper reporter was with the *Chicago Enterprise*, which was supported by the controversial mayor William Hale Thompson during the 1910s. When Rogers relocated to New York in 1921, he became a newspaper columnist and reporter for the *Pittsburgh Courier* and the *Amsterdam News* (New York City), and he wrote many essays and commentaries for the *Messenger* magazine during the 1920s. Rogers worked for the *Pittsburgh Courier* from 1921 to 1966. His weekly comic column "Your History," which began in 1934, became a medium for popularizing African and African diaspora history to the masses of African Americans throughout the United States. Not only did Rogers use the "Your History" column to disseminate history, but he also used it to popularize prominent contemporary people of African descent. In 1962 the column's name was changed to "Facts about the Negro." In addition to this column, Rogers also wrote social commentaries in columns entitled "Rogers Says" and "History Shows."

During the 1920s, while traveling overseas, Rogers did observational international journalism in Africa and Europe for the *Pittsburgh Courier* and *New York Amsterdam News*. While living in Paris during the late 1920s, Rogers wrote a short-lived column entitled the "Paris Pepper Pot," which covered race relations in France and how African Americans fared in Paris compared to America.

The "Paris Pepper Pot" was also syndicated in the *Amsterdam News* and the *Chicago Defender*. In 1930 Rogers attended the coronation of emperor Haile Selassie (Ras Tafari) of Ethiopia, yet his most rewarding international journalistic opportunity came when the *Pittsburgh Courier* sent him to Ethiopia in 1935 to cover the Italo-Ethiopia War (1935–1936). Rogers was the only African American journalist sent to Ethiopia during the conflict; he reported firsthand and secondary accounts of the war, and did a rare exclusive interview with Emperor Haile Selassie.

After leaving Ethiopia in 1936, Rogers traveled to Geneva to attend the League of Nations hearings on the Ethiopian war, and he reported through the *Pittsburgh Courier* what the league's Committee of Thirteen proposed to do about the conflict. Within a week Rogers traveled to London and lectured before Sir Percy Vincent, the Lord mayor of London, and other British dignitaries about the crisis confronting Ethiopia. After settling back in New York, Rogers became a major contributor and advisor for the WPA's *Negroes of New York* (1936–1941). As a historian and journalist, Rogers received one of his biggest compliments from the journalist and social critic H. L. Mencken, who paid Rogers five hundred dollars to publish "The Negro in Europe" in the *American Mercury* (May 1930), and in 1945 Mencken wrote Rogers to commend his book *Sex and Race*.

Although Rogers wrote on a variety of issues concerning people of African descent, he is best remembered for his African diasporic biographical sketches about people of African descent, and his writings about miscegenation between blacks and whites from antiquity to the modern era. The amount of archival research Rogers did during his lifetime is remarkable considering the handicaps of not having a research assistant while traveling throughout Europe, Africa, and America. In Europe, Rogers was able to do extensive archival research that many other black and white Americans could not do because he had mastered several languages, including French, German, Portuguese, and Spanish. Furthermore, without philanthropic or institutional support, Rogers self-published his own works that challenged the conventional racist scholarship about people of African descent. His major works include *Sex and Race*, Volumes I–III (1941–1944), *World's Great Men of Color* Volumes I–II (1946–1947), *Nature Knows No Color Line* (1952), and *Africa's Gift to America* (1961).

At the end of his life Rogers was working on a two projects; the first was a book entitled *Color Mania*, which he addressed mainly to white Americans. Rogers intended to write about the historical aversion and phobia of black skin color in America. Since Rogers was a secular humanist he envisioned a world where people of all different ethnic backgrounds could coexist and appreciate what people of African descent had contributed to humanity from antiquity to the modern era. Shortly before Rogers passed away he suffered a stroke while visiting friends and doing research in Washington, D.C. Rogers had spent the entire day at the National Gallery and the Smithsonian Institute, and he had planned on going to the Library of Congress. Ten years before the appearance of Ivan Van Sertima's controversial *They Came Before Columbus* (1976), Rogers had started research on his second project about Africans making contact with the Olmecs in Mexico during the pre-Columbian era. Unfortunately, Rogers never published *Color Mania*, nor did he have the chance to finish his latest research. He died at St. Clare's Hospital in New York.

FURTHER READING

Rogers, J. A. *World's Great Men of Color.* Vol. 1 (1972).

Asukile, Thabiti. "J. A. Rogers: The Scholarship of an Organic Intellectual," in *The Black Scholar.* Vol. 36, Nos. 2–3 (2006).

Asukile, Thabiti. "My Name is J. A. Rogers: The Making of a Black Intellectual (1880–1936)." Ph.D. dissertation, University of California, Berkeley (2007).

Rogers, Helga. *100 Amazing facts about the Negro with Complete Proof: A short cut to the world history of the Negro by J.A. Rogers: as well as additional information by the author and a biographical sketch by Helga Rogers* (1934, 1995).

Turner, W. Burghardt. "J. A. Rogers: Portrait of an Afro-American Historian," in *The Black Scholar.* Vol. 6, No. 5 (1975).

THABITI ASUKILE

Roker, Roxie (28 Aug. 1929–3 Dec. 1995), actress, was born of Bahamian descent to Albert and Bessie Roker in Miami, Florida, and was raised in Brooklyn, New York. A member of the Alpha Kappa Alpha sorority, she graduated from Howard University in 1952 with a BFA in Drama. Following study at England's Shakespeare Institute in Stratford-on-Avon, Roker returned to the United States, where she worked as a secretary in the New York offices of NBC while auditioning for acting roles. Parts in Off-Broadway productions, such as Jean Genet's *The Blacks*, and a position as the host of a local community television show from 1967 to 1968, soon followed.

Roker's career as a professional stage actress took off when she joined the Negro Ensemble Company and appeared in such plays as *Ododo* and *Rosalie Pritchet*. In 1974 she received an Obie Award and later a Tony Award nomination as Best Supporting or Featured Actress in a Drama for her portrayal of Mattie Williams in *The River Niger* (1974). In 1975, shortly after moving to Los Angeles, she auditioned for the role for which she is best remembered, Helen Willis in Norman Lear's television series *The Jeffersons*. This barrier-breaking role as part of the first interracial married couple on prime-time television (along with the actor Franklin Cover) was almost denied her when the producer commented that Roker did not look believable as an African American woman wedded to a Caucasian man. She quickly overcame this objection by producing a photograph of herself and her husband, the producer Sy Kravitz, a white man to whom she was actually married from 1962 to 1985 and with whom she had a son, the musician Lenny Kravitz, born in 1964.

The Jeffersons ran for 253 episodes before it was canceled in 1983. Additionally Roker guest-starred in other series, including *Punky Brewster; Hangin' with Mr. Cooper; A Different World; Murder, She Wrote;* and *The Love Boat.* She appeared in television movies and the groundbreaking miniseries of Alex Haley's *Roots.* She also appeared in the feature film *Claudine* (1974) with JAMES EARL JONES and DIAHANN CARROLL.

In the 1990s Roker returned to her stage roots, appearing in a theatrical version of *The Jeffersons* and touring with Mary Martin and Carol Channing in *Legends.* She also served as a children's advocate and a board member of the Inter-Agency Council on Child Abuse and Neglect, roles that garnered her two citations from the Los Angeles City Council.

Roker died of breast cancer in 1995. Her name, however, lives on in Roxie Records, her son's label with Warner Music, and the Roxie Roker Repertory Touring Company at Howard University.

FURTHER READING

Bogle, Donald. *Primetime Blues: African-Americans on Network Television* (2002).

Littleton, Darryl J. *Black Comedians on Black Comedy* (2006).

ROXANNE Y. SCHWAB

Rolac, John (1842–23 Sept. 1864), slave, Union soldier, and Andersonville prisoner, was born in Windsor,

North Carolina, to unknown parents. His surname sometimes appears as Rolack. His physical description was that of a man five feet six inches tall with hazel eyes, brown hair, and a light complexion. Though historians have done much to illuminate the roles of black soldiers in black regiments, the U.S. Colored Troops (USCT), little has been done to document the experience and contributions of those who served with white regiments.

When Union regiments penetrated the Southern states to blockade Confederate access to the Atlantic coast for the exchange of cotton and tobacco for European guns and ammunition, slaves began to abscond from nearby towns and plantations to seek out the Union troops whose presence promised freedom. Not satisfied with being merely paid laborers behind Yankee lines, some "contrabands" like Rolac chose to enlist in the Union army. According to his military records housed at the National Archives in Washington, D.C., Rolac, a twenty-one-year-old runaway slave who enlisted on 12 November 1863, was mustered into the Union army at Plymouth, North Carolina, on 27 January 1864 and was assigned the job of undercook in the Eighty-fifth New York Infantry, Company C. Cook and undercook were the jobs most often allotted runaways who enlisted in white regiments.

Before the battle that raged at Plymouth from 17 to 20 April 1864, eleven "Col'd" cooks, all ranked as privates, served in three of the regiments garrisoned there: the Twenty-fourth and Eighty-fifth New York Volunteers and the 103d Pennsylvania Volunteers. The surprise Sunday afternoon Rebel attack was extremely dangerous for the black soldiers in blue uniform because many Confederates had sworn to kill any they found. Some Rebels even went into battle waving black flags to signal "No quarter," meaning indiscriminate killing without any mercy shown.

Questions remain unanswered still in regard to what happened to an undetermined number of blacks at Plymouth after the battle ended. Numerous stories circulated about their having been massacred, as were the ill-fated black soldiers at Fort Pillow, Tennessee, just nine days earlier. The rumors of a massacre at Plymouth were refuted by both the Union and the Confederacy, even though a number of eyewitnesses claimed otherwise. Many stories were contradictory, and since no concrete proof has ever been offered, the episode remains an enigma.

The "Col'd" cooks, as well as black recruits of the Tenth and Thirty-seventh Colored Troops and the Second Colored Cavalry, were waiting at Plymouth before joining their regiments. No regiment of the USCT was present. Knowing not to expect the same treatment accorded white soldiers, the blacks knew that by whatever means possible they needed to elude being captured. The three "Col'd" cooks serving in the Eighty-fifth New York were Henry Pugh, who managed to escape, Alec Johnson, said by a witness to have been riddled by bullets, and John Rolac, who was captured.

President Jefferson Davis had given orders to the Confederate army stating that any captured black soldiers who were runaway slaves would be returned to their masters if claimed. Otherwise the blacks would be remanded into slavery and put to work for the Rebels building military fortifications. Rolac's military records stated that he had been a slave. Therefore, if President Davis's directives were followed correctly, Rolac upon capture would have been remanded into slavery. Fortunately, his captors did not possess such information about him. If they had he might have been killed instead, especially if he were wearing a uniform. However, he was not killed, nor was he returned to slavery, because in the eyes of his captors his physical characteristics were those of a white man. They had no idea that Rolac was not a New York Yankee soldier, but rather a mulatto and a former North Carolina slave.

Instead Rolac was sent to Andersonville Prison in Georgia along with the surviving members of his regiment and other defeated "Plymouth Pilgrims." Surely some of the Eighty-fifth New York Volunteers knew who he was. His racial identity remained, however, a well-kept secret. Rolac was captured at Plymouth on 20 April 1864. Three days after his admission to the Andersonville Prison hospital he succumbed to the ravages of dysentery and scorbutus (scurvy), and he died five months later. The information concerning the death of Private John Rolac of the Eighty-fifth New York Volunteers was furnished in a report from the roll of the commander general of Andersonville Prison.

No racial identification is found on the Confederate record because, of course, he was presumed to be a white man. However, when the report of Private John Rolac's death was sent to the Union, his racial identification already was on record. Thus Private John Rolac has the unique distinction of being the only known runaway slave buried at the infamous Andersonville Prison in Georgia, where his body lies in grave 9549, one of the forgotten black soldiers who served in white regiments rather than in the USCT.

FURTHER READING

Jordan, Weymouth T., Jr., and Gerald W. Thomas. "Massacre at Plymouth: April 20, 1864," *North Carolina Historical Review* (Apr. 1995).

JUANITA PATIENCE MOSS

Rolark, Wilhelmina Jackson (12 Sept. 1916–14 Feb. 2006), community activist and lawyer, was born Margaret Wilhelmina Jackson in Portsmouth, Virginia, to Margaret and John Jackson. One of three children, she had two siblings, Gwendolyn E. Bowie, a public school teacher, and Horace Jackson, a physician. Until the seventh grade, she attended Truxon Elementary School in Truxon, Virginia, and in 1933 she graduated from J. C. Norco High School in Portsmouth.

Upon high school graduation Rolark attended Howard University from 1933 until 1937, earning bachelor of arts and master's degrees in Political Science while studying under RALPH BUNCHE, a civil rights leader and later a member of President Harry Truman's "black cabinet." As a young political scientist Rolark was one of several researchers who went to the Deep South to collect data for the Swedish economist Gunnar Myrdal, for his seminal book *An American Dilemma: The Negro Problem and Modern Democracy*, published in 1944. The 1,500-page *American Dilemma* was considered the definitive study of "the American Negro" and of race relations. Myrdal had been chosen by the Carnegie Foundation, which funded the project, to author the study because members of the foundation felt that he, as a non American, could offer a more unbiased opinion of race relations in America.

Rolark continued her education as a night student, earning her bachelor of law degree from Washington, D.C.'s, Robert H. Terrell Law School in 1944. She was granted an honorary doctor of law degree from the University of the District of Columbia School of Law and was a member of the Unified Bar of the District of Columbia.

After graduation from law school Rolark became a practicing attorney and worked on employment discrimination cases against the federal and city government. Throughout her career Rolark mentored many African American attorneys either through employment in her law firm or through her work as a legislator on the Washington, D.C., city council, a seat she held for sixteen years beginning in 1977.

In 1963 she married Dr. Calvin W. Rolark, a publisher and prominent leader in the black community, and in 1964 she assisted her husband in establishing the *Washington Informer*, the leading newspaper serving the African American community in Washington, D.C. Dr. Rolark published the first edition of the *Washington Informer* on 16 October 1964, which was made possible by a generous investment from his wife. In 2004 the *Informer* celebrated forty years of service to the Washington, D.C., area.

To meet what they saw as the underfunding of African American community–based organizations in the Washington, D.C., area, in 1969 Rolark and her husband founded the United Black Fund (UBF). Wilhelmina Rolark served as the group's general counsel and fought city and federal officials to secure tax-exempt status for the organization. She pursued legal action against the U.S. Civil Service Commission and the Health and Welfare Council. As a result of her efforts UBF became the first black fund-raising organization in the United States to be granted rights to federal payroll deductions.

In 1970 Rolark founded the National Association of Black Women Attorneys (NABWA) out of a desire to foster and unite African American women lawyers. The organization became a network that supports its members through professional development and sisterhood.

Meanwhile Rolark continued her work on the city council, representing the residents of Ward Eight, the poorest, most isolated part of the city. During her tenure she chaired the committees on Employment and Economic Development, Public Service and Consumer Affairs, and the Judiciary, the final one from 1982 until 1992. She was also a member of the Committee on Human Services, Housing, Labor, Self-determination, and Economic Development. Rolark served on the Sentencing Guidelines Commission of the D.C. Superior Court and the Public Safety Committee of the Council of Governments and the Juvenile Justice Committee. She served as chairperson of the Air Quality Committee of the Council of Governments. As a member of the Superior Court Sentencing Guidelines Commission, she made decisions about whether to increase penalties for crimes in some areas or decrease them in others. While on the city council she addressed the needs of the elderly, as well as the welfare of children in the juvenile justice system.

As a council member Rolark was instrumental in establishing Washington, D.C.'s, MARTIN LUTHER KING JR. parade even before a national holiday was created to honor the civil rights leader. Under her leadership Washington, D.C., became one of the first cities in the country to hold such an event in tribute to King. In 1992 the popular former mayor MARION BARRY, her one-time political ally, unseated Rolark from her Ward Eight position when he won the Democratic primary by a ratio of 3 to 1.

Upon the death of her husband in 1994 Rolark was unanimously elected president and CEO of the United Black Fund, which by that time had grown to become the largest African American charitable fund-raising organization, a global institution with twenty-five member agencies serving the District of Columbia and suburban counties in Virginia and Maryland, and thirty-two national affiliates and five international affiliates. Rolark also served on the national board of the Southern Christian Leadership Conference (SCLC).

Rolark was the recipient of numerous awards and citations for her leadership, devotion, and commitment to the welfare and protection of children, youth, seniors, and the incarcerated. She was inducted into some of the most prestigious legal associations and institutions, including AARP, Washington Highlands Chapter #4879, and the Board of the National Association of University Women. She was a lifetime member of the NAACP. Some of her awards specifically cited her inspiring and contagious enthusiasm for worthy causes. However, central to all the accolades she received was her sense of justice, which transcended age, race, nationality, color, creed, rank, and wealth. A full list of Rolark's accolades would make for tedious reading, but a few of them include Legislator of the Year from the National Child Support Enforcement Association, Hall of Fame Award for Forty Years of Continuous Service from the National Bar Association, and the Charles Houston Award from the Washington Bar Association for her commitment to justice. Rolark was also a founding member of the National Congress of Black Women, Inc.

Rolark died at the Greater Southeast Community Hospital in Washington, D.C., following a struggle with colon cancer.

FURTHER READING

Rolark, Wilhelmina Jackson. "Reminiscing in Memory of a Crusading Editor-Publisher," *Washington Informer*, 1 Nov. 1995.

Loeb, Vernon. "Barry's Tenure Was a Roller-Coaster Ride," *Washington Post*, 22 May 1998.

Rolark-Barnes, Denise. "40 Years … and the Best Is Yet to Come!," *Washington Informer*, 15 Oct. 2004.

Obituary: *Washington Times*, 19 Feb. 2006.

ELIZABETH K. DAVENPORT

Rolle, Esther (8 Nov. 1920–17 Nov. 1998), movie, stage, and television actress, was born in Pompano Beach, Florida, the tenth of eighteen children of Jonathan Rolle and Elizabeth, vegetable farmers. She was the first of her siblings born in Florida after her parents moved there from the Bahamas. When Rolle was a young child, she and her family spent many hot and humid days working in the fields picking vegetables. Early on, her father instilled in her the importance of determination, perseverance in following one's dreams, and striving for a better life. Rolle's father told her that he did not want any of his children to become domestic workers. Ironically, Rolle became a famous actress primarily portraying maids and housekeepers.

Rolle's talent for acting developed during her childhood. Her older siblings were actors, and she often entertained her younger siblings by performing skits written by her older brothers and sisters. She studied at BOOKER T. WASHINGTON High School in Miami and aspired to become a journalist. After graduating from high school at the age of eighteen, she left her parents' farm to attended Spelman College in Atlanta, Georgia. Rolle was also a member of Zeta Phi Beta sorority at Spelman. Later she moved to New York and lived in Harlem with her two sisters, who were actresses. She took drama classes at George Washington Carver High School and also attended the New School for Social Work. Initially Rolle wanted to be a writer, but she ended up on the stage, first as a dancer and later as an actress. During the 1940s she found steady work as a dancer in the Asadata Dafora dance troupe, were she performed for over a decade; later she joined the Calypso Carousel dance company. In 1955 Rolle met Oscar Robinson, who worked as a pants presser in New York. The two married and had no children. After seven years of marriage, the relationship ended in divorce, and Rolle returned to acting. At this time Rolle landed more acting work, which was the result, the actress observed, of a weight gain that more closely fit America's image of black women as overweight.

Rolle made her acting debut in 1962 in a production of Jean Genet's *The Blacks*. During the 1960s Rolle performed extensively on the stage, and her theatrical credits include *Ride a Black Horse*, *The Crucible*, *Ballet behind the Bridge*, *Blues for Mister Charlie*, *Amen Corner*, and *Day of Absence*. In 1967 she became a founding member of the Negro Theater Ensemble, and between 1968 and 1971 she appeared in several of the company's productions. While appearing in MELVIN VAN PEEBLES's, *Don't Play Us*

Esther Rolle won an Emmy Award for her role in the television movie *Summer of My German Soldier* in 1978; in 1990 she was the first woman to win the Chairman's Civil Rights Leadership Award from the NAACP for her achievements in film and television. (AP Images.)

Cheap, Rolle was discovered by the television producer Norman Lear, who offered her the role of a housekeeper named Florida in the television sitcom *Maude*. Rolle was opposed to Hollywood's practice of typecasting black performers but was lured away from Broadway after Lear promised her a fully developed character, not "just a Hollywood maid" (Associated Press, 19 Nov. 1998).

Maude, a spin-off of Lear's successful *All in the Family*, proved to be Rolle's big break. She was a huge success as Florida Evans, a bright and witty maid. The first episode aired in 1972, and the controversial show was rated one of the top ten shows by the Nielson ratings. Although a sitcom, the show addressed a variety of political issues, including women's rights and abortion, which were rarely mentioned at that time on television. Two years later, Lear created the spin-off *Good Times*, a sitcom focused on the struggles of a black family in a Chicago housing project. Lear offered Rolle a lead role, in which she would play a single mother who worked as a housekeeper. Feisty and politically

engaged, the actress demanded that the television family also include a father. The part went to John Amos, who had played her husband on *Maude*. According to Rolle, "I told them I couldn't compound the lie that black fathers don't care about their children. I was proud of the family life I was able to introduce to television" ("Ester Rolle Interview," Associated Press 1987).

Good Times premiered in 1974 and was an immediate success. The show, one of the first sitcoms to feature African American characters and stories, ran from 1974 to 1979 and attracted both white and black viewers. Although a sitcom, *Good Times* gave white America a view of the plight and struggles of the inner-city black family. It also provided African American television audiences with a sense of pride and inclusion during a time when broadcast entertainment was predominantly white. Rolle's character was a symbol of strength, mixing humor and with compassion. Despite the show's success, Rolle left in 1977 because she felt the role of her television son J.J., played by the actor and comedian Jimmie Walker, had been reduced to a clownish stereotype by the show's writers and producers and served as a poor role model for black youths. She later returned for the show's final year in 1979, after the producers agreed to revamp and cast a more positive image of J.J.'s character.

Rolle's struggle against Hollywood typecasting was rewarding and lasting. After *Good Times* she portrayed a maid or housekeeper in many more theatrical and film productions. She played a retired maid in the stage classic *A Raisin in the Sun* and a housekeeper in the critically acclaimed *Driving Miss Daisy*, a film based on the Pulitzer Prize–winning play about the relationship between an aged white widow and her black driver. In 1978 Rolle won an Emmy for her role in the television movie *The Summer of My German Soldier*, and she won acclaim in 1979 for her part in the television adaptation of MAYA ANGELOU's *I Know Why the Caged Bird Sings*.

During her later life, Rolle was a highly sought activist and inspiring motivational speaker; her topics were often women's issues. She addressed domestic violence and was a spokesperson for the National Council of Negro Women's Black Family Reunion. She received three NAACP Image Awards, and in 1990 she became the first woman to receive the Civil Rights Leadership Award for helping raise the image of African Americans.

Rolle died from complications of diabetes at the age of seventy-eight. She is buried in the West View Community Cemetery in Pompano Beach, Florida.

During her talented career, Rolle's pioneering efforts helped increase awareness of Hollywood's typecasting of minority actors. Her work opened the way for future entertainment projects featuring predominantly minority casts and stories about minority issues.

FURTHER READING

Rolle's career memorabilia, including an Emmy and her *Good Times* scripts, are in the African American Research Library in Ft. Lauderdale, Florida.

Contemporary Theater, Film, and Television, vol. 20 (1998).

KEVIN ALAN WHITTINGTON

Rollin, Charlotte (1849–?), political and civil rights activist, suffragist, and feminist, was born free in Charleston, South Carolina. The second daughter born to William and Margarette Rollin, her family and friends called her Lottie. Her parents were among the elite free Charleston families of color. Very little is known about her mother except that she was a free person of color and probably from Saint Dominque. Her father was a descendant of a French family, the De Caradeucs, who were wealthy aristocrats who left Saint Dominque in 1792 and relocated to Charleston. The De Caradeucs became involved in the lumber trade and because of his family connections, William Rollin also entered the lumber business, amassing wealth, political power, valuable real estate, and a few slaves.

To ensure that his daughters, FRANCES ROLLIN (1845–1901), Charlotte Rollin (b. 1849), KATE ROLLIN (1851–1876), and Louisa Rollin (b. 1858) received the finest education available, William Rollin hired the best private local tutors to teach them. His daughters also attended private school in South Carolina because an 1834 law prohibited the governance of schools by and for free people of color and bondsmen (Holt, 53). Furthermore, he wanted his daughters' refinement to reflect their educational excellence, since their ancestry was one of French nobility. When his daughters attained the highest level of education they could in South Carolina, he sent them north for their secondary education. In 1858 Rollin attended Dr. Dio Lewis's Family School for Young Ladies in Boston for a brief period, and around 1860 she followed her eldest sister Frances to Philadelphia, Pennsylvania, to attend the Institute for Colored Youth.

By 1860 William Rollin's business ambitions had paid off. He was a wealthy businessman and was prominent among the free black community of Charleston; but by the close of the Civil War the Rollin family had lost most of their Charleston property, which was confiscated and destroyed by the Union Army. Shortly after the war around 1867, the Rollin sisters moved to Columbia, South Carolina, the state capital and seat of Republican power. Along with her sisters, Rollin became influential in Reconstruction politics in South Carolina during the late 1860s and 1870s.

Universal suffrage was a recurring theme with the Rollin sisters. In 1869 Rollin began her commitment to the movement as she spoke for women's rights on the floor of the South Carolina State House of Representatives. Her speech is claimed to be the first published argument for African American women's suffrage and is documented in *History of Women's Suffrage* (1922). During her speech she exhorted: "It had been so universally the custom to treat the idea of woman suffrage worth ridicule and merriment that it becomes necessary in submitting the subject for earnest deliberation that we assure the gentlemen present that our claim is made honestly and seriously. We ask suffrage not as a favor, nor as a privilege, but as a right based on the ground that we are human beings as such, entitled to all human rights" (Stanton, 827). During the 1870s, Rollin was a member of the American Woman Suffrage Association (AWSA), which included FRANCES ELLEN WATKINS HARPER, Charlotte Forten, JOSEPHINE ST. PIERRE RUFFIN, SOJOURNER TRUTH, and her sisters Louisa Rollin and Frances Rollin Whipper. The AWSA's platform included woman's suffrage, universal suffrage, and other feminist issues. Historians have noted that the AWSA was based on strategies that included the pro-Republican Party and the abolitionist movement. As an outgrowth of the AWSA, the South Carolina Woman's Rights Association was a Republican affiliate and included female and male members and officers. In 1869 Susan B. Anthony and Elizabeth Cady Stanton founded the National Woman Rights Association (NWSA), which was the more radical of the two suffrage groups. In 1870 Rollin addressed the chair of the convention held in Charleston. She made the following argument: "While we concede that woman's enabling influence should be confined chiefly to home and society, we claim that public opinion has had a tendency to limit woman's sphere to too small a circle, and until woman has the right of representation this will last and other rights will be held by an insecure tenure" (Stanton, 828). As Rollin voiced her support for the suffrage movement, she became the first delegate chosen to attend the National Woman Suffrage Convention in South Carolina. In 1870 she was elected secretary of the South Carolina Woman's Rights Association, an affiliate of the AWSA. Rollin continued to make her position clear about her support for the rights of women when she was interviewed by a reporter for the *New York Sun*, who was writing an article about the political power of the Rollin sisters. In the article she noted that "we all believe in woman's rights and had the assistance of the best and purest … of our sex" (*New York Sun*, 15). Rollin's comment reflected the principles that she and her sisters felt about women's rights.

In 1871 Rollin spoke out for women's rights and promoted women's suffrage on the floor of the State House of Representatives. The reputation of the Rollin sisters was well known throughout South Carolina. Their political power-brokering skills were unmatched, and they ran a radical salon where the most powerful politicians gathered.

The Rollin sisters were also known for their culture and refinement. According to an 1871 article in the *New York Sun*, Rollin, along with her sisters, attended the Great Military Ball in Columbia, South Carolina, an affair that was attended by the elite black society of Columbia as well as by several whites. The sisters' social refinement, sophistication, culture, and commitment to civil rights impressed members of both races. They were prominent in the political life of the state and knowledgeable about world events. The Rollin mansion was known as the Republican headquarters, and notable politicians met in the mansion's parlor almost nightly.

Fearful of the activities of the Ku Klux Klan, in 1871 Rollin made her intentions known to the *Sun* reporter that she intended to move to Brooklyn, New York. By the 1880s Rollin had left South Carolina and moved to Brooklyn with her mother, Margarette, and her sister Louisa to an area where she felt safe from the racially charged violence in the South. There exists no extensive biographical account of Rollin. Her date of death is unknown, and it is assumed that she died in Brooklyn.

FURTHER READING

Gatewood, Willard B., Jr. "The Remarkable Misses Rollin": Black Women in Reconstruction South Carolina," *South Carolina Historical Magazine* (July 1991).

Holt, Thomas. *Black Over White: Negro Political Leadership in South Carolina during Reconstruction* (1977).

Ione, Carole. *Pride of Family: Four Generations of American Women of Color* (1991).

Stanton, Elizabeth Cady, et al., eds. *History of Woman Suffrage, 1876–1885*. vol. 3 (1922).

Terborg-Penn, Rosalyn. *African American Women in the Struggle for the Vote, 1850–1920* (1998).

VIVIAN NJERI FISHER

Rollin, Frances (Frank) (19 Nov. 1845–17 Oct. 1901), writer, feminist, and educator, was born Frances Anne Rollin in Charleston, South Carolina. She was the oldest of five daughters born to William Rollin, a businessman whose family migrated from Saint Domingue (now Haiti) in 1792, and Margarette, a woman whose family was also from the Caribbean. Frances and her sisters—CHARLOTTE (LOTTIE) ROLLIN (b. 1849); KATHERINE E. ROLLIN (b. 1851); Louisa Rollin (b. 1858); and Florence Rollin (b. 1861)—grew up in a small middle-class free black community in Charleston, where their father was well known as a successful property owner, slave owner, lumber trader, and member of the prominent French-Creole De Caradeuc family. The Rollins were members of the Brown Fellowship Society, an elite organization for freed people of color that was founded in 1790, and they lived within a community of about 120 educated and politically active free families. Additionally, the girls' father, who was so fair that he could pass for white, worked to maintain his familial connections and ties, particularly in the founding of his lumber business. As a result of his background and economic success and despite the fact that he was not allowed to vote, he wielded substantial local political influence.

The girls received their early years of education in Charleston at a private Catholic parish school for free people. Although it was illegal for black people to learn how to read and write, the girls attended school in the South up until the eve of the Civil War. Frances Rollin, who received her first instruction from an old French family, was fluent in French long before she was fully fluent in English. As a young girl she sometimes traveled north with her father on his business trips, and because of his connections they were able to travel safely despite the Fugitive Slave Act. In 1859, once the family realized that war was inevitable and there were public discussions about re-enslaving free and freed black residents, Rollin's parents decided to send her to study in Paris. She declined their offer and instead chose to relocate to Philadelphia to attend the Quaker Institute for Colored Youth (now Cheyney University) under the direction of GRACE A. MAPPS, the first black woman to receive a college degree (Sterling, 202) and a cousin of SARAH MAPPS DOUGLASS, who founded the first high school for black girls. All of her sisters except Florence soon joined her in Philadelphia after attending Dr. Dio Lewis's Family School for Young Ladies for a short time in Boston. Although Lottie and Katie were definitely enrolled at the school, it is not clear whether Louisa attended with them or joined them in Philadelphia.

Rollin remained in Philadelphia for six years and became friends with CHARLOTTE FORTEN GRIMKÉ, a fellow activist and granddaughter of the Revolutionary War veteran, sailmaker, and former slave JAMES FORTEN, and attended the first black church in the United States, St. Thomas's Episcopal Church. Although she was raised Catholic, Rollin soon became a member of the Episcopal Church, though she did not receive her membership card until the 1880s. While the war raged in the South, Rollin immersed herself in the institute's "Black Nationalist" curriculum; befriended members of the Banneker Society, a black literary organization; and attended the local sewing meetings (Ione, 148). During this time Rollin briefly lost contact with her parents, who had chosen to remain in South Carolina for the duration of the war, presumably to protect their economic interests.

In 1865 Rollin was offered a job to work on the Sea Islands, near Charleston, teaching freedmen and women. While there, she met MARTIN ROBISON DELANY, a subassistant commissioner with the Freedman's Bureau, a co-founder of the *North Star* with FREDERICK DOUGLASS, and one of the few blacks to travel to Africa to meet with tribal leaders. Delany helped her to file and win one of the earliest civil rights cases in the country. At that time, because Charleston was still bound by martial law, Rollin, who had been denied first-class accommodations on a steamer ship, was able to file a suit against the ship's captain. Once the case was settled, Delany offered Rollin the job of writing his biography. Rollin quickly agreed and relocated to Boston to begin her work. It was there that she began to grow as an intellectual, a feminist, a writer, and an activist. She spent her Sundays visiting white churches throughout the city; attended readings by the writers Charles Dickens (she was the only black person in attendance) and Ralph Waldo Emerson; spent time with the abolitionists William Lloyd Garrison and LEWIS HAYDEN, a runaway slave who worked as both a conductor

on the Underground Railroad and a messenger to the Massachusetts secretary of state; and was courted by a number of suitors, including RICHARD THEODORE GREENER, the first African American to graduate from Harvard.

Rollin kept a diary, and her surviving journals begin in January 1868, her last year in Boston. Delany, who had promised to pay her, had fallen on difficult times, and as a result Rollin had worked small jobs to support herself while she finished the book. In July the *Life and Public Services of Martin R. Delany*, the first biography about a freeborn black man, was published, and Rollin returned home to South Carolina to work as a law clerk for WILLIAM J. WHIPPER, who recently had been elected to represent Beaufort County in the state legislature in Columbia. Twelve days after she arrived, Whipper, an older (ten years her senior) widower with two children, proposed to her. Over the objections of her family Rollin agreed, and one month later they were married. Rollin Whipper gave birth to four children in relatively rapid succession: Alicia, who was born and died in 1869, was followed by Winifred (1870–1907), Ionia Rollin (1872–1953), Mary Elizabeth (1874–1875), and Leigh (1876–1975). At the same time, the other Rollin sisters were making a political and cultural name for themselves throughout the North and South, having been profiled in both the *New York Sun* and the *New York Tribune*.

Over the years, despite her husband's known drinking, gambling, and political problems, Rollin Whipper worked to maintain their family. Although Whipper was elected to serve as a judge in 1875, the governor refused to sign the commission and the family relocated to Beaufort. By 1880 Rollin Whipper had moved to Washington, D.C., with her children but without her husband. She continued to support her husband's efforts while working as copyist with the U.S. Department of Lands. Although Whipper joined the family in 1882, he left in 1885 and was soon elected as Beaufort County probate judge. As a result of his election, Rollin Whipper lost her job and began working as a recorder of deeds for Washington, D.C., with Frederick Douglass. By 1889, after seeing all of her children graduate from Howard University and begin their respective careers, Rollin Whipper's health began to fail, and she returned to Beaufort and to Whipper. Two years later, at the age of fifty-seven, Rollin Whipper died of tuberculosis. Although her diaries and letters have never been published in their entirety, her work stands as one of the few primary sources to detail the life and experiences of a young woman who experienced the Civil War, Reconstruction, and Jim Crow.

FURTHER READING

Rollin's great-granddaughter, Carol Ione, is in possession of her surviving diary (which begins in 1868) and some of her memorabilia, including photos and oral testimonies from her children. Additional items are housed at the Schomburg Center for Research on Black Culture in New York City, and in the Leigh Whipper Collections of the Moorland-Spingarn Research Center in Washington, D.C.

Ione, Carol. *Pride of Family: Four Generations of American Women of Color* (1991).

Shockley, Ann Allen, ed. *Afro-American Women Writers: 1746–1933* (1988).

Smith, Jessie Carney, ed. *Notable Black American Women, Book II* (1991).

Sterling, Dorothy, ed. *We Are Your Sisters: Black Women in the Nineteenth Century* (1984).

K. WISE WHITEHEAD

Rollin, Katherine E. (1851–4 Mar. 1876), political and civil rights activist, suffragist, and educator, was born free in Charleston, South Carolina, as Katherine Euphrosyne Rollin, the third daughter of William Rollin, wood factor, and Margarette, housekeeper. Her mother's maiden name is unknown. Family and friends referred to her as Katie. Rollin and her parents were listed as mulatto in the 1850 U.S. census. Her parents wanted their four daughters to have a fine education. A law passed in 1834 in Charleston, however, "prohibited the maintenance of schools by and for free people of color and slaves." As a result of this legislation, free blacks were forced to find other ways to educate their children (Holt, 53). Like her older sisters FRANCES ROLLIN and CHARLOTTE ROLLIN, Katie was privately tutored, and she attended private schools in Charleston. She also enrolled in secondary schools in Boston and in Philadelphia, Pennsylvania, during the antebellum period. In Boston she attended Dio Lewis's Family School for Youth on Essex Street, where social graces were taught in addition to an advanced educational curriculum. In Philadelphia it is likely that she attended the Institute for Colored Youth for a brief period.

After the Civil War, around 1868, the Rollin sisters moved to Columbia, South Carolina, the seat of Republican power. Staunch Republicans, like many African Americans during this period who affiliated with the Republican Party during the late 1850s and 1860s because of the party's platform and stance against slavery and proequality, the sisters actively worked for women's rights. In 1871 Rollin spoke with a journalist from the *New York Sun* about her race and her principles for equal rights. She noted: "We can assure you that we do represent the greater portion of all that is now good for anything in South Carolina—and that is the colored population who are determined to exert every effort on behalf of the equal rights to our race. We were educated in Boston, and we drank in those principles of liberty, which are now so dear to us" (*New York Sun*, 29 Mar. 1871). The suffrage movement began at Seneca Falls, New York, in 1848, and the issue of woman suffrage was a debated political topic until women received the right to vote in 1920. In South Carolina the Rollin sisters devoted themselves to women's rights and equal rights and joined the quest to get a constitutional amendment to support the rights of women.

In the 1870s Rollin became an active member of the American Woman Suffrage Association (AWSA), an organization that split with the National Woman Suffrage Association (NWSA) over the enfranchisement of black males. The AWSA's abolitionist membership and moderation proved more representative of her beliefs and principles. Her concern for fair and equal treatment of women won her the support of her peers and the few African American men who supported woman suffrage.

The AWSA argued that universal suffrage should be the goal of the suffrage movement. To further this philosophy, in 1870 Lucy Stone and her husband Henry Browne Blackwell created *Woman's Journal*, which became the official organ of the AWSA. Initially the NWSA strategy focused on efforts to challenge the Fourteenth Amendment while attempting to vote. The NWSA's ultimate goal was to work toward achieving a constitutional amendment to enfranchise women, while the AWSA focused on achieving woman suffrage on a state level through local legislatures and continuing to petition Congress for a constitutional amendment.

The South Carolina Woman's Rights Association's mission was similar to the AWSA's. As an affiliate of the AWSA, the South Carolina Woman's Rights Association included male as well as female members and officers. In 1871 the *Woman's Journal* reported that Rollin gave a short speech at a meeting in Columbia, South Carolina, endorsing the women's movement and wishing it victory. The following year Rollin became treasurer of the South Carolina Women's

Rights Association in Columbia, an organization closely aligned with the Republican Party. Several members of the South Carolina House and Senate and Governor Robert Kingston Scott sent a message to Rollin and her sister Charlotte wishing them goodwill in their efforts. Among those assembled at the meeting were Lieutenant Governor ALONZO JACOB RANSIER, Speaker of the House Franklin J. Moses, Secretary of State FRANCIS LOUIS CARDOZO, the Honorable WILLIAM J. WHIPPER, State House of Representatives, and the husband of Frances Rollin, and other members of the general assembly.

Because of her commitment to the cause of women's rights, Rollin was selected to work on the committee to amend the South Carolina state constitution to include provisions for woman suffrage. She and her sisters were troubled by the heated debates and eventual defeat of their efforts to challenge the constitutional law of South Carolina that did not support woman suffrage.

Another important issue for the Rollin sisters was the equality of education for African Americans and the establishment of a family school. With the help of Bishop JAMES LYNCH, an African Methodist Episcopal Church missionary who was posted in South Carolina after serving a congregation in Baltimore, Maryland, the Rollin Family School was established in Charleston to teach the children of former slaves. To help finance their school, a model for teaching and uplifting African American children, they needed to acquire private financial support. In 1873 Katie and Charlotte Rollin traveled to Philadelphia with the hopes of raising funds to support their Rollin Family School. The two sisters met with friends of the social activist Lucretia Mott. The sisters, however, never received the type of financial support that they needed to sustain the school.

According to various sources, Rollin was engaged to marry a white South Carolina senator, George F. McIntyre, from Colleton County. There is no record that she ever married the senator. Very little information exists about Rollin after 1873. By 1875 she was living in Madison County, Florida. On 4 March 1876, only twenty-five years old, she died of "consumption of the lungs" (Ione, 176). At the time of her death, she lived in Brunson, South Carolina, a short distance from Charleston.

FURTHER READING

Gatewood, Willard B., Jr. "'The Remarkable Misses Rollin': Black Women in Reconstruction South Carolina," *South Carolina Historical Magazine* 92 (July 1991).

Holt, Thomas. *Black over White: Negro Political Leadership in South Carolina during Reconstruction* (1977).

Ione, Carole. *Pride of Family: Four Generations of American Women of Color* (1991).

Terborg-Penn, Rosalyn. *African American Women in the Struggle for the Vote, 1850–1920* (1998).

VIVIAN NJERI FISHER

Rollin, Louisa (1858–Mar. 1943), activist, was born in Charleston, South Carolina, one of the five daughters of Margarette Rollin and William Rollin, a free man of color. Rollin's father owned a lumber factory and was a man of considerable wealth and influence in Charleston. Louisa Rollin and her sisters enjoyed great educational opportunities as a result of their father's social standing. Although not much is known of her formal education, Rollin is said to have attended school in Philadelphia. Her eldest sister, FRANCES ROLLIN WHIPPER, a celebrated social activist and author of *Life and Public Services of Martin R. Delany*, is noted as having attended the Institute for Colored Youth, an elite academic institution founded by Quakers in Philadelphia. Considering her family's social standing and the documented education of her sister, Louisa Rollin is assumed to have received a strong and largely uncommon academic education for her time.

Although much is unknown about Louisa's early life, evidence abounds of the degree of influence she and her sisters yielded within the elite political circles of Columbia, the state's capital, during Rollin's early adulthood. The Rollin sisters occupied a position of great access within the Republican-dominated political sphere of South Carolina. Reporters of the time described the women as operating a salon that was frequented by political and social elites. Those who encountered the Rollin sisters and engaged in conversation with them noted their exceptionally well-rounded knowledge of society, literature, and politics. They were especially known for their intimate knowledge of the inner-workings of state politics, as well as for their strong opinions on matters pertaining to women in particular. From 1869 until the formal disenfranchisement of blacks in the state's constitution of 1895, black men in South Carolina could actively vote and participate in state politics. With many black men exercising their right to vote and participating in state politics in significant roles, Louisa Rollin and her sisters championed the rights of women. Louisa Rollin joined the American Woman Suffrage Association (AWSA) along with her sisters FRANCIS E. ROLLIN,

CHARLOTTE (LOTTIE) ROLLIN, and Frances Rollin Whipper. As a part of this association, the sisters interacted with significant suffragists of the period, most notably Lucy Stone, a famous white abolitionist and advocate for universal suffrage.

Affiliated with AWSA and utilizing the social resources garnered through her salon, Louisa Rollin influenced politics in her state throughout Reconstruction. In 1869, she spoke before the South Carolina House of Representatives on the issue of women's suffrage, urging the body to grant women the same voting rights afforded men in the state. This moment was her most well documented in the formal public sphere.

Although little remains in the way of formal documentation of Louisa Rollin's work and political influence, her commitment to women's rights and racial equality during a moment of significant political and social progress in South Carolina remains a significant part of the larger historical narrative of African Americans in the state.

FURTHER READING

Bennett, Lerone. *Black Power U.S.A.: The Human Side of Reconstruction* (1967).

Gatewood, Willard. "The Remarkable Misses Rollin: Black Women In Reconstruction South Carolina." *South Carolina Historical Magazine* 92, no. 3 (1991): 172–188.

Sterling, Dorothy. *We Are Your Sisters* (1984).

Terborg-Penn, Rosalyn. *African American Women in the Struggle for the Vote, 1850–1920* (1998).

DOROTHY BROWN

Rollins, Charlemae Hill (20 June 1897–3 Feb. 1979), librarian, author, developer of curricula in multicultural children's literature, and one of the first bibliographers of African American children's books, was born in Yazoo City, Mississippi, the daughter of Allen G. Hill, a farmer, and Birdie Tucker, a teacher. During her early childhood, Rollins's family moved to the Oklahoma territory. Although Rollins was denied access to her local library as a child because of her race, she credited her family with encouraging her to seek as much education as possible, and her grandmother, a former slave, with instilling in her a love of books. She explained: "Grandma told wonderful stories of her life as a slave. I've always loved books because of her.... I would read anything and everything" (Hopkins, 300). Rollins attended segregated schools in Beggs, Oklahoma; St. Louis, Missouri; and Holly Springs, Mississippi; and in 1916 she graduated from high

school in Quindoro, Kansas. As she grew older few educational opportunities existed for blacks, so she moved to places that let blacks attend schools.

Rollins briefly taught school in Oklahoma; however, her yearning for more education led her to Howard University. She matriculated at Howard for one year, in 1917, before returning to Oklahoma. On 8 April 1918 she married Joseph Walter Rollins. They had one child. Shortly after their marriage, Joseph, a U.S. Army serviceman, was sent to France to serve in World War I. When he returned from overseas, the couple settled in Chicago.

In Chicago, Rollins embarked on a distinguished career in librarianship. Starting as a junior assistant in 1927 at the Chicago Public Library, Rollins secured funding from the library system to attend the School of Library Service at Columbia University in the summer of 1932, and the Graduate Library School at the University of Chicago from 1932 to 1936, in order to be professionally trained as a librarian. When the George C. Hall Branch of the Chicago Public Library opened in 1932, she accepted a position that made her the first black head of a children's department in Chicago.

Working at the first branch library designed to serve a primarily black Chicago neighborhood, Rollins used her creativity to encourage children, parents, and educators to use the library resources, particularly as they related to child development. She and her co-workers felt a responsibility to serve this community where "Negro readers include every social and economic level from the successful writer, checking material for his latest book, to the kitchenette dwelling child who stays every night until nine o'clock because there is no place at home to read or do homework" (Rollins, 92). One of Rollins's work responsibilities, storytelling, led her to a project that examined how African Americans were presented in children's books. She recognized there were few books on the black experience and once said of many children's books that "blacks were stereotyped as pickaninnies, barefooted, grinning and with pigtails sticking out all over their heads" (*Chicago Sun Times*, 7 Feb. 1979). To combat these misconceptions she began a crusade for honest ethnic portrayals in literature for children.

Under the direction of Agatha L. Shea, the director of work with children at the Chicago Public Library, Rollins compiled a list of books that accurately depicted blacks as a guide to be used by publishers, librarians, and educators. From this initial effort evolved one of the first significant publications of African American literature geared toward children, *We Build Together: A Reader's Guide to Negro Life and Literature for Elementary and High School Use* (1941), which was published by the National Council of Teachers of English. This publication, with revised editions in 1948 and 1967, included criteria necessary to evaluate literature concerned with the black experience and an annotated bibliography of recommended books arranged by subject.

In 1957 Rollins became the first black to be elected president of the Children's Services Division of the American Library Association; she served until the following year. She remained at the Hall Branch of the Chicago Public Library until her retirement in 1963. In retirement she continued to publish books about African American literature for children, including *Christmas Gif': An Anthology of Christmas Poems, Songs, and Stories, Written by and about Negroes* (1963); *They Showed the Way: Famous American Negro Leaders* (1964); *Famous Negro Entertainers of Stage, Screen, and TV* (1967); and *Black Troubadour: Langston Hughes* (1971).

In retirement Rollins received invitations to lecture at national conferences about children's literature, in particular how to evaluate African American children's books, and was sought by publishers and authors to review manuscripts. She received numerous awards, including the American Brotherhood Award (1952), Zeta Phi Beta's Woman of the Year (1956), the Women's National Book Association's Constance Lindsay Skinner Award (1970), and the Coretta Scott King Award (1971). The American Library Association also extended its highest award, Honorary Membership, to Rollins in 1972. In 1974, Columbia College in Chicago awarded Rollins a doctorate of humane letters.

Rollins died at the age of eighty-one in Chicago. On 12 October 1989 Mayor Richard M. Daley rededicated the Hall Branch Library Children's Room in her remembrance. As of 2007, a biennial conference continued to be held in her honor at the School of Library and Information Science at North Carolina Central University and the American Library Association Library Service to Children division continued to present the Charlemae Rollins President's Program at its annual convention.

FURTHER READING

The records and papers of Charlemae Hill Rollins are in the Research Collection of the Woodson Regional Library in Chicago.

Rollins, Charlemae. "Library Work with Negroes," in *Illinois Libraries* 25 (Feb. 1945).

Hopkins, Lee Bennett. *More Books by More People: Interviews with Sixty-five Authors of Books for Children* (1974).

Shaw, Spencer G. "Charlemae Hill Rollins (1897–1979), Librarian, Storyteller, Author" in *Notable Black American Women*, ed. Jessie Carney Smith (1992).

Obituary: *Chicago Sun Times*, 7 Feb. 1979.

BILLIE E. WALKER

Rollins, Howard E., Jr. (17 Oct. 1950–8 Dec. 1996), film, television, and stage actor, was born in Baltimore, Maryland, the youngest child of four to Howard E. Rollins Sr. (a steelworker) and Ruth Ann Rollins (a domestic worker). After graduating from Baltimore's Northern High School, he attended Towson State College for two years, where he studied theater arts and French. In 1970 Rollins dropped out of college and joined the cast of "Our Street," the nation's first black soap opera, produced by Maryland Public Television.

Despite his family's protestations that an African American could not support himself on an acting career, Rollins headed to New York City to follow his dream of becoming an actor in 1974. At first he performed in off-Broadway plays, including his role as Vietnam veteran Dale Jackson in Tom Cole's *Medal of Honor Rag*, and then he broke into two television miniseries, playing civil rights leader Andrew Young in *King* in 1978 and George Haley in *Roots: The Next Generation* in 1979.

Rollins's biggest break came in 1981 when he landed a role in *Ragtime*, Michael Weller's screen adaptation of E. L. Doctorow's Pulitzer-prize-winning novel. In this epic story about racial and class hatred in New York at the turn of the twentieth century, Rollins played the pivotal role of the young, proud piano player, Coalhouse Walker Jr., whose maltreatment at the hands of racist white firemen leads him to armed rebellion against a corrupt criminal justice system in the name of justice. For this riveting performance, Rollins earned an Oscar nomination for best supporting actor.

Three years later, in 1984, Rollins played Captain Richard Davenport, a Washington, D.C., attorney, in *A Soldier's Story*, the screen adaptation of CHARLES FULLER's prize-winning play *A Soldier's Play*. Directed by Norman Jewison and set at the Fort Neal Army base in Louisiana near the end of World War II, *A Soldier's Story* explores an investigation into the murder of the well-hated Sergeant Waters. Rollins's performance not only illuminated how enlisted men navigated discrimination within the segregated military, but also in a larger sense illustrated the insidiousness of racial prejudice. After *A Soldier's Story*, Rollins became "emblematic" of actors who worked during the period after the well-known SIDNEY POITIER but before the meteoric rise of DENZEL WASHINGTON, who played the murderer in *A Soldier's Story* (author interview with Steve Yeager, 14 April 2009).

Despite his film successes, Rollins is perhaps best known for his television roles. In 1982 he was nominated for an Emmy for besting supporting actor in the television daytime drama "Another World." The following year, he was the starring role in the PBS American Playhouse television movie, *For Us the Living: The Medgar Evers Story*, a dynamic production of the Mississippi civil rights leader's achievements and assassination. Three years later, in 1986, he played Otis Travis, a cocaine dealer, in a made-for-television movie, *The Children of Times Square*, about recruiting teenage boys into criminal gangs. Rollins enjoyed playing Otis Travis because the role of "the bad guy" was an unusual part for him (author interview with Hattie Fields, 8 April 2009).

In 1988 Rollins and Carroll O'Connor starred in the television remark of the 1967 film *In the Heat of the Night* that had originally co-starred SYDNEY POITIER and Rod Steiger. Rollins was exceptional as chief of detectives, Virgil Tibbs, and O'Connor was outstanding as sheriff, Bill Gillespie, and together they demonstrated insights into prejudices in the South. Rollins was thrilled to join the cast and he particularly liked working with O'Connor (author interview with Steve Yeager, 14 April 2009). Unfortunately, the show, which became a long-running hit television series, was shot in small towns in Louisiana and Georgia, where Rollins felt especially isolated as a gay black man.

In 1993 Rollins was written out of *In the Heat of the Night* because of the effects of illegal drug use on his work. He had been arrested for possession of cocaine, driving under the influence of a tranquilizer, and reckless driving, and subsequent brief incarcerations followed. Nonetheless, Rollins worked hard to get his life and acting career back on track. He checked himself into a number of alcohol and drug rehabilitation programs, most notably the Betty Ford Clinic (author interview with Hattie Fields, 8 April 2009).

Ironically, Rollins's last feature screen performance was in 1995 for the theatrical film *Drunks* about an Alcoholics Anonymous meeting in a church basement. Written by Gary Lennon and based on his play *Blackout*, *Drunks* included an ensemble of actors from Faye Dunaway to Richard Lewis to Spaulding Gay. Rollins played the role of Joseph, a father tormented by a blackout he had while driving that left his five-year-old son severely injured.

Rollins also created a powerful audiotape of his favorite author, JAMES BALDWIN's, masterful novel *Another Country*, produced by G. Goodwin and J. Dunn in 1987. In that same year he lent his voice to the emotionally gripping television documentary, *Dear America: Letters Home from Vietnam*, written and produced by Bill Couturie.

In 1996 Rollins died in New York City in Saint Luke's Hospital from complications from AIDS-related lymphoma. He was forty-six years old.

Ten years later Rollins was the first person from Baltimore inducted into the National Great Blacks in Wax Museum in Baltimore, Maryland, where he took his place alongside other talented African Americans, including writer LANGSTON HUGHES and saxophonist Mickey Fields.

For the evening of the induction at Baltimore's Senator Theater, Steve Yeager, his friend and mentor, showed *An Evening with Howard*, a documentary that he had produced as a tribute to his friend. Through a montage of clips and interviews, the film captured Rollins's versatility as an actor and portrayed the courage he possessed to follow his dreams. In light of Rollins's tenacity of spirit, his family created the Howard E. Rollins, Jr. Foundation, a nonprofit based in Baltimore, Maryland, whose mission is "to continue Howard's legacy by awarding scholarships and providing cultural and educational programs in the performing or film media arts for aspiring inner city, minority, and disadvantaged youth."

FURTHER READING

Blumenthal, Ralph. "Howard Rollins Is Dead at 46; Star in TV's 'Heat of the Night.'" *New York Times*, 10 Dec. 1996.

Brenda, Eady. "Howard Rollins' Stalled Career Marches on with 'A Soldier's Story.'" *People*, 1 Oct. 1984, Vol. 22, No. 14.

Grimes, William. "Tom Cole, Writer for Film and Stage, Dies at 75." *New York Times*, 5 Mar. 2009.

Norment, Lynn. "'Ragtime's Star Is Rich In Talent.'" *Ebony*, Feb. 1982.

Howard E. Rollins at The National Great Blacks in Wax Museum, http://www.ngbiwm.com/Exhibits/Howard_Rollins.htm.

The Howard E. Rollins Jr. Foundation, http://www.howarderollinsfoundation.org/index.htm.

THERESA C. LYNCH

Rollins, Ida Gray Nelson (c. Mar. 1867–3 May 1953), dentist, was born in Clarkesville, Tennessee. To escape continuing antiblack discrimination and poverty after the Civil War, her family moved to Cincinnati, Ohio, when Gray was a youngster. She attended Cincinnati's racially segregated public schools, including Gaines High School, Ohio's first public high school for black students. Opened in 1866 the school was named for the black educator John I. Gaines and was administered by his nephew, the political activist and educator PETER HUMPHRIES CLARK. Gaines High School provided classical as well as vocational instruction, and teacher training was added to the curriculum in 1868. The school gained a national reputation for academic excellence, and during the mid-1880s it produced scores of qualified black teachers annually.

Gray was determined to study dentistry. She found a willing and powerful mentor in Jonathan Taft, dean of the College of Dental Surgery at the University of Michigan. Until 1875 Taft had served as the dean of the Ohio College of Dental Surgery in Cincinnati, and although he was based in Ann Arbor, Michigan, in the late 1880s, Taft maintained strong ties in Cincinnati. He was a popular lecturer on public health issues, and he continued to practice dentistry on a limited basis from an office in Cincinnati. Gray worked in his office while still a student at Gaines High School, and after her graduation Taft served as her preceptor when she applied for admission to the University of Michigan's College of Dental Surgery. Gray graduated from Gaines High School in 1887, and Cincinnati's board of education ordered the school closed in 1889.

As the dean of the University of Michigan's College of Dental Surgery, Taft had introduced an exacting medical curriculum that by 1885 had gained international recognition. Gray was admitted to the college, and she studied under Taft during her years as a student in Ann Arbor. She completed the rigorous dentistry training and graduated from the University of Michigan with a DDS degree in 1890, thereby becoming the first African American woman to earn a degree in dentistry.

Gray returned to Cincinnati in 1890 and opened her own dental practice. In 1895 she married James S. Nelson, and the couple moved to Chicago, where they became part of that city's growing black professional elite. Dr. Nelson, as she preferred to be called, opened a successful dental practice and was periodically active in the African American women's club movement in the city. She was not an advocate of either black militancy or direct competition between white and black specialists in the same professions, although many of her African American friends and professional associates in Chicago were. Her husband died in 1926 after having served in the U.S. military in both the Spanish-American War and World War I. She married again in 1929, to William A. Rollins.

In 1916, along with the African American surgeon DANIEL HALE WILLIAMS, Nelson became one of the first black professionals from the Chicago area to purchase real estate and build a summer home in the small black resort community of Idlewild, near the village of Baldwin in Lake County, Michigan. Other Idlewild property owners soon included W. E. B. DuBois, MADAME C. J. WALKER, and the novelist CHARLES WADDELL CHESTNUTT. Nelson's modest cottage, located at the corner of Lake Drive and Palm Street near a small lake at the center of Idlewild, served as her retreat from the summertime heat of Chicago, and she often hosted friends and professional acquaintances there.

During the 1920s Idlewild emerged as a key social enclave for black elites from Chicago, Detroit, and other cities in the Midwest. It was also an important stop on the summertime "Chitlin Circuit" for black entertainers, including LOUIS ARMSTRONG, WILLIAM "COUNT" BASIE, SARAH VAUGHAN, Della Reese, and the Mills Brothers. At the height of its popularity in the late 1930s, Idlewild attracted as many as twenty thousand African Americans each summer. They came to the small town in rural northern Michigan for the entertainment, the social atmosphere, and to enjoy the mild climate, unspoiled lakes and woods, and fresh air of what came to be known as "Black Eden."

Rollins retired from the practice of dentistry around 1926 and for several years thereafter divided her time between her homes in Chicago and Idlewild. She died in Chicago on 3 May 1953 at the age of eighty-seven. Her accomplishments are commemorated by the University of Michigan's School of Dentistry, which in the 1990s created the annual Ida Gray Awards for faculty, staff, and students who-make "distinguished contributions to diversity matters in the University of Michigan's School of Dentistry."

FURTHER READING
Biographical information on and a photograph of Ida Gray Nelson Rollins is held in the University of Michigan's Bentley Historical Library in Ann Arbor, Michigan.

Adams, John Henry. "Rough Sketches: A Study of the Features of the New Negro Woman," *Voice of the Negro* (Aug. 1904).

Obituary: *Baldwin (Michigan) Lake County Star*, 22 May 1953.

LAURA M. CALKINS

Rollins, Sonny (9 Sept. 1930–), tenor saxophonist, was born Theodore Walker Rollins in Harlem, New York City, the son of Walter Theodore Rollins and Valborg Solomon Rollins. His parents were both from the West Indies and loved music; they often played Enrico Caruso 78s, and they brought Sonny to see a performance of the *Pirates of Penzance* when he was two. Sonny spent time as a child with an uncle from Georgia who played records by bluesmen like LONNIE JOHNSON and the jump blues saxophonist LOUIS JORDAN. He also spent a good deal of time with his grandmother, a follower of MARCUS GARVEY, and she also brought him to the local Sanctified church, exposing him to the sect's jubilant and rhythmically powerful worship.

Rollins began to study piano at age nine, taking up the alto saxophone at age eleven and the tenor at fourteen. Although he grew up in a neighborhood soaked in musical atmosphere, he studied saxophone at the New York School of Music and at the YMCA and studied harmony and theory in high school. The pianists BUD POWELL and THELONIOUS MONK lived nearby, and Rollins led a high school group called The Countsmen that included future stars: the altoist JACKIE MCLEAN, the pianist Kenny Drew, and the drummer Art Taylor. In 1948 Rollins led a trio at the Club Barron in Harlem, playing opposite Monk, and he began to hang out and rehearse at Monk's home. Rollins also made his first recording that year, with the vocalist Babs Gonzalez. In August 1949 he appeared on a Blue Note date with Powell. Rollins began to develop a more personal style during these years, moving from the early influence of COLEMAN HAWKINS and through the influences of LESTER YOUNG, DON BYAS, and, finally, CHARLIE PARKER. Like so many other young players of the period, Rollins also began to use drugs. In 1950 he was arrested for armed robbery and spent ten months at Rikers Island prison, drifting back into the world of drugs and petty crime after his release. Musically he continued to progress, appearing on several notable MILES DAVIS sessions of the early 1950s and releasing his first complete session under his own name in 1951. Rollins's confident, substantial tenor sound is already well in evidence in this session, in stark contrast to McLean's Parkerish alto and Davis's own sparse, introspective playing. But in 1952 Rollins was sent back to Rikers on a parole violation involving drug use. It took an encounter with Parker in 1953, when Parker himself expressed his dismay at Rollins's continued drug use, to motivate Rollins to quit drugs. In the interim Rollins appeared on November 1953 sessions with Monk and, most famously, on 1954 sessions with ART FARMER and Davis, with Davis recording the Rollins compositions "Airegin," "Doxy," and "Oleo" on an album released as *Dig*.

From November 1954 to November 1955 Rollins took the first of several career sabbaticals, entering and successfully completing an experimental methadone program at the federal prison in Lexington, Kentucky. He worked for a while as a day laborer in Chicago and returned to the scene to win his first regular job with a working group, as a member of the CLIFFORD BROWN–MAX ROACH quintet. Though he appeared on only two albums with the group, *Sonny Rollins plus Four* and *The Clifford Brown and Max Roach Quintet at Basin Street East*, both released in 1956, the musical and personal experience marked a decisive turning point in his life. Rollins found a musical equal in the drummer Roach and a personal role model in Brown. The self-effacing trumpeter showed him that it was possible to lead a clean, creative life in music.

At the same time Rollins embarked as a leader on a string of recordings that have become jazz classics. For Prestige Records he released *Worktime* in 1955 and *Tenor Madness* (with JOHN COLTRANE), *Saxophone Colossus*, *Rollins Plays for Bird*, and *Tour de Force* in 1956, and for Blue Note he released *Sonny Rollins, Volume 1*. He followed this stunning series of recordings with 1957's *Way Out West* (Contemporary Records), *Sonny Rollins, Volume 2* (Blue Note), *The Sound of Sonny* (Riverside), and *Newk's Time* and *A Night at the Village Vanguard*, both for Blue Note. Finally in 1958 he released *Freedom Suite* and *Sonny Rollins and the Contemporary Leaders*, both for Riverside. The highlights in this astounding series of recordings are many, but a few deserve particular mention.

On *Saxophone Colossus*, with Tommy Flanagan on piano, Doug Watkins on bass, and Max Roach on drums, Rollins began a lifelong affinity for calypso rhythms in his performance of "St. Thomas," a song that his mother sang that actually has roots as a Scandinavian folk song. The album also contains his edgy, melodic reading of "Moritat," otherwise known as "Mack the Knife." And in "Blue

7" he constructed an approach to improvisation that Gunther Schuller later analyzed as the origins of "thematic improvisation ... in which the soloist develops motifs extracted from his theme." Rollins himself was a bit put off by this intellectual analysis; he regarded his playing as more organically conceived and in fact had already learned from Monk how to get inside of a theme in this way and to "abstract it as a basis for variations."

Way Out West, a pianoless trio with Ray Brown on bass and Shelly Manne on drums, is filled with witty improvisations on the hokiest of Western songs, such as "I'm an Old Cowhand." Indeed, the ability to transform such popular, Tin Pan Alley tunes into imaginative, rhythmically elastic jazz statements quickly became a signal characteristic of Rollins's playing; *Newk's Time*, with Wynton Kelly on piano and Philly Joe Jones on drums, has another example in "Surrey with the Fringe on Top."

On *A Night at the Village Vanguard* (1957) Rollins unveiled the spontaneous, fiery, intellectually probing live performances that remain the hallmark of his career and reputation. Again recorded as a trio album without piano (there are two different trios), these performances further reveal the freedom Rollins discovered by abandoning the chordal restrictions of the piano. Freedom, musically and racially, was the theme of Rollins's boldest statement of this period, *The Freedom Suite* (with Roach and Oscar Pettiford on bass). The album consists of connected sections, all based on a common melodic figure, differentiated by shifts in tempo, mood, or rhythm. Rollins's own comments on the album cover address the music's philosophic roots: "America is deeply rooted in Negro culture; its colloquialisms, its humor, its music. How ironic that the Negro, who more than any other people can claim America's culture as his own, is being persecuted and repressed, that the Negro, who has exemplified the humanities in his very existence, is being rewarded with inhumanity."

Rollins had clearly established himself as the most accomplished, stylistically imaginative tenor player in jazz (Coltrane had not yet reached his peak), and he also found personal fulfillment. He married his first wife, Dawn Finney, in 1957, but that same year he met Lucille Pearson. He married Pearson within two years; she later became his manager, and he relied on her wisdom and support for the rest of their years together (she died in December 2004). Yet Rollins remained intensely self-critical. Health problems and a desire to escape the pervasive atmosphere of drugs and alcohol

Sonny Rollins, tenor saxophonist and composer, August 1972. (AP Images.)

prompted him to take his most famous sabbatical, from August 1959 to November 1961. As he later noted, "I needed to brush up on various aspects of my craft. I felt I was getting too much, too soon." He studied harmony and took piano lessons during these years, but fans have always focused on the somewhat mythical image that emerged at the time—the lonely jazzman, pursuing creative freedom in the middle of the night on the Williamsburg Bridge. In reality, as Rollins himself later recounted, he just wanted a place to practice the basics of his music without disturbing his neighbors or attracting attention to himself.

Rollins returned to the jazz scene with a 1962 album titled, appropriately, *The Bridge*. The new group included the guitarist Jim Hall and the bassist Bob Cranshaw, the latter to remain Rollins's musical partner for more than forty years. Rollins unveiled a richer tenor tone and a music that was more tonally and harmonically nuanced, thanks in part to Hall's influential presence. Though *The Bridge* was entirely within the jazz tradition, Rollins also began to play with freer improvisers like Don Cherry, Henry Grimes, and Paul Bley; he recorded *Our Man in Jazz* in 1962 with the trumpeter Cherry and the drummer Billy Higgins (both had played with Ornette Coleman, an inspiration for this album).

Rollins's 1963 recording *Sonny Meets Hawk* (with Hawkins) was again a more mainstream effort, but he followed this by refusing to record from 1963 to 1965, traveling to Japan and India and studying yoga, to improve his wind capacity and mental concentration. He returned to recording with the 1966 release *East Broadway Rundown*, the furthest he was to travel toward the avant-garde, a recording that showed that Rollins could play "out" with as much confidence and inspiration as he could "in." The personnel reflected the album's intent—Freddie Hubbard on trumpet, Jimmy Garrison on bass, and Elvin Jones on drums. But after recording the soundtrack for the movie *Alfie*, Rollins embarked on a five-month spiritual journey to India in 1968, and from 1969 to 1972 he took another sabbatical from performance. Music, he said, had started to become a chore.

Rollins returned to jazz in 1972, beginning the most controversial period of his career. Over the next decade he recorded a dozen albums for Milestone, as notable for their occasional brilliance as for their frustratingly uneven quality. There were occasional exceptions—at times 1978's *Don't Stop the Carnival* provides a reasonable approximation of the power and energy of a Rollins live performance. For the most part, though, the studio recordings seemed to show him reaching for something more "primitive … less industrialized, more basic … closer to nature" (Nisenson, 212). Some accused him of selling out in an attempt to play in a more popular style. At the same time his concert performances remained the stuff of legends, showcasing inspired, powerful, imaginative playing.

Then almost abruptly Rollins seemed to reconnect with his muse. Beginning in 1988 with *Dancing in the Dark*, and later with 1993's *Old Flames*, he began to explore his romantic side. *Sonny Rollins plus Three* (1996), conceived as a tribute to the singers ETHEL WATERS, NAT KING COLE, and DINAH WASHINGTON, was his best studio effort in years and is one of the great Rollins albums. The personnel is fresh—with Cranshaw on bass, Flanagan or a young Stephen Scott on piano, and the veterans Al Foster or JACK DEJOHNETTE on drums—and once again Rollins magically transforms standards like "What a Difference a Day Makes," "Cabin in the Sky," and "Mona Lisa."

Global Warming, from 1998, is a conscious plea for the environment; a mix of quartets and sextets, it contains some of his most powerful playing of the past twenty years, in addition to the rhythmically powerful title tune. *This Is What I Do* (2000), a most appropriately titled recording, presents an immediate, stripped-down Rollins, his playing and phrasing as idiosyncratic as ever but still more powerfully concise. Finally, in 2005 Rollins released "Without a Song: The 9/11 Concert," recorded in concert at the Berkelee School of Music four days after the tragic events of 11 September 2001. Rollins had been in his apartment, six blocks away, when the planes hit the World Trade Center.

Sonny Rollins is considered the most important jazz saxophonist between Charlie Parker and John Coltrane. Though his originality may have peaked earlier, his playing remains largely unequaled even among the younger generations. He plays a variety of bop harmonic formulas, with "rhythmic imagination, harmonic subtlety, and freedom of design that have been surpassed only by Charlie Parker" (Kernfeld, 446). During the latter years of his career Rollins has spent most of his time enjoying the solitude of his farm in Upstate New York, practicing every day. Music for Rollins seems the wellspring of life. It is, he has remarked, "a beautiful way of bringing people together, a little bit of an oasis in this messed-up world."

FURTHER READING

Davis, Francis. *In the Moment: Jazz in the 1980s* (1986).
Kernfeld, Barry. "Sonny Rollins," in *The New Grove Dictionary of Jazz*, 2d ed. (2001).
Nisenson, Eric. *Open Sky: Sonny Rollins and His World of Improvisation* (2000).
Williams, Martin. *The Jazz Tradition*, rev. ed. (1983).
Wilson, Peter Niklas. *Sonny Rollins: The Definitive Musical Guide* (2001).

RONALD P. DUFOUR

Romain (c. 1776–1803), a slave whose death was the subject of the first graphic illustration of slave suicide in American literature, was likely born into slavery in the French Caribbean. By the time of his adolescence he was the property of a plantation owner in the French colony of St. Domingue. During the early 1790s Romain was brought by his master, M. Salaignac, to Trenton, New Jersey, when Salaignac fled the slave insurrection in St. Domingue. By 1800 Romain had married another "French negro," Marie Naval, and fathered two children, Anna and Garcin, one of whom was sent to live as a house slave in Philadelphia, Pennsylvania. In 1803 Salaignac received news that the revolution's leader, Toussaint Louverture, had been captured and that Napoleon's army was restoring order—and, many expected, slavery—to St. Domingue. Salaignac made preparations to return to the island, a decision that would return Romain and his family to the horrors of plantation slave labor.

Romain and his wife knew firsthand the wretchedness of life as slaves in the Caribbean, so on each step of their journey from Trenton to the ship waiting for them beyond Philadelphia their dejection and horror grew. En route to Delaware to be shipped to the West Indies, the party—Romain, his wife and child, a constable, and an envoy of his master—spent the night in Philadelphia. After just a few hours' rest at Howell's Inn on Second Street, the constable and the envoy were preparing to move the family on again. A coachman had brought the carriage to the door of the inn and the family was being escorted out when Romain's wife, Marie, took a chance and darted out into the street with her child. They disappeared into the morning bustle before the constable could catch them. Angry and humiliated, the envoy bellowed at Romain to get into the carriage. "Must I go alone?" Romain asked. "Yes," came the furious reply. Maddened by the thought and with no other prospects for freedom, Romain took a pruning knife from his pocket, "and dreading a spark of life should remain, whereby he might be restored, he three times cut his throat across, and fell dead on the pavement" (Humanitas, 14). Days later, when the coroner eventually brought in the verdict of inquest, it confirmed what every witness that morning already knew: Romain had committed suicide, "occasioned by the dread of slavery, to which the deceased knew himself devoted" (17).

One eyewitness recorded these events, the coroner's verdict, and his own lengthy commentary in a pamphlet, titled *Reflections on Slavery* (1803), published pseudonymously soon afterward—it is the only source available for the lives of Romain and his family. Directing his pamphlet to the attention of the Pennsylvania Abolition Society (PAS), the author, who called himself "Humanitas," hoped that its contents would excite moral outrage and legal action from the members of the society—the first organized antislavery organization in America. To amplify the power of the story of Romain's death, Humanitas provided a graphic illustration of his suicide.

Reflections on Slavery presented Romain's desperate circumstances—he was being forced to return to Caribbean bondage, the harshest system of slavery he knew—in a way that made clear that his suicide was a reasonable cause for sympathy. Describing Romain's suicide as an act of self-emancipation, an act of revolution, and an act worthy of divine mercy, Humanitas framed Romain's death as the deed of a virtuous man who had been degraded and numbed by the burden of his slave status. In an accompanying critique of the legal rulings that allowed slaves like Romain to be transported across state lines, Humanitas beseeched the members of the PAS to use their influence to repeal laws he considered cruel and unconstitutional.

While his imprecations apparently caused few ripples within the PAS or elsewhere, Humanitas's reflections served to shine a brief spotlight on slave suicide. While its urban, northern location set Romain's suicide apart from many of the hundreds of thousands of other suicides committed by enslaved people in the decades before the Civil War, in many ways it was typical. First, by taking his own life to escape transportation to a harsher system of labor than that in which he lived at the time, Romain's death echoed the suicides that took place on slave ships as they made the Middle Passage. Suicides also occurred when masters on estates in Virginia and Maryland sold slaves south to exhaustive plantation labor in Georgia, South Carolina, and further south and west. Narratives by former slaves such as CHARLES BALL, MOSES ROPER, and JAMES WILLIAMS testify to the frequency of suicidal thoughts and actions on those long journeys southward. Second, Romain's death followed his forcible separation from his family, another circumstance that often propelled slaves to suicide. While in this case Romain's wife had not been sold away from her husband but had escaped, the notion that slaveholders were uninterested in the preservation of black families would become a recurrent theme in abolitionist moral critiques of slavery in the decades after Romain's death. His suicide, like others that were recorded in antislavery writing in the nineteenth century, underlined the strength of emotional bonds between members of black families and the despairing depths to which individuals sunk when these bonds were forcibly broken by the institution of slavery.

Romain, who cut his throat in 1803, was one of only a handful of enslaved men and women whose individual circumstances were recorded before former slave autobiographers such as Charles Ball and FREDERICK DOUGLASS and white activists such as Theodore Dwight Weld and Lydia Maria Child brought dozens of similarly dramatic tales to national attention in the 1830s and 1840s. Romain's story was thus one of the first attempts to use testimony from eyewitnesses, descriptions of bodies in pain, and a focus on the circumstances of individual slaves to shame Americans into outrage and action against slavery.

FURTHER READING

Humanitas. *Reflections on Slavery; with Recent Evidence of Its Inhumanity. Occasioned by the Melancholy Death of Romain, a French Negro* (1803).

Blackburn, Robin. *The Making of New World Slavery: From the Baroque to the Modern, 1492–1800* (1997).

Dubois, Laurent. *Avengers of the New World: The Story of the Haitian Revolution* (2004).

RICHARD J. BELL

Roman, Charles Victor (4 July 1864–25 Aug. 1934), physician and medical educator, was born in Williamsport, Pennsylvania, the son of James William Roman, a former slave, and Anna Walker McGuinn, the child of a former slave. Charles's parents met in Canada, where his father had fled about twenty years before the Civil War. After the Emancipation Proclamation, a year and a half before his birth, they had moved back to the United States, but making a living there was difficult and by the time Charles was six the family had returned to Ontario, where his father worked as a broom maker. From an early age Charles knew he wanted to be a physician. Soon after the move to Canada he apprenticed himself to a local herbalist, possibly his grandmother. His practice ended when one of his patient's parents became nervous about the treatment Roman had administered and called in the local doctor, who pronounced the child cured and predicted that one day the young herbalist would himself become a physician.

At the age of twelve Roman moved with his family to Dundas, Ontario, and started working in a cotton mill to supplement the family's meager income. He continued this grueling work until an accident left him lame for life. He entered the Hamilton Collegiate Institute as its first black student and supported himself by selling small items. Despite these obstacles, he took only two years to finish a course of studies that usually took four. Later in life he would describe himself as "a factory boy—the product of the night school and public library, a triumph of democracy and a justification of its creed" (Cobb, 301). After graduating from the Canadian school, he wanted to attend McGill University's School of Medicine, but he did not have the money to pay tuition. At the advice of one of his teachers, he headed south and started teaching school.

After five months teaching first grade in Trigg County, Kentucky, Roman decided to spend another year teaching in the South. He still planned to return to Canada one day for medical school, but he happened to board with a physician who was an alumnus of Meharry Medical College. This doctor persuaded Roman to apply to his alma mater in Nashville, Tennessee, and in 1887 Roman entered Meharry. An able and popular teacher, he continued teaching during the day to fund his night medical classes. The Nashville board of education required its applicants for teaching jobs to take a competitive examination, and Roman finished first among one hundred white and seventy black teachers who took the test. After apprenticing with a local physician in his third year of medical school, he decided to give up teaching and pursue a career in medicine. He set to work completing a required graduate thesis on prophylaxis, or preventive medicine.

In 1890 Roman received his medical degree from Meharry and moved to Clarksville, Tennessee, where he opened a medical practice. In 1891 he married Margaret Voorhees, a Tennessee native, with whom he later had one child. The young couple moved to Dallas in 1893, and Roman practiced there. Like many physicians of that time, after a few years in practice, Roman decided he needed additional training. In 1899 he went to Chicago for a year of postgraduate study, and in 1904 he traveled to England's Royal Ophthalmic Hospital and the Central London Ear, Nose, and Throat Hospital for specialty training in ophthalmology and otolaryngology.

When Roman returned from abroad he contemplated opening a private practice specializing in diseases of the eye, ear, nose, and throat, but George Hubbard, dean of Meharry Medical College, made him a more attractive offer. While in Chicago, Roman had encountered the noted African American physician DANIEL HALE WILLIAMS, who had written to his good friend Hubbard of the younger physician's great promise. When the National Medical Association, the professional society for black physicians, gathered in Nashville in 1903, Hubbard met with Roman and tried to woo him back to Meharry. The following year Roman accepted Hubbard's offer and came to Meharry as the first chair of the ophthalmology and otolaryngology department, a post he retained until 1931.

At Meharry Roman lobbied for the construction of a teaching hospital attached to the university. Meharry used Mercy Hospital as a teaching hospital, but it was becoming increasingly crowded, and the school had no control over its operation. The faculty had long planned to build a hospital to honor Hubbard while he was still alive but had been uncertain where to start construction and how to fund the project. Roman presented a definitive schedule for construction. When the doors of Hubbard Hospital opened in 1912 he was considered one of the key forces behind its rapid completion. His influence in medical circles in Nashville extended beyond Meharry. From 1904 to 1933 he served as director of health at Fisk University, and he started and for a while conducted medical inspections in the city's black public schools.

Throughout his career Roman played an active role in the National Medical Association, founded in 1895. He served a year as its president, but perhaps his greatest contribution was founding and for ten years editing its house organ, the *Journal of the National Medical Association*. His leadership role in the national organization of black medical professionals attests directly to the respect he was accorded within this community—respect that was well earned. In 1904, the year he became president, the association had only 250 members; four years later Roman proposed that the group start the journal to help raise professional standards and attract more members, and by 1912 membership had more than doubled. Roman described the group in a 1908 speech: "Conceived in no spirit of racial exclusiveness, fostering no ethnic antagonisms, but born of the exigencies of the American environment, the National Medical Association has for its object binding together for mutual cooperation and helpfulness the men and women of African descent who are legally and honorably engaged in the cognate professions of medicine, surgery, pharmacy, and dentistry."

Roman did not restrict his activities to medicine; in the later years of his life he became increasingly involved with the humanities and the state of blacks in America. During World War I, for instance, he lectured to black troops about social hygiene. Over the course of his life he wrote more than forty journal articles and two books, which cemented his intellectual reputation among both blacks and whites. After he stepped down as chair of the medical department in 1934, he became professor of medical history and ethics at Meharry.

Roman wrote a number of pamphlets and papers on health, race, and Christian ethics. In 1921 he published a book, *American Civilization and the Negro: The Afro-American in Relation to National Progress*. In this well-received work he discussed the nature of race relations in the United States and the place of blacks in American society. In the introduction he summarized his point of view, saying, "The writer of this volume believes that the differences in mankind are the differences between charcoal and diamonds—differences of *condition* and not of *composition.*"

A resonant orator, Roman did not confine his opinions to the printed page. His 1913 speech before the Southern Sociological Congress was described in one local newspaper as the "most significant utterance on the race question" of that year. A devout member of the African Methodist Episcopal (AME) Church for his entire life, he was one of the pillars of Nashville's St. Paul AME Church community. He taught an adult Sunday school class that was so popular that the pastor invited him to address the entire congregation. Roman's lay sermons, as they came to be called, were imitated in other congregations throughout the country.

Throughout his life Roman enjoyed the respect of his peers, black and white, physicians and humanists. In a world rarely sympathetic to black men he managed without compromising his ideals to pursue the work that interested him and to help others. He was aware, however, that few black men shared his experiences. In *A History of Meharry Medical College*, published in the year of his death, he wrote, "The young professional man of my race needs to be learned in the lore of the past and wholeheartedly committed to the principles of noblesse oblige. Without these virtues, scientific knowledge will become an individual delusion and a group danger—apples of Sodom that will turn to ashes in the hour of need." Roman continued writing and speaking until his death in Nashville.

FURTHER READING

Cobb, William Montague. *Journal of the National Medical Association* 45 (1953).
Summerville, James. *Educating Black Doctors: A History of Meharry Medical College* (1983).
Obituary: *Journal of the National Medical Association* 26 (1934).

This entry is taken from the *American National Biography* and is published here with the permission of the American Council of Learned Societies.

SHARI RUDAVSKY

Romney, Lionel (26 Dec. 1912–26 June 2004), merchant mariner who was interned in the Nazi concentration camp system, was born in San Pedro de Macoris, in the Dominican Republic, to Alfred and Marie Louise Illidge Romney. He was of African and Dutch ancestry, and later immigrated to the United States; in the 1980s, he applied for citizenship.

The extremist, racist policies of Nazi Germany during the period 1933–1945 frequently extended to both its own black populace and prisoners of war. African Europeans and nationals living in occupied African territories were also singled out for persecution. In some cases, captive black soldiers were first segregated from white soldiers and then summarily executed. According to the United States Holocaust Memorial Museum, in addition to European blacks, blacks from the Americas were also detained in the Nazi concentration camp system (Carr, 47).

Romney, whose surname has also been recorded erroneously as "Rommney" (Taylor) and "Rombley" ("War"), was one such African American survivor of Nazi brutality. In his *African American Troops in World War II* (2007), Alexander Bielakowski recounted how tens of thousands of African Americans served in segregated military units. Although the U.S. Navy and Marine Corps were reluctant to either commission African Americans as officers or to permit them combat roles, they did make up two complete ships' companies by 1945. In accordance with the Merchant Marine Act of 1936, during World War II civilian merchant mariners were regarded as military personnel. In a 1945 military debriefing report filed by U.S. Navy Lieutenant Jack Taylor, an agent of the Office of Strategic Services during World War II, Romney is reported to have served as a firefighter with a merchant marine unit, a naval auxiliary in wartime, as early as 1940.

According to Taylor's account, Romney's vessel, the Greek-registered freighter SS *Makis*, was damaged in an Italian minefield and sank on 14 June 1940 near the Isle of Pantelleria (*New York Times*, 20 June 1940). Having survived the shipwreck, Romney was subsequently captured by the Italian armed forces.

After enduring four years as an Italian prisoner of war, Romney was handed over to the Nazis in 1944 and detained for a year in the infamous Mauthausen-Gusen concentration camp near Linz, Austria. In 1941 Mauthausen had been designated by SS Commander Heinrich Himmler as a *Stufe III Ausmerzungslager* [Category III Eliminating-camp], an exclusive label designated for sites commissioned to incarcerate "hardened criminals and antisocial elements incapable of rehabilitation" (Pike, 14). The notorious death camp Auschwitz II, alternately known as Birkenau, was also in this classification. Nazis described category III prisoner policy as both *Rückkehr unerwünscht* (return undesired) and *Vernichtung durch arbeit* (extermination through labor).

The daily living conditions of slave labor at Mauthausen were insufferable and, while there, Romney performed duties as a forest lumberjack in order to receive extra rations. Some controversy exists over inaccuracies in previously published— and often reprinted—accounts of Romney's experiences. For example, although Romney's nationality remained Dutch throughout the war, it is unclear why Lieutenant Taylor listed him as a Negro serviceman in the U.S. Merchant Marine in his debriefing. Until recently, little was known about Romney's life after this period of the war; political scientist Clarence Lusane, writing about Romney in *Hitler's Black Victims* (2003), was unsure if he had even survived (158). In 2006 a two-part series for "Law in Focus," a St. Maarten–produced television program about wartime infringements on human rights for residents of the Netherlands Antilles, disclosed that Romney was finally freed when American soldiers liberated the Mauthausen camp on 5 May 1945, the same date reported by Lieutenant Taylor.

After the war, it appears that Romney had at least one child, named Mary. Forty years after his liberation, Romney's daughter recorded his testimony and used it as a basis for the aforementioned documentary film. Romney died in Queens, New York, at the age of ninety-two.

The documentation of Romney's presence at Mauthausen is significant for several reasons. One is because scholars such as David Wing Pike, author of *Spaniards in the Holocaust*, have claimed that Spanish Moroccan Carlos Gray Key was "the only Negro in Mauthausen" (75). Romney's presence makes this assertion untrue. Another reason is because the Nazi leadership, in retreat from the advancing Allied armies, destroyed so much of the physical evidence associated with their death camps. The late Robert Kestling, an archivist for the United States Holocaust Memorial Museum, wrote that for blacks in the Holocaust, of whom there were about 55,000 victims and prisoners, there is a "lack of documentation as compared to the abundance of archival and published materials that exist about the plight of other victims" (84). The data destroyed by Nazis attempting to mask their crimes against humanity might have revealed a more complete historical representation of other African American, Caribbean American, and Afro-Caribbean experiences in the Holocaust.

FURTHER READING

Bard, Mitchell Geoffrey. *Forgotten Victims: The Abandonment of Americans in Hitler's Camps* (1994).

Carr, Firpo W. *Germany's Black Holocaust, 1890–1945: The Untold Truth!* (2003).

Friedman, Ina R. *The Other Victims: First-Person Stories of Non-Jews Persecuted by the Nazis* (1990).

Lusane, Clarence. *Hitler's Black Victims: The Historical Experiences of Afro-Germans, European Blacks, Africans, and African Americans in the Nazi Era* (2003).

Pike, David Wingeate. *Spaniards in the Holocaust: Mauthausen, Horror on the Danube* (2000).

"War and Human Rights Topic of Law in Focus," *The Daily Herald*, 26 Oct. 2006.

BURGSBEE L. HOBBS

Roper, Moses (1815–?), fugitive slave, antislavery agitator, memoirist, and farmer, was born in Caswell County, North Carolina, the son of a white planter, Henry H. Roper, and his mixed-race (African and Indian) house slave, Nancy. Moses Roper's light complexion and striking resemblance to his father proved embarrassing to the family. The animosity of the wife of his father, coupled with the death of Moses's legal owner, probably a man named John Farley, led to Henry Roper's decision to trade mother and son to a nearby plantation when Moses was six years of age. Soon after, he was sold to a "Negro trader" and shipped south. He never saw his mother again. Over the next twelve years he was sold repeatedly in North and South Carolina, Georgia, and Florida.

Moses Roper's light skin had an impact on his value on the slave market. Unable to secure a buyer, various slave traders found it necessary to hire the young boy out. Before the age of eleven, he worked first as a waiter and then as a tailor's apprentice. When he was eleven, Roper was sold to a Dr. Jones, a planter from Georgia, beginning a remarkable period during which, by his own accounting, he was sold at least thirteen times. It was his last owner, John Gooch, a cotton planter from Kershaw ("Cashaw" in Roper's narrative) County, South Carolina, who proved the worst. Gooch was a brutal man who flogged Roper mercilessly for minor offenses. Roper claimed that when Gooch was away on business, his wife stood in, whipping him with impunity. After repeated torture, the fourteen-year-old Roper could take no more and attempted to escape. He was soon captured near the Gooch plantation and harshly flogged. But this began a period during which Roper ran away whenever the opportunity presented itself. Once he made it as far as Charlotte, North Carolina, before being captured and returned to Gooch, who always stood ready to make his slave pay for the transgression.

In 1833 Roper's life changed for the better when Gooch sold him to a northern Florida slave trader whose economic travails soon led to bankruptcy. To pay his debts, the trader sold Roper to a local planter with a reputation for extreme brutality. Rather than endure that abuse, Roper once again took to the roads and swamps, eventually making his way to Savannah, Georgia, where he convinced a sea captain to take him on as a steward. After a period of extreme anxiety for Roper, the ship set sail for New York.

Roper took advantage of an escape network along the eastern seaboard that the historian David Cecelski has characterized as the "maritime underground railroad." Coastal geography as well as demography made this region of the slaveholding South more porous than most. In North Carolina alone, blacks comprised 45 percent of the population of the tidewater counties. Black watermen worked as stevedores, stewards, and pilots. Many lived and worked as squatters and swampers. Their world was the "underside of slavery," where the institution was anything but stable. Their actions betrayed the "complex, tumultuous, and dissident undercurrent to coastal life in the slavery era" (Cecelski, "Shores of Freedom," 176). Runaway slaves like Roper found a ready-made network of allies willing to assist them on their way northward. Roper estimated that he had traveled nearly five hundred miles to get to Savannah from Florida along the tangle of rivers and creeks that crisscross the region.

In August 1834 Roper arrived in New York City. His euphoria was short-lived, however, when he was informed that he could easily be recaptured. He continued up the Hudson River toward Poughkeepsie, New York, battling both a racist crew who claimed to know his true identity and a cholera outbreak that nearly killed him. Roper eventually journeyed into Vermont, securing work as a farmhand. Soon after his arrival, he was informed that he was being "advertised" in area newspapers. He fled Vermont for New Hampshire and after a short while went to that hotbed of abolitionist agitation, Boston, Massachusetts, where he made contact with local abolitionists, including William Lloyd Garrison. Roper's name appears as one of the signatories of the constitution of the American Anti-Slavery Society. But even in Boston, life for a fugitive slave was precarious. After several weeks of working for a Brookline shopkeeper, Roper was told by two of his black neighbors that a "gentleman" had been inquiring for a person matching his description. He left Boston, hiding first in the Green Mountains and then making his way to New York City, where he was able to secure passage on a ship, the *Napoleon*, bound for England.

Roper arrived in Liverpool, England, in November 1835, armed with letters of recommendation to the noted British abolitionists John Morrison, John Scoble, and George Thompson, who quickly embraced the young fugitive and pressed him into service as an antislavery lecturer. When Roper expressed an interest in getting an education, his patrons convinced Dr. Francis Cox to assume the financial burden for sending him to boarding school, first at Hackney and then at Wallingford. Roper also attended University College in London for a short while in 1836. All the while he continued lecturing to reform audiences across the country, becoming one of the first former slaves to play such a role.

In 1837 Roper published in London a narrative of his life as a slave, *A Narrative of the Adventures and Escape of Moses Roper from American Slavery*; it was published in the United States one year later. The publication was accompanied by an extensive lecture tour. In 1839 he married Ann Stephen Price, an Englishwoman from Bristol who assisted him in carrying on the antislavery work. In 1844, after nine years of lecturing, Roper estimated that he had given two thousand lectures. He informed the British Anti-Slavery Society that he was going to retire and asked that they assist him in putting together the funds to purchase a farm in the British colony on the Cape of Good Hope in southern Africa. There he hoped to put the agricultural knowledge that he had gleaned during his labors as a slave to better use. Roper never made it to Africa, but he did secure the capital to purchase a farm in western Canada. He returned to England twice, in 1846 to supervise another edition of his narrative, and in 1854 to lecture. Unfortunately, historians have been unable to determine how Roper spent the remainder of his life.

Given the intense suffering of Roper's early years, his is a remarkable tale of resilience that ultimately illuminates the network that was the "maritime underground railroad." If Roper is a minor character in the history of American slavery and abolitionism, it is important to note that he was also a key transatlantic connection in the early stages of an international movement to abolish slavery.

FURTHER READING

Roper, Moses. *A Narrative of the Adventures and Escape of Moses Roper from American Slavery* (1838, repr. in William L. Andrews, ed., *North Carolina Slave Narratives* [2003], 21–76).
Cecelski, David S. "The Shores of Freedom: The Maritime Underground Railroad in North Carolina, 1800–1861," *North Carolina Historical Review* 71 (Apr. 1994).
Cecelski, David S. *The Waterman's Song: Slavery and Freedom in Maritime North Carolina* (2001).
Ripley, C. Peter, et al., eds. *The Black Abolitionist Papers*, vol. 1, *The British Isles, 1830–1865* (1985).
MARK ANDREW HUDDLE

Rose, Arthur (26 May 1921–13 Feb. 1995), artist, educator, and community activist, was born in Charleston, South Carolina, the son of Edward Rose Sr. and Mary Marshall. Arthur Rose attended the segregated public schools in Charleston. In 1942 Rose enlisted as a ship serviceman in the U.S. Navy; he served until 1945. A member of Company 1621, 18th Regiment, 28th Battalion of the U.S. Naval Reserve Corps, Rose entered basic training in Chicago and was later stationed at the naval base in Norfolk, Virginia, for the duration of the war, and did not see combat. He returned to Charleston and graduated from Burke High School in 1946. He later matriculated at Claflin University, South Carolina's oldest historically black institution of higher learning, established in 1869.

Rose was among the first students in Claflin's history to major in fine arts. During his college tenure Rose met and married fellow Claflin student Elizabeth McMillan in 1948, at first secretly since McMillan had promised her mother not to marry until after her graduation. Rose went on to teach at Holmes Elementary School in Florence, South Carolina, for one year. In the summer of 1951 the Roses moved to New York City, where Arthur attended New York University and studied with the artists HALE WOODRUFF, William Baziotes, Peter Busa, and James Podzez. Rose earned his master of arts in Education in 1952 and returned to his native South Carolina to head the department of art at Claflin. He served as its chair from 1952 until 1976.

Functioning at first virtually as a department of one at Claflin, Rose provided instruction for all levels of the art curriculum and served as an inspirational mentor for his students, not solely in the visual arts. Rose was also an important local activist and strategic planner for demonstrations, sit-ins, marches, and protests in the civil rights movement.

In 1953 Rose and his students implemented the annual Fence Exhibition at Claflin, which showcased the productivity of the art program and its students. It was a public demonstration of their commitment to an enviable work ethic and was a discernible presentation of instructional standards for the group. During this time the Fence Exhibition was the only local art activity that attempted to bridge the community's racial divide, and people came from across the state to support the art program and purchase student works. The exhibition raised the profile of the art department at Claflin, and its reputation grew considerably.

Rose was a founding member of the National Conference of Artists (NCA), an organization established in 1958 (originally as the National Conference of Negro Artists, or NCNA) specifically to promote and encourage creative expression among Americans of African descent. Rose served as the NCA regional representative for the state of South Carolina from 1959 until 1962.

During the late 1950s through the early 1960s Rose and his wife, Elizabeth, were among the first local African American families to petition and formally protest the institutional segregation by race in the Orangeburg, South Carolina, public schools. The Roses' interest in quality education for their growing family created the foundation for much of their activism. Their daughter Patricia Ann was born in 1951, followed in 1953 by Arthur Jr. In the following decade, Bernard Henry was born in 1960 and Marcia Lorraine in 1963. Rose's name appears first on the petition to the courts submitted in 1955. He was an active agent for social change through his participation as a strategist in the NAACP and the civil rights movement in Orangeburg. Rose, supported by his family, fought fearlessly against the injustices of segregation, and gained a reputation as a daring and innovative experimental artist among his peers. Generally Rose's works dealt more with formalist concerns, evading overtly political themes, with the exception of a painting created as a commemorative response to the Orangeburg massacre of 7 February 1968.

Prior to the mid-1960s Claflin's art program offered the only opportunity in South Carolina for African American students interested in visual culture to major in fine arts. Many talented students from across the state were drawn to the program, and a number of Rose's students completed their curriculum at Claflin and continued with postgraduate study, some founding art departments in other state venues or achieving prominence as artists, artist-educators, or arts administrators. In this group were the batik artist LEO TWIGGS, MacArthur Goodwin (former president of the National Art Education Association), the award-winning painter Alvin Staley, and the internationally exhibited sculptor Winston Wingo. From 1966 to 1968 Rose pursued postgraduate studies at Indiana University, Bloomington, and following this period the University Foundation purchased his welded-steel sculpture *Bison* (c. 1969).

A teacher and mentor remembered for his paradoxically demanding and supportive approach to the young people in his charge, Rose was also an avid, lifelong fisherman. He was well known for taking his students on fishing excursions, as well as for his invitations to join his family for meals. He held animated discussions with them about art, politics, and civil rights.

Rose actively engaged his students in the exploration of new media and formal experimentation, using his infectious enthusiasm for the creative process. He encouraged creativity and innovation among his students, providing the consummate example through his experiments in unusual materials. His work ranged from paintings that he sought to infuse with a "primitive" simplicity to unusual works of collage, mixed-media assemblage, and whimsical, welded-metal sculptures. For Rose, the primitivist approach was an aesthetic reconciliation of his African heritage, southern folk traditions, Western figurative representation, and modernist conceptualism. He also developed a personal approach to expressionism and abstraction.

In the oil painting *The Old Man Who Came to Dinner* (c. 1972), Rose combined eloquent social commentary with compositional élan. This image emphasizes the flat, planar qualities of his subject and is articulated by its thickly applied impasto, a heavy buildup of paint pigment within the image, which draws the observer into the artwork, and its surface patterning energized by bright color. The theme of the painting, alluding to the process of aging and its too often attendant poverty, is characteristic of Rose's socially conscious themes. In other works he entirely relinquished figuration, and Rose was among a small group of southern African American artists who worked before the 1970s in either a non-objective or figurally abstract manner.

From the 1960s through the early 1970s Rose often experimented with unusual materials such as asphalt, tar, acrylic house paint, and found objects to create quixotic works in the French avant-garde tradition. Yet the works maintained nuanced references to African American heritage. The power of these abstract works often spilled over into his marginally representational sculpture. In the well-known piece *Killer Whale* (c. 1969), a chaotic, tiered tumult of welded steel, Rose imparted the recognizable essential forms of a streamlined, surging sea creature.

In the 1970s Rose received considerable attention and acclaim in South Carolina. He was included in J. Edward Atkinson's *Black Dimensions in Contemporary American Art* (1971) and was profiled in John W. Faust's 1971 article for *Sandlapper* magazine. In it Rose was quoted as saying: "Art is a concentration of self into an expression ... a definition of what you yourself want to say in any medium whether it's oils, stone, pastels, watercolor or metalwork.... I've got to like it and if only one other person likes what I've created, then I feel I've accomplished something worthwhile" (Faust, 77–78). In 1977 Rose left Claflin to be an artist-in-residence at Vorhees College in Denmark, South Carolina. He returned to Claflin in 1985, and in that same year the exhibition Arthur Rose: A Retrospective was held at South Carolina State University's I. P. Stanback Museum in Orangeburg. Rose died in his adoptive community of Orangeburg. In recognition of his life and work, the Arthur Rose Museum at Claflin University was opened and dedicated in 1999. In 2000 his works were included in the exhibition 100 Years, 100 Artists, sponsored by the South Carolina Arts Commission and the South Carolina State Museum in celebration of the new millennium.

FURTHER READING

Cederholm, Theresa Dickason. *Afro-American Artists: A Bio-bibliographical Directory* (1973).

Faust, John W. "Teacher-Artist Arthur Rose," *Sandlapper* 4.2 (Feb. 1971): 77–79.

FRANK MARTIN

Rose, Edward (?–1833?), mountain man and Indian interpreter, may have been born in Kentucky, near Louisville, most likely of African, Indian, and white ancestry. The year and date of his birth remain unknown, as do the names and occupations of his parents. It is possible that Rose was born a slave. The details of Rose's life have been gleaned from the narratives and records of others, including Washington Irving, who claimed that after leaving home as a teenager, Rose became a kind of roving bandit, "one of the gangs of pirates who infested the islands of the Mississippi, plundering boats as they went up and down the river ... waylaying travelers as they returned by land from New Orleans ... plundering them of their money and effects, and often perpetuating the most atrocious murders" (*Astoria*, ch. 24). It appears that Rose left New Orleans after the police broke up his gang, eventually settling in St. Louis, where, in the spring of 1806, the local newspaper described him as big, strong, and hot-tempered, with a swarthy, fierce-looking face.

That same year Rose traveled up the Osage River with a group of hunters, after which he must have returned to St. Louis, because in the spring of 1807 he left from there with Manuel Lisa's fur-trading expedition up the Missouri River, the first major expedition organized after Lewis and Clark's return to St. Louis. Led by Lisa, a St. Louis businessman, the party traveled north, up the Missouri River through present-day North and South Dakota, and then southwest, along the Yellowstone River to the mouth of the Bighorn River, where they established the first trading post on the upper river, Fort Manuel (also called Fort Lisa), in what became Montana. After trading jewelry, tobacco, liquor, weapons, and blankets for pelts with the local Crow Indians (Absaroke or Sparrowhawk people), Lisa and his men returned to St. Louis. Rose, however, chose to remain behind. Living with the Crow in what is now southern Montana and northern Wyoming, Rose learned their culture and language. Because of his appearance, Rose was known as Nez Coupe ("Scarred Nose") and later, after a particularly fierce battle, as Five Scalps.

It has been suggested that during this time Rose partnered with the French frontiersman and husband of Sacagawea, Toussaint Charbonneau, in escorting Arapaho women captured by Snake Indians to European trappers willing to pay for Indian women. In any event, in the spring of 1809 Rose joined an expedition organized for the purpose of escorting Sheheke (also known, by whites, as Big White), the principal chief of Matootonha, a lower Mandan village, through hostile territory back to his tribe. In 1806 Sheheke, along with his wife and children, had accompanied Lewis and Clark to St. Louis and Washington, D.C., via Monticello, where they met Thomas Jefferson. The first attempt to return Sheheke in 1807, led by Nathaniel Pryor, had failed because of resistance from the Sioux and Arikara. Two years later, with a contract for seven thousand dollars paid to the Missouri Fur Company by the U.S. government, twenty men, including Rose, spent three months traveling with the chief and his family northwest, up the Missouri River to Matootonch, in present-day North Dakota. On the way back to St. Louis, Rose elected to rejoin the Crow.

In 1811 Rose was hired by the "Astorians"—John Jacob Astor's Pacific Fur Company—as a guide for the first expedition to the Pacific Ocean since Lewis and Clark had returned six years earlier. Led by Wilson Price Hunt, a merchant from New Jersey with no experience as a hunter or trapper, the party included sixty-four men and eighty-four horses. Rose joined the party on the plains near the Arikara villages just north of the present-day border between North and South Dakota and guided the expedition through Crow territory. Suspicious of his loyalty to the Crow, Hunt never trusted Rose. Predisposed to believe reports that Rose was organizing a mutiny, Hunt fired him as soon as the party reached the Black Hills of South Dakota, an error in judgment that contributed to many of the expedition's failures. Immediately after dispatching Rose, in an indication of what lay ahead, Hunt and his group became lost as they tried to pass through mountains. A few days later Rose returned with several Crow and helped the party find a pass.

Washington Irving's description of Rose in his 1836 book *Astoria; or, Anecdotes of an Enterprise beyond the Rocky Mountains* must have been typical of attitudes toward Rose, whom Irving describes as "one of those anomalous beings found on the frontier, who seem to have neither kin nor country … and was, withal, a dogged, sullen, silent fellow, with a sinister aspect, and more of the savage than the civilized man in his appearance" (*Astoria*, ch. 22). "This fellow it appears," Irving continues, "was one of those desperadoes of the frontiers, outlawed by their crimes, who combine the vices of civilized and savage life, and are ten times more barbarous than the Indians with whom they consort" (*Astoria*, ch. 24).

A year later, in 1812, Manuel Lisa found Rose living with the Arikaras and hired him as a scout. Rose, however, never made it to their meeting place in New Orleans, having attached himself to an Omaha Indian woman, with whom he remained in her tribe until he was arrested for drinking and fighting and was taken to St. Louis. Records show that Rose was released in 1813 by Superintendent of Indian Affairs William Clark in exchange for Rose's promise to stay out of Indian territory.

Historians are unsure of Rose's activities in the following decade, until 10 March 1823, when he left St. Louis with one hundred men on the ill-fated trapping expedition of William Henry Ashley and Andrew Henry, owners of the Rocky Mountain Fur Company. From the outset Ashley dismissed Rose's counsel against bartering for horses with the Arikara and against mooring company boats on the same side of the river as the tribe. More disastrously, Ashley ignored Rose's warning of an impending Arikara attack, and when the ambush came, the company's losses were heavy. Attacks on the traders continued until Colonel Henry Leavenworth arrived from Fort Atkinson with two hundred fur traders, frontiersmen, and Lakota and Tankton warriors organized into a frontier militia known as the Missouri Legion. Rose was made an ensign, and the militia attacked the Arikara villages in August 1823. In his official report submitted to General Henry Atkinson and dated 20 October 1823, Leavenworth singled out Rose: "I had not found anyone willing to go into those villages, except a man by the name of Rose…. He appeared to be a brave and enterprising man, and was well acquainted with those Indians…. He was with General Ashley when he was attacked. The Indians at that time called to him to take care of himself, before they fired upon General Ashley's party" (quoted in Burton, 11).

Trying to salvage the expedition, Ashley assembled a small party of men, described by Harrison Clifford Dale in the *Ashley-Smith Explorations* (1941) as "the most significant group of continental explorers ever brought together." This group included Rose and other such noted frontiersmen as James Clyman, David Jackson, William Sublette, Jim Bridger, Hugh Glass, and Thomas Fitzpatrick. Led by Jedediah Smith, the party traveled up the Grand River and through the Black Hills to the Rockies. From Clyman's diary we learn that Rose's familiarity with the Indian language and customs saved the party from disaster.

Rose served with Smith for the next two years, leaving in May 1825 to join a large treaty-making expedition up the Missouri under the command of General Atkinson and Major Benjamin O'Fallon. Forty men on horseback, under the command of a Lieutenant Armstrong, went with Rose by land; the rest traveled up the river in nine boats. The Yellowstone expedition, as it came to be known, succeeded in signing peace treaties with all the tribes of the river except the Blackfoot. Reports of the expedition by several authors delight in recounting Rose's mythmaking adventures. A clerk whose expedition journal was published in 1929 in the *North Dakota Historical Society Quarterly* documented one oft-repeated tale of Rose's heroics and skill: "Thursday 30 June. Rose, an interpreter, one of the party, we understand, covered himself with bushes and crawled into the gang of 11 Bulls [buffalo] and shot down 6 on the same ground before the others ran off."

Much of the information we know about Rose comes from a biographical sketch of him that Captain Ruben Holmes, a member of the Atkinson-O'Fallon expedition, published in the *St. Louis Beacon* in 1828 (reprinted in the *St. Louis Reveille* in

1848). In "The Five Scalps" (1848), Holmes describes Rose's confrontation with a band of six hundred hostile Crow warriors: "One foot was on the pile of muskets, to prevent the Indians from taking any from it … his eye gleamed with triumphant satisfaction. There was an expression about his mouth, slightly curved and compressed, and a little smiling at the curves, indicative of a delirium of delight— his eye, his mouth, the position of his head, and scars on his forehead and nose all united in forming a general expression, that, of itself, seemed to paralyze the nerves of every Indian before him."

Rose apparently rejoined the Crow after the 1825 expedition, and nine years later he rode alongside them in their battles with the Blackfoot. "The old Negro," Zenas Leonard wrote in his autobiography, *Adventures of Zenas Leonard, Fur Trader* (1839), "told them that if the red man was afraid to go among his enemy, he would show them that a black man was not." Rose was one of first black frontiersmen to earn a wide reputation, preceding JIM BECKWOURTH, who was born around 1800, by a generation. Indeed, Beckwourth, who in his autobiography, *The Life and Times of James P. Beckwourth* (1856), called Rose "one of the best interpreters ever known in the whole Indian country," may have claimed some of the older man's exploits for himself.

When and how Rose—whom Harold Felton describes as "a mountain man's mountain man, a trail blazer's trail blazer" (vii)—died remains unknown. Legend has it that Rose, Hugh Glass, and a third mountain man named Menard were killed and scalped on the frozen Yellowstone River in the winter of 1832–1833 by a band of Arikaras hostile to the Crow. A site called Rose's Grave is located at the junction of the Milk and Missouri rivers, on the Milk River near the Yellowstone River.

FURTHER READING

Burton, Art T. *Black, Buckskin, and Blue: African-American Scouts and Soldiers on the Western Frontier* (1999).

Felton, Harold W. *Edward Rose: Negro Trail Blazer* (1967).

Irving, Washington. *Astoria; or, Anecdotes of an Enterprise beyond the Rocky Mountains* (1836).

LISA E. RIVO

Ross Barnett, Marguerite (22 May 1942–26 Feb. 1992), political scientist, educator, scholar, and university president, was born Marguerite Ross in Charlottesville, Virginia, the daughter of George Dewey Ross and Mary Douglass, but she was raised and educated in Buffalo, New York. A stellar student, Ross Barnett graduated from Bennett High School in 1959 and then continued her education at Antioch College. Although she originally planned to pursue a career in the sciences, Ross Barnett realized that teaching was her true calling while an undergraduate student at Antioch. She graduated from Antioch in 1964 with an AB in Political Science and then earned an M.A. from the University of Chicago an in 1966 and a Ph.D. in Political Science in 1972.

Given her outstanding academic talents, it is not surprising that Ross Barnett served as a lecturer at the University of Chicago in 1969 before completing her doctoral studies. Over the next decade, she rose rapidly through the faculty ranks with appointments at some of the most prestigious universities in the United States. She joined the faculty at Princeton University in 1972 and was appointed the James Madison Bicentennial Preceptor from 1974 until 1976. As her reputation as a brilliant scholar grew, Ross Barnett moved to Howard University, where she served as chair of the political science department from 1977 to 1980. At the age of thirty-four, when most academics are struggling for recognition as junior faculty, Ross Barnett became a full professor at Howard. It was not long before she was lured to Columbia University, where she was also appointed a full professor. In 1980 she married Walter King, a former member of the Bermuda parliament.

Ross Barnett continued to gain national and international recognition for scholarly contributions to her discipline. She served as the primary author or editor of five books and some forty articles. She won the American Political Science Association's coveted prize for the best work on ethnic and cultural pluralism for *The Politics of Cultural Nationalism in South India* (1976) and received the RALPH BUNCHE Award in 1981 in recognition for her scholarship in political science. In 1986 she was recognized again by the American Political Science Association, a rare honor, for excellence in scholarship and service to the profession. Ross Barnett married Stephen A. Barnett, with whom she had a daughter before they divorced.

It was not long before Ross Barnett's administrative talents were recognized and as highly regarded as her scholarship. In 1983 she was selected to serve as vice chancellor of academic affairs at the City University of New York, one of the country's largest public university systems with more than nineteen colleges. In 1986 she assumed the position of chancellor at the University of Missouri–Saint Louis, where she served until 1990. Her appointment in 1990 as president of the University of Houston solidified Ross-Barnett's reputation as a national leader in higher education. She was the first African American and the first woman appointed president of that teaching and research institution. While Ross Barnett only held the position for a year and a half, she proved an effective leader and fund-raiser. She established the nationally recognized Bridge Program, which helps disadvantaged youth make the transition to college-level study. In addition she raised more than $150 million for the university and established the Texas Center for Environmental Studies and the Texas Center for University–School Partnerships. Her unyielding focus on excellence in education and her commitment to building "bridges" for disadvantaged youth were evident throughout her career. Ross Barnett's influence and accomplishments went far beyond higher education to include seats on the board of directors at the Monsanto Corporation, the Council on Foreign Relations, the American Council on Education, the President's Commission on Environmental Quality, and the Houston Grand Opera, among others.

As Ross Barnett's professional career was soaring, her physical health declined. In 1991 she was diagnosed with cancer and took a leave of absence to seek medical treatment. In a matter of months, she had succumbed to the disease. Yet her vision for the future of higher education did not end.

Following Ross Barnett's death, several memorial and scholarship funds were established in her name. The Marguerite Ross Barnett Memorial Scholarship Program was established to provide financial assistance to students who are employed while attending a college or university part-time. The American Political Science Association and the Women's Caucus for Political Science established the Marguerite Ross Barnett Endowment Fellowship, which provides postdoctoral fellowships for political scientists beginning their careers. Her legacy lives on in the academic institutions she helped strengthen, in the programs she created, and in the lives of the students she influenced.

FURTHER READING

The Marguerite Ross Barnett Papers, including speeches, correspondence, and other documents from September 1990 to March 1992, are at the University of Houston Libraries.

"Marguerite Ross Barnett." *Notable Black American Women*, ed. Jessie Carney Smith (1992).

ROBIN M. DASHER-ALSTON

Ross, Diana (26 Mar. 1944–), singer and actress, was born in Detroit, Michigan, the second of six children of Fred Ross, a college-educated factory worker, and Ernestine Moten. Although Fred and Ernestine had intended to name their daughter Diane, a clerical oversight at the hospital altered the name to Diana. She was known as Diane to family and close friends, and the use of this familiar name has remained an indicator throughout her life of those among her inner circle. The family lived in a black middle-class neighborhood where, as she ironed her family's laundry, she could see from her window fifteen-year-old SMOKEY ROBINSON singing with his friends on his front porch (Taraborrelli, 36). When Ross turned fourteen the family moved to the Brewster projects, a low-income development that had not yet warranted the stigmatizing nomenclature of "ghetto" or "slum." The Rosses had an affordable three-bedroom home and attended Olivet Baptist Church, where Ross sang in the junior choir with her siblings, while her parents sang in the adult choir.

Ross attended Cass Technical High School, an esteemed public school, where she registered high marks in cosmetology and dress design; upon graduating in 1962 she was voted the best dressed in her class. In high school many of Ross's peers had begun singing at parties and on street corners. One of these groups, the Primes, would eventually become the Temptations—but in the meantime their manager wanted a sister group to complement their local performances. The manager began with his girlfriend's husky-voiced sister, FLORENCE BALLARD, as the centerpiece; recruited two of her friends, MARY WILSON and Betty McGlown; and searched exhaustively for the final voice. The Primes' singer Paul Williams finally suggested Ross, and the Primettes—undaunted by McGlown's leaving the group to get married—quickly established themselves on the Detroit scene, earning fifteen dollars a week in local clubs and signing a deal with LuPine records, with whom they recorded two singles that were never released. But BERRY GORDY JR. at Motown Records, heeding the advice of his young star in the making, Smokey Robinson, was ready on 15 January 1961 to sign the four women. (They had recruited Barbara Martin to replace McGlown.) Gordy renamed the group the Supremes and began processing them through the Motown Artists Development Department, where they were schooled in style, public speaking, and overall deportment. Hardly an immediate success, the Supremes floundered for three years,

Diana Ross keeps singing despite a heavy downpour during her free concert in New York's Central Park to an audience of approximately 80,000 people, 21 July 1983. (AP Images.)

one album, and eight mediocre singles, in addition to weathering the first of many personnel changes. Ballard briefly departed in 1962 to tour with the Marvelettes, and Martin quit in order to have a baby. Ross sang lead only about half the time, and, at that point, the Supremes were attempting to succeed as a trio that sang songs with four-part harmonies. They toured briefly in 1962 under the auspices of a Motown revue, but it was not until another tour in June 1964, when Motown released "Where Did Our Love Go?," that the Supremes had their first number-one hit. Written by LAMONT DOZIER and Brian and Eddie Holland—three of Motown's premier writers and producers—the single was the first of a string of hits that helped define the Motown sound as a successful crossover hybrid of gospel, rock and roll, rhythm and blues, and pop.

The Supremes made numerous television appearances, most often on *The Ed Sullivan Show*, where their glamorous evening gowns and dashing wigs projected an image of black womanhood rarely seen by white Americans. During the mid-1960s the Supremes could boast a yearly income of $250,000 each. Ross literally took center stage by this point, singing lead and prompting Gordy to change the group's name to Diana Ross and the Supremes. By 1969 they had hit number one with eleven singles, registering about a half dozen in the pop music canon: "Baby Love" (1964), "Come See about Me" (1964), "Stop! In the Name of Love" (1965), "I Hear a Symphony" (1965), and "You Can't Hurry Love" (1966). They finished the decade with their twelfth hit, titled "Someday We'll Be Together." Ironically, on 14 January 1970, almost nine years to the day after signing with Motown, Ross left to pursue a solo career. The Supremes continued shuffling personnel for another seven years before disbanding in 1977, never again hitting number one.

Ross continued manufacturing hit after hit for Motown, starting with 1970's "Ain't No Mountain High Enough." She would eventually score seven more number-one hits as a solo artist, first with Motown and then with RCA, with whom she signed in 1981 for $20 million. But the most dynamic element of her career to develop in the 1970s was her acting. She landed the lead in the BILLIE HOLIDAY biopic *Lady Sings the Blues* (1972) and was nominated for an Academy Award for Best Actress. Her next project, the Motown-backed vehicle *Mahogany* (1975), attempted to capitalize on her superstar status. The film's production was notoriously troubled, as rumors surfaced about Ross's demanding personality and Gordy's curious decision to direct the film himself. *Mahogany* garnered hardly any positive reviews, but Ross did gain another number-one hit from the soundtrack, "The Theme from *Mahogany* (Do You Know Where You're Going To?)."

In 1978 she again compelled her critics to claim that she was overbearing—and her supporters to praise her business acumen—by purchasing the movie rights to the Broadway smash *The Wiz* and reworking the story so that she could play the lead of Dorothy. The ensemble cast of MICHAEL JACKSON, RICHARD PRYOR, and LENA HORNE was not nearly enough to salvage this African American retelling of *The Wizard of Oz* from more sternly negative reviews.

The 1970s were also tumultuous personally for Ross. In 1970 she married Robert Silberstein, a music manager, with whom she had three children (though the first, she later admitted, was fathered by Gordy). They divorced in 1975; two years later, Ross married an international businessman named Arne Naess Jr., with whom she had two more children, but they divorced in 2000. Musically she seemed to fall into a rut, always staying even with the latest trend, as with her tepid disco tracks, rather than innovating, as she had with the Supremes earlier in her career. In 1989 she returned to Motown as both a performer and a director of the company. She continued releasing albums but seemed to drift further and further from mainstream pop success. Ross wrote her autobiography, *Secrets of a Sparrow*, in 1993. In 2000 a "reunion" tour for the Supremes was cancelled after poor ticket sales. The tour received widespread criticism from conception since the two living Supremes with whom Ross had sang Mary Wilson and Cindy Birdsong, declined to participate, allegedly because of the relatively small fees they were offered. Subsequently, Ross was a frequent tabloid target as reports of alcohol problems emerged. Nevertheless, she returned to the album charts in 2007 with *I Love You*.

FURTHER READING

Ross, Diana. *Secrets of a Sparrow* (1993).
Haskins, James. *Diana Ross* (1985).
Itkowitz, Leonore K. *Diana Ross* (1974).
Taraborrelli, J. Randy. *Call Her Miss Ross* (1989).

DAVID F. SMYDRA JR.

Ross, Eunice (1823–1895), educator and catalyst for the successful integration of Nantucket public schools and for the passage of the first law in the United States to guarantee equal access to education, was born on the island of Nantucket. She was the youngest child born to Jam, a laborer, and Mary Ross, and had one brother and three sisters. Her father was one of the few people on the island listed in the census of having been born in Africa.

During Eunice Ross's childhood, Nantucket was a thriving whaling community. African Americans lived on the outskirts of town in a segregated neighborhood known as Newtown or New Guinea. During her childhood, the black and white population of the island increased steadily, and by the time she was seventeen, the Newtown community had doubled in size to around six hundred residents. The community was self-sufficient with its own shops, inns, and cemetery. The African Meeting House, a Baptist church and community center, was organized near the time of her birth. Many Newtown families, like the Rosses, owned their own houses and paid taxes.

As the population on the island grew, the demand for public education grew as well. However, there was resistance among the white male voting population to using tax money to support schools, and it took a court case in 1826 to force Nantucket to provide public instruction. However, the Newtown community was at least one year in advance of the rest of the town; it had created a school that met at the African Meeting House. Generally, about forty students attended the multi-graded, one-room school. When the town did establish a public school system, it funded the African School and hired its teachers. Black students were barred from all the other schools. Nantucket continued, however, to violate Massachusetts's law, as it did not establish a high school. It took eleven more years of steady pressure before one was finally created. Eunice Ross at age seventeen had outgrown the curriculum of the African School. Under the tutelage of the school's abolitionist teacher, Anna Gardner, Ross prepared for the examination to enter the new high school. She passed the examination along with seventeen white students, but the School Committee turned her down because of her race.

At the time of Ross's application to the high school, other racial issues divided the island. The local library had closed its doors to blacks and to abolitionist groups. Some churches had barred their doors to abolition speakers, and many Quaker abolitionists, such as Anna Gardner, were disowned. As a result, the African Meeting House stopped renting space to the School Committee, and the town had to erect a new building in Newtown to keep the schools segregated. From 1840 to 1847, the issue of school integration and the denial of Eunice Ross to the high school dominated each of Nantucket's annual town meetings and letters to the editor in the *Inquirer*, the local paper. One series of racist letters referred to her as being an "obnoxious" color and compared it to measles and other "contagious diseases" (*Inquirer*, 4 May 1843).

The African Americans in Nantucket turned to political action in an attempt to integrate the schools. In 1842 they wrote an "Address to the Town," which was printed locally and in William Lloyd Garrison's abolitionist paper, the *Liberator*. The letter documented their grievances concerning the state of public education on the island, which included the denial of "having their youth educated in the same schools which are common to the more favored members" of the town (*Liberator*, 18 March 1842). African Americans in the community also ran for office. While they never won an election, they continually put their names forward. For example, James Ross, Eunice's father, ran for the

School Committee in 1843, along with nine other African Americans.

Meanwhile, during the 1840s, the Anti-Slavery Society held yearly conventions on the island, which were attended by well-known speakers such as William L. Garrison and FREDERICK DOUGLASS. The issue of Nantucket's school segregation provided a flash point for their debate about emancipation and the ways the northern society helped sustain the slave economy. In 1842, there were several days of riots, with fighting against black and white abolitionists, and the convention had to change its location three times for safety reasons. Many local white leaders blamed off-island radicals for the violence and for encouraging Nantucket abolitionists in their pursuit of school integration.

In 1843, abolitionists dominated the School Committee and integrated the schools contrary to a vote of the town. About fifteen black students were placed into two grammar schools, but there is no evidence that twenty-year-old Eunice Ross was admitted to the high school. However, the integration was short-lived. At the next annual town meeting there was a backlash, and the abolitionists were swept from office. The next School Committee ordered the schools to be re-segregated, and black students were physically removed from their seats in the midst of their lessons. Abolitionists rented a schoolroom, staffed by volunteers, for the black students, but it did not offer a full curriculum.

The expulsion of their children prompted drastic action by the Newtown community, and it embarked upon an unprecedented boycott of the school system that lasted for almost two years. Finally, having exhausted their political options on the island, the black community appealed to the state government. A petition, signed by a cross-section of the Newtown's children and adults, was submitted to the Massachusetts legislature in January 1845 by "Edward J. Pompey and 104 others" (Vaults of Massachusetts Archives, 1845); it stated that up to forty of their children were being deprived of an equal education. Several days later, four more petitions followed. Two were signed by white Nantucketers in support of the Pompey petition, and two defended segregation. The sixth, and final, petition presented to the Massachusetts legislature is a unique and poignant document written and signed by one person, Eunice F. Ross, in which she told her own story:The undersigned respectfully requests that the prayer of the petition of E.J. Pompey and others may be granted— The undersigned has good reason to feel on this subject, as she was examined in 1840 by the School Committee and found amply qualified for admission into the High School at Nantucket and was refused admittance by a vote of the Town, instructing the School Committee not to admit her, on account of her colour.As a result, the state legislature passed the groundbreaking Chapter 214 of the Acts of 1845 that prohibited discrimination in public schools and guaranteed equal education to all students. It also gave parents or guardians the right to sue their towns for damages. It soon became evident, however, that Nantucket intended to disregard the new law. As a result, Captain ABSALOM F. BOSTON, the wealthiest African American on the island, began legal proceedings against the town on behalf of his daughter, Phebe Ann. His suit was dropped, however, when abolitionists were voted onto the 1846 School Committee, which re-integrated the schools.

Eunice Ross, then twenty-four years old, never entered the school system, but she had been instrumental in the passage of a significant civil rights law. Little is known about the rest of her life, but there is evidence that she remained friendly with her former teacher, Anna Gardner. A reference in the New England Freedman's Aid Society Records in 1865 shows that Ross was asked to teach in the Freedmen's Bureau schools in Maryland, but she was unable to do so. That she was even considered implies that she was well educated. She lived quietly in her own house on York Street, in the heart of the Newtown community, until her death in 1895 at age seventy-two. Her obituary in the *Inquirer* on 2 March 1895 refers to her role in the segregation "outrage," and that she was "fond of the study of French, in which language she became proficient."

FURTHER READING
Johnson, Robert Jr., ed. *Nantucket's People of Color: Essays on History, Politics, and Community* (2006).
Karttunen, Francis. *The Other Islanders: People who Pulled Nantucket's Oars* (2005).
Massachusetts State House Vaults. Seven petitions presented to the House, 1845.
Nantucket Historical Association Archives. Available online at www.nha.org
White, Barbara. *The African School: The African School and the Integration of Nantucket Public Schools, 1825–1847* (1978, 1997, 2006).

BARBARA A. WHITE

Ross, Fran (25 June 1935–17 Sept. 1985), author, was born Frances Delores Ross in Philadelphia, Pennsylvania, the eldest child of Bernetta Bass, a store clerk, and Gerald Ross, a welder. The Ross family, which included Fran's two younger brothers, lived on Pearl Street in Philadelphia in a home owned by the children's maternal grandmother, Lena Bass. Ross attended George Brooks Elementary School and Shoemaker Junior High School, both predominantly white and Jewish. In spite of attending schools where she was one of few blacks, Ross was an active participant in West Philadelphia's black community, attending church five blocks from her home. As a member of Mount Carmel Baptist Church, located at 5732 Race Street, she played basketball for different church and youth centers. Just prior to her sixteenth birthday, Ross graduated with honors from Overbrook High School, where the famed professional basketball player WILT CHAMBERLAIN played varsity basketball. She enrolled at Temple University on a full scholarship and graduated in 1956 with a degree in communications, journalism, and theater.

Ross then worked at Curtis Publishing Company, home of the *Saturday Evening Post*, while still living in Philadelphia. In search of better opportunities, she moved to New York in 1960. While in New York, Ross worked as a proofreader and copy editor, first at McGraw-Hill. Then she worked at Simon and Schuster, where she proofread the first book by New York City's mayor Ed Koch.

Ross published her first and only novel, *Oreo*, in 1974 with Greyfalcon House. However, sales were low, and Ross's novel soon went out of print despite Gregory Peterson's positive review in the April 1975 issue of *Essence* magazine. In the introduction to the reprinted edition in 2000, Harryette Mullen, the scholar responsible for the republication of *Oreo* with Northeastern University Press, offers possible reasons for the virtual ignorance of this text. Ross was not in sync with the aesthetics of the Black Arts Movement, a literary movement during the 1960s that privileged the black vernacular and departed from European literary conventions, in that she does not examine the separateness or roots of black culture but, rather, focuses on the ways cultures merge, especially in the sphere of language. Ross proves herself an accomplished linguist, moving in and out of different dialects (Yiddish, black vernacular, and academic prose as well as some invented dialects) in *Oreo* as a means of demonstrating hybridity and diversity within the African American community. Mullen believes the blend of languages possibly alienated Ross's potential readership.

Oreo is structured on the Greek legend of Theseus, which tells the story of the grandson of the king of Troezen who searches for his father.

The novel examines issues of race, class, and gender through its protagonist Christine "Oreo" Clark, who functions as a modern-day Theseus. Oreo is a coming-of-age biracial girl who, like Theseus, is in search of her father and the secret behind her birth. The polished use of vernacular helps situate Oreo between two worlds and offers her a deep-seated cultural immersion to complete her quest. Ross suggests, through her dialect switching, the plethora of influences shaping African Americans, thus dismissing the ideal of a singular African American experience. The diversity of African Americans and the acknowledgement that African Americans exist outside a vacuum are apparent from the first pages of the novel. *Oreo* is divided in two parts: "Troezen," being between two worlds, describes Oreo's relatives and provides a solid example of cultural immersion, and "Meandering," a lengthy or roundabout journey, follows Oreo's quest into the labyrinth to find her father.

Growing into adulthood with her extended family affords Oreo a myriad opportunities that prepare her for her quest. This moving in and out of different vernaculars flavored with hysterical satire characterizes the "Troezen" section of the novel. "Mishpocheh" (family), the first chapter in "Troezen," begins with descriptions of the grandparents, situating the text between two worlds where orality transmits racial stereotypes or prejudices. Upon learning her son was marrying a black girl, Frieda Schwartz suffered a fatal heart attack, and James Clark has a debilitating stroke. Racial discrimination, reverse racial discrimination, sexual puns, and skirmishes shape the novel and reveal the complexity of race, gender, and sexuality in America.

Eager to publish a second book, Ross moved to Los Angeles to work as a writer on *The Richard Pryor Show*, a controversial variety sitcom starring the popular black comedian and actor RICHARD PRYOR. The show initially aired in 1977 on the NBC network against the shows rated number one and number two, *Happy Days* and *Laverne and Shirley*. Because the show was slotted at eight o'clock, the designated family hour, Pryor found himself censored and decided he would only tape four of the ten contracted shows. After the cancellation of *The Richard Pryor Show*, Ross declined an opportunity to write for *Laverne and Shirley*, and she returned to New York and the publishing industry. She worked as a freelance writer, submitting articles to *Essence*, *Playboy*, and *Titters*, an early feminist publication. She never married and had no children. Ross died in New York City. Despite only writing one novel, Ross contributed significantly to African American literature as one of few black women satirists.

FURTHER READING

Foreman, Gabrielle, and Michelle Stein-Evers. "Review of *Oreo*, by Fran Ross," *Women's Review of Books* (July 2001).

Mullen, Harryette. "'Apple Pie with Oreo Crust': Fran Ross's Recipe for an Idiosyncratic American Novel," *Melus* 27 (Spring 2002).

Peterson, Gregory. "Review of *Oreo*, by Fran Ross," *Essence* (Apr. 1975).

LISA C. LAKES

Ross, Frank K. (9 July 1943–), cofounder and first president of the National Association of Black Accountants, was born in St. Kitts, West Indies, the youngest of four sons of Reginald Ross, a plantation overseer, and Ruby Swanston, a nurse. When he was nine months old, his father died after a short illness. He and his three brothers moved to Yonkers, New York, in 1950 to live with their aunt and uncle, Annette Swanston, a seamstress, and Henry Phipps, a retired carpenter.

Ross's eighth grade guidance counselor tried to steer him into a trade or commercial high school, as she did with other black students (including his three brothers), but Ross was determined to attend the academic high school with his friends, who were mostly white. Despite his good school record, the white counselor refused to approve the academic high school until, in desperation, Ross told her that the real reason that he wanted to attend the academic high school was to play on its superior football team.

Ross's youthful ambitions coincided with the early years of the civil rights movement. He was well aware that students across the South were standing up for their rights, and he knew that he would have to do the same to achieve his own goal of becoming an attorney. After graduating from high school in 1962 he entered Long Island University the same year, and took business classes, expecting that this would provide an excellent background for a corporate lawyer. Instead, he found himself enjoying and excelling at accounting, and he became president of the university's accounting society. Like many young African Americans in the 1960s, his first professional job was with one of President Lyndon B. Johnson's Great Society Anti-Poverty programs. While in college, he worked as a bookkeeper for Bedford Stuyvesant Youth in Action.

Many of his professors and classmates told him that he would never get a job with any of the major accounting firms and that he would be stuck being a glorified bookkeeper for the rest of his career. Some told him he was wasting his time, because the major accounting firms in New York did not hire African Americans. Ross thought: "Maybe if I got out of college today, I wouldn't get a job, but I'm not graduating today. I'm going to graduate four years from now. Four years from now I will be able to get a job" (Interview with author, 16 Aug. 1997).

Ross was right, and when he graduated in 1966 he got a job in the New York office of Peat, Marwick, Mitchell, one of the eight largest certified public accounting (CPA) firms in the United States. To his knowledge he was the only black person hired in that year. Only a trickle of African Americans had been hired to work for major CPA firms since the first, Robert Hill, was hired in Los Angeles in 1961. This changed in 1968, after the New York Human Rights Commission filed a suit charging that the accounting firms had discriminatory employment policies. In 1968 the eight large firms had eighteen African American employees in their New York offices; two years later they employed over one hundred.

Ross became the first African American regional managing partner of a major office and geographical area—Washington, D.C., and the Mid-Atlantic—in the firm that later became known as KPMG. He was also the first African American elected to the firm's board of directors and its management committee. He reasoned that had he graduated in 1964, the firms would not have hired a black person. Had he graduated two years later, he believed he would have fallen through the cracks as the firm hired many African Americans under massive government pressure and gave no attention to any individual employee, resulting in a high turnover rate. In contrast, when he was hired, the firm took an interest in his progress and was determined that he was going to be successful. He was assigned to the firm's first Jewish partner, who provided him with developmental opportunities. In this way Ross's experience was like that of many of the early African American CPAs. Before the Civil Rights Act of 1964, virtually every white person who played a major role in helping an African American become a CPA was Jewish. This partner ensured that Ross was challenged and mentored.

In 1969 Ross and a group of eight friends, who also worked for major public accounting firms, started the National Association of Black Accountants (NABA). The other eight founders were Ronald

Benjamin, Earl Biggett, Donald Bristow, Kenneth Drummond, Bertram Gibson, Richard McNamee, George Wallace, and Michael Winston. The men began the organization because the big accounting firms had begun hiring African Americans but had provided no support system for these new employees. Once a name for the organization had been chosen, the group strove to gain credibility and acceptance within the CPA firms. The firms were experiencing a tremendous amount of turnover among their new black employees and thus were interested in their message. They were suddenly recruiting at the historically black colleges, which meant that they were recruiting from a number of schools that did not have fully developed accounting programs. Many students were from the South, but the first offices to integrate were in the North, which meant that many recruits were far from home in their first year of work. Until the late 1960s there were few job opportunities for African Americans with accounting training. As a result many black colleges did not develop their accounting programs until the 1970s.

At NABA's first major event, a reception and panel on integration held at the Biltmore Hotel in midtown Manhattan, the firms sent not only recruiting personnel but also senior partners. That event was funded by member dues, but NABA grew to be funded by the major public accounting firms and other major employers of accountants. Although the early meetings were held in members' homes, within the first year meetings were held downtown in the various firms' offices.

While the firms adapted quickly to the new organization, NABA experienced some recalcitrance on the part of African Americans who were involved in minority-recruitment committees of the New York State Society of Certified Public Accountants and the American Institute of Certified Public Accountants. Some believed that there was no need to begin a "separatist" organization and that the members of NABA should work within existing professional structures. NABA members successfully resisted this effort at assimilation, maintaining that the various organizations each played an important role.

With two of his friends from NABA, Ross explored a detour on his way to becoming partner at KPMG. In 1973 Ross and his friends started their own firm, Ross, Stewart, and Benjamin. Ross stayed with the firm, which peaked at twenty employees and $4 million in revenue, for three years before deciding to rejoin KPMG after that firm aggressively

courted him for over a year. After returning to the firm, he became a partner in 1977, and in 1996 he became managing partner of the Washington, D.C., office and the Mid-Atlantic area.

Ross married Cecelia Mann on 23 December 1967, and they had two children. Ross not only succeeded in his own career, he also taught at Howard University while working for the firm and helped many of its students land jobs in the major public accounting firms. In addition he was active in the United Negro College Fund, the Gallaudet University Board of Advisors, and the Urban League. In retirement Ross reactivated the Howard University School of Business Center for Accounting Education, which works to improve opportunities for African Americans in the field.

FURTHER READING

Hammond, Theresa A. *White-Collar Profession: African American Certified Public Accountants since 1921* (2002).

Ross, Frank K. (as told to Janis F. Kearney). *Quiet Guys Can Do Great Things, Too: A Black Accountant's Success Story* (2006).

THERESA A. HAMMOND

Ross, Loretta (16 Aug. 1953–), feminist and activist, was born Loretta June Ross in Temple, Texas, the sixth of eight children of Alexander Ross, a mailman and military serviceman who was born in Jamaica, and Lorene Burton, a domestic worker who later became a full-time homemaker. Because of Alexander Ross's career in the army, the Ross family moved around a lot, living in Oklahoma, California, and Texas. In 1963 the family eventually settled in San Antonio, Texas, where Loretta Ross attended Sam Houston High School. She was always a conscientious student. While in middle school in California she skipped two grades because of her high marks in the state's mandatory testing system. Loretta Ross was an honors student in high school, where she was identified, groomed, and subsequently offered a scholarship to Radcliffe College in Cambridge, Massachusetts, by a program for promising minority students.

At the age of fourteen Ross became pregnant from the sexual abuse of a close male relative. Upon learning about the pregnancy Radcliffe rescinded its scholarship offer. Although her admission into the college was still good, Ross could not afford to attend Radcliffe and had to act quickly to gain admission and secure financial aid to attend another college. On 9 April 1969 Ross gave birth to a son, Howard Michael Ross. In 1970 she earned a full scholarship and began undergraduate studies at Howard University in Washington, D.C., majoring in the sciences. Attending the university as a single mother and sole breadwinner was a challenge. After three years Ross lost her scholarship and left school.

Ross's career as a political activist resulted from a confluence of social forces and personal experience. Her politicization, or radicalization, was a slow process that evolved from her educational enlightenment as a student at Howard and her involvement in several social and political movements. As a student at Howard, Ross was influenced by the works of TONI CADE BAMBARA and MALCOLM X and by the radical politics that took place on Howard's campus in the late 1960s and early 1970s. After leaving Howard, Ross continued her political education by participating in the D.C. Study Group, a Marxist-Leninist reading group started by Jimmy Garrett, a radical professor at Howard.

Her first direct involvement in politics was in 1971 with the Citywide Housing Association, a tenants' association in Washington, D.C., organized to fight condominium conversions, including those affecting Ross's apartment building. Ross and other tenants banded together to prevent the conversion of their apartments into condominiums and eventually won a ten-year fight. Spurred by this initial activism, Ross became involved in the black liberation, antiapartheid, and prisoners' rights movements. In the 1970s Ross became an advocate of women's and consumers' rights when she became one of the ten thousand plaintiffs who filed and won class-action lawsuits against A. H. Robbins, the manufacturer of the Dalkon Shield intrauterine device (IUD), after suffering pelvic inflammatory disease while using the device. In the end the company was forced to pay $520 million in damages.

Ross's involvement in feminist politics did not officially begin until her involvement with the D.C. Rape Crisis Center, for which she served as executive director from 1979 to 1982. During her tenure at the center Ross began to connect the instances of sexual assault and abuse she had experienced as a teenager and college student with the larger social and political context of violence against women. Although the center was founded by two white women from working-class backgrounds, the center's staff was predominantly African American, which reflected the demographics of its clientele. During her tenure there Ross came into contact with such black feminist luminaries as BELL HOOKS, AUDRE LORDE, and

BARBARA SMITH. Although it was an exciting time for black feminism, Ross did not start to think of herself as a feminist until the mid-1980s.

After leaving the D.C. Rape Crisis Center in 1982, Ross worked for the National Organization for Women (NOW), directing the organization's programs for women of color, including organizing delegations of women of color to two national reproductive rights marches on Washington, D.C., in 1986 and 1989. During this period Ross also became involved with the Black Women's Self-Help Collective, which was the precursor of the National Black Women's Health Project, an organization started by BYLLYE AVERY in 1984 and with which Ross later worked briefly in the late 1980s.

In the 1990s Ross shifted gears a bit. It was around this time that she began to adopt a human rights framework in her political activism. After working for the Center for Democratic Renewal, a group that monitored the activities of hate groups on the far right such as the Ku Klux Klan, Ross founded in 1996 the National Center for Human Rights Education, an Atlanta-based organization that trained community leaders and social activists in how to use a human rights framework in their political organizing around issues of racism, sexism, and class. Ross created the group in order to bring together and improve cooperation among the many progressive social-justice movements within the United States.

Since the early 1980s Ross had been involved in and greatly influenced by several international conferences for women organized by the United Nations that approached women's rights, including reproductive rights, as issues of human rights. Influenced by a series of symposiums in New York City and Atlanta in the late 1990s, Ross help establish the SisterSong Women of Color Reproductive Health Collective, a network comprising more than thirty local, regional, and national grassroots organizations in the United States that represented four racial and ethnic groups, including Native American/Indigenous, African American, Latina, and Asian and Pacific Islander. Using a human rights framework and rejecting the singular focus on women's individual legal rights to abortion, SisterSong linked reproductive health to other social issues such as poverty, economic justice, welfare reform, access to health care, housing, environmental justice, child care, and immigration policy.

A sought-after speaker, Ross was awarded an honorary degree in civil law from Arcadia University in 2003. In 2004 she was the national co-director for the March for Women's Lives, a rally in support of reproductive rights held in Washington, D.C. In an effort to document the history and contributions of women of color in activist movements, Ross co-authored the book *Undivided Rights: Women of Color Organize for Reproductive Justice* in 2004.

FURTHER READING

Silliman, Jael, and Anannya Bhattacharjee, eds. *Policing the National Body: Race, Gender, and Criminalization* (2002).

Solinger, Rickie, ed. *Abortion Wars: A Half Century of Struggle, 1950–2000* (1998).

Springer, Kimberly, ed. *Still Lifting, Still Climbing: African American Women's Contemporary Activism* (1999).

KIMALA PRICE

Roudanez, Louis Charles (12 June 1823–11 Mar. 1890), physician, newspaper proprietor, and Republican Party activist, was born in St. James Parish, Louisiana, the son of Louis Roudanez, a wealthy French merchant, and Aimée Potens, a free woman of color. Roudanez was raised in New Orleans as a member of the city's free black elite, but in 1844 he left to pursue a professional education in France. In 1853 the faculty of medicine at the University of Paris awarded him a degree in medicine. He graduated with a second medical degree from Dartmouth College in 1857, and soon after he returned to New Orleans to open his own office. In the same year he married Louisa Celie Seulay; their union produced eight children.

Roudanez continued to build his medical practice during the Civil War and Reconstruction, but, like other free men of color in New Orleans, upon federal occupation of south Louisiana in the spring of 1862 he became deeply interested in the issues of Reconstruction in his state. He was one in a group of investors who made possible the creation of the *New Orleans Union*, the wartime political voice of the city's French-speaking free black elite. The paper proved short-lived, and just weeks after its failure in July 1864 Roudanez and his brother Jean-Baptiste Roudanez founded the *New Orleans Tribune*. A bilingual publication, the *Tribune* sought to bring together former slaves and free black people in the cause of racial equality. This first black daily newspaper in the nation reported primarily on politics, and the reform program it promoted bore the ideological imprints of Roudanez and the paper's chief editor, white Belgian radical Jean-Charles Houzeau.

It called for universal suffrage, office-holding rights for black men, the right of jury duty, and economic independence for former slaves through a federally sponsored division of plantations. Roudanez also used the paper to aid in the 1869 campaign to end discrimination in public accommodations in New Orleans. The *Tribune* served as the official organ of Louisiana's Republican Party, although it was at times highly critical of both the state and national party. The paper rejected the 1864 state constitution because it did not extend suffrage to black men, and it was at odds with Andrew Johnson's administration over its lenient southern policy. Eventually it was Roudanez's opposition to the selection of Henry Clay Warmoth as the Republican gubernatorial candidate in 1868 and Roudanez's role in the nomination of a more radical splinter ticket that caused the party to cut its ties to the *Tribune*. His bolt from the party did much to sully his reputation among many of the black and white activists whom he previously had helped to establish the state party. His insistence on a competing ticket also prompted Houzeau to resign his post, a move that helped to undermine the already financially strapped newspaper. Consequently it ceased publication in April 1868, although Roudanez's continuing opposition to Governor Warmoth led him to resurrect it the following year for a brief period.

Roudanez disappeared from the public spotlight until 1873, when he and other propertied New Orleanians began a political reform movement under the banner "Unification." Motivated by the perceived deleterious effect of political instability on the city's businesses, this group advocated honest government, racial cooperation in politics and government and an end to political violence, equal civil and political rights for all citizens, desegregation on public conveyances, and an equal distribution of public offices between the races. Roudanez was on the "Committee of One Hundred" that drew up the movement's platform in June of that year. Unification failed as a movement ultimately because it did not garner significant support in Louisiana's country parishes, and ironically because of persistent mistrust between white and black participants within the movement itself.

In addition to his activity in politics and journalism, Roudanez was involved in black community affairs. He had a well-earned reputation for philanthropy. In 1865, for example, he donated some of the funds for the building of the Providence Asylum, an institution that was operated by the Louisiana Association for the Benefit of Colored Orphans. He also strongly supported higher education, and he served for a time on the Examining Committee of Straight (later Dillard) University.

Despite his activity in the public realm, his primary professional commitment throughout his life remained in the field of medicine. In the 1870s and 1880s Roudanez ran a large and prosperous practice, reportedly treating both black and white patients. He devoted his final years to maintaining his practice. Roudanez died in New Orleans.

Roudanez's public life was brief but had a significant effect on the course of Reconstruction in Louisiana. His newspaper was instrumental in the formation and growth of the Republican Party in the state. Its editorials undoubtedly helped to focus attention on the critical issues of Reconstruction, though its position on some matters proved too extreme for most policymakers. Roudanez himself exemplified the intense interest of black men in postbellum politics and the hopes that free men and freedmen alike invested in the Reconstruction experiment. Moreover, his conflicts with other activists highlighted the disunity that plagued Reconstruction leaders in his and in other Southern states, a problem that contributed to their demise.

FURTHER READING

Valuable information about Roudanez's life and career can be found in manuscript collections located at Louisiana State University, Baton Rouge; the Roman Catholic Diocese of Baton Rouge; the University of New Orleans; the Amistad Research Center; the Louisiana Collection at Tulane University; and the Louisiana Division of the New Orleans Public Library.

Blassingame, John W. *Black New Orleans, 1860–1880* (1973).

Everett, Donald E. "Demands of the New Orleans Free Colored Population for Political Equality, 1862–1865," *Louisiana Historical Quarterly* 38 (Apr. 1955).

Houzeau, Jean-Charles. *My Passage at the "New Orleans Tribune"* (1984).

Vincent, Charles. *Black Legislators in Louisiana during Reconstruction* (1976).

Warmoth, Henry Clay. *War, Politics and Reconstruction* (1930).

Obituaries: *New Orleans Picayune,* 12 Mar. 1890; *New Orleans Abeille,* 13 Mar. 1890; and *New Orleans Daily Crusader,* 22 Mar. 1890.

This entry is taken from the *American National Biography* and is published here with the permission of the American Council of Learned Societies.

CONNIE MEALE

Roundtree, Dovey (17 April 1914–), lawyer, minister, Army veteran, and activist, was born Dovey Mae Johnson in Charlotte, North Carolina, the second oldest of four daughters of James Eliot Johnson, an AME Church printer, and Lela Bryant Johnson, a seamstress and domestic servant. The primary formative influence of Roundtree's childhood was her maternal grandmother, Rachel Bryant Graham, who took the family to live with her and her husband, the Rev. Clyde Graham, an AME Church minister, after the death of Roundtree's father in the 1919 influenza epidemic. While Roundtree's burning academic ambition derived largely from her mother and her grandfather, who refused to see the family's poverty as an obstacle to the children's educational advancement, her "Grandma Rachel's" courage and sense of justice shaped Roundtree spiritually. A woman with only a third-grade education, Rachel Graham was nevertheless an influential and highly respected figure in the black community of Charlotte, and through her work with the colored women's club movement, she forged a friendship with the renowned educator and activist MARY MCLEOD BETHUNE whom she entertained in her home and held up to her granddaughters as the supreme role model. Bethune became for Roundtree a mentor, an ally, and a lifelong emblem of infinite possibility.

Determined to embark on a medical career, Roundtree managed to work her way through Spelman College in Atlanta at the height of the Great Depression and to graduate in 1938, but her economic situation forced her to abandon her medical school plans and take a teaching position in a small South Carolina town. In the summer of 1941, however, world events conspired to move her into the sweep of history. With America's "war preparedness" industry opening its doors to blacks, she sought out Mary McLeod Bethune in Washington, D.C., for assistance in obtaining a job. Impressed with Roundtree's educational background, Bethune tapped her in May 1942 for the select group of forty African American women who would become the first to train as officers in the newly created Women's Army Auxiliary Corps. As a black woman within a rigidly Jim Crow military, Roundtree found her voice as an activist. She publicly challenged the overt racial discrimination she confronted in the Army even as she traveled the country on assignment from 1942 to 1944, recruiting other young black women to join the military. Traveling alone without Army protection while canvassing the Deep South, Roundtree was evicted

Dovey Roundtree, 86, sits for a portrait on 20 April 2000, in Spotsylvania, Virginia. (AP Images.)

from a Miami bus while in uniform. She pressed onward nevertheless, aggressively recruiting African American women and laying the groundwork for an interracial Army four years before President Truman mandated the desegregation of the military in 1948.

Transformed by her military experience into an advocate for social justice, Roundtree threw herself into the battle for civil rights in a nine-month postwar stint with black labor leader A. PHILIP RANDOLPH in his campaign for a permanent Fair Employment Practices Committee. During her 1945 to 1946 assignment in the FEPC's West Coast office, she met constitutional lawyer and activist PAULI MURRAY, who persuaded her that the greatest instrument for racial reform was the law. Inspired by Murray, Roundtree set her sights on Howard University Law School. She struggled during this period to reconcile her activism with her equally strong desire to marry and raise a family. In December 1945 she married William A. Roundtree, a Morehouse College graduate and Army engineer she had known during her Spelman years. The marriage foundered under the strain of her

growing commitment to the cause of civil rights, and by the time she entered Howard Law in 1947, she and William Roundtree had divorced.

Despite the gender discrimination she faced as one of only five women in her Howard Law class, Roundtree moved quickly to the center of the legal assault upon the Supreme Court's 1896 *Plessy v. Ferguson* ruling, which had enshrined 'separate but equal' in law. Inspired by such giants as THURGOOD MARSHALL, JAMES MADISON NABRIT, JR., and GEORGE E. C. HAYES, who were mounting the attack on *Plessy* that would culminate in the historic 1954 *Brown v. Board of Education* decision, Roundtree went on to carve out her own place in history. In November 1955, one month before ROSA PARKS ignited the protest movement led by the REV. MARTIN LUTHER KING JR., Roundtree and her law partner Julius W. Robertson wrested from the notoriously segregationist Interstate Commerce Commission a bus desegregation ruling in behalf of a young WAC named Sarah Keys, who had been subjected to the same indignities as Roundtree while traveling in uniform. In its ruling in *Sarah Keys v. Carolina Coach Company* 64 MCC 769 (1955), and in a companion railway ruling handed down the same day, the ICC expressly rejected the concept of 'separate but equal,' extending the logic of the Supreme Court's 1954 *Brown* decision to the field of interstate transportation. The *Keys* case, invoked by Attorney General Robert F. Kennedy at the height of mob violence in the South during the Freedom Riders' campaign of 1961, moved the recalcitrant ICC to enforce its own regulations and brought an end to Jim Crow in travel across state lines. Along with the Supreme Court's 1960 *Boynton v. Virginia* 364 U.S. 454 (1960) decision banning segregation in bus terminals and restaurants, the *Keys* case stands as a milestone in the legal battle for civil rights in the field of public transportation.

Even as she fought on the national level, Roundtree led the charge for justice in the segregated courtrooms of the Washington, D.C. In an era when African American lawyers had to leave the courthouses to use the bathrooms, she successfully pressed the cases of black clients, first with her partner Julius Robertson, and then, after his death in 1961, alone. The first woman of color to be admitted to the Women's Bar of the District of Columbia in 1962, Roundtree became one of the city's most respected criminal defense attorneys, the voice for Washington's black poor, and the inspiration to two generations of African American attorneys of both genders who followed her. She was the founding partner of the D.C. law firm of Roundtree Knox Hunter and Parker, special consultant for legal affairs to the AME Church, and, in tribute to her mentor Mary McLeod Bethune, General Counsel *pro bono* for nearly fifty years to the National Council of Negro Women.

In 1961 Roundtree became one of the first women ordained to the ministry of the AME Church, and in 1963 she was given full ministerial status as an itinerant elder. She served for thirty-five years as an associate pastor at Allen Chapel AME Church in Washington, D.C., where she fought from the pulpit, as she had in the courtroom, for families and children. She began in the 1980s to shift the focus of her law practice to family law, directing her efforts toward what she perceived as a crisis within the black community in the disintegration of the family. The quest for social justice that had begun in the civil rights era of the 1950s gave way during the latter years of her career to a hands-on role as advocate for women and their children. Roundtree has been the recipient of numerous honors and awards, including the THURGOOD MARSHALL Award of Excellence,

the National Bar Association CHARLOTTE E. RAY Award, and the 2000 Margaret Brent Award for Women Lawyers of Achievement from the American Bar Association. In 2009 the University of Mississippi Press published Roundtree's memoir, *Justice Older than the Law: The Life of Dovey Johnson Roundtree*.

FURTHER READING

Dovey Roundtree's papers are housed in the Mary McLeod Bethune Archives, Washington, D.C.

McCabe, Katie and Dovey Johnson Roundtree. *Justice Older than the Law: The Life of Dovey Johnson Roundtree* (2009).

Barnes, Catherine. "A Legal Breakthrough," in *Journey from Jim Crown: The Desegregation of Southern Transit* (1983).

McCabe, Katie. "She Had a Dream," *Washingtonian Magazine* (March 2002).

Putney, Martha. *When the Nation Was in Need: Blacks in the Women's Army Corps during World War II* (1992).

KATIE MCCABE

Roumania, Matilda. *See* Peters, Margaret and Matilda Roumania Peters.

Roundtree, Richard (9 July 1942–), actor and model, was born Richard Roundtree in New Rochelle, New York. His father, John, was a garbage collector and caterer; his mother, Kathryn, worked as a housekeeper. Even while attending New Rochelle High School, Roundtree's physical prowess, affable personality, and good looks made him a standout. In high school he was captain of the track team and played end on the nation's third-ranked high school football team; he graduated in 1961. While on a football scholarship at Southern Illinois University, Roundtree became a model for an *Ebony* Fashion Fair tour. Upon returning to New York he began acting lessons, and then joined the Negro Ensemble Company in 1967 for a series of Off-Broadway roles for two years. That experience paved the way for him to star as boxer JACK JOHNSON in the stage presentation of *The Great White Hope*.

Roundtree's struggle to find work as a stage actor ended when filmmaker GORDON PARKS SR. selected him to portray private detective John Shaft in the 1971 film *Shaft*. Matched with an unforgettable soundtrack by ISAAC HAYES, John Shaft became a cultural benchmark, spawning two more movies, *Shaft's Big Score* (1972) and *Shaft in Africa* (1973), and a short-lived television show. In the process it launched Roundtree to international fame, putting him on par with such white actors as Peter O'Toole and Clint Eastwood. It marked the first time a black man was cast as an urban crime-fighting hero who always got both the criminal and the woman.

While many other actors such as FRED WILLIAMSON, JIM BROWN, and PAM GRIER emerged from "blaxploitation" films, Roundtree became one of the more legendary figures associated with the genre, something he later grew to regret: "It's bitter-sweet," Roundtree reminisced, "I will defend that character till the death, but at this point in life, it's getting a little tiresome to constantly be hearing, they say that cat Shaft is a bad mother.... Shut your mouth" (Rohan, Virginia, in *The Bergen County Record*, 11 Sept. 1997).

Over the years, as a new generation of actors came on the scene, Roundtree disappeared from the spotlight, working mostly in small television roles and minor films during the 1980s. He worked consistently, appearing in more than 120 film and television roles, the most noteworthy being ABC's *Roots* (1977), *Once Upon a Time ... When We Were Colored* (1996), CBS's *Having Our Say* (1999), and *Seven* (1995). In 1996 he worked with a number of former blaxploitation stars, including Grier, Williamson, Jim Brown, Ron O'Neal and with other major black actors such as PAUL WINFIELD and ISABEL SANFORD, in *Original Gangstas*. Later, in 2000, he appeared in John Singleton's remake of *Shaft*, this time as the lead character's uncle. Roundtree's most recent television work has included recurring roles on *Grey's Anatomy*, *Desperate Housewives*, and *Heroes*.

Roundtree was married in 1980; he and his wife Karen had two sons, Morgan and John James, and one daughter, Tayler-Marie. In 1993 Roundtree was diagnosed with breast cancer, an illness he hid from the public for years, fearing it would undermine his acting opportunities. He underwent a mastectomy and six months of chemotherapy that left him bedridden. Years later he began to speak out about his experiences with breast cancer and he even helped raise funds and awareness. While not acting or participating in fundraising for breast-cancer research, Roundtree spends his time championing children's causes.

FURTHER READING

Bogle, Donald. *Blacks in American Films and Television* (1989).

Katz, Ephraim. *The Film Encyclopedia*, 5th ed. (2005).

SAMUEL AUTMAN

Rouse, Carl Albert (14 July 1926–), astrophysicist, was born in Youngstown, Ohio. His father owned and operated an auto repair shop and his mother was a homemaker. After finishing high school in 1944, he was drafted into the U.S. Army and sent to study engineering at Howard University, Penn State University, and New York University. Discharged in 1946 without a degree, he worked as an engineering draftsman before entering Case Institute of Technology (later Case-Western Reserve University) in Cleveland, where he received a B.S. in Physics in 1951. He then entered the California Institute of Technology (Caltech) and became a research assistant to Carl D. Anderson, who won the 1936 Nobel Prize in physics for discovering the positron, a subatomic particle with the same mass as an electron but with a positive charge. Anderson had made his discovery in a cloud chamber, a closed vessel filled with supersaturated steam through which charged particles leave a minute but visible trail that can be photographed. For his doctoral research, Rouse modified Anderson's cloud chamber by adding a device known as a gated proportional counter. This device permitted him to photograph particles with relatively low energy levels; consequently, he was able to offer evidence for the existence of the particle known today as the K meson.

Rouse received an M.S in Physics in 1953, and two years later married Lorraine Moxley. He received a Ph.D. in Particle Physics in 1956, and went to work as a research physicist at Caltech's Lawrence Livermore National Laboratory, one of the world's foremost research facilities for the study of nuclear physics. One of his first assignments was to study the near-instantaneous transition of a solid to a gas resulting from exposure to the extremely hot temperatures caused by the explosion of an atomic bomb. Since the sun and other stars are fueled by nuclear reactions similar to the ones that take place in an atomic explosion, Rouse soon developed an interest in the behavior of extremely hot stellar gases. He was particularly interested in pulsating variable stars such as the Cepheids; these stars expand and contract cyclically, causing them to pulsate rhythmically in brightness and size. He concluded that this phenomenon results from the nonlinear effects of ionization and excitation of the atoms in the atmospheres of these stars. In his spare time he developed a computer model appropriate for highly ionized gases, and then he ran the model in a program that had been designed to model supernovas, or stars whose brightness increase hundreds of millions of times when they explode violently. When his model reproduced the observed variation in star pulsations, Rouse began to construct a model for a more typical star like the sun.

Although little solar modeling had been done by the mid-1960s, there was a considerable degree of consensus in the astrophysical community concerning the nature of the sun's interior. This consensus was based on estimates of the sun's central temperature and density and some knowledge concerning the relative abundances of hydrogen and helium in the solar atmosphere, which made it possible to guess intelligently at the internal abundances of hydrogen and helium. But when Rouse plugged these assumptions into his own computer model, the result was a star that bore no resemblance to the sun in terms of mass, brightness, or radius, values which were well known at the time. Conversely, when he modeled the sun's interior with a higher abundance of heavier elements such as iron, the model yielded a star that looks very much like the sun. Consequently, Rouse advanced the theory that the sun's core is composed of solid iron rather than a mixture of hydrogen and helium gases.

Rouse's theory was received with a great deal of skepticism by the astrophysical community for several reasons. The first concerned his total lack of formal training in astrophysics, even though his training in particle physics made him perhaps more qualified to study stellar nuclear phenomena. The second was that Rouse's iron core theory challenged existing assumptions about the origins of the sun and the solar system. The solar system is commonly thought to have formed between four and five billion years ago from a homogeneous, well-mixed nebula composed of 71 percent hydrogen, 27 percent helium, and only 2 percent heavier elements. Rouse's theory implies that the solar system was formed, at least in part, from the remnants of one or more supernovas, because the cores of supernovas are believed to consist of iron and even heavier elements such as uranium. Rouse's iron core theory was received with a particular lack of enthusiasm at Lawrence Livermore, whose management seems to have been embarrassed by Rouse's extracurricular research. In 1968 he left Lawrence Livermore for a small company in San Diego, known today as General Atomics, where he was granted a bit more leeway to pursue his theories. His official duties at General Atomics were to develop practical applications for nuclear energy, and in this regard he developed several improvements in the material used to build protective shielding for nuclear power plants. Meanwhile, he continued to develop his solar model by using the computers at San Diego State College in his spare time.

Although the iron core theory has yet to be accepted by the astrophysical community, several subsequent developments have offered support for Rouse's theory. The first came in the 1990s, when the Nobel Prize winner Raymond Davis demonstrated that the sun produces only about one-third of the number of solar neutrinos, subatomic particles with no charge and virtually no mass, that it was assumed to produce. A number of interesting theories have been advanced to explain this discrepancy, but one of the most convincing explanations is Rouse's iron core theory. The second involved the development after 1970 of helioseismology, the study of sound waves on the sun's surface caused by the oscillations of solar gases. Rouse was able to incorporate helioseismology into his solar model so that the model can reproduce the observed spectrum of oscillations when a small core of solid iron is assumed.

In 1992 Rouse left General Atomics to found Rouse Research, an atomic energy consulting firm, and to devote more time to his solar models and theories.

FURTHER READING

Kessler, James H., et al. *Distinguished African American Scientists of the 20th Century* (1996).

Krapp, Kristine M., ed. *Notable Black American Scientists* (1999).

Spangenburg, Ray, and Kit Moser. *African Americans in Science, Math, and Invention* (2003).

CHARLES W. CAREY JR.

Rouse, Charlie (6 Apr. 1924–30 Nov. 1988), jazz tenor saxophonist, was born Charles Rouse in Washington, D.C. His parentage is unknown. Having admired a local big band led by Bill Hester, he took up clarinet around age ten or eleven. He studied privately before joining bands and orchestras in junior high school and at Armstrong High School, where he doubled on alto saxophone. For three years he again took private lessons on clarinet, studying with a member of the Howard University faculty. For his last two years of high school he switched from alto to tenor saxophone, and during his senior year he worked in the pianist John Malachi's band at the Crystal Caverns club. By this time Rouse had become friends with the jazz tenor saxophonist BEN WEBSTER, who encouraged his striving for a huge and personalized instrumental tone. Rouse also played football and after graduating from high school, apparently at age twenty, he faced a choice between college athletics and music. He had married at age eighteen. Details are unknown, but an obituary noted that he was survived by Mary Ellen Rouse and a son, presumably from this marriage.

By his own account Rouse joined BILLY ECKSTINE's bop big band in St. Louis in June 1944. According to Malachi, who was Eckstine's pianist at the time, Rouse sat next to CHARLIE PARKER and was so mesmerized by Parker's alto saxophone playing that he was unable to concentrate on his own parts. Soon his chair in the band was given to GENE AMMONS. Rouse became a member of DIZZY GILLESPIE's bop big band in 1945. While participating in jam sessions at Minton's Playhouse in New York City, he first played with the pianist and composer THELONIOUS MONK. Performing alongside the trumpeter FATS NAVARRO in the pianist TADD DAMERON's sextet, Rouse made his first soloist recordings, "The Squirrel" and "Our Delight," in 1947.

Rouse's work in rhythm and blues bands included brief stays with LOUIS JORDAN and Eddie "Cleanhead" Vinson and an extended period in a quintet that he founded with the drummer Jimmy Cobb in New York. The group returned to Washington, where DUKE ELLINGTON, searching for a tenor saxophonist, heard Rouse and hired him in late 1949. He performed in the film short *Salute to Duke Ellington* (1950), but soon thereafter he was obliged to leave the band when it embarked for Europe because he had failed to locate his birth certificate and could not get a passport. Resuming freelance work he briefly joined COUNT BASIE's octet in May 1950.

Rouse took part in the trumpeter CLIFFORD BROWN's first recordings, issued as *New Star on the Horizon* (1953). He worked with the trombonist Bennie Green in 1955 and also played in the bassist OSCAR PETTIFORD's sextet, which included the French horn player JULIUS WATKINS. Subsequently Watkins and Rouse led Les Modes—soon to be renamed the Jazz Modes—a group that presented a gentle version of bop. Making its debut at Birdland in New York in 1956, it worked mainly as a quintet, with French horn added to the conventional mix of tenor saxophone, piano, string bass, and drums. For recordings and concerts Watkins and Rouse added a singer, a harpist, the Latin percussionist Chino Pozo (heard on their album *The Most Happy Fella*, 1957), and—for the group's last studio session in November 1958—the baritone saxophonist Sahib Shihab.

By the autumn of 1958 Rouse was rehearsing with Monk, often at the New Jersey home of Monk's patron, Baroness Pannonica de Koenigswarter. The two jazz musicians were traveling with the baroness when she was arrested in October 1958 for marijuana possession in Wilmington, Delaware, in a widely publicized incident. Later that same month or early in November Rouse substituted for SONNY ROLLINS in Monk's quartet for a Sunday afternoon concert at the Five Spot in New York, and he joined Monk again for a performance at Town Hall on 28 November.

The Jazz Modes had no work after January 1959, by which time Rouse had formally joined Monk's quartet. He stayed with Monk until 1970. Apart from his unusual tolerance of Monk's eccentricities (owing in no small part to his recognition of Monk's musical genius), the most obvious reason that Rouse's tenure lasted far longer than that of any of Monk's other sidemen was his willingness to adapt his style to Monk's work. He improvised with more deliberation than many bop instrumentalists and restated melodies often. This distinctive approach may be heard on "Shuffle Boil," from the album *It's Monk's Time* (1964), in which he reiterates the principal thematic motif, alternating with formulaic bop runs. "Many people try to interpret Thelonious' compositions their own way and it doesn't work," Rouse said. "I know how he wanted them, and when you play them like he wanted, it's very effective. Otherwise it won't go, because his composition is so personal" (Franklin, *Cadence*, 10).

Other recordings of note included the albums *Five by Monk by Five* (1959), *Monk's Dream* (1962), *Criss Cross* (1963), *Monk Misterioso* (1963–1965), and *Underground* (1967–1968). Rouse appeared with Monk on the BBC television series "Jazz Goes to College" (1966 or 1967), and he figured prominently in the acclaimed documentary film *Thelonious Monk: Straight, No Chaser* (1989). Numerous sessions apart from Monk included trumpeter DONALD BYRD's album *Byrd in Hand* (1959), Rouse's own *Yeah!* and *Takin' Care of Business* (both 1960), the pianist SONNY CLARK's *Leapin' and Lopin'* and Benny Carter's *Further Definitions* (both 1961), and Rouse's *Bossa Nova Bacchanal* (1962).

After leaving Monk, Rouse stopped playing and studied acting. Returning to jazz he formed a group with the cellist Calo Scott, who suffered a stroke that ended the project. Rouse then worked as a freelancer, led a sextet oriented toward Latin jazz in 1975, and recorded three albums as a leader, including *Moment's Notice* (1977). From 1979 until his death he belonged to the cooperative quartet Sphere, with the pianist KENNY BARRON, the bassist Buster Williams, and the drummer Ben Riley. Their first album, *Four in One*, recorded in 1982, the year Monk died, was dedicated to Monk's music. But Rouse claimed that his group's name, Sphere, was selected without realizing that it was Monk's middle name, and he argued that the connection to Monk's music was thus overemphasized in most accounts of the band. Apart from Sphere, Rouse worked regularly with his own band. In 1984 he recorded the album *Social Call*, leading a quintet that included the trumpeter Red Rodney. Also during his last years Rouse and the pianist Mal Waldron co-led a quartet. These groups worked frequently at the Village Vanguard in Greenwich Village.

Rouse performed in WYNTON MARSALIS's group at the Concord (California) Jazz Festival in 1987. Early in 1988 he performed Monk's compositions with the singer CARMEN McRAE in San Francisco; two "live" tracks are included on the ensuing disc, *Carmen Sings Monk*.

Throughout his career Rouse was extremely hardworking and devoted to jazz as an artistic endeavor, and he kept his problems to himself. Suffering from lung cancer, he played in a trio for a tribute to Dameron at Lincoln Center in August 1988, and he led a tribute to Monk in San Francisco in October, seven weeks before his death in Seattle. His outstanding performance in San Francisco was recorded for broadcast and issued as *Epistrophy: The Last Concert* (1989).

FURTHER READING

Franklin, A. David. "Charlie Rouse," *Cadence* (June 1987).

Gourse, Leslie. *Straight, No Chaser: The Life and Genius of Thelonious Monk* (1997).

Van Der Bliek, Rob. *The Thelonious Monk Reader* (2001).

Obituaries: *New York Times*, 2 Dec. 1988; *Washington Post*, 4 Dec. 1988; *San Francisco Chronicle Datebook*, 12 Feb. 1989; *Down Beat* (Apr. 1989).

This entry is taken from the *American National Biography* and is published here with the permission of the American Council of Learned Societies.

BARRY KERNFELD

Rowan, Carl Thomas (11 Aug. 1925–23 Sept. 2000), journalist, diplomat, and United States Information Agency director, was born in Ravenscroft, Tennessee. He was one of three children of Thomas David Rowan, a lumberyard worker with a fifth-grade education who had served in World War I, and Johnnie Bradford, a domestic worker with an eleventh-grade education. When Rowan was an infant, his family left the dying coal-mining town of his birth to go to McMinnville, Tennessee, lured by its lumberyards, nurseries, and livery stables. But there, in the midst of the Great Depression, they remained mired in poverty. The elder Rowan sometimes found jobs stacking lumber at twenty-five cents an hour and, according to his son, probably never made more than three hundred dollars in a single year. Meanwhile his mother worked as a domestic, cleaning houses and doing the laundry of local white families.

The family lived in an old frame house along the Louisville and Nashville Railroad tracks; Rowan and his siblings slept on a pallet on a wooden floor. In his 1991 autobiography, *Breaking Barriers*, Rowan recalled a traumatic incident in 1933 when he, at age eight, awakened to his sister's screams after she had been bitten on the ear by a rat. "We had no electricity, no running water, and, for most of the time, no toothbrushes," Rowan wrote in *Breaking Barriers*. "Toilet paper was a luxury we did not know when second-hand newspapers were good enough for our outhouse" (*Breaking Barriers*, 10). He also recalled staving off hunger by hunting for rabbit. "I survived the Depression eating fried rabbit, rabbits and dumplings, broiled rabbit, rabbit stew and a host of similar dishes made possible because Two-Shot Rowan so often came home with a rabbit or two draining blood down his pants leg," he said, referring to his father (*Breaking Barriers*, 11). Rowan credited his mother, who often praised his abilities, and Bessie Taylor Gwynn, a teacher in his segregated high school, for rescuing him from a life of poverty. They instilled in him a love of academics, and because blacks were not allowed to use the local library, Gwynn smuggled books out of the white library for Carl. "This frail looking woman, who could make sense of the writings of Shakespeare, Milton, Voltaire, and bring to life BOOKER T. WASHINGTON and W. E. B. DuBois, was a towering presence in our classrooms," he once wrote. During forty-seven years of teaching, Gwynn also taught Rowan's mother and siblings. Rowan praised her for immersing him in a "wonderful world of similes, metaphors, alliteration, hyperbole, and even onomatopoeia. She acquainted me with dactylic verse, with the meter and scan of ballads, and set me to believing that I could write sonnets as good as any ever penned by Shakespeare, or iambic pentameter that would put Alexander Pope to shame" (*Breaking Barriers*, 31–32). Gwynn insisted that Rowan keep up with world affairs, so he became a delivery boy for the *Chattanooga Times*, which afforded him the opportunity to read the newspaper each day. "'If you don't read, you can't write, and if you can't write, you can stop dreaming,' Miss Bessie told me. So I read whatever she told me to read and tried to remember what she insisted that I store away."

While a student at Tennessee State University, an historically black college in Nashville, Rowan, at age nineteen, became one of the first twenty African Americans commissioned as officers in the United States Navy during World War II. Rowan was the only African American in a unit of 335 sailors. With the assistance of the GI Bill, he went on to earn a college degree in Mathematics from Oberlin College in Ohio and a master's degree in Journalism from the University of Minnesota. In 1950 he married Vivien Murphy, the college-educated daughter of a Norfolk Navy Yard worker. The couple had three children: Carl Jr., Jeffrey, and Barbara.

Rowan began his journalism career in 1948 as a copy editor at the *Minneapolis Tribune*, and in 1950 the paper hired him as one of only a handful of black general-assignment reporters in the country. While African Americans had worked on mainstream newspapers as far back as the Civil War, black reporters were still a rarity in the early 1950s. His first major assignment was a series of articles on African American life in the Deep South, for which he traveled six thousand miles in six weeks. Flying out of Nashville, he said, "I was shocked in 1951 to see signs on two airport chairs proclaiming: FOR COLORED PASSENGERS ONLY. I was even more shocked to see four airport toilets marked WHITE MEN, COLORED MEN, then WHITE LADIES, and the last inviting COLORED WOMEN." For his series he garnered an award for best newspaper reporting by the Sidney Hillman Foundation, and the Minneapolis Junior Chamber of Commerce named him Outstanding Young Man of 1951. He also secured a book contract for his first book, *South of Freedom* (1953). He went on to cover the Supreme Court's historic school desegregation ruling, *Brown v. Board of Education* (1954), and some of the other major civil rights battles of the 1950s, including the Montgomery bus boycott, which formed the basis for his third book, *Go South to Sorrow*.

In 1961 President John F. Kennedy appointed Rowan assistant secretary of state for public affairs, which at the time was the highest position held by an African American in the State Department. He later became a delegate to the United Nations during the Cuban missile crisis and served as the U.S. ambassador to Finland from 1963 to 1964. In

Carl Rowan, director of the United States Information Agency (USIA), in his office in Washington, D.C., 27 February 1964. (AP Images.)

1964 President Lyndon Johnson chose Rowan to replace Edward R. Murrow as director of the U.S. Information Agency, which, through its Voice of America radio broadcasts, provided information about the policies and culture of the United States. Though Rowan was picked for the job on his merits, his selection was also a major cold war propaganda coup for the United States; the Soviets, in their efforts to woo decolonizing nations in Africa and elsewhere, had long highlighted racial discrimination in the United States. In appointing Rowan and other African Americans like ROBERT C. WEAVER (secretary of housing and urban development) and THURGOOD MARSHALL (U.S. solictor-general and later Supreme Court justice), to prominent positions in government, President Johnson was seeking to counter such Soviet claims. As a result of these two appointments, Rowan became the first African American to sit in on cabinet and National Security Council meetings.

Rowan returned to journalism after more than four years in government and became one of the most widely known journalists, black or white, in the nation when he signed with Westinghouse Broadcasting to deliver three commentaries a week. He simultaneously signed with the *Chicago Daily News* and Publishers Newspaper Syndicate to write three columns a week, which would appear in more than one hundred newspapers. That made him the first syndicated black columnist, a position he used to highlight racial injustice and policies injurious to the poor. Rowan broke another racial barrier in 1972 when he became the first African American elected to membership in the Gridiron Club, a prestigious organization of Washington journalists established in 1885. Inclusion in elite circles, however, did not cause him to temper his outspoken views on racial injustice. In 1974, as the nation marked the twentieth anniversary of *Brown v. Board of Education*, Rowan noted that "we are still a racist society," and added that some of the litigants in the decision never enjoyed even one day of integrated education. Instead, Rowan notes, "they saw evasion, circumvention, massive resistance and a generation of litigation."

Rowan also was, for three decades, a regular panelist on the PBS talk show *Inside Washington* until he retired in 1996. During three decades he earned many awards and wrote eight books, including *Dream Makers, Dream Breakers: The World of Justice Thurgood Marshall* and *The Coming Race War in America*, which took aim at the state of race relations in America.

In 1987 Rowan founded Project Excellence, a nonprofit group that by the time of his death in April 2000 had provided millions of dollars in scholarships to some three thousand black teenagers in Washington, D.C.

FURTHER READING

The Carl T. Rowan Papers are housed at the Oberlin College Archives in Oberlin, Ohio.

Rowan, Carl T. *Breaking Barriers* (1991).

Matusow, Barbara. "Visible Man," *Washingtonian* 30 (Fall, 1995): 44–49.

Zehnpfennig, Gladys. *Carl T. Rowan: Spokesman for Sanity* (1971).

Obituary: *New York Times*, 24 Sept. 2000.

PAMELA NEWKIRK

Rowe, George Clinton (1 May 1853–3 Oct. 1903), poet, minister, and editor, was born in Litchfield, Connecticut, to Adeline Agnes Starr Ferguson Rowe and Solomon D. Rowe, sexton of St. Michael's Episcopal Church, 1865–1880. He was descended on his mother's side from Robin Starr, enslaved and brought to Danbury, Connecticut, from Guinea in West Africa in the late 1600s, and on his father's side from grandfather Phillip Rowe, enslaved in Litchfield until the early 1800s (Smith, pp. 37–40).

At the age of seventeen, Rowe obtained an apprenticeship with the weekly Litchfield *Enquirer*, earning a certificate in the printing trade after three years. Gifted with an inquiring mind, he next began a study of natural history and theology, collecting, identifying, and labeling specimens of minerals, bird eggs, and reptiles.

He married Miranda Jackson, who was born in 1857 to Richard and Mary Ward Jackson of Salisbury, Connecticut, on 8 July 1874; they had nine children. The Rowes were members of the First Congregational Church of Litchfield and maintained their connection with that church after moving south. Rowe studied theology privately in Litchfield until 1876. In 1877 Rowe moved with his family to Hampton, Virginia, to work in the printing department at Hampton Normal and Agricultural Institute.

He began a Sunday school soon after his arrival, when he invited three children playing on the beach near his temporary home to come in and led them in singing hymns. The next Sunday, seventeen children arrived, and after a few months the number had grown to forty-five. It became known as Ocean Cottage Sunday School. By the following year, attendance swelled to seventy-five, then over one hundred, so that a large outdoor arbor had to be erected to seat everyone, and five or more teachers assisted. His first book of poetry, *Sunbeams*, was published the same year.

During his time in Hampton, Virginia, he worked on production of the *American Missionary*, the *Southern Workman*, the *Alumni Journal*, and the *African Repository* (Haley, p. 589). After five years, he moved to Cypress Slash, Georgia. There he was ordained as a minister by the Georgia Association (of congregational churches) in 1881, pastored the local church for three years, and began writing *Thoughts in Verse*, which was published in 1887. This volume included poems to daughters Agnes, Adeline, Wilhelmina, and Mary, while part 3 was dedicated to, among others, Wendell Phillips, a leading New England abolitionist, and the Reverend Allan McLean, a congregational minister in Litchfield, whom Rowe recognized as a mentor. Rowe also sold stationery, fancy goods, and picture frames to supplement the family income (Smith, p. 46).

Around 1886 Rowe became the pastor of Plymouth Congregational Church in Charleston,

South Carolina, formed in 1867 by colored members of the older Circular Congregational Church. The custom of that church was that "white" and "colored" members worshipped in common, but only freedmen among those designated "colored" had a vote in church business. A fire that destroyed the church building in 1861, a seven-year period in which the church had no fixed location to meet, and the upheavals of the Civil War inspired a six-year process during which a new and separate church was formed by the colored congregants. A new building was dedicated in 1872. Rowe successfully endeavored to make Plymouth financially self-sufficient, also completing the building of a new parsonage.

During twelve years at this pulpit, Rowe published several pamphlets, including *The Aim of Life*, *A Noble Life*, and *Decoration*. Plymouth Church was spared significant damage from the earthquake that struck Charleston in 1886, which allowed Rowe to take a leading role in relief efforts organized by black clergy. About 1892 he become owner and editor of the weekly *Charleston Inquirer*, located on King Street, described in a contemporary account as "doing excellent service for the race" (Haley, p. 590). He published the paper until 1901, supporting prohibition of alcohol and Republican politics (Smith, p. 58). Two of Rowe's sons, Phillip and Blyden, worked on the presses with their father. In 1890 he published *Our Heroes: Patriotic Poems on Men, Women, and Sayings of the Negro Race*, including a lengthy tribute to Toussaint Louverture, and "The Old Flag" in memory of the 54th Massachusetts regiment in the Civil War.

Rowe served in many leadership positions in councils of the Congregational Church, including several years as Statistical Secretary and Treasurer of the Georgia Association, and as a delegate at two of the denomination's National Councils (Haley, p. 590). At the October 1892 council in Minneapolis, Rowe was appointed to the committee on nominations and elected second assistant moderator, chairing sessions on three days. Coverage of the council in the *New York Times* described Rowe as "a negro" and "a man of marked ability. At the Worcester meeting three years ago he made an address of great power" (13 Oct. 1892).

From 1890 to at least 1895 he was president of the Preachers Union of Negro Ministers in Charleston and served as a trustee and as treasurer of the Frederick Deming Jr. Industrial School, outside of Charleston. In preparation for the Atlanta Exposition of 1895, Rowe was appointed to the Literary Congress of the Negro department (Haley, p. 590). This department, headed by Dr. I. GARLAND PENN of Lynchburg, Virginia, oversaw a building at the exposition set aside to display, as BOOKER T. WASHINGTON put it, "what the Negro had accomplished since emancipation" (Winton, Ruth M., "Negro Participation in Southern Expositions, 1881–1915," *The Journal of Negro Education*, 16, no. 1, 1947, p. 35).

In 1898 Rowe resigned his position at Plymouth to become minister at the Battery Congregational Church, originally a mission of the Plymouth Church. He remained in that pulpit until his death of heart disease in 1903.

FURTHER READING

Haley, James T. *Afro-American Encyclopedia* (1895). http://docsouth.unc.edu/church/haley/haley.html

Sherman, Joan R. *African-American Poetry of the Nineteenth Century: An Anthology* (1992).

Smith, Alene Jackson, and Adeline Jackson Tucker. *Live, Labor, Love: The History of a Northern Family, 1700–1900* (2005).

CHARLES ROSENBERG

Roye, Edward James (3 Feb. 1815–28? Oct. 1871), fifth president of the Republic of Liberia, was born in Newark, Ohio, the son of John Roye, a wealthy merchant. His mother's name is unknown. His father died in 1829, leaving some personal property and land to Roye. He went to public schools in Ohio, attended Oberlin College, and taught for a few years in Chillicothe. He also tried his hand as a sheep trader and shopkeeper in various parts of the Midwest. After his mother died in 1840 he was influenced by the emigration movement to escape American prejudice. He rejected the idea of going to Haiti and instead traveled to Liberia in 1846 just before an independent republic was installed there in July 1847, taking with him a stock of goods.

At the time of Roye's arrival the new republic faced a variety of ills. The dominant Americo-Liberians remained a small minority threatened by the local tribes; Liberia was in financial straits; the colony's international position was in doubt; the colonists were involved in disputes with the Colonization Society; and various social divisions had developed. The more conservative element consisted mainly of light-skinned blacks, many of them adherents of the Colonization Society and some of them prominent traders and ship owners. The light-skinned immigrants tended to be better educated than were their darker-skinned neighbors, and some biracial settlers had inherited property from their white fathers. They regarded themselves as a social elite entitled to the better jobs in commerce and government and defended their political interests by founding the True Liberian Party, later known as the Republican Party. The darker-skinned settlers, who, in the main, made up the less affluent and lower class of immigrant population, were assigned land outside Monrovia, the main settlement, and they accused the Colonization Society's white agents of discrimination. In the 1850s the dark-skinned elements formed the National True Whig Party (NTWP), led by Roye, JAMES S. SMITH, and EDWARD WILMOT BLYDEN, in the upriver settlement of Clay Ashland. They called for the unification of all tribes and classes in the country and professed a more democratic outlook than did the rival party.

The colonists faced all manner of difficulties: lack of capital, markets, and military resources; a difficult climate and soil; and tropical diseases for which no remedy was known. From the beginning they fought numerous wars with tribes of the coast and the hinterland. European colonial powers also threatened the new republic.

Roye became a leading merchant and ship owner and challenged the biracial mercantile monopoly. Becoming one of the wealthiest men in the republic, he started the first shipping line to fly the Liberian flag and had a distinguished public career. He was a journalist, a member of the House of Representatives in Liberia, and a government official in many capacities, including chief justice from 1865 to 1868, before being elected president in 1870 on his third attempt. A leader of the True Whigs, Roye was the first pure-blooded black elected to the presidency. According to Blyden, Roye had married "a pure Negro woman" from the United States, and she was the first woman who was not a biracial to live in the presidential mansion.

With Roye's election, lower-class and darker-skinned Americo-Liberians and Congoes, freed slaves from ships captured by the American African Squadron, gained power at the expense of the light-skinned, upper-class Monrovian traders; Roye was the major architect of the political change that propelled the government into economic development. He had become acquainted with Blyden, "the brilliant and controversial West Indian born Liberian" who spent "his entire life championing his race" in 1850, and they both resented the dominance of light-skinned Americo-Liberians in the country's government and mercantile life. With Blyden's help Roye set forth a program of development for

Edward J. Roye, Liberian senator and fifth president of the Republic of Liberia, c. 1856. (Library of Congress/American Colonization Society Records, 1792–1964.)

Liberia that called for a national banking system, education of the indigenous people, building of railroads to open the interior, incorporation of the native peoples contiguous to Liberia, and the formation of an alliance with distant interior tribes.

Roye's predecessor, James S. Payne, had seized the British ship *Elizabeth*, had been involved in border disputes with Sierra Leone, and was forced to pay an indemnity to Britain. After his election Roye faced the problems of acquiring a loan to pay off the indemnity and settling the border disputes. He went to England in 1870 to request a loan of $500,000 from a London banking firm, offering future customs receipts as security. Consul General David Chinery, Speaker of the House of Representatives William S. Anderson, and Secretary of the Interior Hiliary Johnson carried out the negotiations. The terms were onerous—$150,000 discount, 7 percent interest, and repayment in fifteen years—and Liberia only received about $90,000 from the loan. Roye sanctioned the terms of the loan but failed to win the border dispute with Sierra Leone, a British colony. His biracial Republican Party opponents claimed he profited from the loan and gave away land.

Roye's troubles increased dangerously when he tried to extend his presidential term from two to four years. In 1869 the Republicans had maneuvered to keep Payne in office by amending the constitution to allow an additional two-year term. In 1870 Roye won a vote in the Liberian House to amend the constitution to allow for a four-year term, but the Republicans in the Liberian Senate refused to accept the amendment. In May 1871 a referendum was held, but the legislature ignored the electoral vote and, without a two-thirds majority, declared the constitution not amended. Angered, Roye in October 1871 issued a proclamation declaring the constitution amended on the basis of the 1869 vote and the presidential term extended to four years. A crisis developed when the Republicans claimed the proclamation was unconstitutional and nominated former president J. J. Roberts to take over when Roye's term ended. Believing he had a four-year term, Roye forbade the holding of the election.

Fighting broke out in Monrovia on 21 October 1871. A mob led by biracial attackers stormed Roye's house and imprisoned him and the other True Whig Party leaders. Roye was deposed on 26 October 1871, and though he did manage to escape from prison, he was soon recaptured. Some accounts hold that Roye, carrying a portion of the loan money, tried to escape in a boat and was drowned when the boat capsized. Blyden later claimed a biracial assailant shot Roye while he was waiting for the boat. Roye's wife stated that, after his attempted escape, Roye was captured, beaten, then dragged through the streets and left to die in prison in Monrovia, the date unknown. It is unlikely that Roye had any of the loan money on him when he escaped. He was reportedly the richest man in Liberia, and most of his money was in British banks. He could have lived comfortably, had he escaped. Any money he carried on his person during the escape attempt, therefore, would probably have been his own cash.

Vice President J. S. Smith did not complete Roye's term. Instead, a junta that had helped stage the coup took over. The legislature proclaimed Roberts president in December 1871, and he served until 1875. He was succeeded by Payne, who served until 1877, when once again the True Whig Party won the presidency. When Britain took over the customs offices (until 1912) to collect the loan, Liberia lost some of its legitimacy, and Roye was unjustly blamed for the loan and the political trouble. In fact the crisis was the work of the light-skinned elite who did not want to share power with black-skinned Americo-Liberians.

Despite Roye's failings his short administration marked a watershed. Although he was deposed he had encouraged dark-skinned people to gain a share of government and to challenge the light-skinned politicians. He introduced the politics of patronage to the dark-skinned Americo-Liberians and the Congoes, and when the True Whig Party returned to power in 1877 it remained in control until 1980. Patronage was thereafter extended to all Americo-Liberians, but the indigenous people continued to be excluded, except for a select few youths from the interior who were provided an education. Finally in 1980 the sons and daughters of the original settlers were overthrown.

FURTHER READING

Archival materials on Roye are in the U.S. Consulate, Monrovia: *Dispatches from U.S. Consuls in Monrovia, 1852–1906*; the National Archives, Washington, D.C.

Cassell, C. Abayomi. *Liberia: History of the First African Republic* (1970).

Johnston, Sir Harry Hamilton. *Liberia*, vol. 1 (1906).

Lynch, Hollis R. *Edward Wilmot Blyden: Pan-Negro Patriot 1832–1912* (1967).

Webster, James Bertin, and A. A. Boahen. *The Revolutionary Years: West Africa Since 1800* (1967).

This entry is taken from the *American National Biography* and is published here with the permission of the American Council of Learned Societies.

PETER J. DUIGNAN

Ruby, George Thompson (1841–31 Oct. 1882), politician and journalist, was born in New York and was living in the Portland, Maine, area by 1850. He was the son of Reuben and Rachel (Humphrey) Ruby, although some scholars have mistakenly asserted that he was the son of his first cousin Ebenezer and Jemima Ruby, who, with their daughter Margaret and son Arthur, were free black farmers in Cumberland County, Maine. Born in Gray, Maine, on 28 December 1798, Reuben Ruby was a free African American trader who moved to Portland, Maine, before 1821. He moved to New York in about 1839, returning to Portland in 1849 after a four-month trip to California where he reportedly mined $3,000 in gold. Reuben and Rachel, his second wife, are listed in the 1850 Portland census with sons Frederic B., William W., George T., and Horatio F. living in the home of Reuben's sister, Sophia Ruby Manuel. George T. was the first African American male to attend the Portland High School for Boys, where he was graduated with high honors. In the 1860 census of Bangor, Maine, George T. was living with his brother William W. George's occupation is listed as "confectionary," while his brother's is "baker."

William Wilberforce Ruby became involved in politics, serving on what is now the Portland City Council, and was deputy fire chief in the city. He is credited with sounding the first alarm of the Great Portland Fire on 4 July 1866, which destroyed much of Portland and was the largest fire in the United States until Chicago went up in flames. The youngest brother, Horatio Ruby, was politically active in the Greenback Party in Maine, lived briefly in Texas and Kansas, and testified before the U.S. Senate hearing on the Exoduster Movement.

By 1861 George T. Ruby began working with the journalist James Redpath. Redpath had already begun his storied career: he was well known for his abolitionist writing and also for his editing of the antislavery Kansas publication *Crusader of Freedom,* and his biography of John Brown had just been published. He had toured Haiti in 1859 and early 1860 and actively lobbied the United States on behalf of the Haitian government. As part of these efforts he worked actively for African American emigration to Haiti, and the organ of these efforts, *Pine and Palm*, was where Ruby found his entry into journalism. Ruby himself traveled to Haiti as one of Redpath's correspondents, writing his first "Letter from Hayti," from Port-au-Prince on 22 April 1861.

Returning to the United States, Ruby taught at a school for newly freed African American adults in New Orleans, where he was also correspondent for the *Anti-Slavery Standard,* owned by William Lloyd Garrison, and the *New York Tribune*. He "was an occasional correspondent also for the *New York Times* and the *Toledo Blade.*" When the war ended Ruby established and taught in various schools in Louisiana and began an important association with the Freedmen's Bureau." However, when he was beaten by a white mob for attempting to start a black school near Jacksboro, Louisiana, and economic hardship closed Louisiana's schools in September of 1866, he left for Texas, where he received an appointment from the school superintendent Edwin Wheelock (with whom he had worked in Louisiana) to organize black schools in and around Galveston.

Ruby was both fairly popular and respected in postwar Galveston and left the bureau in late 1867 to turn his energies fully to politics while becoming editor of *The Freedman*, which appeared intermittently in Austin and Galveston throughout 1868 and 1869, and then the *Galveston Standard*, published in the island city from 1870 to 1873. He used the opportunities provided by Reconstruction, along with his own considerable political savvy, to move from a largely figurehead position to a key player in Texas politics. Initially he became the president of Galveston's local chapter of the Union League, a semisecret organization (with rituals echoing Masonic orders) that worked for the full enfranchisement of black men and against attempts by former Confederates to take control of the government. Scholars have argued that he may have initially been a convenient choice for Republican whites, who knew him from his work with the Freedmen's Bureau. In turn, with these connections and his background as an educator and writer, Ruby was able to position himself as a spokesperson for area African Americans, who joined the league in significant numbers.

White leaders perhaps realized too late how much local power Ruby had been able to create through the league. When he successfully fought for a role at the convention to draft a new Texas state constitution in late 1867 and early 1868 and was then able in June 1868 to take the state presidency of the Union League, they recognized that his local power had statewide implications. Ruby parlayed his position into a delegate's seat at the 1868 Republican National Convention, as well as into an appointment as a notary public in Galveston; such work also allowed him to attend the December 1868 Colored National Labor Convention, which further shaped his ideas on organizing and economic power.

Texas's white Republicans were already becoming factionalized by this time, and Ruby used this to his advantage, eventually strengthening his ties to Edmund J. Davis, a white radical who secured the Texas governorship. Ruby received a patronage appointment as the powerful deputy collector of customs at Galveston in 1869 that lasted four years. More important, Ruby was elected to the Texas state senate that same year. One of two African American senators, he secured positions on most of the senate's major committees and became a power broker not only for Galveston but also for much of the state.

On 14 April 1868, Ruby was refused cabin accommodations aboard the steamship *Morgan* on a route from Galveston to Brashar City, Texas, although he was willing to pay the $18 fare. Ruby sued and won, a United States District Court judge awarding him $250.

Ruby's relationship with his district was always complex. Whites—especially former Confederates—often depicted him as a carpetbagger. Among Galveston's native blacks he was sometimes seen as a tool of opportunistic white Republicans. As his term went on he realized that he would have to court the votes of now reenfranchised planters, whose desires were far from those of the Union League. He was also certainly self-interested, and this led to even more complications—most notably when he sided with William T. Clark, an incumbent Texas congressman, against the much more radical Republican Louis Stevenson, who had actively questioned Ruby's integrity. Galveston's black community split over this race, and the African American writer FRANK J. WEBB, now living in Galveston and a staunch Stevenson supporter, angered Ruby so much that Ruby called for his arrest.

Still, Ruby's record in the state senate and his role in the creation of Texas's constitution show a man deeply conscious of his race and actively striving for civil, economic, and educational rights for African Americans. Perhaps equally important, his role in helping form the Labor Union of Colored Men—which cinched the black control of employment in and shipment through the Galveston docks—created a base for one of the few post-Reconstruction pockets of black power. NORRIS WRIGHT CUNEY, who succeeded Ruby as Union League president, controlled the docks for most of the rest of the nineteenth century and used this power to advance the sociopolitical agenda of Galveston's African Americans with skill and acumen.

Still, after 1871 Ruby's local role and power became limited, and he refused to run for reelection in 1873—perhaps predicting the rise of Texas Democrats and the victory of Richard Coke over Davis in 1873. Ruby left Texas soon after and moved back to Louisiana, where he settled in New Orleans.

The late 1870s saw Ruby—still a relatively young man—attempt to regain his role as a voice for African Americans, but by journalism and activism rather than by running for office. He gained a clerkship with the Port of New Orleans—probably through the patronage of old allies in the Republican Party. He also worked for a succession of newspapers—P. B. S. PINCHBACK's *State Register*, the *New Orleans Observer*, and the *Republic*—all strongly Republican papers with ties to African American readers. Ruby's break with Pinchback seems to have been over Ruby's support of the Exoduster movement, which arguably hearkened back to his flirtation with Haitian emigration and certainly echoed his lifelong calls for black land ownership and economic self-sufficiency. This work led Ruby to speak at a major convention on the movement in 1879 and to testify before the U.S. Senate in 1880. However, this second attempt at achieving prominence and his own vision of black empowerment was cut short by malaria, and he died in New Orleans.

On 19 September 1870 he married a Virginian who lived in Washington, DC, Lucy Nalle, a light-skinned mulatto who many thought was white.

The newlywed's first public outing was at Cooper Institute (now Union) in New York City at a reception for the Hon. E. D. Bassett, who was the first African American diplomat for the United States as Minister to Hayti. In its report of the reception, the *Boston Post* newspaper reported that "Mrs. Ruby... is a white blonde." The couple then traveled to Portland where the city honored Ruby with a reception. The *Portland Daily Press* called Mrs. Ruby "white and very attractive." Their first child, Mabel, was born in Texas in 1872; their second, George, in Washington, D.C., in 1875; and their third, Victor T., in New Orleans in 1879. Both Lucy Ruby and the children are difficult to trace after George Ruby's death.

After the death of George T., Lucy and the three children moved to Washington, DC, where her family still lived. Lucy worked for the U.S. Government's printing office before she died on 14 February 1925. Mabel Ruby was a teacher in Washington, DC, where she died in 1927. George N. was a printer for newspapers in Portland, Maine, and later in Boston. He died in Boston in 1945. Victor was living in Washington as late as 1935.

FURTHER READING

Some of Ruby's letters survive in the archives of Texas politicians, most notably the James P. Newcomb Papers at the University of Texas and the Governor's Papers Collection at the Texas State Archives.

Additional material on Ruby, taken from Ruby family papers and other manuscript sources, was added to this essay by Bob Greene in 2011.

Moneyhon, Carl H. "George T. Ruby and the Politics of Expediency in Texas," in *Southern Black Leaders of the Reconstruction Era*, ed. Howard N. Rabinowitz (1982).

Moneyhon, Carl H. *Republicanism in Reconstruction Texas* (1980).

Price, H. H. and Gerald E. Talbot. *Maine's Visible Black History: The First Chronicle of Its People* (2006).

ERIC GARDNER

Ruby, Reuben (28 Dec. 1798–3 July 1878), activist, coachman, cook and waiter, was born in Gray, Cumberland County, Maine. His parents are unknown, but they could have been Boston Reuben and Zeruiah Lewis, who were married 6 December 1783 in New Gloucester, Cumberland County, Maine. Boston Reuben could have been the

"Boston Black" listed in the 1790 federal census as living in New Gloucester, Maine, with four "other free persons" and the "Moston Ruby" in the 1800 federal census living in Gray with seven "other free persons."

Reuben Ruby moved to Portland, Cumberland County, Maine, where he married Jennett C. Pierre (1805–1827) on 23 October 1821. Their only child, William, died at the age of three. Two years after the death of first wife, Ruby married Rachel Humphrey (1805–1861) in Boston, Massachusetts, on 23 December 1829. They had at least six children, with three living to adulthood, and all of whom were involved in politics. Reuben was married a third time, to Ann Mayo of Middlebury, Vermont, in Boston on 10 November 1864.

Ruby was one of Portland's most prominent African American businessmen, and he used his earnings to acquire a considerable amount of land. He is listed in the 1823 Portland City Directory as a waiter, while an advertisement in an 1834 Portland newspaper "informs the public that he has two good Coaches, one or the other of which may generally be found at his old Stand, at the Elm Tavern, where he will be happy to attend to any calls which are made upon him."

Ruby joined with his brother-in-law, Christopher Christian Manuel, along with Caleb Jonson, Clement Thompson, Job L. Wentworth and John Sigs in signing a letter that appeared in the 15 September 1826 issues of the *Eastern Argus* (Portland, Maine) condemning the local churches of treating its non-white members as second-class citizens. He then joined Sigs, Thompson, Ephraim Small, and Titus Skillings in 1828 to petition the State of Maine for incorporation of the Abyssinian Religious Society to enable "them to receive a deed for a lot of land to erect a house of public worship thereon." Ruby paid $250 for the land. While most members of the religious society pledged up to two dollars, Ruby donated one hundred dollars toward constructing the building, and on 3 June 1839 was chosen moderator of the Society. The building, which later became the Abyssinian Church, was the third-oldest African American worship house still standing in the United States in 2008, the year a restoration project was begun.

In 1828 Ruby was an authorized agent for *Freedom's Journal*, the first African American owned and operated newspaper published in the United States. The *Journal* was edited by JOHN B. RUSSWORM, who had graduated from Bowdoin College in Brunswick, Cumberland County, Maine. Ruby also was heavily involved with *The Liberator*, the abolitionist newspaper published in Boston by William Lloyd Garrison. While on a visit to Portland in September 1832, Garrison was driven around on a sightseeing tour by Ruby and entertained at Ruby's home where he also met with twenty African Americans.

Extremely active in many areas, Ruby in 1834 volunteered to represent Portland at the state Whig convention in Augusta. Later that year he was present in Augusta when the Maine Antislavery Society was formed. And Ruby was one of two men nominated to represent Portland at the Fifth Annual Convention of the Free People of Color held in Philadelphia the first Monday in June 1835. The other was George H. Black, and what happened to the two illuminates the problems African Americans endured in moving about the United States at that time.

Ruby joined with other black men from Massachusetts, Rhode Island, and New York to write a letter to *The Liberator* tendering "their thanks to Capt. Vanderbelt, of the steamboat Lexington, for his kind treatment to them while on board of his boat, and would recommend their colored friends, who have occasion to travel from Providence to New York, to patronize his boat in preference to all others." Right below the recommendation the newspaper printed a notice from George Black saying he "was refused the liberty of the cabins on account of my color, but was told I could not be permitted on board of the boat, unless I consented to take quarters on the forward deck. This, in respect to myself and my character, I could not do, though obliged to postpone my trip at considerable inconvenience and disappointment."

Ruby also served as president of the 1835 convention. In the late 1830s Ruby moved his family to New York City where he opened a restaurant and became even more active in the abolitionist movement. He was listed as president and chair of a group that met in New York City's Philomathean Hall on 16 November 1840 "to adopt efficient measures for petitioning the legislature of the state to extend the elective franchise to all her citizens irrespective of color or condition." Among others in the group were THOMAS VAN RENSAELAER, Lewis Bodine, Jeffrey Van Cleef, and Samuel Hardenburgh. Ruby was a vice president of the American Moral Reform Society. The organization, based in Philadelphia with JAMES FORTEN as president, emphasized education, temperance, economy, and university liberty.

In 1849 Ruby joined the gold rush and went to California. The Portland *Argus* newspaper reported in its 6 December 1849 edition that Ruby had returned to Maine with his family after mining for four months and collecting about $3,000 worth of gold.

After being embroiled in several lawsuits with the Abyssinian Church—Ruby said he had loaned the church money, the church said it was a donation—Reuben Ruby joined a new black congregation, the Mountfort Street AME Church, where he again was one of the leaders. In a way, it was the beginning of the end for the Abyssinian, which saw its membership dwindle as congregants aged and died and the younger people joined the AME church.

Ruby named his children after abolitionists. The three who survived to adulthood became prominent in local and national politics. One of his sons, William Wilberforce Ruby, became a deputy fire chief in Portland and is credited with helping save the Abyssinian building when fire destroyed much of the city on 4 July 1866. William also was a restaurant owner. Another son, GEORGE THOMPSON RUBY, became a foreign correspondent in Haiti for the *Pine and Palm*, a newspaper edited by the radical Scottish American abolitionist, James Redpath. George T. Ruby also wrote for several other newspapers, including the *Anti-Slavery Standard*, the *New York Tribune, Toledo Blade*, and the *New York Times*. Following the Civil War, George Ruby taught former slaves in New Orleans, was an agent for the Freedmen's Bureau in both Louisiana and Texas; was editor and publisher of newspapers in both Galveston, Texas, and New Orleans; served two terms in the Texas state senate and was a delegate from Texas to the National Republican Conventions in 1868 and 1872.

Reuben's youngest son, Horatio, was involved with the Greenback Party in Maine, giving one of the seconding speeches in 1880 for General Harris M. Plaisted, who went on to win the governorship. Horatio Ruby made several trips to South America where he died while searching for gold.

FURTHER READING

Information on Reuben Ruby's activities in the National Negro Convention is contained in the *Minutes of the Fifth Annual Convention of the Free People of Colour in the United States, Held by Adjournments, in the Wesley Church, Philadelphia, from the First to the Fifth of June, Inclusive, 1835* (1835).

Colesworthy, D. C. *School Is Out* (1876).

Lapp, Rudolph M. *Blacks in Gold Rush California* (1995).

Quarles, Benjamin. *Black Abolitionists* (rpt. 1991).

Rose, James M. and Alice Eichholz. *Black Genesis: A Resource Book for African-American Genealogy* (2003).

Young, David C., and Benjamin Lewis Keene. *The Maine Farmer Abstracts of Death Notices (1833–1852) and Miscellaneous News Articles (1833–1924) from The Maine Farmer* (1997).

BOB GREENE

Rucker, Benjamin H. "Black Herman" (June 1890–17 Apr. 1934), magician, ventriloquist, and entrepreneur, was born in Amherst, Virginia, one of eight children of Peticus Rucker, a farm laborer, and Louise A. Rucker, a cook. In his teens Rucker worked as a cook and then as a contractor building houses. When Harry Kellar ("Kellar the Great"), one of the foremost magicians of his time, came through the area on tour, Rucker performed some handyman tasks for him and became his assistant.

Rucker studied stage magic under Kellar and eventually began performing on his own, taking the stage name "Black Herman." This pseudonym linked him with earlier black magicians, such as Prince Herman, a traveling medicine show magician, whom Rucker also claimed as a mentor, and James A. Willis and Alonzo Moore, whose stage names included "Herman" in some combination or else billed themselves as "the black Hermann" (or "the black Herman"), implying that they possessed abilities and could perform wonders equaling those of the famous Herrmann family of magicians, who had been international stars for some eighty years.

As Black Herman, Rucker soon became the most renowned African American magician of his time. His act also included ventriloquism, and he was famous for making a handkerchief talk and making his voice appear to come from the back of the auditorium. After establishing his reputation in the Midwest with major shows in St. Louis, Chicago, and Detroit, he relocated permanently to Harlem in New York City at the end of a successful eastern tour in March 1923. His arrival was highlighted by sell-out performances during a two-month booking at the four-thousand-seat Liberty Hall, the headquarters of MARCUS GARVEY's Universal Negro Improvement Association (UNIA). Black Herman's imposing physique and self-made success neatly fit Garvey's ideal image of the black man and proved his assertion that skin color should be no handicap to personal success. To add to his mystique, Rucker claimed that he had been born near a small village in Africa and brought to Amherst, Virginia, when he was ten; this African connection, however spurious, also resonated with Garvey's own connections with Africa. Black Herman became an associate and supporter of Garvey and regularly appeared in his UNIA parades.

The highlight of Black Herman's act was hypnotizing a young woman, burying her alive for a few hours, and then "resurrecting" her unharmed. When he performed this trick as the chief act at the 1923 Independence Day Jubilee and Aviation Carnival and Athletic Meet in Hasbrouck Heights, New Jersey, it further involved the Garvey supporter HUBERT FAUNTLEROY JULIAN, one of the first African Americans to receive a pilot's license in the United States, parachuting onto the "grave." In later years on tour, Black Herman arrived in a town a few days ahead of his booking and had himself buried in a preselected plot of ground near the theater. Then on the night of the performance he was dug up and led a procession of fans to the theater.

Despite public suspicions of magicians, considered by some preachers and other religious leaders as being in league with the devil or black magic, and despite the religious connotations and resonances of his most distinctive illusion, Black Herman maintained a good relationship with the African American religious community. He first came to national attention when he was the star attraction at a weeklong fair in St. Louis sponsored by the St. Paul AME Church and the Metropolitan AME Zion Church. Throughout his career, he appeared at various church functions to help raise money to pay off mortgages on church properties. He also counted as a friend the Reverend Will Banks, the "black Billy Sunday" of Washington, D.C., who punctuated his services with a walk across the backs of pews with his eyes closed, a trick Rucker taught him.

Rucker was a significant figure in Harlem during the 1920s not only because of his professional renown but also for his general support of education and culture. He held regular salons in his home that were attended by black business and society leaders, and he presented well-attended Chautauquas (educational tent shows named after Lake Chautauqua, where the movement originated in 1874) for the general public. He also performed at various schools, including Tuskegee University, where he met BOOKER T. WASHINGTON, who, Rucker claimed after the educator's death, highly commended his skills. His links with two such disparate African American leaders as Garvey and Washington attest to his charisma, showmanship, political savvy, and ability to read his audiences—all skills he demonstrated throughout his career.

In 1925 Rucker wrote a book that combined a fictionalized version of his autobiography, astrology, and dream interpretation (as well as numbers guides for gamblers in some editions) with instructions on how to do simple magic tricks. Under various titles, it went through at least fifteen editions, including at least one posthumous edition in 1938 titled *Black Herman's Secrets of Magic: Mystery & Legerdemain.*

Like his contemporary Harry Houdini, Black Herman included in his performances a general debunking of psychics and spiritualists. Conversely, he also used his act to sell his herbal remedies, his books on dream interpretation and astrology, and lucky numbers, a sideline for which some African American newspapers—especially the Philadelphia *Tribune*—repeatedly took him to task. He established herb gardens in Harlem, Chicago, Indianapolis, St. Louis, and other cities to produce Black Herman's Body Tonic, and he also sold beauty products. Prescribing and selling herbal remedies from his home, where he also conducted private fortune-telling sessions, led to his arrest and conviction in 1927 for practicing medicine without a license, and he was sentenced to an indefinite period in the New York State Penitentiary in Ossining (more commonly known as Sing Sing).

After his release from prison, Rucker returned to touring with his magic act, employing the catchphrase "Black Herman comes through only once every seven years" in all his publications. During an April 1934 appearance in Louisville, Kentucky, he died unexpectedly from what was diagnosed as "acute indigestion." Because of the nature of his signature "resurrection" trick, local audiences either doubted the report of his death or expected him to come back to life; his assistant capitalized on the situation by charging admission to view his body in a local mortuary. After Rucker's death, various African American magicians imitated his tricks and used his name or some variation on it to attract audiences. And he appears in fictionalized form as a detective in ISHMAEL REED's highly respected novel *Mumbo Jumbo* (1972).

FURTHER READING

Cullen, Frank. *Vaudeville Old & New: An Encyclopedia of Variety Performers in America* (2007). This work, like most about Rucker, contains interesting information about his act but also some dubious material—such as, for example, an 1892 birth date and the claim that he could neither read nor write (both contradict U.S. Census records).

Early, Gerald. "'Black Herman Comes through Only Once Every Seven Years': Black Magic, White Magic, and American Culture," in *The Black Columbiad: Defining Moments in African American Literature and Culture*, edited by Werner Sollors and Maria Diedrich (1994).

Haskins, Jim, and Kathleen Benson. *Conjure Times: Black Magicians in America* (2001).

RICHARD J. LESKOSKY

Darius Rucker performs on *The Tonight Show with Jay Leno* on 27 October 2008. (AP Images.)

Rucker, Darius (13 May 1966–), musician, singer, and songwriter, was born Darius Rucker in Charleston, South Carolina, one of three sons and three daughters of Carolyn Rucker, a nurse.

He was raised by his mother and grandmother; his father belonged to a gospel band named The Rolling Stones and was absent with the exception of Sunday morning visits before church. Rucker lived, at times, in a three bedroom house with his mother, grandmother, two aunts and fourteen children. As a young boy he was exposed to the music of AL GREEN, OTIS REDDING, and GLADYS KNIGHT played by his mother around the house. Rucker was fond of singing the tunes his mother played in addition to other genres of music he heard on the radio and at school; he had early aspirations of becoming a singer and would mimic playing a guitar with the household broomstick. Upon graduating from Middleton High School, Rucker began his college career at the University of South Carolina. There he sang in the college choir and joined up with his friend Mark Bryan to perform R.E.M. cover songs at bars around Columbia, South Carolina as the Wolf Brothers. The duo convinced Dean Felber to join them in 1986 to form a band that was named for two college friends; one with an owl-like appearance and the other with huge round cheeks; Hootie and the Blowfish. Initially a joke, the name stuck, and soon the trio was joined by Jim Sonefeld, from a rival band. Rucker was the lead singer for Hootie and the Blowfish, in addition, he plays harmonica and guitar; just as much as he was known for his mellow baritone voice, he was novel as an African American lead singer of an otherwise all white pop-rock band. The band sold t-shirts at their concerts in high numbers as their popularity grew. In 1991 the band produced and financed their first EP, "Kootchypop," which sold fifty thousand copies despite only being available at Hootie and the Blowfish concerts. the Hootie and the Blowfish Foundation was established in 2000 to benefit children in South Carolina through education and music programs.

Rucker and the band soon caught the attention of Atlantic Records and were signed to a deal and on 5 July 1994 they released *Cracked Rear View Mirror*, which achieved number one on the U.S. charts, certified platinum sixteen times and classified as the best-selling album of 1995. In October 1995, Rucker was invited to sing the national anthem at the World Series. Six months later Hootie and the Blowfish released the album *Fairweather Johnson*, which also reached number one in the United States and was certified platinum three times. Also in 1996 the band won a Grammy Award for Best New Artist, and began their own label, Breaking Records, a subsidiary of Atlantic Records; however, the label folded four years later. Their 1998 release, *Musical Chairs*, scaled to number four on the U.S. charts and achieved platinum status. Rucker and his band did not have as much success with subsequent albums; their self-titled release in 2003 reached number 46 in the United States and only 161 in the U.K., where before they had always charted in the top twenty. Two years later, *Looking for Lucky* topped the U.S. charts at forty-seven and failed to rank in the U.K. Despite the ranking of latter albums, Hootie and the Blowfish with Rucker at the helm had achieved record success and garnered a solid cult following with their listener-friendly pop tunes and laid-back appeal. Even more, Rucker and members of Hootie and the Blowfish maintain an annual agenda for charitable performances in Charleston, and in October 2006 members and crew went to New Orleans, after Hurricane Katrina had devastated the area, to assist with the construction of homes in 'Musician's Village.'

Rucker welcomed his first solo album on July 2002, *Back to Then*, an R&B release on Hidden Beach Records featuring the singer Jill Scott on the tune "Hold On." His debut reached number one on the U.S. Heat charts and forty-three on the R&B chart. Rucker sang at the wedding of his longtime friend Tiger Woods in 2004, and at the funeral of his father two years later. In 2005 Rucker starred as a singing cowboy in a Burger King commercial, plucking away at a guitar and singing a jingle to the tune of "Big Rock Candy Mountain," to advertise their newest sandwich. In 2008 Rucker announced that he would be leaving Hootie and the Blowfish to pursue a solo career in country music. He had signed a contract with Capitol Records Nashville and temporarily made the city his home. In May 2008 Rucker entered the Billboard chart for Hot Country songs at number fifty-one with his first single, "Don't Think I Don't Think about It." The single continued to scale the charts and by July, Rucker had become the first African American singer with a top twenty country music single since CHARLEY PRIDE in 1988; he made his debut at the famed Grand Ole Opry the same month. In September 2008, the first country album from Rucker, *Learn to Live*, was released and his single had achieved number one and certified gold status, making Rucker at the first African American with a number one country hit since Pride in 1983. The album was certified gold in February 2009 and certified platinum in August 2009. Subsequent releases from the album also charted at number one on the country music charts, "I Won't Be Like This for Long," and "Alright," respectively; Rucker was the first country music artist since Wynonna Judd in 1992 with this accomplishment. In November 2009 Rucker became the first African American to be awarded the Country Music Association's New Artist of the Year Award, and the second African American to win a CMA award since Pride won in 1971 and 1972.

In 2000 Rucker married Beth Leonard, with whom he has a daughter, Daniella Rose, and a son, Jack. He also has a daughter, Carolyn Pearl Phillips, born in 1995 from a previous relationship.

FURTHER READING

Mukherjee, Tiarra, and Maggie Murphy. "Give a Hootie." *Entertainment Weekly*, 19 April 1996, 10.

Puterbaugh, Parke. "Fish out of Water." *Rolling Stone*, 15 June 1995, 74.

Tucker, Ken. "New Kid on the Block.' *Billboard*, 27 Sept. 2008, 39.

SAFIYA DALILAH HOSKINS

Rucker, Henry Allan (14 Nov. 1852–11 May 1924), businessman and federal officeholder, was born in Washington, Georgia, the older son of slaves owned by Dr. William King. After the Civil War, Rucker's parents moved to Atlanta, where his father, Edward, became a skilled plasterer and whitewasher and his mother, Betsy, ran a boarding house. As a youth, Rucker attended the city's first school for freedmen in the Tabernacle Church Building on Armstrong Street.

Rucker briefly attended Atlanta University, founded by the American Missionary Association in

1865, where he financed his tuition by tutoring other students. He later devoted his primary energies to a series of business ventures, acquiring a profitable barbershop and an eleven-room house, which he purchased jointly with his father, and to civic and political affairs. In the late 1870s he joined one of Atlanta's black militia companies, and in 1880 was chosen as a delegate from the state's Fifth Congressional District to the Republican national convention in Chicago.

In 1881 he obtained the first of many federal patronage appointments, working first as a gauger for the Internal Revenue Service and then as a clerk, under the Republican James A. Garfield and Chester A. Arthur administrations. Replaced during the Democratic administration of Grover Cleveland, Rucker was reappointed by Republican Benjamin Harrison in 1889, and rose to the position of deputy collector for Georgia by 1893, when he was again dismissed by Cleveland.

His tenure as statewide collector was marred by racial issues. Many whites resigned rather than work for him, and one of Georgia's Democratic U.S. Senators Alexander Clay succeeded in stripping Rucker of appointment and supervision rights for most internal revenue employees (Mixon, p. 490). Despite the setback, Rucker served creditably for the next fourteen years, and twice more served as a delegate to the party's national conventions, again as an at-large delegate (1900) and representing his congressional district in 1904. He exerted considerable power within the party ranks until at least 1904, described by one biographer as "for a brief time … boss of Georgia republican politics" (Mixon, p. 503).

Rucker's reappointment in December 1901 by the Republican president Theodore Roosevelt surprised some observers, who had expected the new president to appoint a "lily-white" Republican instead. According to the *Atlanta Constitution* (22 Dec. 1901), Roosevelt "said he had looked into the matter very fully, and also saying that Rucker came fully up to his—the president's—standard of qualification for office." The newspaper noted that Rucker had won without the endorsement of the state's most influential white Republican, Major John F. Hanson of Macon, the "referee" in such matters. In 1910 Rucker submitted his resignation to Roosevelt's Republican successor President William Howard Taft, after it became apparent that he would not be reappointed as collector, and stepped down in 1911.

An active member of both the Niagara Movement and the early NAACP, Rucker also remained active in Atlanta business affairs. In 1904 he constructed the Rucker Building on Atlanta's

Henry A. Rucker, internal revenue collector, Atlanta, Georgia, seated in his office, c. 1899. (Library of Congress/Daniel Murray Collection.)

Auburn Avenue, a three-story brick office building for black professionals which remained in use until its demolition in 2001, after structural damage caused by an automobile crash. He died in Atlanta at age seventy-one.

FURTHER READING

Bacote, Clarence A. "Negro Officeholders in Georgia under President McKinley," in *Journal of Negro History* 44 (July 1959).

Hornsby, Ann R. Henry A. Rucker. In *Dictionary of Georgia Biography*, vol. 2 (1983).

Mixon, Gregory. "The Making of a Black Political Boss: Henry A. Rucker, 1897–1904." *Georgia Historical Quarterly* 89 (2005).

BENJAMIN R. JUSTESEN

Rudd, Daniel (7 Aug. 1854–4 Dec. 1933), newspaper editor and Catholic lay leader, was born in Bardstown, Kentucky, the son of Robert Rudd, a slave on the Rudd estate, and Elizabeth "Eliza" Hayden, a slave of the Hayden family in Bardstown. He was baptized a Catholic when an infant. Although little information exists about his early life, it may be conjectured that his Catholic upbringing came chiefly from his mother, who acted as sexton in the local church for more than sixty years. After the Civil War, he went to Springfield, Ohio, where an older brother had already established himself, to get a secondary-school education.

There is little information about Rudd until 1884, when he began a black newspaper, the *Ohio State Tribune*. In 1886 Rudd changed the name of the weekly newspaper to the *American Catholic Tribune*, proudly displaying on the editorial page the words "The only Catholic Journal owned and published by Colored men." The newspaper's focus was the Catholic Church and the African American. Rudd's purpose was to demonstrate to African Americans that the Catholic Church was truly the best hope of black Americans. He was convinced that Catholicism would elevate the cultural level of the black race and thus attract an enormous influx of black converts to the Catholic Church. Believing that the authority structure of the church could change racist behavior and influence racist thought, he asserted: "The Catholic Church alone can break the color line. Our people should help her to do it." Although black Catholics could point to the Catholic Church's teaching on the dignity of the person as inherently antiracist, Rudd made the case more directly for the usefulness of Roman Catholicism in changing the moral and religious status of African Americans. He published the following on the front page of his paper: "The Holy Roman Catholic Church offers to the oppressed Negro a material as well as spiritual refuge, superior to all the inducements of other organizations combined.... The distinctions and differences among men are unrecognized within the pale of the Church.... The Negro and the Caucasian are equally the children of one Father and as such, are equally welcomed, with equal rights, equal privileges."

At the same time, Rudd used the newspaper to speak out forcefully against racial discrimination. He editorialized in favor of an integrated school system in Cincinnati, Ohio, and against segregated schools and institutions. Race pride was important to him, so he used his newspaper to highlight the achievements of leading African Americans of his day.

By 1887 Rudd had moved his weekly newspaper to Cincinnati, where he had a small staff of assistant editors and traveling correspondents who doubled as sales representatives. The paper in most editions ran to four pages. Front-page articles carried religious news from various black Catholic communities along with other items related to African Americans. A column or two was often dedicated to an exposition of Catholic belief or practice. Many articles were reprints from other newspapers, including items from the Catholic press and the African American press. According to some estimates, the newspaper had as many as ten thousand subscribers in the period prior to the move to Detroit, Michigan. Rudd received the approbation of some members of the church hierarchy and some small contributions, but there is no indication of any long-term subsidy from Catholic leaders or laypeople.

Rudd also traveled across the country as a tireless lecturer. The message was usually the same: "The Catholic Church is not only a warm and true friend to the Colored people but is absolutely impartial in recognizing them as the equals of all." He spoke to varied audiences in places like Lexington, Kentucky, and Fort Wayne, Indiana (1887); Natchez, Mississippi, and Nashville, Tennessee (1891); Syracuse, New York (1895); and Lewiston, Maine (1896). Fluent in German, he spoke to German organizations such as the Central Verein in Toledo, Ohio, in 1886 and to students at a German orphanage in Linwood, Ohio, in 1890.

In the summer of 1889 Rudd was sent to Europe to participate in the Anti-Slavery Conference organized by Cardinal Charles-Martial Lavigerie, the primate of Africa. The trip was made possible, it seems, by a subvention from William Henry Elder, the archbishop of Cincinnati. Rudd was already in Germany when the conference which was to be held in Lucerne, Switzerland, was postponed; he nevertheless continued his trip to Lucerne, where he met with Cardinal Lavigerie, and to London, where he visited Cardinal Henry Edward Manning before returning to America.

Rudd was responsible for the five black Catholic lay congresses that were held between the years 1889 and 1894. He first called for a congress of black Catholics in the columns of his newspaper as early as 1888, writing: "Colored Catholics ought to unite.... Let leading Colored Catholics gather together from every city in the Union [where] they may get to know one another and take up the cause of the race." The first nationwide assembly of black Catholics, meeting in Washington, D.C., in early January 1889, was well attended and widely acclaimed. The second congress was held in Cincinnati in 1890 and the third in Philadelphia, Pennsylvania, in 1892. Rudd published the proceedings of these congresses on his own press. His influence in the last two congresses, held in Chicago, Illinois, in 1893 and in Baltimore, Maryland, in 1894, is less evident.

Rudd played other significant roles in American Catholicism and black journalism. He was on the steering committee for the first national Lay Catholic Congress held in Baltimore in November 1889 and was a founding member of the Catholic Press Association (1890) and the Afro-American Press Association and was actively involved in both. By 1894 he had moved the publication of the *American Catholic Tribune* to Detroit for unknown reasons. There are no extant copies of the newspaper dating after 1894, but only after 1897 did Rudd's name cease to appear as a publisher in the Detroit City Directory.

Under circumstances that are not clear Rudd had, according to census records, moved to Bolivar

County in Mississippi by 1910. He later moved to eastern Arkansas, where he acted as accountant and business manager for two well-to-do black farmers. He seemingly had little contact with the small black Catholic community in Arkansas centered around Pine Bluff. The black Catholic congresses had ceased to meet after 1894 for reasons that remain unclear, and Rudd thereafter was no longer an influential leader in the black Catholic movement. In his correspondence with John B. Morris, the bishop of Little Rock, he alluded to his former role and indicated his continued interest in the cause of black Catholics, even expressing a desire to represent the diocese at a meeting of the National Association for the Advancement of Colored People. In 1917 Rudd was the coauthor of a biography of SCOTT BOND, one of the successful black farmers of the region for whom he worked as an accountant (*From Slavery to Wealth, the Life of Scott Bond: The Rewards of Honesty, Industry, Economy, and Perseverance*, 1917, 1971). Rudd's attention in his later years seemingly centered on the furtherance of black business. After suffering a stroke, he returned to Bardstown in 1932, where he died.

A member of the first generation of postslavery African Americans, Rudd was one of the more significant figures in the history of black Catholics in the United States. Here was a former slave welcomed by two cardinals, a black man lecturing to white audiences both in the North and in the South. He began the longest, running African American Catholic newspaper in the country and singlehandedly launched a black Catholic lay movement when he began the black lay congresses. From this effort emerged other black Catholic lay leaders from whom came the first articulation of a black Catholic theological position. As the first African American Catholic layman to call publicly for the Catholic Church to live up to its teachings on social justice and social equality, Rudd opened the way for later black Catholic activists in the civil rights movement.

Rudd never married. He could be difficult; many ecclesiastics and white lay leaders saw him as "pushy" because he would not accept circumstances that he deemed disrespectful to the black race. Among Catholic laymen of his time, he was unique; among black leaders of his generation, he was extraordinary; in the light of recent American Catholic history, he was prophetic.

FURTHER READING
Copies of Rudd's newspaper are in the Archdiocese of Philadelphia Archives in Overbrook, Pennsylvania

His correspondence is in the Archdiocese of Cincinnati Archives, the Little Rock Diocesan Archives, and the Josephite Archives in Baltimore.

Davis, Cyprian. *The History of Black Catholics in the United States* (1990).

Lackner, Joseph H. "Daniel Rudd, Editor of the *American Catholic Tribune*, from Bardstown to Cincinnati," *Catholic Historical Review* 80 (1994): 258–281.

Spalding, Thomas. "The Negro Catholic Congresses, 1889–1894," *Catholic Historical Review* 55 (1969): 337–357.

This entry is taken from the *American National Biography* and is published here with the permission of the American Council of Learned Societies.

CYPRIAN DAVIS

Rudd, Wayland (1900?–4 July 1952), actor, was born in Nebraska and raised in a foster home from the age of nine. He eventually held menial jobs in the countryside, working in the mines and delivering messages, before becoming enamored of the theater. Rudd moved east to earn a spot on the stage, and began performing regularly in Philadelphia in the early 1920s. Though he was initially disgruntled by the lack of opportunities given to him even on stage, Rudd was soon "discovered" by Jasper Deeter, a director and founder of Hedgerow, a white theater in Moylan-Rose Valley, Pennsylvania. Deeter began using Rudd as part of his repertory company, most notably as the eponymous character in a critically acclaimed production of *The Emperor Jones*. In 1930, the same year PAUL ROBESON famously played Othello in London, Rudd was said to have performed it at Hedgerow, in America.

Along with the roles supplied to him in Pennsylvania, Rudd also found—albeit limited—success in New York, appearing in four Broadway plays, including the revival of *Porgy* in 1929. In the spring of 1932, Rudd was invited to join the "Black and White" project, or the "Cooperating Committee for Production of a Soviet Film on Negro Life." Funded by the Meschrabpom Film Corporation of the Workers International, the project and its American representative, JAMES A. FORD (the three-time Communist Party vice presidential candidate), recruited African American performers and intellectuals to create a propaganda film in Russia that would exhibit the evils of American racism and highlight the plight of black Americans. For Rudd, the appeal of filming a movie, getting away from stereotypical parts he was offered in America, and

Wayland Rudd on a postcard photograph with fellow USSR entertainer Irene Yvanova. (Courtesy of the Southern California Library for Social Studies and Research.)

seeing the promise of the Soviet state was too great to refuse.

Along with the late addition LANGSTON HUGHES (who had been hired to write dialogue) and a handful of other African American representatives, Rudd sailed to Moscow in June 1932, and was impressed at the huge reception the "delegation" received when they arrived in Leningrad weeks later. Though the film shoot itself was ultimately scrapped because of artistic and business misunderstandings, Rudd remained in Moscow briefly to study acting, fencing, and dancing.

Rudd soon married a white woman with whom he had been in love in America; the two had a child, Lolita, and in 1934 the three moved back to the states. Not long after, Rudd again became disillusioned with the treatment of blacks, and returned to Russia, alone. This time, he renounced his citizenship and became a naturalized Soviet.

Rudd penned an article for the NAACP's *The Crisis* magazine, expounding on the difference between Russian and American theater. In it he wrote that, "there has never been anything in my histrionic experiences so thrilling and absorbing as the moments the theatre afforded me [in Moscow] unless it is my present imagination of what the theatre in America could be like if it were liberated as the Russian theatre is liberated." Noting the problem with censorship and patriotic duty in a Communist state, Rudd added, "[This] is the glorified privilege of the Russian director: to work unhampered by expense limitations, though he must worry about what the play says" (Rudd, "Russia and America Theatre" *The Crisis*, September 1934).

In Moscow, Rudd attended the Theatrical Art Institute, and later joined the Meyerhold Theatre. When the Stalinist government began investigating the artistic director Vsevolod Meyerhold and shut down his theater, Rudd joined the Stanislavsky Opera and Drama Theatre, despite the opposing artistic viewpoints of the respective founders.

After the German invasion of Russia, Rudd joined a theater on the front lines to entertain the troops. After the war, he returned to Moscow to act, direct, and found his own theater company. Rudd met his second wife, a Jewish American woman who had emigrated to Europe with her Communist father, at an arts conservatory in Moscow; after they married, they had two children, Wayland Jr. and Victoria.

Wayland Jr., who was born in 1947, later noted the elder Rudd's disillusionment with his Soviet dream: "Though he was able to find enough movie roles to keep busy, he was treated more like a circus attraction than a professional" (Hiatt, *Washington Post*). Though Soviet Russia may not have turned out to be the race-blind utopia he had originally envisioned, Rudd did find more success in Russia than in America, gaining popularity from roles including his portrayal of a black war veteran struggling with American racism in *Deep Are the Roots*, and the character of Jim in a film adaptation of *Tom Sawyer*. Rudd also made history when he became the first black actor to perform Othello in the Russian language.

Rudd died in 1952.

FURTHER READING

Carew, Joy Gleason. *Blacks, Reds, and Russians* (2008).

Hiatt, Fred. "The Ambivalent American." *Washington Post*, 10 July 1994.

ADAM W. GREEN

Wilma Rudolph hits the tape to win the gold medal in the women's 4 x 100-meter relay at the Summer Olympics in Rome, 8 September 1960. (AP Images.)

Rudolph, Wilma (23 June 1940–12 Nov. 1994), track-and-field athlete, was born Wilma Glodean Rudolph in St. Bethlehem, Tennessee, the daughter of Edward Rudolph, a railroad porter, and Blanche (maiden name unknown), a domestic. Born nearly two months premature and weighing only four and a half pounds, Rudolph was a sickly child who contracted both double pneumonia and scarlet fever, which resulted in her left leg being partially paralyzed. Her doctors doubted that she would ever regain the use of her leg. Undaunted, Rudolph's mother made a ninety-mile bus trip once a week with her to Nashville, Tennessee, so she could receive heat, water, and massage treatments. At age five she began wearing a heavy steel brace and corrective shoes to help straighten her leg. After years of physical therapy, at age twelve she was finally able to move about without her leg brace.

When she entered a racially segregated high school in Clarksville, Tennessee, Rudolph tried out for the basketball team and, in recognition of her abilities, made the all-state team four times. As an outstanding athlete she came to the attention of ED TEMPLE, the premier women's track coach at Tennessee State University. Though Rudolph was still in high school, Temple invited her to spend the summer with other track athletes at the university training camp. In 1956 she participated in the national Amateur Athletic Union track-and-field competition, winning the 75-yard and 100-yard events as well as anchoring the winning relay team. Encouraged by her coach, she traveled with the Tennessee State team to the tryouts for the 1956 Olympic Games in Melbourne, Australia. At sixteen Rudolph became the youngest member of the U.S. women's track-and-field team. Though she did not make the Olympic finals in the 200-meter event, she and her team won a bronze medal in the 400-meter relay event.

Rudolph returned home to complete her last two years of high school and looked forward to going to college. However, in her senior year of high school she became pregnant and gave birth to a daughter. Her boyfriend wanted to marry her, but Rudolph was unwilling to give up her fledgling track career. Her daughter was sent to live with a married older sister in St. Louis. In 1957 Rudolph enrolled at Tennessee State on a track scholarship and continued to train for the 1960 Olympic Games in Rome, Italy. During the 1960 Olympics, temperatures in

Rome hovered around 100 degrees. Rudolph contended not only with the weather, but with an ankle injury she suffered the day before the first race. Despite her impairment she won three gold medals: one in the 100-meter event, setting a world record with a finishing time of 11.0 seconds; another in the 200-meter dash with a time of 23.2 seconds; and her third as anchor of the women's 400-meter relay team. She thus became the first American woman to win three gold medals in a single Olympics.

In 1961 Rudolph competed in the previously all-male Millrose Games, tying her own world record in the 60-yard dash with a time of 6.9 seconds. She also became the first woman to compete in the heralded New York Athletic Club meet, the Los Angeles Times Games, and the Penn Relays. That year she received the Sullivan Award as the nation's top amateur athlete.

In 1962 Rudolph was awarded the coveted Babe Didrikson Zaharias Award as the most outstanding female athlete in the world. That same year she competed in a meet against the Soviet Union held at Stanford University. She won the 100-meter dash and overcame a 40-yard deficit to win the women's 400-meter relay. When Rudolph recalled the race she said: "That was it. I knew it. The crowd in the stadium was on its feet, giving me a standing ovation, and I knew what time it was. Time to retire, with a sweet taste."

After retiring from competition, Rudolph returned to college and graduated from Tennessee State University in 1963 with a degree in education. She first took a job teaching second grade and coaching basketball. She coached track for a brief time at DePauw University in Greencastle, Indiana. Over the next several years she worked in a variety of positions as a goodwill ambassador to French West Africa, a radio show cohost, an administrative assistant at the University of California, Los Angeles, and an executive for a hospital in Nashville. In 1982 Rudolph established the Wilma Rudolph Foundation, a nonprofit organization dedicated to educating and inspiring underprivileged children. In so doing she said, "If I have anything to leave, the foundation is my legacy."

In 1961 Rudolph had married William Ward, but the marriage dissolved the next year. In 1963 she married Robert Eldridge, who was the father of her first child. They would have one more daughter and two sons before they divorced in 1976.

In July 1994, while giving a speech, Rudolph fainted. Diagnosed with brain cancer, she died at her home in Brentwood, Tennessee. Overcoming physical challenges and racial barriers, Rudolph became a world-class athlete whose legacy inspired successive generations. In an earlier interview she remarked, "I just want to be remembered as a hardworking lady with certain beliefs."

FURTHER READING
Rudolph, Wilma. *Wilma* (1977).
Bernstein, Margaret. "That Championship Season," *Essence* (July 1984).
Davis, Michael D. *Black American Women in Olympic Track and Field* (1992).
Jackson, Tenley-Ann. "Olympic Mind Power," *Essence* (July 1984).
Rhoden, William C. "The End of a Winding Road," *New York Times*, 19 Nov. 1994.
Obituary: *New York Times*, 13 Nov. 1994.
This entry is taken from the *American National Biography* and is published here with the permission of the American Council of Learned Societies.

GAYNOL LANGS

Ruffin, David (18 Jan. 1941–1 June 1991), singer and songwriter with the Temptations, was born Davis Eli Ruffin in Whynot, Mississippi, a rural unincorporated community near Meridian in southeastern Lauderdale County. He was the youngest of five children, and the third son, of Eli Ruffin and Ophelia Davis Ruffin. His father was a Baptist minister; Ruffin never knew his mother, who had died during his earliest stages of infancy; his sister Rosetta died as a child. In 1942 his father married a woman named Earline, a schoolteacher. Eli Ruffin was strict and at times abusive, even though he reared young Ruffin and his other children in the church. As a young boy Ruffin was sickly and suffered with asthma; yet, he maintained an active childhood. The Ruffin family was musically inclined; Ruffin, together with his father, stepmother, and three siblings—Quincy, Jimmy, and Rita Mae—traveled throughout Mississippi as a gospel singing group, The Spiritual Trying Four. As a young boy he had the privilege of performing as the opening act on the same stage as acclaimed gospel artists such as MAHALIA JACKSON and The Five Blind Boys of Mississippi. Ruffin was member of the choir at Salem Methodist Church; together with his brother Jimmy he performed with various gospel groups and participated in school choir competitions and talent shows, often winning the prize. In 1955, Ruffin went to Memphis, Tennessee—where the "Memphis sound" or rockabilly was peaking—in order to study ministry under the guardianship of a minister, with the objective to follow in his father's footsteps. Yet, with a passionate desire to sing, Ruffin was soon participating in talent shows around Memphis, ultimately making the acquaintance of Elvis Presley, then a rising rockabilly star in the city. Following his heart, at age fifteen, Ruffin went to Hot Springs, Arkansas, where he performed at the Fifty Grand Ballroom and Casino with the jazz musician Phineas Newborn Sr., who led the band and played drums. He had a job working with horses at a jockey club and became a member of the Dixie Nightingales gospel group, touring with the Staple Singers, the Dixie Hummingbirds, the Womack Brothers, and the Swan Silvertones; and he met the already popular rock and roll artist and musician LITTLE RICHARD. Ruffin also performed with The Soul Stirrers after Johnnie Taylor left the gospel group for a secular career, as had SAM COOKE before him. At age sixteen, Ruffin was at a racetrack in New Orleans, Louisiana, when he met a minister, Father Eddie Bush, who also worked as a pimp. Bush filed papers to adopt Ruffin in order to establish custody and travel authorization.

In 1957, Reverend Bush and Dorothy Helen took Ruffin to Detroit, Michigan, where he began his foray into secular music. Ruffin had already developed a style that showcased his strong voice, which has been described as brassy and soulful, as well as his dance moves, which were smooth, swift, precise, and energetic. In 1958, he recorded songs for Vega Records under the name Little Davis Bush, having adopted the last name of his guardian, including "You and I" and "Believe Me." In Detroit, Bush and Helen introduced Ruffin to Gwen Gordy and Billy Davis, who were influential on the burgeoning Detroit music scene as owners of Anna Records, a Chess subsidiary, with Ana Gordy, and having to their credit hit songs written for JACKIE WILSON and ETTA JAMES. In 1961, Ruffin recorded as an artist on the Ana label, a subsidiary of Motown Records, with The Voice Masters—a group that also included LAMONT DOZIER and Ruffin's distant cousin, Melvin Franklin—the songs "I'm in Love" and "One of These Days." It was through Gwen Gordy that Ruffin met her brother, BERRY GORDY JR., founder of the Motown record label, who orchestrated what became known as the Motown sound with his artists and defined an era in American music. The same year Ruffin joined Davis on his newly established Check-Mate Records label; he was featured with The Voice Masters singing background vocals on "You Can Get What I Got" and "Actions Speak Louder

Than Words." The following year he recorded "Mr. Bus Driver Hurry," which found local success, and the song, "Knock You Out with Love." Meanwhile, his brother Jimmy had arrived in Detroit before him and signed with Miracle Records, a subsidiary of Motown, as an artist; three years later he was drafted into the army. When Jimmy returned from the army, in 1964, he reenlisted at Motown and was soon thereafter invited by Otis Williams to join The Temptations when the founding member Elbridge "Al" Bryant was dismissed from the group. Jimmy wanted to pursue a solo career and suggested his brother. Ruffin expressed his interest to Williams, who was a nearby neighbor, and won over the group with his audition. Furthermore, Ruffin had already established ties with the Gordy family.

On 9 January 1964, Ruffin, performed in his first recording session as a member of The Temptations, alongside Eddie Kendricks, Paul Williams, Melvin Franklin, and Otis Williams. Until Ruffin joined the group they had known minimal success but the first single he appeared on, "The Way You Do the Things You Do," was nationally acclaimed and rose to number eleven on the music charts. SMOKEY ROBINSON wrote many of the songs for artists on the Motown level and he wanted to create a something special for the newest member of The Temptations. In November 1964, Ruffin sang lead on "My Girl," written by Robinson and released a month later. Ruffin was solidly established as the lead singer and front man for The Temptations with the huge success of "My Girl," which became the first number one single for the group. Ruffin's lead vocals issued in a string of nationally acclaimed hits for The Temptations and Motown, including in 1965 "It's Growing," "Since I Lost My Baby," and "My Baby"; in 1966 "Ain't Too Proud to Beg," "Beauty Is Only Skin Deep," and "(I Know) I'm Losing You"; in 1967 "All I Need," "(Loneliness Made Me Realize) It's You That I Need," and "I Wish It Would Rain." Ruffin shared lead vocals with Eddie Kendricks on "You're My Everything" and "I Could Never Love Another (After Loving You)" in 1968. In 1967, Ruffin was celebrating his success with luxury items including a mink lined limousine; he had become addicted to cocaine and oftentimes had violent disagreements with his girlfriend and fellow label mate at Motown, Tammi Terrell; all of which were affecting his relationship with the group. Even more, Motown had begun changing group names to feature the lead singer, like DIANA ROSS and the Supremes and Smokey Robinson and the Miracles; Ruffin desired this same designation. Otis Williams did not like that Ruffin desired to set himself apart from The Temptations; in April 1968, Williams finally received the support of group members determining that Ruffin's overall behavior was too detrimental to the whole and collectively voted to have him fired. Ruffin was replaced by Dennis Edwards, who had belonged to The Contours. Upon release from The Temptations, Ruffin filed a suit against Motown Records for an audit of his finances and a separation from the label; Motown issued a countersuit obligating the artist to remain with the label to honor his initial contract.

On 1 May 1969 Ruffin released his first album, *My Whole World Ended*, as a solo artist on Motown; and, the first single, "My Whole World Ended (The Moment You Left Me)" was widely successful and the album reached number 1 on the U.S. R&B Charts. Ruffin released a second album on Motown the same year, *Feelin' Good*, which achieved number 9 on the U.S. R&B Charts. Ruffin collaborated for another Motown release with his brother Jimmy on the album, *I Am My Brothers Keeper*, released in 1970, acclaimed for their rendition of the BEN E. KING hit "Stand by Me." In 1971 he recorded the album *David* for Motown, but it was shelved until 2005, when Hip-O Records released it. *David Ruffin*, the album, only reached number 34 on the 1973 U.S. R&B Charts, followed by *Me 'N Rock 'N Roll Are Here to Stay*, released December 1974, and *Who Am I*, which reached number 5 on the charts in 1975. Ruffin recorded his last two albums for Motown in 1976 and 1977 *Everything's Coming Up Love*, and *In My Stride*, respectively. Ruffin was dissatisfied with the level of commitment he received from Motown and in 1979 went to Warner Bros. Records. The artist recorded two albums for Warner Bros. *So Soon We Change* and *Gentleman Ruffin* in 1979 and 1980; neither album delivered a hit. In 1982, Ruffin was invited to perform on The Temptations Reunion Tour with the original Temptations, minus Paul Williams who had committed suicide, plus Richard Street and Glenn Leonard, who had since been added. The same year, Ruffin together with The Temptations recorded "Standing on the Top" with the recording artist Rick James. In 1985, Ruffin joined forces with Kendricks, who had left the group in 1970, and they struck out on tour as a duo act. Additionally, in 1985, Ruffin and Kendricks performed with the blue-eyed soul duo Hall & Oates for a reopening event at the world famous Apollo Theater in New York and again in Philadelphia on 13 July for the Live Aid concert to raise funds and awareness of the devastating Ethiopian famine. They also appeared in the video, *Sun City*, with numerous artists for the Artists United Against Apartheid effort; and in 1987 they recorded the album *Ruffin*

& *Kendrick* for RCA Records. In 1989, Ruffin and Kendricks united with Edwards, who had been fired from The Temptations in 1977, for a Temptation revue appropriately showcasing themselves as former lead vocalists for The Temptations.

In 1991, Ruffin, Kendricks, and Edwards had just returned to the United States after a month-long tour in England; when on 1 June Ruffin, aged fifty, was pronounced dead after an overdose of cocaine. It is believed that he had visited a "crack house" and consumed ten vials of the drug; controversy surrounds $40,000 that was missing from his person. The Ruffin family lacked the financial resources to cover his funeral services, so a casket was donated by the Atlanta company that made one for DR. MARTIN LUTHER KING JR. ARETHA FRANKLIN paid for printing, and MICHAEL JACKSON, then at the peak of his fame and musical powers, paid for the funeral. Among those who attended the memorial service for Ruffin were STEVIE WONDER, Aretha Franklin, MARY WILSON, Martha Reeves, The Temptations, The Four Tops, The Miracles, and Minister LOUIS FARRAKHAN.

Ruffin was first married to Sandra Ruffin with whom he had three daughters: Cheryl, Nedra, and Kimberly. His second marriage was to Joy Hamilton. Ruffin had a son, David Ruffin Jr., with his longtime girlfriend Genna Sapia, who later added the last name Ruffin to her own.

In 1989, Ruffin, along with other members of The Temptations, was inducted into the Rock and Roll Hall of Fame.

FURTHER READING

Graff, Gary. "The Temptations: Otis Tells the Group's Tale," *Detroit Free Press*, 29 Aug. 1988.

n.a. "Probe into the $40,000 Missing from Singer David Ruffin Continues," *Jet Magazine*, 24 June 1991.

Ribowsky, Mark. *Ain't Too Proud to Beg: The Troubled Lives and Enduring Soul of The Temptations* (2010).

Obituary: *New York Times*, 2 June 1991.

SAFIYA DALILAH HOSKINS

Ruffin, George Lewis (16 Dec. 1834–20 Nov. 1886), judge, politician, and activist, was born in Richmond, Virginia. He was the oldest son of George W. Ruffin, a barber, and Nancy Lewis, both free African Americans. Because the Ruffins valued education highly, they hired a tutor to teach their eight children English literature, as well as Latin and the classics, despite the financial strain of this instruction's cost. The Ruffins owned a small amount of property in Richmond, but they decided to abandon it and move to Boston in 1853 after the Virginia legislature prohibited African Americans from learning to read. In Boston, George W. worked as a barber, as he had in Richmond, while Nancy made a profitable living selling fish and fruit that her relatives shipped to her from Richmond. The eight Ruffin children entered the segregated Boston public school system. At the Chapman Hall school nineteen-year-old George excelled. The move to Boston also signaled the beginning of Ruffin's political life, because here he began his steadfast affiliation with the Republican Party.

In 1858 Ruffin married sixteen-year-old Josephine St. Pierre, the well-educated daughter of a prominent black Boston family. JOSEPHINE ST. PIERRE RUFFIN later became a well-known activist whose legacy eventually eclipsed her husband's. The couple became so disillusioned by American slavery and the racial discrimination that supported it—especially as this discrimination was manifested in the DRED SCOTT decision of 1857—that they decided in 1858 to move to Liverpool, England. They returned to Boston only six months later, however, and Ruffin followed in his father's footsteps, beginning work as a barber.

During the Civil War, Ruffin was anxious to enlist in the Fifty-fifth Massachusetts Colored Regiment, but his nearsightedness prevented him from realizing his dream of becoming a soldier. Still, George and Josephine worked tirelessly for the war effort by helping to recruit soldiers. Both worked at the Twelfth Street Baptist Church, an influential Boston congregation, to aid the U.S. Sanitary Commission, an organization that sought to bring comfort to Union soldiers by improving their living conditions. Because of their dedication to community service, both George and Josephine earned reputations as committed social activists and reformers. Ruffin gained further fame by writing for the *New York Anglo-African* a scathing review in 1863 that criticized WILLIAM WELLS BROWN's *The Black Man: His Antecedents, His Genius, and His Achievements*. Ruffin also served as a delegate at the 1864 National Negro Convention in Syracuse, New York. This convention, attended by such leaders as FREDERICK DOUGLASS, HENRY HIGHLAND GARNET, and JONATHAN GIBBS, was the first since the war's beginning. It addressed its delegates' concerns about recent Republican Party actions and presidential policy decisions—especially those regarding slavery, African American civil liberties, and colonization.

Between barbering and activism, Ruffin, known always to have a book with him, began to study law

under the tutelage of the law firm of Harvey Jewell. Ruffin was admitted to Harvard Law School, which at the time did not require an undergraduate degree for admission. Ruffin is said to have completed the rigorous three-year program in just one year, becoming in 1869 the first African American to earn a law degree from Harvard University. Many scholars also believe him to be the first African American to graduate from any American university law school. Admitted to the Suffolk County bar on 18 September 1869, Ruffin joined a small group of pioneering African American lawyers in Boston by signing on with Jewell's firm. There he specialized in criminal law, serving both black and white clients. Ruffin and Jewell were both elected to the Massachusetts state legislature in 1869 and 1870, Ruffin as only the second African American ever elected to that body.

Ruffin became more politically popular and better known in Massachusetts as he continued vehemently to condemn racial discrimination and violence against African Americans in the South. The Ruffins also became more prominent in Boston's black social scene. They befriended such influential abolitionists as William Lloyd Garrison and Frederick Douglass, who asked Ruffin to write the introduction to the 1881 edition of *Life and Times of Frederick Douglass*. In this introduction Ruffin declared, "America will be the field for the demonstration of truths not now accepted and the establishment of a new and higher civilization." He also called for healing and progressivism, asserting thatAll Americans, no matter what may have been their views on slavery, now that freedom has come and slavery is ended, must have a restful feeling and be glad that the source of bitterness and trouble is removed. The man who is sorry because of the abolition of slavery, has outlived his day and generation; he should have insisted upon being buried with the "lost cause" at Appomattox.In 1876 and 1877 Ruffin was elected to the Boston Common Council. In November 1883 he became Massachusetts's first black judge when Governor Benjamin Butler appointed him to the post for the municipal court in Charlestown. The executive council unanimously accepted Ruffin's nomination, though Butler's other appointees had been rejected. In the same year Ruffin was also named Boston's consul resident for the Dominican Republic. While a judge Ruffin remained a fiery civil rights leader. He attended the Massachusetts Colored League's first meeting in 1883 and in 1885 spoke out publicly, most notably in the *A.M.E. Church Review*, in favor of Douglass's marriage to Helen Pitts, a white woman, and in support of interracial marriage in general. Ruffin also served as the first president of the Wendell Phillips Club of Boston, as president of the Banneker Literary Club, and for twelve years as Sunday school superintendent of the Twelfth Street Baptist Church.

In 1886, three years after his appointment to the Charlestown bench, Ruffin succumbed to Bright's disease, a kidney condition, after weeks of illness. Though well established and successful, Ruffin left little money to his widow and four children because he had given so much to support social reform efforts. Ruffin's family kept his legacy strong. Josephine Ruffin did not waiver in her pioneering work for African American civil liberties. Their son Hulbert became a partner in a law firm, and their daughter Florida taught public school and edited the *Women's Era*, a magazine—once also edited by her mother—that advanced the causes of women's suffrage and equal rights.

Though Ruffin's reputation has been in eclipse, and accounts of his life vary widely, the George Lewis Ruffin Society, a group of Massachusetts criminal justice professionals, memorializes his importance to Massachusetts jurisprudence. Founded in 1984 and affiliated with Northeastern University, the society through its Minority Fellowship Program assisted minority students seeking advanced degrees in criminal justice.

FURTHER READING

Most of Ruffin's papers are available at the Moorland-Spingarn Research Center, Howard University, but other notable documents can be found in the Heslip-Ruffin Family papers at the Amistad Research Center at Tulane University.

Simmons, William J. *Men of Mark: Eminent, Progressive, and Rising* (1887).

Stanford, Peter Thomas. *The Tragedy of the Negro in America: A Condensed History of the Enslavement, Sufferings, Emancipation, Present Condition, and Progress of the Negro Race in the United States of America* (1887).

JENNIFER LARSON

Ruffin, Josephine St. Pierre (31 Aug. 1842–13 Mar. 1924), editor and woman's club organizer, was born in Boston, Massachusetts, the daughter of Eliza Matilda Menhenick of Cornwall, England, and John St. Pierre, a clothing seller whose father was a French immigrant from Martinique. Though Josephine's complexion was very light, public schools in Boston were closed to people of color until 1855, so she received her early education at nearby Salem and Charlestown. Later she attended Boston's Bowdoin School and took two years of private tutoring in New York. In 1858 she married GEORGE LEWIS RUFFIN, who made his living as a barber but later became a prominent Boston legislator and judge. The marriage produced five children.

Because of the slavery issue in the United States, Ruffin and her family moved briefly to Liverpool, England, in 1858 but soon returned to Boston to fight for civil rights when the Civil War began. Even at her young age, Ruffin was beginning to demonstrate her organizational and leadership skills. Despite the demands of raising a family, she was soon busy recruiting soldiers for the war effort and working for the U.S. Sanitary Commission. She also worked with other charitable groups, such as the Boston Kansas Relief Association, which helped freed slaves who migrated west, and the Massachusetts School Suffrage Association.

In 1890 Ruffin used what little was left of her husband's resources (he died in 1886 nearly destitute because he gave much of his money to charitable and civil rights work) to embark on a new adventure. With her family's help, she founded the *Woman's Era*, a monthly magazine devoted almost exclusively to issues affecting African American women. The publication covered society news but also dealt with more serious social issues like abolition, suffrage, and living conditions in the cities. Though the articles were written by a staff, Ruffin acted as editor, layout person, and editorial writer—she even became her own advertising executive. Besides editing and publishing her own magazine, she supplemented her income in 1891 by acting as editor in chief of the *Boston Courant*, a black weekly newspaper. She gave up this work, though, in 1893 to devote more time to the *Woman's Era*, and she also joined the New England Women's Press Association in 1893. Though the *Woman's Era* gave Ruffin a decent living for several years, it suffered from insufficient advertising revenue, as did most of the African American periodical press of the time. Also the *Woman's Era* catered to the elite African American society of Boston, and its one-dollar-per-year subscription price was more than most ordinary African American women could afford. The last issue was dated January 1897. Ruffin's work as an editor and her friendship with many influential people aroused in her an interest in the field for which she is best remembered. In 1894, influenced by Julia Ward Howe and others, she organized with her friend, MARIA BALDWIN, and her daughter, FLORIDA RUFFIN RIDLEY, the Woman's Era Club. Using the *Woman's Era* as its official publication, the club devoted itself to the education of young

African American women and to charitable causes. The Woman's Era Club became so successful under Ruffin's leadership that it grew in 1896 from a sixty-member Boston club into the National Association of Colored Women, with thousands of members. Ruffin tried to gain more support from the white women's clubs by joining the Massachusetts State Federation of Women's Clubs, and she also joined the all-white General Federation of Women's Clubs and was asked to serve on its executive committee. Not realizing that she was president of a black club, the federation had accepted her membership. When she arrived at the biennial convention in Milwaukee in 1900, however, the situation was quite different. What happened there was one of the defining moments of Josephine Ruffin's career and one of the most unfortunate incidents in the history of the women's club movement. Southern delegates were outraged that an "octoroon" wanted to become a member of the General Federation, and they insisted that the membership remain white. The executive board of the federation claimed that she had violated the rules by not revealing that the Woman's Era Club was a black club. The federation was fearful of losing southern members, and despite protests from Ruffin's supporters, it refused to recognize her organization or seat her as a delegate to a black club, although it was willing to seat her as a member of the two white clubs to which she already belonged, the New England Women's Press Association and the Massachusetts State Federation of Women's Clubs. Never one to compromise her principles, however, Ruffin refused its offer.

Ruffin remained president of the Woman's Era Club until 1903, but her activities in it gradually began to dwindle, although her involvement in the community remained strong. Among other organizations to which she gave her time were the Association for the Promotion of Child Training in the South and the American Mount Coffee School Association, which helped raise funds for a school in Liberia. She was also instrumental in establishing the Boston chapter of the National Association for the Advancement of Colored People, of which she remained a member for many years.

Advanced age did not stop Josephine Ruffin from giving her time and energy to worthy causes. Her daughter, Florida Ridley, recalled that Ruffin attended the "Women's Day" celebration in Boston when she was seventy-nine, and, at the age of eighty-two, she took a taxi on a stormy night to attend a meeting of the League of Women for Community Service. Less than a month later she died of nephritis at her home in Boston.

FURTHER READING

The Ruffin Family Papers are at the Amistad Research Center, Tulane University. Incomplete files of the *Woman's Era* are in the Moorland-Spingarn Research Center at Howard University and at the Boston Public Library.

Brown, Hallie Quinn. *Homespun Heroines and Other Women of Distinction* (1926).

Bullock, Penelope. *The Afro-American Periodical Press, 1838–1909* (1981).

Logan, Rayford W. *The Betrayal of the Negro from Rutherford B. Hayes to Woodrow Wilson* (1965).

Wesley, Charles H. *The History of the National Association of Colored Women's Clubs* (1984).

This entry is taken from the *American National Biography* and is published here with the permission of the American Council of Learned Societies.

ROGER A. SCHUPPERT

Ruggles, David (15 Mar. 1810–26 Dec. 1849), abolitionist and journalist, was born in Norwich, Connecticut, the son of David Ruggles and Nancy (maiden name unknown), both free blacks. Educated at the Sabbath School for the Poor, he moved to New York City at the age of seventeen. In 1829 he opened a grocery, selling goods of "excellent quality" but no "spirituous liquors." He later served as an officer in the New York City Temperance Union.

In 1833 Ruggles sharpened his speaking skills as an agent for the *Emancipator and Journal of Public Morals*, the organ of the American Anti-Slavery Society. He attacked colonization and spoke in support of the black national convention movement and the newly established Phoenix Society, organized to nurture black education. The society sponsored the Phoenix High School for Colored Youth, which by 1837 employed thirteen teachers.

With HENRY HIGHLAND GARNET, Ruggles organized the Garrison Literary and Benevolent Association, named after the famed abolitionist William Lloyd Garrison, which sponsored a reading room. In 1834 he opened the first known African American–owned bookshop, which served the abolitionist and black community. An antiabolitionist mob destroyed the store, however, in 1835.

Ruggles became well known to white abolitionists through his numerous articles in the *Emancipator*. In 1834 he published his first pamphlet, the anticolonization satire *Extinguisher, Extinguished … or David M. Reese, M.D. "Used Up."* He expanded his abolitionist arguments in 1835 in *The Abrogation of the Seventh Commandment by* the American Churches. Published by Ruggles's own press, another African American first, the pamphlet stood on their heads proslavery arguments that the abolition of slavery would lead to interracial sex. He charged slave owners with violating the Seventh Commandment by forcing slave women to surrender "to their unbridled lusts," thus offending "every principle of feminine sensibility and Christian morals." In this appeal to the emerging northern feminist movement, Ruggles beseeched northern women to shun their southern white sisters who brought their slaves north "while on a summer tour." Those same women, he thundered, passively allowed their husbands to father children in the slave quarter or used as domestics "the spurious offspring of their own husbands, brothers, and sons." He found these actions of southern white women "inexcusably criminal" and demanded that northern women close their churches to them. ANGELINA WELD GRIMKÉ used Ruggles's arguments in a speech before the Anti-Slavery Convention of American Women held in New York City in 1837.

In 1835 Ruggles founded and headed the New York Committee of Vigilance, which sought to shield the growing number of fugitive slaves from recapture and protect free blacks from kidnapping. Cooperating with the white abolitionists Lewis Tappan and Isaac T. Hopper, Ruggles and other black leaders were daring conductors on the Underground Railroad and harbored nearly one thousand blacks, including FREDERICK DOUGLASS, before transferring them farther north to safety. A fearless activist, he raised funds for the committee, served writs against slave catchers, and directly confronted suspected kidnappers. In frequent columns for the Colored American, he exposed kidnapping incidents on railroads. In 1839 he published the Slaveholders Directory, which identified the names and addresses of politicians, lawyers, and police in New York City who "lend themselves to kidnapping." His bold efforts often led to his arrest and imprisonment, which contributed to his failing health and eyesight.

Between 1838 and 1841 Ruggles published five issues of the Mirror of Liberty, the first African American magazine. Circulated widely throughout the East, Midwest, and the South, the magazine reported on the activities of the Committee of Vigilance, kidnappings and related court cases, antislavery speeches, and the activities of black organizations. Despite its irregular appearances, its publication was a significant achievement. In 1844 Ruggles attempted unsuccessfully to establish

a second magazine, entitled the Genius of Freedom. In 1838 he attacked colonization once more in An Antidote for a Poisonous Combination.

Ruggles's antislavery zeal caused a fractious dispute with the editor SAMUEL CORNISH in 1838. Without the permission of Cornish, Ruggles published the accusation in the Colored American that John Russell, a local black and landlord of a home for African American seamen, trafficked in slaves. Russell successfully sued Ruggles and the newspaper for libel, and Cornish blamed Ruggles for the subsequent upheaval that split the black community. By 1839, stung by the divisive battle with Cornish, accused of mishandling funds by the Committee of Vigilance, and suffering from poor health and near-blindness, Ruggles moved to Northampton, Massachusetts. There Lydia Maria Child and the Northampton Association of Education and Industry gave him succor in the 1840s while he continued his activities on the Underground Railroad. In 1841 he showed his old grit when he pioneered protest against segregation on public transit by refusing to leave his seat in a New Bedford, Massachusetts, railroad car.

Beset by illness and weary of failed cures, Ruggles in the 1840s tried successfully the watercure treatments made famous by Vincent Priessnitz of Austrian Silesia. In Northampton, Ruggles overcame his poor health and built a prosperous practice as a doctor of hydropathy. In 1846, with the help of the Northampton Association, he refurbished an old watermill and opened the first establishment devoted to water cures in the United States. Using "cutaneous electricity" treatments, Ruggles became nationally known. He assisted a variety of patients, from the wife of a southern slave owner to William Lloyd Garrison and SOJOURNER TRUTH. He died in Northampton from a severe bowel inflammation. As an abolitionist, journalist, and physician, Ruggles gave selflessly to help others.

FURTHER READING
The most complete collection of Ruggles's writings is in C. Peter Ripley et al., eds., The Black Abolitionist Papers (1981–1983), microfilm.
Porter, Dorothy B., ed. Early Negro Writing, 1760–1837 (1971).
Ripley, C. Peter. Black Abolitionist Papers, vol. 3 (1991).
This entry is taken from the American National Biography and is published here with the permission of the American Council of Learned Societies.

GRAHAM RUSSELL HODGES